Webster's

21st CENTURY™

Spanish/English Dictionary

NELSON/REGENCY

Nashville, Tennessee

Copyright© 1993, Thomas Nelson Publishers, Nashville, Tennessee.

Library of Congress Cataloging-in-Publication Data

Webster's 21st Century Spanish/English Dictionary.
   p.   cm.
   ISBN 0-8407-4850 - 7 (pb)
   1. Spanish language--Dictionaries--English.
   PC4640.W4 1993
   463'.21--dc20

                            93-483
                               CIP

Printed in the United States of America

94 95 96 97 ---- 5 4 3 2 1

Pronunciation Key

a　　　amar, andar, pata
As in pat or patter

e　　　eso, pelo, agredir
As in set, wet, deck

i　　　filosofía, iris, image
As in fidelity, figure.

o　　　oso, otro, óseo
As in over, oven, other

u　　　pulula, luna, aquella, guerra
As in rule, food. It is silent after g, in syllables gue, gui, unless accented
with (ü) as in *vergüenza, antigüedad, agüero*

ch(a) *ch*(e) *ch*(i) *ch*(o) *ch*(u) chance, cheche, chico, chocolate, chusma
As in channel, Chevrolet, chimney, chocolate, shoe

ll(a) *ll*(e) *ll*(i) *ll*(o) *ll*(u) llama, lleve, lligues, llorar, llueve
As in jazz, jet, jingle, job, juice.

ñ(a) as in *nya,* ñame
ñ(e) as in *nye,* muñeca
ñ(i) as in *nyi,* ñipe
ñ(o) as in *nyo,* ñoño
ñ(u)as in *nyu,* ñuto

Abbreviations

abbr, abr	abreviatura	abbreviation
Acad	Academia	Academy
adj	adjetivo	adjective
adv	adverbio	adverb
Agr	agricultura	agriculture
Anat	anatomía	anatomy
Archit, Arquit	arquitectura	architecture
art	artículo	article
Astron	astronomía	astronomy
Aut	automóviles	automobile
Bib	bíblico	biblical
Bio	biología	biology
Bot	botánica	botany
Chem	química	chemistry

Comm, Com	comercio	commerce
Culin	clinario, cocina	cookery
dat	dativo	dative
def	definido	definite
dem	demostrativo	demonstrative
Dep	deportes	sport
Eccl, Ecl	eclesiástico	ecclesiastical
Econ	economía	economics
Educ	educación	education
Elec	electricidad	electricity
etc	etcétera	etceteras
f	femenino	feminine
Fil	filosofía	philosophy
Fin	finanzas	finance
Geog	geografía	geography
ind	indicativo	indicative
interj	interjección	interjection
interrog	interrogativo	interrogative
Jur	derecho, jurídico	law, legal
m	masculino	masculine
Math, Mat	matemáticas	mathematics
Med	medicina	medicine
Mus, Mús	música	music
n	nombre, sustantivo	noun
Naut	náutica	nautical
neg	negativo	negative
Opt	óptica	optics
pl	forma plural	plural
Pol	política	politics
poss	posesivo	possessive
pref	prefijo	prefix
prep	preposición	preposition
pron	pronombre	pronoun
Rel	religión	religion
subj	subjuntivo	subjunctive
superl	superlativo	superlative
Teat, Theat	teatro	theater
TV	televisión	television
Typ	tipografía	typography
US	Estados Unidos	United States
v	verbo	verb
vi	verbo intransitivo	intransitive verb
vr	verbo reflexivo	reflexive verb
vt	verbo transitivo	transitive verb
Zool	zoología	zoology

Spanish\English

A

A, a, *nf* (letter) A, a.

a, *prep* to, at, for.

abacado, *nm* avocado pear.

abacero, *nm/f* grocer, provision merchant.

abacorar, *vt* **1.** harass, plague bother to catch, surprise; **2.** to undertake boldly, to entice away; **3.** monopolize.

abajo, *adv* down, below, down below, underneath, downstairs down, downwards.

abaldonar, *vt* to degrade, debase, to affront.

abalear, *vt* to shoot, fire at, to shoot to death, execute, to shoot off guns, fire in the air.

abanderado, *nm* standard-bearer, champion, leader.

abanderar, *vt* to register, to take a leading role in.

abandonado, *adj* abandoned; deserted, forsaken.

abandono, *nm* abandonment, dereliction, desertion, giving up, renunciation, relinquishment.

abanicar, *vt* to fan; to tell off.

abanico, *nm* fan, fan-shaped object.

abaratar, *vt* to make cheaper, reduce the price of.

abaratarse, *vr* to get cheaper, come down.

abarcar, *vt* to include, embrace, take in; to span, to contain, comprise; to extend to, to monopolize.

abarrotar, *vt* to bar, fasten with bars; overstock.

abarrote, *nm* packing food item, foodstuff; food supplies; groceries.

abastecer, *vt* to supply, provide (with).

abastecimiento, *nm* provisions, supplies.

abatido, *adj* depressed, dejected, downcast, crestfallen low, contemptible, despicable.

abatir, *vt* knock down, take apart; discourage, humble.

abatirse, *vr* to drop, fall; to swoop, dive; to swoop on, pounce on.

abdicar, *vt* to renounce, relinquish; to give up.

abdomen, *nm* abdomen.

abdominal, *adj* abdominal.

abecedario, *nm* alphabet, spelling book.

abeto, *nm* fir-tree.

abigarrar, *vt* to paint in a variety of colors.

abigeo, *nm* rustler.

abismal, *adj* abysmal; vast, enormous.

abismarse, *vr* to be amazed, be astonished.

abismo, *nm* abyss, trough, hell.

abjurar, *vt* to abjure, forswear.

ablandarse, *vr* to soften, soften up, get soft(er).

ablusado, *adj* loose garment.

abnegado, *adj* self-denying, self-sacrificing; unselfish.

abnegarse, *vr* to deny oneself, act unselfishly.

abobar, *vt* to make stupid; to daze, bewilder.

abocado, *adj* smooth, pleasant.

abocar, *vt* to seize (or catch) in one's mouth; to bring nearer, bring up, to pour out, decant.

abochornado, *adj* embarrassed.

abochornar, *vt* to make flushed, overheat.

abofarse, *vr* to stuff.

abofetear, *vt* to slap, hit (in the face).

abogado(a), *nm/f* lawyer, solicitor; attorney-at-law.

abogar, *vt* to plead, defend, to advocate.

abolengo, *nm* ancestry, lineage, inheritance.

abolir, *vt* to abolish; to cancel, annul, revoke.

abolsado, *adj* full of pockets, baggy.

abolsarse, *vr* to form pockets, be baggy.

abolladura, *nf* dent; bump; bruise; embossing.

abollar, *vt* to dent; to raise a bump on, to bruise.

abominación, *nf* abomination, loathing, detestation.

abominar, *vt* to loathe, detest, abominate.

abonado(a), *adj* **1.** reliable, trustworthy, to be ready to; **2.** *nm/f* subscriber; season-ticket holder.

abonar, *vt* **1.** to vouch for, support, guarantee, confirm; **2.** to pay, to pay money into an account, credit money to an account; **3.** to fertilize, manure.

abono, *nm* **1.** guarantee; in support of, in justification of; as confirmation of; **2.** payment; installment; credit, down payment, deposit; **3.** fertilizer, manure; **4.** subscription; **5.** receipt.

aboquillado, *adj* (cigarette) tipped, filter-tipped.

abordaje, *nm* collision, fouling, boarding; accosting, approach.

abordar, *vt* **1.** to come alongside; to board; **2.** to accost, approach; to stop and speak to; to tackle; to undertake, get down to, start on.

aborigen, *adj* **1.** aboriginal; indigenous; **2.** *nm/f* aborigine.

aborrecer, *vt* to hate, loathe, detest; bored by; to desert.

aborrecido, *adj* hated, loathed; boring.

abortar, *vt* to abort, cause to miscarry; to have an abortion.

aborto, *nm* miscarriage; abortion.

abotonar, *vt* **1.** to button up, do up; **2.** to block, obstruct; **3.** to bud.

abovedado, *adj* **1.** vaulted; arched; **2.** vaulting.

abovedar, *vt* to vault, arch.

aboyar, *vt* **1.** to buoy, mark with buoys; **2.** to float.

abra, *nf* cave, small bay, inlet; dale, gorge; fissure; clearing; mountain pass.

abrasador, *adj* burning, scorching; withering.

abrasar, *vt* to burn, burn up, to dry up, to sear; to cut, nip.

abrasivo, *adj nm* abrasive.

abrazar, *vt* to embrace; to hug, take in one's arms; to include; comprise, take in; to adopt, enter.

abrevar, *vt* (animal) to water, give a drink to; to water, irrigate; (pieles) to soak.

abrevarse, *vr* to drink, quench its thirst.

abreviación, *nf* abbreviation; abridgment, shortening.

abreviar, *vt* to abbreviate; to abridge, reduce; to shorten, cut short; to hasten; to advance, bring forward.

abreviatura, *nf* abbreviation.

abridor, *nm* bottle opener; can opener.

abrigar, *vt* to shelter, protect; to keep warm, protect, cover; to wrap up; to help, support.

abrigarse, *vr* to take shelter; to cover oneself up (warmly), wrap oneself up; warm oneself.

abrigo, *nm* shelter; protection; help, support; covering.

abril, *nm* April.

abrillantado, *adj* **1.** polished; glazed; **2.** *nm* glaze.

abrillantar, *vt* to cut into facets; to polish, burnish, brighten; to glaze; to enhance.

abrir, *vt* to open; to open up.

abrirse, *vr* to open; spread (out); to expand; confide.

abrochar, *vt* to button (up); to do up, fasten (up).

abrocharse, *vr* to struggle, wrestle.

abroncar, *vt* to shame, to make ashamed, ridicule.

abroncarse, *vr* to get angry.

abrumador(a), *adj* overwhelming, crushing.

abrumar, *vt* to crush, overwhelm, to oppress, weigh down; to wear out, exhaust.

abrupto, *adj* steep, abrupt; rough, rugged.

absceso, *nm* abscess.

absolución, *nf* absolution; acquittal; pardon.

absolutizar, *vt* to pin down, be precise about.

absolutorio, *adj* verdict of acquittal, not guilty.

absolver, *vt* to absolve, to acquit, clear of a charge.

absorbente, *adj* absorbent.

absorber, vt to absorb, to soak up, to suck in.
absorto, adj absorbed; engrossed.
abstemia, nf abstainer; teetotaler.
abstención, nf abstention, nonparticipation.
abstenerse, vr to abstain; to refrain; to abstain from.
abstraer, vt to abstract; to remove, consider separately, exclude.
abstraído, adj absentminded; preoccupied.
absurdo, adj 1. absurd, ridiculous, preposterous; farcical; 2. n m/f absurdity; farce.
abuchear, vt to boo, hoot at; to howl down, jeer at.
abucheo, nm booing, hooting; jeering.
abuela, nf grandmother, old woman, old lady.
abuelo, nm grandfather.
abultado, adj bulky, large, massive; unwieldy.
abundante, adj abundant, plentiful, copious provision, generous an abounding in.
abundar, vi to abound, be plentiful, abound in.
aburrición, nf revulsion, repugnance.
aburrido, adj boring, tedious, dull; monotonous.
aburrimiento, nm boredom, tedium, monotony.
aburrir, vt to bore, to tire, weary.
abusador, adj abusive.
abusar, vi to go too far, exceed one's rights, take advantage, to ask too much, to presume upon, take unfair advantage of, to impose upon.
abuso, nm abuse, imposition.
acá, adv here, over here, round here.
acabado, adj 1. finished, complete; perfect; consummated, masterly, polished; 2. old, worn out; ruined in health, wrecked.
acabar, vt to finish, stop.
acabarse, nm to come to an end, to run out of something; to die.
academia, nf academy; (private) school.
académico, adj, 1. academic; 2. nm/f academician, member (of an academy); fellow (of a learned society), full member of an academy.
acaecer, vi to happen, occur; to take place; to befall.
acalambrarse, vr to get a cramp.
acalaminado, adj rough, uneven, bumpy.
acalenturarse, vr to get feverish.
acalorado, adj heated, hot; tired; excited; passionate.
acalorar, vt to make hot, warm up; to overheat.
acallar, vt to silence, quieten, hush; to assuage, pacify.
acampada, nf camp.
acampadora, nm camper.
acampar, vi to camp; to encamp.
acanalado, adj grooved, fluted; corrugated.
acanalar, vt to groove, furrow, to flute, to corrugate.
acanallado, adj disreputable, low; worthless.
acanelado, adj cinnamon flavored (or colored).
acantilado, adj steep, sheer.
acantonamiento, nm cantonment, billeting.
acantonar, vt to billet, quarter.
acaparador, adj acquisitive.
acaparador(a), nm/f monopolizer, monopolist; profiteer, hoarder.
acaparar, vt to monopolize; to corner.
acápite, nm paragraph; subheading; caption.
acaracolado, adj spiral, winding, twisting.
acaramelado, adj toffee-covered; (color) toffee-colored; sugary, oversweet; cloying; overpolite.
acardenalar, vt to bruise.
acardenalarse, vr to get bruised, go black and blue.
acariciador, adj caressing.
acariciar, vt to caress, fondle, stroke; to pat, stroke; to brush, touch lightly.
acarrear, vt to transport, haul, cart, carry, to lug about, lug along, to carry along, bring down.
acarreo, nm transport, haulage, cartage, carriage.

acartonado, adj wizened, shriveled; like cardboard.
acartonar, vt to get like cardboard; to become wizened; to shrivel up.
acaso, adv 1. perhaps, maybe; by chance; 2. nm chance, accident, coincidence.
acatar, vt 1. to respect; to hold in awe, revere; to defer to, treat with deference, to obey, respect, observe; 2. to notice, observe; 3. to annoy.
acatarrar, vt to harass, pester.
acaudalado, adj well-off, affluent.
acaudalar, vt to acquire, accumulate, to hoard.
acaudillar, vt to lead, command, head.
acceder, vi to accede, agree.
accesible, adj accessible; approachable; open to access.
acceso, nm 1. entry, access; 2. way, approach.
accesorio, adj 1. accessory dependent, subordinate; incidental; 2. nm attachment, accessory.
accidentado, adj uneven, broken, rugged.
accidentado(a), nm/f injured person; casualty; person involved in an accident.
accidentarse, vr to have an accident.
accidente, nm accident, misadventure.
acción, nf 1. act, deed; 2. action, stock share.
accionar, 1. vt to work, drive, propel; to set off, detonate; 2. vi to wave one's hands about.
accionista, nm/f shareholder, stockholder.
acechador(a), adj spy, watcher, observer.
acechar, vt to spy on, watch, observe; to lie in wait for.
acéfalo, adj headless; leaderless.
aceitada, nf bribe, backhanded.
aceitar, vt to oil, lubricate.
aceite, nm oil.
aceitoso, adj oily.
aceituna, nf olive.
acelerado, adj jumpy, nervous: impatient.
acelerador, nm accelerator, gas pedal.
acelerar, vt to accelerate, to speed up, hasten, expedite.
acelerarse, vr to make haste, hurry oneself up.
acento, nm accent, stress, emphasis; tone, inflection.
acentuación, nf accentuation.
acentuado, adj accented, stressed.
acentuar, vt to accent, stress; to highlight.
acepción, nf 1. sense, meaning; 2. preference.
acepilladora, nf planer, planing machine.
acepillar, vt to brush, to plane, shave.
aceptar, vt to accept, to approve, take on, undertake.
acepto, adj acceptable, agreeable, welcomed.
acequia, nf irrigation ditch, irrigation channel.
acera, nf pavement, sidewalk (US); row (of houses).
acerado, adj made of steel, steely; steel-tipped.
acerbo, adj sharp, bitter, sour.
acerca de, prep about, on, concerning.
acercar, vt to bring nearer, to bring over.
acercarse, vt to approach, come near, come close to.
acerería, nf steelworks, steel mill.
acero, nm steel, crude steel.
acérrimo, adj very strong, staunch.
acertado, adj correct, right, successful.
acertar, vt to hit (target), (solución) to get, get right, guess correctly; to find, succeed in tracing; to achieve, succeed in reaching.
acertijo, nm riddle, puzzle.
acervo, nm heap, pile, stock, store.
acetileno, nm acetylene.
acetona, nf acetone.
aciago, adj ill-fated, ill-omened, fateful.
aciano, nm cornflower.
acíbar, nm aloes, sorrow, bitterness.
acicalado, adj (metal) polished, bright and clean, smart, neat, spruce, dapper, overdressed.

acicalar, *vt* metal to polish, burnish, clean; to dress up, bedeck, adorn.

acicate, *nm* spur, incentive, stimulus.

acidificar, *vt* to acidify.

ácido, *adj* sharp, sour, acid.

acidófilo, *adj* acidophilus.

acierto, *nm* success, good shot, hit, good guess, good idea.

acizañar, *vt* to stir things, cause trouble.

aclamación, *nf* acclamation applause, acclaim.

aclamar, *vt* to acclaim, to applaud.

aclaración, *nf* 1. rinse, rinsing; 2. clarification, explanation, elucidation; 3. brightening, clearing up.

aclarar, *vt* 1. to rinse, to thin, thin down; to clear; (bosque) to clear, thin (out); 2. to clarify, cast light on, explain; to resolve, remove.

aclararse, *vr* to catch on, get it.

aclimatación, *nf* acclimatization, acclimation.

aclimatizar, *vt* to acclimatize, acclimate.

acobardar, *vt* to daunt, intimidate, cow, unnerve.

acobardarse, *vr* to be frightened, get frightened, to flinch, shrink back.

acobrado, *adj* copper-colored, coppery.

acocear, *vt* to kick, to ill-treat, trample on, to insult.

acodado, *adj* bent, elbowed.

acodar, *vt* to lean, rest.

acogedor, *adj* welcoming, friendly, hospitable, warm snug, cozy.

acoger, *vt* to welcome, receive, to take in, give refuge to, to receive, to accept, admit.

acogida, *nf* welcome, reception, acceptance.

acogotar, *vt* to fell, kill (with a blow on the neck) to knock down, lay out.

acojinar, *vt* to cushion.

acolchado, *adj* quilted, padded.

acomedido, *adj* helpful, obliging concerned, solicitous.

acomedirse, *vr* to offer to help.

acometedor, *adj* energetic, enterprising.

acometer, *vt* 1. to attack, to set upon, rush on, assail; 2. to undertake, attempt, to tackle, deal with; 3. to overcome; to seize, take hold of.

acometida, *nf* 1. attack, assault; charge; 2. aggression, connection.

acomodación, *nf* accommodation; adaptation.

acomodado, *adj* 1. suitable, moderate; moderately priced; 2. well-to-do, well-off.

acomodar, *vt* 1. to adjust, accommodate, adapt; 2. to fit in, find room for, accommodate; take in, lodge; 3. to suit, adapt, to match.

acomodo, *nm* arrangement; compromise; agreement, understanding; secret arrangement, secret deal.

acompañamiento, *nm* accompaniment.

acompañante, *nm/f* companion, chaperon, escort; accompanist (Music).

acompañar, *vt* to accompany, go with; to attend; to escort, to keep company with someone, stay with someone, not leave someone.

acompasado, *adj* rhythmic, regular, measured; slow, deliberate, leisurely.

acompasar, *vt* 1. to measure with a compass; 2. to mark the rhythm of, to speak with a marked rhythm.

acomplejado, *adj* full of complexes; gravely embarrassed, much put out.

acomplejar, *vt* to cause complexes in, give a complex to; to embarrass gravely, cause to be much put out.

acondicionado, *adj* nice; in good condition.

acondicionador, *adj* conditioner; air conditioner.

acondicionar, *vt* 1. to arrange, prepare, make suitable; to condition; 2. to air-condition.

acongojado, *adj* distressed, anguished.

acongojar, *vt* 1. to distress, grieve; 2. *vr* to become distressed, get upset.

aconsejado, *adj* sensible; well-advised.

aconsejar, *vt* 1. to advise, counsel; to advise someone to do; 2. recommend; to preach.

aconsejarse, *vr* to seek advice, take advice; to consult; major to think better of it.

acontecer, *vi* to happen, occur, come about.

acontecimiento, *nm* event, happening, occurrence; incident; happening.

acopiar, *vt* to gather (together), collect; to buy up, get a monopoly of; to collect, hive.

acopio, *nm* 1. gathering, collecting; 2. collection; store.

acoplado, 1. *adj* a well coordinated team; 2. *nm* trailer, hanger on, sponger; gatecrasher.

acoplar, *vt* to couple; to join, fit together, to connect, to dock, link up, to yoke, hitch; (zool) to mate, pair, to associate, bring together; to reconcile; to coordinate.

acoquinar, *vt* to scare, intimidate, cow.

acorazonado, *adj* heartshaped.

acordada, *nf* decree.

acordado, *adj* agreed; has been agreed (upon).

acordar, *vt* 1. to decide, resolve, agree on; 2. to grant, accord; 3. to reconcile; to tune; to blend, harmonize; 4. to remind someone of something; 5. *vi* to agree; to correspond.

acordarse, *vr* 1. to agree, come to an agreement 2. to remember, recall, recollect.

acorde, *adj* 1. with identical feelings; agreed; 2. harmonious, in tune, in harmony.

acordonado, *adj* ribbed; cordoned.

acordonar, *vt* 1. to tie up, tie with string; to lace up; 2. to cordon off, rope off, surround with a cordon; to surround; 3. (borde) to mill.

acornar, *vt* to butt; to gore.

acorralar, *vt* to round up, pen, corral, to corner, bring to bay; to corner to intimidate.

acortar, *vt* to shorten, cut down, reduce; to shorten; to cut short, abbreviate.

acortarse, *vr* to be slow; to be shy, falter.

acostar, *vt* 1. to lay down; 2. to put to bed; 3. to bring alongside.

acostarse, *vr* to lie down; to go to bed.

acostumbrado, *adj* usual, customary.

acostumbrar, *vt* to get someone used to something; to inure someone to hardships.

acotación, *nf* 1. boundary mark; elevation mark; 2. marginal note; stage direction.

acotar, *vt* to survey, mark out; to limit, set bounds to; to fence in, protect, preserve.

acotejar, *vt* to arrange, put in order.

acreedor, *adj* a worthy of, deserving of; eligible for, creditor, mortgagee.

acribillado, *adj* pitted, pockmarked; a riddled with, peppered with; filled with; honeycombed with.

acribillar, *vt* 1. to riddle with bullets, pepper with shots; to cover with stab wounds; 2. to pester, badger; to harass; to pester someone with questions.

acrisolado, *adj* pure; tried, tested; unquestionable.

acrisolar, *vt* to purify, refine; to purify, purge; to bring out, clarify.

acristalado, *adj* glazed.

acróbata, *nm/f* acrobat.

acta, *nf* minutes, record; certificate of election.

actitud, *nf* 1. posture, pose; 2. attitude; outlook.

activar, *vt* to activate; to expedite, speed up.

actividad, *nf* 1. activity, liveliness; promptness; 2. occupation; activity.

activo, *adj* 1. active; lively; prompt; energetic; busy; 2. *nm* assets; circulating assets.

acto, *nm* act; action, deed; ceremony, function.

actor, *nm* actor, protagonist; plaintiff.

actriz, *nf* actress; leading lady.

actuación, *nf* action; conduct, behavior.

actualidad, *nf* 1. present, present time; at present, at the present time; nowadays, now; 2. present importance, current importance; 3. (*pl*) current events; contemporary issues.

actualización, *nf* modernization, bringing up to date; refresher course, course of retraining; updating, updating.

actualizar, *vt* to bring up to date, update, modernize, to add topicality to.

actuar, *vt* to work, actuate, operate; to set in motion.

acuarela, *nf* watercolor.

acuario, *nm* aquarium.

acuartelamiento, *nm* quartering, billeting.

acuartelar, *vt* to quarter; to confine to barracks.

acuático, *adj* aquatic, water.

acuatizar, *vi* to come down on the water, land on the sea.

acuciar, *vt* to urge on, goad, prod; to hasten; to harass.

acucioso, *adj* diligent, zealous, keen; eager.

acuchillado, *adj* 1. slashed 2. wary, schooled by bitter experience.

acuchillar, *vt* to cut, slash, hack; to slash; to stab (to death), knife.

acudir, *vi* 1. to come, come along, come up; to turn up; 2. to come (or go) to the rescue, go to help.

acuerdo, *nm* agreement, accord, decision, agreement, pact; understanding; perfect harmony.

aculturación, *nf* acculturation.

aculturar, *vt* to acculturate.

acullá, *adv* over there, yonder.

acumulador, *adj* 1. accumulative; 2. *nm* accumulator, storage battery.

acumular, *vt* to accumulate; to amass, gather collect; to pile (up).

acumularse, *vr* to accumulate, gather, pile up; to collect, put together.

acunar, *vt* to rock (to sleep).

acuñación, *nf* coining, minting; wedging.

acuñar, *vt* 1. to strike; to coin; 2. to finish successfully.

acupuntura, *nf* acupuncture.

acurrucarse, *vr* to squat, crouch; to huddle up, curl up.

acusación, *nf* accusation; accusation, charge, indictment.

acusar, *vt* 1. to accuse (of), charge (with), indict (on a charge of); 2. to denounce; to point to, proclaim the guilt of.

acusarse, *vr* to confess.

acusativo, *nm* accusative.

acústica, *nf* acoustics.

achacoso, *adj* sickly, ailing.

achantado, *adj* bashful, shy.

achantar, *vt* 1. to close 2. to intimidate; to take down; 3. *vi* to be quiet, shut up.

achaparrado, *adj* stunted; stocky, thickset, stumpy.

achaque, 1. *nm* sickliness, infirmity, weakness; ailment, malady; period; 2. defect, fault, weakness.

acharolado, *adj* patent leather.

achatar, *vt* to flatten.

achatarse, *vr* 1. to get flat; 2. to grow weak, decline; to lose heart, feel down.

achicado, *adj* chidlike, childish.

achicar, *vt* 1. to make smaller; to dwarf; to reduce; to shorten, take in; to minimize, diminish the importance of; 2. to scoop, bale (out); to pump out.

achicharrar, *vt* 1. to scorch, overheat; to fry crisp; to overcook, burn; 2. to bother, plague; 3. to shoot, riddle with bullets; 4. to flatten, crush.

achicharrarse, *vr* to scorch, get burnt.

achicharronar, *vt* to flatten, crush.

achiquillado, *adj* childish.

achispado, *adj* tight, tipsy.

achocolatado, *adj* 1. chocolate; like chocolate 2. dark brown, chocolate-colored, tan; 3. tar to be canned.

achuchar, *vt* 1. to crush, squeeze flat; 2. to shove, jostle; to harass, pester; 3. to urge on.

achucharse, *vr* to catch malaria; catch a chill.

adagio, *nm* adage, proverb.

adalid, *nm* leader, champion.

adamado, *adj* effeminate, soft; elegant, chic.

adán, *nm* slovenly fellow; lazy chap.

adaptable, *adj* adaptable; versatile.

adaptador, *nm* adapter.

adaptar, *vt* to adapt; to fit, make suitable; to adjust.

adaptarse, *vr* to adapt oneself; to be able to adapt oneself to the circumstances, know how to adjust to circumstances.

adecentar, *vt* to tidy up, clean up, make decent.

adecentarse, *vr* to tidy oneself up.

adecuado, *adj* adequate; fit, suitable; sufficient; appropriate; satisfactory.

adecuar, *vt* to adapt, fit, make suitable; to prepare.

adefesio, *nm* 1. piece of nonsense, absurdity; rubbish; 2. queer bird; 3. outlandish dress, ridiculous attire; 4. unwanted object.

adelantado, *adj* 1. advanced; 2. well-advanced, ahead of one's age, precocious; 3. *nm* governor (of a frontier province), captain-general.

adelantar, *vt* 1. to move forward, move on, advance; 2. to speed up, hurry along; 3. pay in advance; to lend; 4. put forward; 5. to get ahead of; 6. *vi* to go ahead, get on, make headway; to improve, progress; overtake.

adelante, *adv* forward, onward; ahead; further on.

adelanto, *nm* progress; advancement, loan, advance.

adelgazador, *adj* slimming.

adelgazar, *vt* 1. to make thin, make slender; whittle; to slim, reduce, slenderize; 2. *vi* to grow thin, lose weight; to slim, to split hairs.

además, *adv* besides; moreover, furthermore; also.

adentellar, *vi* to sink one's teeth into.

adentrarse, *vr* to go into, get into, get inside.

adentro, *adv* within, inside.

aderezar, *vt* to prepare, get ready, dress; to make beautiful, dress up, deck; to embellish, adorn; to prepare; to season, garnish; to dress; mix; to blend; to repair.

aderezo, *nm* 1. preparation; (salad) dressing; embellishment; mixing; blending; repair; 2. seasoning.

adeudado, *adj* 1. in debt, to owe; to be liable for; to charge a sum to an account, debit an account for a sum; 2. *vi* to become related by marriage.

adeudar, *vt* 1. to owe, to be liable for; 2. become related by marriage.

adeudarse, *vr* to run into debt.

adherencia, *nf* adherence, adhesion, bond connection; road holding, road holding qualities.

adherir, *vi* to adhere, stick to, espouse, follow.

adhesión, *nf* adhesion; adherence, support; membership; message of support.

adicción, *nf* addiction.

adición, *nf* 1. addition; adding up; 2. bill, check.

adicional, *adj* additional, extra, supplementary.

adicionar, *vt* to add; to add, add up.

adicto(a), *adj* 1. devoted to; 2. addicted to; 3. *nm/f* follower; supporter, fan; addict.

adiestrado, *adj* trained.

adiestrar, *vi* to train, teach, coach; to drill, to guide.

adinerado, *adj* wealthy, moneyed, well-off.

aditamento, *nm* complement, addition, accessory.

adivinar, *vt* to prophesy, foretell, guess; puzzle to solve; to guess correctly.

adivino(a), *nm/f* fortune-teller.

adjetivo, *adj* 1. adjectival 2. *nm* adjective.

adjudicar, vt 1. to award (to); 2. vr to appropriate something

adjuntar, vt to append, attach; to enclose.

adjunto, adj 1. joined on; attached (to); attached, enclosed 2. assistant.

administración, nf administration; management.

administrar, vt to manage, to run.

administrarse, vr to manage one's own life.

administrador, nm administrator, administrative officer, manager.

admiración, nf 1. admiration; 2. wonder, wonderment; amazement; 3. exclamation mark.

admirador, adj admirer.

admirar, vt 1. to admire; to respect, look up to; 2. to astonish, surprise.

admisión, nf admission (to); acceptance; intake, inlet.

admitido, adj accepted, allowed, agreed.

admitir, vt to admit (to, into); to accept, allow; to recognize.

adobar, vt to prepare, dress; to cook; to season.

adobo, nm preparation, dressing; cooking; pickling.

adoctrinador, adj indoctrinating, indoctrinatory.

adoctrinar, vt to teach, instruct, to indoctrinate.

adolecer, vi to be ill, fall ill, to be ill with.

adolescencia, nf adolescence.

adolescente, 1. adj adolescent; 2. nm/f adolescent; youngster, teenager.

adónde, conj where.

adopción, nf adoption.

adoptado, adj adopted child.

adoptar, vt to adopt.

adoración, nf adoration; worship.

adorar, vt to adore, to worship.

adormecedor, adj that sends one to sleep, soporific, sedative, dreamy.

adormecer, vi to make sleepy, send to sleep, to calm.

adornar, vt to adorn; to decorate, embellish; bedeck.

adorno, nm adornment; decoration, embellishment.

adquirir, vi to acquire, to obtain; to procure; to buy; to purchase.

adquisición, nf acquisition; procurement; purchase.

adrenalina, nf adrenalin.

aduana, nf customs, custom-house; custom-duty.

aduanero(a), nm/f customs officers.

aducir, vt to adduce, bring forward, to offer as proof, to provide, furnish.

adueñarse, vr to take possession of; to appropriate.

adulador(a), adj 1. flattering; 2. nm/f flatterer.

adular, vt to flatter.

adulto, adj adult; grown-up.

adusto, adj scorching hot; austere; severe; grim, stern; sullen.

advenedizo, adj foreigner; from outside; newcomer, newly arrived.

adversario(a), nm/f adversary; opponent.

adverso, adj opposite; facing; adverse, untoward, bad.

advertencia, nf warning; piece of advice; reminder.

advertido, adj sharp, wide-awake.

advertir, vi to notice, observe, to become aware of, to point out, to draw attention, to advise; to warn.

adyacente, adj adjacent.

aéreo, adj aerial; air; overhead; elevated.

aerobic, nm/f aerobics.

aerodinámico, adj aerodynamic; streamlined.

aeródromo, nm airdrome (US), airfield.

aerolínea, nf airline.

aerolito, nm meteorite.

aeromoza, nf air hostess, stewardess, flight attendant.

aeronáutica, nf aeronautics.

aeroplano, nm airplane.

aeropuerto, nm airport.

aerosol, nm aerosol.

afable, adj affable, good-natured; easy, pleasant.

afamado, adj famous, noted (for).

afamar, vt to make famous.

afamarse, vr to become famous, make a reputation.

afán, nm 1. hard work; 2. anxiety; solicitude; 3. desire, urge; zeal, eagerness.

afanar, vt to press, harass, bother; to hustle; to jostle.

afanoso, adj hard, heavy, laborious; tough, uphill; industrious; solicitous.

afear, vt 1. to make ugly, deface, spoil, disfigure; 2. to condemn, censure, decry.

afección, nf affection, fondness; inclination.

afectado, adj affected; stilted, precious.

afectante, adj disturbing, distressing.

afectar, vt 1. to affect, have an effect on; 2. move; 3. pretend.

afecto, adj 1. affectionate; attached to, fond of; inclined towards; 2. nm afection, fondness (for), attachment (to); 3. feeling, emotion.

afectuoso, adj affectionate.

afeitadora, nf electric razor, electric shaver.

afeitar, vt 1. to shave; to trim; 2. (women) to make up, paint, apply cosmetics to; 3. to brush, shave.

afeitarse, vr to shave, have a shave.

aferrado, adj stubborn, obstinate.

aferrar, vt to grasp, seize, grapple.

aferrarse, vr 1. to grapple; to anchor, moor; to grapple (together); 2. to stick to, stand by.

afianzar, vt 1. to strengthen, fasten, secure; to support; 2. to guarantee, vouch for; to stand surety for.

afianzarse, vr to steady oneself; to become strong, become established, to make oneself secure.

afición, nf 1. fondness, liking (for); taste (for), inclination; 2. hobby, pastime; interest.

aficionado, adj 1. enthusiastic; 2. keen on, fond of; 3. amateur.

aficionarse, vr to get fond of something.

afiche, nm poster; illustration, picture.

afidávit, nm affidavit, sworn statement.

afiebrado, adj feverish.

afilado, adj (borde) sharp; tapering, sharp.

afilador, nm knife grinder; steel sharpener; strop, razor strop.

afiladura, nf sharpening.

afilar, vi 1. to sharpen, put an edge on; to put a point on; to whet, grind; to strop. 2. to court; seduce.

afiliado, adj affiliated, member; subsidiary.

afinado, adj finished, polished; in tune.

afinar, 1. vt to perfect, put the finishing touch to; to refine, make more precise; to purify, to tune; 2. to sing in tune, play in tune.

afincado, nm farmer.

afincarse, vr (in a town, etc.) to establish oneself, settle.

afinidad, nf affinity; relationship, similarity, kinship.

afirmar, vt 1. to make firm, steady, secure, strengthen; 2. to affirm.

afirmativo, adj affirmative, positive.

aflicción, nf affliction; grief, sorrow.

afligido, adj grieving, sorrowing, heartbroken; stricken with.

afligir, vi 1. to afflict, to grieve, pain; 2. to beat, hit.

afligirse, vr to grieve.

aflojar, vt to slacken; to loosen, undo; to relax, to loosen, let go, to release, take off.

aflojarse, vr to slacken (off, up); to come loose, work loose; to abate; to cool (off), diminish.

afluencia, nf influx, flow; press; crowd, jam; attendance, number present, abundance, eloquence.

afluente, adj 1. flowing; 2. fluent; 3. nm tributary.

afluir, vi to flow.

afonía, nf hoarseness, state of having lost one's voice.

afónico, *adj* 1. hoarse, voiceless; 2. mute.

afortunado, *adj* fortunate, lucky.

afrenta, *nf* affront, insult, outrage.

afrentar, *vt* to affront, insult, outrage; to dishonor.

afrodisíaco, *adj* 1. aphrodisiac; 2. *nm* afrodisiac.

afrontar, *vt* 1. to bring face to face; 2. to confront, face; to deal with, tackle.

afuera, *adv* out, outside; Out of the way!, Get out!, Clear the way!; (*pl*) outskirts, outer suburbs.

agachar, *vt* to bend, bow.

ágape, *nm* banquet, feast.

agarradera, *nf* drawer pull, handle, pot-holder.

agarrar, *vt* grasp, grip; catch, hold of, pick up.

agencia, *nf* agency, office.

agenda, *nf* agenda, diary, notebook.

agente, *nm/f* agent.

agilidad, *nf* agility, nimbleness.

agilizar, *vt* 1. to speed up, improve, make more flexible; 2. *vr* to speed up.

agitado, *adj* agitated, upset, nervous.

agitar, *vt* wave (brazo, bandera); shake, sit; excite.

aglomeración, *nf* aglomeration, crowd, mass.

agobiar, *vt* weigh down, exhaust, oppress.

agobio, *nm* burden, strain; nervous strain, anxiety.

agonía, *nf* agony, death agony.

agonizar, *vt* 1. bother, pester; 2. *vi* in throes of death.

ágora, *nf* main square.

agorar, *vt* to predict, prophesy.

agorero(a), *adj* 1. prophetic; ominous; 2. *nm/f* soothsayer, fortuneteller, forecaster.

Agosto, *nm* August.

agotado, *adj* (with estar) to be exhausted, be worn out, to be finished, be sold out; to be out of stock; to be flat.

agotador, *adj* exhausting.

agotar, *vt* to exhaust, use up; finish.

agotarse, *vr* to become exhausted; to be finished, be used up; run out; to sell out; to go out of print; to exhaust oneself, wear oneself out.

agraciado, *adj* 1. graceful; nice, attractive; charming; 2. lucky.

agraciar, *vt* 1. to grace, adorn; to make more attractive; 2. pardon; 3. bestow something on someone, reward someone with something.

agradable, *adj* pleasant, agreeable, nice; enjoyable.

agradar, *vt* 1. to please, be pleasing to, be to the liking of; 2. *vi* to please; 3. *vr* to be pleased (with).

agradecer, *vt* to thank; to be grateful for.

agradecido, *adj* grateful; appreciative.

agrado, *nm* 1. affability; 2. taste, liking.

agrandar, *vt* to make bigger, enlarge, expand.

agrandarse, *vr* to get bigger.

agravado, *nm* robbery with aggravation.

agravante, *adj* 1. aggravating; 2. *nf* additional burden; unfortunate circumstances.

agravar, *vt* to weigh down, make heavier; to increase; to make worse; to aggravate, to oppress, burden (with).

agravarse, *vr* to worsen, get worse; to get more difficult.

agraviar, *vt* to wrong; to offend, insult.

agraviarse, *vr* to be offended, take offense.

agravio, *nm* wrong, injury; offense, insult.

agredir, *vt* to attack, assault, set upon.

agregada, *nf* 1. attached, assistant professor; 2. person newly added to a group; thing newly added to a collection.

agregar, *vt* 1. to add (to), to join; 2. to gather, collect; 3. to appoint, attach.

agremiar, *vt* to form into a union, unionize.

agremiarse, *vr* to form a union, to join a union

agresión, *nf* aggression, attack, assault.

agresivo, *adj* aggressive; forceful, vigorous.

agresor(a), *adj* 1. aggressor; attacker, assailant; 2. *nm/f* aggressor country.

agreste, *adj* 1. wild; 2. rough, uncouth.

agriado, *adj* 1. sour, sharp; 2. resentful; angry.

agriar, *vt* 1. to sour, turn sour; 2. to vex, annoy.

agriarse, *vr* 1. to turn sour. 2. to get cross, get exasperated; to become embittered.

agricultura, *nf* agriculture, farming.

agrietado, *adj* cracked; chapped.

agrietar, *vt* to crack, crack open; to chap.

agrietarse, *vr* to get cracked, get covered in cracks; to get chapped.

agrimensor(a), *nm/f* surveyor.

agrio, *adj* sour, tart, sour, disagreeable.

agripado, *adj* to have flu.

agriparse, *vr* to catch a cold; to get flu.

agro, *nm* farming, agriculture.

agronomía, *nf* agronomy, agriculture.

agrónomo(a), *adj* 1. agricultural, farming; 2. *nm/f* agronomist, agricultural expert.

agropecuario, *adj* farming, stock-breeding.

agrupación, *nf* 1. group, grouping; association; gathering; union; ensemble; 2. grouping.

agrupar, *vt* to group; to gather, to crowd together.

agruparse, *vr* to form a group; to gather, come together.

agua, *nf* water; fluid, liquid.

aguacate, *nm* avocado pear, avocado pear tree.

aguacero, *nm* shower (heavy), downpour.

aguador, *nm* water carrier, water seller.

aguajirado, *adj* withdrawn, timid.

aguantadero, *nm* hide-out.

aguantar, *vt* 1. to bear, endure, stand, put up with; to endure, bear; 2. *vi* to last, hold out; to resist.

aguantarse, *vr* 1. to restrain oneself, hold oneself back, sit tight; to put up with it; 2. to keep one's mouth shut, to hold back from doing something

aguar, *vt* 1. to water (down); 2. to spoil.

aguardadero, *nm* aguardado, hunter's blind.

aguardar, *vt* 1. to wait for, await; to expect; 2. *vi* to hold on; to wait.

aguardentería, *nf* liquor store.

aguardentero(a), *nm/f* liquor seller.

aguardiente, *nm* brandy, liquor.

aguarrás, *nm* turpentine.

agudeza, *nf* 1. acuteness, sharpness; 2. wit, wittiness; 3. witticism, witty saying.

agudización, *nf* sharpening; worsening.

agudizar, *vt* to sharpen, make more acute.

agudo, *adj* 1. sharp, pointed; acute; 2. high-pitched; shrill; piercing; 3. smart, clever; ready, lively.

agüero, *nm* omen, sign; prediction, forecast.

aguerrido, *adj* hardened, veteran.

aguijón, *nm* 1. point, goad, sting; prickle, spine; 2. stimulus.

águila, *nf* eagle.

aguileño, *adj* aquiline; sharp-featured; hawk-nosed.

aguilillo(a), *nm/f* fast horse.

aguilucho, *nm* eaglet, harrier; hawk, falcon.

aguinaldo, *nm* 1. Christmas, New Year gift; tip; (salary) bonus; 2. Christmas carol.

agujereado, *adj* full of holes, pierced with holes.

agujerear, *vt* to make holes in, pierce; to perforate.

agujero, *nm* 1. hole; 2. needle case; pincushion; 3. hide-out, safe house.

aguzado, *adj* sharp, on the ball.

aguzar, *vt* 1. to sharpen; 2. to incite, stir up.

aherrojar, *vt* to put in irons, fetter, shackle; to oppress.

ahí, *adv* there.

ahijada, *nf* goddaughter; protégée.

ahijado, *nm* godson; protégé.

ahijar, *vt* to adopt; mother.

ahilar, vt 1. to line up; 2. vi to go in single file.

ahitar, vt to cloy, surfeit.

ahito, adj stuffed.

ahogador, nm (Auto) choke.

ahogar, vt 1. to drown; to suffocate; to smother; to put out; to kill. 2. to afflict, oppress, crush.

ahondar, vt 1. to deepen, make deeper, dig out. 2. vi to study thoroughly, examine in depth.

ahondarse, vr to go (or sink) in more deeply.

ahora, adv now; just now; a moment ago; in a little while.

ahorcado(a), adj 1. flat broke; 2. nm/f hanged person.

ahorcajarse, vr to sit astride; straddle.

ahorcar, vt to hang.

ahorcarse, vr to hang oneself.

ahorita, adv right now, this very minute; a moment ago, just now; in a moment.

ahorrador, adj thrifty.

ahorrar, vt to save; to put by; to avoid.

ahorro, nm economy, saving; thrift; (pl) savings.

ahoyar, vt to dig holes in.

ahuecar, vt 1. to hollow (out), make a hollow in, to cup one's hand; 2. vi beat it!.

ahuecarse, vr to give oneself airs.

ahuesarse, vr 1. to go out of fashion; to go off (or rotten); to become unsaleable; 2. to get thin.

ahumado, adj smoked, cured with smoke.

ahumar, vt 1. to smoke, cure; 2. to make smoky.

ahuyentar, vt 1. drive away, frighten away; to put to flight; to keep off; 2. banish, dispel.

airar, vt to anger.

airarse, vr to get angry.

aire, nm 1. air; wind, draft; 2. appearance; 3. resemblance; family likeness; 4. humor, mood; 5. elegance; 6. tune, air.

airear, vi 1. to air, ventilate; 2. discuss at length.

airoso, adj 1. airy; drafty; windy; blowy; 2. graceful, elegant; jaunty; successful.

aislado, adj 1. isolated; cut off, shut off; lonely; 2. insulated.

aislante, adj 1. insulating; 2. nm insulator, insulating material.

aislar, vt 1. to isolate; to separate, detach, to cut off, shut off; 2. to insulate.

ajedrecista, nm/f chessplayer.

ajedrez, nm chess; chess set.

ajeno, adj 1. somebody else's, other people's; 2. outside; alien, foreign; inconsistent; 3. unaware (of), unsuspecting.

ajetreo, nm bustle; fuss; drudgery, hard work.

ají, nm chili, red pepper.

ajillo, nm chopped garlic, (alimento) cooked in garlic.

ajo, nm garlic; clove of garlic; garlic sauce.

ajuar, nm household furnishings; trousseau; dowry, bridal portion; layette.

ajustado, adj 1. right, fitting; in accordance with the law; 2. close.

ajustar, vt 1. to fit, to fasten, engage; 2. to adjust.

ajusticiar, vt to execute.

ala, nf wing.

alabador, adj approving, eulogistic.

alabanza, nf praise, eulogy.

alabar, vt to praise.

alabarse, vr to boast, to be pleased, be satisfied.

alacena, nm food cupboard, larder, closet.

alacrán, nm scorpion; gossip, scandalmonger.

alado, adj winged, with wings, swift.

alambicado, adj 1. distilled; 2. given sparingly, given grudgingly; 3. subtle, precious, refined.

alambicar, vt 1. to distil; 2. to polish, to overrefine; 3. scrutinize, investigate.

alambrada, nf wire netting, wire fence, barbed-wire fence, barbed-wire entanglement.

alambrar, vt to wire, to fence.

alambre, nm wire.

alameda, nf poplar grove, avenue, boulevard, tree-lined walk.

alancear, vt to spear.

alarde, nm review, show, display, parade; supreme effort, sprint.

alardear, vi to boast, brag.

alargador, nm extension lead.

alargar, vt to lengthen, prolong, extend, to stretch.

alarido, nm shriek.

alarma, nf alarm, signal, warning bell.

alarmar, vt to alarm; to frighten, to alert, to rouse.

alazán, adj 1. sorrel; 2. nm sorrel horse.

alba, nf dawn, daybreak; at dawn, at daybreak.

albacea, nm/f executor, executrix.

albañal, nm drain, sewer; dung heap, mess, muck.

albañil, nm bricklayer, mason, building worker.

albañilería, nf brickwork, masonry, bricklaying.

albaricoque, nm apricot.

albedrío, nm (libre) free will, whim, fancy, pleasure.

alberca, nf cistern, tank, reservoir, swimming pool.

albergar, vt to shelter, give shelter to; to lodge, put up.

albergarse, vr to shelter; to lodge, stay.

albo, adj white.

albóndiga, nf meatball.

alborada, nf dawn; reveille, dawn song.

alborear, vi to dawn.

albornoz, nm burnous(e), bathing wrap, bathrobe.

alborotado, adj 1. agitated, excited, noisy, rough; 2. hasty, rash; reckless.

alborotador(a), adj 1. turbulent, rebellious; boisterous, noisy; 2. nm/f agitator, troublemaker, mischief-maker, rioter.

alborotar, vt 1. to disturb, agitate, stir up; 2. vi to make a racket, make a row.

alboroto, nm disturbance, racket, row, uproar.

alborotoso(a), adj 1. troublesome, riotous; 2. nm/f troublemaker.

alborozar, vt to gladden, fill with joy.

alborozo, nm joy, merriment.

álbum, nm album; (Music) long-playing record.

albur, nm 1. bleak; 2. chance, risk.

alcachofa, nf artichoke.

alcaide, nm governor; warder, jailer.

alcalde, nm mayor.

alcaldía, nf mayoralty, office of mayor.

alcance, nm 1. reach; 2. range; scope; grasp.

alcancía, nf moneybox; collection box, poorbox.

alcantarilla, nf drain; sewer.

alcantarillado, nm sewer system, drains.

alcantarillar, vt to lay sewers in, provide drains for.

alcanzado, adj 1. hard up, broke; 2. tired; slow, late.

alcanzar, vt 1. to catch, catch up; 2. to hit, strike.

alcayata, nf meat hook, spike; hook.

alcázar, nm fortress, citadel; royal palace.

alce, nm (Zool) elk, moose.

alcoba, nf bedroom; sleeping compartment.

alcohol, nm alcohol.

alcohólico(a), adj, nm/f alcoholic.

alcoholizado(a), nm/f alcoholic.

alcoholizarse, vr to drink heavily.

alcuza, nf olive-oil bottle.

aldaba, nf door-knocker; bolt, latch, crossbar.

aldabilla, nf latch.

aldabón, nm large door-knocker; large handle.

aldea, nf village, hamlet.

aldeano(a), adj 1. village; rustic, rude; 2. provincial, parish-pump; 3. nm/f villager; peasant.

aleación, *nf* alloy.
aleado, *adj* alloyed, alloy.
alear, *vt* to alloy.
alebrestar, *vt* to distress, disturb; to excite.
aleccionar, *vt* to instruct, enlighten, teach a lesson to; to train.
alegación, *nf* declaration (in court); citation; argument.
alegador, *adj* argumentative.
alegar, *vt* **1.** to cite, invoke; to state; to bring forward as an argument; **2.** to argue against, dispute.
alegato, *nm* **1.** claim; **2.** bill (of indictment); plea.
alegrar, *vt* to cheer (up), gladden; to make merry, make happy.
alegrarse, *vr* to be glad, be happy, rejoice.
alegre, *adj* happy, merry, glad; cheerful.
alegría, *nf* happiness, joy; gladness; cheerfulness.
alejado, *adj* distant, remote (from).
alejar, *vt* to remove, move away (from).
alemán(ana), *adj, nm/f* German.
alentador, *adj* encouraging.
alentar, *vt* to encourage, cheer, inspire.
alergia, *nf* allergy.
alérgico, *adj* allergic.
alergista, *nm/f* allergist, specialist in allergies.
alerta, *interj* **1.** watch out!; **2.** *adv* y *adj* alert.
alertar, *vt* **1.** to alert, warn, put on one's guard; **2.** *vi* to be alert, keep one's eyes open.
aleta, *nf* small wing; fin.
aletargar, *vt* to make drowsy, make lethargic.
aletargarse, *vr* to grow drowsy, become lethargic; to get numb.
aletear, *vi* to flutter, flap its wings; (fish) to move its fins.
aleudar, *vt* to leaven, ferment with yeast.
alfabético, *adj* alphabetic(al).
alfabetización, *nf* teaching literacy (or reading and writing).
alfabetizador(a), *nm/f* literacy tutor.
alfabetizar, *vt* **1.** to alphabetize, arrange alphabetically; **2.** to teach someone to read and write.
alfabeto, *nm* alphabet.
alfarería, *nf* pottery; pottery shop.
alfarero(a), *nm/f* potter.
alferecía, *nf* epilepsy.
alférez, *nm* second lieutenant.
alfiler, *nm* pin; brooch, clip.
alfiletero, *nm* needle case; pincushion.
alfombra, *nf* carpet; rug, mat.
alfombrilla, *nf* rug, mat.
alforja, *nf* saddlebag; knapsack.
alforza, *nf* pleat, tuck; slash, scar.
alforzar, *vt* to pleat, tuck.
alga, *nf* seaweed, alga.
algarabía, *nf* arabic; gibberish; gabble; din.
álgebra, *nf* algebra.
algebraico, *adj* algebraic.
algo, *pron* something; anything.
algodón, *nm* cotton; wadding; swab.
algodonal, *nm* cotton plantation.
algodonar, *vt* to stuff with cotton wool, wad.
algodonero, *adj* **1.** cotton; **2.** *nm* cotton grower; cotton dealer, cotton plant.
alguacil, *nm* governor; bailiff, constable.
alguien, *pron* someone, somebody; anybody.
alguno, *adj* some, any; (*pl*) a few.
alhaja, *nf* jewel, gem; precious object, treasure.
alhajera, *nf* jewel box.
aliado(a), *adj* **1.** allied; **2.** *nm/f* ally.
alianza, *nf* alliance.
aliar, *vt* to ally, bring into an alliance.
alicatar, *vt* to shape, cut.

alicates, *nm/f* pliers, pincers; wire-cutters.
aliciente, *nm* incentive, inducement; lure; attraction.
alienación, *nf* alienation; mental derangement.
alienado(a), *adj* **1.** alienated; insane, mentally ill; **2.** *nm/f* alienated person; lunatic, mad person.
aliento, *nm* **1.** breath; breathing, respiration; **2.** courage, spirit; strength.
aligerar, *vt* to lighten; to ease, relieve, alleviate.
aligerarse, *vr* **1.** to get lighter; **2.** to beat it, get out.
alimentación, *nf* **1.** feeding, nourishment; **2.** supply.
alimentador, *nm* feeder.
alimentar, *vt* to feed, nourish.
alimento, *nm* food; nourishment.
alindar, *vt* **1.** (land) to mark off, mark out; **2.** to embellish, make pretty, make look nice; **3.** *vi* to adjoin, be adjacent.
alinderar, *vt* to mark out the boundaries of.
alineación, *nf* alignment.
alinear, *vt* to align; to line up, put into line.
alinearse, *vr* to line up; to fall in, form up.
alisador, *nm* polisher; smoothing tool.
alisar, *vt* to smooth (down); to polish, burnish.
alistamiento, *nm* enrolment; enlistment.
alistar, *vt* **1.** to list, put on a list; **2.** to prepare.
aliviar, *vt* to lighten; to ease, relieve.
aliviarse, *vr* to diminish, become more bearable.
alivio, *nm* alleviation, relief; mitigation.
alma, *nf* soul; spirit.
almacén, *nm* warehouse, store; depository.
almacenar, *vt* to store, put into storage, keep in store.
almácigo, *nm* seedbed, nursery.
almanaque, *nm* almanac.
almeja, *nf* shellfish, cockle, clam.
almenara, *nf* beacon, chandelier.
almendra, *nf* almond.
almendrada, *nf* almond milk shake.
almendrado, *adj* almond-shaped, pear-shaped.
almendrera, *nf* almond tree.
almíbar, *nm* syrup.
almidón, *nm* starch; paste.
almidonar, *vt* to starch.
almirante, *nm* admiral.
almirez, *nm* mortar.
almohada, *nf* pillow; bolster; cushion.
almohadón, *nm* large pillow, bolster; hassock.
almorzar, *vt* **1.** to have for lunch, lunch on; **2.** *vi* to lunch, have lunch.
almuerzo, *nm* lunch, luncheon; wedding breakfast.
alocado, *adj* crazy, mad.
alocarse, *vr* to go crazy.
alocución, *nf* allocution; speech, address.
alojado(a), *nm/f* guest, lodger.
alojar, *vt* to lodge, accommodate, put up, house.
alojarse, *vr* to lodge, be lodged; to stay.
alpargata, *nf* rope-soled sandal, canvas sandal.
alpinista, *nm/f* mountaineer, climber.
alquilador(a), *nm/f* renter, hirer; tenant, lessee.
alquilar, *vt* to rent (out), let; to hire.
alquiler, *nm* letting, renting; hire.
alquimista, *nm* alchemist.
alquitrán, *nm* tar.
alquitranar, *vt* to tar.
alrededor, *adv* around, about.
alta, *nf* discharge from hospital.
altanería, *nf* **1.** haughtiness, disdain, arrogance; **2.** hawking, falconry.
altanero, *adj* haughty, disdainful, arrogant.
altar, *nm* altar.
altavoz, *nm* loudspeaker; amplifier.

alteración, *nf* **1.** alteration, change; **2.** upset, disturbance; irregularity.

alterar, *vt* to alter, to change.

altercado, *nm* argument, altercation.

altercar, *vi* to argue, quarrel, wrangle.

alternación, *nf* alternation.

alternador, *nm* alternator.

alternar, *vt* **1.** to alternate; to vary; **2.** *vi* to alternate.

alternativa, *nf* alternative, option, choice.

alteza, *nf* **1.** height; **2.** sublimity; **3.** (Su Alteza) His (or Her) Royal Highness.

altísimo, *adj* very high.

altitud, *nf* height; altitude, elevation.

altivez, *nf* haughtiness, arrogance.

altivo, *adj* haughty, arrogant.

alto, *adj* **1.** high; tall; **2.** lofty, elevated; high; **3.** loud; sharp; **4.** *nm* halt; stop; pause.

altoparlante, *nm* loudspeaker.

altruísmo, *nm* altruism, unselfishness.

altruísta, *adj,* *nm/f* altruistic, unselfish.

altura, *nf* height; altitude.

alucinación, *nf* hallucination, delusion.

alucinador, *adj* hallucinatory, deceptive.

alucinar, *vt* to hallucinate, delude, deceive.

alud, *nm* avalanche.

aludido, *adj* aforesaid, above-mentioned.

aludir, *vi* to allude to, mention.

alumbrado, *adj, nm* lighting, lighting system.

alumbramiento, *nm* **1.** lighting; **2.** childbirth.

alumbrar, *vt* **1.** to light (up), illuminate, shed light on; **2.** to give birth, have a baby.

aluminio, *nm* aluminum.

alumnado, *nm* pupils, roll; student body.

alumno(a), *nm/f* pupil, student.

alunizaje, *nm* landing on the moon.

alunizar, *vi* to land on the moon.

alusión, *nf* allusion, mention, reference.

alusivo, *adj* allusive.

alverja, *nf* **1.** vetch; **2.** pea.

alverjilla, *nf* sweet pea.

alza, *nf* rise.

alzado, *adj* raised, elevated.

alzar, *vt* **1.** to lift (up), raise (up); to hoist (up); **2.** to remove; to steal.

alzarse, *vr* **1.** to rise, get up, stand up; **2.** to revolt.

allá, *adv* there, over there; up there, down there.

allanamiento, *nm* levelling, flattening; smoothing.

allanar, *vt* **1.** to level (out), flatten, make even, to smooth (down); **2.** to force an entry into, break into, burgle.

allegado, *adj* **1.** near, close; allied; **2.** closely related.

allegar, *vt* to gather (together), collect.

allegarse, *vr* to arrive, approach.

allí, *adv* there.

amabilidad, *nf* kindness; niceness.

amable, *adj* kind; nice; lovable.

amado(a), *adj* dear, beloved.

amador(a), *adj* **1.** loving, fond; **2.** *nm/f* lover.

amaestrado(a), *adj* trained.

amaestrar, *vt* to train.

amagar, *vt* to threaten, portend; to show signs of.

amago, *nm* threat; threatening gesture.

amalgamar, *vt* to amalgamate; to combine, mix.

amamantar, *vt* to suckle, nurse.

amanecer, *nm* dawn, daybreak.

amanezca, *nf* dawn; breakfast.

amansador(a), *nm/f* tamer; horse breaker.

amansar, *vt* to tame; to break in.

amanuense, *nm/f* scribe, copyist; secretary.

amañado, *adj* **1.** skillful, clever; **2.** fake, faked.

amañar, *vt* to do skillfully, perform cleverly.

amar, *vt* to love.

amaraje, *nm* landing (on the sea); splashdown.

amargo, *adj* bitter; sharp, tart.

amargura, *nf* bitterness; sharpness, tartness.

amarillear, *vi* to go yellow, turn yellow.

amarillento, *adj* yellowish, sallow, pale.

amarillo, *adj* yellow.

amarradera, *nf* mooring; rope, line, tether.

amarrado, *adj* mean, stingy.

amarrar, *vt* to fasten, hitch, tie up.

amartillar, *vt* to hammer; (escopeta) to cock.

amasado, *adj* doughy.

amasador(a), *nm/f* **1.** kneader, baker; **2.** kneading machine.

amasar, *vt* to knead; to mix; massage.

amasijo, *nm* kneading; mixing; mashing.

amateur, *adj, nm/f* amateur.

amatista, *nf* amethyst.

amazona, *nf* Amazon; horsewoman, rider.

ambición, *nf* ambition; ambitiousness, egotism.

ambicionar, *vt* to aspire to, seek; strive after.

ambicioso, *adj* ambitious.

ambidextro, *adj* ambidextrous.

ambientador, *nm* air-freshener.

ambiente, *adj* ambient; enviroment; atmosphere.

ambigüedad, *nf* ambiguity.

ambiguo, *adj* ambiguous; doubtful; uncertain.

ámbito, *nm* compass, field; scope, range, area.

ambos, *adj, pron* both.

ambulancia, *nf* ambulance.

ambulante, *adj* walking; roving; itinerant.

ambulatorio, *nm* out-patients department.

amedrentador, *adj* frightening, menacing.

amedrentar, *vt* to scare, frighten; to intimidate.

amenaza, *nf* threat, menace.

amenazador, *adj* threatening; menacing.

amenazar, *vt* to threaten, menace.

amenguar, *vt* to lessen, diminish.

amenidad, *nf* pleasantness, agreeableness; grace.

amenizar, *vt* to make pleasant, make more agreeable to.

América, *nf* America (_ Central), Central America (_ del Norte), North America; (_ del Sur), South America.

americana, *nf* coat, sports jacket.

americanizar, *vt* to americanize.

americano, *adj* American.

ameritar, *vt* to deserve.

ametralladora, *nf* machine gun.

amiba, *nf* amoeba.

amiga, *nf* friend; girlfriend.

amigarse, *vr* to get friendly; to set up house together.

amigo, *adj* **1.** friendly; to be fond of; **2.** *nm* friend; boyfriend.

amilanar, *vt* to scare, intimidate.

aminorar, *vt* to lessen, diminish.

amistad, *nf* friendship; friendly relationship.

amistar, *vt* to bring together, make friends of; to bring about a reconciliation between.

amistoso, *adj* friendly, amicable; friendly.

amnesia, *nf* amnesia; loss of memory.

amnistía, *nf* amnesty.

amnistiar, *vt* to amnesty, grant an amnesty to.

amo, *nm* **1.** master; **2.** owner; proprietor.

amodorrarse, *vr* to get sleepy, get drowsy; to fall into a stupor; to go to sleep.

amoladera, *nf* whetstone, grindstone.

amolador, *adj* **1.** boring, tedious; **2.** *nm* knife-grinder.

amoladura, *nf* grinding, sharpening.

amolar, *vt* to grind, sharpen.

amoldar, *vt* to mold; to fashion; to adapt, adjust.

amonestación, *nf* warning; piece of advice.

amonestador, *adj* warning, cautionary.

amonestar, *vt* to warn; to advise, admonish.

amontonado, *adj* heaped (up), piled up.

amontonar, *vt* to heap (up), pile (up).

amor, *nm* love.

amoral, *adj* amoral.

amoratado, *adj* purple, purplish; livid.

amorcillo, *nm* flirtation, light-hearted affair.

amordazar, *vt* to gag; to muzzle, silence.

amorfo, *adj* amorphous, formless, shapeless.

amorío, *nm* love affair, romance.

amoroso, *adj* loving, affectionate, tender.

amortajar, *vt* to lay out; to shroud.

amortecer, *vt* (ruido) to deaden, muffle.

amortiguador, *adj* deadening, muffling; softening; shock abosrber.

amortizar, *vt* to amortize; to redeem.

amotinado(a), *adj* 1. riotous, violent; mutinous; 2. *nm/f* rioter, mutineer.

amotinar, *vt* to stir up, incite to riot.

amotinarse, *vr* to riot; to rise up, revolt, rebel.

amparador(a), *adj* 1. helping, protecting, protective; 2. *nm/f* protector.

amparar, *vt* to protect (from), shelter, help.

ampararse, *vr* to seek protection, seek help.

ampliación, *nf* enlargement, extension; expansion.

ampliado, *nm* general meeting; mass meeting.

ampliar, *vt* to enlarge, extend.

amplificador, *nm* amplifier.

amplio, *adj* spacious, wide; extensive; roomy.

ampolla, *nf* bubble; blister; flask.

ampollarse, *vr* to blister, form blisters.

ampolleta, *nf* small bottle; hourglass, vial.

amputación, *nf* amputation.

amputado(a), *nm/f* amputee.

amputar, *vt* to amputate, cut off.

amueblado, *adj* furnished.

amueblar, *vt* to furnish (with).

amularse, *vr* to get stubborn, dig one's heels in.

amuleto, *nm* amulet, charm.

amurallado, *adj* (ciudad) walled.

amurallar, *vt* to wall, wall in, fortify.

anacarado, *adj* pearly, mother of-pearl.

anacronía, *nf* timelessness.

anacrónico, *adj* anachronistic.

anagrama, *nm* anagram.

analfabeto, *adj* illiterate.

analgesia, *nf* analgesia.

analgésico, *nm* analgesic, pain killer.

análisis, *nm* analysis; breakdown.

analítico, *adj* analytic(al).

analogía, *nf* analogy; similarity.

analógico, *adj* analogical.

análogo, *adj* analogous, similar.

anaquel, *nm* shelf.

anaranjado, *adj* orange (colored).

anarquía, *nf* anarchy.

anarquista, *adj* 1. anarchist(ic); 2. *nm/f* anarchist.

anatema, *nm* anathema.

anatomía, *nf* anatomy.

anatómico, *adj* anatomical.

anca, *nf* 1. haunch; rump; 2. toasted maize.

ancestral, *adj* ancient.

ancestro, *nm* ancestor; ancestry.

anciano(a), *adj* 1. old, aged; 2. *nm* old man; 3. *nf* old woman.

ancla, *nf* anchor.

ancladero, *nm* anchorage.

anclar, *vi* to anchor, drop anchor.

ancho, *adj* wide, broad.

anchoa, *nf* anchovy.

andaderas, *nf* baby-walker.

andadero, *adj* passable, easy to traverse.

andado, *adj* worn, well-trodden.

andador, *adj* fast-walking; a good walker.

andamio, *nm* scaffold; stage, stand.

andanada, *nf* broadside; big rocket; reprimand.

andante, *adj* walking; errant.

andanza, *nf* fortune, fate.

andar, *vt* to go, cover, travel; walk.

ándele, *interj* come on!

andino, *adj* Andean, of the Andes.

anécdota, *nf* anecdote, story; incident.

anegación, *nf* drowning; flooding.

anegar, *vt* to drown, flood.

anemia, *nf* anemia.

anémico, *adj* anemic.

anestesia, *nf* anesthesia.

anestesiar, *vt* to anesthetize, give an anesthetic to.

anexar, *vt* to annex; to append.

anexo, *adj* 1. attached; dependent, 2. *nm* annex.

anfibio, *adj* amphibious; amphibian.

anfiteatro, *nm* amphitheater.

anfitrión, *nm* host.

anfitriona, *nf* hostess.

ánfora, *nf* amphora; ballot box.

ángel, *nm* angel.

angelito, *nm* little angel.

angina, *nf* angina, tonsil.

anglicano(a), *adj*, *nm/f* Anglican.

anglosajón(ona), *adj*, *nm/f* Anglo-Saxon.

angostar, *vt* to narrow; to make smaller.

angosto, *adj* narrow.

anguila, *nf* eel.

ángulo, *nm* angle; corner; bend, turning.

anguloso, *adj* angular, sharp; tortuous, full of bends.

angurria, *nf* voracious hunger, greed.

angustia, *nf* anguish, distress.

angustiado, *adj* anguished, distressed; anxious.

angustiar, *vt* to distress, grieve, cause anguish to.

anhelante, *adj* 1. panting; 2. eager; longing, yearning.

anhelar, *vt* to be eager for; to long for, yearn for, crave.

anhelo, *nm* eagerness; longing, yearning.

anillar, *vt* to make into a ring, make rings in, to fasten with a ring.

anillo, *nm* ring; cigar band; wedding ring.

animación, *nf* liveliness, life; bustle, activity, movement, animation; sprightliness.

animado, *adj* 1. lively, gay; bustling, busy, animated; sprightly; merry, in high spirits; 2. well-attended, popular; 3. animate; 4. (Med) recovering, improving.

animador, *nm* master of ceremonies; presenter; cheerleader.

animal, *adj* 1. animal; 2. stupid; 3. *nm* pet.

animalada, *nf* 1. group (or herd) of animals; 2. foolishness, stupidity; silly thing; coarse thing.

animar, *vt* 1. to animate, give life to; 2. to enliven; 3. to cheer up; to encourage.

anímico *adj* mental.

ánimo, *nm* 1. mind; soul, spirit. 2. courage, pluck; nerve; energy. 3. intention, purpose.

aniquilación, *nf* annihilation, destruction.

aniquilar, *vi* to annihilate, destroy, obliterate.

aniversario, *nm* anniversary.

anoche, *adv* last night.

anochecer, *vt* 1. to get dark. 2. to arrive at night fall; 3. *nm* dusk, nightfall.

anomalía, *nf* anomaly.

anonimato, *nm* anonymity.

anónimo, *adj* anonymous; nameless.

ante, *adv* 1. before; first; once, previously, formerly; sooner, before now; 2. *prep* before, in the presence of, in the face of; 3. *pref* ante. . .

anteayer, *adv* the day before yesterday.

antebrazo, *nm* forearm.

antecedente, *adj* 1. previous, preceding, foregoing; 2. *nm* antecedent.

anteceder, *vt* to precede, go before.

antecesor(a), *adj* 1. preceding, former; 2. *nm/f* predecesor, ancestor, forbear.

antedicho, *adj* aforesaid, aforementioned.

antelación, *nf* precedence, in advance, beforehand.

antena, *nf* antenna.

anteojo, *nm* eyeglass, spyglass, telescope.

antepasado, *nm* ancestor, forbear, forefather.

anteponer, *vt* 1. to place in front; 2. to prefer.

anterior, *adj* 1. front, fore; 2. preceding, previous.

antes, *adv* 1. before; first, formerly; 2. sooner, rather.

antesala, *nf* anteroom, antechamber, lobby.

antiácido, *adj, nm* antiacid.

antiaéreo, *adj* 1. antiaircraft; 2. *nm* antiaircraft gun.

antiamericano, *adj* anti-American, un-American.

antibiótico, *adj* 1. *antibiótico;* 2. *nm* antibiotic.

anticipación, *nf* anticipation; foretaste.

anticipado, *adj* future, early; advance, beforehand.

anticipar, *vt* to bring forward, advance; to anticipate.

anticipo, *nm* an advance payment.

anticoagulante, *adj* 1. anticoagulant; 2. *nm* anticoagulant.

anticonceptivo, *adj* 1. birth-control, family-planning, contraceptive; 2. *nm* birth-control methods, contraceptive devices, contraceptive pill.

anticuado, *adj* antiquated.

anticuerpo, *nm* antibody.

antidepresivo, *adj* 1. antidepressant; 2. *nm* stimulant.

antídoto, *nm* antidote.

antifaz, *nm* 1. mask; veil; 2. condom.

antigás, *adj* gasmask.

antigripal, *adj* flu vaccine.

antigüedad, *nf* antiquity.

antiguo, *adj* old; ancient; vintage, classic.

antihigiénico, *adj* unhygienic, unsanitary.

antihumano, *adj* inhuman.

antílope, *nm* antelope.

antillano, *adj* West Indian, of the Antilles.

antiniebla, *nm* fog-lamp.

antinuclear, *adj* antinuclear.

antipatía, *nf* antipathy, dislike; unfriendliness.

antipático, *adj* disagreeable, unpleasant, antipathetic; uncongenial.

antirrobo, *adj* 1. (sistema) anti-theft system; 2. *nm* anti-theft device.

antiséptico, *adj, nm* antiseptic.

antisocial, *adj* antisocial.

antiterrorista, *adj* against terrorism.

antojado, *adj* taken by, hankering after; craving for.

antojo, *nm* 1. caprice, whim, passing fancy, notion; 2. craving.

antología, *nf* anthology.

antológico, *adj* selective exhibition; a goal for the history books.

antorcha, *nf* torch; lamp.

antropólogo(a) *nm/f* anthropologist.

anual, *adj* annual.

anualidad, *nf* 1. annuity; annual payment; 2. annual occurrence.

anudar, vt to knot, tie; to join, link, unite.

anulación, *nf* annulment, cancellation; repeal.

anular, *vt* to annul, cancel; to overrule.

anularse, *vr* to lose one's identity; to renounce everything.

anunciador, *nm* announcer.

anunciante, *nm/f* advertiser.

anunciar, *vt* to announce; to proclaim; foreshadow.

anuncio, *nm* 1. announcement; sign, omen; notice; 2. advertisement; placard, poster.

anzuelo, *nm* hook, fish hook; bait.

añadidura, *nf* addition, extra; thing added.

añadir, *vt* to add; to increase; to add, lend.

año, *nm* year.

añojo(a) *nm/f* yearling.

añorar, *vt* 1. to long for, yearn for, to grieve for, to mourn; 2. *vi* to yearn, pine, grieve.

apacentadero, *nm* pasture, pasture land.

apacentar, *vt* to pasture, graze, feed.

apacible, *adj* gentle, mild.

apaciguador, *adj* pacifying, calming, soothing.

apaciguar, *vt* to pacify, appease, mollify; to calm down; to appease.

apadrinar, *vt* to sponsor, to back.

apagado, *adj* 1. extinct, to be out; to be off; 2. muted, muffled, dull; timid. 3. quiet, lusterless, lifeless; listless, spiritless, colorless.

apagador, *nm* 1. extinguisher. 2. silencer, muffler; damper; on-off switch.

apagar, *vt* 1. put out, extinguish, quench, to put out, turn off, to switch off, to snuff; to empty, discharge; to slake; to quench; 2. to silence, muffle, deaden; to mute, damp; 3. to dull, tone down, soften.

apalancado, *adj* settled, established.

apalancar, *vt* 1. lever up, move (lift) with a crowbar; 2. to support; 3. to keep; 4. *vi* to hide; to settle down, to find a place.

apalear, *vt* to beat, thrash; to beat; to winnow.

apañado, *adj* 1. skilful, clever, handy; 2. suitable.

apañar, 1. *vt* to take hold of, grasp, seize, to pick up; 2. to dress, dress up; to wrap up; to mend, patch up.

aparador, *nm* showcase; shop window; workshop.

aparato, *nm* apparatus, device; piece of equipment, machine; (domestic) appliance.

aparcamiento, *nm* 1. parking; 2. parking lot.

aparcar, *vt* to park.

aparear, *vt* 1. to pair, match; to level up; 2. (animal) to mate, pair.

aparecer, *vi* to appear; to show up, turn up; to come into sight; to loom up; to come out.

aparecido, *nm* ghost.

aparejado, *adj* suitable, ready.

aparejar, *vt* to prepare, prime; harness.

aparejarse, *vr* to get ready; to equip oneself.

aparejo, *nm* 1. preparation; 2. equipment, tackle; 3. rig; 4. lifting gear; 5. harness; saddle.

aparentar, *vt* to feign, affect.

aparente, *adj* 1. apparent, seeming; unreal; deceptive; 2. visible, evident; outward.

aparición, *nf* 1. appearance; public appearance; 2. apparition, specter.

apariencia, *nf* 1. appearance, aspect, look(s); 2. outward appearance, seemingly; 3. probability.

apartado, *adj* 1. separated; remote, out-of-the-way; 2. *nm* spare room; side room; 3. post-office box.

apartar, *vt* to separate, divide, take away (from); to remove, move away, put aside; to extract; cut out; to sort; to shunt; to set aside, waive.

apartarse, *vr* 1. to part, separate; to become separated; 2. to move away, withdraw, retire (from); to keep away (from), stand aside.

aparte, *adv* apart, aside; separately; besides; aside.

apasionado(a), *adj* 1. passionate; intense, emotional; fervent, enthusiastic; 2. biased, partial; 3. *nm/f* admirer, devotee.

apasionar, *vt* 1. to fill with passion; make a strong appeal to; to stir; 2. to afflict, torment.

apasionarse, *vr* 1. to get excited, be roused, work oneself up; 2. to become biased.

apatía, *nf* apathy; listlessness.

apátrida, *adj* stateless; unpatriotic, unpatriotic person.

apedrear, *vt* 1. to stone, pelt with stones; to stone to death; 2. *vi* to hail.

apedrearse, *vr* to be damaged by hail.

apegado, *adj* attached to, devoted to, fond of.

apego, *nm* attachment to, devotion to, fondness for.

apelación, *nf* 1. appeal; 2. remedy.

apelar, *vi* to appeal (against), have recourse to, call on.

apellidar, *vt* to name, surname, call.

apellidarse, *vr* to be called, have as a surname.

apellido, *nm* name; surname; maiden name.

apenado, *adj* ashamed, embarrassed; sad, sorry; timid.

apenarse, *vr* 1. to grieve, sorrow, distress oneself; 2. to feel embarrassed, feel ashamed; to be sorry.

apenas, *adv* hardly, scarcely.

apéndice, *nm* appendix; appendage; appendix.

apendicitis, *nf* appendicitis.

apercibir, 1. *vi* to prepare, make ready, to furnish, provide; 2. to warn, advise.

aperitivo, *nm* appetizer, snack; aperitif.

apero, *nm* tools, gear; equipment; implement.

apertura, *nf* 1. opening. openness, liberalization; 2. opening, start.

apesadumbrado, *adj* grieved, sad, distressed.

apestado, *adj* stinking; infected.

apestar, *vt* 1. to infect (with the plague); 2. to corrupt, spoil, vitiate. 3. to stink.

apestoso, *adj* 1. stinking; awful, pestilential; 2. annoying; sickening, nauseating.

apetecer, *vt* 1. to crave, long for, yearn for; 2. to appeal, to attract.

apetencia, *nf* hunger, appetite; hunger, craving, desire (for); inclination.

apetito, *nm* 1. appetite (for); 2. desire, relish (for).

apiadar, *vt* to move to pity.

apiadarse, *vr* to take pity on, express pity for.

apilar, *vt* to pile up, heap up, stack.

apiñado, *adj* 1. crowded, packed, congested (with); 2. cone shaped, pyramidal.

apiñar, *vt* to crowd together, bunch together; to pack in, squeeze together; to overcrowd.

apio, *nm* celery.

apisonadora, *nf* steamroller, road roller.

apisonar, *vt* to roll, roll flat; to tamp down, ram down.

aplacar, *vt* to appease; to soothe, calm down; to satisfy.

aplanar, *vt* 1. to smooth, level, make even; to roll, flat, flatten; to iron; 2. to knock out, bowl over with surprise.

aplanarse, *vr* 1. to collapse, cave in, fall down; 2. to get discouraged; to become lethargic.

aplastante, *adj* overwhelming, crushing.

aplastar, *vt* 1. flatten (out), squash, crush (flat); 2. crush, overwhelm; 3. flatten, leave speechless.

aplaudir, *vi* to applaud, cheer, clap; to approve.

aplauso, *nm* applause; approval, acclaim; cheering.

aplazar, *vt* 1. to postpone, put off, defer; hold over; 2. to set another time for, set a date for; to summon, convene.

aplicación, *nf* 1. application; 2. industry.

aplicado, *adj* 1. applied; 2. studious; diligent.

aplicar, *vt* to apply (to); to devote, assign (to), earmark (for); to attribute, impute (to).

aplomar, *vt* to plumb, test with a plumb line; to make perpendicular, make straight.

aplomarse, *vr* 1. to collapse, cave in, fall down; 2. to gain confidence. 3. to get embarrassed.

aplomo, *nm* self-possession, assurance, aplomb; gravity, seriousness; nerve.

apócrifo, *adj* apocryphal; false, spurious.

apodar, *vt* to nickname, dub, call; to label.

apoderado, *nm* agent, representative; proxy, attorney; manager.

apoderar, *vt* 1. to authorize, empower; 2. to grant power of attorney to.

apoderarse, *vr* (de) to get hold of, seize, take possession of.

apologética, *nf* apologetic.

apología, *nf* defense; eulogy; apology.

aporcar, to earth up.

aporrear, *vt* 1. to beat, club; to beat up; 2. to thump (on), pound (on), bang away at; 3. crush completely (in an argument); 4. bother, pester.

aporrearse, *vr* to slave away, slog, toil.

aporreo, *nm* 1. beating; beating-up. 2. humping, pounding, banging. 3. bother, nuisance.

aportar, *vt* 1. to bring; to furnish, to contribute; 2. *vi* to reach port; 3. to arrive, show up, come.

aporte, *nm* contribution.

aposentar, *vt* to lodge, put up.

aposento, *nm* room; lodging; main bedroom.

apostador(a), *nm* better, backer, punter; bookmaker.

apostar, *vt* 1. to station, post; 2. lay, stake, bet (on).

apostarse, *vr* 1. to station oneself in (at); 2. to compete (with), be rivals.

apóstata, *nm*/ apostate.

apóstol, *nm* apostle.

apóstrofe, *nm* 1. apostrophe; 2. insult; rebuke.

apóstrofo, *nm* inverted comma, apostrophe.

apoyador, *nm* 1. support, bracket; 2. seconder.

apoyar, *vt* 1. to lean, rest (on); to hold up, support; to prop up; 2. to back; to stand by; to abet; to second, to uphold; 3. *vi* to rest on, be supported by.

apoyo, *nm* 1. support; prop; 2. backing; approval.

apreciar, *vt* 1. to value, assess, estimate, to evaluate, 2. to esteem, be fond of; 3. to appreciate; 4. to become aware of; 5. to add value to; 6. to be grateful for.

aprecio, *nm* 1. valuation, appraisal; estimate; 2. appreciation; esteem, regard.

apremio, *nm* 1. urgency, pressure; compulsion. 2. writ, judgment; summons; 3. oppression; harassment

aprender, *vt* to learn; to learn to do.

aprenderse, *vr* to learn by heart.

aprendiz(a), *nm* 1. learner; beginner, novice; 2. apprentice; trainee.

aprendizaje, *nm* apprenticeship.

aprensión, *nf* apprehension, fear, worry; nervousness; fear of being ill.

aprensivo, *adj* apprehensive, worried; nervous, timid, fearful of being ill, squeamish.

apresar, *vt* 1. to seize, clutch, grab, grasp; 2. to capture; 3. to seize.

aprestado, *adj* ready; to be ready.

aprestar, *vt* to prepare, make ready; to prime.

apresto, *nm* 1. preparation. 2. outfit, equipment, 3. size, primer.

apresurar, *vt* to hurry (along); to hustle; to speed up, accelerate, expedite.

apretadera, *nf* 1. strap, rope; 2. pressure, insistence.

apretado, *adj* 1. tight; 2. tense, thick, compact, 3. tight-fisted, stingy; 5. (money) broke, flat.

apretar, *vt* 1. to tighten (up); to clasp, grip, to press, press down; squeeze; to pressurize; to pack in, pack tight; 2. intensify; 3. *vi* be too tight; to pinch, hurt; 4. to get worse, get more severe.

aprieto, *nm* (apretón) difficulty, jam, fix; distress.

aprisa, *adv* quickly, hurriedly.

aprisionar, *vt* to imprison; to bind, tie; to trap.

aprobación, *nf* 1. approval; consent; 2. passing mark.

aprobar, *vt* to approve, approve of, consent to.

apropiado, *adj* appropriate (to), suitable, fitted (for).

apropiar, *vt* to adapt, fit (to), make suitable (for); to apply (to).

aprovechado(a), *adj* **1.** industrious, diligent, hard-working; **2.** thrifty; **3.** unscrupulous, selfish; grasping; **4.** well-spent time; **5.** *nm/f* selfish person.

aprovechar, *vt* **1.** to make (good) use of, use, utilize; to develop, exploit; to take up, take advantage of; to profit by, profit from; **2.** *vi* to be of use, be useful, be profitable; **3.** to progress, improve; to make progress in one's work.

aprovisionador(a), *nm/f* supplier.

aprovisionar, *vt* to supply.

aproximado, *adj* approximate, rough.

aproximar, *vt* to bring near(er), bring up, draw up (to).

aptitud, *nf* **1.** suitability, fitness; **2.** aptitude, ability.

apto, *adj* suitable, fit; pass, approved.

apuesta, *nf* bet, wager; (Bridge) bid.

apuesto(a), *adj* **1.** neat, elegant, spruce; **2.** handsome.

apuntado, *adj* **1.** pointed, sharp; **2.** (drunk) tight.

apuntar, *vt* **1.** to aim, level, point (at); **2.** point to; to point out; **3.** to note, make (or take) a note of; to score; to enter, to record; **4.** to sharpen, put a point on.

apuntarse, *vr* to score a point, to score a win.

apunte, *nm* **1.** note, jotting, memorandum, entry; **2.** debit; **3.** sketch.

apuñalar, *vt* to stab; to knife.

apuñar, *vt* to seize (in one's fist); to knead (with the fist).

apurado, *adj* **1.** needy, hard up; **2.** difficult; **3.** hurried, rushed.

apurar, *vt* **1.** to purify, refine; **2.** to drain, drink up; **3.** to hurry, to hustle.

apuro, *nm* **1.** (económico) want, financial need, hardship; **2.** fix, difficulty, tight spot; **3.** haste, hurry.

aquejar, *vt* to distress, grieve, afflict.

aquel(la), *adj dem* that, those.

aquél(la), *pron dem* that, those; that one, those (ones).

aquello, *pron dem* that (that picture)

aquí, *adv* here, in here, right here.

aquietar, *vt* to calm (down); to pacify.

aquilatar, *vt* to assay, to value, grade, to examine.

ara, *nf* altar.

arado, *nm* plow.

araña, *nf* spider.

arañar, *vt* to scratch, to scrape.

arañazo, *nm* scratch.

arar, *vt* to plow; to till, to cultivate.

arbitraje, *nm* arbitration.

arbitrar, *vt* to arbitrate in, to umpire, to referee.

árbitro, *nm* arbiter, arbitrator, umpire, referee.

árbol, *nm* tree.

arbolado, *adj* wooded, tree-covered; wood land.

arbolar, *vt* to put up, place upright, raise.

arboleda, *nf* grove, plantation, coppice.

arbusto, *nm* shrub, bush.

arca, *nf* chest, box, coffer; safe.

arcada, *nf* arcade.

arcaico, *adj* archaic.

arce, *nm* maple, maple tree.

arcilla, *nf* clay.

arco, *nm* arch; archway.

arcón, *nm* large chest, bin, bunker.

archiduque(a), *nm/f* archduke, archduchess.

archipiélago, *nm* archipelago.

archivado, *adj* **1.** out-of-date, old-fashioned **2.** filed.

archivo, *nm* **1.** archive(s); registry; **2.** files, records.

ardentía, *nf* heartburn.

arder, *vt* **1.** to burn; to sting; **2.** *vi* to blaze.

ardid, *nm* ruse, devise, stratagem.

ardiente, *adj* burning, shining, blazing.

ardor, *nm* **1.** heat, warmth; **2.** ardor, eagerness, zeal.

arduo, *adj* arduous, hard, tough.

área, *nf* area.

arena, *nf* sand, grit, gravel.

arenal, *nm* sandy spot, sandy ground, sandpit.

arenga, *nf* harangue, speech; lecture.

arenilla, *nf* stone gravel.

arenque, *nm* herring; kipper.

arepa, *nf* large tortilla (or maize cake).

argolla, *nf* ring; door-knocker.

argollar, *vt* to ring.

argot, *nm* slang.

argüir, *vt* **1.** to argue, contend, to indicate; **2.** to accuse.

argumentación, *nf* argumentation.

argumentar, *vt* to argue.

argumento, *nm* **1.** argument, reasoning, thinking; **2.** plot, story-line.

árido, *adj* arid, dry.

ariscar, *vt* to pacify, control.

arisco, *adj* (animal) shy; wild, vicious.

aristócrata, *nm/f* aristocrat.

aristocrático, *adj* aristocratic.

aritmética, *nf* arithmetic.

aritmético, *adj* **1.** arithmetical; **2.** *nm/f* arithmetician.

arma, *nf* arm, weapon.

armada, *nf* fleet, navy.

armado, *adj* **1.** armed; **2.** mounted, assembled.

armadura, *nf* **1.** armor; **2.** frame, (Zool) armature.

armamento, *nm* **1.** arms, armament; **2.** framework.

armar, *vt* **1.** to arm; **2.** to fix, to load; **3.** to prepare, arrange, to assemble, put together, to set up.

armario, *nm* cupboard, bookcase, wardrobe.

armería, *nf* **1.** armory; **2.** gunsmith's shop, gun shop; **3.** the art of gunsmith; **4.** heraldry.

armero, *nm* **1.** gunsmith, gunmaker, armorer; **2.** gun rack, stand for weapons.

armiño, *nm* (Zool) stoat; ermine.

armisticio, *nm* armistice.

armonía, *nf* harmony.

armonizar, *vt* to harmonize, bring into harmony.

aro, *nm* ring, hoop, rim.

aroma, *nf* aroma, scent, fragance; bouquet.

aromático, *adj* aromatic, sweet-scented.

aromatizar, *vt* to scent, give fragance to; to spice.

arpillar, *vt* to pile up.

arpillera, *nf* sacking, sackcloth.

arpista, *nm/f* harpist.

arpón, *nm* harpoon; gaff.

arquear, *vt* to arch, to bend.

arqueo, *nm* **1.** arching; **2.** checking.

arqueología, *nf* archaeology.

arqueólogo(a), *nm/f* archaeologist.

arquero, *nm* **1.** archer; **2.** cashier; **3.** goalkeeper.

arquitecto(a), *nm/f* architect.

arquitectura, *nf* architecture.

arraigado, *adj* **1.** firmly rooted, well-rooted, deep-rooted; **2.** established.

arraigar, *vt* **1.** to establish; to strengthen; **2.** *vi* to take root, strike root.

arraigo, *nm* rooting, settling, establishment.

arrancadero, *nm* starting point.

arrancado, *adj* **1.** broke, penniless; **2.** *nm* starting, ignition.

arrancar, *vt* **1.** to pull up, root out, to extract; **2.** to snatch, wrest; **3.** *vi* (automóvil) to start, set off.

arranque, *nm* **1.** sudden start, jerk, jolt, wrench; **2.** starting point; **3.** start, starting, ignition.

arrasar, *vt* **1.** to level, flatten; raze, demolish; **2.** to fill up; **3.** *vi* to clear; **4.** to triumph.

arrastrar, *vt* **1.** to drag, drag along, to haul, pull; **2.** to carry away, trail on the ground.

arrastrarse, vr to crawl, to drag oneself along.

arrastre, nm 1. drag, pulling, haulage; 2. influence.

arreada, nf rustling, cattle-thieving; round-up.

arrear, vt 1. to drive, urge on; 2. to harness; 3. to steal.

arrebatado, adj hasty, sudden, violent.

arrebatar, vt 1. to snatch, to seize, to wrench; 2. to move deeply, stir, to captivate, enrapture.

arrebatarse, vr to get carried away; to get excited.

arrebato, nm 1. fit of rage, fury; 2. ecstasy, rapture.

arreciar, vi to grow worse, get more severe, to intensify; to get stronger.

arrecife, nm reef, coral reef.

arreglado, adj neat, ordely, proper, moderate.

arreglador(a), nm/f arranger.

arreglar, vt to arrange, to settle; to adjust, fix up.

arreglarse, vr to come to terms with, reach an understanding.

arreglo, nm 1. arrangement, settlement; adjustment; 2. agreement, understanding; compromise.

arrellanarse, vr to lounge, sprawl, loll.

arremeter, vt to attack, assail.

arremetida, nf attack, assault, onrush; push.

arremolinarse, vr to crowd around, swirl.

arrendador, nm/f 1. landlord; lessor; 2. tenant.

arrendar, vt 1. lease, to hire out; 2. to rent, to hire.

arrendatatio(a), nm/f tenant, lessee, leaseholder.

arreo, nm harness, trappings; gear, equipment.

arrepentido(a), adj 1. regretful, repentant, sorry; 2. nm/f penitent.

arrepentimiento, nm regret, repentance, sorrow.

arrepentirse, vr to repent, be repentant; to regret something.

arrestado(a), adj 1. bold, daring; 2. arrested, detained

arrestar, vt to arrest; to imprison.

arresto, nm arrest; imprisonment, confinement.

arriba, adv 1. above, overhead, on top; 2. the upper part, the top side.

arribar, vi to arrive; reach port.

arriesgado, adj risky, dangerous, hazardous, daring.

arriesgar, vt to risk, expose oneself to danger, to dare to do something.

arrimadero, nm support.

arrimado(a), adj 1. close; 2. nm/f parasite.

arrimar, vt to bring close, move up, draw up.

arrinconado, adj forgotten; neglected, abandoned.

arrinconar, vt to put in a corner; to lay aside, put away, ignore.

arroba, nf measure of weight = 25 lbs.

arrobador, adj entrancing, enchanting.

arrodillarse, vr to kneel, be kneeling.

arrogancia, nf arrogance; pride.

arrogante, adj arrogant, haughty; proud.

arrogarse, vr to assume something.

arrojado, adj daring, dashing, boldly.

arrojar, vt to throw, fling, hurl, cast.

arrojo, nm daring, dash, fearlessness.

arrollador, adj sweeping, overwhelming.

arrollar, vt to roll up, to coil, wind.

arropar, vt to cover, to wrap up, to tuck up.

arrostrar, vt to face, to stand up to.

arroyada, nf 1. gully, stream bed; 2. flood, flooding.

arroyo, nm 1. stream, brook; 2. gully, ravine.

arroyuelo, nm small stream, brook.

arroz, nm rice.

arruga, nf wrinkle, line; crease, fold.

arrugado, adj wrinkled, lined; creased; crumpled.

arrugar, vt to wrinkle, line; to knit, pucker up; to crease; to crumple, screw up.

arruinado, adj ruined.

arruinar, vt to ruin; to wreck, destroy.

arrullar, vt 1. to lull to sleep, rock to sleep; 2. to whisper endearments to, say sweet nothings to.

arrullo, nm cooing; billing.

arrumar, vt to stow; to pile up.

arrumbar, vt 1. to put aside, put on one side, discard; to neglect, forget; 2. vi to take one's bearings.

arsenal, nm 1. dockyard, naval dockyard; 2. storehouse, mine.

arsénico, nm arsenic.

arte, nm art.

artefacto, nm appliance, device, contrivance.

artejo, nm knuckle, joint.

artería, nf cunning, artfulness.

arteria, nf artery.

arterio(e)sclerosis, nf arteriosclerosis.

artero, adj cunning, artful.

artesa, nf trough, kneading trough.

artesanal, adj craft.

artesanía, nf craftsmanship; handicraft, skill.

artesano(a), adj 1. home-made, home-produced; 2. nm/f craftsman.

ártico, adj Arctic.

articulación, nf articulation; joint.

articulado(a), adj 1. articulate; 2. articulated, jointed.

artículo, nm 1. article, thing; commodity; 2. (Ling) article.

artífice, nm/f artist, craftsman; maker; inventor.

artificial, adj artificial.

artificioso, adj 1. skilful, ingenious; artistic; 2. cunning, artful.

artillería, nf 1. artillery; anti-aircraft guns; field guns; 2. forward line.

artillero, nm artilleryman, gunner; explosives expert.

artimaña, nf trap, snare.

artista, nm/f artist; actor, actress.

artístico, adj artistic.

artritis, nf arthritis.

arzobispo, nm archbishop.

asa, nf handle; grip; lever; pretext.

asadera, nf baking tin.

asado, adj roast, roasted.

asador, nm 1. spit, roasting-jack; 2. carvery.

asalariado(a), adj 1. paid; wage-earning; 2. nm/f wage earner, employee.

asalariar, vt to hire, put on the payroll.

asaltador(a) nm/f attacker, assailant, raider.

asaltar, vt 1. to attack, assail; to rush; to storm; to break into, raid; to loot, sack; 2. to fall upon.

asamblea, nf assembly; meeting; congress, conference.

asar, vt 1. to roast; to bake; to broil, grill. 2. to pester.

ascendencia, nf 1. ancestry, descent, origin; 2. ascendancy; hold, influence.

ascender, vt 1. to promote; 2. vi to ascend, rise; 3. be promoted, go up; 4. to amount to, add up to.

ascendiente, nm/f 1. ancestor; 2. ascendancy, influence, power (over).

ascenso, nm promotion.

ascensor, nm lift, elevator.

asco, nm loathing, disgust, revulsion.

ascua, nf live coal, ember.

aseado, adj clean, neat, tidy; smart.

asear, vt 1. to adorn, embellish; 2. to clean up, tidy up.

asechanza, nf trap, snare.

asechar, vt to waylay, ambush; to set a trap for.

asediar, vt 1. to besiege, lay siege to; to blockade; 2. to bother, pester; to chase.

asedio, nm siege, blockade.

asegurado(a), adj 1. insured; 2. nm/f the insured, the insured person.

aseguradora, nf insurer; underwriter.

asegurar, *vt* 1. to secure, fasten, to make firm, settle securely; 2. strengthen the defenses of; 3. to safeguard, guarantee, assure; 4. to assure, affirm.

asentar, *vt* to seat, sit down; to place, to found; to make firm, to seat.

asentir, *vi* 1. to assent, agree; 2. to agree to, consent to; to approve, grant; to accept.

aseo, *nm* cleanliness, neatness, tidiness.

aséptico, *adj* aseptic; germ-free, free from infection.

aserradero, *nm* sawmill.

aserradora, *nf* power saw.

aserrar, *vt* to saw, saw through; to saw up.

aserrín, *nm* sawdust.

asertar, *vt* to assert, affirm.

asertivo, *adj* assertive.

asesinado, *nm/f* murder victim, murdered person.

asesinar, *vt* to murder; to assassinate.

asesinato, *nm* murder; assassination.

asesino, *adj* murderous killer.

asesor(a), *nm/f* adviser, consultant.

asesorar, *vt* to advise.

asesoría, *nf* advising, task of advising, legal advice.

asestar, *vt* 1. to aim (at, in the direction of) to fire, shoot; 2. tó deal, give, strike.

aseveración, *nf* assertion, contention.

aseverar, *vt* to affirm, assert.

asfaltado, *adj* 1. asphalt, asphalted; 2. *nm* asphalting; 3. pavement, asphalt surface.

asfixia, *nf* suffocation, asphyxiation, asphyxia.

así, *adv* so, in this way, thus; by this means, thereby.

asiento, *nm* seat, chair; place; saddle.

asignar, *vt* to assign, to allot, apportion, to allocate.

asignatura, *nf* subject, course.

asilado, *nm/f* inmate; refugee.

asilar, *vt* to take in, give shelter to; to give political asylum to.

asilo, *nm* asylum; sanctuary; shelter, refuge.

asimilar, *vt* to assimilate.

asir, *vi* to seize, grasp, catch, take hold of.

asirse, *vr* to take hold; to fight, grapple.

asistencia, *nf* 1. attendance, presence; 2. people present, those attending; audience; 3. help, assistance; service; care; 4. allowance, maintenance.

asistente(s), *nm/f* assistant; orderly, servant.

asistir, *vt* 1. to attend; to serve, wait on; 2. to help, assist; care for; 3. to represent, appear for; 4. *vi* to be present (at); to witness, be a witness of.

asma, *nf* asthma; bronquid; bronchial asthma.

asmático(a), *adj* asthmatic.

asna, *nf* female donkey.

asno, *nm* donkey.

asociación, *nf* association; society; partnership; union.

asociarse, *vr* to associate; to become partners, form a partnership, join forces with someone.

asolador, *adj* destructive, devastating.

asolar, *vt* 1. to dry up, parch; 2. *vi* raze, destroy.

asoleada, *nf* sunstroke.

asoleado, *adj* 1. stupid 2. tired out.

asolear, *vt* to put in the sun; to dry in the sun.

asomada, *nf* 1. brief appearance; 2. glimpse.

asomar, *vt* 1. (cabeza) to show, put out, stick out; to put one's head out; 2. *vi* to begin to show, appear, become visible.

asombrar, *vt* 1. to amaze, astonish; to frighten; 2. to shade, cast a shadow on; to darken.

asombro, *nm* a amazement, astonishment, surprise; fear, fright; wonder.

asomo, *nm* 1. appearance; 2. sign, indication.

aspaviento, *nm* exaggerated display of feeling.

aspecto, *nm* look, appearance; looks, aspect.

áspero, *adj* 1. tough; ragged; 2. sour, tart, bitter; 3. hard; 4. harsh, rasping; gruff; unpolished.

aspersión, *nf* sprinkling; spray, spraying.

aspersor, *nm* sprinkler.

áspid, *nm* asp.

aspillera, *nf* loophole.

aspiración, *nf* 1. breath; breathing in, inhalation; 2. aspiration, air intake.

aspiradora, *nm/f* vacuum-cleaner.

aspirar, *vt* 1. to breathe in, inhale, to suck in, suck up; 2. to aspirate.

aspirina, *nf* aspirin.

asquearse, *vr* to be nauseated, feel disgusted.

asqueroso, *adj* 1. disgusting, loathsome, sickening; awful, vile; 2. squeamish.

asta, *nf* lance, spear; pole, shaft, handle; flagstaff, flagpole; horn, antler.

asterisco, *nm* asterisk.

astilla, *nf* splinter, chip; firewood, kindling.

astillero, *nm* shipyard, dockyard.

astro, *nm* star, heavenly body, leading light.

astrología, *nf* astrology.

astronauta, *nm/f* astronaut.

astronomía, *nf* astronomy.

astucia, *nf* cleverness; guile, cunning.

astuto(a), *nm/f* clever, smart; crafty, cunning.

asumir, *vt* 1. to assume, take on; to take over; to take up; 2. to assume, suppose; to take for granted.

asunción, *nf* assumption.

asunto, *nm* matter, subject; topic; affair, business.

asustar, *vt* to frighten, scare; to alarm, startle.

atacado, *adj* fainthearted.

atacador(a), *nm/f* ramrod, attacker, assailant.

atacar, *vt* to attack, to assail, assault, impugn.

atado, *adj* tied, shy, inhibited, irresolute; bundle; bunch.

atadura, *nf* 1. tying, fastening; 2. string, cord, rope; tether; bond, limitation, restriction.

atajar, *vt* to stop, intercept; to head off, cut off.

atajo, *nm* short cut.

atalaya, *nf* 1. watchtower; observation point; 2. vantage point; 3. *nm* lookout observer, sentinel.

ataque, *nm* attack; strike; raid.

atar, *vt* to tie, tie up; to bind; to fasten.

atardecer, *vi* 1. to get dark; 2. *nm* late afternoon; dusk, evening.

atareado, *adj* busy, rushed; to be very busy.

atarear, *vt* to give a job to, assign a task to.

atarearse, *vr* to work hard, keep busy; to be busy.

atarugarse, *vr* 1. to swallow the wrong way, choke; 2. to get confused, be in a daze.

atascadero, *nm* 1. mire, bog, muddy place; 2. stumbling block, obstacle; dead end.

atascar, *vt* to stop; to block, plug; to clog, obstruct.

atascarse, *vr* get stuck (in the mud), get bogged down; to get into a jam; to stall.

ataúd, *nm* coffin; bier.

ataviar, *vt* to deck, array; to dress up; to adapt, adjust, accommodate.

atavío, *nm* attire, dress; rig, get-up; finery.

atemorizar, *vt* to frighten, scare.

atemperar, *vi* 1. to temper, moderate; 2. to adjust, accommodate.

atenazar, *vt* to grip.

atención, *nf* 1. attention; care, heed; 2. kindness, civility, courtesy.

atender, *vt* to attend to, pay attention to; to heed; to service, maintain; care for; to comply with.

atentado, *adj* 1. prudent, cautious; moderate; 2. *nm* illegal act, crime; assault, attack; attempt.

atento(a), *adj* 1. attentive, observant, watchful; 2. polite; thoughtful, kind; obliging.

atenuante, *adj* extenuating.

atenuarse, *vr* to weaken.

aterrador, *adj* frightening, terrifying; appalling.

aterrar, *vt* 1. to pull down, demolish, destroy; 2. to cover with earth; to earth up; 3. *vi* to reach land; 4. to terrify, frighten; to appall.

aterrarse, *vr* to be terrified, be frightened; to be appalled, to panic.

aterrizaje, *nm* landing.

aterrizar, *vi* to land; to get out (of an airplane).

aterrorizar, *vt* to terrorize.

atesar, *vt* to smooth.

atestado, *nm* 1. affidavit, statement; 2. *adj* obstinate, stubborn; 3. *adj* packed; crammed with.

atestiguar, *vt* to testify to, bear witness to, give evidence of; to attest, vouch for.

atiborrar, *vt* to fill, stuff (with).

ático, *nm* attic; penthouse.

atinado, *adj* accurate, correct; wise, sensible, judicious; pertinent.

atinar, *vi* 1. to guess right, be right; 2. *vt* hit the target, hit the mark

atirantar, *vt* to tighten, tauten; to stretch.

atizador, *nm* poker.

atizar, *vt* to poke, stir; to stoke; to snuff, trim.

Atlántico, *nm* the Atlantic.

Atlántida, *nf* Atlantis.

atlas, *nm* atlas.

atleta, *nm/f* athlete.

atlético, *adj* athletic.

atocinar, *vt* to cut up; to make into bacon; to cure.

atolondrado, *adj* scatterbrained; silly; bewildered; stunned, amazed.

atolondrar, *vt* to bewilder; to stun, amaze.

atolladero, *nm* 1. muddy place; mire, morass; 2. awkward spot, jam; embarrassing situation.

atollarse, *vr* 1. to get stuck in the mud, get bogged down; 2. to get into a jam, get stuck.

atómico, *adj* atomic.

atomizador, *nm* atomizer; spray, scent spray.

átomo, *nm* atom; particle, speck.

atontado, *adj* 1. stunned, bewildered; 2. silly, dim-witted.

atontar, 1. *vi* to stun, stupefy; 2. to stun, bewilder.

atorar, *vt* 1. to stop up, choke, obstruct; to stop, immobilize; 2. to block, impede.

atorarse, *vr* to choke, swallow the wrong way.

atormentador(a), *adj* 1. tormenting; 2. *nm/f* tormentor.

atormentar, *vt* to torture; torment; to plague, harass.

atornillador, *nm* screwdriver.

atrabancar, *vt* to rush, hurry over.

atrabancarse, *vr* to be in a fix, get into a jam.

atracadero, *nm* berth, wharf, landing place.

atracador, *nm* hold-up man, bandit, gangster.

atracar, *vt* 1. to hold up; to attack, waylay; to hijack; 2. to tie up, moor, bring along side.

atracción, *nf* 1. attraction; attractiveness, appeal, charm; 2. amusement; entertainment.

atraco, *nm* hold-up, robbery.

atractivo, *adj* attractive; *nm* attraction; attractiveness, appeal, charm.

atragantarse, *vr* 1. to choke (on), swallow the wrong way; 2. to get mixed up, lose the thread of what one is saying.

atramparse, *vr* 1. to fall into a trap; to get stuck, get oneself into a jam; 2. to clog; to get blocked up.

atrancar, *vt* to bar, bolt; block up; to batten down.

atrapar, *vt* to trap; to catch, overtake; to get.

atrás, *adv* back!, get back!; behind.

atrasado, *adj* slow, late, behind; overdue.

atrasar, *vt* to slow down, slow up, retard; to delay, to put back.

atraso, *nm* delay, time lag.

atravesada, *nf* crossing, passage.

atravesado, *adj* 1. crossed, laid across, oblique; 2. squinting, cross eyed; 3. crossbred.

atravesar, *vt* 1. to cross, cross over, go over; 2. to pierce, transfix; 3. to cross, span.

atrayente, *adj* attractive.

atreverse, *vr* to dare.

atrevido, *adj* 1. bold, daring; 2. insolent, disrespectful; impudent, forward; daring.

atrevimiento, *nm* 1. boldness, daring; audacity; 2. insolence; impudence, forwardness.

atribuir, *vi* to attribute to; to put down to, impute to.

atribuirse, *vr* to assume something.

atribulado, *adj* afflicted, suffering.

atribularse, *vr* to grieve, be distressed.

atributo, *nm* attribute; emblem, sign of authority.

atrincherar, *vt* to surround with a trench, fortify with trenches.

atrio, *nm* atrium, inner courtyard; vestibule, porch.

atrocidad, *nf* atrocity, outrage.

atrochar, *vi* to go by the byways; to take a short cut.

atrofia, *nf* atrophy.

atronar, *vt* 1. to deafen. 2. to stun, daze; to fell with a blow on the neck; 3. to bewilder, confuse.

atropellado, *adj* hasty, abrupt; violent.

atropellar, *vt* to trample underfoot; to knock down; to push violently past.

atropellarse, *vr* to act hastily.

atropello, *nm* accident; knocking down, running over.

atroz, *adj* cruel, inhuman, outrageous, huge, terrific, dreadful, awful.

atún, *nm* tuna fish.

aturdido, *adj* bewildered, dazed, stunned.

audacia, *nf* boldness, audacity.

audaz, *adj* bold, audacious.

audición, *nf* hearing, audition.

audiencia, *nf* 1. audience, hearing; 2. audience chamber; high court.

audífono, *nm* hearing-aid, receiver; (*pl*) headphones.

audiovisual, *adj* audio-visual.

auditivo, *adj* 1. auditory, hearing; 2. *nm* earpiece, receiver.

auditor(a), *nm/f* 1. judge-advocate; 2. auditor; firm of auditors, accountancy firm.

auditorio, *nm* 1. audience; 2. auditorium, hall.

auge, *nm* peak, summit, zenith; apogee, increase.

aula, *nf* classroom; lecture room, assembly hall, main hall.

aullido, *nm* howl; yell; to howl.

aumentar, *vt* to increase, add to.

aumento, *nm* increase; increase, raise.

aun, *adv* even.

aún, *adv* yet, still.

aunque, *conj* though, although, even though.

auricular, *adj* auricular, aural, of the ear.

aurora, *nf* dawn; aurora borealis.

ausencia, *nf* absence.

ausente, *adj* 1. absent; 2. *nm/f* absentee.

auspiciar, *vt* 1. to back, sponsor; 2. to wish good luck to.

auspicios, *nm* auspices; protection, patronage; sponsorship.

austeridad, *nf* austerity; sternness, severity; economic, austerity.

auténtica, *nf* certificate, certification; authorized copy.

auténtico, *adj* authentic; genuine, real.

auto, *nm* car, automobile; edict, judicial decree; written order.

auto, *pref* self-sufficient.

autoacusarse, *vr* to accuse oneself.

autoadministrarse, *vr* 1. to take a drug; 2. to govern oneself, be self-governing.

autoanálisis, *nm* self-analysis.

autobiografía, *nf* autobiography.

autobús, *nm* bus, coach; long-distance bus.

autoclave, *nm* pressure cooker; sterilizing apparatus.

autoconfesado, *adj* self-confessed.

autocontrol, *nm* 1. self-control, self-restraint; 2. self-monitoring.

autoconvencerse, *vr* to convince oneself.

autocrítica, *nf* self-criticism, self-examination.

autodisciplina, *nf* self-discipline.

autoempleo, *nm* self-employment.

autoengaño, *nm* self-deception, self-delusion.

autogobierno, *nm* self-government.

autógrafo, *nm* autograph.

automatizado, *adj* automated.

automóvil, *adj* motor car, automobile; self-propelled.

automovilista, *nm/f* motorist, driver.

autonomía, *nf* autonomy; self-government.

autónomo, *adj* autonomous; self-governing; independent, self-employed.

autopatrulla, *nm* patrol car.

autopista, *nf* motorway; expressway.

autoprotegerse, *vt* to protect oneself

autopsia, *nf* post mortem, autopsy.

autor, *nm/f* author, writer; creator, originator, inventor; perpetrator.

autoridad, *nf* 1. authorship; 2. *nf* authority; jurisdiction.

autoritario, *adj* authoritarian; peremptory; dogmatic.

autorización, *nf* authorization; permission, license.

autorizado, *adj* authorized, official; authoritative.

autosuficiencia, *nf* 1. self-sufficiency; 2. smugness.

auxilio, *nm* help, aid, assistance; relief; welfare, first aid.

avalancha, *nf* avalanche.

avalar, *vt* to guarantee; to support, endorse.

avalorar, to enhance; to set off, to encourage.

avaluar, *vt* to value, appraise (at).

avance, *nm* 1. advance; rise, in advance; 2. attack, raid; 3. advance payment; estimate.

avanzado, *adj* advanced; avant-garde, progressive.

avanzar, *vt* 1. to advance, move forward; 2. (Fin.) to advance; 3. to promote; 4. put forward.

avaricia, *nf* miserliness, avarice; greed, greediness.

avaro, *adj* miserly, mean; to be sparing in one's praise, be mean with one's praises.

avasallador, *adj* overwhelming; domineering.

avasallar, *vt* 1. to subdue, subjugate; to dominate; to enslave; 2. to steamroller someone.

ave, *nf* bird, chicken.

avecinar, *vt* to approach, come near.

avejentar, *vi* to age.

avellana, *nf* hazelnut.

avenar, *vt* to drain.

avenencia, *nf* agreement; compromise; bargain, deal.

avenida, *nf* avenue.

avenir, *vi* to reconcile, bring together.

aventajado, *adj* outstanding, excellent, advanced.

aventajar, *vt* to surpass, beat, excel; to outstrip.

aventar, *vt* to fan, blow (on); to winnow.

aventura, *nf* adventure; bold venture, daring enterprise; escapade; love affair.

aventurarse, *vr* to dare, take a chance, risk it, to venture.

aventurero(a), *adj* 1. adventurous; enterprising; 2. *nm/f* adventurer; adventuress; mercenary.

avergonzado, *adj* shamefaced; embarrassed; to be ashamed.

avergonzar, *vt* to shame, put to shame; to abash, embarrass.

avergonzarse, *vr* to be ashamed, to be embarrassed, look embarrassed.

avería, *nf* 1. aviary; flock of birds; 2. damage; breakdown, fault, failure.

averiar, *vt* to damage, spoil; to cause a breakdown in, cause a failure in.

averiguación, *nf* ascertainment, discovery; establishment; investigation; inquiry; check.

averiguar, *vi* to find out, ascertain, discover; to look up; to investigate, inquire into.

aversión, *nf* aversion; distaste, disgust, loathing.

avestruz, *nm* ostrich.

avezado, *adj* accustomed; inured, experienced.

aviación, *nf* 1. aviation; 2. air force.

aviador(a), *nm/f* aviator, airman, airwoman, pilot.

avícola, *adj* chicken, poultry; chicken farm, poultry farm.

avicultor, *nm* chicken farmer, poultry farmer.

ávido, *adj* avid, eager; greedy (for).

avión, *nm* airplane, plane, aircraft.

avisado, *adj* sensible, wise.

avisador(a) *nm/f* informant; messenger.

avisar, *vt* to warn; to inform, tell.

avispa, *nf* wasp.

avispado, *adj* sharp, clever, wide-awake.

avispar, to spur on, urge on.

avispero, *nm* wasp's nest.

avistar, *vt* to sight, make out, glimpse.

avivado, *adj* forewarned, alerted.

avivar, *vt* to stoke; to brighten.

avizorar, *vt* to watch, spy on.

axila, *nf* axilla, armpit.

axioma, *nm* axiom.

ayer, *adv* yesterday.

ayuda, *nf* a help, aid, assistance.

ayudar, *vt* to help, aid, assist; to help out; to be of use to.

ayunar, *vi* to fast (on); to go without.

azafata, *nf* air hostess, stewardess, flight attendant.

azafrán, *nm* saffron, crocus.

azahar, *nm* orange blossom.

azalea, *nf* azalea.

azar, *nm* chance, fate, accidentally, by chance.

azaroso, *adj* risky, hazardous, chancy.

ázimo, *adj* unleavened.

azogado, *adj* restless, shaking like a leaf, trembling all over.

azogue, *nm* mercury, quicksilver.

azorado, *adj* alarmed, upset, embarrassed, excited.

azotaina, *nf* beating, spanking.

azotar, *vt* to whip, flog, beat; to scourge; to thrash, spank.

azotea, *nf* a flat roof, terrace roof; flat-roofed adobe house.

azúcar, *nm* sugar.

azucarero, *adj* sugar, sugar basin, sugar bowl.

azufre, *nm* sulphur; brimstone.

azul, *adj* blue.

azulado, *adj* blue, bluish.

azulejo, *nm* tile, glazed tile, ornamental tile.

B

B, b, *nf* (letter) B, b.

babear, *vi* to drool, slobber.

babel, *nm* bedlam; mess.

babilla, nf (Vet) stifle.

babor, nm on the port side; the sea to port; land to port; to turn to port.

babosa, adj fool, idiot.

bacalao, nm codfish.

bacilar, adj bacillary.

bacilarse, vr to have a good time.

bacilo, nm bacillus, germ.

bacteria, nf bacterium, germ.

bactericida, adj 1. germ-killing; 2. nm germicide, germ killer.

bacteriología, nf bacteriology.

bache, nm hole, pothole; bad spot, air pocket.

bacheado, adj bumpy, uneven, full of pot-holes.

bachiller, adj 1. talkative; 2. nm/f person who holds certificate of higher education, bachelor.

bachillerato, nm school-leaving examination, baccalaureate; bachelor's degree.

bagaje, nm 1. baggage; equipment; luggage; 2. beast of burden; 3. knowledge, experience.

bagatela, nf trinket, mere nothing, bagatelle.

bagazo, nm chaff, husks; pulp; husks of sugar cane.

bahía, nf bay.

bailar, vt to dance; to spin.

bailarín(a), nm/f professional dancer; ballet dancer, tap-dancer.

baile, nm 1. dance; dancing; 2. ball.

baja, nf 1. drop, fall; cut; slump, recession; decline; 2. casualty; vacancy; cancelled subscription.

bajada, nf 1. slope; 2. descent, going down.

bajar, vt to lower, let down; to bring down, carry down.

bajista, adj 1. tendency to lower prices; 2. nm (Fin) bear; 3. nm/f bass guitar player, bassist.

bajo, adj low; short, small; shallow.

bala, nf 1. bullet; cannonball; 2. cotton bale.

balacera, nf exchange of shots, shooting; shoot-out.

balada, nf ballad, ballade.

balance, nm 1. to-and-fro motion, oscillation; rocking, swinging; 2. rocking chair; 3. balance.

balancear, vt to balance.

balandra, nf sloop; yacht.

balanza, nf balance, scale; weighing machine.

balar, vi to bleat, baa.

balazo, nm shot; bullet wound.

balbuceo, nm stammering, stuttering; babbling.

balcón, nm balcony; balcony window; railing, vantage point.

baldado(a), adj 1. crippled, disabled; 2. nf cripple, disabled person.

baldar, vt 1. to cripple, maim, disable; 2. to harm, cripple; to trump.

balde, nm bucket, pail; trash-can.

baldeo, nm wash, hosing down.

baldío, adj 1. waste; 2. lazy, idle; 3. vain, useless; 4. nm uncultivated land; waste land.

baldón, nm affront, insult; blot, stain, disgrace.

baldosar, vt to tile; to pave (with flagstones).

balneario, adj 1. spa, health; 2. nm spa, health resort.

balompié, nm football.

balón, nm 1. ball, football; bag (for gas); balloon; drum, canister; beach-ball; 2. bale, brandy glass.

baloncesto, nm basketball.

balsa, nf 1. balsa; balsa wood; 2. craft; ferry; life-raft.

bálsamo, nm 1. balsam, balm; 2. comfort.

báltico, adj Baltic; the Baltic (Sea); the Baltic states.

baluarte, nm bastion; bulwark.

ballena, nf whale; blue whale.

ballenear, vi to whale, hunt whales.

ballesta, nf 1. crossbow; 2. spring; suspension.

ballet, nm troupe of dancers.

bambalina, nf drop (Theat), cloth border.

bambolear, vi to swing, sway; to sway, roll, reel; to wobble, be unsteady; to sway.

banana, nf banana; banana tree.

bananera, nf banana plantation.

bananero, adj 1. banana, related to banana; 2. vulgar, coarse; 3. third-world, backward.

banca, nf 1. stand, stall; bench; 2. the banks, banking.

bancada, nf stone bench; bed, bed-plate; thwart.

bancarrota, nf bankruptcy; failure.

banco, nm 1. bench, seat; work table; 2. alluvial soil; raised ground; 3. stratum, layer; 4. (peces) shoal, school.

banda, nf band, strip; ribbon; sash, fan-belt.

bandada, nf flock; flight; shoal.

bandeja, nf tray, large serving dish.

bandera, nf banner, standard; marker, flag.

bandido, nm bandit; outlaw; desperado; rascal.

bando, nm edict, proclamation; faction, party; side.

banquear, vt 1. bank; 2. level, flatten out.

banquero(a), nm/f banker.

banqueta, nf 1. stool; low bench; piano stool; 2. pavement, sidewalk.

banquete, nm banquet, feast; formal dinner, dinner party.

banquillo, nm bench; footstool, team bench.

bañadera, nf bathtub.

bañador, nm 1. tub, trough; 2. bathing costume, swimsuit; trunks.

bañar, vt to bathe, immerse, dip.

baptista, nm/f Baptist.

baptisterio, nm baptistery, font.

baqueteado, adj experienced, used to.

bar, nm bar.

barahúnda, nf uproar, hubbub; racket, din.

baraja, nf pack of cards.

barajar, vt 1. to shuffle; 2. to fumble up, mix up, shuffle; 3. to see the point of something.

barajuste, nm stampede, rush.

baranda, nf rail, railing; handrail; (Billar) cushion.

barandilla, nf balustrade; handrail; altar rail.

barata, nf 1. sale, bargain sale; 2. bargain counter; cut-price store.

baratillo, nm 1. cheap goods; 2. second-hand shop, junk-shop; bargain counter; 3. bargain sale; gimcrack article; 4. flea market.

barato, adj 1. cheap; inexpensive, economical; 2. adv cheaply; inexpensively.

barba, nf 1. chin; 2. beard, whiskers.

barbacoa, nf 1. barbecue; barbecued meat, meat; 2. bed made with a hurdle supported on sticks.

barbaridad, nf 1. barbarity; barbarism; atrocity, barbarous act; 2. awful!, shocking! 3. terrible things, naughty things; nonsense.

barbería, nf barber's shop.

barbero, nm barber, hairdresser.

barca, nf boat, small boat.

barcaza, nf barge, lighter; ferry; landing-craft.

barco, nm boat; ship, vessel.

barda, nf 1. protective covering on a wall; high hedge, fence, wall; top of a wall, walls; 2. jacket.

barítono, nm baritone.

barniz, nm varnish; glaze; gloss, polish.

barométrico, adj barometric.

barómetro, nm barometer.

barquilla, nf basket; gondola.

barquillo, nm horn, rolled wafer; ice-cream cornet.

barra, nf bar; rail, railing; bar, counter; rod; lever.

barracón, nm 1. hut; farm-worker's living quarters; 2. large booth, stall; side show.

barracuda, nf barracuda.

barranco, nm 1. gully, ravine; 2. cliff; steep riverbank.

barredor, *nm* sweeper.

barrena, *nf* drill, auger; bit; mining drill.

barrenar, *vt* to drill, drill through, bore; to blast.

barrer, *vt* to sweep; to sweep clean, sweep out.

barrera, *nf* barrier; rail, bar; barricade; parapet.

barricada, *nf* barricade.

barriga, *nf* belly, rounded part; bulge.

barril, *nm* barrel, cask, keg.

barrio, *nm* quarter, district, area (of a town); suburb; slum quarter, shanty-town

barro, *nm* 1. mud; 2. clay; potter's clay, baked clay.

barrote, *nm* heavy bar, thick bar; crosspiece; rung.

basar, *vt* to base; found, ground to be based on, rest on.

báscula, *nf* scales; weighing machine.

bascular, *vi* to tilt, tip up; to seesaw; to rock to and fro.

base, *nf* base; mounting, bed; base line; foundation.

básico, *adj* basic.

basta, *nf* tacking stitch, basting stitch.

bastante, *adj* 1. enough, too much; 2. more than enough; 3. *adv* sufficiently.

bastardo(a), *adj* 1. bastard; 2. base; 3. hybrid, mixed.

bastidor, *nm* frame, framework; case; stretcher; chassis, spring mattress.

bastón, *nm* stick; staff; walking stick.

basura, *nf* rubbish, refuse, garbage; litter; dust; waste.

basurero, *nm* dust-man, garbage man; scavenger.

bata, *nf* housecoat, smock, dressing gown.

batalla, *nf* battle; fight, struggle.

batea, *nf* tray; small trough; round trough, wash-tub; washing pan.

bateador, *nm* batter.

batear, *vt* to hit; to bat.

batería, *nf* battery, battery set; percussion drums; kitchen utensils.

batido, *adj* 1. well-trodden, beaten; 2. *nm* batter; milk-shake.

batidora, *nf* beater, whisk, mixer.

batuta, *nf* baton.

baúl, *nm* trunk; wardrobe trunk; large trunk.

bautismo, *nm* baptism, christening.

bautista, *adj* 1. Baptist Church; 2. *nm* Baptist.

bautizar, *vt* to baptize, christen; name, give a name to.

bayoneta, *nf* bayonet.

bazar, *nm* bazaar; large retail store, toy shop.

bazuca, *nf* bazooka.

bebedero, 1. *adj* drinkable, good to drink; 2. *nm* drinking trough; drinking place, watering hole; 3. establishment selling alcoholic drinks.

bebedor, *adj* hard-drinking, given to drinking.

bebida, *nf* 1. drink, beverage; 2. (alcoholic) drink, liquor.

beca, *nf* scholarship, grant; fellowship; award.

becar, *vt* to award a scholarship to.

becerrillo, *nm* calfskin.

becerro, *nm* 1. yearling calf, bullock; 2. calfskin.

beisbol, *nm* baseball.

beldad, *nf* beauty.

belén, *nf* nativity scene, crib.

belicoso, *adj* warlike; bellicose, aggressive; militant.

belleza, *nf* beauty, loveliness.

bello, *adj* beautiful, lovely.

bendecir, *vt* to bless; to consecrate; to praise, call down a blessing on.

benefactor, *adj* salutary; beneficent.

beneficencia, *nf* beneficence, doing good; charity; charitable organization.

beneficio, *nm* benefit, profit, gain, advantage

benevolencia, *nf* benevolence, kindness, kindliness; geniality.

bengala, *nf* flare; star shell.

benigno, *adj* kind, kindly, benign; gracious; gentle.

bermejo, *adj* red, bright red; reddish.

berrear, *vi* to bellow, low, to bawl; to screech.

berro, *nm* watercress.

besar, *vt* to kiss; to pay one's humble respects.

beso, *nm* kiss.

bestia, *nf* beast, horse, mule.

bestial, *adj* 1. bestial; 2. marvelous.

betún, *nm* bitumen; asphalt; shoeblack.

biberón, *nm* feeding bottle.

Biblia, *nf* Bible; the Holy Bible.

bíblico, *adj* Biblical.

bibliografía, *nf* bibliography.

biblioteca, *nf* library.

bibliotecario, *nm/f* librarian.

bicarbonato, *nm* bicarbonate of soda; baking soda.

bíceps, *nm* biceps.

bicicleta, *nf* bicycle, cycle, racing bicycle.

bicho, *nm* small animal; unpleasant insect, creepy-crawly, maggot, grub; snake, odd-looking creature.

bidón, *nm* drum; can, tin; oildrum.

bien, *adj* well; properly. right; successfully.

bienaventurado, *adj* happy, fortunate.

bienestar, *nm* wellbeing, welfare; comfort.

bienvenida, *nf* welcome; greeting.

bifocal, *adj* bifocal.

biftec, *nm* steak, beefsteak.

bifurcación, *nf* fork; function; branch.

bigamia, *nf* bigamy.

bígamo, *nm/f* bigamous; bigamist.

bigote, *nm* mustache; whiskers.

bikini, *nm* bikini.

bilateral, *adj* bilateral.

bilingüe, *adj* bilingual.

bilis, *nf* bile.

billar, *nm* billiards; pool.

billete, *nm* 1. ticket; 2. banknote, note, bill (US).

billetera, *nm/f* wallet, pocketbook, billfold.

billón, *nm* a billion, a million millions.

billonario, *nm/f* billionaire.

bimensual, *adj* twice-monthly.

bimotor, *adj* 1. twin-engined; 2. *nm* twin-engine plane.

bingo, *nm* bingo; bingo hall.

binocular, *nm* binoculars, field glasses; opera glasses.

biofísica, *nf* biophysics.

biografía, *nf* biography, life.

biografiar, *vt* to write the biography of.

biógrafo(a), *nm/f* biographer.

biología, *nf* biology.

biológico, *adj* biological.

biopsia, *nf* biopsy.

bioquímica, *nf* biochemistry.

bioquímico, *adj* 1. biochemical; 2. *nm*, biochemist.

biplaza, *nm* two-seater.

birreta, *nf* biretta; cardinal's skull cap.

bisabuelo(a), *nm/f* great-grandfather, great-grandmother.

bisagra, *nf* hinge.

bisecar, *vt* to bisect.

bisemanal, *adj* twice-weekly.

bisexual, *adj* *nm/f* bisexual.

bisiesto, *adj* leap year.

bisnieta, *nf* great-granddaughter.

bisnieto, *nm* great-grandson; great-grandchildren.

bisturí, *nm* scalpel.

bizarro, *adj* 1. gallant, brave; dashing; 2. generous, splendid.

blanca, *nf* 1. white woman; 2. old Spanish copper coin.

blanco, *adj* 1. white; blank; 2. *nm* target.

blancura, *nf* whiteness.

blandear, *vt* to convince, persuade.

blandir, 1. *vt* to brandish, flourish, wave about; **2.** *vi* to wave to and for, swing.

blando, *adj* soft; smooth.

blanqueador(a), *nm* bleacher, bleach.

blanqueo, *nm* whitening; whitewashing; bleaching.

blasfemar, *vi* to blaspheme, to curse, swear.

blasfemia, *nf* blasphemy; insult, swearword.

blindado, *adj* **1.** armored, amor-plated; shielded, protected, encased. **2.** *nm* armored vehicle.

blindar, *vt* to armor, armor-plate; to shield.

bloque, *nm* block.

bloqueante, *adj* **1.** paralyzing; inhibiting; **2.** *nm* inhibitor, anticatalyst.

bloquear, *vt* to block, obstruct; to tackle; to stop, trap; to jam.

blusa, *nf* blouse; overall; smock.

blusón, *nm* smock; jacket.

bobina, *nf* bobbin, spool; reel; drum, cylinder; ignition coil.

bobinar, *vt* to wind.

bobo, *adj* silly, stupid; simple; naive.

boca, *nf* mouth; entrance, opening.

bocacalle, *nf* entrance to a street; intersection.

bocadito, *nm* small bite, morsel.

bocado, *nm* mouthful; morsel, bite.

bocal, *nm* **1.** pitcher, jar; **2.**(Music) mouthpiece.

bocamanga, *nf* **1.** cuff, wristband; **2.** hole for the head (in a cape).

bocanada, *nf* **1.** mouthful, swallow; **2.** puff; gust, blast; **3.** to boast, brag; **4.** crush of people.

bocina, *nf* trumpet; horn; megaphone; speaking trumpet; mouthpiece; informer; foghorn.

bocón, *adj* **1.** big-mouthed; **2.** boastful; loud-mouthed; **3.** indiscreet; **4.** *nm* braggart; bigmouth.

bochorno, *nm* **1.** sultry weather, oppressive weather; stifling atmosphere; sultriness; hot summer breeze; **2.** queer turn; hot flush; blush; **3.** embarrassment, flush, (feeling of) shame; stigma, dishonor.

boda, *nf* wedding, marriage; wedding reception.

bodega, *nf* wine cellar; pantry; storeroom, warehouse, wine shop, bar, tavern; restaurant; grocery store, general store.

bodeguero, *adj* **1.** coarse, common; **2.** *nm* vintner; cellarman; owner of a bodega; **3.** grocer.

bofetada, *nf* slap in the face, punch.

boga, *nf* rowing.

bohío, *nm* hut, shack.

boicot, *nm* boycott.

bola, *nf* ball; marble; signal.

boleadoras, *nf* lasso with balls.

bolear, *vt* **1.** to throw; **2.** to hunt; to catch with; **3.** to reject, blackball; **4.** *vi* play for fun, knock the balls about; **5.** tell fibs; **6.** boast.

bolera, *nf* bowling-alley.

boleta, *nf* **1.** pass, permit; authorization; ticket; first draft of a deed; draft (document); certificate; ballot, voting paper; report; **2.** billet; **3.** small packet of tobacco.

boletín, *nm* bulletin, journal, review; ticket; pay warrant; report.

boleto, *nm* ticket.

bólido, *nm* **1.** meteorite; **2.** racing car, hot-rod, powerboat, speedboat.

bolígrafo, *nm* ball-point pen.

bolívar, *nm* bolívar (Venezuelan unit of currency).

bolo, *nm* ninepins, skittle.

bolsa, *nf* bag; pouch; handbag; purse.

bolsillo, *nm* pocket; purse, moneybag, pocketbook.

bolsista, *nm/f* **1.** stockbroker; **2.** pickpocket.

bolso, *nm* bag, purse (US); handbag, purse (US).

bollería, *nf* baker's (shop), bakery, pastry shop.

bollo, *nm* **1.** bread roll; bun; **2.** dent; bump, lump; puff; **3.** confusion; mix-up; **4.** punch; **5.** troubles.

bomba, *nf* **1.** bomb; shell; charge; **2.** pump; garage, petrol-station; **3.** shade (of a lamp); glass, globe.

bombachas, *nf* **1.** panties; **2.** *nm* baggy trousers, peasant trousers.

bombardeo, *nm* bombardment, shelling; bombing; raid; air attack.

bombardero, *adj* **1.** bombing; **2.** *nm* bomber; bombardier.

bombero, *nm* **1.** fireman; fire brigade; **2.** trouble shooter; **3.** petrol-pump attendant.

bombilla, *nf* (light) bulb; ship's lantern.

bombón, *nm* **1.** chocolate; **2.** beauty, gem; peach.

bonachón, *adj* good-natured, kindly; easy-going.

bonanza, *nf* **1.** fair weather, calm conditions; **2.** pocket of ore, bonanza; **3.** prosperity, boom.

bondadoso, *adj* kind, good; kindly, kind-hearted, good-natured.

boniato, *nm* sweet potato, yam.

bonito, *adj* pretty; nice, nice-looking; handsome.

bono, *nm* voucher, certificate.

boquear, *vt* to say, utter, pronounce.

boquera, *nf* **1.** sluice; **2.** lipsore, mouth ulcer; **3.** *nm* warder.

boquerón, *nm* **1.** wide opening, big hole; **2.** anchovy.

boquete, *nm* gap, opening; hole, breach.

boquilla, *nf* mouthpiece; nozzle; burner; cigarette holder.

borda, *nm* gunwale, rail.

bordado, *nm* embroidery, needlework.

bordar, *vt* to embroider; to do supremely well.

borde, *nm* edge, border; side; brim, rim.

bordear, *vt* to skirt, go along (or round) the edge of.

bordón, *nm* pilgrim's staff; stick.

bordonear, *vt* to strum.

boricua, *adj* Puerto Rican.

borla, *nf* tassel, pompom; tuft.

borne, *nm* (Elect) terminal.

borracho(a), *adj* **1.** drunk, intoxicated; hard drinking, fond of the bottle; **2.** *nm/f* drunkard, drunk.

borrado, *nm* erasure.

borrador, *nm* first draft, rough copy.

borrajear, *vt/i* to scribble, scrawl; to doodle.

borrar, *vt* to erase, rub out; to cross out, score out.

borrarse, *vr* to resign (from a club etc).

borrasca, *nf* storm; squall.

borregaje, *nm* flock of lambs.

borrego(a), *nm/f* (Zool) lamb, yearling lamb.

borreguil, *adj* meek, like a lamb.

borrica, *nf* she-donkey.

borrico, *nm* donkey.

borriquete, *nm* easel; sawhorse.

borrón, *nm* blot, smudge, stain; blemish.

borronear, *vt* to scribble; to doodle.

borroso, *adj* blurred, indistinct, fuzzy; smudgy.

boscoso, *adj* wooded.

bosque, *nm* wood, woodland, forest; woods.

bosquejo, *nm* sketch, outline; rough model; draft.

bosta, *nf* dung, droppings; manure.

bostezo, *nm* yawn.

bota, *nf* boot; leather wine bottle.

botador, *nm* **1.** pole; **2.** spendthrift.

botanas, *nf* snack, appetizer.

botánica, *nf* botany.

botar, *vt* **1.** to throw, hurl; pitch; **2.** to launch.

bote, *nm* **1.** thrust, lunge, blow; **2.** can, tin, canister; pot, jar; **3.** boat.

botella, *nf* bottle.

botellería, *nf* wine shop.

botellero, *nm* wine-rack.

botica, *nf* chemist's (shop), pharmacy, drugstore.

botija, *nf* earthenware jug.

botillero, *nm* shoemaker, cobbler.

botiquín, *nm* medicine chest; first-aid post; first-aid kit.

botón, *nm* button.

botonar, *vt* to button (up).

bóveda, *nf* vault; dome; cave, cavern.

boxeador, *nm* boxer.

boxeo, *nm* boxing.

boyante, *adj* buoyant, light in the water; prosperous.

boyar, *vi* to float.

boyera, *nf* cattle shed.

boyero, *nm* oxherd, drover.

bozal, *adj* 1. new, raw, green; 2. muzzle; halter, headstall.

bracear, *vi* to swing one's arms.

bracero, *nm* laborer, farmhand.

braga, *nf* sling, rope; nappy, diaper; breeches; panties.

bragado, *adj* energetic, tough; wicked, vicious.

bramante, *nm* twine, string.

bramar, *vi* (Zool) to roar, bellow.

bramido, *nm* roar, bellow howl, howling.

branquia, *nf* gill.

brasa, *nf* live coal, hot coal.

brasear, *vt* to braise.

brasería, *nf* grill.

brasero, *nm* brazier (as used for domestic heating); hearth, fireplace.

brava, *nf* dispute, row, fight.

bravear, *vi* to boast, talk big to bluster.

bravo, *adj* brave; tough, spirited.

brazada, *nf* movement of the arms.

brazalete, *nm* bracelet, wristlet.

brazo, *nm* arm; foreleg.

brebaje, *nm* potion, mixture; brew, concoction.

brecha, *nf* breach; gap, opening.

bregar, *vi* to struggle, fight, to quarrel, scrap.

brete, *nm* fetters, shackles.

brevedad, *nf* shortness, brevity; terseness, conciseness.

brida, *nf* bridle; rein.

brigada, *nf* 1. brigade; 2. squad, gang.

brigadier, *nm* brigadier(-general).

brillante, *adj* 1. brilliant, bright, shining; sparkling; glittering, splendid; 2. diamond.

brillar, *vi* to shine; to sparkle, glitter, gleam, glisten.

brillo, *nm* brilliance; brightness, shine; glitter; glow.

brincar, *vt* 1. to jump up and down, bounce, dandle; 2. to skip, miss out.

brinco, *nm* hop, jump, leap, skip; bounce.

brindar, *vt* 1. to offer, present, 2. to dedicate (to).

brindis, *nm* toast; (ceremony of) dedication.

brío, *nm* spirit, dash, verve; determination.

brioso, *adj* spirited, dashing; determined.

brisa, *nf* breeze.

británico(a), *adj* British.

brocado, *nm* brocade.

brocal, *nm* rim, mouth; curb, parapet.

brocha, *nf* brush.

broche, *nm* clip, clasp, fastener; brooch.

brollero, *adj* trouble-making, mischief-making.

broma, *nf* fun, gaiety, merriment; joke.

bromear, *vi* to joke, crack jokes, rag.

bromuro, *nm* bromide.

bronca, *nf* row, scrap, set-to.

bronce, *nm* bronze; brass.

bronceado, *adj* 1. bronze, bronze-colored; 2. tanned, sunburnt.

bronceador, *nm* suntan lotion.

broncear, *vt* 1. to bronze; 2. to tan, brown.

broncearse, *vr* to brown, get a suntan.

bronco, *adj* 1. rough, coarse; 2. wild, untamed.

bronquios, *nm* bronchial tubes.

bronquitis, *nf* bronchitis.

broquero, *nm* brace.

bretar, *vt* 1. to bring forth; to sprout, put out; 2. to spring up, gush forth, flow.

brote, *nm* 1. bud, shoot; 2. outbreak, appearance.

bruja, *nf* witch; sorceress.

brujería, *nf* witchcraft, sorcery, (black) magic.

brujo, *nm* sorcerer; wizard, magician.

brújula, *nf* compass; magnetic needle.

bruma, *nf* mist, fog.

brumoso, *adj* misty, foggy.

bruñido, *adj* polished, burnished.

brusco, *adj* sudden; brusque.

brusquedad, *nf* 1. suddenness; sharpness; 2. brusqueness, abruptness; rudeness.

brutal, *adj* brutal; brutish, beastly.

bruto, *adj* brute, beast, brutish.

buba, *nf* tumor, bubo.

bubónico, *adj* bubonic plague.

bucal, *adj* of the mouth; through the mouth, by mouth, orally.

búcaro, *nm* vase.

buceador(a), *nm/f* diver; underwater swimmer, skindiver.

bucear, *vt* to dive; to swim under water; to skin dive.

bucle, *nm* curl, ringlet.

buchada, *nf* mouthful of liquid.

buche, *nm* 1. crop; (Zool) maw; guts, belly; 2. mouthful (of liquid).

budín, *nm* cake; trifle.

budismo, *nm* Buddhism.

budista, *adj* 1. buddhist; 2. *nm/f* Buddhist.

buenaventura, *nf* 1. good luck; 2. fortune.

buenmozo, *adj* good-looking, handsome.

bueno, *adj* good, fine, fair.

buey, *nm* ox; bullock, steer.

búfalo, *nm* buffalo.

bufanda, *nf* scarf, muffler.

bufet, *nm* buffet supper; sideboard.

búho, *nm* owl.

buitre, *nm* vulture, Griffin vulture.

buje, *nm* axle box, bushing.

bujía, *nf* 1. candle; candlestick; 2. candle-power; 3. spark plug.

bulbo, *nm* bulb; valve, tube (US); electric bulb.

bulto, *nm* size, bulk, bulkiness, volume, massiveness.

bulla, *nf* noise, uproar; racket; bustle; fuss, confusion; quarrel, brawl.

buñuelo, *nm* doughnut, fritter, botched job, mess.

buque, *nm* ship, vessel, boat.

buqué, *nm* bouquet (of wine).

burbuja, *nf* bubble.

burbujeante, *adj* bubbly, fizzy; bubbling.

burdo, *adj* coarse, rough; clumsy.

burguesía, *nf* middle class, bourgeoisie; upper middle class.

burla, *nf* gibe, taunt, jeer; mockery, ridicule.

burlador, *adj* 1. mocking; 2. *nm* scoffer, mocker.

burlar, *vt* to deceive, take in, hoax, trick

buró, *nm* bureau, (roll-top) desk.

burocracia, *nf* bureaucracy.

burócrata, *nm/f* civil servant, administrative official.

burra, *nf* (she-)donkey.

burro, *nm* donkey.

bursátil, *adj* stock-exchange, stock-market.

busca, *nf* search, hunt; pursuit.

buscador(a), *nm/f* searcher, seeker.

buscas, *nf* perks, profits on the side.

buscavida, *nm/f* 1. snooper, meddler, busybody; 2. hustler; social climber, go-getter.

busquéda, *nf* search; inquiry, investigation.

butaca, *nf* armchair, easy chair; orchestra stall.

butacón, *nm* large armchair.
butifarra, *nf* Catalan sausage.
buzo, *nm* diver.
buzón, *nm* letterbox, pillar-box, mailbox.

C

C, c, *nf* (letter) C, c.
C, *abr* (de centígrado) centigrade.
cábala, *nf* 1. cab(b)ala; 2. guess, supposition; intrigues.
cabalgador, *nm* rider, horseman.
cabalgata, *nf* ride; cavalcate, mounted procession.
caballaje, *nm* horse power.
caballería, *nf* 1. steed; horse; mule; 2. cavalry; 3. knighthood.
caballeriza, *nf* stable; stud, horse-breeding establishment.
caballero, *nm* 1. rider, horseman; 2. gentleman; 3. knight; nobleman.
caballerosidad, *nf* gentlemanliness; chivalry.
caballo, *nm* horse.
cabaña, *nf* hut, cabin, hovel, shack; log cabin.
cabaret, *nm* cabaret, nightclub.
cabaretera, *nf* cabaret dancer, cabaret entertainer; nightclub hostess; showgirl.
cabe, *prep* near, next to.
cabecear, *vi* 1. to bind (the edge of); 2. to nod, to shake one's head; 3. to shift, slip.
cabecera, *nf* 1. head, seat of honor; 2. headboard.
cabecilla, *nm/f* 1. hothead, wrong-headed person; 2. ringleader, leader.
cabellera, *nf* hair, head of hair; wig.
cabello, *nm* hair.
cabelludo, *adj* hairy, shaggy.
caber, *vi* to go, fit (in), to be contained; to have enough room.
cabeza, *nf* 1. head; 2. summit; 3. bulb of garlic.
cabezada, *nf* 1. butt; blow on the head; 2. shake of the head, doze.
cabida, *nf* space, room; capacity.
cabildear, *vi* to lobby.
cabildero(a), *nm/f* lobbyist, member of a pressure group.
cabildo, *nm* chapter; town council.
cabina, *nf* cabin; cockpit; locker; projection room.
cable, *nm* cable, rope, hawser, wire.
cablegrafiar, *vi* to cable.
cablegrama, *nm* cable, cablegram.
cabo, *nm* 1. end, extremity, termination, conclusion; 2. bit; stub, stump, butt; 3. cape.
cabotaje, *nm* coasting trade, coastal traffic.
cabra, *nf* 1. (Zool) goat; 2. trick, swindle.
cabrear, *vt* to infurate, make livid.
cabrestante, *nm* capstan, winch.
cabritilla, *nf* kid, kidskin.
cabro, *nm* (Zool) he-goat, billy goat.
cábula, *nf* 1. amulet; 2. intrigue; 3. trick.
cabulear, *vi* to scheme.
cabuya, *nf* agave, pita; pita fiber; rope, cord.
cacahual, *nm* cacao plantation.
cacahuate, *nm* peanut, groundnut.
cacao, *nm* cacao; cocoa.
cacareo, *nm* crowing, cackling; boasting, trumpeting.

cacatúa, *nf* cockatoo.
cacerola, *nf* pan, saucepan; casserole.
caco, *nm* 1. pickpocket, thief; crook; 2. ward.
cacto, *nm* cactus.
cacharrería, *nf* 1. crockery shop; 2. crockery, pots; 3. ironmongery.
cacharro, *nm* 1. earthenware pot, crock; earthenware, crockery, pots, coarse pottery; 2. piece of pottery; 3. useless object, piece of junk.
cachaza, *nf* slowness; calmness, phlegm.
cachemir, *nm/f* cashmere.
cachete, *nm* 1. cheek; 2. punch in the face, slap.
cachimba, *nf* pipe.
cachiporra, *nf* truncheon; club, big stick, cosh.
cachorro(a), *nm/f* puppy; cub.
cachucha, *nf* hat, tile.
cada, *adj* each, every.
cadalso, *nm* scaffold; stand, platform.
cadáver, *nm* body, dead body, corpse, cadaver (US).
cadavérico, *adj* cadaverous; death-like; ghastly, deathly pale.
cadena, *nf* chain; bond, link; series, sequence; network.
cadencia, *nf* cadence, rhythm; measure.
cadenilla, *nf* small chain; necklace.
cadera, *nf* hip.
cadete, *nm* cadet; junior; office-boy; apprentice.
caedizo, *adj* 1. unsteady, about to fall; weak; 2. *nm* shed; sloping roof.
caer, *vi* to fail; to fall down; to tumble (down), collapse; to fall off, fall out; to crash.
café, *nm* coffee.
cafeína, *nf* caffeine.
cafetal, *nm* 1. coffee plantation; 2. coffee tree.
cafetín, *nm* seedy bar, small café.
caída, *nf* fall; tumble, spill; falling, falling-out.
caimán, *nm* cayman, caiman, alligator.
caja, *nf* box; chest; case, crate; coffin, casket (US).
cajero(a), *nm/f* cashier; (bank) teller.
cajetilla, *nf* small box.
cajuela, *nf* car trunk.
cal, *nf* lime.
calabaza, *nf* gourd, squash, pumpkin.
calabozo, *nm* prison; prison cell; dungeon.
caladero, *nm* fishing-grounds.
calado, *adj* 1. to be soaked (to the skin); 2. *nm* openwork; 3. depth of water.
calamar, *nm* squid.
calambre, *nm* cramp.
calamidad, *nf* calamity, disaster.
calamina, *nf* 1. calamine; 2. corrugated iron.
calar, *vt* soak, drench; to penetrate, perforate, pierce, go through.
calavera, *nf* skull.
calcado, *nm* tracing.
calcañal, *nm* heel.
calcáreo, *adj* calcareous; lime.
calcetín, *nm* sock.
calcificar, *vi* to calcify.
calcinar, *vt* 1. to calcine; to burn, reduce to ashes, blacken; 2. to bother, annoy.
calcio, *nm* calcium.
calcomanía, *nf* transfer.
calculador, *adj* 1. calculating; 2. selfish, mercenary.
calculadora, *nf* calculating machine, calculator.
calcular, to calculate, compute; to add up, work out.
cálculo, *nm* calculation; reckoning; estimate; conjecture; calculus.
caldear, *vi* to warm (up), heat (up); to weld.
caldearse, *vr* to get very hot; get overheated.
caldeo, *nm* warming, heating; welding.
caldera, *nf* boiler; boiling-pan; pot, kettle.

calderón, nm 1. large boiler, cauldron; 2. paragraph sign, section mark; 3. musical sign.

caldo, nm broth, bouillon; consommé, clear soup.

calefactor, adj 1. heating; heating system; 2. nm heater.

calendario, nm calendar.

calentador, nm heater.

calentura, nf fever, temperature.

caleta, nf cave, small bay, inlet.

calibre, nm caliber, gauge, bore, diameter.

calibración, nf calibration.

calibrador, nm gauge; calliper(s); wire gauge.

calidad, nf 1. quality; 2. position, capacity.

cálido, adj hot; warm.

caliente, adj warm, hot.

calificación, nf 1. calification; assessment; description, label; 2. standing; grade, mark.

calificado, adj 1. qualified, competent; skilled; 2. well-known, eminent; undisputed.

calificar, vt 1. qualify; 2. assess; to rate; to grade, mark.

cáliz, nm 1. calyx; 2. chalice, communion cup.

calizo, adj lime; limy.

calma, nf calm, inactivity; cessation.

calmar, vt 1. to calm; 2. vi to abate.

calor, nm heat; warmth.

caloría, nf calorie.

calorífero, adj 1. heat-producing, heat-giving, 2. nm heating system; furnace, stove.

calumniar, vt to slander, libel.

caluroso, adj warm, hot; enthusiastic, hearty.

calva, nf bald patch; bare spot.

calvicie, nf baldness.

calvo, adj bald; hairless.

calzada, nf roadway; (paved) road; causeway.

calzado, adj shod, wearing shoes; 2. nm footwear.

calzar, vt to put on; to wear shoes.

calzoncillos, nm pants, underpants, shorts.

callado, adj quiet, reserved, reticent.

callar, vt to keep a secret; to pass over in silence, say nothing about, not mention.

calle, nf street, road.

callejear, vi to wander about the streets, stroll around; to loaf, hang about idly.

callicida, nm corn cure.

callista, nm/f chiropodist.

callo, nm corn; callus.

cama, nf 1. bed; bedstead; 2. bedding, litter.

camaleón, nm chameleon.

cámara, nf room, hall, camber.

camarada, nm/f comrade, companion, pal, mate.

camaradería, nf comradeship, companionship, camaradie, mattines.

camarero(a), nm/f 1. waiter, steward, chamberlain; 2. waitress, maid, chambermaid.

camarógrafo, nm cameraman.

camarón, nm shrimp, prawn.

camaronear, vi to go shrimping.

camarote, nm cabin, state room.

cambiador, nm barterer; moneychanger; switchman.

cambiar, vt 1. to change, alter, convert; 2. to exchange, to shift, to move.

cambio, nm change, alteration, substitution, switch.

camelia, nf camellia.

camello, nm (Zool) camel.

camilla, nf sofa, couch; stretcher.

camillero(a), nm/f stretcher-bearer.

caminata, nf long walk; hike.

camino, nm road; track, path; trail.

camión, nm truck.

camioneta, nf van, light truck; station-wagon.

camisa, nf shirt; chemise, slip.

camisero, nm 1. shirt maker; outfitter; 2. dress shirt.

camiseta, nf vest, undershirt; singlet, T-shirt.

camita, nf small bed, cot.

campamento, nm camp; encampment.

campana, nf bell.

campanario, nm bell tower, church tower.

campanear, vi 1. ring the bells; 2. keep watch.

campanilla, nf small bell, handbell.

campaña, nf 1. countryside; level country, plain; 2. campaign.

campar, vi to camp.

campear, vi 1. to go to graze, go out to pasture; 2. to work in the fields.

campeón(a), nm/f champion.

campeonato, nm championship.

campesina, nf peasant (woman).

campesino, adj country, rural, peasant; rustic.

campiña, nf countryside, open country; flat stretch of farmland, large area of cultivated land.

campo, nm 1. country, countryside; 2. field.

camposanto, nm cemetery, churchyard.

campus, nm (University) campus..

camuflaje, nm camouflage.

can, nm dog, hound.

cana, nf white hair, grey hair.

canal, nm 1. canal; waterway; 2. (TV) channel; 3. conduit, pipe; underground watercourse; 4. gutter, guttering; spout; drainpipe.

canalización, nf 1. canalization, channelling. 2. piping; (Elec) wiring.

canalón, nm gutter, guttering; spout; drainpipe.

canalla, nf rabble, mob, riffraff; 2. nm swiner.

canallada, nf dirty trick, mean thing (to do), despicable act.

canario, adj 1. of the Canary Isles; 2. nm/f native (or inhabitant) of the Canary Isles; 3. nm (Orn) canary.

canasta, nf basket; hamper; crate.

canasto, nm large basket; hamper; crate.

cáncamo, nm eyebolt; ringbolt.

cancán, nm (Music) cancan.

cancanear, vi to loiter, loaf about.

cancelación, nf cancellation; deletion.

cancelar, vt to cancel; to write off, wipe out; to delete.

cáncer, nm cancer.

canceroso, adj cancerous.

canciller, nm chancellor.

cancillería, nf chancery; chancellery.

cancionero, nm (Mús) songbook, collection of songs.

cancha, nf field; ground; open space, tract of level ground; sports-field.

candado, nm padlock.

candela, nf 1. candle; candlestick; 2. fire; light.

candelero, nm candlestick; oil lamp.

candelilla, nf small candle.

candente, adj red-hot, white-hot; glowing, burning.

candidato(a), nm/f candidate (for); applicant (for).

cándido, adj simple, ingenuous, innocent; naïve.

candil, nm oil lamp, kitchen lamp.

candileja, nf oil reservoir of a lamp; small oil lamp.

candor, nm innocence, guilelessness, simplicity; frankness, candidness.

canela, nf cinnamon.

canelero, nm cinnamon tree.

canelo, adj cinnamon, cinnamon-colored.

cangrejo, nm crab.

caníbal, adj 1. cannibal; cannibalistic, man-eating; 2. nm/f cannibal.

canica, nf marble.

canicultura, nf dog-breeding.

canijo, adj weak, frail, sickly.

canilla, *nf* long bone (of arm or leg); (espinilla) shin, shinbone.

canillera, *nf* fear; cowardice.

canino, *adj* (Zool) canine; dog.

canje, *nm* exchange.

cano, *adj* grey-haired, white-haired, white-headed.

canoa, *nf* canoe; boat, launch.

canódromo, *nm* dogtrack.

canon, *nm* (a) rule, canon.

canónico, *adj* canonical; canon law.

canonizar, *vt* to canonize; to consecrate.

canoso, *adj* grey-haired, white-haired.

cansado, *adj* 1. tired, weary (de); 2. tedious, boring; tiresome, trying.

cansancio, *nm* tiredness, fatigue, exhaustion.

cansar, *vt* to tire, tire out, weary; to fatigue, exhaust.

cantadera, *nf* loud singing, prolonged singing.

cantador(a), *nm/f* folksinger, singer of popular songs.

cantante, *adj* 1. singing; 2. *nm/f* singer; vocalist.

cantar, *vt/i* to sing; to chant.

cántara, *nf* large pitcher.

cántaro, *nm* pitcher, jug; jugful.

cantera, *nf* 1. quarry, pit; 2. talent, genius; 3. source of supply.

cántico, *nm* canticle; song.

cantidad, *nf* quantity; amount, number.

cantillos, *nm* jacks.

cantimplora, *nf* water bottle, canteen.

cantina, *nf* buffet, refreshment room; canteen; (snack) snack bar.

cantinero, *nm* barman, publican.

canto, *nm* 1. (Mús) singing; chanting; 2. edge; rim, border.

canturreo, *nm* humming, crooning, soft singing; chanting; droning.

canuto, *adj* super, smashing.

caña, *nf* cane, stem, stalk; walking stick.

cañabrava, *nf* reed; bamboo.

cañada, *nf* gully, ravine; glen.

cañamelar, *nm* sugar-cane plantation.

cáñamo, *nm* hemp; hempen cloth; hempen cord.

cañaveral, *nm* reedbed; sugar-cane plantation.

cañear, *vi* to drink, carouse.

cañengo, *adj* weak, sickly; skinny.

cañería, *nf* pipe, piece of piping.

cañero, *adj* sugar-cane; machete.

cañita, *nf* (drinking) straw.

caño, *nm* tube, pipe; pipe.

cañonear, *vt* 1. to shell, bombard; 2. *vr* to get tight.

cañoneo, *nm* shelling, shellfire, gunfire; bombardment, cannonade.

cañonero(a), *nm/f* 1. embrasure; 2. gunboat.

caoba, *nf* mahogany.

caos, *nm* chaos.

caótico, *adj* chaotic.

capa, *nf* cloak, cape; raincape, waterproof cloak.

capacidad, *nf* capacity.

capacitación, *nf* capacitation; training, education.

capar, *vt* to castrate, geld.

capataz, *nm* foreman, overseer.

capaz, *adj* capacious, roomy, large.

capcioso, *adj* wily, deceitful.

capeador, *nm* bullfighter who uses the cape.

capear, *vt* to play with the cape.

capellán, *nm* chaplain; priest, clergyman.

capellanía, *nf* chaplaincy.

capero, *nm* hallstand, hatstand.

capilar, *adj* capillary; hair; capillary.

capilla, *nf* chapel.

capítulo, *nm* chapter.

capón, *adj* 1. castrated; 2. *nm* capon; eunuch.

caporal, *nm* chief, leader, foreman, head man.

capotar, *vi* to turn over, turn turtle; to somersault; to fall down, collapse.

capote, *nm* long cloak, cloak with sleeves; bullfighter's cape.

capotear, *vt* to play with the cape.

capricho, *nm* whim, caprice, keen desire, sudden urge.

caprichoso, *adj* capricious: full of whims, having odd fancies; full of one's own pet notions.

cápsula, *nf* capsule.

captador, *nm* sensor.

captar, *vt* to captivate; apoyo to win, gain, attract.

captura, *nf* capture; seizure; arrest.

capturar, *vt* to capture; to seize; to arrest.

capuchino, *nm* 1. Capuchin; 2. capuccino (coffee).

capuchón, *nm* capuchin, lady's hooded cloak.

capujar, *vt* to catch in (or snatch out of) the air.

capullo, *nm* 1. cocoon; 2. bud; cup; rosebud.

cara, *nf* face.

carabina, *nf* carbine, rifle.

caracol, *nm* snail; snail shell, sea shell.

carácter, *nm* 1. character; nature, kind, condition; 2. personage; 3. type, typeface.

característica, *nf* characteristic; trait, quality, attribute.

caracterizado, *adj* distinguished, of note; special, peculiar, typical.

caracterizarse, *vr* to make up, dress for the part.

caramba, *interj* well!, good gracious!; very odd!, how strange!.

caramelo, *nm* sweet, toffee; candy caramel.

carapacho, *nm* shell, carapace.

caraqueño(a), *adj* 1. of Caracas; 2. *nm/f* native (or inhabitant) of Caracas; the people of Caracas.

carátula, *nf* 1. mask; the stage, the theater; 2. face, dial; 3. title page; cover (of a magazine).

caravana, *nf* caravan; group, band.

caray, *interj* gosh!, good heavens!.

carbohidrato, *nm* carbohydrate.

carbón, *nm* coal.

carboncillo, *nm* charcoal; small coal, slack.

carbonera, *nf* coalmine.

carbonería, *nf* coalyard.

carbonero, *adj* 1. coal; charcoal; 2. *nm* coal merchant; charcoal burner.

carbonizar, *vt* to carbonize; to char.

carburador, *nm* carburetor.

carburante, *nm* fuel.

carburar, *vi* 1. to go, work; 2. to think, ponder.

carburo, *nm* carbide.

carcajada, *nf* laugh, peal of laughter, guffaw.

carcajear, *vi* to roar with laughter, have a good laugh (at).

cárcel, *nf* prison, jail.

carcelero, *adj* 1. prison; 2. *nm* warder, jailer.

carcomer, *vt* to bore into; eat into, eat away.

carcomerse, *vr* to get worm-eaten.

carcomido, *adj* worm-eaten, wormy, infested with wood-worm; rotten.

cardán, *nm* propellor shaft; axle.

cardar, *vt* to card, comb.

cardenal, *nm* 1. cardinal; 2. bruise, mark, weal; 3. cardinal bird.

cárdeno, *adj* purple, violet; livid; opalescent.

cardíaco, *adj* cardiac, heart.

cardinal, *adj* cardinal.

cardiograma, *nm* cardiogram, cardiograph.

cardiología, *nf* cardiology.

cardiólogo(a), *nm/f* cardiologist, heart specialist.

cardiovascular, *adj* cardiovascular.

carear, *vt* 1. to bring face to face; to compare, collate, check against each other; 2. *vi* to face towards, look on to.

carecer, *vi* to lack, be in need of, be without.

carencia, *nf* lack (of), shortage (of), need (for); scarcity.

carente, *adj* lacking (in), devoid of.

careo, *nm* confrontation, meeting (face to face); comparison, collation.

carero, *adj* expensive, dear, pricey.

carestía, *nf* scarcity, shortage, dearth; famine.

careta, *nf* mask; breathing apparatus, respirator.

carga, *nf* load; freight; burden, weight.

cargadero, *nm* loading point; loading bay.

cargador, *nm* loader; carrier, haulier; docker, stevedore, longshoreman.

cargamento, *nm* 1. loading; 2. load;

cargar, *vt* 1. to load burden, weigh down (with); 2. to stoke; 3. to impose, lay (on); 4. to impute, ascribe; 5. to attack; 6. to carry.

carguero, *nm* freighter, cargo boat; freight plane.

cariado, *adj* bad, rotten, decayed, carious.

cariadura, *nf* caries, decay.

cariar, *vt* to cause to decay, cause decay in.

caribe, *adj* Caribbean.

caricatura, *nf* caricature; cartoon.

caricia, *nf* caress; pat, stroke.

caridad, *nf* charity; charitableness.

carie, *nf* dental decay, caries.

cariño, *nm* affection, love; fondness.

cariñoso, *adj* affectionate, loving, fond; tender.

carioca, *adj* 1. of Rio de Janeiro, of the State of Guanabara; 2. *nm/f* native (or inhabitant) of Rio de Janeiro, native (or inhabitant) of the State of Guanabara.

carisma, *nm* charisma.

carismático, *adj* charismatic.

carmelita, *adj* 1. Carmelite; light brown, tan; 2. *nm/f* Carmelite; discalced Carmelite.

carmesí, *adj* 1. crimsonm; 2. *nm* crimson.

carmín, *nm* carmine; rouge, lipstick.

carnada, *nf* bait.

carnal, *adj* 1. carnal, of the flesh. 2. full, blood; full brother.

carnaval, *nm* carnival.

carne, *nf* 1. flesh; 2. meat; 3. carnality.

carnear, *vt* to slaughter; to murder, butcher.

carnero, *nm* sheep, ram.

carnet, *nm* carnets; notebook; identity card.

carnicería, *nf* butcher's (shop); meat market; slaughterhouse.

carnicero, *adj* 1. carnivorous, flesh-eating; 2. person fond of meat; 3. savage, cruel, bloodthirsty; 4. *nm* butcher.

caro, *adj* 1. dear, beloved; 2. expensive.

carótida, *nf* carotid (artery).

carpa, *nf* 1. carp; goldfish; 2. tent; marquee; awning

carpeta, *nf* folder, file; portfolio; briefcase.

carpintería, *nf* 1. carpentry, joinery, woodwork, 2. carpenter's shop,

carpintero, *nm* 1. carpenter; woodworker; 2. woodpecker.

carrera, *nf* run, running, chase; (beisbol) homerun; race; career, profession.

carrerilla, *nf* non-stop, continuously.

carreta, *nf* wagon, low cart; wheelbarrow.

carrete, *nm* reel, spool; bobbin.

carretear, *vt* to cart, haul.

carretera, *nf* road, highway.

carretilla, *nf* truck; handcart, barrow; wheelbarrow.

carril, *nm* rut, track.

carrilera, *nf* 1. rut, track, lane; 2. siding.

carrito, *nm* 1. trolley, shopping cart; 2. taxi.

carro, *nm* cart, wagon; chariot, trolley, shopping cart.

carrocería, *nf* 1. coachbuilder's; carriage repair shop; 2. bodywork, coachwork.

carromato, *nm* covered wagon, (gipsy) caravan.

carroña, *nf* carrion.

carroñero, *adj* rotten; vile, foul; 2. animal which feeds on carrion.

carroza, *nf* coach, carriage.

carruaje, *nm* carriage; vehicle.

carrusel, *nm* 1. merry-go-round, roundabout; 2. carrousel, circular slide-tray.

carta, *nf* 1. letter; 2. document, 3. map; 4. playing card.

cartabón, *nm* square, set-square-triangle; quadrant.

cartear, *vi* to play low.

cartearse, *vr* to correspond (with).

cartel, *nm* poster, placard; bill.

cartelera, *nf* billboard; notice board.

cartelón, *nm* large notice; sign.

carteo, *nm* correspondence, exchange of letters.

cartera, *nf* 1. wallet, pocketbook; 2. ministerial post.

carterista, *nm* pickpocket.

cartero, *nm* postman, mailman.

cartílago, *nm* cartilage.

cartilla, *nf* first reader; spelling book.

cartografía, *nf* cartography, mapmaking.

cartográfico, *adj* cartographic(al).

cartógrafo(a), *nm/f* cartographer, mapmaker.

cartomancia, *nf* fortune-telling (with cards).

cartomante, *nm/f* fortune-teller (who uses cards).

cartón, *nm* cardboard, pasteboard; board; cartoon; box; carton.

cartuchera, *nf* cartridge belt.

cartucho, *nm* 1. cartridge; cartridge case; 2. paper cone, paper cornet.

cartulina, *nf* thin cardboard.

casa, *nf* house; flat, apartment.

casaca, *nf* frock coat; zip jacket; riding coat.

casada, *nf* married woman.

casadero, *adj* marriageable, of an age to be married.

casado, *adj* 1. married; 2. *nm* married man.

casamiento, *nm* marriage, wedding.

casar, *vt* 1. to marry, join in marriage, join in wedlock; 2. *vi* to match, harmonize.

cascabel, *nm* bell.

cascabelear, *vt* 1. to take in, raise the hopes of, beguile; 2. *vi* to jingle, tinkle.

cascabeleo, *nm* jingle, jingling, tinkling.

cascabelero(a), *adj* 1. scatterbrained; 2. *nm/f* scatterbrain.

cascada, *nf* waterfall; cascade.

cascado, *adj* 1. broken (down); infirm, decrepit, worn out; 2. weak, unmelodious, cracked;

cascajo, *nm* gravel; rubble; fragments, shards.

cascar, *vt* 1. to crack, split, break (open); to crunch; 2. *vi* to chatter, talk too much.

cáscara, *nf* shell; husk, rind, peel, skin.

cascarón, *nm* eggshell.

cascarrabias, *nm/f* quick-tempered person, irritable sort.

casco, *nm* helmet; crown.

cascote, *nm* rubble, debris.

casera, *nf* landlady (owner); housekeeper.

caserío, *nm* 1. country house; 2. hamlet, settlement, group of dwellings.

casero, *adj* 1. domestic, household; home-made; 2. persona home-loving; 3. *nm* landlord; caretaker; porter, concierge, janitor.

caseta, *nf* stall, stand, booth.

caset(t)e, *nm/f* 1. cassette; 2. *nm* cassette-player.

casi, *adv* almost, nearly.

casilla, nf hut, cabin, shed.
casillero, nm pigeonholes; luggage-locker; sorting-rack; score-board.
casino, nm club; social club, casino.
casita, nf small house; cottage.
casona, nf large house.
caspa, nf dandruff, scurf.
casquete, nm skullcap; helmet; cap.
casquillo, nm tip, cap; bottle-top.
casquivano(a), adj 1. scatterbrained; 2. nm/f scatterbrain.
casta, nf caste; breed, race.
castaña, nf chestnut.
castañar, nm chestnut grove.
castañero(a), nm chestnut seller.
castañetear, vt 1. to snap; 2. vi to snap; to click.
castañeteo, nm snapping; clicking; rattling.
castaño, adj 1. chestnut(-colored), brown; 2. nm chestnut, chestnut tree.
castañuela, nf castanet.
castellano(a), adj 1. Castilian; Spanish; 2. nm/f Castilian Spaniard; 3. nm Castilian, Spanish.
casticidad, nf 1. purity, correctness; 2. traditional character; thoroughbred character.
castigar, vt to punish; to penalize (for).
castigo, nm punishment; penalty.
castilla, nf Castilian, Spanish.
castillo, nm castle.
castizo, adj 1. pure, correct; 2. thoroughbred; true-born.
casto, adj chaste, pure.
castor, nm beaver.
castra, nf pruning; pruning season.
castración, nf 1. castration, gelding; 2. pruning; 3. extraction of honeycombs.
castrado, adj 1. castrated; 2. nm eunuch.
castrar, vt 1. to castrate, geld; 2. to prune, cut back; 3. to extract honeycombs from.
castrense, adj army, military.
casualidad, nf chance, accident; coincidence.
cata, nf tasting, sampling; wine-tasting; parrot.
cataclismo, nm cataclysm.
catadura, nf tasting, sampling, blending.
catalejo, nm spyglass, telescope.
catalizador, nm catalyst; catalytic converter.
catalogar, vt to catalogue.
catálogo, nm catalogue.
catapulta, nf catapult.
catapultar, vt to catapult.
catar, vt 1. to taste, sample, try; 2. to examine, inspect, have a look at.
catarata, nf waterfall, falls; cataract.
catarro, nm cold; catarrh.
catarroso, adj subject to colds; having catarrh, suffering from catarrh.
catástrofe, nf catastrophe.
catastrófico, adj catastrophic.
cate, nm 1. punch, bash; 2. nm/f teacher.
catear, vt to investigate; to try, sample.
catecismo, nm catechism.
cátedra, nf 1. chair, professorship; senior teaching post; 2. adj wonderful, marvellous, excellent.
catedral, nf cathedral.
catedrático(a), nm/f professor.
categoría, nf category; class, group.
categorizar, vt to categorize.
caterva, nf host, throng, crowd.
catéter, nm catheter.
cátodo, nm cathode.
catolicismo, nm Catholicism.
católico, adj Catholic.

catorce, adj fourteen; fourteenth.
catre, nm cot; bed; bedstead.
cauchal, nm rubber plantation,
cauchar, nm 1. rubber plantation; 2. vi to tap (trees for rubber).
cauchera, nf rubber plant, rubber tree.
cauchero, adj 1. rubber; 2. nm rubber tapper, rubber worker.
caucho, nm 1. rubber; 2. raincoat, mac.
caudal, nm 1. volume, flow; 2. plenty, abundance, wealth; fortune.
caudaloso, adj 1. large, carrying much water; 2. copious, abundant; wealthy, rich.
caudillo(a), nm/f leader, chief; strong man.
causa, nf cause; reason, motive; snack, light meal.
causal, adj 1. causal; 2. nf reason, grounds.
causante, adj 1. causing, originating; 2. nm/f causer, originator; 3. nf cause.
causar, vt to cause; to create, entail, make; to create.
cáustico, adj caustic.
cautela, nf caution, cautiousness, caginess, wariness.
cauteloso, adj cautious, cagey, wary, careful.
cauterizar, vt to cauterize.
cautivar, vt to capture, take prisoner.
cautiverio, nm captivity; bondage, serfdom.
cautivo(a), adj, nm/f captive.
cauto, adj cautious, wary, careful.
cava, nf 1. digging and hoeing; 2. closed truck; 3. winecellar; sparkling wine.
cavar, vt to dig.
caverna, nf cave, cavern.
cavernícola, adj 1. cave-dwelling, cave; 2. nm/f cave dweller, caveman, troglodyte.
caviar, nm caviar(e).
cavidad, nf cavity; hollow, space.
cavilación, nf deep thought, rumination.
cavilar, vt to ponder, consider closely; to brood over.
cayado, nm staff, stick; crook; crozier.
cayo, nm islet, key.
caza, nf hunting; shooting, trapper.
caza-bombardero, nm fighter-bomber.
cazadero, nm hunting ground.
cazador, nm hunter; huntsman.
cazadora, nf hunter, huntress.
cazar, vt to hunt; to trap; to chase, pursue.
cazo, nm saucepan.
cazoleta, nf pan; bowl; boss; cup.
cazuela, nf pan, cooking-pot, casserole.
ceba, nf 1. fattening; 2. charge, priming.
cebadero, nm 1. barley dealer; 2. feeding place.
cebado, adj 1. man-eating; 2. nm fattening.
cebar, vt 1. to fatten (up), feed (up); 2. vi to grip, catch, go on.
cebiche, nm marinated fish salad; marinated shellfish.
cebolla, nf onion.
cebollino, nm young onion, spring onion, onion for transplanting; onion seed.
cebra, nf zebra.
ceceoso, adj lisping, having a lisp.
ceda, nf priority, right of way.
ceder, vt 1. to hand over, give up; to yield (up); 2. vi to give in, yield.
cedro, nm cedar.
cédula, nf certificate, document.
cefalea, nf severe headache, migraine.
cegador, adj blinding; blinding glare.
cegarse, vr to become blinded (by).
ceguera, nf blindness.
ceiba, nf silk-cotton tree, bombax.
ceja, nf eyebrow.
cejar, vi to move back, back; to give way, back down.

celada, nf ambush, trap; trick, ruse.

celador(a), nm/f watchman, guard.

celar, vt 1. to watch over, keep a watchful eye on; 2. to conceal, cover, hide; 3. vi to watch over.

celda, nf cell.

celdilla, nf cell; cavity, hollow; pigeonhole; niche.

celebración, nf celebration; holding.

celebrar, vt 1. to celebrate; to hold; to praise; to applaud; 2. vi to say mass.

celebrarse, vr occur; be celebrated; take place.

célebre, adj famous, celebrated, noted (for); remarkable.

celebridad, nf celebrity, fame.

celeridad, nf speed, swiftness; quickly, speedily.

celeste, adj celestial, heavenly; heavenly; sky blue.

célico, adj heavenly, celestial.

celo, nm 1. zeal, fervor, ardor; **religious fervor**, piety; 2. (Zool) rut, heat; 3. jealousy.

celofán, nm cellophane.

celosía, nf lattice; slatted shutter; lattice window.

celoso, adj 1. zealous (for), keen (about, on); eager; fervent; 2. jealous, suspicious.

célula, nf cell.

celular, adj cellular.

celuloide, nm celluloid.

cellisca, nf sleet; sleet storm.

cellisquear, vi to sleet.

cementar, vt to case-harden, cement.

cementerio, nm cemetery, graveyard.

cemento, nm cement; concrete

cena, nf evening meal; dinner.

cenador, nm arbor; pavilion; summerhouse.

cenagal, nm bog, quagmire, morass; tricky situation.

cenagoso, adj muddy, boggy.

cenar, vt 1. to have for supper, sup on, sup off; 2. vi to have one's supper, have dinner, dine.

cenceño, adj thin, skinny.

cenefa, nf edging, trimming, border; stripe, band.

cenicero, nm ashtray; ash pan; ash pit, ash tip.

cénit, nm zenith.

ceniza, nf ash, ashes; cinder.

cenizo, adj ashen, ash-colored.

censar, vt to take a census of.

censo, nm census.

censor(a), nm/f censor.

censurable, adj censurable, blameworthy.

censurar, vt 1. to censor; 2. to censure, condemn, criticize.

centavo, adj hundredth.

centella, nf spark; flash of lightning.

centelleante, adj sparkling; gleaming, glinting, twinkling; flashing.

centell(e)ar, vi to sparkle; to gleam, glint.

centelleo, nm sparkle, sparkling; gleam(ing); glinting; flashing.

centenar, nm hundred.

centenario, adj 1. centenary, centennial, 2. nm centenary, centennial.

centeno, nm rye.

centésimo, adj 1. hundredth; 2. nm hundredth.

centígrado, adj centigrade.

centímetro, nm centimeter.

céntimo, adj 1. hundredth; 2. nm hundredth part.

centinela, nf sentry, guard, sentinel; look-out man.

central, adj 1. central; middle; 2. nf head office.

centralizar, vt to centralize.

centrar, vt to center; to concentrate, focus (on).

céntrico, adj central, middle; focal point.

centrifuga, nf centrifuge.

centrifugar, vt to centrifuge; to spin.

centro, nm center, middle; mall, hub.

Centroamérica, nf Central America.

centuplicar, vt to increase a hundredfold, increase enormously.

centuria, nf century.

ceñido, adj tight, tight-fitting, close-fitting, clinging.

ceñidor, nm sash, girdle.

ceñir, vt to girdle, encircle, surround; tighten up.

ceñirse, vr 1. to put something on; 2. to reduce expenditure, tighten one's belt.

ceño, nm frown, scowl.

cepa, nf stump; stock; vine.

cepillado, nm brushing, brush; planing.

cepillar, vt 1. to brush; to plane (down); 2. to flatter.

cepo, nm 1. branch, bough; 2. trap, snare; stocks.

cera, nf wax.

cerámica, nf ceramics, pottery.

cerbatana, nf blowpipe; peashooter.

cerca, adv 1. near, nearby, close; 2. nf fence, wall.

cercado, nm 1. enclosure; enclosed, fenced.

cercanía, nf nearness, closeness, proximity.

cercano, adj near, close, neighboring.

cercar, vt 1. to fence in, wall in, hedge; to enclose; 2. to surround, besiege; cut off, encircle.

cercenar, vt to clip; to cut, trim the edges of.

cerciorar, vt to inform, assure.

cerciorarse, vr to find out; to make sure.

cerco, nm enclosure; fence, hedge.

cerda, nf 1. sow, 2. bristle; horsehair; snare, noose.

cerdo, nm pig.

cereal, adj cereal; grain.

cerebelo, nm cerebellum.

cerebral, adj cerebral, brain.

cerebro, nm brain; cerebrum; intelligence.

ceremonia, nf ceremony.

cereza, nf cherry.

cerezo, nm cherry tree; cherry wood.

cerilla, nf match; wax taper.

cerillero(a), nm/f street vendor of tobacco.

cerillo, nm match.

cernedor, nm sieve.

cerner, vt 1. to sift, sieve; 2. to scan, watch.

cernerse, vr to hover; to soar; to circle; be poised over, hang over; to threaten.

cernido, nm sifting; drizzle.

cero, nm nothing; nought; zero.

cerquillo, nm fringe of hair round the tonsure.

cerquita, adv quite near, close by.

cerradero, adj 1. locking, fastening; 2. nm locking device; clasp, fastener.

cerrado, adj closed, shut; locked.

cerrajería, nf 1. locksmith's craft (or trade); 2. locksmith's (shop).

cerrajero, nm locksmith.

cerrar, vt to close, shut; to lock (up); to bolt.

cerrero, adj wild; untamed, unbroken; rough, uncouth.

cerril, adj 1. rough; mountainous. 2. wild; untamed, unbroken; rough, uncouth.

cerro, nm hill.

cerrojo, nm bolt, latch.

certamen, nm competition, contest.

certero, adj accurate, sure, certain.

certeza, nf certainty.

certidumbre, nf certainty; conviction.

certificación, nf certification; registration.

certificado, adj 1. certified; registered; 2. nm certificate.

certificar, vt 1. to certify; to guarantee, vouch for; 2. to register.

cervecera, nf brewery.

cervecero, adj 1. beer; the brewing industry; 2. nm brewer.

cerveza, nf beer.

cervical, adj neck, cervical.

cerviz, nf 1. neck, nape of the neck; 2. cervix.

cesante, adj out of a job, out of office; discharged.

cesantear, vt to dismiss, sack.

cesantía, nf redundancy; suspension; dismissal, unemployment.

cesar, vi 1. to cease, stop; suspend; 2. to dismiss, sack, fire.

cese, nm 1. cessation; suspension, stoppage; 2. dismissal, compulsory retirement; sacking, firing.

césped, nm grass, lawn, turf.

cesta, nf basket.

cestero(a), nm/f basketmaker; basket seller.

cianuro, nm cyanide.

ciático, adj sciatic.

cicatero, adj stingy, mean.

cicatriz, nf scar.

cicatrizar, vt to heal.

ciclismo, nm cycling; cycle racing.

ciclista, nf 1. cycle, cycling; 2. nm/f cyclist.

ciclo, nm cycle.

ciclón, nm cyclone.

cicuta, nf hemlock.

cidra, nf citron.

ciego, adj 1. blind; 2. nm blind man, blind person.

cielo, nm sky; heavens, firmament.

cien, adj a hundred.

ciénaga, nf marsh, bog, swamp.

ciencia, nf science; knowledge, learning.

ciencia-ficción, nf science fiction.

cieno, nm mud, mire; silt, ooze; slime.

científico(a), adj 1. scientific; 2. nm/f scientist.

ciento, adj, nm hundred, (one) hundred.

cierne, nm 1. blossoming, budding; 2. in blossom; in its infancy.

cierre, nm 1. closing, shutting; locking; 2. closing device, locking device; snap fastener.

cierto, adj sure, certain; positive.

ciervo, nm deer; stag.

cifra, nf number, numeral.

cifrado, adj coded, in code.

cifrar, vt to code, write in code; to encode.

cigarra, nf cicada.

cigarrera, nf 1. cigar case; 2. cigar maker; cigar seller.

cigarrero, nm cigar maker; cigar-seller.

cigarrillo, nm cigarette.

cigarro, nm cigar; cigarette.

ciguato, adj simple, stupid.

cigüeña, nf 1. stork; 2. crank, handle; winch, capstan.

cigüeñal, nm crankshaft.

cilantro, nm coriander.

cilindrada, nf cylinder capacity.

cilindrar, vt to roll, roll flat.

cilíndrico, adj cylindrical.

cilindro, nm cylinder; roller; top hat; barrel-organ.

cilla, nf tithe barn, granary.

cima, nf top; peak, summit.

cimarrón, adj wild, untamed.

címbalo, nm cymbal.

cimbrar, vt to shake, swish, swing; to bend.

cimbreo, nm swaying, swinging; shaking; bending.

cimentación, nf foundation.

cimentar, vt to lay the foundations of; establish.

cimera, nf crest.

cimero, adj top, topmost, uppermost; finest.

cimiento, nm foundation, groundwork; basis, source.

cinc, nm zinc.

cincel, nm chisel.

cincelar, vt to chisel; to carve, engrave, cut.

cinco, adj 1. five; fifth; 2. nm five.

cincuenta, adj fifty; fiftieth.

cincuentón(a), adj 1. fifty-year-old, fiftyish. 2. nm/f person of about fifty.

cincha, nf girth, saddle strap.

cine, nm cinema; film(s), movies.

cineasta, nm/f 1. film fan, movie fan; 2. film buff; film critic; film maker, director.

cinema, nm cinema.

cinemateca, nf film library, film archive.

cinematografía, nf films, film-making, cinematography.

cínico, adj 1. cynical. 2. brazen, shameless, impudent; unprincipled.

cinta, nf band, strip; tape; ribbon, tape.

cintillo, nm hatband; hairband.

cinto, nm belt, girdle, sash.

cintura, nf waist; waistline; waist.

cinturón, nm belt; girdle; sword belt.

cipote, adj stupid, thick.

ciprés, nm cypress (tree).

circense, adj circus, of the circus.

circo, nm circus, amphitheater.

circuito, nm circuit; circumference.

circulación, nf 1. circulation; propagation; 2. traffic; movement of traffic.

circular, adj 1. circular, round; 2. nf circular; 3. vt to circulate; to pass round, send round; to put into circulation; 4. vi to be in circulation.

círculo, nm circle; club, group..

circuncidar, vt to circumcise.

circuncisión, nf circumcision.

circunciso, adj circumcised.

circundante, adj surrounding.

circundar, vt to surround.

circunferencia, nf circumference.

circunstancia, nf circumstance.

circunstancial, adj circumstantial.

circunvalación, nf bypass, ring road.

cirio, nm candle.

cirquero(a), nm/f circus performer, acrobat.

cirrosis, nf cirrhosis.

ciruela, nf plum.

ciruelo, nm plum tree.

cirugía, nf surgery.

cirujano(a), nm/f surgeon.

cisma, nm schism; split; discord, disagreement.

cisne, nm swan.

cisterna, nf cistern; tank; reservoir.

cistitis, nf cystitis.

cita, nf 1. appointment, engagement; meeting; 2. quotation; reference.

citación, nf 1. quotation; 2. summons.

citado, adj aforementioned.

citar, vt 1. to make an appointment with; to make a date with; 2. to call, summon; 3. to quote, cite.

citarse, vr to arrange to meet someone.

citrato, nm citrate.

cítrico, adj 1. citric; 2. nm citrus fruits.

ciudad, nf city, town.

ciudadanía, nf 1. citizens, citizenry; 2. citizenship.

ciudadano(a), adj 1. civic, city; 2. nm/f city dweller, townsman; 3. citizen.

cívico, adj 1. civic; domestic; public-spirited, patriotic; 2. nm policeman.

civil, adj 1. civil; 2. courteous, polite.

civilización, nf civilization.

civilizar, vt to civilize.

cizañero(a), nf troublemaker, mischief-maker.

clamar, vt 1. to cry out for; to proclaim; 2. vi to cry out, clamor.

clamor, *nm* cry, shout; noise, clamor.

clan, *nm* clan; faction, group.

clandestino, *adj* secret, clandestine; stealthy.

clara, *nf* 1. white of an egg; 2. bald spot; bare patch.

claraboya, *nf* skylight.

clarear, *vt* 1. to brighten; to light up;(color) to make lighter; 2. to clarify, make clear(er); 3. *vi* to clear up, brighten up; 4. to dawn, break; to grow light.

claridad, *nf* brightness; light.

clarificación, *nf* 1. illumination, lighting (up); 2. clarification.

clarificar, *vt* to illuminate, light (up); to brighten.

clarín, *nm* bugle; clarion.

clarinada, *nf* uncalled-for remark.

clarinazo, *nm* trumpet call.

clarinete, *nm* 1. clarinet; 2. *nm/f* (persona) clarinettist.

clarividencia, *nf* 1. clairvoyance; 2. farsightedness; discernment; intuition.

clarividente, *adj* 1. far-sighted, far-seeing; discerning; gifted with intuition; 2. *nm/f* clairvoyant(e).

claro, *adj* bright;light, well-lit .

clase, *nf* class; kind, sort.

clásico, *adj* 1. classical; 2. classic; outstanding, remarkable; 3. *nm* classic.

clasificación, *nf* classification; sorting.

clasificarse, *vr* to win a place.

claudicación, *nf* giving way, abandonment of one's principles.

claudicar, *vi* to limp; act deceitfully.

claustro, *nm* cloister.

claustrofobia, *nf* claustrophobia.

cláusula, *nf* clause.

clausura, *nm/f* closing, closure; formal closing.

clausurar, *vt* to close, bring to a close; to adjourn, close.

clavada, *nf* dive.

clavadista, *nm/f* diver.

clavado, *adj* 1. nailed; stuck fast, firmly fixed; 2. *nm* dive.

clavar, *vt* to knock in, drive in, to fasten, fix; to pin.

clave, *nf* 1. key; code; 2. *nf* harpsichord.

clavel, *nm* carnation.

clavetear, *vt* to stud, decorate with studs.

clavícula, *nf* collar bone, clavicle.

clavija, *nf* peg, dowel, pin; pintle; peg.

clavo, *nm* nail; tack; stud; spike.

clemencia, *nf* mercy, clemency, leniency.

clemente, *adj* merciful, clement; lenient.

cleptómano(a), *nm/f* kleptomaniac.

clerical, *adj* 1. clerical; 2. *nm* clergyman, minister.

clérigo, *nm* priest; clergyman; minister.

cliente, *nm/f* client, customer.

clima, *nm* climate; atmosphere.

climatología, *nf* climatology; weather.

clímax, *nm* climax.

clínica, *nf* clinic.

clínico, *adj* clinical.

cloaca, *nf* sewer; drain.

cloacal, *adj* sewage system.

cloración, *nf* chlorination.

clorhídrico, *adj* hydrochloric.

clorinar, *vt* to chlorinate.

cloro, *nm* chlorine.

clorofila, *nf* chlorophyll.

cloroformo, *nm* chloroform.

clorure, *nm* chloride.

coacción, *nf* coercion, compulsion; duress.

coaccionador, *adj* constraining, compelling.

coadjutor(a), *nm/f* assistant, coadjutor.

coadjuvar, *vt* to help, assist.

coagulación, *nf* coagulation; clotting; curdling.

coagular, *vt* to coagulate; to clot.

coágulo, *nm* coagulated mass.

coalición, *nf* coalition.

coartada, *nf* alibi.

coartar, *vt* to limit, restrict.

coba, *nf* fib; neat trick.

cobalto, *nm* cobalt.

cobarde, *adj* cowardly; fainthearted, timid.

cobertizo, *nm* shed, outhouse, shelter; covered passage.

cobertor, *nm* bedspread, coverlet.

cobertura, *nf* cover, covering.

cobijar, *vt* 1. to cover (up), close in; 2. to protect, shelter; to take in, give shelter to, harbor.

cobijarse, *vr* to take shelter.

cobra, *nf* (Zool) cobra; (hunt) retrieval.

cobrador, *nm* collector.

cobradora, *nf* conductress.

cobrar, *vt* to collect, receive; to cash

cobrarse, *vr* to recover, get well; to come to.

cobre, *nm* copper.

cobro, *nm* 1. recovery, retrieval; 2. collection.

coca, *nf* head, nut; coca tree (or bush); Coca-Cola

cocaína, *nf* cocaine.

cocal, *nm* coconut plantation.

cocción, *nf* cooking; cooking time.

cocear, *vt/i* to kick.

cocer, *vt/i* to cook; to boil.

cocido, *adj* boiled, cooked.

cociente, *nm* quotient.

cocina, *nf* 1. kitchen; 2. stove, cooker; 3. cooking, cookery; 4. cuisine.

cocinado, *nm* cooking.

cocinar, *vt* to cook.

coco, *nm* coconut.

cocodrilo, *nm* crocodile.

cocotero, *nm* coconut palm.

cóctel, *nm* cocktail.

coctelera, *nf* cocktail shaker.

cocuyo, *nm* firefly.

coche, *nm* 1. car, motorcar, automobile; 2. coach, carriage.

cochecillo, *nm* small carriage.

cochera, *nf* 1. coach house; livery stable; 2. garage, carport; 3. engine-shed.

cochero, *adj* 1. carriage entrance; 2. *nm* coachman.

cochina, *nf* sow.

cochinada, *nf* filth, filthiness.

cochino, *adj* 1. filthy, dirty; 2. *nm* pig.

cochiquera, *nf* pigsty.

codazo, *nm* jab, poke, nudge (with one's elbow).

codear, *vt* to elbow, nudge, jostle .

codearse, *vr* to hobnob with, rub shoulders with.

codeína, *nf* codeine.

codera, *nf* elbow patch; elbow guard.

códice, *nm* manuscript, codex.

codicia, *nf* greed, covetousness; greed for.

codiciado, *adj* widely desired; much in demand; sought after, coveted.

codiciar, *vt* to covet.

codificador, *nm* encoder.

codificar, *vt* to codify; to scramble.

código, *nm* code; law, statute; rules, set of rules.

codo, *nm* elbow; angle-iron; elbow joint.

codorniz, *nf* quail.

coedición, *nf* joint publication; joint publishing.

coeditar, *vt* to publish jointly.

coeducación, *nf* coeducation.

coerción, *nf* coercion, constraint; restraint.

coestrella, *nm/f* co-star.

coexistir, *vi* to coexist (with).

cofia, *nm/f* cap, white cap; coif; bonnet.

cofinanciar, *vt* to finance jointly.

cofradía, *nf* brotherhood, fraternity.

cofre, *nm* chest; case.

cofundador(a), *nm/f* co-founder.

cogedero, *adj* 1. ripe, ready to be picked; 2. *nm* handle.

cogedor, *nm* small shovel, ash shovel; dustpan.

coger, *vt* to take hold of, catch hold of; to seize, grasp; pick up.

cognoscitivo, *adj* cognitive.

cogollo, *nm* shoot, sprout; heart; top.

cogote, *nm* back of the neck, nape; scruff of the neck.

cohabitar, *vi* to live together, cohabit; to coexist.

cohechar, *vt* to bribe, offer a bribe to.

cohecho, *nm* bribe, bribery.

coherente, *adj* coherent; logical; right.

cohesión, *nf* cohesion.

cohete, *nm* rocket.

cohibición, *nf* restraint; inhibition.

cohibido, *adj* restrained, restricted; inhibited.

cohibir, *vt* to restrain, check, restrict; to inhibit.

cohorte, *nf* cohort.

coincidencia, *nf* coincidence, agreement.

coincidir, *vi* 1. to coincide (with); 2. to coincide, agree.

cointérprete, *nf* fellow actor.

cojear, *vi* to limp, hobble; to be lame.

cojín, *nm* cushion.

cojo, *adj* lame; crippled; limping.

cola, *nf* tail; glue, gum, Coca-Cola.

colaboración, *nf* collaboration.

colaborador(a), *nm/f* collaborator, helper, co-worker; contributor.

colaborar, *vi* to collaborate; to help, assist.

colación, *nf* 1. collation, comparison; 2. collation; light meal, snack; buffet meal.

colada, *nf* 1. wash, washing; 2. intruder; uninvited guest, gatecrasher.

coladera, *nf* 1. strainer, 2. sewer.

coladero, *nm* strainer; colander.

colador, *nm* sieve.

colapsar, *vt* to overthrow, cause to collapse.

colapso, *nm* collapse; breakdown.

colección, *nf* collection.

coleccionar, *vt/i* to collect.

coleccionista, *nm/f* collector.

colecta, *nf* 1. collection (for charity); 2. collect.

colectar, *vt* to collect.

colectividad, *nf* collectivity; group as a whole.

colectivo, *adj* collective; joint action, group action, communal action.

colega, *nm/f* colleague; pal, mate, buddy.

colegiada, *nf* doctor; referee.

colegial, *adj* 1. school, college; 2. *nm* schoolboy; inexperienced person; callow youth.

colegiarse, *vr* to become a member of one's professional association.

colegio, *nm* 1. independent secondary school, private (or fee-paying) high school; 2. college.

colegir, *vt* to collect, gather.

cólera, *nf* anger, rage.

colérico, *adj* angry.

colesterol, *nm* cholesterol.

colgadero, *nm* hook, hanger, peg.

colgadizo, *adj* hanging, loose.

colgado, *adj, ptp* uncertain, doubtful.

colgante, *adj* 1. hanging; droopy, floppy; dangling; 2. *nm* drop, pendant, earring.

cólico, *nm* colic.

coliflor, *nf* cauliflower.

colina, *nf* hill.

colindante, *adj* adjacent, adjoining, neighbouring.

colirio, *nm* eye-drops.

colisión, *nf* collision; crash, smash.

colisionar, *vt* to collide; to clash with, conflict with.

colitis, *nf* colitis.

colmado, *adj* 1. abundant, copious; full, overflowing; 2. *nm* cheap seafood restaurant; grocer's shop.

colmar, *vt* fill to the brim, fill right up.

colmena, *nf* beehive; hive.

colmenar, *nm* apiary.

colmenero(a), *nm/f* beekeeper.

colmillo, *nm* eye tooth, canine (tooth).

colmo, *nm* height, summit; extreme.

colocar, *vt* to place, put, position; to arrange.

colonia, *nf* colony; eau-de-Cologne.

coloniaje, *nm* colonial period; system of colonial government; slavery, slave status.

colonización, *nf* colonization; settlement.

colonizar, *vt* to colonize; to settle; to inhabit, live in.

colono, *nm* colonist, settler; colonial.

coloquiar, *vi* to talk, discuss.

coloquio, *nm* conversation, talk; conference.

color, *nm* color; hue, shade.

colorado, *adj* 1. red; rosy, ruddy; 2. *nm* bread; money.

colorante, *adj* 1. coloring; 2. *nm* coloring (matter).

colorar, *vt* to color; to dye, tint, stain.

coloreado, *adj* 1. colored; tinted; 2. *nm* coloring.

colorete, *nm* rouge.

colorido, *nm* color(ing); local color.

colosal, *adj* colossal; splendid.

columbrar, *vt* 1. to glimpse, spy; make out; 2. to guess; to begin to see.

columna, *nf* column; pillar.

columpiar, *vt* to swing.

columpio, *nm* swing.

collado, *nm* hill, height; hillock.

collar, *nm* necklace.

collera, *nf* 1. horse-collar; 2. cufflinks.

coma, *nf* comma.

comadre, *nf* kinswoman, woman relative of godparents.

comadrona, *nf* midwife.

comandancia, *nf* 1. command; 2. commander's headquarters (or office).

comandante, *nm* commandant, commander.

comandar, *vt* to command, lead.

comando, *nm* command; leadership; control.

comarca, *nf* region, area, part.

comarcar, *vi* to border, be adjacent (to).

comatoso, *adj* comatose.

combar, *vt* to bend, curve.

combate, *nm* combat, engagement; battle, struggle.

combatir, *vt* to attack; to combat, fight, oppose.

combatirse, *vr* to fight, struggle (against).

combinación, *nf* combination.

combinado, *nm* cocktail.

combinar, *vt* to combine; to join, unite, put together.

combustible, *adj* 1. combustible; 2. *nm* fuel.

combustión, *nf* combustion.

comebolas, *nm* simple soul, gullible individual.

comedia, *nf* comedy; play, drama; 2. farce; pretense.

comediante, *nm/f* 1. actor; actress; 2. hypocrite.

comedido, *adj* moderate, restrained; courteous.

comediógrafo(a), *nm/f* playwrighter.

comedirse, *vr* to behave moderately, be restrained, restrain oneself.

comedor, *adj* 1. greedy, gluttonous; 2. *nm* dining-room.

comején, *nm* termite, white ant.

comensal, *nm/f* fellow guest, diner guests.

comentador(a), *nm/f* commentator.

comentar, *vt* to comment on; to expound; to discuss.

comentario, *nm* comment, remark, observation.

comenzar, *vt/i* to begin, start, commence.

comer, *vt* to eat.

comerse, *vr* to eat up.

comercial, *adj* commercial; business, trading.

comerciante, *nm/f* trader, dealer, merchant.

comerciar, *vi* to trade; to do business with.

comercio, *nm* commerce; trade; business.

cometa, *nm* comet; kite; delta, hang-glider.

cometer, *vt* to commit; to make.

cometido, *nm* task, assignment; commitment.

comezón, *nf* itch, itching; tingle.

cómica, *nf* actress; comedienne.

comicios, *nm pl* elections, voting.

cómico, *adj* 1. comic(al), funny, amusing; 2. comedy; 3. *nm* comedian.

comida, *nf* food.

comienzo, *nm* beginning, start.

comillas, *nf* quotation marks, inverted commas, quotes.

comino, *nm* cumin, cumin seed.

comisaría, *nf* 1. police station; 2. administrative office.

comisario(a), *nm/f* commissioner; administrative officer.

comisión, *nf* assignment, task, commission; mission.

comisionar, *vt* to commission.

comisura, *nf* join; corner, angle; commissure.

comité, *nm* committee.

comitiva, *nf* suite, retinue; train; procession.

como, *adv* 1. as, like; such as; as it were; 2. *conj* as, since; because.

cómo, *adv interrog* 1. how?; why?, how is it that ...?; how does he do it?; 2. *interj* I beg your pardon?, what?, eh?; what was that?.

cómoda, *nf* chest of drawers; bureau.

comodidad, *nf* comfort; comfortableness; convenience.

comoquiera, *conj* que ... since ..., in view of the fact that ....

compadecer, *vt* to pity; be sorry for, to sympathize with.

compadrazgo, *nm* kinship, relationship through one's godparents.

compadre, *nm* godfather o father (with respect to each other), frien, pal.

compaginación, *nf* continuity.

compaginar, *vt* to arrange, put in order.

compaginarse, *vr* to agree, tally.

compañerismo, *nm* fellowship, companionship.

compañero(a), *nm/f* companion; partner.

compañía, *nf* company.

comparación, *nf* comparison.

comparar, *vt* to compare; to liken (to).

comparecencia, *nf* appearance (in court).

comparecer, *vi* to appear (in court); to appear before a judge.

comparsa, *nf* group, procession; masquerade.

compartim(i)ento, *nm* 1. division, sharing; distribution; 2. compartment.

compartir, *vi* to divide (up), share (out).

compás, *nm* 1. measure, beat, rhythm; 2. compass.

compasión, *nf* pity, compassion; sympathy.

compasivo, *adj* compassionate, full of pity; sympathetic, understanding.

compatibilidad, *nf* compatibility.

compatriota, *nm/f* compatriot, fellow countryman, fellow countrywoman.

compeler, *vt* to compel.

compendiar, *vt* to abridge, condense, summarize.

compenetración, *nf* mutual understanding, fellow feeling, natural sympathy.

compensación, *nf* compensation.

compensar, *vt* to compensate; make up (for).

competencia, *nf* 1. competition; rivalry; competitiveness; 2. aptitude; adequacy; suitability.

competente, *adj* 1. competent; proper, appropriate; 2. fit, adequate, suitable.

competir, *vi* 1. to compete; 2. to rival, vie with.

compilación, *nf* compilation.

compilador(a), *nm/f* compiler.

compilar, *vt* to compile.

complacencia, *nf* pleasure, satisfaction.

complacer, *vt* to please.

complacido, *adj* pleased, satisfied.

complejidad, *nf* complexity.

complejo, *adj* complex.

complementar, *vt* to complement; to complete, make up, round off.

complemento, *nm* complement.

completar, *vt* to complete; to round off, make up.

completo, *adj* complete; perfect, rounded, finished.

complexión, *nf* constitution, make-up.

complicación, *nf* complication, complexity.

complicado, *adj* complicated, complex.

complicar, *vt* 1. complicate; 2. to involve (in).

cómplice, *nm/f* accomplice.

complotado, *nm/f* plotter, conspirator.

complotar, *vi* to plot, conspire.

componedor(a), *nm/f* bonesetter.

componenda, *nf* 1. compromise; settlement, arrangement; 2. shady deal.

componer, *vt* 1. to compose, put together, constitute; 2. mend, fix, repair.

componerse, *vr* to consist of, be composed of, be made up of.

comportamiento, *nm* behavior, conduct.

comportar, *vi* to bear, endure, put up with.

comportarse, *vr* to behave; to comport oneself, conduct oneself.

compostura, *nf* 1. composition; structure; make-up; 2. mending, repair, repairing; overhauling.

compota, *nf* stewed fruit, preserve.

comprador(a), *nm/f* buyer, purchaser; shopper, customer.

compraventa, *nf* buying and selling, dealing.

comprender, *vt/i* 1. comprise, include; to take in; 2. extend to; to consist of; 3. understand; to see.

comprensión, *nf* 1. comprehension, commprehensiveness, inclusiveness; inclusion; 2. understanding.

compresa, *nf* compress; sanitary towel, sanitary napkin.

compresión, *nf* compression.

compresor, *nm* compressor.

comprimido, *adj* 1. compressed; 2. *nm* pill, tablet.

comprimir, *vt* compress, squeeze down, press down, condense.

comprobación, *nf* checking, verification; proof.

comprobador, *nm* tester.

comprobante, *adj* supporting document; documents in proof thereof.

comprobar, *vt* check, verify; to prove; to confirm.

comprometer, *vi* to compromise; to embarrass, put in an awkward situation.

compromiso, *nm* obligation; commitment; undertaking, pledge, promise; engagement, date.

compulsión, *nf* compulsion.

compungir, *vt* to make remorseful, arouse feelings of contrition in.

computador(a), *nm/f* computer.

computadorizado, *adj* computerized.

computar, *vt* to calculate, compute, reckon.

cómputo, *nm* calculation, computation, reckoning.

comulgante, *nm/f* communicant.

comulgar, *vt* 1. to administer communion to; 2. *vi* to take communion, receive communion; 3. to like, accept, agree with.

comulgatorio, *nm* communion rail, altar rail.

común, *adj* common; joint; public, belonging to all, held in common.

comunicación, *nf* communication; contact.

comunicado, *adj* 1. (cuarto) connected, interconnecting; 2. *nm* communique.

comunicador(a), *nm/f* communicator.

comunicar, *vt* to communicate, tell, pass on; to convey, to tell.

comunidad, *nf* community; society, corporation.

comunión, *nf* communion.

comunismo, *nm* communism.

comunista, *adj* communist(ic).

comunitario, *adj* community; communal.

con, *prep* with.

concatenar, *vt* to link together, concatenate.

concavidad, *nf* concavity, hollow, cavity.

cóncavo, *adj* 1. concave; hollow; 2. *nm* hollow, cavity.

concebir, *vt* to conceive; to imagine.

conceder, *vt* to concede, grant, admit; to confer, bestow.

concejal(a), *nm/f* town councillor.

concejo, *nm* council.

concentración, *nf* concentration; gathering, meeting, rally.

concentrado, *adj* concentrated.

concepción, *nf* conception.

concepto, *nm* concept, conception; idea, notion; thought.

conceptualizar, *vt* to conceptualize.

conceptuar, *vt* to think, judge, deem.

concerniente, *adj* concerning, relating to.

concertación, *nf* harmonizing; coordination; reconciliation; social harmony.

concertado, *adj* methodical, systematic; orderly.

concertar, *vt* harmonize, bring into harmony.

concesión, *nf* concession; grant(ing); allowance; award.

concesionario(a), *nm/f* concessionaire, concessionary, licensee, authorized dealer.

conciencia, *nf* 1. conscience; moral sense; 2. knowledge, awareness, consciousness.

concierto, *nm* 1. concert, agreement; order; harmony; to be in agreement with regard to; 2. concert; song recital; symphony concert.

conciliación, *nf* 1. conciliation; reconciliation; 2. afinity, similarity.

conciliar, *vt* to reconcile; to harmonize, bring into line, blend.

concitar, *vt* 1. stir up, incite; 2. gather, assemble, bring together.

conciudadano(a), *nm/f* fellow citizen.

concluir, *vt* 1. conclude, finish; 2. infer, deduce; to reach, arrive at.

concordar, *vt* to reconcile; to bring into line; to make agree.

concordia, *nf* 1. concord, harmony, agreement; conformity; 2. double finger-ring.

concretar, *vt* to make concrete, make specific.

conculcar, *vt* to infringe (on); to break, violate.

concupiscencia, *nf* 1. greed, acquisitiveness; 2. lustfulness, sinfulness, concupiscence.

concurrencia, *nf* 1. concurrence; simultaneity, coincidence; 2. gathering, assembly; spectators, public, audience; 3. competition.

concurrente, *adj* 1. concurrent; 2. competing; 3. *nm* person presen; 4. competitor.

concurrido, *adj* crowded; much frequented; calle busy, crowded; popular, well-attended.

concurrir, *vi* 1. to meet, come together (at); 2. gather, assemble.

concursante, *nm/f* competitor; contestant, participant.

concursar, *vt* 1. declare insolvent, declare bankrupt; 2. compete in, compete for; 3. participate.

concha, *nf* shell; shellfish, scallop, scallop shell.

condecoración, *nf* decoration, medal, badge.

condecorar, *vt* to decorate.

condena, *nf* sentence; conviction.

condenación, *nf* condemnation; disapproval, censure; damnation.

condenado, *adj* 1. condemned; convicted; damned; 2. doomed; mischievous, naughty.

condensación, *nf* condensation.

condensador, *nm* condenser.

condensar, *vt* to condense.

condescendencia, *nf* helpfulness, willingness; affability; acquiescence; submissiveness.

condescender, *vi* to acquiesce, comply, agree, say yes.

condición, *nf* 1. condition; temperament, character; 2. social class, rank; status, position.

condicionante, *nm* determining factor, determinant.

condicionar, *vt* to condition; to determine; to prepare; to shape, mold.

condolencia, *nf* condolence, sympathy.

condolerse, *vr* to sympathize with, feel sorry for.

condominio, *nm* 1. joint ownership; condominium; 2. apartment (owned by the occupant).

condonar, *vt* to condone.

cóndor, *nm* condor.

conducción, *nf* 1. leading; guiding; management; transport(ation); conveyance; piping; conduction; 2. driving.

conducir, *vt* 1. to take, convey; to pass; transport; 2. drive; to steer; 3. to take lead (to); to guide, conduct (to).

conductor(a), *nm/f* 1. leader; guide; 2. driver; motorist.

conectado, *adj* connected; to be on; to be live.

conectar, *vt* 1. to connect (up); to switch on, plug in; to put through; 2. put someone in touch with someone else.

coneja, *nf* doe rabbit.

conejera, *nf* warren, burrow; rabbit hutch.

conejillo, *nm* young rabbit; bunny.

conexión, *nf* 1. connection; plug; coupling; joint; 2. relationship.

conexo, *adj* connected, related.

confabulación, *nf* plot; intrigue; dubious scheme; ring.

confabularse, *vr* to plot, conspire, scheme.

confeccionado, *adj* ready-made, ready-to-wear.

confeccionador, *nm* layout man.

confeccionar, *vt* to make out; to prepare, write up; to make (up).

confederación, *nf* confederation, confederacy, league.

confederado(a), *adj, nm/f* confederate.

conferencia, *nf* conference, meeting; lecture.

conferenciar, *vi* to confer (with); to be in conference.

conferir, *vt* to award (a to); honor to grant (to), confer (on), bestow (on).

confesar, *vt* to confess, admit, acknowledge; to own up to.

confesarse, *vr* to confess, own up; to confess (to), make one's confession.

confes(i)onario, *nm* confessional box.

confesor, *nm* confessor.

confiable, *adj* reliable, trustworthy.

confiado, *adj* 1. trusting; unsuspecting, gullible; 2. confident; selfconfident, self-reliant.

confiar, *vt* to entrust something to someone, commit something to the care of someone.

confidente(a), *nm/f* 1. intimate friend; 2. informer, secret agent; police informer.

configuración, *nf* shape, configuration.

configurar, *vt* to shape, form, fashion.

confín, *nm* limit, boundary; horizon; confines.

confinar, *vt* 1. to confine; to banish, exile (to); to arrest; to shut away; 2. *vi* to border on.

confirmar, *vt* to confirm; to corroborate; to endorse.

confiscación, *nf* confiscation.

confiscar, *vt* to confiscate.

confiscado, *adj* mischievous, naughty.

conflictivo, *adj* troubled, filled with conflict; unstable; controversial; fraught with conflict; tense.

conflicto, *nm* 1. conflict; struggle; 2. clash of interests; labor dispute; 3. difficulty, jam.

confluencia, *nf* confluence.

confluir, *vi* to meet, join, come together; to gather.

conformación, *nf* shape, form, structure.

conformado, *adj* 1. well-made, well-shaped; 2. patient, resigned, long-suffering; 3. *nm* molding, shaping, forming.

conformar, *vt* 1. to shape, fashion; to mold; 2. adjust.

conformidad, *nf* 1. similarity; correspondence; uniformity (between); 2. agreement; approval, consent; 3. resignation (to); forbearance; to bear something with resignation, resign oneself to putting up with something.

conformista, *adj* 1. conformist; 2. *nm/f* conformist.

confortar, *vt* 1. comfort, console; to encourage; 2. strengthen, invigorate, act as a tonic to.

confraternidad, *nf* fraternity, brotherhood.

confraternizar, *vi* to fraternize (with).

confrontación, *nf* 1. confrontation; 2. comparison.

confrontar, *vt* 1. to confront, face; to face up to; 2. bring face to face; to confront someone with someone else; 3. compare, collate.

confundir, 1. *vi* to blur, confuse; 2. mistake (for), confuse (with), mix up (with).

confusión, *nf* confusion.

confuso, *adj* confused; mixed up, jumbled up, in disorder.

congelación, *nf* 1. freezing; congealing; freeze-frame; 2. frostbite.

congelado, *adj* 1. frozen, chilled; 2. frostbitten.

congelador, *nm* deepfreeze, freezer, freezing unit.

congelar, *vt* freeze; to congeal.

congeniar, *vi* to get on.

congénito, *adj* congenital.

congestionado, *adj* 1. congested; 2. congested, chesty.

congestionar, *vt* to congest, produce congestion in.

conglomerado, *nm* conglomerate; conglomeration.

conglomerar, *vt* to conglomerate.

congoja, *nf* anguish, distress, grief.

congraciador, *adj* ingratiating.

congraciar, *vt* to win over.

congratulaciones, *nf* congratulations.

congratular, *vt* to congratulate (on).

congregación, *nf* gathering, assembly; brotherhood; guild; congregation.

congregarse, *vr* to gather, congregate.

congreso, *nm* congress; assembly, convention; conference; parliament.

congruencia, *nf* congruence, congruity.

congruente, *adj* 1. congruent, congruous (with); in keeping (with); related (to); 2. suitable.

cónico, *adj* conical; conic.

conjetura, *nf* guess, conjecture, surmise; by guesswork.

conjeturar, *vt* to guess (at), conjecture, surmise.

conjugar, *vt* 1. conjugate; 2. combine, bring together, fit together blend.

conjunción, *nf* conjunction.

conjuntivitis, *nf* conjunctivitis.

conjunto, *adj* 1. joint; united; combined operations; 2. allied, related; 3. *nm* music group.

conjura, *nf* plot, conspiracy.

conjurado(a), *nm/f* plotter, conspirator.

conjurar, *vt* 1. to conjure, to exorcise; 2. stave off, ward off.

conjuro, *nm* incantation, conjuration, exorcism; spell.

conmemoración, *nf* commemoration.

conmemorar, *vt* to commemorate.

conmigo, *pron* with me; with myself.

conminar, 1. *vt* to threaten (with); 2. warn someone to do something, instruct someone to do something; 3. to challenge.

conmiseración, *nf* pity, sympathy; commiseration.

conmoción, *nf* 1. shock; tremor, earthquake; 2. concussion.

conmocionar, *vt* 1. to move, affect deeply; to shake profoundly, cause an upheaval in; 2. to put into shock.

conmover, *vt* 1. to shake, disturb; 2. to move, touch, stir, affect; to disturb, upset.

conmutación, *nf* commutation.

conmutador, *nm* switch; switchboard; telephone exchange.

conmutar, *vt* 1. to exchange; to convert (into); 2. to commute (to).

connotación, *nf* 1. connotation; 2. distant relationship.

connotado, *adj* famous; outstanding.

conocer, *vt* to know; to know about, understand; to meet, get to know; to become acquainted with.

conocido, *adj* known; well-known; notorious; famous.

conocimiento, *nm* knowledge

conquistar, *vt* 1. to conquer (a from); to overcome; 2. win, succeed in attracting.

consabido, *adj* 1. well-known, familiar; usual; 2. over-mentioned.

consagración, *nf* consecration, dedication.

consagrado, *adj* consecrated (to); dedicated (to) .

consagrar, *vt* consecrate, hallow; to dedicate (to); to deify.

consagrarse, *vr* to devote oneself to.

consciencia, *nf* 1. consciousness; awareness; realization; 2. *adj* conscious; be aware of.

consecución, *nf* obtaining, acquisition; attainment; achievement.

consecuente, *adj* 1. consistent (with); 2. consequent.

consecutivo, *adj* consecutive.

conseguido, *adj* successful.

conseguir, *vt* 1. get, obtain, secure; to bring about; to succeed in; 2. attain, achieve.

consejería, *nf* 1. council, commission; 2. ministry in a regional government.

consejero(a), *nm/f* adviser; consultant; member (of a board); minister in a regional government.

consejo, *nm* 1. a piece of advice; a hint; 2. council; board; tribunal; court.

consenso, *nm* accord; assent; consensus.

congresista, *nm/f* delegate, member (of a congress).

consentido, *adj* 1. spoiled, pampered; 2. complaisant.

consentimiento, *nm* consent.

consentir, *vt* 1. to consent to; to allow, permit; to tolerate; 2. admit; to bear, put up with.

conserje, *nm* porter; doorman; caretaker.

conserva, *nf* 1. preserving; 2. preserved foods; preserve(s); jam.

conservación, *nf* conservation; preservation; maintenance, upkeep.

conservar, *vt* 1. preserve; to tin, can; to conserve; to preserve; 2. keep, retain; to keep up, maintain.

conservatorio, *nm* conservatory.

considerable, *adj* considerable; substantial; sizeable; worthy of consideration.

consideración, nf 1. consideration; thought; reflexion; 2. respect, regard.

considerado, adj respected, esteemed; well-regarded.

considerar, 1. vt consider; to think about, reflect on; 2. take into account; 3. consider; to think, deem.

consigna, nf instruction; watchword, slogan, motto.

consignación, nf 1. consignment, shipment; 2. appropriation; earmarked sum.

consignar, vt 1. send, dispatch, to consign; to deposit (with); 2. assign, earmark.

consignatario(a), nm/f consignee; agent; assign(ee); recipient, addressee.

consistencia, nf consistence, consistency.

consistente, adj consistent, sound, valid.

consistir, vi consist of; to be made of, be composed of.

consolación, nf consolation.

consolador(a), adj 1. consoling, comforting; 2. nm/f consoler, comforter.

consolar, vt to console, comfort.

consolidación, nf consolidation.

consonancia, nf 1. consonance, harmony; in accordance with, in harmony with; 2. rhyme.

consonar, vi 1. be in harmony with; 2. to rhyme (with).

consorte, nm/f 1. consort, spouse; prince consort; 2. partner, companion.

conspicuo, adj eminent, famous.

conspiración , nf conspiracy.

conspirar, vi to conspire, plot.

constancia, nf 1. constancy; steadiness; firmness, steadfastness, loyalty; 2. certainty; proof, evidence; 3. documentary proof, written evidence.

constante, adj constant; unchanging; steady; firm, steadfast; loyal, faithful, staunch.

constar, vi be clear from, be evident from.

consternación, nf consternation, dismay.

consternado, adj to be dismayed; to be aghast.

consternar, vt to dismay, shatter. shock.

constipado, adj 1. having a cold; 2. nm cold, catarrh.

constitución, nf constitution.

constitucional, adj constitutional.

constreñir, vt 1. to restrict; 2. compe, constrain.

construcción, nf construction; building; structure.

constructor, adj 1. building; 2. nm builder.

constructora, nf construction company.

construir, vt 1. to construct; to build, erect, put up; 2. construe.

consuelo, nm consolation, solace, comfort.

cónsul, nm consul.

consulado, nm consulship; consulate.

consulta, nf 1. consultation; popular referendum; 2. consulting room; outpatients department; 3. examination.

consultar, vt consult; to consult a doctor, see a doctor.

consultoría, nf consultancy; management consultancy.

consultorio, nm information bureau; surgery.

consumación, nf consummation; extinction.

consumado, adj consummate, perfect; accomplished.

consumido, adj 1. consumed, wasted; shrivelled, shrunken; 2. timid; fretful, easily upset.

consumidor(a), nm/f consumer.

consumir, vt consume, eat.

consumo, nm consumption.

contabilidad, nf accounting, book-keeping.

contabilizar, vt enter in the accounts; to tabulate.

contactar, vt to contact, get in touch with.

contacto, nm 1. contact; touch; ignition; 2. switch, contact breaker; plug.

contaduría, nf 1. accountancy; 2. accountant's office; cashier's office.

contagiar, vt 1. pass on, transmit, give (to); to spread; to infect (with); 2. infect, contaminate; to corrupt others.

contaminación, nf 1. contamination; corruption; 2. infection; defilement.

contaminador(a), nm/f polluter.

contaminar, vt to contaminate; to pollute; to soil; to influence, affect.

contaminarse, vr to be(come) contaminated.

contar, vt count, to number off.

contemplación, nf 1. contemplation; meditation, reflexion; 2. indulgence; leniency, gentle treatment.

contemplar, vt 1. to look at, gaze at, to contemplate; 2. show consideration for, treat indulgently, be lenient with; 3. take account of, deal with.

contemporáneo(a), adj 1. contemporary; contemporaneous; 2. nm/f contemporary.

contemporizador, adj excessively compliant; temporizing; lacking firm principles.

contemporizar, vi to be compliant, show oneself ready to compromise; to lack firm principles.

contencioso, adj 1. contentious; argumentative, captious; 2. litigious; 3. nm dispute, problem; point of disagreement.

contender, vi to contend; to compete, be rivals (in); to fight.

contenedor, nm container; container ship.

contener, vt hold, contain.

contenido, adj 1. restrained, controlled; moderate; equable; 2. suppressed; 3. nm content, contents.

contentar, vt to satisfy, content; make happy.

contento, adj happy, pleased, glad, satisfied.

conteo, nm count, counting; count.

contestación, nf 1. answer, reply; defense plea; sharp retort, piece of backchat; 2. protest.

contestar, vt/i to answer, reply; to answer back.

contextualizar, vt to provide a context for, set in a context.

contextura, nf 1. contexture; 2. build, physique; constitution; make-up.

contienda, nf contest; struggle, fight.

contigo, pron with you.

contigüidad, nf nearness, closeness, continuity.

contiguo, adj next; adjacent (to); contiguous (to), adjoining.

continente, adj 1. continent; 2. nm continent; 3. container.

contingencia, nf contingency; risk; hazard, danger.

continuación, nf continuation; sequel.

continuar, vt to continue, go on with; to resume; to carry on.

continuo, adj 1. continuous; endless; direct; 2. continual, constant.

contoneo, nm swagger, strut; hip-swinging, waggle; affected gait.

contorno, nm outline, contour; perimeter; shape; edge, rim.

contorsión, nf contortion.

contorsionarse, vr to contort oneself.

contra, adv against.

contra(a)tacar, vt/i to counter-attack.

contra(a)taque, nm counter-attack.

contrabajo, nm 1. double bass; bass guitar; 2. bass, contrabass.

contrabandear, vi to smuggle, live by smuggling.

contrabando, nm smuggling.

contracción, nf contraction; shrinkage; wasting.

contracepción, nf contraception.

contraceptivo, adj nm contraceptive.

contradecir, vt to contradict.

contradicción, nf contradiction; incompatibility.

contraer, vt 1. contract; to shrink; to make smaller (or tighter etc); to condense; 2. (Med) to contract, to acquire, pick up, get into.

contrahecho, adj 1. counterfeit; fake, faked, forged; spurious, pirated; 2. hunchbacked deformed.

contraído, adj 1. contracted; shrunken, wasted; 2. diligent, industrious.

contrainteligencia, nf counter-intelligence.

controlar, vt to control.

controlador, nm comptroller; treasury inspector.

contralto, adj 1. contralto; 2. nm counter tenor.

contraluz, nm view against the light; against the light.

contramaestre, nm warrant officer; boatswain; foreman.

contramarcha, nf 1. countermarch; 2. reverse; to reverse, go into reverse.

contraofensiva, nf counter-offensive.

contraoferta, nf counter-offer.

contraorden, nf counter-order.

contrapartida, nf 1. balancing entry; 2. compensation.

contrapeso, nm counterpoise, counterweight.

contraponer, vi to compare, set against each other.

contraportada, nf inside cover (of book).

contraposición, nf comparison; contrast, clash.

contraproducente, adj self-defeating; counter-productive.

contrapunteo, nm argument. quarrel.

contrariado, adj upset, annoyed, put out.

contrariar, vi to oppose, be opposed to, go against; to contradict.

contrariedad, nf obstacle; setback, misfortune; snag, trouble.

contrario, adj opposite, opposed, different.

contrarrestar, vr to counteract, offset, balance; to counter.

contrarrevolución, nf counter-revolution.

contrasentido, nm contradiction; illogicality; inconsistency; piece of nonsense.

contrata, nf contract(ing).

contratación, nf signing-up; hiring, contracting; trade.

contratante, nm/f contractor; contracting party.

contratar, vt to contract for; to negotiate for; to sign a contract for.

contratiempo, nm 1. setback, reverse, contretemps; mishap, accident; 2. offbeat, syncopated.

contratista, nm/f contractor; building contractor, builder.

contrato, nm contract, agreement.

contravenir, vi to contravene, infringe, violate.

contribución, nf contribution, make use of, put to use.

contribuir, vt/i to contribute.

contribuyente, nm/f contributor, taxpayer.

contrincante, nm opponent, rival.

contristar, vt 1. to sadden; 2. vr to grow sad, grieve.

contrito, adj contrite.

control, nm control, inspection.

controlador(a), nm/f controller, inspector.

controlar, vt to control; to inspect, check.

controversia, nf controversy.

controvertir, vt to dispute, question; to argue about.

contubernio, nm ring, conspiracy; collusion.

contumacia, nf obstinacy, stubborn disobedience, contumaciousness; perversity.

contundente, adj 1. offensive, blunt instrument; 2. forceful, convincing, powerful.

contundir, vt to bruise, contuse.

conturbar, vt to trouble, dismay, perturb.

conturbarse, vr to be troubled, be dismayed, become perturbed.

convalecencia, nf convalescence.

convalecer, vi to convalesce, get better, recover.

convencer, vt/i to convince, to persuade.

convencerse, vr to become convinced.

convención, nf convention.

conveniencia, nf suitability, fitness, usefulness, advantageousness.

conveniente, adj suitable, fitting, proper, profitable.

convenio, nm agreement, treaty, convenant.

convenir, vi to agree, to suit.

convergente, adj convergent, converging.

converger, vi to converge (on); be in accord.

conversación, nf conversation, talk.

conversador(a), adj, nm/f talkative, chatty, conversasionalist.

conversar, vt 1. to tell, relate, to chat up, 2. vi to talk, converse.

convertidor, nm converter.

convertir, vt to convert, to transform, turn (into).

convicción, nf conviction.

convicto, adj convicted, found guilty, condemned.

convidado(a), nm/f guest.

convidar, vt to invite.

convincente, adj convincing.

convivencia, nf 1. living together, life together, good fellowship; 2. coexistence.

convivir, vi to live together, life together, to share the same life.

convocar, vt to summon, call (together), convoke.

convoyar, vt to convoy; to guard, escort.

convoyarse, vr to connive together, plot.

convulsión, nf convulsion; upheveal

convulsionar, vt to produce convulsion in; to convulse, cause an upheaval in.

conyugal, adj conjugal; married.

cónyuge, nm/f spouse, partner; husband, wife.

cooperación, nf cooperation.

cooperador(a), adj 1. cooperative; collaborating, participating; 2. nm/f collaborator, co-worker.

cooperar, vi to cooperate, work together, take part in.

cooperativa, nf cooperative, mutual association.

coordinación, nf coordination.

coordinador(a), nm/f coordinator.

copa, nf glass; goblet; cup, trophy.

copar, vt to surround, cut off, to corner.

coparticipación, nf joint participation (in).

copartícipe, nm/f partner, fellow participant, joint owner, collaborator.

copia, nf copy, replica, reproduction, duplicate.

copiador(a), nm/f 1. (persona) copier, copyist; 2. (máquina) copying machine, photocopier.

copiar, vt to copy (from); to imitate; to duplicate.

copiloto, nm/f co-driver, co-pilot.

copioso, adj copious, abundant, plentiful.

copla, nf verse, popular song, folksong, ballad.

coproducción, nf joint production.

coproducir, vt to co-produce, produce jointly.

copropiedad, nf co-ownership.

copropietario(a), nm/f co-owner, joint owner.

cópula, nf copulation, sexual intercourse.

coqueta, adj flirtatious, flighty, coquettish.

coquetear, vi to flirt (with).

coraje, nm fighting spirit; toughness, courage.

coral, adj 1. (Mus) choral; 2. nm/f chorale, choir, choral group; 3. nm (Zool) coral; 4. coral snake.

corazón, nm heart.

corazonada, nf presentiment, hunch.

corbata, nf tie, necktie, bow-tie.

corcovar, vt to bend (over); to crook.

corcovear, vi to prance along, cut capers; (horse) to buck, plunge.

corcho, nm cork.

cordel, nm cord, line, thin rope.

cordelería, *nf* cordage, ropes, rigging.
cordero(a), *nm/f* (Zool) lamb.
cordialidad, *nf* warmth, cordiality.
cordillera, *nf* range, chain (of mountains).
córdoba, *nf* monetary unit of Nicaragua.
cordón, *nm* cord, string; strand, lace.
cordura, *nf* good sense, prudence, wisdom.
corear, *vt* to say in a chorus, to shout (in unison); to sing in a chorus.
coreografía, *nf* choreograph.
coreógrafo(a), *nm/f* choreographer.
corista, *nm/f* chorister, member of a chorus.
cornada, *nf* butt, thrust (with the horns), goring.
cornalina, *nf* cornelian, carnelian.
cornamenta, *nf* horns; antlers; cuckold's horns.
córnea, *nf* cornea.
cornear, *vt* to butt, gore.
córneo, *adj* horny, corneous.
corneta, *nf* bugle; horn.
cornetista, *nm/f* bugler.
coro, *nm* chorus; choir.
corolario, *nm* corollary.
corona, *nf* crown; coronet.
coronación, *nf* 1. coronation; 2. crowning, completion.
coronel, *nm* colonel.
coronilla, *nf* crown, top of the head.
corpiño, *nm* bodice; brassière, bra.
corporación, *nf* corporation; company.
corpulencia, *nf* burliness, heavy build; stoutness.
corpulento, *adj* burly, heavily-built.
corpúsculo, *nm* corpuscle.
corral, *nm* yard, farmyard; stockyard, cattlepen, corral (US).
correa, *nf* strap; leather strap, thong; belt; leash.
corrección, *nf* 1. correction; adjustment; 2. rebuke, reprimand; punishment; 3. correctness; courtesy, politeness; good manners; propriety.
correccional, *nm* reformatory.
correctivo, *adj, nm* corrective.
correcto, *adj* 1. correct, accurate, right.
corrector(a), *nm/f* proofreader; copy editor.
corredero, *nm* racetrack.
corredizo, *adj* sliding; travelling; running, slip.
corredor(a), *nm/f* 1. runner; athlete; 2. broker.
corregible, *adj* which can be corrected.
corregidor, *nm* chief magistrate; mayor.
corregir, *vt* 1. to correct; to put right, adjust; to revise, look over, read; 2. rebuke, reprimand; to punish.
correlación, *nf* correlation.
correlacionar, *vt* to correlate.
correligionario(a), *nm/f* co-religionist, person of the same faith; fellow supporter, sympathizer.
correo, *nm* 1. courier; postman, mailman; 2. mail.
correr, 1. *vt* (terreno, distancia) to traverse, cover travel over; to pass over; 2. to overrun; to raid, invade; to lay waste; 3. to race, run.
correrse, *vr* 1. slide, move along; to shift.
correspondencia, *nf* correspondence, letters; post, mail.
corresponder, *vi* correspond to, belong to.
corresponsal, *nm* (newspaper) correspondent.
corretaje, *nm* brokerage.
corretear, *vi* 1. to pursue, harass; 2. scare off.
corrida, *nf* 1. run, dash, sprint; 2. bullfight.
corriente, *adj* 1. flowing, fluent, easy, smooth; current, valid, accepted; 2. ordinary, normal.
corro, *nm* ring, circle; huddle, knot; round enclosure (in the stock exchange).
corroboración, *nf* corroboration.
corroborar, *vt* to corroborate.

corroer, *vi* to corrode; to erode; to corrode, eat away.
corromper, *vi* rot; to turn bad; to spoil, ruin, cause damage to.
corrosión, *nf* corrosion; rust; erosion.
corrugación, *nf* contraction, shrinkage.
corrupción, *nf* 1. rot, decay; stink, stench; 2. corruption; perversion, graft, bribery; seduction.
corrupto, *adj* corrupt.
corruptora, *nf* corrupter, perverter.
corsario, *nm* privateer, corsair.
corta, *nf* felling, cutting.
cortacésped, *nm* lawnmower.
cortacircuitos, *nm* circuit breaker.
cortada, *nf* cut, slash; trench; short cut, slice.
cortado, *adj* 1. cut; clipped; steep, 2. disjointed.
cortador, *adj* cutting.
cortadora, *nf* cutter; slicer; lawnmower.
cortante, *adj* cutting, sharp.
cortapisa, *nf* restriction, limitation (attached to a concession).
cortar, *vt* cut; to hack, chop, slash.
corte, *nm* 1. cutting, deletion; 2. (Juris) court.
cortejar, *vt* to court, woo.
cortejo, *nm* 1. entourage, suite, retinue; 2. procession; solemn gathering; wedding procession, wedding party; 3. courting; courtship; 4. beau.
cortés, *adj* 1. courteous, polite; gracious; 2. courtly love.
cortesano, *adj* of the court; courtly; court.
cortésmente, *adv* courteously, politely; graciously.
corteza, *nf* 1. peel, skin, rind; cortex; crust; 2. outside, outward appearance; hide, exterior.
cortijo, *nm* farm, farmhouse.
cortina, *nf* curtain; screen, flap.
corto, *adj* short; brief, short.
cortocircuito, *nm* short-circuit.
corva, *nf* back of the knee.
corza, *nf* doe.
corzo, *nm* roe deer, roebuck.
cosa, *nf* thing; matter.
cosecha, *nf* crop, harvest; harvesting, gathering.
cosechar, *vt* to harvest, gather; to pick; to cut, reap.
cosechero(a), *nm/f* harvester, reaper; picker.
coser, *vt* 1. to sew; to stitch; 2. to unite, join closely.
cosido, *nm* sewing, needlework.
cosignatario(a), *nm/f* cosignatory.
cosmético, *adj* 1. cosmetic; 2. cosmetic.
cosmetólogo(a), *nm/f* cosmetician.
cósmico, *adj* cosmic.
cosmonauta, *nm/f* cosmonaut.
cosmopolita, *adj* 1. cosmopolitan; 2. *nm/f* cosmopolitan.
cosquillar, *vt* to tickle.
cosquilloso, *adj* 1. ticklish; 2. touchy, easily offended.
costa, *nf* coast; coastline; shore, seashore.
costal, *nm* sack, bag.
costanera, *nf* side, flank; slope.
costanero, *adj* 1. sloping; steep; 2. coastal.
costear, *vt* 1. to pay for, defray the cost of; to endow; to back, sponsor; 2. to sail along the coast; to skirt, go along the edge; to pass close to.
costilla, *nf* 1. bone, rib; 2. pork chop, pork cutlet; 3. shoulders; 4. better half.
costo, *nm* 1. cost; direct cost; price; 2. trouble, effort.
costoso, *adj* costly, expensive.
costumbre, *nf* custom, habit; customs, ways.
costumbrista, *adj* of (local) customs and manners.
costura, *nf* sewing, needlework, dressmaking.
costurera, *nf* dressmaker, seamstress.
costurero, *nm* sewing box, sewing case; sewing room.
coteja, *nf* equal, match.
cotejar, *vt* to compare, collate; to check; arrange.

cotidiano, *adj* daily.

cotilla, *nm/f* busybody, gossip.

cotillear, *vi* to gossip.

cotización, *nf* 1. quotation, price; 2. subscription, assessment (for tax); taxation.

cotizar, *vt* 1. to quote, price (at); 2. collect dues ; pay dues; 3. value (at).

cotorra, *nf* parrot, cockatoo; magpie.

cotorrear, *vi* to chatter, gabble.

coyuntura, *nf* 1. joint; 2. juncture, occasion; opportunity.

cráneo, *nm* skull, cranium.

crápula, *nf* 1. drunkenness; 2. dissipation.

craso, *adj* 1. fat; 2. greasy, thick; 3. crass, stupid.

cráter, *nm* crater.

creación, *nf* creation.

creador(a), *adj* 1. creative; 2. *nm/f* creator; inventor, originator.

crear, *vt* to create; to make official; to invent, originate; to found, establish, institute.

crecer, *vi* to grow; to increase; to rise; to get longer.

crecido, *adj* full-grown; grown-up.

crédito, *nm* 1. credit; belief; to believe (in); 2. authority, standing, reputation.

crédulo, *adj* credulous.

creencia, *nf* belief.

creer, 1. *vi* to think, believe; 2. consider.

creíble, *adj* believable.

crema, *nf* cream; custard.

cremación, *nf* cremation; incineration.

cremallera, *nf* (cierre de _) zipfastener, zipper.

cremoso, *adj* creamy.

crepuscular, *adj* twilight, crepuscular.

crepúsculo, *nm* twilight, dusk.

crespo, *adj* curly; kinky.

cresta, *nf* 1. crest, comb; tuft; 2. toupée.

cría, *nf* 1. rearing, keeping, breeding; 2. baby animal, young creature.

criada, *nf* servant, maid.

criadero, *nm* 1. nursery; 2. feeding ground, breeding place.

criado, *adj* bred, reared, brought up.

criar, *vt* to suckle, feed; to breast-feed; raise, bring up.

criatura, *nf* 1. creature, being; 2. infant, baby, small child.

crimen, *nm* crime.

criminal, *adj* 1. criminal; of murder, murderous; 2. *nm* criminal.

criminalista, *nm/f* 1. criminologist; 2. criminal lawyer.

criminología, *nf* criminology.

crío, *nm* kid, child; brat.

crisis, *nf* crisis.

crisol, *nm* crucible; melting pot.

crispado, *adj* tense, on edge.

crispar, *vt* 1. cause to twitch (or contract); to set on edge; 2. to annoy someone intensely, get on someone's nerves.

cristal, *nm* 1. crystal; 2. glass; 3. mirrors.

cristalera, *nf* window.

cristalería, *nf* 1. glasswork; glass making; 2. glassware shop; 3. glasses (collectively), glassware.

cristalino, *adj* crystalline; clear, limpid, translucent; transparent.

cristalizar, *vt/i* to crystallize.

cristiandad, *nf* Christendom; Christianity.

cristiano(a), *adj* 1. christian; 2. *nm/f* Christian.

Cristo, *nm* Jesus Christ .

criterio, *nm* criterion; yardstick, standard of judgment.

crítica, *nf* criticism.

crítico, *adj* critical.

cromosoma, *nm* chromosome.

crónica, *nf* 1. cronicle; account; 2. news report; feature, article.

crónico, *adj* chronic; ingrained.

cronista, *nf* 1. chronicler; 2. writer, columnist.

cronograma, *nm* timetable, schedule.

cronología, *nf* chronology.

cronometrar, *vt* to time.

cronómetro, *nm* chronometer; stopwatch.

cruce, *nm* 1. crossing; near miss; 2. (point of) intersection; 3. crossing, intersection.

crucero, *nm* cruiser.

crucial, *adj* crucial.

crucificar, *vt* to crucify; to torment, torture.

crucifijo, *nm* crucifix.

crucifixión, *nf* crucifixion.

crucigrama, *nm* crossword (puzzle).

crudeza, *nf* 1. raowness; unripeness; 2. digestibility; 3. hardness; 4 . harshness.

crudo, *adj* raw, half-cooked, uncooked; unripe.

cruel, *adj* cruel.

crueldad, *nf* cruelty.

cruento, *adj* bloody, gory.

crujir, *vi* to rustle; to creak; to crack; to crunch; to grind, gnash; to chatter.

cruz, *nf* cross.

cruzado, *adj* 1. crossed; 2. (Cost) double-breasted; 3. crossbred, hybrid.

cruzar, *vt* 1. to cross: to cut across, intersect; 2. cruise; 3. to cross.

cuaderna, *nf* timber; rib, frame.

cuaderno, *nm* notebook; exercise book; folder.

cuadra, *nf* stable; racing stable.

cuadrado, *adj* square.

cuadrante, *nm* 1. quadrant; 2. face; sundial.

cuadrar, 1. *vt* to square; 2. square (off), make square.

cuadrilla, *nf* party, group; gang; armed patrol.

cuadro, *nm* 1. square; 2. frame; 3. picture, painting; 4. scene.

cuadrúpedo, *nm* quadruped; four-footed animal.

cuajada, *nf* curd; cottage cheese; cheese tart.

cuajar, *vt* to thicken, curdle; (blood) coagulate, clot, to become set or firm.

cual, *adj* such as, of the kind (that); said.

cuál, *pron interrog* which (one).

cualidad, *nf* quality; attribute, trait, characteristic; property.

cualquier(a), *adj* any.

cuando, *adv* when.

cuantioso, *adj* large, substantial; abundant; numerous; considerable.

cuanto, *adj* all that, as much as, whatever.

cuánto, *adj interr* how much?

cuarenta, *adj* forty; fortieth.

cuaresma, *nf* Lent.

cuarta, *nf* quarter, fourth, fourth part.

cuartel, *nm* barracks.

cuartería, *nf* bunkhouse (on a ranch).

cuarterón, *nm* 1. quarter; quarter pound; 2. panel.

cuartilla, *nf* sheet (of paper); manuscript, copy; notes, jottings.

cuarzo, *nm* quartz.

cuatrero, *adj* 1. treacherous, disloyal; 2. *nm* cattle rustler; horse thief.

cuatro, *adj* four; fourth.

cuatrocientos, *adj* four hundred.

cubano(a) *adj* 1. cuban, 2. *nm/f* Cuban.

cubeta, *nf* keg, small cask; pail; tray.

cúbico, *adj* cubic.

cubículo, *nm* cubicle.

cubierta, *nf* cover, covering; paper cover, jacket.

cubierto, *nm* covered, cutlery set, (knife, fork, spoon etc.)

cubo, *nm* cube.

cubrecama, *nf* coverlet, bedspread.

cubrir, *vt* cover (up, over, with); put a roof on; (Mil) protect, defend.

cubrirse, *vr* to cover oneself.

cucaracha, *nf* cockroach; crock.

cucarachero, *nm* parasite, hanger-on; flatterer, creep.

cuchara, *nf* spoon; scoop; ladle; bucket.

cucharada, *nf* spoonful.

cuchilla, *nf* large, (kitchen) knife; chopper, cleaver.

cuchillería, *nf* 1. cutlery; 2. cutler's shop.

cuchillero, *adj* 1. quarrelsome; 2. *nm* cutler.

cuchillo, *nm* knife.

cuello, *nm* neck; bottleneck.

cuenca, *nf* 1. hollow; eye socket; 2. wooden bowl, begging bowl; 3. deep valley; basin.

cuenta, *nf* 1. account, counting; calculation; 2. account, bill.

cuento, *nm* story, tale; short story; funny story, joke.

cuerda, *nf* rope, string, cord; lead; fishing line.

cuerdo, *adj* 1. sane; 2. sense, sensible, prudent.

cuerear, *vt* 1. skin, flay; 2. whip, beat.

cuerno, *nf* 1. horns; antlers; 2. drinking horn.

cuero, *nm* 1. skin, hide; pelt; leather; 2. whip.

cuerpo, *nm* body; corpse.

cuervo, *nm* raven; crow; cormorant.

cuesta, *nf* slope; hill.

cuestación, *nf* charity collection; flag day.

cuestión, *nf* 1. matter, question, issue; problem; 2. quarrel, dispute; trouble.

cuestionar, *vt* 1. to question, dispute, argue about; 2. *vi* to argue.

cueva, *nf* cave; cellar, vault.

cuidado, *adj* 1. elegant; 2. *nm* care, worry, concern; solicitude.

cuidador, *nm* care-taker trainer; groundsman.

cuidadora, *nf* nursemaid, nanny.

cuidar, *vt* to look after, care for; pay attention.

cuidarse, *vr* to look after oneself.

culebra, *nf* snake.

culero, *adj* 1. lazy; 2. *nm* diaper (US).

culinario, *adj* culinary; cooking.

culminante, *adj* highest; topmost; culminating.

culminar, *vt* 1. to conclude, put the finishing touches to; 2. *vi* to reach its highest point.

culpabilidad, *nf* guilt.

culpable, *adj* 1. person to blame, the person at fault; the guilty person; 2. condemned blameworthy; 3. *nm/f* culprit; offender, guilty party.

culpar, *vt* to blame, accuse; to condemn.

cultivador(a), *nm/f* farmer, grower.

cultivar, *vt* cultivate, work, till; to culture (Bio).

cultivo, *nm* cultivation, growing.

culto, *adj* 1. cultivated, cultured, refined; educated; 2. learned; 3. *nm* worship; cult; divine service.

cultura, *nf* culture; refinement; education; elegance.

culturización, *nf* education, enlightenment.

culturizar, *vt* to educate, enlighten.

cumbre, *nf* summit, top; height, pinnacle.

cumplidor, *adj* reliable, trustworthy.

cumplimentar, *vt* to pay one's respects to, pay a courtesy call on; to congratulate (on).

cumplimiento, *nm* fulfilment; completion.

cumplir, *vi* to carry out, fulfil; to comply with.

cúmulo, *nm* 1. heap; accumulation; lot; 2. cumulus.

cuna, *nf* cradle; cot.

cundir, *vi* to spread; expand, increase.

cuñado(a), *nm/f* brother-in-law, sister-in-law.

cuño, *nm* 1. stamp, die-stamp; 2. mark; official stamp.

cuota, *nf* 1. quota; share; 2. instalment, payment.

cupón, *nm* coupon; trading stamp.

cúpula, *nf* 1. cupola; 2. turret.

cura, *nm* 1. priest; father; 2. *nf* cure, healing; treatment; remedy.

curación, *nf* cure, healing; treatment.

curador(a), *nm/f* healer.

curandero, *nm* quack; bonesetter.

curar, *vt* to cure (of); to treat.

curarse, *vr* to recover, get better.

curiosear, *vt* to glance at, look over; to look round.

curiosidad, *nf* curiosity; inquisitiveness.

currículo, *nm* curriculum.

cursante, *nm/f* student.

cursar, *vt* 1. to send, dispatch; (order) to send out; to pass on, dispatch, deal with; 2. study; to take, attend (a course).

cursi, *adj* in bad taste, vulgar; pretentious.

cursilería, *nf* bad taste, vulgarity; pretentiousness.

cursillista, *nm/f* member (of a course).

cursillo, *nm* short course; short series (of lectures).

cursiva, *nf* italics; cursive writing.

curso, *nm* 1. curse; direction; flow; fluvial watercourse; 2. school year.

cursor, *nm* slide; cursor.

curtido, *adj* 1. tanned; hardened, weather-beaten; 2. be expert at, be skilled in.

curtir, *vt* 1. to tan; 2. harden; inure.

curva, *nf* curve; graph, bend.

curvatura, *nf* curvature.

curvo, *adj* curved; crooked, bent.

cúspide, *nf* summit, peak; tip, apex; top, pinnacle.

custodia, *nf* care, safekeeping, custody.

custodio, *nm* guardian, keeper, custodian.

cutis, *nm* skin, complexion.

cuyo, *adj rel* whose; of whom, of which.

Ch

Ch, ch, *nf* (letter) Ch, ch.

chabacanear, *vi* to say (or do) coarse things.

chabacanería, *nf* 1. vulgarity, bad taste; commonness; shoddiness; 2. coarse thing (to say), vulgar remark, platitude; shoddy piece of work.

chabacanizar, *vt* to trivialize.

chabacano, *adj* 1. vulgar, coarse, in bad taste; 2. *nm* apricot.

chabola, *nf* shack, shanty; shanty-town.

chabolista, *nm/f* shanty-town dweller.

chacal, *nm* jackal.

chacanear, *vt* 1. to spur violently; 2. to pester, annoy; 3. to use daily.

chacinería, *nf* pork butcher's.

chacinero, *adj* pork; pigmeat industry.

chacota, *nf* noisy merriment, fun (and games).

chacra, *nf* 1. small farm, smallholding, market garden; 2. truck farm (US); 3. country estate; large orchard, fruit-farming estate; cultivated land; 4. farmhouse.

chacha, *nf* maid, nursemaid; cleaning lady; low-class girl.

chachal, *nm* charm necklace.

cháchara, *nf* chatter, idle talk, small talk.

chacharear, 1. vt to deal in, sell; 2. vi to chatter, jaw.

chacho, nm lad; servant.

chaflán, nm 1. bevel (surface), chamfer; 2. street corner, road junction; 3. corner house.

chal, nm shawl.

chalado, adj dotty; cranky.

chaladura, nf crankiness.

chalanear, vt 1. to haggle successfully with, beat down; to handle cleverly, bring off; 2. to break in, tame; 3. to pester; 4. make fun of.

chalarse, vr to go crazy, go off one's rocker; to be crazy about.

chalecito, nm little place in the country, country retreat.

chaleco, nm waistcoat, vest; sweater.

chalet, nm chalet, cottage; bungalow.

chalina, nf 1. floppy bow tie; 2. small shawl, headscarf.

chalupa, nf launch, boat; ship's boat, lifeboat.

chamaca, nf girl; girlfriend, sweetheart.

chamaco, nm boy, lad; boyfriend.

chamberga, nf coat.

chamarra, nf jacket; short jacket.

chambergo, nm cocked hat; broad-brimmed soft hat; coat.

chambonada, nf 1. awkwardness, clumsiness; 2. stroke of luck, lucky shot; 3. blunder.

chambra, nf housecoat; blouse; loose jacket.

chamiza, nf thatch, thatch palm; brushwood.

champaña, nm champagne.

champiñón, nm mushroom.

champú, nm shampoo.

champurrar, vt to mix, make a cocktail of.

champurreado, nm hastily-prepared dish; hash, botch.

chamuscar, vt 1. to scorch, sear, singe; 2. to sell cheap.

chance, nm 1. chance; prospects; 2. good luck.

chancear, vi to joke, make jokes (about); to fool about, play around (with).

chancillería, nf chancery.

chancla, nf old shoe, broken shoe.

chancleta, nf slipper.

chanchería, nf pork-butcher's shop.

chanchero, nm pork butcher.

chancho, adj 1. dirty, filthy; 2. nm pig, hog; pork; wild boar.

chanchullo, nm fiddle, wangle; crooked deal; piece of graft, dirty business.

chantaje, nm blackmail(ing).

chantajista, nm/f blackmailer.

chapa, nf 1. plate, sheet; 2. panel, veneer.

chapar, vt 1. to plate, cover (or line) with sheet metal (or veneer); to tile; 2. to throw out, come out with an observation.

chaparral, nm thicket (of kermes oaks), chaparral.

chaparro, adj 1. squat, short and chubby; 2. nm kermes oak, dwarf oak.

chaparrón, nm downpour, cloudburst.

chapear, vt 1. to weed; 2. vi to clear the ground.

chapetón, adj 1. awkward, clumsy; 2. nm Spaniard in America.

chapistería, nf car-body works, panel-beating shop.

chapotear, vt 1. to sponge (down); to wet, moisten; 2. vi to splash about; to paddle; to dabble.

chapoteo, nm 1. sponging; moistening; 2. splashing; paddling; dabbling.

chapucear, vi 1. botch, bungle, make a mess of; to do in a slapdash way; 2. swindle.

chapucería, nf 1. shoddiness; 2. shoddy piece of work, mess.

chapucero, adj rough, crude, shoddy.

chapuzar, vt to duck, dip, plunge.

chapuzón, nm 1. dip, swim; ducking; to go for a dip; 2. splashdown.

chaqueta, nf jacket.

chaquetón, nm long jacket, reefer, shooting jacket; three-quarter coat.

charanga, nf 1. brass band; band of street musicians; cavalry band; 2. formal dance, hop.

charca, nf pond, pool.

charcutería, nf 1. cooked pork products; 2. delicatessen store.

charla, nf talk, chat; chatter.

charlar, vi to chat, talk (about); to chatter, gossip.

charlatán, adj talkative; gossipy, trickster.

charol, nm varnish; patent leather.

charola, nf tray.

charolado, adj polished, shiny.

charolar, vt to varnish, japan.

charra, nf 1. peasant woman; lowclass woman, coarse woman; 2. broad brimmed hat.

charrada, nf 1. coarse thing, piece of bad breeding; example of bad taste; 2. flashy ornament, vulgar adornment.

charranada, nf dirty trick.

charro, adj 1. rustic; coarse, vulgar, ill-bred; 2. rude, gaudy; flashy, showy; overornamented, decorated in bad taste; 3. cowboy; 4. skilled in horsemanship.

chasco, nm 1. disappointment; failure, letdown; 2. sick joke; prank.

chasis, nm chassis; plateholder.

chasquido, nm click; snap; crack; crunch; creak.

chatarra, nf scrap iron, junk; coppers, small change.

chatarrero, nm scrap dealer, scrap merchant.

chayote, nm chayote, fruit of the chayotera.

chelista, nm/f cellist.

chelo, nm 1. cello; 2. cellist.

cheque, nm check (US).

chequeo, nm check; checking-up; checkup; service, overhaul(ing).

chequera, nf checkbook.

chica, nf girl; maid, servant; bar-girl.

chicle, nm chewing gum.

chico, 1. adj small, little, tiny; 2. nm boy; child, youngster, lad.

chícharo, nm pea, chickpea.

chicharrón, nm piece of burnt meat, to be burnt to a cinder.

chiflado, adj daft, barmy; cranky.

chiflar, vt 1. hiss, boo, whistle, to blow; 2. to drink, knock back; 3. vi to whistle, hiss; to sing.

chiflido, nm whistle, shrill sound, hiss.

chile, nm chili, red pepper.

chilindrón, nm cooked with tomatoes and peppers.

chillar, vi 1. howl; to squeak; to squeal; to screech, squawk; to yell; to shriek, scream; 2. scream, be loud, clash; 3. shout, protest.

chillería, nf row, hubbub.

chillido, nm howl; squeak; squeal; screech; squawk; yell, shriek, scream; blare; creak.

chimenea, nf 1. chimney; funnel; smokestack; shaft; 2. fireplace; mantelpiece; chimney piece.

chimpancé, nm chimpanzee.

china, nf 1. china; porcelain; 2. china silk.

chinche, nf 1. bug, bedbug; 2. drawing pin, thumbtack (US); 3. nuisance; annoying person, pest, bore; naughty child.

chinchilla, nf chinchilla.

chinchín, nm drizzle.

chinchorro, nm 1. dragnet, trawl; 2. rowing boat, dinghy; 3. hammock; poor tenement.

chinela, nf slipper, mule; clog.

chinero, nm china cupboard.

chino(a), *adj* 1. Chinese; 2. *nm/f* Chinese.

chiquear, *vi* to spoil, indulge; to flatter, suck up to.

chiquero, *nm* pigsty; bull pen.

chiquilín, *nm* tiny tot, small boy.

chiquillada, *nf* 1. childish prank; childish thing (to do); 2. kids, youngsters.

chiquillería, *nf* a crowd of youngsters, a mob of kids.

chiquillo(a), *nm/f* kid, youngster, child.

chirimoya, *nf* 1. stard apple; 2. head.

chirola, *nf* jug , jail.

chirriar, *vi* to chirp, sing; to chirp, cheep; to screech, squawk; to creak, squeak.

chisme, *nm* 1. contrivance, jigger, things, gear, tackle; 2. piece of gossip, tale; tittletattle, tales.

chismear, *vi* to gossip, tell tales, spread scandal.

chismoso, *adj* gossiping, scandalmongering.

chispa, *nf* spark; sparkle, gleam.

chispita, *nf* a drop of wine.

chistar, *vi* to speak, say something.

chistoso, *adj* funny, amusing; witty.

chivatazo, *nm* tip-off; to inform; give a tip-off.

chivero, *nm* 1. busdriver; 2. brawler; intriguer.

chivo, *nm* 1. goat; billy goat; 2. fraud, intrigue; smuggling; contraband, smuggled goods.

chocante, *adj* 1. startling, striking; odd, strange; noteworthy; 2. shocking, scandalous.

chocolate, *adj* 1. chocolate-colored; dark red; 2. *nm* drinking chocolate, cocoa.

chocolatero, *adj* 1. fond of chocolate; 2. *nm* chocolate pot.

choque, *nm* impact, jolt, jar; crash, collision; (Med) shock.

choquezuela, *nf* kneecap.

chorizo, *nm* hard pork sausage, salami.

chorrear, *vt* 1. soak; 2. *vi* gush forth, spurt out, drip, trickle.

chorreo, *nm* gushing, spouting, dripping.

chorrera, *nf* (pico) spout; channel.

chorro, *nm* jet, spurt, stream, trickle.

chotear, *vt* 1. to make fun of; 2. spoil, pamper.

choteo, *nm* joking, amusement.

choza, *nf* hut, shack.

chubasco, *nm* 1. shower, squall; 2. setback.

chula, *nf* 1. flashy female, brassy girl; 2. girlfriend.

chulada, *nf* funny thing; mean trick.

chulear, *vi* to pinch, nick.

chuleta, *nf* chop, cutlet.

chumacera, *nf* ball bearing, journal bearing; rowlock, oarlock (US).

chupada, *nf* suck; pull, puff; sip.

chupar, *vt* suck; to suck out, suck up; to absorb, take in, take up; to sip.

chupete, *nm* pacifier (US); teat; lollipop.

churrasco, *nm* barbecue, barbecued-meat; steak.

churrasquear, *vi* to eat steak.

churrasquería, *nf* barbecue stall.

churre, *nf* thick grease; filth.

churrería, *nf* fritter stall.

churrero(a), *nf* fritter maker, fritter seller.

churro, *adj* 1. coarse; coarse-wooled; 2. *nm* fritter.

churruscar, *vi* to burn, scorch.

chuscada, *nf* funny remark, joke; coarse joke.

chusco, *adj* funny, droll.

chusma, *nf* rabble, mob, riffraff.

chuzar, *vt* to prick; to sting, hurt.

chuzo, *nm* pike; spiked stick, metal-tipped stick.

D

D, d, *nf* (letter) D, d.

dable, *adj* possible, feasible, practicable.

dactilar, *adj* finger.

dactilografía, *nf* typing.

dactilografiar, *vt* to type.

dactilógrafo(a), *nm/f* typist.

dadista, *nm* gambler.

dadito, *nm* small cube.

dádiva, *nf* gift, present; sop.

dadivoso, *adj* generous, lavish with gifts.

dado, *nm* cube, dice.

daga, *nf* dagger, stiletto; machete.

dálmata, *nm/f* dalmatian (dog).

daltonismo, *nm* color blindness.

dama, *nf* 1. lady; gentle woman; 2. (ajedrez) queen.

damasco, *nm* damask.

damisela, *nf* damsel; courtesan, prostitute.

damnificar, *vt* to injure, harm; to disable.

dantesco, *adj* 1. relating to Dante; 2. dantesque; horrific, weird, macabre; hellish, infernal.

danza, *nf* dancing.

danzar, *vt* to dance.

danzarín(ina), *nm/f* dancer; artistic dancer, professional dancer.

dañar, *vt* to damage; to harm, hurt; to spoil.

daño, *nm* damage; hurt, harm, injury.

dar, *vt* to give.

dardo, *nm* dart, shaft.

datar, 1. *vt* to date, put a date on; 2. *vi* to date from, date back to.

dátil, *nm* 1. date; 2. mussel.

datilera, *nf* date palm.

dato, *nm* fact, datum, piece of information.

de, *prep* 1. (possession) of; 2. origin, (distance) from; 3. (nature) made of, (acerca de) about.

debajo, *adv* underneath, below; on the underside.

debatir, *vi* 1. to debate; to discuss, argue about; 2. *vi* to struggle; to writhe; to flail about.

deber, *vt* to owe.

debido, *adj* 1. due, just; right, correct; 2. due to, because of.

debilidad, *nf* weakness; feebleness; faintness; dimness; senility, senile decay.

debitar, to debit.

débito, *nm* 1. debit; 2. duty.

debú, *nm* debut.

debutar, *vi* to make one's debut.

década, *nf* decade.

decadencia, *nf* decadence, decline, decay.

decaer, *vi* decay, decline; to flag, weaken; to wane; to fall off; to sink, fail.

decaído, *adj* downcast, crestfallen; to be down.

decálogo, *nm* decalogue.

decantar, *vt* 1. to praise, laud; 2. *vi* to decant; to pour off; to leave behind, form, deposit.

decapitar, *vt* to behead, decapitate.

decena, *nf* ten; about ten.

decencia, *nf* 1. decency; seemliness, decorum; respectability; modesty; 2. cleanness, tidiness.

decente, *adj* 1. decent; seemly, proper; respectable; modest; 2. clean, tidy.

decepción, *nf* disappointment.

decepcionar, *vt* to disappoint.
deceso, *nm* passing, death; fatality.
decidido, *adj* decided, determined; emphatic.
decidir, 1. *vi* decide, persuade, convince; 2. decide, settle, resolve
décima, *nf* tenth, tenth part.
decimal, *nm* decimal.
decir, *vt/i* to say, to tell, to speak, indicate, show.
decisión, *nf* decision; (Jur) judgment.
declamación, *nf* declamation; recitation; delivery.
declamar, *vt* 1. to declaim; to recite; 2. *vi* to speak out, hold forth (against).
declaración, *nf* declaration; pronouncement, statement.
declarado, *adj* confessed, declared.
declarar, *vt* to declare, state; to explain, expound.
declinación, *nf* decline, falling-off; decay.
declinar, *vt* 1. to decline, refuse; to reject; 2. *vi* to decline, fall off, fall away; to decay.
declive, *nm* slope, incline, declivity; pitch.
decolorado, *adj* discolored.
decolorante, *nm* bleaching agent.
decolorar, *vt* to discolor, affect the color of.
decomisar, *vt* to seize, confiscate.
decomiso, *nm* seizure, confiscation.
decongestionante, *nm* decongestant.
decoración, *nf* decoration.
decorador(a), *nm/f* decorator; interior designer.
decorar, *vt* to decorate, adorn (with); to memorize.
decoro, *nm* decorum, propriety, decency; proprieties.
decrecer, *vi* to decrease, diminish; to get shorter.
decrecimiento, *nm* decrease, diminution; fall; shortening.
decrépito, *adj* decrepit.
decreto, *nm* decree, order; act.
dechado, *nm* sampler; model, example, epitome.
dedicación, *nf* dedication; devotion (to).
dedicado, *adj* dedicated.
dedicar, *vt* to dedicate (to); to consecrate.
dedicatoria, *nf* inscription, dedication.
dedo, *nm* finger; (del pie) toe.
deducción, *nf* deduction; inference.
deducir, *vt* to deduce, infer (from); derive.
defección, *nf* defection, desertion.
defectible, *adj* fallible, imperfect; faulty.
defecto, *nm* fault, defect, flaw; shortcoming, failure.
defectuoso, *adj* defective, faulty.
defender, *vt* to defend (against, from); to protect.
defensa, *nf* defense; protection, shelter.
defensiva, *nf* defensive.
defensivo, *adj* 1. defensive; 2. *nm* defense, safeguard.
deferencia, *nf* deference.
deferir, *vt* 1. to refer, relegate (to); 2. *vi* to defer to.
deficiencia, *nf* deficiency, shortcoming, defect.
deficiente, *adj* deficient, wanting (in); defective.
definición, *nf* definition.
definido, *adj* definite; defined.
deformante, *adj* distorting.
deformar, *vt* to deform; to disfigure; to distort; to strain.
deforme, *adj* deformed, misshapen; abnormal.
defraudar, *vt* to cheat, defraud; to deceive.
degeneración, *nf* degeneration (into).
degenerar, *vi* to degenerate (into); to decline, decay.
deglutir, *vt/i* to swallow.
degolladero, *nm* throat, neck, throttle.
degollador, *nm* executioner.
degradación, *nf* degradation; humiliation; reduction in rank.
degradar, *vt* to degrade, debase; to humiliate.
deidad, *nf* deity; divinity.

deificación, *nf* deification; apotheosis.
deificar, *vt* to deify; to apotheosize.
dejado, *adj* untidy, slovenly; abandoned; unkempt.
dejar, *vt* 1. to leave; to forget, leave out; abandon, desert, forsake; 2. *vi* to stop; leave off.
delación, *nf* accusation; denunciation.
delantal, *nm* apron.
delantera, *nf* front, front part.
delatar, *vt* to denounce, inform against; to betray.
delator(a), *nm/f* informer, accuser; betrayer.
delegación, *nf* delegation.
delegado(a), *nm/f* delegate; agent, representative.
delegar, *vt* to delegate.
deleitar, *vt* to delight, charm.
deleite, *nm* delight, pleasure; joy; delights.
deletrear, *vt* to spell (out); to decipher, interpret.
deletreo, *nm* spelling, spelling-out.
delfín, *nm* (Zool) dolphin.
delgado, *adj* thin; slim, slender; slight.
deliberación, *nf* deliberation.
deliberado, *adj* deliberate.
deliberar, *vt* 1. to debate, discuss; 2. *vi* to deliberate.
deliberativo, *adj* deliberative.
delicadeza, *nf* weakness; hypersensitiveness, touchiness, susceptibility.
delicado, *adj* delicate; dainty; sensitive.
delicia, *nf* delight; delightfulness.
delimitar, *vt* to delimit.
delincuencia, *nf* delinquency, criminality.
delincuente, *adj* 1. delinquent; criminal; guilty; 2. *nm/f* criminal, offender; guilty person.
delineación, *nf* delineation.
delineador, *nm* eyeliner.
delineante, *nm* draftsman.
delinear, *vt* to delineate; to outline; to draw.
delinquir, *vi* to commit an offense; to offend.
delirante, *adj* delirious; light-headed; raving.
delirar, *vi* to be delirious, rave; rant, talk nonsense.
delito, *nm* crime, offense.
demacrado, *adj* emaciated, wasted away.
demanda, *nf* demand, request; inquiry; claim.
demandante, *nm/f* claimant; plaintiff.
demandar, *vt* to demand, ask for; to claim; to sue.
demarcación, *nf* demarcation; demarcation line.
demás, *adj* 1. the other ..., the rest of the...; 2. *pron* the rest; the others, the rest (of them).
demasiado, *adj* too much; overmuch, excessive.
demencia, *nf* madness, insanity, dementia.
demérito, *nm* demerit, fault; disadvantage.
democracia, *nf* democracy.
demócrata, *nm/f* democrat.
demoledor, *adj* powerful, overwhelming; shattering, devastating.
demoler, *vt* to demolish; pull down.
demoníaco, *adj* demoniacal, demonic.
demonio, *nm* devil; demon; evil spirit.
demora, *nf* delay.
demorar, *vt* 1. to delay; to hold up, hold back; 2. *vi* to stay on, linger on; to delay, waste time.
demostración, *nf* demonstration, show, display; gesture.
demostrar, *vt* to demonstrate, show; to show off; to prove.
demostrativo, *adj, nm* demonstrative.
demudado, *adj* pale.
demudar, *vt* rostro to change, alter.
denegar, *vt* to refuse; to reject; to deny.
denigración, *nf* denigration.
denigrante, *adj* insulting; degrading.
denigrar, *vt* to denigrate, revile, run down; to insult.
denominación, *nf* designation; denomination.

denominado, *adj* named, called; so-called.

denominar, *vt* to name, call, designate.

denotar, *vt* to denote; to indicate, show; to express.

densidad, *nf* density; compactness; thickness; heaviness, dryness; solidity.

denso, *adj* dense; compact.

dentado, *adj* having teeth; cogged, toothed; jagged.

dentadura, *nf* set of teeth, denture.

dental, *adj* 1. dental; 2. *nf* dental.

dentar, *vt* to put teeth on, furnish with teeth.

dentellear, *vt* to bite, nibble, sink one's teeth into.

dentífrico, *adj* tooth.

dentista, *nm/f* dentist.

dentro, *adv* inside; indoors; inwardly.

denudar, *vt* to denude (of); to lay bare.

denunciación, *nf* denunciation; accusation.

denunciador(a), *nm/f* accuser; informer.

denunciar, *vt* to report (to); to proclaim, announce.

deparar, *vt* to provide, furnish with; to present.

departamento, *nm* department, section; office.

departir, *vi* to talk, converse (with, about).

depauperar, *vt* to impoverish; to weaken, deplete, exhaust.

depender, *vi* to depend; to depend on.

dependienta, *nf* salesgirl, saleswoman, shop assistant.

dependiente, *adj* 1. dependent (on); 2. *nm* employee; salesman, shop assistant.

deponente, *adj* 1. deponent; 2. *nm/f* deponent, person making a statement.

deponer, *vt* 1. to lay down; to lay aside; to remove, take down; 2. *vi* (Jur) to give evidence.

deportación, *nf* deportation.

deportar, *vt* to deport.

deporte, *nm* sport; game; recreation.

deportivo, *adj* sporting, sportsmanlike.

deposición, *nf* deposition, removal.

depositar, *vt* to deposit; to place; to lay aside.

depositario(a), *nm/f* depository, trustee; receiver.

depósito, *nm* deposit; sediment.

depravación, *nf* depravity, depravation, corruption.

depravado, *adj* depraved, corrupt.

depravar, *vt* to deprave, corrupt.

depreciación, *nf* depreciation.

depreciar, *vt* to depreciate, reduce the value of.

depredación, *nf* depredation; outrage, excess; pillage.

depredador, *nm* predator.

depredar, *vt* to pillage, commit outrage against; take a prey.

depresión, *nf* 1. depression; hollow; dip; recess, niche; 2. wering; drop, fall; 3. slump, recession, nervous depression.

deprimente, 1. *adj* depressing; 2. *nm* depressant.

deprimido, *adj* depressed.

deprimir, *vt* depress, press down; to flatten.

depurado, *adj* pure, refined.

depurador, *nm* water purifier.

depuradora, *nf* purifying plant; water-treatment plant.

depurar, *vt* 1. purify; to cleanse, purge; 2. debug.

derecha, *nf* right hand; right side, righthand side.

derechista, 1. *adj* rightist, right-wing; 2. *nm/f* rightist, right-winger.

derecho, 1. *adj* right; right hand; 2. straight; upright, erect, standing; 3. earnest.

deriva, *nf* drift; leeway.

derivación, *nf* 1. derivation; origin, source; 2. etymology, word formation; compounding.

derivado, *adj* 1. derived; derivative; 2. *nm* derivative; 3. by-product.

derivar, *vt* 1. derive; 2. direct, diver; 3. *vi* derive from, be derived from; 4. drift; to lead to, end up as.

dermatología, *nf* dermatology.

dermatólogo(a), *nm/f* dermatologist.

dérmico, *adj* skin.

derogación, *nf* repeal, abolition.

derogar, *vt* to repeal, abolish.

derramadero, *nm* spillway; rubbish dump.

derramar, *vt* 1. spill; to pour out, pour away; to weep, shed; 2. scatter, spread (about); to scatter, lavish, pour out.

derredor, *adv y prep* around, about.

derrengado, *adj* 1. bent, twisted, crooked; 2. crippled, lame.

derrengar, *vt* bend, twist, make crooked.

derretido, *adj* 1. melted; molten; thawed; 2. be crazy about someone.

derretir, *vi* melt; to liquefy; to thaw.

derribar, *vt* nock down, pull down, demolish; to tear down.

derrocamiento, *nm* 1. bringing down; 2. demolition; 3. overthrow, toppling; ousting.

derrocar, *vt* 1. fling down, hurl down; 2. knock down, demolish; 3. overthrow, topple; to oust (from).

derrochador(a), *adj* 1. spendthrift; 2. *nm/f* spendthrift, wastrel.

derrochar, *vt* to squander, waste; to lavish, pour out.

derroche, *nm* squandering, waste; lavish expenditure; extravagance.

derrota, *nf* 1. road, route, track; 2. curse; 3. defeat; rout; débacle, disaster.

derrotado, *adj* defeated, beaten, losing.

derrotar, *vt* 1. defeat; to rout, put to flight; 2. to tear, ruin.

derrotero, *nm* course, plan of action.

derrumbamiento, *nm* 1. plunge, headlong fall; 2. demolition; collapse; fall, cave-in.

derrumbar, *vt* 1. fling down; to throw headlong; 2. knock down, demolish; 3. upset, overturn.

desabotonar, *vt* to unbutton.

desabrido, *adj* tasteless, insipid, flat.

desabrigado, *adj* 1. to lightly dressed, without adequate clothing; 2. unprotected, exposed; defenceless.

desabrigar, *vt* 1. remove the clothing of; to leave bare, uncover; 2. leave without shelter, deprive of protection.

desabrigo, *nm* 1. descovering; 2. undress; exposure; lack of clothing, unprotectedness; poverty, destitution.

desabrochar, *vt* 1. undo, unfasten, unbutton; to loosen the clothing of; 2. uncover, expose.

desaceleración, *nf* deceleration, slowing down, slowdown; downturn, reduction.

desacelerar, *vi* 1. to slow down; 2. *vi* to decelerate, slow down; to slow down, decline.

desacertar, *vi* to be mistaken, be wrong; to get it wrong; to act unwisely.

desacoplar, *vt* to disconnect; to take apart, uncouple.

desacostumbrado, *adj* unusual; unaccustomed.

desacostumbrar, *vt* to break someone of the habit of, wean someone away from.

desacreditar, *vt* 1. discredit, damage the reputation of, bring into disrepute; 2. cry down, disparage, run down.

desactivar, *vt* to defuse, make safe, render harmless; to deactivate, neutralize.

desacuerdo, *nm* discord, disagreement.

desafiador, *adj* 1. defiant; challenging; 2. *nm/f* challenger.

desafiante, *adj* challenging; defiant.

desafiar, vt to challenge.

desafiliarse, vr to disaffiliate (from).

desafinar, vi to be (or play, sing) out of tune; to go out of tune.

desafío, nm challenge.

desafortunado, adj unfortunate, unlucky, inopportune, untimely.

desagradable, adj disagreeable, unpleasant.

desagradar, vt 1. to displease; to bother, upset; 2. vi to be unpleasant.

desagradecido, adj ungrateful.

desagrado, nm displeasure; dislike; dissatisfaction.

desaguar, vt 1. to drain, empty, run off; 2. vi to drain away, drain off.

desahogado(a), adj 1. roomy, large; clear, free, unencumbered; 2. nm/f brazen person, shameless individual.

desahogar, vt to ease, relieve; to console.

desahogo, nm comfort, ease; comfortable circumstances.

desahuciado, adj hopeless.

desahuciar, vt to evict, eject; to oust, remove, get out; deprive of hope.

desahucio, nm eviction, ejection; dismissal.

desajustado, adj ill-adjusted, poorly adjusted.

desajustar, vt to disarrange, disturb the order of.

desajuste, nm disorder, disarrangement; breakdown.

desalentar, vt 1. to make someone breathless, make someone gasp for breath; 2. to discourage.

desaliento, nm discouragement; depression, dejection; dismay.

desalmado, adj cruel, heartless.

desalojar, vt 1. to eject, oust, remove; to dislodge; to evict; 2. vi to move out.

desalojo, nm ejection, removal; evacuation; abandonment.

desalquilado, adj vacant, untenanted.

desalquilar, vt to vacate, move out of.

desamar, vt to cease to love, to dislike, detest.

desamarrar, vt to untie; (Naut) cast off.

desarmar, vt 1. to disarm; 2. to take apart, take to pieces, dismantle; to strip down; to ship; to remove, take down.

desarme, nm 1. disarmament; 2. removal of tariff barriers; industrial removal of trade tariffs, lifting of protectionist barriers.

desarraigar, vt 1. uproot, root out, dig up; 2. eradicate; to extirpate.

desarreglar, vt to disarrange; to disturb, mess up, upset; to put out of order.

desarreglo, nm disorder, confusion, chaos; untidiness; irregularity.

desarrollado, adj well-developed.

desarrollar, 1. vt to unroll, unwind; to unfold, open (out); 2. expand; 3. develop; to evolve; to explain, expound; to carry out.

desarrollo, nm development; evolution; unfolding; expansion; growth.

desarticular, vt to take apart, take to pieces; to separate.

desatado, adj wild, violent, uncontrolled.

desatar, vt untie, undo, unfasten; to loosen, slacken; to detach, separate.

desatender, vi to disregard, pay no attention to; to ignore; to neglect; to slight, offend.

desatento, adj heedless, careless; neglectful; inattentive.

desatinado, adj silly, foolish; wild, reckless.

desatinar, vt 1. to perplex, bewilder, 2. vi to act foolishly; to talk nonsense, rave; to get rattled, begin to act wildly.

desatino, nm 1. foolishness, folly, silliness; tactlessness; 2. silly thing, foolish act; blunder, mistake.

desautorización, nf 1. discrediting; disapproval; repudiation; 2. denial.

desautorizado, adj unauthorized; unofficial; unwarranted.

desautorizar, 1. vt deprive of authority, declare without authority; to discredit; to disapprove of; to disown, repudiate; 2. deny, issue a denial of.

desayunar, vr to have breakfast, breakfast.

desazón, nf tastelessness, lack of flavor.

desazonar, vt 1. make tasteless, take the flavor out of; 2. annoy, upset, displease.

desbandada, nf rush (to get away).

desbandarse, vr to disband; to flee in disorder; disperse in confusion.

desbande, nm rush (to get away).

desbaratar, vt to ruin, spoil, destroy; to mess up.

desbarbar, vt to shave; to trim.

desbarrancar, vt to fling over a precipice.

desbarrar, vi to talk rubbish; to be very wide of the mark.

desbastar, vt to rough-hew; to plane (down), smooth (down).

desbloquear, vt to break the blockade of.

desbocar, vt to chip.

desbocarse, vr (horse) to bolt, run away; to rush off.

desbordamiento, nm overflowing, flooding; spilling.

desbordar, vt to pass, go beyond; to exceed, surpass.

descabellado, adj wild, crazy, preposterous.

descabellar, vt to dishevel; to ruffle, rumple.

descabezar, vt to behead; cut the head off.

descafeinado, adj decaffeinated; diluted, watereddown.

descafeinar, vt to decaffeinate; to dilute, water down.

descalabrar, vt to smash, damage; to hit, hurt.

descalabro, nm blow, setback; disaster, misfortune.

descalificación, nf discrediting; rejection, relegation; dismissal.

descalificar, vt to discredit; to write off, reject, relegate to oblivion; to dismiss.

descalzo, adj refoot(ed); shoeless.

descansadero, nm stopping place, resting place.

descansado, adj 1. rested, refreshed; 2. restful; tranquil, unworried, free from care.

descansar, vt 1. rest, support, lean; 2. take a rest.

descanso, nm rest; repose; relief; break.

descarado, adj shameless, brazen, barefaced; cheeky, saucy; blatant.

descargadero, nm wharf.

descargador, nm unloader; docker, stevedore.

descargar, vt 1. unload, to empty; to download; 2. fire, discharge, shoot.

descaro, nm shamelessness, brazenness.

descarriar, vi misdirect, put on the wrong road.

descarriarse, vi lose one's way; go astray.

descarrilamiento, nm derailment.

descarrilar, vi to be derailed, run off the rails, jump the track.

descartar, vt to discard; to put aside, lay aside.

descascarar, vt to peel; to shell, take the shell off.

descendencia, nf descent, origin; offspring, descendants.

descendente, adj descending, downward; downward sloping.

descender, vt to lower, let down; to get down, lift down.

descenso, nm descent; going down; demotion.

descentrado, adj off-center; out of focus; wrongly adjusted, maladjusted.

descentralizar, vt to decentralize.

descifrador(a), nm/f decipherer; decoder.

descifrar, *vt* escritura to decipher, read; to decode.

descinchar, *vt* (caballo) to loosen the girths of.

desclavar, *vt* to pull out the nails from, unnail.

descobijar, *vt* to uncover, leave exposed.

descodificar, *vt* to decode; (TV) to unscramble, descramble.

descolgado(a), *nm/f* backslider.

descolgar, *vt* to take down, get down; to unhook.

descolonizar, *vt* to decolonize.

descompasado, *adj* excessive, disproportionate, out of all proportion.

descompensar, *vt* to unbalance.

descomponer, *vi* separate into its constituent parts.

descomposición, *nf* 1. splitting up, breakdown; decomposition; 2. rotting; 3. stomach upset, diarrhea; 4. discomposure.

descompresión, *nf* decompression.

descomprometido, *adj* lacking in commitment, uncommitted.

descompuesto, *adj* broken, out of order, faulty; twisted, distorted; loose.

desconcertante, *adj* disconcerting, upsetting; embarrassing; bewildering, puzzling.

desconcertar, *vt* put out of order, damage; to dislocate.

desconcertarse, *vr* to get out of order, develop a fault; be dislocated; be disconcerted.

desconectar, *vt* to disconnect; to uncouple; (Elec); to switch off, turn off.

desconfianza, *nf* distrust, mistrust, lack of confidence.

desconfiar, *vi* to be distrustful; to lack confidence; mistrust, suspect.

descongelar, *vt* to defrost; to deice; unfreeze.

descongestión, *nf* relief, relieving.

descongestionar, *vt* to relieve; to clear.

desconocido(a), *adj* 1. unknown, not known; strange, unfamiliar; 2. *nm/f* (persona no conocida) stranger; unknown person; newcomer.

desconocimiento, *nm* ignorance; disregard, repudiation.

desconsideración, *nf* inconsiderateness, thoughtlessness.

desconsiderado, *adj* inconsiderate, thoughtless.

desconsolado, *adj* disconsolate; sad, woebegone.

desconsolar, *vt* to distress, grieve.

desconsuelo, *nm* affliction, distress, grief; sadness; despair.

descontar, *vt* to take away; to discount, deduct.

descontentar, *vt* to displease.

descontento(a), *adj* 1. dissatisfied, discontented (with); disgruntled; unhappy; 2. *nm/f* malcontent.

descontinuar, *vt* to discontinue.

descontrol, *nm* decontrol; lack of control, loss of control.

descontrolado, *adj* wild, undisciplined, out of control.

descontrolarse, *vr* lose control.

descorrer, *vt* to draw back.

descortesía, *nf* discourtesy, rudeness, impoliteness.

descoser, *vt* to unstitch, unpick; to rip, tear.

descoyuntado, *adj* dislocated, out of joint.

descoyuntar, *vt* to dislocate; put out of joint.

descrédito, *nm* discredit; disrepute.

descremar, *vt* to skim.

describir, *vt* to describe.

descripción, *nf* description.

descriptivo, *adj* descriptive.

descruzar, *vt* (legs) to uncross.

descuartizar, *vt* to carve up, cut up.

descubierta, *nf* reconnoitring, patrolling.

descubierto, *adj* open, exposed; bare, uncovered.

descubridor(a), *nm* 1. scout, 2. *nm/f* discoverer.

descubrimiento, *nm* discovery; detection; disclosure, revelation; unveiling.

descubrir, *vt* to discover; criminal, to find, detect, spot.

descuidar, *vt* deber etc to neglect; to disregard.

descuido, *nm* carelessness; slackness; negligence; forgetfulness.

desde, *prep* from, since.

desdicha, *nf* unhappiness, wretchedness; misfortune misery.

desdichado(a), *adj* 1. unhappy; unlucky; unfortunate; wretched; 2. *nm/f* poor devil, wretch.

desdoblado, *adj* split; (road) two-lane.

desdoblamiento, *nm* widening; breaking down, reduction.

desdoblar, *vt* to unfold, spread out; to untwist, straighten.

deseable, *adj* desirable.

desear, *vt* to want, desire, wish (for).

desecación, *nf* desiccation; draining.

desecar, *vt* to dry up, desiccate.

desechable, *adj* disposable, throwaway.

desechar, *vt* to throw out; to scrap, get rid of.

desecho, *nm* residue; waste, rubbish; scrap, junk.

desembarazar, *vt* to clear, free (of).

desembarcadero, *nm* quay, landing stage, pier.

desembarcar, *vt* personas to land; put ashore; to land, unload.

desembargar, *vt* to free; to remove the embargo on, remove the impediments from.

desembarrar, *vt* to clear of mud, remove the silt from.

desembocadura, *nf* outlet, exit; (river) mouth.

desembocar, *vi* to flow into, run into, empty into.

desembolsar, *vt* to pay out; to lay out.

desembolso, *nm* payment; disbursement; outlay, expenditure.

desembuchar, *vt* to disgorge; to tell, reveal, let out.

desempacar, *vt* to unpack.

desempapelar, *vt* (paquete) to unwrap; to remove (or strip).

desempaquetar, *vt* to unpack, unwrap.

desempatar, *vi* to break a tie.

desempedrar, *vt* to take up the paving stones of.

desempeñar, *vt* to redeem, recover, get out of pawn.

desempeño, *nm* 1. redeeming, redemption; 2. payment; 3. occupation; performance, discharge

desempleo, *nm* unemployment.

desempolvar, *vt* to dust, remove the dust from.

desencadenar, *vt* to unchain; to unleash, let loose.

desencajado, *adj* twisted, contorted; (ojos) wild.

desencajar, *vt* to throw out of joint; to dislocate.

desencallar, *vt* to refloat, get off.

desencantar, *vt* to disillusion, disenchant.

desenchufar, *vt* to disconnect, unplug.

desenfadado, *adj* free, uninhibited; free-and-easy; carefree.

desenfadar, *vt* to pacify, calm down.

desenfocado, *adj* out of focus; in soft focus.

desenfoque, *nm* lack of focus; state of being out of focus.

desenfrenado, *adj* wild, uncontrolled; immoderate.

desenfreno, *nm* wildness; lack of self-control; lack of moderation; licentiousness.

desenganchar, *vt* to unhook, undo, unfasten.

desengañar, *vt* to disillusion; to disappoint.

desenlace, *nm* outcome; ending.

desenlatar, *vt* to open, take out of a can.

desenlazar, *vt* to untie, unlace, undo.

desenmarañar, *vt* to disentangle, unravel.

desenmascarar, *vt* to unmask, expose.

desenredar, *vt* to unravel; to straighten out; to resolve, clear up.

desenrollar, *vt* to unroll, unwind.

desenroscar, *vt* to unscrew; to unwind.

desensillar, *vt* to unsaddle.

desentablar, *vt* to break up.

desenterrar, *vt* to exhume, disinter.

desentonar, *vi* to be out of tune.

desenvainar, *vt* espada to draw, unsheathe.

desenvoltura, *nf* ease, naturalness; confidence.

desenvolver, *vt* to unwrap; to unwind.

deseo, *nm* wish, desire.

deseoso, *adj* anxious for, desirous of.

desequilibrar, *vt* to unbalance; to overbalance, throw off balance.

deserción, *nf* desertion; defection.

desertar, *vi* to desert; to desert.

desertor(a), *nm/f* deserter; defector.

desescalar, *vt/i* to de-escalate.

desescamar, *vt* to descale.

desesperación, *nf* despair, desperation.

desesperanzar, *vt* to deprive of hope.

desesperar, *vt* to deprive of hope, drive to despair.

desespero, *nm* despair, desperation.

desestabilizar, *vt* to destabilize; to subvert.

desestimar, *vt* to have a low opinion of; to scorn, belittle, disparage.

desfachatez, *nf* brazenness, impudence.

desfalcar, *vt* to embezzle.

desfallecer, *vt* 1. to weaken; 2. *vi* to get weak, weaken; to faint.

desfallecido, *adj* weak; faint.

desfavorable, *adj* unfavorable.

desfavorecer, *vt* to cease to favor, withdraw support from.

desfigurado, *adj* disfigured; deformed; distorted, twisted.

desfigurar, *vt* cara to disfigure; to deform.

desfiladero, *nm* pass; gorge.

desfilar, *vi* to parade; to march past; to file by, file out.

desfondado, *adj* bankrupt.

desfondar, *vt* to knock the bottom out of, stave in.

desforestar, *vt* to deforest.

desgajado, *adj* separated, unconnected.

desgajar, *vt* to tear off, break off, split off.

desgana, *nf* 1. lack of appetite, loss of appetite; 2. unwillingness, disinclination, reluctance.

desganarse, *vr* lose one's appetite; lose interest, get fed up.

desgarrado, *adj* torn; tattered, in tatters.

desgarrador, *adj* heartbreaking, heartrending.

desgarrar, *vt* to tear, rip (up), rend; to shatter, crush.

desgastar, *vt* to wear away, wear down; to erode.

desgobernar, *vt* to misgovern, misrule; to mismanage.

desgracia, *nf* misfortune; mishap; accident; (piece of) bad luck.

desgraciado, *adj* unlucky, unfortunate; luckless, hapless; wretched.

desgraciar, *vt* to spoil, ruin (the appearance of).

desgranar, *vt* to remove the grain from.

desgrasado, *adj* fat-free.

desgrasar, *vt* to remove the fat, take out the grease.

desgreñado, *adj* dishevelled, tousled.

desgreñar, *vt* to dishevel, rumple, tousle.

deshabitado, *adj* uninhabited; deserted; empty, vacant.

deshabitar, *vt* to move out of, leave empty; to desert, quit.

deshacer, *vt* to undo, unmake; to spoil, ruin, damage, destroy; unpack, unwrap, dissolve.

desheredar, *vt* to disinherit.

deshidratación, *nf* dehydration.

deshidratar, *vt* to dehydrate.

deshojar, *vt* to strip the leaves off; to defoliate.

deshonesto, *adj* indecent, improper, lewd.

deshonor, *nm* dishonor, disgrace, insult, affront.

deshonrar, *vt* to dishonor, disgrace, bring disgrace on.

deshonroso, *adj* dishonourable, disgraceful, ignominious.

desierto, *adj* desert; desolate; empty.

desigual, *adj* unequal, different; unfair, inequitable.

desilusión, *nf* disillusion(ment), disappointment.

desilusionar, *vt* to disillusion; to disappoint, let down.

desinfectante, *nm* disinfectant.

desinfectar, *vt* to disinfect.

desinflado, *adj* (neumático) flat.

desinflar, *vt* to deflate, let the air out of.

desinformar, *vt* to misinform.

desintegración, *nf* disintegration; fission.

desintegrar, *vt* to disintegrate; to split, smash.

desinterés, *nm* disinterestedness; impartiality; unselfishness, generosity.

desinteresado, *adj* disinterested, impartial.

desintoxicar, *vt* to cure of poisoning; to cure of drug addiction (or alcoholism).

desistir, *vi* to stop, desist.

desleal, *adj* disloyal (to); unfair; foul, dirty.

desligar, *vt* to untie, undo, unfasten; to unbind.

deslizador, *nm* scooter; small speedboat.

deslizamiento, *nm* slide, sliding, slipping.

deslizar, *vt* to slide, slip.

deslucido, *adj* tarnished; worn out, old and useless.

deslucir, *vt* to tarnish; to damage, spoil, ruin.

deslumbrar, *vt* to dazzle; to blind.

deslustrado, *adj* frosted, ground; unglazed.

deslustrar, *vt* to frost; to remove the glaze from.

desmadejar, *vt* to enervate, weaken, take it out of.

desmallar, *vt* to pull out; to make a run.

desmantelar, *vt* to dismantle, raze; to strip down.

desmarcar, *vt* to disassociate (from).

desmayado, *adj* unconscious; weak, faint; languid.

desmayar, *vi* to lose heart, get discouraged, get depressed; to falter, flag.

desmayarse, *vr* to faint (away), swoon.

desmayo, *nm* faint, fainting fit, swoon; unconsciousness.

desmedido, *adj* excessive, disproportionate, out of all proportion.

desmedirse, *vr* to forget oneself, go too far.

desmejorar, *vt* to impair, spoil, damage; to cause to deteriorate.

desmejorarse, *vr* to be impaired, be spoiled; to decline, deteriorate, go downhill.

desmembración, *nf* dismemberment, break-up.

desmembrar, *vt* to dismember, separate, break up.

desmentir, *vt* to deny, refute, give the lie to.

desmentirse, *vr* to contradict oneself; to go back on one's word.

desmenuzar, *vt* 1. to crumble (up), break into small pieces; to chop, shred, mince; to grate; 2. to examine minutely, take a close look at.

desmerecedor(a), *nm/f* undeserving person.

desmerecer, *vt* 1. to be unworthy of; 2. *vi* to deteriorate, go off, be less good; to lose value.

desmesurado, *adj* disproportionate, excessive, inordinate; enormous.

desmilitarizado, *adj* demilitarized.

desmilitarizar, *vt* to demilitarize.

desmochar, *vt* to lop, cut off the top of; to pollard.

desmolado, *adj* toothless.

desmoldar, *vt* to remove from its mold.

desmontar, *vt* to dismantle, strip down; to take apart, take to pieces; to knock down, demolish.

desmoralización, *nf* demoralization.

desmoralizar, *vt* to demoralize; to corrupt.

desmoronado, *adj* tumbledown, ruinous, dilapidated.

desmoronar, *vt* to wear away, destroy little by little.

desmovilización, *nf* 1. demobilization; 2. demoralization.

desmovilizar, *vt* 1. demobilize; 2. demoralize.

desnivelado, *adj* 1. uneven; 2. unbalanced, badly adjusted, unequal.

desnivelar, *vt* 1. make uneven; 2. unbalance, upset the balance of.

desnucar, *vt* to break the neck of; to fell.

desnucarse, *vr* to break one's neck.

desnudar, *vt* to strip; undress.

desnudo, *adj* naked, nude; unclothed, bare.

desnutrición, *nf* malnutrition, undernourishment.

desobedecer, *vt/i* to disobey.

desobediencia, *nf* disobedience.

desocupado, *adj* 1. empty, vacant, unoccupied; 2. spare, free; leisure; 3. not busy; idle; unemployed.

desocupar, *vt* to vacate, move out of; to leave empty.

desodorante, *nm* deodorant.

desoír, *vt* to ignore, disregard; to turn a deaf ear to.

desojarse, *vr* to strain one's eyes.

desolación, *nf* desolation; grief, distress.

desolador, *adj* distressing, grievous; bleak, cheerless; devastating.

desolar, *vt* to lay waste, ruin, desolate.

desorbitado, *adj* disproportionate, excessive; exorbitant.

desorbitar, *vt* to carry to extremes; to exaggerate.

desorbitarse, *vr* to go to extremes, lose one's sense of proportion; to get out of hand.

desorden, *nm* disorder; confusion; turmoil; disarray.

desordenar, *vt* to disarrange, mess up.

desorganización, *nf* disorganization, disruption.

desorganizar, *vt* to disorganize, disrupt.

desorientación, *nf* disorientation.

desorientar, *vt* to direct someone wrongly, to make someone lose his way; to disorient someone.

desorientarse, *vr* to lose one's way, lose one's bearings.

despabilado, *adj* wide-awake; alert, watchful; quick, sharp.

despabilar, *vt* 1. to snuff; to trim; 2. to sharpen; to wake up; liven up, brighten up.

despacio, *adv* slowly; gently; (poco a poco) gradually.

despachado, *adj* resourceful, quick; businesslike; practical.

despachar, *vt* to complete; to do, dispatch, settle.

despachurrar, *vt* to squash, crush; to squelch; to mash.

desparramar, *vt* to scatter, spread; to spill.

desparramarse, *vr* to scatter, spread out; to spill, be spilt.

despavorido, *adj* to be utterly terrified.

despechado, *adj* angry, indignant; spiteful.

despechar, *vt* 1. to anger, enrage; to drive to despair; 2. (child) to wean.

despecharse, *vr* to get angry; to fret; to despair.

despectivo, *adj* contemptuous, scornful; derogatory; pejorative.

despedazar, *vt* to tear apart, tear to pieces; to cut into bits.

despedida, *nf* farewell; leave-taking; send off; dismissal.

despedir, *vt* 1. to see off; to see out; to say goodbye to; 2. to dismiss, sack, discharge.

despegar, *vt* 1. to unglue, unstick; to detach, loosen; 2. *vi* to take off; to lift off, blast off.

despeinado, *adj* dishevelled, tousled; unkempt.

despeinar, *vt* to tousle, ruffle; to mess up, muss.

despejar, *vt* to clear, disencumber, free from obstructions.

despellejar, *vt* to skin, flay; criticize unmercifully.

despeluznar, *vt* 1. to dishevel, tousle, rumple; 2. to horrify someone, make someone's hair stand on end; 3. to ruin, leave penniless.

despensa, *nf* pantry, larder; food store; storeroom.

despeñadero, *nm* cliff, precipice.

despeñar, *vt* to fling down, hurl from a height, throw over a cliff.

despeñarse, *vr* to hurl oneself down, throw oneself over a cliff; to fall headlong.

despercudir, *vt* to clean, wash.

desperdiciado, *adj* wasteful.

desperdiciar, *vt* to waste, squander, fritter away.

desperfecto, *nm* flaw, blemish, imperfection; slight damage.

despersonalizar, *vt* to depersonalize.

despertador, *nm* alarm clock.

despertamiento, *nm* awakening; revival, rebirth.

despertar, *vt* to wake (up), awaken.

despiadado, *adj* cruel; merciless, relentless; heartless.

despido, *nm* dismissal.

despierto, *adj* awake.

despilfarrar, *vt* to waste, squander.

despintar, *vt* to take the paint off.

despistado(a), *adj* 1. vague, absent-minded; unpractical; hopeless; 2. *nm/f* absent-minded person, vague individual; unpractical type.

desplante, *nm* 1. wrong stance; 2. bold statement, outspoken remark; impudent remark, cutting remark.

desplazado(a), *adj* 1. displaced, wrongly placed, off-center; 2. *nm/f* misfit; ill-adjusted person; outsider; displaced person.

desplazar, *vt* to displace, move.

desplegar, *vt* to unfold, open (out), spread (out).

despliegue, *nm* unfolding, opening; deployment.

desplomarse, *vr* 1. to lean, tilt, get out of vertical; to bulge; 2. to collapse, tumble down, come crashing down.

despojar, *vt* to strip of, clear of, leave bare of.

despojarse, *vr* to undress; to take off, remove, strip off.

despojo, *nm* spoliation, despoilment; plundering.

despolvorear, *vt* to dust.

desposado, *adj* newly-wed, recently married.

desposar, *vt* to marry.

desposarse, *vr* to become engageg; to get married (to).

desposeer, *vt* to dispossess (of); to oust; to remove someone's authority, strip someone of his authority.

déspota, *nm/f* despot.

despreciable, *adj* despicable, contemptible; worthless, trashy.

despreciar, *vt* to scorn, despise, look down on; to underestimate.

desprecio, *nm* scorn, contempt, disdain.

desprender, *vt* to unfasten, loosen; to detach, separate.

desprendido, *adj* 1. loose, detached; unfastened; 2. disinterested; generous.

desprendimiento, *nm* loosening, detachment; unfastening.

despreocupación, *nf* 1. unconcern; carefree nature; nonchalance, casualness; 2. indifference, apathy; broad-mindedness.

desprestigiar, *vt* to disparage, run down; to smear.

desprestigio, *nm* disparagement; discredit; loss of prestige (or caste, standing).

desprevenido, *adj* unready, unprepared; unaware.

desprogramar, *vt* to deprogram.

desproporción, *nf* disproportion, lack of proportion.

desproporcionado, *adj* disproportionate, out of proportion.

desprotección, *nf* lack of (legal) protection; vulnerability, defenselessness.

desprotegido, *adj* unprotected, vulnerable, defenseless.

desproveer, *vt* to deprive someone of something.

desprovisto, *adj* devoid of, bereft of, without; to lack, be lacking in.

después, *adv* afterwards, later; since, since then.

despuntar, *vi* 1. to blunt; dull; 2. *vi* to sprout, bud, begin to show.

desquiciado, *adj* deranged, unhinged.

desquiciar, *vt* 1. to unhinge, take off its hinges; 2. to upset, disturb, turn upside down, make a mess of.

desquitar, *vt* to make good, make up.

desquitarse, *vr* to obtain satisfaction; to recover a debt, get one's money back.

desregular, *vt* to free, deregulate, remove controls from.

desrizar, *vt* to straighten.

destacado, *adj* notable, outstanding, distinguished; important.

destacamento, *nm* detachment; landing party.

destacar, *vt* to make stand out; to emphasize, show up, point up.

destacarse, *vr* to stand out.

destajo, *nm* piecework; contract work.

destapador, *nm* bottle opener.

destapar, *vt* to uncover; to open, uncork; take the lid off.

destaparse, *vr* to get uncovered; to undress, strip off.

destartalado, *adj* untidy, in disorder; large and rambling; ruinous.

destechar, *vt* to unroof, take the roof off.

destellar, *vi* to sparkle, to glint, gleam.

destello, *nm* sparkle; flash; glint, gleam.

destemplado, *adj* out of tune; harsh, unpleasant.

desteñir, *vt* to fade, discolor, take the color out of.

desterrado(a), *nm/f* exile; outlaw; outcast.

desterrar, *vt* to exile, banish.

destierro, *nm* exile; banishment; to live in exile.

destiladera, *nf* still, distilling vessel; filter.

destilar, *vt* to distil; to exude, ooze.

destilería, *nf* distillery.

destinar, *vt* to destine; to assign (to); to design (for).

destinatario(a), *nm/f* addressee.

destino, *nm* 1. destiny, fate; 2. destination.

destitución, *nf* dismissal, removal.

destituir, *vt* to dismiss, remove, sack (from).

destorcer, *vt* to untwist; to straighten.

destornillador, *nm* screwdriver.

destornillar, *vt* to unscrew.

destrabar, *vt* to loosen, detach.

destreza, *nf* skill, dexterity; cleverness; handiness.

destripador, *nm* butcher; murderer.

destripar, *vt* to gut, draw, paunch.

destronar, *vt* to dethrone; to overthrow.

destroncar, *vt* 1. chop off; to uproot; 2. maim, mutilate; to tire out, exhaust; to wear out.

destrozado, *adj* smashed, shattered, ruined.

destrozar, *vt* to smash, shatter, ruin; to break up, break in pieces; to destroy.

destrozo, *nm* destruction; smashing, annihilation, rout.

destrucción, *nf* destruction.

destruir, *vt* to destroy; to ruin, wreck; to damage.

desusado, *adj* obsolete, antiquated, out of date.

desusar, *vt* to stop using, discontinue the use of, give up.

desunir, *vt* to separate, sever, detach.

desunión, *nf* 1. separation; disconnection; 2. disunity; rift.

desuso, *nm* disuse; to fall into disuse; become obsolete.

desvainar, *vt* to shell.

desvalido, *adj* helpless; destitute; underprivileged.

desvalijar, *vt* to rob, plunder; to ransack.

desvalorar, *vt* to devaluate; to devalue.

desvalorizar, *vt* to devalue.

desvanecer, *vt* to cause to vanish, make disappear.

desvanecido, *adj* faint; giddy, dizzy; to fall in a faint.

desvariar, *vi* to be delirious; to rave, talk nonsense.

desvelar, *vt* to keep awake.

desvelo, *nm* lack of sleep; sleeplessness, insomnia.

desventaja, *nf* disadvantage; handicap, liability.

desventura, *nf* misfortune.

desvergonzado, *adj* shameless; impudent, brazen; unblushing.

desvestir, *vt* to undress.

desviación, *nf* deviation (from); deviance; deflection.

desviar, *vt* to turn aside; to deflect; divert (from).

desvío, *nm* deflection, deviation (from); detour; bypass.

desvirtuar, *vt* to impair, spoil; to detract from.

desvivirse, *vr* to crave something, yearn for something, long for something.

detallar, *vt* to detail, list in detail, specify, itemize.

detalle, *nm* detail, particular; item; retail.

detallista *adj* 1. retail; retail trade; 2. *nm/f* retailer, retail trader.

detectar, *vt* to detect.

detective, *nm/f* detective.

detector, *nm* detector.

detención, *nf* 1. stopping; stoppage, holdup; delay; 2. arrest, detention.

detener, *vt* to stop; to hold up, check, delay.

detenido, *adj* 1. arrested, under arrest; 2. detailed; careful.

detentar, *vt* to hold.

detentor(a), *nm/f* holder.

detergente, *adj, nm* detergent.

deteriorado, *adj* spoiled, damaged; worn.

deteriorar, *vt* to spoil; damage; to worsen, make worse; to impair.

deterioro, *nm* deterioration; impairment; damage; worsening.

determinación, *nf* determination; decision.

determinar, *vt* to determine, fix, settle.

detestable, *adj* detestable; odious, hateful; damnable.

detestar, *vt* to detest, hate, loathe.

detonación, *nf* detonation; report, explosion, bang.

detonador, *nm* detonator.

detonar, *vi* to detonate, explode, go off.

detracción, *nf* detraction, disparagement; knocking; slander; vilification.

detraer, *vt* to remove, separate, take away.

detrás, *adv* behind; at the back, in the rear.

detrimente, *adj* detrimental.

deuda, *nf* indebtedness, debt.

deudor(a) , *adj* 1. debit balance, adverse balance; 2. *nm/f* debtor; slow payer, defaulter.

devaluación, *nf* devaluation.

devaluar, *vt* to devalue.

devastación, *nf* devastation.

devastar, vt to devastate.

devengar, vt to earn; to draw, receive.

devengado, nm amount earned; income.

devenir, vi to develop into, become, evolve into.

devoción, nf devotion; devoutness, piety; piously.

devolución, nf return; repayment, refund.

devolver, vt to return; to give back, send back; to hand back.

devorar, vt to devour; to eat up, gobble up.

devoto(a), adj 1. devout; pious; 2. nm/f devout person.

día, nm day.

diabetes, nf diabetes.

diabético(a) adj, nm/f diabetic.

diablo, nm evil; devil

diabólico, adj diabolical, devilish.

diáfano, adj diaphanous, transparent; filmy.

diafragma, nm diaphragm.

diagnosticar, vt to diagnose.

diagrama, nm diagram.

dialéctica, nf dialectic(s).

dialecto, nm dialect.

dialogar, vt to set down (or compose) as a dialogue.

diálogo, nm dialogue.

diamante, nm diamond.

diamantista, nm/f diamond cutter; diamond merchant.

diámetro, nm diameter.

diana, nf 1. reveille; 2. center, bull's-eye.

diapositiva, nf slide; transparency.

diario, adj daily; everyday; day-to-day.

diarrea, nf diarrhea.

diáspora, nf diaspora; dispersal, migration.

diatriba, nf diatribe, tirade.

dibujante, nm/f sketcher; cartoonist, draftsman.

dibujar, vt to draw, sketch.

dibujo, nm drawing; sketching; art of design.

diccionario, nm dictionary.

diciembre, nm December.

dictador(a), nm/f dictator.

dictadura, nf dictatorship.

dictamen, nm opinion, dictum; judgment; report.

dictaminar, vt 1. to pass; 2. vi to pass judgment, give an opinion.

dictar, vt 1. to dictate (to); 2. to pass, pronounce.

dicha, nf happiness.

dicharacho, nm coarse remark, rude thing (to say).

dicho nm 1. (susodicho) above-mentioned, afore-mentioned; 2. saying, proverb; tag.

dichoso, adj happy.

didáctica, nf didactics; education department.

didáctico, adj didactic.

diecinueve, adj nineteen; nineteenth.

dieciocho, adj eighteen; eighteenth.

dieciséis, adj sixteen; sixteenth.

diecisiete, adj seventeen; seventeenth.

diente, nm tooth.

diestro, adj right; dexter.

dieta, nf diet.

dietética, nf 1. dietetics; 2. nf dietician.

diez, adj ten; tenth.

diezmar, vt to decimate.

difamación, nf slander, defamation; libel (on).

difamador(a), adj 1. slanderous, defamatory, libel-lous; 2. nm/f slanderer, defamer; scandalmonger.

difamar, vt to slander, defame; to libel.

diferencia, nf difference.

diferenciable, adj distinguishable.

diferenciar, vt 1. to differentiate between; to make a difference between; 2. vi to differ (from), be in disagreement (with).

difícil, adj difficult, hard; awkward.

dificultad, nf difficulty; trouble; objection.

dificultar, vt to obstruct, impede, hinder.

difteria, nf diphtheria.

difuminado, adj slurred, husky; sketchy, vague, barely outlined.

difuminar, vt to blur.

difundir, vt to diffuse; to spread, disseminate; to divulge.

difundirse, vr to spread; to become diffused.

difunto(a), adj 1. dead, deceased; 2. nm/f dead person.

difusión, nf diffusion; spread(ing), dissemination.

difuso, adj diffused; widespread, widely extended.

digerir, vt to digest; to swallow.

digestión, nf digestion.

digitalizar, vt to digitalize.

dígito, nm digit.

dignatario(a), nm/f dignitary.

dignidad, nf dignity; honor; self-respect.

dignificar, vt to dignify.

digno, adj worthy; fitting; proper, appropriate; worthy of.

dilación, nf delay.

dilapidación, nf squandering, waste.

dilapidar, vt to squander, waste.

dilatación, nf dilation; expansion, enlargement, widening, stretch.

dilatado, adj dilated; vast, extensive, spacious.

dilatar, vt to dilate; to expand; to enlarge, widen.

dilatarse, vr to delay, to be slow.

dilema, nm dilemma.

diletante, nm/f dilletante.

diligencia, nf diligence, care; assiduity; speed, dispatch.

diligente, adj diligent; industrious, assiduous; quick.

dilucidar, vt to elucidate, explain, clarify.

dilución, nf dilution.

diluir, vt to dilute; to water down, weaken.

diluviar, vi to pour with rain, rain in torrents.

diluvio, nm deluge, flood.

dimensión, nf dimension; size.

diminuto, adj tiny, minute, exceedingly small.

dimisión, nf resignation.

dimitir, vt to resign; to give up, relinquish.

dinámica, nf dynamic(s).

dinamita, nf dynamite.

dinamitar, vt to dynamite.

dinamizador, adj revitalizing.

dínamo, nf dynamo.

dinastía, nf dynasty.

dinero, nm money; currency, coinage.

dinosaurio, nm dinosaur.

Dios, nm God.

diosa, nf goddess.

diploma, nm diploma.

diplomacia, nf diplomacy.

diplomado, adj qualified, trained, having a diploma.

diplomático(a), adj 1. diplomatic; 2. nm/f diplomat; diplomatist.

diputado(a), nm/f delegate, representative; deputy; member of parliament.

disparada, nf sudden flight, stampede, wild rush.

disparadero, nm trigger, trigger mechanism.

disparador, adj 1. lavish; 2. nm trigger; release.

disparar, vt to shoot, fire, to throw, hurl, let fly.

disparatado, adj absurd, crazy, nonsensical.

disparatar, vi to talk nonsense, to do something silly, blunder.

disparate, nm foolish remark, silly idea, absurd thing (to do).

disparo, *nm* shot, firing.

dispendiador, *adj* free-spending, big-spending.

dispensa, *nf* exemption, excusal; dispensation.

dispensación, *nf* dispensation.

dispensador, *nm* dispenser.

dispensar, *vt* to dispense; to give out, distribute.

dispensario, *nm* dispensary; clinic.

dispersar, *vt* disperse, scatter.

dispersión, *nf* dispersion, dispersal.

disponer, *vi* 1. arrange, dispose; to lay out, to put in order; to line up; 2. prepare, get ready; 3. order, decide.

disposición, *nf* arrangement, disposition; order; layout.

dispositivo, *nm* device, mechanism; appliance.

disputa, *nf* dispute; argument; controversy.

disputador, *adj* disputatious, argumentative.

disputar, *vt* to dispute, question, challenge; to debate.

distancia, *nf* distance.

distanciador, *adj* distancing effect.

distanciar, *vt* to space out, separate; to put further apart.

distanciarse, *vr* become estranged.

distante, *adj* distant; far-off; remote.

distender, *vt* to distend; to stretch.

distendido, *adj* distended, relaxed.

distensión, *nf* distension; stretching; relaxation.

distinción, *nf* distinction, difference.

distinguir, *vt* to distinguish, discern, make out.

distintivo, *adj* 1. distinctive, distinguishing; 2. *nm* distinguishing mark, characteristic, typical feature.

distinto, *adj* clear, distinct, plain.

distorsión, *nf* sprain, distortion.

distorsionar, *vt* to distort.

distracción, *nf* distraction, amusement, relaxation.

distraer, *vt* to distract, divert, lead away.

distribución, *nf* distribution, giving out, sending out.

distribuidor, *nm* distributor, agent, dealer.

distriguir, *vt* to distribute, to hand out, to give out.

distrito, *nm* district, region, zone.

disturbio, *nm* disturbance; riot, commotion.

disuadir, *vt* to dissuade, deter, discourage.

disuación, *nf* dissuasion, deterrent.

divagación, *nf* digression; wanderings, ramblings.

divagar, *vi* to digress, to wander, ramble.

diván, *nm* divan, sofa; couch.

divergencia, *nf* divergence.

divergente, *adj* divergent; contrary, opposite.

divergir, *vi* to diverge; to differ, be opposed, clash; to differ, disagree.

diversidad, *nf* diversity, variety.

diversificación, *nf* diversification.

diversificar, to diversify.

diversión, *nf* amusement, entertainment.

divertir, *vt* 1. amuse, entertain; 2. to divert, distract (the attention of).

dividendo, *nm* dividend.

dividir, *vi* to divide (up); to split (up), separate; to share out, distribute.

divinizar, *vt* to deify; to exalt, extol.

divino, *adj* divine, wonderful; great.

divisa, *nf* 1. emblem, badge; device, motto; 2. foreign exchange; hard currency.

divisar, *vt* to make out, spy, descry.

divisoria, *nf* dividing line.

divorciado, *adj* divorced.

divorciar, *vt* to divorce.

divorcio, *nm* divorce, separation.

divulgacion, *nf* spreading, circulation; dissemination.

divulgar, *vt* to spread, circulate, publish; to disseminate.

doblado, *adj* double; doubled over, folded.

doblador, *nm* roll-your-own, hand-rolled cigarette.

doblar, *vt/i* to double; to fold (up, over), crease.

doble, *adj* double.

doce, *adj* twelve; twelfth.

docena, *nf* dozen.

docencia, *nf* teaching.

docente, *adj* educational; teaching.

dócil, *adj* docile; obedient; gentle, mild.

docilidad, *nf* docility; obedience; gentleness; mildness.

doctor, *nm* doctor.

doctorado, *nm* doctorate.

doctorar, *vt* to confer a doctor's degree on.

doctorarse, *vr* to take one's doctor degree on.

doctrina, *nf* doctrine; learning; teaching; religious instruction.

doctrinar, *vt* to teach.

documentación, *nf* documentation; papers, documents.

documental, *nm* documentary.

documentar, *vt* to document, establish with documentary evidence.

documento, *nm* document; paper; record.

dogma, *nm* dogma.

dogmático, *adj* dogmatic.

dolencia, *nf* ailment, complaint, affliction.

doler, *vt/i* to hurt, pain; to ache.

dolido, *adj* to be distressed, be upset.

dolor, *nm* pain; ache.

dominación, *nf* domination; dominance.

dominante, *adj* dominant, predominant.

dominar, *vt* to dominate; to rule (over).

domingo, *nm* Sunday.

dominio, *nm* dominion; power, sway, authority; ascendancy.

dominó, *nm* a set of dominoes.

donación, *nf* donation; gift.

donar, *vt* to donate; to grant, bestow.

donativo, *nm* donation, contribution.

doncella, *nf* maid, lady's maid, maidservant.

donde, *interrog adv* where?

dondequiera, *adv* anywhere; everywhere, all over the place.

dorado, *adj* golden; gold-plated.

dorar, *vt* to gild; to brown.

dormidero, *nm* sleeping place.

dormilón, *adj* sleepy; much given to sleeping.

dormir, *vt* to have one's afternoon nap, have a doze, have a siesta.

dormitar, *vi* to doze, snooze.

dormitorio, *nm* bedroom, dormitory.

dorso, *nm* back.

doscientos, *adj* two hundred.

dosel, *nm* canopy.

dosclera, *nf* valance.

dosificación, *nf* dosage.

dosificador, *nm* dispenser.

dosificar, *vt* to measure out, put up in doses.

dotación, *nf* 1. endowment; amount of the prize; 2. staff, establishment, personnel; crew.

dotado, *adj* gifted.

draga, *nf* dredge; dredger.

dragado, *nm* dredging.

dragar, *vt* to dredge; to sweep.

dragón, *nm* dragon.

drama, *nm* drama.

dramática, *nf* drama, dramatic art.

dramático, *adj* dramatic.

dramatizar, *vt* to dramatize.

drástico, *adj* drastic.

droga, *nf* drug; medicine; hard drug.

drogadicción, *nf* drug addiction.

drogadicto(a), *nm/f* drug addict.

drogar, *vt* to drug.

dualidad, *nf* duality.

dubitativo, *adj* doubtful, uncertain, hesitant.

ducha, *nf* shower, shower bath.

ductilidad, *nf* ductility.

dudar, *vi* to doubt.

dudoso, *adj* doubtful, dubious, uncertain.

duelo, *nm* 1. duel; 2. grief, sorrow; bereavement, sufferings, hardships; mourning.

dueño, *nm* owner, proprietor; landlord.

dulcería, *nf* confectioner's, sweetshop, candy store.

dulcificante, *nm* sweetener.

dulcificar, *vt* to sweeten; to soften, make more gentle; to play down; to make more pleasant, make more tolerable.

duplicar, *vt* to double.

duplo, *adj* double.

duración, *nf* duration; period, length of time.

durante, *prep* during; (during the whole time)

duraznero, *nm* peach-tree.

durazno, *nm* peach; peach-tree.

dureza, *nf* 1. hardness, toughness; stiffness; 2. harshness; callousness; roughness.

durmiente, *adj* 1. sleeping. 2. *nm/f* sleeper.

duro, *adj* hard, rough.

E

E, e, *nf* (letter) E, e.

ebanista, *nm* cabinetmaker; carpenter.

ebanistería, *nf* 1. cabinetmaking; woodwork, carpentry; 2. cabinetmaker's (shop), carpenter's (shop).

ébano, *nm* ebony.

ebrio, *adj* 1. intoxicated, drunk; 2. beside oneself with joy.

ebullición, *nf* 1. boiling; boiling point; come to the boil; 2. movement, activity.

eccema, *nm* eczema.

eclesial, *adj* church (atr).

eclesiástico, *adj* 1. ecclesiastic(al), church; 2. *nm* clergyman priest, ecclesiastic.

eclipsar, *vt* to eclipse; to eclipse, outshine, overshadow.

eclipse, *nm* eclipse.

eco, *nm* 1. echo; 2. echo response.

ecología, *nf* ecology.

ecologista, *adj* 1. conservation; environmental; 2. *nm/f* conservationist; environmentalist.

ecólogo(a), *nm/f* ecologist.

economato, *nm* cooperative store; cut-price store; company store.

economía, *nf* 1. economy; 2. saving; thrift, thriftiness; 3. economics.

economista, *nm/f* economist; accountant.

economizar, *vt* to economize, save; to save up.

ectópico, *adj* ectopic.

ectoplasma, *nm* ectoplasm.

ecuación, *nf* equation.

ecualizar, *vt* to equalize.

ecuánime, *adj* level-headed, equable; calm, composed.

ecuanimidad, *nf* equanimity, level-headedness; calmness, composure; impartiality.

ecuatorial, *adj* equatorial.

ecuestre, *adj* equestrian.

ecuménico, *adj* ecumenical.

ecumenismo, *nm* ecumenicism.

eczema, *nm* eczema.

echadizo, *adj* spying, sent to spy.

echado, *adj*, *ptp* 1. to lie, be lying (down); 2. well-placed, in a good position.

echador, *adj* 1. boastful, bragging, 2. *nm* boaster, braggart.

echar, *vt* 1. to throw; to cast, fling, pitch, toss; 2. to put in, add; 3. to pour out; 4. to emit, send forth, discharge; 5. to eject, throw out, chuck out; to turn out.

edad, *nf* age.

edicto, *nm* edict, proclamation.

edificación, *nf* 1. construction, building; 2. edification.

edificante, *adj* edifying; improving; uplifting, ennobling.

edificar, *vt* 1. to build, construct; 2. to edify; to improve; to uplift, ennoble.

edificio, *nm* building; edifice; structure.

editar, *vt* 1. to publish; 2. to edit, correct.

editor, *adj* publishing; publishing house.

editora, *nf* 1. publisher; 2. editor, compiler.

editorial, *adj* 1. publishing; publishing house; 2. leading article, editorial.

editorializar, *vi* to write editorials.

edredón, *nm* eiderdown; feather pillow; duvet.

educable, *adj* educable, teachable.

educación, *nf* 1. education; training; upbringing; 2. manners, (good) breeding; politeness, civility.

educacional, *adj* educational.

educado, *adj* well-mannered, polite; nicely behaved; cultivated, cultured.

educando(a), *nm/f* pupil.

educar, *vt* to educate; to train; to raise, bring up.

educativo, *adj* educative; educational.

efectividad, *nf* effectiveness.

efectivo, *adj* 1. effective; to make something effective; 2. actual, real; 3. permanent, established; 4. cash.

efecto, *nm* 1. effect; 2. result; 3. purpose.

efectuar, *vt* to effect, carry out, bring about.

efervescencia, *nf* 1. effervescence; fizziness; 2. commotion, agitation; high spirits.

efervescente, *adj* effervescent; fizzy, bubbly.

eficaz, *adj* 1. efficacious, effective; telling; 2. efficient.

eficiencia, *nf* efficiency.

eficiente, *adj* efficient.

efímero, *adj* ephemeral, fleeting, short-lived.

efusión, *nf* 1. outpouring; shedding; 2. effusion, warmth, effusiveness.

efusivo, *adj* effusive.

Egipto, *nm* Egypt.

egiptología, *nf* Egyptology.

ego, *nm* ego.

egocéntrico, *adj* egocentric, self-centered.

egocentrista, *nm/f* egocentric, self-centered person.

egoísmo, *nm* egoism; selfishness.

egoísta, *adj* egoistical; selfish.

egresado(a), *nm/f* graduate.

egresar, *vi* 1. to go out, go away, leave; 2. to graduate, take one's degree.

egreso, *nm* 1. departure, leaving, going away; 2. exit; 3. graduation; 4. outgoings, expenditure.

eje, *nm* 1. axis; 2. axle; 3. shaft, spindle.

ejecución, *nf* 1. execution, performance, carrying out; fulfillment; enforcement; 2. performance, rendition; 3. execution.

ejecutante, *nm/f* performer.

ejecutar, vt 1. to execute, carry out; 2. to perform, render, play; 3. to execute.

ejecutivo, adj executive.

ejecutor(a), nm/f executor.

ejemplar, adj exemplary; model.

ejemplarizar, vt to set an example to; to exemplify, demonstrate by example, set an example of.

ejemplo, nm example, instance; object lesson.

ejercer, vt to exercise; to exert, use.

ejercicio, nm exercise; practice; drill.

ejercitar, vt to exercise; to practice; to drill, train.

ejército, nm army.

él, pron he.

elasticidad, nf elasticity; spring, sponginess.

elástico, adj elastic; flexible.

elección, nf choice, selection; option.

electivo, adj elective.

electo, adj elect.

elector(a), nm/f elector; voter.

electorado, nm electorate, voters.

electricidad, nf electricity; static electricity.

electricista, nm/f electrician.

eléctrico, adj electric(al).

electrificación, nf electrification.

electrificar, vt to electrify.

electrizar, vt to electrify.

electrocardiograma, nm electrocardiogram.

electrocutar, vt to electrocute.

electrochoque, nm electroshock.

electrodo, nm electrode.

electrodoméstico, adj home electrical appliance.

electroencefalograma, nm electroencephalogram.

electroimán, nm electromagnet.

electromagnético, adj electromagnetic.

electromotor, nm electric motor.

electrón, nm electron.

electrónica, nf electronics.

electronuclear, adj central nuclear power station.

elefante, nm/f elephant.

elefantino, adj elephantine.

elegancia, nf elegance; gracefulness; stylishness.

elegante, adj elegant; graceful.

elegible, adj eligible.

elegido, adj 1. chosen, selected; 2. elect, elected.

elegir, vt to choose, select; to opt for.

elemental, adj elementary; elemental, fundamental.

elemento, nm 1. element; 2. ingredient, constituent(part); 3. factor.

elenco, nm catalogue, list; staff, team; cast.

elevación, nf 1. elevation, raising, 2. height, altitude; 3. exaltation, loftiness; conceit, pride.

elevado, adj elevated, raised; high, lofty.

elevador, nm elevator, hoist; lift, elevator.

elevar, vt 1. to raise, lift (up), elevate; 2. to present, submit.

eliminación, nf elimination; removal.

eliminar, vt to eliminate; to remove.

eliminatoria, nf heat, preliminary round, qualifying round; knockout competition.

elipsis, nf ellipsis.

elíptico, adj elliptic(al).

elixir, nm elixir.

elocuencia, nf eloquence.

elocuente, adj eloquent; telling; significant.

elogiar, vt to praise, eulogize.

elogio, nm praise, eulogy; tribute.

elucidación, nf elucidation.

elucidar, vt to elucidate.

eludir, vt to elude, evade, avoid, escape.

elusivo, adj evasive, tricky.

ella, pron she.

emanación, nf emanation; smell.

emanar, vi to emanate from, come from.

emancipación, nf emancipation; freeing.

emancipado, adj emancipated; independent, free.

emancipar, vt to emancipate; to free.

embajada, nf 1. embassy; 2. ambassadorship; 3. errand, message.

embajador, nm ambassador.

embajadora, nf (woman) ambassador; ambassador's wife.

embalado, adj 1. randy; 2. high; 3. nm packing, packaging.

embalador(a), nm/f packer.

embalar, vt to pack, parcel up, wrap.

embaldosado, nm tiled floor, tiling.

embaldosar, vt to tile, pave with tiles.

embalsadero, nm boggy place.

embalsamar, vt to embalm.

embalsar, vt to dam, dam up; to retain, collect.

embalse, nm damming; dam; reservoir.

embarazada, adj pregnant.

embarazar, vt 1. to obstruct, hamper, hinder; 2. to make pregnant, put in the family way.

embarazo, nm 1. obstacle, obstruction, hindrance; 2. pregnancy.

embarazoso, adj awkward, inconvenient, troublesome; embarrassing.

embarcación, nf boat, craft, vessel.

embarcadero, nm 1. pier, landing stage, jetty; 2. goods station; platform.

embarcar, vt to embark, put on board; to ship.

embargar, vt to impede, hinder; to restrain, put a check on.

embargo, nm 1. seizure, distraint; 2. indigestion.

embarque, nm 1. embarkation; shipment, loading; 2. emotional affair.

embarrado, adj muddy.

embarrancamiento, nm running aground, beaching, stranding.

embarrancar, vt/i 1. to run aground; 2. to run into a ditch.

embarrar, vt 1. to smear, to splash with mud; 2. to cover with mud; to plaster; 3. to set someone up.

embate, nm sudden attack; brunt of the attack.

embaucador(a), nm/f trickster, swindler; impostor.

embaucar, vt to trick, swindle; to fool, lead up the garden path.

embeber, vt 1. to absorb, soak up; to saturate, soak; 2. to take in, gather in; 3. to imbibe; to insert, introduce.

embelesado, adj spellbound, enraptured.

embelesador, adj enchanting, entrancing.

embelesar, vt to enchant, entrance, enrapture.

embeleso, nm enchantment, rapture, delight.

embellecedor, nm hubcap; stripes.

embellecer, vt to embellish, beautify.

embestida, nf assault, onrush, onslaught; charge, rush.

embestir, vt to assault, attack, to rush at; to charge.

embetunar, vt to tar (over), pitch; to black.

emblema, nm emblem.

embobar, vt to amaze; to fascinate.

embobecer, vt to make silly.

embocadura, nf 1. narrow entrance; mouth; passage, narrows; 2. mouthpiece; tip; bit.

emboinado, adj wearing a beret.

embolia, nf clot; embolism.

émbolo, nm plunger; piston.

embolsar, vt to pocket, put into one's pocket.

embolsillar, vt to put one's hands in one's pockets.

emboquillado, *adj* tipped.

emboquillar, *vt* to tip; to point, repoint.

emborrachar, *vt* to intoxicate, make drunk; to get drunk.

emborracharse, *vr* to get drunk.

emborronar, *vt* to blot, make blots on; to scribble on.

emboscada, *nf* ambush.

embotado, *adj* dull, blunt.

embotamiento, *nm* 1. dulling, blunting; 2. dullness, bluntness.

embotar, *vt* 1. to dull, blunt; 2. to dull, to weaken, enervate.

embotellado, *adj* bottled; prepared (beforehand).

embotellador(a), *nm/f* bottler.

embotellamiento, *nm* 1. traffic jam; 2. bottleneck.

embotellar, *vt* 1. to bottle; 2. to bottle up.

embovedar, *vt* to arch, vault.

embozar, *vt* to muffle; to cloak, disguise, conceal.

embragar, *vt* to engage; to connect, couple; to sling.

embrague, *nm* clutch.

embravecer, *vt* to enrage, infuriate.

embravecido, *adj* 1. rough; wild; 2. furious, enraged.

embriagador, *adj* intoxicating; heady, strong.

embriagar, *vt* 1. to make drunk, intoxicate; to get drunk; 2. to enrapture, delight, intoxicate.

embriaguez, *nf* 1. drunkenness, intoxication; 2. rapture, delight, intoxication.

embriología, *nf* embryology.

embriólogo(a), *nm/f* embryologist.

embrión, *nm* embryo.

embrionario, *adj* embryonic.

embrocar, *vt* 1. to wind; to tack; 2. to pour from one container into another; 3. to turn upside down, invert.

embrollar, *vt* to muddle, confuse, complicate; to mess up.

embrollo, *nm* muddle, tangle, confusion.

embromado, *adj* annoying; difficult.

embromar, *vt* to tease, make fun of, rag.

embrujado, *adj* bewitched; haunted.

embrujar, *vt* to bewitch, put a spell on.

embrujo, *nm* 1. bewitching; 2. curse; 3. spell, charm.

embrutecer, *vt* to brutalize, deprave; to coarsen.

embuchado, *nm* sausage; pretext, blind.

embuchar, *vt* 1. to stuff with minced meat; 2. to wolf, bolt.

embudo, *nm* 1. funnel; hopper; 2. trick, fraud; 3. bottleneck.

embullar, *vt* to excite; disturb; to put to flight.

embullo, *nm* noise, excitement, bustle; revelry.

emburujar, *vt* 1. to jumble together, jumble up; to pile up; 2. to bewilder.

embuste, *nm* 1. trick, fraud, imposture; lie; 2. trinkets.

embustero(a), *adj, nm/f* deceitful, rascally.

embutido, *nm* 1. sausage; 2. inlay, inlaid work, marquetry.

embutir, *vt* 1. to insert; to pack tight, stuff; 2. to inlay; to hammer, work.

emergencia, *nf* 1. emergence; appearance; 2. emergency.

emerger, *vi* to emerge; to appear; to surface.

emigración, *nf* emigration; migration.

emigrante, *adj, nm/f* emigrant.

emigrar, *vi* to emigrate; to migrate.

eminencia, *nf* 1. height, eminence; loftiness; 2. prominence.

eminente, *adj* 1. high, lofty; 2. eminent, distinguished; prominent.

emisario, *nm* emissary.

emisión, *nf* 1. emission; issue; output; 2. broadcasting.

emisora, *nf* radio station; broadcasting station.

emitir, *vt* 1. to emit, give off, give out; 2. to issue; to put into circulation, utter; 3. to express; give; cast.

emoción, *nf* 1. emotion; feeling; 2. excitement; thrill; tension.

emocionado, *adj* deeply moved, deeply stirred.

emocionante, *adj* exciting, thrilling; touching, moving; stirring.

emocionar, *vt* to excite, thrill; to touch, move; to stir.

emotividad, *nf* emotive nature.

emotivo, *adj* emotive.

empacar, *vt* to bale, crate, pack up.

empachado, *adj* 1. clogged; overloaded; upset, uncomfortable; 2. embarrassed; 3. awkward, clumsy.

empachar, *vt* to stop up, clog; to overload; to upset, make uncomfortable.

empacho, *nm* 1. hindrance, obstacle; 2. indigestion; 3. embarrassment; awkwardness.

empadronamiento, *nm* 1. census; register; 2. census-taking; registration.

empadronar, *vt* to take a census of.

empajar, *vt* to cover (or fill) with straw.

empalagar, *vt* to pall on.

empalago, *nm* cloying, palling.

empalizada, *nf* fence; palisade, stockade.

empalmar, *vt* 1. to join, connect; 2. to combine, put together.

empanada, *nf* 1. meat pie, patty; 2. fraud, piece of shady business.

empanado, *adj* done (or rolled) in breadcrumbs, breaded.

empanar, *vt* 1. to do (or roll) in breadcrumbs; to roll in pastry; 2. to sow with wheat.

empantanado, *adj* flooded, swampy.

empantanar, *vt* 1. to flood, swamp; 2. to obstruct; to bog down.

empañado, *adj* misty, steamy, steamed-up; dim, blurred.

empañar, *vt* 1. to put a diaper on; 2. to mist, steam up; to dim, blur.

empapar, *vt* to soak, saturate, drench; to steep.

empapelado, *nm* papering, paperhanging.

empapelar, *vt* 1. to wrap in paper; 2. to lay a charge against someone.

empaque, *nm* 1. packing; 2. look, appearance; manner.

empaquetadura, *nf* packing; filling; gasket.

empaquetar, *vt* to pack; to pack up, parcel up; to package.

emparedado, *nm* sandwich.

emparedar, *vt* to immure; confine.

emparejar, *vt* 1. to pair, match; 2. to level, make level; to make flush; to even up.

emparentado, *adj* related (by marriage) (to).

emparentar, *vi* to become related by marriage (to).

empastado, *adj* 1. clothbound, bound; 2. filled.

empastar, *vt* 1. to paste; 2. to bind in boards, bind in stiff covers, bind in cloth; 3. to fill, stop.

empatar, *vt* 1. to join, connect, tie firmly together; 2. to bother, harass.

empate, *nm* 1. draw tie; dead heat; 2. joint, connection.

empavonar, *vt* 1. to blue; 2. to grease, cover with grease.

empecinado, *adj* stubborn, pigheaded.

empecinamiento, *nm* stubbornness, pigheadedness.

empedernido, *adj* 1. heartless; obdurate; flinty, stony; 2. hardened, inveterate; strongly addicted.

empedernir, *vt* to harden.

empedrado, *adj* 1. paved; 2. pitted; pockmarked; 3. *nm* paving; cobbled street.

empedrar, *vt* to pave.

empegado, *nm* tarpaulin.

empeine, nm 1. groin; instep. 2. cotton flower.

empellón, nm push, shove.

empeñado, adj 1. pawned; 2. pledged; 3. determined; completely set on.

empeñar, vt 1. to pawn, pledge; 2. to engage, compel.

empeñero(a), nm/f pawnbroker, moneylender.

empeño, nm 1. pledge; 2. obligation, undertaking; 3. determination; insistence.

empeorar, vt to make worse, worsen; to impair.

empeorarse, vr to get worse, worsen, deteriorate.

empequeñecer, vt 1. to dwarf, make smaller; 2. to minimize; to belittle.

emperador, nm 1. emperor; 2. swordfish.

emperatriz, nf empress.

emperifollar, vt to adorn, deck; to doll up.

empernar, vt to bolt, secure with a bolt; to fit a bolt to.

empero, conj but, yet, however.

empertigar, vt to hitch up.

empezar, vt/i to begin, start.

empilonar, vt to pile up.

empinada(a), nm/f 1. steep climb, zoom upward; 2. adj steep; high, lofty.

empinar, vt 1. to raise, lift; 2. to straighten.

empizarrado, nm slate roof.

empizarrar, vt to roof with slates, slate.

emplantillar, vt 1. to put insoles into; 2. to fill with rubble.

emplastar, vt 1. to put a plaster on, poultice; 2. to make up, paint.

emplasto, nm 1. plaster, poultice; 2. makeshift arrangement.

emplazamiento, nm 1. summons, summoning; 2. site, location; emplacement.

emplazar, vt 1. to summon, convene; to summons; to subpoena; 2. to site, locate place.

empleado(a), nm/f employee.

emplear, vt to use, employ; to give a job to, engage, hire.

empleo, nm use, employment; work; occupation.

emplumar, vt 1. to adorn with feathers; to tar and feather; 2. to swindle, con; 3. to nick, arrest.

empobrecer, vt to impoverish.

empolvado, adj powdery; dusty.

empolvar, vt to powder; to cover with dust, make dusty.

empollar, vt 1. to incubate, sit on; to hatch; 2. to grind up; 3. vi brood; 4. to breed.

emponzoñar, vt to poison; to poison; to taint, corrupt.

emporio, nm emporium, mart, trading center; department store.

emporrado, adj to be high (on drugs).

empotrado, adj built-in; integral.

empotrar, vt to embed, fix; to build in.

empotrerar, vt 1. to pasture, put out to pasture; 2. to convert into fenced pasture, enclose.

emprendedor, adj enterprising; go-ahead, pushy, aggressive; entrepreneur.

emprender, vt 1. to undertake; to take on, tackle; 2. to start, set out; have it out with someone; to attack someone.

empresa, nf enterprise; undertaking, venture.

empresario, nm businessman; employer; manager.

empréstito, nm loan.

empujar, vt 1. to push, shove; to push thrust; to drive, move, propel; 2. to sack, give the push to.

empuje, nm 1. pressure; thrust; 2. shove; 3. push, drive.

empujón, nm push, shove; dig, poke, jab.

empuntar, vt 1. to put a point on; 2. to run away.

empuñadura, nf 1. hilt; grip, handle; 2. start, traditional opening.

empuñar, vt 1. to grasp, clutch, grip, take hold of; 2. to take up arms; 3. to take command.

emulación, nf emulation.

emuladora, nf rival.

emular, vt to emulate, rival.

emulsión, nf emulsion.

emulsionar, vt to emulsify.

enajenación, nf 1. alienation; transfer; 2. estrangement; 3. absentmindedness; rapture, trance.

enajenar, vt 1. to alienate, transfer; to dispose of; 2. to alienate, estrange; 3. to enrapture, carry away; to drive mad.

enaltecer, vt to exalt; to praise, extol.

enamoradizo, adj amorous, that falls in love easily.

enamorado, adj 1. in love, lovesick; 2. in love (with).

enamorada, nf lover.

enamorar, vt to inspire love in, win the love of.

enanito(a), nm/f dwarf.

enano, adj dwarf, small, tiny; stunted; midget.

enarbolar, vt to hoist, raise.

enarcar, vt 1. to hoop, put a hoop on; 2. to arch; to raise, arch.

enardecer, vt to fire, inflame; to fill with enthusiasm.

enarenar, vt to sand, cover with sand.

encabestrar, vt to put a halter on; to lead by a halter.

encabezado, adj 1. heading; headline; 2. foreman.

encabritar, vt to rile, upset.

encabuyar, vt to tie up.

encadenamiento, nm 1. chaining (together); 2. linking, connection, concatenation.

encadenado, nm fade, dissolve.

encadenar, vt 1. to chain (together); to put chains on, fetter, shackle; 2. to shackle, paralyze.

encajar, vt 1. to insert, to push in, thrust in, force in; 2. to get in, put in, intrude.

encaje, nm 1. insertion, fitting; fitting together, joining; 2. socket, cavity; groove; housing; 3. inlay, inlaid work, mosaic; lace.

encajera, nf lacemaker.

encajetillar, vt to pack in boxes, box.

encajonado, nm cofferdam.

encajonar, vt 1. to box (up), put in a box, crate, pack; 2. to confine (between banks), canalize.

encalar, vt 1. to whitewash; 2. to lime.

encalladero, nm shoal, sandbank.

encalladura, nf stranding, running aground.

encallar, vi to run aground, run ashore, get stranded.

encallecer, vi to harden, form corns.

encallecido, adj hardened.

encamar, vt to take to hospital, hospitalize.

encaminar, vt to guide, direct, set on the right road.

encampanar, vt to raise, raise on high.

encanado(a), nm/f prisoner.

encanalar, vt to pipe; to channel, canalize.

encanallarse, vr to degrade oneself; to become coarse, acquire coarse habits.

encanar, vt to throw into jail.

encandilado, adj high, erect.

encandilar, vt 1. to dazzle; 2. to stir, poke; 3. to daze, bewilder.

encanecer, vi to go grey; look old.

encantado, adj 1. bewitched; haunted; 2. delighted, pleased, charmed.

encantador, adj charming, delightful, lovely, enchanting.

encantadora, nf magician, enchanter.

encantar, vt 1. to bewitch, cast a spell on (or over); 2. to charm, delight, enchant, captivate, fascinate.

encanto, nm 1. charm, spell, enchantment; 2. delight.

encañar, vt 1. (water) to pipe; 2. to stake, prop up.

encañoñar, vt 1. (water) to pipe; 2. to stick up, hold up; to cover (with a gun).

encapotado, adj 1. cloaked, wearing a cloak; 2. cloudy, overcast.

encapotar, vt to cover with a cloak.

encapricharse, vr to persist in one's foolishness; to dig one's heels in, insist on having one's way.

encapuchado, adj hooded.

encapuchar, vt to cap a well.

encarado, adj good-looking, with nice features.

encaramar, vt 1. to raise, lift up; 2. to praise, extol.

encarar, vt 1. to aim, point; 2. to face (up to), confront; 3. to bring face to face.

encarcelación, nf imprisonment.

encarcelar, vt to imprison, jail.

encarecer, vt to put up the price of, make more expensive.

encargado, adj the employee in charge of.

encargar, vt to entrust; to charge, commission.

encargo, nm assignment, job, post.

encariñarse, vr to grow fond of, get attached to.

encarnación, nf incarnation; embodiment.

encarnado, adj 1. incarnate, 2. red, bloodred; flesh-colored; ruddy.

encarnar, vt 1. to embody, personify; to embod; 2. to bait.

encarnecer, vi to put on flesh.

encarnizado, adj red, inflamed; bloodshot.

encarnizar, vt to enrage, infuriate; to make cruel.

encarpetar, vt to file away; to pigeonhole.

encarrilar, vt 1. to put back on the rails; 2. to put on the right track, start off again on the right lines.

encartado(a), nm/f accused, defendant.

encartar, vt to enroll, register.

encartonar, vt to cover with cardboard; to bind in boards.

encasillamiento, nm 1. pigeonholing; sorting, classification; 2. type-casting.

encasillar, vt 1. to pigeonhole; to sort out, classify; to file; 2. to type-cast.

encasquetar, vt 1. to pull on, pull down tight, jam on; 2. to typecast.

encastillar, vt to fortify; defend with castles.

encauchado, nm rubberized cloth; waterproof cape.

encauchar, vt to rubberize, waterproof.

encausado(a), nm/f accused, defendant.

encausar, vt to prosecute, sue; to put on trial.

encauzar, vt to channel.

encefalitis, nf encephalitis.

enceguecer, vt to blind.

encelar, vt to make jealous.

encenagado, adj 1. muddy, mud-stained; 2. sunk in vice, depraved.

encendedor, nm lighter.

encender, vt to light; to set fire to, ignite; to kindle.

encendida, nf beating; telling-off.

encendido, adj to be alight, be on fire, be burning; to be on fire.

encenizar, vt to cover with ashes.

encerado, adj waxed; waxy, wax-colored.

encerador(a), nm/f polisher.

encerar, vt to wax; to polish.

encerrar, vt 1. to shut in, shut up; to lock in, lock up; 2. to include, contain, comprise.

encerrona, nf detention; sit-in.

enciclopedia, nf encyclopedia.

enciclopédico, adj encyclopedic.

encierro, nm 1. shutting-in, shutting-up, locking, closing; confinement; 2. enclosure; prison, lock-up.

encima, adv above, over; overhead; at the top; on top.

encinta, adj pregnant.

enclavar, vt to nail; to pierce, transfix.

enclave, nm enclave.

encofrado, nm form, plank mold.

encofrar, vt to plank, timber.

encoger, vt to shrink, contract, shorten.

encogido, adj 1. shrunken; shrivelled; 2. shy, timid, bashful.

encogimiento, nm shrinking, contraction; shrinkage.

encogollado, adj stuck-up, snobbish.

encogollarse, vr to get conceited, be haughty.

encolar, vt to glue, gum, paste; to size; to stick down, stick together.

encolerizar, vt to anger, provoke.

encomendar, vt to entrust, commend.

encomiar, vt to praise, extol, pay tribute to.

encomienda, nf 1. command (of a military order); 2. charge, commission; 3. protection; patronage.

encomio, nm praise, eulogy, tribute,

enconado, adj 1. inflamed, angry; sore; 2. angry, bitter; 3. ardent, fervent.

enconar, vt 1. to inflame; to make sore; 2. to anger, irritate, provoke.

encono, nm 1. rancor, spite(fulness); ill-feeling, bad blood; 2. inflammation, soreness.

encontrado, adj contrary, conflicting, hostile; opposed.

encontrar, vt to find; meet, encounter.

encopetarse, vr to get conceited, give oneself airs.

encorar, vt to cover with leather.

encorbatado, adj wearing a tie.

encorchar, vt 1. to cork; 2. to hive.

encordelar, vt to tie (with string).

encornar, vt to gore.

encorralar, vt to pen, corral.

encorvado, adj curved, bent; stooping; crooked.

encorvar, vt to bend, curve; to bend (down, over); to hook; to make crooked.

encrespado, adj (hair) curly; choppy.

encrespador, nm curling tongs.

encrespar, vt to curl, frizzle; to ruffle; to make rough, produce waves on.

encrucijada, nf crossroads; intersection, junction.

encuadernación, nf 1. binding; 2. bindery, binder's.

encuadernador(a), nm/f bookbinder.

encuadernar, vt to bind; to cover.

encuadrar, vt to frame, put in a frame, make a frame for.

encubierta, nf fraud.

encubierto, adj hidden, concealed; underhand; undercover.

encubridor(a), adj 1. concealing; 2. nm/f harborer; receiver of stolen goods; accessory after the fact, abettor.

encubrimiento, nm concealment, hiding; receiving of stolen goods; complicity, abetment.

encubrir, vt to conceal, hide, cover (up), cloak; to harbor, shelter.

encuentro, nm 1. meeting; encounter; 2. skirmish, action, fight.

encuerar, vt 1. to strip (naked); 2. to skin, fleece.

encuesta, nf inquiry, investigation; probe; inquest.

encuestador(a), nm/f pollster

encuestar, vt to poll, take a poll of.

encumbrado, adj 1. lofty, towering, high; 2. exalted, eminent.

encumbrar, *vt* to raise, elevate; exalt; to extol.

encurtidos, *nm* pickles; appetizers, savories.

encurtir, *vt* to pickle.

enchapado, *nm* plating; veneer.

enchapar, *vt* to plate, overlay; to veneer.

enchaquetarse, *vr* to put one's jacket on.

encharcado, *adj* still, stagnant.

encharcar, *vt* to swamp, flood; to cover with puddles, turn into pools.

enchilada, *nf* stuffed tortilla.

enchilado, *adj* 1. seasoned with chili; spicy, hot. 2. bright red; 3. *nm* stew with chili sauce.

enchilar, *vt* 1. to season with chili; 2. to annoy, vex; to disappoint; 3. *vi* to sting, burn.

enchufado(a), *nm/f* well-connected person, person with pull.

enchufar, *vt* to join, connect, fit together, fit in; to plug in.

endeble, *adj* feeble, weak, frail; feeble, flimsy.

endémico, *adj* endemic; rife, chronic.

endemoniado, *adj* 1. possessed of the devil. 2. devilish, fiendish; perverse; furious, wild.

endemoniar, *vt* 1. to bedevil; 2. to rile, anger.

enderezar, *vt* 1. to straighten, straighten out (or up), to unbend; 2. to set upright, stand vertically; to right.

endeudarse, *vr* to get into debt.

endiablado, *adj* devilish, diabolical, fiendish.

endiablar, *vt* 1. to bedevil, bewitch; 2. to pervert, corrupt.

endilgar, *vr* 1. to send, direct; to guide; 2. to fetch.

endiosado, *adj* stuck-up, conceited; high and mighty.

endiosar, *vt* to deify; to make a god out of.

endocrina, *nf* endocrine.

endocrino, *adj* endocrine.

endorsar, *vt* to endorse, support, back; to confirm.

endosante, *nm/f* endorser.

endosar, *vt* to endorse.

endoso, *nm* endorsement.

endulzante, *nm* sweetening, sweetener.

endulzar, *vt* 1. to sweeten; 2. to soften, mitigate.

endurecer, *vt* to harden, make hard; to toughen; to stiffen.

endurecido, *adj* hard; tough; stiff; hardened, caked, set.

endurecimiento, *nm* hardening; stiffening; setting.

enema, *nf* enema.

enemiga, *nf* enemy; foe, adversary, opponent.

enemigo, *adj* enemy, hostile; unfriendly.

enemistad, *nf* enmity.

enemistar, *vt* to make enemies of, cause a rift between, set at odds.

energético, *adj* energy, fuel, power.

energía, *nf* 1. energy; vigor, drive; push, go; 2. power; current.

enérgico, *adj* energetic; vigorous; forceful, forthright.

energizar, *vt* to energize.

enero, *nm* January.

enervante, *adj* enervating.

enervar, *vt* 1. to enervate; 2. to anger, upset.

enfadar, *vt* to anger, irritate, annoy; to offend.

enfado, *nm* annoyance, irritation, anger.

enfangar, *vt* to cover with mud.

énfasis, *nm* emphasis; stress.

enfático, *adj* emphatic; positive; discurso heavy, pompous, ponderous.

enfatizar, *vt* to emphasize, stress.

enfermar, *vt* 1. to make ill, cause illness in; 2. *vi* to fall ill, be taken ill.

enfermedad, *nf* illness; sickness.

enfermera, *nf* nurse.

enfermería, *nf* infirmary; sanatorium.

enfermero, *nm* male nurse.

enfermo, *adj* ill, sick, unwell; sickly.

enfilar, *vt* to enfilade; line up, put in row.

enfisema, *nm* emphysema.

enflaquecer, *vt* to make thin; to weaken, sap the strength of.

enflaquecido, *adj* thin, extenuated.

enflaquecimiento, *nm* 1. loss of weight; emaciation; 2. weakening.

enfocar, *vt* to focus.

enfoque, *nm* 1. focus; focusing; 2. grasp; approach.

enfrascar, *vt* to bottle.

enfrascarse, *vr* to bury oneself in, become absorbed in; get deeply involved in a problem.

enfrentamiento, *nm* clash, confrontation.

enfrentar, *vt* 1. to put face to face; 2. confront.

enfriadero, *nm* cold storage, cold room.

enfriador, *nm* cooler, cooling plant.

enfriar, *vt* to cool, chill; to cool down, take the heat out of.

enfundar, *vt* to sheathe; to put away, put in its case.

enfurecer, *vt* to enrage, madden.

engalanar, *vt* to adorn, deck.

engallado, *adj* arrogant, haughty; confident; boastful.

engallinar, *vt* to cow, intimidate.

enganchado(a), *nm/f* drug-addict; hooked.

enganchar, *vt* to hook; to hitch; to hang up.

engañador(a), *adj,nm/f* deceiving, cheating; deceptive.

engañar, *vt* to deceive; to cheat, trick, swindle, fool.

engaño, *nm* deceit; deception, fraud, trick, swindle.

engarce, *nm* 1. setting, mount; 2. linking, connection.

engarrotarse, *vr* to get stiff, go numb.

engarzar, *vt* to set, mount; to thread; to curl.

engastar, *vt* to set, mount.

engaste, *nm* setting, mount.

engatado, *adj* thievish.

engatusar, *vt* to coax, wheedle, soft-soap.

engendrar, *vt* to beget, breed; to have as offspring, to generate.

engendro, *nm* fetus; malformed creature, abortion; freak.

englobar, *vt* to include, comprise, to lump together, put all together.

engomar, *vt* to gum, glue, stick.

engordar, *vt* 1. to fatten (up); 2. to swell, increase; 3. *vi* to get fat.

engorde, *nm* fattening (up).

engorrar, *vt* to annoy.

engorro, *nm* bother, nuisance.

engorroso, *adj* bothersome, vexatious, trying; cumbersome, awkward.

engrampador, *nm* stapler.

engrampar, *vt* to clip together, staple.

engranaje, *nm* gear; gearing; mesh.

engranar, *vt* to gear; to put into gear.

engrandecer, *vt* 1. to enlarge, magnify; 2. to extol, magnify; to exalt; to exaggerate.

engrane, *nm* 1. mesh, meshing; 2. seizing, jamming.

engrasado, *nm* greasing, lubrication.

engrasador, *nm* greaser, lubricator; grease point; grease nipple; grease cup.

engrasar, *vt* to grease, lubricate, oil.

engreído, *adj* vain, conceited, stuck-up.

engreír, *vt* to make vain, make conceited.

engriparse, vr to catch the flu.
engrosar, vt to enlarge; to increase, swell; to thicken.
engrudo, nm paste.
enguantado, adj gloved, wearing a glove.
enguantarse, vr to put one's gloves on.
engullir, vt to gobble, bolt, gulp (down); to devour.
enhebrar, vt to thread.
enigma, nm enigma; puzzle; mystery.
enigmático, adj enigmatic; puzzling; mysterious.
enjabonar, vt to soap; to lather.
enjambre, nm swarm.
enjaular, vt to cage, put in a cage; to coop up, pen in.
enjoyar, vt to adorn with jewels; set with precious stones; to set precious stones in.
enjuagado, nm rinsing.
enjuagar, vt to rinse, rinse out; to wash out.
enjugar, vt to wipe (off), wipe the moisture from; to dry.
enjuiciar, vt to judge, pass judgement on.
enjuto, adj dry; dried; pie; shrivelled up; wizened.
enlace, nm link, tie-up, connection; bond; relationship.
enladrillado, nm brick paving.
enladrillar, vt to pave with bricks.
enlatado, adj canned, tinned.
enlatar, vt to can, tin.
enlazar, vt to link, connect; to tie, bind (together); to knit together.
enlodar, vt to muddy, cover in mud.
enloquecedor, adj maddening; splitting; excruciating.
enloquecer, vt to drive mad; to madden, drive crazy.
enloquecerse, vr to go mad, go out of one's mind.
enlosado, nm flagstone pavement, tiled pavement.
enlosar, vt to pave (with flagstones or tiles).
enlozado, adj enamelled, glazed.
enlozar, vt to enamel, glaze.
enlutado, adj in mourning, wearing mourning.
enlutar, vt to put into mourning; to dress in mourning.
enmaderado, adj timbered; boarded.
enmaderar, vt to timber; to board (up).
enmarcarse, vr to place oneself in (the context of).
enmascarado(a), nm/f masked man, masked woman.
enmascarar, vt to mask; disguise.
enmendar, vt to emend, correct; to amend.
enmohecer, vt to rust; (Bot etc) to make moldy.
enmohecido, adj rusty, rust-covered; moldy, mildewed.
enmudecer, vt to silence.
ennegrecer, vt to blacken; to dye black; to darken, obscure.
ennoblecer, vt to ennoble; to embellish, adorn; to dignify.
ennoviarse, vr to get engaged.
enojadizo, adj irritable, peevish, short-tempered.
enojado, adj angry, cross.
enojar, vt to anger; to upset, annoy, vex.
enorgullecer, vt to fill with pride.
enorme, adj enormous, huge, vast; tremendous.
enormidad, nf enormousness; hugeness.
enquistar, vt to seal off, shut off, enclose.
enrachado, adj lucky; enjoying a run of luck.
enraizar, vt to take root.
enramada, nf arbor, bower.
enramar, vt to cover with branches.
enrarecer, vt 1. to rarefy; 2. to make scarce, cause to become rare.

enrarecimiento, nm 1. (air) rarefaction; thinness; 2. scarceness, rareness; 3. deterioration; tension.
enredadera, nf climbing plant, creeper; bindweed
enredador, adj trouble-making, mischief-making.
enredadora, nf gossip; busybody, meddler; troublemaker.
enredar, vt to net, catch in a net.
enriquecer, vt to make rich, enrich.
enriquecido, adj enriched.
enriquecimiento, nm enrichment.
enrizar, vt to curl.
enrojecer, vt to redden, turn red; to make blush; to make red-hot.
enrollamiento, nm 1. rolling up; 2. coiling.
enrollar, vt to roll, wind; to coil.
enroscado, adj coiled; twisted; kinky.
enroscar, vt to coil (round), wind; to twist.
ensacar, vt to sack, bag, put into bags.
ensalada, nf salad.
ensalzamiento, nm exaltation, extolling.
ensalzar, vt to exalt; to praise, extol.
ensamblado, nm assembly.
ensamblador(a), nm/f joiner; fitter; assembler.
ensamblaje, nm assembly; docking, link-up; assembly plant.
ensamblar, vt to join; to assemble.
ensanchar, vt to enlarge, widen, extend; to stretch; to expand.
ensangrentado, adj bloodstained; bloody, gory.
ensangrentar, vt to stain with blood, cover in blood.
ensañado, adj furious; cruel, merciless.
ensartador, nm roasting spit.
ensartar, vt to string; to thread; to spit.
ensayar, vt 1. to test, try, try out; 2. to rehearse, practice.
ensayo, nm 1. test, trial; experiment; attempt; practice; 2. assay; 3. essay; 4. rehearsal.
enseguida, adv immediately, in a short time, in a moment.
ensenada, nf inlet, cove; creek.
enseña, nf ensign, standard.
enseñado, adj trained; informed; educated.
enseñanza, nf 1. education; teaching; instruction, training; schooling; 2. doctrine.
enseñar, vt 1. to teach, instruct, train; to educate; 2. to show; to point out.
enseñorearse, vr to take possession of, take over.
enseres, nm utensils, household goods.
ensillar, vt to saddle (up), put a saddle on.
ensoberbecer, vt to make proud.
ensombrecer, vt to darken, cast a shadow over; to overshadow, put in the shade.
ensoñación, nf fantasy, fancy, dream.
ensoñador(a), adj 1. dreamy dreamer 2. nm/f dreamy; dreamer.
ensopar, vt to dip, dunk; to soak, drench; to saturate.
ensordecedor, adj deafening.
ensordecer, vt 1. to deafen; to muffle; 2. vi to go deaf.
ensortijar, vt (hair) to curl, put curls into.
ensuciar, vt to soil, dirty; to foul; to mess up, make a mess of.
entablado, nm boarding, planking; wooden flooring.
entablar, vt to board, plank, cover with boards.
entable, nm 1. boarding, planking; 2. (chess) position; 3. order, arrangement, disposition.
entablillar, vt to splint, put in a splint.
entallado, adj waisted, with a waist.
entallador(a), nm/f sculptor; engraver.

entallar, vt 1. to sculpt, carve; to engrave; 2. to notch, cut a slot in, cut a groove in; 3. to cut, tailor.

entapizado, adj upholstered; covered.

entapizar, vt 1. to upholster; to hang with tapestries; 2. to grow over, cover, spread over.

entarimar, vt to board, plank; to put an inlaid floor on.

entechar, vt to roof.

entejar, vt to tile.

entenada, nf stepdaughter.

entenado, nm stepson; stepchild.

entendederas, nf brains.

entender, vt/i 1. to understand; 2. to intend, mean; 3. to think, believe; to infer.

entendimiento, nm understanding; grasp, comprehension.

entenebrecer, vt to darken, obscure.

enterado, adj knowledgeable; well-informed.

enterar, vt to inform (about, of), acquaint, tell.

entereza, nf 1. entirety; completeness; perfection; 2. integrity; decency, honesty; strength of mind.

enterizo, adj in one piece.

enternecedor, adj affecting, touching, moving.

enternecer, vt to soften; to affect, touch, move.

entero, adj 1. entire, complete; whole; 2. whole, integral; 3. not castrated.

enterradero, nm burial ground.

enterrado, adj buried; (fingernail) ingrown.

enterrador, nm gravedigger.

enterrar, vt to bury, inter.

entibiar, vt to cool; to take the chill off.

entidad, nf entity; body, organization.

entierro, nm burial, interment.

entintar, vt to ink; to ink in; to stain with ink.

entizar, vt to chalk.

entoldado, nm awning(s).

entoldar, vt 1. to put an awning over, fit with an awning; 2. to decorate (with hangings).

entonación, nf intonation.

entonado, adj toned; harmonious; in tune.

entonar, vt to intone; to modulate; to sing in tune.

entonces, adv then; at that time; since then; at that time.

entongado, adj cross, riled.

entongar, vt to pile up, pile in layers.

entono, nm intonation, intoning; being in tune, singing in tune.

entontecer, vt to make silly.

entorchar, vt 1. to twist. 2. to braid.

entornado, adj half-closed; ajar.

entornar, vt to half-close.

entorno, nm setting, milieu, ambience; environment; climate.

entorpecer, vt 1. to dull, benumb, stupefy; to make torpid, make lethargic; 2. to obstruct, hinder; to set back.

entrada, nf entrance, way in; income, admission ticket.

entrampar, vt to trap, catch, snare; to snare, trick.

entrante, adj next, coming; next week.

entraña, nf core, root, essential part.

entrañable, adj close, intimate; beloved, dearly loved.

entrañar, vt 1. to bury deep; 2. to contain, carry within; to entail, mean.

entrar, vt 1. to introduce; to bring in, show in; to access, enter; 2. to get at, approach; to tackle.

entre, prep among, amongst, between.

entreabrir, vt to half-open, open halfway; to leave ajar.

entrecerrar, vt to half-close, close halfway; to leave ajar.

entrecoger, vt to catch, intercept; to seize.

entrecortado, adj labored; faltering, hesitant, confused.

entrecortar, vt 1. to cut into, partially cut, cut halfway through; 2. to cut off, interrupt.

entrecruzar, vt 1. to interlace, interweave; 2. to cross, interbreed.

entrechocar, vi (teeth) to chatter.

entredicho, nm prohibition, ban, interdict; injunction.

entregado, adj committed, devoted; absorbed in.

entregar, vt to deliver; to hand, give.

entrelazado, adj entwined, interlaced crisscrossed; interlocking.

entrelazar, vt to entwine, interlace, interweave; to interlock.

entrelucir, vi 1. to show through; 2. to gleam, shine dimly.

entremeter, vt to insert, put in; to put between.

entremezclar, vt to intermingle.

entrenador(a), nm/f trainer, training plane.

entrenamiento, nm training, coaching.

entrenar, vt to train, coach; to exercise.

entresacar, vt to pick out, select; to sift.

entretanto, adj meanwhile, meantime.

entretecho, nm attic, garret.

entretejer, vt to interweave; insert, put in.

entretela, nf interlining.

entretener, vt to entertain, amuse; to distract.

entretenido, adj entertaining, amusing.

entretenimiento, nm entertainment, amusement; diversion, distraction; recreation.

entretiempo, nm period between seasons.

entrever, vt 1. to glimpse, catch a glimpse of; make out ; 2. to guess, suspect.

entrevista, nf interview; meeting.

entrevistado(a), nm/f interviewee, person being interviewed.

entrevistador(a), nm/f interviewer.

entrevistar, vt to interview.

entristecer, vt to sadden, grieve.

entrometerse, vr to meddle, interfere, intrude.

entrometido, adj meddlesome, interfering.

entroncar, vt to connect, establish a relationship between.

entronización, nf enthronement.

entronizar, vt 1. to enthrone; 2. to exalt.

entronque, nm relationship, connection, link.

entuerto, nm wrong, injustice.

entumecer, vt to numb, benumb.

entumecido, adj numb, stiff.

entumido, adj 1. numb, stiff; 2. timid.

enturbiar, vt to muddy; to disturb, make cloudy.

entusiasmar, vt to fill with enthusiasm; to fire, excite; to delight.

entusiasmarse, vr to get excited.

entusiasmo, nm enthusiasm.

entusiasta, adj enthusiastic; keen; zealous.

enumeración, nf enumeration; count, reckoning.

enumerar, vt to enumerate; to count, reckon up.

enunciado, nm principle.

enunciar, vt to enunciate; to state, declare.

envainar, vt to sheathe, put in a sheath.

envalentonar, vt to embolden; courage.

envanecer, vt to make conceited.

envanecerse, vr to grow vain, get conceited, give oneself airs; to swell with pride.

envanecido, adj conceited, stuck-up.

envarar, vt to stake; to stiffen, to numb.

envasado, *nm* packing, packaging.

envasador(a), *nm/f* packer.

envasar, *vt* to pack, wrap; to package; to bottle; to can, tin.

envase, *nm* packing, wrapping; packaging; bottling; canning.

envejecer, *vt* to age, make (seem) old.

envejecimiento, *nm* ageing.

envenenamiento, *nm* poisoning.

envenenar, *vt* to poison; to poison, embitter.

envergadura, *nf* expanse, spread, extent; breadth, beam; wingspan.

enviado(a), *nm/f* envoy; special correspondent.

enviar, *vt* to send.

enviciador(a), *nm/f* drug-pusher.

enviciar, *vt* to corrupt; to vitiate.

envidia, *nf* envy, jealousy; desire; bad feeling.

envidiar, *vt* to envy; to desire, covet.

envilecer, *vt* to debase, degrade.

evilecerse, *vr* to grovel, lower oneself.

envío, *nm* sending, dispatch; shipment.

enviudar, *vi* to become a widow(er), be widowed.

envoltura, *nf* cover; wrapper, wrapping.

envolver, *vt* to wrap (up), pack (up), tie up, do up.

enyerbar, *vt* to bewitch.

enyesado, *nm* plastering; plaster cast.

enyesar, *vt* to plaster; to put in a plaster cast.

enyugar, *vt* to yoke.

enyuntar, *vt* to put together, join.

enzima, *nf* enzyme.

épica, *nf* epic poetry.

épico, *adj* epic.

epidemia, *nf* epidemic.

epidémico, *adj* epidemic.

epidermis, *nf* epidermis.

epiglotis, *nf* epiglottis.

epígrafe, *nm* epigraph; inscription; title, headline.

epilepsia, *nf* epilepsy.

epiléptico(a), *adj nm/f* epileptic.

epílogo, *nm* epilogue.

episcopado, *nm* **1.** bishopric; **2.** episcopate; **3.** bishops (collectively), episcopacy.

episcopal, *adj* episcopal.

episodio, *nm* episode; incident; instalment, part.

epístola, *nf* epistle.

epistolario, *nm* collected letters.

epitafio, *nm* epitaph.

época, *nf* period, time; age, epoch.

equidad, *nf* equity; justice, fairness, impartiality.

equilátero, *adj* equilateral.

equilibrado, *adj* balanced.

equilibrar, *vt* to balance; to poise.

equilibrio, *nm* balance, equilibrium.

equino, *adj* equine, horse.

equipaje, *nm* luggage, baggage.

equipar, *vt* to equip, furnish, fit up.

equiparación, *nf* comparison.

equiparar, *vt* to put on the same level, consider equal; to compare.

equipo, *nm* equipment; outfit, kit; gear, tackle.

equis, *nf* (name of the) letter x.

equitación, *nf* riding; horsemanship.

equitativo, *adj* equitable, fair; reasonable.

equivalente, *adj* equivalent.

equivaler, *vi* to be equivalent, be equal.

equivocación, *nf* mistake, error; oversight.

equivocado, *adj* wrong, mistaken.

equivocar, *vt* to mistake.

equivocarse, *vr* to be wrong, to make a mistake.

erección, *nf* erection, raising; establishment, foundation.

erguido, *adj* erect, straight; proud.

erguir, *vt* to raise, lift.

erigir, *vt* to erect, raise, build; to establish, found.

erizado, *adj* bristly.

erizo, *nm* hedgehog; sea urchin.

erogar, *vt* to distribute.

erosión, *nf* erosion; graze.

erosionar, *vt* to erode.

erótico, *adj* erotic.

erotismo, *nm* eroticism.

erotizar, *vt* to eroticize; to stimulate.

errabundear, *vi* to wander, rove.

errabundo, *adj* wandering, roving.

erradamente, *adj* mistakenly.

erradicación, *nf* eradication.

erradicar, *vt* to eradicate.

errado, *adj* mistaken, wrong.

errante, *adj* wandering, roving; itinerant; nomadic.

errar, *vt* to miss with, aim badly.

erróneo, *adj* mistaken, erroneous; false, untrue.

error, *nm* error, mistake; fault.

eructar, *vi* to belch.

erudición, *nf* erudition, learning, scholarship.

erudito, *adj* erudite, learned, scholarly.

esbeltez, *nf* slimness, slenderness; litheness; gracefulness.

esbelto, *adj* slim, slender; lithe, willowy; graceful.

esbirro, *nm* henchman, minion; killer.

esbozar, *vt* to sketch, outline.

escabeche, *nm* pickle, brine, sauce of vinegar, oil, garlic, etc.

escabroso, *adj* rough, rugged; uneven.

escabuche, *nm* weeding hoe.

escafandra, *nf* diving suit; scuba suit.

escafandrista, *nm/f* underwater fisherman; deep-sea diver.

escala, *nf* **1.** ladder; **2.** scale; **3.** stop (airline, etc.)

escalador(a), *nm/f* climber; mountaineer.

escalafón, *nm* roll, list, register; list of officials, establishment.

escalamiento, *nm* burglary, housebreaking.

escalante, *adj* escalating.

escalar, *vt* **1.** to climb, scale; **2.** to burglarize, break into.

escalarse, *vr* to scalate.

escaldadura, *nf* scald, scalding.

escaldar, *vt* to scald.

escalera, *nf* stairs, staircase, stairway;

escalerilla, *nf* small ladder; low step; gangway.

escalinata, *nf* steps, flight of steps; outside staircase.

escalofriante, *adj* bloodcurdling, hair-raising; chilling, frightening.

escalofrío, *nm* chill, feverish chill.

escalón, *nm* step, stair; rung; tread; (rocket) stage.

escalonar, *vt* to spread out at intervals.

escalpar, *vt* to scalp.

escalpelo, *nm* scalpel.

escama, *nf* scale; flake.

escamado, *adj* wary, cautious.

escamar, *vt* to scale, remove the scales from.

escamoso, *adj* scaly; flaky.

escamoteador(a), *nm/f* conjurer, juggler; swindler.

escamotear, *vt* to whisk away, whisk out of sight, snatch away, make vanish.

escampar, *vt* to clear out.

escanciador, *nm* wine waiter; cupbearer.

escanciar, *vt* to pour, serve; to drain.

escandalizar, *vt* to scandalize, shock.

escándalo, *nm* 1. scandal; outrage; 2. row, uproar, commotion, fuss; 3. sense of shock; astonishment.

escáner, *nm* scanner.

escapado, *adj* at top speed, in a rush.

escapar, *vt* 1. to ride hard, drive hard; 2. to escape, flee, run away.

escaparate, *nm* shop window; showcase, display case.

escapatoria, *nf* 1. escape, flight; getaway; 2. (gas) leak, leakage.

escapulario, *nm* scapular(y).

escara, *nf* crust, slough.

escarabajo, *nm* 1. beetle; 2. dwarf, runt. 3. scrawl; scribble.

escaramuza, *nf* skirmish, brush.

escarbador, *nm* scraper.

escarbar, *vt* to scratch; to poke; to pick, clean.

escarcear, *vi* to prance.

escarcha, *nf* frost, hoarfrost.

escarchado, *adj* covered in hoarfrost, frosted.

escarchar, *vt* to frost, cover in hoarfrost.

escardador, *nm* weeding hoe.

escardar, *vt* to weed, weed out.

escariar, *vt* to ream.

escarlata, *adj* scarlet.

escarlatina, *nf* scarlet fever.

escarmentado, *adj* wary, cautious.

escarmentar, *vt* to punish severely, teach a lesson to.

escarmiento, *nm* punishment; lesson, warning, example.

escarnecedor, *adj* mocking.

escarnecedora, *nf* scoffer, mocker.

escarnecer, *vt* to scoff at, mock, ridicule.

escarnio, *nm* jibe, taunt; derision, ridicule.

escarpado, *adj* steep, sheer; craggy.

escasear, *vt* to be sparing with, give out in small amounts, skimp.

escasez, *nf* scarcity, shortage, lack; poverty, want.

escaso, *adj* scarce; scant, scanty; limited; slight.

escatimar, *vt* to curtail, cut down.

escena, *nf* scene.

escenario, *nm* stage; setting; scenery.

escénico, *adj* scenic.

escenificación, *nf* staging; dramatization.

escenificar, *vt* to stage; to dramatize.

escenografía, *nf* scenography; stage design.

esclarecedor, *adj* illuminating.

esclarecer, *vt* 1. to light up, illuminate; 2. to explain, elucidate.

esclarecido, *adj* illustrious, distinguished.

esclarecimiento, *nm* 1. illumination; 2. explanation, elucidation, clarification; 3. enlightenment.

esclava, *nf* 1. slave; drudge; 2. slave bangle, bracelet.

esclavitud, *nf* slavery, servitude, bondage.

esclavizar, *vt* to enslave.

esclavo, *nm* slave.

escoba, *nf* 1. broom; brush; 2. sweeper.

escobada, *nf* brush, sweep.

escocedor, *adj* painful, hurtful.

escocer, *vt* to annoy, hurt.

escofina, *nf* rasp, file.

escofinar, *vt* to rasp, file.

escoger, *vti* to choose, select, pick (out).

escogido, *adj* chosen, selected; choice, select.

escolar, *adj* 1. scholastic; school; 2. *nm* pupil.

escolta, *nf* escort.

escoltar, *vt* to escort; to guard, protect.

escollar, *vi* to hit a reef, strike a rock.

escollo, *nm* reef, rock.

escombrar, *vt* to clear out, clean out, clear of rubbish.

escombrera, *nf* dump, rubbish heap; slag heap.

escombro, *nm* 1. rubbish; debris; wreckage, rubble; waste, slag; 2. mackerel.

esconder, *vt* to hide, conceal.

escondite, *nm* hiding place.

escondrijo, *nm* hiding place, hideout.

escopera, *nf* shotgun.

escopetazo, *nm* gunshot; gunshot wound.

escopeteo, *nm* shooting.

escopetero, *nm* gunsmith; rifleman.

escorar, *vt* to shore up.

escoria, *nf* slag.

escorpión, *nm* scorpion; Scorpio.

escote, *nm* low neck.

escotilla, *nf* hatch, hatchway; floodgates.

escozor, *nm* smart, sting; burning pain.

escriba, *nm* scribe.

escribano, *nm* court clerk; lawyer's clerk; notary; (municipal) town clerk.

escribiente, *nm* copyist, amanuensis; clerk.

escribir, *vt/i* 1. to write; 2. to spell.

escritor(a), *nm/f* writer; copywriter.

escritorio, *nm* 1. desk, bureau; 2. office.

escritura, *nf* 1. handwriting; 2. writing, script; alphabet; 3. (Jur) deed, document.

escriturar, *vt* to execute by deed, formalize legally.

escroto, *nm* scrotum.

escrúpulo, *nm* 1. scruple; doubt, hesitation; 2. scrupulousness.

escrupuloso, *adj* scrupulous; exact, particular, precise.

escrutador, *adj* searching, penetrating.

escrutar, *vt* 1. to scrutinize, examine; 2. (votes) to count.

escrutinio, *nm* 1. scrutiny, examination, inspection; 2. count, counting; voting, ballot.

escuadra, *nf* carpenter's square, draftman's square; bracket.

escuadrar, *vt* to square.

escuadrón, *nm* squadron; troop.

escucha, *nf* listening; listening-in; monitoring.

escuchar, *vt* to listen to; to hear.

escucho, *nm* whispered secret.

escudar, *vt* to shield; protect.

escudero, *nm* squire; page.

escudilla, *nf* bowl, basin.

escudo, *nm* shield; coat of arms.

escudriñar, *vt* to inquire into, investigate; to examine, scan, scrutinize.

escuela, *nf* school.

esculpir, *vt* to sculpt, sculpture; carve, engrave.

escultor(a), *nm* 1. sculptor; 2. *nf* sculptress.

escultura, *nf* sculpture, carving; wood carving.

escupidera, *nf* 1. spittoon; 2. chamberpot.

escupidor, *nm* 1. spitter; 2. spittoon; 3. round mat, doormat.

escupir, *vt/i* to spit.

escurridero, *nm* draining board, drainboard.

escurrir, *vt* to wring; to drain; to press dry, squeeze dry.

ese(a), *adj demm* that.

esos(as), *adj demm (pl)* those.

esencia, *nf* essence; heart, core.

esencial, *adj* essential; chief, main.

esfera, *nf* sphere; globe.

esférico, *adj* 1. spherical; 2. *nm* ball, football.

esfinge, *nf* 1. sphinx; 2. hawk moth.

esforzado, *adj* vigorous, brave, strong; tough; enterprising.

esforzar, *vt* to strengthen; to invigorate.

esfumar, *vt* to shade; to tone down, soften.

esfumarse, *vr* to fade away, melt away.

esgrima, nf fencing; swordsmanship,

esgrimir, vt to wield; to brandish; to use.

esgrimista, nm/f fencer.

eslabón, nm link; steel; shackle.

eslabonar, vt to link, join; interlink.

eslora, nf length.

esmaltar, vt metal to enamel; to varnish, paint.

esmalte, nm enamel; enamelwork, smalt.

esmerado, adj 1. careful, neat; polished, elegant; 2. careful, painstaking, conscientious.

esmeralda, nf emerald.

esmerar, vt to polish, brighten up.

esmerarse, vr to do one's best, exercize great care.

esmeril, nm emery.

esmerilar, vt to polish with emery.

esmero, nm care, carefulness; neatness; polish, elegance; refinement.

esmoquin, nm dinnerjacket, tuxedo.

eso, pron demm neuter that.

espabilar, vt to snuff.

espaciado, nm spacing.

espaciador, nm spacing key, spacing bar.

espacial, adj spatial.

espaciar, vt to space; to spread, expand.

espacio, nm space; room; distance; period, interval.

espacioso, adj spacious, roomy, big.

espada, nf sword.

espadazo, nm sword thrust, slash with a sword.

espaguetis, nm spaghetti.

espalda, nf back, shoulder(s).

espaldar, nm 1. (chair) back; 2. trellis, espalier.

espaldarazo, nm slap on the back; pat on the back; accolade.

espaldera, nf trellis, espalier.

espaldero, nm bodyguard, henchman.

espaldilla, nf shoulder blade; shoulder of pork.

espantada, nf 1. sudden scare, sudden fear; 2. stampede, panic.

espantado, adj frightened, scared, terrified.

espantador, adj frightening.

espantar, vt to frighten, scare; to frighten off, scare away; to appall, horrify.

espanto, nm fright, terror; consternation, dismay; amazement, astonishment.

espantoso, adj frightful, dreadful; terrifying; shocking; appalling; amazing.

español(a), adj 1. Spanish; 2. nm/f Spanish.

españolizar, vt to make Spanish, hispanicize; to give a Spanish flavor.

esparcido, adj 1. scattered; widespread; 2. merry, jolly, cheerful; open, frank.

esparcimiento, nm 1. spreading, scattering; 2. relaxation; amusement.

esparcir, vt 1. to spread, scatter, to sow; to disseminate; 2. to amuse, divert.

espárrago, nm asparagus.

espasmo, nm spasm.

espasmódico, adj spasmodic.

especia, nf spice.

especiado, adj spiced, spicy.

especial, adj 1. special, especial; 2. particular, fussy.

especialidad, nf speciality, specialty; special branch, special field.

especialista, nm/f 1. specialist; 2. stuntman, stuntwoman.

especializado, adj specialized; skilled, trained.

especiar, vt to spice.

especie, nf species.

especificación, nf specification.

especificar, vt to specify; to particularize; to list, itemize.

específico, adj specific.

espécimen, nm specimen.

espectacular, adj spectacular.

espectáculo, nm spectacle; sight; show; function, performance.

espectador(a), nm/f spectator; onlooker, looker-on.

espectral, adj 1. spectral; 2. ghostly; unearthly.

espectro, nm 1. (Fis) spectrum; 2. specter, ghost.

especulación, nf speculation; contemplation, meditation.

especular, vt to examine, inspect; to speculate about, contemplate.

especulativo, adj speculative.

espejado, adj glossy, bright, shining, mirror-like.

espejear, vi to shine, gleam, glimmer, glint.

espejo, nm mirror, looking-glass.

espeluznante, adj hair-raising, horrifying, blood-curdling; lurid.

espera, nf wait, period of waiting; waiting; delay.

esperable, adj to be hoped for; to be expected.

esperanza, nf hope; expectation; prospect.

esperanzador, adj hopeful, encouraging; promising.

esperanzar, vt to give hope to, buoy up with hope.

esperar, vt 1. to hope for; to expect.

esperma, nf 1. sperm; 2. candle.

esperpento, nm fright, sight; scarecrow.

espesar, vt 1. to thicken; to make dense; 2. to weave tighter; to knit tighter.

espeso, adj 1. thick; dense; deep; 2. dirty, untidy.

espesura, nf thickness; density.

espía, nm/f spy.

espiga, nf ear; spike.

espigar, vt to glean; to look closely at, scrutinize.

espigón, nm 1. ear; spike; 2. sting; 3. sharp point, spike.

espina, nf 1. thorn, prickle; splinter; 2. bone.

espinaca, nf spinach.

espinaso, nm spine, backbone.

espionaje, nm spying, espionage.

espiral, adj spiral; winding; helical; corkscrew.

espirar, vt to breathe out, exhale.

espíritu, nm spirit; ghost.

espiritual, adj 1. spiritual; 2. unworldly; ghostly.

espiritualizar, vt to spiritualize.

esplendidez, nf splendor; magnificence, grandeur; pomp.

espléndido, adj 1. splendid; magnificent, grand; 2. lavish; liberal, generous.

esplendor, nm splendor; magnificence, grandeur; brilliance.

espolear, vt 1. to spur; 2. stimulate; to stir up, enliven.

espoleta, nf 1. fuse; 2. wishbone.

espolvorear, vt to dust, sprinkle.

esponja, nf sponge.

esponjado, adj spongy; fluffy.

espontaneidad, nf spontaneity.

espontáneo, adj spontaneous; impromptu, unprepared.

esporádico, adj sporadic; desultory.

esposa, nf 1. wife; 2. handcuffs; manacles.

esposar, vt to handcuff.

esposo, nm husband.

espuela, nf 1. spur; 2. feminine charm.

espuelear, vt 1. to spur, spur on; 2. to test, try out.

espulgar, vt to delouse.

espuma, nf foam, spray; surf; froth.

espumadera, nf skimmer, skimming ladle.

espumajear, vi to foam at the mouth.
espumar, vt 1. to skim off; 2. vi to froth, foam; to sparkle (wine).
espúreo, adj spurious; adulterated; illegitimate.
esputar, vt/i to spit (out), hawk (up).
esputo, nm spit, spittle, sputum.
esquela, nf 1. note; short letter; 2. notice, announcement.
esqueleto, nm 1. skeleton; 2. framework.
esquema, nm diagram, plan; scheme; sketch, outline.
esquemático, adj schematic; diagrammatic.
esquiador(a), nm/f skier.
esquiar, vi to ski.
esquilador, nm shearer.
esquilar, vt to shear; to clip, crop.
esquilmar, vt 1. to harvest; 2. to exhaust, impoverish.
esquilmo, nm harvest, crop; yield.
esquimal, adj nm/f Eskimo.
esquina, nf corner.
esquinado, adj having corners; sharp-cornered.
esquinar, vt 1. to form a corner with; to be on the corner of; 2. to square (off); 3. to put in a corner.
esquinazo, nm 1. corner; 2. serenade.
esquivada, nf dodge, evasion.
esquivar, vt to avoid, shun; to elude, dodge, side-step.
esquivarse, vr to withdraw.
esquizofrenia, nf schizophrenia.
esquizofrénico(a), adj nm/f schizophrenic.
estabilizador, nm stabilizer.
estabilizar, vt to stabilize; to make stable, steady.
estable, adj stable; firm.
establecer, vt to establish; to set up, found.
establecimiento, nm establishment, setting-up, founding; institution; settlement.
establero, nm stableboy, groom.
establo, nm cowshed, stall; barn.
estaca, nf stake, post, paling; peg; stick.
estacar, vt 1. to stake (out, off), mark with stakes; to fence with stakes; 2. to tie to a post.
estación, nf 1. station; 2. season.
estacional, adj seasonal.
estacionamiento, nm 1. stationing, placing; 2. parking.
estacionar, vt to station, place; to park.
estacionario, adj stationary; motionless; stable.
estadía, nf 1. demurrage; 2. length of stay.
estadio, nm 1. stage, phase; 2. furlong; 3. stadium.
estadista, nm statesman; statistician.
estadística, nf 1. statistics; 2. figure.
estado, nm 1. state, condition; 2. status; rank, class.
Estados Unidos, nm United States (of America).
estafa, nf swindle, trick; racket, fraud.
estafador(a), nm/f swindler, trickster.
estafar, vt to swindle, defraud.
estafilococo, nm staphylococcus.
estalactita, nf stalactite.
estalagmita, nf stalagmite.
estallar, vi to burst, explode, go off.
estallido, nm explosion, report; crash, crack.
estambre, nm worsted, woollen yarn.
estampa, nf 1. imprint; footprint, track; 2. engraving; picture.
estampado, adj 1. printed; 2. nm printing; stamping.
estampar, vt to print; to stamp; to engrave.
estampida, nf stampede.
estampido, nm report; detonation; bang, boom.
estampilla, nf 1. rubber stamp; 2. (mail) stamp.
estancado, adj 1. stagnant; 2. static.
estancamiento, nm 1. stagnation; 2. blockage, stoppage, suspension; deadlock.

estancar, vt 1. to hold up, hold back, stem; 2. block, to stop, suspend.
estancia, nf 1. stay; 2. dwelling, abode.
estanco, adj watertight.
estándar, adj, nm standard.
estandar(d)izar, vt to standardize.
estandarte, nm banner, standard; royal standard.
estanque, nm 1. pool, pond, small lake; 2. tank.
estanquillo, nm booth, kiosk, stall.
estante, nm rack, stand; piece of furniture with shelves; bookcase.
estañar, vt to tin; to solder.
estaño, nm tin; solder.
estar, vi to be; to be in (at).
estatal, adj state; national, nationwide.
estatua, nf statue.
estatuaria, nf statuary (art).
estatuario, adj statuesque.
estatuir, vt 1. to establish, enact, ordain; 2. to prove.
estatura, nf stature, height.
estatuto, nm statute; by-law.
este(a), adj dem m/f this.
esto(a)s, adj dem m/f pl these.
éste(a), pron dem m/f this; this one; the latter.
ésto(a)s, pron dem m/f pl, these; the latter; this.
estela, nf wake; trail.
estelar, adj 1. stellar, sidereal; 2. star.
estepa, nf 1. steppe; 2. (Bot) rockrose.
estera, nf mat, matting.
estercolar, vt to manure.
estercolero, nm manure heap, dunghill.
estéreo, nm stereo.
estereofónico, adj stereophonic, stereo.
estereotipar, vt to stereotype.
estereotipo, nm stereotype.
estéril, adj 1. sterile, barren; 2. vain, futile, unproductive.
esterilidad, nf 1. sterility, barrenness; 2. futility, uselessness.
esterilización, nf sterilization.
esterilizar, vt to sterilize.
esternón, nm breastbone, sternum.
estertor, nm death rattle.
estética, nf aesthetics.
estético, adj aesthetic.
estetoscopio, nm stethoscope.
estiba, nf stowage; loading.
estibador, adj 1. shipping company; 2. nm stevedore.
estibar, vt to stow, put; to load; to house, store.
estigma, nm stigma; mark, brand.
estigmatizar, vt to stigmatize.
estilar, vt 1. to draw up (in due form); 2. to use, be in the habit of using; to wear, adopt.
estilarse, vr to be in style.
estilizar, vt to stylize; to design, style.
estilo, nm style; manner; fashion.
estima, nf esteem, respect.
estimación, nf estimation; valuation; forecast.
estimado, adj esteemed, respected.
estimar, vt 1. to estimate; to appraise; 2. to esteem, respect.
estimulante, adj 1. stimulating; 2. nm stimulant.
estimular, vt to stimulate; to encourage.
estímulo, nm stimulus, incentive.
estipulación, nf stipulation, condition.
estipular, vt to stipulate.
estirada, nf dive, stretch.
estirado, adj stretched.
estirador, nm stretcher.

estiraje, nm stretching.

estirar, vt to stretch, pull out, draw out; to extend.

estirpe, nf stock, lineage; race.

esto, pron dem (neutro), this.

estofado, adj 1. stewed; 2. quilted; 3. nm stew.

estofar, vt 1. to stew; 2. to quilt.

estoico(a), adj 1. stoic(al); 2. nm/f stoic.

estola, nf stole; cape.

estomacal, adj stomachic; stomach.

estómago, nm stomach.

estoque, nm 1. rapier, sword; 2. gladiolus.

estoquear, vt to stab, run through.

estorbar, vt to hinder, obstruct, impede, be (or get) in the way of.

estorbo, nm hindrance, obstruction, impediment, obstacle; drag; nuisance.

estornudar, vi to sneeze.

estornudo, nm sneeze.

estrado, nm stage, platform; bandstand.

estragado, adj ruined; corrupted, spoiled, perverted; depraved.

estragar, vt to ruin: to corrupt, spoil, pervert; to deprave.

estrambótico, adj odd, outlandish, eccentric.

estrangulado, adj strangulated.

estrangulador, nm strangler.

estrangular, vt to strangle.

estratagema, nf stratagem.

estratega, nm/f strategist.

estrategia, nf strategy; generalship.

estratégico, adj strategic(al).

estratificación, nf stratification.

estratificar, vt to stratify.

estrato, nm 1. stratum, layer; 2. stratus.

estratósfera, nf stratosphere.

estrechar, vt 1. to narrow; to make smaller, reduce; 2. to squeeze; to hug, embrace.

estrechez, nf narrowness, tightness; cramped nature, lack of room.

estrecho, adj narrow; tight; cramped, small.

estregar, vt to scrub, scour.

estrella, nf 1. star; 2. asterisk.

estrellado, adj 1. starred; star-shaped; 2. smashed, shattered.

estrellar, vt 1. to star, spangle, cover with stars; 2. to smash, shatter; to dash to pieces.

estremecedor, adj alarming, disturbing, shattering.

estremecer, vt to shake.

estremecerse, vr shiver, shudder, tremble.

estremecimiento, nm tremor, vibration; shiver, shudder; shaking, trembling; tingling.

estrenar, vt 1. to wear for the first time; 2. to show for the first time.

estrenarse, vr to make one's début, appear for the first time; to start to do some work.

estreñido, adj constipated, costive.

estreñimiento, nm constipation.

estreñir, vt to constipate, bind.

estrépito, nm noise, racket, row; din.

estrepitoso, adj noisy; loud, deafening.

estriado, adj grooved;fluted; striate, striated.

estriar, vt to groove, to flute; to striate.

estribación, nf spur; foothills.

estribar, vi to rest on, be supported by.

estribillo, nm refrain; chorus; pet phrase.

estribo, nm stirrup; running board, step, footboard.

estribor, nm starboard.

estricnina, nf strychnine.

estricto, adj strict; severe.

estridencia, nf stridency; raucousness.

estridente, adj strident, raucous, unpleasant sounding.

estrógeno, nm estrogen.

estropajo, nm 1. scourer, scouring pad, scrubber; 2. dirt, rubbish; worthless object.

estropajoso, adj 1. tough, leathery, gristly; 2. stammering; indistinct.

estropeado, adj damaged, spoiled; ruined; crumpled, torn.

estropear, vt to damage, spoil; to ruin; to mess up.

estropearse, vr to deteriorate, to fail.

estructura, nf structure; frame, framework.

estructural, adj structural.

estructurar, vt to construct; to arrange, organize.

estruendo, nm 1. noise, clamor, din; crash, clatter, racket; thunder; 2. uproar, turmoil, confusion.

estrujado, nm pressing.

estrujar, vt to squeeze; to press, crush; to bruise, mash.

estuche, nm box, case, container.

estudiado, adj studied, elaborate.

estudiante, nm/f student.

estudiar, vti to study; to work; to think about, think over, ponder.

estudioso(a), adj 1. studious; bookish; 2. nm/f scholar.

estudio, nm study, research; (room) study; (Mus) etude.

estufa, nf stove, heater; cooker.

estupefacción, nf stupefaction.

estupefacto, adj astonished, speechless, thunderstruck.

estupendo, adj stupendous; marvellous, wonderful.

estupidez, nf stupidity, silliness.

estúpido, adj stupid, silly.

estupor, nm 1. stupor; 2. astonishment, amazement.

etapa, nf stage; leg; lap.

eternidad, nf eternity.

eternizar, vt to etern(al)ize, perpetuate; to make everlasting.

eterno, adj eternal, everlasting.

ética, nf ethics.

ético, adj ethical.

etileno, nm ethylene.

etiqueta, nf 1. etiquette; formality; formal, full-dress; 2. ticket, label, tag.

etiquetar, vt to label.

etnia, nf ethnic group; race.

étnico, adj ethnic.

E. U. A., abr United States of America.

eucalipto, nm eucalyptus, gum-tree.

euforia, nf euphoria; exuberance, elation.

eufórico, adj euphoric; exuberant.

eunuco, nm eunuch.

Europa, nf Europe.

europeo(a), nm/f European.

evacuación, nf 1. evacuation. 2. bowel movement.

evacuado(a), nm/f evacuee.

evacuar, vt 1. to evacuate; to move out of, leave empty, vacate; 2. to have a movement of the bowels.

evadido(a), nm/f fugitive, escaped prisoner.

evadir, vt 1. to evade, avoid; 2. to pass, get away with.

evadirse, vr to escape, breack out, slip away.

evaluación, nf evaluation; assessment; appraisal.

evaluador(a), nm/f assessor; appraiser; referee.

evaluar, vt to evaluate, assess.

evangélico, adj evangelic(al).

Evangelio, nm gospel.

evangelista, nm/f gospeller; revivalist evangelist.

evansgelizador(a), nm/f evangelist.

evangelizar, *vt* to evangelize.

evaporación, *nf* evaporation.

evaporar, *vt* to evaporate.

evaporizar, *vt* to vaporize.

evasión, *nf* escape, flight; evasion.

evasivo, *adj* evasive, non-committal, ambiguous.

evento, *nm* 1. unforeseen happening; contingency; eventuality; 2. event; sporting event.

eventual, *adj* 1. fortuitous; possible; conditional upon circumstances; 2. temporary, casual; eventual.

evidencia, *nf* evidence, proof.

evitar, *vt* to avoid; to prevent.

evocación, *nf* evocation; invocation.

evocador, *adj* evocative; reminiscent.

evocar, *vt* to evoke, call forth, conjure up.

evocativo, *adj* evocative.

evolución, *nf* 1. evolution; 2. change, development; (Med) progress.

evolucionar, *vi* 1. to evolve; 2. (point of view) to change, develop; to progress.

evolutivo, *adj* evolutionary.

exabrupto, *nm* broadside; sudden attack.

exacerbante, *adj* irritating, provoking; aggravating.

exacerbar, *vt* to irritate, provoke; to aggravate, exacerbate.

exactitud, *nf* exactness; accuracy.

exacto, *adj* exact; accurate; precise; punctual.

exageración, *nf* exaggeration.

exagerado, *adj* exaggerated; excessive, exorbitant.

exagerar, *vt* to exaggerate; to overdo, overstate, make too much of.

exaltado, *adj* 1. exalted; 2. over-excited, worked up; elated.

exaltar, *vt* 1. to exalt; to elevate, raise; 2. to extol, praise.

exaltarse, *vr* to get excited, very intense.

examen, *nm* examination; exam; inquiry.

examinado(a), *nm/f* examinee, candidate.

examinador(a), *nm/f* examiner.

examinar, *vt* to examine; to test; to inspect.

exánime, *adj* lifeless; weak, exhausted.

exasperación, *nf* exasperation.

exasperar, *vt* to exasperate, infuriate.

excarcelación, *nf* release (from prison).

excarcelado(a), *nm/f* ex-prisoner, former prisoner.

excarcelar, *vt* to release (from prison).

excavación, *nf* excavation.

excavador(a), *nm/f* excavator, digger.

excavar, *vt* to excavate, dig (out); to hollow out.

exedente, *adj* 1. excess, surplus; 2. *nm* excess, surplus.

exceder, *vt* to exceed, surpass; to pass, outdo, excel.

exederse, *vr* to go to extremes, go to far.

excelencia, *nf* 1. excellence; superiority.

excelente, *adj* excellent; superior.

excelso, *adj* lofty, exalted, sublime.

excéntrico(a), *adj nm/f* eccentric.

excepción, *nf* exception.

excepcional, *adj* exceptional.

excepto, *prep* except (for), excepting.

exceptuar, *vt* to except, exclude, leave out of account; to exempt.

excesivo, *adj* excessive; unreasonable, over-generously.

exceso, *nm* excess; surfeit; surplus.

excitación, *nf* 1. excitement; 2. excitation.

excitante, *adj* 1. exciting; 2. stimulating.

excitar, *vt* 1. to excite; arouse, stir up; 2. to incite, urge on.

exclamación, *nf* exclamation; cry.

exclamar, *vi* to exclaim; to cry out.

excluir, *vt* to exclude (from de); to shut out.

exclusión, *nf* exclusion.

exclusiva, *nf* sole right, sole agency.

excomulgado, *adj* 1. excommunicated; 2. cursed.

excomunión, *nf* excommunication.

excoriar, *vt* to skin, flay; to graze, take the skin off.

excremento, *nm* excrement, excreta.

excretar, *vt* to excrete.

exculpación, *nf* exoneration; acquittal.

exculpar, *vt* to exonerate, exculpate; to acquit.

excursión, *nf* excursion, outing, trip.

excursionar, *vi* to go on a trip, have an outing.

excusa, *nf* excuse; apology.

execración, *nf* execration.

execrar, *vt* to execrate, loathe, abominate.

excusado, *adj* 1. unnecessary, superfluous; 2. to be exempt from; 3. reserved, private.

excusar, *vt* 1. to excuse; 2. to exempt (from).

exención, *nf* exemption; immunity, freedom.

exento, *adj* exempt; free (from, of).

exhalación, *nf* exhalation; fumes, vapor.

exhalar, *vt* to exhale, breathe out.

exhausto, *adj* exhausted.

exheredar, *vt* to disinherit.

exhibición, *nf* exhibition, display, show.

exhibir, *vt* to exhibit, display, show.

exhortar, *vt* to exhort.

exhumación, *nf* exhumation, disinterment.

exhumar, *vt* to exhume, disinter.

exigencia, *nf* demand, requirement.

exigir, *vt* 1. to exact, levy (from); 2. to demand, require (of, from).

exilado(a), *adj nm/f* exiled, in exile.

exilio, *nm* exile.

eximio, *adj* distinguished, eminent.

eximir, *vt* to exempt (from); to free, excuse.

existencia, *nf* existence; being; life.

existente, *adj* in existence, in stock.

existir, *vi* to exist, be.

exitazo, *nm* great success; smash hit.

éxito, *nm* 1. result, outcome; 2. success.

exoneración, *nf* exoneration; freeing, relief.

exonerar, *vt* 1. to exonerate; to exempt; 2. to dismiss.

exorbitante, *adj* exorbitant.

exorcizar, *vt* to exorcise.

exótico, *adj* exotic.

expandible, *adj* expandible.

expandir, *vt* to expand; to spread out.

expatriación, *nf* expatriation; exile.

expatriado(a), *nm/f* expatriate; exile.

expectación, *nf* expectation, expectancy, anticipation.

expectativa, *nf* expectation; hope, prospect.

expectorar, *vti* to expectorate.

expedición, *nf* expedition.

expedicionario, *adj* expeditionary.

expedidor, *nm* shipper, shipping agent.

expediente, *nm* expedient; means; device.

expedir, *vt* to send, ship off, forward.

expedito, *adj* expeditious, prompt, speedy.

expeler, *vt* to expel, eject.

expendedor(a), *nm/f* dealer, retailer; agent.

expendeduría, *nf* retail shop.

expender, *vt* 1. to expend, spend; 2. to sell (retail).

expendio, *nm* expense, outlay.

experiencia, *nf* 1. experience; 2. experiment.

experimentado, *adj* experienced.

experimentar, *vt* 1. to test, try out; to experiment with; 2. to experience, undergo, go through.

experto, *adj* expert; skilled, experienced.

expiación, *nf* expiation, atonement.
expiar, *vt* to expiate, atone for.
expiración, *nf* expiration.
expirar, *vi* to expire.
explicación, *nf* explanation; reason (or).
explicar, *vt* to explain; to expound.
explicitar, *vt* to state, assert, make explicit.
explícito, *adj* explicit.
exploración, *nf* exploration; reconnaissance, scouting.
explorador(a), *nm/f* explorer; pioneer; scout.
explorar, *vt* to explore; to pioneer, open up.
explosión, *nf* 1. explosion; blast; 2. outburst.
explosivo, *adj* explosive.
explotación, *nf* exploitation; running, operation.
explotador, *adj* 1. exploitative; 2. *nm/f* exploiter.
explotar, *vt* to exploit; to run, operate.
exponente, *nm/f* exponent.
exponer, *vt* 1. to expose; to show, exhibit; 2. to risk.
exportación, *nf* export, exportation.
exportador(a), *nm/f* exporter; shipper.
exportar, *vt* to export.
exposición, *nf* exposing, exposure; display.
expositor(a), *nm/f* exhibitor; exponent.
expresado, *adj* above-mentioned.
expresar, *vt* to express; to voice.
expresión, *nf* expression.
expresividad, *nf* expressiveness.
expresivo, *adj* expressive.
exprimir, *vt* to squeeze; to wring out, squeeze dry.
expropiación, *nf* expropriation.
expropiar, *vt* to expropriate.
expulsar, *vt* to expel, eject, turn out.
expulsión, *nf* expulsion, ejection; sending-off.
expurgar, *vt* to expurgate.
exquisito, *adj* exquisite; delicious, delightful; excellent.
extasiar, *vt* to entrance, enrapture, captivate.
éxtasis, *nm* ecstasy; rapture.
extático, *adj* ecstatic, rapturous
extender, *vt* to extend; to enlarge, make bigger.
extenderse, *vr* to stretch out.
extensión, *nf* extension; stretching; spreading.
extenuación, *nf* emaciation, weakness; exhaustion.
extenuar, *vt* to emaciate, weaken; to exhaust.
exterior, *adj* exterior, external; outer.
exteriorizar, *vt* to express outwardly; to show, reveal.
exterminar, *vt* to exterminate.
extinción, *nf* extinction.
extinguido, *adj* 1. to be out, be extinguished; 2. extinct.
extinguir, *vt* 1. to extinguish, put out; 2. to exterminate, wipe out.
extinto, *adj* 1. extinct; 2. dead, deceased.
extirpar, *vt* to extirpate, eradicate, root out.
extorsión, *nf* extortion, exaction; blackmail.
extorsionador(a), *nm/f* extortioner.
extorsionar, *vt* to extort, extract.
extracción, *nf* extraction; draw.
extractar, *vt* 1. to make extracts from; 2. to abridge
extracto, *nm* 1. extract; 2. abstract, summary.
extractor, *nm* extractor.
extradición, *nf* extradition.
extraditar, *vt* to extradite.
extraer, *vt* to extract, take out, pull out.
extranjero, *adj* 1. foreign; alien; 2. *nm/f* foreigner.
extrañar, *vt* 1. to find strange, find odd, wonder at; 2. to miss; to feel the lack of, regret the absence of.
extrañarse, *vr* to be surprised at.
extrañeza, *nf* strangeness, oddness, oddity.

extraño, *adj* 1. strange, odd, queer; singular; 2. foreign.
extraordinario, *adj* extraordinary; unusual; outstanding.
extraterrestre, *adj* extraterrestrial.
extravagancia, *nf* extravagance.
extravagante, *adj* extravagant; outlandish, eccentric.
extraviado, *adj* lost; missing.
extraviar, *vt* 1. to mislead, misdirect; to lead astray; 2. to lose, mislay, misplace; 3. to embezzle.
extraviarse, *vr* to get sost, go stray.
extravío, *nm* loss, misplacement, straying; wandering.
extremado, *adj* extreme; excessive; intense.
extremar, *vt* to carry to extremes.
extremidad, *nf* 1. end, tip, extremity; outermost part; 2. extremities.
extrovertido(a), *adj nm/f* extrovert; outgoing.
exuberancia, *nf* exuberance.
exuberante, *adj* exuberant.
exudación, *nf* exudation.
exudar, *vt* to exude, ooze.
exultar, *vi* to exult.
eyaculación, *nf* ejaculation
eyacular, *vt/i* to ejaculate.

F

F, f, *nf* (letter) F, f.
fabada, *nf* rich stew of beans, pork, etc.
fábrica, *nf* factory; works, plant; mill.
fabricante, *nm/f* manufacturer; maker; factory owner, mill owner.
fabricar, *vt* 1. to manufacture, make; 2. to fabricate; falsify.
fábula, *nf* fable; myth; tale.
fabuloso, *adj* fabulous; mythical; imaginary, fictitious.
facción, *nf* faction; breakaway group.
facial, *adj* facial; face value.
fácil, *adj* easy; simple, straightforward; easy to do.
facsímil(e), *adj* facsimile.
factible, *adj* feasible; workable.
factor, *nm* factor.
factoría, *nf* 1. trading post; agency; 2. factory.
factura, *nf* bill, invoice.
facturar, *vt* to invoice; to bill.
facultad, *nf* faculty.
facultar, *vt* to authorize, empower.
facultativo, *adj* 1. optional; 2. faculty; 3. *nm/f* professional; doctor, practitioner.
facha, *nf* look, appearance; face, sight.
fachada, *nf* façade, front; frontage.
faena, *nf* 1. task, job, piece of work; duty; 2. dirty trick.
faisán, *nm* pheasant.
faja, *nf* strip, sash, belt, girdle.
fajar, *vt* 1. to wrap; to swathe; to bandage; 2. to attack, lay into; to bash, beat.
fajo, *nm* bundle, sheaf; roll, wad.
falacia, *nf* deceit, fraud; fallacy, error.
falda, *nf* 1. skirt; flap, fold; 2. slope, hillside.
faldear, *vt* to skirt.

faldón, *nm* tail, skirt; coat-tails; flap.

falibilidad, *nf* fallibility.

falible, *adj* fallible.

falo, *nm* phallus.

falsario(a), *nm/f* 1. falsifier; liar; 2. forger, counterfeiter.

falsear, *vt* to falsify; to forge, counterfeit, fake.

falsedad, *nf* falseness; falsity; unsoundness.

falsificación, *nf* falsification, forging.

falsificador(a), *nm/f* forger, counterfeiter.

falsificar, *vt* to falsify; to counterfeit

falso, *adj* false; counterfeit, bad.

falta, *nf* lack, want, need; absence; shortage.

faltar, *vt* 1. show disrespect for; 2. *vi* to be lacking, to be without.

falla, *nf* fault, defect; failure; lack.

fallar, *vt* 1. to trump; 2. *vi* to fail, go wrong.

fallecer, *vi* to pass away, die; expire.

fallecido, *adj* 1. late; 2. *nm/f* deceased.

fallido, *adj* unsuccessful; disappointed.

fallo, *adj* 1. to be out of; have a void in; 2. *nm* shortcoming, defect; failure, trouble, breakdown; 3. sentence, verdict; decision, ruling.

familia, *nf* family, household.

familiar, *adj* 1. family; 2. familiar (to); 3. homely, domestic.

familiaridad, *nf* familiarity; homeliness; informality, familiarities.

famoso, *adj* 1. famous; 2. great, splendid.

fanal, *nm* lighthouse; beacon; lantern; headlight.

fanático(a), *adj*, *nm/f* fanatical; fanatic; fan, supporter, admirer.

fanatizar, *vt* to arouse fanaticism in.

fanfarria, *nf* bluster, bravado, bragging.

fanfarrón, *adj* blustering, boastful; flashy.

fanfarronada, *nf* bluster, bravado.

fanfarronear, *vi* to bluster, boast.

fango, *nm* mud, mire.

fangoso, *adj* muddy, miry; slushy.

fantasear, *vi* to fantasize, daydream.

fantasía, *nf* 1. fantasy, imagination, fancy; 2. fantastic tale; work of the imagination.

fantasma, *nm* ghost, phantom, apparition.

fantasmagoría, *nf* phantasmagoria.

fantasmagórico, *adj* phantasmagoric.

fantasmal, *adj* ghostly; phantom.

fantástico, *adj* fantastic; weird, unreal; fanciful.

fantoche, *nm* puppet, marionette.

farallón, *nm* steep rock, cliff; headland; bluff.

farándula, *nf* troupe of strolling players; the theater world.

farero, *nm* lighthouse-keeper.

faringe, *nf* pharynx.

faringitis, *nf* pharyngitis.

fariseo, *nm* Pharisee, hypocrite.

farmacéutico, *adj* pharmaceutical.

farmacia, *nf* pharmacy; chemist's (shop), drugstore.

farmacología, *nf* pharmacology.

faro, *nm* lighthouse; beacon.

farola, *nf* street lamp; lamppost.

farolear, *vi* to swank, strut around; to brag.

farolero, *adj* 1. vain, stuck-up; 2. *nm* lamp-maker; lamplighter.

farsante, *nm* humbug, fraud, pseud.

farsear, *vi* to joke.

fascinación, *nf* fascination.

fascinador, *adj* fascinating.

fascinar, *vti* to fascinate; to captivate.

fase, *nf* phase, stage; half.

fastidiar, *vt* 1. to annoy, bother, vex; 2. to harm, damage.

fastidio, *nm* annoyance, bother, nuisance.

fastuoso, *adj* magnificent; splendid; lavish; pompous.

fatal, *adj* fatal; ill-fated, disastrous.

fatalidad, *nf* 1. fate; fatality; 2. mischance, misfortune, ill-luck.

fatalista, *adj* fatalistic.

firma, *nf* signature; signing.

firmamento, *nm* firmament.

firmar, *vti* to sign.

firme, *adj* firm; steady, secure, stable; hard.

firmeza, *nf* firmness; steadiness, stability; solidity, compactness.

fiscal, *adj* fiscal, financial; tax.

fiscalía, *nf* office of the public prosecutor.

fiscalizar, *vt* to control, oversee, inspect.

fisco, *nm* treasury, exchequer.

fisgar, *vt* 1. to spear, harpoon; 2. to pry into, spy on.

fisgón, *adj* snooping, prying, nosey.

fisgonear, *vt* to be always prying into, spy continually on.

física, *nf* physics, physicist.

físico, *adj* 1. physical; 2. finicky, affected.

fisiología, *nf* physiology.

fisiológico, *adj* physiological.

fisión, *nf* fission.

franqueo, *nm* postage; franking.

franqueza, *nf* frankness, openness, forthrightness, candidness.

franquicia, *nf* exemption (from).

frasco, *nm* 1. flask, bottle; 2. liquid measure.

frase, *nf* 1. sentence; 2. phrase, expression.

fraseología, *nf* phraseology; verbosity, verbiage.

fraternal, *adj* brotherly, fraternal.

fraternidad, *nf* brotherhood, fraternity.

fraternizar, *vi* to fraternize.

fraterno, *adj* brotherly, fraternal.

fratricida, *adj* fratricidal.

fraude, *nm* 1. dishonesty, fraudulence; 2. fraud, swindle; deception.

frazada, *nf* blanket.

frecuencia, *nf* frequency.

frecuentar, *vt* to frequent; to haunt.

frecuente, *adj* frequent; common; usual, prevalent.

fregadero, *nm* kitchen sink.

fregar, *vt* to rub, scrub; to scour; to mop, scrub.

fregona, *nf* kitchen maid, dishwasher.

frenar, *vt* to brake; to put the brake on, apply the brake to.

frenazo, *nm* sudden braking; sudden halt; squeal of brakes.

frenesí, *nm* frenzy.

freno, *nm* brake.

fresa, *nf* strawberry; strawberry plant.

fresadora, *nm* milling machine; thread cutter.

fresal, *nm* strawberry bed.

fresar, *vt* to mill.

fresca, *nf* fresh air, cool air; cool part of the day.

fresco, *adj* 1. fresh; new, recent; 2. cool.

frescura, *nf* freshness; coolness.

fresno, *nm* ash, ash tree.

freza, *nf* 1. spawn; spawning; 2. dung, droppings.

frezar, *vi* to spawn.

frialdad, *nf* coldness, cold, chilliness.

fricción, *nf* rub, rubbing; massage; friction.

friccionar, *vt* to rub; to rub, massage.

frigorífico, *adj* refrigerating, cold-storage.

frío, *adj* cold; chilly.

friolera, *nf* trifle, mere nothing.

frisa, *nf* frieze.

frisar, *vt* to frizz, rub.

fritada, *nf* fry, fried dish.

frito, *adj* fried.

fritura, *nf* **1.** fry, fried dish; **2.** fritter.

frivolidad, *nf* frivolity, frivolousness.

frívolo, *adj* frivolous.

fronda, *nf* frond; foliage, leaves.

frondoso, *adj* leafy; luxuriant.

frontal, *adj* frontal; front; front-end.

frontera, *nf* frontier, border.

frontón, *nm* **1.** pediment; **2.** court.

frotación, *nf* rub, rubbing; friction.

frotar, *vt* to rub; to strike.

fructífero, *adj* **1.** productive, fruit-bearing; **2.** fruit-ful.

fructificación, *nf* fruition.

fructificar, *vi* to produce, yield a crop, bear fruit.

frugal, *adj* frugal; thrifty; parsimonious.

frugalidad, *nf* frugality; thrift, thriftiness; parsimony.

fruición, *nf* enjoyment; satisfaction, delight.

fruncir, *vt* to contract, pucker; to ruffle; to pleat, gather; to wrinkle.

frustración, *nf* frustration.

frustrar, *vt* to frustrate, thwart.

fruta, *nf* fruit.

frutal, *adj* fruit-bearing tree.

frutera, *nf* fruit-dish, fruit-bowl.

fruticultor(a), *nm/f* fruit-farmer, fruit-grower.

fuego, *nm* fire; conflagration.

fuelle, *nm* bellows; blower; footpump.

fuente, *nf* **1.** fountain, spring; **2.** serving dish, platter.

fuera, *adv* outside; out.

fuero, *nm* **1.** municipal charter; local (or regional); **2.** jurisdiction, authority; **3.** inwardly, in our hearts.

fuerte, *adj* strong; tough, sturdy; robust; vigorous; solid.

fuerza, *nf* strength; toughness, sturdiness; vigor; solidity; power, force.

fuga, *nf* flight, escape; (Mus) fugue.

fugado, *nm* escapee.

fugar, *vi* to flee, escape; to run away.

fugaz, *adj* fleeting, short-lived, transitory, brief.

fugitivo, *adj* fugitive, fleeing.

fulgir, *vi* to glow, shine; to glitter.

fulgor, *nm* brilliance, radiance, glow; splendor.

fulgurante, *adj* **1.** bright, shining; **2.** shattering, stunning.

fulgurar, *vi* to shine, gleam, glow; to flash.

fulminador(a), *adj, nm/f* fulminator (against), thunderer.

fulminante, *adj* **1.** fulminating; **2.** fulminant; sudden.

fulminar, *vt* **1.** to fulminate; to utter, thunder; **2.** to strike with lightning.

fumadero, *nm* smoking room.

fumador(a), *nm/f* smoker.

fumar, *vt/i* to smoke.

fumigación, *nf* fumigation; crop-dusting, cropspraying.

fumigar, *vt* to fumigate; to dust, spray.

función, *nf* **1.** function; functioning, operation; **2.** duties.

funcional, *adj* functional.

funcionamiento, *nm* functioning, operation; working, running.

funcionar, *vi* to function; to go, work, run.

funcionario(a), *nm/f* official, functionary; employee.

funda, *nf* case, cover, sheath; sleeve, jacket.

fundación, *nf* foundation.

fundado, *adj* firm, well-founded, justified.

fundador(a), *nm/f* founder.

fundamental, *adj* fundamental.

fundamentar, *vt* to lay the foundations of.

fundamento, *nm* **1.** foundation(s); **2.** basis; groundwork; grounds, reason.

fundar, *vt* to found; to institute, set up, establish.

fundición, *nf* **1.** fusing, fusion; smelting, founding; **2.** nm foundry, forge, smelting plant.

fundido, *adj* ruined, bankrupt.

fundir, *vt* to fuse (together); to join, unite.

fúnebre, *adj* funeral; mournful, lugubrious.

funeral, *adj* funeral.

funeraria, *nf* undertaker's, undertaker's establishment, funeral parlor.

funesto, *adj* ill-fated, unfortunate; baneful; fatal, disastrous.

fungicida, *nm* fungicide.

fungir, *vi* to act; to substitute, stand in.

furgón, *nm* wagon, van, truck.

furgoneta, *nf* van; transit van, pick-up truck.

furia, *nf* fury; rage, violence.

furibundo, *adj* furious; frenzied.

furioso, *adj* furious; violent; frantic, raging.

furor, *nm* fury, rage; frenzy; passion.

furtivo, *adj* furtive; clandestine; sly, stealthy.

fuselaje, *nm* fuselage.

fusible, *nm* fuse.

fusil, *nm* rifle, gun.

fusilamiento, *nm* **1.** shooting, execution; **2.** pinching, plagiarism; piracy, illegal copying.

fusilar, *vt* to shoot, execute; to kill.

fusilero, *nm* rifleman.

fusión, *nf* fusion; joining, uniting; merge; melting.

fusionar, *vt* to fuse; to merge; amalgamate.

fusta, *nf* long whip; riding whip.

fuste, *nm* **1.** wood, timber; wooden; **2.** shaft.

fustigar, *vt* **1.** to whip, lash; **2.** to upbraid, lash (with one's tongue).

fútil, *adj* trifling, trivial.

futileza, *nf* trifle, bagatelle.

futilidad, *nf* triviality, trifling nature, unimportance.

futuro, *adj* future.

G

G, g, *nf* (letter) G, g.

gabán, *nm* overcoat, topcoat; jacket.

gabarda, *nf* wild rose.

gabardina, *nf* gabardine; raincoat, mackintosh.

gabear, *vt* to climb.

gabela, *nf* tax, duty; burden.

gabinete, *nm* study, library; office; cabinet.

gaceta, *nf* gazette, official journal; newspaper.

gacetero(a), *nm/f* newswriter, journalist.

gacetilla, *nf* gossip column; section of local news, section of miscellaneous news items.

gacho, *adj* bent down, turned downward; downcurved; slouch hat.

gafa, nf grapple; clamp; glasses, spectacles; goggles.

gafar, vt to hook, claw, latch on to.

gafo, adj footsore, dog-tired; numb.

gago(a), adj stammering, stuttering.

gaguear, vi to stammer, stutter.

gaguera, nf stammer, stutter, speech defect.

gaita, nf flute, flageolet; hurdy-gurdy; bagpipe.

gaitero, adj gaudy, flashy.

gaje, nm emoluments; perquisite; reward, bonus.

gajo, nm branch, bough; small cluster, bunch.

galán, nm handsome fellow, attractive young man; ladies man; young gentleman, courtier.

galante, adj gallant; charming, attentive (to women); polite, urbane.

galantear, vt to court, woo; to flirt with.

galantería, nf gallantry; attentiveness (to women); politeness, urbanity.

galardón, nm reward, prize; award.

galardonado(a), nm/f prize-winner, award-winner.

galardonar, vt to reward, recompense.

galaxia, nf galaxy.

galera, nf 1. galley; 2. wagon; 3. hospital ward.

galería, nf gallery; passage, corridor.

galerna, nf violent north-west wind.

galgo, nm greyhound.

galimatías, nm rigmarole; gibberish, nonsense.

galón, nm 1. braid; stripe, chevron; 2. gallon.

galopar, vi to gallop; to break into a gallop.

galope, nm gallop.

galvanizado, adj galvanized.

galvanizar, vt to galvanize, electroplate.

gallardía, nf gracefulness, elegance; bravery; gallantry, dash; nobleness.

gallardo, adj graceful, elegant; fine, splendid; brave; gallant, dashing; noble.

gallego, adj Galician.

gallería, nf cockpit.

gallero, adj 1. fond of cockfighting; 2. nm man in charge of gamecocks (or cockfighting); cockfighting enthusiast.

galleta, nf 1. biscuit; cracker; cookie; wafer; 2. slap.

galletero, nm 1. biscuit barrel, biscuit tin; 2. quick-tempered person; argumentative sort, brawler.

gallina, nf 1. hen, fowl; 2. coward.

gallinería, nf 1. flock of hens; 2. poultry shop; chicken market; 3. cowardice.

gallinero, nm 1. henhouse, coop; poultry basket; 2. chicken farmer; poulterer, poultry dealer.

gallo, nm 1. cock, cockerel, rooster; 2. boss; expert, master.

gama, nf 1. scale; range, gamut; 2. gamma; 3. doe (of fallow deer).

gambado, adj knock-kneed.

gamo, nm buck (of fallow deer).

gamuza, nf 1. chamois; 2. chamois leather.

gana, nf desire, wish; appetite; inclination, longing for.

ganadería, nf 1. cattle raising, stockbreeding; ranching; 2. stock farm; cattle ranch; 3. livestock; strain, breed, race (of cattle).

ganadero, adj stockbreeder, rancher; cattle dealer.

ganado, nm stock, livestock; cattle.

ganador, adj winner, victorious.

ganancia, nf gain; increase; earnings; profits, winnings.

ganar, vt to gain; to get, acquire, obtain; to earn; to profit; to win.

gancho, nm hook; hanger; stump.

gandido, adj greedy.

gandinga, nf 1. thick stew; 2. sloth.

gandul, adj idle, lazy, slack; good-for-nothing.

ganga, nf bargain.

ganglio, nm ganglion; swelling.

gangosear, vi to talk through one's nose, whine.

gangoso, adj twanging.

gangrena, nf gangrene.

gangrenar, vt 1. to make gangrenous, cause gangrene in; 2. to infect, destroy.

gangrenoso, adj gangrenous,

gán(g)ster, nm gangster, gunman.

gan(g)sterismo, nm gangsterism.

ganguear, vi to talk with a nasal accent, speak with a twang.

gansa, nf 1. goose; 2. silly girl.

ganso, nm 1. goose, gander; 2. idiot, dimwit, dolt.

ganzúa, nf picklock, skeleton key.

gañán, nm farmhand, laborer.

gañir, vi to yelp, howl; to croak, to wheeze.

garabatear, vt to scribble, scrawl.

garabato, nm 1. hook; grapnel; grappling iron; 2. scribble, scrawl.

garaje, nm garage.

garajista, nm garage owner; garage man, garage attendant.

garante, adj 1. guaranteeing, responsible; 2. nm/f guarantor; surety.

garantía, nf guarantee: pledge, security.

garantizado, adj guaranteed; genuine, authentic.

garantizar, vt to guarantee, warrant; to vouch for.

garapiña, nf 1. sugar icing, sugar coating; 2. iced pineapple drink.

garapiñar, vt to freeze; to clot; to ice, coat with sugar.

garbanzo, nm chickpea.

garceta, nf egret.

gardenia, nf gardenia.

garfio, nm hook; gaff; grapple, grappling iron, claw.

garganta, nf 1. throat, gullet; neck; 2. gorge, ravine; narrow pass.

gargantear, vi to warble, quaver, trill.

gargantilla, nf necklace.

gárgara, nf gargle, gargling.

gargarismo, nm gargling solution.

garita, nf cabin, hut, box; sentry box; cab.

garitero(a), nm/f keeper of a gaming house; gambler.

garito, nm gaming house, gambling-den.

garnacha, nf 1. (Jur) gown, robe; 2. judge; 3. tortilla with filling.

garra, nf claw; talon; paw.

garrafa, nf carafe; cylinder.

garrafal, adj enormous, terrific; monumental, terrible.

garrafón, nm demijohn.

garrapata, nf tick.

garrapatear, vi to scribble, scrawl.

garrido, adj 1. neat, elegant, smart; 2. handsome; pretty.

garrocha, nf goad; spear; vaulting pole.

garrotazo, nm blow with a stick (or club).

garrote, nm 1. stick, club, cudgel; 2. tourniquet.

garrotero, adj stingy.

garrotillo, nm croup; summer hail.

garrudo, adj tough, muscular.

garúa, nf drizzle, row, din.

garuar, vi to drizzle.

garza, nf heron.

gas, nm gas; fumes.

gasa, nf gauze; lint; crepe.

gaseado, adj carbonated, aerated.

gasear, vt to gas, kill with gas.

gaseosa, nf mineral water; fizz, fizzy drink.

gaseoso, adj gaseous; carbonated; gassy.

gasificación, nf 1. gasification; 2. supply of piped gas.
gasoducto, nm gas pipeline.
gasolina, nf gasoline.
gasolinera, nf 1. motorboat; 2. gas station.
gastado, adj 1. spent; used up; 2. worn out; shabby, threadbare.
gastador, adj extravagant, lavish; wasteful.
gastar, vt 1. to spend; 2. to use up, consume.
gasto, nm 1. spending, expenditure; 2. cost.
gástrico, adj gastric.
gastritis, nf gastritis.
gastronomía, nf gastronomy.
gastronómico, adj gastronomic.
gastrónomo(a), nm/f gastronome, gourmet.
gatear, vt 1. to scratch, claw; 2. to pinch, steal; 3. to creep, crawl, go on all fours.
gatera, nf 1. cat-lover; 2. cat hole; catflap.
gatería, nf cats, collection of cats.
gatillo, nm trigger; dental forceps; clamp.
gato, nm cat, tomcat.
gauchear, vi to live as a gaucho.
gaucho, nm/f good horseman.
gaveta, nf drawer, till; locker.
gavilán, nm sparrowhawk.
gaviota, nf seagull, gull.
gayo, adj 1. merry, gay; 2. bright, showy.
gaza, nf loop.
gazapa, nf fib, lie.
gazapera, nf 1. rabbit hole, warren; 2. den of thieves.
gazapo, nm 1. young rabbit; 2. sly fellow; cat burglar; liar; 3. blunder, blooper.
gaznatada, nf smack, slap.
gaznate, nm 1. gullet; windpipe, throttle; 2. fritter.
gazpacho, nm gazpacho (Andalusian cold soup).
gelatina, nf gelatin(e), jelly.
gelatinoso, adj gelatinous.
gema, nf gem, jewel.
gemelo, adj twin.
gemido, nm groan, moan; wail, howl.
gemidor, adj groaning, moaning; wailing, howling.
gemir, vi to groan, moan; to wail, howl; to whine.
gen, nm gene.
genciana, nf gentian.
gendarme, nm policeman, gendarme.
gene, nm gene.
genealogía, nf genealogy; family tree; pedigree.
genealógico, adj genealogical.
generación, nf 1. generation; 2. progeny, offspring; succession.
generador, adj 1. generating; 2. nm generator.
general, adj 1. general; wide; common, prevailing, rife; 2. nm military rank.
generalización, nf generalization.
generalizar, vt to generalize; to make more widely known, bring into general use.
generar, vt to generate.
genérico, adj generic.
género, nm 1. class, kind, type, sort; 2. genus; 3. genre.
generosidad, nf generosity; nobility, magnanimity.
generoso, adj generous; noble, magnanimous.
génesis, nf 1. genesis; 2. nm Genesis (First book of the Bible)
genética, nf genetics.
genético, adj genetic.
genial, adj 1. inspired, brilliant, of genius; 2. pleasant, cheerful, genial; cordial, affable.
genio, nm 1. disposition, nature, character; 2. bad temper.
genital, adj genital.

genitivo, adj generative, reproductive.
genocida, nm/f person accused (or guilty) of genocide.
genocidio, nm genocide.
gente, nf people, folk, race, nation.
gentil, adj elegant, graceful, attractive; charming; courteous.
gentileza, nf elegance, gracefulness; charm; courtesy.
gentío, nm crowd, throng; lots of people.
genuino, adj genuine; real, pure, true.
geofísica, nf geophysics.
geografía, nf geography.
geología, nf geology.
geólogo(a), nm/f geologist.
geometría, nf geometry.
geométrico, adj geometric(al).
geranio, nm geranium.
gerencia, nf 1. management; 2. managership, post of manager.
gerente, nm/f manager, director; executive.
geriatría, nf geriatrics.
geriátrico(a), adj, nm/f geriatric.
germen, nm germ.
germicida, adj 1. germicidal; 2. nm germicide, germ killer.
germinación, nf germination.
germinar, vi to germinate; to sprout, shoot.
gerundio, nm gerund.
gesta, nf heroic deed, epic achievement.
gestación, nf gestation.
gestante, adj pregnant woman, expectant mother.
gestar, vt to gestate; to prepare, hatch.
gesticulación, nf gesticulation.
gesticular, vi to gesticulate, gesture.
gestión, nf 1. management, conduct; 2. negotiation.
gestionar, vt 1. to manage, conduct; 2. to negotiate; 3. to try to arrange, strive to bring about, work towards.
gesto, nm face; expression on one's face.
gestora, nf committee of management.
giba, nf hump; hunchback.
gibado, adj with a hump, hunchbacked.
gibar, vt to bother, annoy.
gigante, adj giant, gigantic.
gigantesco, adj gigantic, giant.
gil, adj stupid, silly.
gilar, vt to watch, keep tabs on.
gimnasia, nf gymnastics; physical training.
gimnasio, nm gymnasium, gym.
gimnasta, nm/f gymnast.
gimotear, vi to whine, whimper; to wail.
gimoteo, nm whine, whining; whimpering.
ginebra, nf gin.
ginecología, nf gynecology.
ginecólogo(a), nm/f gynecologist.
gira, nf tour; trip.
giralda, nf weathercock.
girar, vt 1. to turn, turn round, rotate; to twist; to spin; 2. to swing, swivel.
girasol, nm sunflower.
giratorio, adj revolving, rotatory; gyratory.
giro, nm 1. turn; revolution, rotation; gyration; 2. turn of phrase, expression; 3. commercial draft.
gitana, nf Gypsy; fortuneteller.
gitanear, vt to wheedle, cajole.
gitanería, nf band of Gypsies.
gitano, adj 1. Gypsy; 2. wheedling, cajoling; smooth, flattering.
glacial, adj 1. glacial; icy, bitter, freezing; 2. cold, stony.
glaciar, nm glacier.

gladiador, *nm* gladiator.

gladíolo, *nm* gladiolus.

glándula, *nf* gland.

glandular, *adj* glandular.

glaseado, *adj* glazed, glossy; glacé.

glasear, *vt* to glaze; to glacé, glaze.

glaucoma, *nm* glaucoma.

glicerina, *nf* glycerin(e).

glicina, *nf* wisteria.

global, *adj* global; total, complete, comprehensive.

globalizar, *vt* 1. to encompass, include; 2. to make universal, extend world-wide.

globo, *nm* 1. globe, sphere; 2. balloon.

globular, *adj* globular, spherical.

glóbulo, *nm* globule, red corpuscle; blood cell.

gloria, *nf* glory; heaven; delight.

gloriarse, *vr* to boast of something, be proud of something; to glory in something, rejoice in something

glorieta, *nf* arbor; traffic circle.

glorificar, *vt* to glorify, extol, praise.

glorioso, *adj* glorious.

glosa, *nf* gloss; comment, note, annotation; telling off.

glosar, *vt* to gloss; to comment on, annotate.

glosario, *nm* glossary.

glotis, *nf* glottis.

glotón, *adj* gluttonous, greedy.

glotonear, *vi* to be greedy, be gluttonous.

glotonería, *nf* gluttony, greediness.

gobernación, *nf* governing, government.

gobernador, *adj* 1. governing, ruling; 2. *nm/f* governor, ruler; civil governor.

gobernar, *vt* to govern, rule, to guide, direct; to control, manage, run.

gobierno, *nm* government.

gol, *nm* goal.

golear, *vt* to score a goal against.

goleta, *nf* schooner.

golf, *nm* golf; golf-course.

golfear, *vi* to loaf, idle; to live like a street urchin.

golfería, *nf* loafers, street urchins.

golfo, *nm* gulf, open sea.

golondrina, *nf* swallow.

golosina, *nf* tidbit, delicacy, dainty; sweet.

goloso, *adj* 1. sweet-toothed, fond of dainties; 2. greedy.

golpe, *nm* blow; hit, punch, knock; smack.

golpeador, *nm* door knocker.

golpear, *vt* to strike, knock, hit; to beat.

golpiza, *nf* bash, bashing, beating-up.

goma, *nf* gum; rubber.

gomal, *nm* rubber plantation.

gomero, *adj* 1. gum; rubber; 2. *nm* gum-tree; rubber tree; 3. rubber planter, rubber producer.

gomina, *nf* haircream; (hair) gel.

gomita, *nf* rubber band, elastic band.

gónada, *nf* gonad.

góndola, *nf* gondola; goods wagon, freight truck.

gondolero, *nf* gondolier.

gonorrea, *nf* gonorrhea.

gorda, *nf* fat woman; darling.

gordo, *adj* fat; stout, plump; big; thick, coarse.

gordura, *nf* fat, fatness; corpulence, stoutness.

gorgojo, *nm* grub; weevil.

gorgotear, *vi* to gurgle.

gorgoteo, *nm* gurgle.

gorila, *nm* 1. gorilla; 2. henchman, bodyguard; strong-arm man.

gorjear, *vi* to chirp, twitter, trill.

gorjeo, *nm* chirping, twittering, trilling; crowing, gurgling.

gorra, *nf* 1. cap; bonnet; 2. bearskin, busby.

gorrero(a), *nm/f* cap maker.

gorrino(a), *nm/f* small pig, sucking pig.

gorrión, *nm* sparrow.

gota, *nf* a drop.

goteado, *adj* speckled, spotted.

gotear, *vi* to drip, dribble; to trickle; to leak.

goteo, *nm* dripping, dribbling; trickle, trickling; leak; drip.

gotera, *nf* drip; trickle; leak.

gotero, *nm* drip, drip-feed; dropper.

gótico, *adj* Gothic; noble, illustrious.

gozar, *vt* to enjoy; have a good time.

gozo, *nm* enjoyment, pleasure; delight; joy.

gozoso, *adj* glad, joyful, delighted.

grabación, *nf* recording.

grabado, *adj* recorded.

grabador, *nm/f* 1. tape-recorder; 2. engraver.

grabadora, *nf* 1. graver, cutting tool; 2. recorder; 3. recording company.

grabar, *vt* 1. to engrave; to etch; 2. to record.

gracejo, *nm* wit; charm, gracefulness.

gracia, *nf* 1. grace, gracefulness; attractiveness; 2. favor, kindness.

grácil, *adj* graceful; slender; small, delicate.

gracioso, *adj* 1. graceful; pleasing, elegant; 2. funny, amusing; witty.

gradación, *nf* gradation; graded series.

gradar, *vt* to harrow; to hoe.

gradería, *nf* 1. steps; 2. terrace, tiers; rows.

grado, *nm* 1. step; 2. degree; stage, step; measure; rate.

graduación, *nf* 1. grading; graduation; 2. rating.

graduado(a), *nm/f* graduate.

gradual, *adj* gradual.

graduar, *vt* 1. to grade, classify to appraise; to gauge, measure; to calibrate; to graduate; 2. to confer a degree on; to confer a rank on.

gráfica, *nf* graph; diagram.

gráfico, *adj* 1. graphic; pictorial, illustrated; 2. vivid, lively.

grafito, *nm* graphite, black lead.

gragea, *nf* small colored sweets; pill.

grajear, *vi* to caw; to gurgle.

grama, *nf* grass; lawn.

gramatical, *nf* grammar.

gramático, *adj* grammatical; 2. *nm/f* grammarian.

gramo, *nm* gram.

granada, *nf* 1. pomegranate; 2. shell; grenade.

granadero, *nm* grenadier; riot police.

granar, *vi* to seed, run to seed.

grande, *adj* 1. big, large; tall; 2. great; 3. grand, grandiose, impressive.

grandeza, *nf* 1. bigness: size, magnitude; 2. greatness; 3. grandeur, magnificence.

grandioso, *adj* grand, impressive, magnificent; grandiose.

granear, *vt* to sow.

granel, *nm* heap of corn; bulk commodity.

granero, *nm* granary, barn; corn-producing area.

granete, *nm* punch.

granito, *nm* 1. granite; 2. small grain; granule; pimple.

granizada, *nf* 1. hail, hailstorm; 2. shower, volley; vast number.

granizado, *nm* iced drink.

granizar, *vi* to hail; to rain, shower.

granizo, *nm* hail.

granja, *nf* farm.

granjear, *vt* to gain, earn; to win.

grano, *nm* grain; seed; berry.

granoso, *adj* granular; granulated; grainy.

granulación, *nf* granulation.

granular, *adj* 1. granular; 2. *vt* to granulate.

gránulo, *nm* granule.

grapa, *nf* 1. staple; clip, fastener; 2. grape liquor, grappa.

grapadora, *nf* stapler, stapling machine.

grapar, *vt* to staple.

grasa, *nf* grease; fat.

grasiento, *adj* greasy, oily; slippery; filthy.

grasoso, *adj* fatty; greasy; oily.

gratificación, *nf* reward, recompense; tip; gratuity.

gratificador, *adj* gratifying; pleasurable, satisfying.

gratificar, *vt* 1. to reward, recompense; to tip, give a gratuity to; to give a bonus to; 2. to gratify; to give pleasure to, satisfy.

gratinado, *adj* au gratin, with cheese.

gratis, *adv* free, for nothing.

gratitud, *nf* gratitude.

grato, *adj* pleasing, pleasant; agreeable; welcome, gratifying.

grava, *nf* gravel; crushed stone.

gravamen, *nm* burden, obligation; lien, encumbrance; tax.

gravar, *vt* to burden, encumber, to place a lien upon, to assess for tax.

grave, *adj* 1. heavy, weighty; 2. grave, serious; critical; important.

gravedad, *nf* gravity; seriousness.

gravitación, *nf* gravitation.

gravitar, *vi* 1. to gravitate (towards); 2. to rest on; to bear down on.

gravoso, *adj* 1. burdensome, oppressive, onerous; 2. costly, expensive.

graznar, *vi* to squawk; to caw, croak; to cackle.

graznido, *nm* squawk; caw, croak; cackle; quack.

gregario, *adj* 1. gregarious; 2. servile, slavish.

gremial, *adj* 1. guild; 2. trade union, trades union.

gremio, *nm* 1. guild, corporation, company; 2. union.

greña, *nf* shock of hair, mat of hair, matted hair.

grey, *nf* flock, congregation.

grieta, *nf* fissure, crack; chink.

grifo, *adj* 1. person with kinky or curly hair; 2. *nm* tap, faucet; cock; fire hydrant.

grillo(a), *nm/f* cricket.

grillete, *nm* fetter, shackle.

grima, *nf* loathing, disgust; aversion, reluctance.

gripar, *vi* to seize up.

gripe, *nf* influenza, flu.

gris, *nm* grey.

grisáceo, *adj* greyish.

grita, *nf* uproar, hubbub; shouting; catcalls, booing.

gritadera, *nf* loud shouting, clamour.

gritar, *vti* to shout, yell; to scream, shriek, cry out.

grito, *nm* shout, yell; scream, shriek, cry.

gritón, *adj* loud-mouthed; screaming, shouting.

groncho, *nm* worker.

grosella, *nf* currant; gooseberry.

grosellero, *nm* currant bush.

grosería, *nf* rudeness, discourtesy; coarseness, crudeness, vulgarity.

grosor, *nm* thickness.

grosura, *nf* fat, suet.

grotesca, *nf* sans serif.

grotesco, *adj* grotesque; bizarre, absurd.

grúa, *nf* crane; derrick; tow-truck, towing vehicle.

gruesa, *nf* gross, twelve dozen.

grueso, *adj* thick; bulky, stout, massive, solid.

gruñido, *nm* grunt, growl; snarl.

gruñir, *vi* to grunt, growl; to snarl.

gruñón, *adj* grumpy, grumbling.

grupa, *nf* hindquarters, rump (of horse).

grupo, *nm* group; cluster, clump.

gruta, *nf* cavern, grotto.

guacarnaco, *adj* silly, stupid.

guadaña, *nf* scythe.

guadañar, *vt* to scythe, mow.

guadañero, *nm* mower.

guagua, *adj* 1. small, little; 2. baby; 3. trifle, small thing; 4. *nf* bus.

guajiro(a), *nm/f* countryman; outsider; (Cuba) peasant.

guanábana, *nm* custard apple; fool.

guanajada, *nf* silly thing, foolish act.

guanajo(a), *nm/f* 1. turkey; 2. fool, idiot.

guanear, *vt* to fertilize with guano.

guanera, *nf* guano deposit.

guano, *nm* guano; artificial manure: dung, manure; palm tree; palm leaf.

guante, *nm* glove.

guantelete, *nm* gauntlet.

guantera, *nf* glove compartment.

guapear, *vi* 1. dress flashily; 2. to bluster, swagger.

guapo(a), *adj* 1. good-looking; pretty, attractive; handsome; 2. smart, elegant, well dressed; 3. bold, dashing; brave.

guara, *nf* lot, heap.

guaracha, *nf* popular song; folk dance.

guarachear, *vi* to revel; to let one's hair down.

guarapo, *nm* sugar-cane liquor; palm wine; watered-down drink.

guarda, *nm/f* 1. guard; keeper, custodian; 2. safekeeping; custody.

guardacostas, *nm* coastguard vessel, revenue cutter.

guardaespaldas, *nm* bodyguard, henchman; minder.

guardafango, *nm* fender.

guardar, *vt* to guard; to keep, to watch over, protect, take care of, keep safe.

guardería, *nf* day nursery, day-care center.

guardia, *nf* custody, care; defense, protection.

guardián(ana), *nm/f* guardian, custodian, keeper; warden; watchman.

guardilla, *nf* attic, garret; attic room,

guarecer, *vt* to protect, give shelter to, take in.

guargüero, *nm* throat, throttle.

guarida, *nf* den, lair, hideout; refuge, shelter, hideout.

guarnecer, *vt* to equip, provide; to adorn, embellish.

guarnecido, *nm* plaster, plastering; upholstery.

guarnición, *nf* 1. equipment, provision; fitting; adorning, embellishing; garnishing; 2. adornment; trimming, edging, binding.

guata, *nf* raw cotton; padding; twine, cord.

guataca, *nf* small hoe; wooden shovel.

guateque, *nm* party, celebration, binge.

guayaba, *nf* guava.

guayabera, *nf* loose shirt with large pockets.

guayabo, *nm* guava tree.

guayar, *vt* to grate.

guayo, *nm* grater; bad street band.

gubernamental, *adj* governmental.

guedeja, *nf* long hair, lock; mane.

güero, *adj* blond(e), fair; light-skinned.

guerra, *nf* war; warfare; struggle, fight, conflict.

guerrear, *vi* to wage war, fight; to put up a fight.

guerrera, *nf* trench coat; combat jacket; military jacket.

guerrero, *adj* 1. fighting; war; 2. *nm* warrior.

guerrilla, *nf* 1. guerrilla band; group of partisans; guerrilla forces; 2. guerrilla warfare.

guerrillero(a), *nm/f* guerrilla; partisan; irregular.

guía, nf 1. guidance, guiding; 2. guidebook; handbook; directory; 3. nm/f guide; leader; adviser.

guiar, vt to guide; to lead, direct; to manage; to advise.

guijarral, nm stony place; shingle, pebbles, pebbly part.

guijarro, nm pebble; cobble, cobblestone.

guillotina, nf guillotine; paper-cutter; sash window.

guillotinar, vt to guillotine.

guindar, vt to hoist, hang up (high); string up.

guindilla, nf hot pepper, red chili pepper.

guiñar, vt to wink; to blink.

guiño, nm wink; grimace, wry face.

guiñol, nm art of the puppeteer, puppet theater.

guión, nm 1. leader; 2. summary, outline; explanatory text; script.

guionista, nm/f scriptwriter; writer of subtitles.

guirnaldo, nm garland; funeral wreath.

guisador(a), nm/f cook.

guisante, nm pea.

guisar, vt 1. to prepare; to arrange. 2. to cook; to stew.

guiso, nm cooked dish; stew.

guitarra, nf guitar.

guitarrista, nm/f guitarist.

gula, nf greed, gluttony.

guloso, adj greedy, gluttonous.

gusanera, nf nest of maggots; breeding ground for maggots.

gusanillo, nm small maggot, small worm.

gusano, nm maggot, grub, worm; caterpillar; earthworm.

gustado, adj esteemed, well-liked, popular.

gustar, vt 1. to taste, try, sample; 2. vi to please, be pleasing.

gustazo, nm great pleasure.

gustillo, nm suggestion, touch, tang; aftertaste.

gusto, nm taste; flavor; pleasure.

gustoso, adj tasty, savory, nice.

gutural, adj guttural; throaty.

H

H, h, nf (letter) H, h.

haba, nf 1. bean; 2. tumor.

habanero, adj of Havana.

habano, adj Havana cigar.

habeas corpus, nm habeas corpus.

haber, vt 1. to have, possess; 2. to get; to catch, lay hands on.

haberse, vr to behave, comport oneself.

habichuela, nf kidney bean.

hábil, adj clever; skillful; able, capable, proficient.

habilidad, nf cleverness; skill; ability, proficiency.

habilitación, nf 1. qualification, entitlement; 2. equipment, fitting out.

habilitar, vt 1. to qualify, entitle; to enable, to empower, authorize; 2. to equip, fit out, set up.

habitación, nf habitation; dwelling, abode.

habitado, adj inhabited; lived-in.

habitante, nm/f inhabitant; resident; occupant, tenant.

habitar, vt to inhabit, live in, dwell in.

hábitat, nm habitat.

hábito, nm 1. habit, custom; 2. monastic habit.

habituar, vt to accustom.

habla, nf 1. speech; 2. language.

habladera, nf talking, noise of talking.

hablador, adj 1. talkative; chatty; voluble; 2. gossipy, given to gossip.

hablante, adj 1. speaking; 2. nm/f speaker.

hablar, vt to speak, talk.

hacedor(a), nm/f maker.

hacendado, adj 1. landed, property-owning; 2. nm land-owner; gentleman farmer; rancher.

hacendoso, adj industrious, hard-working; busy, bustling.

hacer, vt to make, create; to do, to cause.

hacerse, vr to become, grow, turn into.

hacia, prep towards, in the direction of; about, near.

hacienda, nf property; country estate, large farm.

hacinado, adj crowded.

hacinar, vt to pile (up), heap (up); to stack, to accumulate.

hacha, nf axe; chopper; hatchet.

hachador, nm woodman, lumberjack.

hachazo, nm axe blow, stroke with an axe; hack, cut.

hache, nf the (name of the) letter h.

hachear, vt 1. to hew, cut; 2. vi to wield an axe.

hachero, nm woodman, lumberjack; sapper.

hachís, nm hashish.

hada, nf fairy; good fairy.

hado, nm fate, destiny.

halagar, vt 1. to show affection to, make up to; 2. to please, gratify; to allure.

halago, nm pleasure, delight; gratification; allurement.

halagüeño, adj pleasing, gratifying; alluring, attractive.

halcón, nm falcon, hawk.

halda, nf 1. skirt; 2. sackcloth, coarse wrapping material.

hálito, nm breath; vapor, exhalation.

halógeno, adj halogenous, halogen.

hallador(a), nm/f finder.

hallar, vt to find; to discover; to locate.

hallazgo, nm finding, discovery.

hamaca, nf 1. hammock; 2. swing; rocking chair.

hamacar, vt to rock, swing.

hambre, nf hunger; famine; starvation.

hambrear, vt to starve.

hambriento, adj starving, hungry, famished.

hambruna, nf ravenous hunger.

hamburguesa, nf hamburger.

hampa, nf underworld, low life, criminal classes.

hampón, nm tough, rowdy, thug.

hangar, nm hangar.

haragán, adj idle, lazy, good-for-nothing.

haraganear, vi to idle, waste one's time; to lounge about, loaf around.

haraganería, nf idleness, laziness.

harapiento, adj ragged, tattered, in rags.

harapo, nm rag, tatter.

harén, nm harem.

harina, nf flour, meal; powder.

harinear, vi to drizzle.

harinero, nm flour merchant.

harpillera, nf sacking, sackcloth.

hartar, vt to satiate, surfeit, glut; to weary, get tired of.

harto, adj full (of), satiated; glutted (with).

hartón, adj greedy, gluttonous.

hasta, adv 1. even; 2. prep as far as; up to, down to; 3. till, until; as late as.

hastiar, vt to weary, bore; to sicken, disgust.

hastío, *nm* weariness; boredom; disgust, loathing.
hato, *nm* 1. clothes, set of clothing; 2. provisions; 3. flock, herd; group, crowd.
hazaña, *nf* feat, exploit, deed, achievement.
hebilla, *nf* buckle, clasp.
hebra, *nf* thread; piece of thread, length of thread.
hebreo, *adj* Hebrew; Israeli.
hectárea, *nf* hectare (= 2.471 acres).
hechicera, *nf* sorceress, enchantress, witch.
hechicero, *adj* 1. magic(al); bewitching, enchanting; 2. *nm* wizard, sorcerer, enchanter.
hechizar, *vt* 1. to bewitch, cast a spell on; 2. charm, enchant, fascinate; to bedevil.
hechizo, *adj* 1. artificial, false, fake; 2. *nm* magic witchcraft.
hechura, *nf* 1. making, creation; 2. product.
heder, *vi* 1. to stink, smell, reek (of); 2. to annoy, be unbearable.
hedor, *nm* stink, stench, smell.
hegemonía, *nf* hegemony.
helada, *nf* frost; freeze, freeze-up.
heladera, *nf* refrigerator, icebox.
heladería, *nf* ice-cream stall, ice-cream parlor.
helado, *adj* 1. frozen; freezing, icy; 2. *nm* ice cream
helar, *vt* to freeze; to ice (up).
helénico, *adj* Hellenic, Greek.
hélice, *nf* 1. spiral; helix; 2. propeller, airscrew.
helicóptero, *nm* helicopter.
helio, *nm* helium.
hematología, *nf* hematology.
hematoma, *nm* bruise.
hembra, *nf* female.
hemiciclo, *nm* semicircular theater; chamber; floor.
hemisferio, *nm* hemisphere.
hemofilia, *nf* hemophilia.
hemofílico(a), *adj* hemophiliac.
hemoglobina, *nf* hemoglobin.
hemorragia, *nf* hemorrhage; bleeding, loss or blood.
hemorroides, *nf* hemorrhoids, piles.
henchir, *vt* to fill (up), stuff, cram (with).
henchirse, *vr* to swell; to stuff oneself with food.
hendedura, *nf* crack, fissure, crevice; cleft, split.
hender, *vt* to crack; to cleave, split, slit.
hendija, *nf* crack, crevice.
heno, *nm* hay.
hepático, *adj* hepatic, liver.
hepatitis, *nf* hepatitis.
heráldico, *adj* heraldic.
heraldo, *nm* herald.
herbáceo, *adj* herbaceous.
herbazal, *nm* grassland, pasture.
herbívoro, *adj* herbivorous.
heredad, *nf* landed property; country estate, farm.
heredar, *vt* to inherit; to be heir to.
heredera, *nf* heiress.
heredero, *nm* heir.
hereditario, *adj* hereditary.
hereje, *adj* 1. disrespectful; 2. excessive.
herejía, *nf* heresy.
herencia, *nf* 1. inheritance, estate, legacy; heritage; 2. heredity.
herida, *nf* 1. wound, injury; 2. insult, outrage.
herido, *adj* 1. injured; hurt; wounded; 2. offended.
herir, *vt* to injure, hurt; to wound.
hermana, *nf* sister.
hermanar, *vt* to match, put together; to join.
hermanastra, *nf* stepsister.
hermanastro, *nm* stepbrother.

hermandad, *nf* 1. brotherhood; close relationship, intimacy; 2. fraternity; sisterhood.
hermano, *nm* brother.
hermético, *adj* hermetic; airtight, watertight.
hermetismo, *nm* tight secrecy, close secrecy; silence, reserve; hermeticism.
hermetizar, *vt* to seal off, close off.
hermosear, *vt* to beautify, embellish, adorn.
hermoso, *adj* beautiful, lovely; fine, splendid.
hermosura, *nf* beauty, loveliness; splendor; lavishness; handsomeness.
héroe, *nm* hero.
heroicidad, *nf* heroism; heroic deed.
heroico, *adj* heroic.
heroína, *nf* 1. heroine; 2. (drug) heroin.
heroísmo, *nm* heroism.
herpes, *nm* herpes, shingles.
herrador, *nm* farrier, blacksmith.
herradura, *nf* horseshoe.
herramienta, *nf* tool; implement, appliance.
herranza, *nf* (horses) branding.
herrar, *vt* (horses) to shoe; to brand; to bind with iron.
herrería, *nf* smithy, forge, blacksmith's (shop).
herrero, *nm* blacksmith, smith.
hervidero, *nm* boiling; bubbling, seething.
hervidor, *nm* kettle; boiler.
hervir, *vt* to boil; to cook.
hervor, *nm* boiling; seething.
heterogéneo, *adj* heterogeneous.
hexagonal, *adj* hexagonal.
hexágono, *nm* hexagon.
hez, *nf* sediment, dregs; slops; feces.
hibernación, *nf* hibernation; to be dormant.
hibernar, *vi* to hibernate.
hibridizar, *vt* to hybridize; to lend a mixed appearance to.
híbrido(a), *adj, nm/f* hybrid.
hidalgo, *adj* noble; illustrious.
hidalguía, *nf* nobility; gentlemanliness, honorableness; generosity.
hidratante, *adj* moisturizing cream.
hidratar, *vt* to hydrate; to moisturize.
hidráulico, *adj* hydraulic, water, water power, hydraulic power.
hidroavión, *nm* seaplane, flying boat.
hidrocarburo, *nm* hydrocarbon.
hidroeléctrico, *adj* hydroelectric.
hidrofobia, *nf* hydrophobia; rabies.
hidrógeno, *nm* hydrogen.
hidroplano, *nm* hydroplane.
hidroterapia, *nf* hydrotherapy.
hiedra, *nf* ivy.
hiel, *nf* gall, bile.
hielera, *nf* ice tray; refrigerator.
hielo, *nm* ice.
hiena, *nf* hyena.
hierba, *nf* grass.
hierro, *nm* iron.
hígado, *nm* liver.
higiene, *nf* hygiene.
higiénico, *adj* hygienic; sanitary.
higienizar, *vt* to clean up, cleanse.
higo, *nm* fig.
higuera, *nf* fig tree.
hija, *nf* daughter; child.
hijastra, *nf* stepdaughter.
hijastro, *nm* stepson.
hijo, *nm* son; child.
hijuela, *nf* little girl; small daughter.

hijuelo, *nm* little boy; small son; small children.

hilacha, *nf* loose thread, hanging thread; shred; fiber, filament.

hilada, *nf* row, line; course.

hilador, *nm* spinner.

hilar, *vt* 1. to spin; 2. to reason, infer.

hilarante, *adj* hilarious; merry, mirthful.

hilaridad, *nf* hilarity; merriment, mirth.

hilazón, *nf* connection.

hilera, *nf* row, line; string.

hilo, *nm* thread, yarn; fiber, filament.

hilván, *nm* tacking, basting; basting thread.

hilvanar, *vt* to tack, baste.

himnario, *nm* hymnal, hymnbook.

himno, *nm* hymn.

hincada, *nf* 1. thrust; 2. genuflection; 3. sharp pain, stabbing pain.

hincadura, *nf* thrust, thrusting, driving.

hincapié, *nm* to make a stand, take a firm stand; to insist on.

hincar, *vt* to thrust (in), drive (in), push (in).

hincarse, *vr* to kneel, kneel down.

hinchado, *adj* 1. swollen; 2. pompous.

hinchador, *nm* tire inflator.

hinchar, *vt* to swell; to distend, enlarge.

hincharse, *vr* to swell (up); to get distended.

hinchazón, *nf* 1. swelling; bump, lump; 2. arrogance, vanity, conceit.

hipar, *vi* to hiccup.

hiperactividad, *nf* hyperactivity.

hiperactivo, *adj* hyperactive.

hipermetropía, *nf* long-sight, long-sightedness.

hipersensibilidad, *nf* hypersensitivity; over-sensitiveness, touchiness.

hipertensión, *nf* hypertension; high blood pressure.

hípico, *adj* horse; equine.

hipismo, *nm* horse-racing.

hipnosis, *nf* hypnosis.

hipnotismo, *nm* hypnotism.

hipnotizar, *vt* to hypnotize, mesmerize.

hipo, *nm* hiccup(s).

hipocondria, *nf* hypochondria.

hipocondríaco, *adj* hypochondriac(al).

hipocresía, *nf* hypocrisy.

hipócrita, *adj* hypocritical.

hipodérmico, *adj* hypodermic.

hipódromo, *nm* racetrack, racecourse; hippodrome.

hipopótamo, *nm* hippopotamus.

hipoteca, *nf* mortgage.

hipotecar, *vt* to mortgage.

hipotenusa, *nf* hypotenuse.

hipótesis, *nf* hypothesis; supposition; theory, idea.

hipotético, *adj* hypothetic(al).

hirviente, *adj* boiling, seething.

hisopear, *vt* to sprinkle with holy water, asperse.

hisopo, *nm* (Rel) sprinkler; (Bot) aspergillum.

hispánico, *adj* Hispanic, Spanish.

hispanidad, *nf* Spanishness; Spanish quality, Spanish characteristics.

hispanizar, *vt* to hispanicize.

hispano, *adj* Spanish, Hispanic.

Hispanoamerica, *nf* Spanish America, Latin America.

histerectomía, *nf* hysterectomy.

histeria, *nf* hysteria.

histérico, *adj* hysterical.

histerismo, *nm* hysteria; hysterics.

historia, *nf* 1. story; tale; 2. history.

historiador(a), *nm/f* historian; chronicler, recorder.

historiar, *vt* 1. to tell the story of; to write the history of; to record, chronicle, write up; 2. to paint, depict.

histórico, *adj* historical; historic.

historieta, *nf* short story, tale; anecdote.

histrión, *nm* actor, player; playactor; buffoon.

histriónico, *adj* histrionic.

hito, *nm* 1. boundary post, boundary mark; 2. landmark, milestone.

hocicar, *vt* (pigs) to root among; (Pers) to nuzzle.

hocico, *nm* 1. snout, muzzle, nose; 2. angry face, grimace.

hogar, *nm* 1. fireplace, hearth; furnace; 2. home, house.

hogareño, *adj* home, family; home-loving.

hogaza, *nf* large loaf, cottage loaf.

hoguera, *nf* bonfire; blaze.

hoja, *nf* 1. leaf; petal; blade; 2. (paper, metal) sheet.

hojalata, *nf* tin, tinplate.

hojalatero, *nm* tinsmith.

hojaldre, *nm* puff-pastry.

hojarasca, *nf* dead leaves, fallen leaves.

hojear, *vt* to turn the pages of, leaf through.

hojuela, *nf* 1. leaflet, little leaf; 2. flake; (metal) foil.

holgado, *adj* loose, full, comfortable; roomy; baggy.

holganza, *nf* idleness; rest.

holgar, *vi* to rest, take one's ease, be at leisure.

holgazán, *adj* 1. idle, lazy, slack; 2. *nm/f* idler, loafer.

holgazanear, *vi* to laze around, be idle, slack, loaf.

holocausto, *nm* holocaust, burnt offering; sacrifice.

hollar, *vt* to tread, tread on; to trample down, trample underfoot.

hollejo, *nm* skin, peel.

hollín, *nm* soot.

hombrada, *nf* manly deed, brave act.

hombre, *nm* man; mankind.

hombrear, *vi* to play the man, act grown-up; to act tough, try to be somebody.

hombrera, *nf* shoulder strap; shoulder pad.

hombría, *nf* manliness; honesty, uprightness, worthiness.

hombro, *nm* shoulder.

homenaje, *nm* 1. homage; allegiance; 2. tribute, testimonial.

homenajeado(a), *nm/f* the person being honored, the guest of honor.

homenajear, *vt* to honor, pay tribute to.

homeópata, *nm/f* homeopath.

homeopatía, *nf* homeopathy.

homicida, *adj* 1. murderous, homicidal; 2. *nm* murderer; 3. *nf* murderess.

homicidio, *nm* murder, homicide; manslaughter.

homilía, *nf* homily.

homogeneización, *nf* levelling, equalization, unification.

homogéneo, *adj* homogeneous.

homogen(e)izar, *vt* to homogenize; to level, equalize, unify.

homólogo, *adj* equivalent.

homosexual, *adj*, *nm/f* homosexual.

honda, *nf* sling; catapult.

hondear, *vt* to hit with a slingshot, kill with a sling; to hit with a catapult.

hondo, *adj* deep; low.

hondonada, *nf* 1. hollow, dip, depression; gully, ravine; 2. lowland.

hondura, *nf* 1. depth; profundity; 2. depth; deep place.

honestidad, *nf* 1. decency, decorum; honesty; 2. modesty; purity, chastity.

hongo, *nm* fungus; mushroom; toadstool.

honor, *nm* honor; virtue, good name.

honorable, *adj* honorable, worthy,

honorario, *adj* 1. honorary, honorific; 2. *nm* honorarium; fees, charges.

honorífico, *adj* honorable; honorific.

honra, *nf* self-esteem, sense of personal honor, dignity.

honradez, *nf* honesty; honorableness, uprightness, integrity.

honrado, *adj* 1. honest; honorable, upright; 2. *nm* honest man, decent man, honorable man.

honrar, *vt* to honor, revere, respect; to do honor to.

honroso, *adj* honorable; respectable, reputable.

hora, *nf* hour; time.

horadar, *vt* to bore (through), pierce, drill, perforate; to tunnel.

horario, *adj* 1. hourly; hour, time; 2. *nm* timetable.

horca, *nf* 1. gallows, gibbet; 2. pitchfork; hayfork.

horcón, *nm* 1. pitchfork; 2. forked prop; prop, support.

horizontal, *adj* horizontal.

horizonte, *nm* horizon; skyline.

horma, *nf* form, mold.

hormiga, *nf* ant.

hormigón, *nm* concrete.

hormiguear, *vi* to itch; to have pins and needles; to have a feeling as though insects were crawling over one.

hormigueo, *nm* itch, itching; tingling, prickly feeling, pins and needles.

hormiguero, *adj* 1. ant-eating; 2. *nm* ant hill.

hormona, *nf* hormone.

hormonal, *adj* hormonal.

hornada, *nf* batch (of loaves), baking.

hornear, *vt* to cook, bake.

hornero(a), *nm/f* baker.

horno, *nm* oven; furnace; kiln.

horóscopo, *nm* horoscope.

horqueta, *nf* pitchfork; fork of a tree; bend in the road.

horquilla, *nf* hairpin, hairclip; pitchfork; fork.

horrendo, *adj* horrible; hideous; dire, frightful.

horrible, *adj* horrible, dreadful, ghastly.

horripilante, *adj* hair-raising, horrifying; harrowing; grisly; creepy.

horripilar, *vt* to make someone's hair stand on end, horrify someone, give someone the creeps.

horror, *nm* horror, dread, terror; abhorrence; enormity; frightfulness.

horrorizar, *vt* to horrify; to terrify, frighten.

horrorizarse, *vr* to be horrified, be aghast.

horroroso, *adj* 1. horrifying, terrifying; horrible, frightful; 2. ghastly, dreadful, awful; hideous, ugly.

hortícola, *adj* horticultural; garden.

horticultor(a), *nm/f* horticulturist; gardener; nurseryman.

horticultura, *nf* horticulture; gardening.

hospedador, *nm* host.

hospedaje, *nm* lodging; board and lodging.

hospedar, *vt* to put up, lodge, give a room to; to receive as a guest, entertain.

hospedería, *nf* hostelry, inn.

hospedero, *nm* innkeeper, landlord.

hospicio, *nm* poorhouse; orphanage; old people's home.

hospital, *nm* hospital; infirmary.

hospitalidad, *nf* hospitality.

hospitalización, *nf* hospitalization.

hospitalizar, *vt* to send (or take) to hospital.

hostelería, *nf* hotel trade, hotel business; catering company.

hostelero, *nm* innkeeper, landlord.

hostería, *nf* inn, hostelry; tourist hotel.

hostigamiento, *nm* harassment.

hostigar, *vt* 1. to lash, whip, scourge; 2. to harass, plague, pester; to bore.

hostil, *adj* hostile.

hostilidad, *nf* hostility.

hostilizar, *vt* to harry, harass, worry.

hotel, *nm* hotel.

hotelería, *nf* hotels (collectively); hotel trade.

hoy, *adv* today, now, nowadays.

hoya, *nf* pit, hole; grave; bunker.

hoyo, *nm* hole, pit; hollow, cavity; grave.

hoyuelo, *nm* dimple.

hoz, *nf* sickle.

hozar, *vt* to root in, root among.

hucha, *nf* chest, bin; moneybox.

hueco, *adj* hollow; empty; soft, spongy.

huelga, *nf* 1. rest, repose; leisure; idleness; recreation; 2. strike; stoppage, walkout.

huelguear, *vi* to strike, be on strike.

huelguista, *nm/f* striker.

huella, *nf* tread, treading; trace, mark, sign, imprint.

huérfano(a), *adj, nm/f* orphaned; orphan.

huerta, *nf* vegetable garden, kitchen garden.

huertero(a), *nm/f* market gardener.

huerto, *nm* kitchen garden.

huesa, *nf* grave.

huesecillo, *nm* small bone,

hueso, *nm* bone.

huesoso, *adj* bony.

huesped, *nm* guest; lodger, boarder, resident.

hueste, *nf* host, army.

huesudo, *adj* bony; big-boned, raw-boned.

hueva, *nf* roe; eggs, spawn.

huevada, *nf* nest of eggs, clutch of eggs.

huevera, *nf* eggcup.

huevo, *nm* egg.

huida, *nf* 1. flight, escape; 2. shy(ing), bolt(ing).

huido, *adj* 1. fugitive, on the run; 2. very shy, easily scared.

huir, *vt* to run away from, flee (from), escape (from); to avoid.

hular, *nm* rubber plantation.

hule, *nm* 1. rubber; 2. oilskin, oilcloth.

hulear, *vi* to extract rubber.

hulla, *nf* coal, soft coal.

hullera, *nf* colliery, coalmine.

humanar, *vt* to humanize.

humanidad, *nf* humanity, mankind.

humanista, *nm/f* humanist.

humanitaria, *nf* humanitarian.

humanizar, *vt* to humanize, make more human.

humano, *adj* human.

humareda, *nf* cloud of smoke.

humeante, *adj* smoking, smoky; steaming.

humear, *vt* 1. to fumigate; 2. to beat, thrash; 3. to smoke, give out smoke.

humectante, *adj* moisturizing.

humedad, *nf* humidity; dampness; moisture.

humedecedor, *nm* humidifier.

humedecedor, *vt* to dampen, wet, moisten; to humidify.

húmedo, *adj* humid; damp, wet; moist.

humidificar, *vt* to wet; to dampen, moisten.

humildad, *nf* humbleness, humility; meekness.

humilde, *adj* humble; meek; small.

humillación, *nf* humiliation; humbling.
humillar, *vt* to humiliate; to humble; to bow.
humo, *nm* smoke; fumes; vapor, steam.
humor, *nm* mood, humor; temper, disposition.
humorada, *nf* joke, witticism, pleasantry.
humorista, *nm/f* humorist.
hundido, *adj* sunken; deep-set, hollow.
hundimiento, *nm* sinking.
hundir, *vt* to sink; to submerge, engulf.
huracán, *nm* hurricane.
huracanado, *adj* hurricane wind, violent wind.
hurgar, *vt* to poke, jab; to stir up; to rake.
hurgarse, *vr* to pick one's nose.
hurgón, *nm* poker, fire rake.
hurgonear, *vt* to poke, rake.
hurón, *adj* 1. shy, unsociable; 2. greedy; 3. *nm* ferret.
huronear, *vt* to ferret out; to pry into.
huronera, *nf* ferret hole; den, lair; hiding place.
hurtadillas, *adv* stealthily, by stealth, on the sly.
huntar, *vt* to steal; to plagiarize, pinch.
husmear, *vt* to scent, get wind of, sniff out.
husmeo, *nm* 1. scenting; 2. spying, snooping.
huso, *nm* spindle; bobbin, drum.
huyente, *adj* receding.
huyón, *adj* cowardly; shy, unsociable.

I

I, i, *nf* (letter) I, i.
Iberia, *nf* Iberia.
ibérico, *adj* Iberian; the Iberian Peninsula.
Iberoamérica, *nf* Latin America.
ibis, *nf* ibis.
ícaro, *nm* hang-glider.
iceberg, *nm* iceberg.
iconoclasta, *adj* iconoclastic.
iconoclas(t)ia, *nf* iconoclasm.
ictericia, *nf* jaundice.
ida, *nf* 1. going, departure; 2. track, trail.
idea, *nf* idea, notion; intention.
ideal, *adj, nm* ideal.
idealizar, *vt* to idealize.
idear, *vt* to think up; to contrive, invent, devise; to plan, design.
ídem, *pron* ditto, the same, idem.
idéntico, *adj* identical; the same, the very same.
identidad, *nf* identity; sameness, similarity.
identificación, *nf* identification.
identificador, *adj* 1. identifying; 2. *nm* identifier.
identificar, *vt* to identify; to recognize, spot, pick out.
ideología, *nf* ideology.
ideólogo(a), *nm/f* ideologue, ideologist.
idílico, *adj* idyllic.
idilio, *nm* idyll; romance, love-affair.
idioma, *nm* language.
idiomático, *adj* language, linguistic; idiomatic.
idiosincrasia, *nf* idiosyncrasy.
idiota, *adj* 1. idiotic, stupid; 2. *nm/f* idiot.
idiotizar, *vt* to reduce to a state of idiocy, make an idiot of.
ido, *adj* 1. absent-minded; 2. crazy.

idólatra, *adj* 1. idolatrous; 2. *nm/f* idolater, idolatress.
idolatrar, *vt* to worship, adore; to idolize.
idolatría, *nf* idolatry.
ídolo, *nm* idol.
idoneidad, *nf* suitability, fitness; aptitude, ability.
idoneizar, *vt* to make suitable.
idóneo, *adj* suitable, fit, fitting; genuine.
iglesia, *nf* church.
iglú, *nm* igloo.
ígneo, *adj* igneous.
ignición, *nf* ignition.
ignominia, *nf* ignominy, shame, disgrace; disgraceful act.
ignorado, *adj* unknown; obscure, little-known.
ignorancia, *nf* ignorance.
ignorante, *adj* 1. ignorant; uninformed; 2. *nm/f* ignoramus.
ignorar, *vt* to ignore, not to know, be ignorant of, be unaware of.
igual, *adj* 1. same; alike, similar; 2. *nm* equal.
iguala, *nf* 1. equalization; 2. agreement; agreed fee.
igualación, *nf* equalization; evening up, levelling; equating.
igualar, *vt* to equalize, make equal; to equate.
igualatorio, *nm* insurance group.
igualdad, *nf* equality; sameness.
iguana, *nf* iguana.
ijar, *nm* flank, side.
ilación, *nf* inference; connection, relationship.
ilativo, *adj* inferential; illative.
ilegal, *adj* illegal, unlawful.
ilegalidad, *nf* illegality, unlawfulness.
ilegalizar, *vt* to outlaw, declare illegal, ban.
ilegible, *adj* illegible, unreadable.
ilegitimar, *vt* to make illegal.
ilegítimo, *adj* illegitimate; unlawful; false, spurious.
ileso, *adj* unhurt, unharmed; untouched.
iletrado, *adj* uncultured, illiterate.
ilíada, *nf* Iliad.
iliberal, *adj* illiberal.
ilícito, *adj* illicit, illegal, unlawful.
ilimitado, *adj* unlimited, limitless, unbounded.
iliterato, *adj* illiterate.
ilógico, *adj* illogical.
iluminacion, *nf* illumination, lighting; floodlighting.
iluminado(a), *adj* 1. illuminated, lighted, lit; enlightened; 2. *nf* visionary.
iluminador, *adj* illuminating.
iluminar, *vt* 1. to illuminate, light, light up; 2. to enlighten.
ilusión, *nf* 1. illusion; delusion; 2. hope, dream; piece of wishful thinking.
ilusionado, *adj* hopeful; excited, eager.
ilusionante, *adj* exciting.
ilusionar, *vt* to deceive; to give false hopes to, encourage falsely.
ilusionarse, *vr* to have unfounded hopes, indulge in wishful thinking.
ilusionista, *nm/f* conjurer, illusionist.
iluso(a), *adj* 1. easily deceived; deluded; 2. *nf* dreamer, visionary.
ilustración, *nf* illustration.
ilustrado, *adj* 1. illustrated; 2. learned, erudite; enlightened.
ilustrador(a), *adj* 1. illustrative; enlightening; 2. *nf* illustrator.
ilustrar, *vt* to illustrate; to explain, elucidate, make clear; to instruct, enlighten.

ilustrarse, *vr* to acquire knowledge, become enlightened.

ilustre, *adj* illustrious, famous.

imagen, *nf* 1. image; picture; likeness; 2. statue.

imaginación, *nf* imagination; fancy.

imaginar, *vt* to imagine; to visualize; to think up, invent.

imaginaria, *nf* reserve guard, night guard.

imaginario, *adj* imaginary.

imaginativo, *adj* imaginative.

imán, *nm* magnet.

imantación, *nf* magnetization.

imantar, *vt* to magnetize.

imbatido, *adj* unbeaten.

imbécil, *adj* imbecile, feeble-minded.

imbecilidad, *nf* imbecility, feeble-mindedness.

imbecilizar, *vt* to reduce to a state of idiocy; to stupefy.

imberbe, *adj* beardless.

imborrable, *adj* ineffaceable, indelible; unforgettable.

imbuir, *vt* to imbue, infuse.

imitación, *nf* imitation; mimicry.

imitador(a), *adj* 1. imitative; 2. *nm/f* imitator; follower; impersonator; impressionist.

imitar, *vt* 1. to imitate; to mimic, to follow; 2. to counterfeit.

impaciencia, *nf* impatience.

impacientar, *vt* to make impatient; to irritate, exasperate.

impacientarse, *vr* lose patience, get impatient.

impaciente, *adj* impatient; anxious; fretful.

impactante, *adj* striking, impressive; shattering; crushing, overwhelming.

impactar, *vt* to impress, have an impact on; to please, delight.

impactarse, *vr* to be overawed by.

impacto, *nm* 1. impact; incidence; hit; blow; 2. impression; shock.

impar, *adj* odd; unique, exceptional.

imparable, *adj* unstoppable.

imparcial, *adj* impartial, unbiased, fair.

imparcialidad, *nf* impartiality, lack of bias, fairness.

impartición, *nf* teaching.

impartir, *vt* to impart, give, convey.

impavidez, *nf* intrepidity; dauntlessness.

impávido, *adj* intrepid, dauntless, undaunted.

impecable, *adj* impeccable, faultless.

impedido(a), *adj* 1. crippled, disabled, handicapped; 2. *nm/f* cripple, handicapped person.

impedimento, *nm* 1. impediment, obstacle, hindrance; 2. disability, handicap.

impedir, *vt* to impede, obstruct, hinder, hamper; to deter.

impeler, *vt* 1. to drive, propel; 2. to impel; to urge.

impenetrable, *adj* impenetrable; impervious; obscure, incomprehensible.

impenitencia, *nf* impenitence.

impenitente, *adj* impenitent, unrepentant.

impensado, *adj* unexpected, unforeseen.

imperante, *adj* ruling; prevailing.

imperar, *vi* to rule, reign; to be in command.

imperceptible, *adj* imperceptible, undiscernible.

imperdible, *nm* safety pin.

imperecedero, *adj* imperishable, undying; immortal.

imperfección, *nf* imperfection; flaw, fault, blemish.

imperfecto, *adj* imperfect, faulty.

imperial, *adj* imperial.

imperialismo, *nm* imperialism.

imperialista, *adj* imperialist(ic).

impericia, *nf* unskillfulness; lack of experience, inexperience.

imperio, *nm* empire.

imperioso, *adj* imperious; lordly; urgent; imperative, overriding.

impermeabilización, *nf* waterproofing; undersealing.

impermeabilizar, *vt* to waterproof, make waterproof; to underseal.

impermeable, *adj* 1. waterproof; 2. *nm* raincoat.

impersonal, *adj* impersonal.

impertérrito, *adj* unafraid, unshaken, undaunted, fearless.

impertinencia, *nf* irrelevance; fussiness; peevishness.

impertinente, *adj* 1. irrelevant, not pertinent; uncalled for; 2. touchy, fussy; peevish.

ímpetu, *nm* impetus, impulse; momentum.

impetuosidad, *nf* impetuousness, impulsiveness; violence; haste, hastiness.

impiadoso, *adj* impious.

impiedad, *nf* impiety, ungodliness.

implantación, *nf* implantation; introduction.

implantar, *vt* to implant; to introduce.

implante, *nm* implant.

implementar, *vt* to implement.

implemento, *nm* means; tool, implement.

implicación, *nf* 1. contradiction (in terms); 2. involvement, implication, complicity.

implicar, *vt* to implicate, involve.

implícito, *adj* implicit, implied.

imploración, *nf* supplication, entreaty.

implorar, *vt* to implore, beg, beseech.

imponderable, *adj* imponderable, priceless.

imponencia, *nf* imposing character, impressiveness; stateliness, grandness.

imponente, *adj* imposing, impressive; stately, grand.

imponer, *vt* to impose; to exact.

impopular, *adj* unpopular.

impopularidad, *nf* unpopularity.

importación, *nf* importation, importing.

importador(a), *nm/f* importer.

importancia, *nf* importance; significance.

importante, *adj* important; significant.

importar, *vt* 1. to import; to amount to, to cost, be worth; 2. to involve, imply; 3. to be important, to matter.

importunar, *vt* to importune, bother, pester.

importunidad, *nf* importunity, pestering.

importuno, *adj* importunate, troublesome, annoying.

imposibilidad, *nf* impossibility.

imposibilitado, *adj* disabled, crippled; helpless, without means.

imposibilitar, *vt* to disable; to make unfit, incapacitate.

imposible, *adj* impossible; intolerable, unbearable.

imposición, *nf* imposition.

impositiva, *nf* tax office.

impostergable, *adj* that cannot be delayed.

impostor(a), *nm/f* 1. impostor, fraud; 2. slanderer.

impostura, *nf* imposture, fraud; sham.

impotencia, *nf* impotence, powerlessness, helplessness.

impracticable, *adj* impracticable, unworkable.

imprecación, *nf* imprecation, curse.

imprecar, *vt* to curse.

imprecisión, *nf* lack of precision, vagueness.

impreciso, *adj* imprecise, vague.

impredecible, *adj* unpredictable.

impregnación, *nf* impregnation.

impregnar, *vt* to impregnate; to saturate; to pervade.

impremeditado, *adj* unpremeditated.

imprenta, *nf* 1. printing, art of printing. 2. press; printer's shop, printing house.

imprescindible, *adj* essential, indispensable, vital.

impresentable, *adj* unpresentable; disgraceful.

impresión, *nf* impression; imprint.

impresionable, *adj* impressionable.

impresionado, *adj* impressed.

impresionante, *adj* impressive; striking; moving, affecting; awesome, frightening.

impresionar, *vt* 1. (record) to cut; (photo) to expose; 2. to impress, to move, affect; to shock.

impresionista, *adj* impressionist(ic).

impreso, *adj* printed.

impresor, *nm* printer.

imprevisible, *adj* unforeseeable.

imprevisión, *nf* improvidence; lack of foresight.

imprevisor, *adj* improvident; lacking foresight.

imprevisto, *adj* unforeseen, unexpected.

imprimir, *vt* to imprint, impress, stamp, to print.

improbabilidad, *nf* improbability, unlikelihood.

improbable, *adj* improbable, unlikely.

improbar, *vt* to fail to approve, not approve.

improbo, *adj* dishonest, corrupt.

improcedente, *adj* wrong, not right; inappropriate, inapplicable.

improductividad, *nf* unproductiveness.

improductivo, *adj* unproductive; non-productive.

impronunciable, *adj* unpronounceable.

improperio, *nm* insult, taunt.

impropiedad, *nf* inappropriateness, unsuitability.

impropio, *adj* improper; inappropriate, unsuitable.

improvisación, *nf* improvisation; extemporization.

improvisado, *adj* improvised; makeshift.

improvisar, *vti* to improvise; to extemporize.

imprudencia, *nf* imprudence; carelessness.

imprudente, *adj* unwise, imprudent, rash.

impuesto, *nm* tax, duty, levy.

impugnar, *vt* to oppose, contest, challenge.

impulsador, *nm* booster.

impulsar, *vt* to stimulate, promote; to drive.

impulsivo, *adj* impulsive.

impulso, *nm* impulse; drive, thrust; impetus, momentum.

impune, *adj* unpunished.

impunidad, *nf* impunity.

impureza, *nf* impurity.

impurificar, *vt* to adulterate, make impure; to corrupt, defile.

impuro, *adj* impure; unchaste, lewd.

imputación, *nf* imputation, charge.

imputar, *vt* to impute to, attribute to, charge with.

inacabado, *adj* unfinished, (problem) unresolved.

inaccesibilidad, *nf* inaccessibility.

inaccesible, *adj* inaccessible.

inacción, *nf* inaction; inactivity, idleness; drift.

inaceptable, *adj* unacceptable.

inactividad, *nf* inactivity; laziness, idleness; dullness.

inactivo, *adj* inactive, lazy, idle; dull.

inadaptable, *adj* unadaptable.

inadaptación, *nf* maladjustment.

inadaptado, *adj* maladjusted.

inadecuado, *adj* inadequate; unsuitable, inappropriate.

inadvertido, *adj* unobservant, inattentive; careless.

inagotable, *adj* inexhaustible, tireless.

inaguantable, *adj* intolerable, unbearable.

inalámbrico, *adj* wireless; cordless.

inalcanzable, *adj* unattainable.

inalienable, *adj* inalienable; not transferable.

inalterable, *adj* unalterable, unchanging; immutable.

inalterado, *adj* unchanged, unaltered.

inamovible, *adj* fixed, immovable; undetachable.

inanición, *nf* starvation, inanition.

inanimado, *adj* inanimate.

inánime, *adj* lifeless.

inapetencia, *nf* lack of appetite, loss of appetite.

inapetente, *adj* to be suffering from loss of appetite.

inaplazable, *adj* which cannot be postponed, pressing, urgent.

inaplicable, *adj* inapplicable, not applicable.

inapreciable, *adj* imperceptible; invaluable, inestimable.

inarrugable, *adj* crease-resistant, which does not crease.

inasequible, *adj* unattainable, out of reach.

inaudible, *adj* inaudible.

inaudito, *adj* unheard-of; unprecedented; outrageous.

inauguración, *nf* inauguration; opening; unveiling.

inaugurar, *vt* to inaugurate.

inca, *nm/f* Inca.

incalculable, *adj* incalculable.

incandescencia, *nf* incandescence; white heat; glow.

incansable, *adj* tireless, untiring, unflagging.

incapacidad, *nf* incapacity; unfitness; inadequacy, incompetence.

incapacitado, *adj* incapacitated; unfitted; disabled, handicapped.

incapacitar, *vt* to incapacitate, render unfit, to disqualify.

incapturable, *adj* unattainable.

incautación, *nf* seizure, confiscation.

incauto, *adj* unwary, incautious; gullible.

incendiar, *vt* to set on fire.

incendiario, *adj* incendiary; inflammatory.

incendio, *nm* fire; conflagration.

incentivar, *vt* to encourage, stimulate, provide incentives for.

incentivo, *nm* incentive.

incertidumbre, *nf* uncertainty, doubt.

incesto, *nm* incest.

incestuoso, *adj* incestuous.

incidencia, *nf* incidence.

incidentado, *adj* unruly, riotous, turbulent.

incidental, *adj* incidental.

incidente, *adj* 1. incidental; 2. *nm* incident.

incidir, *vt* to incise, cut.

incienso, *nm* incense.

incierto, *adj* uncertain, doubtful; inconstant.

incineración, *nf* incineration; cremation.

incinerador(a), *nm/f* incinerator.

incinerar, *vt* to incinerate, burn; to cremate.

incipiente, *adj* incipient.

incircunciso, *adj* uncircumcised.

incisión, *nf* incision.

incisivo, *adj* sharp, cutting; incisive.

incitación, *nf* incitement; provocation.

incitante, *adj* provoking, provocative, inviting.

incitar, *vt* to incite, rouse, spur on.

incivilizado, *adj* uncivilized.

inclemencia, *nf* harshness, severity, inclemency.

inclemente, *adj* harsh, severe, inclement.

inclinación, *nf* inclination; slope.

inclinado, *adj* inclined, sloping, leaning, slanting.

inclinar, *vt* to incline; to slope, slant, tilt.

incluir, *vt* to include; to comprise, contain; to incorporate, enclose.

inclusión, *nf* inclusion.

inclusive, *adv* inclusive, inclusively.

incluso, *adj* included; enclosed.

incógnita, *nf* unknown quantity.

incógnito, *adj* unknown.

incoloro, *adj* colorless; clear.

incólume, *adj* safe; unhurt, unharmed.

incomodar, *vt* to inconvenience, trouble, put out.

incómodo, *adj* inconvenient; uncomfortable.

incomparable, *adj* incomparable, matchless.

incompatibilidad, *nf* incompatibility.

incompatible, *adj* incompatible.

incompetencia, *nf* incompetence.

incompetente, *adj* incompetent.

incompletamente, *adv* incompletely.

incompleto, *adj* incomplete, unfinished.

incomprendido, *adj* misunderstood; not appreciated.

incomprensible, *adj* incomprehensible.

incomprensión, *nf* incomprehension, lack of understanding; lack of appreciation.

incomunicación, *nf* isolation; lack of communication.

incomunicado, *adj* isolated, cut off.

incomunicar, *vt* to cut off the communications of.

inconcebible, *adj* inconceivable, unthinkable.

inconcluso, *adj* unfinished, incomplete.

inconcreto, *adj* vague.

incondicional, *adj* unconditional; implicit, complete, unquestioning.

incondicionalidad, *nf* unconditional support; unquestioning loyalty.

inconfesable, *adj* which cannot be told; shameful, disgraceful.

inconfundible, *adj* unmistakable.

incongruencia, *nf* incongruity.

incongruente, *adj* incongruous.

inconmensurable, *adj* immeasurable, vast; incommensurate; fantastic.

inconmovible, *adj* unshakeable.

inconsciencia, *nf* unconsciousness; unawareness.

inconsciente, *adj* unconscious.

inconsecuente, *adj* inconsistent; inconsequent.

inconsistencia, *nf* lack of firmness; unevenness; weakness; looseness; flimsiness.

inconsistente, *adj* lacking firmness, not solid; uneven.

inconsolable, *adj* inconsolable.

inconstancia, *nf* inconstancy; fickleness.

inconstitucional, *adj* unconstitutional.

inconsumible, *adj* unfit for consumption.

incontable, *adj* countless, innumerable.

incontinencia, *nf* incontinence.

incontinente, *adj* incontinent.

incontrastable, *adj* insuperable; unanswerable; unshakeable, unyielding.

incontrolable, *adj* uncontrollable.

incontrolado, *adj* uncontrolled; unauthorized; violent, wild.

incontrovertible, *adj* incontrovertible.

incontrovertido, *adj* undisputed.

inconveniencia, *nf* unsuitability, inappropriateness; inadvisability; inconvenience.

inconveniente, *adj* unsuitable, inappropriate; inadvisable; inconvenient.

incorporación, *nf* incorporation, embodiment; inclusion.

incorporar, *vt* to incorporate.

incorpóreo, *adj* incorporeal, bodiless; intangible.

incorrección, *nf* 1. incorrectness, inaccuracy; irregularity; 2. discourtesy.

incorregible, *adj* incorrigible.

incorruptible, *adj* incorruptible.

incorrupto, *adj* incorrupt; uncorrupted, pure, chaste, undefiled.

incredibilidad, *nf* incredibility.

incredulidad, *nf* incredulity, unbelief.

incrédulo, *adj* incredulous, unbelieving, sceptical.

incrédula, *nf* unbeliever, sceptic.

increíble, *adj* incredible, unbelievable.

incrementar, *vt* to increase; to promote.

increpar, *vt* to reprimand severely, upbraid.

incriminación, *nf* accusation.

incriminar, *vt* to accuse; to incriminate.

incruento, *adj* bloodless.

incrustar, *vt* to incrust; to inlay.

incubación, *nf* incubation.

incubadora, *nf* incubator.

incubar, *vt* to incubate; to hatch.

inculcar, *vt* to instill, inculcate.

inculpar, *vt* to charge, accuse; to blame.

inculto, *adj* 1. uncultivated, unworked, untilled; 2. uncultured; uncivilized; uncouth.

incultura, *nf* lack of culture; uncouthness.

incumplimiento, *nm* non-fulfillment; non-completion.

incumplir, *vt* to break, disobey, fail to observe.

incurable, *adj* incurable; hopeless, irremediable.

incurrir, *vi* to commit; incur.

incursión, *nf* raid, incursion, attack.

incursionar, *vt* to make a raid into, penetrate into.

indagación, *nf* investigation, inquiry.

indagar, *vt* to investigate, inquire into; to find out.

indagatorio(a), *adj* 1. investigatory; 2. *nf* investigation, inquiry.

indecencia, *nf* indecency; obscenity.

indecente, *adj* indecent, improper; obscene.

indecible, *adj* unspeakable, indescribable.

indecisión, *nf* indecision, hesitation; indecisiveness.

indeciso, *adj* undecided; hesitant, irresolute; vague.

indeclinable, *adj* indeclinable; unavoidable.

indefenso, *adj* defenseless, helpless.

indefinible, *adj* indefinable; inexpressible.

indefinido, *adj* indefinite; undefined, vague.

indeleble, *adj* indelible.

indemnización, *nf* 1. indemnification; 2. indemnity, compensation.

indemnizar, *vt* to indemnify, compensate (for).

independencia, *nf* independence.

independiente, *adj* independent; self-sufficient.

independizar, *vt* to emancipate, free; to make independent, grant independence to.

independizarse, *vr* to become free, become independent.

indescifrable, *adj* undecipherable, indecipherable.

indescriptible, *adj* indescribable.

indeseable, *adj* undesirable.

indeseado, *adj* unwanted.

indestructible, *adj* indestructible.

indeterminado, *adj* indeterminate; inconclusive.

indexar, *vt* to index-link.

indicación, *nf* indication, sign; symptom.

indicador, *nm* indicator; gauge, meter, dial.

indicar, *vt* to indicate, show; to register, record.

indicativo, *adj* indicative.

índice, *nm* index; catalogue; table of contents.

indicio, *nm* indication, sign; token; evidence.

indiferencia, *nf* indifference; apathy.

indiferente, *adj* indifferent, unconcerned, apathetic.

indígena, *adj* indigenous, native.

indigencia, *nf* poverty, destitution, indigence.

indigente, *adj* destitute, poverty-stricken, indigent.

indigestar, *vt* to cause indigestion to.

indisgesto, *adj* undigested; indigestible, hard to digest.

indignación, *nf* indignation, anger.

indignar, *vt* to anger, make indignant; to provoke, stir up.

indigno, *adj* unworthy; contemptible, mean, low.

indio, *adj* Indian.

indirecta, *nf* hint; insinuation, innuendo.

indirecto, *adj* indirect; roundabout.

indisciplina, *nf* lack of discipline; insubordination.

indisciplinado, *adj* undisciplined; lax.

indiscreción, *nf* indiscretion; tactless thing (to do), tactless remark.

indiscreto, *adj* indiscreet; tactless.

indiscriminado, *adj* indiscriminate.

indisoluble, *adj* indissoluble; inseparable.

indispensable, *adj* indispensable, essential.

indisponer, *vt* upset; make ill, make unfit.

indisposición, *nf* indisposition, slight illness.

indispuesto, *adj* indisposed, unwell, slightly ill.

indisputable, *adj* indisputable, unquestioned.

individual, *adj* individual; peculiar, special.

individualidad, *nf* individuality.

individualizar, *vt* to individualize.

individuo, *adj* individual.

indivisible, *adj* indivisible.

indiviso, *adj* undivided.

indocto, *adj* ignorant, unlearned.

indoctrinar, *vt* to indoctrinate.

indocumentado(a), *adj* 1. without identifying documents; 2. *nm/f* one who carries no identity papers.

índole, *nf* 1. nature; character, disposition; 2. class, kind, sort.

indolencia, *nf* indolence, laziness; listlessness.

indolente, *adj* indolent, lazy; listless.

inducción, *nf* (Elec) induction; inducement.

inducido, *nm* armature.

inducir, *vt* to induce, to infer.

inductivo, *adj* inductive.

indulgencia, *nf* indulgence; forbearance.

indulgente, *adj* indulgent, lenient.

indultar, *vt* to pardon, reprieve (from).

indumentaria, *nf* clothing, apparel, dress.

indumentario, *adj* clothing.

industria, *nf* industry.

industrialización, *nf* industrialization.

industrializar, *vt* to industrialize.

industrioso, *adj* industrious.

inédito, *adj* unpublished.

ineducado, *adj* uneducated.

inefable, *adj* indescribable, inexpressible, ineffable.

inefectivo, *adj* ineffective.

ineficacia, *nf* ineffectiveness; inefficiency.

ineficaz, *adj* ineffective, ineffectual; inefficient.

ineficiencia, *nf* inefficiency.

ineficiente, *adj* inefficient.

inelegancia, *nf* inelegance, lack of elegance.

inelegante, *adj* inelegant.

inelegible, *adj* ineligible.

inenarrable, *adj* inexpressible.

inepcia, *nf* ineptitude, incompetence; stupidity.

ineptitud, *nf* ineptitude, incompetence; unsuitability.

inepto, *adj* inept, incompetent; stupid.

inequívoco, *adj* unequivocal, unambiguous; unmistakable.

inercia, *nf* inertia; passivity; sluggishness, slowness.

inescrupuloso, *adj* unscrupulous.

inescrutable, *adj* inscrutable.

inesperado, *adj* unexpected; unforeseen; sudden.

inestabilidad, *nf* instability, unsteadiness.

inestabilizar, *vt* to destabilize.

inestable, *adj* unstable, unsteady.

inestimable, *adj* inestimable, invaluable.

inevitable, *adj* inevitable, unavoidable.

inexactitud, *nf* inaccuracy; incorrectness.

inexacto, *adj* inaccurate; incorrect, untrue.

inexcusable, *adj* inexcusable, unforgivable.

inexistencia, *nf* non-existence.

inexistente, *adj* non-existent; defunct.

inexorable, *adj* inexorable.

inexperiencia, *nf* inexperience; unskillfulness, lack of skill.

inexperimentado, *adj* inexperienced.

inexperto, *adj* inexperienced; unskilled, inexpert.

inexplicable, *adj* inexplicable, unaccountable.

inexplicado, *adj* unexplained.

inexplorado, *adj* unexplored; uncharted.

inexpresividad, *nf* inexpressiveness; flatness.

inexpresivo, *adj* inexpressive; dull, flat, wooden.

inexpuesto, *adj* unexposed.

inexpugnable, *adj* impregnable; firm, unyielding.

inextinguible, *adj* inextinguishable, unquenchable.

inextirpable, *adj* ineradicable.

infalibilidad, *nf* infallibility; certainty.

infalible, *adj* infallible; certain, sure; foolproof; unerring.

infamación, *nf* defamation.

infamador(a), *adj* 1. defamatory, slanderous; 2. *nm/f* slanderer.

infamante, *adj* offensive, rude; slanderous; shameful, degrading.

infamar, *vt* to dishonor, discredit; to defame, slander.

infamatorio, *adj* defamatory, slanderous.

infamia, *nf* infamy; disgrace.

infancia, *nf* infancy, childhood.

infantería, *nf* infantry; marines.

infanticida, *nm/f* infanticide, child-killer.

infanticidio, *nm* infanticide.

infantil, *adj* infant; child's, children's.

infarto, *nm* heart attack; coronary thrombosis.

infatigable, *adj* tireless, untiring.

infatuar, *vt* to make conceited.

infausto, *adj* unlucky; ill-starred, ill-fated.

infección, *nf* infection.

infeccioso, *adj* infectious.

infectar, *vt* to infect; to contaminate, corrupt.

infecundo, *adj* infertile; sterile, barren.

infelicidad, *nf* unhappiness; misfortune.

infeliz, *adj* unhappy; unfortunate, miserable.

inferencia, *nf* inference.

inferior, *adj* lower; inferior.

inferioridad, *nf* inferiority.

inferir, *vt* to infer, deduce.

infestación, *nf* infestation.

infestante, *adj* invasive, pervasive.

infestar, *vt* to infect; to overrun, invade.

infidelidad, *nf* infidelity, unfaithfulness.

infiel, *adj* unfaithful, disloyal.

infierno, *nm* hell; inferno.

infiltración, *nf* infiltration.

infiltrado(a), *nm/f* infiltrator.

infiltrar, *vt* to infiltrate; to inculcate.

ínfimo, *adj* lowest; very poor, of very poor quality; vile.

infinidad, *nf* infinity; great quantity.

infinitivo, *adj* infinitive.

infinito, *adj* infinite; boundless, limitless, endless.

inflable, *adj* inflatable.

inflación, nf 1. inflation; swelling; 2. pride, conceit.

inflacionario, adj inflationary.

inflamabilidad, nf inflammability.

inflamable, adj inflammable, flammable.

inflamación, nf 1. ignition, combustion; 2. inflammation.

inflamar, vt 1. to set on fire, ignite; 2. to inflame; excite, arouse.

inflamatorio, adj inflammatory.

inflar, vt 1. to inflate, blow up, pump air into; 2. exaggerate; to make conceited.

infligir, vt to inflict (on).

influencia, nf influence.

influenciar, vt to influence.

influenza, nf influenza.

influir, vt to influence.

influjo, nm influence.

influyente, adj influential.

información, nf 1. information; news; intelligence; 2. report, account; reference.

informado, adj informed.

informador(a), nm/f informant; informer.

informalidad, nf unreliability, incorrectness; unconventionality.

informar, vt 1. to inform, tell to announce; 2. to form, shape.

informarse, vr inquire into, find out.

informativo, adj informative; news.

informe, adj 1. shapeless; 2. nm report, statement; announcement.

infortunado, adj unfortunate, unlucky.

infortunio, nm misfortune, ill luck, mishap.

infracción, nf infraction, infringement; breach; offense.

infractor(a), nm/f offender.

infra(e)structura, nf infrastructure.

infrahumano, adj subhuman.

infranqueable, adj impassable; unsurmountable.

infrarrojo, adj infrared.

infrecuencia, nf infrequency.

infrecuente, adj infrequent.

infringir, vt to infringe, break, contravene.

infructuoso, adj fruitless, unsuccessful; unprofitable.

ínfulas, nf conceit; pretentious nonsense.

infundado, adj unfounded, baseless, groundless.

infundio, nm fairy tale, lie; malicious story.

infundir, vt to infuse; to instill.

infusión, nf infusion.

ingeniar, vt to devise, think up, contrive.

ingeniería, nf engineering.

ingeniero(a), nm/f engineer.

ingenio, nm 1. ingenuity, inventiveness; talent; creativeness; 2. apparatus, engine, machine, device; 3. mill, plant; sugar mill, sugar refinery.

ingenioso, adj ingenious, clever, resourceful.

ingente, adj huge, enormous.

ingenuidad, nf ingenuousness, naïveté; candor.

ingerir, vt to swallow; to ingest, consume, take in.

ingestión, nf swallowing; ingestion.

ingle, nf groin.

inglés, adj English.

ingratitud, nf ingratitude.

ingrato, adj ungrateful.

ingravidez, nf weightlessness.

ingrávido, adj weightless; very light.

ingrediente, nm ingredient.

ingresar, vt 1. to deposit, pay in; to receive, take in; 2. to admit someone (as a patient).

ingreso, nm 1. entry, joining; admission; 2. income; revenue; receipts, takings.

inhábil, adj unskillful, inexpert, clumsy.

inhabilidad, nf unskillfulness; clumsiness; incompetence.

inhabilitar, vt to disqualify; to remove (from office).

inhabitable, adj uninhabitable.

inhabitado, adj uninhabited.

inhalación, nf inhalation.

inhalador, nm inhaler.

inhalar, vt to inhale; to sniff.

inherente, adj inherent.

inhibir, vt to inhibit; to restrain, stay.

inhibitorio, adj inhibitory.

inhospitalidad, nf inhospitality.

inhóspito, adj inhospitable.

inhumación, nf burial, inhumation.

inhumanidad, nf inhumanity.

inhumano, adj inhuman; dirty, disgusting.

inhumar, vt to bury, inter.

inicializar, vt to initialize.

iniciar, vt 1. to initiate; 2. to begin, start, to originate.

iniciativa, nf initiative, enterprise; lead, leadership.

inicio, nm start, beginning.

inigualable, adj unsurpassable.

inimaginable, adj unimaginable, inconceivable, incredible.

inimitable, adj inimitable.

ininteligente, adj unintelligent.

ininteligible, adj unintelligible.

ininterrumpido, adj uninterrupted; continuous, without a break; steady; prolonged, sustained.

iniquidad, nf wickedness, iniquity; injustice.

injerencia, nf interference, meddling.

injerir, vt 1. to insert, introduce (into); 2. to interfere, meddle (in).

injertar, vt to graft.

injerto, nm grafting.

injuria, nf insult, offense, affront; outrage, injustice.

injuriar, vt to insult, abuse, revile; to wrong.

injurioso, adj insulting, offensive; outrageous.

injusticia, nf injustice; unfairness.

injustificable, adj unjustifiable.

injustificado, adj unjustified, unwarranted.

injusto, adj unjust, unfair; wrong, wrongful.

inmadurez, nf immaturity.

inmaduro, adj immature; unripe.

inmediaciones, nf neighborhood, surroundings.

inmediatez, nf immediacy.

inmediato, adj immediate; prompt.

inmenso, adj immense, huge, vast.

inmensurable, adj immeasurable.

inmerecido, adj undeserved; uncalled-for.

inmergir, vt to immerse.

inmersión, nf immersion; dive, plunge.

inmigración, nf immigration.

inmigrado(a), nm/f immigrant.

inmigrar, vi to immigrate.

inminencia, nf imminence.

inminente, adj imminent, impending.

inmiscuirse, vr to interfere, meddle.

inmisericorde, adj insensitive, hard-hearted, pitiless.

inmisericordioso, adj merciless.

inmoble, adj immovable; motionless.

inmolar, vt to immolate.

inmoral, adj immoral; unethical.

inmoralidad, nf immorality; unethical nature.

inmortal, adj, nm/f immortal.

inmortalidad, *nf* immortality.
inmortalizar, *vt* to immortalize.
inmovible, *adj* immovable.
inmóvil, *adj* immovable; immobile; motionless, still.
inmovilidad, *nf* immovability; immobility; stillness.
inmovilización, *nf* immobilization; stopping.
inmovilizar, *vr* to immobilize; to stop, paralyze, bring to a standstill.
inmundicia, *nf* filth, dirt; nastiness.
inmundo, *adj* filthy, dirty; foul, nasty.
inmune, *adj* 1. immune; 2. exempt, free.
inmunidad, *nf* 1. immunity; 2. exemption.
inmunizar, *vt* to immunize.
inmunología, *nf* immunology.
inmunológico, *adj* immune.
inmutabilidad, *nf* immutability.
inmutable, *adj* immutable, changeless.
inmutarse, *vr* to change countenance, turn pale, lose one's self-possession.
innato, *adj* innate, inborn; inbred.
innecesario, *adj* unnecessary.
innegable, *adj* undeniable.
innocuo, *adj* innocuous, harmless.
innovación, *nf* innovation; novelty, new thing.
innovador, *adj* innovative, innovatory.
innovar, *vt* 1. to introduce; 2. *vi* to innovate, introduce something new.
innumerable, *adj* innumerable, countless.
inocencia, *nf* innocence.
inocentada, *nf* 1. naïve remark; blunder; 2. practical joke, April Fool joke.
inocente, *adj* 1. innocent; harmless; 2. simple, naïve.
inocuidad, *nf* innocuousness, harmlessness.
inoculación, *nf* inoculation.
inocular, *vt* to inoculate.
inofensivo, *adj* inoffensive, harmless.
inolvidable, *adj* unforgettable.
inoperante, *adj* inoperative; unworkable; ineffective, impotent.
inopia, *nf* indigence, poverty.
inopinado, *adj* unexpected.
inoportuno, *adj* inopportune, untimely, ill-timed.
inorgánico, *adj* inorganic.
inoxidable, *adj* rustless, rustproof; stainless.
inquebrantable, *adj* unbreakable; unshakeable, unyielding, unswerving.
inquietante, *adj* worrying, disturbing.
inquietar, *vt* to worry, disturb, trouble, upset.
inquieto, *adj* anxious, worried, uneasy.
inquietud, *nf* anxiety, worry, uneasiness, disquiet.
inquirir, *vt* to inquire into, investigate, look into.
inquisición, *nf* inquiry, investigation.
inquisidor, *nm* inquisitor.
insaciable, *adj* insatiable.
insalubre, *adj* unhealthy, insalubrious; unsanitary.
insalubridad, *nf* unhealthiness.
insalvable, *adj* insuperable.
insania, *nf* insanity.
insano, *adj* insane, mad, unhealthy.
insatisfacción, *nf* dissatisfaction.
insatisfecho, *adj* unsatisfied; dissatisfied.
inscribir, *vt* to inscribe; to list, to enroll; to register.
inscripción, *nf* inscription; enrollment; registering.
insecticida, *nm* insecticide.
insecto, *nm* insect.
inseminación, *nf* insemination.
inseminar, *vt* to inseminate, fertilize.
insensatez, *nf* folly, foolishness, stupidity.

insensato, *adj* senseless, foolish, stupid.
insensibilizar, *vt* to render insensitive, make callous.
insensible, *adj* insensitive; unfeeling; callous.
inseparable, *adj* inseparable.
inserción, *nf* insertion.
insertar, *vt* to insert.
inservible, *adj* useless; unusable.
insigne, *adj* distinguished; notable, famous.
insignia, *nf* badge, device, emblem; decoration.
insignificante, *adj* insignificant; trivial, tiny, petty.
insinceridad, *nf* insincerity.
insincero, *adj* insincere.
insinuación, *nf* insinuation.
insinuador, *adj* insinuating.
insinuar, *vt* to insinuate, hint at, imply.
insistencia, *nf* insistence; persistence.
insistente, *adj* insistent; persistent.
insistir, *vi* to insist; to persist.
insobornable, *adj* incorruptible.
insociable, *adj* unsociable.
insolar, *vt* to expose to the sun, put in the sun.
insolarse, *vr* to get sunstroke.
insolencia, *nf* insolence, effrontery.
insolente, *adj* insolent, rude; unblushing.
insólito, *adj* unusual, unwonted.
insolvencia, *nf* insolvency, bankruptcy.
insolvente, *adj* insolvent, bankrupt.
insomne, *adj* 1. sleepless; 2. *nm/f* insomniac.
insomnio, *nm* sleeplessness, insomnia.
insondable, *adj* bottomless; unfathomable.
insoportable, *adj* unbearable, intolerable.
inspección, *nf* inspection, examination; check; survey.
inspeccionar, *vt* to inspect, examine; to check.
inspector(a), *nm/f* inspector; superintendent, supervisor.
inspiración, *nf* 1. inspiration; 2. inhalation.
inspirador, *adj* inspiring; inspirational.
inspirar, *vt* 1. to inspire; 2. to inhale, breathe in.
instalación, *nf* installation, installment.
instalador, *nm* installer; fitter; electrician.
instalar, *vt* to install; to set up, erect.
instalarse, *vr* settle down, establish oneself.
instantánea, *nf* snap, snapshot.
instante, *nm* instant, moment.
instar, *vt* to urge, press.
instauración, *nf* 1. restoration, renewal; 2. establishment, setting-up.
instaurar, *vt* 1. to restore, renew; 2. to establish.
instigación, *nf* instigation.
instigador(a), *nm/f* instigator.
instigar, *vt* to instigate; to abet.
instilar, *vt* to instill.
instintivo, *adj* instinctive.
instinto, *nm* instinct; impulse, urge.
institución, *nf* institution, establishment.
instituir, *vt* to institute, establish; to found, set up.
instituto, *nm* institute, institution.
instrucción, *nf* instruction; education, teaching; training.
instructor(a), *nm/f* instructor, teacher; coach.
instruir, *vt* to instruct, teach; to educate; to train.
instrumentar, *vt* to score, orchestrate.
instrumento, *nm* instrument; tool, implement.
insubordinación, *nf* insubordination; turbulence, unruliness.
insubordinado, *adj* insubordinate; turbulent, rebellious, unruly.
insubordinar, *vt* to stir up, rouse to rebellion.
insubordinarse, *vr* to become unruly; to rebel.

insuficiencia, nf insufficiency, lack, shortage.
insuficiente, adj insufficient, inadequate.
insuflar, vt to breathe into, introduce by blowing.
insufrible, adj unbearable, insufferable.
insular, adj insular.
insularidad, nf insularity.
insulina, nf insulin.
insulso, adj tasteless, insipid.
insultante, adj insulting; abusive.
insultar, vt to insult.
insulto, nm insult.
insuperable, adj insuperable, unsurmountable; unsurpassable.
insurgencia, nf rebellion, uprising.
insurgente, adj, nm/f insurgent.
insurrección, nf revolt, insurrection.
insurreccionar, vt to rouse to revolt, incite to rebel.
insurrecto(a), adj, nm/f rebel, insurgent.
intacto, adj untouched; whole, intact, undamaged; pure.
integración, nf integration.
integrado, adj integrated; in one piece, all of a piece.
integral, adj integral; built-in.
integrar, vt 1. to make up, compose, form; 2. to integrate.
integridad, nf 1. wholeness, completeness; 2. uprightness, integrity.
intelecto, nm intellect; understanding; brains.
intelectual, adj nm/f intellectual.
intelectualidad, nf intellectuality; intellectual character.
inteligencia, nf intelligence; mind, wits, understanding; ability.
inteligente, adj intelligent; clever, brainy, talented.
intemperie, nf inclemency (of the weather); bad weather, rough weather.
intención, nf intention; purpose; plan.
intencionado, adj meaningful, deliberate.
intensidad, nf intensity; power, strength; vividness.
intensificación, nf intensification.
intensificar, vt to intensify.
intenso, adj intense, powerful, strong.
intento, nm intention, intent, purpose.
interacción, nf interaction, interplay.
interaccionar, vi to interact.
intercalación, nf intercalation, insertion.
intercalar, vt to intercalate, insert; to merge.
intercambiar, vt to change over, interchange.
interceder, vi to intercede.
interceptar, vt to intercept, cut off.
interceptor, nm 1. interceptor; 2. trap; separator.
intercesión, nf intercession; mediation.
intercomunicación, nf intercommunication.
intercomunicador, nm intercom.
intercomunicar, vt to link.
interconectar, vt to interconnect.
interconexión, nf interconnection.
interdecir, vt to forbid, prohibit.
interdependencia, nf interdependence.
interdependiente, adj interdependent.
interés, nm 1. interest; concern; 2. share, part.
interesado, adj interested; concerned.
interesante, adj interesting; useful, convenient.
interesar, vt to interest, be of interest to; to appeal to.
interesarse, vr to be interested, take an interest.
interferir, vt to interfere with, jam.
interín, adv meanwhile.
interinar, vt to occupy temporarily, occupy in an acting capacity.

interior, adj interior, inner, inside.
interioridad, nf inwardness; inner being; innermost thoughts.
interiorizar, vt 1. to internalize; 2. to look into, investigate closely.
interiorizarse, vr to familiarize oneself with.
interjección, nf interjection.
interlinear, vt to interline, write (or print) between the lines.
interlocutor(a), nm/f speaker, interlocutor.
interludio, nm interlude.
intermediación, nf mediation; brokerage.
intermediario, adj 1. intermediary; 2. mediating.
intermedio, adj 1. intermediate, halfway (between); 2. intervening; the period between.
intermitente, adj 1. intermittent; 2. nm directional light, flashing light, indicator.
internacional, adj international.
internacionalizar, vt to internationalize.
internar, vt to intern; to admit.
internarse, vr to penetrate, to advance deeply.
interno, adj internal, interior; inside.
interpelación, nf appeal, plea, interpellation.
interpelante, nm/f questioner.
interpelar, vt to implore, beseech; to interpellate; to beg for the aid of.
interpersonal, adj interpersonal.
interplanetario, adj interplanetary.
interpolación, nf interpolation.
interpolar, vt 1. to interpolate; 2. to interrupt briefly.
interponer, vt to interpose, put in, insert.
interposición, nf insertion.
interpretación, nf 1. interpretation; 2. translation.
interpretar, vt to interpret.
intérprete, nm/f 1. interpreter, translator; 2. performer; exponent; artist(e).
interracial, adj interracial.
interrelación, nf interrelation.
interrelacionar, vt to interrelate.
interrogación, nf interrogation; question; inquiry.
interrogador(a), nm/f interrogator; questioner.
interrogante, adj 1. questioning; 2. nm/f interrogator; questioner.
interrogar, vt to question, interrogate; to examine.
interrogatorio, nm questioning; debriefing; examination, questionnaire.
interrumpir, vt to interrupt.
interrupción, nf interruption; break; stoppage, holdup; disturbance; termination.
interruptor, nm switch.
intersección, nf intersection; crossing junction.
intersticio, nm interstice; crack; interval, gap.
intérvalo, nm interval; break; gap.
intervención, nf supervision, control; government takeover; audit.
intervenir, vt to supervise, control; audit.
interventor(a), nm/f inspector, supervisor; auditor.
intestinal, adj intestinal.
intestino, adj 1. internal; domestic, civil; 2. nm intestine.
intimación, nf intimation, announcement, notification.
intimar, vt to intimate, announce, notify; to order, require.
intimidación, nf intimidation.
intimidad, nf intimacy, familiarity.
intimidador, adj intimidating.
intimidar, vt to intimidate, overawe, to bully, scare.
íntimo, adj intimate; close; inner, innermost.
intocable, adj untouchable; sacrosanct.

intolerable, *adj* intolerable, unbearable.

intolerancia, *nf* intolerance; narrow-mindedness, bigotry.

intoxicación, *nf* poisoning.

intoxicador, *adj* intoxicating.

intoxicar, *vt* to poison.

intramuros, *adv* within the city, within the walls.

intranquilidad, *nf* worry, uneasiness, disquiet.

intranquilizar, *vt* to worry, disquiet, make uneasy.

intranquilizarse, *vr* to get worried, feel anxious, be uneasy.

intranquilo, *adj* worried, uneasy, anxious; restless.

intra(n)scendencia, *nf* unimportance, insignificance.

intransferible, *adj* untransferable, not transferable.

intransigencia, *nf* intransigence; uncompromising attitude, intolerance.

intransigente, *adj* intransigent; uncompromising, intolerant; diehard.

intransitable, *adj* impassable.

intrauterino, *adj* intrauterine.

intravenoso, *adj* intravenous.

intrepidez, *nf* intrepidity, fearlessness.

intrépido, *adj* intrepid, dauntless, fearless.

intriga, *nf* intrigue; plot, scheme.

intrigar, *vt* to intrigue, interest, puzzle.

intrigarse, *vr* to be intrigued, be puzzled.

intrincar, *vt* to entangle; to confuse, complicate.

intrínseco, *adj* intrinsic; inherent.

introducción, *nf* introduction; insertion; creation.

introducir, *vt* to introduce; to bring in, show in.

introductor, *adj* introductory.

intromisión, *nf* 1. introduction, insertion; 2. interference, meddling.

introspección, *nf* introspection.

introspectivo, *adj* introspective.

introversión, *nf* introversion.

intrusión, *nf* intrusion; trespass; hacking, computer piracy.

intruso, *adj* intrusive.

intuición, *nf* intuition.

intuir, *vt* to know by intuition; to sense, feel.

intuirse, *vr* that can be guessed.

inundación, *nf* flood, flooding.

inundar, *vt* to flood, inundate, swamp.

inusitado, *adj* unusual, unwonted, rare.

inusual, *adj* unusual.

inútil, *adj* useless; vain, fruitless.

inutilidad, *nf* uselessness.

inutilizable, *adj* unusable, unfit for use.

inutilización, *nf* disablement; spoiling; cancellation.

inutilizar, *vt* to make useless, render useless.

invadir, *vt* to invade; to overrun.

invalidar, *vt* to invalidate, nullify.

inválido, *adj* invalid, disabled; unfit.

invariable, *adj* invariable.

invasión, *nf* invasion; attack.

invencible, *adj* invincible; unsurmountable, insuperable.

invención, *nf* invention; discovery, finding; fabrication.

inventar, *vt* to invent; to devise; to make up, fabricate.

inventariar, *vt* to inventory, make an inventory of.

inventario, *nm* inventory; stocktaking.

inventiva, *nf* inventiveness; ingenuity, resourcefulness.

inventivo, *adj* inventive; ingenious, resourceful.

invento, *nm* invention.

inventor(a), *nm/f* inventor.

invernal, *adj* wintry, winter.

inversión, *nf* inversion; reversal; reversing.

inversionista, *nm/f* investor.

inverso, *adj* inverse, inverted; reverse, contrary.

invertebrado, *adj, nm* invertebrate.

invertido(a), *adj* 1. inverted; reversed; 2. *nm/f* homosexual.

invertir, *vt* to invert, turn upside down; to reverse, put the other way round.

investidura, *nf* investiture; vote of confidence.

investigación, *nf* investigation; inquiry.

investigador(a), *adj* 1. investigative; researcher; 2. *nm/f* investigator.

investigar, *vt* to investigate; to inquire.

invicto, *adj* unconquered, unbeaten.

invidencia, *nf* sightlessness.

invidente, *adj* 1. sightless, blind; 2. *nm/f* sightless person, blind person.

invierno, *nm* winter, wintertime.

inviolable, *adj* inviolable.

invisible, *adj* invisible.

invitación, *nf* invitation.

invitado(a), *adj* 1. guest; 2. *nm/f* guest.

invitar, *vt* to invite.

invocación, *nf* invocation.

invocar, *vt* 1. to invoke, call on; 2. to beg for, implore.

involucrar, *vt* 1. to involve; 2. to jumble up, mix up;

involucrarse, *vr* to meddle, interfere (in); to get involved.

involuntario, *adj* involuntary; unintentional.

invulnerabilidad, *nf* invulnerability.

invulnerable, *adj* invulnerable.

inyectable, *nm* serum, vaccine, injection.

inyección, *nf* injection, shot.

inyectar, *vt* to inject.

inyectarse, *vr* to give oneself an injection.

ionizar, *vt* to ionize.

ionósfera, *nf* ionosphere.

ir, *vi* to go; to move; to travel.

irse, *vr* to go away.

ira, *nf* anger, rage, wrath; fury, violence.

iracundo, *adj* irate; irascible.

irascible, *adj* irascible.

iris, *nm* rainbow, iris.

irisación, *nf* iridescence.

irisado, *adj* iridescent.

irisar, *vi* to be iridescent, iridesce.

ironía, *nf* irony.

irónico, *adj* ironical.

ironizar, *vt* 1. to ridicule; 2. *vi* to speak ironically.

irracional, *adj* irrational; unreasoning.

irracionalidad, *nf* irrationality; unreasonableness.

irradiación, *nf* irradiation.

irradiar, *vt* to irradiate, radiate.

irrazonable, *adj* unreasonable.

irreal, *adj* unreal.

irrealidad, *nf* unreality.

irrealizable, *adj* unrealizable; unworkable.

irrebatible, *adj* unanswerable, irrefutable, unassailable.

irreconciliable, *adj* irreconcilable; inconsistent, incompatible.

irrecuperable, *adj* irrecoverable, irretrievable.

irrechazable, *adj* irresistible.

irreducible, *adj* irreducible; irreconcilable.

irreflexión, *nf* thoughtlessness; rashness.

irreflexivo, *adj* thoughtless, unthinking; rash, impetuous; ill-considered.

irrefutable, *adj* irrefutable, unanswerable.

irregular, *adj* irregular; abnormal.

irregularidad, *nf* irregularity; abnormality.

irregularmente, *adv* irregularly; abnormally.
irrelevante, *adj* irrelevant.
irremisible, *adj* unpardonable; irretrievable.
irreparable, *adj* irreparable.
irrepetible, *adj* one-and-only, unique.
irreprensible, *adj* irreproachable.
irreprimible, *adj* irrepressible.
irreprochable, *adj* irreproachable.
irresistible, *adj* irresistible; unbearable, insufferable;
    impossibly strong.
irresoluble, *adj* unsolvable; unresolved.
irresolución, *nf* irresolution, hesitation.
irresoluto, *adj* irresolute, hesitant, undecided.
irrespetuoso, *adj* disrespectful.
irrespirable, *adj* unbreathable.
irresponsabilidad, *nf* irresponsibility.
irresponsable, *adj* irresponsible.
irreverencia, *nf* irreverence; disrespect.
irreverente, *adj* irreverent; disrespectful.
irreversible, *adj* irreversible.
irrevocable, *adj* irrevocable, irreversible.
irrigación, *nf* irrigation.
irrigador, *nm* sprinkler.
irrigar, *vt* to irrigate.
irritar, *vt* to irritate, anger, exasperate.
irrompible, *adj* unbreakable.
irrumpir, *vi* to burst into, rush into; to invade.
irrupción, *nf* irruption; inrush; invasion.
isla, *nf* island; isle.
islámico, *adj* Islamic.
islandés, *adj* Icelandic.
isleño(a), *adj* 1. island; 2. *nm/f* islander.
islote, *nm* small island, rocky isle.
istmo, *nm* isthmus; neck.
italiano(a), *adj*, *nm/f* Italian.
itinerante, *adj* itinerant, roving, travelling.
itinerario, *nm* itinerary, route; timetable.
izado, *nm* raising the flag.
izar, *vt* to hoist, haul up; to raise.
izquierda, *nf* left hand; left side, left-hand side.
izquierdista, *adj* leftist, left-wing.
izquierdo, *adj* left; left-hand; left-handed.

J

J, j, *nf* (letter) J, j.
jaba, *nf* 1. straw basket; crate; 2. beggar's bag.
jabado, *adj* white with brown patches.
jabalí, *nm* wild boar; warthog.
jabalina, *nf* 1. wild sow, female wild boar; 2.
    javelin.
jabón, *nm* soap; piece of soap, bar of soap.
jabonadura, *nf* 1. soaping; 2. lather, soapsuds.
jabonar, *vt* to soap; to wash; to lather.
jabonera, *nf* soapdish.
jabonería, *nf* soap factory.
jabuco, *nm* large basket, big crate; bag.
jaca, *nf* pony, cob, small horse; mare.
jacinto, *nm* hyacinth; jacinth.
jactancia, *nf* boasting, bragging; boastfulness.
jactancioso, *adj* boastful.

jactarse, *vr* to boast, brag; to boast about, boast of.
jadeante, *adj* panting, gasping, breathless.
jadear, *vi* to pant, gasp for breath.
jadeo, *nm* panting, gasping.
jaguar, *nm* jaguar.
jagüey, *nm* pool; well, cistern.
jaiba, *nf* 1. crab; 2. mouth.
jaladera, *nf* handle.
jalador, *nm* door-handle.
jalapeño, *nm* chili.
jalar, *vt* 1. to pull, haul; to heave; to draw, attract,
    win; 2. to work hard at; 3. to pull; tug at.
jalea, *nf* jelly.
jalear, *vt* 1. to urge on; to encourage; 2. to jeer at.
jaleo, *nm* spree, binge.
jalón, *nm* stake, pole; surveying rod.
jalonar, *vt* to stake out, mark out; to mark.
jalonear, *vt* to pull at, yank out.
jamás, *adv* never; (not) ever.
jamba, *nf* jamb; door post.
jambado, *adj* greedy, gluttonous.
jamelgo, *nm* wretched horse, nag.
jamón, *nm* ham.
jamona, *nf* buxom woman.
janearse, *vr* 1. to leap into the saddle; 2. to come
    to a complete stop.
japonés(esa), *adj*, *nm/f* Japanese.
jaque, *nm* (chess) check.
jaquear, *vt* (chess) to check; to harass.
jaqueca, *nf* headache, migraine.
jarabe, *nm* syrup; sweet drink.
jarana, *nf* spree; binge; rumpus, row.
jaranear, *vt* to cheat, swindle.
jaranero, *adj* merry, roistering, rowdy; deceitful.
jardín, *nm* garden, flower garden.
jardinera, *nf* 1. gardener; 2. window box.
jardinería, *nf* gardening.
jardinero, *nm* gardener.
jarra, *nf* jar, pitcher; churn.
jarrete, *nm* back of the knee; hock; heel.
jarro, *nm* jug, pitcher.
jarrón, *nm* vase; urn.
jaspeado, *adj* mottled, speckled, marbled; streaked.
jaspear, *vt* to speckle, marble; to streak.
jauría, *nf* pack of hounds.
jazmín, *nm* jasmine.
jefa, *nf* (woman) head, (woman) boss; manager(ess).
jefatura, *nf* 1. leadership; chieftainship; 2. head-
    quarters; central office.
jefe, *nm/f* chief, head, boss; leader; manager.
Jehová, *nm* Jehovah.
jengibre, *nm* ginger.
jenízaro, *adj* mixed, hybrid.
jerarca, *nm* chief, leader; important person; big shot.
jerarquía, *nf* hierarchy; rank.
jerez, *nm* sherry.
jerga, *nf* 1. coarse cloth, sackcloth; 2. jargon;
    slang, cant; gibberish.
jerigonza, *nf* silly thing, piece of folly.
jeringa, *nf* syringe.
jeringar, *vt* to syringe; to inject; to squirt.
jeringuilla, *nf* syringe.
jeroglífico, *adj* hieroglyphic.
Jesucristo, *nm* Jesus Christ.
jesuita, *adj* 1. Jesuit; 2. hypocrite, sly person.
Jesús, *nm* Jesus.
jíbaro, *adj* country, rustic; sullen.
jícara, *nf* 1. small cup (for drinking-chocolate,
    coffee, etc.); 2. gourd, calabash.
jicarazo, *nm* poison, poisonous drink; cupful.

jícaro, nm calabash tree.

jijona, nm soft nougat (made in Jijona, Spain).

jimagua, adj twin; identical twin.

jineta, nf horsewoman, rider; genet.

jinete, nm horseman, rider; cavalryman.

jinetear, vt (horses) to break in; to ride.

jipato, adj pale, wan; sickly, frail; tasteless.

jipi, nm 1. straw hat; 2. nm/f hippy.

jipijapa, nf straw for weaving.

jira, nf excursion, outing; picnic.

jirafa, nf giraffe.

jirón, nm rag, shred, tatter; in shreds.

jobo, nm cedar (tree).

jocosidad, nf humor; jokiness; joke.

jocoso, adj humorous, comic, jocular.

jolgórico, nm riotous, hilarious, rowdy.

jornada, nf 1. day's journey; stage (of a journey); 2. working day; hours of work.

jornal, nm (day's) wage; day's work.

jornalero, nm laborer.

joroba, nf 1. hump, hunched back; 2. nuisance, bother, annoyance.

jorobado(a), adj, nm/f hunchbacked.

jorobar, vt to annoy, pester, bother.

jorobón, adj annoying.

jota, nf 1. the (name of the) letter j; 2. Spanish dance and tune (esp Aragonese)

joven, adj 1. young; youthful; 2. nm young man, youth; young people.

jovencito(a), nm/f youngster.

jovial, adj jolly, cheerful, jovial.

jovialidad, nf cheerfulness, joviality.

joya, nf jewel, gem, piece of jewelry.

joyería, nf 1. jewelry, jewels; 2. jeweler's (shop).

joyero, nm 1. jeweler; 2. jewel case.

juanete, nm bunion; prominent cheek-bone; ball of the foot.

jubilación, nf 1. retirement; 2. pension, retirement pension.

jubilado, adj retired; pensioner.

jubilar, vt to pension off, retire.

jubilarse, vr to retire, take one's pension.

jubileo, nm jubilee.

júbilo, nm joy, jubilation, rejoicing.

jubiloso, adj jubilant.

judaico, adj Jewish, Judaic.

judaismo, nm Judaism.

judas, nm peephole.

judia, nf 1. Jewess, Jewish woman; 2. kidney bean; haricot bean.

judicatura, nf 1. judicature; 2. judgeship.

judicial, adj judicial.

judio, adj 1. Jewish; 2. nm Jew.

judo, nm judo.

juego, nm play, playing; sport; fun, amusement.

juerga, nf binge, spree, carousal; good time.

jueves, nm Thursday.

juez, nm/f judge.

jugada, nf play; playing.

jugador(a), nm/f player; gambler; speculator.

jugar, vi 1. to play; 2. to gamble, stake.

jugarse, vr to gamble (away), risk.

juglar, nm minstrel, tumbler, entertainer.

jugo, nm 1. juice; sap; 2. essence, substance.

jugosidad, nf 1. juiciness, succulence; 2. substantial nature, pithiness.

juguera, nf liquidizer, blender.

juguete, nm toy; plaything.

juguetear, vi to play, romp, sport.

juguetería, nf toy trade, toy business; toyshop.

juicio, nm 1. judgement, reason; 2. sanity, reason; good sense, prudence, wisdom; 3. opinion; 4. trial.

juicioso, adj judicious, wise, prudent, sensible.

julio, nm July.

juncal, adj rushy, reedy.

juncar, nm ground covered in rushes; reed bed.

junco, nm rush, reed; rattan; junk.

jungla, nf jungle.

junio, nm June.

junquillo, nm jonquil; reed.

junta, nf meeting, assembly; session.

juntar, vt to join, unite; to assemble, put together; to collect, gather (together).

junto, adj joined, united; together.

juntura, nf join, junction; seam; coupling.

jura, nf oath, pledge.

jurado, adj 1. qualified, chartered; 2. nm jury; panel (of judges); 3. juror, juryman; member of a panel.

juramentar, vt to swear in, administer the oath to.

juramentarse, vr to be sworn in, take the oath.

juramento, nm oath.

jurar, vti to swear.

jurídico, adj juridical; legal.

jurisdicción, nf 1. jurisdiction; 2. district, administrative area.

jurisperito(a), nm/f jurist, legal expert.

jurisprudencia, nf jurisprudence, law.

jurista, nm/f jurist, lawyer.

justa, nf joust, tournament; contest.

justicia, nf justice; fairness; equity, rightness.

justiciero, adj just, righteous.

justificación, nf justification.

justificar, vt to justify; to verify, substantiate; to clear, vindicate.

justipreciar, vt to evaluate, appraise.

justo, adj just, fair, right.

juvenil, adj youthful; young-looking, youthful in appearance.

juventud, nf 1. youth; early life; 2. young people.

juzgado, nm court, tribunal.

juzgar, vti to judge.

K

K, k, nf (letter) K, k.

kaki, nm khaki.

kamikaze, nm kamikaze.

kárate, nm karate.

kartins, nm go-carting.

Katar, nm Qatar.

kayac, nm kayak.

kebab, nm kebab.

kéfir, nm type of yogurt.

Kenia, nf Kenya.

keniano(a), adj, nm/f Kenyan.

kepi(s), nm kepi.

kermes, nm charity fair, bazaar.

kerosén, nm kerosene, paraffin.

kilo, nm kilo; kilogram.

kilociclo, nm kilocycle.

kilogramo, nm kilogram.

kilojercio, nm kilohertz.

kilolitro, nm kiloliter.

kilometraje, *nm* 1. distance in kilometers, mileage; 2. mileage allowance.

kilometrar, *vt* to measure (in kilometers).

kilométrico, *adj* kilometric.

kilómetro, *nm* kilometer.

kiloocteto, *nm* kilobyte.

kilotón, *nm* kiloton.

kilovatio, *nm* kilowatt.

kimon(a), *nm/f* kimono.

kínder, *nm* kindergarten.

kión, *nm* ginger.

kiwi, *nm* kiwi; kiwi fruit.

klínex, *nm* tissue, Kleenex.

Kurdistán, *nm* Kurdistan.

kurdo, *adj* 1. kurdish; 2. *nm/f* Kurd; Kurdish.

Kuwait, *nm* Kuwait.

kuwaití, *adj, nm/f* Kuwaiti.

L

L,l, *nf* (letter) L, l.

la, *art def fem* 1. of el; 2. *pron pers fem* her, it, you; 3. *pron dem* that, the, one.

laberíntico, *adj* labyrinth; rambling.

laberinto, *nm* 1. labyrinth, maze; tangle; 2. row, racket.

labia, *nf* fluency, blarney; glibness.

labial, *adj* labial.

labio, *nm* lip; edge, rim.

labiolectura, *nf* lip-reading.

labor, *nf* 1. labor, work; job, task, piece of work; 2. needlework, sewing; embroidery; knitting.

laboral, *adj* labor; technical.

laboratorio, *nm* laboratory.

laborar, *vt* 1. to work, till; 2. to work to scheme, plot.

laboriosidad, *nf* 1. industry; painstaking skill; 2. laboriousness.

laborioso, *adj* 1. hard-working, industrious, painstaking. 2. tough, hard, laborious, difficult.

laborismo, *nm* labor movement.

laborista, *adj* 1. Labor Party; Labor member; 2. *nm/f* small farmer, smallholder.

labra, *nf* carving, working, cutting.

labradío, *adj* arable.

labrado, *adj* worked; wrought; carved; patterned, embroidered.

labrador, *nm* farmer; farm labourer; plowman; peasant; lumberjack.

labradora, *nf* peasant (woman).

labrantío, *adj* arable.

labranza, *nf* 1. farming; cultivation; 2. farm; farmland.

labrar, *vt* to work; to fashion, shape; carve; to fell and smooth.

labriego, *nm* farmhand, laborer; peasant.

laca, *nf* shellac; lacquer; hair-spray; nail polish, nail varnish.

lacar, *vt* to lacquer.

lacayo, *nm* footman; lackey.

laceada, *nf* whipping.

lacear, *vt* to beribbon, adorn with bows.

laceración, *nf* laceration; damage, spoiling.

lacerante, *adj* wounding, hurtful.

lacerar, *vt* to lacerate, tear, mangle; to damage.

laciar, *vt* to straighten.

lacio, *adj* withered, faded; straight; limp, languid.

lacón, *nm* shoulder of pork.

lacónico, *adj* laconic, terse.

lacra, *nf* 1. mark, trace, scar; sore, ulcer; 2. blot, blemish.

lacrar, *vt* 1. to injure the health of; to infect, strike (with a disease); 2. to injure, harm, cause damage to; 3. *vt* to seal (with sealing wax).

lacre, *adj* 1. bright red; 2. *nm* sealing wax.

lacrimógeno, *adj* 1. tear-producing; 2. tearful, highly sentimental; weepy.

lactación, *nf* breast-feeding.

lactante, *adj* (woman) nursing mother.

lactar, *vt* to breast-feed, nurse, to feed on milk.

lácteo, *adj* lacteal, dairy; milky, lacteous.

lactico, *adj* lactic.

lactosa, *nf* lactose.

lacado, *nm* lacquer.

lacar, *vt* to lacquer.

lacayo, *nm* footman; lackey.

laceración, *nf* laceration; damage, spoiling.

lacerante, *adj* wounding, hurtful.

lacerar, *vt* to lacerate, tear, mangle; to damage.

lacio, *adj* withered, faded; straight; limp, languid.

lacón, *nm* shoulder of pork.

lacónico, *adj* laconic, terse.

lacra, *nf* 1. mark, trace, scar; sore, ulcer; 2. blot, blemish.

lacrar, *vt* 1. to injure the health of; to infect, strike (with a disease); 2. to injure, harm, cause damage to; 3. *vt* to seal (with sealing wax).

lacre, *adj* 1. bright red; 2. *nm* sealing wax.

lacrimógeno, *adj* 1. tear-producing; 2. tearful, highly sentimental; weepy.

lactante, *adj* (woman) nursing mother.

lactar, *vt* to breast-feed, nurse, to feed on milk.

lácteo, *adj* lacteal, dairy; milky, lacteous.

láctico, *adj* lactic.

lactosa, *nf* lactose.

ladeado, *adj* 1. tilted, leaning, inclined; 2. slovenly.

ladear, *vt* to tilt, tip; to incline (to one side); to bank, turn; go round the side of.

ladeo, *nm* tilting, inclination, leaning; banking, turning.

ladera, *nf* slope, hillside.

ladino, *adj* cunning, wily; smart, shrewd.

lado, *nm* 1. side; 2. flank.

ladrar, *vi* to bark; to rumble.

ladrido, *nm* bark, barking; slander, scandal.

ladrillar, *nm* 1. brickworks; 2. *vt* to brick, pave with bricks.

ladrillo, *nm* brick; tile; block.

ladrón(a), *adj* 1. thieving; 2. *nm/f* thief.

ladronera, *nf* den of thieves.

lagar, *nm* winepress; oil press.

lagarta, *nf* lizard.

lagartija, *nf* small lizard, wall lizard.

lagarto, *nm* lizard; alligator.

lago, *nm* lake.

lágrima, *nf* tear.

lagrimal, *nm* corner of the eye.

lagrimar, *vi* to cry.

lagrimear, *vi* to shed tears easily, be tearful.

laguna, *nf* 1. pool; lagoon; 2. gap, blank; break.

laico, *adj* 1. lay; 2. *nm* layman.

laja, *adj* sandstone.

lama, *nf* 1. mud, slime, ooze; 2. mold, mildew; moss; 3. *nm* (Rel) lama.

lamentable, *adj* regrettable; lamentable; pitiful.

lamentación, *nf* lamentation; sorrow.

lamentar, *vt* to be sorry about, regret; to lament, bemoan, bewail; to mourn.

lamento, *nm* lament; moan, wail; lamentation.

lamer, *vt* to lick; to lap, lap against; to graze.

lamido, *adj* very thin, emaciated; pale.

laminado, *adj* laminated.

laminador, *nm* rolling mill.

laminar, *vt* to laminate; to roll.

lamiscar, *vt* to lick greedily, lick noisily.

lámpara, *nf* 1. lamp, light; bulb; valve, tube; 2. *nm/f* thief.

lamparilla, *nf* 1. small lamp; nightlight; 2. aspen.

lampiño, *adj* hairless; beardless.

lana, *nf* 1. wool; fleece; 2. dough, money.

lanar, *adj* wool-bearing.

lancear, *vt* to spear.

lancero, *nm* lancer; dreamer, blind optimist.

lanceta, *nf* 1. lancet; 2. goad; sting.

lancinar, *vt* to lance, pierce.

lancha, *nf* 1. launch; (small) boat; lighter, barge; 2. police car.

lanchar, *vi* to become overcast; to freeze.

lanchero, *nm* 1. boatman; lighterman; 2. Cuban refugee.

lanero, *adj* wool; woolen; woolman, wool dealer.

langosta, *nf* 1. lobster; crayfish; 2. locust.

langostera, *nf* lobster pot.

languidecer, *vi* to languish, pine (away).

lánguido, *adj* languid; weak, listless, drooping.

lanilla, *nf* nap; thin flannel cloth.

lanudo, *adj* 1. woolly, fleecy; 2. rustic, uncouth; 3. well off.

lanza, *nf* 1. lance, spear; 2. pole; 3. nozzle.

lanzada, *nf* spear thrust; spear wound.

lanzadera, *nf* shuttle; missile-launcher.

lanzador, *nm* thrower; pitcher.

lanzamiento, *nm* 1. throw, cast; hurling; drop; 2. launch, launching.

lanzar , *vt* 1. to throw, cast; fling, hurl; 2. to launch.

lanzarse, *vr* undertake, launch into; throw oneself into.

lápida, *nf* stone, stone tablet, memorial tablet.

lapidar, *vt* to stone, throw stones at; to stone to death.

lapidario, *adj* lapidary; immortal phrase.

lápiz, *nm* pencil; crayon.

lapso, *nm* lapse; interval of time, passage of time.

lapsus, *nm* lapse, mistake; slip of the pen; slip of the tongue; lapse of memory.

laqueado, *adj* lacquered; varnished.

laquear, *vt* to lacquer; to varnish, paint.

largada, *nf* start.

largar, *vt* 1. to let go, let loose, release; 2. to give, fetch, deal; 3. to let fly; to let out.

largo, *adj* long; long, lengthy.

largura, *nf* length.

laringe, *nf* larynx.

laringitis, *nf* laryngitis.

larva, *nf* grub, maggot.

larvado, *adj* hidden, latent; embryonic.

lasca, *nf* chip, stone chips; slice.

lascar, *vt* 1. to slacken; 2. to graze, bruise; to chip.

lascivia, *nf* lewdness, lasciviousness; lust, lustfulness; playfulness.

lascivo, *adj* lewd, lascivious; lustful; playful, wanton.

láser, *nm* laser.

lástima, *nf* pity; compassion; shame.

lastimador, *adj* harmful, injurious.

lastimar, *vt* 1. to hurt, harm, injure; to wound; to bruise; 2. to offend, distress.

lastrar, *vt* to ballast; to burden, weigh down.

lastre, *nm* 1. ballast; 2. dead weight, useless load.

lata, *nf* tinplate; tin, can.

latear, *vi* 1. to be a nuisance, be annoying; 2. to talk a lot, chatter away pointlessly.

latente, *adj* latent, alive, intense, vigorous; fresh.

lateral, *adj* lateral, side.

laterío, *nm* tinned goods, canned goods.

latero, *nm* 1. tinsmith; 2. bore, drag.

latido, *nm* 1. beat, beating; throb, throbbing; palpitation; 2. bark, yelp.

latigazo, *nm* 1. lash; crack (of a whip); 2. harsh reproof; verbal lashing.

látigo, *nm* whip; crack.

Latín, *nm* Latin (language).

latinización, *nf* latinization.

latinizar, *vti* to latinize.

Latinoamérica, *nf* Latin America.

latir, *vt* to beat, throb, palpitate.

latitud, *nf* latitude; breadth; area, extent.

lato, *adj* broad, wide, extensive.

latón, *nm* brass; big tin, large tin container.

laureado(a), *adj* honored, distinguished, famous.

laurear, *vt* to crown with laurel; to honor, reward.

laurel, *nm* 1. laurel; honor, reward; 2. bay (leaves).

lava, *nf* lava.

lavabo, *nm* washbasin; lavatory, washroom.

lavacara, *nf* washbasin.

lavadero, *nm* laundry, wash-house; washing place; utility room.

lavanda, *nf* lavender; lavender water.

lavandera, *nf* laundress, washerwoman.

lavar, *vt* to wash.

lavarse, *vr* to wash oneself, have a wash.

laxante, *adj*, *nm* laxative.

laxar, *vt* to ease, relax, slacken.

laxitud, *nf* laxity, slackness.

lazar, *vt* 1. to lasso, rope; 2. *vi* to connect.

lazarillo, *nm* blind man's guide.

lazarino(a), *adj* leprous; leper.

lazo, *nm* 1. bow, knot; loop; lasso, lariat; 2. snare, trap; 3. bend, loop.

leal, *adj* loyal, faithful, trustworthy; fair.

lealtad, *nf* loyalty, fidelity; trustworthiness.

lección, *nf* lesson; class, lecture, example.

lector(a), *adj* 1. the reading public; 2. *nm/f* reader.

lectura, *nf* reading; reading matter; read-out.

lechada, *nf* 1. whitewash; paste; grout; pulp; 2. milking.

lechar, *vt* 1. to milk; to suckle; 2. to whitewash.

leche, *nf* 1. milk; 2. milky juice; rubber.

lechera, *nf* 1. milkmaid, dairymaid; 2. milk can, milk churn.

lechería, *nf* 1. dairy, creamery; 2. cows, herd.

lechero, *adj* 1. milk; dairy; dairy herd; 2. *nm* dairyman; milkman.

lecho, *nm* bed; couch; bedding.

lechón, *nm* 1. piglet, suckling-pig; 2. filthy person.

lechucero, *nm* nightshift worker; night driver.

lechuga, *nf* lettuce.

lechuguilla, *nf* frill, flounce, ruff.

lechuza, *nf* owl.

leer, *vti* to read.

legación, *nf* legation.

legado, *nm* 1. legate; 2. legacy, bequest.

legajar, *vt* to file.

legajo, *nm* file, bundle (of papers).

legal, *adj* 1. legal, lawful; 2. trustworthy, truthful; loyal, reliable.

legalidad, *nf* legality, lawfulness.
legalización, *nf* legalization; authentication.
legalizar, *vt* to legalize, make lawful; to authenticate.
legaña, *nf* rheum, sleep.
legar, *vt* to bequeath, leave (to).
legendario, *adj* legendary.
legión, *nf* legion.
legionario, *adj* legionary.
legislación, *nf* legislation.
legislador(a), *nm/f* legislator, lawmaker.
legislar, *vi* to legislate.
legislativo, *adj* legislative.
legislatura, *nf* term; session; period of office; legislature, legislative body.
legítima, *nf* legitimate, genuine, authentic.
legitimar, *vt* to legitimize; to legalize.
legitimarse, *vr* to establish one's identity; to establish one's title.
legítimo, *adj* legitimate, rightful; just.
legua, *nf* league.
legumbre, *nf* vegetable.
leguminoso, *adj* leguminous.
lejía, *nf* bleach.
lejos, *adv* far, far away, far off.
lema, *nm* motto, device; theme; slogan, watchword.
lengua, *nf* 1. tongue; 2. language.
lenguaje, *nm* language; speech.
lengüeta, *nf* tab, small tongue.
lengüetear, *vt* to lick.
lengüilargo, *adj* foul-mouthed.
lenidad, *nf* lenience, softness.
lenitivo, *adj* 1. lenitive; 2. *nm* lenitive, palliative.
lente, *nm* lens; eyeglass; spectacles.
lenteja, *nf* lentil.
lentejuela, *nf* spangle, sequin.
lentillas, *nf* contact lenses.
lentitud, *nf* slowness.
lento, *adj* slow.
leñar, *vt* to make into firewood, cut up for firewood.
leñera, *nf* woodshed.
leño, *nm* log; timber, wood, piece of wood.
león, *nm* lion; puma.
leonera, *nf* 1. lion's cage; lion's den; 2. gambling den, dive.
leontina, *nf* watch chain.
leopardo, *nm* leopard; cheetah.
leotardo, *nm* leotard, tights.
leporino, *adj* leporine; hare-like.
lepra, *nf* leprosy.
leprosario, *nm* leper colony.
leproso(a), *adj* 1. leprous; 2. *nm/f* leper.
lesbiana, *nf* lesbian.
lesión, *nf* wound, lesion; injury.
lesionado, *adj* hurt, injured; unfit.
lesionar, *vt* to hurt, injure; to wound.
lesionarse, *vr* to get hurt.
letal, *adj* deadly, lethal.
letanía, *nf* litany; tedious recitation.
letárgico, *adj* lethargic.
letargo, *nm* lethargy.
letra, *nf* letter.
letrado, *adj* 1. learned; pedantic; 2. *nm/f* counsel, legal representative.
letrero, *nm* sign, notice; placard, poster; label.
letrina, *nf* latrine; sewer, sump.
letrista, *nm/f* lyricist, songwriter.
leucemia, *nf* leukemia.
leucémico(a), *nm/f* person suffering from leukemia.
leucocito, *nm* leucocyte.

leudar, *vt* to leaven.
leudarse, *vr* to rise.
leva, *nf* 1. weighing anchor; 2. levy; 3. lever; cam; 4. trick, swindle, ruse.
levadura, *nf* yeast, leaven.
levantar, *vt* to raise, lift; to elevate.
levantarse, *vr* to rise; to get up, stand up, rise to one's feet.
levante, *nm* east; uprising.
levar, *vt* to weigh anchor.
leve, *adj* light; slight; trivial, small, unimportant.
levita, *nf* 1. frock coat; 2. *nm* Levite.
levitación, *nf* levitation.
levitar, *vi* to levitate.
Levítico, *nm* Leviticus.
léxico, *adj* 1. lexical; 2. *nm* lexicon, dictionary; vocabulary; word list.
ley, *nf* law; act, bill, measure; rule.
leyenda, *nf* legend; inscription; key.
liana, *nf* liana.
liar, *vt* to tie, tie up, do up; to bind.
liarse, *vr* to get tied up; to entwine; to get involved (with), get embroiled.
libación, *nf* libation.
libar, *vt* to suck; to sip; to taste.
libelo, *nm* lampoon, satire.
liberación, *nf* liberation; release.
liberal, *adj* 1. liberal, generous; lavish; 2. *nm/f* liberal.
liberalidad, *nf* liberality, generosity, lavishness.
liberalizador, *adj* liberalizing.
liebre, *nf* hare.
lienzo, *nm* linen; canvas.
liga, *nf* league.
ligado, *nm* slur, tie; ligature.
ligamento, *nm* ligament.
ligar, *vt* to tie, bind; to alloy; to mix.
ligerear, *vi* to walk fast, move quickly.
ligereza, *nf* lightness; thinness.
ligero, *adj* 1. light; lightweight; 2. swift, quick, rapid.
liguero, *adj* 1. league; league leader; 2. *nm* suspender belt, garter belt.
lija, *nf* 1. dogfish; 2. sandpaper; emery paper.
lijadora, *nf* sander, sanding machine.
lijar, *vt* to sand, sandpaper.
lila, *nf* lilac.
lima, *nf* 1. lime, sweet-lime tree. 2. (Tool) file; 3. filing, polishing.
limar, *vt* to file, file down, file off; to smooth, to polish (up).
limitación, *nf* limitation, restriction.
limitado, *adj* limited.
limitar, *vt* to limit, restrict; to cut down, reduce.
limitarse, *vr* to limit oneself, restrict oneself.
límite, *nm* limit; end; boundary, border.
limítrofe, *adj* bordering, neighboring.
limón, *nm* lemon; lime.
limonada, *nf* lemonade; lemon juice.
limonar, *nm* lemon grove.
limonero, *nm* lemon-tree.
limosina, *nf* limousine.
limosna, *nf* alms; charity.
liberalizar, *vt* to liberalize; to deregulate.
liberar, *vt* to free, liberate; to release from a duty.
libertad, *nf* liberty, freedom.
libertador(a), *adj* 1. liberating; 2. *nm/f* liberator.
libertar, *vt* to set free, liberate, release, to exempt, to save, deliver.
libra, *nf* pound.
librado(a), *nm/f* (Com) drawee.
librar, *vt* to save, free, rescue, deliver.

libre, *adj* free.

librea, *nf* livery, uniform.

librepensador(a), *nm/f* freethinker.

librería, *nf* bookshop.

librero, *nm* bookcase; bookseller.

libreta, *nf* notebook.

libreto, *nm* libretto; film script.

libro, *nm* book.

licencia, *nf* license, permission.

licenciado(a), *nm/f* licensiate, bachelor; lawyer.

licenciar, *vt* to license, grant a permit (or license) to.

licenciarse, *vr* to graduate, take one's degree.

licenciatura, *nf* degree, licentiate.

licitación, *nf* bidding (at auction).

licitador(a), *nm/f* bidder; auctioneer.

licitar, *vt* 1. to bid for; 2. to sell by auction.

lícito, *adj* lawful, legal, licit; permissible.

licor, *nm* 1. liquid; 2. (alcoholic) liquor, spirits.

licorería, *nf* distillery, liquor shop.

licorero, *nm* distiller.

licuado, *nm* milk shake.

licuadora, *nf* blender, liquidizer.

licuar, *vt* to liquefy, turn into liquid; to melt.

lid, *nf* fight, combat; dispute, controversy.

líder, *adj* 1. top, leading, foremost; 2. *nm/f* leader.

liderar, *vt* to lead; to head.

liderato, *nm* leadership; top position.

lidia, *nf* 1. bullfight; 2. trouble, nuisance.

lidiar, *vt* to fight.

liebre, *nf* hare.

lienzo, *nm* linen; canvas.

liga, *nf* league.

ligado, *nm* slur, tie; ligature.

ligamento, *nm* ligament.

ligar, *vt* to tie, bind; to alloy; to mix.

ligerear, *vi* to walk fast, move quickly.

ligereza, *nf* lightness; thinness.

ligero, *adj* 1. light; lightweight; 2. swift, quick, rapid.

liguero, *adj* 1. league; league leader; 2. *nm* suspender belt, garter belt.

lija, *nf* 1. dogfish; 2. sandpaper; emery paper.

lijadora, *nf* sander, sanding machine.

lijar, *vt* to sand, sandpaper.

lila, *nf* lilac.

lima, *nf* 1. lime, sweet-lime tree. 2. (Tool) file; 3. filing, polishing.

limar, *vt* to file, file down, file off; to smooth, to polish (up).

limitación, *nf* limitation, restriction.

limitado, *adj* limited.

limitar, *vt* to limit, restrict; to cut down, reduce.

limitarse, *vr* to limit oneself, restrict oneself.

límite, *nm* limit; end; boundary, border.

limítrofe, *adj* bordering, neighboring.

limón, *nm* lemon; lime.

limonada, *nf* lemonade; lemon juice.

limonar, *nm* lemon grove.

limonero, *nm* lemon-tree.

limosina, *nf* limousine.

limosna, *nf* alms; charity.

limosnero(a), *adj* 1. charitable; 2. *nm/f* almoner; beggar.

limpia, *nf* cleaning; clearing; clean-up.

limpiabarros, *nm* scraper; doormat.

limpiabotas, *nm* bootblack.

limpiador(a), *nm/f* cleaner.

limpiar, *vt* to clean; to cleanse; to wipe, wipe off, wipe clean.

limpieza, *nf* clean; cleaning, cleansing; shine; integrity, honesty.

limpio, *adj* clean, pure, neat, honest.

limusina, *nf* limousine.

lina, *nf* skein of coarse wool.

linaje, *nm* lineage, family.

linaza, *nf* linseed.

lince, *nm* 1. lynx; 2. shrewdness, intelligence.

linchamiento, *nm* lynching.

linchar, *vt* to lynch.

lindante, *adj* bordering, adjoining, adjacent.

lindar, *vi* to adjoin, be adjacent; to border on.

lindero, *adj* 1. adjoining, bordering; 2. *nm* edge, border; boundary.

lindo(a), *adj* pretty; exquisite, elegant, delicate; good-looking.

línea, *nf* line; cable.

lineal, *adj* linear; on-line.

linear, *vt* to line, draw lines, outline.

lingote, *nm* ingot.

lingüista, *nm/f* linguist, language specialist.

lingüística, *nf* linguistics.

linimento, *nm* liniment.

lino, *nm* 1. flax; 2. linseed; 3. linen; canvas.

linóleo, *nm* lino, linoleum.

linterna, *nf* lantern; lamp; headlight.

lío, *nm* 1. bundle; package, parcel; 2. row, fuss; mess, mix-up, confusion, muddle; jam.

lipidia, *nf* poverty, nuisance, pest.

lipidiar, *vt* to annoy, bother, pester.

líquida, *nf* liquid.

liquidación, *nf* 1. liquefaction; 2. liquidation; winding-up; settlement; 3. sale, clearance sale.

liquidador(a), *nm/f* liquidator.

liquidar, *vt* 1. to liquefy; 2. to liquidate; to settle; to wind up; clear; to sell off, sell up.

líquido, *adj* liquid; fluid.

lira, *nf* 1. lyre; 2. (Fin) lira.

lírica, *nf* lyrical poetry, lyric.

lisiado(a), *adj* 1. injured, hurt; lame, crippled; 2. *nm/f* cripple.

lisiar, *vt* to injure (permanently), hurt (seriously); to cripple, maim.

liso, *adj* smooth, even.

lisonja, *nf* flattery.

lisonjear, *vt* to flatter; to please, delight.

lisonjero(a), *adj* 1. flattering; gratifying; pleasing, agreeable; 2. *nm/f* flatterer.

lista, *nf* 1. list, catalogue; roll call; 2. strip; stripe.

listar, *vt* to list, enter on a list.

literal, *adj* literal.

literario, *adj* literary.

literatura, *nf* literature.

litografía, *nf* lithography.

litografiar, *vt* to lithograph.

litoral, *adj* 1. coastal, littoral, seaboard; 2. *nm* seaboard, littoral, coast.

litro, *nm* litre, liter.

liturgia, *nf* liturgy.

litúrgico, *adj* liturgical.

liviandad, *nf* 1. fickleness; frivolity, triviality; 2. lightness.

liviano, *adj* 1. fickle; frivolous, trivial; 2. light.

lívido, *adj* 1. livid; black and blue; 2. pale, pallid.

loar, *vt* to praise.

loba, *nf* she-wolf.

lobato, *nm* wolf cub.

lobito, *nm* otter.

lobo, *adj* 1. shy; 2. *nm* wolf.

lóbrego, *adj* dark, murky, gloomy.

lobreguez, *nf* darkness, murk(iness), gloom(iness).

lóbulo, *nm* lobe.

loca, *nf* madwoman, lunatic.

local, *adj* 1. local; home team; 2. *nm* place; site, scene; rooms; premises.

localidad, *nf* 1. locality; location; place, town; 2. seat, ticket.

localización, *nf* location; placing, siting; finding.

localizador, *nm* pager, paging device, beeper.

localizar, *vt* to locate; to place, to find, track down.

localizarse, *vr* to be located; to be localized.

locería, *nf* china; pottery; crockery.

locero(a), *nm/f* potter.

loción, *nf* lotion; wash.

loco, *adj* 1. mad, crazy; wild, mad; 2. *nm* madman; lunatic, maniac.

locomoción, *nf* locomotion; transport.

locomotora, *nf* engine, locomotive.

locuaz, *adj* talkative, loquacious, voluble.

locución, *nf* expression, idiom, phrase.

locura, *nf* madness, lunacy, insanity.

locutor(a), *nm/f* radio announcer, commentator; newscaster, newsreader.

lodazal, *nm* muddy place, mudhole.

lodo, *nm* mud, mire; sludge.

logia, *nf* lodge; loggia.

lógica, *nf* logic; logician.

lógico, *adj* logical; natural, right, reasonable.

logo, *nm* logo.

logrado, *adj* successful.

lograr, *vt* to get, obtain; to achieve, attain.

logro, *nm* achievement, attainment; success.

loma, *nf* hillock, low ridge.

lombriz, *nf* worm, earthworm.

lomería, *nf* series of ridges.

lomillo, *nm* 1. cross-stitch; 2. pads (of a pack saddle).

lomo, *nm* back; loin.

lona, *nf* canvas; sailcloth; sackcloth

loneta, *nf* canvas.

longaniza, *nf* long pork sausage.

longevidad, *nf* longevity

longevo, *adj* long-lived.

longitud, *nf* length; longitude.

lonja, *nf* 1. market, exchange; 2. grocer's (shop).

loor, *nm* praise.

loquear, *vi* to play the fool; to make merry.

loquera, *nf* madhouse, lunatic asylum.

lora, *nf* 1. (female) parrot; 2. chatterbox.

loro, *nm* 1. parrot; 2. thieves, lookout man.

losa, *nf* slab, flagstone.

loseta, *nf* carpet square, carpet tile; floor tile.

lote, *nm* portion, share; lot; batch; building site

lotería, *nf* lottery.

lotero(a), *nm/f* seller of lottery tickets.

lotificar, *vt* to divide into lots.

loza, *nf* crockery; earthenware; china, chinaware.

lozanear, *vi* to flourish, do well, grow strongly; to grow profusely.

lozanía, *nf* lushness, luxuriance; vigor; liveliness.

lozano, *adj* lush; luxuriant; rank; profuse; vigorous, lusty; lively, sprightly.

lubricación, *nf* lubrication.

lubricante, *adj* 1. lubricating; 2. *nm* lubricator.

lubricante, *adj* lubricant; lubricating.

lubricar, *vt* to lubricate, oil, grease.

lucero, *nm* bright star; venus.

lucidez, *nf* lucidity, clarity.

lúcido, *adj* lucid, clear.

lucido, *adj* splendid, brilliant; sumptuous, magnificent; elegant.

luciente, *adj* bright, shining, brilliant.

lucimiento, *nm* brilliance, luster, splendor.

lucir, *vt* 1. to illuminate, light up; 2. to show off, display; to sport.

lucirse, *vr* to dress up, dress elegantly.

lucrarse, *vr* to do well out of a deal; to enrich oneself.

lucrativo, *adj* lucrative, profitable, remunerative.

lucro, *nm* profit.

lucha, *nf* fight, struggle ; conflict; contest, dispute.

luchador(a), *nm/f* fighter; wrestler.

luchar, *vi* 1. to fight, struggle; 2. to wrestle.

luego, *adv* then, next; presently, soon; later, afterwards.

lugar, *nm* 1. place; spot; position; 2. room, space.

lugareño(a), *adj* 1. village; 2. local, regional; native; 3. *nm/f* villager.

lúgubre, *adj* mournful.

lujo, *nm* luxury; sumptuousness, lavishness.

lujuria, *nf* lust, lechery; lewdness.

lujuriante, *adj* 1. luxuriant, lush; 2. lustful.

lujuriar, *vi* to lust.

lumbago, *nm* lumbago.

lumbar, *adj* lumbar.

lumbre, *nf* 1. fire; 2. light.

lumbrera, *nf* 1. luminary; skylight; 2. vent, port; 3. leading light; authority.

luminaria, *nf* sanctuary lamp.

lumínico, *adj* light.

luminosidad, *nf* 1. brightness, luminosity; 2. brightness, brilliance.

luminoso, *adj* bright, luminous, shining; brilliant.

luminotecnia, *nf* lighting.

luminotécnico, *adj* lighting; lighting effects.

luna, *nf* moon; mirror.

lunar, *nm* mole, spot; defect, flaw, blemish; (moral) stain, blot; black spot.

lunático(a), *adj* 1. lunatic; 2. *nm/f* lunatic.

lunes, *nm* Monday.

lupa, *nf* lens, magnifying glass.

lupanar, *nm* brothel.

lustrada, *nf* shoeshine.

lustrador(a), *nm/f* 1. polisher; 2. shoeshine boy; shoeshine girl.

lustrar, *vt* to shine, polish.

lustre, *nm* 1. polish, shine, gloss; 2. glory.

lustro, *nm* lustrum, period of five years.

lustroso, *adj* glossy, bright, shining.

luteranismo, *nm* Lutheranism.

luterano(a), *adj*, *nm/f* Lutheran.

luto, *nm* mourning; grief, sorrow.

luxación, *nf* dislocation.

luz, *nf* light.

Ll

Ll, ll, *nf* (letter) Ll, ll.

llaga, *nf* wound; ulcer, sore; affliction, torment.

llagar, *vt* to wound, to injure.

llama, *nf* 1. llama; flame; blaze; 2. passion, ardor.

llamada, *nf* 1. call; knock, ring; 2. signal, sign, gesture.

llamado, *adj* so-called.

llamador, *nm* 1. caller; 2. door-knocker; bell.

maestre

llamamiento, *nm* call; (vocation) calling.

llamar, *vt* 1. to call, to name; 2. to summon; to invoke, call upon.

llamarse, *vr* to be called, be named.

llamarada, *nf* flare-up, sudden blaze; sudden flush.

llamativo, *adj* gaudy, flashy, showy; loud.

llame, *nm* bird trap.

llameante, *adj* blazing.

llamear, *vt/i* to blaze, flame, flare.

llana, *nf* plain; flat ground; mason's trowel.

llanear, *vi* to cruise, coast along.

llanero(a), *nm/f* plainsman, plainswoman.

llano, *adj* 1. level, flat, smooth, even; 2. plain, simple, unadorned; clear, easy, straightforward; open, frank; 3. *nm* plain.

llanta, *nf* tire; rim; inner tube.

llantén, *nm* plantain.

llantería, *nf* weeping and wailing.

llanto, *nm* weeping, crying; tears; lamentation; dirge.

llanura, *nf* 1. superficie flatness, smoothness, evenness; 2. plain; prairie.

llave, *nf* 1. key; 2. tap, faucet; 3. lock; hold; 4. (Mus) key.

llavero, *nm* key ring.

llavín, *nm* latchkey.

llegada, *nf* arrival, coming.

llegar, *vt* 1. to bring up, bring over, draw up; to gather together; 2. *vi* to arrive, come.

llegarse, *vr* to come near, draw near, approach.

llenador, *adj* filling, satisfying.

llenar, *vt* 1. to fill; to cover (with); occupy, take up; 2. to fulfill.

llenarse, *vr* to fill, fill up.

lleno, *adj* 1. full, filled; full up; 2. *nm* abundance, plenty; 3. full house, sellout.

llevadero, *adj* bearable, tolerable.

llevar, *vt* 1. to carry, take, transport, convey; 2. to wear.

llevarse, *vr* to carry off, take away, remove.

llorar, *vt* 1. to weep over, weep for, cry about; to bewail, lament; 2. *vi* to cry, weep.

llorera, *nf* sobbing, fit of crying.

lloretas, *nm/f* crybaby.

lloriquear, *vi* to snivel, whimper.

lloriqueo, *nm* snivelling, whimpering.

llorón, *adj* weeping, tearful; snivelling, whining.

llorón(a), *nm/f* tearful person, weepy sort; crybaby.

lloroso, *adj* weeping, tearful; sad.

llover, *vi* to rain.

llovida, *nf* rain, shower.

llovido, *nm* stowaway.

llovizna, *nf* drizzle.

lloviznar, *vi* to drizzle.

lloviznoso, *adj* drizzly.

lluvia, *nf* rain; shower; rainfall.

M

M, m, *nf* (letter) M, m.

macabí, *nm* 1. shrewd person; 2. bandit.

macabre , *adj* macabre.

macana, *nf* 1. club, cudgel; truncheon; 2. stupid comment.

macanazo, *nm* blow.

macanero, *adj* given to talking nonsense, silly; given to telling tall stories.

macanudo, *adj* 1. smashing, great; 2. swollen, overlarge; disproportionate; 3. strong, tough.

macarrón, *nm* 1. macaroon; 2. macaroni.

macear, *vt/f* 1. to hammer, pound; 2. to bet.

maceración, *nf* softening, soaking; maceration.

macerar, *vt/f* to soften, soak, macerate.

macero, *nm* macebearer.

maceta, *adj* 1. slow, thick; 2. flowerpot; bouquet, bunch of flowers; 3. mallet, small hammer; stone-cutter's hammer.

macetero, *nm*. flowerpot stand; flowerpot.

macillo, *nm* (Mus) hammer.

maciza, *nf* chipboard.

macizar, *vt* pack solid.

macizo, *adj* massive; solid; solidly made, stoutly made.

macrocosmo(s), *nm* macrocosm.

macroeconomía, *nf* macroeconomy.

mácula, *nf* 1. stain, spot, blemish; sunspot; 2. trick, fraud.

macular, *vt* to stain, spot.

macha, *nf* mannish woman.

machacadora, *nf* crusher, pounder.

machacante, *adj* insistent; monotonous.

machacar, *vt/f* 1. to crush, pound; to grind (up); to mash; 2. to knock to bits; to maul, crush.

machacón, *adj* 1. tiresome, wearisome; insistent; monotonous, repetitive; 2. *nm/f* pest, bore.

machetazo, *nm* 1. large machete; 2. blow (or slash) with a machete.

machete, *nm* machete, cane knife, big knife.

machetear, *vt* 1. to cut down with a machete; to slash (or wound, stab) with a machete; 2. to sell cheap.

machetero, *nm* 1. cane cutter; 2. porter; 3. revolutionary.

machihembrar, *vt* (joint) to dovetail.

machista, *adj* full of male pride, very masculine; male chauvinistic.

macho, *adj* 1. male; 2. masculine; strong, tough.

machucar, *vt* to bruise, crush, dent.

machucón, *nm* bruise.

madama, *nf* madame; brothel-keeper.

madeja, *nf* skein, hank; mass.

madera, *nf* 1. wood; woodwind section (of the orchestra); 2. timber.

maderero, *adj* wood, timber.

madero, *nm* 1. beam; log; (piece of) timber; 2. ship, vessel.

madrastra, *nf* stepmother.

madre, *adj* 1. mother; 2. *nf* mother, matron.

madreperla, *nf* pearl oyster; mother-of-pearl.

madrigal, *nm* madrigal.

madriguera, *nf* den; burrow; den.

madrileño(a), *adj* 1. of Madrid; typical of Madrid; 2. *nm/f* native (or inhabitant) of Madrid.

madrina, *nf* godmother.

madrugada, *nf* early morning; dawn; daybreak.

madrugador(a), *adj* 1. early rising, who gets up early; 2. *nm/f* early riser; early bird.

madrugar, *vt* to get up early.

maduración, *nf* ripening; maturing.

madurar, *vt* 1. to ripen; 2. to mature.

madurez, *nf* 1. ripeness; 2. maturity; sageness, wisdom.

maduro, *adj* 1. ripe; 2. mature.

maestra, *nf* teacher.

maestre, *nm* grand master (of a military order).

maestría, *nf* 1. mastery; skill, expertise; 2. master's degree.

maestro, *adj* 1. masterly; skilled, expert; 2. *nm* teacher; authority, master.

mafia, *nf* mafia, criminal gang, ring.

mafioso, *nm* member of the Mafia; gangster.

magia, *nf* magic.

mágico, *adj* magic, magical.

magisterio, *nm* teaching; teaching profession.

magistrado(a), *nm/f* magistrate; judge.

magnanimidad, *nf* magnanimity.

magnánimo, *adj* magnanimous.

magnate, *nm* magnate; tycoon.

magnavoz, *nm* loudspeaker.

magnesia, *nf* magnesia.

magnesio, *nm* magnesium; flash, flashlight.

magnético, *adj* magnetic.

magnetizar, *vt* to magnetize.

magneto, *nm* magnet.

magnetofón, *nm/f* tape recorder.

magnicida, *nm/f* assassin (of an important person).

magnificar, *vt* to praise, extol.

magnificencia, *nf* 1. splendor, magnificence; 2. lavishness, generosity.

magnífico, *adj* splendid, wonderful, superb, magnificent.

magno, *adj* great.

mago, *nm* magician, wizard.

magra, *nf* lean part (of meat).

magro, *adj* 1. thin, lean; 2. lean; low-fat; 3. (land) poor, thin.

magulladura, *nf* bruise.

magullar, *vt* to bruise; to hurt, damage; to batter, bash; to crumple, rumple.

maicena, *nf* blancmange; cornflour, corn starch.

maicero, *adj* maize, corn.

maíz, *nm* maize, corn.

maizal, *nm* maize field, cornfield.

majaderear, *vt* to bother, annoy.

majadería, *nf* 1. silliness; absurdity; 2. silly thing, absurdity; nonsense.

majadero, *adj* 1. silly, stupid; 2. *nm* idiot, fool.

majar, *vt* 1. to pound, crush, grind; to mash; to bruise; 2. to bother, pester.

majestad, *nf* majesty; stateliness.

majestuoso, *adj* majestic, stately, imposing.

majete, *adj* nice, likeable.

majeza, *nf* 1. good looks, attractiveness; loveliness; 2. smartness, nattiness; flashiness, gaudiness.

majo, *adj* 1. nice; pretty, attractive, handsome; lovely; 2. smart, natty; flashy, gaudy.

mal, *nm* 1. evil, damage, harm; 2. *adv* badly, poorly, wrong.

mala, *nf* bad luck.

malabarismo, *nm* 1. juggling, conjuring; 2. balancing act.

malabarista, *nm/f* juggler, conjurer.

malaconsejado, *adj* ill-advised.

malaconsejar, *vtf* to give bad advice to.

malacostumbrado, *adj* 1. having bad habits, vicious; 2. spoiled, pampered.

malacostumbrar, *vt* to get someone into bad habits.

malagradecido, *adj* ungrateful.

malanga, *nf* 1. thick; 2. *nf* tuber resembling a sweet potato.

malaria, *nf* malaria.

malbaratar, *vtf* to sell off cheap, sell at a loss; to squander.

malcasarse, *vr* to make an unhappy marriage.

malcriado, *adj* rude, bad-mannered, coarse.

malcriar, *vt* to spoil, pamper.

maldad, *nf* 1. evil, wickedness; 2. wicked thing.

maldecir, *vt* 1. to curse; 2. to loathe, detest; 3. *vi* speak ill of; to slander.

maldición, *nf* curse.

maldito(a), *adj* damned, accursed.

maleado, *adj* corrupt.

maleante, *adj* 1. wicked; villainous, rascally; unsavory; 2. *nm/f* malefactor, unsavory character.

malear, *vt* to damage, spoil, harm.

malecón, *nm* pier, jetty, mole.

maleducado, *adj* ill-bred, bad-mannered.

maleducar, *vt* to spoil.

maleficiar, *vt* 1. to bewitch, cast an evil spell on; 2. to harm, damage.

maleficio, *nm* curse, spell; witchcraft.

malestar, *nm* 1. discomfort; indisposition; 2. uneasiness, malaise; unrest.

maleta, *nf* 1. case, suitcase; traveling bag; 2. trunk; 3. saddlebag.

maletero, *nf* saddlebag; boot, trunk.

maletín, *nm* small case, bag; briefcase; satchel.

malevolencia, *nf* malevolence, malice, spite.

maleza, *nf* weeds.

malformación, *nf* malformation.

malformado, *adj* malformed.

malgastar, *vtf* to waste, squander.

malgenio(so), *adj* bad-tempered.

malhabido, *adj* ill-gotten.

malhablado, *adj* coarse, rude; foul-mouthed.

malhecho, *adj* 1. ugly; misshapen; 2. *nm* misdeed.

malhechor(a), *nm/f* malefactor, criminal, wrongdoer.

malhumorado, *adj* bad-tempered, cross.

malicia, *nf* 1. wickedness; 2. evil intention; spite, malice, maliciousness.

malicioso(a), *adj* wicked, evil; ill-intentioned; spiteful; malicious.

malignidad, *nf* malignancy.

maligno, *adj* malignant; pernicious.

malinformar, *vt* to misinform.

malinterpretar, *vt* to misinterpret, misunderstand.

malo(a), *adj* 1. bad; poor; wretched, dreadful; 2. hard, difficult.

malogrado, *adj* abortive; ill-fated.

malograr, *vt* to spoil, upset, ruin.

malpagar, *vt* to pay badly, underpay.

malparar, *vt* to damage; to harm, impair, wreck; to ill-treat.

malparir, *vt* to have a miscarriage, miscarry.

malpensado, *adj* nasty, evil-minded.

malsano, *adj* 1. unhealthy, bad; 2. sickly; morbid.

malsufrido, *adj* impatient; abused.

maltirar, *vi* to get by with difficulty, scrape a living.

maltratado, *adj* battered, abused.

maltratar, *vt* 1. to ill-treat, maltreat; 2. to abuse, insult.

maltrato, *nm* ill-treatment, maltreatment; rough handling, damage; abuse, insults.

maltrecho, *adj* battered, damaged; injured.

malva, *adj* mauve.

malvado, *adj* 1. evil, wicked, villainous; 2. *nm* evil-doer.

malversación, *nf* embezzlement; misappropriation.

malversador(a), *nm/f* embezzler.

malversar, *vt* to embezzle, misappropriate; to distort.

malla, *nf* mesh; network; wire mesh, wire netting.

mamá, *nf* 1. mamma, mom; 2. mother.

mamada, *nf* suck; milk; feeding time.

mamadera, *nf* rubber teat; feeding-bottle.

mamantear, *vt* 1. to nurse, feed, suckle. 2. to spoil, pamper.

mamar, *vt* 1. to suck; 2. to absorb, assimilate; to acquire in infancy.

mestizo, *adj* half-breed.

mamífero, *adj* 1. mammalian; 2. *nm/f* mammal.

mamografía, *nf* mammography.

mampara, *nf* screen; partition.

mampostería, *nf* masonry; rubblework.

maná, *nm* manna.

manada, *nf* 1. herd, flock; pack; 2. crowd, mob.

manadero, *nm* shepherd, herdsman, drover.

manantial, *adj* 1. running water, flowing water; 2. *nm* spring, fountain; 3. source, origin; cause.

manar, *vt* 1. to run with, flow with; 2. to pour out, stream, gush forth.

manatí, *nm* manatee.

mancar, *vt* to maim, cripple.

manceba, *nf* lover, mistress; concubine.

mancebía, *nf* brothel.

mancebo, *nm* 1. youth, young man; 2. bachelor; 3. clerk; assistant.

mancillar, *vt* (honor) to stain, sully.

manco(a), *adj* 1. one-handed; one-armed; armless; crippled; 2. defective, faulty.

mancomunar, *vt* to unite, associate, bring together; to combine.

mancornar, *vt* 1. to seize by the horns; to hobble; 2. to join, couple.

mancha, *nf* spot, mark; speckle; fleck; stain.

manchado(a), *adj* spotty; spotted; dappled; speckled; smudged.

manchar, *vt* to spot, mark; to soil, dirty, stain; to smudge, to stain.

mancharse, *vr* to get dirty.

mandadero, *nm* messenger; errand boy, office boy.

mandado, *nm* order; commission; errand.

mandamiento, *nm* order, command; (Bib) commandment.

mandar, *vt* to order.

mandarina, *nf* tangerine, mandarin.

mandatario, *nm* 1. agent, attorney; 2. leader; political figure; head of state.

mandato, *nm* 1. order; writ, warrant; command; 2. mandate; mandated territory; 3. term (of office); period of rule.

mandíbula, *nf* jaw, mandible.

mando, *nm* command; rule; control; authority; leadership.

mandolina, *nf* mandolin(e).

mandón, *adj* bossy, domineering.

mandril, *nm* mandrill; mandrel.

manecilla, *nf* 1. pointer, (clock) hand; 2. clasp.

manejable, *adj* manageable; handy, easy to use; maneuverable.

manejador(a), *nm/f* driver, motorist.

manejar, *vt* to handle; to run, work, operate; manage.

manejo, *nm* handling; running, working.

manera, *nf* way, manner, fashion; way of going about things.

manga, *nf* 1. sleeve; shirtsleeve; 2. hose, hosepipe.

manganeso, *nm* manganese.

mangar, *vt* 1. to pinch, lift; 2. to beg (for), scrounge; 2. *vi* to pilfer; to shoplift.

manglar, *nm* mangrove swamp.

mangle, *nm* mangrove.

mango, *nm* 1. mango; 2. good-looking lad.

manguera, *nf* hose, hosepipe; pipe, tube.

maní, *nm* peanut; groundnut plant.

manía, *nf* mania; rage, craze, whim, fad.

maníaco, *adj* maniac(al).

maníaca, *nf* maniac; sex maniac.

maniatar, *vt* to tie the hands of; to handcuff.

maniático, *adj* 1. maniacal; fanatical; 2. crazy; odd, eccentric, peculiar; cranky.

manicero(a), *nm/f* peanut seller.

manicomio, *nm* lunatic asylum, mental hospital.

manida, *nf* lair, den.

manido, *adj* 1. high, gamy; smelly; 2. trite, stale.

manifestación, *nf* 1. manifestation; show; sign; 2. statement, declaration; 3. demonstration; mass meeting; rally.

manifestar, *vt* to show, manifest, demonstrate, reveal.

manifiesto, *adj* clear, manifest; evident.

manigueta, *nf* handle, haft; crank.

manija, *nf* handle.

manilla, *nf* 1. bracelet; handcuffs, manacles; 2. door handle.

manillar, *nm* handlebar(s).

maniobra, *nf* handling; maneuvering; operation, control.

maniobrar, *vt* to handle, operate; to maneuver; to shunt.

manipulación, *nf* manipulation.

manipulado, *nm* handling.

manipulador(a), *nm/f* manipulator; handler.

manipular, *vt* to manipulate; to handle; to interfere with.

manipulativo, *adj* manipulative.

maniqueo, *adj* Manichean.

maniquí, *nm* 1. dummy; 2. puppet; 3. mannequin, model.

manir, *vtf* to hang.

manirroto, *adj* 1. lavish, extravagant, prodigal; 2. *nm* spendthrift.

manita, *nf* little hand.

manjar, *nm* dish, special dish.

mano, *nf* hand; foot, forefoot, paw.

manojo, *nm* handful, bunch.

manómetro, *nm* pressure-gauge, manometer.

manoseado, *adj* hackneyed, well-worn.

manosear, *vt* to handle, finger, touch; to rumple, mess up.

manoseo, *nm* handling, fingering, touching; rumpling.

manotada, *nf* slap, smack.

manoteador, *nm* thief; bag-snatcher; gesticulator.

manotear, *vt* 1. to slap, smack, cuff; 2. *vi* to gesticulate, move (or use) one's hands.

manoteo, *nm* gesticulation; theft, robbery.

manquear, *vi* to be maimed, be crippled; to pretend to be crippled; to limp.

mansalva, *adv* without risk, without any danger.

mansedumbre, *nf* 1. gentleness, meekness; 2. tameness.

mansión, *nf* mansion.

manso, *adj* 1. gentle, mild, meek; 2. tame.

manta, *nf* 1. blanket; shawl; 2. calico; poncho.

manteca, *nf* fat; butter.

mantecada, *nf* small cake, iced bun.

mantecado, *nm* ice cream; buttery cake.

mantel, *nm* tablecloth; altar cloth.

mantelería, *nf* table linen.

mantenedor, *nm* chairman, president.

mantener, *vt* to hold up, support.

mantenido, *nm* kept man, gigolo; sponger.

mantenimiento, *nm* maintenance.

mantequera, nf 1. churn; 2. butter dish.
mantequería, nf dairy, creamery; grocer's (shop).
mantequilla, nf butter.
mantequillera, nf butter-dish.
mantillón, nm 1. horse-blanket; 2. kept man, kept woman, mistress; sponger.
manto, nm 1. cloak; robe, gown; 2. mantle.
mantón, nm shawl.
manual, adj 1. manual, hand; 2. nm handbook, guide; stylebook.
manualidad, nf manual craft; handicraft.
manubrio, nm 1. handle, crank; winch; 2. handlebar(s); steering-wheel.
manufactura, nf 1. manufacture; 2. factory.
manufacturar, vt to manufacture.
manufacturero, adj 1. manufacturing; 2. nm manufacturer; 3. nm/f manufacturing company.
manuscrito, adj handwritten, manuscript.
manutención, nf maintenance; support; upkeep.
manzana, nf apple.
manzanilla, nf camomile; camomile tea.
manzano, nm apple tree.
maña, nf skill, dexterity; ingenuity; craft.
mañana, adv 1. tomorrow; 2. nm future; 3. nf morning.
mañanero(a), adj 1. early-rising, who gets up early; 2. nm/f early riser.
mañoso, adj clever, ingenious, skillful; sharp, crafty, wily.
mapa, nm map.
mapear, vt to map.
maqueta, nf model; scale model
maquetear, vt to lay out, design.
maquetista, nm/f model-maker.
maquilar, vt to assemble.
maquillador(a), nm/f make-up artist.
maquillaje, nm make-up; making-up.
maquillar, vt to make up.
maquillarse, vr to make up.
máquina, nf machine; engine.
maquinación, nf machination, scheme, plot.
maquinador(a), nm/f schemer, plotter.
maquinal, adj mechanical, automatic.
maquinar, vti to plot, machinate.
maquinaria, nf machinery.
maquinilla, nf small machine.
maquinista, nm engine-driver, engineer; operator, machinist.
mar, nf sea, ocean.
maraca, nf maraca, rattle.
maraña, nf thicket; tangle of plants.
marañero, adj 1. scheming; 2. nm/f schemer.
maraquear, vt to shake, rattle.
maraquero, nm maraca player.
maratón, nm marathon.
maravilla, nf marvel, wonder.
maravillar, vt to astonish, amaze.
maravilloso, adj wonderful, marvelous.
marca, nf mark; stamp; name tab; footprint; brand name, make.
marcación, nf 1. bearing; 2. dialing.
marcado, adj 1. marked, strong, pronounced; 2. nm branding.
marcador, nm marker; bookmark; scorer.
marcapasos, nm pacemaker.
marcar, vt to mark; to brand, stamp.
marcial, adj martial.
marco, nm frame; framework.
marcha, nf march.
marchante(a), nm/f 1. dealer, merchant; 2. client, customer.

marchar, vi to go; to move, travel; to march.
marchitar, vt to wither, fade, shrivel, dry up.
marchito, adj 1. withered, faded; 2. faded; in decline.
marea, nf tide.
mareado, adj dizzy; seasick, nauseated.
marear, vt to sail, navigate.
marearse, vr to get faint, dizzy.
marejada, nf swell, heavy sea; surge.
maremoto, nm tidal wave.
mareo, nm sick feeling; travel sickness, seasickness.
marfil, nm ivory.
marfileño, adj ivory, like ivory.
margarina, nf margarine.
margarita, nf pearl.
margen, nm border, edge, fringe.
marginación, nf exclusion, rejection.
marginado, adj excluded, left out; neglected; pushed aside.
marginal, adj marginal.
marginar, vt to exclude, leave out, push aside; to reject; to isolate.
mariachi, nm mariachi music.
maridaje, nm conjugal life; marriage ties.
marido, nm husband.
marijuana, nf marijuana.
marimba, nf kind of drum; marimba.
marina, nf 1. coast, coastal area; 2. seamanship; 3. ships; navy; 4. (Art) seascape.
marinar, vt to marinade, marinate.
marinero, adj 1. seafaring; 2. seaworthy; 3. nm sailor, seaman; mariner, seafarer.
marino, adj sea, marine.
marioneta, nf marionette, puppet.
marionetista, nm/f puppeteer.
mariposa, nf butterfly.
mariposear, vif to flutter about, flit to and fro.
mariquita, nf 1. ladybird; 2. parakeet.
mariscada, nf seafood dish.
mariscal, nm blacksmith, farrier; major-general.
mariscos, nm shellfish, seafood.
marital, adj marital.
marítimo, adj maritime; marine, sea.
mármol, nm marble.
marmóreo, adj marble; marmoreal.
marmota, nf marmot.
maroma, nf rope; tightrope; acrobatic performance.
maromear, vi to walk (on) a tightrope; to do acrobatic stunts.
maromero, nm tightrope walker, acrobat.
marqués(a), nm/f marquis; marchioness.
marquesina, nf glass canopy, porch; glass roof, cantilever roof.
marranada, nf filthiness; dirty trick, vile deed.
marrano, adj 1. filthy, dirty; 2. nm pig, boar.
marrón, adj chestnut, brown.
marsopa, nf porpoise.
marsupial, adj, nm marsupial.
martes, nm Tuesday.
martillar, vt to hammer; to pound.
martillazo, nm blow with a hammer.
martilleante, adj insistent, repetitious.
martilleo, nm hammering; pounding.
martillo, nm hammer; gavel.
martinete, nm drop hammer; pile driver.
mártir, nm/f martyr.
martirio, nm martyrdom.
martirizador, adj agonizing, excruciating.
martirizar, vt to martyr; to torture, torment.
marzo, nm March.

más, *adv, adj* more; most.

mas, *conj* but.

masa, *nf* 1. dough; 2. mortar, plaster; 3. mass; bulk; volume, quantity.

masacrar, *vt* to massacre.

masacre, *nf* massacre.

masaje, *nm* massage.

masajear, *vt* to massage.

mascada, *nf* plug of chewing tobacco.

mascar, *vt* to chew; to mumble, mutter.

máscara, *nf* mask.

mascarada, *nf* mask, masquerade.

mascota, *nf* mascot.

masculino, *adj* masculine; manly; male.

masilla, *nf* putty; filler.

masillo, *nm* plaster.

masita, *nf* small bun, teacake, pastry.

masivo, *adj* massive.

masón, *nm* (free)mason.

masonería, *nf* (free)masonry.

masónico, *adj* masonic.

masoquista, *adj* 1. masochistic. 2. *nmf* masochist.

mastectomía, *nf* mastectomy.

masticación, *nf* mastication.

masticar, *vt* to masticate, chew.

mástil, *nm* pole, post; support; flagpole.

mastín, *nm* mastiff; Great Dane.

mastodonte, *nm* mastodon; elephantine person.

mata, *nf* bush, shrub; plant.

matadero, *nm* slaughterhouse, abattoir, drudgery.

matador(a), *adj* 1. killing; 2. *nm/f* killer; 3. bullfighter.

matadura, *nf* sore.

matanza, *nf* 1. slaughter, killing; slaughtering; 2. slaughterhouse; butcher's (shop).

matar, *vt* to kill; to slay; to slaughter.

matarse, *vr* to kill oneself, commit suicide; to be killed, overwork oneself.

matarife, *nm* butcher, slaughterman.

matasanos, *nm* quack (doctor).

mate, *adj* 1. dull, matte, unpolished; 2. *nm* mate, checkmate; 3. maté, Paraguayan tea (herb and drink similar to tea).

matemáticas, *nf* mathematics.

matemático(a), *adj* 1. mathematical; 2. *nm/f* mathematician.

materia, *nf* matter; material; stuff.

material, *adj* 1. material; 2. physical.

materialista, *adj* 1. materialist(ic); 2. *nm/f* materialist.

materializar, *vt* to materialize.

maternal, *adj* motherly; maternal.

maternidad, *nf* motherhood maternity.

matinal, *adj* morning.

matinée, *nm* matinée.

matiz, *nm* shade, hue, tint.

matizar, *vt* to blend; to tinge, tint.

matón, *nm* bully, lout, thug.

matorral, *nm* thicket; brushwood, scrub.

matrero, *adj* cunning, sly, knowing.

matricida, *nm/f* matricide (person).

matricidio, *nm* matricide.

matrícula, *nf* register, list, roll.

matricular, *vt* to register; to enrol; to license.

matrimonial, *adj* matrimonial.

matrimoniar, *vi* to marry, get married.

matrimonio, *nm* marriage, matrimony; married state.

matriz, *nf* womb, uterus; matrix.

matutino, *adj* morning.

maullar, *vi* to mew, meow

maullido, *nm* mew, meow.

maxilar, *adj* 1. maxillary; 2. *nm* jaw, jawbone.

máxima, *nf* maxim.

maximizar, *vt* to maximize.

máximo, *adj* maximum; top; highest, greatest.

maya, *nf* 1. daisy; 2. *adj* Mayan.

mayo, *nm* May.

mayonesa, *nf* mayonnaise.

mayor, *adj* 1. main, major, larger; 2. principal; 3. grown up, adult; of age; elderly.

mayordomo, *nm* steward, butler.

mayorear, *vi* to be in charge, be the boss.

mayoreo, *nm* wholesale (trade).

mayoría, *nf* majority, greater part, larger part.

mayorista, *nmf* wholesaler.

mayúscula, *nf* capital (letter); upper case letter

mayúsculo, *adj* big, tremendous.

maza, *nf* mace; war club; bat.

mazmorra, *nf* dungeon.

mazo, *nm* club; mallet; pestle.

mazorca, *nf* (Bot) spike; cob, ear.

mecánica, *nf* mechanics.

mecánico, *adj* 1. mechanical; 2. *nm/f* mechanic; machinist.

mecanización, *nf* mechanization.

mecanizar, *vt/f* to mechanize.

mecanografía, *nf* typing, typewriting.

mecanografiar, *vt* to type.

mecanógrafo(a), *nm/f* typist.

mecedor, *adj* 1. rocking; swinging; 2. *nm* swing.

mecedora, *nf* rocking-chair.

mecer, *vt* to swing; to rock.

mecha, *nf* wick; fuse.

mechar, *vt* to lard; to stuff.

mechero, *nm* cigarette lighter; burner.

mechón, *nm* tuft, lock, bundle.

medalla, *nf* medal.

medallón, *nm* medallion.

media, *nf* stocking; sock.

mediación, *nf* mediation; intercession.

mediado, *adj* half full.

mediador(a), *nm/f* mediator.

mediano, *adj* middling, medium, average; medium-sized.

medianoche, *nf* midnight.

mediar, *vi* to be in the middle; to get to the middle, get halfway; intervene.

medializar, *vt* to interfere with, obstruct; to affect adversely, influence for the worse.

medicamento, *nm* medicine, drug; patent medicine.

medicinar, *vt* to treat, prescribe for.

medición, *nf* measurement, measuring; to take measurements.

médico, *adj* 1. medical; 2. *nm/f* doctor; medical practitioner, physician.

medida, *nf* measurement, size.

medir, *vt* to measure, to gauge.

medidor, *nm* meter; gauge.

medieval, *adj* medieval.

medio, *adj* 1. half; 2. mid, midway, middle; 3. mean, average.

mediocre, *adj* middling, average; mediocre, rather poor.

mediodía, *nm* noon, midday.

meditar, *vt* to ponder, think over, meditate.

mediterráneo, *adj* Mediterranean; land-locked.

medrar, *vi* to increase, grow; to improve, do well, do better.

médula, *nf* marrow; medulla.

medular, *adj* central, fundamental, essential.

mejicano(a), *adj, nm/f* Mexican.

Méjico, *nm* Mexico.

mejilla, *nf* cheek.

mejor, *adj* better; best.

mejorar, *vt* to improve, make better, to upgrade; to enhance.

mejoría, *nf* improvement; recovery.

melado, *adj* 1. honey-colored; 2. *nm* treacle, syrup; cane syrup.

melancolía, *nf* melancholy, gloom(iness), sadness.

melancólico, *adj* melancholy, gloomy, sad; dreamy.

melaza, *nf* molasses; treacle.

melcochado, *adj* candied; golden, honey-colored.

melena, *nf* long hair; loose hair, flowing hair.

melenudo, *adj* long-haired.

melindre, *nm* sweet cake, iced bun; honey fritter.

melindrear, *vi* to be affected; be fussy.

melindroso, *adj* affected; squeamish; prudish; finicky, fussy.

melocotón, *nm* peach; peach-tree.

melodía, *nf* melody; tune, air.

melódico, *adj* melodic.

melón, *nm* melon, watermelon.

melonada, *nf* silly thing, idiotic remark.

melonar, *nm* bed of melons, melon plot.

mellado, *adj* jagged, nicked, ragged.

mellar, *vt* to nick, dent, notch; to take a chip out of.

mellizo(a), *adj, nm/f* twin.

membresía, *nf* membership.

membrete, *nm* letterhead, heading.

memo, *adj* 1. silly, stupid; 2. *nm* idiot; 3. memo, memorandum.

memorable, *adj* memorable.

memoria, *nf* memory.

memorial, *nm* memorial, petition; brief.

memorización, *nf* memorizing.

memorizar, *vt* to memorize.

mención, *nf* mention.

mencionado, *adj* aforementioned.

mencionar, *vt* to mention, refer to; to name.

mendacidad, *nf* mendacity, untruthfulness.

mendaz, *adj* mendacious; lying, untruthful.

mendicante, *adj* mendicant.

mendigar, *vt* to beg (for).

mendigo(a), *nm/f* beggar.

meneado, *adj* drunk.

menear, *vt* to move, shift.

menearse, *vr* to move; to shake; to wag; to sway, swing, waggle.

meneo, *nm* movement; shake, toss; wag; sway(ing), swing(ing); waggle; jerk, jolt.

menester, *nm* to be necessary; when it is necessary.

mengua, *nf* decrease, diminishment; dwindling; decay, decline.

menguado, *adj* decreased, diminished.

menguante, *adj* decreasing, diminishing; dwindling; decaying.

menguar, *vt* to lessen, diminish, reduce; to decrease.

meningitis, *nf* meningitis.

menor, *adj* 1. minor; 2. *adj comp* smaller; less, lesser; 3. younger; junior.

minoría, *nf* 1. minority; 2. inferiority; subordination.

minorista, *adj* 1. retail; 2. *nm/f* retailer.

menos, *adj* 1. minus; 2. less; fewer.

menoscabar, *vt* to lessen, reduce, diminish; to damage, harm, impair; descredit.

menoscabo, *nm* lessening, reduction; damage; harm; loss.

menospreciar, *vt* to scorn, despise; to slight.

menosprecio, *nm* scorn, contempt.

mensaje, *nm* message.

mensajero(a), *nm/f* messenger; courier.

menstruación, *nf* menstruation.

menstruar, *vi* to menstruate.

mensual, *adj* monthly.

mensualidad, *nf* monthly payment.

menta, *nf* mint.

mental, *adj* mental; intellectual.

mentalidad, *nf* mentality, mind.

mentar, *vt* to mention, name.

mente, *nf* mind; intelligence, understanding.

mentecato(a), *adj* 1. silly, stupid; 2. *nm/f* idiot, fool.

mentir, *vt* to feign, pretend, to lie.

mentiroso(a), *adj* 1. lying, deceitful, untruthful; deceptive, false; 2. *nm/f* liar; deceiver.

mentol, *nm* menthol.

mentolado, *adj* mentholated.

mentón, *nm* chin.

mentor, *nm* mentor.

menú, *nm* menu.

menudear, *vt* to repeat frequently, do repeatedly; to sell retail.

menudo, *adj* small, tiny, minute; slight, petty, insignificant; giblets.

meñique, *adj* 1. tiny, very small; 2. *nm* little finger.

meollo, *nm* marrow, brains; core, essence.

mercadear, *vt* 1. to market; to haggle over; 2. *vi* to deal, trade.

mercader, *nm* merchant.

mercadería, *nf* commodity; goods, merchandise.

mercado, *nm* market.

mercancía, *nf* commodity; goods, merchandise.

mercante, *adj* 1. merchant, trading; 2. *nm* merchantman, merchant ship.

mercantil, *adj* mercantile, trading, commercial.

mercantilizar, *vt* to commercialize.

mercenario(a), *adj* 1. mercenary; 2. *nm/f* mercenary.

mercurio, *nm* mercury.

merecedor, *adj* deserving, worthy.

merecer, *vt* to deserve, be worthy of, merit.

merecido, *adj* well deserved, fully deserved.

merendar, *vt* to have as an afternoon snack.

merendero, *nm* open-air café, snack bar.

meridiana, *nf* divan, couch; chaise lounge, day bed.

meridiano, *adj* 1. midday; 2. *nm* meridian.

meridional, *adj* 1. southern; 2. *nm/f* southerner.

merienda, *nf* afternoon snack.

merino, *adj* 1. merino; 2. *nm* merino.

mérito, *nm* merit; worth, value.

meritorio, *adj* 1. meritorious, worthy, deserving; 2. *nm* unpaid employee, apprentice, unpaid trainee.

merluza, *nf* hake, cod.

merma, *nf* decrease; shrinkage; wastage, loss.

mermar, *vt* to reduce, lessen; to deplete.

mermelada, *nf* jam.

mero, *adj* 1. mere, pure, simple; 2. precise, exact; 3. right.

merodeador, *adj* 1. marauding; prowling; 2. *nm* prowler.

merodear, *vi* to maraud; to prowl, rove about.

merodeo, *nm* marauding; prowling, roving.

mes, *nm* month.

mesa, *nf* table; desk; counter.

mesana, *nf* mizzen.

mesero(a), *nm/f* waiter; waitress.

meseta, *nf* tableland, plateau.

mesiánico, *adj* messianic.

Mesías, *nm* Messiah.

mesilla, *nf* small table, side table, occasional table.

mesón, *nm* meson; inn.

mesonero(a), *nm/f* innkeeper; landlord, landlady; waiter, waitress.

mestizo(a), *adj* (person) of mixed-race; hybrid.

mesura, *nf* 1. gravity, dignity, calm; 2. moderation, restraint; 3. courtesy.

mesurado, *adj* 1. grave, dignified, calm; 2. moderate, restrained; 3. courteous.

mesurar, *vt* to restrain, temper.

mesurarse, *vr* to act with restraint, to restrain oneself.

meta, *nf* goal; winning post, finishing-line.

metafísica, *nf* metaphysics.

metafísico, *adj* 1. metaphysical; 2. *nm/f* metaphysician.

metáfora, *nf* metaphor.

metal, *nm* metal.

metálico, *adj* metallic; metal.

metalizado, *adj* 1. metallic; 2. mercenary, dedicated to making money; who sees everything in terms of money.

metalizarse, *vr* to become mercenary.

metamorfosis, *nf* metamorphosis, transformation.

metedura, *nf* putting, placing; insertion.

meteórico, *adj* meteoric.

meteorito, *nm* meteor, meteorite.

meteoro, *nm* meteor.

meteorología, *nf* meteorology.

meter, *vt* to put, place; to insert, introduce.

meticuloso, *adj* meticulous, scrupulous, thorough.

metido, *adj* to be deeply involved in a matter.

metódico, *adj* methodical.

metodista, *adj* 1. Methodist; 2. *nm/f* Methodist

método, *nm* method.

metodología, *nf* methodology.

metralla, *nf* shrapnel.

metralleta, *nf* submachine gun, tommy gun.

métrica, *nf* metrics.

métrico, *adj* metric(al).

metro, *nm* 1. meter; 2. subway.

metrópolis, *nf* metropolis; mother country.

mezcla, *nf* mixture.

mezclado, *nm* mixture.

mezclador, *nm* mixing bowl, mixer.

mezclar, *vt* to mix, mix up; combine.

mezquinar, *vif* to be stingy with, give sparingly.

mezquindad, *nf* meanness, stinginess.

mezquino, *adj* mean, stingy.

mezquita, *nf* mosque.

miaja, *nf* crumb.

mica, *nf* mica.

micada, *nf* flourish.

mico(a), *nm/f* monkey.

micro, *nm* 1. mike, microphone; 2. minibus, bus; coach; 3. micro, microcomputer.

microbio, *nm* microbe.

microbiología, *nf* microbiology.

microcosmo(s), *nm* microcosm.

microficha, *nf* microfiche.

microfilm, *nm* microfilms.

micrófono, *nm* microphone; mouthpiece.

microonda, *nf* microwave; microwave oven.

microscopio, *nm* microscope.

miedo, *nm* fear, dread; apprehension.

miedoso, *adj* fearful, fainthearted; timid, nervous, shy.

miel, *nf* honey.

miembro, *nm* limb, member, penis.

mientras, *conj* 1. while; as long as; 2. whereas; 3. *adv* meanwhile, meantime; all the while.

miércoles, *nm* Wednesday.

mies, *nf* 1. corn, wheat, grain; 2. harvest time.

miga, *nf* crumb; bit; fried breadcrumbs.

migajas, *nf* crumbs; bits; leavings, scraps.

migración, *nf* migration.

migraña, *nf* migraine.

migrar, *vi* to migrate.

migratorio, *adj* migratory.

mil, *adj, nm* thousand.

milagro, *nm* miracle; wonder.

milagroso, *adj* miraculous.

milenario, *adj* millennial; very ancient.

milenio, *nm* millennium.

milicia, *nf* militia; military, soldiery.

miliciano, *nm* militiaman; conscript.

miligramo, *nm* milligram.

mililitro, *nm* milliliter.

milímetro, *nm* millimeter.

militante, *adj* 1. militant; 2. *nm/f* militant.

militar, *adj* 1. military; 2. *nm* soldier, military man; serviceman; 3. *vi* to serve.

militarizar, *vt* to militarize; to put under military discipline.

milpa, *nf* maize field, cornfield, maize, indian corn.

milla, *nf* mile.

millar, *nm* thousand.

millo, *nm* millet.

millón, *nm* million.

millonario(a), *nm/f* millionaire.

mimado, *adj* spoiled.

mimar, *vt* to spoil, pamper, indulge.

mimeografiar, *vt* to mimeograph.

mimeógrafo, *nm* mimeograph.

mímica, *nf* 1. sign language; gesticulation; 2. mimicry.

mímico, *adj* mimic; imitative.

mimo, *nm* 1. mime; mimic; 2. affectionate caress; nice remark; pampering, indulgence.

mina, *nf* mine; underground passage; gallery.

minador, *nm* sapper; mining engineer.

minar, *vt* 1. to mine; 2. to undermine, sap, wear away.

mineral, *adj* mineral.

mineralogía, *nf* mineralogy.

minería, *nf* mining.

minero, *adj* 1. mining; 2. *nm/f* miner.

miniatura, *adj* miniature.

miniaturizar, *vt* to miniaturize.

minicalculadora, *nf* pocket calculator.

minicoche, *nm* minicar.

minifalda, *nf* miniskirt.

minifundio, *nm* small holding, small farm.

minimizar, *vt* to minimize.

mínimo, *adj* minimum; minimal; smallest, slightest, least.

minino(a), *nm* puss, pussy-cat.

ministerio, *nm* ministry.

ministro(a), *nm/f* minister.

minoración, *nf* reduction, diminution.

minorar, *vt* to reduce, diminish.

minoría, *nf* minority.

minorista, *nm* retailer, retail trader.

minoritario, *adj* minority.

minucioso, *adj* thorough, meticulous; very detailed; minute.

minúscula, *nf* small letter; lower case letter.

minúsculo, *adj* tiny, minute, minuscule; small.

minusválido, *adj* (physically) handicapped, disabled.

minuta, *nf* 1. rough draft, first draft; 2. note, memorandum; lawyer's bill; 3. menu; list.

minutar, *vt* 1. to draft; 2. to bill.

minutero, *nm* minute-hand; timer.

minuto, *nm* minute.

mío, *adj, pron* mine, of mine.

miope, *adj* 1. short-sighted, myopic; 2. *nm/f* short-sighted person.

miopía, *nf* short-sightedness, myopia.

mirada, *nf* look, glance; gaze.

miradero, *nm* look-out, vantage point.

mirador, *nm* bay window; balcony; viewpoint, vantage point.

miramiento, *nm* 1. considerateness; courtesy; 2. caution, circumspection, care.

mirar, *vt* to look at; to gaze at; to watch.

miríada, *nf* myriad.

mirilla, *nf* peephole, spyhole; viewer.

misa, *nf* mass.

misal, *nm* missal.

misceláneo, *adj* miscellaneous.

miserable, *adj* 1. mean, stingy; miserly; miserable, paltry, pitifully small; 2. rotten, vile, contemptible, despicable.

miseria, *nf* 1. poverty, destitution; want; 2. squalor, squalid conditions.

misericordia, *nf* 1. pity, compassion; 2. forgiveness; mercy.

mísero, *adj* wretched.

misión, *nf* mission; job, task; (Ecl) missionary work.

misionero(a), *nm/f* missionary.

misiva, *nf* missive.

mismo, *adj* same.

misterioso, *adj* mysterious; mystifying, puzzling.

místico(a), *adj* 1. mystic(al); 2. *nm/f* mystic.

mistificar, *vt* 1. to hoax, play a practical joke on; to hoodwink, take in; 2. to mix up, make a mess of.

mitad, *nf* half.

mítico, *adj* mythical.

mitigar, *vt* to mitigate, allay; to relieve; to quench.

mito, *nm* myth.

mitología, *nf* mythology.

mixto, *adj* mixed.

mixturar, *vt* to mix.

mobiliario, *nm* furniture; household goods.

moca, *nf* coffee-flavored cake (or biscuit).

mocasín, *nm* moccasin.

mocear, *vi* to play around, live a bit wildly, sow one's wild oats.

mocerío, *nm* young people.

mocetón, *nm* strapping youth.

mocetona, *nf* big girl, hefty wench.

moción, *nf* 1. motion, movement; 2. motion (to propose a motion).

mocionar, *vti* to move, propose.

moco, *nm* mucus.

mocoso(a), *adj* 1. snivelling; ill-bred, rude; 2. *nm/f* brat; child.

mochila, *nf* rucksack, knapsack, back-pack.

mochilero(a), *nm/f* back-packer.

moda, *nf* fashion; style.

modal, *adj* 1. modal; 2. *nm* manners.

modalidad, *nf* form, kind, variety; fashion; way.

modelado, *nm* modeling.

modelador(a), *nm/f* modeler.

modelaje, *nm* modeling.

modelar, *vt* to model.

modelizar, *vt* to model, create a model of.

modelo, *nm* model; pattern; standard.

moderado, *adj* moderate.

moderador(a), *nm/f* presenter.

moderar, *vt* to moderate; to restrain, control.

moderarse, *vr* to control oneself; to calm down.

modernista, *adj* 1. modernist(ic); 2. *nm/f* modernist.

modernización, *nf* modernization.

modernizador(a), *adj* 1. modernizing; 2. *nm/f* modernizer.

modernizar, *vt* to modernize.

moderno(a), *adj* 1. modern; present-day; up-to-date; 2. *nm/f* trendy.

modestia, *nf* modesty.

modesto, *adj* modest.

módico, *adj* reasonable, moderate.

modificación, *nf* modification.

modificar, *vt* to modify.

modista, *nf* dressmaker, modiste.

modisto, *nm/f* fashion designer.

modo, *nm* way, manner; fashion; mode, method.

modorro, *adj* drowsy, heavy.

modulación, *nf* modulation.

modulado, *adj* modulated.

modulador, *nm* modulator.

modular, *adj* 1. modular; 2. *vt* to modulate.

módulo, *nm* module.

mofa, *nf* 1. mockery, ridicule, derision; 2. jibe, taunt, sneer.

mofador, *adj* mocking, scoffing, sneering.

mofar, *vi* to mock, scoff, sneer.

mogote, *nm* flat-topped hillock; heap, pile.

mohín, *nm* (wry) face, grimace; pout.

moho, *nm* rust; mold, mildew.

mohoso, *adj* rusty; moldy, mildewed; musty.

mojada, *nf* wetting, soaking.

mojado, *adj* wet; damp, moist; drenched, soaked.

mojadura, *nf* wetting, soaking.

mojar, *vt* to wet; to damp(en), moisten; to drench, soak.

mojo, *nm* garlic sauce.

mojón, *nm* landmark; boundary stone.

molar, *nm* molar.

molde, *nm* mold, shape; cast.

moldear, *vt/f* to mold, shape; to cast.

moldura, *nf* molding; side stripe.

mole, *nf* mass, bulk; pile.

molécula, *nf* molecule.

molecular, *adj* molecular.

moledor, *adj* grinding, crushing.

moledora, *nf* grinder, crusher; mill.

moler, *vt* to grind; to crush; to pound.

molestar, *vt* to annoy; to bother, inconvenience.

molestarse, *vr* to go to trouble, put oneself out.

molestia, *nf* bother, trouble, nuisance; inconvenience; discomfort.

molesto, *adj* troublesome, annoying; trying, tiresome; inconvenient.

molido, *adj* ground, crushed; powdered.

molienda, *nf* grinding; milling.

molinero, *nm* miller.

molino, *nm* mill; grinder.

molote, *nm* 1. ball of wool; 2. riot, commotion.

molusco, *nm* mollusk.

mollera, *nf* crown of the head.

momentáneo, *adj* momentary.

momento, *nm* moment; instant.

momia, *nf* mummy.

momificación, *nf* mummification.

momificar, *vt* to mummify.

mona, *nf* female monkey.

monaguillo, *nm* acolyte, altar-boy.
monarca, *nm/f* monarch, ruler.
monarquía, *nf* monarchy.
monasterio, *nm* monastery; convent.
monda, *nf* pruning, lopping, trimming; peeling.
mondar, *vt* to prune, lop, trim; to peel, skin.
monear, *vi* to act like a monkey; to make monkey faces.
moneda, *nf* currency, money, coinage.
moned(e)ar, *vt* to coin, mint.
monedero, *nm* purse.
monetario, *adj* monetary, financial.
mongolismo, *nm* mongolism, Down's syndrome.
monigote, *nm* rag doll; puppet; grotesque figure.
monitor, *nm* monitor.
monitoreado, *nm* monitoring.
monitorear, *vt* to monitor.
monitorizar, *vt* to monitor.
monja, *nf* nun; sister.
monje, *nm* monk.
mono, *nm* monkey, ape.
monocarril, *nm* monorail.
monocolor, *adj* of a single color.
monocromo, *adj* monochrome; black-and-white.
monogamia, *nf* monogamy.
monógamo, *adj* monogamous.
monolítico, *adj* monolithic.
monologar, *vi* to soliloquize.
monólogo, *nm* monologue.
mononucleosis, *nf* glandular fever.
monopartidismo, *nm* single-party system.
monoplaza, *nm* single-seater.
monopolio, *nm* monopoly.
monopolización, *nf* monopolization.
monopolizar, *vt* to monopolize.
monoteísmo, *nm* monotheism.
monoteísta, *adj* monotheistic.
monotonía, *nf* monotone.
monótono, *adj* on one note; monotonous.
monóxido, *nm* monoxide.
monseñor, *nm* monsignor.
monstruo, *nm* monster; giant.
monstruosidad, *nf* monstrosity; freak.
monstruoso, *adj* monstrous, huge, monster.
montado, *adj* mounted.
montador, *nm* mounting block.
montaje, *nm* assembly; fitting-up; erection; set-up.
montaña, *nf* mountain; mountains, mountainous area.
montañero(a), *adj* 1. mountain; 2. *nm/f* mountaineer, climber.
montañés(esa), *adj* 1. mountain; hill; highland; 2. *nm/f* highlander.
montañoso, *adj* mountainous.
montar, *vt* 1. to mount, get on; to ride; 2. to assemble, fit (up), put together, set up.
monte, *nm* 1. mountain; 2. woodland; wilds, wild country.
montear, *vt* to hunt.
montería, *nf* hunting; hunt, chase.
montero, *nm* huntsman, hunter; beater.
montés, *adj* wild.
monto, *nm* total, amount.
montón, *nm* heap, pile.
montuno, *adj* 1. mountain; forest; 2. wild, untamed, rustic.
montura, *nf* 1. mount; 2. saddle, harness, trappings.
monumental, *adj* monumental.
monumento, *nm* monument; memorial.
monzón, *nm* of monsoon.

moquear, *vi* to have a runny nose.
moquero, *nm* handkerchief.
moqueta, *nf* moquette; carpet.
morada, *nf* dwelling, abode, home.
morado, *adj* purple, violet.
morador(a), *nm/f* inhabitant.
moradura, *nf* bruise.
moral, *adj* 1. moral; 2. *nf* morals, morality.
moralidad, *nf* morals, morality, ethics.
moralista, *nf* moralist.
moralizador, *adj* moralizing; moralistic.
moralizar, *vt* to moralize; to improve ethical standards in.
morar, *vi* to live, dwell; to stay.
moratoria, *nf* moratorium,
morbosidad, *nf* morbidity, morbidness; unhealthiness.
morboso, *adj* morbid; unhealthy, likely to cause disease(s); diseased.
morcilla, *nf* blood sausage, black pudding.
mordacidad, *nf* sharpness, pungency; bite.
mordaz, *adj* biting, scathing, pungent.
mordaza, *nf* gag; (Tec) clamp, jaw.
morder, *vt* to bite.
mordicar, *vi* to smart, sting.
mordida, *nf* bite; bribe.
mordiscar, *vt* to nibble at; to gnaw at; to nip.
mordisco, *nm* bite, nip; nibble.
morena, *nf* dark girl, brunette.
morenear, *vi* to tan, brown.
morenearse, *vr* to tan, brown.
moreno, *adj* (dark) brown; dark-haired; tanned.
morera, *nf* mulberry tree.
moretón, *nm* bruise.
morfina, *nf* morphia, morphine.
morfinomanía, *nf* morphine addiction, opium addiction.
morfinómano(a), *adj* addicted to morphine, addicted to opium.
morgue, *nf* morgue.
moribundo(a), *adj* dying; moribund; dying person.
morir, *vt* 1. to kill; 2. *vi* to die.
morirse, *vr* to die.
morisqueta, *nf* fraud, dirty trick.
mormón(ona), *nm/f* Mormon.
moro, *adj* Moorish.
moroso(a), *adj* slow, sluggish; dilatory.
morra, *nf* top of the head.
morrada, *nf* butt; bang on the head.
morral, *nm* haversack, knapsack; pouch, gamebag.
morro, *nm* snout, nose; lip, thick lip.
morrudo, *adj* thick-lipped.
morsa, *nf* walrus.
mortadela, *nf* bologna sausage.
mortaja, *nf* shroud; mortise.
mortal, *adj* mortal; fatal; deadly.
mortalidad, *nf* mortality.
mortecino, *adj* weak, failing; dim, fading.
mortero, *nm* mortar.
mortífero, *adj* deadly, lethal.
mortificación, *nf* mortification; humiliation.
mortificar, *vt* to damage, affect seriously.
morza, *nf* carpenter's vise.
mosaico, *adj* 1. Mosaic, of Moses; 2. *nm* mosaic; tessellated pavement; marquetry.
mosca, *nf* fly.
moscatel, *adj*, *nm* muscatel.
mosqueado, *adj* spotted; angry, resentful.
mosquete, *nm* musket.
mosquetero, *nm* musketeer; groundling.

mosquitero, *nm* mosquito net.

mosquito, *nm* mosquito; gnat.

mostacera, *nf* mustard pot.

mostaza, *nf* mustard.

mosto, *nm* must, unfermented grape juice.

mostrador, *nm* counter; bar.

mostrar, *vt* to show; to display, exhibit; to point out; to explain.

mote, *nm* motto, device; nickname, by-name.

moteado, *adj* speckled, mottled, dappled; flecked, dotted.

motear, *vt* to speck; to speckle, dapple.

motel, *nm* motel.

motín, *nm* revolt, rising; riot, disturbance.

motivación, *nf* motivation.

motivar, *vt* to cause, motivate, give rise to.

motivo, *adj* 1. motive; 2. *nm* motive, reason, cause.

motocicleta, *nf* motorcycle.

motoneta, *nf* motor scooter.

motor, *adj* 1. motive; 2. *nm* motor, engine.

motora, *nf* motorboat, speedboat.

motorización, *nf* motorization; mechanization.

motorizado, *adj* motorized; mechanized.

motorizar, *vt* to motorize; to mechanize.

motriz, *adj* motive, driving.

mover, *vt* to move; to shift.

movible, *adj* movable; mobile.

movida, *nf* (chess) move.

movido, *adj* 1. blurred; 2. active; restless, always on the go.

movilización, *nf* mobilization.

movilizar, *vt* to mobilize; to unblock, free.

movimiento, *nm* movement; motion.

mozo, *adj* young; single, unmarried; servant, waiter.

mozuela, *nf* girl; wench.

mozuelo, *nm* (young) lad.

mucosa, *nf* mucous membrane; mucus.

mucosidad, *nf* mucus.

mucoso, *adj* mucous.

múcura, *nf* earthenware jug.

muchacha, *nf* girl.

muchachada, *nf* childish prank.

muchacho, *nm* boy, lad.

muchedumbre, *nf* crowd, mass, throng; mob.

mucho, *adj* 1. a lot of; much, great; 2 *adv* a lot, a great deal, much; more, a lot more.

mudanza, *nf* 1. change; 2. move, removal.

mudar, *vt* to change, alter; to change into, transform into.

mudez, *nf* dumbness.

mudo, *adj* dumb; silent, mute.

mueble, *adj* 1. movable; 2. *nm* piece of furniture.

mueblería, *nf* furniture factory; furniture shop.

mueca, *nf* face, grimace.

muela, *nf* tooth, molar, back tooth.

muelle, *adj* 1. soft; delicate; 2. springy, bouncy. 3. *nm* spring; 4. wharf, quay; pier.

muerte, *nf* death.

muerto, *adj* dead, lifeless.

muesca, *nf* notch, nick; groove, slot.

muestra, *nf* indication, sign; example; sample.

muestrario, *nm* collection of samples (or specimens); pattern book.

mugido, *nm* moo, lowing; bellow; roar, howl.

mugir, *vi* to moo, low; to bellow; to roar, howl.

mugre, *nf* dirt, filth; grease, grime.

mugriento, *adj* dirty, filthy; greasy, grimy.

mujer, *nf* 1. woman; 2. wife.

mujeriego, *adj* fond of women, given to chasing the girls, wolfish.

mula, *nf* mule.

mulada, *nf* drove of mules.

muladar, *nm* dungheap, dunghill, midden.

mulato(a), *adj, nm/f* mulatto.

mulero(a), *nm* 1. muleteer; 2. *nm/f* liar.

muleta, *nf* 1. crutch; 2. matador's stick with red cloth attached.

mulo, *nm* mule.

multa, *nf* fine; penalty.

multicolor, *adj* multicolored, many-colored; motley, variegated.

multimillonario(a), *nm/f* multimillionaire.

múltiple, *adj* multiple; many-sided.

multiplicación, *nf* multiplication.

multiplicar, *vt* to multiply.

múltiplo, *adj* multiple.

multitud, *nf* multitude; crowd.

mullido, *adj* soft, sprung; fluffy; springy.

mullir, *vt* to make fluffy, fluff up; to soften.

mundanal, *adj* worldly, of the world.

mundano, *adj* worldly, of the world.

mundial, *adj* world-wide, universal.

mundo, *nm* world.

munición, *nf* ammunition, munitions.

municipal, *adj* municipal; town; public.

municipio, *nm* municipality; town, township.

muñeca, *nf* 1. wrist; 2. doll, dummy.

muñeco, *nm* figure; doll; scarecrow; puppet, marionette.

muñequero(a), *nm/f* puppeteer.

mural, *adj* mural, wall.

muralla, *nf* wall, rampart.

murciélago, *nm* bat.

murmullo, *nm* murmur(ing), whisper(ing), mutter(ing).

murmuración, *nf* gossip; slanderous talk, backbiting, constant complaining.

murmurador, *adj* gossip; backbiting; critical; complaining, grumbling.

murmurar, *vi* to murmur, whisper; to mutter.

muro, *nm* wall.

musaraña, *nf* shrew; (any) small creature, bug creepy-crawly.

muscular, *adj* muscular.

musculatura, *nf* muscles, musculature.

músculo, *nm* muscle.

musculoso, *adj* muscular; tough, brawny

museo, *nm* museum; gallery.

musgo, *nm* moss.

música, *nf* music.

musical, *adj, nm* musical.

musicalizar, *vt* to set to music.

músico(a), *adj* 1. musical; 2. *nm/f* musician, player.

musitar, *vti* to mumble, mutter.

muslo, *nm* thigh.

mustiarse, *vr* to wither, wilt.

mustio, *adj* withered, faded; sad, gloomy.

mutación, *nf* change; mutation.

mutilación, *nf* mutilation.

mutilado, *adj* crippled, disabled.

mutismo, *nm* dumbness; silence, uncommunicativeness.

mutual, *nf* friendly society.

mutuo, *adj* mutual, reciprocal; joint.

muy, *adv* very; greatly, highly; too.

N

N, n, *nf* (letter) N, n.
naba, *nf* swede.
nabab, *nm* nabob.
nabina, *nf* rapeseed.
nabo, *nm* turnip; root vegetable, thick root.
nácar, *nm* mother-of-pearl, nacre.
nacarado, *adj* mother-of-pearl, pearly, nacreous.
nacedera, *nf* hedge.
nacer, *vi* 1. to be born; to hatch; to sprout, bud; 2. to be born; to begin, originate.
nacido, *adj* born; newborn.
naciente, *adj* 1. nascent; new, recent; growing; 2. *nm* east.
nacimiento, *nm* birth; hatching.
nación, *nf* nation; people.
nacional, *adj* national; home.
nacionalidad, *nf* nationality.
nacionalizacion, *nf* naturalization.
nacionalizar, *vt* to nationalize.
nada, *pron* 1. nothing; 2. *adv* not at all.
nadador(a), *nm/f* swimmer.
nadar, *vi* to swim; to float.
nadie, *pron* nobody, no one.
nailon, *nm* nylon.
naipe, *nm* playing card.
naipeador, *adj* fond of cards.
naipear, *vi* to play cards.
nalga, *nf* buttock; buttocks, backside, rump.
nalgada, *nf* 1. ham; 2. smack on the bottom.
nana, *nf* 1. grandma, granny; 2. nursemaid; 3. mummy.
naranja, *nf* orange.
naranjada, *nf* orangeade.
naranjado, *adj* orange, orange-colored.
naranjal, *nm* orange grove.
naranjo, *nm* orange tree.
narcótico, *adj* 1. narcotic; 2. *nm* sleeping pill.
narcotizar, *vt* to narcotize.
narcotraficante, *nm/f* drug dealer.
narcotráfico, *nm* drug traffic, traffic in drugs.
naricear, *vt* to smell (out); to poke one's nose into.
narigón, *adj* 1. big-nosed; 2. *nm* nose ring.
nariz, *nf* nose; nostril.
narración, *nf* narration, account.
narrador(a), *nm/f* narrator.
narrar, *vt* to tell, narrate, recount.
narrativa, *nf* 1. narrative, story; 2. narrative skill, skill in storytelling.
nasal, *adj, nf* nasal.
nata, *nf* cream; whipped cream.
natación, *nf* swimming.
natal, *adj* natal; native; home.
natalicio, *adj* birthday.
natalidad, *nf* birth rate.
natillas, *nf* custard; egg custard.
natividad, *nf* nativity.
nato, *adj* born.
natural, *adj* 1. natural; 2. *nm/f* native, inhabitant.
naturaleza, *nf* nature.
naturalidad, *nf* naturalness.
naturalización, *nf* naturalization.
naturalizar, *v* to naturalize.

naturalizarse, *vr* to become naturalized.
naufragar, *vi* to be wrecked, sink; to be shipwrecked.
naufragio, *nm* shipwreck.
náufrago, *adj* shipwrecked; shipwrecked person.
náusea, *nf* nausea, sick feeling; repulsion.
náutica, *nf* navigation, seamanship.
náutico, *adj* nautical.
navaja, *nf* clasp knife, jack-knife; razor.
naval, *adj* naval; ship, sea.
nave, *nf* 1. ship, vessel; 2. spacecraft; 3. large building, large shed; factory.
navegable, *adj* navigable; seaworthy.
navegación, *nf* 1. navigation; sailing; 2. sea voyage.
navegante, *nm* navigator.
navegar, *vt* to sail; to navigate.
Navidad, *nf* Christmas; Christmas Day.
naviera, *nf* shipping company.
naviero, *adj* 1. shipping; 2. *nm* shipowner.
navío, *nm* ship.
nazarenas, *nf* large gaucho spurs.
nazareno(a), *adj* 1. Nazarene; 2. *nm/f* Nazarene, penitent in a Holy Week procession.
nazi, *adj, nm/f* Nazi.
neblina, *nf* mist; mistiness; fog.
nebulosa, *nf* nebula.
nebulosidad, *nf* nebulosity; cloudiness; mistiness; gloominess.
necedad, *nf* foolishness, silliness.
necesario, *adj* necessary.
neceser, *nm* toilet case, dressing case; holdall.
necesidad, *nf* necessity; need.
necesitado(a), *adj* 1. in need of; 2. *nf* needy person.
necesitar, *vt* to need, want; to necessitate, require.
necio(a), *adj* 1. silly, stupid; 2. *nm/f* fool.
néctar, *nm* nectar; fruit essence.
nectarina, *nf* nectarine.
nefasto, *adj* pernicious; harmful; unlucky, ill-fated; dreadful, terrible.
negación, *nf* negation; refusal, denial.
negado, *adj* dull, stupid.
negar, *vt* to deny; reject, refuse.
negativa, *nf* negative; denial, refusal.
negativo, *adj* negative; against, contrary.
negligencia, *nf* negligence; neglect, slackness, carelessness.
negligente, *adj* negligent; neglectful, slack, careless.
negociación, *nf* negotiation; deal, transaction.
negociado, *nm* 1. department, section; 2. shop, store; 3. illegal transaction, shady deal.
negociador, *adj* negotiating.
negociar, *vi* to negotiate.
negocio, *nm* affair; business; deal, transaction.
negrear, *vi* to go black, turn black.
negrero, *nm* slave trader; slave driver.
negrita, *nf* bold face; bold type, in heavy type.
negrito, *nm* black coffee.
negro, *adj* 1. black; dark; 2. *nm/f* black person.
negrura, *nf* blackness.
nene(a), *nm/f* baby, small child.
neófito(a), *nm/f* neophyte.
neón, *nm* neon; neon light.
neonatal, *adj* postnatal, neonatal.
neonatólogo(a), *nm/f* neonatologist.
neoyorquino, *adj* 1. of New York; 2. *nm/f* New Yorker.
nervio, *nm* 1. nerve; 2. tendon, sinew.
nerviosismo, *nm* nervousness; nervous anticipation.
nervioso, *adj* nerve, nervous.
nervudo, *adj* tough, strong.
nesgado, *adj* flared.

neto, *adj* clear; clean, pure; neat; net.

neumático, *adj* 1. pneumatic; air; 2. *nm* tire; balloon tire.

neumonía, *nf* pneumonia.

neuralgia, *nf* neuralgia.

neurastenia, *nf* 1. neurasthenia; nervous exhaustion. 2. excitability, highly-strung nature, nerviness.

neuritis, *nf* neuritis.

neurocirugía, *nf* neurosurgery.

neurólogo(a), *nm/f* neurologist.

neurosis, *nf* neurosis.

neurótico(a), *adj*, *nm/f* neurotic.

neutral, *adj*, *nm/f* neutral.

neutralidad, *nf* neutrality.

neutralización, *nf* neutralization.

neutralizar, *vt* to neutralize; to counteract.

neutro, *adj* neutral; neuter, sexless.

neutrón, *nm* neutron.

nevada, *nf* snowstorm; snowfall.

nevado, *adj* snow-covered.

nevar, *vt* 1. to cover with snow; to whiten; 2. *vi* to snow.

nevera, *nf* refrigerator, icebox.

nexo, *nm* link, connection; nexus.

ni, *conj* nor, neither.

nicotiana, *nf* tobacco plant.

nicotina, *nf* nicotine.

nicho, *nm* niche; recess; hollow.

nidal, *nm* nest; nesting box.

nidificar, *vi* to nest.

nido, *nm* nest.

niebla, *nf* fog, mist.

nieta, *nf* granddaughter.

nieto, *nm* grandson; grandchild.

nieve, *nf* 1. snow; 2. ice-cream.

nimiedad, *nf* triviality; fussiness; smallmindedness; long-windedness.

nimio, *adj* insignificant, trivial, tiny.

ninfa, *nf* nymph.

ningún, *adj* none, no-one.

ninguno, *adj* 1. no; no man; 2. *pron* nobody, no-one; none; neither.

niña, *nf* girl, little girl, child.

niñera, *nf* nursemaid, nanny.

niñería, *nf* childishness; childish thing; silly thing.

niñero, *adj* fond of children.

niñez, *nf* childhood; infancy.

niño, *adj* 1. young; immature, inexperienced; 2. *nm* boy, little boy, child.

níquel, *nm* 1. nickel; 2. small coin.

niquelado, *adj* nickel-plated.

niquelar, *vt* to nickel-plate.

niquelera, *nf* purse.

nitidez, *nf* brightness; spotlessness; clarity, sharpness.

nítido, *adj* bright, clean; spotless.

nitrato, *nm* nitrate.

nitrogenado, *adj* nitrogenous.

nitrógeno, *nm* nitrogen.

nitroglicerina, *nf* nitroglycerin(e).

nivel, *nm* 1. level, height; 2. standard.

nivelación, *nf* leveling.

nivelado, *adj* 1. level, flat; 2. *nm* leveling.

niveladora, *nf* bulldozer.

nivelar, *vt* 1. to level, to grade; 2. to equalize, even (out, up), make even.

níveo, *adj* snowy, snow-white.

no, *adv* no, not.

nobilizar, *vt* to enhance, dignify, ennoble.

noble, *adj* noble; honest, upright.

nobleza, *nf* nobility; honesty, uprightness.

noción, *nf* notion.

nocivo, *adj* harmful, injurious.

nocturnidad, *nf* evening hours, night hours.

nocturno, *adj* night; evening.

noche, *nf* night; night-time; evening; dark, darkness.

Nochebuena, *nf* Christmas Eve.

nodriza, *nf* wet-nurse.

nodular, *adj* nodular.

nódulo, *nm* nodule.

nogal, *nm* walnut; walnut tree.

nómada, *adj* 1. nomadic; 2. *nm/f* nomad.

nomadear, *vi* to wander.

nombrado, *adj* 1. aforementioned; 2. famous, renowned.

nombramiento, *nm* naming; designation, nomination; appointment; commission.

nombrar, *vt* to name; to designate, to mention; nominate, appoint.

nombre, *nm* name.

nómina, *nf* list, roll; payroll.

nominación, *nf* nomination.

nominal, *adj* 1. nominal, titular, in name only; 2. face value; 3. noun, substantival.

nominar, *vt* to nominate.

nominativo, *adj*, *nm* nominative.

nonato, *adj* not born naturally; unborn.

noqueada, *nf* knockout.

noqueado, *adj* shattered.

noquear, *vt* to knock out, K.O.

noratlántico, *adj* north-Atlantic.

norcoreano(a), *adj*, *nm/f* North Korean.

nordeste, *adj* northeast, northeastern.

noria, *nf* waterwheel, chain pump.

norma, *nf* standard, norm, rule; pattern.

normal, *adj* normal; regular, usual, natural.

normalidad, *nf* normality, normalcy; calm.

normalización, *nf* normalization.

normalizado, *adj* standard(ized).

normalizar, *vt* to normalize, restore to normal; to standardize.

normar, *vt* to lay down rules for, establish norms for.

normativa, *nf* rules, regulations; guideline.

noroeste, *adj* northwest, northwestern.

nororiental, *adj* northeastern.

norte, *adj* north, northern, northerly.

Norteamérica, *nf* North America.

norteamericano(a), *adj*, *nm/f* North American, American.

norteño, *adj* 1. northern; 2. *nm/f* northerner.

nos, *pron pers pl* us.

nosotros(as), *pron pers pl* we; us; ourselves.

nostalgia, *nf* nostalgia, homesickness; longing.

nostálgico, *adj* nostalgic, homesick; longing.

nota, *nf* 1. note; memorandum; 2. grade, mark, class; 3. (Mus) note.

notabilidad, *nf* noteworthiness, notability.

notable, *adj* 1. noteworthy, notable; remarkable; 2. outstanding.

notar, *vt* 1. to note, notice; to feel, perceive; to see; 2. to note down; to mark, indicate.

notaría, *nf* 1. profession of notary; 2. notary's office.

notario(a), *nm/f* notary, notary public.

noticia, *nf* piece of news; news item.

noticiar, *vt* to notify.

noticiero, *adj* 1. news; 2. news-bearing, news-giving; 3. *nm/f* reporter.

notición, *nm* bombshell.

noticioso, *adj* well-informed; newsworthy.

notificación, *nf* notification.

notificar, *vt* to notify, inform.

notoriedad, *nf* fame, renown; wide knowledge.

notorio, *adj* well-known, publicly known.

novatada, *nf* 1. rag, ragging, hazing; 2. beginner's mistake, elementary, blunder.

novato, *adj* 1. (rookie) raw, green, new; 2. *nm* beginner.

novecientos, *adj* nine hundred.

novedad, *nf* newness, novelty.

novedoso, *adj* novel; new; full of novelties.

novela, *nf* novel.

novelista, *nm/f* novelist.

noveno, *adj*, *nm* ninth.

noventa, *adj* ninety; ninetieth.

novia, *nf* sweetheart: fiancée; bride.

noviazgo, *nm* engagement.

noviciado, *nm* apprenticeship, training; novitiate.

novicio(a), *nm/f* beginner, novice; apprentice.

noviembre, *nm* November.

novilla, *nf* heifer.

novillada, *nf* bullfight with young bulls (and novice bullfighters).

novillo, *nm* young bull, bullock, steer.

novio, *nm* sweetheart; fiancé; bridegroom.

nubarrada, *nf* downpour, sudden shower.

nubarrón, *nm* storm cloud.

nube, *nf* cloud; raincloud.

nublado, *adj* 1. cloudy, overcast; 2. *nm* storm cloud, black cloud.

nublar, *vt* to darken, obscure.

nublarse, *vr* to become cloudy.

nuboso, *adj* cloudy.

nuca, *nf* nape (of the neck), back of the neck.

nuclear, *adj* nuclear.

nuclearizarse, *vr* to build nuclear power stations, go nuclear.

núcleo, *nm* nucleus; core; kernel; center.

nudillo, *nm* knuckle.

nudismo, *nm* nudism.

nudista, *nm/f* nudist.

nudo, *nm* knot.

nudoso, *adj* knotty, full of knots.

nuera, *nf* daughter-in-law.

nuestro, *adj pos* 1. our; of ours; 2. *pron pos* ours, of ours.

nueve, *adj* 1. nine; ninth; 2. *nm* nine.

nuevo, *adj* new; fresh; novel.

nuez, *nf* nut, walnut; pecan nut.

nulidad, *nf* nullity; incompetence, incapacity.

nulo, *adj* 1. void, null, invalid, without force; 2. useless.

numeración, *nf* numeration, numbering.

numerador, *nm* numerator.

numeral, *adj* 1. numeral, number; 2. *nm* numeral.

numerar, *vt* to number.

numérico, *adj* numerical; numeric.

número, *nm* 1. number; 2. size; 3.(magazine) issue.

numeroso, *adj* numerous.

numismata, *nm/f* numismatist.

nunca, *adv* never; ever.

nuncio, *nm* 1. nuncio; 2. messenger; herald, harbinger.

nupcial, *adj* wedding, nuptial.

nupcias, *nf* wedding, nuptials.

nutrición, *nf* nutrition.

nutricional, *adj* nutritional.

nutrido, *adj* nourished; vigorous.

nutriente, *nm* nutrient.

nutrir, *vt* 1. to feed, nourish; 2. to strengthen; to support, foment, encourage.

nutritivo, *adj* nourishing, nutritious.

Ñ

Ñ, ñ, *nf* (letter) Ñ, ñ.

ñácara, *nf* ulcer, sore.

ñaco, *nm* popcorn.

ñame, *nm* yam.

ñandú, *nm* rhea, South American ostrich.

ñagada, *nf* nip, bite.

ñagado, *adj* knock-kneed; bow-legged.

ñágara, *nm/f* guerrilla.

ñango, *adj* awkward, clumsy; short-legged.

ñangotarse, *vr* to squat, crouch down; to lose heart.

ñaña, *nf* elder sister, nursemaid.

ñaño, *adj* spoiled, pampered; silly.

ñapa, *nf* extra; bonus; tip.

ñapango, *nm* mulatto, mestizo, half-breed.

ñata, *nf* death.

ñato, *adj* flat-nosed; snub-nosed.

ñeque, *adj* strong; vigorous; clever; brave.

ñique, *nm* butt with the head; punch.

ñiquiñaque, *nm* trash, junk, rubbish.

ñisca, *nf* bit, small piece.

ñoco, *adj* lacking a finger; one-handed.

ñongo, *adj* stupid; good-for-nothing.

ñoñería, *nf* inispidness; spinelessness; shyness, fussiness.

ñoño, *adj* characterless, insubstantial, spineless.

ñuco, *adj* dehorned; limbless.

ñufla, *nf* 1. piece of junk; 2. *adj* worthless

ñutir, *vi* to grunt.

ñuto, *adj* crushed, ground.

O

O, o, *nf* (letter) O, o.

oasis, *nm* oasis.

obcecación, *nf* blindness, blind obstinacy; mental blockage, disturbance.

obcecado, *adj* blind; mentally blinded; stubborn, disturbed.

obcecar, *vt* to blind (mentally), disturb the mind of.

obedecer, *vti* to obey.

obediencia, *nf* obedience.

obediente, *adj* obedient.

obelisco, *nm* obelisk; (Tip) dagger.

oberol, *nm* overalls.

obesidad, *nf* obesity.

obeso, *adj* obese.

óbice, *nm* obstacle, impediment.

obispo, *nm* bishop.

óbito, *nm* decease, demise.

obituario, *nm* 1. decease, demise; 2. obituary; obituary section.

objeción, *nf* objection.

objetar, *vt/i* to object.

objetivizar, *vt* to objectify; to put in objective terms.

objetividad, *nf* objectivity.
objetivo, *adj* 1. objective; 2. clear, obvious.
objeto, *nm* object, thing.
oblea, *nf* wafer; very thin slice.
oblicuar, *vt* to slant, place obliquely, cant, tilt.
oblicuo, *adj* oblique; slanting; sidelong.
obligación, *nf* obligation; duty; responsibility.
obligacional, *adj* compulsory; binding.
obligado, *adj* obligatory, unavoidable.
obligar, *vt* to force, compel, oblige.
obligatorio, *adj* obligatory, compulsory; binding.
obliteración, *nf* obliteration.
obliterar, *vt* 1. to obliterate; 2. to obliterate, efface, destroy.
óbolo, *nm* mite, small contribution.
obra, *nf* work; piece of work.
obradera, *nf* diarrhea.
obrador, *nm* workroom, workshop.
obrajero, *nm* foreman, overseer.
obrar, *vt* to work.
obrero, *adj* 1. working; labor; 2. *nm* worker, workman; man, hand laborer.
obscenidad, *nf* obscenity.
obsceno, *adj* obscene.
obseder, *vt* to obsess.
obsequiar, *vt* to lavish attentions on, make a fuss of.
obsequio, *nm* present, gift; presentation.
obsequioso, *adj* obliging, helpful, attentive.
observable, *adj* observable.
observación, *nf* 1. observation; observance; 2. remark, comment; objection.
observador(a), *adj* 1. observant; 2. *nm/f* observer.
observar, *vt* to observe, watch; to see, notice, spot.
observatorio, *nm* observatory.
obsesión, *nf* obsession.
obsesionar, *vt* to obsess, haunt.
obsesivo, *adj* obsessive; obsessional.
obseso, *adj* obsessed, haunted.
obsoleto, *adj* obsolete.
obstaculizar, *vt* to hinder, hamper, hold up; to prevent, stand in the way of.
obstáculo, *nm* obstacle; hindrance; handicap.
obstetra, *nmf* obstetrician.
obstetricia, *nf* obstetrics.
obstinación, *nf* obstinacy, stubbornness.
obstinado, *adj* obstinate, stubborn.
obstinarse, *vr* to be obstinate; to dig one's heels in.
obstrucción, *nf* obstruction.
obstruccionar, *vt* to obstruct.
obstruir, *vt* to obstruct; to block.
obtención, *nf* obtaining, securing.
obtener, *vt* to get, obtain, secure; to achieve.
obtenible, *adj* obtainable, accessible; achievable.
obturador, *nm* plug, stopper; choke; shutter.
obturar, *vt* to plug, stop (up); to seal off.
obtuso, *adj* blunt, dull, obtuse.
obús, *nm* howitzer; shell.
obviar, *vt* to obviate, remove.
obviedad, *nf* obvious nature, obviousness.
obvio, *adj* obvious.
ocasión, *nf* 1. occasion, time; 2. chance, opportunity; 3. cause, motive.
ocasional, *adj* chance, accidental; incidental.
ocasionar, *vt* to cause, produce, occasion.
ocaso, *nm* sunset; setting.
occidental, *adj* 1. western; 2. *nm/f* westerner.
occidentalizado, *adj* westernized.
occidentalizar, *vt* to westernize.
occidente, *nm* west; the West.

occiso(a), *nm/f* murdered person, murder victim.
océano, *nm* ocean.
oceanografía, *nf* oceanography.
oceanográfico, *adj* oceanographic.
ocio, *nm* 1. leisure, idleness; 2. pastime, diversion.
ociosidad, *nf* idleness.
ocioso, *adj* idle; at leisure; inactive.
oclusión, *nf* occlusion; glottal stop.
ocre, *nm* ochre; yellow ochre; red ochre.
octagonal, *adj* octagonal.
octágono, *nm* octagon.
octanaje, *nm* octane number; high-octane.
octano, *nm* octane.
octava, *nf* octave.
octavo, *adj* eighth.
octeto, *nm* octet(te); byte.
octogenario, *adj* octogenarian, eighty-year old.
octubre, *nm* October.
ocular, *adj* ocular; eye.
oculista, *nm/f* oculist.
ocultar, *vt* to hide, conceal; to screen, mask.
ocultista, *nm/f* occultist.
oculto, *adj* hidden, concealed.
ocupación, *nf* occupation.
ocupado, *adj* occupied, taken; busy.
ocupante, *nm/f* occupant; squatter.
ocupar, *vt* to occupy, fill, take up.
ocurrencia, *nf* 1. occurrence; incident, event; 2. idea, bright idea.
ocurrente, *adj* witty; bright, clever.
ocurrir, *vi* to happen, occur
ochenta, *adj* eighty; eightieth.
ocho, *adj* eight; eighth.
odiar, *vt* to hate.
odio, *nm* hatred; ill will; dislike.
odioso, *adj* odious, hateful, detestable; nasty, unpleasant.
odisea, *nf* odyssey, epic journey.
odómetro, *nm* milometer.
oeste, *adj* west, western; westerly.
ofender, *vt* to offend; to slight, insult.
ofenderse, *vr* to take offense.
ofendido, *adj* offended.
ofensa, *nf* offense; slight; wrong.
ofensiva, *nf* offensive.
ofensor, *adj* 1. offending; 2. *nm/f* offender.
ofertar, *vt* to offer.
oficial, *adj* official.
oficializar, *vt* to make official, give official status to.
oficiar, *vt* to inform officially; (Ecl) officiate, celebrate.
oficina, *nf* office.
oficinista, *nm/f* office worker, clerk; white-collar worker.
oficio, *nm* job, profession, occupation; craft, trade.
ofrecer, *vt* to offer; to present.
ofrenda, *nf* offering, gift; tribute.
ofrendar, *vt* to offer, give as an offering.
oftálmico, *adj* ophthalmic.
oftalmología, *nf* ophthalmology.
oftalmólogo(a), *nm/f* ophthalmologist.
ofuscar, *vt* 1. to dazzle; 2. to bewilder, confuse, mystify.
oída, *nf* hearing; by hearsay.
oído, *nm* hearing.
oidor, *nm* judge.
oír, *vti* to hear; to listen (to).
ojal, *nm* buttonhole.
ojalá, *interj* if only it were so!, if only it would! (etc); let's hope so!.

ojeada, *nf* glance; take a quick look at.
ojeador, *nm* (hunting) beater; talent scout, talent spotter.
ojear, *vt* to eye; to stare at.
ojera, *nf* ring under the eye.
ojeroso, *adj* with rings under the eyes; tired, haggard.
ojete, *nm* eyelet.
ojiva, *nf* ogive, pointed arch, warhead.
ojo, *nm* 1. eye; 2. *interj* hazard!, beware!, careful!
ola, *nf* wave.
oleada, *nf* big wave; surge, swell.
oleaginosa, *nf* oil product.
oleaginoso, *adj* oily, oleaginous.
oleaje, *nm* swell, surge; surf.
olear, *vi* to wave, flutter.
óleo, *nm* oil.
oleoducto, *nm* (oil) pipeline.
oler, *vt* to smell.
oletear, *vt* to pry into.
olfatear, *vt* to smell, sniff.
olfato, *nm* 1. (sense of) smell; 2. instinct, intuition.
olimpíada, *nf* Olympiad; the Olympics.
olímpica, *nf* Olympic athlete
oliscar, *vt* to smell, sniff, to investigate, look into.
oliva, *nf* olive; olive tree.
olivar, *nm* olive grove.
olivero, *adj* olive, olive-growing.
olivo, *nm* olive tree.
olmo, *nm* elm, elm tree.
olor, *nm* smell; odor, scent.
olorcillo, *nm* faint smell; delicate aroma.
oloroso, *adj* sweet-smelling, scented, fragrant.
olvidadizo, *adj* forgetful; absent-minded.
olvidado, *adj* forgotten.
olvidar, *vt* to forget; to leave behind; to leave out, omit.
olvido, *nm* 1. oblivion; 2. forgetfulness; omission, oversight; slip.
olla, *nf* pot, pan; kettle.
ollero(a), *nm/f* maker of (or dealer in) pots and pans.
ombligo, *nm* navel.
ominoso, *adj* awful, dreadful; ominous.
omisión, *nf* omission; oversight.
omitir, *vt* to leave out, miss out, omit.
ómnibus, *nm* omnibus; bus.
omnímodo, *adj* all-embracing; absolute.
omnipotencia, *nf* omnipotence.
omnipotente, *adv* omnipotent, all-powerful.
omnipresencia, *nf* omnipresence.
omnipresente, *adj* omnipresent.
omnisapiente, *adj* omniscient, all-knowing.
omnisciente, *adj* omniscient, all-knowing.
omóplato, *nm* shoulder-blade.
once, *adj* 1. eleven; eleventh; 2 *nm* eleven.
oncear, *vi* to have an afternoon snack.
onceavo, *adj; nm* eleventh.
onceno, *adj* eleventh.
onda, *nf* wave.
ondear, *vt* 1. to wave; 2. *vi* to wave (up and down), undulate; to be wavy.
ondulación, *nf* undulation; wavy motion.
ondulado, *adj* wavy; undulating, uneven, waved.
ondular, *vt* to wave.
ondulatorio, *adj* undulatory, wavy.
oneroso, *adj* onerous, burdensome.
ónice, *nm* onyx.
onomástica, *nf* onomastics.

onomástico, *adj* onomastic, name, birthday.
ontología, *nf* ontology.
ontológico, *adj* ontological.
opacar, *vt* to make opaque; to darken; to mist up.
opacidad, *nf* opacity, opaqueness.
opaco, *adj* opaque; dark.
opado, *adj* pale.
ópalo, *nm* opal.
opción, *nf* option, choice.
opcional, *adj* optional.
opear, *vi* to act the fool, fool about.
ópera, *nf* opera.
operación, *nf* operation; management.
operacional, *adj* operational.
operador(a), *nm/f* operator; operating surgeon.
operante, *adj* operating.
operar, *vt* 1. to produce, bring about, effect; to work; 2. to operate on; 3. to use, to manage, run.
operario(a), *nm/f* operative; worker.
operativo, *adj* operative.
opereta, *nf* operetta, light opera.
operista, *nm/f* opera singer.
opinable, *adj* debatable, open to a variety of opinions.
opinar, *vi* to think; to give one's opinion.
opinión, *nf* opinion, view.
opio, *nm* opium.
opiómano(a), *nm/f* opium addict.
opíparo, *adj* sumptuous.
oponente, *adj* opposing, contrary.
oponer, *vt* to oppose, put up resistance to; be against.
oponerse, *vr* to resist, be opposed to.
oportunidad, *nf* opportunity; occasion; timeliness; appropriateness; expediency.
oportunismo, *nm* opportunism.
oportunista, *adj* opportunist; opportunistic.
oportuno, *adj* 1. opportune, timely; appropriate, suitable; convenient; 2. witty, quick.
oposición, *nf* opposition.
opositor(a), *adj* 1. opposing; opposition, ot the opposition; 2. *nm/f* competitor, opponent.
opresión, *nf* oppression; oppressiveness.
opresivo, *adj* oppressive.
opresor(a), *adj* 1. oppressive, tyrannical; 2. *nm/f* oppressor.
oprimente, *adj* oppressive.
oprimir, *vt* 1. to squeeze, press, exert pressure on; to compress; 2. to oppress; to burden, weigh down.
oprobio, *nm* shame, ignominy, opprobrium.
oprobioso, *adj* shameful, ignominious.
optar, *vi* to choose, decide.
optativo, *adj* 1. optional; 2. optative.
óptica, *nf* 1. optics; 2. optician's (shop); 3. *nm/f* optician.
óptico, *adj* optic(al).
optimismo, *nm* optimism.
optimista, *adj* 1. optimistic, hopeful; 2. *nm/f* optimist.
optimización, *nf* optimization; improvement, perfection.
optimizar, *vt* to optimize; to improve, perfect.
óptimo, *adj* very good, very best; optimal, optimum.
optometrista, *nm/f* optometrist.
opuesto, *adj* opposite.
opulencia, *nf* opulence; luxury; affluence.
opulento, *adj* opulent, rich; luxurious; affluent.
opúsculo, *nm* booklet; short work, tract.
oquedad, *nf* hollow, cavity; void; emptiness.

ora, *adv* sometimes; some other times.

oración, *nf* 1. oration, speech; 2. prayer; 3. sentence; clause.

oráculo, *nm* oracle.

orador(a), *nm/f* speaker, orator,

oral, *adj* oral.

orar, *vi* to pray; to orate, speak.

orangután, *nm* orangutan.

orate, *nm/f* lunatic.

orático, *adj* crazy, lunatic.

oratoria, *nf* oratory.

oratorio, *adj* 1. oratorical; 2. *nm* oratory, chapel.

orbe, *nm* orb, sphere; world.

órbita, *nf* orbit.

orbital, *adj* orbital.

orbitar, *vi* to orbit.

orca, *nf* grampus, killer whale.

ordalías, *nf* ordeal, trial by ordeal.

orden, *nm* order; arrangement.

ordenación, *nf* 1. order; arrangement; ordering, arranging; 2. ordination.

ordenada, *nf* ordinate.

ordenado, *adj* orderly; tidy; well arranged.

ordenador, *nm* computer.

ordenamiento, *nm* ordering, arranging.

ordenanza, *nf* 1. ordinance, decree; 2. *nm* office boy, messenger; errand boy; orderly.

ordenar, *vt* to arrange, put in order.

ordeña, *nf* milking.

ordeñadero, *nm* milking pail.

ordeñadora, *nf* milking machine.

ordeñar, *vt* to milk.

ordinal, *adj*, *nm* ordinal.

ordinariez, *nf* commonness, coarseness, vulgarity.

ordinario, *adj* 1. ordinary; usual; current; 2. common, coarse, vulgar; rude.

orear, *vt* to air.

orégano, *nm* marjoram.

oreja, *nf* 1. ear; 2. tab; tag.

orejear, *vi* 1. to eavesdrop; 2. to suspect, be distrustful.

orejera, *nf* earmuff.

orejudo, *adj* big-eared, with big ears.

orfanato, *nm* orphanage.

orfebre, *nm* goldsmith, silversmith.

orfebrería, *nf* gold work, silver work, craftsmanship in precious metals.

orfelinato, *nm* orphanage.

orfeón, *nm* glee club, choral society,

orgánico, *adj* organic.

organigrama, *nm* flow chart; organization chart.

organillero, *nm* organ-grinder.

organillo, *nm* barrel organ, hurdy-gurdy.

organismo, *nm* 1. organism; 2. organization; body, institution.

organista, *nm/f* organist.

organización, *nf* organization.

organizador(a), *nm/f* organizer.

organizar, *vt* to organize.

organizarse, *vr* to manage one's affairs, organize one's life; to get one's priorities right.

órgano, *nm* 1. organ; 2. (Mús) organ.

orgásmico, *adj* orgasmic.

orgasmo, *nm* orgasm.

orgía, *nf* orgy.

orgullo, *nm* pride; arrogance.

orgulloso, *adj* proud; haughty.

orientación, *nf* 1. orientation, position(ing); direction, course; 2. guidance; training.

orientador(a), *nm/f* career adviser.

oriental, *adj* oriental; eastern.

orientar, *vt* 1. to orientate, position; to point (towards); to give a direction to, direct; 2. to guide, to train.

oriente, *nm* east, the East.

orificación, *nf* gold filling.

orificar, *vt* to fill with gold.

orificio, *nm* orifice, hole; vent.

origen, *nm* origin; source.

original, *adj* original; novel; odd, eccentric, strange.

originar, *vt* to originate; to start, cause, give rise to.

orilla, *nf* edge, border; bank; side, shore.

orillar, *vt* to edge, trim (with).

orina, *nf* urine.

orinal, *nm* chamberpot; bedpan.

orinar, *vti* to urinate.

orines, *nm* urine.

oriundo(a), *adj* native to; to be a native of, come from, hail from.

orla, *nf* border; fringe; trimming; coastal strip.

orlar, *vt* to border, edge, trim (with).

ornamental, *adj* ornamental.

ornamentar, *vt* to adorn (with).

ornamento, *nm* ornament, adornment; vestments.

ornar, *vt* to adorn (with).

ornato, *nm* adornment, decoration.

oro, *nm* gold.

orondo, *adj* 1. big, big-bellied, rounded; fat, pot-bellied; 2. smug, self-satisfied; pompous.

oropel, *nm* tinsel; flashy, bright but tawdry.

orquesta, *nf* orchestra.

orquestación, *nf* orchestration.

orquestar, *vt* to orchestrate.

orquídea, *nf* orchid, orchis.

ortodoncia, *nf* orthodontics.

ortodoncista, *nm/f* orthodontist.

ortodoxia, *nf* orthodoxy.

ortodoxo, *adj* orthodox.

ortografía, *nf* spelling; orthography.

ortográfico, *adj* spelling; orthographic(al).

ortopeda, *nm/f* orthopedist.

ortopedia, *nf* orthopedics.

ortopédico, *adj* orthopedic.

oruga, *nf* 1. caterpillar; 2. rocket.

orzuelo, *nm* stye.

osa, *nf* she-bear.

osadía, *nf* daring, boldness.

osado, *adj* daring, bold.

osamenta, *nf* bones; skeleton.

osar, *vi* to dare; to dare to do.

oscilación, *nf* 1. oscillation; swing, sway, to and fro movement; rocking; 2. fluctuation; 3. wavering.

oscilador, *adj* 1. oscillating; 2. *nm* oscillator.

oscilante, *adj* oscillating; swinging.

oscilar, *vi* 1. to oscillate; to swing, sway, move to and fro; to rock; to wink, blink; 2. to fluctuate; to vary.

osciloscopio, *nm* oscilloscope.

oscular, *vt* to osculate, kiss.

ósculo, *nm* osculation, kiss.

oscurecer, *vt* 1. to obscure, darken; to dim; to black out; 2. to confuse, cloud, fog.

oscuridad, *nf* darkness, obscurity; gloom, gloominess; obscurity.

oscuro, *adj* dark; dim, gloomy, obscure; confused.

óseo, *adj* bony, osseous.

osificación, *nf* ossification.

osificar, *vt* to ossify.

ósmosis, *nf* osmosis.

oso, *nm* bear.

ostentación, *nf* ostentation, display; pomp.

ostentar, *vt* to show; to show off, display, make a parade of, flaunt.

ostentoso, *adj* ostentatious.

osteópata, *nm/f* osteopath.

osteopatía, *nf* osteopathy.

ostión, *nm* large oyster.

ostra, *nf* 1. oyster; 2. dull person; retiring individual.

ostrero, *nm* 1. oyster bed; 2. oyster catcher.

otate, *nm* cane, stick; reed, rush.

oteadero, *nm* look-out post.

otear, *vt* to descry, make out, glimpse; to look down on; to watch; to scan, spy on.

otero, *nm* low hill, hillock, knoll.

otitis, *nf* earache.

otoñal, *adj* autumnal, autumn, fall.

otoño, *nm* autumn, fall, maturity.

otorgamiento, *nm* granting, conferring; consent.

otorgar, *vt* 1. to grant, give (to); 2. to consent, agree to.

otorrino(laringólogo), *nm/f* ear, nose and throat specialist.

otro, *adj* another, other.

otrora, *adv* formerly, in olden times.

ovación, *nf* ovation.

ovacionar, *vt* to acclaim.

oval, *adj* oval.

óvalo, *nm* oval; (Med) pessary.

ovario, *nm* ovary.

oveja, *nf* sheep, ewe.

ovejera, *nf* sheepfold.

ovejero, *nm* sheepdog.

ovejuno, *adj* sheep.

overear, *vt* to cook to a golden color, brown.

ovillar, *vt* to wind, wind into a ball.

ovillo, *nm* ball.

ovino, *adj* ovine; sheep.

ovíparo, *adj* oviparous.

ovulación, *nf* ovulation.

ovular, *vi* to ovulate.

óvulo, *nm* ovule, ovum.

oxidación, *nf* rusting; oxidation.

oxidar, *vt* to rust; to oxidize.

óxido, *nm* rust; oxide.

oxigenación, *nf* oxygenation.

oxigenado, *adj* oxygenated.

oxigenar, *vt* to oxygenate.

oxígeno, *nm* oxygen.

oyente, *nm/f* 1. listener; hearer; 2. unregistered student, occasional student, auditor.

ozono, *nm* ozone.

ozonósfera, *nf* ozonosphere, ozone layer.

P

P, p, *nf* (letter) P, p.

pabellón, *nm* 1. bell tent; 2. canopy, hangings; pavilion; summerhouse, hut.

pabilo, *nm* wick; snuff (of candle).

pacer, *vt* 1. to eat, graze; 2. pasture.

paciencia, *nf* patience; forbearance.

paciente, *adj, nm/f* patient.

pacificación, *nf* pacification.

pacificador(a), *adj* 1. pacifying, peace-making; 2. *nm/f* peace-maker.

pacificar, *vt* to pacify; to calm; to appease.

Pacífico, *nm* Pacific (Ocean).

pacífico, *adj* pacific; peace-loving.

pacotilla, *nf* 1. trash, junk; 2. rabble, crowd, mob.

pacotillero, *adj* 1. rude, uncouth; 2. *nm* peddler, hawker.

pactar, *vt* to agree to, agree on; to stipulate, contract for.

pacto, *nm* pact; agreement, covenant.

pachorrada, *nf* blunder, gaffe.

pachorrear, *vi* to be slow, be sluggish.

padecer, *vt* to suffer; to endure, put up with; be a victim of.

padecimiento, *nm* suffering; ailment.

padrastro, *nm* stepfather; harsh father.

padre, *nm* 1. father; sire; 2. priest.

padrino, *nm* 1. godfather; 2. best man.

padrón, *nm* list of inhabitants, roll; census; register.

paella, *nf* paella.

paellera, *nf* paella dish; dish aerial, TV satellite dish.

paellero, *nf* paella cook.

paga, *nf* 1. payment; 2. pay, wages; allowance.

pagadero, *adj* payable, due.

pagador(a), *nm/f* 1. payer; 2. teller, cashier; paymaster.

paganismo, *nm* paganism, heathenism.

pagano(a), *adj, nm/f* pagan, heathen.

pagar, *vti* 1. to pay; pay off; 2. to repay.

pagaré, *nm* promissory note, IOU; Treasury bill, Treasury bond.

página, *nf* page.

paginación, *nf* pagination.

paginar, *vt* to paginate, number the pages of.

pago, *nm* 1. payment; repayment; 2. return, reward.

paila, *nf* 1. large pan; frying-pan; 2. meal of fried foods.

país, *nm* country; land, region, landscape; state; nation.

paisaje, *nm* landscape, countryside, scenery.

paisanada, *nf* group of peasants.

paisanaje, *nm* civil population.

paisano, *adj* 1. of the same country; 2. *nm* civilian; 3. compatriot, fellow countryman.

paja, *nf* 1. straw; dried brushwood; 2. trash, rubbish.

pájara, *nf* 1. hen, hen bird; hen partridge; 2. kite.

pajarería, *nf* 1. pet shop; 2. large flock of birds.

pajarero, *adj* 1. bird; 2. fun-loving person; facetious, waggish.

pajarito, *nm* baby bird, fledgling; birdie.

pájaro, *nm* bird.

paje, *nm* page; cabin boy.

pajilla, *nf* straw hat.

pajizo, *adj* straw.

pajonal, *nm* scrubland.

pala, *nf* shovel, spade; scoop.

palabra, *nf* word, speech.

palabrería, *nf* wordiness; verbiage, hot air.

palabrota, *nf* rude word, swearword.

palacete, *nm* small palace.

palacial, *adj* palatial.

palaciego, *adj* 1. palace, court; 2. *nm* courtier.

palacio, *nm* palace; mansion, large house.

palada, *nf* 1. shovelful, spadeful; 2. stroke.

paladar, *nm* palate, roof of the mouth; palate, taste.

paladear, *vt* to taste; to relish, savor.

paladeo, *nm* tasting; relishing, savoring; sipping.

paladín, *nm* paladin; champion.

palanca, *nf* lever; crowbar; influence, pull.

palanganear, *vi* to brag; to show off.

palanganero, *nm* washstand.

palanquear, *vt* to lever; move with a lever.

palanquero, *nm* brakeman; lumberman; burglar, housebreaker.

palatino, *adj* palace, court, palatine.

palco, *nm* 1. box; director's box; 2. balcony.

palear, *vt* 1. to punt, pole; 2. to shovel; to dig; to thresh.

palestino, *adj, nm/f* Palestinian.

palestra, *nf* arena.

paleta, *nf* 1. small shovel, small spade; scoop; 2. palette; 3. shoulder-blade; wooden paddle for beating clothes; 4. lollipop.

paletada, *nf* shovelful, spadeful.

paletear, *vt* to pat; to flatter; to be out of work.

paletilla, *nf* shoulder blade.

paliar, *vt* 1. to palliate, mitigate, alleviate; to relieve; 2. to lessen, cushion; conceal.

paliativo, *adj* 1. palliative; mitigating; concealing; 2. *nm* palliative.

palidecer, *vi* to pale, turn pale.

palidez, *nf* paleness, pallor; wanness; sickliness.

pálido, *adj* pale, pallid ; wan; sickly.

palillo, *nm* 1. small stick; toothpick; drumstick; knitting needle; penholder; castanets; 2. very thin person.

paliza, *nf* 1. beating, thrashing; beating-up; 2. beating, drubbing.

palizada, *nf* 1. fence, stockade, palisade; 2. fenced enclosure.

palma, *nf* 1. palm; applaud; 2 . palm tree; palm leaf.

palmada, *nf* 1. slap, pat; 2. clapping, applause.

palmar, *nm* palm grove, cluster of palms.

palmear, *vi* to clap.

palmera, *nf* palm, palm tree.

palmista, *nm/f* palmist.

palmo, *nm* span; few inches, small amount.

palmotear, *vi* to clap, applaud.

palmoteo, *nm* clapping, applause.

palo, *nm* 1. stick; post, pole; 2. mast; spar; mainmast; 3. tree; wood; 4. golf club.

paloma, *nf* dove, pigeon; carrier pigeon.

palomilla, *nf* 1. moth; grain moth; nymph, chrysalis, 2.wing nut; 3. wall bracket, angle iron.

palomino, *adj* 1. white; 2. *nm* young pigeon; 3. palomino (horse).

palomitas, *nf* popcorn.

palpar, *vt* to touch, feel; caress, fondle.

palpitación, *nf* palpitation, throb(bing), beat(ing).

palpitante, *adj* palpitating, throbbing.

palpitar, *vi* to palpitate; to throb, beat; to quiver; to flutter.

pálpito, *nm* hunch, presentiment.

palúdico, *adj* marshy; malarial.

paludismo, *nm* malaria.

pamela, *nf* picture hat, sun hat.

pampa, *nf* 1. pampa(s), prairie; 2. region of nitrate deposits.

pámpano, *nm* vine shoot, vine tendril.

pampear, *vi* to travel over the pampas.

pampero, *adj* 1. of (or from) the pampas; 2. *nm* inhabitant of the pampas, plainsman.

pamplina, *nf* chickweed; silly remark; nonsense.

pamplinero, *adj* 1. silly, nonsensical; 2. fussy, emotional, given to making a great fuss.

pamplonada, *nf* triviality; silly thing, piece of nonsense.

pan, *nm* bread; loaf.

pana, *nf* 1. velveteen, corduroy; 2. breakdown; 3. liver; guts, courage.

panacea, *nf* panacea, cure-all.

panadería, *nf* bakery, bakehouse; baker's shop.

panadero, *nm* baker.

panal, *nm* honeycomb.

panamá, *nm* panama hat.

panamericano, *adj* Pan-American.

pancarta, *nf* placard, banner.

páncreas, *nm* pancreas.

pancreático, *adj* pancreatic.

panda, *nm/f* 1. panda; 2. pandeo.

pandear, *vi* to bend, warp; to sag; to bulge.

pandereta, *nf* tambourine.

panderetear, *vi* to play the tambourine.

pandero, *nm* 1. tambourine; 2. kite.

pandilla, *nf* set, group; clique, coterie, set; gang.

pandillero, *nm* member of a clique; gangster.

pando, *adj* 1. sagging; bulging; 2. shallow; flat.

panecillo, *nm* roll.

panel, *nm* 1. panel; 2. panelling; display panel.

panela, *nf* 1. brown sugar; sugar loaf; 2. straw hat.

panelería, *nf* panelling.

panera, *nf* bread basket.

pánico, *nm* panic, fear;

panificadora, *nf* bakery.

panorama, *nm* view, scene; outlook, prospect.

panorámica, *nf* general view, survey.

panorámico, *adj* panoramic.

pantaleta, *nf* bloomers, drawers panties.

pantalón, *nm* trousers, pants slacks, trousers.

pantalla, *nf* 1. screen; 2. shade, lampshade.

pantanal, *nm* marshland.

pantano, *nm* 1. marsh, swamp, bog; wetland; 2. reservoir, dam.

pantanoso, *adj* 1. marshy, swampy; boggy; 2. difficult, problematic.

panteón, *nm* 1. pantheon; family vault, the burial place of the royal family; 2. cemetery; 3. ore, mineral.

pantera, *nf* 1. panther; jaguar, ocelot; 2.risk taker.

pantomima, *nf* pantomime, dumb show.

pantorrilla, *nf* 1. (of the leg) calf; 2. vanity.

pantufla, *nf* slipper.

panza, *nf* belly; belly, paunch.

pañal, *nm* diaper; shirttail.

pañero, *nm/f* draper, dry-goods dealer, clothier.

paño, *nm* 1. cloth; stuff, material; 2. duster, rag, cleaning cloth.

pañol, *nm* store, storeroom.

pañuelo, *nm* handkerchief; scarf, headscarf, shawl.

papá, *nm* dad, daddy, papa.

papa, *nm* 1. (Ecl) pope; 2. *nf* potato.

papada, *nf* double chin; dewlap.

papado, *nm* papacy.

papalote, *nm* kite; windmill.

papalotear, *vi* to wander about; to give one's last gasp.

papar, *vt* to swallow, gulp (down).

papaya, *nf* 1. pawpaw; 2. papaya (tree).

papel, *nm* paper; (Theat) role; stocks and shares.

papelear, *vi* 1. to rummage through papers; 2. to make a splash, draw attention to oneself.

papeleo, *nm* paperwork; red tape,

papelera, *nf* 1. litter bin; wastepaper basket; 2. desk; 3. paper-mill.

papelería, *nf* stationery; mass of papers, heap of papers; sheaf of papers.

papelero, *adj* 1. stationer; 2. paper manufacturer; 3. paper-boy.

papeleta, *nf* slip of paper, bit of paper; voting paper, ballot paper.

papera, *nf* goit; mumps.

papilla, *nf* 1. baby food; 2. deceit.

paprika, *nf* paprika.

paquete, *nm* packet, parcel, package.
papujo, *adj* 1. swollen, puffed up; fat-cheeked; 2. wan, sickly, anemic.
paquete, *nm* packet, parcel, package.
paquetear, *vi* to be very smart.
paquetero, *nm* card sharper.
paquidermo, *nm* pachyderm.
paquetear, *vi* to be very smart.
par, *adj* 1. like, equal; even; 2. *nm* pair; couple; 3. equally; together, jointly.
para, *prep* to, for, intended for.
parábola, *nf* parable.
parabrisas, *nm* windscreen, windshield.
paracaídas, *nm* parachute.
parachoques, *nm* bumper, fender.
parada, *nf* stop; stopping; stopping place; shutdown.
paradero, *nm* 1. whereabouts; 2. stopping place; lodging.
parado, *adj* 1. to be motionless, be standing still; 2. to be unemployed, be idle; 3. to be standing (up); to be on one's feet.
paradoja, *nf* paradox.
paradójico, *adj* paradoxical.
parador, *nm* inn.
parafina, *nf* paraffin wax.
parafinado, *adj* waxed, waterproofed.
parafrasear, *vt* to paraphrase.
paráfrasis, *nf* paraphrase.
paraguas, *nm* umbrella.
paraíso, *nm* paradise, heaven.
paralela, *nf* parallel (line); parallel bars.
paralelo, *adj* parallel.
parálisis, *nf* paralysis; cerebral palsy.
paralítico(a), *adj*, *nm/f* paralytic.
paralización, *nf* paralysis; stagnation.
paralizar, *vt* to paralyze; to stop; block.
paramédico, *adj* paramedical.
parámetro, *nm* parameter.
paramilitar, *adj* paramilitary.
páramo, *nm* 1. bleak plateau, high moor; 2. waste land; 3. drizzle; storm of wind and snow; 4. mountain heights.
parapetarse, *vr* to protect oneself, shelter (behind).
parapeto, *nm* parapet, breastwork; defense, barricade.
parapsicología, *nf* parapsychology.
parar, *vt* 1. to stop; 2. cut off; to come to rest; to come to an end.
pararse, *vr* to stop; pull up, to come to a halt.
pararrayos, *nm* lightning conductor.
parasitar, *vt* to parasitize.
parásito, *adj* 1. parasitic; 2. *nm* parasite.
parasol, *nm* parasol, sunshade.
paratifoidea, *nf* paratyphoid.
parcela, *nf* plot, portion, piece of ground.
parcelar, *vt* to divide into plots.
parcial, *adj* partial; part; (opinion) prejudiced, biased.
parcialidad, *nf* partially, prejudice, bias.
parco, *adj* frugal, sparing; parsimonious; moderate.
parchar, *vt* to patch, put a pacth on.
parche, *nm* sticking plaster; patch.
parcheo, *nm* temporary remedies, stopgap solutions.
parchís, *nm* board game.
pardo, *adj* 1. (color) dun; drab, dark grey; 2. *nm* mulato, half-breed.
pareado, *nm* couplet; (slogan) jingle.
parear, *vt* to match, to put together, to form a pair.
parecer, *vt* opinion, view.

parecido, *adj* similar, alike.
pared, *nf* wall.
paredón, *nm* thick wall.
pareja, *nf* pair, couple.
parejero, *adj* cheeky; cocky, over-confident.
parejo, *adj* equal; similar, alike, the same.
paréntesis, *nm* parenthesis; digression; aside.
paria, *nm/f* pariah.
parida, *nf* woman who has recently given birth.
paridad, *nf* 1. parity, equality; similarity; 2. comparison.
paridora, *adj* fertile productive.
pariente, *nm* relative, relation.
parir, *vi* to give birth to, have a baby; to be delivered.
paritorio, *nm* maternity ward.
parlador, *adj* talkative.
parlamentar, *vi* to converse, talk; to parley.
parlamentario(a), *adj* 1. parliamentary; 2. *nm/f* parliamentarian; member of parliament.
parlante, *adj* 1. talking; 2. *nm* loudspeaker, speaker.
parlar, *vi* to chatter, talk (a lot), gossip.
parlotear, *vi* to chatter, prattle.
parloteo, *nm* chatter, prattle.
paro, *nm* 1. stoppage (of work); standstill; strike; 2. unemployment.
parodia, *nf* parody, travesty, takeoff.
parodiar, *vt* to parody, travesty, take off.
parpadear, *vi* to blink, wink; flicker.
parpadeo, *nm* blinking, winking; flickering; twinkling.
párpado, *nm* eyelid.
parque, *nm* park.
parqueadero, *nm* parking lot; parking place.
parquear, *vti* to park.
parquedad, *nf* frugality, sparingness; parsimony; moderation.
parquímetro, *nm* parking meter.
parra, *nf* grapevine; climbing vine, trained vine.
párrafo, *nm* paragraph.
parral, *nm* vine arbor.
parranda, *nf* spree, party.
parrilla, *nf* grating, broiler, grill; shelf.
parrillada, *nf* 1. grill; barbecue; 2. steak house.
párroco, *nm* parish priest.
parroquia, *nf* parish; parish church.
parte, *nm* 1. message; report; dispatch; 2. *nf* piece, a piece of, part.
partear, *vt* (woman) to deliver.
partera, *nf* midwife.
partero, *nm* gynecologist.
partición, *nf* division, sharing-out; partition.
participación, *nf* 1. participation, taking part; 2. share.
participante, *nm/f* participant; entrant.
participar, *vt* 1. to notify, inform; to notify someone; 2. *vi* to take part, participate.
partícipe, *nm/f* participant.
participio, *nm* participle.
partícula, *nf* particle.
particular, *adj* 1. particular, special; peculiar; 2. private, personal; 3. individual.
particularizar, *vt* 1. to distinguish, characterize, mark out; 2. to particularize, specify.
partida, *nf* 1. departure; 2. register;certificate; 3. consignment, shipment; 4. game, hand.
partidario, *adj* 1. partisan; 2. *nm/f* supporter, follower.
partido, *nm* 1. political party; 2. game, match; fixture.

partir(la), vt 1. to split, divide; to break open; 2. to share (out), distribute; 3. to start, set off, set out, depart.

partisano(a), adj, nm/f partisan.

partitura, nf (Mus) score.

parto, nm birth, childbirth; delivery; labor; to be in labor.

parturienta, nf woman in labor; woman who has just given birth.

párvulo, nm child, infant.

pasada, nf 1. passing; 2. clean, polish.

pasadera, nf stepping stone,

pasadizo, nm passage, passageway, alley; arcade.

pasado, adj 1. past; 2. overripe; 3. past (tense).

pasador, nm bolt, fastener; pin; hairclip.

pasaje, nm 1. passage, passing; voyage, crossing; fare; 2. passageway, alleyway.

pasajero, adj passing, fleeting, transient.

pasaporte, nm passport.

pasar, vt 1. to pass; to hand, give; 2. to transfer; 3. to cross, go over; 4. to swallow; 5. to tolerate.

pasarse, vr get overripe, stale; go to far, overdo it.

Pascua, nf 1. Easter; Christmas; Whitsun; 2. Passover.

pascual, adj paschal.

pase, nm pass; permit.

pasear, vt to take a turn, walk.

paseo, nm stroll, walk; outing; ride;

paseíto, nm little walk, gentle stroll.

pasillo, nm passage, corridor; lobby.

pasión, nf passion.

pasional, adj 1. passionate; crime of passion; 2. temperamental.

pasividad, nf passiveness, passivity.

pasivo, adj 1. passive; inactive; 2. nm liabilities, debts.

pasmado, adj astonished, amazed.

pasmar, vt to amaze, astonish.

pasmo, nm amazement, astonishment; awe; wonder, marvel, prodigy.

paso, nm passing, passage; crossing; overtaking.

pasquín, nm skit, satire, lampoon; wall poster.

pasta, nf paste.

pastar, vti to graze.

pastel, nm cake; pie.

pastelillo, nm small cake.

pasteurización, nf pasteurization.

pasteurizado, adj pasteurized.

pasteurizar, vt to pasteurize.

pastilla, nf tablet; cake.

pastizal, nm pasture.

pasto, nm 1. grass, herbage, fodder; grazing; 2. food, feed for cattle.

pastor, nm 1. shepherd; herdsman; goatherd; cowman; 2. minister, clergyman, pastor,

pastoral, adj 1. pastoral, 2. nf idyll; 3. pastoral letter.

pastorear, vt to pasture, graze, shepherd; to look after; to guide, lead.

pastoreo, nm grazing.

pastoso, adj 1. doughy; soft; pasty; 2. rich, mellow, pleasant.

pata, nf foot, leg; paw.

patada, nf kick; stamp.

patadón, nm big kick; long kick, long ball.

patalear, vi 1. to stamp; 2. to protest; to make a fuss.

pataleo, nm stamping; kicking.

pataleta, nf tantrum; fit, convulsion.

patán, nm rustic, yokel; lout.

patata, nf potato.

patatal, nm potato field, potato patch.

pateador, nm kicker.

pateadura, nf stamping, kicking.

patear, vt to stamp on, trample (on); to kick, boot.

patear, vi to putt.

patentado, adj patent; proprietary.

patentar, vt to patent.

patente, adj 1. patent, obvious, evident; 2. superb great; 3. grant; warrant; license.

patentizar, vt to show, reveal, make evident.

paternal, adj fatherly, paternal,

paternidad, nf fatherhood, parenthood.

paterno, adj paternal.

patético, adj pathetic, moving, poignant.

patilla, nf 1. bench; 2. watermelon.

patín, nm skate; runner; skid.

patinador(a), nm/f skater.

patinar, vi to skate; to skid, slip.

patinazo, nm skid; blunder.

patio, nm court, courtyard.

pato, nm duck; drake.

patraña, nf story, fib; hoax; rigmarole.

patria, nf native land, mother country; fatherland.

patriarca, nm patriarch.

patriarcado, nm patriarchy.

patricio(a), adj, nm/f patrician.

patrimonio, nm 1. inheritance; 2. heritage; birthright; 3. net worth, capital resources.

patrio, adj native, home.

patriota, nm/f patriot.

patriótico, adj patriotic.

patrocinado(a), nm/f client.

patrocinar, vt to sponsor, act as patron to; to back, support.

patrocinio, nm sponsorship, patronage; backing, support; sponsorship.

patrón, nm patron; master; boss, chief; skipper; landlord.

patrona, nf patron(ess); employer, owner; landlady.

patronear, vt to skipper.

patronizar, vt to patronize.

patrono, nm patron; sponsor; protector, supporter.

patrulla, nf patrol.

patrullar, vt to patrol, police.

patrullero, nm 1. patrol car; 2. patrol boat; 3. patrolman, policeman.

paulatino, adj gradual, slow.

pausa, nf pause; break, respite; interruption; rest.

pausado, adj slow, deliberate.

pausar, vt to slow down; to interrupt.

pauta, nf 1. line, guideline; 2. ruler.

pautado, adj 1. ruled paper; 2. nm (Music) stave.

pautar, vt 1. to rule; 2. to mark, to establish a norm for.

pavimentar, vt to pave; to floor.

pavimento, nm pavement, paving; flooring.

pavo, nm turkey; peacock.

pavón, nm 1. peacock; 2. bluing, bronzing.

pavonearse, vr to swagger, strut; show off.

pavor, nm dread, terror.

paz, nf peace; peacefulness, tranquility.

peatón, nm pedestrian, person on foot; walker.

peca, nf freckle.

pecado, nm sin.

pecador(a), adj 1. sinful, sinning; 2. nm/f sinner.

pecar, vi to sin; to err, go astray.

pececillos, nm (fish) fry.

pecera, nf fishbowl, fishtank.

pecoso, adj freckled.

pectina, *nf* pectin.
pectoral, *adj* pectoral.
pecuario, *adj* cattle.
peculiar, *adj* special, peculiar; typical, characteristic.
peculio, *nm* one's own money; modest savings.
pechar, *vti* to pay (as a tax).
pechera, *nf* shirt front; bosom; chest protector.
pecho, *nm* 1. chest; 2. breast.
pechuga, *nf* breast; bosom; cleavage.
pedagogía, *nf* pedagogy.
pedagógico, *adj* pedagogic(al).
pedagogo(a), *nm/f* teacher; educator; pedagogue.
pedal, *nm* pedal.
pedalear, *vi* to pedal; to tread water.
pedante, *adj* pedantic; pompous, conceited.
pedantería, *nf* pedantry; pompousness, conceit.
pedazo, *nm* piece, bit; scrap; morsel.
pediatra, *nm/f* pediatrician.
pediatría, *nf* pediatrics.
pediátrico, *adj* pediatric.
pedigree, *nm* pedigree.
pedigüeño, *adj* insistent, importunate; demanding.
pedimento, *nm* petition; claim, bill.
pedir, *vt* 1. to ask for, request; 2. to order.
pedrada, *nf* throw of a stone; hit (or blow) from a stone.
pedregal, *nm* stony place, rocky ground.
pedrería, *nf* precious stones, jewels.
pedrero, *nm* quarryman, stone cutter.
pega, *nf* sticking; beating; beating-up.
pegada, *nf* 1. fib, lie; 2. exchange of punches.
pegadizo, *adj* 1. sticky; 2. i nfectious, catching.
pegajoso, *adj* 1. sticky, adhesive; viscious; 2. infectious, catching.
pegar, *vt* to stick (on, together, up); glue, paste.
pegote, *nm* sticking plaster.
peinada, *nf* combing.
peinador(a), *nm/f* hairdresser.
peinar, *vt* to comb; to do, arrange, style;
peine, *nm* comb.
peineta, *nf* back comb, ornamental comb.
pelado, *adj* shorn; hairless; bare; peeled.
pelador, *nm* peeler.
pelaje, *nm* (Zool) fur, coat.
pelambre, *nm* thick hair, long hair, mop of hair.
pelar, *vt* to cut the hair of, shear; (fruits, etc) peel, pare.
pelarse, *vr* to peel off.
peldaño, *nm* step, stair; rung.
pelea, *nf* fight, tussle, scuffle; quarrel, row.
peleador, *adj* brawling; combative, quarrelsome.
pelear, *vi* to fight; to scuffle, brawl; to struggle.
pelele, *nm* guy, dummy, figure of straw; puppet.
peletería, *nf* furrier's, fur shop; shoe shop.
peletero, *nm* furrier.
peliagudo, *adj* tricky, ticklish.
pelícano, *adj* 1. grey-haired; 2. *nm* pelican.
pelicorto, *adj* short-haired.
película, *nf* film; thin covering; movie, motion picture.
peligrar, *vi* to be in danger.
peligro, *nm* danger, peril; risk; menace, threat.
peligroso, *adj* dangerous; risky; ugly, nasty.
pelo, *nm* hair; whisker; fur, coat.
pelón, *adj* 1. hairless, bald; closecropped, with a crew cut; 2. poor; broke, penniless.
pelona, *nf* 1. baldness; 2. death.
pelota, *nf* ball.
pelotera, *nf* row, scrap, set-to.
pelotón, *nm* 1. big ball; 2. squad, party, detachment.

peluca, *nf* wig.
peluche, *nm* felt; plush.
peludo, *adj* hairy, shaggy; long-haired, furry.
peluquería, *nf* hairdresser, barber's (shop).
peluquero, *nm* hairdresser; barber.
pelusa, *nf* down; fuzz; fluff; dust.
pélvico, *adj* pelvic.
pelvis, *nf* pelvis.
pellejo, *nm* skin, hide, pelt.
pellizcar, *vt* to pinch, nip; to take a small bit of.
pellizco, *nm* pinch, nip, small bit.
pena, *nf* grief, sadness, sorrow; distress.
penacho, *nm* tuft, crest; plume.
penal, *adj* 1. penal; criminal; 2. *nm* prison.
penalidad, *nf* 1. trouble, hardship; 2. penalty, punishment.
penalización, *nf* penalty; penalization.
penalizar, *vt* to penalize.
penar, *vt* 1. to penalize; to punish; 2. *vi* to suffer; to be in torment.
penco, *adj* 1. hard-working; 2. *nm* horse.
pendencia, *nf* quarrel; fight, brawl; to fight.
pendenciero, *adj* quarrelsome, argumentative.
pender, *vi* to hang; to hang down, dangle; to droop.
pendiente, *adj* 1. hanging; to be hanging; to hang, dangle; 2. *nm* earring; pendant; 3. *nf* slope, incline; hill; 4. pending, unfinished.
péndulo, *nm* pendulum.
penetración, *nf* penetration.
penetrante, *adj* 1. deep; 2.sharp; biting; penetrating, piercing.
penetrar, *vt* 1. to penetrate, pierce; to permeate; 2. *vi* to go in; to sink in, soak in; 3. to enter; 4. understand, grasp (idea).
penetrarse, *vr* to become imbued with.
penicilina, *nf* penicillin.
península, *nf* peninsula.
penitencia, *nf* 1. penitence; 2. penance.
penitenciar, *vt* to impose a penance on.
penitenciaría, *nf* prison, penitentiary.
penoso, *adj* 1. painful, distressing; 2. arduous, laborious, difficult.
pensador(a), *nm/f* thinker.
pensamiento, *nm* thought.
pensante, *adj* thinking.
pensar, *vt* to think.
pensión, *nf* pension; allowance; alimony.
pensionado(a), *nm* 1. boarding school; 2. *nm/f* pensioner.
pensionar, *vt* to pension, give a pension to.
pentágono, *nm* pentagon; the Pentagon.
pentagrama, *nm* stave, staff.
Pentateuco, *nm* Pentateuch.
penúltimo, *adj* penultimate, last but one, next to last.
penumbra, *nf* penumbra; half-light, semi-darkness; shadows.
penuria, *nf* shortage, dearth; poverty, penury.
peón, *nm* unskilled workman; assistant; laborer, farmhand; apprentice.
peonar, *vi* to work as a laborer.
peor, *adj*, *adv* worse; worst.
pepinillo, *nm* gherkin.
pepino, *nm* cucumber.
pepsina, *nf* pepsin.
péptico, *adj* peptic.
pequeñez, *nf* 1. smallness, littleness, small size; shortness; infancy; 2. pettiness, small-mindedness.
pera, *nf* pear.
peral, *nm* pear-tree.
percance, *nm* misfortune, mishap; accident.

percatarse, *vr* to notice, take note of; to heed; to guard against; to realize, come to understand.

percepcion, *nf* perception.

percibir, *vt* to perceive, notice, detect; to see, observe.

percudir, *vt* to tarnish, dull; to dirty, mess up.

percusión, *nf* percussion.

percutor, *nm* striker, hammer.

percutir, *vt* to strike, tap.

percha, *nf* pole, support; rack; coatstand, hallstand.

perchero, *nm* clothes rack, hallstand.

perdedor(a), *adj* 1. losing; 2. *nm/f* loser.

perder, *vt* to lose; (time) waste; (train, etc.) to miss.

perderse, *vr* to get lost, lose oneself; to stray; to lose one's way.

perdición, *nf* perdition, undoing, ruin.

perdido, *adj* lost; stray.

perdigar, *vt* to half-cook, brown.

perdigón, *nm* 1. young partridge; 2. pellet.

perdón, *nm* pardon, forgiveness.

perdonador, *adj* forgiving.

perdonar, *vti* to pardon, forgive, excuse.

perdurar, *vi* to last, endure, survive; to stand.

perecedero, *adj* perishable.

perecer, *vi* to perish, die; to shatter.

peregrinación, *nf* long tour, travels; peregrination.

peregrinar, *vi* 1. to go to and fro; to travel extensively; 2. to go on a pilgrimage.

peregrino, *adj* wandering; traveling.

perejil, *nm* parsley.

perenne, *adj* everlasting, constant, perennial.

perezosa, *nf* deckchair.

perezoso, *adj* slothful, lazy; slow, sluggish, idle.

perfeccion, *nf* perfection; completion.

perfeccionar, *vt* to perfect; to improve.

perfecto, *adj* perfect.

perfidia, *nf* perfidy, treachery.

pérfido, *adj* perfidious, treacherous.

perfil, *nm* profile; silhouette, outline.

perfilado, *adj* well-shaped, well-finished.

perfilador, *nm* lip pencil.

perfilar, *vt* to outline; to shape, give character to.

perfilarse, *vr* to show one's profile, give a side view.

perforación, *nf* perforation; piercing, drilling, punching.

perforadora, *nf* punch; drill.

perforar, *vt* to perforate; to pierce; to puncture.

perfumado, *adj* scented; sweet-smelling.

perfumar, *vt* to scent, perfume.

perfume, *nm* scent, perfume.

pericia, *nf* skill, skillfulness, expertness, expertise.

periferia, *nf* periphery; outskirts.

periférico, *adj* peripheral; marginal.

perilla, *nf* pear-shaped ornament, drop.

perímetro, *nm* perimeter.

periódico, *adj* 1. periodic(al); recurrent; 2. *nm* newspaper.

periodismo, *nm* journalism.

periodista, *nm/f* 1. journalist; 2. *nm* pressman, newsman; newspaperman.

período, *nm* period.

peripecia, *nf* vicissitude; sudden change, unforeseen change.

periquito, *nm* parakeet.

periscopio, *nm* periscope.

peritar, *vt* to judge expertly, give an expert opinion on.

perito, *adj* skilled, skillful; expert; experienced, seasoned.

perjudicar, *vt* to damage, harm, impair.

perjuicio, *nm* damage, harm.

perjurar, *vi* to perjure oneself, commit perjury.

perjurio, *nm* perjury.

perla, *nf* pearl.

perlífero, *adj* pearl-bearing; pearl oyster.

permanecer, *vi* to stay, remain.

permanencia, *nf* permanence; stay.

permeabilidad, *nf* permeability, pervious nature.

permiso, *nm* permission.

permitir, *vt* to permit, allow.

permitirse, *vr* to be permitted, be allowed.

permuta, *nf* barter, exchange; interchange.

permutar, *vt* to permute; to exchange; to interchange.

pernicioso, *adj* pernicious; wicked, evil.

perno, *nm* bolt.

pernoctar, *vi* to spend the night, stay for the night.

pero, *conj* but; yet.

peroné, *nm* fibula.

perorar, *vi* to make a speech; to orate, spout.

perorata, *nf* long-winded speech; violent speech, harangue.

peróxido, *nm* peroxide.

perpendicular, *adj* perpendicular.

perpetración, *nf* perpetration.

personalidad, *nf* 1. personality; 2. legal entity.

personalizar, *vt* 1. to personalize; to embody, personify; 2. *vi* to make a personal reference.

personarse, *vr* to appear in person; to present o.s. at; to report to.

personificar, *vt* to personify; to embody.

perspectiva, *nf* 1. perspective; 2. view, scene, panorama.

perspicacia, *nf* keen-sightedness; shrewdness.

perspicaz, *adj* 1. keen; keen-sighted; 2. perspicacious, shrewd, discerning.

persuadir, *vt* to persuade; to convince, prevail upon.

persuasión, *nf* 1. persuasion; 2. conviction.

persuasivo, *adj* persuasive; convincing.

pertenecer, *vi* 1. to belong (to); 2. to concern; to apply to, pertain to.

pertenencia, *nf* ownership.

pertinaz, *adj* 1. persistent; long-lasting, prolonged; 2. pertinacious, obstinate.

pertinencia, *nf* relevance, pertinence; appropriateness.

pertinente, *adj* relevant, pertinent; appropriate.

pertrechar, *vt* to supply; to equip (with); to supply with ammunition and stores.

pertrechos, *nm* implements, equipment; gear; supplies and stores, provisions; ammunitions.

perturbación, *nf* disturbance; upset, perturbation.

perturbado(a), *adj* 1. mentally unbalanced; 2. *nm/f* mentally unbalanced person.

perturbador(a), *adj* 1. perturbing, disturbing; 2. *nm/f* disturber.

perturbar, *vt* to disturb; ruffle, upset.

perversión, *nf* 1. perversion; deviance; 2. wickedness; corruption.

perverso, *adj* perverse; depraved; wicked.

pervertido(a), *adj* 1. perverted, deviant; 2. *nm/f* pervert; deviant.

pervertir, *vt* to pervert, corrupt; to distort.

pervertirse, *vr* to become perverted.

pesa, *nf* weight.

pesadez, *nf* 1. heaviness; weight; 2. slowness, ponderousness; sluggishness.

pesadilla, *nf* 1. nightmare, bad dream; 2. worry, obsession.

pesado, *adj* heavy, weighty.

pesador, *nm* butcher.

pésame, *nm* expression of condolence, message of sympathy.

pesar, *vt* 1. to weigh; 2. *nm* regret; grief, sorrow.

pesaroso, *adj* sorrowful, regretful, sad.

pesca, *nf* fishing.

pescado, *nm* fish.

pescador(a), *nm/f* fisherman, fisherwoman.

pescar, *vt* 1. to catch; to land; 2. to fish for, try to catch.

pescuezo, *nm* neck.

pesebre, *nm* manger; stall.

peseta, *nf* peseta (Spain's currency).

pesetero, *adj* money-grubbing, mercenary.

pesimista, *adj* 1. pessimistic; 2. *nm/f* pessimist.

pésimo, *adj* abominable, wretched, vile.

peso, *nm* 1. weight; weightiness, heaviness; 2. unit of currency of certain Latin American countries.

pespuntear, *vt/i* to backstitch.

pespunte, *nm* backstitch(ing).

pesquería, *nf* fishing-ground, fishery.

pesquero, *adj* 1. fishing; 2. *nm* fishing boat.

pesquisa, *nf* investigation, inquiry; search.

pesquisador(a), *nm/f* investigator, inquirer; member of the secret police; detective.

pestaña, *nf* eyelash.

pestanar, *vi* to blink, wink.

pestañeo, *nm* blink(ing), wink(ing).

peste, *nf* 1. plague, epidemic; 2. stink, stench.

pesticida, *nm* pesticide.

pestilencia, *nf* 1. pestilence, plague; 2. stink, stench.

pestilente, *adj* 1. pestilent; 2. smelly, foul.

pestillo, *nm* bolt, latch; catch, fastener.

pétalo, *nm* petal.

petardo, *nm* firework, firecracker, explosive device, incendiary device.

petición, *nf* request, plea; petition.

peto, *nm* bodice; bib; breastplate.

pétreo, *adj* stony; rocky.

petrificación, *nf* petrifaction.

petrificado, *adj* petrified.

petrificar, *vt* to petrify, turn to stone.

petrificarse, *vr* to petrify, become petrified, turn to stone.

petróleo, *nm* oil, petroleum.

petrolífero, *adj* petroliferous, oil-bearing.

petroquímica, *nf* petrochemistry, petrochemical company.

petulancia, *nf* vanity, self-satisfaction, opinionated nature.

petulante, *adj* vain, self-satisfied, opinionated.

petunia, *nf* petunia.

peyorativo, *adj* pejorative.

pez, *nm* fish.

pezón, *nm* teat, nipple.

piadoso, *adj* pious, devout.

pianista, *nm/f* pianist.

piano, *nm* piano.

piar, *vi* to cheep; to talk, chatter.

pibe(a), *nm/f* kid, child; boy.

pica, *nf* 1. magpie; 2. pike; goad; prick.

picacho, *nm* peak, summit.

picada, *nf* prick; sting; bite; peck.

picadillo, *nm* mince, minced meat.

picado, *adj* pricked, perforated; with a row of holes.

picadora, *nf* mincer, mincing machine.

picadura, *nf* prick; puncture; sting, bite.

picante, *adj* 1. hot; peppery; spicy; 2. sharp, stinging, cutting.

picaporte, *nm* door-handle; latch; door-knocker.

picar, *vt* 1. to prick, puncture; 2. to sting; to bite; 3. to peck; pick at.

picardía, *nf* 1. villainy, knavery; slyness, craftiness; naughtiness; 2. dirty trick; naughty thing (to do), mischievous act.

picaresca, *nf* picaresque novel.

pícaro, *adj* villainous, knavish; sly, crafty, naughty, mischievous.

picazón, *nf* 1. itch; sting; 2. annoyance, uneasy feeling.

picnic, *nm* picnic.

pico, *nm* 1. beak, bill; mouth, lips; 2. corner, peak, sharp point; 3. pick, pickaxe.

picotazo, *nm* peck; sting, bite.

picotear, *vt* to peck.

pictórico, *adj* pictorial.

picuda, *nf* 1. woodcock; 2. barracuda.

pichón, *nm* 1. young pigeon; pigeon; chick, young bird; 2. novice, greenhorn; tyro.

pie, *nm* 1. foot; 2. unit of measure (12 inches long).

piedad, *nf* 1. piety, devotion, devoutness; respect; 2. mercy.

piedra, *nf* stone; rock; flint.

piel, *nf* 1. skin; 2. hide, pelt; fur; leather.

pienso, *nm* feed, fodder; grub.

pierna, *nf* leg.

pieza, *nf* piece; roll; part.

pigmento, *nm* pigment.

pigmeo(a), *adj*, *nm/f* pigmy.

pijama, *nm* pajamas.

pila, *nf* 1. heap, pile; stack; 2. sink; trough; drinking trough; 3. font; 4. battery; cell.

pilar, *nm* 1. post, pillar; milestone; 2. column, pier; 3. prop, support, mainstay; 4. basin, bowl.

píldora, *nf* pill.

pileta, *nf* basin, bowl; sink; trough.

pilotar, *vt* 1. to pilot; to drive; to steer; 2. to guide, direct.

piloto, *nm/f* 1. pilot; 2. first mate; navigator, navigation officer.

pillada, *nf* 1. dirty trick; 2. surprise revelation; surprise encounter.

pillar, *vt* to pillage, plunder, sack.

pillería, *nf* 1. dirty trick. 2. gang of scoundrels.

pillete, *nm* young rascal, scamp.

pillín(ina), *nm/f* little rascal.

pillo, *adj* 1. villainous, blackguardly; sly, crafty; 2. *nm* rascal, rogue, scoundrel; rotter.

pimentón, *nm* cayenne pepper, red pepper; paprika.

pimienta, *nf* pepper.

pináculo, *nm* pinnacle.

pinaza, *nf* pinnace.

pincel, *nm* paintbrush, artist's brush.

pincelada, *nf* brush-stroke.

pinchante, *adj* piercing.

pinchar, *vt* to prick, pierce, (tire) puncture.

pinche, *nm* 1. kitchen-boy, scullion; 2. minor office clerk.

pincho, *nm* point; prickle, thorn; pointed stick, spike.

pingüe, *adj* 1. greasy, fat; 2. abundant; lucrative.

pingüino, *nm* penguin.

pino, *nm* pine, pine tree.

pinta, *nf* 1. spot, dot; mark; 2. pint.

pintada, *nf* graffiti, daub; slogan.

pintado, *adj* spotted; mottled, dappled.

pintar, *vt* to paint; to draw.

pintarse, *vr* to put on makeup.

pinto, *adj* spotted; mottled, dappled; marked.

pintor(a), *nm/f* painter.

pintoresco, *adj* picturesque.

pintura, *nf* painting; depiction.

pinza, *nf* clothes-peg, clothespin; forceps.

piña, *nf* pineapple.

piñal, *nm* pineapple plantation.

piñata, *nf* brawl, scrap.

piñón, *nm* pine nut, pine seed.

pío, *nm* pious, devout; sanctimonious.

pionero, *adj* pioneering.

piorrea, *nf* pyorrhea.

pipa, *nf* 1. pipe; smoke a pipe; 2. cask, barrel; 3. pip, seed, edible sunflower seed.

pique, *nm* resentment; ill will; grudge; rivalry, competition.

piquera, *nf* 1. hole, vent; 2. taxi rank.

piquete, *nm* 1. prick, jab, slight wound; 2. small hole; 3. squad, party; picket.

pirámide, *nf* pyramid.

piraña, *nf* piranha.

pirata, *nm/f* pirate.

piratear, *vt* to hijack; to pirate; to hack into; to steal.

piratería, *nf* piracy; theft, stealing.

piromanía, *nf* pyromania.

pirómano(a), *nm/f* arsonist, fire-raiser, pyromaniac.

piropear, *vt* to pay an amorous compliment to, make a flirtatious remark to.

piropo, *nm* amorous compliment, flirtatious remark.

pirueta, *nf* pirouette; caper.

piruleta, *nf* lollipop.

pirulí, *nm* lollipop.

pisa, *nf* 1. treading; 2. beating.

pisada, *nf* footstep, footfall, tread;footprint.

pisadera, *nf* carpet.

pisar, *vt* to tread (on), walk on; to step on; to flatten, crush, trample.

pisca, *nf* maize harvest, corn harvest.

piscar, *vi* to harvest maize (or corn).

piscina, *nf* 1. swimming-pool; 2. fishpond, fishtank.

piso, *nm* floor; flooring.

pisotear, *vt* to tread down, trample; to stamp on.

pisoteo, *nm* treading, trampling; stamping.

pista, *nf* 1. track, trail; 2. clue.

pistero, *adj* mercenary, fond of money.

pisto, *nm* 1. chicken broth; 2. fried vegetable hash.

pistola, *nf* pistol; (spray) gun.

pistolera, *nf* holster.

pistolero, *nm* gunman, gangster.

pistoletazo, *nm* pistol shot; starting signal.

pistón, *nm* piston.

pitada, *nf* whistle; hiss.

pitandero(a), *nm/f* smoker.

pitar, *vt* to blow; to whistle at.

pitcher, *nm* pitcher.

pitido, *nm* whistle.

pitillera, *nf* cigarette case.

pitillo, *nm* 1. cigarette; 2. drinking-straw.

pito, *nm* whistle; (auto) horn.

pitón, *nm* 1. python; 2. bump, lump, protuberance.

pitonisa, *nf* fortune-teller; witch, sorceress.

pituitario, *adj* pituitary.

piyama, *nm* pajamas.

pizarra, *nf* 1. slate; shale; 2. blackboard; notice board.

pizarrón, *nm* blackboard; scoreboard.

pizarroso, *adj* slaty.

pizca, *nf* pinch, spot; crumb.

pizcar, *vt* to pinch, nip.

pizpireta, *nf* bright girl, lively (little) girl.

pizza, *nf* pizza.

placa, *nf* plate; thin piece of material, sheet; tab; plaque, tablet.

placenta, *nf* placenta.

placentero, *adj* pleasant, agreeable.

placer, *nm* 1. pleasure; enjoyment, delight; 2. sandbank; 3. ground prepared for sowing; plot, patch; field.

placero(a), *nm/f* 1. stallholder, market trader; 2. loafer, gossip.

placeta, *nf* plateau.

plácido, *adj* placid.

plaga, *nf* 1. pest, blight; 2. plague; scourge; calamity, disaster; 3. affliction, grave illness.

plagar, *vt* to infest, plague; to fill.

plagiar, *vt* to plagiarize; to pirate, copy illegally.

plagio, *nm* plagiarism; piracy, illegal copying.

plan, *nm* 1. plan; scheme; idea, intention; 2. activity, amusement.

plana, *nf* 1. sheet, page; writing exercises; 2. staff.

plancha, *nf* plate, sheet; slab; iron.

planchado, *adj* ironed; pressed.

planchar, *vt* to iron; to press.

planeador, *nm* glider.

planeadora, *nf* 1. leveller, bulldozer; 2. speedboat, powerboat.

planear, *vt* 1. to plan; to plan to do something; 2. *vi* to glide; to hover (over), hang (over).

planeo, *nm* gliding.

planeta, *nm* planet.

planetario, *adj* 1. planetary; 2. *nm* planetarium.

planicie, *nf* plain; flat area, level ground; flat surface.

planificación, *nf* planning; scheduling.

planificar, *vt* to plan.

planilla, *nf* 1. list; slip of paper; table, 2. form, application form.

plano, *adj* flat, level, even; plane, smooth.

planta, *nf* 1. sole of the foot; 2. floor, story; 3. plant; assembly plant; 4. (Bot) plant.

plantador, *nm* dibber, planter.

plantar, *vt* to plant; to bury.

plante, *nm* stoppage, protest strike.

planteamiento, *nm* (problem) posing, raising; approach.

plantear, *vt* to implant; to get under way; to set up, establish.

plantearse, *vr* to think, reflect.

plantel, *nm* training establishment.

plantilla, *nf* 1. inner sole, insole; 2. pattern, template; stencil; 3. establishment, personnel; list, roster.

plasma, *nm* plasma; blood plasma.

plasmar, *vt* to mold, shape, form; to create.

plástica, *nf* sculpture, modeling.

plasticar, *vt* to cover with plastic, seal in plastic, laminate.

plástico, *adj* plastic.

plata, *nf* 1. silver; 2. money; wealth.

platada, *nf* dish, plateful.

plataforma, *nf* platform; stage.

platanal, *nm* banana plantation.

platanero, *adj* 1. banana; 2. *nm* banana grower; dealer in bananas.

plátano, *nm* 1. plane, plane tree; 2. banana; banana tree; 3. plantain.

platea, *nf* (Theat) pit, orchestra.

plateado, *adj* silver; silvery; silver-plated.

platear, *vt* to silver; to silver-plate.

platería, *nf* 1. silversmith's craft; 2. silversmith's shop, jeweler's.

platero(a), *nm/f* silversmith; jeweler.

plática, *nf* talk, chat; sermon.

platicador, *adj* chatty, talkative.

platicar, *vi* to talk, chat; to say, tell.

platillo, *nm* saucer; small plate; collecting bowl.

platina, *nf* microscope slide.

platino, *nm* platinum; contact points.

plato, *nm* plate, (Cul) dish; course.

platónico, *adj* platonic.

playa, *nf* shore, beach.

playera, *nf* sports shirt, T-shirt.

plaza, *nf* square; public square, open space; market.

plazo, *nm* time, period, term; deadline, time limit.

plazoleta, *nf* small square.

plebe, *nf* the common people, the masses, the mass of the population.

plebeyo(a), *adj* plebeian; coarse, common.

plebiscito, *nm* plebiscite.

plegado, *nm* folding; bending; creasing.

plegar, *vt* to fold; to bend; to crease.

plegaria, *nf* prayer.

pleitear, *vi* 1. to plead, conduct a lawsuit; to go to law; 2. to argue.

pleito, *nm* 1. lawsuit, litigation; 2. dispute, feud; controversy; quarrel, argument; fight.

plenaria, *nf* plenary (session).

plenitud, *nf* plenitude, fullness; abundance.

pleno, *adj* full; complete; plenary.

plétora, *nf* plethora, abundance; excess, surplus.

pleuresía, *nf* pleurisy.

pléyade, *nf* group, gathering.

pliego, *nm* sheet; folder.

pliegue, *nm* fold, crease; pleat.

plisado, *nm* pleating; pleat.

plisar, *vt* to pleat.

plomada, *nf* plumb, plumb line.

plomar, *vt* to seal with lead.

plomazo, *nm* shot; bullet wound.

plomería, *nf* 1. leading, lead roofing; 2. plumbing; plumber's workshop, plumber's shop.

plomero, *nm* plumber.

plomo, *nm* lead.

pluma, *nf* 1. feather; quill; plume; 2. pen.

plumada, *nf* stroke of the pen; flourish.

plumazo, *nm* stroke of the pen.

plumear, *vt* to write, scribble.

plumero, *nm* 1. feather duster; 2. plume; bunch of feathers; 3. penholder.

plumífero(a), *nm/f* poor writer, hack; hack journalist.

plural, *adj* plural.

pluralismo, *nm* pluralism.

pluralista, *adj* pluralist; pluralistic.

plusvalía, *nf* appreciation, added value; unearned increment; capital gain, equity.

pluvial, *adj* rain.

población, *nf* population.

poblada, *nf* revolt, armed, rising.

poblado, *adj* inhabited.

poblador(a), *nm/f* settler, colonist; founder.

poblano, *adj* village, town.

poblar, *vt* to settle, people, colonize.

pobre, *adj* poor.

pobrete, *adj* poor, wretched.

pobreza, *nf* poverty; work, penury.

pócima, *nf* potion, draft; drench.

poco, *adj* little; small; slight, scanty.

poda, *nf* pruning.

podadera, *nf* pruning knife; pruning shears.

podadora, *nf* lawnmower.

podar, *vt* 1. to prune; 2. cut out.

poder, *vi* 1. can, to be able to; 2. *nm* power, authority, strength; power of attorney.

poderío, *nm* power; might; authority, jurisdiction.

poderoso, *adj* powerful.

podiatría, *nf* podiatry.

podio, *nm* podium.

podredumbre, *nf* rottenness, putrefaction; decay, corruption.

podrido, *adj* rotten, bad; putrid.

poema, *nm* poem.

poesía, *nf* poetry.

poeta, *nm/f* poet; writer, author, literary person.

poética, *nf* poetics, art of poetry, theory of poetry.

poetisa, *nf* poetess, poet.

poetizar, *vt* to poeticize; to idealize; to turn into poetry, make poetry out of.

polaco, *adj* Polish.

polar, *adj* polar.

polaridad, *nf* polarity.

polarización, *nf* polarization.

polarizar, *vt* to polarize.

polea, *nf* pulley; fan belt; tackle, tackle block.

polémica, *nf* polemics; controversy.

polémico, *adj* polemic(al); controversial.

polemizar, *vi* to indulge in a polemic, argue.

polen, *nm* pollen.

policía, *nm/f* policeman; policewoman.

policíaco, *adj* police.

policlínico, *nm* general hospital.

poligamia, *nf* polygamy.

polígamo(a), *adj* 1. polygamous; 2. *nm/f* polygamist.

poligloto(a), *nm/f* polyglot.

polígrafo(a), *nm/f* writer on a wide variety of subjects.

polilla, *nf* moth, grub, bookworm.

polínico, *adj* pollen.

polinización, *nf* pollination.

polinizar, *vt* to pollinate.

polio, *nf* polio.

pólipo, *nm* polyp, polypus.

polisón, *nm* 1. bustle; 2. bottom.

político, *adj* 1. political; politic; politician; 2. *nm* polite; courteous.

politiquear, *vi* to play at politics; to talk politics.

politiquero(a), *nm/f* politician, political intriguer.

politización, *nf* politization.

politizar, *vt* to politize.

póliza, *nf* certificate, voucher; draft; insurance certificate.

polizón, *nm* tramp, vagrant, bum; stowaway.

poltrona, *nf* easy chair; chair.

polución, *nf* pollution.

polucionar, *vt* to pollute.

polvareda, *nf* dust cloud, cloud of dust.

polvera, *nf* powder compact, vanity case.

polvo, *nm* dust.

pólvora, *nf* gunpowder.

polvorear, *vt* to powder, dust, sprinkle (with).

polvoriento, *adj* dusty; powdery.

polvorín, *nm* fine gunpowder.

pollera, *nf* hencoop; chicken run; basket for chickens.

pollero, *nm* chicken farmer; poulterer.

pollino(a), *nm/f* donkey.

pollo, *nm* chicken, chick, young bird.

polluelo, *nm* chick.

pomada, *nf* pomade, ointment.

pomo, *nm* pome, scent bottle.

pompa, *nf* bubble.

pomposidad, *nf* splendor, majesty; pomposity.

pomposo, *adj* splendid, magnificent; majestic; pompous.

pómulo, *nm* cheekbone; cheek.

ponchadura, *nf* puncture.

ponchar, *vt* 1. to punch; 2. to puncture.

ponchera, *nf* punch bowl.

poncho, *nm* poncho; blanket.

ponderado, *adj* calm, steady, balanced.
ponderar, *vt* to weigh up, consider.
ponedora, *adj* laying hen, hen in lay.
ponencia, *nf* paper, communication; report.
poner, *vt* to put; to place, set; to lay.
poniente, *adj* west, western.
pontaje, *nm* toll.
pontificado, *nm* papacy, pontificate.
pontifical, *adj* papal, pontifical.
pontificar, *vi* to pontificate.
pontífice, *nm* pope, pontiff.
ponzoña, *nf* poison, venom.
ponzoñoso, *adj* poisonous, venomous.
popa, *nf* stern.
populacho, *nm* populace, plebs, mob.
popular, *adj* popular.
popularidad, *nf* popularity.
popularizar, *vi* to popularize.
populoso, *adj* populous.
popurrí, *nm* potpourri.
póquer, *nm* poker.
poquito, *nm* a little bit.
por, *prep* by, through, over, by way of, for, because.
porcelana, *nf* porcelain; china, chinaware.
porcentaje, *nm* percentage; proportion, ratio; rate.
porcino, *adj* porcine; pig.
porción, *nf* portion; part, share.
porche, *nm* arcade (of shops); porch.
pordiosero(a), *nm/f* beggar.
porfía, *nf* persistence; obstinacy, stubbornness.
porfiado, *adj* persistent; obstinate, stubborn.
porfiar, *vi* to persist, insist; to argue stubbornly.
pormenor, *nm* detail, particular.
pormenorizado, *adj* detailed.
pormenorizar, *vt* to detail, set out in detail.
pornografía, *nf* pornography.
pornográfico, *adj* pornographic.
porosidad, *nf* porousness, porosity.
poroso, *adj* porous.
porque, *conj* because, in order that.
porqué, *interr* why?
porra, *nf* stick, club, cudgel; truncheon.
porrón, *nm* wine jar with a long spout.
porta(a)viones, *nm* aircraft-carrier.
portable, *adj* portable.
portada, *nf* 1. main front; facade; porch, doorway; 2. title page; cover.
portado, *adj* well-dressed; well-behaved; respectable.
portador(a), *nm/f* carrier, bearer.
portafolio(s), *nm* briefcase, attaché case.
portal, *nm* vestibule, hall.
portar, *vt* to carry, bear.
portavoz, *nm* 1. megaphone; 2. *nm/f* spokesperson, spokesman.
portazo, *nm* bang (of a door), slam.
porte, *nm* carriage, transport charges; postage.
porteador, *nm* carrier; porter; bearer.
portento, *nm* marvel, wonder, prodigy.
portentoso, *adj* marvelous, extraordinary.
porteo, *nm* carriage, transport, conveyance.
portería, *nf* 1. porter's office; 2. (Sport) goal.
portero, *nm* 1. porter, janitor; doorman; 2. (Sport) goal-keeper.
pórtico, *nm* portico, porch; gateway.
portillo, *nm* gap, opening; breach.
portón, *nm* large door; main door.
portuario, *adj* port, harbor; dock.
porvenir, *nm* future.
posada, *nf* 1. shelter, lodging; 2. inn; house, dwelling, abode.

posadero, *nm* innkeeper.
posar, *vt* to lay down, put down; pose.
pose, *nf* pose; time exposure.
poseedor(a), *nm/f* owner, possessor; holder.
poseer, *vt* to have, possess, own.
poseído, *adj* possessed; maddened, crazed.
posesión, *nf* possession; tenure, occupation.
posesivo, *adj* nm possessive.
posgrado, *nm* postgraduate course.
posgraduado(a), *adj*, *nm/f* postgraduate.
posguerra, *nf* postwar period.
posibilitar, *vt* to make possible, facilitate, permit.
posición, *nf* position; status, standing.
posicionado, *nm* positioning.
posicionar, *vt* to position.
positiva, *nf* (Phot) positive, print.
positivar, *vt* to develop.
positivo, *adj* positive.
posnatal, *adj* postnatal.
posponer, *vt* to postpone.
posposición, *nf* postposition; relegation; subordination; postponement.
posta, *nf* relay; team; stage.
postal, *adj* 1. postal; 2. *nf* postcard.
posdata, *nf* postscript.
poste, *nm* post, pole; pillar; stake.
postema, *nf* abscess, tumor; pus.
postergación, *nf* passing over, ignoring; delaying.
postergar, *vt* to pass over, disregard; to ignore, to delay; to defer, postpone.
posteridad, *nf* posterity.
posterior, *adj* back, rear.
postizo, *adj* false, artificial.
postor(a), *nm/f* bidder.
postración, *nf* prostration; nervous exhaustion.
postrado, *adj* prostrate.
postrar, *vt* to cast down, overthrow; to humble.
postre, *nm* sweet course; dessert.
postrero, *adj* last; rear, hindermost.
postrimerías, *nf* dying moments; final stages, closing stages.
postulación, *nf* postulation.
postulado, *nm* postulate, proposition; assumption, hypothesis.
postular, *vt* to postulate, to seek, demand.
póstumo, *adj* posthumous.
postura, *nf* posture, position; stance; pose.
potaje, *nm* broth; vegetable stew.
potasio, *nm* potassium.
pote, *nm* pot; jar; jug.
potencia, *nf* power; potency.
potencial, *adj* potential.
potente, *adj* powerful.
potestad, *nf* power, authority, jurisdiction.
potrero, *nm* pasture; paddock.
potro, *nm* colt.
poza, *nf* puddle, pool.
pozo, *nm* well.
practicante, *adj* 1. practicing; 2. *nm/f* practitioner.
practicar, *vt* to practice, exercise.
práctico, *adj* practical; handy; convenient.
pradera, *nf* meadow, meadowland.
pradería, *nf* meadowlands, grasslands.
prado, *nm* meadow, field; pasture; green grassy area.
pragmático, *adj* pragmatic.
preámbulo, *nm* preamble, introduction.
precalentar, *vt* to preheat; to warm up.
precario, *adj* precarious; doubtful, uncertain.
precaución, *nf* precaution; preventive measure.

precaver, *vt* to guard against, try to prevent.

precaverse, *vr* to be on one's guard, take precautions.

precavido, *adj* cautious, wary.

precedente, *adj* 1. preceding, foregoing; 2. *nm* precedent.

preceder, *vt* to precede, go before.

precepto, *nm* precept; order, rule.

preceptor(a), *nm/f* teacher; tutor.

preceptuar, *vt* to lay down, establish; to state as an essential requirement.

preciado, *adj* esteemed, valuable.

precintar, *vt* to seal; to seal off.

precio, *nm* price; cost; value, worth.

preciosidad, *nf* preciousness; value, worth.

precioso, *adj* 1. precious; valuable; 2. pretty, lovely, beautiful; charming.

precipicio, *nm* cliff, precipice.

precipitación, *nf* 1. haste; rashness; 2. precipitation, rainfall.

precipitado, *adj* headlong; hasty, sudden.

precipitar, *vt* to hurl down, cast down throw.

precisar, *vt* 1. to need, require; 2. to determine exactly, fix; to pinpoint.

precisión, *nf* precision; accuracy, exactness.

preciso, *adj* precise; exact, accurate.

precitado, *adj* above-mentioned.

precocinar, *vt* to precook.

preconcebido, *adj* preconceived.

preconización, *nf* 1. recommendation; favoring; 2. (future) visualizing.

preconizar, *vt* to praise.

precoz, *adj* precocious; forward.

precursor(a), *nm/f* predecessor, forerunner.

predador, *nm* predator.

predecesor(a), *nm/f* predecessor.

predecir, *vt* to predict, foretell, forecast.

predestinación, *nf* predestination.

predestinado, *adj* predestined.

predeterminar, *vt* to predetermine.

prédica, *nf* sermon; preaching.

predicado, *nm* predicate.

predicador(a), *nm/f* preacher.

predicar, *vti* to preach.

predicción, *nf* prediction; forecast.

predicho, *adj* aforementioned.

predilección, *nf* predilection.

predilecto, *adj* favorite.

predio, *nm* property, estate.

predisponer, *vt* to predispose; to prejudice, bias (against).

predisposición, *nf* predisposition, inclination.

predominante, *adj* predominant; major, prevailing.

predominar, *vt* to dominate, predominate over.

predominio, *nm* predominance; prevalence.

preeminencia, *nf* pre-eminence; superiority.

preescolar, *adj* preschool; preschool education.

preestrenar, *vt* to preview, give a preview of.

preexistir, *vi* to pre-exist, exist before.

prefabricar, *vt* to prefabricate.

prefacio, *nm* preface, foreword.

preferencia, *nf* preference.

preferible, *adj* preferable (a to).

preferido, *adj* favorite.

preferir, *vt* to prefer.

prefigurar, *vt* to foreshadow, prefigure.

prefijar, *vt* 1. to fix beforehand, arrange in advance, prearrange; 2. to prefix.

prefijo, *nm* prefix.

pregón, *nm* proclamation, announcement.

pregonar, *vt* to proclaim, announce.

pregonero, *nm* town crier; auctioneer.

pregrabado, *adj* prerecorded.

preguntar, *vt* to ask, ask question.

prehistórico, *adj* prehistoric.

prejuiciado, *adj* prejudiced (against).

prejuicio, *nm* 1. prejudgement; 2. prejudice, bias.

prejuzgar, *vt* to prejudge.

prelado, *nm* prelate.

preliminar, *adj, nm* preliminary.

preludio, *nm* prelude.

premarital, *adj* premarital.

prematuro, *adj* premature.

premeditado, *adj* premeditated, deliberate; willful.

premeditar, *vt* to premeditate; to plan, think out (in advance).

premiar, *vt* to reward; to give a prize to, make an award to.

premier, *nm/f* prime minister, premier.

premio, *nm* reward, recompense.

premisa, *nf* premise.

premonitorio, *adj* indicative, warning, premonitory.

premura, *nf* pressure; haste, urgency.

prenda, *nf* pledge; token.

prendar, *vt* to captivate, enchant.

prendedor, *nm* clasp, brooch.

prender, *vt* 1. to catch, capture; arrest; 2. to fasten; to pin.

prensa, *nf* press; printing press.

prensado, *nm* pressing; sheen, shine, gloss.

prensador, *nm* press, pressing machine.

prensar, *vt* to press.

preñada, *adj* pregnant.

preñar, *vt* to get pregnant; to impregnate, fertilize.

preñez, *nf* pregnancy.

preocupación, *nf* worry, anxiety, concern, preoccupation.

preocupado, *adj* worried, anxious, concerned, preoccupied.

preocupar, *vt* to worry, preoccupy; to bother.

preparación, *nf* 1. preparation; 2. preparedness, readiness; 3. training.

preparado, *adj* 1. prepared; ready to serve; 2. competent, able; qualified; well-informed.

preparar, *vt* 1. to prepare, get ready; process, treat; 2. to teach, train.

preponderante, *adj* preponderant; superior.

preponente, *adj* boastful, conceited.

preponer, *vt* to place before.

preposición, *nf* preposition.

prepotencia, *nf* power, dominance, superiority; arrogance; abuse of power.

prepotente, *adj* powerful, supreme; arrogant, overbearing, domineering; given to abusing power.

prepucio, *nm* foreskin, prepuce.

prerrequisito, *nm* prerequisite.

prerrogativa, *nf* prerogative, right, privilege.

presagiador, *adj* ominous.

presagiar, *vt* to betoken, forebode, presage.

presagio, *nm* omen, portent.

presbiteriano(a), *adj, nm/f* Presbyterian.

presbiterio, *nm* presbytery, chancel.

presbítero, *nm* priest.

presciencia, *nf* prescience, foreknowledge.

presciente, *adj* prescient.

prescindible, *adj* dispensable.

prescindir, *vi* (de) to do without, go without.

prescribir, *vt* to prescribe.

prescripción, *nf* prescription.

prescrito, *adj* prescribed.

presea, *nf* jewel; treasure, precious thing.

presencia, *nf* presence.
precenciar, *vt* to be present at; to attend; to see, witness, watch.
presentación, *nf* presentation; introduction.
presentador(a), *nm/f* presenter; host, hostess.
presentar, *vt* to present; to offer; to show, display.
presentarse, *vr* introduce oneself; appear.
presente, *adj* present.
presentimiento, *nm* premonition, presentiment.
presentir, *vt* to have a premonition of.
preservación, *nf* protection, preservation.
preservar, *vt* to protect, preserve.
presidencia, *nf* presidency.
presidencial, *adj* presidential.
presidente, *nm/f* president.
presidiario, *nm* convict.
presidio, *nm* prison, penitentiary.
presidir, *vt* to preside at, preside over.
presilla, *nf* fastener, clip.
presión, *nf* pressure.
presionar, *vt* to press.
prestador(a), *nm/f* lender.
prestamista, *nm/f* moneylender; pawnbroker.
préstamo, *nm* loan, lending, borrowing.
prestancia, *nf* distinction, excellence; elegance, dignity.
prestar, *vt* to lend, loan.
presteza, *nf* speed, promptness.
prestigiar, *vt* to give prestige (or distinction, status) to, to make famous; to honor, to enhance.
prestigio, *nm* prestige; good name.
prestigioso, *adj* worthy, estimable, prestigious; reputable; famous.
presto, *adj* quick, prompt.
presumido, *adj* conceited.
presumir, *vt* 1. to presume, conjecture, surmise; 2. to court; to flirt with.
presunción, *nf* supposition, presumption; suspicion.
presuntuoso, *adj* conceited, presumptuous; pretentious.
presuponer, *vt* to presuppose.
presuposición, *nf* presupposition.
presupuestal, *adj* budgetary, budget.
presupuestar, *vt* to budget for, to estimate the cost of.
presupuesto, *nm* budget.
presusrizado, *adj* pressurized.
presuroso, *adj* quick, prompt, speedy.
pretemporada, *nf* pre-season.
pretensioso, *adj* pretentious, presumptuous.
pretender, *vt* to try to, to claim, to seek, to expect.
pretendido, *adj* supposed, pretended; alleged.
pretendiente, *nm* suitor; claimant, candidate, applicant.
preterir, *vt* to leave out, omit, pass over.
pretérito, *adj* 1. past, former; 2. *nm* preterite.
pretextar, *vt* to plead, use as an excuse.
pretexto, *nm* pretext; excuse, plea.
prevalecer, *vi* to prevail (over); to triumph, to come to dominate.
prevaleciente, *adj* prevaling, prevalent.
prevención, *nf* preparation; readiness; preparedness.
prevenido, *adj* to be cautious; to be far-sighted, to be prepared.
prevenir, *vt* to prepare, get ready, make ready.
preventivo, *adj* preventive, precautionary.
prever, *vt* to foresee.
previo, *adj* previous, prior, earlier.
previsión, *nf* foresight, farsightedness; caution.

previsor, *adj* far-sighted; prudent.
prieto, *adj* blackish, dark.
prima, *nf* cousin.
primar, *vt* to give priority to; to place a high value on.
primario, *adj* primary.
primavera, *nf* spring; springtime.
primero, *adj* first; former.
primicia, *nf* novelty; first appearance.
primitivo, *adj* early; first, original; primitive.
primo, *adj* 1. prime; 2. (materials) raw; 3. *nm* cousin.
primogénito, *adj* first-born.
primogenitura, *nf* primogeniture; birthright.
primor, *nm* exquisiteness, beauty.
primordial, *adj* basic, fundamental, essential.
primoroso, *adj* exquisite, line, delicate, elegant; neat, skillful.
princesa, *nf* princess.
principal, *adj* 1. principal, chief, main; foremost; 2. head, chief, principal.
príncipe, *nm* prince.
principiante, *adj* 1. who is beginning; 2. *nm* beginner, novice.
principiar, *vti* to begin.
principio, *nm* 1. beginning, start; origin; 2. rudiments, first notions; 3. principle; element, constituent.
prioridad, *nf* priority; seniority, greater age.
priorizar, *vt* to give priority to, treat as a priority.
prisa, *nf* hurry, haste; speed; urgency.
prisión, *nf* prison.
prisionero(a), *nm/f* prisoner.
prisma, *nm* prism.
prismático, *adj* 1. prismatic; 2. *nm* binoculars, field glasses.
privacidad, *nf* privacy; secrecy.
privación, *nf* deprivation, deprival.
privado, *adj* private; personal.
privar, *vt* take something away from someone.
privatizar, *vt* to privatize.
privilegiado, *adj* privileged; exceptionally good.
privilegiar, *vt* to grant a privilege to; to favor.
privilegio, *nm* privilege; concession.
proa, *nf* bow, bows; prow; nose.
probabilidad, *nf* probability, likelihood.
probado, *adj* proven.
probador, *nm* 1. taster; 2. fitting room.
probar, *vt* 1. to prove; to show, demonstrate; to establish; 2. to test, taste, try (out); to try on.
problema, *nm* problem; difficulty.
problemático, *adj* problematic.
probo, *adj* honest, upright.
procedencia, *nf* source, origin; provenance.
procedente, *adj* coming from, proceeding from, originating in.
proceder, *vi* to proceed.
procedimiento, *nm* procedure; process; means, method.
prócer, *nm* worthy, notable; important person.
procesador, *nm* processor.
procesadora, *nf* food processor.
procesar, *vt* to try, put on trial; to prosecute.
procesión, *nf* procession.
procesional, *adj* processional.
proceso, *nm* process.
proclama, *nf* proclamation; address; manifesto.
proclamación, *nf* proclamation.
proclamar, *vt* to proclaim.
procreación, *nf* procreation, breeding.
procrear, *vti* to procreate, breed.

procurar, vt to get, obtain; to secure; to yield, produce.

prodigar, vt to lavish, give lavishly; to squander.

prodigio, nm prodigy; wonder, marvel.

pródigo, adj 1. bountiful; rich; 2. lavish, generous; 3. prodigal; extravagant, wasteful.

producción, nf production; output.

producir, vt to produce; to make; to cause, bring about.

productividad, nf productivity.

productivo, adj productive; profitable.

producto, nm product.

profanación, nf desecration.

profanar, vt to desecrate, profane.

profecía, nf prophecy.

proferir, vt to utter.

profesar, vt to profess; to declare.

profesión, nf profession, declaration; avowal; (Ecl) taking of vows.

profesionalismo, nm professionalism.

profesor(a), nm/f teacher; instructor.

profeta, nm prophet.

profético, adj prophetic.

profetisa, nf prophetess.

profetizar, vti to prophesy.

prófugo, nm fugitive; deserter.

profundidad, nf depth.

profundizar, vt to deepen; to go deeper.

profusión, nf profusion; wealth, extravagance.

profuso, adj profuse; lavish, extravagant.

progenie, nf progeny, offspring.

progenitor, nm ancestor; father.

programa, nm program; scheme, plan.

programación, nf programming.

programado, adj programmed; planned.

programador(a), nm/f programmer.

programar, vt to plan; to draw up a program for.

progresar, vi to progress, make progress.

progresión, nf progression.

progresivo, adj progressive; gradual.

progreso, nm progress; advance.

prohibición, nf prohibition.

prohibir, vt to prohibit, forbid, stop, ban.

prohibitivo, adj prohibitive.

prohijar, vt to adopt.

prójimo, nm fellow man, fellow creature; neighbor.

prole, nf offspring; brood, spawn.

proliferación, nf proliferation.

proliferar, vi to proliferate.

prolífico, adj prolific.

prolijo, adj prolix, long-winded; tedious.

prologar, vt to preface, write an introduction to.

prólogo, nm prologue; preface, introduction.

prolongación, nf prolongation, extension.

prolongar, vt to prolong, extend.

promediar, vt 1. to divide into two halves; divide equally; 2. to work out the average of, average (out).

promedio, nm average.

promesa, nf promise.

prometedor, adj promising.

prometer, vt to promise; to pledge.

prometida, nf fiancée.

prometido, adj 1. promised; 2. engaged.

prominencia, nf protuberance; swelling, bump; prominence.

prominente, adj prominent, that sticks out.

promiscuidad, nf mixture, jumble, confusion.

promiscuo, adj mixed (up), in disorder.

promoción, nf promotion, advancement.

promocionar, vt to promote; to give rapid promotion to.

promocionarse, vr to improve oneself, better oneself.

promontorio, nm promontory, headland.

promotor(a), nm/f promoter.

promover, vt to promote, advance, further.

promulgación, nf promulgation; announcement, publication.

promulgar, vt to promulgate; to proclaim.

pronto, adj prompt, quick.

pronunciación, nf pronunciation.

pronunciar, vt to pronounce; to make, utter.

pronunciarse, vr to declare oneself, state one's opinion; to make a pronouncement.

propagación, nf propagation.

propaganda, nf propaganda; advertising.

propagar, vt to propagate; spread, disseminate.

propalación, nf disclosure; dissemination.

propalar, vt to divulge, disclose; to disseminate.

propasarse, vr to go too far, overstep the bounds; to take liberties.

propela, nf propeller; outboard motor.

propender, vi to tend towards, incline to.

propiciador(a), nm/f sponsor.

propiciar, vt to propitiate, to win over.

propiciatorio, adj propitiatory.

propicio, adj propitious, auspicious.

propiedad, nf possession; ownership.

propietario(a), adj 1. proprietary; 2. nm/f owner, proprietor.

propina, nf tip, gratuity.

propinar, vt 1. buy someone a drink; 2. to deal, hit.

propio, adj own, of one's own.

proponer, vt to propose, put forward; to suggest.

proporción, nf proportion; ratio; relationship.

proporcionado, adj proportionate.

proporcional, adj proportional.

proporcionar, vt to give, supply, provide, furnish; to get.

proposición, nf proposition; proposal.

propósito, nm purpose; aim, intention, objective.

propuesta, nf proposal.

propugnar, vt to advocate, propose, suggest.

propulsar, vt 1. to drive, propel; 2. to promote, encourage.

propulsión, nf propulsion.

propulsor, nm propellent, fuel; motor, engine.

prorratear, vt to share out, apportion, distribute proportionately.

prorrateo, nm sharing, apportionment.

prórroga, nf deferment; extension.

prorrogación, nf deferment, prorogation.

prorrogar, vt 1. to prorogue; 2. adjourn; to extend.

prorrumpir, vi to burst forth, break out.

proscribir, vt to prohibit, ban.

proscripción, nf prohibition (of), ban (on); proscription.

prosecución, nf continuation; pressing; pursuit.

proseguir, vt to continue, carry on, go on with, proceed with.

prosista, nm/f prose writer.

prospeccionar, vt to look to; examine.

prospecto, nm prospectus; leaflet, sheet of instructions.

prosperar, vi to prosper, thrive, flourish; to be successful.

prosperidad, nf prosperity; success.

próspero, adj prosperous, thriving, flourishing; successful.

próstata, nf prostate.

prostático, *adj* prosthetic.
prostitución, *nf* prostitution.
prostituir, *vt* to prostitute.
prostituta, *nf* prostitute; streetwalker.
protagónico, *adj* leading, major.
protagonista, *adj* 1. important, leading, influential; 2. *nm/f* protagonist; main character.
protagonizar, *vt* to take the chief role in, play the lead in.
protección, *nf* protection.
proteccionista, *adj* protectionist; protective.
protector, *adj* protective, protecting.
protectorado, *nm* protectorate.
proteger, *vt* to protect, to shield; to defend.
protegido(a), *adj* 1. protected; 2. *nm/f* protégé.
proteína, *nf* protein.
protesta, *nf* protest; grumble.
protestante, *adj*, *nm/f* Protestant.
protestar, *vt* to protest, declare, avow; to profess.
protocolo, *nm* protocol.
protoplasma, *nm* protoplasm.
prototipo, *nm* prototype.
protuberancia, *nf* protuberance.
protuberante, *adj* protuberant.
provecto, *adj* aged; elderly.
provecho, *nm*, advantage, benefit, profit.
proveedor(a), *nm/f* supplier, purveyor; dealer.
proveer, *vt* to provide, supply, furnish.
provenir, *vi* to come from, arise from, stem from.
proverbial, *adj* proverbial.
proverbio, *nm* proverb.
providencia, *nf* foresight; forethought, providence.
próvido, *adj* provident.
provincia, *nf* province.
provincial, *adj* provincial.
provinciano(a), *adj* provincial; country.
proviniente, *adj* coming from, arising out of.
provisión, *nf* provision; supply.
provisional, *adj* provisional.
provisionar, *vt* to cover.
provisorio, *adj* provisional.
provocación, *nf* provocation.
provocador, *adj* provocative; provoking.
provocar, *vt* to provoke; to rouse, stir up; to tempt.
proximidad, *nf* nearness, closeness, proximity.
próximo, *adj* near, close; neighboring.
proyección, *nf* projection.
proyectar, *vt* 1. to hurl, throw; to cast, shed; 2. to project; to screen, show.
proyectil, *nm* projectile, missile; shell.
proyecto, *nm* plan, design; project.
proyector, *nm* 1. projector; 2. searchlight; spotlight.
prudencia, *nf* wisdom, prudence; care; soundness, sound judgement.
prudenciarse, *vr* to be cautious; to hold back, control oneself.
prudente, *adj* sensible, wise, prudent.
prueba, *nf* 1. proof; evidence; exhibit; 2. test, examination.
prurito, *nm* itch, pruritis.
psicoanálisis, *nm* psychoanalysis.
psicoanalista, *nm/f* psychoanalyst.
psicoanalizar, *vt* to psychoanalyze.
psicología, *nf* psychology.
psicológico, *adj* psychological.
psicólogo(a), *nm/f* psychologist.
psicópata, *nm/f* psychopath.
psicosis, *nf* psychosis.
psicosomático, *adj* psychosomatic.

psicoterapia, *nf* psychotherapy.
psique, *nf* psyche.
psiquiatra, *nm/f* psychiatrist.
psiquiatría, *nf* psychiatry.
psíquico, *adj* psychic.
púa, *nf* sharp point; prickle, spike.
púber, *adj* adolescent.
pubertad, *nf* puberty.
publicación, *nf* publication.
publicar, *vt* to publish; to publicize.
publicidad, *nf* publicity.
publicista, *nm/f* publicist.
publicitar, *vt* to publicize; to advertise.
público, *adj* public.
puchero, *nm* cooking-pot.
pudiente, *adj* wealthy; powerful, influential.
pudín, *nm* pudding.
pudor, *nm* modesty; shyness; chastity.
pudrición, *nf* rotting.
pudrir, *vt* to rot; to upset, vex, annoy, exasperate.
pueblo, *nm* 1. people, nation; common people; 2. village; small town, country town.
puente, *nm* bridge.
puentear, *vt* to bypass, pass over.
puerca, *nf* sow.
puerco, *nm* pig, hog; wild boar.
puerta, *nf* door; gate; doorway.
puerto, *nm* port, harbor; seaport.
pues, *adv* 1. then, well, well then, so; 2. *conj* for, since, because.
puesta, *nf* putting, placing; bet, sunset.
puesto, *nm* place, position, office, booth, stall.
púgil, *nm* boxer.
pugilato, *nm* boxing.
pugilista, *nm* boxer.
pugna, *nf* battle, struggle, conflict.
pugnar, *vi* 1. to fight; 2. to struggle, strive.
puja, *nf* attempt, effort.
pujante, *adj* strong, vigorous; powerful; forceful.
pujar, *vi* to bid, bid up; to struggle, strain.
pujo, *nm* 1. difficulty in relieving oneself; 2. longing, strong urge.
pulcritud, *nf* neatness, tidiness, smartness, exquisiteness, delicacy.
pulcro, *adj* neat, tide, smart, delicate.
pulga, *nf* flea.
pulgada, *nf* inch.
pulgar, *nm* thumb.
pulgarada, *nf* flick, flip.
pulido, *adj* neat, tidy.
pulidor(a), *nm/f* polisher.
pulimentar, *vt* to polish.
pulimento, *nm* polishing; polish, shine; gloss.
pulir, *vt* to polish; to put a gloss on, put a shine on.
pulirse, *vr* spruce oneself, up, refine oneself.
pulmón, *nm* lung.
pulmonar, *adj* pulmonary, lung.
pulmonía, *nf* pneumonia.
pulpa, *nf* pulp; soft mass.
púlpito, *nm* pulpit.
pulpo, *nm* octopus.
pulsación, *nf* beat, pulsation.
pulsador, *nm* button, push-button; switch.
pulsar, *vt* (key) beat, pulsate, throb; to strike, touch, tap, to press.
pulsera, *nf* wristlet, bracelet.
pulso, *nm* pulse.
pulverización, *nf* pulverization.
pulverizador, *nm* spray, sprayer, spray-gun.

pulverizar, *vt* to pulverize; to powder, convert into powder.

punción, *nf* puncture.

pundonor, *nm* self-respect, pride; honor; face.

pundonoroso, *adj* honorable; punctilious, scrupulous.

punta, *nf* end; tip, point, sharp end.

puntada, *nf* stitch.

puntal, *nm* prop, shore, support.

puntapié, *nm* kick.

puntera, *nf* toe cap.

puntería, *nf* aim, aiming.

puntero, *adj* top, leading.

punto, *nm* 1. dot, spot; fleck; spot, speckle; 2. (Gram) period; place, point.

puntuación, *nf* punctuation; marking.

puntualidad, *nf* reliability, conscientiousness; punctuality.

puntualizar, *vt* to fix, specify, state in detail; to settle, determine.

punzada, *nf* 1. puncture, prick; jab; 2. pain, spasm.

punzante, *adj* shooting, sharp.

punzar, *vt* to puncture, prick, pierce.

puñado, *nm* handful.

puñal, *nm* dagger.

puñalada, *nf* stab.

puño, *nm* fist.

pupila, *nf* 1. pupil; 2. inmate; boarder.

pupilo, *nm* 1. inmate; boarde; 2. ward.

pupitre, *nm* desk; console.

puré, *nm* purée, soup.

pureza, *nf* purity.

purga, *nf* purge, cathartic, purgative.

purgante, *nm* purgative.

purgar, *vt* to purge, cleanse.

purgatorio, *nm* purgatory.

purificación, *nf* purification.

purificar, *vt* to purify; to cleanse.

puro, *adj* pure; unadulterated.

púrpura, *adj* purple.

pus, *nm* pus, matter.

putativo, *adj* putative, supposed.

putrefacción, *nf* rotting, putrefaction; decay.

putrefacto, *adj* rotten, putrid; decayed.

pútrido, *adj* putrid, rotten.

Q

Q, q, *nf* (letter) Q, q.

quáker, *nm* porridge.

quántum, *nm* quanta; quantum.

quark, *nm* quarks quark.

quásar, *nm* quasar.

que, *pron rel* (*pers: sujeto*) who, that; (*acusativo*) whom, that; (*cosa*) that, which; (*conj*) that; for, because,

qué, *interj* 1. What?; 2. *adj* which?

quebrada, *nf* gorge, ravine; gap, pass; mountain stream.

quebrado, *adj* broken, rough, uneven; irregular, zigzag; bankrupt; (Math) fraction.

quebradura, *nf* fissure, slit, crack, rupture.

quebrantamiento, *nm* breaking; cracking; weakening; forcing; violation.

quebrantar, *vt* to break; to crack; to shatter.

quebrantarse, *vr* to be shattered, be broken.

quebranto, *nm* damage, harm; severe loss.

quebrar, *vt* to break, smash.

quedar, *vi* to stay, remain.

quedo, *adj* still; quiet, soft, gentle.

quehacer, *nm* job, task; household job, chore.

queja, *nf* complaint; protest; grumble, grouse; grudge, resentment.

quejarse, *vr* to complain; grumble; to protest.

quejido, *nm* moan, groan.

quema, *nf* burning, combustion; burning-off (of scrub).

quemado, *adj* burned, burnt.

quemador, *nm* burner; hob; lighter.

quemadura, *nf* burn; scald; sunburn; (fuse) blowing, blow-out.

quemar, *vt* to burn, burn up, set on fire; (fuse) burn out.

querella, *nf* complaint; charge, accusation; suit, case.

querellarse, *vr* to complain; to file a complaint, bring an action.

querer, *vt/i* 1. to want, wish (for); 2. love, desire; 3. *nm* affection, liking, fondness.

querido(a), *adj*, *nm/f* dear, darling, beloved.

querosén, *nm* kerosene, paraffin.

querubín, *nm* cherub.

quesera, *nf* dairymaid; cheesemaker.

quesería, *nf* dairy; cheese factory.

quiebra, *nf* 1. crack, fissure; slit; 2. bankruptcy; failure; slump, crash.

quiebre, *nm* breaking, rupture.

quieto, *adj* still, motionless.

quietud, *nf* stillness; quietude; calm.

quijada, *nf* jaw, jawbone.

quijote, *nm* quixotic person; dreamer, hopelessly unrealistic person.

quilate, *nm* carat.

quilo, *nm* kilo, kilogram.

quimbo, *nm* knife, machete.

quimera, *nf* chimera; hallucination; fancy.

quimérico, *adj* fantastic, fanciful; impossible.

quimerizar, *vi* to indulge in fantasy, indulge in pipe dreams.

química, *nf* 1. chemistry; 2. chemist.

químico, *adj* chemical.

quimioterapia, *nf* chemotherapy.

quimono, *nm* kimono.

quina, *nf* quinine.

quincalla, *nf* hardware, trinket.

quincallero(a), *nm* hardware dealer.

quince, *adj* fifteen.

quinceañero(a), *adj* 1. fifteen-year old, teenager; 2. *nm/f* fifteen-year old, teenager.

quinceavo, *adj, nm* fifteenth.

quincena, *nf* fortnight.

quincenal, *adj* fortnightly.

quiniento, *adj* five hundred.

quinina, *nf* quinine.

quinqué, *nm* oil lamp.

quinquenio, *nm* quinquennium, five-year period.

quinta, *nf* 1. villa, country house; small estate on the outskirts of a town; 2. draft, call-up; 3. (Mus) fifth.

quintal, *nm* measure of weight, = 25 lbs., = 100 kg.

quintería, *nf* farmhouse.

quintero, *nm* farmer; farmhand, laborer.

quinteto, *nm* quintet(te).

quintillizo(a), *nm/f* quintuplet.

quinto, *adj* fifth.

quíntuplo, *adj* quintuple, fivefold.

quiosco, *nm* kiosk, stand, stall; summerhouse, pavilion.

quiosquero(a), *nm/f* proprietor of a newsstand, newspaper seller.

quirófano, *nm* operating theater.

quiromancia, *nf* palmistry.

quiromántico(a), *nm/f* palmist.

quirúrgico, *adj* surgical.

quisicosa, *nf* conundrum; puzzle.

quisquilla, *nf* trifle, triviality.

quisquilloso, *adj* touchy, oversensitive, irritable.

quiste, *nm* cyst.

quitamanchas, *nm* cleaning material, stain remover.

quitar, *vt* to take away, remove; (cloth) take off; (Math) subtract.

quitasol, *nm* sunshade, parasol.

quite, *nm* removal.

quitrín, *nm* trap (vehicle).

quizá(s), *adv* perhaps, maybe.

quórum, *nm* quorum.

R

R, r, *nf* (letter) R, r.

rabada, *nf* hindquarter, rump.

rábano, *nm* radish; horseradish.

rabear, *vi* to wag its tail.

rabí, *nm* rabbi.

rabia, *nf* 1. rabies; 2. fury, rage, anger; bad feeling.

rabiar, *vi* 1. to have rabies; 2. to suffer terribly, be in great pain; 3. to rage, rave, be furious; to storm at, rave about.

rabieta, *nf* fit of temper; paddy, fly into a rage.

rabillo, *nm* small tail.

rabino, *nm* rabbi.

rabioso, *adj* 1. rabid, suffering from rabies; mad dog; 2. furious; raging, violent.

rabo, *nm* tail.

rabón, *adj* 1. short-tailed; bobtailed; tailless; 2. short, small; 3. stark naked.

racial, *adj* racial, race.

racimo, *nm* bunch, cluster; raceme.

raciocinar, *vi* to reason.

raciocinio, *nm* 1. reason; 2. reasoning.

ración, *nf* 1. ratio; 2. portion.

racional, *adj* 1. rational; 2. reasonable, sensible.

racionalización, *nf* rationalization.

racionalizador, *adj* rationalizing; streamlining.

racionalizar, *vt* to rationalize; to streamline.

racionamiento, *nm* rationing.

racionar, *vt* to ration; to be rationed, to ration out.

racista, *adj* 1. racial, racialist; 2. *nm/f* racist.

racha, *nf* 1. gust of wind; squall; 2. string, series; run.

rada, *nf* roads, roadstead; natural bay.

radar, *nm* radar; radar station.

radiación, *nf* radiation.

radiactivo, *adj* radioactive.

radiado, *adj* radiate.

radiador, *nm* radiator.

radial, *adj* 1. radial. 2. radio, broadcasting.

radiante, *adj* radiant.

radiar, *vt* 1. to radiate; to irradiate; 2. to broadcast; 3. to treat with X-rays.

radical, *adj* 1. radical; 2. *nm* root; squareroot sign; 3. *nm/f* (Politician) radical.

radicar, *vi* to take root.

radicarse, *vr* to establish oneself, put down one's roots (in).

radio, *nm* 1. radius; 2. spoke; 3. radium; 4. *nf* radio, wireless; broadcasting.

radiodifusión, *nf* broadcasting.

radiodifusora, *nf* radio station, transmitter.

radioescucha, *nm/f* listener.

radiofónico, *adj* radio (atr).

radiografía, *nf* radiography, X-ray photography.

radiografiar, *vt* to X-ray.

radiología, *nf* radiology.

radiólogo(a), *nm/f* radiologist.

radiorreceptor, *nm* radio, wireless, receiver.

radioscopía, *nf* radioscopy.

radiotelegrafía, *nf* radiotelegraphy, wireless (telegraphy).

radioyente, *nm/f* listener.

raedura, *nf* scrape, scraping; abrasion.

raer, *vt* to scrape; to erase; to abrade, graze.

ráfaga, *nf* gust, squall; sudden blast.

raicear, *vi* to take root.

raicero, *nm* mass of roots, root system.

raído, *adj* frayed, threadbare; shabby.

raíz, *nf* 1. root; 2. root cause; source.

raja, *nf* 1. slit, split; crack; 2. sliver, splinter, thin piece, slice.

rajado, *nm* 1. swine; 2. coward.

rajador, *adj* fast.

rajar, *vt* to split, split; crack; to cleave; to slit.

rala, *nf* birdlime.

ralea, *nf* kind, sort, breed.

ralear, *vi* to become thin, become sparse; to thin out; to become less dense.

rallado, *adj* grated.

rallador, *nm* grater.

rallar, *vt* to grate.

rallón, *adj* bothersome, irritating.

rama, *nf* branch.

ramada, *nf* branches, foliage.

ramal, *nm* 1. strand (of a rope); halter. 2. branch road; branch line.

ramificación, *nf* ramification.

ramificarse, *vr* to ramify, divide, branch (out).

ramillete, *nm* bouquet, bunch of flowers, posy; corsage.

ramo, *nm* branch; bunch of flowers, bouquet.

rampa, *nf* ramp, incline.

rampla, *nf* trailer.

rana, *nf* frog.

rancio, *adj* old, mellow; rank, rancid, stale; musty.

ranchera, *nf* 1. typical Mexican song; 2. station wagon.

ranchero, *adj* 1. uncouth; ridiculous, silly; 2. *nm* rancher, farmer; peasant.

rancho, *nm* hut, thatched hut, shed; country house, villa.

ranfla, *nf* ramp, incline.

ranura, *nf* groove; slot; expansion slot.

rapar, *vt* 1. to shave; to crop, cut very close; 2. to snatch; to pinch.

rapaz, *adj* rapacious, greedy; thieving, predatory.

rape, *nm* quick shave; close haircut.

rapé, *nm* snuff.

rápida, *nf* chute.

rapidez, *nf* rapidity, speed; speediness, swiftness.

rápido, *adj* rapid, fast, quick, swift; express.

rapiña, *nf* robbery (with violence); V ave.

rapiñar, *vt* to steal.

rapsodia, *nf* rhapsody.

raptar, *vt* to kidnap, abduct; to carry off.

rapto, *nm* 1. kidnapping, abduction; carrying-off; 2. sudden impulse; a sudden fit of jealousy.

raptor(a), *nm/f* kidnapper.

raqueta, *nf* racquet.

raquetazo, *nm* shot, hit, stroke.

raquítico, *adj* 1. rachitic; weak, stunted; 2. small, inadequate, miserly.

rareza, *nf* rarity, rareness, scarcity.

raro, *adj* 1. rare, scarce, uncommon; 2. odd, peculiar, strange; eccentric; remarkable.

ras, *nm* levelness, evenness; flush.

rasado, *adj* level.

rasante, *adj* low; low shot; low-level flight.

rasar, *vt* 1. to level (with the rim); 2. to skim, graze.

rascacielos, *nm* skyscraper.

rascadera, *nf* scraper; currycomb.

rascado, *adj* drunk.

rascador, *nm* scraper; flle, rasp.

rascar, *vt* to scrape, rasp; to scratch.

rasco, *adj* common, low; low-class.

raseado, *adj* level.

rasgadura, *nf* tear, rip, slash.

rasgar, *vt* to tear, rip, slash.

rasgo, *nm* 1. stroke, flourish; adornment; 2. features; appearance; 3. characteristic.

rasgón, *nm* tear, rent.

rasguear, *vt* to strum; to write with a flourish.

rasgunar, *vt* 1. to scratch; 2. to sketch, draw in outline.

rasguño, *nm* 1. scratch; 2. sketch, outline drawing.

raso, *adj* 1. flat, level; clear, bare, open; smooth; 2. *nm* satin.

raspa, *nf* beard; stalk.

rastra, *nf* 1. rake; harrow; 2. sledge (for removing heavy objects); 3. trawl; dredge.

rastreador, *nm* tracker.

rastrear, *vt* to track, trail, follow the trail of.

rastreo, *nm* dredging, dragging; trawling; tracking.

rastrero, *adj* 1. creeping, crawling; 2. mean, despicable.

rastrillar, *vt* to rake.

rastrillo, *nm* rake.

rastro, *nm* track, trail; mark on the ground; scent.

rastrojear, *vi* to glean; to feed in the stubble.

rastrojera, *nf* stubble field.

rastrojo, *nm* 1. stubble; ploughed field; 2. *(pl)* waste, remains, left-overs.

rasurado, *nm* shave.

rasurador(a), *nm/f* shaver, razor.

rasurar, *vt* to shave; to scrape.

rata, *nf* 1. rat; 2. *nm* sneak thief.

ratear, *vt* to steal, pilfer; to filch.

ratera, *nf* rat-trap.

ratería, *nf* petty larceny, small-time thieving, pilfering.

ratero, *adj* 1. thievish, light-fingered; 2. *nm* pickpocket; sneak thief, small-time thief; burglar.

ratificación, *nf* ratification; confirmation; support.

ratificar, *vt* to ratify; to confirm; to support.

rato, *nm* time, while; spell, period.

ratón, *nm* 1. mouse; 2. squib, cracker.

ratonar, *vt* to gnaw, nibble.

ratonera, *nf* mousetrap; mouse-hole.

raudal, *nm* torrent, flood, plenty, abundance; great quantity.

raudo, *adj* swift; rushing, impetuous.

raya, *nf* 1. line; streak; scratch, mark; 2. boundary, limit; 3. stripe; 4. ray, skate.

rayado, *adj* ruled; crossed; striped.

rayar, *vt* to line, rule lines on; to cross· to scratch.

rayo, *nm* ray, beam; shaft; beam.

raza, *nf* race; breed, strain; stock.

razón, *nf* 1. reason; 2. right, rightness; justice.

razonable, *adj* reasonable.

razonado, *adj* reasoned; detailed.

razonamiento, *nm* reasoning.

razonar, *vt* to reason, argue.

reabastecer, *vt* to refuel.

reabastecimiento, *nm* refuelling.

reabrir, *vt* to reopen.

reacción, *nf* reaction; response.

reaccionar, *vi* to react; to respond.

reaccionario(a), *adj*, *nm/f* reactionary.

reacio, *adj* stubborn; reluctant.

reacondicionar, *vt* to recondition; to reorganize, restructure.

reactivación, *nf* reactivating; recovery, upturn.

reactivar, *vt* to reactivate.

reactivo, *nm* reagent.

reactor, *nm* reactor; nuclear reactor, (motor) jet engine.

readmisión, *nf* readmission.

readmitir, *vt* to readmit.

reafirmación, *nf* reaffirmation; reassertion.

reafirmar, *vt* to reaffirm; to reassert.

reagrupar, *vt* to regroup.

reajustar, *vt* to readjust; to reshuffle.

reajuste, *nm* readjustment.

real, *adj* 1. real; 2. royal.

realar, *vt* to round up.

realce, *nm* 1. raised work, embossing; 2. highlight; lustre, splendour; importance, significance.

realidad, *nf* reality; truth.

realinear, *vt* to realign.

realismo, *nm* realism.

realista, *adj* realistic.

realización, *nf* 1. realization; sale, clearance sale; 2. realization; fulfillment, carrying out; achievement.

realizado, *adj* fulfllled.

realizador(a), *nm/f* (TV, Radio, Theater) director.

realizar, *vt* 1. to realize; 2. to attain, achieve, fulfill, carry out.

realizarse, *vr* to come true; to materialize; to be carried out.

realzar, *vt* to emboss, raise; to highlight.

reanimación, *nf* revival; resuscitation.

reanimar, *vt* to revive; to resuscitate.

reanudación, *nf* renewal; resumption.

reanudar, *vt* to renew.

reaparecer, *vi* to reappear; to return; to recur.

reapertura, *nf* reopening.

reaprovisionamiento, *nm* replenishment, restocking.

reaprovisionar, *vt* to replenish, restock.

rearmar, *vt* to rearm.

reasumir, *vt* to resume, reassume.

reata, *nf* rope.

reavivar, *vt* to revive.

rebaja, *nf* lowering, lessening, reduction; discount, rebate.

rebajar, *vt* to lower, lower the level of; to reduce, lower, cut (down).

rebanada, *nf* slice.

rebanar, *vt* to slice, cut in slices.

rebasar, *vi* to exceed, surpass; to overtake, leave behind.

rebatir, *vt* 1. to repel; to parry, ward off; 2. to reject, rebut, refute; to resist.

rebelarse, *vr* to revolt, rebel, rise.

rebelde, *adj* 1. rebellious; 2. unruly; unmanageable, uncontrollable; stubborn; 3. *nm/f* rebel.

rebeldía, *nf* rebelliousness; defiance, disobedience.

rebelión, *nf* revolt, rebellion, rising.

reblandecer, *vt* to soften.

reblandecido, *adj* soft in the head; senile.

rebobinado, *nm* rewind(ing).

rebobinar, *vt* to rewind.

reborde, *nm* ledge; flange, rim; border.

rebosadero, *nm* overflow.

rebosante, *adj* brimming with, overflowing with.

rebosar, *vi* to overflow, run over.

rebotar, *vt* to bounce; to repel; to send back, turn back.

rebote, *nm* bounce, rebound.

rebozado, *adj* 1. fried in batter (or breadcrumbs); 2. *nm* batter.

rebozar, *vt* 1. to muffle up, wrap up; 2. to roll in batter, fry in batter.

rebozo, *nm* muffler, wrap; shawl.

rebullicio, *nm* hubbub, uproar; agitation.

rebullir, *vt* to stir up.

rebusca, *nf* search.

rebuscado, *adj* recherché; out-of-the-way; studied, elaborate; affected, stuck-up.

rebuscar, *vt* to search carefully for, search out; to glean.

recabar, *vt* to obtain by entreaty, manage to get; to collect.

recadero, *nm* messenger; errand boy, delivery-man; carrier.

recado, *nm* message; errand; gift, small present.

recaer, *vi* 1. to suffer a relapse; 2. to fall back, to backslide.

recaída, *nf* relapse; backsliding.

recalar, *vt* 1. to saturate, soak. 2. *vi* to sight land, reach port.

recalcar, *vt* 1. to press down, press in, squeeze in; 2. to stress, emphasize; to make great play with.

recalentamiento, *nm* overheating; warming.

recalentar, *vt* to overheat.

recamado, *nm* embroidery.

recamar, *vt* to embroider.

recámara, *nf* side room; dressing room; bedroom.

recapacitar, *vt* to think over; reflect on.

recapitular, *vti* to recapitulate, sum up, summarize.

recargado, *adj* overloaded.

recargar, *vt* to overload.

recargo, *nm* new burden; extra load, additional load.

recatado, *adj* modest, shy, demure; cautious, circumspect.

recatar, *vt* to hide.

recato, *nm* modesty, shyness, demureness, caution, circumspection; reserve, restraint.

recaudación, *nf* collection; recovery.

recaudador(a), *nm/f* tax collector; tax office.

recaudar, *vt* to collect; take (in), receive.

recelar, *vt* to suspect that ..., fear that ....

recelo, *nm* suspicion; fear, apprehension; distrust, mistrust.

recepción, *nf* reception, receiving; reception; admission.

recepcionar, *vt* to receive, accept.

recepcionista, *nm/f* receptionist, desk clerk.

receptáculo, *nm* receptacle; holder.

receptar, *vt* to receive.

receptivo, *adj* receptive.

receptor, *nm* 1. receiver; 2. catcher.

recesar, *vi* to recess, go into recess.

recesión, *nf* recession; slump; slide, fall.

receso, *nm* recess.

receta, *nf* recipe; prescription.

recetar, *vt* to prescribe.

recetario, *nm* collection of recipes, recipe book.

recibidor, *nm/f* entrance hall; receiver, recipient.

recibimiento, *nm* reception, welcome.

recibir, *vt* 1. to receive; 2. to welcome, greet.

recibirse, *vr* to qualify; to graduate.

reciclado, *adj* recycled.

reciclar, *vt* to recycle; to retrain; to modify, adjust.

recién, *adv* newly, recently.

recién casado, *adj* newlywed; the newlyweds.

recién llegado, *adj* newly arrived.

recién nacido, *adj* newborn; newborn child.

reciente, *adj* recent; new, fresh, newly-made.

recinto, *nm* enclosure; precincts.

recio, *adj* thick, strong; tough, robust

recipiente, *nm* 1. recipient; 2. container, vessel.

recíproca, *nf* reciprocal.

reciprocar, *vt* to reciprocate.

reciprocidad, *nf* reciprocity; mutual character.

recíproco, *adj* reciprocal, mutual.

recitado, *nm* recitation; recitative.

recital, *nm* recital; reading; poetry reading.

recitar, *vt* to recite.

reclamación, *nf* 1. reclamation; 2. claim, demand; objection.

reclamar, *vt* to claim, demand.

reclamo, *nm* 1. call, bird call; decoy, lure; 2. claim, statement; complaint, protest.

reclinar, *vt* to lean, recline.

reclinarse, *vr* to lean; to recline, lean back.

recluir, *vt* to shut away; to confine; to imprison.

reclusión, *nf* seclusion; imprisonment, confinement.

recluta, *nf* 1. recruitment; 2. *nm/f* recruit.

reclutar, *vt* to recruit.

recobrar, *vt* to recover, get back, retrieve.

recobrarse, *vr* to recover, convalesce, get better; to come to, regain consciousness.

recobro, *nm* recovery, retrieval; recapture.

recocer, *vt* to cook again, warm up; to overcook.

recogedor, *nm* picker, harvester; gleaner.

recoger, *vt* to pick up; to gather (up).

recogida, *nf* 1. withdrawal, retirement; 2. harvest; collection.

recoleccion, *nf* harvesting, picking; collection; gathering.

recolector(a), *nm/f* picker; collector.

recolocar, *vt* to relocate.

recomendación, *nf* (recommendation; suggestion.

recomendado, *adj* registered.

recomendar, *vt* 1. to recommend; to suggest; to advise; 2. to entrust; 3. to praise, commend.

recomenzar, *vti* to begin again, recommence.

recomerse, *vr* to bear a secret grudge, harbor resentment.

recompensa, *nf* recompense, reward; compensation.

recompensar, *vt* to reward, recompense; to compensate.

recomponer, *vt* to mend, repair; to reset.

recomprar, *vt* to repurchase, buy back.

reconcentrar, *vt* to concentrate (on), devote.

reconcentrarse, *vr* to concentrate hard, become totally absorbed.

reconciliación, *nf* reconciliation.

reconciliar, *vt* to reconcile.

reconducir, vt to take back, bring back (to).

reconfortante, adj 1. comforting; cheering; heart-warming; 2. nm tonic.

reconfortar, vt to comfort; to cheer, encourage.

reconocer, vt to recognize; to identify, know, tell, distinguish.

reconocido, adj recognized, accepted.

reconocimiento, nm 1. recognition; identiflcation; 2. admission, acknowledgement.

reconquista, nf reconquest; recapture.

reconquistar, vt to reconquer; to recapture (from); to recover, win back.

reconsideración, nf reconsideration.

reconsiderar, vt to reconsider.

reconstitución, nf reconstitution, reforming; reconstruction.

reconstituir, vt to reconstitute, reform; to reconstruct.

reconstituyente, nm tonic, restorative, pick-me-up.

reconstrucción, nf reconstruction; reshuffle.

reconstruir, vt to reconstruct.

reconvenir, vt to reprimand; to expostulate with, remonstrate with.

reconvertir, vt to reconvert; to restructure, reorganize.

recopilación, nf summary; compilation.

recopilador(a), nm/f compiler.

recopilar, vt to compile, gather, collect, to summarize.

recordación, nf recollection; remembrance.

recordar, vt to remember; to recollect, recall.

recordativo, adj reminiscent; certa record'tiva reminder.

recordatorio, nm 1. reminder; 2. in memoriam card

recorrer, vt to go over, go across, go through, traverse.

recorrido, nm run, journey; route, course, path.

recortada, nf sawn-off shotgun.

recortado, adj 1. jagged; uneven, irregular; 2. short and stocky.

recortar, vt to cut away, cut off, cut back, trim.

recortarse, vr to stand out, be outlined, be silhouetted.

recoser, vt to patch up, darn.

recosido, nm patch, darn.

recostado, adj reclining, recumbent; to be lying down.

recostar, vt to lean (on).

recreación, nf recreation.

recrear, vt 1. to recreate; 2. to amuse, divert, entertain.

recreativo, adj recreative; recreational.

recreo, nm 1. recreation, relaxation; amusement; 2. break, playtime, recreation.

recriminación, nf 1. recrimination; 2. countercharge.

recriminar, vt 1. to reproach; to countercharge; 2. vi to recriminate.

recriminarse, vr to reproach each other, indulge in mutual recrimination.

recrudecer, vi to recrudesce, break out again; to worsen.

recta, nf straight line.

rectángulo, adj rectangular, oblong; right angled.

rectificación, nf rectiflcation; correction.

rectificador(a), nm/f rectifier.

rectificar, vt to straighten (out).

rectilíneo, adj rectilinear.

recto, adj straight.

rector, adj leading person; governing, managing.

rectora, nf head, chief, leader; principal.

rectorado, nm rectorship, presidency; rector's office.

recubrir, vt to cover (with); to coat (with).

recuento, nm count, recount; inventory, survey.

recuerdo, adj 1. awake; 2. nm memory; recollection; reminiscence.

recuperación, nf recovery, recuperation, retrieval.

recuperar, vt to recover, recuperate, retrieve.

recuperativo, adj recuperative.

recurrencia, nf recurrence; recourse, appeal.

recurrente, adj recurrent.

recurrir, vt to appeal against.

recurso, nm recourse, resort; means.

recusar, vt to reject, refuse.

rechace, nm rejection; rebound.

rechazamiento, nm 1. repelling, beating off; driving back; reflection; 2. rejection; refusal; resistance.

rechazar, vt 1. to push back, push away; to repel, beat off; 2. to reject.

rechazo, nm bounce, rebound; recoil; rejection.

rechinamiento, nm creaking, grating; squeaking; clanking, clattering.

rechinar, vi to creak, grate; to squeak.

rechoncho, adj thickset, stocky, squat; plump.

red, nf net.

redacción, nf 1. writing, redaction; editing; 2. wording; 3. newspaper office; 4. editorial staff.

redactar, vt to write; to draft, draw up; to word.

redactor(a), nm/f writer, drafter.

redada, nf 1. cast, casting; throw; 2. sweep, raid; 3. catch, haul.

redargüir, vt to impugn, hold to be invalid.

redención, nf redemption.

redentor, adj 1. redeeming; 2. nm redeemer; the Redeemer, Saviour (Jesus Christ)

redescubrir, vt to rediscover.

redesignar, vt to rename.

redimensionar, vt to remodel; to rationalize, streamline, cut back.

redimir, vt to redeem.

rédito, nm interest, yield, return.

redituar, vt to yield, produce, bear.

redoblado, adj reinforced, extra strong.

redoblar, vt 1. to bend back, bend over, bend down; 2. to redouble.

redoble, nm drumroll, drumbeat.

redomado, adj sly, artful

redondear, vt to round, round off.

redondearse, vr to acquire money, become wealthy.

redondez, nf roundness.

redondo(a), adj round; rounded.

reducción, nf reduction; diminution, lessening.

reducido, adj reduced; limited.

reducir, vt to reduce; to diminish, lessen, cut (down).

reductivo, adj slimming.

reducto, nm redoubt.

redundancia, nf redundancy, superfluity.

redundante, adj redundant, superfluous.

reedición, nf reissue, reprint(ing).

reedificación, nf rebuilding.

reedificar, vt to rebuild.

reeditar, vt to reissue, republish, reprint.

reeducación, nf re-education.

reeducar, vt to re-educate.

reelección, nf re-election.

reelegir, vt to re-elect.

reembalar, vt to repack.

reembolsar, vt to reimburse; to repay.

reembolso, nm reimbursement; repayment, refund.

reemplazable, *adj* replaceable.
reemplazar, *vt* to replace.
reemplazo, *nm* replacement.
reemprender, *vt* to resume.
reencarnación, *nf* reincarnation.
reencender, *vt* to light again, rekindle.
reenvasar, *vt* to repack, rewrap.
reenviar, *vt* to forward, send on; to send back.
reestructuración, *nf* restructuring, reorganizing.
reestructurar, *vt* to restructure, reorganize.
reevaluación, *nf* reappraisal.
reevaluar, *vt* to reappraise.
reexaminación, *nf* re-examination.
refacción, *nf* 1. light refreshment, refection; 2. running costs; 3. short-term loan, financial assistance.
refajo, *nm* flannel underskirt; slip.
referencia, *nf* reference.
referenciar, *vt* to index.
referendo, *nm* referendum.
referente, *adj* relating to, about, concerning.
referir, *vt* to recount, report; to tell.
referirse, *vr* to refer to.
refinación, *nf* refining.
refinador, *nm* refiner.
refinamiento, *nm* refinement.
refinanciar, *vt* to refinance.
refinar, *vt* to refine, to perfect; to polish.
refinería, *nf* refinery.
reflector, *nm* reflector.
reflejar, *vt* to reflect.
reflejo, *adj* 1. reflected; 2. reflex.
reflexión, *nf* reflection.
reflexionar, *vt* to reflect on, think about, think over.
reflexivo, *adj* 1. reflexive; 2. thoughtful, reflective.
reforma, *nf* reform; reformation; improvement.
reformado, *adj* reformed.
reformador(a), *nm/f* reformer.
reformar, *vt* to reform; to change, alter; to improve.
reformarse, *vr* to reform, mend one's ways.
reformatear, *vt* to reformat.
reformatorio, *nm* reformatory; remand home.
reformista, *adj* 1. reforming; 2. *nm/f* reformist, reformer.
reforzar, *vt* to reinforce, strengthen.
refractar, *vt* to refract.
refractario, *adj* 1. fireproof, heat-resistant; ovenproof; 2. refractory, recalcitrant; stubborn.
refractor, *nm* refractor.
refrán, *nm* proverb, saying.
refrenar, *vt* to rein back, rein in; to hold back; restrain, hold in check.
refresco, *nm* cool drink, soft drink, non-alcoholic drink.
refresquería, *nf* refreshment stall.
refriega, *nf* scuffle, set-to; affray, brawl.
refrigeración, *nf* refrigeration; cooling; air conditioning.
refrigerado, *adj* cooled; air-conditioned.
refrigerador, *nm* refrigerator; cooling unit, cooling system.
refrigerante, *adj* cooling, refrigerating.
refrigerar, *vt* to cool, refresh.
refrigerio, *nm* snack; cooling drink.
refuerzo, *nm* strengthening; reinforcement.
refugiado(a), *adj, nm/f* refugee.
refugiarse, *vr* to take refuge; to shelter; to go into hiding; seek asylum in a neighbouring country.
refugio, *nm* refuge, shelter; asylum; sanctuary.
refulgencia, *nf* brilliance, refulgence,
refulgente, *adj* brilliant, refulgent,
refulgir, *vi* to shine.

refundir, *vt* to recast.
refundirse, *vr* to get lost, be mislaid.
refutación, *nf* refutation.
refutar, *vt* to refute.
regadera, *nf* sprinkler; watering-can; shower.
regadío, *nm* irrigated land, irrigation land.
regador, *nm* watering can.
regalar, *vt* to give, present; to give away.
regalía, *nf* 1. royal prerogatives; 2. privilege, prerogative; 3. gift, present.
regalo, *nm* gift, present.
regalón, *adj* spoiled, pampered; comfort-loving, soft, lapped in luxury.
regañar, *vt* to scold; to tell off, reprimand; to nag (at).
regaño, *nm* snarl, growl, scowl; grumble, scolding, telling-off.
regar, *vt* to water; irrigate; wash; to bathe.
regarse, *vr* to scatter (in all directions).
regata, *nf* 1. irrigation channel; 2. race, boat-race; regatta;
regatear, *vi* 1. to race; 2. *vt* to haggle over, bargain over.
regatón, *adj* 1. haggling; bickering, niggling, argumentative 2. *nm* tip, ferrule.
regazo, *nm* lap.
regeneración, *nf* regeneration.
regenerado, *adj* regenerate.
regenerador, *adj* regenerative.
regenerar, *vt* to regenerate.
regentar, *vt* 1. to occupy, hold; to run, manage, administer; 2. to domineer, boss.
regente, *adj* 1. regent; 2. managing; 3. *nm/f* regent.
régimen, *nm* rule.
regimiento, *nm* 1. administration, government, organization; 2. regiment; 3. mass, crowd.
regio, *adj* royal, regal; kingly.
región, *nf* region; district, area, part.
regional, *adj* regional.
regionalista, *adj, nm/f* regionalist.
regir, *vt* to rule, govern; to run, be in charge of, to manage, run, control,
registrado, *adj* registered.
registrar, *vt* to register, record; to enter; to file.
reglable, *adj* adjustable.
reglamentación, *nf* regulation; rules.
reglamentar, *vt* to regulate; to make rules for, establish regulations for.
reglamento, *nm* rules, regulations; standing order(s); by-law.
reglar, *vt* 1. to rule; 2. to check, overhaul; to adjust; 3. to regulate, make regulations for.
regocijado, *adj* jolly, cheerful, merry.
regocijar, *vt* to gladden, delight, cheer (up).
regocijo, *nm* joy, happiness; rejoicing; delight, elation.
regresar, *vt* to give back, send back, return.
regresión, *nf* regression; retreat; backward step.
regreso, *nm* return; return trip, homeward.
regulación, *nf* regulation; adjustment; control.
regulador(a), *adj* 1. regulating, regulatory; 2. *nm/f* regulator, throttle, governor.
regular, *adj* 1. regular; normal, usual, customary; (corriente) ordinary; 2. middling, medium, average; fair.
regularización, *nf* regularization; standardization.
regularizar, *vt* to regularize; to standardize, bring into line.
regustado, *adj* well-satisfied.
regustar, *vt* to taste, relish, savor.
rehabilitación, *nf* rehabilitation; reinstatement.

rehabilitar, vt to rehabilitate; to reinstate; to discharge.

rehacer, vt to redo, do again; to repeat.

rehacerse, vr to recover; to regain one's strength.

rehecho, adj thickset, chunky; rested.

rehén, nm hostage.

rehuir, vt to shun, avoid; to shrink from.

rehusar, vt to refuse, decline.

reidor, adj merry, laughing.

reimplantar, vt to re-establish, reintroduce.

reimpresión, nf reprint(ing).

reimprimir, vt to reprint.

reina, nf queen.

reinante, adj reigning.

reincidencia, nf relapse; recidivism.

reincidente, nm/f recidivist; hardened offender; backslider.

reincidir, vi to relapse; to repeat an offense; to backslide.

reingresar, vi to re-enter.

reinicializar, vt to reset.

reiniciar, vt to begin again; to resume.

reinicio, nm new beginning; resumption.

reino, nm kingdom.

reinsertar, vt to rehabilitate, assimilate into society.

reinstalar, vt to reinstall; to reinstate.

reintegrar, vt to make whole again, reintegrate.

reintegro, nm refund, repayment, reimbursement; withdrawal.

reinvertir, vt to reinvest.

reír, vi to laugh at.

reiterado, adj repeated.

reiterar, vt to reiterate, reaffirm; to repeat.

reivindicación, nf claim; grievance; vindication; restoration of rights.

reivindicar, vt 1. to claim (the right to); 2. to vindicate; to restore; 3. to recover.

rejado, nm grille, grating.

rejar, vt to jail, put in jail.

rejilla, nf grating, grille; lattice; screen.

rejón, nm pointed iron bar; spike; lance.

rejonear, vt to wound the bull with the lance.

rejuvenecedor, adj rejuvenating; refreshing, stimulating.

rejuvenecer, vt to rejuvenate.

relación, nf relation, relationship.

relacionado, adj a well-connected person.

relacionar, vt 1. to relate (to), connect (with); 2. to list.

relajación, nf relaxation.

relajado, adj 1. relaxed; 2. dissolute, loose.

relajante, adj relaxing; 2laxative.

relajar, vt to relax.

relajo, nm laxity, dissipation, depravity; lewdness.

relamido, adj prim and proper; affected; overdressed.

relámpago, nm lightning, flash of lightning; flash.

relampagueo, nm twinkle; flicker, gleam.

relampaguear, vi to lighten; to flash.

relanzar, vt 1. to relaunch; 2. to repel, repulse.

relatar, vt to relate, tell; to report.

relativizar, vt to play down, (seek to) diminish the importance of.

relativo, adj relative; a relative to; regarding, relating to.

relato, nm story, tale; account, report.

relator(a), nm/f teller, narrator; court reporter.

releer, vt to reread.

relegación, nf relegation; exile, banishment.

relegar, vt to relegate; to banish something from one's mind; to consign something to oblivion.

relevación, nf 1. relief; replacement; exoneration.

relevante, adj outstanding; relevant.

relevar, vt 1. to emboss; to carve (or paint) in relief; 2. to free someone from the obligation to; to relieve someone of his post, replace someone in his post.

relevo, nm relief, change.

religión, nf religion.

religioso(a), adj 1. religious; 2. nm/f religious, member of a religious order, monk, nun.

relinchar, vi to neigh, whinny, snort.

reloj, nm clock; watch.

relojería, nf watchmaking, clockmaking; watchmaker's (shop).

relojero, nm watchmaker, clockmaker.

reluciente, adj shining, brilliant; glittering, gleaming, sparkling; bright.

relucir, vi to shine; to glitter, gleam, sparkle; to be bright.

rellano, nm landing.

rellenar, vt to refill, replenish; to refuel.

rellenarse, vr to stuff oneself (with).

relleno, adj packed, stuffed, crammed (with); very full.

remachado, adj quiet, reserved.

remachador, nm riveter.

remachar, vt to clinch; to rivet.

remada, nf stroke.

remador, nm/f rower.

remalladora, nf mender, darner,

remanente, adj 1. remaining; remanent; surplus; 2. nm remainder; retained earnings.

remanso, nm 1. pool; backwater; 2. quiet place, peaceful area.

remar, vi 1. to row; 2. to toil, struggle; to suffer hardships.

remarcar, vt 1. to notice, observe, remark on; 2. to distinguish; 3. to emphasize, underline.

rematado, adj hopeless; complete, out-and-out; raving lunatic.

rematador(a), nm/f 1. goal-scorer; 2. auctioneer, auction house, auctioneer's.

rematar, vt 1. to finish off, to kill off; to shoot dead, kill instantly; 2. bring to a conclusion; round off; 3. to buy at an auction, to sell at auction.

remecer, vt to rock, swing (to and fro); to shake; to wave.

remedar, vt to imitate, copy; to ape; mimic.

remediar, vt to remedy; to make good, repair.

remedio, nm remedy; cure; help.

rememorar, vt to remember, recall.

remendar, vt to mend, repair; to patch, darn.

remero, nm 1. oarsman; 2. rowing machine.

remesa, nf remittance; shipment, consignment.

remesar, vt to remit, send; ship, consign,

remeter, vr to put back; to tuck in.

reminiscencia, nf reminiscence.

remirar, vt to look at again; to look hard at.

remisión, nf 1. sending; shipment, consignment; 2. postponement; adjournment.

remiso, adj slack, slow, remiss.

remisor(a), nm/f sender.

remite, nm sender's name and address.

remitente, nm/f sender.

remitido, nm 1. paid insert; 2. shipment, consignment.

remitir, vt to send; dinero to remit; ship, consign.

remo, nm 1. oar; 2. rowing; 3. arm, leg; wing.

remodelación, nf remodeling; refurbishment; restyling.

remodelar, vt to remodel; to restyle; to reshuffle, restructure.

remojar, vt to steep, soak (in); to dip (in, into).

remojo, *nm* steeping, soaking; drenching; dip, dipping.

remolacha, *nf* beet, beetroot.

remolcador, *nm* tow car, breakdown lorry.

remolcar, *vt* to tow, tow along; to take in tow.

remoler, *vt* to grind up small.

remolón, *adj* stubborn; awkward, cantankerous.

remolonear, *vi* to be stubborn, refuse to budge; to hold out on someone.

remolque, *nm* **1.** towing; a on tow, being towed.

remontar, *vt* **1.** to mend; repair, resole; **2.** to soar (up), to go up.

remontarse, *vr* to rise, soar.

rémora, *nf* (Zoo) remora; drawback; hindrance.

remorder, *vt* persona to grieve, distress; to cause remorse to.

remoto, *adj* remote.

remover, *vt* **1.** to turn over, dig up; **2.** to remove; to excise, cut out.

remozado, *nm* rejuvenation; renovation.

remozamiento, *nm* rejuvenation; renovation.

remozar, *vt* to rejuvenate; to brighten up, polish up.

remuneración, *nf* remuneration.

remunerador, *adj* remunerative; rewarding, worthwhile.

remunerar, *vt* to remunerate; to pay; to reward.

renacer, *vi* to be reborn; to appear again, come up again.

renacimiento, *nm* rebirth, revival; Renaissance.

renal, *adj* renal, kidney.

rencilla, *nf* quarrel; feud; dissension; arguments.

renco, *adj* lame.

rencor, *nm* rancour, bitterness; ill feeling, resentment.

rendición, *nf* **1.** surrender; **2.** yield, profit(s), return.

rendido, *adj* **1.** submissive; obsequious; **2.** to be exhausted, be all in.

rendija, *nf* crack, cleft, crevice; chink; aperture.

rendimiento, *nm* **1.** usable part, proportion of usable material; **2.** efficiency, performance; capacity; **3.** yield, profit(s), return.

rendir, *vt* to produce, yield, bear.

renegado, *adj* renegade; apostate.

renegar, *vt* **1.** to deny vigorously, deny repeatedly; **2.** to abhor, detest; **3.** *vi* to turn renegade, go over to the other side, be a traitor; to apostatize.

renegociar, *vt* to renegotiate.

renegrido, *adj* very black, very dark.

renglón, *nm* line (of writing).

renguear, *vi* to limp, hobble.

renguera, *nf* limp, limping; lameness.

reno, *nm* reindeer.

renombrado, *adj* renowned, famous.

renombre, *nm* renown, fame; renowned.

renovación, *nf* renewal; restoration; redecoration.

renovado, *adj* renewed, redoubled.

renovar, *vt* to renew; to renovate; to restore; to redecorate.

renquear, *vi* to limp, hobble.

renta, *nf* income; interest, return, yield.

rentabilizar, *vt* to make (more) profitable; to promote; to exploit to the full, cash in on.

rentado, *adj* paid.

rentar, *vt* to produce, yield.

renuncia, *nf* renunciation; resignation; relinquishment; abdication.

renunciar, *vt* to renounce, surrender, relinquish.

reñidero, *nm* cockpit.

reñido, *adj* bitter; hard fought.

reñir, *vt* **1.** to scold; to tell off, reprimand; **2.** to fight, wage; **3.** *vi* to quarrel, fall out.

reo, *nm/f* **1.** culprit, offender; criminal; defendant; **2.** sea-trout.

reordenación, *nf* realignment.

reordenar, *vt* to realign.

reorganización, *nf* reorganization.

reorganizar, *vt* to reorganize; to reshuffle.

reorientación, *nf* reorientation; new direction; re-adjustment.

reparación, *nf* repairing, mending.

reparador, *adj* **1.** critical, faultfinding; **2.** fortifying, strengthening, restorative; refreshing; **3.** *nm* repairer.

reparar, *vt* to repair, mend.

reparo, *nm* **1.** repair; restoration; **2.** parry; defense, protection; **3.** remedy; restorative; **4.** objection; criticism.

repartición, *nf* distribution; sharing out, division.

repartido, *nm* delivery; round.

repartidor, *nm* distributor; roundsman, delivery-man.

repartimiento, *nm* distribution; division; assessment.

repartir, *vt* to distribute; to divide (up), share (out); to parcel out; to allot, assign.

repasar, *vt* to pass (by) again; check, revise.

repaso, *nm* review, revision; check.

repatriación, *nf* repatriation.

repatriar, *vt* to repatriate; to deport; to send home, send back to one's country of origin.

repelar, *vt* to leave completely bare, shear.

repelencia, *nf* revulsion, disgust.

repelente, *adj* repellent, repulsive, disgusting.

repeler, *vt* to repel, repulse, drive back; to push away.

repellar, *vt* to plaster, stucco; to whitewash.

repello, *nm* whitewash(ing).

repensar, *vt* to rethink, reconsider, think out again.

repente, *nm* sudden movement, start, jerk.

repercusión, *nf* repercussion; (reverberación) reverberation.

repercutir, *vt* **1.** to contradict; **2.** *vi* to rebound, bounce off; **3.** to have repercussions on, have effects on.

repertoriar, *vt* to catalogue, list.

repertorio, *nm* list, index, compendium;

repetidor, *nm* booster station.

repetidora, *nf* repeater rifle,

repetir, *vt* to repeat; to say again; to do again.

repicar, *vt* **1.** to chop up small; **2.** to prick (again); **3.** to ring, peal (merrily).

repintar, *vt* to repaint; to paint hastily, paint roughly.

repisa, *nf* ledge, shelf; (wall) bracket.

replantar, *vt* to replant.

replantear, *vt* to raise again, reopen.

replegar, *vt* to fold over; to fold again, refold.

repletar, *vt* to fill completely, stuff full, pack tight.

repleto, *adj* replete, full up; de filled with, absolutely full of.

réplica, *nf* **1.** answer; retort, rejoinder; rebuttal; **2.** replica, copy.

replicar, *vi* to answer, retort, rejoin; to argue, answer back.

repliegue, *nm* **1.** fold, crease; **2.** withdrawal, retirement.

repoblación, *nf* repopulation, repeopling; (re)forestation.

repoblar, *vt* to repopulate, repeople; to (re)forest.

reponer, *vt* **1.** to replace, put back; **2.** to revive, put on again; to repeat.

reportaje, *nm* report, article, news item.

reportar, vt to bring, fetch, carry.

reporte, nm report, piece of news.

reportear, vt to report; to interview (for the purpose of writing an article).

reportero(a), nm/f reporter.

reposado, adj quiet; gentle, restful.

reposar, vi 1. let one's meal go down, settle one's stomach; 2. vi to rest, repose; to lie.

reposición, nf replacement.

repositorio, nm repository.

reposo, nm rest, repose.

repostar, vt to replenish; renew.

repostero(a), nm/f confectioner, pastrycook.

repregunta, nf cross-examination, cross-questioning.

repreguntar, vt to cross-examine, cross-question.

reprender, vt to reprimand, tell off, take to task.

reprensión, nf reprimand, rebuke; scolding; criticism, reproach.

represa, nf 1. recapture; 2. check, stoppage; 3. dam; weir; pool, reservoir.

represalia, nf reprisal.

represaliar, vt to take reprisals against; to victimize.

represar, vt 1. to recapture. 2. to repress; to check, put a stop to; 3. to dam, to stem.

representación, nf representation.

representante, nm/f representative; agent.

representar, vt to represent; to act for; to stand for.

represión, nf repression; suppression.

reprimenda, nf reprimand, rebuke.

reprimido, adj repressed.

reprimir, vt to repress, suppress; to curb, check; hold in.

reprobación, nf reproval, reprobation.

reprobador, adj reproving, disapproving.

reprobar, vt to reprove, condemn; to blame; to damn.

reprocesar, vt to reprocess.

reprochar, vt to reproach: to condemn, censure.

reproche, nm reproach (for).

reproducción, nf reproduction,

reproducir, vt to reproduce; to breed.

reproductor, adj reproductive.

reptar, vi to creep, crawl; to snake along.

reptil, adj reptilian.

república, nf republic.

republicano(a), adj, nm/f republican.

repudiar, vt to repudiate; to disown, disavow; to renounce.

repudio, nm repudiation.

repugnancia, nf disgust, loathing, repugnance; aversion (to).

repugnante, adj disgusting, loathsome, revolting.

repugnar, vt to disgust, revolt, nauseate.

repugnarse, vr to conflict, be in opposition; to contradict each other.

repujar, vt to emboss, work in relief.

repulsa, nf check; rejection, refusal; rebuff.

repulsar, vt to repulse; to check; to reject, refuse; to rebuff.

repuntar, vt 1. to round up; 2. to (begin to) make itself felt, give the first signs.

reputación, nf reputation; standing.

reputado, adj highly reputed, reputable.

reputar, vt to repute; to esteem; to deem, consider.

requemado, adj scorched; parched; overdone.

requemar, vt to scorch; to parch, scorch, dry up; to overdo, burn.

requerir, vt to need, require.

requesón, nm cottage cheese; curd(s).

requiebro, nm amorous compliment, remark.

requintar, vt to tighten, make taut.

requisa, nf survey, inspection.

requisar, vt to requisition.

requisito, nm requirement, requisite; qualification.

resaca, nf undertow, undercurrent; backward movement (of the waves).

resacar, vt to distill (a second time).

resalado, adj lively, vivacious, attractive.

resaltar, vi to jut out, stick out, stick up, project.

resanar, vt to restore, repair, make good.

resarcir, vt to repay; to indemnify, compensate.

resbaladero, nm slippery place; slide, chute.

resbaladizo, adj slippery.

resbalar, vi to slip, slip up, to slide, skit.

rescatar, vt to ransom; to recapture, recover.

rescate, nm ransom; recapture, recovery; redemption; rescue.

rescindir, vt to rescind, cancel; to withdraw.

resecar, vt to dry off, dry thoroughly.

reseco, adj very dry, too dry; parched.

resembrar, vt to re-sow, re-seed.

resentido, adj resentful; bitter; sullen.

resentimiento, nm resentment; bitterness.

resentirse, vr to recent something, be offended about something.

resolver, vt to solve, resolve.

resollar, vi to breathe heavily, breathe noisily; to puff and blow; to wheeze.

resonancia, nf resonance.

resonante, adj resonant; ringing, echoing, resounding.

resonar, vi to resound, ring, echo (with).

resoplar, vi to snort; to pant.

resoplido, nm heavy breathing, noisy breathing.

resorber, vt to reabsorb.

resorte, nm spring.

respaldar, vt 1. to endorse; 2. to back, support; 3. to ensure; to guarantee, safeguard.

respaldo, nm 1. back; 2. endorsement.

respecto, nm in the matter, with regard to the subject under discussion.

respetar, vt to respect; to win respect.

respeto, nm respect, regard, consideration;.

respetuoso, adj respectful.

respingado, adj nose snub, turned-up.

respingar, vi to shy, balk; to start.

respingo, nm shy; start; wince.

respiración, nf breathing, respiration; breath.

respiradero, nm 1. vent, valve; 2. respite, breathing space.

respirador, nm breathing tube, snorkel.

respirar, vt to breathe.

respiratorio, adj respiratory; breathing.

respiro, nm 1. breathing; 2. rest; extension of time, period of grace.

resplandecer, vi to shine; to gleam, to blaze.

resplandor, nm brilliance, brightness, radiance; gleam, glitter.

responder, vt to answer; to reply to.

respondón, adj cheeky, insolent.

responsabilidad, nf responsibility.

responsable, adj responsible; the person in charge.

responsorio, nm response.

respuesta, nf answer, reply; response.

resquebrajar, vt to crack, split.

resquebrar, vi to begin to crack.

resquicio, nm chink, crack.

restablecer, vt to re-establish; to restore.

restablecimiento, nm re-establishment; restoration; recovery.

restallido, nm crack; click; crackle.

restante, adj remaining; lo the rest, the remainder.

restar, vt to take away, reduce; to deduct.

restauración, *nf* restoration.
restaurador(a), *nm/f* restorer.
restaurán, *nm* restaurant.
restaurar, *vt* to restore,
restitución, *nf* return; restoration,
restituir, *vt* to return, give back, restore (to).
resto, *nm* rest, remainder; (*pl*) left-overs.
restricción, *nf* restriction; limitation; restraint.
restrictivo, *adj* restrictive, limiting.
restrillar, *vt* to crack; creak.
restringido, *adj* restricted, limited.
restringir, *vt* to restrict, limit (to).
resucitación, *nf* resuscitation.
resucitador, *nm* respirator.
resucitar, *vt* to resuscitate, revive.
resudar, *vti* to sweat a little, to leak slightly.
resuello, *nm* breath; breathing.
resultado, *nm* result, outcome, sequel; effect.
resultar, *vi* to prove (to be), turn out to be.
resumen, *nm* 1. summary, résumé; 2. brief concluding appearance; exposición.
resumir, *vt* to sum up; summarize; to abridge, shorten, cut down.
resurgimiento, *nm* resurgence; revival.
resurgir, *vi* 1. to reappear, revive; to be resurrected. 2. to acquire a new spirit, pick up again; to recover.
resurrección, *nf* resurrection.
retador(a), *adj* 1. challenging; 2. *nm/f* challenger.
retaguardia, *nf* rearguard; in the rear.
retama, *nf* broom.
retar, *vt* to challenge; to defy.
retardar, *vt* to slow down, slow up, retard.
retardo, *nm* delay; time lag.
retazar, *vt* to cut up, snip into pieces; to divide up.
retazo, *nm* remnant; snippet; bit, piece, fragment.
retén, *nm* stop, catch; lock; oil-seal.
retención, *nf* retention, deduction, stoppage.
retener, *vt* to retain; to keep, hold back; to deduct; to withhold (part of).
retentiva, *nf* memory, capacity for remembering.
reteñir, *vt* to redye.
reticencia, *nf* 1. insinuation, suggestion; implication; 2. half-truth, misleading statement; 3. reticence, reserve; unwillingness, reluctance.
retícula, *nf* reticle; screen.
reticular, *adj* reticulated.
retina, *nf* retina.
retinto, *adj* very dark.
retiñir, *vi* to tinkle; to jingle, jangle.
retirada, *nf* retreat, withdrawal.
retirar, *vt* to move away, move back; to put away.
retirarse, *vr* 1. to move back, move away (from); to retreat, withdraw; 2. to retire; go off into retreat, withdraw from active.
retiro, *nm* retirement; withdrawal.
reto, *nm* challenge; threat, defiant statement.
retobado, *adj* wild, untamed; unruly; rebellious; obstinate.
retocar, *vt* to retouch, touch up.
retomar, *vt* to take up again.
retonar, *vi* to sprout, shoot, to reappear, recur.
retoque, *nm* retouching, touching-up; finishing touch.
retorcer, *vt* to twist.
retorcimiento, *nm* twisting; wringing; entwining; writhing.
retórica, *nf* rhetoric; affectedness, windiness.
retórico, *adj* rhetorical; affected, windy; grandiloquent.
retornar, *vt* to return, give back.

retorno, *nm* return.
retorta, *nf* retort.
retostar, *vt* to burn, overcook.
retozar, *vi* to romp, frolic, frisk about; to gambol.
retozo, *nm* romp, frolic, gambol; romping, frolics.
retractación, *nf* retraction, recantation.
retractar, *vt* to retract, withdraw.
retráctil, *adj* retractable; retractile.
retraer, *vt* 1. to draw in, retract; 2. to bring back, bring again.
retraimiento, *nm* withdrawal, retirement; seclusion.
retranca, *nf* brake.
retrancar, *vt* to brake.
retransmisión, *nf* repeat (broadcast), rebroadcast.
retransmitir, *vt* to relay, pass on; (Rad, TV) to repeat, rebroadcast, retransmit.
retrasar, *vt* to delay, put off, postpone; to retard, slow down; to hold up.
retraso, *nm* 1. delay; time lag; slowness, lateness; 2. underdevelopment; subnormality, mental deficiency.
retratar, *vt* to portray; to paint a picture of, paint the portrait of.
retrato, *nm* portrait; photograph, portrayal, depiction, description.
retreta, *nf* retreat; tattoo, display.
retrete, *nm* lavatory.
retribución, *nf* pay, payment; reward; compensation.
retribuir, *vt* to pay; to reward, compensate.
retroactivo, *adj* retroactive, retrospective.
retroceder, *vi* to move back; to draw back, stand back.
retrógrado, *adj* retrograde, retrogressive; reactionary.
retrogresión, *nf* retrogression.
retropropulsión, *nf* retropropulsion; jet propulsion.
retrospección, *nf* retrospection.
retrospectiva, *nf* retrospective.
retrotraer, *vt* to carry back (in timel; take back).
retrovisión, *nf* hindsight; flashback.
retrovisor, *adj* rearview mirror; wing mirror.
retumbar, *vi* to boom, roll, thunder, rumble.
retumbo, *nm* boom, roll, thunder, rumble; reverberation.
reúma, *nm* rheumatism.
reumático, *adj* rheumatic.
reumatoide(o), *adj* rheumatoid.
reunificación, *nf* reunification.
reunificar, *vt* to reunify.
reunión, *nf* meeting, gathering.
reunir, *vt* to reunite, join (together).
reutilización, *nf* reuse; recycling.
reutilizar, *vt* to reuse.
reválida, *nf* resit.
revalidar, *vt* to confirm, ratify; to resit.
revalorar, *vt* to revalue; to reassess.
revancha, *nf* revenge.
revanchista, *adj*, *nm/f* revanchist.
revelación, *nf* revelation; disclosure.
revelar, *vt* 1. to reveal; to disclose; show; to give away; 2. to develop.
revendedor(a), *nm/f* retailer; speculator.
revender, *vt* to resell; to retail; to speculate in.
reventar, *vt* to burst, explode, pop.
reverberación, *nf* reverberation.
reverberador, *nm* reverberator.
reverberar, *vi* to play, be reflected; to shimmer, shine.

reverbero, *nm* 1. play, reilection; shimmer, shine; glare; 2. reverberation; 3. reflector; 4. small spirit stove.

reverdecer, *vt* 1. to renew, reawaken; 2. *vi* to grow green again; 3. to come to life again, revive, acquire new vigour.

reverencia, *nf* reverence.

reverenciar, *vt* to revere, venerate.

reverendo, *adj* respected, revered; reverend.

reverente, *adj* reverent.

reversa, *nf* reverse.

reversible, *adj* reversible.

reversión, *nf* reversion.

reverso, *nm* back, other side; wrong side.

revertir, *vi* to revert (to).

revés, *nm* 1. back; other side; 2. setback; to suffer a setback.

revestir, *vt* to put on, don; to wear.

revirar, *vt* to turn (round), twist (round).

revisar, *vt* to revise, look over, go through.

revisión, *nf* revision; check, checking; re-examination, review.

revisor(a), *nm/f* reviser; inspector.

revista, *nf* 1. review, revision; inspection; 2. journal, magazine.

revista, *vt* to review, inspect.

revitalizador, *adj* revitalizing; stimulant.

revitalizar, *vt* to revitalize.

revivificar, *vt* to revitalize.

revivir, *vt* 1. to revive memories of; to relive, live again; 2. *vi* to revive, be revived; to come to life again.

revocación, *nf* revocation, repeal; reversal.

revocar, *vt* to revoke, repeal; to cancel; to reverse.

revolar, *vi* to take to flight again; to flutter about, fly around.

revolcadero, *nm* mudhole, mudbath.

revolcar, *vt* to knock down, knock over, send flying; to knock down and trample on.

revolear, *vt* to whirl, twirl.

revolotear, *vi* to flutter, fly about; to flit; to wheel, circle; to hover.

revoloteo, *nm* fluttering; flitting; wheeling, circling; hovering.

revolución, *nf* revolution.

revolucionar, *vt* to revolutionize, cause a revolution in.

revolucionario(a), *adj, nm/f* revolutionary.

revolver, *vt* to move about; to turn round, turn over, turn upside-down.

revólver, *nm* revolver.

revuelo, *nm* flutter(ing).

rey, *nm* king.

reyerta, *nf* quarrel; fight, brawl, affray.

rezagado, *adj* to be left behind; to be late, be behindhand.

rezagar, *vt* to leave behind; to outpace, outdistance; to postpone.

rezago, *nm* 1. left-over goods unused material; 2. group of straggling cattle; 3. unclaimed letters.

rezar, *vt* 1. to say; 2. to call for, plead for; 3. *vi* to pray; to say one's prayers.

rezo, *nm* prayer(s); devotions.

rezongar, *vt* 1. to tell off, scold; 2. *vi* to grumble; to mutter; to growl.

rezumar, *vt* to ooze, exude; to leak.

riachuelo, *nm* brook, stream.

riada, *nf* flood.

ribera, *nf* bank; beach, shore; riverside.

ribete, *nm* edging, border, trimming.

ribetear, *vt* to edge, border, trim.

ricamente, *adv* richly.

ricino, *nm* castor-oil plant.

ricito, *nm* ringlet, kiss-curl.

rico, *adj* 1. rich, wealthy; 2. valuable, precious; 3. delicious, tasty.

ricura, *nf* tastiness, delicious quality.

ridiculez, *nf* absurdity.

ridiculizar, *vt* to ridicule, deride; to mock, guy, parody.

ridículo, *adj* ridiculous, absurd, ludicrous.

rienda, *nf* rein; restraint.

riesgo, *nm* risk, danger.

riesgoso, *adj* risky, dangerous.

rifa, *nf* raffle.

rifar, *vt* to raffle.

rifle, *nm* rifle.

riflero, *adj* 1. ace, crack; 2. *nm* rifleman; marksman, crack shot.

rigidez, *nf* rigidity, stiffness.

rígido, *adj* rigid, stiff; to go rigid;

rigor, *nm* severity, harshness, strictness; toughness, stringency.

riguroso, *adj* severe, harsh.

rima, *nf* 1. rhyme; 2. poems, verse, poetry.

rimador(a), *nm/f* rhymester.

rimar, *vti* to rhyme (with).

rimbombancia, *nf* 1. resonance, echo; 2. pomposity, bombast; 3. showiness, flashiness.

rimbombante, *adj* 1. resounding, echoing; 2. pompous, bombastic; 3. showy, flashy.

rincón, *nm* corner; nook; retreat; niche.

rinconera, *nf* corner-piece (of furniture); corner-cupboard, dresser.

rinoceronte, *nm* rhinoceros.

riña, *nf* quarrel, argument; fight, brawl, scuffle.

riñonera, *nf* money belt, money pouch.

río, *nm* river; stream, torrent.

ripiado, *adj* ragged; wretched, down-at-heel.

ripiar, *vt* 1. to fill with rubble; 2. to shred, cut into shreds; to crumble.

ripio, *nm* refuse, waste; rubble; debris; roadstone.

riqueza, *nf* wealth, riches.

risa, *nf* laugh; laughter.

risible, *adj* ludicrous, laughable.

risión, *nf* derision, mockery.

risotada, *nf* guffaw, loud laugh.

ristra, *nf* string; string of garlic.

risueño, *adj* 1. smiling; smiling all over; 2. cheerful, sunny.

rítmico, *adj* rhythmic(al).

ritmo, *nm* 1. rhythm; 2. rate, pace; speed.

ritual, *adj, nm* ritual.

ritualista, *adj* 1. ritualistic, ritual; 2. *nm/f* ritualist.

rival, *adj* rival, competing.

rivalizar, *vi* to vie, compete, contend.

rizado, *adj* curly; ridged, crinkly.

rizador, *nm* curling iron, hair-curler.

rizadura, *nf* ripple.

rizar, *vt* to curl; to ruffle; to ridge, crinkle.

róbalo, *nm* sea-bass.

robar, *vt* to rob; to steal; to break into, burgle.

roble, *nm* oak, oak tree.

roblonar, *vt* to rivet.

robo, *nm* theft; robbery, thieving.

robot, *nm* robot.

robótica, *nf* robotics.

robotizar, *vt* to automate; to turn into a robot.

robustecer, *vt* to strengthen.

robusto, *adj* strong, tough, robust.

roca, *nf* rock.

rocalloso, *adj* pebbly, stony.

roce, *nm* 1. rub, rubbing; friction; 2. close contact; familiarity.

rociada, *nf* shower, spray, sprinkling; dash, splash.

rociadera, *nf* watering can.

rociado, *nm* sprinkling; spraying.

rociador, *nm* spray; sprinkler.

rociar, *vt* to sprinkle, spray.

rocío, *nm* dew; light drizzle.

roceso, *adj* rocky.

rodada, *nf* 1. rut, wheel track; 2. fall (from a horse).

rodadero, *nm* cliff, precipice.

rodado, *adj* wheeled, on wheels.

rodaja, *nf* 1. small wheel; small disc; 2. slice.

rodaje, *nm* 1. wheels, set of wheel;. 2. shooting, filming.

rodante, *adj* rolling; rolling stock.

rodar, *vt* 1. to wheel (along); to roll, drag (along); 2. to shoot, to film; 3. to travel.

rodear, *vt* to surround; to ring, encircle, enclose, shut in.

rodeo, *nm* 1. long way round, roundabout way; 2. circumlocution; evasion; 3. round-up, rodeo.

rodilla, *nf* knee; kneeling.

rodillera, *nf* knee guard; kneepad, patch on the knee.

rodillo, *nm* roller; rolling pin; ink roller.

roedor, *adj* gnawing.

roer, *vt* to gnaw; to nibble at.

rogar, *vt* to beg; to plead with; to ask for.

rojear, *vi* to redden, turn red.

rojillo, *adj* pink; suspicious, subversive.

rojizo, *adj* reddish; ruddy.

rojo, *adj* red.

roldana, *nf* pulley wheel.

rolo, *nm* stick, truncheon.

rollizo, *adj* 1. round, cylindrical; 2. plump; stocky; chubby.

rollo, *adj* 1. boring, tedious; 2. *nm* roll; coil; scroll.

romana, *nf* steelyard; to heap the blame on somebody else.

romance, *adj* 1. (language) Romance; 2. *nm* romance, love-affair.

romancear, *vt* 1. to translate into Spanish; 2. *vi* to waste time chatting; 3. to flirt.

romancero, *nm* collection of ballads.

románico, *adj* 1. (Language) Romance; 2. Romanesque, Romanic; Norman.

romántico(a), *adj, nm/f* romantic.

romería, *nf* pilgrimage; gathering at a local shrine.

romero(a), *nm/f* pilgrim.

romo, *adj* blunt; snub-nosed.

rompecabezas, *nm* puzzle; riddle; jigsaw.

rompedero, *adj* 1. breakable, delicate, fragil; 2. *nm* puzzle, brain teaser.

rompeolas, *nm* breakwater.

romper, *vt* 1. to break, smash, shatter; 2. to wear out, wear a hole in.

rompiente, *nm* reef, shoal.

rompimiento, *nm* breaking, smashing; shattering; breaching; snapping.

roncar, *vi* 1. to snore. 2. to roar.

ronco, *adj* hoarse; throaty, husky; harsh, raucous.

ronda, *nf* 1. night patrol, night watch; beat; 2. group of serenaders; 3. round.

rondar, *vt* 1. to patrol; to inspect, go the rounds of; 2. to hang round; to harass, pester; to court.

ronquear, *vi* to be hoarse, talk hoarsely.

ronquera, *nf* hoarseness; huskiness.

ronquido, *nm* snore; snoring; roar(ing); snort.

ropa, *nf* clothes, clothing; dress.

ropería, *nf* clothier's, clothes shop.

ropero, *adj* 1. for clothes, clothes; 2. wardrobe, clothes cupboard.

ropita, *nf* baby clothes.

ropón, *nm* long robe; loose coat, housecoat.

roque, *nm* rook, castle.

roqueño, *adj* rocky.

rosa, *nf* rose.

rosado, *adj* pink, rosy, roseate.

rosal, *nm* rosebush, rosetree.

rosario, *nm* rosary; chaplet; beads.

rosca, *nf* 1. coil, spiral, ring; 2. thread; turn.

roseta, *nf* small rose.

rosquete, *nm* bun.

rosquilla, *nf* 1. ring; 2. grub, small caterpillar; 3. ring-shaped pastry, doughnut.

rostro, *nm* face.

rotación, *nf* rotation; turn, revolution.

rotar, *vt* to rotate.

rotativo, *adj* 1. rotary, revolving; 2. *nm* rotary press; newspaper; 3. revolving light.

roto, *adj* broken, smashed; torn; ragged; shattered.

rotonda, *nf* rotunda; circular gallery; roundhouse; traffic circle.

rótula, *nf* 1. kneecap; 2. ball-and-socket joint.

rotulación, *nf* labelling; lettering; sign painting.

rotulador, *nm* felt-tip pen, marking pen.

rotular, *vt* to label, put a label on.

rotulista, *nm/f* sign painter.

rótulo, *nm* label, ticket, tag; lettering; inscription; sign, notice.

rotundo, *adj* 1. round; 2. flat, forthright; clear, convincing.

rotura, *nf* 1. breaking; 2. breach;crack; tear, rip, hole.

roturación, *nf* breaking-up, ploughing.

roturar, *vt* to break up, plough.

roza, *nf* groove, hollow (in a wall).

rozado, *adj* worn, grazed.

rozador, *nm* machete.

rozadura, *nf* mark of rubbing, chafing mark; abrasion, graze, sore place.

rozagante, *adj* showy, gorgeous; striking.

rozar, *vt* to rub (on), rub against; to scrape (on); to chafe

rubéola, *nf* German measles, rubella.

rubí, *nm* ruby; jewel.

rubia, *nf* blonde.

rubio, *adj* fair, fair-haired; blond(e); light-coloured, golden.

rubor, *nm* 1. bright red; 2. blush, flush.

ruborizado, *adj* blushing; flushed; ashamed.

ruborizar, *vt* to cause to blush, make blush.

rúbrica, *nf* 1. red mark; 2. paraph, flourish; 3. title, heading, rubric.

rubricar, *vt* to sign with a flourish, sign with one's paraph; to sign and seal.

rubro, *nm* heading, title; headline; section heading.

rudeza, *nf* simplicity; plainness; roughness, coarseness, commonness.

rudimento, *nm* rudiment.

rueda, *nf* wheel; tyre.

ruedecilla, *nf* small wheel; roller, castor.

ruedo, *nm* 1. turn, rotation; 2. edge, circumference; border; 3. bullring, arena.

ruego, *nm* request, entreaty.

rufianesca, *nf* criminal underworld.

rufo, *adj* sandy-haired, red-haired; curly-haired.

ruibarbo, *nm* rhubarb.

ruido, *nm* noise, sound; din, row.

ruidoso, *adj* noisy, loud.

ruin, adj mean, despicable, low, contemptible.
ruindad, nf meanness, lowness; shabbiness; callousness; piece of villainy.
ruiseñor, nm nightingale.
rumba, nf 1. rumba; 2. party, celebration.
rumbar, vt 1. to throw. 2. vi to get one's bearings.
rumbear, vi 1. to dance the rumba; 2. to follow a direction.
rumbero, adj 1. tracking, pathfinding; 2. party-going, fond of a good time.
rumbo, nm 1. route, direction; course; bearing; 2. course of events; line of conduct.
rumiante, adj 1. ruminant; 2. ruminant.
rumiar, vt 1. to chew; 2. to chew over; to brood over, ponder.
rumor, nm murmur, mutter; confused noise, low sound.
rumoreo, nm murmur(ing).
rumoroso, adj full of sounds; murmuring, musical.
rupestre, adj rock.
ruptor, nm contact-breaker.
ruptura, nf rupture; split; breaking.
rural, adj rural, country.
ruso(a), adj, nm/f Russian.
rústica, nf unbound, in paper covers; paperback (book).
rústico, adj 1. rustic, rural, country; 2. coarse, uncouth, crude; unmannerly.
ruta, nf route.
rutilante, adj shining, sparkling, glowing.
rutilar, vi to shine, sparkle, glow.
rutina, nf routine; daily round.
rutinario, adj routine; ordinary, everyday.
rutinizarse, vr to become routine, become normal.

S

S, s, nf (letter) S, s.
sábado, nm Saturday; Sabbath.
sábalo, nm shad.
sábana, nf sheet; cloth.
sabandija, nf bug, insect, creepy-crawly, creature.
sabanero(a), adj plain, savannah; of (or from) the plains (or savannah).
sabático, adj sabbatical; Saturday.
sabedor, adj to know about; to be aware of.
saber, vti 1. to know; de to know about, be aware of; to know of; 2. to taste; 3. nm (learning) knowledge
sabiduría, nf wisdom; learning, knowledge.
sabio, adj learned; expert; know-all; wise, sensible, judicious.
sable, nm 1. sabre, cutlass; 2. sable.
sablear, vt 1. to scrounge something from someone; 2. vi to live by sponging; to ask for a loan.
sabor, nm taste, flavour; savour, savouriness.
saborcillo, nm slight taste, after-taste.
saborear, vt to savour, relish (the savour of); to taste; to enjoy.
sabotaje, nm sabotage.
saboteador, nm saboteur.
sabotear, vt to sabotage.
sabroso, adj tasty, delicious; nice, pleasant, agreeable.

sabrosura, nf 1. tastiness; 2. pleasantness, delightfulness, sweetness; delight, enjoyment.
sabueso, nm bloodhound.
saca, nf 1. big sack; 2. taking out; withdrawal.
sacacorchos, nm corkscrew.
sacamanchas, nm cleaning material, stain remover.
sacamuelas, nm/f 1. dentist, tooth-puller; 2. quack; chatterer.
sacapuntas, nm pencil sharpener.
sacar, vt to take out, get out; to pull out, draw out, extract.
sacarina, nf saccharin(e).
sacerdocio, nm priesthood.
sacerdote, nm priest.
sacerdotisa, nf priestess.
saciado, adj sated with; steeped in, saturated in, full of.
saciar, vt to satisfy, satiate, sate; to quench.
saco, nm 1. bag; sack; kitbag; 2. sack; loot, plunder.
sacralizar, vt to consecrate, canonize; to give official approval to.
sacramental, adj sacramental.
sacramentar, vt to administer the last sacraments to.
sacramento, nm sacrament.
sacrificar, vt 1. to sacrifice; 2. to slaughter; destroy, put to sleep.
sacrificio, nm sacrifice.
sacrilegio, nm sacrilege.
sacrílego, adj sacrilegious.
sacristán, nm verger, sacristan; sexton.
sacristía, nf vestry, sacristy.
sacro, adj 1. sacred, holy; 2. nm sacrum.
sacrosanto, adj most holy; sacrosanct.
sacudido, adj ill-disposed, unpleasant.
sacudir, vt to shake; to beat, thrash.
sacudirse, vr to shake off a burden, get rid of a burden.
sádico, adj sadistic.
sadista, nm/f sadist.
saeta, nf arrow, dart.
saetera, nf loophole.
safari, nm safari.
saga, nf 1. saga; 2. clan, dynast; family.
sagacidad, nf shrewdness, cleverness, sagacity; astuteness.
sagaz, adj shrewd, clever, sagacious.
sagrado, adj 1. sacred, holy; 2. nm santuary, refuge.
sahumar, vt to perfume; to smoke.
sajar, vt to cut open, lance.
sal, nf salt.
saladar, nm salt marsh, saltings.
saladería, nf meat-salting plant.
saladito, nm nibble, snack.
salado, adj salt, salty; savory.
salamanca, nf cave, grotto; dark place.
salame, nm idiot, thickhead.
salami, nm salami.
salar, nm 1. salt mine; salt pan; 2. vt to put salt in, add salt to.
salarial, adj wage.
salario, nm wages, pay.
salazón, nf salting.
salcochar, vt to boil in salt water.
salchicha, nf sausage.
salchichería, nf pork butcher's (shop).
salchichón, nm sausage.
saldar, vt 1. to pay; to pay off; 2. to settle, resolve.
saledizo, adj projecting.
salero, nm salt cellar, salt store.

saleta, nf small room; vestibule.

salida, nf leaving, going out, exit; departure.

salidor, adj restless, roving; party-going.

saliente, adj projecting, protuberant; raised, overhanging.

salina, nf salt mine.

salinizar, vt to salinify, make salty.

salino, adj saline; salty.

salir, vi to come out, go out; to leave; to appear, emerge.

salita, nf small room; small auditorium.

saliva, nf saliva, spit.

salivación, nf salivation.

salivar, vi to salivate; to spit.

salivera, nf spittoon.

salmón, nm salmon.

salmonela, nf salmonella.

salmonete, nm red mullet.

salmuera, nf pickle, brine.

salobre, adj salt, salty; brackish.

salón, nm drawing-room, lounge; hall, assembly-room.

saloncillo, nm private room; restroom.

salpicadera, nf mudguard.

salpicadero, nm dashboard.

salpicado, adj splashed with, spattered with; sprinkled with.

salpicar, vt to splash, spatter, to sprinkle.

salpullido, nm rash, skin disease.

salsa, nf 1. sauce; gravy; dressing; 2. seasoning, spice; appetizer.

salsero(a), adj 1. salsa-loving; salsa rhythm; 2. nm/f music player.

saltado, adj 1. to be chipped, be damaged; 2. bulging.

saltador(a), nm/f skipping rope; jumper; diver; highjumper.

saltar, vt to jump (over), leap (over), vault.

salteador, nm holdup man; highway man, footpad.

saltear, vt to hold up; to rob, assault, attack.

salterio, nm psalter; Book of Psalms.

salto, nm jump, leap; bound, spring; vault.

salubre, adj healthy, salubrious.

salubridad, nf 1. healthiness, salubrity, salubriousness; 2. health; welfare, wellbeing.

saludador(a), nm/f quack doctor.

saludar, vt 1. to greet; to bow to; take off one's hat to; 2. to salute; hail, welcome.

saludo, nm greeting; bow; salute.

salutación, nf greeting, salutation.

salvación, nf 1. rescue, delivery, salvation. 2. eternal salvation.

Salvador, nm the Saviour.

salvador(a), nm/f rescuer, saviour; life-saver.

salvaguardar, vt to safeguard; to backup, make a backup copy of.

salvajada, nf savage deed, piece of savagery; barbarity, atrocity; brutal.

salvaje, adj 1. wild; wildcat; 2. savage.

salvamento, nm rescue; delivery; salvage; salvation.

salvar, vt to save, rescue (from); to salvage.

salvavidas, nm 1. lifeguard, lifebelt; 2. adj life-saving; lifeboat.

salvia, nf sage.

salvo, adj safe.

salvoconducto, nm safe-conduct.

samaritano(a), adj, nm/f Samaritan.

sanaco, adj silly.

sanar, vt 1. to heal; to cure (of); 2. vt to recover, get well.

sanativo, adj healing, curative.

sanatorio, nm sanatorium; nursing-home.

sanción, nf sanction; punishment, penalty.

sancionado(a), nm/f guilty person.

sancionar, vt to sanction; to penalize.

sancochar, vt to parboil; to throw together, rustle up.

sancocho, nm (a) (comida malguisada) undercooked food;

sándalo, nm sandal, sandalwood.

sandez, nf 1. foolishness; 2. stupid thing, piece of stupidity; to talk nonsense.

sandía, nf watermelon.

saneamiento, nm draining; drainage.

sanear, vt 1. to drain; to remove the dampness from; to instal drainage (or sewerage) in, lay sewers in; 2. to remedy, repair.

sangradura, nf 1. inner angle of the elbow; 2. cut made into a vein; bleeding, blood-letting; 3. outlet, drainage channel.

sangrante, adj bleeding.

sangrar, vt 1. to bleed; 2. to drain, drain the water from.

sanguijuela, nf leech.

sanguinario, adj bloodthirsty, cruel, callous.

sanguíneo, adj blood; blood-red.

sanidad, nf health, healthiness; salubrity.

sanitario, adj sanitary; health; sanitation.

santo(a), adj 1. saint, consecrated; 2. nm/f saint.

santería, nf 1. shop selling religious images; 2. religion of African origin.

santero(a), nm 1. maker (or seller) of religious images, prints; 2. nm/f person excessively devoted to the saints.

santiaguero(a), nm/f faith-healer.

santificación, nf sanctification.

santificar, vt to sanctify, make holy, hallow.

santiguar, vt to make the sign of the Cross over; to bless.

santo, adj holy; sacred; consecrated.

santoral, nm calendar of saints' days.

santuario, nm sanctuary, shrine.

santurrón(a), adj 1. sanctimonious; hypocritical; 2. nm/f sanctimonious person; hypocrite.

sapo, nm toad; small animal, bug, creature.

saque, nm service, serve.

saqueador, nm looter.

saquear, vt to sack; to loot, plunder, pillage.

saqueo, nm sacking; looting, plundering; ransacking.

sarampión, nm measles.

sarcasmo, nm sarcasm.

sarcástico, adj sarcastic.

sarcoma, nm sarcoma.

sardina, nf sardine; pilchard; herring.ked) like sardines.

sardinero, adj sardine.

sargentear, vt to command; to boss about.

sargento, nm sergeant; bossy female.

sarmiento, nm vine shoot.

sarna, nf itch, scabies; mange.

sarracina, nf quarrel; brawl, free fight.

sarro, nm incrustation, deposit; tartar, scale, plaque.

sartén, nf frying-pan.

sastre, nm tailor.

sastrería, nf 1. tailoring, tailor's trade; 2. tailor's (shop)

satánico, adj satanic; devilish, fiendish.

satélite, nm satellite.

satín, nm sateen, satin.

satinado, adj 1. glossy, shiny; 2. nm gloss, shine.

satinar, vt to gloss, make glossy.

sátira, nf satire.

satírico, *adj* satiric(al).

satirizar, *vt* to satirize.

satisfacción, *nf* satisfaction.

satisfacer, *vt* to satisfy; to gratify, please.

satisfactorio, *adj* satisfactory.

satisfecho, *adj* satisfied; content(ed).

saturación, *nf* saturation; permeation,

saturado, *adj* saturated.

saturar, *vt* to saturate; to permeate; to flood.

sauce, *nm* willow (tree).

sauna, *nf* sauna.

saurio, *nm* saurian.

savia, *nf* sap.

saxo, *nm* sax; saxist.

saxofón, *nm* 1. saxophone; 2. *nm/f* saxophonist.

saya, *nf* skirt; petticoat; dress.

sayo, *nm* smock, tunic; loose garment, long loose gown.

sayuela, *nf* long shirt, smock.

sazón, *nf* 1. good heart; proper condition (of land); 2. ripeness, maturity; 3. seasoning.

sazonado, *adj* 1. ripe; mellow; tasty; 2. seasoned with, flavoured with.

sazonar, *vt* 1. to ripen, bring to maturity; 2. to season, flavour; 3. *vi* to ripen.

sebo, *nm* grease, fat; tallow; suet.

seboso, *adj* greasy, fatty; tallowy.

seca, *nf* drought; dry season.

secadero, *nm* drying place; drying shed.

secador, *nm* 1. place where clothes are hung to dry; 2. hair-driver

secar, *vt* to dry, dry up, dry off; to wipe dry.

sección, *nf* section; cross-section.

seccionar, *vt* to divide up, divide into sections; to cut (off); to dissect.

secesión, *nf* secession.

secesionisea, *adj, nm/f* secessionist.

seco, *adj* dry; dried.

secreción, *nf* secretion.

secretaría, *nf* 1. secretariat; secretary's offIce; 2. secretaryship.

secretario(a), *nm/f* secretary.

secretear, *vi* 1. to talk confidentially, exchange secrets; 2. to whisper unnecessarily; to whisper ostentatiously.

secreto, *adj* secret; hidden; confidential, classified.

secta, *nf* sect; denomination.

sectario, *adj* sectarian; denominational.

sector, *nm* sector; section.

secuaz, *nm* follower, supporter; underling, hireling.

secuela, *nf* consequence; sequel.

secuencia, *nf* sequence.

secuencial, *adj* sequential.

secuenciar, *vt* to arrange in sequence.

secuestrador(a), *nm/f* kidnapper.

secuestrar, *vt* to kidnap; abduct; to hijack.

secuestro, *nm* kidnapping, abduction; hijack(ing).

secular, *adj* secular; lay.

secularizar, *vt* to secularize.

secundar, *vt* to second, help, support; to take part in, join.

secundario, *adj* secondary; minor, of lesser importance.

sed, *nf* thirst; thirstiness.

sedante, *adj* 1. sedative; soothing, calming. 2. *nm* sedative.

sedar, *vt* to sedate.

sede, *nf* seat; headquarters, central offIce.

sedentario, *adj* sedentary,

sedería, *nf* silk raising; silk manufacture, sericulture; silk trade.

sedición, *nf* sedition.

sediento, *adj* thirsty, eager (for).

sedimentación, *nf* sedimentation.

sedimentar, *vt* (to deposit.

sedimento, *nm* sediment, deposit.

sedosidad, *nf* silkiness.

sedoso, *adj* silky, silken.

seducción, *nf* seduction.

seducir, *vt* to seduce.

seductor, *adj* 1. seductive; 2. charming, captivating, fascinating; 2. *nm* seducer.

segadera, *nf* sickle.

segador, *nm* harvester, reaper.

segadora, *nf* 1. harvester, reaper; 2. mower, reaper, mowing machine; lawn mower.

segar, *vt* to reap, cut, harvest.

seglar, *adj* secular, lay; 2. n m/f layman, laywoman.

segmento, *nm* segment; sector, group.

segregación, *nf* 1. segregation; 2. secretion.

segregar, *vt* 1. to segregate, separate; 2. to secrete.

seguido, *adj* continuous, unbroken.

seguidor(a), *nm/f* follower; fan, supporter.

seguimiento, *nm* chase, pursuit; continuation; follow-up.

seguir, *vt* 1. to follow; to follow on, come next to, come after; 2. to chase, pursue; to hound.

según, *adv* 1. according to circumstances; 2. *prep* according to.

segundar, *vt* 1. to do again; 2. to return.

segundero, *nm* second hand (of a watch).

segundo, *adj* second; secondary.

seguridad, *nf* 1. safety; security; safeness; 2. certainty; 3. confidence, self-confidence; 4. trustworthiness; reliability; 5. firmness; stability, steadiness.

seguro, *adj* safe; secure.

seis, *adj* six, sixth.

seiscientos, *adj* six hundred.

selección, *nf* selection.

seleccionado, *nm* team.

seleccionador(a), *nm/f* selector; team manager.

seleccionar, *vt* to pick, choose, select.

selectivo, *adj* selective.

selecto, *adj* select; choice, fine.

selenizar, *vi* to land on the moon.

selva, *nf* forest, woods; jungle.

selvático, *adj* woodland, sylvan; jungle; rustic, wild.

sellado, *adj* sealed; stamped.

selladora, *nf* primer, sealant.

sellar, *vt* to seal; to stamp.

sello, *nm* seal; stamp; signet.

semáforo, *nm* semaphore; signal; traffic-lights.

semana, *nf* week.

semanal, *adj* weekly.

semanario, *adj* 1. weekly; 2. *nm* weekly (magazine).

semántica, *nf* semantics.

sembrado, *nm* sown fIeld.

sembrador(a), *nm/f* sower.

sembradura, *nf* sowing.

sembrar, *vt* to sow; to sow with, to plant.

semejante, *adj* similar; alike, the same.

semejanza, *nf* similarity, resemblance.

semejar, *vi* to seem like, resemble, seem to be.

semental, *adj* stud, breeding.

sementera, *nf* sowing; seedtime, sowing season.

semestral, *adj* half-yearly, biannual.

semestre, *nm* period of six months; semester.

semicírculo, *nm* semicircle.

semidesnudo, *adj* half-naked.

semidormido, *adj* half-asleep.

semifinal, *nf* semifinal.

semilla, *nf* seed.
semillero, *nm* seedbed; nursery; seedbox.
seminal, *adj* seminal.
seminario, *nm* 1. seedbed; nursery; 2. seminary.
semioficial, *adj* semiofficial.
semítico, *adj* Semitic.
sémola, *nf* semolina.
sempiterno, *adj* everlasting.
senado, *nm* senate; assembly, gathering.
senador(a), *nm/f* senator.
senatorial, *adj* senatorial.
sencillez, *nf* simplicity, plainness.
sencillo, *adj* simple, plain, unadorned.
senda, *nf* path, track; path; lane.
sendero, *nm* path, track.
senectud, *nf* old age.
senil, *adj* senile.
seno, *nm* 1. bosom, bust; breasts; 2. hollow, cavity.
sensación, *nf* sensation, feeling; sense; feel.
sensacional, *adj* sensational.
sensatez, *nf* good sense, sensibleness.
sensato, *adj* sensible.
sensibilidad, *nf* sensitivity, sensitiveness; sensibility.
sensibilizar, *vt* to sensitize; to alert (about, to), make aware.
sensible, *adj* feeling, sentient; sensitive, tender, sore.
sensitiva, *nf* 1. mimosa; 2. highly sensitive person, delicate flower.
sensor, *nm* sensor.
sensual, *adj* 1. sensual; sensuous; 2. alluring, sexy.
sensualidad, *nf* 1. sensuality; sensuousness; 2. attractiveness, allure, sexiness.
sentada, *nf* sitting; sit-down.
sentadera, *nf* seat (of a chair).
sentadero, *nm* seat.
sentado, *adj* sit, be sitting (down), be seated.
sentador, *adj* smart, elegant.
sentar, *vt* to sit, seat; set in place, settle, establish.
sentencia, *nf* sentence: decision, ruling.
sentenciar, *vt* to sentence (to).
sentido, *adj* 1. regrettable; deeply felt; 2. *nm* sense, meaning, direction; feeling.
sentimental, *adj* sentimental; emotional; soulful.
sentimiento, *nm* feeling, emotion, sentiment.
sentir, *vt* 1. to feel; to perceive, sense; to hear; 2. feel sorry for, regret; 3. *nm* opinion, judgement.
señal, *nf* sign; symptom; token, indication.
señaladero, *nm* signalman.
señalado, *adj* to be marked down as, be known to be.
señalador, *nm* bookmark.
señalar, *vt* 1. to mark, to denote, betoken; 2. to stamp.
señalarse, *vr* to distinguish oneself, make one's mark.
señalizador, *nm* roadsign, signpost.
señalizar, *vt* to put up signs on; to signpost.
señor, *nm* 1. man; gentleman; 2. owner, master.
señorear, *vt* to rule, control; to domineer, lord it over.
señorío, *nm* 1. manor, feudal estate; domain; 2. rule, sway, dominion; 3. lordliness; majesty, stateliness.
señorita, *nf* young lady.
separación, *nf* separation; division; removal.
separado, *adj* separated; separate; detached.
separador, *nm* separator; delimiter.
separar, *vt* to separate; take away, remove.
separatista, *adj* 1. separatist; 2. *nm/f* separatist.
sepelio, *nm* burial.
septentrional, *adj* north, northern.
séptico, *adj* septic.
se(p)tiembre, *nm* September.
septillizo(a), *nm/f* septuplet.

séptimo, *adj* 1. seventh; 2. *nm* seventh
séptuplo, *adj* sevenfold.
sepulcral, *adj* sepulchral; gloomy, dismal.
sepulcro, *nm* tomb, grave; sepulchre;
sepultar, *vt* 1. to bury; to bury, entomb; 2. to hide away, bury, conceal.
sepultura, *nf* 1. burial; to bury; 2. grave, tomb.
sepulturero, *nm* gravedigger, sexton.
sequedad, *nf* dryness; bluntness; brusqueness, bareness.
sequía, *nf* drought; dry season.
séquito, *nm* 1. retinue, suite, entourage; 2. group of supporters, adherents, devotees.
ser, *vi* to be.
serafín, *nm* 1. angel; cherub; 2. clip, fastener.
serenar, *vt* to calm; to clarify.
serenata, *nf* serenade.
serenidad, *nf* calmness, serenity; peacefulness, quietness.
sereno, *adj* 1. calm, serene; 2. settled, cloudless, clear.
serie, *nf* series; set, sequence, succession.
seriedad, *nf* 1. seriousness; gravity, solemnity; 2. dignity; properness; seriousness, (sense of) responsibility.
serio, *adj* serious, grave, solemn.
sermón, *nm* sermon.
sermonear, *vt* to lecture, read a lecture to.
serpentear, *vi* to wriggle, to creep.
serpenteo, *nm* 1. wriggling; creeping; 2. winding, twisting; meandering.
serpentina, *nf* serpentine, streamer.
serpiente, *nf* snake; serpent.
serrado, *adj* serrated; toothed; jagged.
serranía, *nf* mountainous area, hilly country.
serrano, *adj* highland, hill, mountain.
serrar, *vt* to saw (off, up)
serrería, *nf* sawmill
serrín, *nm* sawdust
serruchar, *vt* to saw (off, up)
serrucho, *nm* saw, handsaw
servicial, *adj* helpful, obliging.
servicio, *nm* service.
servidor(a), *nm/f* servant; waiter, waitress.
servidumbre, *nf* servitude; serfdom.
servil, *adj* 1. slave; 2. servile; obsequious, grovelling.
servilleta, *nf* serviette, napkin.
servir, *vt* to serve; to do a favour to, oblige.
servo, *nm* servo.
sesenta, *adj* sixty; sixtieth.
sesera, *nf* brainpan; brains, intelligence.
sesgado, *adj* slanted.
sesgar, *vt* to slant, slope, place obliquely.
sesión, *nf* session, sitting, meeting.
sesionar, *vi* to sit; to be in session; to hold a meeting.
seso, *nm* brain.
sesudo, *adj* 1. sensible, wise; 2. brainy, stubborn, pig-headed.
seta, *nf* mushroom; toadstool.
setecientos, *adj* seven hundred.
setenta, *adj* seventy; seventieth.
setiembre, *nm* September.
seto, *nm* fence; hedge.
severidad, *nf* severity, harshness; strictness; stringency.
severo, *adj* severe, harsh; strict.
sexagenario, *adj* sexagenarian, sixty-year old.
sexo, *nm* sex.
sexología, *nf* sexology.
sexólogo(a), *nm/f* sexologist
sextante, *adj*, *nm* sextant

sexto, *adj* 1. sixth; 2. *nm* sixth

séxtuplo, *adj* sixfold

sexual, *adj* sexual; sex ; sex life

sexualidad, *nf* sexuality, sex.

si, *conj* 1. if, whether; 2. *nm* (Mus) B.

sí, *adv* yes, indeed, certainly.

siamés(esa), *adj, nm/f* siamese.

sicario, *nm* hired assassin.

sicote, *nm* foot odor.

sideral, *adj* astral, space.

siderurgia, *nf* iron and steel industry.

siderúrgico, *adj* iron and steel.

siembra, *nf* sowing, sowing time.

siempre, *adv* always: all the time; ever.

sien, *nf* temple.

sierpe, *nf* snake, serpent.

sierra, *nf* saw.

siervo(a), *nm/f* slave.

siesta, *nf* 1. hottest part of the day, afternoon heat; 2. siesta, nap; to have one's afternoon nap.

siete, *adj* seven; seventh.

sífilis, *nf* syphilis.

sifilítico(a), *adj, nm/f* syphilitic

sifón, *nm* trap, U-bend; siphon.

siga, *nf* pursuit; to chase after sth.

sigilo, *nm* secrecy; discretion; stealth.

sigiloso, *adj* secret; discreet; stealthy, sly.

sigla, *nf* symbol; abbreviation; acronym.

siglo, *nm* century.

significación, *nf* significance, importance; meaning.

significado, *adj* 1. well-known; outstanding; 2. *nm* significance; meaning.

significar, *vt* 1. to mean; to signify; 2. to make known, express.

siguiente, *adj* following; next.

sílaba, *nf* syllable.

silabear, *vt* to syllabify, syllabicate, divide into syllables.

silábico, *adj* syllabic.

silbato, *nm* whistle.

silbido, *nm* whistle, whistling; hiss; wheeze; whine, whizz.

silenciador, *nm* silencer.

silenciar, *vt* to hush up; to keep silent about, pass over in silence.

silencio, *nm* silence; quiet, hush; (Mus) rest.

silente, *adj* silent, noiseless.

silo, *nm* silo; underground store; storage pit.

silueta, *nf* silhouette; outline.

siluetear, *vt* to outline; to shape, mould.

silvestre, *adj* wild; rustic, rural.

silla, *nf* seat; chair.

sillero, *nm* chairmaker.

sillín, *nm* saddle, seat.

sillón, *nm* armchair; easy chair; rocking-chair.

sima, *nf* abyss, chasm; pit; deep fissure, pothole.

simbólico, *adj* symbolic(al); token.

simbolizar, *vt* to symbolize; to represent, stand for, be a token of; to typify.

símbolo, *nm* symbol.

simbología, *nf* symbols; system of symbols.

simetría, *nf* symmetry; harmony.

simetrizar, *vt* to make symmetrical; to bring into line, harmonize

simiente, *nf* seed.

símil, *adj* similar.

similar, *adj* similar.

simpatía, *nf* liking; affection.

simpático, *adj* nice, likeable, genial, pleasant; kind; charming, attractive.

simpatizar, *vi* to get on (well together).

simplada, *nf* simplicity, stupidity; stupid thing (to do o to say).

simple, *adj* simple; uncomplicated, unadorned, bare.

simplicidad, *nf* simplicity, simpleness.

simplificación, *nf* simplification.

simplificar, *vt* to simplify.

simposio, *nm* symposium.

simulación, *nf* simulation; make-believe; pretense.

simulacro, *nm* 1. simulacrum; image, idol; 2. semblance; sham, pretence.

simulado, *adj* simulated; feigned; mock, sham.

simular, *vt* to simulate; to feign, sham.

simultáneo, *adj* simultaneous.

sin. *prep* without; with no ...; apart from, not counting, not including.

sinagoga, *nf* synagogue.

sincerarse, *vr* to vindicate onself; to tell the truth, be honest.

sincero, *adj* sincere.

sincronía, *nf* synchronous character; simultaneity

sincrónico, *adj* synchronous; synchronized.

sincronización, *nf* synchronization.

sincronizador, *nm* timer.

sincronizar, *vt* to synchronize (with).

sindical, *adj* union, trade-union; syndical.

sindicalizar, *vt* to unionize.

sindicalizarse, *vr* to form a union.

sindicato, *nm* syndicate; to have a shotgun wedding.

síndrome, *nm* syndrome; withdrawal symptoms.

sinfín, *nm* conveyor-belt; spiral conveyor.

sinfonía, *nf* symphony.

sinfónico, *adj* symphonic.

singular, *adj* 1. singular; 2. single, outstanding, exceptional; peculiar, odd.

singularidad, *nf* singularity, peculiarity, oddity.

singularizar, *vt* to single out; to refer specifically to.

siniestrado(a), *adj* 1. involved in an accident; damaged, wrecked, crashed; 2. *nm/f* victim (of an accident), person who has suffered a loss (or damage).

siniestro, *adj* 1. left; 2. sinister; ominous; evil, malign.

sino, *nm* 1. fate, destiny; 2. *conj* not but; 3. except, save; only.

sinónimo, *adj* synonymous (with).

sinopsis, *nf* synopsis.

sinsonte, *nm* mockingbird.

sintaxis, *nf* syntax.

síntesis, *nf* synthesis, summary.

sintetizador, *nm* synthesizer.

sintetizar, *vt* to synthesize; to summarize, sum up.

síntoma, *nm* symptom; sign, indication.

sintonía, *nf* syntony; tuning.

sintonización, *nf* tuning.

sintonizar, *vt* to syntonize; to synchronize.

sinvergüenza, *nm/f* scoundrel, villain, rascal; shameless person.

sinvergüenzura, *nf* shamelessness.

sión, *nm* zion.

sionista, *adj, nm/f* zionist.

siquiera, *adv* at least; once, at least, just once.

sirena, *nf* siren; mermaid; bathing beauty.

sirope, *nm* syrup.

sirvienta, *nf* servant, maid.

sirviente, *nm* servant; waiter.

sísmico, *adj* seismic.

sismografía, *nf* seismography.

sismógrafo, *nm* seismograph.

sismología, *nf* seismology.

sistema, *nm* system; method.
sistemático, *adj* systematic.
sistematización, *nf* systematization.
sistematizar, *vt* to systematize.
sitial, *nm* seat of honor; ceremonial chair.
sitiar, *vt* to besiege, lay siege to; to surround.
sitio, *nm* place; spot, site, location.
sito, *adj* situated, located (at, in).
situación, *nf* situation, position; standing.
situado, *adj* situated, placed.
situar, *vt* to place, put, set, to locate, situate, site; to post, station.
soba, *nf* 1. kneading; 2. slap, punch; hiding.
sobado, *adj* 1. worn, shabby; rumpled, crumpled, 2. well-worn; hoary, corny; 3. short.
sobar, *vt* to handle, finger, to massage, rub.
soberanía, *nf* sovereignty
soberano(a), *adj* 1. sovereign, supreme; 2. *nm/f* sovereing, king; queen.
soberbia, *nf* pride; haughtiness, arrogance.
soberbio, *adj* 1. proud; haughty, arrogant; 2. magnificent, grand, superb.
sobornar, *vt* to bribe, suborn; to buy off.
soborno, *nm* bribe; bribery, graft.
sobra, *nf* excess, surplus; s leavings, left-overs, scraps.
sobrante, *adj* spare, remaining, extra, surplus.
sobrar, *vt* 1. to exceed, surpass; 2. *vi* to remain, be left (over).
sobre, *nm* 1. envelope; 2. over, more than; in addition to, on top of.
sobreabundar, *vi* to superabound, be very abundant.
sobrealimentar, *vt* to overfeed; to supercharge.
sobrecama, *nm* bedspread.
sobrecarga, *nf* extra load; excess weight; new burden.
sobrecargar, *vt* to overload; to overcharge; overburden.
sobrecoger, *vt* to startle, take by surprise; to scare, frighten.
sobredosis, *nf* overdose.
sobre(e)stimar, *vt* to overestimate.
sobre(e)xcitar, *vt* to overexcite.
sobre(e)xponer, *vt* to overexpose.
sobregirar, *vti* to overdraw.
sobrehumano, *adj* superhuman.
sobrellevar, *vt* to carry, help to carry, help with.
sobremanera, *adv* exceedingly.
sobremarcha, *nf* overdrive.
sobrenatural, *adj* supernatural; weird, unearthly.
sobrenombre, *nm* by-name, extra name; nickname.
sobrepasar, *vt* to exceed, surpass, outdo.
sobrepeso, *nm* extra load; excess weight, overweight.
sobreponer, *vt* to put on top (of), superimpose (on).
sobreprecio, *nm* surcharge; increase in price.
sobreprotección, *nf* over-protection.
sobrepujar, *vt* to outdo, excel, surpass.
sobresaliente, *adj* 1. projecting; overhanging; 2. outstanding, excellent; first class.
sobresalir, *vi* to project, jut out; to overhang; to stick out, protrude.
sobresaltar, *vt* to startle, scare, frighten.
sobretodo, *nm* overcoat.
sobrevalorar, *vt* to overvalue; to overrate, put too high a value on.
sobrevenir, *vi* to happen (unexpectedly), come up, supervene; to follow.
sobrevivir, *vi* survive
sobrevolar, *vt* to fly over, overfly.

sobriedad, *nf* soberness; moderation, restraint; quietness.
sobrina, *nf* niece.
sobrino, *nm* nephew.
sobrio, *adj* sober; moderate, temperate, restrained.
socavar, *vt* to undermine; to dig under, dig away.
sociable, *adj* sociable, friendly.
social, *adj* social.
socialista, *adj* socialist(ic).
socializar, *vt* to socialize; to nationalize.
sociedad, *nf* society.
socio(a), *nm/f* 1. associate; member; fellow members; 2. partner; 3. buddy, mate.
sociología, *nf* sociology.
sociológico, *adj* sociological.
sociólogo(a), *nm/f* sociologist.
socorrer, *vt* persona to help; to relieve.
socorrista, *nm/f* lifeguard, life-saver.
socorro, *nm* help, aid, assistance; relief.
soda, *nf* 1. soda; 2. soda water.
sodio, *nm* sodium.
sofá, *nm* sofa, settee.
sofisticado, *adj* sophisticated; affected, over refined.
sofocación, *nf* suffocation.
sofocado, *adj* to be out of breath; to feel stifled.
sofocante, *adj* stifling, suffocating.
sofocar, *vt* to suffocate, stifle.
sofoco, *nm* 1. suffocation; stifling sensation; 2. embarrassment; (ira) anger, rage, feeling of indignation.
sofreír, *vt* to fry lightly.
soga, *nf* rope, cord; halter.
sojuzgar, *vt* to conquer; to subdue; to rule despotically.
sol, *nm* 1. sun; 2. (Music) G; G major.
solapa, *nf* lapel; flap.
solar, *nm* 1. lot, piece of ground, site; building site; 2. ancestral home, family seat; 3. *vt* to floor, tile; to sole; 4. *adj* solar, sun.
solariego, *adj* family seat, ancestral home.
solaz, *nm* recreation, relaxation; solace.
solazar, *vt* to provide relaxation for.
soldado, *adj* 1. welded; 2. *nm/f* soldier.
soldador, *nm* 1. soldering iron; 2. welder.
soldadura, *nf* solder; soldering, welding.
soldar, *vt* to solder, weld.
soleado, *adj* sunny.
solear, *vt* to put in the sun.
soledad, *nf* solitude; loneliness.
solemnidad, *nf* solemnity; impressiveness; formality, gravity, dignity.
solemnizar, *vt* to solemnize, celebrate.
solfear, *vt* to solfa.
solfeo, *nm* solfa, singing of scales, voice practice.
solicitar, *vt* to ask for, request, seek.
solícito, *adj* diligent, concerned; affectionate.
solicitud, *nf* diligence, care; solicitude, concern; affection.
solidarizarse, *vr* to declare one's solidarity with, affirm one's support for.
solidez, *nf* solidity; hardness
solidificar, *vt* to solidify, harden.
sólido, *adj* solid; hard.
solista, *nm/f* soloist
solitario, *adj* lonely, solitary; to live alone.
solo, *adj* alone.
solomillo, *nm* sirloin.
soltar, *vt* to let go of; to drop; to release.
soltera, *nf* single woman, unmarried woman.
soltería, *nf* single state, unmarried state.

soltero, *adj* 1. single, unmarried; 2. *nm* bachelor, unmarried man.

soltura, *nf* looseness, slackness.

solución, *nf* solution.

solucionar, *vt* to solve; to resolve, settle.

solvencia, *nf* solvency.

solventar, *vt* to settle, pay.

solvente, *adj* solvent, free of debt.

sollozar, *vi* to sob.

sollozo, *nm* sob.

sombra, *nf* shadow; shade; shaded part, shaded area, dark part.

sombreado, *adj* 1. shady; 2. *nm* shading; hatching.

sombreador, *nm* eyeshadow.

sombrear, *vt* to shade; to shade; to hatch; to put eyeshadow on.

sombrerera, *nf* 1. milliner; 2. hatbox; 3. hatstand.

sombrerería, *nf* 1. hats, millinery; 2. hat shop; hat factory.

sombrero, *nm* hat; headgear.

sombrilla, *nf* parasol, sunshade.

sombrío, *adj* shaded, in the shade, dark.

somero, *adj* shallow.

someter, *vt* to conquer; to subject to one's will.

sometimiento, *nm* submission, subjection.

somnámbulo(a), *nm/f* sleepwalker, somnambulist.

somnífero, *adj* 1. sleep-inducing; 2. *nm* sleeping pill.

son, *nm* sound, pleasant sound, sweet sound.

sonado, *adj* talked-of; famous; sensational; scandalous.

sonar, *vt* 1. to ring, to play, blow; 2. *vi* to sound. chime, (Mus) to play.

sonda, *nf* 1. sounding; 2. lead; bore, drill; probe.

sondeo, *nm* poll, inquiry, investigation.

soneto, *nm* sonnet.

sonido, *nm* sound.

sonoridad, *nf* sonority, sonorousness.

sonorizar, *vt* to voice.

sonoro, *adj* sonorous; loud, resonant, resounding.

sonreír, *vi* to smile.

sonriente, *adj* smiling.

sonrisa, *nf* smile.

sonrojar, *vt* to make someone blush.

sonrojo, *nm* blush.

sonrosado, *adj* rosy, pink.

sonrosarse, *vr* to turn pink.

sonsacar, *vt* to get by cunning; to remove surreptitiously.

soñador(a), *adj* 1. dreamy; 2. *nm/f* dreamer.

soñar, *vti* to dream.

soñoliento, *adj* sleepy, drowsy, somnolent.

sopa, *nf* soup.

sopapear, *vt* to punch, bash; to slap; to shake violently.

sopapo, *nm* punch, thump.

sopesar, *vt* 1. to try the weight of, try to lift; 2. to weigh, consider; to weigh up.

soplado, *adj* 1. clean; extra smart, overdressed; 2. *nm* air-cooling; glass-blowing.

soplador, *nm* 1. glass blower; 2. fan, ventilator.

soplar, *vt* 1. to blow away, blow off; 2. to inspire.

soplete, *nm* blowlamp, torch; welding torch.

soplido, *nm* strong puff, blast.

soplo, *nm* 1. blow, puff; gust; blast; 2. tip. tip-off, secret warning.

sopor, *nm* drowsiness; torpor, lethargy.

soporífico, *adj* sleep-inducing; soporific.

soportar, *vt* to bear, carry, support, endure.

soporte, *nm* support; base, stand, mounting.

soprano, *nf* soprano.

sorber, *vt* to sip; to suck up.

sorbo, *nm* sip; gulp, swallow.

sordera, *nf* deafness.

sordo, *adj* deaf.

sordomudo(a), *adj* 1. deaf and dumb; 2. *nm/f* deaf-mute.

soriasis, *nf* psoriasis.

sorprendente, *adj* surprising; amazing; startling.

sorprender, *vt* to surprise; to amaze; to startle.

sorpresa, *nf* surprise; amazement.

sortear, *vt* to draw lots for, decide by lot; to draw out of a hat.

sorteo, *nm* draw, drawing lots; raffle.

sortija, *nf* ring.

sosa, *nf* caustic soda.

sosegado, *adj* quiet, calm, peaceful; gentle.

sosegar, *vt* to calm, quieten; to lull.

sosiego, *nm* calm(ness), quiet(ness); peacefulness.

sospecha, *nf* suspicion.

sospechar, *vt* to suspect.

sospechoso, *adj* suspicious; suspect; suspected;

sostén, *nm* support, pillar; brassiere.

sostener, *vt* 1. to hold up, support; to prop up; 2. to support, back; to help; to defend.

sostenido, *adj* steady, continuous; sustained; prolonged.

sostenimiento, *nm* support; holding up; maintenance; upholding.

sotana, *nf* cassock, soutane, hiding.

sótano, *nm* basement; cellar; vault.

soterrar, *vt* to bury; to hide away.

suave, *adj* smooth, even, gentle, mild, soft.

suavidad, *nf* smoothness, evenness; gentleness; softness, mildness; sweetness.

suavizar, *vt* to smooth (out, down); to soften.

subvalorar, *vt* to undervalue.

subalterno, *adj* secondary; minor, auxiliary.

subarrendador(a), *nm/f* subtenant.

subarrendar, *vt* to sublet, sublease.

subasta, *nf* auction, sale by auction.

subastar, *vt* to auction, auction off, sell at auction.

subcomisión, *nf* subcommittee.

subconsciencia, *nf* subconscious.

subconsciente, *adj* subconscious.

subcultura, *nf* subculture.

subdesarrollado, *adj* underdeveloped.

súbdito(a), *adj, nm/f* subject.

subdividir, *vt* to subdivide.

subdivisión, *nf* subdivision.

subestimar, *vt* to underestimate, underrate; to undervalue.

subida, *nf* climb, climbing; ascent.

subir, *vt* 1. to raise, lift up; to put up; to take up, get up; 2. to promote.

súbito, *adj* sudden; unexpected.

sublevación, *nf* revolt, rising; mutiny; riot.

sublevar, *vt* to rouse to revolt, stir up a revolt among.

sublimación, *nf* sublimation.

sublimado, *nm* sublimate.

sublimar, *vt* 1. to exalt, praise; 2. to sublimate.

sublimidad, *nf* sublimity.

submarino, *adj* underwater, submarine.

subordinación, *nf* subordination.

subordinado, *adj* subordinate.

subproducto, *nm* by-product; spin-off.

subrayado, *adj* underlined; italicized.

subrayar, *vt* to underline; to italicize.

subrogar, *vt* to substitute (for), replace (with).

subsanar, *vt* to overlook, excuse; to repair, make good.

subsecuente, *adj* subsequent.

subsede, *nf* secondary venue.

subsidiar, *vt* to subsidize.
subsidiario, *adj* subsidiary; complementary.
subsidio, *nm* (a) subsidy, grant; aid.
subsiguiente, *adj* subsequent.
subsistencia, *nf* subsistence; sustenance.
subterráneo, *adj* underground, subterranean.
subtropical, *adj* subtropical.
suburbio, *nm* suburb, outlying area.
subvencionar, *vt* to subsidize, aid.
subversión, *nf* subversion.
subversivo, *adj* subversive.
subvertir, *vi* to subvert; to overthrow, undermine.
succión, *nf* suction.
succionar, *vt* to suck; to apply suction to; to absorb.
suceder, *vti* 1. to happen; 2. to succeed, follow.
sucesivo, *adj* successive, following; consecutive.
suceso, *nm* event, happening; incident.
sucesor(a), *nm/f* successor; heir.
suciedad, *nf* dirt, filth, grime; dirtiness.
sucio, *adj* dirty; filthy, grimy.
suculencia, *nf* tastiness, richness; succulence, lusciousness, juiciness.
suculento, *adj* tasty, rich; succulent, luscious, juicy.
sucumbir, *vi* to succumb (to).
sucursal, *nf* branch, branch office; subsidiary.
sudadera, *nf* sweatshirt.
sudar, *vt* to sweat.
sudeste, *adj* south-east, south-eastern.
sudoeste, *adj* south-west, south-western.
sudor, *nm* sweat.
suegra, *nf* mother-in-law.
suegro, *nm* father-in-law.
suela, *nf* sole; piece of strong leather.
sueldo, *nm* pay; salary; wage.
suelo, *nm* ground; surface; soil.
suelto, *adj* free; untied, undone.
sueño, *nm* 1. sleep; 2. sleepiness, drowsiness; 3. dream.
suerte, *nf* 1. fate, destiny; chance, fortune; 2. lot; luck.
suficiencia, *nf* 1. sufficiency; adequacy; enough; 2. competence; suitability, fitness; adequacy.
suficiente, *adj* 1. enough, sufficient; adequate; 2. competent; suitable, fit.
sufijo, *nm* suffix.
sufragar, *vt* 1. to aid, help, support; 2. to meet, defray, cover; 3. *vi* to vote (for).
sufragio, *nm* vote.
sufrido, *adj* longsuffering, patient.
sufrimiento, *nm* suffering; misery, wretchedness.
sufrir, *vt* to suffer; experience; sustain; undergo.
sugerencia, *nf* suggestion.
sugerir, *vt* to suggest; to hint.
sugestión, *nf* 1. suggestion; hint; prompting, stimulus; 2. fascination, hypnotic power,
sugestionar, *vt* to influence, dominate the will of, hypnotize.
suicida, *adj* suicidal.
suicidar, *vt* to murder, assassinate.
suicidarse, *vr* to commit suicide, kill oneself.
sujeción, *nf* subjection, fastening; seizure.
sujetador, *nm* fastener; clip, pin, grip.
sujetar, *vt* to subdue, conquer; to hold down.
sujeto, *adj* 1. fastened, secure; tight; 2. subject to; 3. to keep someone under supervision.
sulfato, *nm* sulphate.
sulfurar, *vt* to sulphurate.
sulfuro, *nm* sulphide.
sumadora, *nf* adding machine.
sumar, *vt* to add (up), total; to summarize, sum up.
sumarse, *vr* to join a party; to associate onself. with.

sumario, *adj* 1. brief, concise; summary; 2. *nm* summary; 3. indictment.
sumergible, *adj* 1. submersible; that can go under water; 2. *nm* submarine.
sumergir, *vt* to submerge; to sink; to immerse, dip, plunge (in).
sumidero, *nm* drain, sewer; sink.
suministrador(a), *nm/f* supplier.
suministrar, *vt* to supply, furnish, provide.
suministro, *nm* supply; furnishing, provision.
sumir, *vt* to sink, plunge, submerge; to swallow up, suck down.
sumisión, *nf* 1. submission; 2. submissiveness, docility.
sumiso, *adj* submissive, docile, obedient.
suntuosidad, *nf* sumptuousness, magnificence; lavishness.
suntuoso, *adj* sumptuous, magnificent; lavish, rich.
supeditar, *vt* 1. to subordinate (to); 2. to subdue; to oppress, crush.
súper, *adj* 1. super; 2. *adv* really well, real good.
superabundancia, *nf* superabundance.
superación, *nf* overcoming, surmounting; transcending; excelling.
superar, *vt* to surpass, excel (in), beat, do better than.
superchería, *nf* fraud, trick, swindle.
superdotado, *adj* 1. extremely gifted; 2. *nm/f* extremely gifted person.
superestrella, *nf* superstar.
superficial, *adj* surface, of the surface; flesh.
superficie, *nf* surface; face; outside.
superfino, *adj* superfine.
superfluo, *adj* superfluous,
superintendencia, *nf* supervision, superintendence.
superintendente, *nm/f* supervisor, superintendent, overseer.
superior, *adj* upper; uppermost, top
superiora, *nf* mother superior.
superioridad, *nf* superiority.
superlativo, *adj* *nm* superlative.
supermercado, *nm* supermarket.
superpoblación, *nf* overpopulation, excess of population; overcrosing congestion.
superponer, *vt* to superimpose, superpose, put on top.
superposición, *nf* superposition.
superpotencia, *nf* superpower, great power.
superproduccion, *nf* overproduction.
supersecreto, *adj* top secret.
supersónico, *adj* supersonic.
superstición, *nf* superstition.
supersticioso, *adj* superstitious.
supervigilancia, *nf* supervision.
supervisar, *vt* to supervise.
supervisión, *nf* supervision.
supervisor(a), *nm/f* supervisor; matron.
supervivencia, *nf* survival.
superviviente, *adj* 1. surviving; 2. *nm/f* survivor.
suplantar, *vt* to supplant; to take the place of (fraudulently), impersonate.
suplemento, *nm* supplement.
suplencia, *nf* substitution, replacement.
suplente, *adj* substitute, deputy; supply teacher.
súplica, *nf* request; entreaty, supplication; petition.
suplicar, *vt* to beg (for), plead for, implore.
suplicio, *nm* torture; punishment; execution; torment.
suponer, *vt* 1. to suppose, assume; 2. to think, imagine; to guess.
supositorio, *nm* suppository.
supremacía, *nf* supremacy.
supremo, *adj* supreme.

supresión, nf suppression; abolition; cancellation.

supresor, nm suppressor.

suprimido, adj suppressed, banned.

suprimir, vt to suppress; to abolish; to remove, eliminate.

supuesto, adj supposed, ostensible.

supuración, nf suppuration.

supurar, vi to suppurate, discharge, fester.

sur, adj south, southern.

surcar, vt to plough, furrow; to cut, score, groove.

surgir, vi to arise, emerge, spring up, appear.

surrealista, adj surrealist(ic).

surtido, adj mixed, assorted, varied.

surtidor, nm jet, spout; fountain.

surtir, vi to supply, furnish, provide.

surtirse, vr to provide onself. with.

surto, adj anchored.

susceptibilidad, nf susceptibility (to); sensitivity; touchiness.

susceptible, adj 1. capable of; 2. susceptible; sensitive; touchy; impressionable.

suscitar, vt to stir up; to make, cause, provoke.

suscribir, vt to sign; to make, agree to, ratify.

suscriptor(a), nm/f subscriber.

susodicho, adj above-mentioned.

suspender, vt to hang, hang up, suspend.

suspensión, nf hanging (up), suspension.

suspenso, adj 1. hanging, suspended; hung (from); 2. failed.

suspicacia, nf suspicion, mistrust.

suspicaz, adj suspicious, distrustful.

suspirar, vi to sigh (for).

suspiro, nm sigh;breath, rustle, whisper.

sustancial, adj substantial; essential, vital, fundamental.

sustantivar, vt to use as a noun.

sustantivo, adj 1. substantive; substantival; 2. nm noun, substantive.

sustentación, nf sustenance; support; lift.

sustentar, vt 1. to hold up, support, (bear the weight of); 2. to sustain, nourish, feed, keep going.

sustituir, vt to substitute, replace.

sustituto(a), nm/f substitute, replacement; deputy.

susto, nm fright, scare.

sustracción, nf removal; subtraction, taking away; deduction; extraction.

sustraer, vt to remove, take away; to subtract, to deduct.

susurrante, adj whispering; murmuring; rustling.

susurrar, vi to whisper.

susurro, nm whisper; hum, humming; murmur; rustle.

sutil, adj fine, delicate, tenuous; thin.

sutileza, nf fineness, delicacy; thinness; subtlety, subtleness.

sutura, nf suture.

suturar, vt to suture; to stitch.

suyo, adj y pron pos his, hers, its.

T

T, t, nf (letter) T, t.

tabacal, nm tobacco field; tobacco plantation.

tabacalera, nf cigarette factory.

tabacalero, adj 1. tobacco; 2. nm tobacconist; tobacco grower; tobacco merchant .

tabaco, nm tobacco; cigarettes, cigar; tobacco plant.

tabacón, nm marijuana, grass.

tabasco, nm Tabasco.

taberna, nf bar, pub; tavern.

tabernáculo, nm tabernacle.

tabernero, nm publican, landlord; barman, bartender.

tabicar, vt puerta to wall up; to partition off.

tabique, nm thin wall, partition (wall).

tabla, nf plank, board, shelf; panel.

tablada, nf slaughterhouse.

tablado, nm plank floor, boards; stage, platform; dance-floor.

tablazón, nf planks, planking, boards.

tablao, nm flamenco show; dance-floor (for flamenco dancing)

tablear, vt to cut into boards (or planks).

tableta, nf small board; block; writing-pad.

tablilla, nf small board; splint.

tabloide, nm tabloid.

tabú, adj taboo.

tabulación, nf tabbing.

tabulador, nm tab.

tabular, vt to tabulate; to tab; to tabulate.

taburete, nm stool.

tacañear, vt to tread down; to pound, crush.

tacañería, nf meanness, stinginess.

tacaño, adj mean, stingy.

tacar, vt to shoot at.

tacita, nf small cup.

tácito, adj tacit; unspoken; unwritten; unexpressed, understood.

taciturno, adj taciturn, silent; moody, sullen, sulky; glum.

taco, nm wad, wadding; wooden peg; stopper, plug.

tacómetro, nm tachometer.

tacón, nm heel.

taconazo, nm heel tap; kick with one's heel, blow with the heel.

taconear, vt 1. to pack tight, fill right up; 2. vi to tap (or stamp) with one's heels; to click one's heels.

táctica, nf tactics; move; gambit.

táctico, adj 1. tactical; 2. nm tactician; coach.

táctil, adj tactile.

tacto, nm 1. ouch, sense of touch; 2. touching; feel.

tacha, nf 1. large tack, brad, stud; 2. flaw, blemish, defect.

tachadura, nf erasure, correction.

tachar, vt 1. to cross out, erase; to correct; 2. to criticize, attack, find fault with.

tacho, nm boiler, large boiling pan.

tachón, nm 1. large stud, ornamental stud, boss; 2. erasure, stroke, crossing-out.

tachonar, vt to stud, adorn with studs; to trim.

tachuela, nf tack, tintack; stud; drawing-pin.

tafetán, nm taffeta; sticking plaster.

tafilete, nm morocco leather.

tahur, nm gambler; cardsharper, cheat.

taima, nf slyness, craftiness, slickness.

taimado, adj sly, crafty, slick.

taimarse, vr to get sly, adopt crafty tactics.

taja, nf cut.

tajada, nf slice; slab, chunk.

tajador, nm pencil sharpener.

tajante, adj 1. sharp, cutting; 2. incisive, sharp, emphatic.

tajar, vt to cut, slice, chop.

tajo, nm 1. cut, slash; 2. cleft; steep cliff, sheer drop.

tala, nf tree felling, wood cutting; havoc, destruction.

talabarte, nm sword belt.

talabartería, nf 1. saddlery, harness-maker's shop; 2. leather-goods shop.

talabartero, nm saddler, harness maker.

taladradora, nf drill.

taladrar, vt 1. to bore, drill, punch; 2. to pierce.

taladro, nm 1. drill; auger, gimlet; borer; 2. drill hole.

talaje, nm 1. pasture; 2. grazing.

tálamo, nm marriage bed.

talante, nm 1. mood, disposition, frame of mind; will, willingness; tendency; 2. mien, look, appearance.

talar, vt to fell, cut down.

talco, nm talcum powder; talc.

talego, nm big sack, long sack, poke.

talento, nm talent; ability; gift.

talentoso, adj talented, gifted.

talismán, nm talisman.

talón, nm heel.

talonario, nm receipt book; book of tickets.

talla, nf 1. carving; sculpture; engraving; 2. height, stature; size.

tallado, adj 1. carved; sculpted; engraved; 2. shapely, well-formed; 3. nm carving; sculpting; engraving.

tallador, nm carver; sculptor; engraver.

tallar, vt 1. to carve, shape, work; to sculpt; to engrave; 2. to measure.

talle, nm waist; figure.

taller, nm workshop; mill, factory; studio; work-room.

tallo, nm stem, stalk; blade, sprig.

tamal, nm tamale.

tamarindo, nm tamarind.

también, adv also, as well, too; besides;.

tambor, nm drum; bottle; tambour.

tambora, nf bass drum; brass band.

tamborilear, vt 1. to praise up, boost. 2. vi to drum, play the drum.

tamiz, nm sieve.

tamizar, vt to sieve, sift.

tampoco, adv neither, not.

tampón, nm tampon; plug; buffer.

tanda, nf 1. series, set; batch; layer; 2. shift, turn, spell; job; task, piece of work.

tándem, nm tandem; duo, pair, partnership.

tanga, nf tanga, G-string.

tanganear, vt to beat.

tangencial, adj tangential; oblique.

tangente, nf tangent.

tango, nm tango.

tanguear, vi 1. to tango. 2. to reel drunkenly.

tanque, nm tank; reservoir.

tanquero, nm tanker; tank wagon .

tanteada, nf dirty trick; hoax, swindle.

tanteador(a), nm 1. scoreboard; 2. nm/f scorer.

tantear, vt 1. to reckon (up), work out roughly, try to calculate, guess; 2. to test, try out; to probe.

tanteo, nm 1. reckoning, rough calculation, guess-work; weighing up; 2. trial; trial and error.

tanto, adj so much, as much; so many, as many.

tapa, nf lid, cover, cap.

tapabarro, nm mudguard

tapadero, nm stopper.

tapado, nm buried treasure.

tapaojo, nm blindfold, bandage, patch.

tapar, vt to cover, cover up.

taparse, vr to wrap o. s. up.

taparrabo, nm trunks.

tape, nm cover.

tapete, nm rug; table runner, table cover.

tapia, nf garden wall; mud wall, adobe wall.

tapiar, vt to wall in; to block up; to block, stop up.

tapiz, nm tapestry; carpet.

tapizado, nm tapestries; carpeting; upholstery.

tapizar, vt to hang with tapestries; to upholster, cover; to carpet.

tapón, adj 1. tailless; 2. nm stopper, cap, top; cork, plug.

taponar, vt to stopper, cork, put the cap on; to plug, stop up, block.

taquería, nf taco restaurant, taco stall,

taquicardia, nf abnormally rapid heartbeat, tachy-cardia.

taquigrafía, nf shorthand, stenography.

taquígrafo(a), nm/f shorthand writer, stenographer.

taquilla, nf booking-office, ticket-office, ticket win-dow; box-office.

taquillero(a), adj 1. popular, successful (at the box-office); 2. nm/f clerk, ticket clerk.

tara, nf 1. tare; 2. defect, blemish.

tarado, adj 1. damaged, defective, imperfect; 2. physically impaired, crippled; odd; 3. stupid; crazy.

tarántula, nf tarantula.

tarar, vt to tare.

tararear, vt/i to hum.

tardanza, nf slowness; delay.

tardar, vi to take a long time, be long; to be late.

tarde, adv 1. late; too late; 2. afternoon; evening.

tardío, adj late; overdue, belated, slow to arrive.

tarea, nf job, task; chore; set piece of work.

tareco, nm old thing, piece of junk.

tarifa, nf tariff; rate; price.

tarifar, vt to price.

tarima, nf platform.

tarja, nf tally, tally stick.

tarjeta, nf card.

tarro, nm 1. pot, jar; 2. horn.

tarta, nf cake; tart; flan.

tartamudear, vi to stutter, stammer.

tartamudeo, nm stutter(ing), stammer(ing).

tartamudo(a), adj 1. stuttering, stammering; 2. nm/f stutterer, stammerer.

tarugo, adj 1. stupid; 2. lump, chunk (of wood etc); wooden peg; plug, stopper.

tasa, nf 1. valuation; estimate, appraisal; 2. meas-ure, standard, norm.

tasación, nf valuation, assessment; appraisal.

tasador(a) , nm/f valuer; adjuster; tax appraiser.

tasajear, vt 1. to cut, slash; 2. to jerk.

tasajo, nm dried beef, jerked beef;

tasar, vt 1. to fix a price for, price (at); to regulate; 2. to value, appraise, assess (at).

tatuaje, nm tattoo; tattooing.

tatuar, vt to tattoo.

taumaturgo, nm miracle-worker; wonder-worker.

taurino, adj bullfighting.

taurofobia, nf dislike of bullfighting.

taxi, nm taxi, cab, taxicab.

taxidermia, nf taxidermy.

taxidermista, nm/f taxidermist.

taxímetro, nm taximeter, clock.

taxista, nm/f taxidriver, cabby.

taza, nf 1. cup; 2. basin, bowl.

tazar, vt 1. to cut; to cut up, divide; 2. to fray.

tazón, nm large cup; bowl, basin; washbasin.

té, nm tea.

tea, nf torch; firelighter.

teatral, adj theatre; dramatic.

teatro, nm theatre.

tecla, nf key.

teclado, nm keyboard, keys.

teclear, *vt* to play clumsily, mess about on.

tecleo, *nm* fingering, playing; touch; strumming.

técnica, *nf* technique; technology; method.

técnico(a), *adj* 1. technical; 2. *nm/f* technician; expert, specialist.

tecnología, *nf* technology.

tecnológico, *adj* technological.

tecnólogo(a), *nm/f* technologist.

techar, *vt* to roof (in, over).

techo, *nm* roof; ceiling; lid.

tedio, *nm* boredom, tedium.

teja, *nf* tile.

tejado, *nm* roof, tiled roof; housetop.

tejar, *vt* to tile, roof with tiles,

tejedor(a), *nm/f* weaver.

tejedura, *nf* weaving, weave, texture.

tejer, *vt* to weave; to make; to spin.

tejido, *nm* weave, woven material; web; fabric.

tejón, *nm* badger.

tela, *nf* cloth, fabric, material.

telar, *nm* loom; textile mill.

telaraña, *nf* spider's web, cobweb.

telecámara, *nf* television camera.

telecomedia, *nf* television comedy show.

telecomunicación, *nf* telecommunication.

teledifusión, *nf* telecast.

teleférico, *nm* ski lift; cable railway, cableway.

telefonear, *vti* to telephone.

telefonema, *nm* telephone message.

teléfono, *nm* telephone, phone; telephone number.

telegrafía, *nf* telegraphy,

telegrafiar, *vti* to telegraph.

telégrafo, *adj* telegraphic; telegraph.

telegrama, *nm* telegram.

telemando, *nm* remote control.

telemedir, *vt* to telemeter.

telémetro, *nm* rangefinder.

telenovela, *nf* television serial, soap-opera.

telépata, *nm/f* telepathist.

telepático, *adj* telepathic.

telescopio, *nm* telescope.

telespectador(a), *nm/f* viewer.

teletipo, *nm* teletype, teleprinter.

televidente, *nm/f* viewer, televiewer.

televisar, *vt* to televise.

televisión, *nf* television.

televisor, *nm* television set.

telón, *nm* curtain.

telúrico, *adj* of the earth, telluric; earthy.

tema, *nm* theme; subject, topic; motif.

temario, *nm* set of themes, collection of subjects; programme; topics to be examined.

tembladera, *nf* violent shaking; trembling fit.

temblar, *vi* 1. to tremble, shake; to shiver; 2. to tremble.

temblor, *nm* trembling, shaking; shivering, shuddering.

temer, *vt* to fear, be afraid of; to dread.

temerario, *adj* rash, reckless; hasty.

temeridad, *nf* rashness, recklessness; hastiness.

temeroso, *adj* timid; fearful, frightened.

temor, *nm* fear, dread; mistrust.

témpano, *nm* ice floe.

temperamento, *nm* temperament, nature, disposition.

temperancia, *nf* temperance, moderation.

temperar, *vt* to temper, moderate; to calm; to relieve.

temperatura, *nf* temperature.

tempestad, *nf* storm.

templado, *adj* 1. moderate, restrained; frugal; of sober habits; 2. warm; mild, temperate; 3. in tune, well-tuned.

templanza, *nf* moderation, restraint; frugality; abstemiousness; mildness.

templar, *vt* 1. to temper; to moderate, soften; to restrain, control; 2. to warm up (slightly); 3. to tune (up).

temple, *nm* 1. temper; tempering; 2. tuning; 3. spirit, temper, mettle; courage, boldness.

templo, *nm* temple; church, chapel.

temporada, *nf* time, period, spell; social.

temporal, *adj* 1. temporary; casual; seasonal; 2. *nm* storm; rainy, weather, spell of rough weather.

temporizar, *vi* to temporize.

temprano, *adj* early.

tenacidad, *nf* toughness; tenacity.

tenaz, *adj* tough, durable, resistant.

tenaza, *nf* squeeze, pliers, pincers; tongs; forceps.

tendedera, *nf* clothes-line.

tendencia, *nf* tendency; trend; inclination; dominant trend.

tendencioso, *adj* tendentious.

tender, *vt* 1. to stretch; to spread, spread out, extend; 2. to hang out; to hang (from); 3. *vi* to tend to, tend towards, have a tendency towards.

tendido, *adj* lying down; flat.

tendón, *nm* tendon, sinew; tendon.

tenebrosidad, *nf* 1. darkness; gloom(iness); 2. sinister nature, shadiness; 3. obscurity,

tenedor(a), *nm* 1. fork; 2. *nm/f* holder, bearer; shareholder, book-keeper.

teneduría, *nf* book-keeping.

tenencia, *nf* tenancy, occupancy; tenure; possession.

tener, *vt* to have; to have got; to possess.

tenerse, *vr* to stand, stand up.

teniente, *nm/f* lieutenant; deputy.

tenis, *nm* tennis.

tenista, *nm/f* tennis-player.

tenor, *nm* tenor.

tensado, *nm* tensioning; tension.

tensar, *vt* to tauten; to draw.

tensión, *nf* tension, tautness; stress, strain; rigidity.

tensionar, *vt* 1. to tense, tauten; 2. tense; strained.

tensor, *adj* tensile.

tentación, *nf* temptation.

tentáculo, *nm* tentacle; feeler.

tentador, *adj* tempting.

tentadora, *nf* temptress.

tentar, *vt* 1. to touch, feel; to probe; 2. to try, test, try out; 3. to tempt; to attract, lure, entice.

tentativa, *nf* attempt; effort.

tentativo, *adj* tentative.

tenue, *adj* thin, slim, slender; fine.

teñir, *vt* to dye; to tinge, colour; to stain.

teocracia, *nf* theocracy.

teocrático, *adj* theocratic.

teología, *nf* theology.

teologico, *adj* theological.

teólogo, *nm* theologian.

teorema, *nm* theorem.

teorético, *adj* theoretic(al).

teoría, *nf* theory.

teórico, *adj* theoretic(al).

teorizar, *vi* to theorize.

teosófico, *adj* theosophical.

tequila, *nf* tequila.

terapeuta, *nm/f* therapist.

terapéutica, *nf* therapeutics; therapy.

terapéutico, *adj* therapeutic(al).

terapia, *nf* therapy.

tercero(a), *nf* third.

terceto, *nm* trio, tercet, triplet.

terciada, *nf* plywood.

terciado, *adj* brown sugar.

terciar, *vt* to divide into three.

terciopelo, *nm* velvet.

terco, *adj* obstinate, stubborn.

tergiversar, *vt* to distort, twist of, misrepresent.

termal, *adj* thermal.

térmica, *nf* thermal, hot-air current.

térmico, *adj* thermic, heat.

terminación, *nf* ending, termination.

terminado, *nm* finish, finishing.

terminal, *adj* terminal.

terminar, *vt* to end; to conclude; to finish, complete.

término, *nm* end, finish, conclusion.

termita, *nm/f* termite.

termo, *nm* thermos (bottle, flask); water-heater.

termómetro, *nm* thermometer.

termonuclear, *adj* thermonuclear.

termostato, *nm* thermostat.

ternero(a), *nm/f* calf, bull calf; veal.

terno, *nm* 1. set of three, group of three; trio; 2. curse, swearword.

ternura, *nf* 1. tenderness; fondness; affection; 2. endearment, tender word.

terracota, *nf* terracotta.

terrado, *nm* terrace; flat roof.

terraplén, *nm* embankment; terrace; rampart, bank, earthwork; mound.

terrateniente, *nm/f* landowner.

terraza, *nf* flat roof; balcony; terrace.

terrenal, *nm* 1. clod, hard lump of earth; 2. *adj* earthly, worldly.

terremoto, *nm* earthquake.

terreno, *adj* 1. terrestrial; earthly, worldly; 2. *nm* terrain; soil, earth, ground, land.

terrestre, *adj* terrestrial; earthly; ground, land.

terrible, *adj* terrible, dreadful, awful.

territorial, *adj* territorial.

territorio, *nm* territory; mandated territory.

terrón, *nm* clod, lump, sod.

terror, *nm* terror; pánico panic.

terrorista, *adj, nm/f* terrorist.

terruño, *nm* 1. lump, clod; 2. plot, piece of ground; 3. native soil, home.

terso, *adj* smooth; glossy, polished, shining.

tertulia, *nf* social gathering, informal gathering.

tesar, *vt* to tauten, tighten up.

tesis, *nf* thesis.

tesitura, *nf* attitude, frame of mind.

tesón, *nm* insistence; tenacity, persistence; firmness.

tesonero, *adj* tenacious, persistent.

tesorería, *nf* treasurership, office of treasurer.

tesorero(a), *nm/f* treasurer.

tesoro, *nm* 1. treasure; hoard; 2. treasury.

testamento, *nm* will, testament.

testar, *vi* to make a will.

testarudez, *nf* stubbornness, pigheadedness.

testarudo, *adj* stubborn, pigheaded.

testera, *nf* front, face; forehead.

testículo, *nm* testicle.

testificar, *vt* to attest; to testify to, give evidence of.

testigo, *nm/f* witness.

testimonio, *nm* testimony, evidence; affidavit.

tétanos, *nm* tetanus.

tetera, *nf* 1. teapot, tea urn; 2. feeding bottle; vessel with a spout.

tetero, *nm* feeding bottle.

tétrico, *adj* gloomy, dismal; humor gloomy, pessimistic; sullen.

textil, *adj* textile.

texto, *nm* text.

textual, *adj* 1. textual; 2. exact; literal.

textura, *nf* texture.

tez, *nf* complexion, skin; colouring.

tía, *nf* aunt; abuela great-aunt.

tibia, *nf* tibia.

tibio, *adj* lukewarm, tepid.

tiburón, *nm* shark; pike.

tiempo, *nm* time.

tienda, *nf* shop, store; grocer,s.

tienta, *nf* probe.

tiento, *nm* 1. feel, feeling, touch; 2. tact; care.

tierno, *adj* tender; soft; new, fresh.

tierra, *nf* earth, world.

tierrero, *nm* cloud of dust.

tieso, *adj* stiff, rigid; erect.

tiesura, *nf* stiffness, rigidity; erectness.

tifo, *nm* typhus.

tifoidea, *nf* typhoid.

tifón, *nm* typhoon.

tigre, *nm* tiger, jaguar.

tigresa, *nf* tigress.

tijera, *nf* fork; scissors.

tijeretear, *vt* to snip, snick, cut.

tila, *nf* 1. lime tree; 2. lime(-blossom) tea; 2. hash, pot.

tildar, *vt* to put an accent on; to put a tilde over.

tilde, *nf* accent, tilde.

tilo, *nm* lime, lime tree.

timador(a), *nm/f* swindler, trickster.

timar, *vt* to steal.

timbal, *nm* small drum, kettledrum.

timbrar, *vt* to stamp; to postmark.

timbre, *nm* fiscal stamp, revenue stamp; stamp duty.

timidez, *nf* timidity, shyness, nervousness; bashfulness.

tímido, *adj* timid, shy, nervous; bashful.

timo, *nm* swindle, confidence trick, confidence game.

timón, *nm* rudder; helm.

timonear, *vt* 1. to direct, manage; to guide; 2. *vi* to steer; to drive.

timonel, *nm* steersman, helmsman; cox.

tímpano, *nm* tympanum, eardrum.

tina, *nf* vat, tub; bathtub; washtub.

tinaja, *nf* large earthen jar.

tinieblas, *nf* darkness, dark, shadows, gloom.

tino, *nm* 1. skill, knack, feel, (sureness of) touch; aim, (good) marksmanship; 2. good judgement.

tinta, *nf* ink.

tintado, *adj* 1. tinted; 2. *nm* tinting.

tinte, *nm* dyeing.

tintero, *nm* inkpot, inkwell; inkstand.

tinto, *adj* dyed, stained; tinged.

tintorera, *nf* shark; female shark.

tintorería, *nf* dyeing; dyer's shop; 2. dry cleaner's.

tintura, *nf* 1. dyeing; 2. dye, dyestuff; stain; tincture.

tío, *nm* uncle.

tiovivo, *nm* roundabout, merry-go-round.

tipear, *vt/i* to type.

tipicidad, *nf* genuineness, authenticity.

típico, *adj* typical; characteristic.

tipificar, *vt* to typify; to characterize.

tipo, *nm* type; norm, standard; pattern, model.

tipografía, *nf* typography; printing.

tipógrafo(a), *nm/f* typographer; printer.

tira, *nf* strip; band.

tirabuzón, *nm* corkscrew.

tirada, *nf* cast, throw; shoot.

tiradera, *nf* sash; belt, strap; harness strap, trace.

tiraje, *nm* printing; print run.

tiranía, *nf* tyranny.

tiránico, *adj* tyrannical; despotic.

tiranizar, *vt* to tyrannize, rule despotically; to domineer.

tirano(a), *adj* tyrannical, despotic; domineering.

tirante, *adj* tight, taut; tensed; drawn.

tirantear, *vt* to stretch.

tirantez, *nf* tightness, tautness; tension.

tirar, *vt* to throw; to hurl, fling, cast, to shoot.

tiritar, *vi* to shiver (with).

tiritona, *nf* shivering.

tiro, *nm* 1. throw; 2. shot.

tiroides, *nf* thyroid (gland).

tirón, *nm* pull, tug, sudden jerk; hitch.

tirotear, *vt* to shoot at, fire on; to blaze away at.

tiroteo, *nm* firing, shooting, exchange of shots; skirmish; gunfight.

tisana, *nf* tisane, infusion.

tísico, *adj* consumptive, tubercular.

tisis, *nf* consumption, tuberculosis.

titánico, *adj* titanic.

titanio, *nm* titanium.

títere, *nm* puppet, marionette.

titilar, *vi* to flutter, tremble; to twinkle.

titiritero(a), *nm/f* puppeteer; acrobat; juggler.

titubeante, *adj* tottery; shaky, unsteady.

titubear, *vi* to totter; to stagger; to be unstable, be shaky.

titubeo, *nm* tottering; staggering; instability, shakiness, unsteadiness.

titulación, *nf* degrees and diplomas.

titulado, *adj* entitled; titled, having a degree;

titulada, *nf* graduate.

titular, *adj* 1. titular, official; 2. *nm* headline; 3. *nm/f* holder, occupant; head.

título, *nm* 1. title, section heading; 2. titled person; 3. professional qualification; diploma, certificate; degree.

tiza, *nf* chalk.

tizar, *vt* to plan to design, model, to mark out for cutting.

tizna, *nf* black, grime.

tiznar, *vt* to blacken, black, to smudge, soil.

tizne, *nm* soot, black smear, blackening; grime.

tizo, *nm* burning piece of wood, brand.

tizón, *nm* burning piece of wood, brand; half-burned piece of wood.

tizonazos, *nm* pains of hell.

tizonear, *vt* to poke, stir.

toalla, *nf* towel.

toallero, *nm* towel-rail.

tobar, *vt* to tow.

tobera, *nf* nozzle.

tobillera, *nf* ankle-sock.

tobillo, *nm* ankle.

tobogán, *nm* toboggan.

toca, *nf* headdress; bonnet.

tocadiscos, *nm* record player, phonograph.

tocador, *nm* dressing table.

tocador(a), *nm/f* player.

tocante, *prep* with regard to, about; so far as concerns.

tocar, *vt* to touch; to feel; to handle.

tocayo(a), *nm/f* namesake.

tocinillo, *nm* pudding made with egg yolk and syrup.

tocino, *nm* bacon; salt pork.

tocología, *nf* obstetrics,

tocólogo(a), *nm/f* obstetrician.

todavía, *adv* still, yet; no not yet.

todo, *adj* all; whole, entire; every.

toga, *nf* gown, robe.

togado(a), *nm/f* lawyer.

tolda, *nf* canvas; tent, improvised hut; shelter.

toldillo, *nm* mosquito net.

toldo, *nm* sunshade, awning; sunblind; marquee.

tolerancia, *nf* tolerance; toleration.

tolerante, *adj* tolerant.

tolerar, *vt* to tolerate; to bear, endure.

tolva, *nf* hopper; chute, hopper wagon, hopper car.

tolvanera, *nf* dustcloud.

toma, *nf* 1. taking; 2. capture, taking; seizure.

tomacorriente, *nm* plug.

tomada, *nf* plug.

tomado, *adj* 1. rusty; 2. hoarse; 3. to be drunk.

tomador, *adj* drunken, boozy.

tomar, *vt* to take; to accept; to get.

tomatal, *nm* tomato bed; tomato field.

tomate, *nm* tomato.

tomatero(a), *nm/f* 1. tomato plant; 2. tomato grower; tomato dealer.

tomo, *nm* volume.

tomografía, *nf* scanner.

tonada, *nf* tune, song air.

tonadilla, *nf* little tune; merry tune light-hearted song.

tonalidad, *nf* key; tonality.

tonel, *nm* barrel, cask, vat, keg.

tonelada, *nf* ton.

tonelaje, *nm* tonnage.

tonelero, *nm* cooper.

tonelete, *nm* cask, keg.

tonga, *nf* layer, stratum; pile.

tongada, *nf* layer; coat, covering.

tónica, *nf* 1. tonic; keynote; 2. tone, trend tendency.

tónico, *adj* 1. tonic; stressed, accented; 2. tonic, invigorating, stimulating.

tonificador, *adj* invigorating stimulating.

tonificar, *vt* to tone up; to invigorate, fortify.

tonillo, *nm* singsong, monotone, monotonous voice.

tono, *nm* tone; pitch; key.

tontear, *vi* to fool about, act the fool; to talk nonsense.

tontería, *nf* silliness, foolishness, stupidity.

tonto, *adj* silly, foolish, stupid; imbecile.

topacio, *nm* topaz.

topadora, *nf* bulldozer.

topar, *vt* to butt, horn.

tope, *adj* invar top, maximum.

topetar, *vt* to butt, bump.

tópico, *adj* for external application.

topo, *nm* mole; clumsy person, blunderer.

topografía, *nf* topography.

topográfico, *adj* topographic(al).

topógrafo(a), *nm/f* topographer; surveyor.

toque, *nm* touch.

toquetear, *vt* 1. to touch repeatedly, handle, keep fingering; 2. to fondle, feel up, touch up .

torácico, *adj* thoracic.

tórax, *nm* thorax.

torbellino, *nm* whirlwind; dust cloud.

torcedor, *nm* spindle, torture, torment.

torcedura, *nf* twist(ing); sprain, strain, wrench.

torcer, *vt* to twist; to bend; to warp.

torcida, *nf* wick.

torcido, *adj* twisted; bent; crooked.

tordillo, *adj* dappled, dapple-grey.

tordo, *adj* dappled, dapple-grey.

torear, *vt* to fight, play.

toreo, *nm* bullfighting.

torero, *nm* bullfighter.

torete, *nm* 1. small bull, young bull; 2. strong boy, robust child; rough child.

toril, *nm* bullpen.

tormenta, *nf* storm.

tormento, *nm* torture; torture, torment; anguish.

torna, *nf* return.

tornadera, *nf* pitchfork, winnowing fork.

tornado, *nm* tornado.

tornar, *vt* 1. to give back, return; 2. to change, alter, transform (into).

tornasol, *nm* sunflower.

tornear, *vt* to turn (on a lathe).

torneo, *nm* tournament, competition; tourney, joust.

tornero(a), *nm/f* machinist, turner, lathe operator.

tornillo, *nm* screw; bolt.

torniquete, *nm* turnstile, tourniquet.

toro, *nm* 1. bull; 2. strong man, he-man.

toronja, *nf* grapefruit.

torpe, *adj* clumsy, awkward; slow, ungainly; sluggish, heavy.

torpedear, *vt* to torpedo.

torpedero, *nm* torpedo boat.

torpedo, *nm* torpedo.

torpeza, *nf* clumsiness, awkwardness; slowness, ungainliness; sluggishness, heaviness.

torrencial, *adj* torrential.

torre, *nf* tower.

torrente, *nm* rushing stream, mountain stream, torrent.

tórrido, *adj* torrid.

torrija, *nf* French toast.

torso, *nm* torso; head and shoulder; bust.

torta, *nf* cake; tart, flan; pancake.

tortear, *vt* to flatten, roll.

tortícolis, *nf* crick in the neck, stiff neck.

tortilla, *nf* omelet(te).

tortita, *nf* pancake.

tórtola, *nf* turtledove.

tortuga, *nf* tortoise; turtle.

tortuoso, *adj* winding, tortuous, full of bends; devious.

tortura, *nf* torture.

torturado(a), *nm/f* torture victim.

torturar, *vt* to torture.

toruno, *nm* stud bull.

tosedera, *nf* nagging cough.

toser, *vi* to cough.

tosquedad, *nf* coarseness, roughness, crudeness.

tostada, *nf* toast, piece of toast.

tostado(a), *adj* 1. toasted; dark brown, sunburnt.

tostador, *nm/f* toaster; roaster.

tostar, *vt* to toast; to roast; to brown, to tan.

tostarse, *vr* to tan, brown, get brown.

tostón, *nm* 1. small cube of toast, crouton; 2. toast dipped in oil; toasted chickpea.

total, *adj* total; whole, complete; utter, sheer.

totalitario, *adj* totalitarian.

totalizar, *vt* to totalize, add up.

tóxico, *adj* toxic, poisonous.

toxicología, *nf* toxicology.

toxicológico, *adj* toxicological.

toxicólogo(a), *nm/f* toxicologist.

toxicomanía, *nf* drug-addiction.

toxina, *nf* toxin.

tozudez, *nf* obstinacy.

tozudo, *adj* obstinate.

traba, *nf* bond, tie; crosspiece.

trabajado, *adj* 1. worn out, weary from overwork; 2. carefully worked, elaborately fashioned.

trabajador(a), *adj* 1. hard-working, industrious; 2. *nm/f* worker.

trabajar, *vt* to work, till.

trabajo, *nm* work; job, task.

trabar, *vt* to join, unite, link.

trabarse, *vr* o get entangled, get tangled up.

trabilla, *nf* small strap; clasp; belt loop.

tracción, *nf* traction; haulage.

tractor, *adj* 1. drive wheel; 2. *nm* tractor.

tractorista, *nm/f* tractor-driver.

tradición, *nf* tradition.

tradicional, *adj* traditional.

traducción, *nf* translation; rendering, interpretation.

traducir, *vt* to translate (into, from); to render, interpret.

traductor(a), *nm/f* translator.

traer, *vt* to bring, get, fetch; to carry; to take.

trafagar, *vi* to bustle about; to be on the move, keep on the go.

tráfago, *nm* traffic, trade.

traficante, *nm/f* trader, dealer.

traficar, *vi* to trade, deal (with, in); to buy and sell.

tráfico, *nm* trade, business; trafic.

tragaderas, *nf* throat, gullet, gullibility.

tragadero, *nm* throat, gullet.

tragador(a), *nm/f* glutton; great walker.

tragaluz, *nm* skylight.

tragar, *vt* to swallow; to swallow down, drink up, to gulp down, get down.

tragedia, *nf* tragedy.

trágico, *adj* tragic(al).

tragicomedia, *nf* tragicomedy,

traición, *nf* treachery; treason; betrayal.

traicionar, *vt* to betray.

traicionero, *adj* treacherous.

traído, *adj* worn, old, threadbare.

traidor, *adj* treacherous; treasonable.

traidora, *nf* traitress; betrayer.

trailla, *nf* 1. scraper, leveller; harrow; 2. lead, leash; lash.

traje, *nm* dress, costume; suit.

trajear, *vt* to clothe, dress, to get up, rig out.

trajín, *vt* 1. haulage, carriage, transport, 2. coming and going, movement.

trajinado, *adj* well-worked, overworked.

trajinar, *vt* to carry, cart; to transport.

trama, *nf* weft, woof.

tramar, *vt* to weave.

tramitación, *nf* transaction; negotiation; steps.

tramitar, *vt* to transact; to negotiate.

trámite, *nm* step, stage; transaction.

tramo, *nm* section, stretch; length; span.

tramontar, *vi* to sink behind the mountains.

tramoya, *nf* piece of stage machinery.

tramoyar, *vt* to swindle.

tramoyista, *nm* scene shifter, stagehand, swindler, trickster.

trampa, *nf* 1. trapdoor; hatch; fly; 2. trap; snare; bunker.

trampear, *vt* 1. to cheat, swindle; 2. *vi* to cheat; to get money by false pretences.

trampolín, *nm* springboard, diving-board:

tramposo, *adj* crooked, tricky, swindling.

tranca, *nf* stick, cudgel, club; legs.

trancar, *vt* 1. to bar; 2. to box in, block, shut in.

trancazo, *nm* blow, bang.

trance, *nm* difficult moment, juncture, situation; critical juncture.

tranque, *nm* dam; reservoir.

tranquera, *nf* 1. palisade, fence; 2. cattle-gate.
tranquilidad, *nf* stillness calmness, tranquillity.
tranquilizador, *adj* soothing; lulling; reassuring.
tranquilizar, *vt* to calm, quieten, still; to reassure.
tranquilo, *adj* still, calm. tranquil; peaceful; quiet.
transacción, *nf* transaction; deal, bargain.
transar, *vt* to trade.
transatlántico, *adj* transatlantic.
transbordador, *nm* ferry; shuttle.
transbordar, *vt* to transfer, move across, switch; to tranship.
transbordo, *nm* transfer; move, switch; transhipment; ferrying.
transcribir, *vt* to transcribe; to transliterate.
transcripción, *nf* transcription; transliteration.
transcurrir, *vi* to pass, go by, elapse.
transcurso, *nm* course of time, passing of time, lapse of time.
transferencia, *nf* transference; transfer.
transferir, *vt* 1. to transfer; 2. to postpone.
transfiguración, *nf* transfiguration.
transfigurar, *vt* to transfigure (into).
transformación, *nf* transformation; change, conversion.
transformador, *nm* transformer.
transformar, *vt* to transform; to change, convert.
tránsfuga, *nm/f* deserter; turncoat; defector.
transfundir, *vt* 1. to transfuse; 2. to tell, spread, disseminate.
transfusión, *nf* transfusion; (blood transfusion).
transgredir, *vti* to transgress.
transgresión, *nf* transgression.
transgresor(a), *nm/f* transgressor.
transición, *nf* transition (to, from); transitional period.
transigencia, *nf* compromise; yielding.
transigente, *adj* accommodating, compromising; tolerant.
transigir, *vt* 1. to settle out of court; 2. *vi* to compromise to give way, yield.
transistor, *nm* transistor.
transitar, *vi* to go, go from place to place.
transitivo, *adj* transitive.
tránsito, *nm* transit, passage, movement.
transitorio, *adj* transitory; fleeting; temporary.
transliteración, *nf* transliteration.
transliterar, *vt* to transliterate,
translúcido, *adj* translucent.
transmigrar, *vi* to migrate, transmigrate.
transmisión, *nf* 1. transmission; transfer; 2. (Automobile) transmission; 3. (Radio & TV) broadcast(ing).
transmisor, *adj* transmitting; transmitter.
transmitir, *vt* to transmit; to transfer, to broadcast; to pass on, hand down.
transmutación, *nf* transmutation.
trasmutar, *vt* to transmute (into).
transparencia, *nf* transparency; clarity, clearness.
transparentar, *vt* to reveal, allow to be seen;
transparente, *adj* transparent; clear; plain.
transpiración, *nf* perspiration; transpiration.
transperar, *vi* to perspire; to transpire.
transponer, *vt* to transpose; to switch over, move about, change the places of.
transportación, *nf* transportation.
transportador, *nm* 1. conveyor, transporter; 2. protractor.
transportar, *vt* to transport; to haul, carry, take.
transporte, *nm* transport; haulage, carriage; transportation.

transposición, *nf* transposition.
transversal, *adj* transverse, cross; oblique.
transustanciación, *nf* transubstantiation.
tranvía, *nm* tram, tramcar, streetcar tramway.
trapeador, *nm* floor mop.
trapear, *vt* 1. to mop; 2. to beat, tan, to insult.
trapecio, *nm* trapeze; trapezium.
trapecista, *nm/f* trapeze artist(e).
trapichar, *vt* to smuggle; to deal in.
trapiche, *nm* olive-oil press; sugar mill.
trapichero, *nm* sugar-mill worker.
tráquea, *nf* trachea, windpipe.
traquido, *nm* crack; crack, bang.
tras, *prep* 1. behind; after; 2. across, beyond.
trascendencia, *nf* importance; significance, momentousness; transcendence.
trascender, *vi* 1. to smell; 2. to smack of, be suggestive of; to evoke, suggest; 3. to come out.
trasegar, *vt* to move about, switch round.
trasero, *adj* back, rear; hind.
trasfondo, *nm* background; undertone.
trasiego, *nm* move, switch; reshuffle; decanting; racking.
traslación, *nf* movement, passage; removal.
trasladar, *vt* 1. to move; to remove; 2. to postpone.
traslucir, *vt* to show, reveal, betray.
trasluz, *nf* diffused light; reflected light, glint, gleam.
trasnochado, *adj* stale, old.
trasnochador, *adj* given to staying up late.
trasnochar, *vt* 1. problema to sleep on; 2. *vi* to stay up late, go to bed late;
traspapelar, *vt* to lose, mislay, misplace.
traspasar, *vt* to pierce, penetrate, go through; to transfix.
traspaso, *nm* transfer, sale; conveyance.
traspatio, *nm* backyard.
traspie, *nm* slip, stumble, trip; to slip, trip, stumble.
trasplantar, *vt* to transplant.
trasplante, *nm* transplanting, transplant, transplantation.
trasquiladura, *nf* shearing, clipping.
trasquilar, *vt* to shear, clip; to crop.
trastada, *nf* stupid act, senseless act; mischief, prank.
trastear, *vt* 1. to play; 2. to move around; to mess up, disarrange.
trastera, *nf* lumber room.
trastienda, *nf* back room (of a shop), room behind a shop.
trastornado, *adj* persona mad, crazy.
trastornar, *vt* to overturn, upset.
trastrabillar, *vt* to trip, stumble.
trastrocar, *vt* to switch over, change round; to reverse, invert.
trata, *nf* slave trade.
tratado, *nm* agreement; treaty, pact.
tratamiento, *nm* treatment; processing.
tratar, *vt* 1. to treat, handle; to process; 2. to have dealings with sb.
trato, *nm* intercourse, dealings; relationship.
trauma, *nm* trauma, injury.
traumático, *adj* traumatic.
traumatizante, *adj* traumatic.
traumatizar, *vt* to traumatise; to shock, affect profoundly, shake to the core.
traumatología, *nf* orthopedic surgery.
travesaño, *nm* crosspiece, crossbeam; crossbar.
travesear, *vi* to play around; to play up, be mischievous, be naughty.

travesía, nf 1. cross-street, short street which joins two others; road that passes through a village; 2. crossing, voyage; crossing; distance travelled, distance to be crossed.

travestirse, vr to dress in clothes of the other sex.

travesura, nf prank, lark, piece of mischief.

traviesa, nf crossbeam, rafter.

travieso, adj naughty, mischievous; restless.

trayectoria, nf 1. trajectory, path; 2. course of development, evolution.

traza, nf plan, design; layout.

trazada, nf line, course, direction.

trazado, adj 1. shapely, well-formed; good-looking; 2. nm plan, design; layout; outline, sketch.

trazador, adj tracer; 2. nm planner, designer.

trazadora, nf tracer, tracer bullet.

trazar, vt to plan, design, to lay out; to draw, trace.

trazo, nm line, stroke; 2. sketch, outline.

trébol, nm clover, trefoil.

trece, adj thirteen; thirteenth.

trecho, nm stretch; length, distance.

tregua, nf truce.

treinta, adj thirty; thirtieth.

treintena, nf thirty; about thirty.

tremedal, nm quaking bog.

tremendo, adj 1. terrible, dreadful, frightful; 2. imposing, awesome; 3. tremendous; awful, terrific; 4. inventive, witty, entertaining.

tremolar, vt 1. to wave; 2. to show off, flaunt.

trémulo, adj quivering, tremulous; timid,small; flickering.

tren, nm train.

trencilla, nf braid.

trenista, nm 1. owner of a workshop; company manager; 2. railwayman.

trenza, nf 1. plait; pigtail, ponytail; tress; braid; plait; twist; postizn switch, hairpiece; 2. string; 3. shoelaces.

trenzado, adj plaited; braided; twisted together, intertwined.

trepa, nf climb, climbing.

trepaderas, nf climbing-irons.

trepado, nm 1. drilling, boring; 2. perforation.

trepador, adj 1. climbing, rambling; 2. nm climber, rambler.

trepadora, nf climber, rambler.

trepanar, vt to trepan.

trepar, vti to climb (up), clamber up; to scale.

trepidacion, nf shaking, vibration.

trepidar, vi 1. to shake, vibrate; 2. to hesitate, waver.

treque, adj witty, funny.

tres, adj three; third.

trescientos, adj three hundred.

tresillo, nm 1. three-piece suite; triplet.

treta, nf 1. feint; 2. trick; ruse, stratagem; stunt, gimmick.

triangulación, nf triangulation.

triangular, adj triangular; three-cornered.

triángulo, nm triangle.

tribal, adj tribal.

tribu, nf tribe.

tribulación, nf tribulation.

tribuna, nf 1. platform, rostrum, stand, grandstand.

tribunal, nm court.

tributación, nf 1. payment; 2. taxation.

tributar, vt 1. to pay; to give; 2. vi to pay taxes; 3. taxation.

tributo, nm 1. tribute; 2. tax.

triciclo, nm tricycle.

tricolor, adj tricolour, three-coloured.

tricornio, nm three-cornered hat.

tricota, nf sweater.

tricotar, vti to knit; hand-knitted.

tridente, nm trident.

trienal, adj triennial.

trienio, nm 1. period of three years; 2. monthly bonus for each three-year period worked with the same employer.

trifásico, adj three-phase, triphase.

trifulca, nf row, shindy.

trigal, nm wheat field.

trigésimo, adj thirtieth.

trigo, nm wheat.

trigonometría, nf trigonometry.

trigonométrico, adj trigonometric(al).

trigueño, adj 1. corn-coloured, dark blonde; 2. light brown, golden-brown.

trilogía, nf trilogy.

trilla, nf 1. threshing; 2. thrashing, beating; 3. track; 4. short cut.

trillado, adj 1. threshed; 2. beaten, well-trodden;

trillador, nm thresher.

trilladora, nf threshing machine.

trilladura, nf threshing.

trillar, vt 1. to thresh; 2. to use a lot, wear out by frequent use.

trillizo, nm triplet.

trillo, nm 1. threshing machine; 2. rib, path, track.

trillón, nm trillion.

trimestral, adj quarterly, three-monthly.

trimestre, nm 1. quarter, period of three months.

trinar, vi to trill; to sing, warble.

trincar, vt 1. to tie up, tie firmly; to lash; 2. to pinion, hold by the arms.

trinchador, nm carving-knife, carver.

trinchar, vt to carve, slice, cut up.

trinche, nm 1. fork; 2. sidetable; 3. pitchfork.

trinchera, nf trench, entrenchment; fence, stockade.

trineo, nm sledge, sleigh; bobsleigh; dog sleigh.

trinidad, nf trio, set of three.

trino, nm warble; trill; trill.

trío, nm trio.

tripa, nf 1. intestine, gut; 2. core, seeds.

tripartito, adj tripartite.

tripear, vi to stuff off.

triperío, nm guts, entrails.

tripero, adj greedy.

triple, adj triple; threefold; of three layers.

triplicado, adj triplicate; in triplicate.

triplicar, vt to treble, triple.

trípode, nm tripod.

tripulación, nf crew.

tripulado, adj manned ilight; manned by.

tripulante, nm crew member, crewman.

tripular, vt 1. to man; 2. to drive.

triquiñuela, nf trick, dodge; dodges, funny business.

trisar, vt to crack; to chip.

triunfo, nm 1. uproar, rumpus, row. 2. mockery; private joke.

trisecar, vt to trisect.

trisílabo, adj trisyllabic, three-syllabled.

trisito, nm pinch; scrap, piece.

triste, adj miserable; gloomy; sorrowful; gloomy.

tristeza, nf adj sadness; misery; gloom; sorrow; gloominess, melancholy.

trituración, nf trituration; grinding, crushing.

triturador, nm/f grinder, crushing machine; mincer.

triturar, vt to triturate; to grind, crush, pulverize.

triunfador(a), adj 1. triumphant; winning; 2. nm/f victor, winner.

triunfal, *adj* 1. triumphal; 2. triumphant.

triunfante, *adj* triumphant; winning; to come out the winner, emerge victorious.

triunfar, *vi* to triumph; to win.

triunfo, *nm* triumph; win, victory; success.

trivial, *adj* trivial, trite, commonplace.

triza, *nf* bit, fragment; shred.

trizar, *vt* to smash to bits; to tear to shreds.

trocar, *vt* to exchange, barter; 2. to mix up, confuse; 3. to sell; to buy.

trocear, *vt* to cut up, cut into pieces.

trocha, *nf* 1. by-path, narrow path; short cut; 2. gauge; normal standard gauge.

trochar, *vi* to trot.

trole, *nm* 1. trolley, trolley pole; 2. trolley bus.

tromba, *nf* whirlwind; violent downpour.

trombón, *nm* trombone;

trombonista, *nm/f* trombonist.

trombosis, *nf* thrombosis; cerebral haemorrhage.

trompa, *nf* horn; hunting horn.

trompada, *nf* 1. bump, bang; head-on collision; 2. punch, swipe.

trompeta, *nf* 1. trumpet; bugle clarion.

trompetear, *vi* to play the trumpet.

trompetero, *nm* trumpet player.

trompetilla, *nf* 1. ear trumpet; 2. raspberry .

trompicón, *nm* 1. stumble, trip; 2. with difficulty; blow, punch.

trompo, *nm* 1. spinning top; humming-top; 2. clumsy person.

trompón, *nm* bump, bang; hefty punch, vicious swipe.

tronada, *nf* thunderstorm.

tronca, *nf* bird.

tronco, *nm* 1. trunk; stem, stalk; log; tree stump.

troncha, *nf* slice; chunk, piece.

tronchado, *nm* gold mine , prosperous business.

tronchar, *vt* 1. to bring down; to chop down, 2. to cut off, cut short.

tronera, *nf* 1. loophole, embrasure; small window; 2. pocket; 3. chimney, flue.

tronido, *nm* thunderclap; loud report, bang, detonation; boom.

trono, *nm* to inherit the crown; to ascend the throne, come to the throne.

tronzar, *vt* to cut up; to split, rend, smash.

tropa, *nf* troop, body, crowd; troop, mob.

tropel, *nm* 1. mob, crowd, throng; 2. jumble, mess, litter ; rush, haste.

tropezar, *vti* 1. to trip, stumble on, to run into, run up against.

tropical, *adj* rhetorical, melodramatic, highly-coloured.

trópico, *nm* tropic; tropics.

tropiezo, *nm* 1. slip, blunder, moral lapse; 2. misfortune, mishap; setback.

tropilla, *nf* drove, team.

tropo, *nm* trope, figure of speech.

troquel, *nm* die.

troquelado, *nm* hot-die forging, punching; moulding, shaping.

trotar, *vi* 1. to trot; to travel about, chase around here and there; to hustle.

trote, *nm* trot; jogtrot; to trot, go at a trot.

trovador, *nm* troubadour.

troza, *nf* log.

trozo, *nm* 1. bit, piece; chunk; fragment; 2. passage; section.

truco, *nm* trick, device, dodge; effect, piece of trick.

truculento, *adj* horrifying, terrifying; full of extravagant effects.

trucha, *nf* trout.

truchero, *nm* hawker, vendor.

trueno, *nm* thunder.

trueque, *nm* 1. exchange; switch; barter; 2. in exchange for.

truhán, *nm* 1. jester, buffoon, funny man; 2. rogue, crook.

truhanería, *nf* 1. buffoonery; 2. roguery, crookedness, swindling.

trujal, *nm* winepress; olive-oil press.

truncado, *adj* truncated, shortened; incomplete,

truncar, *vt* to truncate, shorten; to cut off; to cut short, curtail.

trunco, *adj* truncated, shortened; incomplete.

truquero, *adj* tricky; gimmicky.

trusa, *nf* 1. bathing trunks; 2. underpants; panties, knickers; pants.

truzas, *nf* knickers.

tu, *adj* pos your.

tubérculo, *nm* 1. tuber; 2. tubercle

tuberculosis, *nf* tuberculosis.

tuberculoso, *adj* tuberculous, tubercular.

tubería, *nf* pipes, piping; tubes, tubing; pipeline,

tubero, *nm* plumber, pipe-fitter.

tubo, *nm* 1. tube; pipe; set, earpiece; capillary; chimneypot, drainpipe, waste-pipe; alimentary canal; test-tube; 2. tube, underground.

tubular, *adj* 1. tubular 2. *nm* roll-on.

tuerca, *nf* nut; mariposa wingnut; to tighten the screws on sb.

tuerce, *nm* misfortune, setback.

tuerto, *adj* 1. twisted, bent, crooked; 2. one-eyed, blind in one eye; 3. upside-down; back to front. 4. *nm nf* one-eyed person, person blind in one eye; 5. *nm* wrong, injustice.

tueste, *nm* roasting.

tuétano, *nm* 1. marrow; pith; 2. core, essence.

tufillo, *nm* slight smell.

tufo, *nm* 1. vapour, gas, exhalation; 2. bad smell, stink; body odour ; bad breath; fug; 3. *nm* curl, sidelock.

tul, *nm* net.

tulipa, *nf* lampshade.

tulipán, *nm* tulip; hibiscus.

tulipanero, *nm* tulip-tree.

tullido, *adj* crippled; paralysed. paralytic

tullir, *vt* to cripple, maim; to paralyze; to wear out, exhaust. to abuse, maltreat.

tumba, *nf* 1. tomb, grave; 2. shake, jolt; lurch. somersault.

tumbadora, *nf* large conga drum.

tumbar, *vt* 1. to knock down, knock over, knock to the ground; 2. to fall down, to capsize; 3. to lie down; to stretch out; to sprawl, loll; to lie, be lying down. 4. to go flat; 5. to give up, decide to take it easy.

tumbo, *nm* fall, tumble; shake, jolt.

tumefacto, *adj* swollen.

tumido, *adj* swollen, tumid.

tumor, *nm* tumour, growth; cerebral brain tumour; malignant growth.

túmulo, *nm* tumulus, barrow, burial mound; mound.

tumulto, *nm* turmoil, commotion, uproar, tumult; riot, disturbance; popular popular rising.

tumultuoso, *adj* tumultuous; riotous, disorderly; rebellious.

tuna, *nf* student music group.

tunante, *nm* rogue, villain, crook.

tunantería, nf 1. villainy, crookedness; 2. villainy, dirty trick.

tunda, nf 1. beating, thrashing; 2. to wear out.

tundir, vt 1. to beat, thrash; 2. to exhaust, tire out.

tundra, nf tundra.

túnel, nm 1. tunnel; 2. dark passage; dark period.

tunelar, vi to tunnel.

túnica, nf tunic; robe, gown, long dress.

tupé, nm 1. hairpiece; 2. nerve, cheek.

tupición, nf 1. blockage, stoppage, obstruction; 2. dense crowd, throng; 3. blocked, stopped up, obstructed.

tupir, vt 1. to pack tight, press down, compact; 2. to block, stop up, obstruct.

turba, nf 1. crowd, throng; swarm; mob; rabble.

turbación, nf 1. disturbance; 2. perturbation, worry, alarm; embarrassment.

turbado, adj disturbed, worried, upset; embarrassed.

turbador, adj disturbing, alarming; embarrassing.

turbante, nm 1. turban; 2. gourd, calabash.

turbar, vt 1. to disturb; 2. to disturb, worry; 3. to stir up.

turbina, nf turbine.

turbio, adj 1. cloudy, thick, turbid, muddy; 2. misty, blurred; disturbed; unclear confused; 3. restless, unsettled, turbulent.

turbión, nm heavy shower, downpour; squall. shower, torrent; swarm; hail.

turbonada, nf sudden storm, squall.

turbulencia, nf turbulence; troubled nature, unsettled character; storminess.

turbulento, adj turbulent; troubled, unsettled, turbulent; stormy.

turgencia, nf turgidity.

turgente, adj turgid, swollen.

turismo, nm tourism; touring, sightseeing; tourist trade.

turista, nm/f tourist; sightseer, visitor, holidaymaker.

turnar, vi to take (it in) turns.

turno, nm 1. order (of priority); 2. turn; spell, period of duty; shift.

turquesa, nf turquoise,

turquí, adj deep blue.

turrón, nm 1. nougat; 2. cushy government job; sinecure, political plum.

turulato, adj dazed, stunned, flabbergasted.

tusa, nf cob (of corn) corncob.

tutear, vt 1. to address person sing; 2. to be on equal terms with.

tutela, nf guardianship; protection,

tutelado, nm pupil; ward.

tutelar, adj 1. tutelary; 2. to protect, guard; to advise, guide; to supervise, oversee.

tutor(a), nm/f 1. guardian; tutor; form master or mistress; 2. prop, stake.

tutoría, nf 1. guardianship; 2. tutorial, class.

tutorial, adj tutorial.

tuyo, adj yours, of yours; thy, of thine; it is yours.

U, u, nf (letter) U, u.

ubérrimo, adj exceptionally fertile, marvellously productive, very rich.

ubicar, vt 1. to place, put, locate, situate; to site; to find, locate; 2. to instal in a place.

ubicuo, adj ubiquitous.

ufanarse, vr to boast; to be vain, be conceited; to boast of, pride, be vain about.

ufanía, nf pride; vanity, conceit; boastfulness.

ufano, adj 1. proud; gay, cheerful; exultant; vain, conceited; boastful; 2. nf study of unidentified flying objects, ufology.

úlcera, nf ulcer, sore; bedsore; duodenal

ulceración, nf ulceration.

ulcerar, vt 1. to make sore, make a sore on, ulcerate.

ulterior, adj 1. farther, further; 2. later, subsequent; eventual.

ultimación, nf completion, conclusion.

ultimador(a), nm/f killer, murderer.

ultimar, vt 1. to finish, complete, conclude; to finalize; 2. to finish off, grace to; to kill, murder.

ultimato, adj 1. ultimatum.

último, adj 1. last; latest, most recent; latter; 2. furthest, most remote; back; top, topmost; lowest, bottom.

ultra, adj extreme, extremist.

ultracorto, adj ultra-short.

ultrajador, adj outrageous; offensive; insulting.

ultrajar, vt to outrage; to offend; to insult, revile, abuse.

ultraje, nm outrage; insult.

ultramar, nm countries beyond the seas, foreign parts; overseas.

ultrarrápido, adj extra fast.

ultratumba, nf what lies beyond the grave; life beyond the grave, life in the next world.

ultravioleta, adj ultraviolet.

ulular, vi to howl, shriek; to hoot, screech.

umbilical, adj umbilical.

umbral, nm threshold.

unánime, adj unanimous.

unanimidad, nf unanimity; por unanimously.

unción, nf anointing.

uncir, vt to yoke.

undécimo, adj eleventh.

ungido, adj anointed;

ungir, vt to anoint, put ointment on, rub with ointment.

unicameral, adj single-chamber.

unicelular, adj unicellular, single-cell.

único, adj only; sole, single, solitary; unique.

unicolor, adj one-colour, all one colour.

unicornio, nm unicorn.

unidad, nf unity; oneness; togetherness.

unido, adj 1. joined (by), linked (by); 2. united;

unifamiliar, adj single-family .

unificación, nf unification.

unificar, vt to unite, unify.

uniformado, adj 1. uniformed; 2. nm man in uniform.

uniformar, vt 1. to make uniform; to level up; to standardize, make the same; 2. to put into uniform, provide a uniform for.

uniformidad, nf uniformity; levelness, evenness, regularity.

uninigénito, adj only begotten; the Only Begotten Son.

unilateral, adj unilateral, one-sided.

unión, nf 1. union, uniting, joining; 2. unity; closeness, togetherness. 3. marriage; together with, accompanied by.

U

unipersonal, *adj* for one (person); single, individual.

unir, *vt* to join, unite; to tie together; to unite.

unísono, *adj* unisonous, on the same tone.

universal, *adj* universal; world-wide; world history.

universalidad, *nf* universality.

universalizar, *vt* to universalize, make universal; to extend widely, bring into general use.

universidad, *nf* university.

universitario, *adj* university; academic.

universitaria, *nf* (profesor) university teacher; university student;

universo, *nm* universe; world.

uno, *adj* 1. one; one and the same, identical; 2. *pron* somebody; oneself.

untar, *vt* 1. to smear, dab, rub to anoint, dip, soak 2. to bribe, grease 3. untarse vrto smear 4. to take a rake-off,

unto, *nm* soft substance; ointment, unguent; grease

untuoso, *adj* greasy, oily, sticky.

uñada, *nf* nail mark; scratch.

uñalarga, *nm/f* thief.

uñero, *nm* 1. whitlow. 2. ingrowing nail. 3. thumb-notch.

uranio, *nm* uranium; enriched uranium.

urbanidad, *nf* courtesy, politeness, urbanity.

urbanismo, *nm* 1. town planning; urban development. 2. real-estate development .

urbanista, *nm/f* town planner.

urbanita, *nm/f* city dweller.

urbanización, *nf* 1. urbanization; urban development. 2. housing estate, residential development.

urbanizado, *adj* built-up.

urbanizadora, *nf* property development company.

urbanizar, *vt* 1. tierra to develop, build on, urbanize; to lay out and prepare for city development. 2. to civilize.

urbano, *adj* urbane.

urbe, *nf* large city, metropolis; capital city.

urdimbre, *nf* 1. warp. 2. scheme, intrigue.

urdir, *vt* 1. tela to warp. 2. to plot, scheme for, contrive .

urente, *adj* burning, stinging.

urgencia, *nf* 1. urgency; pressure; haste, rush; 2. emergency; 3. pressing need.

urgir, *vi* to be urgent, be pressing;

urinario, *adj* 1. urinary. 2. public lavatory, comfort station

urna, *nf* urn;glass case; ballot-box;

urología, *nf* urology.

urólogo, *nm/f* urologist.

usanza, *nf* usage, custom;

utilitario, *vt* 1. to use, make use of; 2. to be accustomed to 3. to be used, be in use:

uslero, *nm* rolling-pin,

uso, *nm* 1. use; article for personal use; 2. wear, wear and tear; 3. custom, usage; fashion, style;

usted(es), *pron* pers you (polite or formal address).

usual, *adj* usual, customary; ordinary; regular.

usuario, *nm/f* reader; road user; final end-user.

usufructo, *nm* usufruct, use; life interest

usura, *nf* usury;profiteering, racketeering.

usurario, *adj* usurious.

usurero, *nm/f* usurer profiteer, racketeer.

usurpación, *nf* usurpation; seizure, illegal taking; encroachment

usurpador, *nm/f* usurper.

usurpar, *vt* to usurp; to seize, take illegally; to encroach upon, make inroads into.

utensilio, *nm* tool, implement; utensils materials;

uterino, *adj* uterine;children born of the same mother;

útero, *nm* womb, uterus;

útil, *adj* 1. useful; usable, serviceable; handy; 2. working day, weekday; 3. tools, implements; tackle, equipment.

utilidad, *nf* 1. usefulness, utility; benefit. 2. profit, benefit; windfall profits; 3. utility.

utilización, *nf* use, utilization; reclamation.

utilizar, *vt* to use, make use of, utilize;

utopía, *nf* utopia.

uva, *nf* grape; gooseberry:

úvula, *nf* uvula.

uvular, *adj* uvular.

V, v, *nf* (letter) V, v.

vaca, *nf* 1. cow; dairy cow; 2. good business, profitable deal;

vacaburra, *nf* insult.

vacación, *nf* vacation; holiday(s)

vacacional, *adj* vacation holiday; holiday period.

vacacionista, *nm/f* holidaymaker, vacationer

vacada, *nf* herd of cows.

vacaje, *nm* cows, cattle; herd of cows;

vacante, *adj* 1. vacant, empty, unoccupied; 2. *nf* vacancy, place, 3. empty seat.

vacar, *vi* 1. to fall vacant, become vacant; to remain unfilled; 2. to cease work; to be idle. 3. to attend to, engage in, devote 4. to lack, be without.

vaciadero, *nm* 1. sink, drain; sump, rubbish tip, dumping ground.

vaciado, *adj* 1. cast in a mould; hollow-ground; a troquel die-cast; 2. cast, mould(ing).

vaciar, *vt* 1. to empty; drail to empty out; to pour, pour away; to run off; to drink up; 2. to hollow out; to cast. 3. to grind, sharpen.

vacilación, *nf* hesitancy, hesitation,

vacilada, *nf* 1. spree, binge; 2. joke; dirty joke; for a laugh.

vacilante, *adj* 1. unsteady; mueble wobbly, tottery; faltering, halting; uncertain; 2. flickering; 3. hesitant, uncertain,

vacilar, *vt* 1. to make fun of, tease; 2. to trick. to mess about, make difficulties for; 3. *vi* to be unsteady; to wobble, rock, move, shake; to totter; to reel, stagger; to stumble.

vacilón, *adj* 1. teasing, jokey; fun-loving; to be in a jokey mood; 2. *nm* tease, joker.

vacío, *adj* 1. empty; vacant, unoccupied; unfilled; unfurnished; 2. insubstantial; 3. vain; proud; 4. *nm* emptiness; void; vacuum.

vacuna, *nf* 1. vaccine; 2. vaccination.

vacunación, *nf* 1. vaccination; 2. preparation; inuring; forearming.

vacunar, *vt* 1. to vaccinate; 2. to prepare; to inure.

vacuno, *adj* 1. bovine; cow; cattle; 2. *nm* cattle.

vade, *nm* satchel, case.

vadeable, *adj* 1. fordable, which can be forded. 2. not impossible, not insuperable.

vadear, vt 1. to ford, to wade through, wade across; 2. dificultad to surmount, get round, overcome. 3. to sound out.

vado, nm 1. garage entrance; 2. way out, solution, to see no way out,find no solution; to look into possible solutions. respite.

vagabundear, vi to wander, roam, rove; to loaf, idle, bum.

vagabundeo, nm wandering, roving; tramp's life; loafing, idling, bumming.

vagabundo, adj wandering, roving; vagrant; vagabond.

vagación, nf free play.

vagancia, nf 1. vagrancy; 2. idleness, laziness.

vagante, adj 1. wandering, vagrant; 2. free, loose.

vagar, vi to wander (about), roam, rove;

vagina, nf vagina.

vaginal, adj vaginal.

vago, adj 1. vague; ill-defined, indistinct; indeterminate; 2. lazy, slack; unreliable; idle, unemployed; nused; 3. in vain; aimlessly, pointlessly; to loaf around.

vagón, nm coach, carriage, car; truck, wagon; car, van.

vaguedad, nf 1. vagueness; indistinctness; indeterminacy. 2. vague remark; woolly idea;

vaharada, nf puff, gust of breath; whiff; reek; smell.

vahear, vi to steam; to fume, give off fumes, smoke; to whiff,-reek, smell.

vahído, nm dizzy spell, blackout.

vaho, nm 1. vapour, steam; 2. mist, condensation; fumes; breath; whiff, reek, smell.

vaina, nf 1. sheath, scabbard;sheath, case; 2. pod; husk, shell; green beans. 3. problem, snag; nuisance, bother; 4. fluke, piece of luck. 5. swindle.

vainilla, nf vanilla.

vaivén, nm 1. to-and-fro movement, oscillation; rocking, backward and forward movement; 2. coming and going, constant movement; 3. change of fortune.

vajear, vt to fascinate, hypnotize; to bewitch; to win over by flattery, seduce.

vajilla, nf crockery, china; dishes; service.

vale, nm promissory note, IOU; voucher, coupon. warrant.

valedero, adj valid; binding.

valedura, nf help; protection; favour.

valentía, nf 1. bravery, courage; boldness; 2. boastfulness; 3. brave deed, heroic exploit; bold ac; 4. brag, boast.

valentón, adj 1. boastful; blustering, bullying; arrogant; 2. nm braggart; bluster, bully.

valentonada, nf boast, brag; piece of bluster; arrogant act.

valer, vt 1. to aid, protect; to serve; to help, avail; 2. to be equal to; 3. to cause; to earn; to win; to lose, cost; 4. to be worth; 5. to cost, be priced at, be valued at.

valeroso, adj brave, valiant.

valía, nf 1. worth, value; of great worth; 2. influence.

validación, nf validation; ratification.

validar, vt to validate, give effect to; to ratify.

válido, adj 1. valid; 2. strong, robust.

valiente, adj 1. brave; valiant; bold. 2. boastful, blustering; 3. fine, excellent; noble; strong; 4. nm/f brave man, brave woman; hero, heroine.

valija, nf case; suitcase; satchel; mailbag.

valijería, nf travel-goods shop.

valimiento, nm 1. value; benefit; 2. favour, protection; position of royal favourite.

valioso, adj 1. valuable; useful, beneficial; estimable; 2. wealthy.

valona, nf 1. artistically trimmed mane; to shave.

valonar, vt to trim, cut; to shear.

valor, nm 1. value, worth; price; 2. importance; meaning; rate; 3. profit; mark-up; 4. bravery, courage, valour.

valoración, nf 1. valuation; assessment, appraisal; 2. vt to value to price; to assess, appraise; to rate.

valorización, nf valuation; appraisal, assessment,

valorizar, vt to put up the price of.

vals, nm waltz.

valsar, vi to waltz.

valsear, vi to waltz.

valuador(a), nm/f valuer.

valva, nf valve.

válvula, nf valve; relief, escape; vent.

valla, nf 1. fence; 2. barricade; stockade; hurdle; obstacle, hindrance.

valladar, nm defence, barrier.

vallado, adj 1. fenced; 2. defensive wall; deep ditch.

vallar, vt to fence in, put up a fence round, enclose.

valle, nm valley.

vampirizar, vt to sap, milk, bleed dry.

vampiro, nm vampire.

vanagloria, nf vainglory.

vanagloriarse, vr to boast; to be vain, be arrogant; to boast of.

vanarse, vr to shrivel up; to fall through, come to nothing, produce no results.

vandálico, adj Vandal; loutish, destructive.

vandalismo, nm vandalism.

vándalo, adj vandal.

vanidad, nf unreality; groundlessness; uselessness, futility; shallowness.

vanidoso, adj vain, conceited; smug.

vano, adj unreal, imaginary, vain; idle; groundless; able; shallow, superficial; frivolous.

vapor, nm vapour; steam; fumes; mist, haze.

vapora, nf steam launch, steam engine.

vapor(e)ar, vt to evaporate; to give off vapour.

vaporización, nf vaporization.

vaporizador, nm vaporizer; spray.

vaporizar, vt to vaporize, convert into vapour; to spray.

vaporoso, adj 1. vaporous; steamy, misty; 2. airy, diaphanous.

vapulear, vt to beat; to thrash; flog.

vapuleo, nm beating; thrashing, flogging;

vaquerear, vi to play truant.

vaquería, nf 1. dairy, cattle farming, cattle tending.

vaquero, adj 1. cattle; 2. nm cowman; herdsman, cattle tender.

vaqueta, nf cowhide, leather.

vaquetón, adj unreliable, shifty; dim-witted; slow barefaced, brazen.

vara, nf stick, pole; rod, bar; rod; shaft.

varado, adj 1. stranded; to be aground; to be beached. 2. to be without regular work.

varal, nm long pole, stout stick; framework of poles; strut, support; shaft.

varar, vt 1. to launch. 2. vr to be stranded, run aground; to get stuck, get bogged down; to come to a standstill.

varazo, nm blow with a stick.

varazón, nf sticks, bunch of sticks.

varear, vt to beat, hit; to knock down (with poles).

varejón, nm stick, straight branch (stripped of leaves).

vareta, nf twig, small stick; lime twig for catching birds.

varga, nf steepest part of a slope.

variable, adj 1. variable, changeable; variable; 2. nf variable.

variación, *nf* variation; without varying, unchanged.

variado, *adj* varied; mixed; assorted; colores.

variante, *adj* 1. variant; 2. *nm* path; short cut.

variar, *vt* to vary, change, alter; to modify.

varicela, *nf* chickenpox.

várices, *nf* varicose veins.

varicoso, *adj* suffering from varicose veins.

variedad, *nf* variety; variation.

varilla, *nf* stick; twig, wand, switch; rod, bar.

varillaje, *nm* rods, links, linkage; ribs, ribbing.

varillar, *vt* to try out, train.

vario, *adj* varied; variegated, motley.

varita, *nf* wand; mágica de las virtudes magic wand.

varón, *adj* male; male child, boy, son, man.

varonil, *adj* manly, virile; vigorous.

vasallo, *nm* vassal.

vasar, *nm* kitchen dresser.

vasectomía, *nf* vasectomy.

vaselina, *nf* Vaseline, petroleum jelly; calm things down;

vasera, *nf* kitchen shelf, rack.

vasija, *nf* vessel; container, receptacle.

vaso, *nm* 1. glass, tumbler; vessel; container; vase, urn; 2. hoof, hull; boat, ship, vessel.

vastedad, *nf* vastness, immensity.

vasto, *adj* vast, huge, immense.

vaticinador, *nm* seer, prophet; forecaster.

vaticinar, *vt* to prophesy, predict; to forecast.

vaticinio, *nm* prophecy, prediction; forecast.

vecinal, *adj* 1. local; municipal; list of residents. 2. neighbourhood, community.

vecindario, *nm* neighbourhood; local community, residents; population, inhabitants.

vecino, *adj* neighbouring, adjacent, adjoining; near, nearby, close.

veda, *nf* 1. prohibition; imposition of a close season; 2. close season.

vedado, *nm* preserve; game preserve; to poach.

vedar, *vt* to prohibit, forbid, ban; to stop, prevent; idea.

vega, *nf* fertile plain, rich lowland area; water meadow(s).

vegetal, *adj* vegetable, plant.

vegetar, *vi* 1. to grow; 2. to vegetate, live like a vegetable;

vegetariano(a), *adj* 1. vegetarian; 2. *nm/f* vegetarian.

vegetativo, *adj* vegetative.

veguero, *adj* 1. lowland; of the plain; 2. *nm* lowland farmer; 3. tobacco planter.

vehemencia, *nf* vehemence; passion, impetuosity; fervour; eagerness, violence.

vehemente, *adj* vehement; passionate, impetuous; fervent, passionate; strong, eager, violent; orador passionate.

vehicular, *vt* to transport; to transmit, convey.

vehículo, *nm* 1. vehicle; spacecraft.

veinte, *adj* twenty; twentieth; the twenties.

veintena, *nf* twenty, a score; about twenty, about a score.

vejación, *nf* vexation, annoyance; to suffer vexations.

vejamen, *nm* satire, lampoon; shaft, taunt.

vejaminoso, *adj* irritating, annoying.

vejar, *vt* to vex, annoy; to scoff at; to harass.

vejatorio, *adj* 1. vexatious, annoying; humiliating, degrading; 2. peevishness; grouchiness, grumpiness; 3. old story.

vejiga, *nf* 1. bladder; gall-bladder; 2. blister.

vela, *nf* 1. wakefulness, state of being awake; sleeplessness; 2. horn; 3. candle, light; 4. *nf* sail; sailing;

velación, *nf* wake, vigil.

velada, *nf* party, social gathering.

velado, *adj* veiled; fogged, blurred; muffled.

velador, *nm* 1. watchman, caretaker; sentinel; 2. candlestick; 3. pedestal table; night table.

veladora, *nf* candle; table-lamp, bedside lamp.

velar, *vt* 1. to watch, keep watch over; to sit up with, stay by the bedside of; 2. to look covetously at; 3. *vi* to stay awake; to go without sleep; 4. to appear; 5. *vt* to veil; to shroud, hide, veil; to fog, blur.

velarte, *nm* broadcloth.

velatorio, *nm* funeral wake.

veleidoso, *adj* fickle, capricious, flighty.

velero, *adj* 1. fast; 2. *nm* sailing ship; 3. glider; 4. sailmaker.

veleta, *nf* 1. weather-vane, weathercock; 2. float; 3. *nm/f* weathercock, fickle person.

velo, *nm* to take the veil, become a nun; light covering; shroud.

velocidad, *nf* speed; rate, pace; velocity.

velocímetro, *nm* speedometer.

velódromo, *nm* cycle track.

velorio, *nm* 1. party, celebration, dull party; 2. wake, vigil for the dead.

veloz, *adj* fast, quick, swift.

vello, *nm* down, fuzz, hair.

vellón, *nm* 1. fleece; sheepskin; 2. tuft of wool; 3 copper and silver alloy..

vellosidad, *nf* downiness, fuzziness, hairiness; fluffiness.

velloso, *adj* downy, fuzzy, hairy; fluffy.

velludo, *adj* 1. hairy, shaggy; 2. *nm* plush, velvet.

vena, *nf* 1. vein, jugular vein; 2. seam, lode; grain.

venablo, *nm* javelin, dart, to burst out angrily.

venado, *nm* 1. deer, 2. contraband

venal, *adj* venous.

venático, *adj* rather crazy, a bit mad.

venatorio, *adj* hunting .

vencedor, *adj* 1. winning, victorious; successful; 2. *nm* winner, victor; conqueror.

vencer, *vt* enemigo to defeat, beat; to conquer, vanquish, overcome; surpass; to overcome; to win.

vencido, *adj* beaten, defeated; equipo etc losing, out of date.

vencimiento, *nm* 1. breaking, snapping; collapse, 2. expiration; maturity.

venda, *nf* bandage.

vendaje, *nm* dressing, bandaging.

vendar, *vt* 1. to bandage, dress; to cover, put a bandage over; 2. to blind.

vendaval, *nm* gale, strong wind, hurricane; storm.

vendedor, *adj* 1. selling; 2. *nm* seller, vendor; retailer; salesman; ambulante street seller; pedlar.

vendedora, *nf* seller; salesgirl, saleswoman.

vendepatrias, *nm/f* invar traitor.

vender, *vt* 1. to sell; to market; descubierto to sell short; 2. betray, to be sold; to sell at, sell for; to fetch, bring in;

vendimia, *nf* grape harvest, wine harvest.

vendimiar, *vt* 1. to harvest, pick, gather, 2. to take a profit from, to bump off.

venduta, *nf* 1. auction, public sale; 2. small grocery store.

vendutero, *nm* auctioneer, greengrocer.

veneno, *nm* poison, venom.

venenoso, *adj* poisonous, venomous.

venera, *nf* scallop; scallop shell.

veneración, nf veneration; worship.

venerando, adj venerable.

venerar, vt to venerate, revere; to worship.

venéreo, adj venereal disease.

venero, nm 1. lode, seam; 2. spring, source, origin.

vengador(a), adj 1. avenging; 2. nm/f avenger.

venganza, nf vengeance, revenge; retaliation.

vengar, vt 1. to avenge; 2. vr to take revenge offence to retaliate.

vengativo, adj espiritu, vindictive retaliatory.

venia, nf 1. pardon, forgiveness; 2. permission, consent.

venial, adj venial.

venida, nf coming; arrival; return, coming, future generations, posterity, our descendants.

venir, vi 1. to come, to arriv; 2. happen.

venoso, adj 1. venous; 2. veined, ribbed.

venta, nf 1. sale; selling; marketing; 2. country inn.

ventaja, nf 1. advantage; start, odds; 2. profit, gain; to bring in a good profit.

ventajear, vt 1. to outstrip, surpass; 2. to get the advantage of; 3. to better, improve on.

ventajista, adj unscrupulous; self-seeking, grasping; sly.

ventajoso, adj advantageous; profitable.

ventana, nf window.

ventanal, nm large window.

ventanilla, nf 1. small window; 2. bank counter; administrative office,

ventanillero, nm/f counter-clerk.

ventarrón, nm gale, violent wind, blast.

ventear, vt 1. to sniff; 2. to air, put out to dry, expose to the wind; 3. to snoop, pry, to inquire.

ventilado, adj draughty, breezy.

ventilador, nm ventilator; fan.

ventilar, vt 1. to ventilate; 2. to air, dry in the air.

ventisca, nf blizzard, snowstorm.

ventolada, nf strong wind, gale.

ventolera, nf 1. gust of wind, blast; 2. windmill; 3. vanity.

ventorrillo, nm small inn, roadhouse.

ventosa, nf 1. vent, airhole; 2. sucker;

ventosear, vi to break wind.

ventoso, adj 1. windy; windy, flatulent; 2. nm burglar.

ventral, adj ventral.

ventrículo, nm ventricle.

ventrilocuo(a), nm/f ventriloquist.

ventriloquia, nf ventriloquism.

ventrudo, adj fat, potbellied.

ventura, nf happiness; luck,(good) fortune; chance.

venturoso, adj happy; lucky, fortunate.

venus, nf venery, love-making, sexual delights.

ver, vti 1. to see; to look at, watch; 2. understand; 3. to look into, examine, inquire into.

vera, nf edge, verge, border; bank; beside, next to.

veracidad, nf truthfulness, veracity.

veranear, vi to spend the summer (holiday).

veraneo, nm summer holiday,

veraniego, adj summer (atr), slight, trivial.

verano, nm 1. summer; 2. dry season.

veranoso, adj dry.

verás, nf truth, reality; serious things; hard facts.

veráz, adj truthful, veracious.

verbal, adj verbal, oral.

verbalizar, vt to verbalize, express.

verbena, nf 1. verbena; 2. fair.

verbo, nm 1. verb; activo transitive verb; auxiliar verb; defective verb.

verdad, nf truth; truthfulness; reliability, trustworthiness.

verde, adj green.

verdín, nm 1. bright green, fresh green; 2. scum; moss.

verdolaga, nf to spread like wind.

verdugo, nm 1. executioner; hangman; 2. cruel master, slave-driver.

verdugón, nm 1. weal, welt; 2. twig, shoot, sprout.

verdulero(a), nm, nf greengrocer.

vereda, nf 1. path, lane; to fall into place; 2. pavement, sidewalk 3. village, settlement; section of a village.

veredicto, nm verdict.

verga, nf 1. rod, stick; yard, spar. 2. at the back of beyond. 3. penis.

vergel, nm garden; orchard.

vergonzoso, adj 1. persona bashful, shy, timid; modest; 2. disgraceful, shocking;

vergüenza, nf shame; sense of shame; bashfulness, shyness, timidity; embarrassment.

vericueto, nm rough part; rough track, piece of difficult terrain.

verídico, adj true, truthful.

verificable, adj verifiable.

verificación, nf check, checkup, inspection; testing.

verificar, vt to check, inspect; to test.

verja, nf grating, grille; railing(s).

vermicida, nm vermicide.

vernáculo, adj vernacular.

vernal, adj spring.

verosímil, adj (probable) likely; credible.

verosimilitud, nf likeliness, probability; credibility.

verraco, nm boar, male pig; wild boar.

verraquear, vi to grunt, to wail, howl with rage.

verraquera, nf crying spell, fit of rage, tantrum.

versación, nf expertise, skill.

versado, adj versed in, conversant with; expert in, skilled in.

versal, adj 1. capital; 2. nf capital (letter).

versar, vi 1. to go round, turn. 2. to deal with, discuss.

versátil, adj versatile, mobile, loose, easily turned.

versatilidad, nf versatility, mobility, looseness, ease of movement.

versículo, nm (Biblia) verse.

versificación, nf versification.

versificador, nm/f versifier.

versificar, vt 1. to versify, put into verse. 2. vi to write verses, versify.

versión, nf version; translation; adaptation.

versus, prep versus, against.

vértebra, nf vertebra.

vertebración, nf 1. support. 2. structuring, essential structure.

vertebrado, adj, nm vertebrate.

vertebrador, adj unifying force, force making for cohesion; central column; soporte principal support.

vertebrar, vt 1. to hold up, support; 2. to provide the backbone of, be the essential structure of.

vertedero, nm 1. rubbish dump, tip; 2. slope. hillside.

vertedor, nm 1. runway, overflow; drain, outlet; spillway; 2. scoop, bailer; 3. scoop, small shovel.

verter, vt 1. to pour (out); to empty (out); to pour, spill; 2. to translate (a into).

vertical, adj 1. uprigh; 2. nf vertical; straight (up).

vértice, nm 1. vertex, apex; top; 2. crown of the head.

vertido, nm 1. spillage; dumping; pouring; 2. waste; residue; effluent; el de residuos nucleares the disposal of nuclear waste.

vertiente, nf 1. slope; 2. side,

vertiginoso, *adj* 1. giddy, dizzy, vertiginous; 2. dizzy, excessive; very rapid.

vértigo, *nm* 1. giddiness, dizziness, vertigo; dizzy spell; it may cause giddiness; 2. sudden frenzy; fit of madness, aberration; 3. at a giddy speed.

vesania, *nf* rage, fury; insanity.

vesánico, *adj* raging, furious; insane.

vesícula, *nf* vesicle; blister; gall-bladder.

vespertino, *adj* evening .

vestíbulo, *nm* vestibule, lobby, hall; foyer.

vestido, *nm* 1. dress, costume, clothing; 2. dress, frock; costume, suit.

vestidor, *nm* dressing-room.

vestidura, *nf* 1. clothing, apparel; 2. vestments; sacerdotales priestly.

vestigio, *nm* vestige, trace; sign; remains, relics.

vestimenta, *nf* 1. clothing; gear, stuff, things; 2. vestments.

vestir, *vt* 1. to dress, to clothe, cover, drape 2. put on; to wear.

vestuario, *nm* 1. clothes, wardrobe; costumes; uniform; 2. dressing-room, backstage area.

veta, *nf* seam, vein, lode; grain; streak, stripe,

vetar(la), *vt* to veto; to blackball.

veteada, *nf* flogging, beating.

veteado, *adj* veined; grained; streaked, striped; streaky.

vetear, *vt* 1. to grain; to streak; 2. to flog, beat.

veteranía, *nf* status of being a veteran; long service; seniority.

veterano, *adj* veteran.

veterinaria, *nf* veterinary science, veterinary medicine.

veterinario, *nm/f* veterinary surgeon, veterinarian.

veto, *nm* veto; to veto; to have a veto.

vetustez, *nf* great age, antiquity.

vetusto, *adj* very old, ancient, venerable.

vez, *nf* 1. time, occasion; instance; at times; at the same time; sometimes; 2. once; 3. turn; in his turn.

vía, *nf* 1. road; route; track; lane (of a motorway); 2. passage, tube; tract; 3. system; way, means; channel.

viabilizar, *vt* to make viable.

viable, *adj* viable; plan etc feasible.

viada, *nf* speed.

viaducto, *nm* viaduct.

viajante, *adj* 1. travelling; 2. *nm* commercial traveller, salesman.

viajar, *vi* 1. to travel; to journey; to travel through; 2. to trip.

viaje, *nm* 1. trip; 2. voyage; 3. load; cartload, cartful.

viajero(a), *adj* 1. travelling; migratory; 2. *nm/f* traveller.

vial, *adj* road; traffic; road

vianda, *nf* 1. food, vegetables; 2. lunch tin, dinner pail.

viaraza, *nf* 1. fit of anger; 2. bright idea.

viático, *nm* 1. food for a journey; 2. travel allowance; travelling expenses.

víbora, *nf* 1. viper; 2. money belt.

vibración, *nf* vibration; shaking.

vibrador, *nm* vibrator.

vibráfono, *nm* vibraphone.

vibrante, *adj* vibrant, vibrating; ringing;

vibrar, *vt* to vibrate; to shake, rattle.

vibratorio, *adj* vibratory.

vicaria, *nf* woman priest.

vicario, *nm* curate; deputy; general vicar-general.

vice, *nm/f* deputy; second in command; vice-president.

vicealcalde(esa), *nm/f* deputy mayor.

vicealmirante, *nm* vice-admiral.

vicecónsul, *nm/f* vice-consul.

vicedirector(a), *nm/f* deputy director; deputy head-master, deputy headmistress.

vicegerente, *nm/f* assistant manager.

vicepresidencia, *nf* vice-presidency; vice-chairmanship.

vicepresidente, *nm/f* vice-president.

viceversa, *adv* vice versa.

viciado, *adj* 1. foul, thick, stale; 2. to corrupt.

viciar, *vt* 1. to corrupt, pervert, subver; 2. to nullify.

viciarse, *vr* 1. to take to vice, get depraved, become corrupted.

vicio, *nm* 1. vice; viciousness, depravity; bad habit; 2. defect, blemish.

vicioso(a), *adj* 1. vicious; depraved, dissolute; 2. rank, luxuriant, lush; 3. *nm/f* vicious person, depraved person; addict, fiend.

vicisitud, *nf* accident, upset, mishap.

victimar, *vt* to wound; to kill.

victimario(a), *nm/f* 1. person responsible for somebody,s suffering 2. person responsible for wounding (or killing).

victimizar , *vt* to victimize.

victoria, *nf* victory; triumph; moral moral victory.

victorioso, *adj* victorious.

victrola, *nf* gramophone, phonograph.

vid, *nf* vine.

vida, *nf* 1. life; way of life; lifetime, life span;

vidente, *adj* 1. sighted, able to see, 2. *nm/f* person who can see; prophet.

video, *nm* video;

videoaficionado(a), *nm/f* video fan.

videocámara, *nf* video camera.

videocasete, *nm* video cassette.

videoclub, *nm* videoclub.

videocopia, *nf* pirate video.

videograbación, *nf* videotaping, video recording.

videograbadora, *nf* video recorder.

vidriado, *adj* glazed.

vidriera, *nf* stained glass window glass door; glass partition.

vidriería, *nf* glassworks.

vidriero, *nm* glazier.

vidrio, *nm* glass; plate glass.

vieja, *nf* old woman.

viejo, *adj* old.

viento, *nm* wind, breeze.

vientre, *nm* belly; womb.

viernes, *nm* Friday.

viga, *nf* balk, timber; beam, rafter.

vigencia, *nf* operation; validity, applicability.

vigente, *adj* valid, applicable, in force; prevailing.

vigía, *nm* 1. look-out, watchman; the watch, 2. *nf* watchtower.

vigilancia, *nf* vigilance, watchfulness; to escape sb's vigilance.

vigilante, *adj* 1. vigilant, watchful; alert; 2. policeman.

vigilar, *vt* to watch, watch over; to look after, keep on eye on.

vigilia, *nf* 1. wakefulness, being awake; watchfulness.

vigor, *nm* vigour; vitality; toughness, stamina, hardiness.

vigorización, *nf* strengthening; encouragement, stimulation; revitalization.

visera, *nf* visor; peak; eyeshade.

visillo, *nm* lace curtain, net curtain.

visión, *nf* vision, (eye)sight; fantasy; illusion.

visionado, *nm* viewing, inspection.

visita, *nf* visit; call; right of search

visitación, *nf* visitation.

visitador(a), *nm/f* frequent visitor, person much given to calling.

visitante, *adj* 1. visiting; 2. *nm/f* visitor.

visitar, *vt* to visit; to call on, go and see.

visiteo, *nm* frequent visiting, constant calling.

visitero, *adj* fond of visiting, much given to calling.

vislumbrar, *vt* 1. to glimpse, catch a glimpse of, see briefly; 2. see some slight possibility of.

vislumbre(a), *nf* glimpse, brief view.

visión, *nf* vague idea; conjecture; to get an inkling of, get a vague idea of.

viso, *nm* gleam, glint; gloss; appearance.

visón, *nm* mink.

visor, *nm* sight; bombsight;

víspera, *nf* eve, day before, evening before;

vista , *nf* sight, eyesight, vision; look, gaze, glance.

vistar, *vt* to have a look at, look over, look round.

vistazo, *nm* look, glance; at a glance.

visual, *adj* 1. visual; of vision; 2. *nf* line of sight.

visualización, *nf* display(ing); scan(ning).

visualizador, *nm* display.

visualizar, *vt* to see, make out, descry.

vital, *adj* 1. living; 2. vital, essential, fundamental.

vitalicio, *adj* 1. life; for life; 2. *nm* life annuity.

vitalidad, *nf* vitality.

vitalizador, *adj* revitalizing effect.

vitalizar, *vt* to vitalize; to revitalize.

vitamina, *nf* vitamin.

vitaminado, *adj* vitaminized, with added vitamins.

vitaminar, *vt* to vitaminize, add vitamins to.

vitamínico, *adj* vitamin.

vitorear, *vt* to cheer, acclaim.

vitral, *nm* stained-glass window.

vítreo, *adj* glassy, vitreous; glass-like.

vitrina, *nf* glass case, showcase; display cabinet.

vitrola, *nf* gramophone, phonograph.

vitualla, *nf* provisions, victuals.

vituperar, *vt* to condemn, censure, inveigh against.

vituperio, *nm* condemnation; reproach, censure.

viudo(a), *adj* 1. widowed, widow; 2.*nm/f* widowed, widow.

viva, *nm* cheer; to give a cheer.

vivamente, *adv* in lively fashion.

vivaz, *adj* long-lived; enduring, lasting.

vivencia, *nf* experience, knowledge gained from experience.

vivencial, *adj* existential.

víveres, *nm* provisions; stores, supplies.

vivero, *nm* nursery; seedbed.

viveza, *nf* liveliness, vividness; brightness; sharpness.

vívido, *adj* vivid, graphic.

vividor, *adj* sharp, clever; opportunistic; unscrupulous.

vivienda, *nf* 1. housing, accommodation; 2. dwelling.

viviente, *adj* living.

vivificante, *adj* life-giving; revitalizing.

vivificar, *vt* to give life to, vivify.

vivíparo, *adj* viviparous.

vivir, *vt* 1. to live through; to experience, go through; 2. vi to live, to be alive.

vivo, *adj* living; live, alive.

vizcondado, *nm* viscounty.

vocablo, *nm* word; term.

vocabulario, *nm* vocabulary.

vocación, *nf* vocation, calling.

vocacional, *adj* vocational.

vocal, *adj* 1. vocal; 2. *nm/f* member (of a committee, etc).

vocálico, *adj* vocalic, vowel.

vocalizar, *vt* 1. to vocalize; 2. *vt* to hum; to sing scales, practise.

vocativo, *nm* vocative.

voceador, *adj* loud, loud-mouthed, vociferous.

vocear, *vt* 1. to cry; 2. to call loudly to, shout to; 3. to cheer, acclaim.

vocerío, *nm* shouting, yelling; clamour, uproar.

vocero(a), *nm/f* spokesperson.

vociferación, *nf* vociferation.

vociferar, *vt* to shout, scream, vociferate.

volada, *nf* short flight, single flight.

voladura, *nf* blowing up, demolition; blast.

volandero, *adj* loose, movable, not fixed.

volanta, *nf* flywheel; large wheel.

volante, *adj* 1. flying; 2. *nm* flywheel; balance; 3. steering wheel; 4. pamphlet.

volar, *vt* 1. to blow up, demolish; 2. to flight; 3. to irritate, upset, exasperate.

volarse, *vr* 1. to fly away; 2. to get angry, lose one's temper.

volátil, *adj* volatile.

volcán, *nm* volcano.

volcánico, *adj* volcanic.

volcar, *vt* to upset, overturn, tip over, knock over.

volea, *nf* volley.

volear, *vti* to volley.

voleo, *nm* volley.

volición, *nf* volition.

voltaje, *nm* voltage.

volteada, *nf* 1. round-up; 2. defection.

volteado, *nm* deserter; turncoat.

voltear, *vt* to turn over, roll over; to turn upside down.

voltereta, *nf* somersault; roll, tumble; lateral cart-wheel.

voltímetro, *nm* voltmeter.

voltio, *nm* volt.

voluble, *adj* 1. twining, clinging; climbing. 2. fickle, changeable; erratic, unpredictable; unstable.

volumen, *nm* volume; bulk.

voluminoso, *adj* voluminous; sizeable, bulky, massive.

voluntad, *nf* will.

voluntario(a), *adj* 1. voluntary; volunteer. 2. *nm/f* volunteer.

voluntarioso, *adj* headstrong, wilful, unreasonable.

voluptuosidad, *nf* voluptuousness; sensuality.

voluptuoso(a), *adj* 1. voluptuous; sensual; 2. *nm/f* voluptuary; sensualist.

volver, *vt* to turn, turn round; to turn over.

vomitar, *vt* to vomit, bring up, throw up.

vomitivo, *adj* 1. emetic; 2. disgusting; sick-making, repulsive.

vómito, *nm* vomiting, being sick.

voracidad, *nf* voracity, voraciousness.

voraz, *adj* voracious, ravenous; greedy.

vórtice, *nm* 1. whirlpool, vortex; whirlwind; 2. cyclone, hurricane.

vos, pron pers you, yett.

vosotros(as), *pron pers* you.

votante, *adj* 1. voting; 2. *nm/f* voter.

votar, *vt* to 1. vote for; 2. to vow, promise.

voto, *nm* vote.

voz, *nf* voice.

vuelco, *nm* upset, overturning, spill.

vuelo, *nm* 1. flight; 2. lace, frill.

vuelta, *nf* turn; revolution.

vuestro, *adj pos* 1. your, of yours; 2. *pron pos* yours, of yours.

vulcanización, nf vulcanization.
vulcanizar, vt to vulcanize.
vulcanología, nf vulcanology.
vulcanólogo(a), nm/f vulcanologist.
vulgar, adj vulgar; common, ordinary.
vulgaridad, nf ordinariness, commonness; coarseness; vulgarity.
vulgarizar, vt to popularize; to spread a knowledge of.
vulgo, nm common people; lower orders, common herd; mob.
vulnerable, adj vulnerable.
vulneración, nf infringement, contravention.
vulnerar, vt to damage, harm; to interfere with, to break, infringe, contravene.
vulpeja, nf fox; vixen.

X

X, x, nf (letter) X, x.
xeno, nm xenon.
xenofobia, nf xenophobia.
xenófobo, adj 1. xenophobic; 2. nm/f xenophobe.
xenón, nm xenon.
xerocopia, nf photocopy.
xerocopiar, vt to photocopy.
xilófono, nm xylophone.
xilografía, nf 1. xylography; 2. xylograph, wood engraving.
xilográfico, adj xylographic.

Y

y, conj and; so?; well?; why?.
ya, adv 1. already; 2. now; at once, right away; presently.
yacente, adj reclining, recumbent.
yacer, vi to lie.
yacimiento, nm bed, deposit; site.
yagua, nf royal palm; fibrous tissue from the wood of the royal palm.
yámbico, adj iambic.
yana, adj black.
yancófilo, adj pro-American, pro-United States,
yanqui, adj 1. Yankee; 2. nm/f Yank, Yankee.
yantar, nm 1. food; 2. vt to eat, 3. vi to have lunch.
yapa, nf 1. extra, extra bit, bonus; 2. tip.
yapar, vt to give as a bonus, add as an extra.
yarará, nm of rattlesnake.
yarda, nf yard.
yate, nm yacht; pleasure cruiser.
yaya, nm 1. slight wound; scar; slight pain; 2. stick, walking stick; 3. nf nana.
yaz, nm jazz.
yedra, nf ivy.

yegua, nf 1. mare; breeding mare; 2. old bag; whore, slag.
yeguada, nf 1. stud; group of breeding mares; 2. piece of stupidity, foolish act.
yelmo, nm helmet.
yema, nf yolk; egg; egg flip.
yen, nm yens, yen.
yerbabuena, nf mint.
yerbal, nm maté plantation.
yerbatero, nm 1. herbalist; quack doctor; 2. dealer in maté; grower of maté.
yermar, vt to lay waste.
yermo, adj uninhabited; waste, uncultivated.
yerno(a), nm/f son-in-law, daughter-in-law.
yernocracia, nf nepotism.
yeros, nm lentils.
yerro, nm error, mistake.
yerto, adj stiff, rigid.
yesca, nf 1. tinder; flint; 2. fuel; inflammable situation.
yesería, nf plastering, plasterwork.
yesero, nm plasterer.
yeso, nm 1. gypsum; 2. plaster; 3. plaster cast; 4. chalk.
yeta, nf bad luck, misfortune.
yetar, vt to put a jinx on.
yip, nm jeep.
yo, pron pers 1. I; it,s me, it is I; 2. the self, the ego.
yodo, nm iodine.
yodoformo, nm iodoform,
yoga, nm yoga.
yogui, nm yogi.
yogur, nm yoghurt.
yola, nf gig, yawl; sailing boat; shell.
yóquey, nm/f yoqueis jockey.
yuca, nf yucca; manioc root, cassava.
yudo, nm judo.
yugo, nm yoke.
yuguero, nm ploughman.
yugular, adj 1. jugular; 2. vt to slaughter.
yunque, nm 1. anvil; 2. tireless worker.
yunta, nf 1. yoke, team (of oxen); 2. couple, pair; cufflinks.
yute, nm jute.
yuxtaponer, vt to juxtapose.
yuxtaposición, nf uxtaposition.
yuyo, nm weed, wild plant, useless plant.

Z

Z, z, nf (letter) Z, z.
zabordar, vi to run aground.
zacatal, nm pasture.
zacate, nm grass; hay, fodder.
zacatear, vt 1. to beat; 2. vi to graze.
zacatera, nf pasture; haystack.
zafado, adj 1. brazen, shameless; insolent; 2. alert, sharp, wide awake; 3. crazy, nuts .
zafadura, nf dislocation, sprain.
zafar, vt to loosen, untie.
zafarse, vr to escape, run away; to slip away; to break loose.

zafarrancho, nm 1. clearing for action; 2. havoc, destruction; mess.

zafiro, nm sapphire.

zaga, nf rear; behind.

zagal, nm boy, lad, youth; shepherd boy.

zagala, nf girl, lass; shepherdess.

zaguán, nm vestibule, hallway, entry.

zaguero, adj 1. rear, back; 2. slow, laggard.

zahareno, adj wild; shy, unsociable.

zaherir, vt to criticize sharply, attack, lash; to wound.

zalagarda, nf ambush, trap; ruse; skirmish.

zalamerear, vi to flatter, cajole, wheedle.

zalamería, nf flattery; cajolery, wheedling.

zalamero(a), adj 1. flattering; cajoling, wheedling; 2. nm/f flatterer; wheedler.

zamarra, nf sheepskin; sheepskin jacket, fur jacket.

zamarrear, vt 1. to shake, worry; 2. to shake up, knock around; to shove around.

zamarro, nm sheepskin; sheepskin, jacket.

zambal, nf zamba (a dance).

zambo(a), adj 1. knock-kneed; 2. nm/f half-breed; mulatto.

zambra, nf gipsy festivity.

zambullida, nf dive, plunge; dip; ducking.

zambullir, vt to dip, plunge (into); to duck (under).

zampa, nf pile.

zampar, vt to put away hurriedly, whip smartly.

zampoña, nf panpipes.

zanahoria, nf carrot.

zanca, nf shank.

zancada, nf stride.

zancadillear, vt to trip (up); to undermine, put the skids under.

zancajear, vi to rush around.

zancarrón, nm leg bone; big bone.

zanco, nm stilt.

zancudero, nm swarm of mosquitoes.

zancudo, adj 1. long-legged; wader; 2. nm mosquito.

zanganada, nf stupid remark, silly thing (to say).

zanganear, vi to idle, loaf; to fool around, waste one's time.

zángano, nm drone.

zangón, nm big lazy lad, lazy lump.

zanja, nf ditch; drainage channel; trench.

zanjón, nm deep ditch.

zapador, nm sapper.

zapallo, nm gourd, pumpkin.

zapapico, nm pick, pickaxe; mattock.

zapar, vi to sap, mine.

zaparrazo, nm claw, scratch.

zapata, nf boot.

zapatear, vt 1. to tap with one's foot; 2. to kick, prod with one's foot.

zapatería, nf shoemaking; shoeshop; shoe factory.

zapatero, adj 1. shoemaking; 2. nm shoemaker.

zapatilla, nf 1. slipper; pump; 2. washer, gasket.

zapato, nm shoe.

zaque, nm 1. wineskin; 2. boozer, old soak .

zarabanda, nf 1. sarabande; 2. confused movement, rush, whirl.

zaragata, nf bustle, turmoil.

zaranda, nf sieve.

zarandear, vt 1. to sieve, sift; 2. to shake vigorously to and fro, shake up, toss about.

zarcillo, nm earring.

zarco, adj light blue.

zarigüeya, nf opossum.

zarina, nf tsarina.

zarpa, nf claw, paw.

zarpada, nf clawing; blow with the paw.

zarpar, vi to weigh anchor, set sail, get under way.

zarpear, vt to splash with mud.

zarza, nf bramble, blackberry (bush).

zarzal, nm bramble patch, clump of brambles.

zarzamora, nf blackberry.

zarzo, nm hurdle; wattle.

zarzuela, nf light opera, (Spanish-style) musical comedy.

zaya, nf whip.

zepelín, nm zeppelin.

zeta, nf the (name of the) letter z.

zigzag, adj zigzag.

zigzaguear, vi to zigzag.

zigzagueo, nm zigzag, zigzagging movement.

zinc, nm zinc,

zócalo, nm plinth, base.

zocato, adj hard, rubbery; damaged.

zodiaco, nm zodiac.

zollenco, adj big and tough.

zollipar, vi to sob.

zombi, nm zombie.

zona, nf zone; belt, area.

zoncear, vi to behave stupidly.

zoncería, nf silliness, stupidity; dullness.

zonda, nf hot northerly wind.

zonzo, adj silly, stupid.

zoología, nf zoology.

zoológico, adj 1. zoological; 2. nm zoo.

zoólogo(a), nm/f zoologist.

zooplancton, nm zooplankton.

zope, nm vulture.

zoquetada, nf stupidity.

zoquetazo, nm swipe, punch.

zoquete, nm 1. block, piece, chunk (of wood); 2. squat person.

zorra, nf fox; vixen.

zorrera, nf foxhole.

zorrería, nf foxiness, craftiness.

zorrero, adj foxy, crafty.

zorrillo, nm skunk.

zorro, adj foxy, crafty.

zozobra, nf capsizing, overturning; sinking.

zozobrar, vi to be in danger (of foundering); to capsize, overturn; sink.

zueco, nm clog, wooden shoe.

zulú, adj Zulu.

zumba, nf 1. banter, chaff, teasing; 2. beating.

zumbador, nm 1. buzzer; 2. hummingbird .

zumbar, vt 1. to rag, tease; 2. to throw, chuck, toss; to chuck out; 3. to buzz, hum, drone.

zumbido, nm buzz(ing), hum(ming), drone.

zumo, nm juice.

zuncho, nm metal band, hoop.

zurcido, nm darning, mending.

zurcir, vt to darn, mend, sew up.

zurdear, vt to do with the left hand.

zurdo, adj left; left-handed.

zurra, nf dressing, tanning.

zurrador, nm tanner.

zurrapa, nf soft lump, dollop; smudge.

zurrar, vt 1. to dress, tan; 2. to tan, wallop, lay into.

zurrón, nm pouch, bag.

zutano(a), nm/f So-and-so.

English/Spanish

A

A, a, *n* (primera letra *f* del alfabeto) A, a.

a, *art indef* 1. un, una; 2. *(before a vowel)*; **an:** uno, una.

aback, *adv* desconcertar, coger de improviso; quedar desconcertado.

abaft, *adv* 1. en la popa; 2. *prep* detrás de.

abalone, *n* oreja *f* marina.

abandon, *vt* 1. abandonar, desamparar; salir de; descuidar; 2. entregarse; 3. *n* libertad *f*, desenfreno *m*.

abandoned, *adj* 1. abandonado; desierto; 2. libre, desenfadado.

abandonment, *n* desamparo *m*; abandono *m*.

abase, *vt* 1. humillar, rebajar, degradar; envilecer, despreciar; 2. *vr* humillarse; envilecerse.

abasement, *n* humillación *f*, rebajamiento *m*, degradación *f*.

abashed, *adj* avergonzado, confuso, corrido, desconcertado.

abate, *vt* 1. disminuir, reducir; acabar con; suprimir; debilitar; 2. *vi* menguar; moderarse; calmarse, amainar.

abatement, *n* disminución *f*, reducción *f*, moderación *f*.

abattoir, *n* matadero *m*, picadero *m*.

abbess, *n* abadesa *f*.

abbey, *n* abadía *f*; monasterio *m*, convento *m*, cenobio *m*.

abbot, *n* abad *m*.

abbreviate, *vt* abreviar.

abbreviation, *n* abreviatura *f*, abreviación *f*.

abdicate, *vt/i* abdicar; renunciar.

abdication, *n* abdicación *f*; renuncia *f*.

abdomen, *n* abdomen *m*.

abdominal, *adj* abdominal.

abduct, *vt* raptar, secuestrar, plagiar.

abduction, *n* rapto *m*; secuestro *m*; plagio *m*.

abductor, *n* raptor *m*, secuestrador *m*.

abed, *adv* en cama, acostado.

aberrant, *adj* aberrante; anómalo.

aberration, *n* aberración *f*.

abet, *vt* incitar; ayudar; instigar; ser cómplice.

abetment, *n* incitación *f*, instigación *f*.

abetter, *n* instigador(a) *m/f*; autor(a) *m/f*; cómplice *m/f*.

abeyance, *n* suspensión *m*.

abhor, *vt* aborrecer, abominar, detestar, odiar.

abhorrence, *n* 1. aborrecimiento *m*, detestación *f*; 2. abominación *f*.

abhorrent, *adj* aborrecible, detestable, repugnante.

abide, *vt* 1. aguantar, soportar; 2. *vi* morar; permanecer, continuar; atenerse, obrar de acuerdo con, guiarse por.

abiding, *adj* permanente, perdurable.

ability, *n* habilidad *f*; capacidad *f*; talento *m*.

abject, *adj* abyecto, vil; servil; abatido.

abjectness, *n* abyección *f*; vileza *f*; lo humilde.

abjure, *vt* renunciar, abjurar.

ablative, *adj* ablativo; absoluto.

ablaze, *adv* en llamas, ardiendo.

able, *adj* hábil, capaz, talentoso, competente.

able-bodied, *adj* sano, robusto.

ablution, *n* ablución *f*.

ably, *adv* hábilmente, con mucha habilidad.

abnegate, *vt* eludir, evitar, rehuir, abjurar.

abnegation, *n* abnegación *f*.

abnormal, *adj* anormal; anómalo; irregular; deforme, mal formado.

abnormality, *n* anormalidad *f*; irregularidad *f*; deformidad *f*.

abnormally, *adv* anormalmente, de modo anormal.

aboard, *adv* a bordo; (to get a___) embarcarse, ir abordo.

abolish, *vt* suprimir, abolir; anular, revocar; eliminar.

abolishment, *n* supresión *f*, abolición *f*; anulación *f*.

abolitionist, *n* abolicionista *m/f*.

abominable, *adj* abominable; execrable; pésimo.

abominate , *vt* abominar, detestar.

abomination, *n* abominación *f*.

aboriginal, *adj*, *n* aborigen, indígena.

aborigine, *n* aborigen *m/f*.

abort, *vt* 1. abortar; interrumpir; 2. *vi* abortar; malparir; malograrse.

abortion, *n* aborto *m*.

abortionist, *n* abortista *m/f*.

abortive, *adj* abortivo; ineficaz; malogrado.

abortively, *adv* en vano.

abound, *vi* abundar.

about, *adv* 1. alrededor de, más o menos; aproximadamente; 2. *prep* alrededor de; 3. de, acerca de, sobre, con respecto a, respecto de.

above, *adv* 1. encima, por encima, arriba; expuesto; de lo alto; 2. *prep* encima de; más de; superior a; 3. *adj* susodicho, citado arriba, escrito, antedicho.

above-board, *adv* 1. abiertamente, sin rebozo; 2. *adj* legítimo, honrado.

above-mentioned, *adj* sobredicho, susodicho.

abrade, *vt* raer, raspar, desgastar.

abrasion, *n* raedura *f*, raspadura *f*, desgaste *m*.

abrasive, *adj* abrasivo; difícil, brusco; áspero.

abrasiveness, *n* brusquedad *f*; aspereza *f*.

abreast, *adv* de frente, de fondo.

abridge, *vt* compendiar, resumir, condensar abreviar, acortar.

abridged, *adj* resumido, en resumen; abreviado.

abridgement, *n* compendio *m*, resumen *m*; abreviación *f*.

abroad, *adv* en el extranjero, fuera; en el extranjero; fuera del país.

abrogate, *vt* abrogar.

abrogation, *n* abrogación *f*.

abrupt, *adj* repentino, brusco; precipitado; abrupto, escarpado.

abruptness, *n* brusquedad *f*; precipitación *f*.

abscess, *n* absceso *m*.

abscond, *vi* fugarse, huir (de la justicia).

absence, *n* ausencia *f*; carencia *f*.

absent, *adj* 1. ausente, distraído; 2. *vr* ausentarse.

absolute, *adj* absoluto; completo; total, pleno.

absolution, *n* absolución *f*.

absolutism, *n* absolutismo *m*.

absolve, *vt* absolver, perdonar.

absorb, *vt* absorber; amortiguar.

absorbent, *adj* absorbente.

absorption, *n* absorción *f*.

abstain, *vi* abstenerse (de).

abstainer, *n* abstemio *m*, abstinente *m*.

abstemious, *adj* sobrio, abstemio, moderado.

abstention, *n* abstención *f*.

abstinent, *adj* abstinente.

abstract, *adj* 1. abstracto; 2. *n* resumen *m*, sumario *m*; 3. *vt* extraer, quitar; resumir

abstracted, *adj* distraído, ensimismado.

abstraction, *n* abstracción *f;* robo *m;* distraimiento *m,* ensimismamiento *m.*

abstruse, *adj* recóndito, abstruso.

absurd, *adj* absurdo, ridículo, disparatado.

absurdity, *n* absurdo *m,* disparate *m.*

abundance, *n* abundancia *f.*

abundant, *adj* abundante; copioso.

abuse, *n* **1.** improperio *m,* injuria *f;* **2.** abuso *m;* malos *m* tratos; **3.** *vt* maltratar, ultrajar, abusar.

abusive, *adj* ofensivo, injurioso, insultante.

abysmal, *adj* abismal; profundo.

abyss, *n* abismo *m,* sima *f.*

academic, *adj* **1.** académico; universitario; **2.** puramente teórico, sin trascendencia práctica; poco provechoso.

academy, *n* academia *f,* colegio *m.*

accede, *vi* consentir en, acceder a; aceptar.

accelerate, *vt* acelerar; impulsar, apresurar.

acceleration, *n* aceleración *f.*

accelerator, *n* acelerador *m.*

accent, *n* acento *m;* énfasis *m.*

accented, *adj* acentuado.

accentuate, *vt* acentuar.

accentuation, *n* acentuación *f.*

accept, *vt* aceptar; aprobar; admitir; reconocer; recibir, acoger.

acceptability, *n* admisibilidad *f.*

acceptable, *adj* aceptable; admisible; adecuado satisfactorio.

acceptance, *n* aceptación *f;* aprobación *f;* (buena) acogida *f.*

accepted, *adj* aceptado; admisible.

access, *n* acceso *m,* entrada *f.*

accessibility, *n* accesibilidad *f;* lo asequible.

accessible, *adj* accesible, asequible.

accessory, *adj* accesorio; secundario; cómplice.

accident, *n* accidente *m;* percance *m.*

acclaim, *vt* aclamar, ovacionar.

accolade, *n* premio *m;* honor *m;* galardón *m.*

accommodate, *vt* **1.** alojar, hospedar; **2.** concertar; arreglar; reconciliar; complacer, adaptarse.

accommodating, *adj* servicial, complaciente, atento.

accommodation, *n* **1.** alojamiento *m;* **2.** espacio *m,* sitio *m;* **3.** acomodación *f,* convenio *m.*

accompaniment, *n* acompañamiento *m.*

accompanist, *n* acompañante *m/f.*

accompany, *vt* acompañar, adjuntar, enviar adjunto.

accomplice, *n* cómplice *m/f.*

accomplish, *vt* acabar, concluir; llevar a cabo, hacer.

accomplished, *adj* experto, consumado, diestro.

accomplishment, *n* conclusión *f;* efectuación *f,* logro *m;* realización *m.*

accord, *n* **1.** acuerdo, *m* armonía *f;* **2.** *vi* concordar; **3.** *vt* conceder, **4.** *vi* concordar.

accordance, *n* conforme *m;* acuerdo *m.*

according, *adv* según que, a medida que; con arreglo, conforme a.

accordion, *n* acordeón *m.*

accordionist, *n* acordeonista *m/f.*

accost, *vt* abordar, dirigirse a, acercarse a.

account, *n* **1.** cuenta *f;* computación *f;* factura *f;* estado *m* de cuenta; **2.** importancia *f;* **3.** relato *m,* relación *f.*

accountability, *n* responsabilidad *f.*

accountable, *adj* responsable, explicable; responsable de los propios actos.

accountancy, *n* contabilidad *f.*

accountant, *n* contable *m/f,* contador(a) *m/f* fiscal.

accounting, *n* contabilidad *f.*

accredit, *vt* atribuir; reconocer certificar, autorizar.

accreditation, *n* reconocimiento *m* (oficial); autorización *f.*

accredited, *adj* autorizado, acreditado.

accretion, *n* aumento *m;* acrecentamiento *m.*

accrue, *vi* aumentar, acumularse; derivarse de.

acculturate, *vt* aculturar.

acculturation, *n* aculturación *f.*

accumulate, *vi* acumular, amontonar; acopiar, juntar.

accumulation, *n* acumulación *f.*

accumulative, *adv* acumulativo.

accumulator, *n* acumulador *m.*

accuracy, *n* exactitud *f,* precisión *f;* esmero *m.*

accurate, *adj* exacto, preciso, correcto.

accurately, *adv* exactamente, correctamente.

accusation, *n* acusación *m;* cargo *m;* denuncia *f,* delación *f.*

accusative, *adj* acusativo.

accuse, *vt* acusar; denunciar, delatar; echar la culpa a.

accused, *n* acusado *m.*

accuser, *n* acusador *m,* delator *m.*

accustom, *vt* acostumbrar, habituar.

accustomed, *adj* acostumbrado, usual.

acerbic, *adj* acre, aspero.

acerbity, *n* acritud, aspereza.

acetate, *n* acetato *m.*

acetic, *adj* acético.

acetone, *n* acetona *f.*

acetylene, *n* acetileno *m.*

ache, *n* dolor *m.*

achieve, *vt* lograr, conseguir, realizar, llevar a cabo.

achievement, *n* realización *f,* consecución *f;* exito *m,* logro *m,* hazaña *f.*

achromatic, *adj* acromático.

acid, *adj* ácido.

acidifier, *n* acidulante *m.*

acidify, *vt* **1.** acidificar; **2.** *vi* acidificarse.

acidity, *n* acidez *f.*

acknowledge, *vt* reconocer; confesar, admitir.

acknowledgement, *n* reconocimiento *m;* confesión *f;* agradecimiento *m.*

acme, *n* auge *m,* cima *f,* colmo *m.*

acorn, *n* bellota.

acoustic, *adj* acústico; acoplador.

acoustics, *n* acústica *f.*

acquaint, *vt* avisar a uno de, informar a uno sobre; poner a uno al corriente de.

acquaintance, *n* conocimiento *m;* familiaridad *f;* trato *m;* conocido *m.*

acquiescent, *adj* condescendiente, conforme.

acquire, *vt* adquirir; obtener; conseguir; tomar.

acquired, *adj* adquirido.

acquirement, *n* adquisición *f;* obtención *f,* consecución *f.*

acquisition, *n* adquisición *f.*

acquisitive, *adj* codicioso.

acquisitiveness, *n* codicia *f.*

acquit, *vt* absolver, exonerar, exculpar.

acquittal, *n* absolución *f,* exculpación *f.*

acre, *n* acre *m.*

acrimonious, *adj* aspero, cáustico mordaz; amargo.

acrimony, *n* aspereza *f,* acrimonia *f,* acritud *f.*

acrobat, *n* acróbata *m/f.*

acrobatic, *adj* acrobático.

acronym, *n* sigla(s) *f,* acrónimo *m.*

acropolis, *n* acrópolis *f.*

across, *adv* **1.** a través de; de una parte a otra, de un lado a otro; **2.** *prep* através de; **3.** al otro lado de, del otro lado.

acrylic, *adj* acrílico.

act, *n* 1. acto *m*, acción *f*, decreto *m*, hecho *m*; 2. *vt* actuar, funcionar, desempeñar un papel.

acting, *adj* 1. interino, suplente; provisional; 2. *n* representación *f*; desempeño *m*, actuación *f*; 3. profesión *f* de actor.

action, *n* acción *f*, acto *m*, hecho *m*; actuación *f*.

activate, *vt* activar.

activator, *n* activador *m*.

active, *adj* activo.

activism, *n* activismo *m*.

activist, *n* activista *f*.

activity, *n* actividad *f*; vigor *m*.

actor, *n* actor *m*.

actress, *n* actriz *f*.

actual, *adj* verdadero, real; efectivo.

actuality, *n* realidad *f*.

actualize, *vt* realizar; representar de manera realista, describir con realismo.

actuarial, *adj* actuarial.

actuary, *n* actuario *m*.

actuate, *vt* animar; estimular.

acupuncture, *n* acupuntura *f*.

acupuncturist, *n* acupuntor(a) *m/f*.

acute, *adj* agudo.

acuteness, *n* agudeza *f*; perspicacia *f*.

adagio, *n* adagio *m*.

adamant, *adj* inexorable, inflexible.

adapt, *vt* 1. adaptar; acomodar, ajustar; 2. arreglar, refundir; 3. adaptarse.

adaptability, *n* adaptabilidad *f*; capacidad *f* para acomodarse.

adaptable, *adj* adaptable; capaz de acomodarse.

adaptation, *n* adaptación *f*; arreglo *m*, refundición *m*.

adapter, *n* adaptador *m*.

add, *vt* 1. sumar; añadir; 2. agregar.

added, *adj* 1. añadido, adicional; 2. además de.

addict, *n* partidario *m*, entusiasta *m/f*, fanático *m*; adicto *m*.

addicted, *adj* ser adicto a algo; estar enviciado con algo.

addiction, *n* afficción *f*; vicio *m*, dependencia *f*, hábito *m* morboso.

addictive, *adj* adictivo, que conduce al hábito morboso.

addition, *n* suma *f*, adición *f*; cálculo *m*.

additional, *adj* adicional; complementario, supletorio; añadido.

additive, *n* aditivo *m*.

addled, *adj* confuso, débil; desorientado.

address, *n* 1. señas *f*, dirección *f*; 2. tratamiento *m*, título *m*; 3. discurso *m*; 4. *vt* dirigirse a.

addressee, *n* destinatario *m*, consignatario *m*.

adduce, *vt* alegar, aducir, presentar.

adductor, *n* aductor *m*.

adenoids, *n* adenoideas *f*.

adept, *adj* 1. hábil, ducho; 2. *n* experto *m*.

adequacy, *n* suficiencia *f*; idoneidad *f*, propiedad *f*.

adequate, *adj* suficiente, adecuado; proporcionado; idóneo, propio.

adhere, *vi* pegarse; cumplir; observar.

adherence, *n* adherencia *f*, adhesión *f*; observancia *f*.

adherent, *adj* 1. adhesivo; 2. *n* partidario *m*.

adhesive, *adj* adhesivo, pegajoso.

adipose, *adj* adiposo.

adiposity, *n* adiposidad *f*.

adjacent, *adj* contiguo, inmediato; adyacente.

adjective, *n* adjetivo *m*.

adjoin, *vt* estar contiguo, lindar con.

adjoining, *adj* contiguo, vecino, colindante.

adjourn, *vt* aplazar; prorrogar, diferir; suspender.

adjournment, *n* aplazamiento *m*; suspensión *m*, clausura *f*.

adjudge, *vt* juzgar, decidir; adjudicar.

adjudicate, *vt* 1. decidir, juzgar; 2. *vi* ser juez, sentenciar.

adjudication, *n* juicio *m*, sentencia *f*; adjudicación *f*.

adjudicator, *n* juez *m*, árbitro *m*.

adjunct, *n* adjunto *m*, accesorio *m*.

adjure, *vt* ordenar solemnemente; suplicar, implorar.

adjust, *vt* 1. modificar, cambiar; corregir; concertar, componer, resolver; 2. *vi/r* adaptarse.

adjustable, *adj* ajustable, graduable, regulable.

adjustment, *n* modificación *f*, cambio *m*; arreglo *m*.

administer, *vt* administrar, dirigir, regir.

administration, *n* administración *f*, gobierno *m*; dirección *f*, gerencia *f*.

administrator, *n* administrator(a) *m/f*.

admirable, *adj* admirable, digno de admiración.

admiral, *n* almirante *m*.

admiration, *n* admiración *f*.

admire, *vt* admirar, elogiar.

admirer, *n* admirador(a) *m/f*.

admissible, *adj* admisible, aceptable.

admission, *n* entrada *f*; ingreso *m*.

admit, *vt* dejar entrar, dar entrada, admitir.

admittance, *n* entrada *f*; derecho de entrada *f*.

admonish, *vt* reprender, amonestar, prevenir.

admonition, *n* reprensión *f*, amonestación *f*; advertencia *f*.

adolescence, *n* adolecencia *f*.

adolescent, *adj* adolecente.

adopt, *vt* adoptar, aprobar, aceptar.

adoption, *n* adopción *f*.

adoptive, *adj* adoptivo.

adoration, *n* adoración *f*.

adore, *vt* adorar.

adorn, *vt* adornar, ornar, embellecer.

adornment, *n* adorno *m*, decoración *f*.

adrift, *adv* a la deriva, al garete.

adulate, *vt* adular.

adulation, *n* adulación *f*.

adult, *adj* adulto; maduro; mayor de edad.

adulterate, *vt* adulterar.

adultery, *n* adulterio *m*.

adulthood, *n* adultez *f*, mayoría *f* de edad, edad *f* adulta.

advance, *n* avance *m*; progreso *m*, adelanto *m*.

advanced, *adj* avanzado; muy moderno.

advantage, *n* ventaja *f*.

advantageous, *adj* ventajoso, provechoso.

advent, *n* advenimiento *m*, venida *f*, llegada *f*.

adventure, *n* aventura *f*.

adverb, *n* adverbio *m*.

adversary, *n* adversario(a) *m/f*; contrario(a) *m/f*.

adverse, *adj* adverso, contrario, hostil.

adversity, *n* adversidad *f*, infortunio *m*; desgracia *f*.

advertise, *vt* publicar, anunciar, revelar.

advertisement, *n* anuncio *m*.

advertising, *n* publicidad *f*; propaganda *f*, publicidad *f*.

advice, *n* consejo *m*; informe *m*, noticia *f*.

advisable, *adj* aconsejable, conveniente, prudente.

advise, *vt* aconsejar, recomendar, informar.

advised, *adj* sería aconsejable; harías bien.

advisement, *n* consulta *f*, deliberación *f*; guía *f* vocacional.

adviser, *n* consejero(a) *m/f*, abogado(a) *m/f*.

advisory, *adj* consultivo.

advocacy, *n* apoyo *m*; defensa *f*.

advocate, *n* 1. defensor(a) *m/f*, partidario *m*; abogado *m*; 2. *vt* abogar por, recomendar.

aeon, n eón m (eternidad f).

aerate, vt airear; ventilar, oxigenar.

aerated, adj gaseosa.

aeration, n aireación f.

aerial, adj 1. aéreo; 2. n antenna f.

aerobatics, n acrobacia f aérea.

aerobic, adj dances de aerobic, para aerobic.

aerobics, n aeróbica f, aerobic f, aerobismo m.

aerodrome, n aeródromo m.

aerodynamic, adj aerodinámico.

aerodynamics, n aerodinámica f.

aeronautic(al), adj aeronáutico.

aeronautics, n aeronáutica f.

aerosol, n aerosol m.

aerospace, adj aeroespacial.

aesthetic(al), adj estético.

aestheticism, n esteticismo m.

aesthetics, n estética f.

affability, n afabilidad f, amabilidad f.

affable, adj afable, amable.

affair, n 1. acontecimiento m; episodio; m caso m;
2. asunto m; negocios m; 3. amorío m, enredo m.

affect, vt 1. afectar, tener que ver con, perjudicar;
interesar; 2. conmover, enternecer.

affectation, n afectación f; amaneramiento m.

affecting, adj conmovedor, enternecedor.

affection, n afecto m, cariño m; inclinación f.

affectionate, adj cariñoso, afectuoso.

affiance, vt prometer en matrimonio; prometerse a.

affidavit, n declaración f jurada.

affiliate, vi 1. afiliarse; 2. n afiliado m, filial f.

affiliated, adj filial, subsidiario; afiliado.

affiliation, n afiliación f.

affirm, vt afirmar, asegurar, aseverar.

affirmation, n afirmación f, aseveración f.

affirmative, adj afirmativo.

affix, vt poner, añadir; pegar; imprimir.

afflict, vt afligir.

affluence, n riqueza f, opulencia f; prosperidad f.

affluent, adj rico, opulento, acaudalado; próspero.

afford, vt 1. dar, proporcionar; 2. tener con que
comprar algo.

affordable, adj razonable; adquirible.

afforest, vt repoblar de árboles.

afforestation, n repoblación f forestal.

afforested, adj repoblado de árboles.

affray, n refriega f, reyerta f.

affright, vt asustar, espantar.

affront, n 1. afrenta, ofensa; 2. vt afrentar, ofender.

aficionado, n aficionado(a) m/f.

afire, adv quemando, en llamas.

aflame, adv en llamas.

afoul, adv, adj 1. enredado; 2. vr enredarse con uno,
indisponerse con uno.

afraid, adj asustado.

afresh, adv de nuevo, otra vez.

after, adv 1. después; detrás; 2. adj siguiente; 3. prep
después de, según.

afterbirth, n placenta f.

afterlife, n vida f futura; vida f posterior.

aftermath, n consecuencias f, resultados m.

afternoon, n tarde f.

aftershock, n réplica f.

aftertaste, n dejo m, resabio m, gustillo m.

afterthought, n ocurrencia f tardía, idea f adicional.

afterwards, adv después, mas tarde.

afterworld, n mundo m más allá.

again, adv 1. otra vez, nuevamente, de nuevo;
2. además; por otra parte.

against, prep 1. contra; al lado de, junto a, cerca
de; 2. en contraste con eso; 3. en contra de.

age, n 1. edad f; 2. época f, era f, siglo m; 3. vt
madurar, envejecer, añejar.

aged, adj viejo, anciano.

agegroup, n grupo m etario, grupo m de personas
de la misma edad.

ageless, adj eternamente joven; perenne, inmemorial.

age-limit, n edad f mínima or máxima.

agency, n 1. agencia f; 2. organismo m, oficina f.

agenda, n orden f del día, asuntos a tratar.

agent, n representante m/f, delegado m, agenciero
m, intermediario m; apoderado m; agente m/f.

aggrandize, vt agrandar, ampliar; aumentar; engrandecer.

aggrandizement, n agrandamiento, ampliación; en-
grandecimiento.

aggravate, vt agravar, empeorar; irritar, sacar de quicio.

aggravating, adj agravante; irritante, molesto.

aggravation, n agravación f, empeoramiento m; circunstancia f agravante.

aggresion, n agresión f.

aggressive, adj agresivo; dinámico, enérgico, emprendedor.

aggressiveness, n agresividad f, dinamismo m, energía f, empuje m.

aggressor, n agresor(ora) m/f

aggrieved, adj ofendido; apenado.

aghast, adj horrorizado, pasmado.

agile, adj ágil.

agility, n agilidad f.

agitate, vt 1. agitar, 2. inquietar, perturbar; alborotar.

agitation, n inquietud f; perturbación f; nerviosismo
f; agitación f.

agitator, n agitador m; alborotador m; elemento m
revoltoso.

aglow, adv radiante, brillante.

agnostic, adj 1. agnóstico; 2. nm/f agnóstico(a)

agnosticism, n agnosticismo m.

ago, adv hace; (p. ej hace dos días)

agonize, vt 1. atormentar; 2. hacer sufrir muchísimo.

agonized, adj angustioso.

agonizing, adj atroz, muy agudo; angustioso.

agony, n dolor m agudo, dolor m punzante; agonía f.

agoraphobia, n agorafobia f.

agrarian, adj agrario.

agrarianism, n agrarismo m.

agree, vt 1. quedar en hacer algo; reconocer; estar de
acuerdo con que es así; 2. planear, convenir en,
aprobar; 3. concordar, coincidir; corresponder.

agreeable, adj agradable; simpático, amable.

agreed, adj según lo convenido.

agreement, n acuerdo m, pacto m, convenio m;
contrato m; armonía f, concordancia f.

agricultural, adj agrícola; agropecuario.

agriculture, n agricultura f.

agrobiology, n agrobiología f.

agrochemical, adj 1. agroquímico; 2. n sustancia f
agroquímica.

agronomist, n agrónomo m.

agronomy, n agronomía f.

agroproduct, n agroproducto.

aground, adv encallado, varado.

ague, n fiebre f intermitente.

ahead, adv 1. delante; 2. prep delante de; al frente de,
antes de.

aid, n 1. auxilio m, socorro m; asistencia; 2. vt ayudar,
auxiliar, socorrer.

aide, n asistente m/f.

aileron, n alerón m.

ailing, *adj* enfermo, achacoso; decadente, debilitado.

ailment, *n* enfermedad *f*, achaque *m*, dolencia *f*.

aim, *n* **1.** puntería *f*; **2.** propósito, intención, meta, blanco; **3.** *vt* apuntar (arma); ambicionar, pretender.

aimless, *adj* sin propósito fijo, sin objeto.

aimlessness, *n* falta *f* de propósito fijo, carencia *f* de objetivo.

air, *n* **1.** aire *m*; viento *m*; aspecto *m*, ademán *m*; **2.** *vt* airear, ventilar.

air-alert, *n* alerta *f* aérea.

airbag, *n* bolsa *f* de aire.

airbase, *n* base *f* aérea.

airbrush, *n* aerógrafo *m*.

air-bubble, *n* burbuja *f* de aire.

air-chamber, *n* cámara *f* de aire.

air-condition, *vt* climatizar, refrigerar.

air-conditioned, *adj* climatizado, refrigerado, con aire acondicionado, con clima artificial.

air-conditioner, *n* aparato *m* acondicionador de aire.

air-cooled, *adj* refrigerado por aire.

air-corridor, *n* pasillo *m* aéreo.

air-cover, *n* cobertura *f* aérea.

aircraft, *n* avión *m*.

aircraft-carrier, *n* porta(a)viones *m*.

airdrome, *n* aeródromo *m*.

airduct, *n* tubo *m* de aire; tubo *m* de ventilación.

airfield, *n* campo *m* de aviación, aeródromo.

airflow, *n* corriente *f* de aire.

air force, *n* aviación *f*, fuerzas *f* aéreas.

airframe, *n* armazón *f* del avión.

air-freight, *n* flete *m* por avión; mercancías *f* aerotransportadas.

airgun, *n* escopeta *f* de aire comprimido.

airily, *adv* muy a la ligera, sin dar importancia a la cosa; de manera confiada.

airing, *n* ventilación *f*.

airlane, *n* vía *f* aérea, pasillo *m* aéreo.

airlift, *n* **1.** puente *m* aéreo; **2.** *vt* aerotransportar.

airline, *n* línea *f* aérea, compañía *f* de aviación.

airliner, *n* avión *m* de pasajeros.

airplane, *n* avión *m*.

airport, *n* aeropuerto *m*.

air-pressure, *n* presión *f* atmosférica.

air-raid, *n* ataque *m* aéreo.

airship, *n* aeronave *f*, dirigible *m*.

air-show, *n* feria *f* aérea; exhibición *f* aeronáutica.

airsick, *adj* mareado.

airspace, *n* espacio *m* aéreo.

airspeed, *n* velocidad *f* aérea.

airstrike, *n* ataque *m* aéreo.

airstrip, *n* pista *f* de aterrizaje.

airtight, *adj* hermético, estanco al aire.

airworthiness, *n* aeronavegabilidad *f*.

airy, *adj* ventilado; airoso, alegre.

aisle, *n* nave *f* lateral; pasadizo *m*; pasillo *m*.

ajar, *adv* entreabierto, entornado.

akin, *adj* consanguíneo; relacionado, análogo, semejante.

alabaster, *n* **1.** alabastro *m*; **2.** *adj* alabastrino.

alarm, *n* alarma *f*, inquietud *f*, temor *m*.

alarmed, *adj* sobresaltado, asustado.

alarming, *adj* alarmante.

albino, *adj* **1.** albino; **2.** *nm* albino.

album, *n* álbum *m*.

albumin, *n* albúmina *f*.

alchemist, *n* alquimista *m/f*.

alcohol, *n* alcohol *f*.

alcoholic, *adj* alcohólico.

alcove, *n* hueco, nicho.

alder, *n* aliso.

alderman, *n* concejal *m*.

alert, *adj* **1.** alerta; vigilante; listo; **2.** *n* aviso *m*; alarma *f*; **3.** *vt* alertar, avisar.

alertness, *n* vigilancia *f*; listeza *f*.

alfalfa, *n* alfalfa *f*.

alfresco, *adv* **1.** al aire libre; **2.** *adj* de aire libre.

algebra, *n* álgebra *f*.

algebraic, *adj* algebraico.

alias, *n* alias *m*; nombre *m* ficticio, seudónimo *m*.

alien, *adj* **1.** ajeno, extraño; extranjero; **2.** *n* ser *m* extraterrestre.; extranjero *m*.

alienate, *vt* **1.** enajenar, traspasar; **2.** indisponerse con, alejar, ofender; apartar; **3.** perder.

alienation, *n* **1.** enajenación *f*, traspaso *m*; **2.** alejamiento *m*.

alight, *vi* **1.** arder, estar ardiendo, estarse quemando; estar encendido; **2.** pegar fuego a, incendiar; **3.** *vi* bajar, apearse; posarse.

align, *vt* **1.** alinear; **2.** *vr* ponerse al lado de, alinearse con.

alignment, *n* alineación *f*.

alike, *adj* **1.** semejante, parecido, igual; **2.** *adv* del mismo modo, igualmente.

alimentary, *adj* alimenticio.

alimony, *n* alimentos, pensión alimenticia.

alive, *adj* **1.** vivo; **2.** lleno de vida; **3.** activo, enérgico.

alkaline, *adj* alcalino.

all, *adj* **1.** todo, todos; **2.** *pron* todo ; **3.** *adv* completamente, enteramente, del todo.

allay, *vt* aliviar; aquietar, disipar.

allegation, *n* aseveración *f*, alegato *m*; acusación *f*.

allege, *vt* declarar, afirmar, pretender; alegar, pretextar.

alleged, *adj* supuesto, pretendido; presunto.

allegiance, *n* lealtad *f*; fidelidad *f*.

allegro, *n* alegro *m*.

alleluia, *n* aleluya *f*.

allergenic, *adj* alergénico.

allergic, *adj* alérgico.

allergy, *n* alergia; síndrome de alergia.

alleviate, *vt* aliviar, mitigar.

alleviation, *n* alivio *m*, mitigación *f*.

alley, *n* **1.** calleja, callejón; paseo; **2.** bolera.

alliance, *n* alianza *f*.

allied, *adj* aliado; afín, conexo.

alligator, *n* caimán *m*.

alliteration, *n* aliteración *f*.

alliterative, *adj* aliterado.

allocate, *vt* asignar, señalar; repartir, distribuir.

allocation, *n* asignación *f*; reparto *m*; distribución *f*.

allot, *vt* asignar, adjudicar, dar, destinar.

allotment, *n* **1.** asignación *f*; reparto *m*, distribución *f*; **2.** ración *f*, cuota *f*.

allow, *vt* permitir; dar, conceder, asignar; aplicar, dar.

allowable, *adj* permisible; admisible; tolerable; lícito.

allowance, *n* **1.** subsidio *m*, subvención *f*, pago *m*; ración *f*; **2.** descuento *m*, concesión *f*; **3.** tolerancia *f*.

alloy, *n* **1.** aleación *f*, liga *f*; mezcla *f*; **2.** *vt* alear, ligar.

all-powerful, *adj* todopoderoso, omnipotente.

allude, *vi* referirse, aludir.

allure, *n* **1.** atractivo *m*, encanto *m*, fascinación *f*; **2.** *vt* atraer, tentar, fascinar.

allusion, *n* alusión *f*, referencia *f*.

allusive, *adj* alusivo, referente; lleno de alusiones.

alluvial, *adj* aluvial.

alluvium, *n* aluvión *m*, depósito *m* aluvial.

ally, *n* **1.** aliado; **2.** *vr* aliarse con; emparentar con.

almanac, *n* almanaque *m*.

almighty, *adj* omnipotente, todopoderoso; imponente.

almond, *n* almendra.

almost, *adv* casi.

alms, *n* limosna *f.*

aloe, *n* áloe *m;* acíbar *f.*

aloft, *adv* arriba, en lo alto; en vuelo.

alone, *adj* 1. solo; 2. *adv* sólo, unicamente.

along, *adv* 1. desde el principio, todo el tiempo; 2. *prep* a lo largo de.

alongside, *adv* 1. al costado; 2. *prep* junto a, al lado de.

aloof, *adj* 1. reservado, frío; 2. *adv* mantenerse a distancia.

aloud, *adv* en voz alta, alto.

alpaca, *n* alpaca *f.*

alphabet, *n* alfabeto *m.*

alphabetic(al), *adj* alfabético.

alphabetize, *vt* alfabetizar, poner en orden alfabético.

alpine, *adj* alpino.

alpinist, *n* alpinista *m/f.*

already, *adv* ya; ¡basta!, ¡vale ya!, ¡ya está bien!.

also, *adv* también, además.

altar, *n* altar *m.*

alter, *vt* cambiar, modificar, alterar; reformar.

altercation, *n* altercado.

alternate, *adj* 1. alterno; alternativo; 2. *n* suplente *m/f;* 3. *vt/i* alternar.

alternating, *adj* alterno.

alternative, *adj* 1. alternativo; 2. *n* aternativa *f.*

alternator, *n* alternador *m.*

although, *conj* aunque; si bien; a pesar de que.

altimeter, *n* altímetro *m.*

altitude, *n* altura *f,* altitud *f.*

altruist, *n* altruista *m/f.*

altruistic, *adj* altruista.

aluminum, *n* aluminio *m.*

alveolar, *adj* alveolar.

always, *adv* siempre.

amalgam, *n* amalgama *f.*

amalgamate, *vt* 1. amalgamar; 2. *vi* amalgamarse; unirse.

amalgamation, *n* amalgamación *f;* unión *f;* fusión *f.*

amass, *vt* amontonar, acumular.

amateur, *n* amateur *m,* aficionado *m.*

amateurish, *adj* de aficionado.

amatory, *adj* amatorio, erótico.

amaze, *vt* asombrar, pasmar.

amazed, *adj* asombrado.

amazement, *n* asombro *m,* sorpresa *f.*

amazing, *adj* asombroso, pasmoso; extraordinario.

ambassador, *n* embajador *m.*

ambassadorial, *adj* de embajador.

ambassadorship, *n* embajada *f.*

ambassadress, *n* embajadora *f.*

amber, *n* ámbar *m.*

ambidextrous, *adj* ambidextro.

ambience, *n* ambiente *m,* atmósfera *f.*

ambient, *adj* ambiente.

ambiguity, *n* ambiguedad *f.*

ambiguous, *adj* ambiguo.

ambition, *n* ambición *f.*

ambitious, *adj* ambicioso.

ambivalence, *n* ambivalencia *f.*

ambivalent, *adj* ambivalente.

ambrosia, *n* ambrosía *f.*

ambulance, *n* ambulancia *f.*

ambulatory, *adj* no encamado.

ambush, *n* 1. emboscada *f;* 2. *vt* emboscar, tender una emboscada.

ameliorate, *vt* 1. mejorar; 2. *vi* mejorar(se).

amelioration, *n* mejora *f,* mejoramiento *m,* mejoría *f.*

amenable, *adj* sumiso, dócil, tratable; responsable.

amend, *vt* enmendar; rectificar, corregir; modificar; reformar.

amendment, *n* enmienda *f;* rectificación *f,* corrección *f.*

amends, *n* dar cumplida *f;* satisfacción *f,* compensarlo, enmendarlo.

amenity, *adj* 1. ameno, atractivo, agradable; 2. *n* amenidad *f.*

amenities, *n* atractivos *m,* conveniencias *f,* comodidades *f.*

American, *adj* americano, estadounidense.

americanism, *n* americanismo *m.*

americanization, *n* americanización *f.*

americanize, *vt* americanizar.

amethyst, *n* amatista *f.*

amiability, *n* afabilidad *f,* amabilidad *f.*

amiable, *adj* afable, amable, simpático; bonachón.

amicable, *adj* amistoso, amigable.

amid, *prep* en medio de, entre.

amiss, *adv* 1. mal, fuera de lugar, fuera de proposito; 2. *adj* malo; no va todo bien.

amity, *n* concordia *f,* amistad *f.*

ammeter, *n* amperímetro *m.*

ammonia, *n* amoníaco *m.*

ammunition, *n* municiones *f.*

amnesia, *n* amnesia *f.*

amnesiac, *adj* amnésico.

amnesty, *n* amnistía *f,* indulto *m* general.

among(st), *prep* entre, en medio de.

amoral, *adj* amoral.

amorality, *n* amoralidad *f.*

amorous, *adj* enamorado, enamoradizo; cariñoso.

amorphous, *adj* amorfo.

amortization, *n* amortización.

amortize, *vt* amortizar.

amount, *n* cantidad *f;* suma *f,* importe *m.*

amphibian, *adj* 1. anfibio; 2. *n* anfibio *m.*

amphibious, *adj* anfibio.

amphitheater, *n* anfiteatro *m.*

ample, *adj* amplio, ancho, espacioso, extenso; grande.

amplification, *n* amplificación *f.*

amplifier, *n* amplificador *m.*

amplify, *vt* amplificar, explicar.

amputate, *vt* amputar.

amputation, *n* amputación *f.*

amuck, *adv* enloquecer, desbocarse, desmandarse.

amulet, *n* amuleto *m.*

amuse, *vt* 1. divertir, hacer reír; 2. *vr* distraerse.

amusement, *n* diversión *f,* entretenimiento *m;* pasatiempo *m;* risa *f.*

amusing, *adj* divertido, gracioso, entretenido.

anachronism, *n* anacronismo *m.*

anachronistic, *adj* anacrónico.

anagram, *n* anagrama *f.*

anal, *adj* anal.

analgesic, *adj* 1. analgésico; 2. *n* analgésico *m.*

analog, *n* análogo *m.*

analogical, *adj* analógico.

analogous, *adj* análogo.

analyse, *vt* analizar.

analysis, *n* análisis *m.*

analyst, *n* analista *m/f.*

analytic(al), *adj* analítico.

anaphoric, *adj* anafórico.

anarchism, *n* anarquismo *m.*

anarchist, *adj* 1. anarquista; 2. *n* anarquista *m/f.*

anarchy, *n* anarquía *f.*

anathema, *n* anatema *m;* abominación *f.*

anatomical, *adj* anatómico.

anatomist, *n* anatomista *m/f.*

anatomize, *vt* anatomizar; analizar minuciosamente.

anatomy, *n* anatomía *f.*

ancestor, *n* antepasado *m;* abuelos *m/f;* ascendientes *m/f.*

ancestral, *adj* hereditario.

ancestry, *n* ascendencia *f,* abolengo *m,* linaje *m,* estirpe *f.*

anchor, *n* 1. ancla *f,* áncora *f;* 2. *vt* echar anclas; levar anclas; anclar.

anchorite, *n* anacoreta *mf.*

anchor-man, *n* presentador *m;* hombre *m* clave.

anchovy, *n* boquerón *m;* anchoa *f.*

ancient, *adj* 1. antiguo; 2. viejo, anciano.

ancillary, *adj* subordinado, secundario; auxiliar.

andiron, *n* morillo *m.*

androcentric, *adj* androcéntrico.

androcentricity, *n* androcentrismo *m.*

androgen, *n* andrógeno *m.*

androgynous, *adj* andrógino.

android, *n* androide *m.*

anecdotal, *adj* anecdótico.

anemia, *n* anaemia *f.*

anerobic, *adj* anaerobic.

aneroid, *adj* 1. aneroide; 2. *n* barómetro *m.*

anesthesia, *n* anaesthesia *f.*

anesthesiologist, *n* anestesista *m/f.*

anesthetic, *adj* anesthetic.

anesthetist, *n* anesthetist *m/f.*

anew, *adv* de nuevo; otra vez.

angel, *n* ángel *m.*

angelfish, *n* angelote *m,* pez ángel *m.*

angelic(al), *adj* angélico.

angelus, *n* ángelus *m.*

anger, *n* 1. cólera *f,* ira *f;* furia *f;* 2. *vt* enojar, provocar, encolerizar.

angina, *n* angina *f;* angina *f* del pecho.

angiosperm, *n* angiosperma *f.*

angle, *n* 1. ángulo *m;* 2. punto *m* de vista; opinión *f;* criterio *m.*

angler, *n* pescador *m.*

anglerfish, *n* rape *m.*

Anglican, *adj* 1. anglicano; 2. *n* anglicano *m.*

Anglicanism, *n* anglicanismo *m.*

anglicism, *n* anglicismo *m,* inglesismo *m.*

anglicist, *n* anglicista *m/f.*

anglophobia, *n* anglofobia *f.*

anglophone, *adj* anglófono.

angry, *adj* 1. enfadado, enojado, airado; 2. bravo; tormentoso, borrascoso; 3. inflamado.

anguish, *n* dolor *m* agudo, tormentos *m;* angustia *f,* congoja *f.*

anguished, adj acongojado, afligido, angustiado.

angular, *adj* angular; (face, etc) anguloso.

angularity, *n* angularidad *f;* angulosidad *f.*

aniline, *n* anilina *f.*

anima, *n* ánima *f,* alma *f.*

animal, *n* animal *m,* bicho *m;* bestia *f.*

animality, *n* animalidad *f.*

animate, *adj* 1. vivo, que tiene vida; 2. *vt* animar, infundir vida ; vivicar, estimular; alentar.

animated, *adj* animado; vivo, vivaz, vigoroso.

animation, *n* animación *f;* vivacidad *f,* viveza *f.*

animator, *n* animador *m.*

animism, *n* animis mo *m.*

animist, *adj* 1. animista; 2. *n* animista *mf.*

animosity, *n* animosidad *f,* rencor *m,* hostilidad *f.*

animus, *n* odio *m,* rencor *m.*

anise, *n* anís *m.*

aniseed, *n* anís *m;* grano *m* de anís.

anisette, *n* anisete *m.*

ankle, *n* tobillo *m.*

anklebone, *n* hueso *m* del tobillo, taba *f,* astrágalo *m.*

ankle joint, *n* articulación *f* del tobillo.

ankle sock, *n* escarpín *m.*

ankle strap, *n* tirita *f* tobillera.

anklet, *n* brazalete *m* para el tobillo, ajorca *f* para el pie; calcetín *m* corto.

ankylosis, *n* anquilosis *f.*

annalist, *n* analista *mf,* cronista *mf.*

annals, *n* anales *m,* crónica *f.*

anneal, *vt* recocer; templar.

annex, *vt* 1. anexar; 2. adjuntar, añadir; 3. *n* pabellón *m* separado, dependencia *f;* edificio *m* anexo; apéndice *m,* anexo *m.*

annexation, *n* anexión *f.*

annihilate, *vt* aniquilar.

annihilation, *n* aniquilación *f,* aniquilamiento *m.*

anniversary, *n* aniversario *m.*

annotate, *vt* anotar, comentar.

annotation, *n* anotación *f,* apunte *m,* comentario *m.*

announce, *vt* anunciar; informar; proclamar; declarar.

announcement, *n* anuncio *m;* informe *m;* proclama *f;* notificación *f;* declaración *f;* aviso *m.*

announcer, *n* locutor *m,* orador *f,* presentador *m.*

annoy, *vt* molestar, fastidiar, irritar.

annoyance, *n* enojo *m,* irritación *f;* contrariedad *f;* disgusto *m.*

annoying , *adj* molesto, fastidioso, engorroso; pesado, importuno.

annual, *adj* 1. anual; 2. anuario *m.*

annuity, *n* renta *f* vitalicia, pensión *f* vitalicia; anualidad *f.*

annul, *vt* anular, invalidar; cancelar; anular; revocar, abrogar.

annulment, *n* anulación *f,* invalidación *f,* cancelación *f;* revocación *f,* abrogación *f.*

Annunciation, *n* Anunciación *f.*

anodize, *vt* anodizar.

anodyne, *adj* 1. anodino; 2. *n* anodino *m.*

anoint, *vt* untar; ungir.

anointing, *n* unción *f* de los enfermos.

anomalous, *adj* anómalo.

anomaly, *n* anomalía *f.*

anonymity, *n* anonimia *f;* anonimato *m;* anónimo *m.*

anonymous, *adj* anónimo.

anorak, *n* anorac *m,* anorak *m.*

anorexia, *n* anorexia *f.*

anorexic, adj anoréxico(a), *nm/f.*

another, *adj* 1. otro; 2. *pron* otro *m,* otra *f.*

answer, *n* 1. contestación *f,* respuesta *f,* réplica *f;* 2. solución *f;* 3. *vt* contestar a, responder a.

answer back, *vi* replicar; ser respondón.

answer for, *vt* responder de, ser responsable de, responder por.

answerable, *adj* 1. que tiene contestación, que admite solución; 2. responsable.

ant, *n* hormiga *f.*

antacid, *adj* 1. antiácido; 2. *n* antiácido *m.*

antagonism, *n* antagonismo *m;* oposición *f,* hostilidad *f;* rivalidad *f.*

antagonist, *n* adversario(a) *m/f;* antagonista *m/f .*

antagonistic, adj antagónico; contrario, opuesto.

antagonize, *vt* enemistarse con, provocar la enemistad de.

Antarctic, *adj* antártico.

Antarctica, *n* Antártica *f.*

Antarctic Circle, n Círculo m Polar Antártico.
ante..., pref ante...
anteater, n oso m hormiguero.
antecedent, adj antecedente.
antechamber, n antecámara f antesala f.
antediluvian, adj antediluviano; viejísimo.
antelope, n antílope m.
antenatal , adj prenatal, antenatal.
antenna, n antena f.
antepenult, n sílaba f antepenúltima.
antepenultimate, adj antepenúltimo.
anterior, adj anterior.
anteroom, n antesala f antecámara f.
anthem, n himno m nacional.
anther, n antera f.
ant-hill, n hormiguero m.
anthologist, n antologista m/f.
anthologize, vt hacer una antología de.
anthology, n antología f.
anthracite, n antracita f.
anthrax, n ántrax m.
anthropocentric, adj antropocéntrico.
anthropoid, adj antropoide; n antropoideo m.
anthropological , adj antropológico.
anthropologist, n antropólogo(a) m/f.
anthropology, n antropología f.
anthropomorphic, adj antropomórfico.
anthropomorphism, n antropomorfismo m.
anti-abortionist, n antiabortista m/f.
anti-aircraft, adj antiaéreo.
antiballistic, adj mísil m antibalístico.
antibiotic, adj antibiótico; n antibiótico m.
antibody, n anticuerpo m.
Antichrist, n Anticristo m.
anticipate, vt 1. anticiparse a, adelantarse a; prevenir; 2. prever; 3. esperar; contar con; disfrutar de antemano.
anticipation, n 1. anticipación f, prevención f; 2. previsión f; 3. anticipo m; 4. expectación f, ilusión f.
anticlerical, adj anticlerical; n anticlerical m/f.
anticlericalism, n anticlericalismo m.
anticlimactic, adj que marca un descenso de la emoción etc; decepcionante.
anticlimax, n acontecimiento m que marca un descenso de la emoción etc; decepción f, chasco m.
anticoagulant, adj 1. anticoagulante; 2. n anticoagulante f.
anticorrosive, adj anticorrosivo.
anti-dandruff, adj anticaspa.
antidepressant, adj. 1. antidepresivo; 2. n antidepresivo m.
antidote, n antídoto m.
antifeminism, n antifeminismo m.
antifeminist, adj 1. antifeminista; 2. n antifeminista m/f.
antifreeze, adj 1. anticongelante; 2. n anticongelante m.
anti-friction, adj antifriccional, contrafricción.
antigen, n antígeno m.
anti-glare, adj antideslumbrante.
anti-hero, n antihéroe m.
antihistamine, adj 1. antihistamínico; 2. n antihistamínico m.
anti-inflationary, adj antiinflacionista.
anti-knock, adj antidetonante.
anti-lock, adj dispositivo anti-bloque.
antimacassar, n antimacasar m.
antimagnetic, adj antimagnético.
antimalarial, adj antipalúdico.

antimatter, n antimateria f.
antimissile, adj antimísil.
antimony, n antimonio m.
antinomy, n antinomia f.
antinuclear, adj antinuclear.
antiparasitic, adj antiparasitario.
antipathetic, adj antipático.
antipathy, n antipatía f; aversión f, cosa f aborrecida.
antipersonnel, adj destinado a causar bajas.
antiperspirant, adj 1. antiperspirante; 2. n antiperspirante m.
antiphon, n antífona f.
antiphony, n canto m antifonal.
antipodean, adj de las antípodas.
antipodes, n antípodas m .
antipope, n antipapa m.
antiprotectionist, adj antiproteccionista.
antiquarian, adj 1. anticuario; 2. n antiquario(a) m/f, coleccionista m/f de antigüedades.
antiquated, adj anticuado.
antique, adj 1. antiguo, viejo; anticuado; decimonónico, caduco; 2. n antigüedad f, antigualla f.
antiracist, adj 1. antirracista; 2. n antirracista m/f.
antireligious, adj antirreligioso.
anti-riot, adj policía f antidisturbios.
anti-roll, adj barra f estabilizadora, estabilizador m.
anti-rust, adj antioxidante, anticorrosión.
antisegregationist, adj antisegregacionista.
anti-semite, n antisemita m/f.
anti-semitic, adj antisemítico.
anti-semitism, n antisemitismo m.
antiseptic, adj 1. antiséptico; 2. n antiséptico m.
anti-skid, adj antideslizante.
antislavery, adj en contra de la esclavitud.
antisocial, adj antisocial.
anti-strike, adj antihuelga.
anti-submarine, adj antisubmarino.
anti-tank, adj antitanque.
anti-terrorist, adj antiterrorista.
anti-theft, adj sistema m anti-robo.
antithesis, n antítesis f.
antithetic, adj antitético.
antitoxin, n antitoxina f.
anti-trust, adj antimonopolista.
antivivisectionism, n antiviviseccionismo m.
antivivisectionist, n antiviviseccionista m/f.
anti-war, adj antibelicista, antiguerra, pacifista.
anti-wrinkle, adj antiarrugas.
antler, n cuerna f; cornamenta f.
antonym, n antónimo m.
antsy, adj nervioso, inquieto.
anus, n ano m.
anvil, n yunque m.
anxiety, n 1. inquietud f, preocupación f, ansiedad f; 2. ansia f, anhelo m; 3. angustia f.
anxious, adj 1. inquieto, preocupado, angustiado; 2. deseoso.
any, adj 1. algún, alguna; 2. cualquier; 3. (negative sense) ningún, ninguna.
anybody, n 1. alguno, alguna; 2. cualquiera; 3. ninguno, ninguna; nadie, ninguno.
anyhow, adv 1. de todas formas, de todos modos, con todo; 2. a pesar de todo; 3. no importa cómo.
anything, pron algo, alguna cosa; (negative sense) nada.
anywhere, adv en todas partes, en cualquier parte, dondequiera; en cualquier parte del mundo.
aorta, n aorta f.
aortic, adj aórtico.
apache, n apache m.

apart, *adv* aparte, separadamente.

apartheid, *n* apartheid *m* segregación *f* racial.

apartment, *n* cuarto *m* aposento *m;* apartamento *m;* departamento *m.*

apathetic, *adj* apático, indiferente.

apathy, *n* apatía *f,* indiferencia *f;* falta *f* de interés.

ape, *n* mono.

aperient, *adj* laxante.

apéritif, *n* aperitivo *m.*

aperture, *n* abertura *f;* rendija *f;* resquicio *m.*

aphasia, *n* afasia *f.*

aphrodisiac, *adj* afrodisíaco.

Aphrodite, *nf* Afrodita.

apiarist, *n* apicultor.

apiary, *n* colmenar *m.*

apiece, *adv* cada uno; por persona, por cabeza.

aplenty, *adv* abundante.

aplomb, *n* aplomo *m,* sangre *f* fría, serenidad *f.*

Apocalypse, *n* Apocalipsis *m.*

apocalyptic, *adj* apocalíptico.

apolitical, *adj* apolítico.

apologetic, *adj* lleno de disculpas; apenado.

apologize, *vi* disculparse, pedir perdón; presentar sus excusas.

apology, *n* disculpa *f,* excusa *f;* apología *f.*

apoplexy, *n* apoplejía *f.*

apostasy, *n* apostasía *f.*

apostate, *n* apóstata *mf.*

apostle, *n* apóstol *m;* paladín *m.*

apostolate, *n* apostolado *m.*

apostolic, *adj* apostólico.

apostrophe, *n* apóstrofo *m.*

appall, *vt* horrorizar, aterrar; repugnar.

appalling, *adj* espantoso, horroroso; pésimo.

apparel, *n* ropa *f,* vestidos *m;* indumentaria *f.*

apparent, *adj* 1.aparente; 2. claro, evidente, manifiesto.

apparition, *n* aparición *f;* fantasma *m,* aparecido *m.*

appeal, *n* 1. llamamiento *m;* 2. súplica *f,* ruego *m,* petición *f;* 3. apelación *f,* recurso *m;* 4.atractivo *m,* encanto *m;* 5. *vi* atraer, interesar, tener atractivo; apelar.

appear, *vi* aparecer, mostrarse, presentarse; salir a luz.

appearance, *n* aparición *f;* comparecencia *f.*

appease, *vt* apaciguar; satisfacer, saciar; mitigar.

appellant, *n* apelante.

append, *vt* añadir, adjuntar.

appendage, *n* añadidura *f,* apéndice *m;* pegote *m.*

appendectomy, *n* apendectomía *f.*

appendicitis, *n* apendicitis *f.*

appendix, *n* apéndice.

apperception, *n* percepción *f.*

appertain, *vi* relacionarse con, tener quever con.

appetite, *n* apetito *m.*

appetizer, *n* aperitivo *m;* tapa *f.*

appetizing, *adj* apetitoso.

applaud, *vt* 1. aplaudir; celebrar, elogiar; 2. *vi* palmotear.

applause, *n* aplausos *m,* aplauso *m;* aprobación *f.*

apple, *n* manzana *f.*

applesauce, *n* compota de manzanas.

appliance, *n* aparato *m,* instrumento *m,* dispositivo *m.*

applicability, *n* aplicabilidad *f.*

applicable, *adj* aplicable; relevante, pertinente.

applicant, *n* aspirante *m/f;* candidato *m;* solicitante *m/f.*

application, *n* aplicación *f;* solicitud *f,* petición *f.*

applicator, *n* aplicador *m.*

applied, *adj* aplicado.

appliqué, *n* encaje de aplicación.

apply, *vt* aplicar; poner, echar; recurrir.

appoint, *vt* fijar, señalar; nombrar.

appointee, *n* persona *f* nombrada.

appointment, *n* 1. nombramiento *m;* 2. cita, compromiso *m;* 3. puesto *m;* colocación *f.*

apportion, *vt* prorratear; reparti; distribuir; desglosar.

apportionment, *n* prorrateo *m;* repartición *f,* distribución *f,* desglose *m.*

apposite, *adj* apropiado; a propósito, oportuno.

appraisal, *n* tasación *f,* valoración *f,* evaluación *f;* estimación.

appraise, *vt* tasar, valorar, evaluar.

appraiser, *n* apreciador; evaluador *m;* tasador *m.*

appraising, *adj* apreciativo.

appreciable, *adj* sensible, perceptible; importante.

appreciate, *vt* apreciar, valorar, aquilatar; tener un alto concepto de.

appreciation, *n* aprecio *m,* apreciación *f,* estimación.

apprehend, *vt* 1. prender, detener; 2. percibir, comprender; 3. recelar.

apprehension, *n* prendimiento *m,* detención *f.*

apprehensive, *adj* aprensivo, inquieto.

apprentice, *n* 1. aprendiz *m/f,* novicio *m,* principiante *m/f;* 2. *vt* poner de aprendiz.

apprenticeship, *n* aprendizaje *m.*

apprise, *vt* informar, avisar.

approach, *vt* 1. acercarse a; aproximarse a; 2. abordar, enfocar; 3. dirigirse a; 4. *n* acercamiento *m,* aproximación *f,* enfoque *m.*

approachable, *adj* asequible; abordable, tratable, accesible.

approaching, *adj* próximo, venidero; que se acerca, que viene en dirección opuesta.

approbation, *n* aprobación *f.*

appropriate, *adj* 1. apropiado, conveniente, a propósito; adecuado; correspondiente; oportuno; competente; 2. *vt* apropiarse, asignar.

appropriateness, *n* propiedad *f,* conveniencia *f.*

approval, *n* aprobación *f;* consentimiento *m;* visto *m* bueno.

approve, *vt* aprobar; dar por bueno; tener un buen concepto.

approved, *adj* aprobado, acreditado; del modo acostumbrado.

approving, *adj* de aprobación, aprobatorio.

approvingly, *adv* con aprobación.

approximate, *adj* 1. aproximado; 2. *vr* aproximar.

approximation, *n* aproximación *f.*

appurtenance, *n* dependencia *f;* accesorio *m.*

apricot, *n* albaricoque *m,* chabacano.

apropos, *adv* 1. a propósito; 2. *prep* proposito de; 3. *adj* oportuno.

apt, *adj* apto, conveniente, apropiado, oportuno.

aptitude, *n* aptitud *f,* capacidad *f,* habilidad *f.*

aptly, *adv* oportunamente, acertadamente.

aquamarine, *adj* verde mar.

aquanaut, *n* submarinista *m/f.*

aquaplane, *n* hidroavión *m.*

aquarium, *n* acuario *m.*

aquatic, *adj* acuático.

aquatint, *n* acuatinta *f.*

aqueduct, *n* acueducto *m.*

aqueous, *adj* ácueo, acuoso.

aquifer, *n* acuífero *m.*

aquiferous, *adj* acuífero.

aquiline, *adj* aguileño, aquilino.

Arab, *adj* 1. árabe; 2. *n* caballo *m* árabe.

arabesque, *n* arabesco *m.*

Arabian, *adj* árabe, arábigo.

arable, *adj* cultivable, arable; granja *f* agrícola.

arachnid, n arácnido m.

arbiter, n árbitro m.

arbitrariness, n arbitrariedad f.

arbitrary, adj arbitrario; subjetivo; artificial.

arbitrate, vt 1. resolver, juzgar; 2. vi arbitrar.

arbitration, n arbitraje m.

arbitrator, n juez árbitro mf.

arbor, n cenador m, pérgola f, glorieta.

arboreal, adj arbóreo.

arboretum, n arboleda f.

arboriculture, n arboricultura f.

arc, n 1. arco m; 2. vi arquearse, formar un arco.

arcade, n (series of arches) arcada f.

arcane, adj arcano; secreto, misterioso.

arch, n 1. arco m; 2. bóveda f, empeine m; arcada f; 3. vi arquearse, formar un arco; formar una bóveda.

archaeological, adj arqueológico.

archaeology, n arqueología f.

archaic, adj arcaico.

archaism, n arcaísmo m.

archangel, n arcángel m.

archbishop, n arzobispo m.

archbishopric, n arzobispado m.

archdeacon, n arcediano m.

archdiocese, n archidiócesis f.

archduke, n archiduque m.

arched, adj en forma de arco(s); arqueado; abovedado.

archer, n arquero m.

archery, n tiro m con arco.

archetypal, adj arquetípico.

archetype, n arquetipo m.

architect, n arquitecto m/f.

architectural, adj arquitectónico.

architecture, n arquitectura f.

archive, n 1. archivo m; fichero m; 2. vt archivar.

archivist, n archivero m; archivista m/f.

archness, n astucia f; picardía f; malicia f; coquetería f.

archway, n arco m; arcada f.

arctic, adj ártico; glacial.

ardent, adj ardiente, vehemente, apasionado; fervoroso.

ardor, n ardor m; fervor m; vehemencia f; pasión f.

arduous, adj arduo, fuerte, riguroso; penoso, arduo; difícil, trabajoso.

area, n área f, superficie f; extensión f; región f, zona f.

arena, n anfiteatro m, redondel m, arena f; palenque m; plaza f.

Argentinian, adj argentino.

argon, n argón m.

argot, n argot m.

arguable, adj discutible; sostenible; defensible.

argue, vt sostener; razonar acerca de; arguir, indicar; discutir, disputar.

argument, n argumento m, discusión f, disputa f, debate m.

argumentative, adj discutidor.

aria, n aria f.

arid, adj árido.

aridity, n aridez f. ,

aright, adv correctamente, acertadamente.

arise, vi presentarse, porvenir de, resultar de.

aristocracy, n aristocracia f.

aristocrat, n aristócrata mf.

aristocratic, adj aristocrático.

arithmetic, n aritmética f.

arithmetical, adj aritmético; progresión f aritmética.

arithmetician, n aritmético mf.

ark, n arca.

arm, n 1. brazo m; bracete; 2. sección f, división f, departamento m; 3. (Mil) arma; 4. vt armar.

armada, n flota f, armada f.

armadillo, n armadillo m.

armament, n armamento m.

armature, n armadura f; inducido m; armazón f.

armband, n brazal m, brazalete m.

armchair, n sillón m, butaca f.

armed, adj armado.

armful, n brazado m, brazada f.

armistice, n armisticio m.

armlet, n brazal m.

armorer, n armero m.

armory, n armería f; arsenal m.

armpit, n sobaco m, axila f.

armrest, n apoyo m para el brazo, apoyabrazos m.

army, n ejército m; multitud f.

arnica, n árnica f.

aroma, n aroma m.

aromatic, adj aromático.

around, adv 1. alrededor; a la redonda, por todas partes, por todos lados; 2. cerca; por aquí.

arouse, vt despertar, incitar, estimular.

arpeggio, n arpegio m.

arrack, n arac m, aguardiente m de palma.

arrange, vt arreglar, ordenar, disponer, organizar.

arranged, adj concertado.

arrangement, n arreglo m, orden m, disposición f; ordenación f; (Mus) adaptación f.

arrant, adj consumado, de siete suelas; puro disparate m.

array, n orden m, formación f.

arrears, n atrasos m pl.

arrest, n 1. detención f; secuestro m; 2. vt detener, arrestar; obstaculizar.

arresting, adj llamativo, impresionante.

arrival, n llegada f; advenimiento m; persona f que llega; recién llegado.

arrive, vi llegar; aparecer, presentarse, triunfar.

arriviste, n arribista m/f.

arrogance, n arrogancia f, prepotencia f.

arrogant, adj arrogante, prepotente.

arrogate, vt arrogarse algo; atribuirse, apropiarse.

arrow, n flecha f.

arrowhead, n punta f de flecha.

arsenal, n arsenal m.

arsenic, n arsénico m.

arson, n incendio m doloso, incendio m provocado, incendiarismo m.

arsonist, n incendiario m/f; pirómano m/f.

art, n arte m.

arterial, adj arterial.

arteriosclerosis, n arteriosclerosis f.

artery, n arteria f.

artesian, adj pozo m artesiano.

artfully, adv con mucha maña, astutamente.

arthritic, adj artrítico.

arthritis, n artritis f.

artichoke, n alcachofa f.

article, n artículo m, objeto m, cosa f; colaboración f; reportaje m.

articulate, adj 1. articulado, claro, distinto; capaz de hablar; que se expresa bien; 2. vt expresar claramente.

articulation, n articulación f.

artifice, n artificio m; ardid m, estratagema f.

artificial, adj artificial; postizo.

artificiality, n artificialidad f; afectación f.

artillery, n artillería f.

artisan, n artesano m.

artist, n artista m/f.

artiste, n artista m/f.

artistic, adj artístico.

artistry, n arte m; talento m artístico, habilidad f artística.

artwork, n material m gráfico.

as, adv, conj and prep como; hace como; ya que, de modo que.

asbestos, n asbesto m, amianto m.

asbestosis, n asbestosis f.

ascend, vt subir; escalar; ascender.

ascending, adj ascendente.

ascension, n ascensión f.

ascent, n subida f, ascensión f; cuesta f.

ascertain, vt averiguar, determinar, descubrir, indagar.

ascertainable, adj averiguable, comprobable.

ascertainment, n averiguación f, comprobación f.

ascetic, adj 1. ascético; 2. n asceta m/f.

ascorbic, adj ácido m ascórbico.

ascribable, adj atribuible.

ascribe, vt atribuir.

ascription, n atribución f.

aseptic, adj aséptico.

asexual, adj asexual.

ash, n 1. fresno m; 2. de fresno m; 3. ceniza f.

ashamed, adj avergonzado, apenado.

ashcan, n cubo m de la basura, tarro m de basura.

ashlar, n sillar m; sillería f.

ashore, adv en tierra.

ashtray, n cenicero m.

Asiatic, adj 1. asiático; 2. n asiático.

aside, adv aparte, a un lado.

asinine, adj asnal; estúpido.

ask, vt preguntar; pedir; invitar, convidar

askance, adv de soslayo; al sesgo, sospechosamente.

aslant, adv 1. a través, oblicuamente; 2. prep a través de.

asleep, adj dormido.

asp, n áspid m.

asparagus, n esparraguera; espárrago.

aspect, n aspecto m; apariencia f.

aspersion, n calumnia f.

asphalt, n asfalto m.

aspic, n gelatina f.

aspidistra, n aspidistra f.

aspirant, n aspirante m/f, candidato m.

aspirate, adj aspirado.

aspiration, n aspiración f.

aspire, vi aspirar a; ambicionar, anhelar.

aspirin, n aspirina f.

aspiring, adj ambicioso; en ciernes.

ass, n 1. asno m, burro m; 2. imbécil m.

assail, vt acometer, atacar; emprender.

assailant, n asaltador(a) m/f, agresor(a) m/f.

assassin, n asesino m.

assassinate, vt asesinar.

assassination, n asesinato m.

assault, n 1. asalto m (sobre), ataque m (a, contra); 2. atentado m (a, contra), agresión f; 3. vt asaltar, atacar, agredir.

assay, n 1. ensayo m; 2. vt ensayar; intentar, probar.

assemble, vt 1. reunir, juntar; convocar; 2. montar; ensamblar; 3. vi reunirse, juntarse; celebrar una sesión.

assembly, n 1. reunión f; colección f; 2. montaje m; ensambladura f.

assembler, n ensamblador m.

assembly-line, n línea f de montaje, cadena f de montaje.

assemblyman, n miembro m de una asamblea.

assembly-plant, n planta f de montaje.

assembly-shop, n taller m de montaje.

assent, n 1. asentimiento m, consentimiento m, aprobación f; 2. vi consentir (en), asentir (a).

assert, vt 1. afirmar, declarar; sostener, defender; 2. vr imponerse, hacer valer sus derechos.

assertion, n aserto m, afirmación f, declaración f.

assertive, adj asertivo.

assertively, adv de manera asertiva.

assertiveness, n asertividad f.

assess, vt valorar, apreciar; tasar, calcular (en); enjuiciar, juzgar; evaluar.

assessable, adj tasable, calculable.

assessment, n valoración f; tasación f; enjuiciamiento m; evaluación f.

assessor, n asesor(a) m/f; tasador(a) m/f.

asset, n 1. ventaja f; factor m positivo; 2. posesión f; partida f del activo; activo m.

asseverate, vt aseverar.

asseveration, n aseveración f.

assiduity, n asiduidad f, diligencia f.

assiduous, adj asiduo, diligente.

assign, vt asignar; señalar, indicar; destinar.

assignation, n asignación f; traspaso m; atribución f; nombramiento m, designación f.

assignment, n 1. asignación f; 2. cometido m, tarea f; misión f; trabajo m.

assimilate, vt 1. asimilar; 2. vi asimilarse.

assimilation, n asimilación f.

assist, vt 1. ayudar; asistir; 2. vi tomar parte en, participar en.

assistant, adj 1. auxiliar; n subdirector(a) m/f; 2. n ayudante mf, auxiliar mf.

associate, adj 1. asociado; 2. n asociado(a) m/f, colega m/f; compañero(a) m/f; cómplice m/f; 3. vt asociar; relacionar; juntar, unir; 4. vi asociarse (con); juntarse, unirse.

associated, adj asociado; conexo, relacionado.

association, n asociación f, relación f, conexión f.

assonance, n asonancia f.

assonant, adj 1. asonante; 2. n asonante m.

assonate, vi asonar.

assort, vt 1. concordar, convenir; 2. vt clasificar, surtir, surtir con variedad.

assorted, adj surtido, variado.

assume, vt 1. tomar; darse; adoptar, arrogarse; 2. suponer, dar por sentado.

assumed, adj 1. falso, fingido; 2. presunto; 3. n suposición f, supuesto m; presunción f.

assurance, n 1. garantía f, promesa f; 2. confianza f; aplomo m, serenidad f; 3. certeza f, seguridad f; 4. seguro m.

assure, vt 1. asegurar, garantizar; 2. vr asegurarse de algo.

assured, adj 1. confiado, sereno; 2. seguro; 3. n el asegurado, la asegurada.

assuredly, adv seguramente, sin duda.

asterisk, n 1. asterisco m; 2. vt señalar con un asterisco, poner un asterisco a.

asteroid, n asteroide m.

asthma, n asma f.

asthmatic, adj asmático.

astigmatic, adj astigmático.

astigmatism, n astigmatismo m.

astir, adj activo, en movimiento.

astonish, vt asombrar, pasmar; sorprender.

astonished, adj estupefacto, pasmado.

astonishing, *adj* asombroso, pasmoso; sorprendente.

astonishment, *n* asombro *m*, sorpresa *f*, estupefacción *f*.

astounded, *adj* pasmado, estupefacto.

astounding, *adj* asombroso, pasmoso.

astral, *adj* astral.

astray, *adv* (to go a__) extraviarse; equivocarse, descarriar, ir por mal camino.

astride, *adv* 1. a horcajadas; 2. *prep* a caballo, sobre, a horcajadas.

astringency *n* astringencia *f*; adustez *f*, austeridad *f*.

astringent, *adj* astringente; adusto, austero.

astro..., *pref* astro...

astrolabe, *n* astrolabio *m*.

astrologer, *n* astrólogo(a) *m/f*.

astrological, *adj* astrológico.

astrologist, *n* astrólogo *m/f*.

astrology, *n* astrología *f*.

astronaut, *n* astronauta *mf*.

astronautics, *n* astronáutica *f*.

astronomer, *n* astrónomo(a) *mf*.

astronomical, *adj* astronómico.

astronomy, *n* astronomía *f*.

astrophysicist, *n* astrofísico(a) *mf*.

astrophysics, *n* astrofísica *f*.

astute, *adj* listo, inteligente; sagaz.

astutely, *adv* inteligentemente, sagazmente.

asunder, *adv* hacer pedazos, romper en dos.

asylum, *n* 1. asilo *m*; 2. manicomio *m*, hospital *m* psiquiátrico.

asymmetric(al), *adj* asimétrico.

asymmetry, *n* asimetría *f*.

asymptomatic, *adj* asintomático.

asynchronous, *adj* asíncrono.

at, *prep* en.

atavism, *n* atavismo *m*.

atavistic, *adj* atávico.

atheism, *n* ateísmo *m*.

atheist, *n* ateo(a) *m/f*.

atheistic, *adj* ateo, ateísta.

athlete, *n* atleta *mf*.

athletic, *adj* atlético.

athleticism, *n* atletismo *m*.

athwart, *adv* 1. de través, al través; 2. *prep* a través de.

atlas, *n* atlas *m*.

atmosphere, *n* atmósfera *f*; ambiente *m*; clima *m*, atmósfera *f*.

atmospheric, *adj* atmosférico; ambiental.

atoll, *n* atolón *m*.

atom, *n* átomo *m*.

atom-bomb, *n* bomba *f* atómica.

atomic, *adj* atómico(a).

atomic-powered, *adj* impulsado por energía atómica.

atomize, *vt* atomizar, pulverizar.

atomizer, *n* atomizador *m*, pulverizador *m*.

atonal, *adj* atonal.

atone, *vi* expiar.

atonement, *n* expiación *f*.

atonic, *adj* átono.

atop, *adv* 1. encima; 2. *prep* encima de; sobre; en la cumbre de.

atrocious, *adj* atroz.

atrociously, *adv* atrozmente.

atrocity, *n* atrocidad *f*.

atrophy, *n* 1. atrofia *f*; 2. *vt* atrofiar; 3. *vi* atrofiarse.

attach, *vt* 1. sujetar, pegar; atar, prender; unir; acoplar; 2. adjuntar.

attaché, *n* agregado(a) *m/f*.

attache-case, *n* portafolio *m*, cartera *f*; maletín *m*.

attachment, *n* 1. atadura *f*; unión *f*; 2. accesorio *m*, dispositivo *m*; acoplamiento *m*; 3. cariño *m*; apego *m*.

attack, *n* 1. ataque, asalto, atentado; 2. *vt* atacar, agredir, asaltar.

attackable, *adj* atacable, expuesto al ataque.

attacker, *n* agresor(a) *m/f*; asaltante *m/f*, atacante *m/f*.

attain, *vt* 1. alcanzar, lograr, conseguir; 2. *vi* llegar a.

attainable, *adj* alcanzable, realizable.

attainment, *n* logro *m*, consecución *f*, obtención *f*.

attempt, *n* 1. tentativa *f*, intento *m*; 2. atentado *m* contra la vida de uno; 3. *vt* probar, ensayar, intentar; tratar de efectuar.

attend, *vt* 1. asistir a; 2. servir; atender; 3. *vi* prestar atención, poner atención.

attend to, *vt* ejecutar; ocuparse de, atender; prestar atención a.

attendance, *n* asistencia *f*, presencia *f*.

attendant, *adj* 1. relacionado; 2. *n* acompañante *m*; sirviente *m/f*; acomodador(a) *f*.

attention, *n* 1. atención *f*; capacidad *f* de concentración; 2. ¡firme(s)!; ponerse firme(s), cuadrarse; 3. atenciones *f pl*, cortesías *f pl*.

attentive, *adj* 1. atento(a); 2. cortés, obsequioso.

attentiveness, *n* atención *f*; cortesía *f*.

attenuate, *vt* atenuar.

attenuating, *adj* atenuante.

attenuation, *n* atenuación *f*, disminución *f*.

attest, *vt* 1. atestiguar (que); confirmar, autenticar; 2. *vi* dar fe de.

attestation, *n* atestación *f*, testimonio *m*; confirmación *f*, autenticación *f*.

attic, *n* desván *m*, ático *m*, buhardilla *f*.

attire, *n* 1. traje *m*, vestido *m* atavío *m*; 2. *vt* vestir; (de) ataviar (de).

attitude, *n* actitud *f*, postura *f*; ademán *m*.

attorney, *n* 1. apoderado(a) *mf*; 2. abogado *m/f*.

attract, *vt* atraer; llamar.

attraction, *n* atracción *f*; atractivo *m*; aliciente *m*.

attractive, *adj* atractivo; agradable; atrayente, interesante.

attributable, *adj* atribuible a, imputable a.

attribute, *n* 1. atributo *m*; 2. *vt* atribuir; achacar.

attribution, *n* atribución *f*.

attributive, *adj* atributivo.

attrition, *n* desgaste *m*; rozadura *f*, roce *m*.

atypical, *adj* atípico.

atypically, *adv* atípicamente, de manera atípica.

auburn, *adj* castaño rojizo.

auction, *n* 1. subasta *f*, almoneda *f*, licitación *f*, subasta *f*; 2. subastar, poner (vender) en pública subasta.

auctioneer, *n* subastador(a) *mf*, licitador(a) *m/f*.

auction-room, *n* sala *f* de subastas.

audacious, *adj* audaz, atrevido; descarado.

audaciously, *adv* audazmente, atrevidamente; descaradamente.

audacity, *n* audacia *f*, atrevimiento *m*; descaro *m*.

audibility, *n* audibilidad *f*.

audible, *adj* audible, perceptible, que se puede oír.

audience, *n* auditorio *m*, público *m*; audiencia *f*.

audio, *adj* de audio.

audio, *pref* audio...

audiofrequency, *n* audiofrecuencia *f*.

audiometer, *n* audiómetro *m*.

audiotypist, *n* mecanógrafo(a) *f* de dictáfono.

audio-visual, *adj* audiovisual.

audit, *n* 1. revisión *f* de cuentas, intervención *f*; auditoría *f*; 2. *vt* revisar, intervenir, auditar.

auditing, *n* auditoría *f,* censura *f* de cuentas.

audition, *n* 1. audición *f;* 2. *vt* dar audición a.

auditor(a), *n* censor(a) *mf* de cuentas.

auditorium, *n* auditorio *m,* sala *f.*

auditory, *adj* auditivo.

augment, *vt* 1. aumentar; 2. *vi* aumentar(se).

augmentation, *n* aumento *m.*

augmentative, *adj* aumentativo.

augur, *vt* augurar, pronosticar, anunciar.

augury, *n* augurio *m;* presagio *m.*

august, *adj* augusto.

aunt, *n* tía *f.*

aura, *n* emanación *f;* atmósfera *f.*

aural, *adj* aural, auditivo.

aureole, *n* aureola *f.*

au revoir, *adv* hasta la vista.

auricle, *n* aurícula *f.*

aurora borealis, *n* aurora *f* boreal.

auspices, *n* bajo los auspicios de, auspiciado por.

auspicious, *adj* propicio, favorable, de buen augurio.

auspiciously, *adv* propiciamente, favorablemente.

austere, *adj* austero.

austerely, *adv* austeramente.

austerity, *n* austeridad *f.*

authentic, *adj* auténtico.

authenticate, *vt* autenticar; autentificar.

authentication, *n* autenticación *f.*

authenticity, *n* autenticidad *f.*

author, *n* 1. autor(a) *mf;* 2. *vt* escribir, componer.

authoress, *n* autora *f.*

authoritative, *adj* autorizado, autoritativo; autoritario.

authority, *n* autoridad *f.*

authorization, *n* autorización *f.*

authorize, *vt* autorizar.

authorship, *n* autoría *f,* paternidad *f* literaria.

autism, *n* autismo *m.*

autistic, *adj* autístico, autista.

auto, *pref* auto...

auto, *n* coche *m,* automóvil *m,* carro *m.*

autobank, *n* cajero *m* automático.

autobiographic(al), *adj* autobiográfico.

autobiography, *n* autobiografía *f.*

autocracy, *n* autocracia *f.*

autocrat, *n* autócrata *mf.*

autocratic, *adj* autocrático.

autocycle, *n* velomotor *m,* ciclomotor *m.*

autogiro, *n* autogiro *m.*

autograph, *adj* autógrafo.

automate, *vt* automatizar.

automated, *adj* automatizado.

automatic, *adj* automático.

automation, *n* automatización *f.*

automatism, *n* automatismo *m.*

automobile, *n* coche *m;* automóvil *m.*

automotive, *adj* automotor.

autonomous, *adj* autónomo; autonómico.

autonomy, *n* autonomía *f.*

autopilot, *n* piloto *m* automático.

autopsy, *n* autopsia *f;* necropsia *f.*

autosuggestion, *n* (auto)sugestión *f.*

auto-teller, *n* cajero *m* automático.

autotimer, *n* programador *m* automático.

autumn, *n* otoño *m.*

autumnal, *adj* otoñal.

auxiliary, *adj* auxiliar.

avail, *vt* aprovechar(se) de, valer(se) de.

availability, *n* 1. disponibilidad *f;* 2. validez *f.*

available, *adj* disponible; asequible, aprovechable.

avalanche, *n* alud *m,* avalancha *f;* torrente *m.*

avant-garde, *adj* de vanguardia, nueva ola, ultramoderno.

avarice, *n* avaricia *f.*

avaricious, *adj* avaro, avariento.

avenge, *vt* vengar.

avenger, *n* vengador(a) *m/f.*

avenging, *adj* vengador.

avenue, *n* avenida *f;* vía *f,* camino *m.*

aver, *vt* declarar, aseverar.

average, *adj* medio, de término medio; mediano; corriente, regular; promedio.

average down, *vt* promediar hacia abajo.

average out, *vt* calcular el término medio de.

average up, *vt* promediar hacia arriba.

aversion, *n* aversión *f* (hacia), repugnancia *f* (por).

avert, *vt* apartar (de); desviar; quitar; impedir.

aviary, *n* pajarera *f,* avería *f.*

aviation, *n* aviación *f;* industria *f* de la aviación.

aviator, *n* aviador(a) *m/f.*

avid, *adj* ávido, ansioso (de).

avidity, *n* avidez *f,* ansia *f.*

avocado, *n* aguacate *m.*

avocation, *n* diversión *f,* distracción *f,* vocación *f.*

avoid, *vt* evitar; guardarse de; eludir.

avoidable, *adj* evitable, eludible.

avow, *vt* reconocer, confesar, admitir.

avowal, *n* confesión *f;* declaración *f.*

avowed, *adj* declarado, abierto.

await, *vt* esperar, aguardar.

awake, *adj* 1. despierto; 2. *vi* despertar(se).

awaken, *vt* 1. despertar; alertar; 2. *vi* despertar(se).

awakening, *adj* 1. naciente; 2. *n* el despertar, despertamiento *m.*

award, *n* 1. premio *m;* galardón *m;* condecoración *f;* 2. *vt* conceder, otorgar; adjudicar.

award-winning, *adj* premiado.

aware, *adj* 1. enterado; despierto; 2. enterado de, consciente de.

awareness, *n* conciencia *f,* conocimiento *m.*

away, *adv* 1. distante, distancia; 2. lejos, lejos de; 3. *adj* ausente.

awe, *n* 1. temor *m* reverencial, pavor *m* y respeto; 2. *vt* imponer respeto.

awful, *adj* 1. tremendo, imponente, terrible, pasmoso; 2. horrible, malísimo, fatal.

awhile, *adv* un rato, algún tiempo.

awkward, *adj* difícil; violento, inoportuno; delicado, desagradable.

awkwardness, *n* dificultad *f;* incomodidad *f;* molestia *f.*

awning, *n* toldo *m;* entalamadura *f;* toldilla *f.*

awry, *adv* 1. descaminadamente; 2. *adj* torcido, fuera de razón.

axe, *n* hacha *f.*

axial, *adj* axial.

axiom, *n* axioma *m.*

axiomatic, *adj* axiomático.

axis, *n* eje *m.*

azalea, *n* azalea *f.*

Aztec, *adj* 1. azteca; 2. *n* azteca *mf.*

azure, *adj* azul celeste.

B

B, b, n (letra) f B, b.
babble, n 1. parloteo m; barboteo m; murmullo m; 2. vi barbullar, parlotear, hablar indiscretamente.
babbling, adj hablador; balbuceante.
babe, n criatura f; chica f, ricura f, nena f.
babel, n babel.
baboon, n mandril m.
baby, n niño(a), bebé m/f.
babyish, adj infantil.
Babylonian, adj babilónico; babilonio.
baccalaureate, n bachillerato m.
baccarat, n bacará m.
bacchanalia, n bacanales f; bacanal f.
bacchanalian, adj bacanal, báquico.
bachelor, n 1. soltero; 2. licenciado(a).
bachelorhood, n soltería f, estado m de soltero, celibato m.
bacillary, adj bacilar.
back, adj 1. trasero, de atrás; posterior; desde atrás; trasero; 2. adv atrás, hacia atrás; 3. vt apoyar, respaldar; defender; favorecer.
backboard, n tablero m.
backbone, n espinazo m; agallas f.
back-breaking, adj deslomador, matador.
backer, n partidario(a); promotor m, impulsor m.
backfire, n 1. petardeo m; 2. vi petardear; salir el tiro por la culata.
backgammon, n backgamon m.
background, n 1. fondo m; último término m; antecedentes m, historial m, educación f; 2. música de fondo; ruido m de fondo.
backing, n apoyo m; garantía f; respaldo m; reserva f.
backlog, n atrasos m; reserva f de pedidos pendientes; volumen m de trabajo acumulado.
back-pack, n mochila f.
back-packer, n mochilero(a), m/f; persona f que viaja con mochila.
backspace, vt 1. retroceder; 2. n retroceso m, tecla f de retroceso.
backspin, n efecto m de retroceso.
backstage, n bastidores m, espacio m entre bastidores.
backstairs, n escalera f de servicio.
back talk, n respuesta f insolente.
backtrack, vi volver pies atrás; volverse atrás, echarse atrás.
back-up, n apoyo m, respaldo m; reserva f; document copia f de seguridad, copia f de respaldo.
backward, adj hacia atrás; movimiento m de vaivén; atrasado.
backwash, n agua f de rechazo; reacción f, consecuencias f.
backwater, n brazo m de río estancado, remanso m; lugar m atrasado, lugar m de agradable tranquilidad.
backwoods, n región f apartada.
backyard, n patio m trasero, jardín m trasero.
bacon, n tocino m.
bacteria, n bacterias f.
bacterial, adj bacteriano.
bacteriologist, n bacteriólogo(a) m/f.
bacteriology, n bacteriología f.
bacterium, n bacteria.

bad, adj malo, malvado; indecente; podrido, nocivo.
badge, n divisa f, insignia f; distintivo m; chapa f, placa f.
badger, n 1. tejón m; 2. vt acosar, atormentar; fastidiar.
badinage, n chanzas f, bromas f.
badminton, n bádminton m, volante m.
badmouth, vt criticar, insultar; murmurar de.
badness, n maldad f, lo malo, mala calidad f.
bad-tempered, adj de mal genio; de mal humor.
baffle, n 1. deflector m; pantalla f acústica; 2. vt impedir, estorbar; desconcertar; dejar perplejo.
bafflement, n perplejidad f; desconcierto m, confusión f.
baffling, adj de solución nada fácil, misterioso; desconcertante, incomprensible; dificilísimo.
bag, n 1. saco m; talega f; costal m; bolso m, cartera f; maleta f; 2. vt ensacar; cazar, coger, derribar; tomar, apropiarse.
bagatelle, n bagatela f.
bagel, n pan m ácimo; especie de bollo.
bagful, n saco m lleno.
baggage, n equipaje m; bagaje m.
baggy, adj muy holgado; que hace bolsa; con rodilleras; abombachado.
bag lady, n indigente f, mujer f que vive con lo puesto.
bagpipes, n gaita f.
bail, n 1. fianza f; 2. vt archicar.
bail-bond, n fianza f.
bailiff, n alguacil m, corchete m; administrador m.
bairn, n niño(a).
bait, n 1. cebo m, carnada f; aliciente m, anagaza f; 2. vt cebar, poner cebo en; acosar, atormentar.
bake, vt cocer al horno; cocer; endurecer.
baked, adj cocido al horno.
baker, n panadero m.
bakery, n tahona f, panadería f.
baking, n cocción f; hornada f.
bakingsoda, n bicarbonato m de sosa.
balance, n 1. equilibrio m; distribución f de fuerzas; balanza f; balance m; 2. vt equilibrar; contrapesar; saldar; nivelar; hacer balance, cerrar los libros.
balanced, adj equilibrado.
balcony, n balcón m; mirador m.
balding, adj parcialmente calvo.
baldness, n calvicie f; lo escueto, desnudez f.
bale, n 1. bala f; paca f, fardo m; 2. vt embalar; empacar.
baleful, adj funesto, siniestro; cenudo, hosco.
balefully, adv tristemente; funestamente, siniestramente.
baler, n empacadora f, enfardadora f.
balk, n 1. lomo m, caballón m; cabana f; viga f; 2. vt burlar, impedir; perder, no aprovechar; 3. vi detenerse bruscamente; plantarse, repropiarse.
ball, n bola f; globo m, esfera f; pelota f; baile m (gen de etiqueta).
ballad, n balada f, romance m, corrido m.
ballade, n balada f.
ballast, n 1. lastre m; balasto m; en lastre; 2. vt lastrar; balastar.
ballerina, n bailarina f.
ballet, n ballet.
ballet-dancer, n bailarín(ina).
ball game, n partido m de béisbol.
ballistic, adj balístico.
ballistics, n balística f.
balloon, n 1. globo m, bomba f; 2. vi subir en un globo.

balloonist, n ascensionista m/f, aeronauta m/f.

ballot, n votación f; papeleta f.

balloting, n votación f.

ballpark, n estadio m de béisbol; (estimate) cálculo m aproximado.

ballroom, n salón m de baile.

ban, n 1. prohibición f; veda f; 2. vt prohibir, proscribir; vedar; excluir.

banal, adj banal, vulgar.

banality, n banalidad f, vulgaridad f.

banana, n plátano m, banana f.

band, n 1. banda f, tira f, faja f; cinta f; 2. orquesta f; charanga f, banda f; grupo m.

bandage, n venda f.

bandit, n bandido m.

banditry, n bandolerismo m, bandidismo m.

bandmaster, n director m de banda.

bandolier, n bandolera f.

bandstand, n quiosco m de música.

bandy, adj 1. estevado; 2. vt cambiar.

bane, n veneno m; plaga f, azote m.

bang, interj 1. ¡pum!, ¡zas! 2. n golpe, estallido, portazo; 3. vt dar golpes; 4. vi hacer explosión, estallar; hacer estrépito.

bangle, n ajorca f, brazalete m, esclava f.

banish, vt desterrar.

banishment, n destierro m.

banisters, n barandilla f, pasamanos m.

banjo, n banjo m.

bank, n 1. ribera f, orilla f, ribo m, loma f; terraplén m; banco m; montón m; institución bancaria; 2. vt ingresar, depositar.

bankable, adj válido, valedero.

bank-card, n tarjeta f bancaria.

banker, n banquero m.

banknote, n billete m de banco.

bankrupt, adj quebrado, insolvente; en quiebra.

bankruptcy, n quiebra f, insolvencia f, bancarrota f.

banner, n bandera f, estandarte m.

banns, n amonestaciones f, banas f.

banquet, n 1. banquete m; 2. vt festejar; banquetear.

banter, n 1. burlas f, zumba f; comentarios sin importancia; 2. vt chancearse con, tomar el pelo a.

baptism, n bautismo m.

baptismal, adj bautismal.

Baptist, n bautista mf.

baptize, vt bautizar.

bar, n 1. tranca f; palanca f; pastilla f, tableta f; barra, cantina f; 2. vt impedir; prohibir; excluir.

barbarian, adj bárbaro.

barbaric, adj bárbaro, barbárico.

barbarity, n barbaridad f.

barbarous, adj bárbaro.

barbecue, n barbacoa f, asado.

barbed, adj armado de lengüetas; incisivo, mordaz.

barbed wire, n alambre m de espino.

barbel, n barbilla f, cococha f; (Fish) barbo.

barbell, n haltera f, pesas f pl.

barber, n peluquero m, barbero m.

barbershop, n barbería f; cuarteto m vocal armónico.

barbiturate, n barbitúrico m.

bar-code, n código m de barras.

bard, n bardo m.

bare, adj 1. desnudo; descubierto; pelado; raso; 2. vt desnudar; descubrir; descubrirse.

bare-bones, adj muy limitado.

barefaced, adj descarado, fresco.

barefoot(ed), adj, adv descalzo, con los pies desnudos.

barely, adv apenas.

bareness, n desnudez f.

bargain, n 1. pacto m, trato m; negocio m; 2. ganga f; 3. vi negociar; regatear.

bargaining, n negociación f; regateo m; fuerza f en el negocio.

barge, n 1. barcaza f; lancha f a remolque; 2. vt empujar; atajar.

bargepole, n bichero m.

baritone, n barítono m.

barium, n bario m.

bark, n 1. corteza f; 2. ladrido m, 3. barco m; 4. vt descortezar; raer, raspar; 5. ladrar.

barkeeper, n tabernero .

barking, n ladridos m, ladrar m.

barley, n cebada f.

barmaid, n camarera f, moza f de taberna.

barn, n granero m, troje f; establo m, cuadra f.

barnacle, n percebe m.

barndance, n baile m campesino.

barn-owl, n lechuza f.

barnstorm, vi hacer una campaña electoral por el campo.

barnyard, n corral m.

barometer, n barómetro m.

barometric, adj barométrico.

baron, n barón m; magnate m, potentado.

baronet, n baronet m.

baroque, adj barroco; complicado; grotesco.

barracuda, n barracuda f.

barrage, n presa f; cortina f de fuego, barrera f.

barred, adj enrejada, con reja.

barrel, n tonel m, cuba f, barril m.

barren, adj estéril, árido.

barricade, n 1. barricada f; 2. vt cerrar con barricadas.

barrier, n barrera f.

barring, prep excepto, salvo.

barrister, n abogado m/f.

barrow, n túmulo m; carretilla f, carretón m de mano.

barstool, n taburete m (de bar).

barter, n 1. permuta f, trueque m; 2. vt permutar.

basal, adj fundamental, básico, esencial; basal.

basalt, n basalto m.

base, n 1. base f; basa f; 2. campamento m de base; 3. adj bajo, infame, vil; 4. vt basar, fundar en.

baseball, n béisbol m.

baseboard, n (US) rodapié m.

Basel, n Basilea f.

baseless, adj infundado.

baseline, n línea f de base; línea f de saque, línea f de fondo.

basely, adv despreciablemente, bajamente, ruinmente.

baseman, n hombre m de base.

basement, n sótano m.

baseness, n bajeza f, vileza f.

bash, n 1. golpe m, palo m; 2. vt golpear; aporrear; pegar, dar una paliza a.

bashful, adj tímido, vergonzoso, apenado.

bashfully, adv tímidamente.

bashfulness, n timidez f, vergüenza f.

bashing, n tunda f, paliza f.

basic, adj basico, fundamental.

basil, n albahaca f.

basilica, n basílica f.

basilisk, n basilisco m.

basin, *n* tazón *m*, cuenco *m*; jofaina *f*, palangana.
basis, *n* base *f*.
bask, *vi* asolearse; tomar el sol.
basket, *n* cesta *f*; cesto *m*; canasta *f*; banasta *f*, capacho *m*.
basketball, *n* baloncesto *m*, básket *m*.
basketwork, *n* cestería *f*.
bas-relief, *n* bajorrelieve *m*.
bass, *n* róbalo *m*; (Mus) bajo *m*, contrabajo *m*.
basset, *n* perro *m* basset.
bassist, *n* bajista *m/f*, bajo *m*.
bassoon, *n* fagot *m*.
baste, *vt* pringar (Cul); (Cost) hilvanar.
basting, *n* hilván *m*, paliza *f*, zurra *f*.
bastion, *n* bastión *m*, baluarte *m*.
bat, *n* 1. maza *f*, paleta *f*; bate *m*; 2. murciélago *m*; 3. *vt* golpear, **apalear**; **discutir acerca de** algo.
batch, *n* colección *f*, serie *f*, grupo *m*, cantidad *f*, lote *m*, montoncito *m*; lío *m*; hornada *f*; producción *f* por lotes.
bath, *n* baño *m*, bañera *f*, tina *f*.
bathe, *n* 1. baño *m*; 2. *vt* bañarse.
bathhouse, *n* baño *m*.
bathing, *n* baños *m*; el bañarse.
bathing-beauty, *n* sirena *f* de la playa.
bathing-cap, *n* gorro *m* de baño.
bathing-costume, *n* traje *m* de baño, bañador *m*.
bathing-suit, *n* traje *m* de baño, bañador *m*.
bathing-wrap, *n* albornoz *m*.
bathmat, *n* estera *f* de baño.
bathos, *n* paso *m* de lo sublime a lo trivial.
bathrobe, *n* albornoz *m*, bata *f* de baño.
bathroom, *n* cuarto *m* de baño.
bath-towel, *n* toalla *f* de baño.
bathtub, *n* bañera *f*.
batiste, *n* batista *f*.
baton, *n* bastón *m*.
batrachian, *n* batracio *m*.
battalion, *n* batallón *m*.
batten, *n* alfarjí *f*, lata *f*, listón *m*.
batter, *n* batido *m*; bateador *m*.
battered, *adj* magullado; estropeado; maltrecho, malparado; golpeado.
battering, *n* paliza; bombardeo *m*.
battle, *n* 1. batalla *f*; lucha *f*; 2. *vi* luchar por.
battlecry, *n* grito *m* de combate; lema *m*, consigna *f*.
battledore, *n* raqueta *f* de bádminton; antiguo juego predecesor del bádminton.
battlefield, *n* campo *m* de batalla.
battlements, *n* almenas *f*.
battleship, *n* acorazado *m*.
bauble, *n* chuchería *f*.
baud, *n* (Comput) baudio *m*.
baudrate, *n* velocidad *f* de transmisión.
bauxite, *n* bauxita *f*.
bawdiness, *n* lo verde.
bawdy, *adj* verde; indecente, obseno.
bawl, *vt* 1. cantar en voz muy fuerte; 2. *vi* gritar, vocear, desganitarse; llorar muy fuerte.
bay, *n* 1. (Bot) laurel *m*; 2. bahía *f*; 3. caballo *m* bayo; 4. (animal) ladrido *m*, aullido *m*; 5. *vt* aullar.
bayonet, *n* bayoneta *f*.
bayou, *n* pantanos *m*.
bazaar, *n* bazar *m*.
bazooka, *n* bazuca *f*.
beach, *n* 1. playa *f*; 2. *vt* varar; embarrancar.
beachball, *n* pelota *f* de playa.
beach-chair, *n* tumbona *f*.

beach umbrella, *n* sombrilla *f*; parasol *m*, quitasol *m*.
beachwear, *n* traje *m* de playa.
beacon, *n* almenara *f*; faro *m*, fanal *m*; baliza *f*, aerofaro *m*.
bead, *n* cuenta *f*; abalorio *m*; gota *f*; mira *f* globular.
beading, *n* astrágalo *m*, contero *m*.
beadle, *n* bedel *m*; pertiguero *m*.
beak, *n* pico *m*.
beaked, *adj* picudo.
beaker, *n* taza *f* alta; vaso *m* de precipitación.
beam, *n* 1. viga *f*; travesaño *m*; timón *m*; astil *m*; balancín *m*; 2. manga *f*; 3. rayo *m*; 4. *vt* emitir; brillar.
beaming, *adj* sonriente, radiante.
bean, *n* haba *f* gruesa; judía *f*, enana *f*, frijol *m*.
beanbag, *n* saquito que se usa para realizar ejercicios girmnásticos; almohadón *m*, cojín *m*.
beanpole, *n* emparrado *m*; espárrago *m*.
beanstalk, *n* judía *f*.
bear, *n* 1. oso *m*; 2. *vt* llevar; tener; sostener; producir; devengar; parir, soportar, aguantar.
bearable, *adj* soportable, aguantable.
beard, *n* barba *f*; arista *f*.
beardless, *adj* barbilampiño, lampino; imberbe.
bearer, *n* mozo *m*; portador *m*.
bearing, *n* porte *m*, comportamiento *m*.
bearskin, *n* piel *f* de oso.
beast, *n* bestia *f*.
beat, *n* 1. latido; compás *m*, ritmo *m*; 2. *vt* golpear; martillar; pegar; 3. batir; vencer, derrotar; latir, pulsar; ojear.
beatbox, *n* caja *f* de ritmos.
beaten, *adj* batido, martillado.
beater, *n* ojeador *m*, batidor *m*, batidora *f*.
beatific, *adj* beatífico.
beatification, *n* beatificación *f*.
beatify, *vt* beatificar.
beating, *n* golpes *m*, el batir, el azotar; pulsación *f*, latido *m*.
beatitude, *n* Las Bienaventuranzas *f*.
beatnik, *n* beatnik *m/f*.
beat-up, *adj* viejo, destartalado, ruinoso.
beau, *n* pretendiente *m*, novio *m*, galán *m*.
beauteous, *adj* (poet) bello.
beautician, *n* esteticista *mf*.
beautiful, *adj* hermoso, bello; precioso.
beautifully, *adv* maravillosamente, perfectamente.
beautify, *vt* embellecer.
beauty, *n* belleza *f*, hermosura *f*; beldad *f*.
beaver, *n* castor *m*.
becalm, *vt* estar encalmado.
became, *pret* of become.
because, *conj* 1. porque; 2. *prep* causa de, debido a, por motivo de.
beckon, *vt* llamar con señas; atraer.
become, *vt* sentar a, favorecer; convenir a; hacerse, llegar a ser, transformarse en, convertirse en.
bed, *n* 1. cama *f*; lecho *m*; estrato *m*, fondo *m*, cauce *m*; 2. *vt* fijar.
bedclothes, *n* ropa *f* de cama.
bedlinen, *n* ropa *f* de cama, sábanas *f*.
bedpan, *n* chata *f*, silleta *f*, cuna *f*.
bedroom, *n* dormitorio *m*, alcoba *f*, habitación *f*, recámara *f*.
bedsore, *n* úlcera *f* de decúbito.
bedspread, *n* sobrecama *m*, cobertor *m*, cubrecama *f*.
bedtime, *n* hora *f* de acostarse.
bedwetting, *n* enuresis *f*.

bee, n 1. abeja f; 2. reunión f social de vecinos, círculo m social.
beech-tree, n haya f.
beechwood, n hayedo m, hayal m. haya f.
beef, n carne f de vaca, carne f de res.
beefburger, n hamburguesa f.
beefsteak, n biftec m, bistec m.
beehive, n colmena f.
beeline, n salir disparado hacia.
beeper, n localizador m.
beer, n cerveza f.
beeswax, n cera f (de abejas).
beetle, n escarabajo m, coleóptero m.
beetroot, n remolacha f, betabel m.
befit, vt convenir a, venir bien a, corresponder a.
befitting, adj conveniente, decoroso.
befog, vt entenebrecer; ofuscar, confundir.
before, adv 1. delante, adelante; antes; anterior-mente; 2. prep delante de; ante, en presencia de; antes de.
beforehand, adv de antemano, con anticipación.
befoul, vt ensuciar.
befriend, vt ofrecer amistad a; amparar, favorecer.
beg, vt pedir, suplicar, rogar.
beggar, n 1. mendigo m, pordiosero m; 2. vt empobrecer, arruinar, reducir a la miseria.
begin, vt/i comenzar, empezar; iniciar; emprender.
beginner, n principiante mf; novato(a) mf.
beginning, n 1. principio m, comienzo m; 2. origen m.
begonia, n begonia f.
begrime, vt tiznar, ensuciar.
begrudge, vt dar de mala gana; tener envidia a.
beguile, vt engañar; seducir; engatusar; entretener.
beguiling, adj seductor, persuasivo, atractivo.
begun, ptp of begin.
behalf, n de parte de; en nombre de.
behave, vi 1. portarse (con), comportarse, conducirse; 2. vr portarse bien.
behavior, n conducta f; comportamiento m.
behavioral, adj conductual, conductista.
behaviorist, adj 1. conductista; 2. n conductista mf.
behead, vt decapitar, descabezar.
beheld, pret and ptp of behold.
behind, adv 1. detrás; por detrás; atrás; 2. estar atrasado; 3. prep detrás de.
behindhand, adv atrasado, con retraso.
behold, vt contemplar.
beholden, adj estar bajo una obligación a; estar agradecido a.
beholder, n espectador(a) mf, observador(a) mf.
beige, adj 1. (color de) beige; 2. n beige m.
being, n ser m.
bejewelled, adj enjoyado.
belated, adj atrasado, tardío.
belay, vt amarrar (dando vueltas en una cabilla).
belch, n 1. eructo m; 2. vi eructar.
beleaguered, adj sitiado, asediado, cercado.
belfry, n campanario m.
belie, vt desmentir, contradecir; defraudar.
belief, n 1. creencia f (de que); opinión f; 2. fe f.
believable, adj creíble.
believe, vt 1. creer; dar crédito a; 2. vi creer.
believer, n creyente mf, fiel m/f; partidario(a) m/f.
belittle, vt despreciar, minimizar, conceder poca importancia a.
bell, n campana f; campanilla f; cencerro m.
bell-bottomed, adj acampanado, abocinado.
bellboy, n botones m.

belle, n belleza f, beldad f.
bellhop, n botones m.
bellicose, adj belicoso.
bellicosity, n belicosidad f.
belligerence, n beligerancia f; agresividad f.
belligerent, adj 1. beligerante; agresivo; 2. n belig-erante m/f.
bellow, n 1. bramido m; rugido m; 2. vt gritar, vociferar; 3. vi bramar; rugir.
bellows, n fuelle m.
bellpull, n campanilla f.
bellringer, n campanero m; campanólogo(a) m/f.
bell-tower, n campanario m.
belly, n 1. vientre m; barriga f, panza f; 2. vi hacer bolso, llenarse de viento.
bellyache, n 1. dolor m de barriga, dolor m de tripas; 2. vi quejarse constantemente (de).
bellyaching, n quejas f constantes.
belly-button, n ombligo m.
belly-landing, n aterrizaje m de panza.
belly-laugh, n carcajada f, risotada f.
belong, vi pertenecer a.
belongings, n pertenencias f, bártulos m; cosas f; efectos m personales.
beloved, adj 1. querido (de); 2. n querido m, amada f.
below, adv 1. abajo, (por) debajo; 2. prep bajo, debajo de; inferior a.
belt, n 1. cinturón m, faja f; correa f, cinta f; 2. vt zurrar, dar una paliza a.
beltway, n carretera f de circunvalación.
bemuse, vt aturdir, confundir.
bench, n banco m; banquillo m; tribunal m; judica-tura f.
benchmark, n cota f, punto m topográfico; punto m de referencia.
bend, n 1. curva f; recodo m, vuelta f; ángulo m; 2. vt encorvar; doblar; torcer; inclinar; 3. vi encorvarse; doblarse, torcerse.
beneath, adv and prep below.
benediction, n bendición f.
benefaction, n beneficio m.
benefactor, n bienhechor m, benefactor m.
benefactress, n bienhechora f, benefactora f.
beneficence, n beneficencia f.
beneficent, adj benéfico.
beneficial, adj provechoso, beneficioso.
beneficiary, n beneficiario(a) mf; beneficiado(a) mf.
benefit, n 1. beneficio m; provecho m, utilidad f; subsidio m; 2. vt beneficiar, aprovechar; 3. vi aprovecharse; sacar provecho de.
benevolence, n benevolencia f.
benevolent, adj benévolo.
benighted, adj ignorante.
benign, adj benigno, benignant; saludable.
benumb, vt entumecer; entorpecer; paralizar.
benumbed, adj entumecido; paralizado.
benzene, n benceno m.
benzine, n bencina f.
bequeath, vt legar.
bequest, n legado m.
bereave, vt privar de.
bereaved, adj afligido.
bereavement, n aflicción f.
beret, n boina f.
beriberi, n beriberi m.
berm, n arcén m.
berry, n baya f; grano m.
berserk, adj perder los estribos; ponerse como una fiera; volverse loco.

berth, n 1. amarradero m; punto m de atraque; camarote m; 2. vt/i atracar.

beryl, n berilo m.

beryllium, n berilio m.

beseech, vt suplicar.

beseeching, adj suplicante.

beset, vt acosar, perseguir; obstruir, dificultar.

besetting, adj obsesionante; dominante.

beside, prep cerca de, junto a, al lado de.

besides, adv 1. además; 2. prep además de; excepto, fuera de.

besiege, vt asediar, sitiar.

besieger, n sitiador m.

besmear, vt embarrar, embadurnar.

besmirch, vt manchar, mancillar.

besotted, adj entontecido; atortolado; encaprichado, encalabrinado.

bespatter, vt salpicar (de).

bespeak, vt apalabrar; encargar, reservar.

besprinkle, vt salpicar, rociar (de); espolvorear.

best, adj superl 1. el, (la) mejor; 2. adv superior (lo) mejor; 3. n lo mejor; 4. vt vencer.

bestial, adj bestial.

bestiality, n bestialidad f.

bestir, vr menearse.

bestow, vt otorgar, conceder.

bestowal, n otorgamiento m; donación f; ofrecimiento m.

bestraddle, vt montar a horcajadas, estar a horcajadas sobre; estar a caballo sobre.

bestrew, vt desparramar, esparcir; sembrar, cubrir.

bestride, vt montar a horcajadas.

best-seller, n bestseller m, éxito m de librería.

bet, n 1. apuesta f; postura f; 2. vt apostar.

beta, n beta f.

betake, vr dirigirse a, trasladarse a, acudir a.

betel, n betel m.

bethink, vr acordarse de.

betide, vt/i acontecer; presagiar.

betimes, adv 1. temprano, al alba; 2. rápidamente; a tiempo.

betoken, vt presagiar, anunciar.

betray, vt 1. traicionar; 2. revelar, delatar; 3. dejar ver, dar muestras de, descubrir.

betrayal, n 1. traición f; abuso m de confianza; 2. revelación f; 3. descubrimiento m.

betrayer, n traidor(a) m/f.

betroth, vt prometer en matrimonio.

betrothal, n desposorios m, esponsales m.

betrothed, adj 1. prometido; 2. n prometido(a) m/f.

better, adj comp 1. mejor; 2. adv comp mejor; mejor que; tanto mejor (para); 3. n apostador(a) m/f; 4. vt mejorar, superar.

betterment, n mejora f, mejoramiento m.

betting, adj 1. aficionado al juego; 2. n juego m, el apostar.

between, adv 1. en medio; 2. prep entre.

bevel, adj biselado.

beverage, n bebida f.

bewail, vt lamentar.

beware, vi tener cuidado; guardarse de.

bewhiskered, adj bigotudo.

bewilder, vt aturdir, dejar perplejo, aturrullar, desconcertar.

bewildered, adj person desconcertado, perplejo, aturdido.

bewildering, adj desconcertante.

bewilderment, n aturdimiento m, perplejidad f.

bewitch, vt hechizar.

bewitching, adj hechicero, encantador.

beyond, adv 1. más allá, más lejos; 2. prep más allá de.

bi..., pref bi...

biannual, adj semestral.

bias, n 1. sesgo m, diagonal f; 2. propensión f, predisposición f; 3. pasión f, prejuicio m.

bias(s)ed, adj parcial.

bib, n babero m, babador m.

Bible, n Biblia f.

Biblical, adj bíblico.

biblio..., pref biblio...

bibliography, n bibliografía f.

bibliophile, n bibliófilo(a) m/f.

bibulous, adj bebedor, borrachín.

bicameral, adj bicameral.

bicarbonate, n bicarbonato m sódico.

biceps, n bíceps m.

bicker, vi reñir, altercar; murmurar.

bickering, n riñas, altercados m.

bicuspid, adj bicúspide.

bicycle, n bicicleta f.

bid, n 1. oferta f, postura f; 2. apuesta f, declaración f; 3. vt ordenar, mandar; ofrecer, licitar.

bidder, n postor(a) m/f; declarante m/f.

bidding, n 1. orden f, mandato m; 2. licitación f, ofertas f.

bide, vt esperar la hora propicia.

bidet, n bidet m, bidé m.

bidirectional, adj bidireccional.

biennial, adj bienal; bianual.

bier, n féretro m, andas f pl.

bifocal, adj bifocal.

bifurcate, vi bifurcarse.

big, adj grande; abultado, voluminoso; importante.

bigamist, n bígamo(a) m/f.

bigamous, adj bígamo.

bigamy, n bigamia f.

big-boned, adj de huesos grandes; huesudo.

biggish, adj bastante grande.

bighead, n orgulloso(a) m/f, engreído(a) m/f.

bigheaded, adj engreído(a).

big-hearted, adj generoso.

bight, n 1. ensenada f, cala f; recodo m; 2. gaza f, laza f.

big-mouthed, adj 1. de boca grande, de boca ancha, bocudo; 2. bocón; chismoso; soplón.

bigot, n fanático(a) f, intolerante m/f.

bigoted, adj fanático, intolerante.

bigotry, n fanatismo m, intolerancia f.

bike, n 1. bici f; 2. vi ir en bicicleta, ir en moto.

biker, n motorista m/f.

bikeshed, n cobertizo m para bicicletas.

bikeway, n carril m de bicicletas; pista f de ciclismo.

bikini, n bikini m.

bilabial, adj, n bilabial f.

bilateral, adj bilateral.

bile, n bilis f.

bilge, n 1. pantoque m; 2. tonterías f.

bilingual, adj bilingüe.

bilingualism, n bilingüismo m.

bilious, adj bilioso.

bilk, vt estafar, defraudar.

bill, n 1. cuenta f, adición f; factura f; 2. proyecto m de ley; declaración f de derechos; 3. billete m; letra f de cambio; 4. vt facturar, cobrar.

billboard, n cartelera f, valla f publicitaria.

billet, n 1. alojamiento m; colocación f, puesto m; 2. vt alojar.

billfold, n billetero m, cartera f.

billiard-ball, *n* bola *f* de billar.

billiard-cue, *n* taco *m*.

billiards, *n* billar *m*.

billion, *n* billón *m*, (U.S.) mil millones *m*.

billionaire, *n* billonario(a) *f*.

billow, *n* 1. oleada *f*; 2. *vi* ondular, ondear.

billowy, *adj* ondoso; hinchado.

billy, *n* porra *f*.

billy goat, *n* macho *m* cabrío.

bimonthly, *adj* bimestral; bimensual, quincenal.

bin, *n* hucha *f*, arcón *m*; caja *f*.

binary, *adj* binario.

bind, *vt* 1. atar, liar; vendar; 2. obligar; encuadernar.

binder, *n* agavilladora *f*; carpeta *f*; encuadernador(a) *m/f*.

bindery, *n* taller *m* de encuadernación.

binding, *adj* 1. obligatorio (para); 2. *n* encuadernación *f*.

binge, *n* borrachera *f*; comilona *f*, exceso *m* gastronómico.

bingo, *n* bingo *m*.

bin-liner, *n* bolsa *f* de la basura.

binnacle, *n* bitácora *f*.

binocular, *adj* binocular.

binomial, *adj* de dos términos.

binuclear, *adj* binuclear.

bio... *pref* bio...

bioactive, *adj* bioactivo.

biochemist, *n* bioquímico *m/f*.

biochemistry, *n* bioquímica *f*.

biodegradable, *adj* biodegradable.

biodegrade, *n* 1. biodegradar; 2. *vi* biodegradarse.

bioengineering, *n* bioingeniería *f*.

biofuel, *n* combustible *m* biológico.

biogenesis, *n* biogénesis *f*.

biographer, *n* biógrafo(a) *m/f*.

biographic(al), *adj* biográfico.

biography, *n* biografía *f*.

biological, *adj* biológico.

biologist, *n* biólogo(a) *m/f*.

biology, *n* biología *f*.

biomedical, *adj* biomédico.

biometrics, *n* biometría *f*.

bionic, *adj* biónico.

bionics, *n* electrónica *f* biológica.

bioorganic, *adj* bioorgánico; química *f* bioorgánica.

biophysical, *adj* biofísico.

biophysics, *n* biofísica *f*.

biopsy, *n* biopsia *f*.

biostatistics, *n* bioestadística *f*.

biosynthesis, *n* biosíntesis *f*.

biosynthetic, *adj* biosintético.

biotechnology, *n* biotecnología *f*.

biotic, *adj* biótico.

biotype, *n* biotipo *m*.

biowarfare, *n* guerra *f* bacteriológica.

bipartisan, *adj* que tienen en común los dos partidos, bipartido.

bipartite, *adj* bipartido; bipartito.

biped, *n* bípedo *m*.

biplane, *n* biplano *m*.

bipolar, *adj* bipolar.

bipolarize, *vt* bipolarizar.

birch, *n* abedul *m*.

birchwood, *n* bosque *m* de abedules.

bird, *n* ave *f*, pájaro *m*.

birdbrain, *n* casquivano(a) *m/f*.

birdcage, *n* jaula *f* de pájaro; pajarera *f*.

bird-call, *n* reclamo *m*.

bird-dog, *n* perro *m* de caza.

bird-sanctuary, *n* reserva *f* para las aves.

birdseed, *n* alpiste *m*.

bird's-nest, *n* nido *m* de pájaro.

bird-watcher, *n* ornitólogo(a) *m/f*, observador(a) *m/f* de aves.

bird-watching, *n* ornitología *f*, observación *f* de aves.

birth, *n* nacimiento *m*; parto *m*.

birth-certificate, *n* partida *f* de nacimiento, fe *f* de bautismo.

birth-control, *n* control *m* de natalidad.

birthday, *n* cumpleaños *m*; aniversario *m*.

birthdaycake, *n* tarta *f* de cumpleaños.

birthdaycard, *n* tarjeta *f* de cumpleaños.

birthdayparty, *n* fiesta *f* de cumpleaños.

birthdaypresent, *n* regalo *m* de cumpleaños .

birthmark, *n* rosa *f*, antojo *m*, marca *f* de nacimiento.

birthplace, *n* lugar *m* de nacimiento.

birthright, *n* derechos *m* de nacimiento; primogenitura *f*.

biscuit, *n* 1. galleta *f*; 2. bizcocho *m*.

bisect, *vt* bisecar.

bisection, *n* bisección *f*, división *f* en dos partes.

bisexual, *adj* 1. bisexual; 2. *n* bisexual *m/f*.

bisexuality, *n* bisexualidad *f*.

bishop, *n* obispo *m/f*.

bismuth, *n* bismuto *m*.

bison, *n* bisonte *m*.

bisque, *n* sopa *f* de mariscos.

bit, *n* freno *m*, bocado *m*; broca *f*; barrena *f*; trozo *m*, porción *f*, pedacito *m*; (Comput) unidad *f* de información.

bite, *n* 1. mordedura *f*; mordisco *m*; dentellada *f*; picadura *f*; 2. *vi* morder; picar; tragar el anzuelo.

bitter, *adj* amargo; penetrante, cortante.

bitterly, *adv* amargamente.

bitterness, *n* amargor *m*; amargura *f*; encarnizamiento *m*; implacabilidad *f*; agudeza *f*.

bittersweet, *adj* agridulce.

bituminous, *adj* bituminoso.

bivalent, *adj* bivalente.

bivalve, *adj* bivalvo.

bi-weekly, *adj* 1. quincenal; bisemanal; 2. *adv* quincenalmente; bisemanalmente.

bizarre, *adj* extraño, raro; estrafalario.

black, *adj* 1. negro; 2. *n* negro *m*.

blackberry, *n* zarzamora *f*, mora *f*; zarza *f*.

blackbird, *n* mirlo *m*.

blackboard, *n* pizarra *f*.

blackcock, *n* gallo *m* lira *f*.

blacken, *vt* ennegrecer; calcinar; tiznar de negro; denigrar, desacreditar.

blackguard, *n* pillo *m*, canalla *m*.

blackhead, *n* comedón *m*, espinilla *f*.

black-hearted, *adj* malvado, perverso.

blackish, *adj* negruzco.

blackjack, *n* cachiporra.

blacklist, *n* 1. lista *f* negra; 2. *vt* poner en la lista negra.

blackmail, *n* 1. chantaje *m*; 2. *vt* chantajear.

blackmailer, *n* chantajista *m/f*.

blackness, *n* negrura *f*; oscuridad *f*.

blackout, *n* 1. apagón *m*; 2. amnesia *f* temporal, desmayo *m*; 3. bloqueo *m* informativo.

Black Sea, *n* Mar *m* Negro.

blacksmith, *n* herrero *m*.

bladder, n vejiga f.

blade, n hoja f; espada f; paleta f, aleta f.

blah, adj poco apetitoso.

blamable, adj censurable, culpable.

blame, n 1. culpa f; 2. vt culpar, echar la culpa a.

blameless, adj person inocente (de); action intachable, irreprochable.

blameworthy, adj censurable, culpable.

blanch, vt 1. blanquear; 2. vi palidecer.

bland, adj suave.

blandish, vt engatusar, halagar.

blandishments, n halagos m, lisonjas f.

blank, adj en blanco; virgen.

blanket, n 1. manta f, frazada f, manto m, capa f; 2. vt cubrir, envolver.

blare, n 1. estrépito m, sonido m fuerte; trompetazo m; 2. vt vociferar, anunciar a gritos; 3. vi resonar, sonar muy fuerte.

blaspheme, vi blasfemar.

blasphemer, n blasfemador(a) m/f.

blasphemous, adj blasfemo.

blasphemy, n blasfemia f.

blast, n 1. ráfaga f; soplo m; chorro m; trompetazo m; explosión f; 2. vt volar; derribar, destruir.

blast off, vi (rocket) despegar.

blasted, adj condenado, maldito.

blast-furnace, n alto horno m.

blasting, n explosión f controlada.

blatant, adj descarado; agresivo; estrepitoso, vocinglero.

blather, n 1. disparates m; 2. vi charlatanear, decir tonterías.

blaze, n 1. llamarada f, resplandor m; incendio m; hoguera f; 2. vi arder en llamas; brillar, resplandecer; 3. n mancha f, estrella f; señal f.

blazer, n chaqueta f (de deporte, de colegio etc), chaquetilla f.

blazing, adj abrasador; brillante; irreprimible; violento.

blazon, n blasón m.

bleach, n 1. lejía f; blanqueo m; 2. vt blanquear; 3. vi blanquearse.

bleak, adj desierto, desolador, inhóspito; pelado; triste, adusto.

bleakly, adv desoladamente; tristemente, descorazonadoramente.

bleakness, n desolación f; frialdad f; crudeza f.

bleary, adj legañoso.

bleat, n 1. balido m; queja f; 2. vi balar; quejarse tristemente, gimotear.

bleed, vt 1. sangrar; desangrar; 2. vi sangrar; exudar.

bleeder, n hemofílico m.

bleeding, adj 1. sangrante, sangriento, que sangra; 2. liberal m de gran corazón; 3. n sangría f; desangramiento m, hemorragia f.

blemish, n 1. tacha f, mancha f; 2. vt manchar.

blend, n 1. mezcla f, combinación f; 2. vt mezclar, combinar, armonizar; 3. vi combinarse, armonizarse.

blended, adj mezclado.

blender, n 1. catador(a) m/f; 2. licuadora f.

bless, vt bendecir; persignarse, santiguarse.

blessed, adj bendito, bienaventurado.

blessedness, n bienaventuranza f; beatitud f, bendición f; felicidad f.

blessing, n bendición f.

blight, n 1. añublo m, tizón m, polvillo m; plaga f; 2. adj infortunio m; desperfecto m.

blimp, n globo m.

blind, adj 1. ciego; 2. n pretexto m; persiana f; 3. vi cegar; deslumbrar.

blindfold, adj 1. con los ojos vendados; 2. n venda f; 3. vt vendar los ojos a.

blinding, adj intenso, cegador, deslumbrante.

blindly, adv a ciegas, ciegamente.

blindness, n ceguera f, ceguedad f.

blink, n 1. parpadeo m; destello; 2. vt guiñar, cerrar momentáneamente; 3. vi parpadear, pestañear.

blinkers, n anteojeras; (luces) intermitentes m.

blissful, adj bienaventurado;feliz; deleitoso.

blister, n 1. ampolla f; 2. vt ampollar, causar ampollas en; 3. vi ampollarse.

blithe, adj alegre.

blizzard, n ventisca f.

bloated, adj hinchado (de), abotagado.

blob, n gota f; borrón m.

bloc, n bloque m; en en bloque.

block, n 1. bloque m; tarugo m; adoquín m; obstáculo m; cuadra f, manzana f; 2. vt obstruir, cerrar, atorar; estorbar, impedir; 3. vi obstruirse, cerrarse.

blockade, n 1. bloqueo m; 2. vt bloquear.

blockage, n obstrucción f; obstáculo m, estorbo m.

blockbuster, n bomba f revientamanzanas; fulminante; bomba f.

blockhead, n zopenco(a) m/f; imbécil m/f.

blond(e), adj rubio(a) güero(a).

blood, n sangre f; linaje m, parentezco m.

blood bank, n banco m de sangre.

blood bath, n carnicería f, baño m de sangre.

blood brother, n hermano m de sangre.

blood cell, n célula f sanguínea.

blood clot, n coágulo m sanguíneo.

blood count, n recuento m sanguíneo.

blood donor, n donante m/f de sangre.

blood feud, n odio m de sangre, enemistad f mortal (entre clanes, familias).

blood group, n grupo m sanguíneo.

bloodhound, n sabueso m.

bloodless, adj exangüe; incruento, sin efusión de sangre.

bloodlust, n sed f de sangre.

blood plasma, n plasma m sanguíneo.

blood poisoning, n envenenamiento m de la sangre.

blood pressure, n presión f sanguínea, tensión f arterial.

blood relation, n pariente m consanguíneo; parienta f consanguínea.

bloodshed, n efusión f de sangre; mortandad f.

bloodstain, n mancha f de sangre.

bloodstained, adj manchado de sangre.

bloodstream, n corriente f sanguínea, sangre f.

bloodsucker, n sanguijuela f.

blood test, n análisis m de sangre.

bloodthirsty, adj sanguinario.

blood transfusion, n transfusión f de sangre.

blood type, n grupo m sanguíneo.

blood vessel, n vaso m sanguíneo.

bloomer, n plancha f.

bloomers, n (prenda femenina) pantalones m bombachos m.

blooming, adj floreciente; lleno de salud.

blooper, n metedura f de pata.

blossom, n 1. flor f; en flor; 2. vi florecer; transformarse en, convertirse en; alcanzar su plenitud.

blotch, n mancha f; erupción f, rojez f.

blotchy, adj manchado, lleno de manchas.

blotter, n secante m tipo rodillo, secafirmas m; hoja f de papel secante.

blouse, n blusa f.

blouson, n cazadora f.

blow, n 1. golpe m; bofetada f; 2. n soplo m, soplido m; 3. vi soplar; sonar.

blow up, vt 1. inflar, ampliar; volar, hacer saltar, explotar; 2. vi estallar, explotar, reventar.

blow dryer, n secador m de pelo.

blow-dry, vt secar con secador.

blowgun, n cerbatana f.

blowtorch, n soplete m.

blowup, n 1. ampliación f; 2. explosión f de ira; riña f, pelea f.

blubber, n 1. grasa f de ballena; 2. vt decir lloriqueando; 3. vi lloriquear, llorar a lágrima viva.

blubbery, adj fláccido, fofo; labios m carnosos.

bludgeon, n 1. cachiporra f; 2. vt aporrear.

blue, adj azul.

bluebell, n jacinto m silvestre.

blueberry, n arándano m.

bluebird, n pájaro m azul, azulejo m.

blue-blooded, adj de sangre noble, linajudo.

blue-eyed, adj de ojos azules.

bluejay, n arrendajo m azul.

blueness, n azul m, lo azul.

blueprint, n cianotipo m, ferroprusiato m; anteproyecto m.

bluff, n 1. blof m, farol m; escarpa f, risco m; 2. vt hacer un blof a, engañar; 3. vi farolear.

bluffer, n farolero m.

bluish, adj azulado, azulino.

blunder, n 1. patochada f, metedura f de pata; error m garrafal; 2. vt hacer una patochada.

blunderer, n torpe m; metelapata f.

blunt, adj 1. embotado, desafilado; despuntado; directo, franco, abrupto; 2. vt embotar, desafilar.

bluntness, n embotadura f; franqueza f, brusquedad f.

blur, n 1. contorno m borroso, impresión f imprecisa; 2. vt hacer borroso, oscurecer, empañar.

blurb, n propaganda f publicitaria.

blurred, adj borroso, poco nítido.

blush, n 1. rubor m, sonrojo m; color m de rosa; 2. vi ruborizarse, sonrojarse, ponerse colorado.

blusher, n colorete m.

blushing, adj ruboroso; candoroso.

bluster, n 1. jactancia f; fanfarronadas f, bravatas f; 2. vt baladronear; 3. vi fanfarronear.

blusterer, n fanfarrón m.

blustery, adj tempestuoso; day de mucho viento.

boa, n boa f; constrictor boa f.

boar, n verraco m, cerdo m; jabalí m.

board, n 1. tabla f, tablero m, tablón m; 2. junta f, consejo m de administración; 2. vt ir a bordo de; 3. vi hospedarse.

boarder, n huésped(da) m/f; interno(a) m/f.

boarding-party, n pelotón m de abordaje.

boarding-pass, n tarjeta f de embarque, pase m de embarque.

boardroom, n sala f de juntas.

boardwalk, n paseo m entablado.

boast, n 1. fanfarronada f, alarde m; 2. vt enorgullecerse de poseer, ostentar; 3. vi jactarse.

boasted, adj alardeado, cacareado.

boaster, n jactancioso(a) m/f, fanfarrón(ona) m/f, presumido(a) m/f.

boastfulness, n jactancia f.

boat, n barco m; buque m, navío m.

boatbuilder, n constructor m de barcos; astillero m.

boat-deck, n cubierta f de botes.

boating, n canotaje m; paseo m en barca.

boatload, n barcada f.

boatman, n barquero m.

boat people, n refugiados que huyen en barco.

boat-race, n regata f.

bobbin, n carrete m, bobina f.

bobble, n 1. borla f; pifia f; 2. vt pifiar.

bobby pin, n horquilla f, prendedor m.

bobcat, n lince m.

bobtailed, adj rabicorto.

bodice, n corpiño m; almilla f.

bodily, adj corpóreo, corporal.

body, n cuerpo m; cadaver m, armazón f, bastidor m; grupo m.

body-builder, n culturista m.

body-building, n culturismo m.

body count, n número de muertos.

bodywork, n carrocería f; chapistería f.

bog, n pantano m, ciénaga f.

bogey, n duende m, pesadilla f.

boggle, vi sobresaltarse, pasmarse.

boggy, adj pantanoso.

bogus, adj falso, fraudulento; fingido.

boil, n 1. divieso m, furúnculo m, postema f; 2. vt hervir, hacer hervir; 3. vi bullir; estar furioso.

boiler, n caldera m/f; caldero m, calefón m.

boiler-room, n sala f de calderas.

boiling-point, n punto m de ebullición.

boisterous, adj borrascoso; ruidoso, turbulento.

bold, adj valiente, audaz; atrevido, osado.

boldness, n audacia f, osadía f; temeridad f; energía f.

boletus, n seta f.

boll, n cápsula f.

bolognese, adj salsa f boloñesa.

boloney, n tipo de salchicha f.

bolster, n 1. travesaño m, cabezal m; 2. vt reforzar; alentar, dar aliento.

bolt, n 1. cerrojo m; perno m, tornillo m; 2. vt echar el cerrojo a; sujetar con tornillos, empernar; 3. vi salir de golpe.

bomb, n 1. bomba f; 2. vt bombardear; suspender.

bombardier, n bombardero m.

bombardment, n bombardeo m.

bombast, n ampulosidad f, rimbombancia f.

bombastic, adj altisonante, ampuloso, rimbombante; jactancioso, farolero.

bomb-disposal, n desactivación f de bombas, neutralización f de bombas.

bombing, n bombardeo m.

bombproof, adj a prueba de bombas.

bomb-shelter, n refugio m antiaéreo.

bona fide, adj genuino, auténtico, de fiar, fiable.

bona fides, n buena fe f; autenticidad f.

bonanza, n bonanza f.

bond, n 1. lazo m, vínculo m; 2. bono m, obligación f; fianza f; 3. vt liar, vincular.

bondage, n esclavitud f, cautiverio m.

bonding, n vinculación f.

bone, n 1. hueso m; espina f; 2. vt deshuesar, quitar las espinas a.

boned, adj deshuesado; sin espinas.

bone-dry, adj enteramente seco.

bone-marrow, n médula f ósea.

bonfire, n hoguera f, fogata f.

bongo, n (also drum) bongó m.

bonhomie, n afabilidad f.

bonnet, n gorra f, cofia f; papalina f; gorro m.

bonsai, n bonsai m.

bonus, n sobrepaga f, bonificación f, suplemento m, adicional; dividendo m.

bony, n huesudo; óseo, huesoso; descarnado, flaco.

boo, n silbido m, rechifla f, pateo m; abuchear, silbar, rechiflar, patear.

boobtube, n televisor m.

booby-trap, n 1. trampa f; trampa f explosiva; 2. vt poner trampa explosiva.

book, n 1. libro m; libreta, cuaderno m; registro m; 2. vt reservar habitación, contratar.

bookable, adj que se puede reservar.

bookbinder, n encuadernador.

bookbinding, n encuadernación f.

bookcase, n librería f, estante m para libros, librero m.

book club, n club de lectores.

book ends, n sujetalibros m pl, soportalibros m pl.

book fair, n feria f de libros.

booking, n reserva f; contratación f.

book keeper, n contable m/f, contador; tenedor de libros.

book keeping, n teneduría f de libros.

booklet, n folleto m; opúsculo m.

bookmaker, n corredor m de apuestas, apostador m profesional.

bookmark, n señal f, registro m de libro.

bookrest, n atril m.

bookseller, n librero, librería f.

bookshelf, n anaquel m para libros, estantería f.

bookshop, n librería f.

bookstore, n librería f.

boom, n 1. botalón m, botávara f; aguilón m, brazo m; estampido m, trueno m; prosperidad f repentina; 2. vi tronar; resonar.

boomerang, n 1. bumerang m; 2. adj contraproducente; 3. vi tener un resultado contraproducente.

booming, adj resonante, retumbante; próspero, floreciente.

boon, n favor m; ventaja f, beneficio m.

boor, n patán m, hombre m grosero.

boorish, adj palurdo, grosero.

boorishness, n grosería f.

boost, n empujón m, estímulo m, ayuda f.

booster, n elevador m de tensión; elevador m de voltaje; cohete m acelerador.

boot, n 1. bota; 2. vt dar un puntapié a; arrancar, cebar, inicializar.

booth, n puesto m; barraca f, cabina f.

bootleg, adj 1. de contrabando; 2. n whisky m ilegal; 3. vi contrabandear en licores.

bootmaker, n zapatero m que hace botas.

booze, n bebida f alcohólica.

boozer, n bebedor m, tomador m.

boracic, adj bórico.

borage, n borraja f.

borax, n bórax m.

border, n 1. borde m, margen m; orilla; frontera f; 2. vt orlar; 3. lindar con.

bordering, adj contiguo.

borderland, n zona f fronteriza.

borderline, n 1. línea f divisoria; frontera f; 2. incierto, dudoso.

bore, n 1. taladro m, barrena f; calibre m; (person) pelmazo m; 2. vt taladrar, agujerear; aburrir, fastidiar.

boredom, n aburrimiento m, fastidio m.

borehole, n perforación f.

boric, adj ácido m bórico.

boring, adj aburrido, pesado, latoso.

born-again, adj renacido, vuelto a nacer.

boron, n boro m.

borough, n municipio m; distrito m municipal.

borrow, vt pedir prestado, tomar prestado.

borrower, n él (la) que toma prestado; usuario, prestatario.

bosh, n tonterías f.

bosom, n seno m, pecho m; pechera f; inseparable.

boss, n 1. protuberancia f; clavo m; llave f de boveda; 2. jefe m; patrón m; amo, capataz m; gerente m; 3. vt regentar, dar órdenes a, dominar, 4. vt mandonear

bossiness, n carácter m mandón, tiranía f.

bossy, adj mandón, tiránico.

botanic(al), adj botanico.

botanist, n botánico m/f, botanista m/f.

botanize, vi herborizar.

botany, n botánica f.

botch, n 1. chapuza f; 2. vt chapucear, chafullar; remendar (chapuceramente).

both, adj and pron ambos, los dos.

bother, n 1. molestia, lata f; 2. vt molestar, fastidiar, incomodar; poner nervioso; 3. vi molestarse con, preocuparse por.

bothersome, adj molesto.

bottle, n 1. botella f; frasco m; 2. vt embotellar; enfrascar.

bottle brush, n escobilla f, limpiabotellas m.

bottled, adj embotellado.

bottle-fed, adj alimentado con biberón.

bottle-feed, vt criar con biberón.

bottleneck, n gollete m.

bottle opener, n abrebotellas m, destapador m.

bottling, n embotellado m.

bottom, n 1. fondo m; 2. adj part más baja, inferior; último.

bottomless, adj sin fondo, insondable.

bottommost, adj (el) más bajo; último.

botulism, n botulismo m.

boudoir, n tocador m.

bouillon, n caldo m.

boulder, n canto m rodado.

boulevard, n zócalo m.

bounce, n 1. rebote m; fanfarronería f, dinamismo m; 2. vt hacer rebotar; 3. vi recuperarse (de repente).

bouncing, adj robusto, fuerte.

bouncy, adj de mucho rebote, que rebota fuertemente.

bound, adj 1. atado, encuadernado, obligado; (b__ for) con destino a; 2. vt limitar; 3. n límite m.

boundary, n límite m, lindero m; banda f.

boundary line, n límite m, frontera f.

boundless, adj ilimitado.

bounty, n munificencia f, liberalidad f.

bouquet, n 1. ramo m, ramillete m; 2. buqué m, nariz f.

bourgeois, adj burgués.

bourgeoisie, n burguesía f.

bout, n rato m, encuentro m; lucha f; (Med) ataque m.

boutique, n boutique f.

bovine, adj bovino; lerdo, estúpido.

bow, n 1. arco m, nudo m, lazo m; (de barco) proa f; reverencia f; (Mus) arco m; 2. vt inclinar la cabeza; 3. vi hacer una reverencia.

bowdlerize, vt expurgar.

bowel, n intestino m; vientre m.

bowing, n técnica f del arco.

bowl, n 1. escudilla f, tazón m, jofaina f; hornillo m; cuenco m; estadio m; 2. vi rodar, arrojar; jugar al boliche.

bowlegs, n piernas f arqueadas.

bowler, n jugador(a) m/f de bolos.

bowline, n bolina f.

bowling, n bolos m, boliche m.

bowling-alley, n bolera f, boliche m.

bowling-green, n pista f para bochas.

bowman, n arquero m, ballestero m.

bowsprit, n bauprés m.

bowstring, n cuerda f de arco.

bow tie, n corbata f de lazo, pajarita f.

bow window, n mirador m, ventana f saediza.

box, n 1. caja f, cajón m; cofre m, arca f; 2. vt encajonar, poner en una caja; encerrar en una caja.

box camera, n cámara f de cajón.

boxcar, n furgón m.

boxer, n boxeador m; calzones m.

boxing, n boxeo m.

box number, n apartado m, casilla f.

box office, n taquilla f, boletería f.

box spring, n muelle m.

boy, n niño m; muchacho m, chico m.

boycott, n 1. boicoteo m; 2. vt boicotear.

boyfriend, n amigo m, amiguito m; compañero m.

boyhood, n juventud f, niñez f.

boyish, adj juvenil, muchachil, de muchacho.

boy scout, n (muchacho m, o niño m) explorador m.

bra, n sostén m, sujetador m.

brace, n 1. abrazadera f, refuerzo m; riostra f, tirante m; banda f; 2. vt asegurar, reforzar; 3. vr prepararse para resistir (una embestida); fortalecer su ánimo.

bracelet, n pulsera f, brazalete m.

bracing, adj tónico, vigorizante.

bracket, n abrazadera f; soporte m.

bracket off, vt excluir; poner aparte, separar; aislar.

bracket together, vt agrupar, poner juntos.

brad, n puntilla f, clavito m.

brag, n 1. fanfarronada f, bravata f; 2. vi jactarse, fanfarronear.

braggart, n fanfarrón m, jactancioso m.

bragging, n fanfarronadas f.

braid, n 1. trenza f; galón m; 2. vt trenzar; galonear.

Braille, n Braille m.

brain, n 1. cerebro m, sesos m; 2. inteligencia f, cabeza f; capacidad f.

brainchild, n parto m del ingenio, invento m.

brainless, adj estúpido, insensato.

brain power, n fuerza f intelectual.

brainstorm, n frenesí m; idea f genia.

brain teaser, n rompecabezas m.

brainwash, vt lavar el cerebro a.

brainwashing, n lavado m de cerebro.

brainwork, n trabajo m intelectual.

brainy, adj (muy) inteligente, talentudo.

braise, vt brasear; cocer a fuego lento.

brake, n 1. freno m; helecho m; 2. vt/i frenar.

bramble, n zarza f.

branch, n 1. rama f; división f, sección f; sucursal f; 2. vi ramificarse, echar ramas.

branch off, vi salir, separarse.

branch out, vi extenderse, ensanchar el campo de sus operaciones.

branch-office, n sucursal f.

brand, n marca f; hierro m (de marcar).

brandish, vt blandir.

brand-new, adj flamante, completamente nuevo, novísimo.

brandy, n coñac m, brandy m; aguardiente m.

brash, adj inculto, tosco; descarado, respondón.

brashness, n incultura f, tosquedad f; descaro m; impetuosidad f; indiscreción f; presunción f.

brass, n latón m.

brassière, n sostén m, sujetador m.

brassy, adj de latón; metálico.

brat, n mocoso m, crío m.

bravado, n bravatas f, baladronadas f.

brave, adj valiente, valeroso; esforzado; bizarro.

bravery, n valor m, valentía f.

bravo, interj ¡bravo!

bravura, n arrojo m, brío m.

brawling, adj 1. pendenciero, alborotador; 2. n alboroto m.

brawn, n fuerza f muscular.

brawny, adj fornido, musculoso.

bray, n 1. rebuzno m; carcajada f; 2. vi rebuznar; sonar con estrépito.

braze, vt soldar.

brazen, adj 1. descarado, cínico; mentira f descarada; 2. vt defenderse con argumentos descarados.

brazenly, adv descaradamente, con cinismo.

brazenness, n descaro m, desvergüenza f.

brazier, n brasero m.

breach, n 1. abertura f, brecha f; violación f, infracción f; rompimiento m de relaciones; 2. vt romper; abrir brecha en.

bread, n pan m.

bread-crumb, n migaja f; pan m rallado.

breaded, adj empanado.

breadfruit, n fruto m del pan; tree árbol m del pan.

breadknife, n cuchillo m para cortar el pan.

bread-pudding, n pudín m de leche y pan.

breadthwise, adv de lado a lado.

breadwinner, n mantenedor(a) f de la familia.

break, n 1. ruptura f, rompimiento m; quiebro m; sollozo m; 2. abertura f; grieta f; 3. vi romperse, quebrarse, hacerse pedazos; estropearse.

break down, vt 1. derribar, romper, echar abajo; 2. vi perder la salud, sufrir un colapso; averiarse, descomponerse; estropearse, dañarse.

break in, vt 1. forzar, romper; 2. (caballo) domar; 3. vi forzar una entrada; cortar, interrumpir.

break off, vt 1. separar, desgajar; 2. romper; terminar; 3. vi separarse, desprenderse, desgajarse.

break out, vi escaparse, evadirse.

break through, vt 1. penetrar, atravesar, romper; 2. vi abrirse paso, abrirse (un) camino; hacer un descubrimiento importante; empezar a tener éxito.

break up, vt 1. romper, deshacer; desguazar; romper en pedazos; 2. vi romperse, hacerse pedazos; desmenuzarse; disolverse.

breakable, adj frágil, quebradizo.

breakage, n rotura f.

breakdown, n 1. interrupción f; fracaso m, mal éxito m; colapso m, crisis f nerviosa; 2. análisis m, descomposición f; desglose m; informe m detallado.

breaker, n ola f grande, cachón m.

breakfast, n 1. desayuno m; 2. vi desayunar(se).

breaking, n rotura f, rompimiento m.

breaking-point, n punto m de ruptura, carga f de rotura.

breakout, n evasión f, fuga f.

breast, n pecho m, seno m; (aves) pechuga f.

breast-fed, adj criado a pecho.

breastplate, n peto m.

breast stroke, n braza f (de pecho).

breath, n aliento m, respiración f.

breathe, *vt* 1. respirar; 2. *vi* respirar; resollar.

breathe in, *vt/i* aspirar, respirar.

breathe out, *vt* 1. exhalar; 2. *vi* espirar.

breather, *n* respiro *m*, descanso *m*.

breathing, *n* respiración *f*; heavy resuello *m*.

breathless, *adj* falto de aliento, jadeante.

breathtaking, *adj* sight imponente, pasmoso; vertiginoso.

breech, *n* recámara *f*.

breed, *n* 1. raza *f*, casta *f*; 2. *vt* criar, engendrar; 3. *vi* procrear.

breeder, *n* 1. criador(a) *m/f*; ganadero *m*; 2. criadero *m*, paridera *f*.

breeding, *n* 1. reproducción *f*; 2. cría *f*; 3. crianza *f*, educación *f*.

breeze, *n* brisa *f*.

breezily, *adv* jovialmente, despreocupadamente.

brethren, *n* hermanos.

breve, *n* breve *f*.

breviary, *n* breviario *m*.

brevity, *n* brevedad *f*.

brew, *n* 1. poción *f*, brebaje *m*; 2. *vt* hacer, elaborar; urdir, tramar; 3. *vi* prepararse.

brewer, *n* cervecero *m*.

brewery, *n* cervecería *f*, fábrica *f* de cerveza.

briar, *n* escaramujo *m*, rosa *f* silvestre; espino *m*.

bribable, *adj* sobornable.

bribe, *n* 1. soborno *m*, cohecho *m*, mordida *f*; 2. *vt* sobornar, cohechar, miajar, aceitar.

bribery, *n* soborno *m*, cohecho *m*, coima *f*.

brick, *n* 1. ladrillo; 2. *vt* enladrillar.

bricklayer, *n* albañil *m*.

brickwork, *n* enladrillado *m*.

bridal, *adj* nupcial.

bride, *n* novia *f*.

bridegroom, *n* novio *m*.

bridesmaid, *n* dama *f* de honor.

bridge, *n* 1. puente *m*; 2. *vt* tender un puente sobre.

bridgehead, *n* cabeza *f* depuente.

bridge player, *n* jugador(a) *m/f* de bridge.

bridle, *n* brida *f*, freno *m*.

brief, *adj* 1. breve, corto; fugaz, pasajero; 2. *vt* informar de antemano.

briefcase, n cartera *f*, maletín *m*, portafolio *m*.

briefing, *n* reunión en que se dan órdenes; órdenes, instrucciones.

briefly, *adv* brevemente; en resumen, en pocas palabras.

briefness, *n* brevedad.

brig, *n* bergantín *m*.

brigade, *n* brigada *f*.

brigadier, *n* general *m* de brigada.

brigand, *n* bandido *m*, bandolero *m*.

bright, *adj* claro, brillante, luminoso; listo, inteligente.

brighten, *vt* 1. abrillantar, lustrar; alegrar; 2. *vi* animarse, alegrarse.

bright-eyed, *adj* de ojos vivos.

brightly, *adv* brillantemente.

brightness, *n* claridad *f*; brillantez *f*; luminosidad *f*; inteligencia *f*; viveza *f* de ingenio.

brilliance, *n* brillo *m*, brillantez *f*.

brilliant, *adj* brillante; idea genial, luminoso.

brilliantine, *n* brillantina *f*.

brilliantly, *adv* brillantemente.

brim, *n* 1. borde *m*; 2. *vi* desbordarse, rebosar.

brimstone, *n* azufre *m*.

brindled, *adj* manchado, mosqueado.

brine, *n* salmuera *f*.

bring, *vt* traer.

brink, *n* borde *m*; a punto de.

briny, *adj* salado, salobre.

brisk, *adj* enérgico, vigoroso; rápido.

brisket, *n* carne *f* depecho (propia para asar).

briskly, *adv* enérgicamente; rápidamente.

briskness, *n* energía *f*; rapidez *f*; actividad *f*.

brisling, *n* espadín *m*.

bristle, *n* 1. cerda *f*; cepillo *m* de púas; 2. *vi* ofenderse, irritarse.

British, *adj* británico, inglés.

brittle, *adj* frágil, quebradizo.

brittleness, *n* fragilidad *f*, lo quebradizo.

broach, *vt* espitar; abrir.

broad, *adj* 1. ancho; extenso, amplio; 2. comprensivo; tolerante, liberal.

broadcast, *adj* 1. sembrado a voleo; 2. radiodifundido; 3. *n* emisión *f*, programa *m*; 4. *vt* sembrar a voleo; diseminar, divulgar; emitir, radiar.

broadcasting, *n* radiodifusión *f*.

broadcasting station, *n* emisora *f*.

broaden, *vt* 1. ensanchar; 2. *vi* ensancharse.

broad-minded, *adj* de amplias miras, de criterio amplio, tolerante, liberal.

broadness, *n* anchura *f*, extensión *f*.

broadsheet, *n* periódico *m* de gran formato.

broad-shouldered, *adj* ancho de espaldas.

brocade, *n* brocado *m*.

broccoli, *n* brécol *m*, bróculi *m*, broculí *m*.

brochure, *n* folleto *m*.

broil, *vt* asar a la parrilla.

broiler, *n* 1. pollo *m* para asar; 2. parrilla *f*, grill *m*.

broken, *adj* accidentado, roto, quebrado.

broken-down, *adj* agotado; destartalado, desvencijado.

broken-hearted, *adj* traspasado de dolor; tener el corazón partido.

broker, *n* corredor *m*, bolsista *m*; agente *m* de negocios.

brokerage, *n* corretaje *m*.

bromide, *n* bromuro *m*.

bromine, *n* bromo *m*.

bronchitis, *n* bronquitis *f*.

bronchopneumonia, *n* bronconeumonía *f*.

bronchus, *n* bronquio *m*.

bronco, *n* potro *m* cerril.

broncobuster, *n* domador *m* de potros cerriles; domador *m* de caballos; vaquero *m*.

brontosaurus, *n* brontosauro *m*.

bronze, *n* 1. bronce *m*; 2. *adj* de bronce; 3. *vt* broncear.

bronzed, *adj* bronceado.

brood, *n* 1. camada *f*, cría *f*; nidada *f*; 2. *vi* empollar; meditar tristemente.

brooding, *adj* siniestro, amenazador.

broodings, *n* meditaciones *f*.

broody, *adj* clueca; triste, melancólico.

brook, *n* 1. arroyo *m*; 2. aguantar, permitir.

brooklet, *n* arroyuelo *m*.

broom, *n* escoba *f*, pichana *f*.

broomstick, *n* palo *m* de escoba.

broth, *n* caldo *m*.

brothel, *n* prostíbulo *m*.

brother, *n* hermano *m*; compañero *m*, camarada *m*.

brotherhood, *n* fraternidad *f*; hermandad *f*; cofradía *f*.

brother-in-law, *n* cuñado *m*, hermano *m* político.

brotherly, *adj* fraternal.

brow, n ceja f; frente f; cresta f.

browbeat, vt intimidar (con amenazas).

brown, adj moreno; marrón; castaño.

browse, vt 1. curiosear; pasearse; 2. vi pacer.

brucellosis, n brucelosis f.

bruise, n contusión f, cardenal m, magulladura f, moretón m.

brunch, n desayuno-almuerzo m.

brunette, adj 1. moreno; 2. n morena f.

brush, n 1. cepilladura f, cepillado m; 2. cepillo m; brocha f; 3. vt cepillar; limpiar; rozar al pasar.

brushwood, n maleza f, monte m bajo.

brushwork, n pincelada f, técnica f del pincel.

brusque, adj brusco, abrupto, áspero.

brusquely, adv bruscamente, abruptamente; ásperamente.

brusqueness, n brusquedad f, aspereza f; mal humor m; falta f de cortesía.

brutal, adj brutal.

brutality, n brutalidad f.

brutalize, vt brutalizar.

brutally, adv de manera brutal.

brute, adj brutal; bruto; 2. n bruto m; bestia f, hombre m bestial.

brutish, adj bruto.

bubble, n 1. burbuja f, ampolla f; 2. vi burbujear, borbotar.

bubble-gum, n chicle m de globo, chicle m de burbuja.

bubbly, adj burbujeante, gaseoso.

bubonic, n (plaga) peste f bubónica.

buccaneer, n 1. bucanero m; 2. vi piratear.

buck, adj macho (cabrío, gama, etc.).

bucket, n cubo m; balde m.

bucketful, n cubo m (lleno), balde m (lleno).

buckle, n 1. hebilla f; 2. vt abrochar con hebilla.

buckram, n bucarán m.

buckshot, n perdigón m zorrero, posta f.

buckskin , n cuero m de ante.

buckthorn, n espino m cerval.

buckwheat, n alforfón m, trigo m sarraceno.

bucolic , adj bucólico.

bud, n 1. brote m, yema f, capullo m; 2. vt injertar de escudete; 3. vi brotar, echar brotes.

budding, adj en ciernes, en embrión.

buddleia, n budleia f.

buddy, n compañero m, amigote m; compadre m, compinche m.

budge, vt 1. hacer que se mueva; 2. vi moverse; bullir; menearse.

budgerigar, n periquito m.

budget, n 1. presupuesto m, 2. presupuestario; cuenta f presupuestaria; plan m presupuestario.

budgetary, n presupuestario m.

budgeted, adj costos mpl presupuestados .

buff, adj 1. color de ante; 2. n piel f de ante; aficionado m, entusiasta m/f; 3. vt pulir.

buffalo, n búfalo m.

buffer, n amortiguador m (de choques); parachoques m; choques m; memoria f intermedia, buffer m.

buffet, n 1. bofetada f; golpe m; 2. aparador m; cantina f, cafetería f; comida f; buffet m; 3. vt abofetear; golpear.

buffoon, n bufón m, chocarrero m, payaso m.

buffoonery, n bufonadas f.

bug, n 1. chinche f; bicho m, sabandija; microbio m, bacilo m; 2. estorbo m, traba f, pega f; problema m; 3. vt molestar, fastidiar; intervenir.

bugaboo, n espantajo m, coco m.

bugbear, n pesadilla f, obsesión f.

bugging, n intervención f.

buggy, n calesa f; cochecillo, cochecito m de niño.

bugle, n corneta f, clarín m.

bugler, n corneta m.

build, n 1. talle m, figura f; 2. vt construir, edificar, montar.

builder, n constructor m; contratista m; aparejador m.

building, n edificio m; pabellón m; construcción f.

built-in, adj empotrado; interior, incorporado.

built-up, adj zona f edificada.

bulb, n bulbo m, camote m, foco m, bombillo m.

bulbous, adj bulboso.

bulge, n 1. bombeo m, pandeo m; protuberancia f; protuberancia f; 2. vi bombearse, pandearse; sobresalir.

bulk, n 1. bulto m, volumen m; masa f, mole f; suelto; 2. la mayor parte de; 3. adj mercancías f a granel; compra f de cantidad grande.

bulkiness, n volumen m, lo abultado.

bulky, adj voluminoso, abultado, grueso; de gran bulto.

bull, n toro m; macho m; bula f.

bulldog, n bul(l)dog m, perro m, dogo m.

bulldoze, vt nivelar (con motoniveladora).

bulldozer, n motoniveladora f, aplanadora f, bulldozer m.

bullet, n bala f.

bullet-hole, n agujero m de bala.

bulletin, n anuncio m, parte m; boletín m.

bulletin board, n tablón m de anuncios; tablero m de noticias.

bulletproof, adj a prueba de balas; vidrio m antibalas.

bullfight, n corrida f (de toros).

bullfighter, n torero m, matador m de toros.

bullfighting, n toreo m; arte m de torear, tauromaquia f.

bullfrog, n rana f toro.

bullhorn, n megáfono m.

bullion, n oro m en barras, plata f en barras.

bullish, adj optimista; (de tendencia) alcista.

bullock, n toro m castrado, novillo m castrado.

bullring, n plaza f de toros.

bull's-eye, n centro m del blanco, diana f; ojo m de buey.

bull terrier, n bulterrier m.

bully, adj 1. de primera; 2. interj (b__ for you) ¡bravo!; 3. n matón m, valentón m.

bulwark, n baluarte m; macarrón m.

bum, n 1. holgazán m; vagabundo m; 2. vi holgazanear, vagabundear.

bumble, vi andar de forma vacilante, andar a tropezones; trastabillar.

bumblebee, n abejorro m.

bumbling, adj inepto, inútil; que habla a tropezones, que se atropella al hablar.

bump, n 1. golpe m, topetazo m; choque m; 2. vt chocar contra, topetar; 3. vi dar sacudidas.

bumper, n parachoques m.

bumptious, adj engreído, presuntuoso.

bumpy, adj accidentado, lleno de baches; desigual.

bun, n bollo m; pastel m.

bunch, n 1. manojo m, puñado m; 2. vt agrupar, juntar.

bundle, n lío m, bulto m, fardo m; haz f.

bungalow, n casa f de un solo piso, chalet m.

bunghole, n piquera f, boca f (de tonel).

bungle, n 1. chapuza f; 2. vt chapucear.

bungler, n chapucero m.

bungling, adj torpe, desmanado.

bunion, n juanete m.

bunk, *n* litera *f*, camastro *m*.

bunker, *n* **1.** carbonera *f*, pañol *m* del carbón; **2.** refugio *m*, búnker *m*, **3.** *vt* proveer de carbón.

bunting, *n* banderas *f*, empavesado *m*; anilla *f*.

buoy, *n* **1.** boya *f*; guindola *f*; **2.** *vt* aboyar.

buoy up, *vt* mantener a flote; animar, alentar.

buoyancy, *n* boyante, capacidad *f* paraflotar.

buoyant, *adj* boyante, capaz de flotar; ilusionado, optimista.

bur(r), *n* erizo *m*.

burble, *vi* burbujear, hervir; parlotear.

burbot, *n* lota *f*.

burden, *n* **1.** carga *f*; peso *m*; **2.** *vt* cargar.

burdensome, *adj* gravoso, oneroso.

burdock, *n* bardana *f*.

bureau, *n* **1.** escritorio *m*, buró *m*; **2.** cómoda *f*; **3.** oficina *f*, agencia *f*, departamento *m*.

bureaucracy, *n* burocracia *f*.

bureaucrat, *n* burócrata *m/f*.

bureaucratic, *adj* burocrático.

burgeon, *vi* retoñar; empezar a prosperar; florecer.

burgher, *n* burgués(esa) *f*; ciudadano *m*.

burglar, *n* ladrón *m*, escalador *m*.

burglar alarm, *n* alarma *f* antirrobo.

burglar proof, *adj* a prueba de ladrones.

burglary, *n* robo *m* en una casa, robo *m* con escalamiento, allanamiento *m* de morada.

burgle, *vt* robar, escalar, allanar, desvalijar.

burial, *n* entierro *m*.

burial-ground, *n* cementerio *m*, camposanto *m*.

burial service, *n* funerales *m*.

burlap, *n* arpillera r.

burlesque, *adj* **1.** burlesco, paródico; **2.** *n* parodia *f*; **3.** *vt* parodiar.

burly, *adj* fornido, membrudo, corpulento, anchote.

burn, *n* **1.** quemadura *f*; **2.** *vt* quemar; incendiar; incinerar; **3.** *vi* arder; incendiarse.

burn away, *vt* **1.** quemar, consumir. **2.** *vi* consumirse.

burn down, *vt* **1.** incendiar; destruir por incendio, quemar totalmente; **2.** *vi* quedar destruido en un incendio, quemarse hasta los cimientos.

burner, *n* mechero *m*; hornillo *m* quemador *m*, fuego *m*.

burning, *adj* ardiente; candente, palpitante.

burnish, *vt* bruñir.

burnoose, *n* albornoz *m*.

burp, *n* **1.** eructo *m*; **2.** *vi* eructar.

burr, *n* erizo *m*.

burrow, *n* **1.** madriguera *f*; conejera *f*; **2.** *vt* socavar, minar; **3.** *vi* amadrigarse.

burst, *n* **1.** reventón *m*; estallido *m*, explosión *f*; **2.** *vt* reventar; deshacer.

bury, *vt* enterrar; sepultar.

bus, *n* **1.** autobús *m*, colectivo *m*, camión *m*; **2.** *vt* ir en autobús.

bus-driver, *n* chófer *m*.

bush, *n* arbusto *m*; cojinete *m*.

bushed, *adj* agotado, hecho polvo.

bushel, *n* medida de áridos; British = 36,36 litros, US = 35,24 litros.

bushy, *adj* parecido a un arbusto; lleno de arbustos.

busily, *adv* activamente; enérgicamente.

business, *n* **1.** comercio *m*, negocios *m*; **2.** empresa *f*, casa *f*; **3.** oficio *m*, ocupación *f*; **4.** asunto *m*, cuestión *f*.

businesslike, *adj* formal, metódico, serio, práctico.

businessman, *n* hombre *m* de negocios, empresario *m*.

businesswoman, *n* mujer *f* de negocios, mujer *f* empresaria.

bus-service, *n* servicio *m* de autobús.

bus-shelter, *n* refugio *m* de espera, parada *f* cubierta, marquesina *f*.

bus(s)ing, *n* transporte *m* escolar.

bus station, *n* estación *f* de autobuses.

bus stop, *n* parada *f* deautobús.

bust, *n* **1.** busto *m*; pecho *m*, pechos *m*; **2.** *vt* romper, estropear.

bustle, *n* **1.** movimiento *m*, actividad *f*; bullicio *m*, animación *f*; prisa *f*, **2.** *vi* menearse, apresurarse.

busway, *n* carril *m* de autobús.

busy, *adj* **1.** ocupado; atareado; activo; **2.** *vt* ocupar; **3.** *vr* ocuparse en, estar ocupado con.

busybody, *n* entrometido(a) *m/f*, metij(ona) *m/f*.

but, *adv* **1.** sólo, solamente, no mas que; **2.** *prep* and *conj* excepto, menos; salvo; **3.** *conj* pero; **4.** *n* pero *m*, objeción *f*.

butane, *n* butano *m*; gas *m* butano.

butcher, *n* **1.** carnicero *m*; **2.** *vt* matar; dar muerte a, hacer una carnicería con.

butchery, *n* matanza *f*, carnicería *f*.

butler, *n* mayordomo *m*.

butt, *n* **1.** (pistola) culata *f*; colilla *f*; cabezada *f*, topetazo *m*; **2.** *vt* topetar, dar cabezadas.

butter, *n* mantequilla *f*.

butterball, *n* gordo *m*.

butterfly, *n* mariposa *f*.

buttermilk, *n* suero *m* de leche, suero *m* de manteca.

butterscotch, *n* dulce de azucar terciado con mantequilla.

buttocks, *n* nalgas *f*, cachas *f*.

button, *n* **1.** botón *m*; **2.** *vt* abotonar, abrochar.

buttress, *n* **1.** contrafuerte *m*; apoyo *m*, sostén *m*; **2.** *vt* poner contrafuerte a; apoyar, reforzar.

buxom, *adj* rollizo, frescachón.

buy, *n* **1.** compra *f*; **2.** *vt* comprar.

buy up, *vt* comprar todas las existencias de, acaparar.

buyer, *n* comprador(a) *m/f*; encargado *m* de compras.

buzz, *n* **1.** zumbido *m*; rumor *m*; **2.** *vi* zumbar.

buzzard, *n* ratonero *m* común, águila *f* ratonera.

buzzer, *n* timbre *m*.

buzzing, *n* zumbido *m*, zumbar *m*.

bye-bye, *interj* ¡adiós!, ¡hasta luego!

bygone, *adj* pasado.

bylaw, *n* estatuto *m*, reglamento *m* local.

by-line, *n* pie *m* de autor.

by name, *n* sobrenombre *m*; apodo *m*, mote *m*.

bypass, *n* **1.** carretera *f* de circunvalación; desviación *f*; **2.** *vt* evitar, evitar el contacto con; prescindir de.

by-product, *n* subproducto *m*; derivado *m*.

bystander, *n* espectador(a) *m/f*, circunstante *m/f*.

byte, *n* octeto *m*.

C

C, c, *n* (letra) *f* C, c.

cab, *n* taxi *m*; cabriolé *m*, coche *m* de alquiler.

cabal, *n* cábala *f*; camarilla *f*; cabildeo *m*.

cabaret, *n* cabaret *m*.

cabbage, n col f, berza f, repollo m.

cabbalistic, adj cabalístico.

cabbie, n taxista m; cochero m.

cabin, n cabaña f, barraca f; camarote m.

cabin boy, n grumete m.

cabin cruiser, n yate m de motor, motonave.

cabinet, n 1. armal; vitrina, cajal; 2. consejo m de ministros, gabinete m de ministros.

cabinetmaker, n ebanista m.

cabinetmaking, n ebanistería f.

cable, n 1. cable m; cablegrama m; televisión f por cable; 2. vt/i cablegrafiar.

cable-car, n coche m de teleférico.

cablecast, n 1. emisión f de televisión por cable; 2. vt emitir por cable.

cablegram, n cablegrama m.

cable-railway, n teleférico m, funicular aéreo.

cable-stitch, n punto m de trenza.

cableway, n teleférico m, funicular m aéreo.

cabman, n taxista m; cochero m.

caboose, n furgón m de cola.

cacao, n cacao m.

cache, n 1. escondite m, escondrijo m; víveres m; escondidos; 2. vt esconder, ocultar; acumular.

cachet, n caché m, cachet m.

cackle, n 1. cacareo m; risotada; parloteo m; 2. vi cacarear; parlotear.

cacophonous, adj cacofónico.

cacophony , n cacofonía f.

cactus, n cactus m, cacto m.

cadaver, n cadáver m.

cadaverous, adj cadavérico.

caddy, n carrito m de la compra.

cadence, n cadencia f.

cadet, n cadete m/f.

cadmium, n cadmio m.

caesarean, n cesáreo m; operación f cesárea.

caesium, n cesio m.

café, n café m; bar m.

cafeteria, n restáurante m de autoservicio.

caffein(e), n cafeína f.

caftan, n caftán m.

cage, n 1. jaula f; 2. vt enjaular.

cagey, adj cauteloso, reservado.

caginess, n cautela f, reserva f.

caiman, n caimán m.

cajole, vt halagar, camelar; halagar (o engatusar) a uno para que haga algo.

cajolery, n halagos m, marrullería f, engatusamiento m.

cajun, adj cajún; cocina f tipo cajún.

cake, n 1. pastel m; tarta f; pasta f, pastelillo m, queque m; 2. vt endurecer; 3. vi endurecerse, apelmazarse.

calabash, n calabaza f.

calaboose, n jaula, cárcel f.

calamine, n calamina f.

calamitous, adj calamitoso, desastroso.

calamity, n calamidad f, desastre m.

calcification, n calcificación f.

calcify, vt 1. calcificar; 2. vi calcificarse.

calcium, n calcio m.

calculable, adj calculable.

calculate, vt calcular.

calculated, adj calculado, premeditado, estudiado.

calculating, adj astuto.

calculation, n cálculo m, cómputo m.

calculator, n calculadora f.

calculus, n cálculo m.

calendar, n calendario m; lista f (de pleitos).

calf, n ternero, becerro m; (Anat) pantorrilla f.

calibre, n capacidad f, aptitud f, carácter m, valor m.

calibrate, vt calibrar.

calibrated, adj calibrado.

calibration, n calibración f.

calico, n calicó m, indiana f.

caliph, n califa m.

calisthenics, n callisthenics.

call, n 1. llamada f; grito m; canto m, reclamo m; clamo m, chilla f; llamamiento m; 2. visita f; 3. demanda f; 4. vt llamar; convocar; (baraja) declarar, marcar.

calligraphic, adj caligráfo.

calligraphy, n caligrafía f.

calling, n vocación f, profesión f.

calling card, n tarjeta f de visita, tarjeta f comercial.

callipers, n calibrador m; soporte m, corrector m.

callous, adj insensible, cruel; calloso.

calloused, adj calloso, con callos.

callow, adj inexperto, novato; imberbe.

callus, n callo.

calm, adj 1. tranquilo, sosegado; calmoso, sin viento; liso, en calma; 2. n calma f, tranquilidad f; 3. vt calmar, tranquilizar; 4. vi calmarse, tranquilizarse.

calmly, adv con calma, tranquilamente.

calmness, n calma f, tranquilidad f, sosiego m.

caloric, adj calórico; térmico.

calorie, n caloría f.

calumniate, vt calumniar.

calumny, n calumnia f .

calve, vi parir (la vaca).

Calvinism, n calvinismo m.

calypso , n calipso m.

calyx, n cáliz m.

camaraderie, n compañerismo m, camaradería f.

camber, n 1. combadura f; convexidad f; peralte m; 2. vt combar, arquear; 3. vi combarse, arquearse.

camcorder, n cámara f de vídeo y audio, cámcorder m.

camel, n camello m.

camera, n (fotográfica) máquina f; cámara f.

camerawork, n uso m de la cámara.

camisole, n camisola f.

camomile, n camomila f; manzanilla f.

camouflage, n 1. camuflage; 2. vt camuflar.

camp, n 1. campamento m, campo m; 2. grupo m, facción f; 3. vi acampar(se); alojarse temporalmente.

campaign, n 1. campaña f; recorrido m electoral; 2. vi luchar; servir; hacer campaña.

campaigner, n paladín m, partidario m, propagandista m/f (por).

campanile, n campanario m.

camper, n campista m/f, autocaravana f, campero.

campfire, n hoguera f de campamento; reunión f alrededor de la hoguera.

camphor, n alcanfor m.

camphorated, adj alcanforado.

camping, n campismo m.

campion, n colleja f.

campsite, n campamento m.

campus, n campus m.

camshaft, n árbol m de levas.

can, n 1. lata f; 2. vi 1. poder; saber; 3. vt conservar en lata; enlatar, envasar; despedir;

canal, n canal m.

canalize, vt canalizar.

canapé, n canapé m.

canard, n bulo m, noticia f falsa.

canary, n canario m.

canasta, n canasta f.

cancan, n cancán m.

cancel, vt 1. cancelar; suprimir; suspender; retirar, inutilizar; 2. vi (Mat) destruirse, anularse.

cancellation, n cancelación f; supresión f; suspensión f; el retirar; matasellos m.

cancer, n cáncer m.

cancerous, adj canceroso.

candelabra, n candelabro m.

candid, adj franco, sincero, abierto.

candidacy, n candidatura f.

candidate, n aspirante m/f solicitante; candidato m.

candidness, n franqueza f.

candied, adj azucarado.

candle, n vela f, cera f; candela f; cirio m.

candlelight, n luz f de una vela.

candlelit, adj alumbrado por velas.

candlepower, n bujía f.

candlestick, n candelero m; palmatoria f; candelabro m.

candlewick, n pabilo m, mecha f (de vela).

candor, n franqueza f.

candy, n 1. azúcar m cande; bombón m, dulce m; 2. vt almibarar, garapiñar.

candy store, n bombonería f, confitería f.

cane, n caña f; caña f de azúcar; bastón m; palmeta f.

canine, adj canino.

canister, n lata f, bote m.

canker, n 1. llaga f gangrenosa; úlcera en la boca; cancro m; cáncer; 2. vt ulcerar; corromper.

cankerous, n ulceroso.

cannabis, n cánamo m; canabis m.

canned, adj en lata, de lata; enlatado.

cannery, n fábrica f de conservas.

cannibal, adj 1. antropófago; 2. n caníbal m/f.

cannibalism, n canibalismo m.

cannibalize, vt canibalizar.

canning, n enlatado m.

cannon, n 1. cañón m; artillería f; 2. vi hacer carambola.

cannonade, n cañoneo m.

cannonball, n bala f de cañón.

canny, adj astuto.

canoe, n 1. canoa f, chalupa f; piragua; 2. vi ir en canoa.

canoeist, n piragüista m/f; canoero(a) m/f.

canon, n 1. canon m; criterio m; 2. adj canónico.

canonization, n canonización f.

canonize, vt canonizar.

canoodle, vi besuquearse.

can-opener, n abrelatas m.

canopy, n dosel m, toldo m; cielo m; baldaquín m.

cant, n 1. inclinación f, sesgo m; 2. jerga f; hipocresías f; 3. vt inclinar, sesgar.

cantaloup, n cantalupo m.

cantata, n cantata f.

canteen, n cantina f, comedor m; cantimplora f.

canter, n medio galope m; a pasearse a caballo.

cantharides, n polvo m de cantárida.

canticle, n cántico m.

cantilever, n viga f voladiza; puente m voladizo.

canting, adj hipócrita.

canto, n canto m.

canton, n cantón m.

canvas, n 1. lona f; velamen m, velas f; 2. (arte) lienzo m.

canvass, n 1. sondeo m, solicitación f; 2. vt sondear, hacer una encuesta, solicitar votos.

canvassing, n solicitación f (de votos).

canyon, n canón m.

cap, n 1. gorra f; bonete m; 2. tapa f, tapon m; cápsula f; capuchón m; caballete m; casquete; 3. vt coronar; terminar, tapar, superar.

capability, n capacidad f, aptitud f.

capable, adj capaz; competente; ser capaz de.

capably, adv competentemente.

capacious, adj grande, extenso, espacioso.

capacitor, n capacitor m.

capacity, n capacidad f; cabida f; cilindrada f; capacidad f de carga; aptitud f.

cape, n capa f; capotillo m, esclavina f; chubasquero m; capote m; cabo m.

caper, n 1. cabriola f; 2. travesura f; lío m, embrollo m; (Bot) alcaparra f.

capillary, adj 1. capilar; 2. n vaso m capilar.

capital, adj 1. capital; 2. n mayúscula f.

capitalism, n capitalismo m.

capitalist, adj capitalista.

capitalize, vt 1. capitalizar; 2. escribir (o imprimir) con mayúscula; convertir en mayúscula; 3. vi aprovechar, sacar partido de.

capitation, n capitación f; impuesto m por.

Capitol, n Capitolio m.

capitulate, vi capitular, rendirse, entregarse, ceder.

capitulation, n capitulación f, rendición f.

capon, n capón m.

cappuccino, n capuchino m.

caprice, n capricho m.

capricious, adj caprichoso, caprichudo.

capriciously, adv caprichosamente.

capsicum, n pimiento m.

capsize, vt volcar; hacer zozobrar, tumbar.

capstan, n cabrestante m.

capsule, n cápsula f.

captain, n 1. capitán m; 2. vt capitanear.

captaincy, n capitanía f.

caption, n 1. encabezamiento m, título m; leyenda f; 2. vt titular, poner un pie a.

captious, adj criticón, reparón.

captivate, vt cautivar, encantar.

captivating, adj cautivante, encantador, delicioso.

captive, adj 1. cautivo; 2. n cautivo m/f.

captivity, n cautiverio m; cautividad f.

captor, n apresador(a) m/f.

capture, n 1. apresamiento m, captura f; toma f, conquista f; recogida f; 2. vt prender; apresar; 3. (atención) captar, llamar, atraer.

capuchin, n capucho m; mono m capuchino.

car, n coche m, automóvil m, carro m.

carafe, n jarro m.

caramel, n caramelo m; azúcar m quemado.

carapace, n carapacho m.

carat, n quilate m.

caravan, n carricoche m, carromato m; caravana f; remolque m, tráiler m.

caravel, n carabela f.

caraway, n alcaravea f.

carbide, n carburo m.

carbine, n carabina f.

carbohydrate, n hidrato m de carbono.

carbon, n carbono m; copia f al carbón.

carbonate, n carbonato m.

carbonated, adj gaseosa f; agua f mineral.

carbonize, vt carbonizar.

carbon paper, n papel m carbón.

carborundum, *n* carborundo *m.*

carbuncle, *n* carbúnculo *m*, carbunco.

carburetion, *n* carburación *f.*

carcass, *n* cadáver *m*, res *f* muerta.

carburetor, *n* carburador *m.*

card, *n* 1. carda *f;* 2. carta *f*, naipe *m;* tarjeta *f*, postal *f;* 3. *vt* cardar.

cardboard, *n* cartón *m*, cartulina *f.*

cardholder, n miembro *m/f* de carnet; socio *m/f.*

cardiac, *adj* cardíaco; paro *m* cardíaco.

cardigan, *n* rebeca *f;* cárdigan *m.*

cardinal, *adj* 1. cardinal; número *m* cardinal; puntos *m* cardinales; 2. *n* cardenal *m.*

cardiogram, *n* cardiograma *m.*

cardiologist, *n* cardiólogo(a).

cardiology, *n* cardiología *f.*

cardiovascular, *adj* cardiovascular.

card trick, *n* truco *m* de naipes.

care, *n* 1. cuidado *m;* solicitud *f;* 2. *vi* interesarse, preocuparse.

careen, *vt* 1. carena *f;* 2. *vi* inclinarse, escorar.

career, *n* 1. profesión *f*, carrera *f;* 2. *vi* correr a toda velocidad.

careerist, *n* ambicioso(a), arribista *m/f.*

carefree, *adj* despreocupado, libre de preocupaciones, alegre, inconsciente.

careful, *adj* cuidadoso; cauteloso, prudente; esmerado, competente.

careless, *adj* descuidado; negligente; poco atento; imprudente; hecho a la ligera.

carelessly, *adv* descuidadamente; a la ligera.

carelessness, *n* descuido *m;* falta *f* de atención; desaliño *m;* indiferencia *f;* descuido, falta de atención.

caress, *n* 1. caricia *f;* 2. *vt* acariciar.

caret, *n* signo *m* de intercalación.

caretaker, *n* vigilante *m;* guardián *m;* portero *m*, conserje *m*, celador *m*, curador *m.*

careworn, *adj* agobiado de preocupaciones; preocupado.

carfare, *n* pasaje *m.*

cargo, *n* cargamento *m*, carga *f.*

cargo plane, *n* avión *m* de carga.

caricature, *n* 1. caricatura *f;* dibujo *m* cómico; 2. *vt* caricaturizar.

caricaturist, *n* caricaturista *m/f*, dibujante.

caries, *n* caries *f.*

caring, *adj* 1. afectuoso, bondadoso; humanitario; 2. *n* cuidado *m;* afecto *m.*

carnage, *n* carnicería *f*, mortandad *f*, matanza *f.*

carnal, *adj* carnal; tener ayuntamiento carnal con.

carnation, *n* clavel *m.*

carnival, *n* carnaval *m;* fiesta *f*, feria *f;* parque *m* de atracciones.

carnivore, *n* carnívoro *m.*

carnivorous, *adj* carnívoro.

carob, *n* algarroba *f;* algarrobo *m.*

carol, *n* 1. villancico *m;* 2. *vi* cantar alegremente.

carotid, *n* carótida *f.*

carousal, *n* jarana *f*, parranda *f*, juerga *f.*

carouse, *vi* jaranear, estar de parranda, estar de juerga.

carousel, *n* caballitos *m*, tiovivo *m*, carrusel *m.*

carp, *n* (pez) carpa *f.*

carpenter, *n* carpintero *m.*

carpentry, *n* carpintería *f.*

carpet, *n* 1. alfombra *f;* moqueta *f;* 2. *vt* alfombrar; cubrir, revestir.

carpeted, *adj* alfombrado, enmoquetado.

carping, adj criticón, reparón.

carpool, *n* coches *m* de uso compartido.

carport, *n* garaje *m* abierto, cobertizo *m* para coche.

carriage, *n* vagón *m*, coche *m;* carruaje *m.*

carrier, *n* transportista *m;* empresa *f* de transportes; aerotransportista *m*, aerolínea *f.*

carrier pigeon, n paloma *f* mensajera.

carrion, *n* carroña *f;* inmundicia *f.*

carrot, *n* zanahoria *f.*

carroty, *adj* pelirrojo.

carry, *n* 1. alcance *m;* 2. *vt* llevar; traer; transportar, acarrear; transmitir, sostener, conllevar.

carryall, *n* cesto *m* grande.

car sickness, *n* mareo *m* (al ir en coche).

cart, *n* 1. carro *m*, carreta *f;* carretón *m;* carretilla *f*, carro *m* de mano; 2. *vt* llevar, acarrear, carretear.

cartage, *n* acarreo *m*, porte *m.*

carte blanche, *n* carta *f* blanca.

cartel, *n* cartel *m.*

cartilage, *n* cartílago *m.*

cartload, *n* carretada *f.*

cartographer, *n* cartógrafo(a) *m/f.*

cartography, *n* cartografía *f.*

carton, *n* envase *m*, caja *f* de cartón, cartón *m.*

cartoon, *n* dibujo *m* cómico, caricatura *f;* cartón *m;* dibujos *m* animados; tira *f* cómica.

cartoonist, *n* dibujante *m/f*, caricaturista *m/f.*

cartridge, *n* cartucho *m.*

cartwheel, *n* rueda *f* de carro; voltereta *f* lateral, rueda *f.*

carve, *vt* trinchar; esculpir, tallar, labrar.

carver, *n* trinchador *m;* escultor(ora), tallista *m/f.*

carving, *n* arte *m* de trinchar; escultura *f*, obra *f* de talla.

carving-knife, *n* trinchante *m.*

car wash, *n* tren *m* de lavado de coches.

cascade, *n* 1. cascada *f*, salto *m* de agua; chorro *m;* torrente *m;* 2. *vi* caer en cascada.

case, *n* 1. caja *f;* cajón *m;* maleta *f*, valija *f;* 2. caso *m;* asunto *m;* 3. causa *f*, pleito *m*, proceso *m;* 4. *vt* encajonar; enfundar.

case file, *n* historial *m.*

casement, *n* ventana *f* a bisagra; marco *m* de ventana.

case-study, *n* estudio *m* de casos.

casework, *n* asistencia *f* social individualizada, trabajo *m* social con individuos.

caseworker, *n* asistente *m/f* social.

cash, *n* 1. dinero *m* contante; efectivo *m*, metálico *m;* plata *f;* 2. *vt* (cheque) cobrar, hacer efectivo.

cash-and-carry, *n* 1. almacén *m* de venta al contado; 2. *adj* de venta al contado.

cashbox, *n* caja *f.*

cashier, *n* 1. cajero(a); 2. *vt* separar del servicio.

cashless, *adj* sin dinero.

cashmere, *n* cachemir *m*, cachemira *f.*

cash-register, *n* caja *f* registradora.

casing, *n* caja *f*, cubierta *f*, envoltura *f;* revestimiento *m*, carcasa *f* reforzada.

casino, *n* casino *m.*

cask, *n* tonel *m*, barril *m*, barrica *f.*

cassava, *n* mandioca *f*, tapioca *f.*

casserole, *n* cacerola *f*, cazuela *f.*

cassette, *n* casete *f*, cassette *f.*

cassette-recorder, *n* cassette *f* grabadora.

cassock, *n* sotana *f.*

cassowary, *n* casuario *m.*

cast, *n* 1. echada *f;* pieza *f* fundida; forma *f*, molde *m;* vaciado *m;* escayola *f;* facciones *f*, fisonomía *f;* reparto *m;* 2. *vt* echar, lanzar, arrojar; echar.

castanet, *n* castañuela *f.*

castaway, *n* náufrago(a).

caste, n casta f.

castellated, adj almenado.

castigate, vt reprobar, condenar, censurar.

castigation, n reprobación f, censura f.

Castilian, adj 1. castellano; 2. n castellano m, castellano m.

casting, adj 1. voto m de calidad; 2. n pieza f fundida, pieza f de fundición.

cast-iron, adj 1. hecho de hierro fundido; fuerte, duro; inflexible; sólido; 2. n hierro m colado.

castle, n castillo m; (chess) torre f, roque m.

cast-off, adj 1. de desecho; 2. n abandonada f.

castor, n ruedecilla f, castor m.

castrate, vt castrar.

castration, n castración f.

casual, adj fortuito, accidental, casual; despreocupado.

casualty, n 1. baja f; perdidas f; 2. víctima f, herido m, muerto m.

casuist, n casuista m/f.

casuistry, n casuística f; sofismas m.

cat, n gato(a).

cataclysm, n cataclismo m.

cataclysmic, adj de cataclismo.

catacombs, n catacumbas f.

catafalque, n catafalco m.

cataleptic, adj 1. cataléptico; 2. n cataléptico.

catalogue, n catálogo m; fichero m; folleto m; 2. vt catalogar, poner en un catálogo.

catalyst, n catalizador m.

catalytic, adj catalético.

catamaran, n catamarán m.

catapult, n catapulta f; tirador m, tiragomas m.

cataract, n catarata f.

catarrh, n catarro m.

catastrophy, n catástrofe f.

catastrophic, adj catastrófico.

catatonic , adj 1. catatónic; 2. n catatónico(a) m/f.

cat-burglar, n (ladrón) balconero m.

catcall, n 1. silbo m, silbido m, rechifla f; 2. vi silbar.

catch, n 1. cogida m; presa f, captura f; 2. vt coger, agarrar, atrapar; asir; recoger, coger.

catcher, n apañador m, receptor m.

catching, adj contagioso; pegajoso, atrayente, cautivador.

catchy, adj pegadizo, atractivo, fácil de recordar.

catechism, n catecismo m; catequismo m, catequesis f.

catechize, vt catequizar.

categorize, vt clasificar.

category, n categoría f.

cater, vi abastecer a, proveer comida a; atender a, proveer a; satisfacer.

caterer, n abastecedor, proveedor(a) m/f.

catering, n abastecimiento m; servicio m de comidas, servicio m de comedor.

caterpillar, n oruga f, gusano m.

caterwaul, vi chillar, aullar, maullar.

caterwauling, n chillidos m, aullidos m.

catfish, n siluro m, bagre m, perro m del norte .

catharsis, n catarsis f.

cathartic, adj catártico, purgante; 2. n purgante m.

cathedral, n catedral f.

catheter, n catéter m.

catheterize, vt entubar.

cathode, n cátodo m; rayos m católicos m pl.

Catholic, adj 1. católico. 2. n católico.

catholic, adj católico.

Catholicism, n catolicismo m.

catkin, n amento m, candelilla f .

catnap, n siestecita f, sueñecito m.

cat's-cradle, n cuna f.

catsup, n salsa f de tomate, catsup m.

cattle, n ganado m, ganado m vacuno, vacas f.

cattle-breeder, n criador f de ganado.

cattle-breeding, n crianza f de ganado.

catwalk, n pasadizo m, pasarela f.

caucus, n camarilla f junta f secreta; reunión f de un partido.

caudal, adj caudal.

cauldron, n caldera f; calderón m.

cauliflower, n coliflor f.

caulk, vt calafatear.

causality, n causalidad f.

causative, adj causativo.

cause, n 1. causa f, motivo m, razón f; 2. vt causar, motivar, provocar; originar.

causeway, n calzada f elevada; carretera f elevada.

caustic, adj cáustico; sosa f cáustica.

cauterize, vt cauterizar.

caution, n cautela f, prudencia; cuidado, precaución; advertencia f, amonestación f .

cautious, adj cauteloso, prudente, precavido; cauto.

cavalcade, n cabalgata f.

cavalier, adj 1. arrogante, desdenoso; 2. n caballero m; galán m.

cavalry, n caballería f.

cave, n 1. cueva f, caverna f; 2. vi derrumbarse, hundirse; ceder, rendirse.

caveat, n advertencia f; (Jur) advertencia f de suspensión.

caveman, n hombre m prehistórico; machote m.

caver, n espeleólogo.

cavern, n caverna f.

cavernous, adj cavernoso.

cavil, n 1. reparo m; 2. vi sutilizar, critiquizar.

caving, n espeleología f.

cavity, n cavidad f, hueco m, hoyo m; caries f.

cavort, vi dar cabrioladas; divertirse ruidosamente.

caw, n 1. graznido m; 2. vi graznar.

cayenne, n pimienta f de chile.

cayman, n caimán m.

ceaseless, adj incesante, continuo.

ceaselessly, adv incesantemente, sin cesar.

cedar, n cedro m; madera f de cedro.

cede, vt ceder.

ceiling, n techo m, cielo m raso; precio m tope.

celebrant, n celebrante m.

celebrate, vt 1. celebrar; festejar; solemnizar; señalar con una fiesta; 2. vi divertirse, estar (o ir) de parranda.

celebrated, adj célebre, famoso.

celebration, n celebración f; fiesta f, guateque m.

celebrity, n celebridad f.

celeriac, n apio m nabo.

celerity, n celeridad f.

celery, n apio m, panil m.

celestial, adj celestial.

celibacy, n celibato m.

celibate, adj 1. célibe; 2. n célibe m/f.

cell, n celda f; celdilla f; elemento m, vaso m, pila f; célula f.

cellar, n sótano m; bodega f.

cellist, n violonchelista m/f.

cello, n violonchelo m.

Cellophane, n celofán m.

cellular, adj celular; teléfono m celular.

cellulitis, n celulitis f.

celluloid, n celuloide m.

Celsius, *adj* celsius, centígrado.

cembalo, *n* clavicordio *m*, clave *m*.

cement, *n* 1. cemento *m;* cola *f*, pegamento *m;* mixer hormigonera; 2. *vt* cementar, revestir, reforzar.

cemetery, *n* cementerio *m*.

censer, *n* incensario *m*.

censor, *n* 1. censor(a); 2. *vt* censurar; tachar, suprimir.

censorship, *n* censura *f*.

censure, *n* 1. censura *f*; 2. *vt* censurar.

census, *n* censo *m;* empadronamiento *m*.

cent, n centavo *m*.

centaur, *n* centauro *m*.

centenary, *n* centenario *m*.

centennial, *adj* 1. centenario; 2. *n* centenario *m*.

center, *n* 1. centro *m;* 2. *vt* colocar en el centro.

centigrade, *adj* centígrado.

centigram(me), *n* centigramo *m*.

centiliter, *n* centilitro *m*.

centimeter, *n* centímetro *m*.

centipede, *n* ciempiés *m*.

central, *adj* central; céntrico.

centralize, *vt* centralizar; concentrar, reunir en un centro.

centurion, *n* centurión *m*.

century, *n* siglo *m;* cien carreras *f*.

ceramic, *adj* cerámico.

ceramics, *n sing* cerámica *f*.

cereal, *adj* 1. cerea; 2. *n* cereal.

cerebellum, *n* cerebelo *m*.

cerebral, *adj* cerebral; intelectual.

cerebrum, *n* cerebro *m*.

ceremonious, *adj* ceremonioso.

ceremony, *n* ceremonia *f*.

cerise, adj color de cereza.

certain, *adj* seguro, cierto; es verdad que.

certainty, *n* certeza *f*, certidumbre *f*; seguridad *f*.

certificate, *n* certificado *m;* título *m*.

certification, *n* certificación *f*.

certified, *adj* document certificado, atestiguado; titulado.

certify, *vt* certificar; atestiguar, dar fe de.

certitude, *n* certidumbre *f*.

cervical, *adj* cervical.

cervix, *n* cuello *m* del útero.

cessation, *n* cesación *f*, suspensión *f*.

cession, *n* cesión *f*.

cesspool, *n* pozo *m* negro; sentina *f*.

cetacean, *adj* cetáceo.

chafe, *vt* 1. rozar, raer; 2. *vi* desgastarse, impacientarse; 3. *n* roce *m*, fricción *f*.

chaff, *n* barcia *f*, ahechaduras *f*.

chain, n cadena *f*.

chainsaw, *n* sierra *f* de cadena.

chair, *n* 1. silla *f;* cátedra *f;* presidencia *f;* 2. *vt* presidir.

chairback, *n* respaldo *m*.

chairlift, *n* telesilla *m*.

chairman, *n* presidente(a).

chairmanship, *n* presidencia *f;* arte *m* de presidir reuniones.

chairperson, *n* presidente(a).

chairwoman, *n* presidenta *f*.

chaise, *n* tumbona *f*.

chalet, *n* chalet *m*, chalé *m*.

chalice, *n* cáliz *m*.

chalk, *n* creta *f;* tiza *f*.

chalkboard, *n* pizarra *f*.

chalky, *adj* cretáceo; gredoso, cretoso.

challenge, *n* 1. desafío *m*, reto *m;* quién vive *m;* 2. *vt* desafiar, retar; dar el quién vive a; recusar.

challenger, *n* desafiador(a) *m/f;* aspirante *m/f*, concursante *m/f;* contrincante *m/f*.

challenging, *adj* desafiante; de desafío; estimulante, provocador.

chamber, *n* cámara *f;* aposento *m*, sala *f;* cámara *f;* despacho *m*, bufete; recamara.

chambermaid, *n* camarera *f*, sirvienta *f*, recamarera *f*.

champ, *vt* morder, mordiscar; tascar.

champagne, *n* champán *m*.

champion, *adj* campeón.

championship, *n* campeonato *m*.

chance, *adj* 1. fortuito, casual; imprevisto; aleatorio; 2. *n* casualidad *f;* azar *m;* suerte *f;* oportunidad *f;* 3. posibilidad *f*.

chancellery, *n* cancillería *f*.

chancellor, *n* canciller *m;* Ministro(a).

chancy, *adj* arriesgado; dudoso.

chandelier, *n* araña *f* (de luces).

chandler, *n* velero *m*.

change, *n* 1. cambio *m;* modificación *f;* transformación *f;* moneda *f* suelta; 2. *vt* cambiar, trocar; reemplazar; modificar; transformar.

changeless, *adj* inmutable.

changeover, *n* cambio *m*.

changing, *adj* cambiante; mudable, variable.

changing-room, *n* vestuario *m*.

channel, *n* 1. canal *m;* estrecho *m;* conducto *m*, medio *m;* 2. *vt* acanalar; encauzar, dirigir.

chantey, *n* saloma *f*.

chaos, *n* caos *m*, desorden *m*.

chaotic, *adj* caótico, desordenado.

chap, *n* 1. mandíbula *f*, grieta; hendedura *f;* 2. *vt* agrietar; 3. *vi* agrietarse.

chapel, *n* capilla *f*.

chaperon, *n* acompañanta de señorita.

chaplain, *n* capellán *m*.

chaplaincy, *n* capellanía *f*.

chapped, *adj* agrietado.

chaps, *n* zahones *m*, chaparreras *f*.

chapter, *n* capítulo *m*.

char, *vt* carbonizar, chamuscar.

character, *n* carácter *m*, naturaleza, índole *f*, calidad *f*.

characteristic, *adj* característico.

characterization, *n* caracterización *f*.

characterize, *vt* caracterizar.

charade, *n* charada, payasada *f*, farsa *f*, comedia *f*.

charcoal, *n* carbón *m* vegetal; carboncillo *m*.

charge, *n* 1. carga *f;* 2. *vt* embestida *f;* 3. acusación *f;* 4. precio *m*, coste *m;* honorarios *m;* 5. responsabilidad *f;* 6. *vt* atacar, acusar, cobrar.

chariot, *n* carro *m* romano, de guerra etc.

charisma, *n* carisma *m*.

charismatic, *adj* carismático.

charitable, *adj* caritativo; comprensivo, compasivo.

charity, *n* caridad *f;* comprensión *f*.

charlatan, *n* charlatán *m;* curandero *m*.

charm, *n* encanto *m*, atractivo.

charming, *adj* encantador; simpático.

charred, *adj* carbonizado, chamuscado.

chart, *n* tabla *f*, cuadro *m*, esquema *m*, gráfico *m;* gráfica *f;* lista *f*.

charter, *n* 1. carta *f;* 2. alquiler; fletamiento; 3. *vt* alquilar, estatuar.

chary, *adj* cuidadoso, cauteloso, reservado.

chasm, n sima f, abismo m, grieta f; fosa f.

chassis, n chasis m.

chaste, adj casto.

chasten, vt castigar, corregir, escarmentar.

chastening, adj aleccionador.

chastise, vt castigar.

chastisement, n castigo m.

chastity, n castidad f.

chasuble, n casulla f.

chat, n charla f, plática f; conversacion.

chattels, n bienes m; muebles; cosas f, enseres m.

chatter, n charla f, parloteo m.

chauffeur, n chófer m.

chauvinism, n chauvinismo m, patriotería f; machismo, falocracia.

chauvinist, adj chauvinista, patriotero; falócrata m.

cheap, adj barato; económico; de mal gusto, de obra barata.

cheaply, adv barato; a precio económico.

cheat, n 1. trampa f; 2. vt person defraudar, embaucar; estafar algo a uno; 3. vi hacer trampas.

cheating, n trampa f; fraude m; fullerías.

check, n 1. (banco) cheque m; 2. (ajedrez) jaque m; 3. inspección f; 4. repulsa f, restricción f; 5. paño m a cuadros; 6. vt verificar, comprobar, parar, detener.

checked, adj a cuadros.

checker, n verificador m; cajero(a); encargado(a) de guardarropa.

checkerboard, n tablero m de damas.

checkers, n 1. damas f; facturación, mostrador m de embarque; 2. mostrador m de facturación, mostrador m de embarque.

checking, n control m, comprobación f; cuenta f corriente.

checkmate, n mate m, jaque m mate.

check-out, n 1. caja f; 2. caja f (de supermercado).

checkroom, n guardarropa m.

cheek, n 1. mejilla f, carrillo m; 2. descaro m, frescura f, impertinencia f.

cheekbone, n pómulo m.

cheep, n 1. pío m; 2. vi piar.

cheer, n 1. grito m de entusiasmo; aplausos m, alegría f; vítores m, vivas f; 2. vt animar, aclmar..

cheerful, adj alegre; de buen humor.

cheerfulness, n alegría f; buen humor m.

cheerleader, n animador(a).

cheerless, adj triste, sombrío.

cheese, n queso m.

cheeseburger, n hamburguesa f con queso.

cheesecloth, n estopilla f.

cheetah, n leopardo m cazador.

chef, n jefe m de cocina, cocinero m.

chemical, adj 1. químico; 2. n agente m químico.

chemise, n camisa f de señora.

chemist, n químico m/f farmacéutico(a), farmacia f.

chemistry, n química f; laboratorio m de química.

chemotherapy, n quimioterapia f.

cherish, vt querer, apreciar, cuidar, abrigar.

cherry, n cerezo m; rojo m cereza; aguardiente m de cerezas.

cherub, n querubín m, angelito m.

chervil, n perifollo m.

chess, n ajedrez m.

chessboard, n tablero m de ajedrez.

chessplayer, n ajedrecista m/f.

chest, n 1. pecho m; tórax m; 2. cofre m, arca f, cajón m.

chew, vt mascar, masticar.

chewing-gum, n chicle m, goma f de mascar.

chiaroscuro, n claroscuro m.

chic, adj 1. elegante; 2. n chic m, elegancia f.

chicanery, n embustes m, sofismas m.

Chicano, adj chicano.

chick, n pollito m, polluelo m; chavala f.

chicken, n gallina f, pollo m.

chickenpox, n varicela f.

chickpea, n garbanzo m.

chickweed, n pamplina f.

chide, vt reprender.

chief, adj 1. primero, mayor, capital; 2. n director(a) m/f; jefe m/f; jerarca m/f.

chiefly, adj principalmente, sobre todo.

chieftain, n jefe m, cacique m.

chiffon, n gasa f.

child, n niño(a) m/f, hijo(a) m/f.

childbirth, n parto m; alumbramiento m.

childcare, n cuidado m de los niños; servicios m de asistencia al niño.

childhood, n niñez f, infancia f.

childishly, adv de modo pueril.

childless, adj sin hijos.

childlike, adj como de niño, infantil.

child-proof, adj a prueba de niños.

chili, n chile m, ají m; polvos m de chile.

chill, adj 1. frío; 2. n escalofrío m; 3. vt enfriar; helar.

chilling, adj escalofriante.

chilly, adj frío; friolento, friolero.

chime, n 1. juego m de campanas, carillón m; repique m; 2. vt repicar, sonar.

chimera, n quimera f.

chiming, adj 1. (reloj) m de carillón; 2. n repiqueteo m, campanadas f.

chimney, n chimenea f; tubo m de lámpara; olla f.

chimney sweep, limpiachimeneas m.

chimpanzee, n chimpancé m.

chin, n barba f, barbilla f, mentón m.

china, n porcelana f, loza f.

chinaware, n porcelana f.

chinchilla, n chinchilla f.

chink, n 1. grieta f, hendedura f, resquicio m; 2. sonido m metálico, tintineo m.

chintz, n cretona f.

chip, n 1. astilla f, pedacito m; lasca f; patatas f fritas; desportilladura f; ficha f; 2. vt astillar, desportillar; picar; sculpture cincelar; 3. vi astillarse; picarse, desconcharse.

chipboard, n cartón-madera m.

chipmunk, n ardilla f listada.

chiropodist, n pedicuro(a), podólogo (a).

chiropractor, n quiropráctico m.

chirp, n pío m, gorjeo m; chirrido m.

chisel, n 1. formón m, escoplo m; cincel m; 2. vt escoplear; cincelar.

chitchat, n chismes m, habladurías f.

chitterlings, n menudos m de cerdo.

chivalrous, adj caballeroso.

chivalry, n caballería f; caballerosidad f.

chive, n cebollino m.

chlorate, n clorato m.

chloride, n cloruro m; cloruro m de cal.

chlorinate, vt clorinar, clorar, tratar con cloro.

chlorine, n cloro m; monóxido m de cloro.

chlorofluorocarbon, n clorofluorocarbono m.

chloroform, n cloroformo m.

chlorophyl, n clorofila f.

chock, n 1. calzo m, cuña f; 2. vt calzar, acuñar.

chocolate, n chocolate m.

choice, *adj* **1.** selecto, escogido; **2.** *n* elección *f*, selección *f*; preferencia *f*; opción *f*, alternativa *f*; (range to choose from) surtido *m*.

choir, *n* coro *m*; coros *m*; orfeón *m*; coral *f*.

choke, *n* **1.** obturador *m*, cierre *m*; estárter *m*, ahogador; **2.** *vt* atascar, tapar, obstruir; estrangular, ahogar, sofocar.

choking, *adj* **1.** asfixiador, asfixiante. **2.** *n* ahogo *m*, asfixia *f*.

cholera, *n* cólera *m*.

choleric, *adj* colérico.

cholesterol, *n* colesterol *m*.

choose, *vt* elegir, escoger; seleccionar.

choos(e)y, *adj* melindroso, delicado.

chop, *n* **1.** chuleta *f*; golpe *m* cortante; **2.** *vt* cortar, tajar.

choppy, *adj* (mar) picado; agitado.

chopsticks, *n* palillos *m* (de los chinos).

choral, *adj* orfeón *m*.

chorale, *n* coral *m*.

chord, *n* cuerda *f*; acorde *m*.

chore, *n* tarea *f*, trabajo *m* rutinario, quehaceres *m pl*.

choreograph, *vt* coreografiar.

choreographer, *n* coreógrafo(a).

choreography, *n* coreografía.

chorister, *n* corista; director(a).

chorus, *n* **1.** coro *m*; conjunto; **2.** *vt* cantar en coro.

chosen, *adj* preferido, predilecto.

chowder, *n* estofado *m* con almejas y pescado.

christening, *n* bautizo *m*, bautismo *m*.

Christianity, *n* cristianismo *m*.

Christmas, *n* Navidad *f*.

chromatic, *adj* cromático.

chrome, *n* acero *m* al cromo.

chromium, *n* cromo *m*.

chromosome, *n* cromosoma *m*.

chronicle, *vt* historiar; registrar, describir.

chronological, *adj* cronológico.

chronology, *n* cronología *f*.

chronometer, *n* cronómetro *m*.

chrysalis, *n* crisálida *f*.

chuck, *n* **1.** echada *f*, despedido *m*; **2.** *vt* tirar, abandonar.

chuckle, *n* **1.** risita *f*, risa *f* sofocada; **2.** *vi* reírse entre dientes.

chug, *vi* hacer ruidos explosivos repetidos; resoplar.

chum, *n* compinche *m*, compañero, amigo.

chunk, *n* pedazo *m*, trozo; pedazo *m* grueso.

church, *n* iglesia; templo.

churl, *n* patán *m*.

churn, *n* **1.** mantequera; **2.** *vt* batir en una mantequera; **3.** *vi* revolverse, agitarse.

chute, *n* tolva *f*, vertedor *m*, rampa *f* de caída.

chutney, *n* chutney *m*.

cicada, *n* cigarra *f*.

cider, *n* sidra *f*; manzana de sidra.

cigar, *n* puro *m*, cigarro *m*.

cigarette, *n* cigarrillo *m*; pitillo *m*, cigarro *m*.

cinchona, *n* quino *m*; bark quina *f*.

cinder, *n* carbonilla *f*; cenizas *f*.

cinder block, *n* ladrillo *m* de cenizas.

cinema, *n* cine *m*; cine *m* multisalas.

cinematography, *n* cinematografía.

cinnamon, *n* canela *f*.

cipher, *n* cero *m*; cifra *f*.

circle, *n* **1.** círculo *m*; grupo *m*; **2.** *vi* dar vueltas.

circlet, *n* anillo *m*; adorno *m* en forma de círculo.

circuit, *n* circuito *m*; gira *f*; pista *f*; vuelta *f*.

circuit-breaker, *n* cortacircuitos *n*.

circular, *adj* circular.

circulate, *vt* **1.** poner en circulación; hacer circular; anunciar por circular; **2.** *vi* circular.

circulating, *adj* circulante.

circulation, *n* circulación *f*; tirada *f*; circulación *f* de la sangre.

circumcise, *vt* circuncidar.

circumference, *n* circunferencia *f*.

circumnavigate, *vt* circunnavegar.

circumscribe, *vt* circunscribir; limitar, restringir.

circumspect, *adj* circunspecto, prudente.

circumspection, *n* circunspección, prudencia.

circumstance, *n* circunstancia *f*.

circumstantiate, *vt* probar refiriendo más detalles, corroborar, confirmar.

circumvent, *vt* burlar; salvar, evitar.

circus, *n* circo *m*; plaza *f* redonda, glorieta.

cistern, *n* tanque *m*, deposito *m*; cisterna *f*.

citadel, *n* ciudadela *f*; alcázar *m*; reducto *m*.

citation, *n* cita *f*; citación *f*; mención *f*.

cite, *vt* citar; mencionar.

citizen, *n* ciudadano(a), habitante *m/f*, vecino(a).

citizenry, *n* ciudadanos *m*, ciudadanía *f*.

citizenship, *n* ciudadanía *f*.

citric, *adj* ácido *m* cítrico.

citron, *n* cidra *f*; cidro *m*.

citrus, *n* agrios *m*, cítricos *m*.

city, *n* **1.** ciudad *f*; **2.** *adj* municipal, de la ciudad.

civet, *n* algalia *f*.

civic, *adj* cívico; municipal.

civics, *n* cívica *f*; educación *f* cívica.

civil, *adj* civil, amable, cortés.

civilian, *adj* **1.** paisano; civil; **2.** *n* civil *m/f*, paisano(a).

civility, *n* cortesía *f*; urbanidad *f*; amabilidad *f*.

civilization, *n* civilización *f*.

civilize, *vt* civilizar.

clack, *vi* charlar, chismear.

claim, *n* **1.** reclamación *f*; petición *f*; **2.** demanda *f*; **3.** *vt* reclamar, exigir; solicitar; demandar.

claimant, *n* solicitante *m/f*; demandante *m/f*; pretendiente.

clairvoyance, *n* clarividencia *f*.

clairvoyant(e), *n* clarividente *m/f*, vidente *m/f*.

clam, *n* almeja *f*.

clamber, *n* **1.** subida *f*; **2.** *vi* trepar, subir.

clammy, *adj* frío y húmedo, pegajoso.

clamorous, *adj* clamoroso, vociferante, ruidoso.

clamp, *n* **1.** abrazadera *f*; cepo *m*; **2.** *vt* afianzar con abrazadera.

clan, *n* clan *m*.

clang, *n* **1.** sonido *m* metálico fuerte, estruendo *m*, **2.** *vt* hacer sonar. **3.** *vi* sonar, hacer estruendo.

clank, *n* sonido *m* metálico seco, golpeo *m* metálico.

clannish, *adj* exclusivista, con fuerte sentimiento de tribu.

clap, *n* **1.** palmoteo *m*; palmada *f*; trueno *m*, estampido *m* de trueno; **2.** *vt* aplaudir.

clapper, *n* badajo *m*.

clapping, *n* aplausos *m*.

claret, *n* vino *m* tinto.

clarification, *n* aclaración *f*.

clarify, *vt* aclarar.

clarinet, *n* clarinete *m*.

clarinetist, *n* clarinetista *m/f*.

clarion, *n* trompeta *f*; llamada *f* fuerte y sonora.

clarity, *n* claridad *f*.

clash, n 1. estruendo m, fragor m; 2. choque m; enfrentamiento m; encuentro m; desacuerdo m; conflicto m; 3. vi enfrentarse, pelearse.

class, n clase f.

classic, adj 1. clásico; 2. n obra f clásica.

classical, adj clásico.

classification, n clasificación f.

classified, adj information secreto, reservado.

classify, vt clasificar; clasificar como secreto, reservar.

classroom, n aula f, clase f.

clatter, n 1. ruido m, estruendo m; choque m; 2. vi hacer ruido, hacer estruendo.

clause, n cláusula f; oración f.

claustrophobia, n claustrofobia f.

claustrophobic, adj 1. claustrofóbico; 2. n claustrófobo(a) m/f.

clavichord, n clavicordio m.

clavicle, n clavícula f.

claw, n 1. garra f, zarpa f, garfio m, gancho m; 2. vt arañar; desgarrar.

clay, n arcilla f.

clayey, adj arcilloso.

clean, adj limpio; aseado; despejado; decente; inocente.

cleaner, n limpiador(a) m/f.

cleaning, n limpia f, limpieza.

cleanliness, n limpieza.

cleanse, vt limpiar.

cleanser, n agente m de limpieza, producto m para la limpieza.

cleansing, adj limpiador; purificador.

clear, adj 1. claro; despejado; limpio, tranquilo; absoluto, neto; 2. entero, completo; 3. vt salvar, saltar por encima de; despejar, liquidar (deuda).

clearance, n despeje m; desmonte m, holgura f.

clearness, n claridad f.

cleat, n abrazadera f, listón m, fiador m.

cleavage, n escisión f, división f; escote m.

cleave, vi 1. partir, hender, abrir por medio; surcar; 2. vi no separarse de; ser inseparables.

cleaver, n cuchilla f de carnicero.

clef, n clave f.

clemency, n clemencia f.

clement, adj clemente, benigno,

clergyman, n clérigo m.

cleric, n eclesiástico m, clérigo m.

clerical, adj oficinesco, oficinesco, de oficina.

clerk, n oficinista m/f, empleado(a), m/f, secretario(a) m/f.

clever, adj inteligente, listo; hábil; ingenioso.

cleverly, adv hábilmente; ingeniosamente; con destreza.

cleverness, n inteligencia f; habilidad f; ingenio m; destreza f.

cliché, n cliché m, tópico m, frase f hecha.

click, n golpecito m seco; piñoneo m; taconeo m; chasquido m; tecleo m.

clicking, n chasquido m.

client, n cliente m/f.

clientèle, n clientela f.

cliff, n risco m; precipicio m; acantilado m.

climate, n clima m; ambiente m.

climatic, adj climático.

climatology, n climatología f.

climax, n 1. punto m culminante, colmo m, apogeo m, orgasmo m; 2. vi llegar a un clímax.

climb, n 1. subida f, escalada f, ascenso m; 2. vt trepar, escalar.

climber, n montañista m/f, alpinista m/f, trepador(a) m/f.

climbing, adj montañismo.

clime, n clima m; región f.

clinch, n 1. abrazo m; clinch m; 2. vt afianzar; remachar.

clincher, n el punto clave, el argumento irrebatible.

cling, vi adherirse a, pegarse a, quedar pegado a; aferrarse a.

clinging, adj ceñido, muy ajustado; pegajoso; tenaz.

clinic, n clínica f; centro m médico.

clinical, adj clínico.

clinician, n médico(a.).

clink, n 1. tintín m, sonido m metálico; choque m; 2. vt hacer sonar, hacer tintinar.

clip, n 1. tijeretada f; esquila f, sujetapapeles, grapa; fotograma m; golpe m, cachete m; 2. vt sujetar.

clipper, n clíper m.

clippers, n maquinilla f (para cortar el pelo).

clique, n pandilla f; camarilla f, pena f.

cliquish, adj exclusivista.

clitoris, n clítoris m.

cloak, n 1. capa f, manto, pretexto m; 2. vt encapotar; cubrir, encubrir, disimular.

clock, n 1. reloj m; esfera f, cuadrante m; taxímetro m; 2. registrar.

clockmaker, n relojero m.

clockwise, adj en dirección de las agujas del reloj.

cloister, n claustro m.

cloistered, adj conventual.

clone, n clon m; clónico m; 2. vt clonar.

cloning, n clonación f, clonaje m.

close, adv 1. cerca; muy cerca; de cerca; 2. adj cercano, próximo; 3. compacto, tupido; 4. vt cerrar; concluir, terminar.

closely, adv fielmente, exactamente; atentamente; atestado.

closeness, n proximidad f; cercanía f; intimidad f.

closet, n armario m, ropero m.

closure, n cierre m; conclusión f; clausura f.

clot, n 1. grumo m, cuajarón m; embolia f; 2. vi cuajarse, coagularse.

cloth, n paño m, tela f; trapo m; mantel m.

clothe, vt vestir; cubrir; revestir.

clothes, n ropa f, vestidos m.

clothier, n ropero m, sastre m.

clothing, n ropa f, vestidos m; prenda f de vestir.

cloud, n nube; nubarrón m.

cloudless, adj sin nubes, despejado.

cloudy, adj nublado, nuboso; turbio; empañado.

clout, n tortazo m; influencia f, fuerza f (política etc).

clove, n diente m de ajo; clavo m de especie.

clove-hitch, n ballestrinque m.

clover, n trébol m.

clown, n 1. payaso m, clown m; patán m; 2. vi hacer el payaso.

clowning, n payasadas f.

clownish, adj clownesco.

cloy, vt/i empalagar.

cloying, adj empalagoso.

club, n 1. porra f, cachiporra f, garrote m; palo m; 2. tréboles m; 3. club m; casino m.

cluck, n 1. cloqueo m; chasquido m (de la lengua); 2. vi (a)cloquear.

clue, n indicio m; pista f; indicación f.

clump, n 1. grupo m; mata f, macizo m; 2. pisadas f fuertes; 3. vi pisar fuerte.

clumsily, *adv* torpemente; pesadamente; toscamente, chapuceramente.

clumsiness, *n* torpeza *f*, desmaña *f*; tosquedad.

clumsy, *adj* torpe, desmailado; desgarbado, pesado.

clunk, *n* 1. sonido *m* metálico sordo; 2. *vi* sonara hueco.

cluster, *n* 1. grupo *m*; racimo *m*; 2. *vi* agruparse, apiñarse; arracimarse.

clutch, *n* 1. apretón *m*; 2. nidada *f*; 3. embrague *m*; 4. *vt* tener asido en la mano; sujetar, apretar, empuñar.

clutter, *n* 1. desorden *m*, confusión *f*; 2. *vt* llenar desordenadamente, atestar.

coach, *n* 1. coche *m*; diligencia *f*; carroza *f*; coche *m*, vagón *m*; 2. entrenador *m*; autocar *m*; 3. *vt* entrenar, preparar; enseñar.

coagulant, *n* coagulante *m*.

coagulate, *vt* 1. coagular; 2. *vi* coagularse.

coagulation, *n* coagulación *f*.

coal, *n* carbón *m*; hulla *f*.

coalesce, *vi* fundirse; unirse, incorporarse.

coalition, *n* coalición *f*.

coarse, adj basto, burdo; grueso; tosco, torpe.

coarseness, *n* basteza *f*; tosquedad *f*.

coast, n costa *f*; litoral *m*.

coastal, adj costero, costanero.

coastguard, *n* guardacostas *m*.

coat, *n* chaqueta *f*, americana *f*, saco *m*; abrigo *m*.

coax, *vt* halagar, mimar.

coaxial, *adj* coaxial.

cob, *n* 1. cisne *m* macho; 2. jaca *f* fuerte, avellana *f*; 3. (maize) mazorca *f*.

cobalt, *n* cobalto *m*.

cobble, *vt* empedrar con guijarros, enguijarrar.

cobbler, *n* zapatero *m* remendón.

cobra, *n* cobra *f*.

cobweb, *n* telaraña *f*.

cocaine, *n* cocaína *f*.

cochineal, *n* cochinilla *f*.

cock, *n* 1. gallo *m*; 2. *vt* (pistola) amartillar; aguzar.

cockade, *n* escarapela *f*.

cockatoo, *n* cacatúa *f*.

cockcrow, *n* canto *m* del gallo.

cockpit, *n* cabina *f* (del piloto).

cockroach, *n* cucaracha *f*.

cockscomb, *n* cresta *f* de gallo.

cocktail, *n* combinado *m*, copetín *m*, cóctel.

coconut, *n* coco *m*.

cocoa, *n* cacao *m*; (bebida) chocolate.

cocoon, *n* 1. capullo *m*; 2. *vt* envolver.

cod, *n* bacalao *m*.

coda, *n* coda *f*.

coddle, *vt* mimar, hacer mimos a.

code, *n* 1. código *m*, clave *f*, cifra *f*; 2. *vt* cifrar.

coded, *adj* 1. en cifra, en clave.

codeine, *n* codeína *f*.

codeword, *n* palabra *f* en clave.

codfish, *n* bacalao *m*.

codicil, *n* codicilo *m*.

codify, *vt* codificar.

coerce, *vt* forzar; obligar, coaccionar.

coercion, *n* coacción *f*, coerción *f*, compulsión *f*.

coeval, *adj* 1. coetáneo, contemporáneo, coevo; 2. *n* coetáneo(a).

coexist, *vi* coexistir.

coexistence, *n* coexistencia *f*, convivencia *f*.

coexistent, *adj* coexistente.

coffee, *n* café *m*.

coffer, *n* cofre *m*, arca *f*; tesoro *m*.

cofferdam, *n* ataguía *f*.

coffin, *n* ataúd *m*.

cog, *n* diente *m*; rueda *f* dentada.

cogency, *n* fuerza *f*, lógica *f*, convicción *f*.

cogent, *adj* fuerte, lógico, convincente, sólido.

cogitate, *vt/i* meditar, reflexionar.

cogitation, *n* meditación *f*, reflexión *f*.

cognac, *n* coñac *m*.

cognition, *n* cognición *f*.

cognitive, *adj* cognitivo, cognoscitivo.

cogwheel, *n* rueda *f* dentada.

cohabit, *vi* cohabitar.

cohabitation, *n* cohabitación *f*.

cohere, *vi* adherirse, pegarse; formar un conjunto sólido.

coherent, *adj* coherente; lógico, comprensible.

cohesion, *n* cohesión *f*.

cohesive, *adj* cohesivo; unido.

cohort, *n* cohorte *f*.

coiffeur, *n* peluquero *m*.

coiffure, *n* peinado *m*.

coil, *n* 1. rollo *m*; aduja *f*; anillo *m*; espiral *f*; serpentín *m*; bobina *f*, carrete *m*; 2. *vt* arrollar , enrollar; 3. *vi* arrollarse, enrollarse; 4. *vi* enroscarse;subir en espiral.

coiled, *adj* arrollado, enrollado.

coin, *n* 1. moneda *f*; 2. *vt* acuñar; inventar, idear.

coinbox, *n* depósito *m* de monedas.

coincide, *vi* coincidir; estar de acuerdo .

coincidence, *n* coincidencia *f*; casualidad *f*.

coincidental, *adj* coincidente; fortuito, casual.

coincidentally, *adv* por casualidad, casualmente.

coitus, *n* coito *m*.

colander, *n* colador *m*, escurridor *m*.

cold, *adj* 1. frío; 2. *n* frío *m*; resfriado *m*, catarro *m*.

coldly, *adv* fríamente.

coldness, *n* frialdad *f*.

coleslaw, *n* ensalada *f* de col.

colic, *n* cólico *m*.

Coliseum, *n* Coliseo *m*.

colitis, *n* colitis *f*.

collaborate, *vi* colaborar (in, on en; with con).

collaboration, *n* colaboración *f*.

collaborator, *n* colaborador(ora).

collage, *n* collage *m*.

collagen, *n* colágeno *m*.

collapse, *n* 1. colapso *m*; hundimiento *m*, derrumbamiento *m*, desplome *m*; socavón *m*; fracaso *m*; 2. *vi* sufrir un colapso; derrumbarse.

collapsible, *adj* plegable; articulado.

collar, *n* 1. cuello *m*; collar *m*; collarín *m*; 2. *vt* prender por el cuello; apropiarse, pisar.

collarbone, *n* clavícula *f*.

collate, *vt* cotejar.

collateral, *adj* 1. colateral; préstamo *m* colateral, préstamo *m* pignoraticio; 2. *n* seguridad *f* subsidiaria, garantía *f* subsidiaria.

collation, *n* colación *f*; cotejo *m*.

colleague, *n* colega *m*.

collect, *n* 1. colecta *f*; 2. *vt* reunir, acumular; coleccionar; cobrar; 3. *vi* reunirse, acumularse.

collectible, *n* coleccionable *m*.

collection, *n* acumulación *f*, montón *m*; grupo *m*; cobro *m*; recaudación *f*.

collector, *n* recolector(a); coleccionista *m/f*; colección *f*.

college, *n* colegio *m*; colegio *m* mayor.

collegiate, adj colegial, colegiado.
collide, vi chocar, colisionar.
collie, n perro m pastor escocés, collie m.
collision, n choque m, colisión f.
collocate, vi colocarse con.
collocation, n colocación f.
colloquial, adj familiar, coloquial.
colloquialism, n palabra f familiar; estilo m familiar.
collude, vi confabularse.
collusion, n confabulación f; connivencia f; colusión f.
colon, n colon m; (tipografía) dos puntos.
colonel, n coronel m.
colonial, adj colonial.
colonnade, n columnata f; galería f.
colony, n colonia f.
color, n 1. color m; colorido m; code código m de colores; 2. vt colorear, pintar.
colorant, n colorante m.
coloration, n colorido m, colores m.
coloratura, n coloratura f; soprano f de coloratura.
color-blind, adj daltoniano.
colorfast, adj no destenible.
colorful, adj lleno de color; vivo, animado.
coloring, n colorido m; colorante m.
colorless, adj sin color, incoloro.
colossal, adj colosal.
colossus, n coloso m.
colostomy, n colostomía f.
colostrum, n colostro m, calostro m.
colt, n potro m; potranco m.
columbine, n aguileña f.
column, n columna f.
columnist, n columnista m/f, articulista m/f.
coma, n coma f.
comatose, adj comatoso.
comb, n 1. peine m; peineta f; 2. vt peinar, cardar.
combat, n combate.
combatant, n combatiente m/f.
combination, n combinación f.
combine, n 1. asociación, monopolio m; 2. vt combinar.
combo, n grupo m, conjunto.
combustible, adj 1. combustible; 2. combustible m.
combustion, n combustión f.
come, vi venir; pasar; cruzar; avanzar.
comedian, n cómico m.
comedy, n comedia f; comicidad f.
comely, adj gentil; lindo.
comestibles, n comestibles m.
comet, n cometa m.
comfort, n consuelo m; alivio m.
comfortable, adj cómodo, confortable.
comforting, adj consolador, (re)confortante.
comfortless, adj incómodo, sin comodidad.
comic, adj cómico; divertido; libro m de cómics.
comical, adj cómico; divertido, entretenido.
coming, adj 1. que viene; venidero; prometedor; 2. n venida f, llegada f; advenimiento m.
comma, n coma.
command, n 1. orden f mandato m; 2. vt mandar, ordenar.
commandant, n comandante m.
commandeer, vt requisar, expropiar.
commander, n comandante m, jefe m.
commanding, adj dominante; imponente.
commandment, n mandamiento m.
commando, n comando m.
commemorate, vt conmemorar.

commemoration, n conmemoración f; en conmemoración de.
commemorative, adj conmemorativo.
commence, vt comenzar, empezar.
commencement, n comienzo m, principio m; ceremonia f de entrega de diplomas.
commend, vt alabar, elogiar; alabar la acción de uno.
commendable, adj recomendable, encomiable, loable.
commensurate, adj proporcionado; equivalente a, que corresponde a.
comment, n 1. comentario m; observación f; 2. vi hacer comentarios, hacer una observación; comentar.
commentary, n comentario m; reportaje m.
commentate, vt 1. hacer un reportaje sobre; 2. vi hacer un reportaje.
commentator, n comentador(ora).
commerce, n comercio m.
commercial, adj 1. comercial; 2. n anuncio m, emisión f publicitaria.
commercialize, vt comercializar, convertir en comercial.
commiserate, vi expresar su sentimiento; compadecerse de, condolerse de.
commiseration, n conmiseración f.
commisary, n comisario(a) m/f.
commission, n comisión f; comisión f, comité m.
commissioned, adj oficial m/f.
commissioner, n comisario(a) m/f.
commit, vt 1. cometer; hacer, entregar; 2. vr hacer una promesa, declararse; comprometerse.
commitment, n compromiso m, obligación f, cometido m.
committed, adj comprometido.
committee, n comisión f, comité m.
commode, n sillico m; cómoda f.
commodious, adj grande, espacioso.
commodity, n artículo m, mercancía f, mercadería f, producto m.
commodore, n comodoro m.
common, adj común; ordinario; corriente, vulgar.
commonplace, adj vulgar, es frecuente ver que ...
commonsense, adj racional, lógico.
commonwealth, n república f.
commotion, n disturbio; tumulto, confusión, alboroto.
communal, adj comunal.
commune, n 1. comuna f; 2. vi comulgar.
communicable, adj comunicable.
communicant, n comulgante m/f.
communicate, vt 1. comunicar; 2. vi comulgar.
communication, n comunicación f.
communicative, adj comunicativo, expansivo.
communion, n comunión f; comulgar.
communiqué, n comunicado m, parte m.
communism, n comunismo m.
communist, adj comunista.
community, n comunidad f; colectividad f, sociedad f; vecindario m.
commutable, adj conmutable.
commutation, n conmutación f.
commute, vt 1. conmutar; 2. vi viajar a diario.
commuter, n viajero m diario, viajera f diaria.
compact, n 1. pacto m, convenio m; polvera f; 2. adj compacto; apretado, sólido.
companion, n compañero(a) m/f.
companionship, n compañerismo m.
companionway, n escalerilla f.
company, n compañía, tripulación f.
comparable, adj comparable; a case un caso análogo.
compare, vt comparar; cotejar.

comparison, n comparación f; cotejo m.

compartment, n compartimiento m; departamento m.

compartmentalize , vt dividir en categorías; aislar en categorías, compartimentar.

compass, n brújula f; compás m.

compassion, n compasión f.

compassionate, adj compasivo.

compatibility, n compatibilidad f.

compatible, adj compatible, conciliable.

compatriot, n compatriota m/f.

compel, vt obligar; imponer; exigir, hacer inevitable.

compelling, adj irresistible, apremiante, convincente; compulsivo.

compendium, n compendio m.

compensate, vt 1. compensar; recompensar; indemnizar; 2. vi compensar algo.

compensation, n compensación f; recompensa f; indemnización f, resarcimiento.

compère, n 1. presentador m, animador m; 2. vt presentar; 3. vi actuar de presentador.

compete, vi competir, hacer competencia.

competence, n aptitud f, capacidad f, competencia f; incumbencia f.

competent, adj competente, capaz; adecuado, suficiente.

competition, n competencia f, rivalidad f.

competitive, adj spirit competidor, de competencia; de concurso.

competitiveness, n competitividad f.

competitor, n competidor(ora); rival m/f.

compilation, n compilación f, recopilación f.

compile, vt compilar, recopilar.

compiler, n compilador(a) m/f; recopilador(a) m/f.

complacence, n suficiencia f, satisfacción f de sí mismo.

complacent, adj suficiente.

complain, vi quejarse; reclamar; formular una queja; presentar síntomas de, sufrir de.

complement, n 1. complemento m; 2. vt complementar.

complementary, adj complementario;

complete, adj 1. entero, completo; total; 2. vt completar; terminar, acabar, concluir.

completely, adv completamente, enteramente; totalmente; por completo; a fondo.

completion, n terminación f, conclusión f; realización f.

complex, adj 1. complejo, complicado; 2. n complejo m.

complexion, n tez f, cutis m; piel f; cariz m, aspecto m.

complexity, n complejidad f, lo complicado.

compliance, n sumisión f; conformidad f.

compliant, adj sumiso.

complicate, vt complicar.

complicated, adj complicado.

complication, n complicación f.

complicity, n complicidad f.

compliment, n 1. polite expression, cumplido m; saludos m; 2. vt felicitar a uno por algo.

complimentary, adj 1. lisonjero; favorable; de favor; 2. n ejemplar m obsequio.

comply, vi obedecer; acceder; conformarse con.

component, adj 1. componente; 2. n componente m.

comport, vi 1. concordar con; 2. vr comportarse.

comportment, n comportamiento m.

compose, vi 1. componer; constar de, componerse de; 2. vr calmarse.

composed, adj sosegado, tranquilo, sereno.

composer, n compositor(ora).

composite, adj 1. compuesto; propuesta f; 2. n propuesta f.

composition, n composición f.

compost, n abono m.

composure, n serenidad f, calma f.

compote, n compota f.

compound, adj 1. compuesto; 2. vt componer, mezclar.

comprehend, vt comprender, entender; abarcar.

comprehension, n comprensión f.

comprehensive, adj completo, exhaustivo; de gran alcance, de máximo alcance.

compress, n 1. compresa f; 2. vt comprimir; condensar.

compression, n compresión f.

compressor, n compresor m.

comprise, vt comprender; constar de, componerse de; abarcar.

compromise, n 1. transigencia f; contemporización f; transacción f; avenencia f, arreglo m; 2. vt comprometer; poner en peligro; 3. vi intransigir.

compromising, adj situation comprometedor; acomodaticio.

comptometer, n máquina f de calcular; operador m.

comptroller, n interventor(ora) m/f.

compulsion, n obligación f, fuerza f mayor, coacción f.

compulsive, adj compulsivo.

compulsory, adj obligatorio; preceptivo.

compunction, n remordimiento m; compunción f.

computation, n cómputo m, cálculo m.

compute, vt computar, calcular.

computer, n cordenador m, computadora f.

computerize, vt computerizar, informatizar.

comrade, n camarada m/f, compañero.

comradeship, n compañerismo m, camaradería f.

con, n contra f.

concave, adj cóncavo.

conceal, vt ocultar; disimular; encubrir.

concealed, adj oculto; disimulado; indirecto.

concealment, n ocultación f; encubrimiento m; disimulación f.

concede, vt conceder; ceder, entregar.

conceit, n presunción f, engreimiento m, vanidad f.

conceited, adj presumido, engreído, vanidoso.

conceivable, adj concebible.

conceivably, adv posiblemente.

conceive, vt concebir; imaginar, formarse un concepto de; idear.

concentrate, n 1. concentrado m; 2. vt concentrar.

concentrated, adj concentrado.

concentration, n concentración f.

concentric, adj concéntrico.

concept, n concepto m.

conception, n concepción f; idea f, concepto m.

conceptual, adj conceptual.

conceptualize, vt conceptualizar.

concern, n 1. asunto m; interés m; preocupación f; 2. vt tener que ver con.

concerned, adj preocupado; inquieto.

concert, n 1. concierto m; 2. vt concertar.

concerted, adj coordinado, conjunto.

concertina, n concertina f.

concerto, n concierto.

concession, n concesión f; privilegio m.

conch, n concha; cóclea f.

concierge, n conserje m.

conciliate, vt conciliar.

conciliation, n conciliación f; servicio m de conciliación.

concise, adj conciso.

concisely, adv concisamente, con concisión.

conciseness, n concision, n concisión f.

conclave, n cónclave m.

conclude, vt concluir, terminar.

conclusion, n conclusión f, terminación f; en conclusión, para terminar.

conclusive, adj concluyente, decisivo; evidence, decisivo.

concoct, vt confeccionar; inventar; tramar.

concomitant, adj 1. concomitante; 2. n concomitante m.

concord, n concordia f, armonía f.

concordance, n concordancia f.

concourse, n muchedumbre f, concurrencia f.

concrete, adj 1. concreto; específico; 2. n hormigón m.

concretize, vt concretar.

concubine, n concubina f, barragana f, manceba f.

concupiscence, n concupiscencia f.

concupiscent, adj concupiscente.

concur, vi concurrir; coincidir.

concurrence, n acuerdo m, conformidad f.

concussion, n conmoción f cerebral.

condemn, vt condenar; censurar; declarar ruinoso.

condemnation, n condena f, condenación f; censura f.

condensation, n condensación f; forma f abreviada.

condense, vt condensar; abreviar.

condenser, n condensador m.

condescending, adj superior; lleno de superioridad; desdeñoso, altivo.

condescension, n aire f de superioridad, aire m protector.

condiment, n condimento m.

condition, n 1. condición f; estado m; clase f; 2. vt acondicionar.

conditional, adj condicional.

conditioned, adj condicionado.

conditioner, n suavizante m de cabello; crema f suavizante.

conditioning, n acondicionamiento m.

condole, vi condolerse de uno; dar el pésame a uno.

condolence, n pésame m.

condom, n condón m, preservativo m.

condominium, n condominio m; apartamento m.

condone, vt condonar.

condor, n cóndor m.

conduce, vi conducir a.

conducive, adj conducente a, propicio para, que favorece.

conduct, n 1. conducta f, comportamiento m; manejo m, dirección f, administración f; 2. vt conducir, llevar, dirigir.

conduction, n conducción f.

conductor, n director m; cobrador m.

conduit, n conducto m.

cone, n cono m; piña f; cucurucho m, pirucho m.

confection, n 1. confección f, hechura f; 2. dulce m, confite m.

confectioner, n pastelero(a) m/f.

confederacy, n confederación f; complot m.

confederate, adj confederado.

confederation, n confederación f.

confer, vt 1. conceder, otorgar; 2. conferenciar.

conference, n congreso m, conferencia f.

conferment, n concesión f, otorgamiento m.

confess, vt confesar.

confessed, adj declarado.

confession, n confesión f; profesión f.

confessional, n confesonario m.

confessor, n confesor m.

confetti, n confeti m.

confide, vt confiar.

confidence, n confianza f; confidencialidad f.

confident, adj seguro de sí mismo, lleno de confianza.

confidential, adj confidencial.

confidentially, adv en confianza.

confiding, adj confiado; crédulo.

configuration, n configuración.

confine, vt encerrar, limitar.

confinement, n encierro m; confinamiento m, confinación f; prisión f, reclusión f; parto m.

confirm, vt confirmar; ratificar.

confirmation, n confirmación f; ratificación.

confirmed, adj inveterado; confirmado.

confiscate, vt confiscar, incautarse de, requisar.

confiscation, n confiscación f, incautación f, requisa f.

conflict, n 1. conflicto m; incompatibilidad f; 2. vt desavenirse.

conflicting, adj contradictorio; opuesto.

conform, vi conformarse; ajustarse a, estar de acuerdo con, cuadrar con.

conformist, adj conformista.

conformity, n conformidad f.

confound, vt confundir.

confounded, adj confundido.

confront, vt hacer frente a, encararse con; confrontar.

confrontation, n confrontación f; careo m.

confuse, vt confundir; desconcertar, dejar confuso a.

confused, adj confuso.

confusing, adj confuso, desconcertante.

confusion, n confusión f, desorden m.

confute, vt refutar.

congeal, vt congelar, cuajar, coagular.

congenial, adj simpático; agradable, compatible.

congenital, adj congénito.

congested, adj congestionado, superpoblado.

congestion, n congestión, aglomeración f.

conglomerate, n 1. conglomerado m; 2. vt aglomerar.

conglomeration, n conglomeración f.

congratulate, vt felicitar, dar la enhorabuena a.

congratulations, n felicitaciones f.

congregation, n reunión f; congregación f.

congress, n congreso m.

congressional, adj del congreso.

congruence, n congruencia f.

congruent, adj congruente.

conifer, n conífera f.

conjecture, n conjetura f.

conjugal, adj conyugal.

conjugate, vt conjugar.

conjugation, n conjugación f.

conjunction, n conjunción f.

conjunctive, adj conjuntivo.

conjunctivitis, n conjuntivitis f.

conjuncture, n coyuntura f.

conjure, vt suplicar; conjurar.

conjure away, vt conjurar, hacer desaparecer.

conjure up, vt hacer aparecer; evocar, hacer pensar en.

conjurer, n prestidigitador m, mago m.

connect, vt 1. juntar, unir (con); conectar; relacionar, asociar; 2. vi unirse, conectarse; enlazar con.

connecting-rod, n biela f.

connection, n juntura f; unión f; conexión f.

connective, adj 1. conjuntivo; tejido m conjuntivo; 2. n conjunción f.

conniving, adj muy dado a intrigas; manoso, tramposo.

connoisseur, n entendido(a) m/f (en); conocedor(a) m/f (de); experto(a) m/f.

connotation, n connotación f.

connote, vt connotar.

connubial, adj conyugal, connubial.

conquer, vt 1. conquistar; vencer; 2. vi triunfar.

conqueror, n conquistador m; vencedor m.

conquest, n conquista f.

consanguinity, n consanguinidad f.

conscience, n conciencia f.

conscientious, adj concienzudo.

conscientiousness, n diligencia f, escrupulosidad f.

conscious, adj ser consciente de, saber, hacerse cargo de.

consciousness, n conciencia f.

conscript, n 1. recluta m, quinto m, conscripto(a) m/f; 2. vt llamar al servicio militar.

conscripted, adj reclutado a la fuerza.

conscription, n servicio m militar obligatorio; conscripción m/f.

consecrate, vt consagrar.

consecration, n consagración f.

consecutive, adj sucesivo, seguido; consecutivo.

consecutively, adv sucesivamente.

consensus, n consenso m.

consent, n 1. consentimiento m; 2. vi consentir.

consequence, n consecuencia f; resultado m.

consequent, adj consiguiente.

consequential, adj consiguiente, resultante.

conservancy, n conservación f.

conservation, n conservación f, preservación f.

conservationism, n conservacionismo m.

conservationist, n conservacionista m/f.

conservative, adj 1. conservador; 2. n conservador(a) m/f.

conservatory, n invernadero m.

conserve, n 1. conserva f; 2. vt conservar.

consider, vt considerar; pensar, meditar; estudiar.

considerable, adj importante, apreciable; cuantioso.

considerate, adj considerado, atento, comedido.

consideration, n 1. consideración f; 2. retribución f.

considering, adv 1. teniendo en cuenta, a pesar de todo; 2. prep en consideración a, teniendo en cuenta.

consign, vt consignar; enviar; confiar.

consignee, n consignatorio(a) m/f.

consigner, n consignador(a) m/f.

consignment, n consignación f; envío m, remesa f.

consist, vi consistir en, constar de, componerse de.

consistency, n consecuencia f, lógica f; coherencia f; consistencia f.

consistent, adj consecuente, lógico; coherente.

consolation, n consuelo m; consolación f.

consolatory, adj consolador.

console, n 1. consola f; 2. vt consolar.

consolidate, vt 1. consolidar; concentrar; fortalecer; 2. vi consolidarse.

consolidated, adj consolidado.

consoling, adj consolador, reconfortante.

consommé, n consomé m, caldo m.

consonance, n consonancia f.

consonant, adj 1. consonante; de acuerdo con, conforme a; 2. n consonante f.

consort, n 1. consorte m/f; 2. vi asociarse con.

consortium, n consorcio m.

conspicuous, adj visible, llamativo, destacado, sobresaliente; notable.

conspiracy, n conspiración f, complot m.

conspirator, n conspirador(a) m/f.

conspire, vi conspirar.

constancy, n constancia f; fidelidad f.

constant, adj 1. constante, continuo, incesante; 2. n constante f.

constantly, adv constantemente.

constellation, n constelación f.

consternation, n consternación f; consternado.

constipate, vt estreñir.

constipation, n estreñimiento m.

constituency, n distrito m electoral, votantes m.

constituent, adj 1. constitutivo, integrante; 2. n constitutivo m; componente m.

constitute, vt constituir; componer, integrar.

constitution, n constitución f.

constitutional, adj constitucional.

constrain, vt constreñir, restringir.

constraint, n fuerza f; encierro m; reserva f.

constrict, vt apretar, estrechar.

constricted, adj limitado, reducido.

constriction, n constricción f.

construct, vt 1. construir; 2. n construcción f.

construction, n construcción f; edificio m.

constructive, adj constructivo; positivo.

construe, vt interpretar; construir; analizar.

consul, n cónsul m/f.

consular, adj consular.

consulate, n consulado m.

consult, vt consultar.

consultant, n consultor(a) m/f; asesor(a) m/f; consejero(a) m/f técnico(a).

consultation, n consulta f; consultación f.

consume, vt comer(se), beber(se) consumir, utilizar.

consumer, n 1. consumidor(a) f; 2. consumista.

consumerism, n consumismo m.

consuming, adj arrollador, apasionado; dominante, avasallador.

consummate, adj 1. consumado, completo; sumo; 2. vt consumar.

consumption, n consumo m; tisis f.

consumptive, adj tísico.

contact, n 1. contacto m; 2. vt contactar.

contact-breaker, n interruptor m.

contact lens, n lente f de contacto, (micro) lentilla f.

contagion, n contagio m.

contagious, adj contagioso.

contain, vt 1. contener; ser exactamente divisible por; 2. vr contenerse, contener la risa.

container, n recipiente m, receptáculo m; caja f, contenedor m.

contaminant, n contaminante m.

contaminate, vt contaminar; contaminarse con.

contamination, n contaminación f.

contemplate, vt contemplar; pensar.

contemplation, n contemplación f.

contemporaneous, adj contemporáneo.

contemporary, adj contemporáneo; coetáneo.

contempt, n desprecio m; desacato m rebeldía f.

contemptible, adj despreciable, vil.

contemptuous, adj desdeñoso; despectivo.

contend, vt 1. afirmar, sostener (que); 2. vi contender, luchar.

contender, n contendiente m/f.

contending, adj rival, opuesto.

content, adj 1. contento, satisfecho; 2. n contento m, contenido m; 3. vt contentar, satisfacer.

contented, adj satisfecho, contento.

contention, n contienda f; equipos m rivales; argumento m.

contentious, adj contencioso, conflictivo, discutible.

contentment, n contento m.

contest, n 1. contienda f, lucha f; concurso m, prueba f; 2. vt impugnar; 3. vi contender con.

contestant, n contendiente m/f, aspirante m/f.

context, n contexto m.

contextual, adj contextual.

contiguous, adj contiguo (a).

continence, n continencia f.

continent, adj 1. continente. 2. n continente m.

continental, adj continental.

contingency, n contingencia f.

contingent, adj contingente, eventual.

continual, adj continuo, constante.

continue, vt continuar; seguir; proseguir.

continuing, adj irresoluto; continuado.

continuity, n continuidad f.

contort, vt retorcer.

contour, n contorno m.

contraband, n contrabando m.

contrabass, n contrabajo m.

contraception, n contracepción f.

contraceptive, adj, n anticonceptivo m, contraceptivo m.

contract, n 1. contrato m; contrata f; 2. vt contratar; 3. vi contraerse, encogerse.

contraction, n contracción f.

contractor, n contratista m/f.

contradict, vt contradecir; desmentir.

contradiction, n contradicción f.

contradictory, adj contradictorio.

contralto, n contralto.

contraption, n dispositivo m, ingenio m, artilugio m.

contrapuntal, adj de contrapunto.

contrariness, n terquedad f.

contrary, adj 1. contrario; en dirección contraria; 2. adv contrario a; 3. n contrario m.

contrast, n 1. contraste m; 2. vt comparar; 3. vi contrastar (con).

contrasting, adj opuesto.

contribute, vt contribuir, aportar.

contribution, n contribución f; donativo m, colaboración f.

contributor, n donante m/f; colaborador(a) m/f.

contributory, adj contributivo.

contrite, adj arrepentido, contrito.

contrition, n arrepentimiento m.

contrivance, n treta f, estratagema f; invención f.

contrive, vt inventar, idear; efectuar; tramar.

contrived, adj artificial; efectista.

control, n 1. control m, mando m, gobierno m; 2. vt controlar, mandar, gobernar; 3. vr dominarse, controlarse.

controlled, adj contenido; sereno.

controller, n director(a) m/f; inspector(a) m/f; controlador(a) m/f.

controversial, adj discutido, debatido, polémico, controvertido, conflictivo.

controversy, n controversia f.

controvert, vt contradecir.

contumacy, n contumacia f.

contusion, n contusión f.

convalesce, vi convalecer.

convalescence, n convalecencia f.

convalescent, adj convaleciente.

convection, n convección f.

convene, vt 1. convocar; 2. vi reunirse.

convener, n organizador(a) m/f.

convenience, n comodidad f; conveniencia f.

convenient, adj cómodo; práctico, útil; accesible.

convent, n convento m.

convention, n 1. convenio; 2. convención f; asamblea f, congreso m.

conventional, adj convencional.

converge, vi convergir (en); dirigirse todos a.

conversant, adj versado en, enterado de.

conversation, n conversación f.

converse, adj 1. contrario; 2. n inversa f; 3. vt conversar, hablar.

conversely, adv a la inversa.

conversion, n conversión f; apropiación f ilícita; transformación f.

convert, n 1. converso(a) m/f; 2. vt convertir; transformar.

converter, n convertidor m.

convex, adj convexo.

convey, vt transportar, llevar; transmitir; comunicar.

conveyor, n portador m, transportador m.

convict, n 1. presidiario m, recluso m; 2. vt condenar.

conviction, n condena f; creencia f, convicción f.

convince, vt convencer.

convinced, adj convencido, fiel, firme.

convincing, adj convincente.

convoke, vt convocar.

convoy, n 1. convoy m; escolta f; 2. vt convoyar; escoltar.

convulse, vt convulsionar, sacudir.

convulsion, n convulsión f; paroxismo m de risa.

convulsive, adj convulsivo.

cony, n conejo m.

cooing, n arrullos m.

cook, n 1. cocinero(a) m/f; 2. vt guisar, cocer, cocinar.

cooked, adj preparado.

cooker, n cocina f; olla f para cocinar.

cookie, n galleta f; bizcocho m.

cooking, n cocina f, arte m culinario.

cool, adj 1. fresco; 2. tranquilo, imperturbable.

coolant, n refrigerante m.

cooler, n nevera f portátil.

cooling, adj refrescante; refrigerante.

cooling-fan, n ventilador m.

coolness, n frescura f, lo fresco.

coop, n gallinero m.

cooper, n tonelero m.

cooperate, vi cooperar, colaborar.

cooperation, n cooperación f, colaboración f.

cooperative, adj 1. cooperativo; servicial, dispuesto a ayudar; 2. n cooperativa f.

coordinate, n 1. coordenada f; 2. vt coordinar.

coordination, n coordinación f.

coordinator, n coordinador(a) m/f.

coowner, n copropietario(a) m/f.

coownership, n copropiedad f.

copartner, n consocio m/f, copartícipe m/f.

cope, vi 1. arreglárselas; 2. poder con; hacer frente a.

copier, n copiadora f.

co-pilot, n copiloto m/f.

copious, adj copioso, abundante.

copper, n cobre m.

copperhead, n víbora f cobriza.

coppersmith, n cobrero m.

coppery, adj cobreño; cobrizo.

copra, n copra f.

coprocessor, n coprocesador m.

copula, n cópula f.

copulate, vi copularse (con).

copulation, n cópula f.

copy, n 1. copia f; 2. vt copiar, imitar.

copycat, n imitador(a) m/f.

copying-machine, n copiadora f.

copyreader, n corrector(a) m/f.

copyright, adj 1. protegido por los derechos de(l) autor; 2. vt registrar como propiedad literaria.

coquetry, n coquetería f.

coquette, n coqueta f.

coquettish, adj coqueta.

coral, n 1. coral m; 2. adj coralino, de coral.

corbel, n ménsula f, repisa f.

cord, n cuerda f; cordón m.

cordial, adj 1. cordial, afectuoso; 2. n cordial m.

cordiality, n cordialidad f, afecto m.

cordite, n cordita f.

cordon, n 1. cordón m; 2. vt acordonar.

corduroy, n pana f.

core, n centro m, núcleo m; corazón m.

cork, n 1. corcho m; 2. vt tapar con corcho, taponar.

corkscrew, n 1. sacacorchos m; 2. vi subir en espiral.

cork-tree, n alcornoque m.

corn, n granos m, cereales m; maíz m.

corncob, n mazorca f de maíz.

cornea, n córnea f.

cornelian, n cornalina f.

corner, n 1. ángulo m; esquina f; 2. vt acorralar, arrinconar; detener; 3. vi monopolizar.

cornerstone, n piedra f angular.

cornet, n corneta f.

cornfield, n trigal m, maizal m, milpa f.

cornflour, n arina f de maíz.

cornice, n cornisa f.

cornstarch, n almidón m de maíz, maicena.

cornucopia, n cuerno m de la abundancia.

corona, n corona f.

coronary, adj coronario.

coronation, n coronación f.

coroner, n juez m de primera instancia e instrucción (que establece las causas de defunción).

coronet, n corona f; diadema f.

corporal, adj 1. corporal; 2. n cabo m.

corporate, adj corporativo, colectivo.

corporation, n corporación f; sociedad f anónima.

corporeal, adj corpóreo.

corps, n cuerpo m.

corpse, n cadáver m.

corpulence, n gordura f.

corpulent, adj gordo.

corpuscle, n glóbulo m, corpúsculo m.

corral, n 1. corral m; 2. vt acorralar.

correct, adj 1. correcto, exacto, justo; 2. vt corregir.

correction, n corrección f; rectificación f.

correlate, vt correlacionar.

correlation, n correlación f.

correspond, vi corresponder, escribirse; estar en correspondencia con.

correspondence, n correspondencia f.

correspondent, n correspondiente m/f; corresponsal m/f.

corresponding, adj correspondiente.

corridor, n pasillo m; corredor m.

corroborate, vt corroborar, confirmar.

corroboration, n corroboración f, corroborative confirmación f.

corrode, vt 1. corroer; 2. vi corroerse.

corroded, adj corroído.

corrosion, n corrosión f.

corrosive, adj corrosivo.

corrugated, adj ondulado; corrugado.

corrupt, adj 1. corrompido; viciado; estragado; 2. vt corromper; sobornar.

corruption, n corrupción f.

corsage, n cuerpo m; ramillete (en o para el pecho).

corset, n faja f, corsé m.

cortège, n cortejo m, séquito m; cortejo m fúnebre.

cortisone, n cortisona f.

corvette, n corbeta f.

cosignatory, n cosignatario(a) m/f.

cosine, n coseno m.

cosiness, n comodidad f; lo acogedor.

cosmetic, adj 1. cosmético; 2. n cosmético m.

cosmetician, n cosmetólog(a) m/f.

cosmic, adj cósmico.

cosmology, n cosmología f.

cosmonaut, n cosmonauta m/f.

cosmopolitan, adj cosmopolita.

cosmos, n cosmos m.

cost, n precio m; coste m, costo m.

cost-effective, adj rentable, beneficioso.

costume, n traje m; disfraz m.

cosy, adj cómodo, agradable; acogedor.

cot, n cuna f, camita f de niño; cama f plegable.

coterie, n grupo m; tertulia f; (clique) peña f.

cottage, n casita f de campo; vivienda f campestre, quinta f.

cotton, n algodón m.

cottontail, n conejo m (de cola blanca).

cottonwood, n álamo m de virginia.

couch, n canapé m, sofá m; diván m.

cougar, n puma f.

cough, n 1. tos f; 2. vi toser.

cough drop, n pastilla f para la tos.

council, n consejo m, junta f; concilio m.

councillor, n concejal m/f.

councilman, n concejal m/f.

counsel, n 1. consejo m; 2. vt aconsejar; orientar; recomendar.

counseling, n asesoramiento m; asistencia f.

counselor, n asesor(a) m/f consejero(a) m/f.

count, n 1. cuenta f, cálculo m; recuento m; 2. n cuenta f; 3. vt contar; calcular.

countenance, n 1. semblante m, rostro m; 2. vt aprobar tolerar, sancionar.

counter, adj 1. contrario, de sentido opuesto (a); 2. n mostrador m 3. vt contrarrestar; devolver; contestar a.

counter... pref contra...

counteract, vt contrarrestar; neutralizar.

counter attack, n 1. contraataque m; 2. vt contraatacar.

counterbalance, n 1. contrapeso m; compensación f; 2. vt contrapesar; compensar.

countercharge, n recriminación f; contraataque m.

counterfeit, adj 1. falso, falsificado, contrahecho; 2. vt falsificar, contrahacer.

counter-indication, n contraindicación f.

counterintelligence, n contraespionaje m.
countermand, vt revocar, cancelar.
counter-measure, n contramedida f.
counteroffensive, n contraofensiva f.
counter-order, n contraorden f.
counterpart, n homólogo(a) m/f; equivalenten.
counterproductive, adj contraproducente.
countess, n condesa f.
countless, adj incontable, innumerable.
country, n país m; patria f; campo m.
countryman, n campesino m; compatriota m/f.
county, n condado m.
coupé, n cupé m.
couple, n 1. par m, pareja f; 2. vt unir, juntar; asociar; 3. vi copularse.
coupler, n acoplador m; enganche m.
couplet, n pareado m.
coupling, n acoplamiento m.
coupon, n cupón m, vale m.
courage, n valor m, valentía f.
courageous, adj valiente, valeroso.
courier, n estafeta; mensajero m.
course, n 1. dirección f, ruta f; trayectoria f; curso m; rumbo m; 2. vi correr.
court, n 1. patio m; cancha, pista; 2. tribunal m; juzgado m; 3. vt cortejar, hacer la corte; 4. vi solicitar.
courteous, adj cortés, fino, correcto.
courteously, adv cortésmente.
courtesan, n cortesana f.
courtesy, n cortesía f; atención f; gentileza f.
courthouse, n palacio m de justicia.
courtier, n cortesano m.
courtroom, n sala f de justicia; sala f de tribunal.
courtship, n cortejo m, noviazgo m.
courtyard, n patio m.
cousin, n primo(a) m/f.
couturier, n modisto m.
cove, n cala f, ensenada f.
coven, n aquelarre m, asamblea f de brujas.
covenant, n pacto m, convenio m; alianza f.
cover, n 1. cubierta f; tapa f, cobertor m, colcha f; 2. vt cubrir (de); revestir; forrar.
coverage, n alcance m; reportaje m.
covering, n cubierta f, envoltura f.
cover-letter, n carta f (adjunta) de explicación.
covert, adj secreto, disimulado.
cover-up, n encubrimiento m.
covet, vt codiciar.
covetous, adj codicioso.
covetousness, n codicia f.
cow, n 1. vaca f; 2. vt intimidar, acobardar.
coward, n cobarde m.
cowardice, n cobardía f.
cowboy, n vaquero m.
cower, vi encogerse (de miedo).
cowl, n capucha f; sombrerete m.
co-worker, n colaborador(a) m/f.
cowshed, n establo m.
coy, adj tímido; evasivo, reservado.
coyness, n timidez f; coquetería f.
crab, n cangrejo m.
crabby, adj malhumorado, hosco, gruñón.
crack, n 1. crujido m; chasquido m; 2. grieta, hendidura; 3. vt romper, agrietar; 4. vi estallar.
cracker, n galleta f de soda.
crackers, adj lelo, chiflado.
crackle, n 1. crepitación f, chisporroteo m; crujido m; 2. vi crepitar, chisporrotear.
crackpot, adj tonto, estrafalario, excéntrico.

cradle, n cuna f.
craft, n 1. destreza f, habilidad f; atucia f; 2. oficio m; 3. nave f.
craftiness, n astucia f.
craftsman, n artesano m; artífice m.
craftsmanship, n artesanía f.
cram, vt cebar; empollar, aprender apresuradamente.
cramp, n 1. grapa f; pieza f de unión, abrazadera f; calambre m; 2. vt estorbar, restringir.
cramped, adj estrecho; menudo, apretado.
cranberry, n arándano m.
crane, n grulla f; grúa f.
cranial, adj craneal.
cranium, n cráneo m.
crank, n manivela f; manubrio m.
crape, n crespón m.
crash, n 1. estruendo m, estrépito m; estallido m; accidente m, colisión f; choque m, encontronazo m; accidente m de aviación; 2. vi chocar, estrellarse, fracasar.
crass, adj craso, estúpido.
crassness, n estupidez f.
crate, n 1. cajón m de embalaje, jaula f; 2. vt embalar.
crater, n cráter m.
crave, vt suplicar, implorar; anhelar.
craving, n deseo m vehemente, ansia f, sed f; antojo m.
crawl, n 1. arrastramiento m; camino m a gatas; 2. vi arrastrarse; avanzar a rastras.
crayon, n pastel m, lápiz m de tiza.
craze, n manía f; moda f.
crazed, adj loco demente.
craziness, n locura f, chifladura f.
crazy, adj loco, chiflado, tarado.
creak, n 1. crujido m; chirrido m, rechinamiento m; 2. vi crujir; chirriar, rechinar.
cream, adj 1. color de crema; 2. n (de leche) nata f.
creaminess, n cremosidad f.
creamy, adj cremoso.
crease, n pliegue m; (en pantalones) raya f; arruga f; 2. vt paper plegar, doblar; arrugar.
create, vt crear, producir, motivar; inventar.
creation, n creación f; modelo m.
creative, adj creativo; work original.
creativity, n creatividad f.
creator, n creado(r)a m/f; el Creador m.
creature, n criatura f; animal m, bicho m.
comfort, n bienestar m material.
creche, n guardería f infantil.
credentials, n documentos m; referencias f.
credibility, n credibilidad f.
credit, n crédito m.
creditable, adj loable, estimable.
credit card, n tarjeta f de crédito.
creditor, n acreedo(a) m/f.
credulity, n credulidad f.
credulous, adj crédulo.
creed, n credo m.
creek, n cala f, ensenada f; riachuelo m.
creel, n nasa f, cesta f.
creep, vi arrastrarse, andar a gatas.
creeper, n enredadera f.
creepy, adj horripilante, escalofriante.
cremate, vt incinerar.
cremation, n incineración f.
crematorium, n crematorio m.
crescendo, n crescendo m.
crescent, adj 1. creciente; 2. n media luna f.

crest, n 1. cresta f; moco m; cima f; cumbre f; 2. vi llegar al máximo.

crestfallen, adj alicaído, cabizbajo.

cretaceous, adj cretáceo.

cretin, n cretino(a).

cretinous, adj cretino.

cretonne, n cretona f.

crevasse, n grieta f de glaciar.

crevice, n grieta f, hendedura f.

crew, n tripulación f; dotación f; personal m, equipo m.

crib, n cuna.

cribbage, n juego m de cartas.

cricket, n grillo m; (Dep) cricquet.

crime, n crimen m, delito m.

criminal, adj 1. criminal; delictivo; 2. n criminal m/f, delincuente m/f.

criminality, n criminalidad f.

criminology, n criminología f.

crimp, vt rizar, encrespar.

crimped, adj rizado, con rizos, encrespado.

crimson, adj carmesí.

cringe, vi agacharse, encogerse; reptar; encogerse de miedo.

crinkly, adj arrugado; rizado, crespo.

crinoline, n mirinaque m, crinolina f.

cripple, n 1. lisiado(a) m/f, cojo(a) m/f; 2. vt lisiar, tullir.

crippled, adj tullido, lisiado; minusválido; averiado.

crisis, n crisis f.

crisp, adj duro pero quebradizo; crujiente; refrescante.

crispy, adj crujiente.

criterion, n criterio m.

critic, n crítico.

critical, adj crítico.

criticism, n crítica f.

criticize, vt censurar.

critique, n 1. crítica f; 2. vt evaluar una ponencia.

croak, n 1. graznido m cuervo m; 2. vi graznar, croar.

crochet, n croché m, labor f de ganchillo.

crock, n vasija f de barro; carcamal m.

crockery, n loza f, vajilla f, los platos.

crocodile, n cocodrilo m.

crocus, n azafrán m.

croissant, n croissant m, cruasán m, medialuna f.

crone, n vieja f, bruja f.

crony, n compinche m/f, amigote m.

cronyism, n amiguismo m.

croon, vt canturrear, cantar en voz baja.

crooning, n canturreo; tarareo.

crop, n 1. cultivo m; cosecha f; 2. vt cortar; recortar.

croquet, n croquet m.

croquette, n croqueta f.

cross, adj 1. cruzado; transversal, oblicuo; 2. adj malhumarado; 3. vt cruzar, atravesar.

crossbeam, n viga f transversal.

crossbow, n ballesta f.

crossbred, adj cruzado, híbrido.

crossfire, n fuego m cruzado.

crossing, n cruce m; paso m a nivel; paso m para peatones.

crosswalk, n paso m de peatones.

crosswind, n viento m de costado.

crossword, n crucigrama m.

crotch, n horcajadura f; entrepiernas f pl.

crotchety, adj áspero, arisco, antojadizo.

crouch, vi agacharse, acurrucarse.

croup, n crup m, garrotillo m.

croupier, n crupier m, crupié m.

crouton, n cuscurro m.

crow, n 1. cuervo m, grajo m, corneja f; 2. vi cantar, cacarear; gorjearse.

crowbar, n palanca f.

crowd, n 1. multitud f; muchedumbre f, gentío m; 2. vt amontonar; congregarse.

crowded, adj lleno, atestado; muy concurrido.

crown, n 1. corona f; copa f; cumbre f; coronilla f; 2. vt coronar; completar, rematar.

crowning, adj 1. supremo; 2. n coronación f.

crucial, adj decisivo, crítico, crucial.

crucible, n crisol m.

crucifix, n crucifijo m.

crucifixion, n crucifixión f.

cruciform, adj cruciforme.

crucify, vt crucificar.

crude, adj 1. crudo, bruto; tosco; ordinario; 2. n crudo m.

crudeness, n tosquedad f; ordinariez f.

cruel, adj cruel.

cruelty, n crueldad f.

cruet, n vinagrera f, salvilla f.

cruise, n crucero m, viaje m por mar.

cruiser, n crucero m.

cruller, n buñuelo m.

crumb, n migaja f; miga f.

crumble, vt 1. desmenuzar, desmigajar; 2. vi desmenuzarse, desmigajarse; desmoronarse.

crumple, vt deshacer; paper estrujar; arrugar.

crunch, n crujido m; crisis f, punto m decisivo.

crusade, n 1. cruzada f; 2. vt hacer una cruzada.

crusader, n cruzado m.

crush, n 1. agolpamiento m; aglomeración f; 2.vt estrujar; triturar, moler; 3. vt abrumar.

crushing, adj aplastante; abrumador; decisivo.

crust, n corteza f; mendrugo m; costra f.

crusty, adj con corteza; malhumorado, irritable.

crutch, n muleta f.

cry, n 1. grito m; pregón m; lema m; lloro m; 2. vt gritar; llorar.

crying, n lloro m, llanto m.

crypt, n cripta f.

cryptic, adj misterioso; secreto, enigmático.

cryptographer, n criptógrafo(a) m/f.

cryptography, n criptografía f.

crystal, n 1. cristal m; 2. adj cristalino.

crystallize, vt cristalizar.

crystallized, adj escarchado.

cub, n cachorro m; niño m explorador; periodista m novato.

cubbyhole, n chiribitil m.

cube, n cubo m.

cubic, adj cúbico; medida f cúbica; metro m cúbico.

cubicle, n cubículo m; caseta f.

cucumber, n pepino m.

cuddle, n 1. abrazo m; 2. vt abrazar.

cuff, n 1. bofetada f, vuelta f del pantanlón; 2. vt abofetear.

cufflinks, n gemelos m; broches m, mellizos m.

cuisine, n cocina f.

culinary, adj culinario.

culminate, vt culminar.

culminating, adj culminante.

culmination, n culminación f, punto m, colmo m.

culpability, n culpabilidad f.

culpable, adj culpable.

culprit, n persona f culpable.

cult, n culto m.

cultivate, vt cultivar.

cultivated, *adj* culto; cultivado.
cultivation, *n* cultivo *m;* cultura *f.*
cultivator, *n* cultivador(a) *m/f.*
cultural, *adj* cultural.
culture, *n* cultivo *m;* cultura *f.*
cultured, *adj* culto.
culvert, *n* alcantarilla *f.*
cumulative, *adj* cumulativo.
cunning, *adj* 1. astuto, taimado; 2. *n* astucia *f.*
cup, *n* copa *f,* taza *f.*
cupola, *n* cúpula *f.*
curable, *adj* curable.
curate, *n* cura *m;* coadjutor *m.*
curative, *adj* curativo.
curator, *n* director(ora) *f,* conservador(ora).
curb, *n* 1. freno *m,* estorbo *m;* 2. *vt* refrenar, limitar.
curd, *n* cuajada *f,* requesón *m.*
curdle, *vt* cuajar.
cure, *n* cura *f,* curación *f.*
curfew, *n* (toque *m* de) queda *f.*
curing, *n* curación *f.*
curiosity, *n* curiosidad *f.*
curious , *adj* curioso.
curl, *n* 1. rizo *m,* bucle *m;* espiral *f;* 2. *vt* rizar, ensortijar; arrollar; fruncir.
curler, *n* bigudí *m,* chicho *m,* rulo *m.*
curlew, *n* zarapito *m.*
currant, *n* pasa *f* de Corinto.
currency, *n* moneda *f.*
current, *adj* 1. corriente, actual; 2. *n* corriente *f;* flúido *m.*
curriculum, n plan de estudios, programa *m* de estudios, currículo *m.*
curried, *adj* (preparado) con curry.
curse, *n* 1. maldición *f;* palabrota *f,* taco *m;* calamidad *f;* 2. *vt* maldecir; echar pestes de.
cursed, *adj* maldito.
cursive, *adj* cursivo.
cursor, *n* cursor *m.*
cursory, *adj* rápido, superficial.
curt, *adj* brusco, seco, lacónico.
curtail, *vt* acortar, abreviar; restringir.
curtailment, *n* acortamiento *m,* abreviación *f;* restricción *f.*
curtain, *n* cortina; visillo *m;* telón *m;* paneles *m pl.*
curtsy, *n* 1. reverencia *f;* 2. *vi* hacer una reverencia.
curvaceous, *adj* de buen tipo, curvilínea.
curvature, *n* curvatura *f;* escoliosis *f.*
curve, *n* 1. curva *f;* combadura *f;* 2. *vt* encorvar, torcer.
curved, *adj* curvo, encorvado.
curvy, *adj* curvo, encorvado; serpentino, con muchas curvas.
cushion, *n* 1. cojín *m;* banda *f;* colchón *m;* 2. *vt* amortiguar.
cusp, *n* cúspide *f;* corona *f;* cuerno *m.*
custard, *n* natillas *f.*
custodial, *adj* sentence condena *f* de prisión.
custodian, *n* custodio *m,* guardián *m;* conservador *m.*
custody, *n* custodia *f.*
custom, adj 1. aduanal; 2. *n* costumbre *f;* clientela *f,* parroquia *f;* aduanero(a) *m/f,* aduana *f.*
customary, *adj* acostumbrado, de costumbre; normal.
customer, *n* cliente *m.*
cut, *adj* 1. cortado; 2. *n* corte *m;* cortadura *f;* 3. reducción *f,* rebaja *f;* 4. *vt* cortar, partir.
cutback, n recorte *m,* corte *m,* reducción *f.*
cute, *adj* mono, lindo; astuto, listo.

cuticle, *n* cutícula *f.*
cutler, *n* cuchillero *m.*
cutlery, *n* cubiertos *m,* cuchillería *f.*
cutlet, n chuleta *f.*
cutter, *n* cortador(ora) *m/f;* cizallas *f;* guardacostas *m.*
cutting, *adj* 1. cortante; mordaz; 2. *n* recorte *m;* desmonte *m,* trinchera *f.*
cyanide, *n* cianuro *m.*
cybernetic, *adj* cibernético.
cybernetics, *n* cibernética *f.*
cyclamate, *n* ciclamato *m.*
cyclamen, *n* ciclamen *m,* ciclamino *m.*
cycle, *n* ciclo *m.*
cycling, *n* ciclismo *m.*
cyclist, n ciclista *m/f.*
cyclone, *n* ciclón *m.*
cyclotron, *n* ciclotrón *m.*
cygnet, *n* pollo *m* de cisne, cisnecito *m.*
cylinder, *n* cilindro *m.*
cylindrical, *adj* cilíndrico.
cymbal, *n* platillo *m,* címbalo *m.*
cynic, *n* cínico(a).
cynical, *adj* cínico; despreciativo, desengañado.
cynicism, *n* cinismo *m;* desprecio *m,* desengaño *m.*
cypress, *n* ciprés *m.*
cyst, *n* quiste *m.*
cystic, *adj* cístico.
cytology, *n* citología *f.*
cytotoxic, *adj* citotóxico.

D

D, d, *n* (letra *f*) D, d.
dab, *n* 1. golpe *m* ligero; pequeña cantidad *f;* gota *f;* 2. *vt* tocar ligeramente.
dabble, *vt* 1. salpicar, mojar; chapotear los pies; 2. *vi* interesarse en algo por pasatiempo.
dabbler, *n* aficionado(a) *m/f,* diletante *m/f.*
dachshund, *n* perro *m* tejonero.
dagger, *n* puñal *m,* daga *f;* cruz *f.*
dahlia, *n* dalia *f.*
daily, *adj* 1. diario, cotidiano; 2. *adv* diario, cada día; 3. *n* (periódico) diario *m.*
daintily, *adv* delicadamente; elegantemente, primorosamente.
daintiness, *n* delicadeza *f;* elegancia *f;* primor *m.*
dainty, *adj* 1. delicado, fino; elegante, primoroso, precioso; 2. *n* bocado *m* exquisito, golosina *f.*
daiquiri, *n* daiquiri *m.*
dairy, *n* lechería *f;* quesería *f;* vaquería *f.*
dairymaid, *n* lechera *f.*
dairyman, *n* lechero *m.*
dais, *n* estrado *m.*
daisy, *n* maya *f,* margarita *f.*
dale, *n* valle *m.*
dalliance, *n* juegos *m,* diversiones *f;* frivolidad *f;* coquetería *f;* flirteo *m.*
dally, *vi* tardar, perder el tiempo; divertirse.
dalmatian, *n* perro *m* dálmata.
dam, *n* 1. presa *f;* dique *m;* madre *f;* 2. *vt* represar; construir una presa sobre.

damage, n **1.** daño m, perjuicio m; avería f; desperfectos m; **2.** vt dañar, perjudicar; averiar, estropear.

damaging, adj perjudicial.

damask, adj adamascado.

dame, n dama f, señora f.

damn, vt condenar; maldecir; ¡condenación!.

damnation, n condenación f; perdición f.

damned, adj condenado, maldito.

damp, adj **1.** húmedo; mojado; **2.** vt mojar, humedecer.

damper, n (Mus) apagador m, sordina f; regulador m de tiro.

dampness, n humedad f.

damsel, n damisela f, doncella f.

dance, n **1.** baile m; **2.** vt bailar; danzar.

dance-band, n orquesta f de baile.

dance-floor, n pista f de baile.

dance-hall, n salón m de baile, sala f de fiestas.

dance-music, n música f de baile.

dancer, n bailador(a) m/f; bailarín m.

dancing, n baile m.

dancing-shoes, n zapatillas f.

dandelion, n diente m de león.

dandle, vt hacer saltar sobre las rodillas.

dandruff, n caspa f.

dandy, adj **1.** de primera; **2.** n dandi m.

danger, n peligro m; riesgo m.

dangerous, adj peligroso, arriesgado.

dangle, vt **1.** colgar, dejar colgado; **2.** vi estar colgado, pender; bambolearse.

dank, adj húmedo y malsano.

dapper, adj apuesto, pulcro.

dappled, adj moteado, salpicado de manchas.

dare, n **1.** hacer algo en desafío; **2.** vt arriesgar.

daring, adj **1.** atrevido, osado; **2.** n atrevimiento m.

daringly, adv atrevidamente, osadamente.

dark, adj **1.** oscuro; tenebroso; moreno; **2.** n oscuridad f.

darken, vt oscurecer; hacer oscuro.

darkness, n oscuridad f; tinieblas f.

darkroom, n cuarto m oscuro.

dark-skinned, adj de piel morena.

darling, n **1.** querido(a) m/f; **2.** adj muy querido.

darn, n **1.** zurcido m, zurcidura f; **2.** vt zurcir.

darned, adj condenado, maldito.

darning, n zurcidura f.

dart, n **1.** dardo m, saeta f, flecha f; **2.** vt lanzar; **3.** vi lanzarse, precipitarse.

dartboard, n diana f, blanco m.

dash, n **1.** pequeña cantidad f, poquito m; **2.** plumada f; raya f; brío m; **3.** vt romper, estrellar; tirar algo al suelo; **4.** vi ir de prisa.

dashboard, n tablero m de instrumentos.

dashing, adj arrojado; elegante; brioso, vistoso.

dastardly, adj ruin, vil, miserable; cobarde.

data, n datos m.

database, n base f de datos.

datable, adj datable, fechable.

dataphone, n datáfono f.

date, n **1.** fecha f; **2.** cita f; compromiso m; **3.** dátil m; palmera f datilera; **4.** vt fechar, poner la fecha en.

date-stamp, n **1.** fechador m; **2.** vt estampar la fecha en.

dative, adj dativo.

datum, n dato m.

daub, n **1.** mancha f; pintarrajo m; **2.** vt manchar; **3.** vi pintarrajear.

dauber, n pintor m de brocha gorda, mal pintor m.

daughter, n hija f.

daughter-in-law, n nuera f, hija f política.

daunt, vt acobardar, intimidar, desalentar.

dauntless, adj impávido, intrépido.

davenport, n sofá m.

dawdle, vt **1.** malgastar; **2.** vi perder el tiempo, holgazanear.

dawdler, n holgazán(ana) m/f, ocioso(a) m/f; persona f que anda despacio.

dawn, n **1.** alba f, amanecer m; aurora f, nacimiento m; **2.** vi amanecer, alborear, romper el día.

dawning, adj naciente.

day, adj **1.** diurno; **2.** n día m.

daybreak, n amanecer m.

day-care, n guardería f; servicios m de guardería.

daydream, n **1.** ensueño m, ilusión f; **2.** vi soñar despierto.

daylight, n luz f, luz f del día.

daylight-saving, n hora f de verano.

day-nurse, n enfermera f diurna.

day-nursery, n guardería f infantil.

day shift, n turno m de día.

daytime, n día m; de día.

day-to-day, adj cotidiano, rutinario; día por día.

daze, n **1.** estar aturdido; **2.** vt aturdir; deslumbrar.

dazed, adj aturdido.

dazzle, n **1.** lo brillante, brillo m; **2.** vt deslumbrar.

dazzling, adj deslumbrante, deslumbrador.

dazzlingly, adv deslumbradoramente.

deacon, n diácono m.

deaconess, n diaconisa f.

deactivate, vt desactivar.

dead, adj muerto.

deadbolt, n cerrojo m de seguridad.

deaden, vt amortiguar; aliviar.

deadline, n fecha f tope, fecha f, plazo m.

deadliness, n letalidad f; tedio m.

deadlock, n **1.** parálisis f; callejón m sin salida; **2.** vi estancarse.

deadly, adj mortal; exacto, certero; devastador.

deadness, n inercia f, falta f de vida.

deadpan, adj sin expresión, inexpresivo.

deaf, adj sordo.

deaf-aid, n aparato m del oído; audífono m.

deafen, vt ensordecer, asordar.

deafening, adj ensordecedor.

deaf-mute, n sordomudo(a) m/f.

deafness, n sordera f.

deal, n **1.** madera f de pino (o abeto); tablón m; viga f; **2.** transacción f, negocio m, trato m; **3.** pacto m, convenio m; reparto m; **4.** vi comerciar; comprar y vender.

dealer, n comerciante m, tratante m; concesionario(a) m/f.

dean, n decano m.

dear, adj querido, caro, costoso.

dearly, adv tiernamente.

dearth, n escasez f; falta f, ausencia f.

death, n muerte f; fallecimiento m, defunción f.

deathbed, n lecho m de muerte.

deathtrap, n sitio m muy peligroso.

débacle, n debacle f, fracaso m; derrota f.

debar, vt excluir; prohibir a uno hacer algo.

debark, vi desembarcar.

debase, vt degradar, envilecer; alterar, falsificar.

debasement, n degradación f, envilecimiento m; alteración f, falsificación f.

debate, n **1.** discusión f; debate m; **3.** vi discutir (con).

debater, *n* persona *f* que toma parte en un debate; polemista *m/f*.

debauch, *vt* corromper; seducir.

debauchery, *n* libertinaje *m*, corrupción *f*.

debenture, *n* vale *m*, bono *m*, obligación *f*.

debilitate, *vt* debilitar.

debilitating, *adj* debilitante, que debilita.

debility, *n* debilidad *f*.

debit, *n* 1. debe *m;* saldo *m* deudor, saldo *m* negativo; 2. *vt* adudar, cargar.

debris, *n* escombros *m*.

debt, *n* deuda *f*.

debtor, *n* deudor(a) *m/f*.

debunk, *vt* quitar lo falso y legendario de; desacreditar, demoler.

début, *n* debú *m*, presentación *f*; hacer su presentación, estrenarse.

decade, *n* década *f*, decenio *m*.

decadence, *n* decadencia *f*.

decadent, *adj* decadente.

decaffeinated, *adj* descafeinado.

decagram, *n* decagramo *m*.

decal, *n* pegatina *f*; calcomanía *f*.

decalcification, *n* descalcificación *f*.

decalcify, *vt* descalcificar.

decant, *vt* decantar.

decapitate, *vt* decapitar, degollar, descabezar.

decapitation, *n* decapitación *f*, degollación *f* .

decay, *n* 1. decadencia *f*, decaimiento *m*; pudrición *f;* 2. *vt* deteriorar, pudrir; 3. *vi* decaer, desmoronarse; pudrirse.

decayed, *adj* podrido; cariado.

decaying, *adj* en estado de putrefacción.

decease, *n* 1. fallecimiento *m;* 2. *vi* fallecer.

deceased, *adj* difunto.

deceit, *n* engaño *m*, fraude *m;* mentira *f*.

deceitful, *adj* engañoso, falso, fraudulento; mentiroso.

deceive, *vt* 1. engañar; defraudar; 2. *vr* engañarse, equivocarse.

deceiver, *n* impostor(a) *m/f*, embustero(a) *m/f;* seductor *m*.

decelerate, *vt* desacelerar, decelerar.

deceleration, *n* desaceleración *f*.

decency, *n* decencia *f*.

decent, *adj* decente.

decentralization, *n* descentralización *f*.

decentralize, *vt* descentralizar.

deception, *n* engaño *m*, fraude *m*.

deceptive, *adj* engañoso.

decibel, *n* decibel(io) *m*.

decide, *vt* 1. decidir, determinar; 2. *vi* decidir, resolver.

decided, *adj* decidido, resuelto.

deciding, *adj* factor decisivo, concluyente.

deciduous, *adj* de hoja caduca.

decimal, *adj* decimal.

decimalize, *vt* decimalizar.

decimate, *vt* diezmar.

decimation, *n* diezmamiento *m*.

decimeter, *n* decímetro *m*.

decipher, *vt* descifrar.

decipherable, *adj* descifrable.

decision, *n* decisión *f*; fallo *m*.

decisive, *adj* 1. decisivo, concluyente; 2. terminante.

deck, *n* cubierta *f*; piso *m*; suelo *m*, superficie *f*.

declaim, *vt* declamar.

declamation, *n* declamación *f*.

declamatory, *adj* declamatorio.

declaration, *n* declaración *f*.

declare, *vt* declarar, afirmar; anunciar.

declared, *adj* declarado, abierto.

declension, *n* declinación *f*.

decline, *n* 1. declinación *f*, descenso *m*, disminución *f;* 2. *vt* rehusar, negarse a aceptar; 3. *vi* declinar, disminuir; bajar.

declivity, *n* declive *m*.

decode, *vt* descifrar; descodificar.

decoder, *n* descodificador *m*.

decompose, *vt* 1. descomponer; 2. *vi* descomponerse.

decomposition, *n* descomposición *f*.

decompression, *n* descompresión *f*.

decongestion, *n* descongestión *f*.

decontaminate, *vt* descontaminar.

decontamination, *n* descontaminación *f*.

décor, *n* decoración *f*; decorado *m*.

decorate, *vt* adornar, decorar (with).

decorating, *n* decoración *f* del hogar.

decorator, *n* decorador *m*; pintor *m* decorador.

decorous, *adj* decoroso, correcto.

decorum, *n* decoro *m*, corrección *f*.

decoy, *n* 1. señuelo *m;* 2. *vt* atraer (o apartar) con señuelo.

decrease, *n* 1. disminución *f;* 2. *vt* disminuir, reducir; 3. *vi* disminuirse, reducirse.

decreasing, *adj* decreciente.

decree, *n* 1. decreto *m;* 2. *vt* decretar.

decrepit, *adj* decrépito.

decry, *vt* desacreditar, rebajar, censurar.

dedicate, *vt* 1. dedicar, consagrar; 2. *vr* dedicarse a.

dedicated, *adj* totalmente entregado, dedicado.

dedication, *n* dedicación *f*.

deduce, *vt* deducir.

deduct, *vt* restar, descontar, rebajar.

deduction, *n* deducción *f*, conclusión .

deed, *n* 1. hecho *m*, acto *m*, acción *f;* 2. escritura *f;* 3. *vt* transferir por acto notarial.

deem, *vt* juzgar, creer.

deep, *adj* profundo, hondo.

deepen, *vt* 1. ahondar, profundizar; 2. *vi* hacerse más profundo; intensificarse; aumentarse.

deep-fry, *vt* freir en aceite abundante.

deep-rooted, *adj* muy arraigado.

deep-sea, *adj* de altura, de alta mar.

deer, *n* ciervo *m*, venado *m*.

deerskin, *n* piel *f* de ciervo, gamuza *f*.

deface, *vt* desfigurar, mutilar.

defamation, *n* difamación *f*.

defamatory, *adj* difamatorio.

defame, *vt* difamar, calumniar.

default, *n* 1. en ausencia de; 2. incumplimiento; 3. *vi* no pagar, ponerse en mora.

defeat, *n* 1. derrota *f;* 2. *vt* vencer, derrotar.

defeated, *adj* derrotado.

defecate, *vt/i* defecar.

defect, *n* 1. defecto *m;* 2. *vi* desertar.

defection, *n* deserción *f*, defección *f*.

defective, *adj* defectuoso; 2. *n* persona *f* anormal.

defector, *n* desertor(a) *m/f*, tránsfuga *m/f*.

defend, *vt* defender.

defendant, *n* demandado(a) *m/f;* acusado(a) *m/f* .

defender, *n* defensor(a) *m/f;* defensa *m/f* .

defense, *n* defensa *f*.

defenseless, *adj* indefenso; inocente, inofensivo.

defensible, *adj* defendible; justificable.

defensive, *adj* defensivo; 2. *n* defensiva *f*.

defer, *vt* aplazar, diferir, postergar.

deference, *n* deferencia *f*, respeto *m*.

deferential, *adj* respetuoso.

deferral, *n* aplazamiento; prórroga *f.*

defiance, *n* desafío *m;* oposición *f* terca.

defiant, *adj* provocativo, insolente; tone desafiante.

defibrillator, *n* desfibrilador *m.*

deficiency, *n* falta *f;* defecto *m,* deficiencia *f.*

deficient, *adj* deficiente; insuficiente; incompleto.

deficit, *n* déficit *m.*

defile, *n* 1. desfiladero *m;* 2. *vt* manchar, deshonrar; ultrajar, profanar.

defilement, *n* deshonra *f;* ensuciamiento *m,* corrupción *f;* profanación *f.*

define, *vt* definir, determinar.

definite, adj claro, positivo; concreto; definitivo.

definition, *n* definición *f.*

definitive, *adj* definitivo.

deflate, *vt* desinflar.

deflect, *vt* desviar (de).

deflower, *vt* desflorar.

defog, *vt* desempañar.

defoliate, *vt* defoliar.

defoliation, *n* defoliación *f.*

deforest, *vt* deforestar, despoblar de árboles.

deforestation, *n* deforestación .

deform, vt deformar.

deformed, *adj* deforme, mutilado.

deformity, *n* deformidad *f.*

defraud, *vt* defraudar; estafar.

defray, *vt* sufragar, pagar, costear.

defreeze, *vt* descongelar.

defrost, *vt* deshelar, descongelar.

defroster, *n* dispositivo *m* antivaho.

deft, *adj* diestro, hábil.

deftly, *adv* diestramente, hábilmente.

defunct, *adj* difunto; que ya no existe.

defuse, *vt* desactivar; calmar, apaciguar.

defy, *vt* desafiar.

degenerate, *adj* 1. degenerado; 2. *n* degenerado(a) *m/f;* 3. *vi* degenerar.

degeneration, *n* degeneración *f.*

degradable, *adj* degradable; biodegradable.

degrade, *vt* 1. degradar, envilecer; 2. *vr* degradarse, aplebeyarse.

degrading, *adj* degradante, envilecedor.

degree, *n* 1. grado *m;* 2. título *m;* licenciatura *f;* 3. rango *m,* condición *f* social.

dehumanize, *vt* deshumanizar.

dehumidifier, *n* deshumedecedor *m.*

dehumidify, *vt* deshumedecer.

dehydrate, *vt* deshidratar.

dehydration, *n* deshidratación *f.*

deify, *vt* deificar.

deity, *n* deidad *f;* divinidad *f.*

dejected, *adj* abatido, desanimado.

dejection, *n* abatimiento *m,* desaliento *m.*

delay, *n* 1. dilación *f;* retraso *m,* demora *f;* 2. *vt* aplazar, demorar; 3. *vi* tardarse, demorarse.

delectable, *adj* delicioso, deleitable.

delegate, *n* 1. delegado(a) *m/f,* diputado(a) *m/f;* 2. *vt* delegar, diputar.

delegation, *n* 1. delegación *f;* 2. diputación *f.*

delete, *vt* suprimir, tachar; cancelar.

deleterious, *adj* nocivo, perjudicial.

deletion, *n* supresión *f,* tachadura *f,* cancelación *f.*

deliberate, *adj* 1. intencionado, premeditado; 2. *vt* meditar; 3. *vi* deliberar.

deliberation, *n* 1. deliberación *f,* reflexión *f;* 2. prudencia *f.*

delicate, *adj* delicado; fino, exquisito; escrupuloso.

delicatessen, *n* delicatessen *m.*

delicious, *adj* delicioso, exquisito, rico.

delight, *n* placer *m,* deleite *m;* encanto *m,* delicia *f;* 2. *vt* encantar, deleitar; 3. *vi* deleitarse con algo.

delightful, *adj* encantador, delicioso, precioso.

delimit, *vt* delimitar.

delineate, *vt* delinear; bosquejar, pintar; definir.

delineation, *n* delineación *f.*

delinquency, *n* delincuencia *f;* culpa *f.*

delinquent, *adj* 1. delincuente; 2. *n* delincuente *m/f.*

delirious, *adj* delirante.

delirium, *n* delirio *m.*

deliver, *vt* 1. repartir, entregar; 2. librar; 3. *vi* cumplir lo prometido, hacer lo pactado.

deliverance, *n* liberación *f,* rescate *m* (de).

delivery, *n* distribución *f,* entrega *f,* repartido *m.*

delouse, *vt* despiojar, espulgar.

delta, *n* delta *m;* (letra) delta *f.*

deltoid, *adj* deltoideo.

delude, *vt* 1. engañar; 2. *vr* engañarse.

deluded, *adj* iluso, engañado.

deluge, *n* 1. diluvio *m;* inundación *f;* 2. *vt* inundar.

delusion, *n* engaño *m,* error *m,* ilusión *f.*

demagnetize, *vt* desimantar.

demagogue, *n* demagogo(a) *m/f.*

demagoguery, *n* demagogia *f.*

demand, *n* 1. petición *f,* solicitud *f;* demanda *f;* 2. *vt* exigir, reclamar; solicitar perentoriamente.

demanding, *adj* exigente; absorbente; agotador.

demarcate, *vt* demarcar.

demarcation, *n* demarcación *f.*

demean, *vr* degradarse.

demeaning, *adj* degradante.

demeanor, *n* porte *m,* conducta *f.*

demented, *adj* demente; loco.

dementia, *n* demencia *f.*

demerit, *n* demérito *m,* desmerecimiento *m.*

demigod, *n* semidiós *m.*

demilitarization, *n* desmilitarización *f.*

demilitarize, *vt* desmilitarizar.

demimonde, *n* mujeres *f* mundanas.

demise, *n* fallecimiento *m.*

demitasse, *n* taza *f* pequeña, tacita *f.*

demo, *n* 1. manifestación *f,* protesta *f* callejera; 2. modelo *m* de demostración; maqueta *f.*

demobilize, vt desmovilizar.

democracy, *n* democracia *f.*

democrat, *n* demócrata *m/f.*

democratic, *adj* democrático.

demography, *n* demografía *f.*

demolish, *vt* derribar, demoler.

demolition, *n* derribo *m,* demolición *f.*

demon, *n* demonio *m.*

demoniacal, *adj* demoniaco, demoníaco.

demonstrate, *vt* 1. demostrar; 2. *vi* manifestarse.

demonstration, *n* demostración *f,* prueba *f;* manifestación *f.*

demonstrative, *adj* demostrativo.

demonstrator, *n* manifestante *m/f.*

demoralize, *vt* desmoralizar.

demoralizing, *adj* desmoralizador.

demote, *vt* degradar.

demotion, *n* degradación *f.*

demur, *vi* objetar; poner reparos.

demure, adj grave, solemne; recatado.

denial, *n* denegación *f,* negativa *f.*

denigrate, *vt* denigrar.

denigration, *n* denigración *f.*

denim, *n* dril de algodón *m.*

denominate, vt denominar.

denomination, n 1. denominación f. 2. clase f, categoría f; valor m; 3. secta f, confesión f.

denominator, n denominador m común.

denote, vt denotar; indicar, significar.

denounce, vt denunciar; abrogar; censurar.

dense, adj denso; espeso, compacto, tupido.

density, n densidad f; lo espeso, lo compacto.

dent, n 1. abolladura f; mella f; 2. vt abollar, mellar.

dental, adj dental.

dental floss, n hilo m de higiene dental.

dented, adj abollado, con abolladuras.

dentifrice, n dentífrico m.

dentist, n dentista m/f, odontólogo(a) m/f.

dentistry, n odontología f, dentistería f.

denture, n dentadura f; dentadura f postiza.

denuclearize, vt desnuclearizar.

denude, vt denudar; despojar.

denunciation, n denuncia f, denunciación f; censura f.

deny, vt negar; denegar; rechazar; desmentir.

deodorant, n desodorante m.

deodorize, vt desodorizar.

deoxidize, vt desoxidar.

depart, vt 1. partir de esta vida; 2. vi partir, irse, marcharse.

department, n departamento m; sección f.

departure, n partida f, ida f, salida f; desviación f.

depend, vi eso depende, según.

depend on, vt depender de; contar con, confiar en.

dependable, adj seguro; serio, formal.

dependence, n dependencia f, confianza f; subordinación f.

dependent, adj 1. dependiente; 2. n familiar m/f dependiente.

depersonalize, vt despersonalizar.

depict, vt representar, pintar.

depiction, n representación f.

depilatory, adj 1. depilatorio; 2. n depilatorio m.

deplane, vi salir del avión, desembarcar.

deplete, vt agotar; mermar, reducir.

depletion, n agotamiento m; merma f, reducción f.

deplorable, adj lamentable, deplorable.

deplore, vt lamentar, deplorar.

deploy, vt 1. desplegar; 2. vt desplegarse.

deployment, n despliegue m.

depopulate, vt despoblar, desertizar.

deport, vt 1. deportar; 2. vr comportarse.

deportation, n deportación f.

deportment, n conducta f, comportamiento m.

depose, vt 1. deponer; destituir; 2. vi declarar.

deposit, n 1. depósito m, yacimiento m; poso m, sedimento m; 2. vt depositar; poner; sedimentar.

deposition, n deposición f; declaración f.

depositor, n depositante m/f, impositor(a) m/f.

depot, n depósito m, almacén m estación f.

depravation, n depravación f.

depraved, adj depravado, perverso, vicioso.

deprecate, vt desaprobar, lamentar.

deprecating, adj de desaprobación.

depreciate, vt 1. depreciar; desestimar; 2. vi depreciarse, perder valor, bajar de precio.

depreciation, n depreciación f.

depredations, n estragos m.

depress, vt presionar, deprimir; rebajar.

depressed, adj deprimido, abatido, desalentado, pesimista.

depression, n depresión f; crisis f económica, bache m; desaliento m, abatimiento m.

depressurization, n descompresión f.

depressurize, vt despresurizar.

deprive, vt privar a uno de algo; 2. vr privarse de algo.

depth, n profundidad f; fondo m; ancho m.

depth charge, n carga f de profundidad.

deputize, vi sustituir a uno, desempeñar las funciones de uno.

deputy, adj 1. suplente; 2. n sustituto(a) m/f; diputado(a) m/f.

derailment, n descarrilamiento m.

derange, vt desarreglar, descomponer; volver loco, desquiciar.

derangement, n desarreglo m; trastorno m mental.

deregulate, vt desregular.

derelict, adj 1. abandonado; 2. n derrelicto m.

dereliction, n abandono m; negligencia f.

deride, vt ridiculizar, mofarse de.

derision, n irisión f; mofas f pl.

derivative, adj 1. derivado; poco original; 2. n derivado m.

derive, vt 1. derivar; sacar, obtener; 2. vi derivar(se) proceder de, provenir de.

dermatitis, n dermatitis f.

dermatologist, n dermatólogo(a) m/f.

dermatology, n dermatología f.

derogatory, adj despectivo.

derrick, n grua f; torre f de perforación.

dervish, n derviche m.

desalinate, vt desalar.

desalination, n desalación f.

descend, vt 1. descender, bajar; 2. vi descender de, bajar (de).

descendant, n descendiente m/f.

descending, adj descendente; en orden descendente.

descent, n pendiente f, declive m; descendimiento m, bajada f.

describe, vt describir.

description, n descripción f.

descriptive, adj descriptivo.

descry, vt divisar.

desecrate, vt profanar.

desecration, n profanación f.

desegregate, vt desegregar.

desegregation, n desegregación f.

desensitize, vt desensibilizar, insensibilizar.

desert, n, adj 1. desierto; 2. vt desertar, abandonar.

desertion, n deserción f, abandono m.

deserve, vt merecer, ser digno de.

desiccate, vt desecar.

design, n 1. diseño m; 2. vt idear; proyectar; diseñar.

designation, n denominación f; nombramiento m, designación f.

designer, n diseñador m, proyectista m/f.

desirable, adj apetecible, atractivo; deseable.

desire, n 1. deseo m; 2. vt desear.

desist, vi desistir de algo.

desk, n mesa f de trabajo; pupitre m; escritorio m.

desolate, adj 1. solitario; desierto, deshabitado; 2. vt asolar, arrasar; afligir.

desolation, n arrasamiento m; desolación f, soledad f.

despair, n 1. desesperación f; 2. vi desesperar(se).

desperate, adj desesperado.

desperation, n desesperación f.

despicable, adj vil, despreciable.

despise, vt despreciar, desdenar.

despite, prep a pesar de.

despoil, vt despojar (de).

despondent, *adj* abatido, deprimido; de tono triste, pesimista.

despot, *n* déspota *m*.

dessert, *n* postre *m*.

destabilize, *vt* desestabilizar.

destination, *n* destino *m*.

destine, *vt* destinar.

destiny, *n* destino *m*.

destitute, *adj* indigente, desamparado; necesitado.

destitution, *n* indigencia *f*, miseria *f*.

destroy, *vt* destruir; matar; sacrificar.

destroyer, *n* destructor *m*.

destruction, *n* destrucción *f*; ruina *f*, perdición *f*.

destructive, *adj* destructivo, destructor.

desultory, *adj* poco metódico; esporádico *f*.

detach, *vt* separar (de); desvincular, despegar.

detachable, *adj* separable; desprendible; desmontable.

detached, *adj* separado, suelto.

detachment, *n* separación *f*.

detail, *n* 1. detalle *m*, pormenor *m*; 2. *vt* detallar.

detailed, *adj* detallado, pormenorizado.

detain, *vt* detener, tener preso.

detainee, *n* detenido(a) *m/f*.

detect, *vt* descubrir; percibir; detectar.

detectable, *adj* perceptible, detectable.

detective, *n* detective *m/f*.

detector, *n* detector *m*.

detention, *n* detención *f*, arresto *m*.

deter, *vt* desalentar; disuadir, impedir.

detergent, *adj* 1. detergente; 2. *n* detergente *m*.

deteriorate, *vi* empeorar, deteriorarse, degradarse.

deterioration, *n* deterioro *m*, empeoramiento *m*.

determination, *n* determinación *f*.

determine, *vt* determinar; señalar, fijar.

determined, *adj* resuelto.

deterrent, *adj* 1. disuasivo; 2. *n* impedimento *m*.

detest, *vi* detestar, aborrecer.

detestable, *adj* detestable, aborrecible, odioso.

detonate, *vt* 1. hacer detonar; 2. *vi* detonar, estallar.

detonator, *n* detonador *m*, cápsula *f* fulminante.

detour, *n* 1. rodeo *m*, desviación *f*; desvío *m*; 2. *vt* desviarse.

detract, *vi* quitar mérito (o atractivo) a, desvirtuar.

detriment, *n* perjuicio *m*.

detrimental, *adj* perjudicial.

detritus, *n* detrito *m*.

devaluate, *vt* desvalorizar; desvalorar.

devaluation, *n* desvalorización *f*, devaluación *f*.

devastate, *vt* devastar, asolar.

devastating, *adj* devastador.

devastation, *n* devastación *f*.

develop, *vt* desarrollar; idear, crear; desenvolver.

developing, *adj* en (vías de) desarrollo.

development, *n* desarrollo *m*; progreso *m*; evolución *f*.

deviate, *vi* desviarse.

deviation, *n* desviación *f*.

device, *n* aparato *m*, mecanismo *m*, dispositivo *m*.

devil, *n* diablo *m*, demonio *m*.

devilish, *adj* diabólico.

devious, *adj* tortuoso, taimado, sinuoso.

devise, *vt* idear, inventar, imaginar.

devitalize, *vt* debilitar, priar de vitalidad, desvitalizar.

devote, *vt* 1. dedicar; 2. *vr* dedicarse a.

devoted, *adj* leal, fiel, dedicado.

devotion, *n* devoción *f*; dedicación *f*; entrega *f*.

devotional, *adj* piadoso, devoto.

devour, *vt* devorar.

devout, *adj* devoto, piadoso.

dew, *n* rocío *m*.

dexterity, *n* destreza *f*.

dexterous, *adj* diestro.

dextrose, *n* dextrosa *f*.

diabetes, *n* diabetes *f*.

diabetic, *adj* diabético.

diabolic(al), *adj* diabólico.

diacritic, *adj* 1. diacrítico; 2. *n* signo *m* diacrítico.

diadem, *n* diadema *f*.

diaeresis, *n* diéresis *f*.

diagnose, *vt* diagnosticar.

diagnosis, *n* diagnóstico *m*; diagnosis *f*.

diagonal, *adj* 1. diagonal; 2. *n* diagonal *f*.

diagram, *n* esquema *m*, diagrama *m*, gráfico *m*.

diagrammatic, *adj* esquemático.

dial, *n* esfera *f*, cuadrante *m*.

dialect, *n* dialecto *m*.

dialing, *n* marcación *f*, discado *m*.

dialogue, *n* diálogo *m*.

dialysis, *n* diálisis *f*.

diameter, *n* diámetro *m*.

diametrical, *adj* diametral.

diamond, *n* diamante *m*.

diaper, *n* pañal *m*.

diaphanous, *adj* diáfano.

diaphragm, *n* diafragma *m*.

diarist, *n* diarista *m/f*.

diarrhea, *n* diarrea *f*.

diary, *n* diario *m*, agenda *f*, calendario *m*.

diatribe, *n* diatriba *f*.

dice, *n* 1. dados *m pl*; 2. *vt* cortar en cubos.

dichotomy, *n* dicotomía *f*.

dicker, *vi* acilar, titubear.

dictate, *n* 1. mandato *m*, dictados *m*, preceptos *m*; 2. *vt* dictar; mandar, disponer.

dictation, *n* dictado *m*.

dictator, *n* dictador(a) *m/f*.

diction, *n* dicción *f*; lengua *f*, lenguaje *m*.

dictionary, *n* diccionario *m*.

didactic, *adj* didáctico.

die, *n* 1. dado *m*; cuño *m*, troquel *m*; 2. *vi* morir (de; por); marchitarse; desvanecerse, extinguirse.

diehard, *adj* 1. intransigente, empedernido, acérrimo; 2. *n* incondicional *m*, intransigente *m*.

dielectric, *adj* 1. dieléctrico; 2. *n* dieléctrico *m*.

diesel, *n* diesel *m*; gasóleo *m*.

die-sinker, *n* grabador *m* de troqueles.

die-stamp, *vt* grabar.

diet, *n* 1. régimen *m*, dieta *f*; 2. *vi* estar a régimen.

dietician, *n* dietético(a) *m*.

differ, *vi* diferir, diferenciar.

difference, *n* diferencia *f*.

different, *adj* diferente, distinto (de).

differentiate, *vt* 1. diferenciar, distinguir; 2. *vi* diferenciarse.

difficult, *adj* difícil.

difficulty, *n* dificultad *f*; apuro *m*, aprieto *m*.

diffidence, *n* timidez *f*, falta *f* de confianza en sí mismo.

diffident, *adj* tímido.

diffuse, *adj* 1. *n* difuso; prolijo; 2. *vt* difundir; 3. *vi* difundirse.

diffused, *adj* difuso.

diffusion, *n* difusión *f*.

dig, *n* 1. excavación *f*; 2. *vt* cavar, excavar.

digest, *n* 1. resumen *m*; digesto; 2. *vt* digerir; meditar, asimilar.

digestible, *adj* digerible.
digestion, *n* digestión *f.*
digger, *n* cavador(a) *m;* excavador(a) *m.*
digging, *n* cava *f;* excavación *f.*
digit, *n* cifra *f,* número *m;* dígito *m.*
digital, *adj* digital.
dignified, *adj* grave, solemne; majestuoso.
dignify, *vt* dignificar; dar un título altisonante a.
dignitary, *n* dignatario(a) *m.*
dignity, *n* dignidad *f.*
digress, *vi* hacer una digresión; divagar.
digression, *n* digresión *f.*
dike, *n* dique *m;* canal *m,* acequia *f.*
dilapidated, *adj* desmoronado; desvencijado.
dilate, *vt* 1. dilatar; 2. *vi* dilatarse; extenderse.
dilation, *n* dilatación *f.*
dilemma, *n* dilema *m.*
dilettante, *n* diletante *m.*
diligence, *n* diligencia *f.*
diligent, *adj* diligente.
dill, *n* eneldo *m.*
dilly-dally, *vi* vacilar; titubear; perder el tiempo.
dilute, *adj* 1. diluido; 2. *vt* diluir; adulterar.
dilution, *n* dilución *f;* adulteración *f.*
dim, *adj* 1. débil, oscuro, sombrío; 2. *vt* reducir
la intensidad de; 3. *vi* apagarse; difuminarse.
dime, *n* moneda de 10 centavos.
dimension, *n* dimensión *f.*
diminish, *vt* 1. disminuir; 2. *vi* disminuir(se).
diminished, *adj* reducido; oscurecido; disminuido.
diminution, *n* disminución *f.*
diminutive, *adj* 1. diminuto; diminutivo; 2. *n* diminutivo *m.*
dimmer, *n* regulador *m* de intensidad; interruptor *m.*
dimple, *n* 1. hoyuelo *m;* 2. *vt* formar hoyuelos.
din, *n* estruendo *m,* estrépito *m.*
dine, *vt* 1. dar de cenar (o comer) a; 2. *vi* cenar.
diner, *n* comensal *m,* restaurante *m* económico;
cafetería *f* de carretera.
dinette, *n* comedor *m* pequeño, comedorcito *m.*
dinghy, *n* dingui *m,* bote *m;* lancha *f* neumática.
dinginess, *n* lo deslustrado, deslucimiento *m.*
dingy, *adj* deslustrado, deslucido.
dining room, *n* comedor *m.*
dinner, *n* cena *f,* comida *f.*
dinner-dance, *n* cena *f* seguida de baile.
dinnerjacket, *n* esmoquin *m.*
dinner time, *n* hora *f* de cenar (o comer).
dinosaur, *n* dinosaurio *m.*
diocesan, *adj* diocesano.
diocese, *n* diócesis *f.*
diode, *n* diodo *m.*
dioxide, *n* dióxido *m.*
dip, *n* 1. baño *m;* depresión *f;* 2. *vt* bañar, mojar
(en); 3. *vi* inclinarse hacia abajo.
diphtheria, *n* difteria *f.*
diphthong, *n* diptongo *m.*
diploma, *n* diploma *m.*
diplomacy, *n* diplomacia *f.*
diplomat, *n* diplomático(a) *m.*
diplomatic, *adj* diplomático.
dipole, *n* bipolo *m.*
dipper, *n* cazo *m,* cucharón *m.*
dipping, *n* lavado *m.*
dipswitch, *n* interruptor *m.*
dire, *adj* horrendo, calamitoso.
direct, *adj* 1. directo; continuo; claro, inequívoco; 2. *adv* directamente; derecho, en línea
recta; 3. *vt* dirigir.

direction, *n* dirección *f.*
directional, *adj* direccional.
directive, *n* directiva *f,* directriz *f.*
directness, *n* franqueza *f.*
director, *n* director(a) *m.*
directorate, *n* dirección *f,* cargo *m* de director, junta
f directiva.
directory, *n* guía *f* telefónica; guía *f* de calles;
directorio *m.*
dirigible, *adj* 1. dirigible; 2. *n* dirigible *m.*
dirndl, *n* falda *f* acampanada.
dirt, *n* suciedad *f,* mugre *f,* basura *f;* tierra *f.*
dirt-cheap, *adj* tirado, regalado, muy barato.
dirtiness, *n* suciedad *f.*
dirty, *adj* sucio; mugriento; manchado.
disability, *n* incapacidad *f;* invalidez *f,* minusvalidez
f.
disable, *vt* estropear, mutilar; incapacitar, inhabilitar.
disabled, *adj* minusválido, discapaz.
disabuse, *vt* desengañar (de).
disadvantage, *n* desventaja *f,* inconveniente *m;* detrimento *m.*
disadvantageous, *adj* desventajoso.
disaffected, *adj* desafecto.
disaffection, *n* descontento *m,* desafección *f.*
disaffiliate, *vi* desaliarse (de).
disagree, *vi* discrepar (de).
disagreeable, *adj* desagradable: displicente, de mal
genio.
disagreement, *n* desacuerdo *m,* disconformidad *f;*
discrepancia *f.*
disallow, *vt* no aceptar, no sancionar, rechazar.
disappear, *vt* 1. hacer desaparecer; 2. *vi* desaparecer.
disappearance, *n* desaparición *f.*
disappoint, *vt* decepcionar, desilusionar, defraudar.
disappointing, *adj* decepcionante, desilucionante.
disappointment, *n* decepción *f,* desilusión *f.*
disapproval, *n* desaprobación *f.*
disapprove, *vi* desaprobar.
disapproving, *adj* desaprobación.
disarm, *vt* 1. desarmar; desactivar; 2. *vi* desarmarse.
disarmament, *n* desarme *m.*
disarming, *adj* encantador; conciliador.
disarrange, *vt* desarreglar, descomponer.
disarranged, *adj* deshecho; desarreglado.
disarray, *n* desorden *m;* confusión *f;* desarreglo *m.*
disassemble, *vt* desmontar.
disassociate, *vt* separar, desligar.
disaster, *n* desastre *m.*
disastrous, *adj* catastrófico, desastroso, funesto,
nefasto.
disavow, *vt* desconocer, rechazar.
disavowal, *n* negativa *f,* rechazo *m.*
disband, *vt* 1. desmantelar, disolver; 2. *vi* desbandarse; disolverse.
disbar, *vt* excluir del ejercicio de la abogacía.
disbelief, *n* incredulidad *f.*
disbelieve, *vt* 1. no creer, desconfiar de; 2. *vi* no
creer.
disbeliever, *n* incrédulo(a) *m/f.*
disburden, *vt* 1. descargar; 2. *vr* descargarse de.
disburse, *vt* desembolsar.
disbursement, *n* desembolso *m.*
disc, *n* disco *m.*
discard, *n* 1. descarte *m,* desecho *m;* 2. *vt* descartar; descartarse de; rechazar, desechar.
disc brake, *n* frenos *m* de disco.

discern, vt percibir, discernir.

discerning, adj perspicaz.

discernment, n perspicacia f, discernimiento m.

discharge, n 1. descarga f; pago m, descargo m; 2. vt descargar; disparar; despedir.

disciple, n discípulo(a) m.

disciplinarian, n ordenancista m/f.

discipline, n 1. disciplina f; 2. vt disciplinar.

disclaim, vt negar, rechazar; desconocer; renunciar a.

disclaimer, n negación f; renuncia f.

disclose, vt revelar.

disclosure, n revelación f.

discolor, vt de(s)colorar; 2. vi de(s)colorarse.

discolored, adj de(s)colorado.

discomfort, n incomodidad f, malestar m.

disconcert, vt desconcertar.

disconcerting, adj desconcertante.

disconnect, vt separar, desacoplar; desconectar.

disconnected, adj inconexo.

disconsolate, adj inconsolable.

discontent, n descontento m.

discontented, adj descontento, disgustado.

discontinuation, n cesación f, interrupción f.

discontinue, vt suspender, descontinuar, interrumpir, terminar.

discord, n discordia f; disonancia f.

discordant, adj discorde; disonante.

discothèque, n discoteca f.

discount, n 1. descuento m, rebaja f; 2. vt descontar, rebajar.

discourage, vt desalentar, desanimar; desaprobar.

discouragement, n desánimo m.

discouraging, adj desalentador; pesimista.

discourse, n 1. discurso m; plática f; tratado m; 2. vi platicar sobre, disertar sobre.

discourteous, adj descortés, desatento.

discover, vt descubrir.

discoverer, n descubridor(a) m.

discovery, n descubrimiento m.

discredit, n 1. descrédito m; 2. vt desacreditar, deshonrar.

discreditable, adj deshonroso, vergonzoso.

discreet, adj discreto, circunspecto, prudente.

discrepancy, n discrepancia f, diferencia f.

discrete, adj discreto.

discretion, n discreción f, circunspección f.

discriminate, vt 1. distinguir (de); 2. vi discriminar a (contra), hacer una distinción en perjuicio de.

discriminating, adj perspicaz, discernidor.

discrimination, n 1. discernimiento m, perspicacia f; 2. distinción f (entre); parcialidad f, discriminación f.

discursive, adj divagador, prolijo; discursivo.

discus, n disco m.

discuss, vt discutir, hablar de, estudiar, comentar.

discussion, n discusión f.

disdain, n 1. desdén m; 2. vt desdeñar.

disdainful, adj desdeñoso.

disdainfully, adv desdeñosamente.

diseased, adj enfermo; morboso.

disembark, vt/i desembarcar.

disembodied, adj incorpóreo.

disembowel, vt desentrañar, destripar.

disenchanted, adj quedar desencantado.

disenchantment, n desencanto m.

disengage, vt soltar, desasir; desacoplar, desenganchar; desembragar.

disengaged, adj libre, desocupado.

disentangle, vt 1. desenredar, desenmarañar; 2. vr desenredarse (de), librarse.

disfavor, n desaprobación f.

disfigure, vt desfigurar; afear.

disfigured, adj desfigurado.

disfigurement, n desfiguración f; afeamiento m.

disfranchise, vt privar de los derechos civiles.

disgorge, vt vomitar, arrojar; desembuchar.

disgrace, n 1. ignominia f, deshonra f; 2. vt deshonrar, desacreditar.

disgraceful, adj vergonzoso, deshonroso.

disgruntled, adj disgustado, contrariado, malhumorado.

disguise, n 1. disfraz m; 2. vt disfrazar de.

disgust, n 1. repugnancia f, aversión f; 2. vt repugnar, inspirar aversión a.

disgusted, adj asqueado, lleno de asco.

disgusting, adj repugnante, asqueroso.

dish, n plato m; platillo m.

disharmony, n discordia f; disonancia f.

dishearten, vt desalentar, desanimar.

disheartening, adj desalentador.

disheveled, adj despeinado, desmelenado.

dishonest, adj nada honrado, falso, tramposo.

dishonestly, adv fraudulentamente.

dishonesty, n falta f de honradez, falsedad f.

dishonor, n 1. deshonra f, deshonor m; 2. vt deshonrar.

dishonorable, adj deshonroso.

dishrack, n escurridera f de platos.

dishtowel, n trapo m de secar los platos.

dishware, n loza f, vajilla f.

dishwasher, n friegaplatos m/f; lavaplatos m.

disillusion, n 1. desilusión f, desengaño m; 2. vt desilusionar, desengañar.

disillusionment, n desilusión f.

disinclination, n aversión f.

disinclined, adj estar poco dispuesto a hacer algo.

disinfect, vt desinfectar.

disinfectant, n desinfectante m.

disingenuous, adj doble, poco sincero.

disinherit, vt desheredar.

disintegrate, vi disgregarse, desagregarse, desintegrarse.

disintegration, n disgregación f, desagregación f, desintegración f.

disinter, vt desenterrar.

disinterested, adj desinteresado.

disinterment, n exhumación f, desenterramiento m.

disjointed, adj inconexo, descosido, desarticulado.

disk, n disco m; unidad f de disco.

diskette, n disquete m, disco m flexible.

dislike, n aversión f, antipatía f.

dislocate, vt 1. dislocarse, descoyuntar; interceptar; 2. vt desarmar.

dislocation, n dislocación f; interceptación f.

dislodge, vt desalojar (de); desprender; hacer caer.

disloyal, adj desleal.

disloyalty, n deslealtad f.

dismal, adj sombrío, tenebroso; triste, tétrico.

dismantle, vt desmontar, desarmar; desmantelar.

dismay, n 1. consternación f; 2. vt consternar.

dismember, vt desmembrar.

dismemberment, n desmembramiento m, desmembración f.

dismiss, vt 1. despedir; 2. vi romper filas.

dismount, vt 1. desmontar; 2. vi desmontarse.

disobedience, n desobediencia f.

disobedient, adj desobediente.

disobey, vt/i desobedecer.

disorder, n 1. desorden m; desarreglo m; 2. vt desordenar; trastornar.

disorderly, adj desordenado.

disorganization, n desorganización f; confusión f.

disorganize, vt desorganizar; interrumpir.

disorganized, adj poco metódico.

disorientate, vt desorientar.

disown, vt rechazar, desconocer.

disparage, vt menospreciar, denigrar, hablar mal de.

disparaging, adj person despreciativo; despectivo.

disparate, adj dispar.

disparity, n disparidad f.

dispassionate, adj desapasionado, imparcial.

dispassionately, adv de modo desapasionado.

dispatch, n 1. envío m, consignación f; 2. vt consignar, enviar, remitir.

dispatcher, n transportista m.

dispel, vt disipar, dispersar; doubts disipar, barrer; desvanecer.

dispensable, adj prescindible, innecesario.

dispensary, n dispensario m, farmacia f.

dispensation, n dispensación f; administración f.

dispense, vt dispensar; repartir; administrar.

dispersal, n dispersión f.

disperse, vt 1. dispersar; 2. vi dispersarse.

dispirit, vt desalentar, desanimar.

dispirited, adj abatido, deprimido, desanimado.

displace, vt desplazar, sacar de su sitio.

displaced, adj person desplazado(a) m.

display, n 1. exhibición f; exposición f; 2. vt exponer, presentar.

displease, vt desagradar; ofender; enojar, enfadar.

displeasing, adj desagradable.

displeasure, n desagrado m, enojo m, indignación f, disgusto m.

disposable, adj de usar y tirar, desechable.

disposal, n disposición f, colocación f, orden m.

dispose, vt disponer, colocar; decidir.

dispose of, vt disponer de.

disposition, n disposición f, colocación f; orden m.

dispossess, vt tenant desahuciar.

disproportionate, adj desproporcionado.

disprove, vt refutar, confutar.

disputable, adj discutible.

dispute, n 1. disputa f, discusión f, altercado m; 2. vt disputar; cuestionar; 3. vi discutir.

disputed, adj discutible; en litigio.

disqualify, vt inhabilitar, incapacitar (para); descalificar.

disquiet, n 1. inquietud f, desasosiego m; 2. vt inquietar.

disquieting, adj inquietante.

disregard, n 1. indiferencia f; descuido m; 2. vt desatender, descuidar; no hacer caso de.

disreputable, adj de mala fama; vergonzoso.

disrespect, n falta f de respeto, desacato m.

disrespectful, adj irrespetuoso.

disrobe, vt 1. desnudar, desvestir; 2. vi desnudarse.

disrupt, vt romper; desorganizar, interrumpir.

disruption, n rompimiento m; desorganización f, interrupción f.

dissatisfaction, n descontento m, insatisfacción f; disgusto m.

dissatisfied, adj descontento, insatisfecho.

dissect, vt hacer la disección de; anatomizar.

dissection, n disección f; análisis m minucioso.

dissemble, vt 1. disimular, encubrir; 2. vi fingir.

disseminate, vt diseminar, difundir, divulgar.

dissension, n disensión f, discordia f.

dissent, n 1. disentimiento m; disidencia f; 2. vi disentir, disidir.

dissenter, n disidente m.

dissertation, n disertación f; tesis f, tesina f.

disservice, n deservicio m; perjudicar a.

dissident, adj 1. disidente; 2. n disidente m.

dissimilar, adj distinto, diferente (de)

dissimulate, vt disimular.

dissimulation, n disimulación f.

dissipate, vt disipar; desvanecer; derrochar, desperdiciar.

dissipated, adj disoluto.

dissipation, n disipación f; derroche m, desperdicio m.

dissociate, vt separar, desligar.

dissoluble, adj disoluble.

dissolute, adj disoluto.

dissolvable, adj soluble.

dissolve, vt 1. disolver, desleír; 2. vi disolverse; desleírse; desvanecerse.

dissonant, adj disonante.

dissuade, vt disuadir (de); disuadir a uno de hacer algo.

distaff, n rueca f; la rama femenina.

distance, n 1. distancia f; diferencia f; 2. vr distanciarse de.

distant, adj distante, lejano, remoto (de).

distaste, n aversión f, repugnancia f.

distasteful, adj desagradable, repugnante.

distemper, n moquillo m; mal m, destemplanza f.

distend, vt 1. dilatar, hincha; 2. vi dilatarse.

distension, n distensión f, dilatación f, hinchazón f.

distillation, n destilación f.

distillery, n destilería f.

distinct, adj distinto (de).

distinctive, adj distintivo, característico.

distinguish, vt 1. distinguir; 2. vr lucirse.

distinguished, adj distinguido (por), eminente, destacado.

distort, vt deformar; torcer, tergiversar; distorsionar.

distortion, n deformación f; distorsión f, deformación f.

distract, vt distraer, apartar.

distraction, n distracción f, aturdimiento m; confusión f.

distraught, adj muy turbado, loco de inquietud.

distress, n dolor m; angustia f, pena f, aflicción f.

distressing, adj doloroso; penoso, que da pena.

distress-signal, n señal f de socorro.

distribute, vt distribuir, repartir.

distribution, n distribución f, reparto m, repartimiento m; distribución f.

distributor, n repartidor(a) f, distribuidor(a) m.

district, n zona f, región f; barrio m.

distrust, n 1. desconfianza f, recelo m; 2. vt desconfiar de, recelar.

distrustful, adj desconfiado, receloso.

disturb, vt perturbar, disturbar.

disturbance, n perturbación f; alteración f; tumulto m, alboroto m.

disunited, adj desunido.

disunity, n desunión f.

disuse, n desuso m.

disyllabic, adj disílabo.

ditch, n 1. zanja f; cuneta f, arroyo m; 2. vt deshacerse de, abandonar.

ditto, adj ídem, lo mismo; comillas f.

ditty, n cancioneta f.

diuretic, adj **1.** diurético; **2.** n diurético m.
diurnal, adj diurno.
divan, n diván m, cama f turca.
dive, n **1.** zambullida f; salto m; inmersión f; **2.** vi zambullirse; tirarse al agua, saltar al agua.
diver, n buzo m, buceador m.
diverge, vi divergir (de); apartarse de.
divergent, adj divergente.
diverse, adj diverso, variado.
diversify, vt **1.** diversificar; **2.** vi diversificarse.
diversion, n diversión f; desviación f, desvío m.
diversity, n diversidad f.
divert, vt divertir; desviar.
diverting, adj divertido.
divest, vt despojar a uno de algo.
divide, n **1.** divisoria f; **2.** vt dividir; partir; separar.
divided, adj dividido.
dividend, n dividendo m; beneficio m.
dividers, n compás m de puntas.
dividing-line, n línea f divisoria.
divination, n adivinación f.
divine, adj **1.** divino; sublime; estupendo, maravilloso m; **2.** vt advinar.
diviner, n adivinador(a) m; zahorí m.
diving, n el bucear, buceo m.
diving bell, n campana f de buzo.
diving board, n trampolín m.
diving suit, n escafandra f, traje m de buceo.
divinity, n divinidad f; teología f.
division, n división f; separación f; repartimiento m.
divisor, n divisor m.
divorce, n **1.** divorcio m; separación f; **2.** vt divorciar, separar; **3.** vi divorciarse.
divorced, adj divorciado.
divorcee, n divorciado(a) m.
divulge, vt divulgar, revelar.
dizziness, n vértigo m, vértigos m.
do, vt **1.** hacer; preparar; representar; **2.** vi hacer; obrar, actuar, proceder.
docile, adj dócil.
dock, n **1.** dársena f, muelle m; **2.** vt poner en dique, atracar, acoplar.
docket, n certificado m; etiqueta f, marbete m.
doctor, n **1.** médico m; **2.** vt tratar, curar.
doctoral, adj doctoral.
doctorate, n doctorado m.
document, n **1.** documento m; **2.** vt documentar.
documentation, n documentación f.
doe, n gama f; coneja f; liebre f.
doer, n hacedor(a) m; persona f enérgica, persona f dinámica.
doeskin, n ante m; piel f de ante.
doff, vt quitarse.
dog, n **1.** perro m; **2.** vt seguir los pasos de, seguir la pista de.
dog-breeder, n criador(a) m/f de perros.
dogged, adj tenaz, obstinado.
doggedness, n tenacidad f.
doggerel, n versos m ramplones, malos m versos.
dogma, n dogma m.
dogmatic, adj dogmático.
dog show, n exposición f canina.
dog-tired, adj estar rendido.
dogtrack, n canódromo m.
doily, n panito m de adorno.
doing, n hechos m; acciones f.
doleful, adj triste, lúgubre, lastimero.
doll, n muñeca f; gachí f.

dollar, n dólar m.
dollar bill, n billete m de un dólar.
dollop, n porción f, masa f.
dolly, n muñequita f; chica f, jovencita f.
dolomite, n dolomía f, dolomita f.
dolphin, n delfín m.
dolt, n imbécil m.
domain, n heredad f, propiedad f; dominio m.
dome, n cúpula f; bóveda f; colina f redonda.
domed, adj abovedado.
domestic, adj **1.** doméstico; **2.** n doméstico m.
domesticate, vt domesticar.
domesticated, adj domesticado; casero, hogareño.
domicile, n **1.** domicilio m; **2.** vt domiciliarse en.
dominate, vt/i dominar.
dominating, adj dominante, dominador.
domination, n dominación f.
domineer, vi dominar, tiranizar (a alguien).
domineering, adj dominante, dominador, tiránico.
dominion, n dominio m.
domino, n (dominoes) ficha f de dominó..
don, vt ponerse.
donate, vt donar.
donation, n donativo m.
donkey, n burro m, burra f.
donor, n donante m.
donut, n buñuelo m, rosquilla f.
doodle, n **1.** garabatos m; **2.** vi garrapatear, borronear, borrajear.
doom, n **1.** suerte f, hado m; **2.** vt condenar (a muerte etc); predestinar.
doomsday, n día m del juicio final.
doorbell, n timbre m (de llamada).
doorchain, n cadena f de la puerta.
door-handle, n tirador m (de puerta).
doorkeeper, n conserje m, portero m.
doorknob, n pomo m (de puerta), tirador m (de puerta).
doorman, n portero m.
doorstep, n umbral m, peldaño m de la puerta.
doorstop, n tope m.
doorway, n puerta f, entrada f; portal m.
dope, n **1.** barniz m; **2.** droga f, narcótico m; **3.** vt narcotizar, drogar.
dopey, adj aturdido, mareado; imbécil.
dormant, adj inactivo; dormir; latente.
dormitory, n dormitorio m.
dorsal, adj dorsal.
dory, n (fish) gallo m, arenera f.
dosage, n dosificación f, dosis f.
dose, n **1.** dosis f; **2.** vt administrar.
dossier, n expediente m.
dot, n **1.** punto m; **2.** vt poner el punto sobre.
dotage, n chochez f.
dote, vi adorar, idolatrar.
dotted, adj línea f de puntos.
double, adj **1.** doble; ambiguo; **2.** n doble m; **3.** vt doblar; duplicar; **4.** vi doblarse.
double-barrelled, adj de dos cañones.
double-breasted, adj (suit) cruzado, con botonadura doble.
double-check, vt/i **1.** verificar dos veces; **2.** n doble verificación f.
double-cross, n **1.** engaño m, trampa f, traición f; **2.** vt engañar, traicionar.
double exposure, n doble exposición f.
double-park, vt/i aparcar en doble fila.
double-space, vt escribir a doble espacio.
double-talk, n palabras f insinceras.

doubling, n multiplicación f por dos; duplicación f.

doubt, n 1. duda f; incertidumbre f; 2. vt/i dudar; dudar de.

doubter, n escéptico(a) m.

doubtful, adj dudoso, incierto; sospechoso.

douche, n 1. ducha f; jeringa f; 2. vt duchar; 3. vi ducharse.

dough, n masa f, pasta f.

doughy, adj pastoso.

dour, adj austero, severo; terco m.

douse, vt apagar; mojar, lavar.

dove, n paloma f.

dovecote, n palomar m.

dovetail, n 1. cola f de milano; 2. vt ensamblar a cola de milano; 3. vi encajar (con), ajustarse.

dovish, adj blando.

dowdiness, n falta f de elegancia.

dowdy, adj poco elegante, poco atractivo.

dowel, n clavija f.

down, adv abajo, hacia abajo, para abajo.

downcast, adj abatido, alicaído.

downfall, n caída f, ruina f.

downgrade, n 1. en declive m; 2. vt asignar a un grado más bajo.

downhill, adv 1. cuesta abajo; 2. adj en declive.

down payment, n entrada f, pago m al contado; desembolso m inicial.

downplay, vt minimizar la importancia de, quitar importancia a.

downpour, n aguacero m, chaparrón m.

downstairs, adv abajo; en el piso de abajo.

downtown, n 1. hacia el centro (de la ciudad); 2. adj del centro (de la ciudad), céntrico.

doze, n 1. sueño m ligero; sueno m breve; 2. vi dormitar; quedarse medio dormido.

dozen, n docena f.

drab, adj gris, monótono, triste.

drabness, n monotonía f, tristeza f.

draft, n 1. giro m, letra f de cambio; orden f de pago; 2. borrador, versión f preliminar; 3. vt redactar; preparar.

draftman, n dibujante m, delineante m.

drafty, adj airoso.

drag, n 1. rastra f, red f barredera; 2. vt arrastrar, llevar arrastrado; 3. vi arrastrarse por el suelo.

drain, n 1. desaguadero m; boca f de alcantarilla, sumidero m; 2. vt desaguar; drenar; purgar.

drainage, n desagüe m; drenaje m; desecación f.

drainpipe, n tubo m de desagüe.

drake, n pato m (macho).

drama, n drama m.

dramatic, adj dramático; espectacular, sensacional.

dramatize, vt escenificar, dramatizar.

drape, n 1. colgadura f; cortinas f; 2. vt adornar con colgaduras, cubrir (de).

drapery, n colgaduras f, ropaje m; pañería f, mercería f.

drastic, adj drástico; enérgico, fuerte.

draw, n 1. empate m, tablas f; 2. sorteo m; 3. vt tirar; arrastrar; 4. dibujar, trazar, atraer.

drawback, n inconveniente m, desventaja f.

drawbridge, n puente m levadizo.

drawer, n cajón m; gaveta f.

drawing, n dibujo m.

drawing board, n tablero m de delineante.

drawl, n 1. habla f lenta y pesada; 2. vt pronunciar lenta y pesadamente, arrastrar; 3. vi hablar lenta y pesadamente.

drawn, adj 1. (juego) empatado; 2. cansado, ojeroso.

drawstring, n cordón m.

dread, n 1. pavor m, terror m; 2. adj espantoso; 3. vt tener miedo a, temer.

dreadful, adj terrible, espantoso; horrible, fatal.

dream, n 1. sueño m; ensueño m; ilusión f; 2. vt/i soñar (con).

dreamer, n soñador(a) m/f; visionario(a) m/f.

dreamland, n reino m del ensueño.

dreamless, adj sin sueños.

dreamlike, adj de ensueño, como de sueño.

dreamy, adj soñador, distraído, el que está en las nubes.

dreary, adj triste, monótono; aburrido, sombrío.

dredge, n 1. draga f, rastra f; 2. vt dragar, limpiar con draga; 3. (Cul) enharinar.

dregs, n heces f, sedimento m, hez f.

drench, vt mojar, empapar.

dress, n 1. vestido m, indumentaria f; 2. vt vestir.

dressed, adj vestido.

dresser, n aparador m; cómoda f con espejo.

dressmaker, n costurera f, modista f.

dressmaking, n costura f, corte m y confección .

dress up, vi ataviarse, engalanarse (de).

dribble, n 1. gotitas f; 2. vt dejar caer gota a gota.

dribbler, n driblador m.

dried, adj seco; desecado.

drift, n 1. impulso m de la corriente; deriva f; 2. vt llevar; 3. vi ir a la deriva, decaer.

drift away, vi dejarse llevar por la corriente.

drifter, n 1. trainera f; 2. vago m.

drill, n 1. taladro m; broca f; fresadora f; 2. instrucción f; ejercicios m; simulacro m; 3. sembradora f; hilera f, surco m; 4. vt perforar, taladrar, barrenar; sembrar con sembradora.

drilling, n perforación f; instrucción f.

drink, n 1. bebida f; 2. vt beber; tomar.

drinkable, adj bebible.

drinker, n bebedor(a) m.

drip, n 1. gota f; gotera f; 2. vt gotear.

drop, n 1. gota; 2. vi caer, dejar caer; tumbar.

droplet, n gotita f.

drop off, vt 1. dejar; 2. vi desprenderse, separarse.

dropper, n cuentagotas m.

droppings, n excremento m.

dropsy, n hidropesía f.

drought, n sequía f.

drown, vt 1. anegar; ahogar, inundar; apagar; 2. vi perecer ahogado; 3. vr ahogarse.

drowning, n ahogo m.

drowse, vi dormitar, quedar medio dormido.

drowsiness, n somnolencia f; modorra f.

drowsy, adj soñoliento, amodorrado; soporífero.

drudge, n 1. esclavo m del trabajo; esclava f de la cocina; 2. vi trabajar como un esclavo.

drudgery, n trabajo m penoso, faena f monótona.

drug, n 1. droga f, medicamento m, fármaco m, droga f; 2. vt drogar, administrar narcóticos a.

drug abuse, n toxicomanía f.

drug-addict, n drogadicto(a) f, toxicómano(a) m/f.

druggist, n farmacéutico(a) m.

drugstore, n farmacia f.

drum, n 1. tambor m, timbal m; 2. vt tabalear; 3. vi tocar el tambor.

drumbeat, n redoble m.

drummer, n tambor m; batería m.

drumstick, n palillo m baqueta f; pierna f de pavo.

drunk, adj borracho.

drunkenness, n embriaguez f.

dry, *adj* 1. seco; árido; 2. *vt* secar; enjugar.

dry-clean, *vt* limpiar en seco.

dry cleaner's, *n* tintorería *f.*

dryer, *n* secador *m.*

dual, *adj* doble.

duality, *n* dualidad *f.*

dub, *vt* armar caballero a; apodar; doblar.

dubbin, *n* adobo *m* impermeable, cera *f.*

dubbing, *n* doblaje *m;* mezclador(a) *m* de sonido.

dubiously, *adv* con duda; de manera sospechosa.

ducat, *n* ducado *m* (moneda).

duchess, *n* duquesa *f.*

duck, *n* 1. pato(a) *m;* ánade *m;* 2. chapuz *m;* agachada *f,* esquiva *f;* 3. *vt* chapuzar, agachar, bajar; 4. *vi* sumergirse.

duckbill, *n* ornitorrinco *m.*

duckpond, *n* estanque *m* de patos.

duct, *n* conducto *m,* canal *m.*

ductile, *adj* dúctil.

due, *adj* 1. debido; ser pagadero; 2. *n* deuda *f;* lo que merece uno.

duel, *n* 1. duelo *m;* 2. *vi* batirse en duelo.

duet, *n* dúo *m.*

duke, *n* duque *m.*

dull, *adj* 1. apagado; sombrío, pálido; deslustrado; 2. *vt* embotar; deslustrar; aliviar.

dully, *adv* de modo apagado, con brillo apagado.

duly, *adv* debidamente; a su debido tiempo.

dumb, *adj* mudo.

dumbbell, *n* pesa; *f;* bobo(a) *m.*

dumbfound, *vt* dejar sin habla, pasmar.

dumbness, *n* mudez *f;* estupidez *f.*

dumbo, *n* imbécil *m.*

dummy, *adj* 1. falso, postizo; empresa *f;* 2. *n* muñeco *m;* maniquí *m.*

dump, *n* 1. montón *m;* vertedero *m,* basurero *m,* botadero *m;* 2. *vt* descargar, verter, vaciar.

dumpling, *n* pelota *f,* bola *f* de masa hervida.

dun, *adj* 1. pardo; 2. *vt* apremiar a uno para que pague lo que debe.

dune, *n* duna *f.*

dunk, *vt* mojar, remojar, ensopar.

duo, *n* dúo *m.*

duodecimal, *adj* duodecimal.

duodenal, *adj* duodenal.

duodenum, *n* duodeno *m.*

dupe, *n* 1. primo *m,* inocentón *m;* ser víctima de; 2. *vt* engañar, embaucar; timar.

duplex, *adj* 1. doble; 2. *n* casa *f* para dos familias.

duplicate, *adj* 1. duplicado; 2. *n* duplicado *m;* copia *f;* 3. *vt* duplicar; repetir; imitar.

duplication, *n* duplicación *f;* repetición pluralidad *f* (innecesaria).

durability, *n* lo duradero, durabilidad *f.*

durable, *adj* duradero.

duration, *n* duración *f.*

during, *prep* durante.

dusk, *n* crepúsculo *m,* anochecer *m;* al atardecer.

dusky, *adj* oscuro; (complexión) moreno.

dust, *n* polvo *m;* barreduras *f.*

dust-cover, n guardapolvo *m.*

duster, *n* paño *m,* trapo *m,* bayeta *f;* plumero *m.*

dustpan, *n* cogedor *m.*

E

E, e, n *f* (letra) E, e.

each, *adj* 1. cada; todo; cada uno de ellos; 2. *pron* cada uno.

eager, *adj* impaciente; apremiante, vehemente.

eagerness, *n* impaciencia *f;* afán *m,* ansia *f,* deseo.

eagle, *n* águila *f.*

eaglet, *n* aguilucho *m.*

ear, *n* oreja *f;* oído *m;* espiga *f.*

earache, *n* dolor *m* de oídos.

eardrops, *n* gotas *f* para el oído.

eardrum, *n* tímpano *m.*

earl, *n* conde *m.*

early, *adj* 1. temprano; primero, primitivo; 2. *adv* temprano; lo más pronto posible.

earmark, *vt* reservar, destinar.

earn, *vt* ganar(se), percibir; devengar.

earner, *n* persona *f* que gana un sueldo; asalariado.

earnest, *adj* serio, formal; fervoroso.

earnings, *n* ganancias *f;* salario *m.*

earpiece, *n* auricular *m.*

earring, *n* pendiente *m;* arete *m,* zarcillo *m.*

earth, *n* tierra *f;* mundo *m.*

earthly, *adj* terrenal, mundano.

earthquake, *n* terremoto *m.*

earthworm, *n* lombriz *f.*

earthy, *adj* terroso; terrero; práctico.

ease, *n* 1. facilidad *f;* alivio *m;* tranquilidad *f;* 2. *vt* tranquilizar, aliviar; aflojar.

east, *n* este.

Easter, *n* Pascua *f* de Resurrección.

easterly, *adj* este, oriental.

eastern, *adj* del este, oriental.

eastward, *adj* hacia el este, en dirección este.

easy, *adj* 1. fácil; sencillo; 2. lento, pausado; 3. *adv* fácilmente; ¡despacio!.

eat, *vt* comer; tomar; consumir, devorar.

eatery, *n* restaurante *m.*

eaves, *n* alero *m.*

eavesdrop, *vi* escuchar a escondidas.

ebb, *n* 1. reflujo *m;* 2. marea *f* menguante; 3. *vi* bajar; menguar.

ebony, *n* ébano *m.*

ebullience, *n* exaltación *f,* entusiasmo *m,* exuberancia *f,* animación *f.*

ebullient, *adj* entusiasta, exuberante, animado.

eccentric, *adj* excéntrico.

eccentricity, *n* excentricidad *f.*

ecclesiastic, *n* eclesiástico *m.*

echelon, *n* escalón *m.*

echo, *n* 1. eco *m;* 2. *vt* repetir; imitar; hacerse eco de; 3. *vi* resonar, hacer eco.

éclair, *n* relámpago *m* de chocolate.

eclectic, *adj* ecléctico.

eclipse, *n* eclipse *m.*

ecologist, *n* ecólogo(a); ecologista *m/f.*

ecology, *n* ecología *f.*

economics, *n* economía *f* política; ciencia *f* económicas.

economist, *n* economista *m/f.*

economize, *vt* economizar, ahorrar.

economy, *n* economía *f.*

ecosystem, n ecosistema m, sistema m ecológico.

ecstasy, n éxtasis m.

ecstatic, adj extático.

ecumenical, adj ecuménico.

ecumenism, n ecumenismo m.

eczema, n eccema m, eczema m.

eddy, n 1. remolino m; 2. vi arremolinarse.

edema, n edema m.

edge, n 1. filo m, corte m; borde m; margen m; canto m; 2. vt ribetear.

edgewise, adv de canto.

edging, n ribete m, orla f; borde m.

edgy, adj nervioso, inquieto.

edible, adj comestible.

edict, n edicto m.

edification, n edificación f.

edifice, n edificio m (esp grande, imponente).

edify, vt edificar.

edifying, adj edificante.

edit, vt dirigir, preparar (para publicación) una edición de.

editing, n redacción f; dirección f.

edition, n edición f; tirada f.

editor, n director m, redactor m, redactora f; autor(a) m/f.

editorial, adj 1. editorial; 2. n editorial m, artículo de fondo m.

educate, vt educar; formar; instruir.

educated, adj culto.

education, n educación f; enseñanza f; instrucción f.

educator, n educador(ora) m/f.

eel, n anguila f.

eerie, adj misterioso; extraño, fantástico, horripilante.

efface, vt borrar.

effect, n 1. efecto m, consecuencia f, resultado m; 2. vt efectuar, llevar a cabo; efectuar; hacer.

effective, adj eficaz; impresionante.

effectiveness, n eficacia f, efectividad f.

effeminate, adj afeminado.

effervesce, vi estar en efervescencia.

effervescent, adj efervescente.

efficacious, adj eficaz.

efficacy, n eficacia f.

efficiency, n eficiencia f, eficacia f; buena marcha f.

efficient, adj eficiente; eficaz; de buen rendimiento.

effort, n esfuerzo m; resultado m, producto m; obra f.

effusive, adj efusivo.

effusiveness, n efusividad f.

egg, n huevo m.

eggnog, n yema f mejida, ponche m de huevo.

ego, n ego m, el yo; amor m propio.

egotism, n egotismo m.

egotist, n egotista m/f.

egotistic(al), adj egotista.

egregious, adj atroz, enorme; notorio.

egress, n salida f.

egret, n garceta f.

Egypt, n Egipto m.

eight, adj ocho.

eighteen, adj dieciocho.

eighth, adj octavo.

either, adj cualquier ... de los dos; uno u otro.

ejaculate, vt exclamar; proferir, lanzar; eyacular

ejaculation, n exclamación f; eyaculación f.

eject, vt expulsar, echar; tenant desahuciar

ejection, n expulsión f; desahucio m.

elaborate, adj 1. complicado; detallado; 2. vt elaborar.

elapse, vi pasar, transcurrir.

elastic, adj elástico; flexible; goma f elástica.

elasticity, n elasticidad f.

elate, vt regocijar.

elated, adj regocijado.

elation, n alegría f; euforia f, júbilo m.

elbow, n codo m; recodo m.

elder, adj mayor.

elderberry, n baya f del saúco.

elderly, adj de edad, mayor.

eldest, adj mayor; primogénito(a).

elect, vt elegir.

elected, adj elegido.

election(s), n elección f; elecciones f generales.

electric, adj eléctrico.

electrical, adj eléctrico.

electrically, adv por electricidad.

electrician, n electricista m/f.

electricity, n electricidad f.

electrify, vt electrificar.

electrocardiogram, n electrocardiograma m.

electrocute, vt electrocutar.

electrocution, n electrocución f.

electrode, n electrodo m.

electrolysis, n electrólisis f.

electrolyte, n electrolito m.

electromagnet, n electroimán m.

electromagnetic, adj electromagnético.

electron, n electrón m.

electronic, adj electrónico.

electronically, adv electrónicamente.

electronics, n electrónica f.

electroplate, vt galvanizar, electrochapar.

electroplated, adj galvanizado, electrochapado .

elegance, n elegancia f.

elegant, adj elegante.

elegy, n elegia f.

element, n elemento m.

elementary, adj elemental; primitivo; rudimentario.

elephant, n elefante(a) m/f.

elephantiasis, n elefantiasis f.

elephantine, adj elefantino, mastodóntico.

elevate, vi elevar; alzar; exaltar; ascender.

elevated, adj elevado.

elevation, n elevación f; exaltación f.

elevator, n elevador, ascensor.

eleven, adj 1. once; 2. n once m.

eleventh, adj undécimo, onceno.

elf, n duende m; elfo m.

elfin, adj de duende(s), mágico; de elfo(s).

elicit, vt sacar, obtener, provocar.

eligibility, n elegibilidad f.

eligible, adj elegible; deseable; atractivo.

eliminate, vt eliminar; suprimir; suspect.

elimination, n eliminación f; supresión f.

élite, n élite f, minoría f selecta.

elixir, n elixir m.

elk, n alce m, anta m.

ellipse, n elipse f.

ellipsis, n elipsis f; puntos m suspensivos.

elliptic(al), adj elíptico.

elocution, n elocución f.

elongate, vt alargar, extender.

elongated, adj alargado, estirado, extendido.

elope, vi fugarse con su amante.

elopement, n fuga f.

eloquence, n elocuencia f.

eloquent, *adj* elocuente.

else, *adj* 1. otro, más; 2. *adv* más, además de.

elsewhere, *adv* en otra parte.

elucidate, *vt* aclarar, elucidar, esclarecer.

elucidation, *n* aclaración *f*, elucidación *f*.

elude, *vt* eludir, esquivar, evitar; escapar de.

elusive, *adj* fugaz, difícil de encontrar.

emaciated, *adj* demacrado; demacrarse.

emaciation, *n* demacración *f*.

emanate, *vi* emanar, proceder.

emanation, *n* emanación *f*.

emancipate, *vt* emancipar; manumitir.

emancipation, *n* emancipación *f*; manumisión *f*.

embalm, *vt* embalsamar.

embargo, *n* prohibición *f*; embargo *m*; estar prohibido.

embark, *vt* embarcar.

embarkation, *n* embarco *m*, embarque *m*.

embarrass, *vt* desconcertar, turbar, azorar.

embarrassing, *adj* embarazoso, desconcertante.

embarrassment, *n* desconcierto *m*, turbación *f*.

embassy, *n* embajada *f*.

embed, *vt* empotrar; clavar, hincar; incrustar.

embedding, *n* incrustación *f*.

embellish, *vt* embellecer; adornar.

embellishment, *n* embellecimiento *m*; adorno *m*.

embezzle, *vt* malversar, desfalcar.

embezzlement, *n* malversación *f*, desfalco *m*.

embezzler, *n* malversador(ora) *f*, desfalcador(ora) *f*.

embitter, *vt* amargar; envenenar, amargar.

embittered, *adj* resentido, rencoroso.

emblazon, *vt* engalanar, blasonar.

emblem, *n* emblema *m*.

embodiment, *n* encarnación *f*, personificación *f*.

embody, *vt* encarnar, personificar; incorporar.

embolden, *vt* animar, envalentonar.

embolism, *n* embolia *f*.

emboss, *vt* realzar; estampar en relieve.

embrace, *n* 1. abrazo *m*; 2. *vt* abrazar, dar un abrazo a.

embroider, *vt* bordar, recamar; adornar con detalles ficticios.

embroidery, *n* bordado *m*.

embroil, *vt* embrollar, enredar.

embroilment, *n* embrollo *m*.

embryo, *n* embrión *m*; embrión *m*, germen *m*.

emend, *vt* enmendar.

emendation, *n* enmienda *f*.

emerald, *n* esmeralda *f*.

emerge, *vi* salir, aparecer, dejarse ver.

emergency, *n* emergencia *f*; crisis *f*.

emergent, *adj* emergente.

emeritus, *adj* emeritus, jubilado.

emery, *n* esmeril *m*.

emetic, *adj*, *n* emético, vomitivo.

emigrant, *adj* 1. emigrante; 2. *n* emigrante *m/f*.

emigration, *n* emigración *f*.

eminence, *n* eminencia *f*.

eminent, *adj* eminente.

emir, *n* emir *m*.

emissary, *n* emisario *m*.

emission, *n* emisión *f*.

emit, *vt* emitir; arrojar.

emollient, *adj* emoliente.

emolument, *n* emolumento *m*.

emotion, *n* emoción *f*.

emotional, *adj* emocional; afectivo; emotivo.

emotionally, *adv* con emoción.

emotive, *adj* emotivo.

empanel, *vt* seleccionar; inscribir a uno para jurado.

empathize, *vi* sentir empatía.

empathy, *n* empatía *f*.

emperor, *n* emperador *m*.

emphasis, *n* énfasis *m*.

emphasize, *vt* acentuar; dar importancia a, subrayar.

emphatic, *adj* enfático.

emphysema, *n* enfisema *m*.

empire, *n* imperio *m*.

emplacement, *n* emplazamiento *m*.

emplane, *vi* subir al avión; embarcar (en avión).

employ, *vt* emplear.

employee, *n* empleado(a) *m/f*.

employer, *n* empresario(a) *m/f*.

employment, *n* empleo *m*.

emporium, *n* emporio *m*.

empower, *vt* autorizar a uno a hacer algo.

emptiness, *n* vacío *m*, lo vacío.

empty, *adj* 1. vacío desocupado; desierto; 2. *vt* vaciar, verter; descargar.

emulate, *vt* emular.

emulation, *n* emulación *f*.

emulsion, *n* emulsión *f*; emulsionada.

enable, *vt* permitir.

enact, *vt* 1. decretar; promulgar; 2. representar; hacer.

enactment, *n* promulgación *f*; presentación *f*.

enamel, *n* 1. esmalte *m*; 2. pintura *f*.

enamor, *vt* enamorar.

encamp, *vi* acamparse.

encampment, *n* campamento *m*.

encapsulate, *vt* resumir, encerrar, encapsular.

encase, *vt* encerrar; revestir; estar revestido de.

encephalitis, *n* encefalitis *f*.

enchain, *vt* encadenar.

enchant, *vt* encantar.

enchanting, *adj* encantador.

enchantment, *n* encantamiento *m*; encanto *m*.

encircle, *vt* rodear; envolver.

enclave, *n* enclave *m*.

enclose, *vt* cercar; encerrar.

enclosure, *n* cercamiento *m*; cercado *m*, recinto *m*.

encode, *vt* codificar; cifrar.

encomium, *n* elogio *m*, encomio *m*.

encompass, *vt* cercar, rodear; abarcar.

encounter, *n* 1. encuentro *m*; 2. *vt* encontrar, encontrarse con.

encourage, *vt* animar, alentar, fomentar, estimular.

encouragement, *n* estímulo *m*, fomento *m*; aliento *m*.

encouraging, *adj* alentador; favorable.

encroach, *vi* invadir, entrometerse.

encroachment, *n* usurpación *f*; invasión *f*.

encrust, *vt* incrustar.

encumber, *vt* person, estorbar; gravar, cargar.

encumbrance, *n* estorbo *m*; carga *f*, gravamen *m*.

encyclical, *n* encíclica *f*.

encyclopedia, *n* enciclopedia *f*.

end, *n* 1. final *m*; extremo *m*; punta *f*; fin *m*; objeto *m*; 2. *adj* final; 3. *vt* terminar, acabar.

endanger, *vt* poner en peligro; arriesgar.

endearing, *adj* simpático, entrañable.

endeavor, *n* 1. esfuerzo *m*, tentativa *f*; 2. *vi* esforzarse.

endemic, *adj* endémico.

ending, *n* fin *m*, conclusión *f*, desenlace *m*.

endless, *adj* interminable, sin fin.

endocrine, *adj* 1. endocrino; 2. *n* endocrino *m*.

endorse, *vt* endosar, aprobar.

endorsement, *n* endoso *m*; aprobación *f*.

endow, vt dotar.

endowment, n dotación f; fundacion f, dote f.

endurance, n resistencia f, aguante m.

endure, vt soportar, tolerar; resistir.

enemy, n enemigo m.

energetic, adj enérgico.

energize, vt activar; energizar.

energy, n energía f.

enervate, vt enervar.

enfeeble, vt debilitar.

enfold, vt estrechar; abrazar; envolver.

enforce, vt hacer cumplir, aplicar.

enforcement, n ejecucion f.

enfranchise, vt emancipar; manumitir; conceder el derecho de votar a.

engage, vt 1. llamar, atraer; ocupar; 2. vi engranar.

engaged, adj 1. ocupado; comprometido; 2. prometido al matrimonio.

engagement, n contrato m, obligación f; compromiso m.

engaging, adj simpático, atractivo.

engender, vt engendrar; motivar.

engine, n motor m; máquina f; locomotora f.

engineer, n 1. ingeniero m; 2. vt tramar, gestionar.

engineering, n ingeniería f.

English, adj inglés.

English-speaking, adj de habla inglesa.

engrave, vt grabar; burilar.

engraver, n grabador m.

engraving, n grabado m.

engross, vt (atención) absorber.

engrossing, adj absorbente.

engulf, vt tragar; sumergir, hundir.

enhance, vt realzar, intensificar, aumentar.

enhancement, n intensificación f; aumento m.

enigma, n enigma f.

enigmatic, adj enigmático.

enjoin, vt imponer algo a uno.

enjoy, vt disfrutar de, gozar de.

enjoyable, adj agradable; divertido.

enjoyment, n disfrute m; placer m.

enlarge, vt 1. extender, aumentar, ensanchar; 2. (foto) ampliar.

enlargement, n extensión f.

enlighten, vt informar, instruir.

enlightening, adj informativo, lleno de datos útiles.

enlist, vt alistar, reclutar.

enliven, vt avivar, animar.

enmity, n enemistad f.

ennoble, vt ennoblecer.

enormous, adj enorme.

enough, adv 1. bastante, suficientemente; 2. adj bastante, suficiente.

enrage, vt enfurecer, hacer rabiar.

enrapture, vt embelesar, arrebatar, extasiar.

enrich, vt enriquecer; fertilizar.

enriched, adj enriquecido.

enrichment, n enriquecimiento m; fertilización f.

enroll, vt registrar, inscribir; matricular.

ensconce, vr instalarse cómodamente.

ensemble, n conjunto m; impresión f de conjunto.

ensign, n bandera f.

enslave, vt esclavizar.

enslavement, n esclavitud f.

ensue, vt seguirse; sobrevenir.

ensuing, adj consiguiente, subsiguiente, resultante.

ensure, vt asegurar.

entail, n 1. vínculo m; 2. vt imponer; 3. vincular.

entangle, vt enredar, enmarañar.

entanglement, n enredo m, embrollo m.

enter, vt entrar en; penetrar en; ingresar en.

enteritis, n enteritis f.

enterprise, n empresa f.

enterprising, adj emprendedor.

entertain, vt 1. divertir, entretener; 2. considerar.

entertainer, n artista m/f; actriz f; músico m.

entertaining, adj divertido, entretenido.

entertainment, n diversión f.

enthuse, vi entusiasmarse muchísimo por.

enthusiasm, n entusiasmo m.

enthusiastic, adj entusiasta; entusiastico.

entice, vt tentar, atraer; seducir.

enticing, adj atractivo, tentador, seductor.

entire, adj entero, completo; todo.

entirely, adv enteramente, totalmente.

entitle, vt titular; dar derecho a.

entitlement, n derecho m; autorización f.

entity, n entidad f, ente m; persona f.

entomb, vt sepultar.

entomology, n entomología f.

entourage, n séquito m.

entrails, n entrañas f, tripas f.

entrain, vi tomar el tren.

entrance, n 1. entrada f; ingreso m; 2. vt encantar, hechizar.

entrancing, adj encantador, cautivador, delicioso.

entrant, n participante m/f, concurrente m/f.

entrap, vt coger en una trampa.

entreat, vt rogar, suplicar.

entreaty, n ruego m, súplica f.

entrée, n entrada f; plato m fuerte, plato m principal.

entrench, vt atrincherar.

entrepreneur, n empresario m.

entrust, vt confiar algo a uno.

entry, n entrada f; acceso m; participante m/f.

entwine, vt entrelazar, entretejer.

enumerate, vt enumerar.

enunciate, vt pronunciar, articular.

envelop, vt envolver.

envelop(e), n sobre m, envoltura.

envelopment, n envolvimiento m.

envenom, vt envenenar.

enviable, adj envidiable.

envious, adj envidioso.

environment, n medio m ambiente, entorno m.

environmentalist, adj 1. ambiental; 2. n ecologtista m/f, ambientalista m/f.

environs, n alrededores n, inmediaciones f.

envisage, vt prever.

envision, vt imaginar; prever.

envoy, n enviado m.

envy, n envidia f.

enzyme, n enzima f.

ephemeral, adj efímero.

epic, adj 1. épico; 2. n épica f.

epicenter, n epicentro m.

epicure, n epicúreo m, gastrónomo m.

epidemic, adj 1. epidémico; 2. n epidemia f.

epidermis, n epidermis f.

epigram, n epigrama m.

epilepsy, n epilepsia f, alferecía f.

epilogue, n epílogo m.

episcopalian, adj 1. episcopalista; 2. n episcopalista m/f.

episodic, adj episódico.

epistemology, n epistemología f.

epistle, n epístola f.

epitaph, n epitafio m.

epitome, n epítome m, compendio m.

epitomize, vt epitomar, resumir; personificar.

epoch, n época f.

equable, adj uniforme.

equal, adj igual, equitativo.

equality, n igualdad f.

equalize, vt igualar; nivelar.

equally, adv igualmente; por igual; equitativamente.

equanimity, n ecuanimidad f.

equate, vt igualar; considerar equivalente.

equation, n ecuación f.

equator, n ecuador m.

equatorial, adj ecuatorial.

equestrian, adj ecuestre.

equilateral, adj equilátero.

equilibrium, n equilibrio m.

equine, adj equino.

equinox, n equinoccio m.

equip, vt equipar; proveer.

equipment, n equipo m, material m.

equitable, adj equitativo.

equity n equidad f.

equivalence, n equivalencia f.

equivalent, adj equivalente (a); equivalente.

equivocal, adj equívoco, ambiguo.

equivocate, vi usar equívocos, no dar una respuesta clara, soslayar el problema.

equivocation, n equívoco m; evasión f.

era, n época f, era f.

eradicate, vt desarraigar, extirpar.

erase, vt borrar; liquidar.

eraser, n goma f de borrar, borrador m.

erect, adj 1. erguido, derecho; vertical; 2. vt erigir, construir, levantar.

erection, n erección f, construcción f; montaje m.

ergonomics, n ergonomía f.

ergot, n cornezuelo m (del centeno).

ermine, n armiño m.

erode, vt erosionar; corroer, desgastar.

erogenous, adj erógeno.

erosion, n erosión f; desgaste m.

erosive, adj erosivo, erosionante.

erotic, adj erótico; erotómano.

eroticism, n erotismo m; erotomanía f.

err, vi errar, equivocarse; pecar.

errand, n recado m, mandado m; misión f.

errand-boy, n recadero m, mandadero m.

erratic, adj irregular, poco constante; errático.

erratically, adv de modo irregular.

erroneous, adj erróneo.

error, n error m, equivocación f.

erudite, adj erudito.

erudition, n erudición f.

erupt, vi estar en erupción; entrar en erupción; hacer erupción.

eruption, n erupción f; explosión f.

escalate, vi extenderse, intensificarse, escalarse.

escalation, n extensión f, intensificación f.

escalator, n escalera f mecánica.

escapade, n aventura f, travesura f.

escape, n 1. escape m; fuga f, huida f, evasión f; 2. vt evitar, eludir; escapar a.

eschew, vt evitar, renunciar a, abstenerse de.

escort, n 1. acompañamiento m; acompañante m; 2. escolta f; 3. vt acompañar; escoltar; convoyar.

Eskimo, adj 1. esquimal; 2. n esquimal m/f.

esophagus, n esófago m.

esoteric, adj esotérico.

espadrille, n alpargata f.

espalier, n espaldar m.

esparto, n esparto m.

especial, adj especial, particular.

espionage, n espionaje m.

esplanade, n paseo m; paseo m marítimo; explanada f.

espousal, n adherencia f (a); adopción f (de).

espouse, vt adherirse a; adoptar.

espresso, adj café m exprés.

espy, vt divisar.

essay, n 1. ensayo m; composición f; 2. vt probar, ensayar.

essayist, n ensayista m/f; tratadista m/f.

essence, n esencia f.

essential, adj esencial; indispensable, fundamental, imprescindible.

establish, vt establecer, fundar, crear; constituir.

establishment, n establecimiento m, fundación f.

estate, n 1. finca f, hacienda f; 2. propiedad f; 3. bienes m relictos; herencia f, heredad f.

esteem, n 1. estima f, estimación f; consideración f; 2. vt estimar, apreciar.

estimate, n 1. estimación f, apreciación f; cálculo m; presupuesto m; 2. vt estimar, apreciar; calcular, computar, tasar; 3. vi presupuestar.

estimation, n opinión f; juicio m; concepto m, estima f, aprecio m.

estrange, vt enajenar, apartar (de).

estrangement, n enajenación f; alejamiento m.

estrogen, n estrógeno m.

estuary, n estuario m, ría f.

etcetera, adv etcétera.

etch, vt grabar al aguafuerte.

etching, n aguafuerte f.

eternal, adj eterno; sempiterno; de siempre.

eternally, adv eternamente.

eternity, n eternidad f.

ethane, n etano m.

ethanol, n etanol m.

ether, n éter m.

ethereal, adj etéreo.

ethical, adj ético; honrado.

ethics, n ética f; moralidad f.

ethnic, adj étnico.

ethnological, adj etnológico.

ethnology, n etnología f.

ethyl, n etilo m.

ethylene, n etileno m.

etiquette, n etiqueta f.

etymological, adj etimológico.

etymology, n etimología f.

eucalyptus, n eucalipto m.

eugenics, n eugenismo m, eugenesia f.

eulogize, vt elogiar, encomiar.

eulogy, n elogio m, encomio m.

eunuch, n eunuco m.

euphemism, n eufemismo m.

euphemistic, adj eufemístico.

euphoria, n euforia f.

euthanasia, n eutanasia f.

evacuate, vt evacuar; desocupar.

evade, vt evadir, eludir; escaparse de.

evaluate, vt evaluar, calcular; tasar.

evaluation, n evaluación f, cálculo m.

evanescent, adj efímero, evanescente, fugaz.

evangelic(al), adj evangélico.

evangelism, n evangelismo m.

evangelist, n evangelista m/f; evangelizador(a) m/f.

evangelize, vt evangelizar.

evaporate, vt 1. evaporar; 2. vi evaporarse; desvanecerse, esfumarse.

evaporation, n evaporación f.

evasion, n evasiva f, evasión f.

evasively, adv de manera evasiva.

eve, n víspera f; tarde f.

even, adj llano; liso, igual, uniforme; a nivel.

evening, n tarde f, atardecer m, noche f.

evenness, n lisura f; uniformidad f.

event, n suceso m, acontecimiento m; evento m.

eventuality, n eventualidad f.

eventually, adv finalmente, al fin y al cabo, al final.

ever, adv siempre; (since) desde entonces, (after) después de que.

everglade, n tierra baja pantanosa cubierta de altas hierbas.

evergreen, adj de hoja perenne; siempreverde.

everlasting, adj eterno, perdurable, perpetuo; interminable.

evermore, adv eternamente; por siempre jamás,

every, adj cada, todo.

everybody, pron todos, todo el mundo.

everyday, adj diario, cotidiano, de todos los días; corriente, acostumbrado.

everything, pron todo.

everywhere, adv en todas partes, a todas partes.

evict, vt desahuciar, desalojar, expulsar.

eviction, n desahucio m, desalojo m, expulsión f.

evidence, n 1. evidencia f; prueba f; 2. vt patentizar; probar.

evident, adj evidente, manifiesto, claro.

evil, adj 1. malo, pernicioso; malvado, perverso; 2. n mal m, maldad f.

evildoer, n malhechor(a) m/f.

evince, vt dar señales de, mostrar.

eviscerate, vt destripar.

evocative, adj sugestivo, evocador, sugerente.

evoke, vt evocar.

evolution, n evolución f; desarrollo m.

evolutionary, adj evolutivo.

evolve, vt 1. desarrollar, producir; desprender; 2. vi evolucionar, desarrollarse.

ewe, n oveja f.

ewer, n aguamanil m.

exacerbate, vt exacerbar.

exact, adj exacto.

exacting, adj exigente; conditions severo, arduo.

exactness, n exactitud f.

exaggerate, vt exagerar.

exaggerated, adj exagerado.

exaggeration, n exageración f.

exalt, vt exaltar, elevar; ensalzar.

exaltation, n exaltación f, ensalzamiento m.

examination, n examen m; interrogación f; investigación f.

examine, vt examinar; inspeccionar, escudriñar.

examiner, n examinador(a) m/f; inspector(a) m/f.

example, n ejemplo m; ejemplar m; problema m.

exasperate, vt exasperar, irritar, sacar de quicio.

exasperation, n exasperación f, irritación f.

excavate, vt excavar.

excavation, n excavación f.

exceed, vt exceder; pasar de, exceder de.

excel, vi aventajar, superar; sobresalir.

excellence, n excelencia f.

excellent, adj excelente.

except, vt 1. exceptuar, excluir; 2. prep excepto, con excepción de, salvo; sin contar; menos.

exception, n excepción f.

excerpt, n extracto m.

excess, n exceso m; excedente m.

excessive, adj excesivo.

exchange, n 1. cambio m; intercambio m; 2. vt cambiar (por); canjear (por, con).

exchangeable, adj cambiable; canjeable.

excite, vt emocionar, llenar de emoción, entusiasmar; excitar, estimular.

excitement, n emoción f, entusiasmo m; excitación f; ilusión f.

exciting, adj emocionante, apasionante; excitante.

exclaim, vi exclamar.

exclamation, n exclamación f.

exclude, vt excluir; exceptuar; evitar.

exclusive, adj exclusivo; único.

excommunicate, vt excomulgar.

excommunication, n excomunión f.

excrement, n excremento m.

excrescence, n excrecencia f.

excrete, vt excretar.

excruciating, adj agudísimo, atroz; horrible, fatal.

exculpate, vt exculpar.

excursion, n excursión f.

excuse, n 1. disculpa f, excusa f; razón f, defensa f, justificación f; 2. vt disculpar, perdonar.

execrate, vt execrar, abominar.

execute, vt ejecutar; cumplir; llevar a cabo, realizar.

execution, n ejecución f; cumplimiento m.

executioner, n verdugo m.

executive, adj 1. ejecutivo; 2. n ejecutivo m, gerente m/f, directivo m, director(a) m/f.

executor, n albacea m, testamentario m.

executrix, n albacea f, ejecutora f testamentaria.

exemplary, adj ejemplar.

exemplify, vt ejemplificar; ilustrar, demostrar.

exempt, adj 1. exento, libre (de); 2. vt exentar, eximir, dispensar.

exercise, n 1. ejercicio m; 2. vt ejercer; usar de, emplear; 3. vi ejercitarse, hacer ejercicios.

exert, vt ejercer, emplear.

exertion, n esfuerzo m; esfuerzo m excesivo.

exhalation, n exhalación f.

exhale, vt espirar, exhalar.

exhaust, n 1. gases m de escape; 2. vt agotar.

exhausting, adj agotador.

exhaustion, n agotamiento m; postración f nerviosa.

exhibit, n 1. exhibición f; 2. vt mostrar, manifestar; 3. vi exponer, exhibir.

exhibitor, n expositor(a) m/f.

exhilarate, vt estimular, vigorizar; arrebatar.

exhilarating, adj tónico, vigorizador, estimulador,

exhort, vt exhortar.

exhume, vt exhumar, desenterrar.

exigence, n exigencia f, necesidad f.

exigent, adj exigente; urgente.

exile, n destierro m, exilio m.

exiled, adj exiliado.

exist, vi existir; vivir.

existence, n existencia f; vida f.

existing, adj existente, actual.

exit, n salida f.

exodus, n éxodo m.

exonerate, vt exculpar, disculpar (de).

exorbitant, adj excesivo, exorbitante.

exorcise, vt exorcizar, conjurar.

exorcist, n exorcista m/f.

exotic, adj exótico.

expand, vt 1. extender; ensanchar; dilatar; 2. vi extenderse; ensancharse; dilatarse; aumentarse.

expanding, adj dilatable; expandible.

expanse, n extensión f; envergadura f.

expansion, n extensión f; dilatación f.

expansive, adj expansivo.

expatriate, adj 1. expatriado; 2. n expatriado(a) m/f.

expect, vt esperar.

expectant, adj expectante; ilusionado; mujer f encinta, futura madre f.

expectation, n expectación f.

expectorate, vt expectorar.

expedience, n conveniencia f, oportunidad f.

expedient, adj 1. conveniente, oportuno; 2. n expediente m, recurso m.

expedite, vt acelerar; facilitar.

expedition, n expedición f.

expend, vt expender, gastar.

expendable, adj que se puede sacrificar, que no es insustituible; reemplazable.

expense, n gasto m, costo m.

expensive, adj caro, costoso.

experience, n 1. experiencia f; 2. vt experimentar.

experienced, adj experimentado, perito, experto (en).

experiment, n 1. experimento m; experiencia f; prueba f, ensayo m; 2. vi experimentar.

expert, adj 1. experto, perito; 2. n experto(a) m/f; técnico m; especialista m/f.

expiate, vt expiar.

expiration, n 1. terminación f; expiración f; vencimiento m; 2. espiración f.

expire, vi terminar; expirar; cumplirse; vencerse.

explain, vt explicar; exponer; aclarar.

explanation, n explicación f; aclaración f.

expletive, n palabra f expletiva; palabrota f.

explicit, adj explícito.

explode, vt 1. volar, hacer saltar, explotar; 2. vi estallar, hacer explosión.

exploit, n 1. hazaña f, proeza f; 2. vt explotar.

exploitation, n explotación f.

exploration, n exploración f.

explore, vt explorar; examinar, sondar, investigar.

explorer, n explorador(a) m/f.

explosion, n explosión f.

explosive, adj 1. explosivo; 2. n explosivo m.

exponent, n exponente m/f, intérprete m/f.

export, n exportación f, artículo m de exportación.

exporter, n exportador(a) m/f.

expose, vt 1. exponer; descubrir; 2. vr exponerse a.

exposition, n exposición f; explicación f.

expostulation, n protesta f, reconvención f.

exposure, n exposición f; revelación f; desenmascaramiento m; exhibición f.

expound, vt exponer, explicar.

express, adj 1. expreso, explícito, categórico; 2. n rápido m; 3. vt expresar.

expression, n expresión f.

expressionless, adj sin expresión, inexpresivo.

expressive, adj expresivo.

expressway, n autopista f.

expropriate, vt expropiar.

expulsion, n expulsión f.

expurgate, vt expurgar.

exquisite, adj exquisito, primoroso.

extant, adj existente.

extemporary, adj improvisado.

extemporize, vt/i improvisar.

extend, vt 1. extender; alargar; 2. vi extenderse; prolongarse.

extended, adj extendido; ampliado.

extension, n extensión f; ensanche m, ampliación f.

extent, n extensión f; alcance m.

extenuate, vt atenuar, mitigar, disminuir.

extenuating, adj atenuante.

exterior, adj exterior, externo.

exteriorize, vt exteriorizar.

exterminate, vt exterminar.

exterminator, n exterminador m.

external, adj externo, exterior.

extinct, adj extinto, apagado, extinguido.

extinction, n extinción f.

extinguish, vt extinguir, apagar; suprimir.

extinguisher, n extintor m; apagador m.

extirpate, vt extirpar.

extort, vt obtener por fuerza, exigir por amenazas.

extortion, n exacción f; concusión f.

extra, adj adicional; de más, de sobra.

extract, n 1. cita f, trozo m; extracto m; 2. vt sacar; extraer.

extraction, n extracción f; obtención f.

extractor, n extractor m.

extracurricular, adj extracurricular.

extraditable, adj sujeto a extradición.

extradite, vt extraditar.

extradition, n extradición f.

extraneous, adj extraño; ajeno a.

extraordinary, adj extraordinario; excepcional.

extraterrestrial, adj 1. extraterrestre; 2. n extraterrestre m/f.

extraterritorial, adj extraterritorial.

extravagance, n prodigalidad f; derroche m; despilfarro m.

extravagant, adj pródigo; derrochador, despilfarrador.

extreme, adj extremo.

extremity, n extremidad f, punta f.

extremist, adj extremista.

extricate, vt desenredar, soltar.

extrinsic, adj extrínseco.

extrovert, adj extrovertido, extravertido.

extrude, vt sacar; expulsar; estirar.

exuberance, n euforia f; exuberancia f.

exuberant, adj eufórico; exuberante.

exude, vt exudar; rezumar, destilar, sudar.

exultation, n exultación f, júbilo m.

eye, n 1. ojo m; 2. vt ojear, mirar.

eyeball, n globo m del ojo.

eyebath, n ojera f, lavaojos m.

eyebrow, n ceja f.

eyelash, n pestaña f.

eyelid, n párpado m.

eyeliner, n lápiz m de ojos, delineador m de ojos.

eyeshade, n visera f.

eyeshadow, n sombreador m de ojos, sombra f de ojos.

eyesight, n vista f.

eyestrain, n vista f fatigada.

eyewash, n colirio m.

eyewitness, n testigo m/f presencial, testigo m/f ocular.

eyrie, n aguilera f.

F

F, f, n (letra f) F, f.
fable, n fábula f.
fabric, n tejido m, tela f.
fabricate, vt fabricar; inventar; falsificar.
fabrication, n invención f, ficción f.
fabulous, adj fabuloso; estupendo.
façade, n fachada f.
face, n 1. cara f, rostro m, semblante m; 2. vt mirar hacia, estar enfrente de, dar a; 3. vi estar orientado en una dirección.
facecloth, n manopla f, paño m.
facecream, n crema f.
facelift, n estirado m de piel, estiramiento m facial.
facet, n faceta.
facetious, adj chistoso; festivo, gracioso.
facetiously, adv chistosamente; dijo guasón.
facial, adj 1. de la cara, facial; 2. n tratamiento m.
facile, adj fácil, superficial, ligero.
facilitate, vt facilitar.
facility, n facilidad f; (facilities) servicios m.
facing, prep 1. de cara a, frente a; 2. adj opuesto, de enfrente; 3. n revestimiento m.
facsimile, adj facsímil.
fact, n hecho m; realidad f.
faction, n facción f.
factor, n hecho m, elemento m.
factory, n fábrica f, factoría f.
factual, adj objetivo, basado en datos.
factually, adv objetivamente.
faculty, n facultad f.
fad, n manía f; novedad f; una moda f pasajera.
fade, vt 1. descolorar, desteñir; marchitar; 2. vi decolorarse, desteñirse; apagarse gradualmente.
faded, adj marchito, seco; descolorido; marchito.
fail, n 1. suspenso m; falta; 2. vt faltar a, fracasar, fallar, hacer bancarrota.
failing, prep 1. a falta de; 2. n falta f, defecto m; flaqueza f.
failure, n fracaso m; malogro m; fracaso m.
faint, adj 1. débil; color pálido; tenue; 2. n desmayo m; 3. vi desmayarse, perder conocimiento.
fair, adj 1. bello, hermoso; 2. rubio; blanco; 3. justo, equitativo; 4. n feria f.
fairground, n real m; parque m de atracciones.
fairy, n hada f.
faith, n fe f; confianza f.
faithful, adj fiel; leal.
faithfully, adv fielmente; lealmente; con exactitud.
fake, n 1. falsificación f, impostura f; imitación f; impostor m; 2. adj falso, fingido, contrahecho; 3. vt contrahacer, falsificar, fingir.
falcon, n halcón m.
falconer, n halconero m.
fall, n 1. caída f; baja f; disminución f; caída f, toma f; 2. otoño m; 3. vi caer; caerse.
fallacious, adj erróneo, engañoso, falaz.
fallacy, n error m; sofisma m; falacia f.
fallibility, n falibilidad f.
fallout, n polvillo m radiactivo, consecuencias f.
fallow, adj barbecho.
false, adj falso; erroneo.

falsely, adv falsamente.
falsetto, adj con voz de falsete.
falsification, n falsificación f.
falsify, vt falsificar.
falter, vt 1. decir titubeando; 2. vi vacilar, titubear; desfallecer, empañarse.
faltering, adj vacilante; entrecortado.
fame, n fama f.
famed, adj famoso.
familiar, adj familiar; conocido, consabido.
familiarize, vt 1. familiarizar; 2. vt familiarizarse con.
family, n familia f.
famine, n hambre f (general y grave), hambruna f; escasez f, carestía f.
famished, adj hambriento, famélico.
famous, adj famoso, célebre.
fan, n 1. abanico m; aventador m; ventilador m; 2. aficionado(a) m/f, admirador(a) m/f, entusiasta m/f; 3. vt abanicar; ventilar; 4. vr abanicarse, hacerse aire.
fanatic, n fanático(a) m/f.
fancied, adj imaginario; favorito; selecto.
fanciful, adj caprichoso; fantástico; imaginario.
fancy, n 1. quimera f, suposición f arbitraria; fantasía f; capricho, antojo; 2. adj de adorno; 3. vi imaginarse, aficionarse.
fang, n colmillo m.
fanlight, n abanico m.
fantasize, vi fantasear.
fantastic, adj fantástico; estupendo, bárbaro.
fantasy, n fantasía f.
far, adv 1. lejos, a lo lejos; 2. adj lejano, remoto.
fare, n precio m (del viaje, del billete); billete m, boleto m; pasaje m.
farewell, interj 1. ¡adiós!; 2. n despedida f.
farinaceous, adj farináceo.
farm, n 1. granja f; cortijo m, quinta f, estancia f; 2. vt cultivar.
farmer, n agricultor m; cultivador m; hacendado m.
farming, n cultivo m, labranza f; agricultura f.
farmyard, n corral m.
farrago, n fárrago m.
far-reaching, adj trascendental, de gran alcance, de ancha repercusión.
farrier, n herrador m.
far-seeing, adj clarividente, previsor.
fascia, n faja f; tablero m.
fascinate, vt fascinar, encantar.
fascinating, adj fascinador, encantador, sugestivo.
fascism, n fascismo m.
fascist, adj 1. fascista; 2. n fascista m/f.
fashion, n 1. uso m, manera f; estilo m; 2. vt labrar, formar.
fashionable, adj de moda, elegante.
fast, adj 1. rápido, veloz; ligero; 2. n ayuno m; 3. vi ayunar.
fast day, n día m de ayuno.
fasten, vt 1. asegurar, sujetar; 2. vi cerrarse.
fastener, n cerrojo m, pestillo m; cierre m; broche m.
fat, adj 1. gordo; grueso; 2. n grasa f.
fatal, adj fatal; funesto.
fatalistic, adj fatalista.
fatality, n calamidad f, desgracia f; fatalidad f.
fate, n hado m, destino m.
fateful, adj fatal, fatídico; decisivo.
father, n 1. padre m; 2. vt engendrar.
fatherhood, n paternidad f.
fatherly, adj paternal.

fathom, n 1. braza f; 2. vt sond(e)ar; profundizar.
fathomless, adj insondable.
fatigue, n 1. fatiga f, cansancio m; 2. vt fatigar.
fatigued, adj fatigado.
fatness, n gordura f.
fatten, vt engordar.
fattening, adj que hace engordar.
fatty, adj graso; grasoso.
fatuous, adj fatuo, necio.
faucet, n grifo m, llave f.
fault, n 1. defecto m; imperfección f; 2. vt tachar, encontrar defectos en.
faultfinder, n criticón(a) m/f.
faultless, adj impecable, intachable, sin defecto.
faulty, adj defectuoso, imperfecto.
fauna, n fauna f.
favor, n 1. favor m; aprobación f; amparo m; 2. vt favorecer, mostrar parcialidad.
favorable, adj favorable; propicio.
favorite, adj favorito, predilecto.
fawn, n 1. cervato m; 2. vi adular, lisonjear; congraciarse con.
fawning, adj adulador, servil.
faze, vt perturbar; molestar; marear.
fazed, adj pasmado.
fear, n 1. miedo m, temor m; aprensión f; 2. vt temer; tener miedo a; 3. vi temer por.
fearful, adj temeroso (de); aprensivo; tímido.
fearfully, adv con miedo; tímidamente; terriblemente.
fearless, adj intrépido, audaz, sin temor.
feasibility, n factibilidad f, viabilidad f.
feasible, adj factible, hacedero, posible.
feast, n 1. banquete m, festín m; fiesta f; 2. vt banquetear; agasajar, festejar.
feast-day, n fiesta f.
feat, n hazaña f, proeza f.
feather, n pluma f.
featherweight, n peso m pluma.
feature, n 1. rasgo m distintivo, característica f; 2. crónica f especial, reportaje m especial; 3. vt delinear, representar; presentar.
February, n febrero m.
feeckless, adj abatido, sin valor.
federal, adj federal.
federate, vt 1. federar; 2. vi federarse.
federation, n federación f.
fedora, n sombrero m flexible, sombrero m tirolés.
feedback, n regeneration.
fee, n derechos m, honorarios m; cuota f.
feeble, adj débil; flojo; tenue.
feeble-minded, adj imbécil; irresoluto.
feebleness, n debilidad f; tenuidad f; irresolución f.
feed, n 1. comida f; (Agr) pienso m; 2. vt alimentar, nutrir; dar de comer; 3. vi alimentarse de.
fed up, adj harto.
feeding, n alimentación f; comida f, comidas f.
feel, n 1. tacto m; sensación f; 2. vt tocar, palpar, sentir, tentar; 3. vi buscar a tientas.
feeler, n antena f; tentáculo m.
feeling, n sensación f; sentimiento m, emoción f.
feet, n (plural) pies.
feign, vt fingir, aparentar.
feigned, adj fingido.
feint, n treta f, estratagema f; 2. vi hacer una finta.
felicitate, vt felicitar, congratular.
felicitations, n felicitaciones f.
felicitous, adj feliz, oportuno.
feline, adj 1. felino; 2. n felino m.

fell, vt derribar, talar, cortar.
fellow, n compañero(a) m/f; prójimo m.
fellow-being, n prójimo m.
fellow-citizen, n conciudadano(a) m/f.
fellowship, n compañerismo m; asociación f.
fellow-worker, n compañero(a) m/f de trabajo, colega m.
felon, n criminal m, delincuente m/f.
felony, n crimen m; delito m mayor, delito m grave.
felt, n fieltro m.
female, adj hembra; del sexo femenino.
feminine, adj femenino.
femininity, n feminidad f.
feminist, adj 1. feminista; 2. n feminista m/f.
femoral, adj femoral.
femur, n fémur m.
fence, n 1. cerca f, cercado m, valla f; 2. vt cercar; cubrir, proteger.
fenced, adj área zona f cercada con valla.
fender, n guardafuego m.
fennel, n hinojo m.
ferment, n 1. fermento m; fermentación f; 2. vt hacer fermentar; 3. vi fermentar.
fermentation, n fermentación f.
fern, n helecho m.
ferocious, adj feroz, fiero; violento.
ferociously, adv ferozmente.
ferocity, n ferocidad f.
ferret, n 1. hurón m; 2. vi cazar con hurones.
Ferris wheel, n noria f.
ferrous, adj ferroso.
ferry, n 1. balsa f, barca f; transbordador; 2. vt llevara uno a la otra orilla.
ferryman, n balsero m, barquero m.
fertile, adj fértil, fecundo.
fertility, n fertilidad f; fecundidad f.
fertilize, vt fecundar; fertilizar, abonar.
fertilizer, n fertilizante m, abono m.
fervent, adj fervoroso, ardiente, apasionado.
fervor, n fervor m, ardor m, pasión f.
fester, vi ulcerarse, enconarse; amargarse.
festival, n fiesta f; festival m.
festive, adj festivo, regocijado.
festoon, n 1. guirnalda f, festón m; 2. vt adornar, engalanar, enguirnaldar, festonear.
fetch, vt 1. traer; ir por, ir a buscar; 2. vi trajinar.
fetid, adj hediondo, fétido.
fetish, n fetiche m.
fetlock, n espolón m.
fetter, vt poner grillos a, encadenar; trabar.
fetters, n grillos m; trabas f.
feud, n 1. enemistad f heredada (entre dos familias etc), odio m de sangre; disputa f; 2. vi reñir, pelear.
feudalism, n feudalismo m.
fever, n fiebre f; calentura f.
feverish, adj febril, calenturiento.
few, adj pocos; algunos, unos; unos pocos.
fewer, adj comp menos; menos de... menos que...
fez, n fez m.
fiancé, n novio m, prometido m.
fiancée, n novia f, prometida f.
fiasco, n fiasco m.
fiat, n fíat m, autorización f.
fib, n 1. mentirilla f, bola f; 2. vi decir mentirillas.
fibber, n mentirosillo(a) m/f.
fiber, n fibra f; nervio m, carácter m.
fibrous, adj fibroso.
fibula, n peroné m.
fickle, adj inconstante, veleidoso, voluble.

fiction, n ficción f, invención f.

fictional, adj novelesco; relativo a la novela.

fictionalize, vt novelar.

fiddle, n 1. violín m; 2. vi tocar el violín.

fiddler, n 1. violinista m/f; 2. tramposo(a) m/f.

fidelity, n fidelidad f.

fidget, vi ser un azogue, agitarse nerviosamente.

fidgety, adj azogado, nervioso.

fiduciary, adj fiduciario.

field, n 1. campo m; prado m; cancha f; 2. esfera f; especialidad f.

field marshal, n mariscal m de campo.

fieldwork, n labor f de campo.

fiend, n demonio m; diablo m; desalmado m.

fiendish, adj diabolico.

fierce, adj feroz, salvaje; cruel.

fiercely, adv ferozmente; furiosamente; intensamente.

fiery, adj ardiente; rojo; muy picante.

fifteen, adj quince.

fifth, adj quinto.

fiftieth, adj quincuagésimo; cincuenta.

fifty, adj cincuenta.

fig, n higo m; breva f; higuera f.

fight, n 1. disputa f; riña f, pelea f; 2. vi pelear, luchar (contra, por, con); batirse.

fighter, n combatiente m/f; luchador(a) m/f; guerrero m, soldado m; boxeador m.

figment, n quimera f, producto m de la imaginación.

fig tree, n higuera f.

figurative, adj figurado, figurativo.

figure, n 1. figura f, estatua f; 2. tipo m, línea f, talle m; 3. cifra f, número m; 4. vt representar; representarse, figurarse; imaginar; 5. vi figurar (entre, como).

figurine, n figurilla f, estatuilla f.

filament, n filamento m.

filbert, n avellana f.

filch, vt sisar, ratear.

file, n 1. lima f; 2. carpeta f, expediente m; archivador m; 3. fila f, hilera f; 4. vt limar; 5. archivar, clasificar; 6. desfilar.

filial, adj filial.

filigree, n filigrana f.

filing, n clasificación f; formulación f.

filing-cabinet, n fichero m, archivador m.

fill, vt 1. llenar; rellenar; cargar; 2. vi llenarse (de); hincharse.

filler, n 1. rellenador m; embudo m; 2. masilla f.

fillet, n filete m.

filling, adj 1. sólido, que llena el estómago; 2. n relleno m; empaquetadura f, empaste m.

filling station, n gasolinera f, estación f de servicio.

film, n 1. película f; capa f; velo m; 2. vt hacer una película de, filmar; rodar.

filming, n filmación f.

filmstar, n astro m, estrella f (de cine).

filmstrip, n tira f (o cinta f) de película, tira f proyectable.

filmy, adj transparente, diáfano.

filter, n 1. filtro m; 2. vt filtrar; 3. vi filtrarse.

filthy, adj inmundo, sucio, puerco.

filtration, n filtración f.

fin, n aleta f.

final, adj último, final.

finale, n final m.

finalist, n finalista m/f.

finalize, vt ultimar, completar, concluir.

finance, n 1. finanzas f, asuntos m financieros; 2. vt financiar.

financial, adj financiero.

financing, n financiación f.

finch, n pinzón m.

find, n 1. hallazgo m; 2. vt encontrar, hallar; descubrir.

finder, n descubridor(a) m/f.

finding, n 1. descubrimiento m; 2. fallo m.

fine, adj 1. fino, bueno; 2. n multa f; 3. vt multar.

finery, n galas f, adornos m, trajes m vistosos.

finesse, n discriminación f sutil, discernimiento m.

fine-tune, vt poner a punto; hacer más preciso.

finger, n 1. dedo m; 2. vt manosear.

fingering, n digitación f.

fingermark, n huella f.

fingernail, n uña f.

fingerprint, n 1. huella f dactilar; 2. vt tomar las huellas dactilares a.

fingertip, n punta f (o yema f) del dedo.

finicky, adj delicado, melindroso, superferolítico.

finish, n fin m, final m, conclusión f; 2. vt terminar, acabar, concluir; completar.

finishing-line, n línea f de meta.

finite, adj finito, que tiene fin.

fire, n 1. fuego m; incendio m; lumbre f; 2. vt encender, incendiar, quemar; 3. vi despedir.

fire-alarm, n alarma f de incendios.

firearm, n arma f de fuego.

fireball, n bola f de fuego.

fire brigade, n cuerpo m de bomberos.

firecracker, n petardo m.

fire door, n puerta f contra incendios.

fire drill, n (ejercicio m de) simulacro m de incendio.

fire engine, n coche m de bomberos.

fire escape, n escalera f de incendios.

fire extinguisher, n extintor m.

firefly, n luciérnaga f.

fireman, n bombero m; fogonero m.

fireplace, n chimenea f; hogar m.

fireproof, adj incombustible, a prueba de fuego.

firewood, n leña f, astillas f.

fireworks, n fuegos m artificiales; petardos m.

firing, n 1. disparo m, tiroteo m; 2. despido m.

firm, adj 1. firme; 2. n firma f, empresa f, casa f de comercio.

firmament, n firmamento m.

firmness, n firmeza f.

first, adj 1. primero; original; 2. adv primero; en primer lugar.

first born, n primogénito(a) m/f.

fir tree, n abeto m.

fiscal, adj fiscal; monetario; financiero.

fish, n 1. pez m, pescado m; 2. vt/i pescar.

fishcake, n croqueta f de pescado.

fisherman, n pescador m.

fishhook, n anzuelo m.

fishing, n pesca f.

fishing-net, n red f de pesca.

fishing-rod, n caña f de pescar.

fishstore, n pescadería f.

fishtank, n acuario m.

fission, n escisión f; fisión f.

fissionable, adj fisionable.

fissure, n grieta f, hendedura f; fisura f.

fist, n puño m.

fistfight, n lucha f a puñetazos.

fistful, n puñado m.

fit, *adj* 1. adecuado; hábil, apto, sano; 2. *n* acceso *m*, atque *m*, arranque *m* de cólera; 3. *vt* ajustar, acomodar, adaptar a.

fitful, *adj* espasmódico, irregular, intermitente.

fitness, *n* conveniencia *f*, (buen) estado *m* físico.

fitter, *n* ajustador *m*.

fitting, *adj* 1. conveniente, adecuado; digno; 2. *n* prueba *f*; medida *f*.

five, *adj* cinco.

fix, *vt* fijar, asegurar, sujetar; componer, arreglar.

fixation, *n* fijación *f*.

fixed, *adj* fijo.

fixings, *n* accesorios *m*, guarniciones *f*.

fixture, *n* cosa *f* fija.

fizz, *n* efervescencia *f*; ruido *m* sibilante.

flabbergast, *vt* pasmar, dejar sin habla.

flabby, *adj* flojo, fofo, blanducho; gordo.

flag, *n* 1. bandera; 2. *vt* hacer señales con bandera; 3. flaquear.

flagellation, *n* flagelación *f*.

flagpole, *n* asta *f* de bandera.

flagrant, *adj* notorio, escandaloso.

flagship, *n* buque *m* insignia, buque *m* escuadra.

flagstaff, *n* asta *f* de bandera.

flagstone, *n* losa *f*.

flair, *n* instinto *m*, aptitud *f* especial.

flake, *n* escama *f*; hojuela *f*; copo *m*.

flaky, *adj* escamoso; desmenuzable; hojaldre *m*.

flambé, *adj* flameado.

flamboyant, *adj* vistoso, llamativo; rimbombante.

flame, *n* 1. llama *f*; arder en llamas; 2. *vi* llamear.

flame-proof, *adj* a prueba de fuego.

flamingo, *n* flamenco *m*.

flammable, *adj* inflamable.

flange, *n* pestaña *f*, reborde *m*, resalte *m*, brida *f*.

flanged, *adj* con pestaña.

flank, *n* 1. costado *m*; 2. *vt* lindar con.

flannel, *n* franela *f*.

flap, *n* 1. faldilla *f*; cartera *f*; 2. *vt* batir; sacudir; 3. *vi* aletear; sacudirse.

flapjack, *n* torta *f* de avena, hojuela *f*, panqueque *m*.

flare, *n* llamarada *f*; cohete *m* de señales, bengala *f*.

flash, *n* relámpago *m*; destello *m*, ráfaga *f*.

flashback, *n* escena *f* retrospectiva, vuelta *f* atrás.

flash bulb, *n* bombilla *f* fusible.

flask, *n* frasco *m*; redoma *f*; termo *m*.

flat, *adj* llano; plano; horizontal; mate, desinflado.

flatten, *vt* allanar, aplanar; alisar; aplastar.

flatter, *vt* adular, lisonjear, halagar.

flatterer, *n* adulador(a) *m/f*.

flattering, *adj* lisonjero; halagüeño.

flattery, *n* adulación *f*, lisonjas *f*, halago(s) *m*.

flatulence, *n* flatulencia *f*; hinchazón *f*.

flaunt, *vt* ostentar, lucir; hacer gala de.

flautist, *n* flautista *m/f*, flauta *m*.

flavor, *n* 1. sabor *m* (a), gusto *m*; condimento *m*; 2. *vt* sazonar, condimentar.

flavoring, *n* condimento *m*.

flavorless, *adj* insípido, soso.

flaw, *n* desperfecto *m*, imperfección *f*; defecto *m*.

flawed, *adj* imperfecto, defectuoso.

flawless, *adj* intachable, impecable.

flay, *vt* desollar.

flea, *n* pulga *f*.

fleabitten, *adj* infestado de pulgas.

flee, *vt* 1. abandonar; evitar; 2. *vi* huir, fugarse.

fleece, *n* vellón *m*; lana *f*.

fleecy, *adj* lanudo; cloud aborregado.

fleet, *n* 1. flota *f*; 2. *adj* veloz, ligero, rápido.

fleeting, *adj* fugaz, momentáneo, efímero.

flesh, *n* carne *f*; pulpa *f*.

fleshy, *adj* gordo; carnoso.

flex, *vt* 1. doblar; flexionar; 2. *vi* doblarse; flexionarse.

flexibility, *n* flexibilidad *f*.

flexible, *adj* flexible.

flick, *n* 1. golpecito *m* rápido; capirotazo *m*; chasquido *m*; 2. *vt* dar un golpecitoa.

flicker, *n* 1. parpadeo *m*; 2. *vi* parpadear.

flier, *n* 1. aviador(a) *m/f*; 2. folleto *m*.

flight, *n* vuelo *m*; recorrido *m*.

flighty, *adj* frívolo, poco serio; caprichoso.

flimsiness, *n* debilidad *f*, endeblez *f*; delgadez *f*, ligereza *f*.

flimsy, *adj* débil, endeble; muy delgado.

flinch, *vi* acobardarse, arredrarse, retroceder.

fling, *n* 1. echada, tiro; 2. *vt* arrojar, tirar, lanzar; 3. *vr* arrojarse, precipitarse.

flint, *n* pedernal *m*; piedra *f*.

flippant, *adj* poco serio, ligero.

flipper, *n* aleta *f*.

flirt, *n* 1. mariposón *m*, coqueta *f*; 2. *vi* flirtear, coquetear.

flit, *vi* revolotear, volar con vuelo cortado.

flitch, *n* hoja *f* de tocino.

float, *n* 1. corcho *m*; pontón *m*, flotador *m*; 2. *vt* (a) hacer flotar; poner a flote; 3. *vi* flotar.

floating, *adj* flotante.

flock, *n* 1. rebaño *m*; bandada *f*; grey *f*; 2. *vi* congregarse, reunirse.

floe, *n* témpano *m* de hielo.

flogging, *n* azotaina *f*, paliza *f*.

flood, *n* 1. inundación *f*; pleamar *f*, diluvio *m*; 2. *vt* inundar, anegar; 3. *vi* desbordar.

flooding, *n* inundación *f*.

floodlight, *n* 1. foco *m*; 2. *vt* iluminar con focos.

floor, *n* suelo *m*; fondo *m*; pista *f*.

flooring, *n* suelo *m*; solería *f*.

floorplan, *n* planta *f*.

floorshow, *n* espectáculo *m* cabaret *m*.

flop, *n* 1. fracaso *m*; 2. *vi* caerse; fracasar.

floppy, *adj* flojo, colgante *m*; flexible *m*.

flora, *n* flora *f*.

floral, *adj* floral.

florid, *adj* florido.

florist, *n* florista *m/f*.

flotation, *n* flotación *f*.

flounce, *n* 1. volante *m*; 2. *vi* moverse airosamente.

founder, *n* 1. platija; 2. *vt* estar indeciso.

flour, *n* harina *f*.

flourish, *n* 1. rasgo *m*, rúbrica *f*; 2. *vi* florecer, prosperar.

flout, *vt* 1. mofarse de, no hacer caso de; 2. *vi* fluir, correr; subir, crecer; ondear.

flow, *n* 1. corriente *f*, flujo *m*, movimiento *m*; 2. *vt* correr, fluir.

flower, *n* 1. flor *f*; 2. *vi* florecer.

flower-garden, *n* jardín *m* (de flores).

flowering, *adj* floreciente, en flor.

flowerpot, *n* tiesto *m*, maceta *f*.

flowing, *adj* corriente; suelto; fluido.

flu, *n* gripe *f*.

fluctuate, *vi* fluctuar; variar.

fluctuation, *n* fluctuación *f*; variación *f*.

fluency, *n* fluidez *f*; elocuencia *f*.

fluent, *adj* fluido, corriente; elocuente.

fluff, *n* pelusa *f*, lanilla *f*.

fluffy, *adj* velloso, lanudo; encrespado.

fluid, *adj* 1. fluido, líquido; 2. *n* fluido *m*, líquido *m*.

flunk, *vt* 1. suspender; perder; no aprobar, salir mal en; 2. *vi* ser suspendido.

fluoresce, *n* fluorescencia *f*.

fluorescent, *adj* fluorescente.

fluoridation, *n* fluoración *f*, fluorización *f*.

fluoride, *n* fluoruro *m*.

fluorine, *n* flúor *m*.

flurry, *n* 1. agitación *f*; ráfaga *f*; 2. *vt* agitar, hacer nervioso.

flush, *n* 1. rubor *m*; 2. *adj* nivelado; 3. *vt* levantar; limpiar con un chorro de agua; sonrojarse.

fluster, *n* 1. confusión *f*, aturdimiento *m*; conmoción *f*; 2. *vt* aturdir, poner nervioso, aturrullar.

flute, *n* flauta *f*.

fluted, *adj* estriado, acanalado.

flutist, *n* flautista *m/f*.

flux, *n* flujo *m*.

fly, *n* 1. mosca *f*; braqueta *f*; 2. *vt* hacer volar; pilot(e)ar, 3. *vi* volar; ir en avión.

flying, *adj* 1. volador; rápido, veloz; 2. *n* el volar, el ir en avión.

flyleaf, *n* hoja *f* de guarda.

flypaper, *n* papel *m* matamoscas.

flysheet, *n* hoja *f* volante.

flywheel, *n* volante *m* (de motor).

foal, *n* 1. potro *m*; 2. *vi* parir (la yegua).

foam, *n* 1. espuma *f*; 2. *vi* espumar, echar espuma.

focus, *n* 1. foco *m*; centro *m*; 2. *vt* enfocar(a);fijar, concentrar; 3. *vi* enfocar(se).

fodder, *n* pienso *m*, forraje *m*.

foe, *n* enemigo *m*.

fetal, *adj* fetal.

fetus, *n* feto *m*.

fog, *n* niebla *f*; confusión *f*.

fogbank, *n* banco *m* de niebla.

foggy, *adj* nebuloso, brumoso.

foghorn, *n* sirena *f* (de niebla).

foglamp, *n* faro *m* antiniebla.

foil, *n* 1. hoja *f*, hojuela *f*; 2. aluminio *m* doméstico; 3. *vt* frustrar.

foist, *vt* encajar algo a uno.

fold, *n* 1. pliegue *m*, doblez *m*, arruga *f*; redil *m*; aprisco *m*; 2. *vt* plegar, doblar; recoger; 3. *vi* plegarse, doblarse.

folding, *adj* plegable, plegadizo; de tijera.

foliage, *n* hojas *f*, follaje *m*.

folio, *n* folio *m*; infolio *m*, libro *m* en folio.

folk, *n* 1. nación *f*, tribu *f*, pueblo *m*; 2. *adj* folk (lórico), tradicional.

folk dance, *n* baile *m* popular, danza *f* tradicional.

folklore, *n* folklore *m*, foklor *m*.

folk music, *n* música *f* folklórica, música *f* popular, típica.

folktale, *n* cuento *m* popular.

follicle, *n* folículo *m*.

follow, *vt/i* seguir.

follower, *n* partidario(a) *m/f*, seguidor(a) *m/f*.

following, *adj* siguiente.

foment, *vt* fomentar; provocar, instigar.

fondle, *vt* acariciar.

fondly, *adv* con cariño, afectuosamente.

fondness, *n* cariño *m*; afición *f* (a).

font, *n* pila *f*; fundición *f*; fuente *f*, tipo *m* de letra.

food, *n* alimento *m*, comida *f*; comestible *m*.

food poisoning, *n* intoxicación *f* alimenticia.

fool, *n* 1. tonto(a) *m/f*, zonzo(a) *m/f*; 2. *adj* tonto; 3. *vt* engañar, embaucar; confundir.

foolish, *adj* tonto, necio; imbécil; ridículo.

foolishness, *n* tontería *f*, necedad *f*; imbecilidad *f*; ridiculez *f*; estupidez *f*; imprudencia *f*.

foolproof, *adj* seguro; a prueba de impericia.

foot, *n* pata *f*; pie *m*.

footage, *n* distancia *f*, extensión *f* (medida en pies).

football, *n* fútbol *m*; balón *m*.

footbrake, *n* pedal *m* del freno; freno *m* de pie.

foothold, *n* pie *m* firme, asidero *m* para el pie.

footing , *n* pie *m*; posición *f*.

footloose, *adj* libre; andariego.

footnote, *n* nota *f* (al pie de la página).

footpath, *n* senda *f*, sendero *m*.

footprint, *n* huella *f*, pisada *f*.

footstep, *n* paso *m*, pisada *f*.

fop, *n* petimetre *m*, currutaco *m*.

forage, *n* 1. forraje *m*; 2. *vi* forrajear; buscar.

foray, *n* correría *f*, incursión *f*.

forbearance, *n* paciencia *f*.

forbears, *n* antepasados *m*.

forbid, *vt* prohibir.

forbidden, *adj* prohibido.

forbidding, *adj* formidable; imponente.

force, *n* 1. fuerza *f*; 2. *vt* forzar, obligar.

forced, *adj* forzado; forzoso; violento, a la fuerza.

forceful, *adj* enérgico, vigoroso.

forcefulness, *n* energía *f*; vigor *m*.

forceps, *n* fórceps *m*; pinzas *f*, tenacillas *f*.

forcibly, *adv* a la fuerza; enérgicamente.

ford, *n* 1. vado *m*, botadero *m*; 2. *vt* vadear.

fore, *adj* anterior, delantero.

forearm, *n* antebrazo *m*.

forebode, *vt* presagiar, anunciar.

foreboding, *n* presagio *m*; presentimiento *m*.

forecast, *n* 1. pronóstico *m*; previsión *f*; 2. *vt* pronosticar, prever.

forecaster, *n* pronosticador(a) *m/f*; meteorólogo(a) *m/f*.

foreclose, *vt/i* extinguir el derecho de redimir (una hipoteca).

forefathers, *n* antepasados *m*.

forefinger, *n* índice *m*.

forefront, *n* vanguardia *f*.

foregoing, *adj* anterior, precedente.

foregone, *adj* resultado *m* inevitable.

foreground, *n* primer plano *m*, primer término *m*.

forehead, *n* frente *f*.

foreign, *adj* extranjero; exterior.

foreknowledge, *n* presciencia *f*; saber algo de antemano.

foreman, *n* capataz *m*, caporal *m*; mayoral *m*.

foremost, *adj* primero, delantero; principal.

forensic, *adj* forense.

forerunner, *n* precursor(a) *m/f*.

foresail, *n* trinquete *m*.

foresee, *vt* prever.

foreseeable, *adj* previsible.

foreshadow, *vt* prefigurar, anunciar; presagiar.

forest, *n* bosque *m*; selva *f*.

forestall, *vt* anticiparse a, adelantarse a (e impedir).

forestry, *n* silvicultura *f*; ciencias *f* forestales.

foretaste, *n* anticipo *m*, muestra *f*.

foretell, *vt* predecir, pronosticar; presagiar.

forever, *adv* sin cesar.

forewarn, *vt* prevenir; precaverse.

foreword, *n* prefacio *m*.

forfeit, *n* 1. perdida *f*; multa *f*; pena *f*; 2. *vt* perder (el derecho a).

forfeiture, n pérdida f.

forgather, vi reunirse.

forge, n 1. fragua f; herrería f; fundición f; 2. vt forjar, fraguar; 3. falsificar, falsear.

forger, n falsificador(a) m/f, falsario(a) m/f.

forgery, n falsificación f.

forget, vt olvidar, olvidarse de.

forgetfulness, n olvido m, falta f de memoria; descuido m.

forgive, vt perdonar, disculpar.

forgiveness, n perdón m; misericordia f.

forgiving, adj perdonador, misericordioso.

fork, n 1. tenedor m; horquilla f; bifurcación f, empalme m; 2. vt cultivar con horquilla; 3. vi bifurcarse.

forked, adj ahorquillado, bifurcado.

fork-lift, n carretilla f elevadora, carretilla f de horquilla.

forlorn, adj abandonado, desamparado.

form, n 1. forma f, figura f; molde m; 2. hoja f, formulario m; 3. vt formar; adquirir integrar.

formal, adj formal; ceremonioso, protocolario.

formality, n ceremonia f, formalidad f, requisito m.

formalize, vt formalizar.

format, n formato m.

formation, n formación f.

former, adj primero, anterior.

formerly, adv antes, antiguamente.

formidable, adj formidable.

formless, adj informe.

formula, n fórmula f.

formulate, vt formular.

fornicate, vi fornicar.

fornication, n fornicación f.

forsake, vt abandonar, dejar, desamparar.

forswear, vt abjurar de, renunciar a.

fort, n fuerte m, fortín m.

forte, n fuerte m; forte m.

forth, adv y así sucesivamente; adelante.

forthcoming, adj venidero, próximo.

forthright, adj person directo, franco; enérgico.

forthwith, adv en el acto; sin dilación.

fortieth, adj cuadragésimo; cuarenta.

fortification, n fortificación f.

fortify, vt fortalecer.

fortitude, n fortaleza f, entereza f, valor m.

fortress, n fortaleza f; plaza f fuerte, alcázar m.

fortuitous, adj fortuito, casual.

fortunate, adj afortunado; dichoso, feliz.

fortunately, adv afortunadamente, fortune.

fortune, n fortuna f; destino m.

forum, n foro m; tribunal m.

forward, adj 1. delantero; 2. vt enviar.

forward(s), adv adelante, hacia adelante.

fossil, adj fósil.

foster, vt fomentar, promover; favorecer; alentar.

foster-brother, n hermano m de leche.

foster-home, n casa f cuna, familia f adoptiva.

foul, adj sucio, puerco; asqueroso.

foulmouthed, adj malhablado.

found, vt fundar, establecer; crear.

foundation, n 1. fundación f, establecimiento m; creación f; 2. base f, fundamento m; cimientos m.

founder, n fundador(a) m/f.

foundry, n fundición f, fundidora f.

fountain, n fuente f; manantial m; surtidor m.

fountain-pen, n estilográfica f, plumafuente f.

four, adj 1. cuatro; 2. n cuatro m.

fourfold, adj 1. cuádruple; 2. adv cuatro veces.

fourfooted, adj cuadrúpedo.

fourteen, adj catorce.

fourth, adj cuarto; 2. n cuarto m, cuarta parte f.,

fowl, n ave f; ave f de corral, gallina f.

fox, n 1. zorra f; 2. vt engañar con astucia.

foxglove, n dedalera f.

foxhound, n perro m raposero.

foxhunt, n cacería f de zorras.

foxy, adj taimado, astuto.

foyer, n vestíbulo m.

fracas, n gresca f, riña f.

fraction, n fracción f, quebrado m.

fracture, n 1. fractura f; 2. vt fracturar; 3. vi fracturarse.

fragile, adj frágil, quebradizo; delicado.

fragility, n fragilidad f.

fragment, n 1. fragmento m; trozo m; 2. vt fragmentar; 3. vi fragmentarse.

fragmentation, n fragmentación f.

fragrance, n fragancia f.

fragrant, adj fragante, oloroso; dulce.

frail, adj frágil, quebradizo; delicado.

frailty, n fragilidad f; debilidad f; flaqueza f.

frame, n 1. estructura f, esqueleto m; armazón f; (picture) marco m; talle m; 2. vt construir; arreglar; 3. enmarcar.

frame-up, n estratagema f para incriminar a uno.

framing, n enmarcado m; encuadrado m.

franc, n franco m.

franchise, n derecho m de votar, sufragio m; representación f exclusiva.

franco, adj factura f franca.

frank, adj 1. franco; 2. vt franquear.

frankfurter, n salchicha f.

frankincense, n incienso m.

frankness, n franqueza f.

frantic, adj frenético, furioso.

fraternal, adj fraternal, fraterno.

fraternity, n fraternidad f; cofradía f.

fraternization, n fraternización f.

fraternize, vt confraternizar.

fratricide, n fratricidio m.

fraud, n fraude m; estafa f, impostor(a) m/f.

fraudulence, n fraudulencia f, fraude m.

fraudulent, adj fraudulento.

fraught, adj tenso, difícil.

fray, n 1. combate m, refriega f; 2. vt desgastar, raer; destrozar, crispar; 3. vi deshilacharse.

freak , n curiosidad f, rareza f.

freckle, n peca f.

free, adj 1. libre; suelto, desatado; 2. adv gratis; 3. vt poner en libertad, libertar.

freedom, n libertad f; exención f, inmunidad f.

freelance, adj 1. independiente, autónomo; 2. vi tra-bajar por cuenta propia.

freely, adv libremente; liberalmente.

freeway, n autopista f.

freewill, n libre albedrío m.

freeze, n 1. helada f; ola f de frío; congelación f; 2. vt helar; congelar; 3. vi helarse; congelarse.

freezer, n congelador m.

freight, n flete m; carga f; mercancías f.

freightage, n flete m.

freighter, n buque m de carga.

freight forwarder, n agente m expedidor.

french, adj 1. francés; 2. n francé(esa) m/f.

Frenchman, n francés m.

frenetic, adj frenético.

frenzied, adj frenético; enloquecido.

frenzy, *n* frenesí *m*, delirio *m*.

frequency, *n* frecuencia *f*.

frequent, *adj* 1. frecuente; 2. *vt* frecuentar.

frequently, *adv* frecuentemente.

fresh, *adj* nuevo; recién pintado.

freshen, *vt* 1. refresca; 2. *vi* refrescarse.

freshman, *n* estudiante *m* de primer ano, novato *m*.

freshness, *n* frescura *f*; novedad *f*; vigor *m*.

freshwater, *adj* de agua dulce.

fretful, *adj* displicente, quejoso.

fretfulness, *n* displicencia *f*; inquietud *f*.

fretsaw, *n* sierra *f* de calados.

fretwork, *n* calado *m*.

friar, *n* fraile *m*.

fricassee, *n* fricandó *m*, fricasé *m*.

friction, *n* fricción *f*, rozamiento *m*; frote *m*.

Friday, n viernes *m*.

fried, *adj* frito.

friend, *n* amigo(a) *m/f*.

friendliness, *n* simpatía *f*; amabilidad *f*.

friendship, *n* amistad *f*; compañerismo *m*.

frieze, *n* friso *m*.

frigate, *n* fragata *f*.

fright, *n* susto *m*, sobresalto *m*; terror *m*.

frighten, *vt* asustar, espantar, sobresaltar; alarmar.

frightening, *adj* espantoso, aterrador.

frightful, *adj* espantoso, horrible, horroroso.

frigid, *adj* frío; frígido; glacial.

frigidity, *n* frialdad *f*; frigidez *f*.

fringe, *n* franja *f*; orla *f*, borde *m*.

frisk, *vt* 1. cachear, registrar; 2. *vi* retozar.

friskiness, *n* vivacidad *f*.

frisky, *adj* retozón, juguetón; horse fogoso.

frivolity, *n* frivolidad *f*, informalidad *f*.

frivolous, *adj* frívolo, poco formal, ligero.

frizz, *n* rizos *m* pequeños y muy apretados.

frock, *n* vestido *m*.

frock coat, *n* levita *f*.

frog, *n* rana *f*.

frogman, *n* hombre-rana *m*, submarinista *m*.

from, *prep* desde (desde A hasta Z); procedencia.

frond, *n* fronda *f*.

front, *adj* 1. delantero, anterior; primero; 2. *n* frente *m*, parte *f* delantera, parte *f* anterior.

frontage, *n* fachada *f*.

frontal, *adj* frontal.

frontbencher, *n* figura *f* eminente del Gobierno.

frontier, *n* frontera *f*.

frontiersman, *n* hombre *m* de la frontera.

frontispiece, *n* frontispicio *m*.

frontwards, *adv* de frente, con la parte delantera primero.

frost, *n* 1. helada *f*; escarcha *f*; 2. *vt* cubrir de escarcha.

frosting, *n* azúcar *m* glaseado.

froth, *n* espuma *f*.

frothy, *adj* espumoso.

frown, *n* 1. ceño *m*; entrecejo; 2. *vi* fruncir el entrecejo.

frowning, *adj* ceñudo, amenazador, severo.

frozen, *adj* congelado.

fructify, *vi* fructificar.

frugal, adj frugal.

frugality, n frugalidad *f*.

fruit, *n* fruto *m*, fruta *f*; 2. *vi* frutar, dar fruto.

fruit-cake, *n* tarta *f* de frutas.

fruit cocktail, *n* cóctel *m* de frutas.

fruitful, *adj* fructuoso, provechoso.

fruition, *n* cumplimiento *m*; realización *f*.

fruit juice, *n* zumo *m* de fruta, jugo *m* de fruta.

fruitless, *adj* infructuoso, inútil.

fruit-tree, *n* (árbol *m*) frutal *m*.

frumpish, *adj* desaliñado.

frustrate, *vt* frustrar; sentirse frustrado.

frustrating, *adj* frustrante.

frustration, *n* frustración *f*.

fry, *n* 1. fritada *f*; 2. *vt* freír; 3. *vi* freírse.

fuchsia, *n* fucsia *f*.

fudge, *n* 1. dulce *m* de azúcar; 2. *vt* esquivar, rehuir.

fuel, *n* combustible *m*, carburante *m*; 2. *vt* aprovisionar de combustible.

fugitive, *adj* 1. fugitivo; 2. *n* fugitivo(a) *m/f*.

fugue, *n* fuga *f*.

fulfill, *vt* cumplir con; realizar; satisfacer, llenar.

fulfillment, *n* cumplimiento *m*; realización *f*.

full, *adj* lleno; completo; amplio, holgado, completo.

full-time, *adj* professional en plena dedicación, el que trabaja una jornada completa.

fully, *adv* completamente, enteramente.

fulminate, vi tronar contra.

fumble, *vt* manosear desmañadamente.

fume, *vi* humear; estar furioso, rabiar.

fumes, *n* humo *m*, gas *m*, vapor *m*.

fumigate, *vt* fumigar.

fumigation, *n* fumigación *f*.

fun, *n* diversión *f*; alegría *f*; broma *f*.

function, *n* 1. función *f*; 2. *vi* funcionar.

functional, *adj* funcional.

functionary, *n* funcionario *m*.

fund, *n* 1. fondo *m*; 2. *vt* financiar; proveer fondos a.

fundamental, *adj* fundamental; ser esencial para.

funding, *n* fondos *m*, finanzas *f*; financiación *f*.

funeral, *adj* fúnebre; funerario.

fungicide, *n* fungicida *m*.

fungous, *adj* fungoso.

funnel, *n* embudo *m*; chimenea *f*.

funny, *adj* divertido, gracioso, cómico; chiste *m*.

fur, *n* piel *f*; saburra *f*.

furbish, *vt* renovar, restaurar.

furious, *adj* furioso; frenético, violento.

furiously , *adv* con furia.

furnace, *n* horno *m*.

furnish, *vt* 1. proveer, suministrar, proporcionar; 2. amueblar.

furniture, *n* muebles *m*, mobiliario *m*, mueblaje *m*.

furor, *n* furor *m*, ola *f* de protestas; escándalo *m*.

furrier, *n* peletero *m*.

furry, *adj* peludo; juguete *m* de felpa.

further, *adv* 1. más lejos; además; 2. *adj* más lejano.

furthermore, *adv* además.

furtive, *adj* furtivo.

fury, *n* furor *m*, furia *f*; violencia *f*.

furze, *n* aulaga *f*, tojo *m*.

fuse, *n* 1. fusible *m*, mecha *f*; 2. *vt* fundir, fusionar.

fuselage, *n* fuselaje *m*.

fusion, *n* fusión *f*, fundición *f*.

fuss, *n* conmoción *f*, bulla *f*, alharacas *f*.

fusspot, *n* quisquilloso(a) *m/f*.

futile, *adj* inútil, vano, infructuoso.

futility, *n* inutilidad *f*, lo inútil.

future, *adj* 1. futuro; venidero; 2. *n* futuro *m*, porvenir *m*.

fuzz, *n* tamo *m*, pelusa *f*; vello *m*.

G

G, g, n (letra f) G, g.
gab, n 1. cháchara f; charla f; 2. vi parlotear.
gabardine, n gabardina f.
gabble, n 1. torrente m de palabras ininteligibles;
  2. vi hablar atropelladamente; cotorrear.
gabby, adj hablador, locuaz.
gable, n aguilón m.
gad, vi salir mucho, viajar mucho, callejear.
gadabout, n azotacalles m/f, pindonga f.
gadfly, n tábano m.
gadget, n artilugio m, chisme m, aparato m.
gaff, n 1. arpón m, garfio m; 2. vt arponear,
  enganchar.
gag, n 1. mordaza f; broma f; 2. vt amordazar; hacer
  callar.
gaiety, n alegría f, regocijo m.
gaily, adv alegremente.
gain, n 1. aumento m (de); ganancia f, beneficio m;
  2. vt ganar; conseguir; adquirir; 3. vi mejorar.
gainful, adj remunerado, retribuido.
gait, n modo m de andar, paso m.
gala, n fiesta f; certamen m, concurso m.
galaxy, n galaxia f; grupo m brillante.
gale, n ventarrón m, vendaval m; tormenta f.
gall, n 1. bilis f, hiel f; descaro m; 2. vt irritar.
gallant, adj 1. galante, valiente; 2. n galán m.
gallantry, n valentía f, valor m, heroísmo m, galantería f.
gallbladder, n vesícula f biliar.
galleon, n galeón m.
gallery, n galería f; tribuna f; museo m.
galley, n galera f; cocina f, fogón m.
galling, adj mortificante.
gallon, n galón m (= 4,546 litros, US = 3,785
  litros).
gallop, n 1. galope m; galopada f; 2. vi galopar;
  desfilar a galope.
gallstone, n cálculo m biliario.
galvanize, vt galvanizar.
galvanized, adj galvanizado.
gamble, n 1. jugada f; empresa f arriezgada; 2. vt jugar,
  aventurar en el juego.
gambling, n juego m.
gambol, vi brincar, retozar, juguetear.
game, n 1. juego m; deporte m; 2. vi jugar (por
  dinero).
gamecock, n gallo m de pelea.
gamma, n gama f.
gamut, n gama f.
gander, n ganso m (macho).
gang, n pandilla f, cuadrilla f, grupo m.
gangling, adj larguirucho, desgarbado.
ganglion, n ganglio m.
gangrene, n gangrena f.
gangster, n pistolero m, pandillero m.
gang up, vi conspirar, confabularse, obrar de concierto.
gangway, n pasillo m, pasadizo m.

gap, n vacío m, hueco m; abertura f, brecha f.
gape, vi estar muy abierto; estar boquiabierto.
gaping, adj abierto.
garage, n garaje m, cochera f.
garb, n 1. vestidura m; 2. vt vestir (de).
garbage, n basura f, desperdicios m.
garble, vt mutilar, falsear.
garbled, adj mutilado, confundido.
garden, n 1. jardín m; 2. vi cultivar un huerto,
  trabajar en el jardín.
gardener, n jardinero(a) m/f.
gardenia, n gardenia f.
gardening, n jardinería f, horticultura f.
gargle, n 1. gargarismo m; 2. vi gargarizar.
garish, adj chillón, llamativo, charro.
garland, n 1. guirnalda f; 2. vt enguirnaldar.
garlic, n ajo m.
garment, n prenda f (de vestir).
garnet, n granate m.
garnish, n 1. aderezo m; 2. vt adornar; aderezar.
garret, n guardilla f, desván m.
garrison, n 1. guarnición f; 2. vt guarnecer.
garrotte, n 1. garrote m; 2. vt agarrotar.
garter, n liga f; order (organización) f.
gas, n 1. gas m; 2. vt asfixiar con gas, gasear.
gas can, n bidón m de gasolina.
gas-cooker, n cocina f de (a) gas.
gash, n 1. raja f, hendedura f; cuchillada f; 2. vt
  rajar, hender; (herida) acuchillar.
gasket, n junta f.
gaslight, n luz f de gas, alumbrado m de gas.
gasman, n gasista m, empleado m del gas.
gasmask, n careta f antigás.
gas-meter, n contador m de gas.
gasoline, n gasolina f; nafta f, bencina f.
gasp, n 1. boqueada f; grito m sofocado; 2. vi
  boquear, anhelar, respirar con dificultad.
gas pedal, n acelerador m.
gas pipeline, n gasoducto m.
gas pump, n bomba f de gasolina; surtidor m de
  gasolina.
gas station, n gasolinera f.
gas-stove, n cocina f de gas.
gassy, adj gaseoso.
gastritis, n gastritis f.
gastroenteritis, n gastroenteritis f.
gastronomy, n gastronomía f.
gate, n puerta f; verja f; barrera f; compuerta f.
gather, vt 1. reunir, recoger; acumular, acopiar;
  2. vi reunirse, juntarse, amontonarse.
gathered, adj fruncido.
gathering, n reunión f, asamblea f; concurrencia f.
gauche, adj torpe, desmañado.
gaudy, adj chillón, llamativo; vulgar.
gauge, n 1. norma f de medida; calibre m; indicación
  f; 2. vt medir; calibrar; juzgar, estimar.
gaunt, adj flaco, desvaído, severo, adusto.
gauze, n gasa f.
gavel, n martillo m (de presidente o subastador).
gawky, adj desgarbado, torpe.
gay, adj 1. alegre; brillante, vistoso; 2. n homosexual m/f.
gaze, n 1. mirada f fija; 2. vi mirar (con fijeza).
gazelle, n gacela f.
gazette, n gaceta f.
gear, n 1. equipo m, aparejo m; mecanismo m;
  2. engranaje m, rueda f dentada; 3. vt engranar.
gearbox, n caja f de cambios; caja f de engranajes.
gearwheel, n rueda f dentada.

gecko, *n* geco *m*, dragón *m*.

gee, *interj* ¡caramba!; ¡corcholis!

geisha, *n* geisha *f*.

gel, *n* 1. gel *m*; 2. *vi* aglutinarse; cuajar.

gelatin(e), *n* gelatina *f*.

geld, *vt* castrar, capar.

gelding, *n* caballo *m* castrado.

gelignite, *n* gelignita *f*.

gem, *n* joya *f*, piedra *f* preciosa, gema *f*.

gender, *n* género *m*.

gene, *n* gene *m*, gen *m*.

genealogy, *n* genealogía *f*.

general, *adj* general; corriente, usual.

generalization, *n* generalización *f*.

generalize, *vi* generalizar.

generate, *vt* generar; producir.

generation, *n* generación *f*.

generator, *n* grupo *m* electrógeno, generador *m*.

generic, *adj* genérico.

generosity, *n* generosidad *f*.

generous, *adj* generoso; espléndido, dadivoso.

genesis, *n* génesis *f*.

geneticist, *n* geneticista *m/f*; genetista *m/f*.

genetics, *n* genética *f*.

genial, *adj* simpático, afable.

geniality, *n* simpatía *f*; afabilidad *f*.

genie, *n* genio *m*.

genital, *adj* genital.

genitalia, *n* genitales *m*.

genius, *n* genio *m*; genialidad *f*.

genocide, *n* genocidio *m*.

genre, *n* género *m*.

genteel, *adj* fino, elegante; cursi.

gentian, *n* genciana *f*; violet violeta *f* de genciana.

gentile, *adj* no judío; gentil.

gentility, *n* finura *f*, elegancia *f*; buen tono *m*.

gentle, *adj* benévolo, amable; apacible.

gentleman, *n* señor *m*; caballero *m*; gentilhombre *m*.

gentleness, *n* amabilidad *f*; suavidad *f*; dulzura *f*; mansedumbre *f*; docilidad *f*; ternura *f*.

genuflect, *vi* doblar la rodilla.

genuflection, *n* genuflexión *f*.

genuine, *adj* auténtico, legítimo, genuino.

genus, *n* género *m*.

geodesic, *adj* geodésico.

geographical, *adj* geográfico.

geography, *n* geografía *f*.

geologist, *n* geólogo(a) *m/f*.

geology, *n* geología *f*.

geomagnetic, *adj* geomagnético.

geometric(al), *adj* geométrico.

geometry, *n* geometría *f*.

geophysicist, *n* geofísico(a) *m/f*.

geophysics, *n* geofísica *f*.

geopolitics, *n* geopolítica *f*.

geothermal, *adj* geotérmico.

geranium, *n* geranio *m*.

gerbil, *n* gerbo *m*, jerbo *m*.

geriatrics, *n* geriatría *f*.

germ, *n* germen *m*; microbio *m*; bacilo *m*; bacteria *f*.

germane, *adj* relacionado (con); inoportuno.

germanium, *n* germanio *m*.

germicide, *n* germicida *m*, bactericida *m*.

germinate, *vi* germinar.

germination, *n* germinación *f*.

germ-killer, *n* germicida *m*, bactericida *m*.

gerontology, *n* gerontología *f*.

gerund, *n* gerundio *m*; sustantivo *m* verbal.

gestate, *vt* llevar en el útero.

gestation, *n* gestación *f*.

gesticulate, *vi* accionar, gesticular, manotear.

gesticulation, *n* gesticulación *f*; manoteo *m*.

gesture, *n* 1. ademán *m*, gesto *m*; 2. *vi* hacer un ademán; 3. *vt* expresar con un ademán.

get, *vt* obtener, adquirir, lograr, conseguir; comprar.

get back, *vt* 1. recobrar, recuperar; 2. *vi* volver.

get by, *vt* pasar, lograr pasar; eludir.

get together, *vt* 1. reunir, juntar; 2. *vi* reunirse; verse.

get up, *vi* levantarse, ponerse de pie; levantarse.

ghastly, *adj* horrible; pálido; cadavérico.

gherkin, *n* pepinillo *m*.

ghetto, *n* gueto *m*; judería *f*.

ghost, *n* fantasma *m*, espectro *m*.

ghoul, *n* demonio *m* necrófago.

giant, *n* 1. gigante *m*; 2. *adj* gigantesco, gigante.

gibberish, *n* galimatías *m*, guirigay *m*.

gibbon, *n* gibón *m*.

gibe, *n* 1. pulla *f*, dicterio *m*; 2. *vi* mofarse.

giblets, *n* menudillos *m*.

giddiness, *n* vértigo *m*.

giddy, *adj* vertiginoso; atolondrado.

gift, *n* 1. regalo *m*; obsequio *m*; ofrenda *f*; 2. don *m*, talento *m*, prenda *f*; 2. *vt* dar, donar.

giftwrap, *vt* envolver en papel de regalo.

gigantic, *adj* gigantesco.

giggle, *n* 1. risilla *f* sofocada, risilla *f* tonta; 2. *vi* reírse con una risilla sofocada.

gigolo, *n* gigoló *m*.

gild, *vt* dorar.

gill, *n* agalla *f*, branquia *f*.

gimlet, *n* barrena *f* de mano.

gimmick, *n* truco *m* publicitario.

gimp, *n* cojo(a) *m/f*.

gin, *n* 1. ginebra *f*; 2. desmontadora *f* de algodón.

ginger, *n* 1. jengibre *m*; 2. *adj* rojo, bermejo.

gingerbread, *n* pan *m* de jengibre.

gingerly, *adj* 1. cauteloso, 2. *adv* con tiento.

gingery, *adj* hair rojo, bermejo.

gingham, *n* guinga *f*, guingán *m*.

gingivitis, *n* gingivitis *f*.

giraffe, *n* jirafa *f*.

gird, *vt* 1. ceñir; rodear (de); 2. *vr* aprestar.

girder, *n* viga *f*.

girdle, *n* 1. cinto *m*, ceñidor *m*; cinturón *m*; faja *f*. 2. *vt* ceñir, rodear (de).

girl, *n* chica *f*, muchacha *f*; niña *f*; chica *f*, joven *f*.

girlfriend, *n* amiga *f*, amiguita *f*; compañera *f*.

girlhood, *n* juventud *f*, mocedad *f*.

girth, *n* cincha *f*; circunferencia *f*; gordura *f*.

gist, *n* esencia *f*, lo esencial.

give, *vt* 1. dar; regalar; entregar; 2. *vi* dar.

give away, *vt* 1. regalar, obsequiar; 2. revelar, descubrir; traicionar; 3. *vr* venderse, traicionarse.

give in, *vt* 1. entregar, dar; 2. *vi* ceder; rendirse, darse por vencido.

give out, *vt* 1. distribuir, repartir; 2. anunciar; revelar, divulgar.

giver, *n* donante *m/f*.

give up, *vt* 1. ceder; renunciar a; sacrificar; 2. *vi* darse por vencido, rendirse; perder la esperanza.

give-and-take, *n* concesiones *f* mutuas.

gizzard, *n* molleja *f*.

glacial, *adj* glacial.

glacier, *n* glaciar *m*.

glad, *adj* alegre; bueno.

gladden, *vt* alegrar, regocijar.

glade, *n* claro *m*.

gladiator, *n* gladiador *m*.

gladiolus, *n* estoque *m*, gladíolo *m*.

gladly, *adv* alegremente, con satisfacción; con mucho gusto.

gladness, *n* alegría *f*; satisfacción *f*.

glamorize, *vt* embellecer; hacer más atractivo.

glamorous, *adj* encantador, atractivo, hechicero.

glance, *n* 1. ojeada *f*, vistazo *m*; mirada *f*; 2. *vi* mirar.

glance away, *vi* apartar los ojos.

gland, *n* glándula *f*.

glare, *n* 1. luz *f* deslumbradora, reverbero *m*, brillo *m*, luminosidad *f*; 2. *vi* relumbrar, deslumbrar.

glaring, *adj* deslumbrador, fuerte.

glass, *n* 1. vidrio *m*, cristal *m*; 2. vaso *m*; copa *f*; 3. *n* gafas *f*, lentes *m*; anteojos *m*.

glassblower, *n* soplador *m* de vidrio.

glasscutter, *n* cortador *m* de vidrio.

glassware, *n* artículos *m* de vidrio, cristalería *f*.

glassy, *adj* vítreo; liso; espejado; vidrioso.

glaucoma, *n* glaucoma *m*.

glaze, *n* 1. vidriado *m*, barniz *m*, lustre *m*; 2. *vt* poner vidriosa.

glazier, *n* vidriero *m*.

gleam, *n* 1. rayo *m*, destello *m*; viso *m*; vislumbre *m*; 2. *vi* brillar, relucir, destellar.

glean, *vt* 1. espigar; recoger; 2. *vi* espigar.

glee, *n* alegría *f*, júbilo *m*, regocijo *m*.

gleeful, *adj* alegre, regocijado.

glen, *n* cañada *f*, valle *m* estrecho.

glib, *adj* person de mucha labia, poco sincero.

glide, *n* 1. deslizamiento *m*; planeo *m*; ligadura *f*; 2. *vi* deslizarse; volar sin motor.

glider, *n* planeador *m*, deslizador *m*.

gliding, *n* planeo *m*.

glimmer, *n* 1. luz *f* trémula, luz *f* tenue, vislumbre *f*; 2. *vi* brillar con luz trémula (o tenue).

glimpse, *n* 1. vislumbre *f*; 2. *vt* vislumbrar, entrever.

glint, *n* 1. destello *m*, chispa *f*; 2. *vi* destellar.

glisten, *vi* relucir, brillar.

glitter, *n* 1. brillo *m*, resplandor *m*; 2. *vi* relucir, brillar, rutilar.

gloating, *adj* sonriendo satisfecho.

glob, *n* gotita *f*, glóbulo *m*.

global, *adj* mundial; global.

globe, *n* globo *m*, esfera *f*; esfera terrestre.

globule, *n* glóbulo *m*.

gloom, *n* tinieblas *f*, lobreguez *f*; tristeza *f*.

gloomy, *adj* oscuro, lóbrego, tenebroso; triste.

glorify, *vt* glorificar; alabar, ensalzar.

glorious, *adj* glorioso.

glory, *n* 1. gloria *f*; esplendor *m*; 2. *vi* gloriarse de.

gloss, *n* 1. glosa *f*; 2. lustre *m*, brillo *m*; 3. *vt* glosar, lustrar, pulir.

glossary, *n* glosario *m*.

glossy, *adj* surface lustroso, brillante.

glottal, *adj* glotal; oclusión *f* glotal.

glottis, *n* glotis *f*.

glove, *n* guante *m*.

glow, *n* 1. luz *f*; brillo *m*; calor *m* vivo; 2. *vi* brillar.

glower, *vi* mirar con ceño.

glowering, *adj* ceñudo.

glowing, *adj* candente, incandescente; entusiasta.

glow-worm, *n* luciérnaga *f*.

gloxinia, *n* gloxínea *f*.

glucose, *n* glucosa *f*.

glue, *n* 1. cola *f*, goma *f*; 2. *vt* encolarpegar.

gluey, *adj* pegajoso, viscoso.

glum, *adj* taciturno, melancólico; triste, abatido.

glumly, *adv* sombríamente; tristemente.

glut, *n* 1. superabundancia *f*; 2. *vt* hartar, saciar.

glutenous, *adj* glutenoso.

glutton, *n* glotón(a) *m/f*.

glycerin(e), *n* glicerina *f*.

glycol, *n* glicol *m*.

gnostic, *adj* gnóstico.

go, *vi* ir; andar, viajar.

goad, *n* 1. aguijada *f*, aguijón *m*; estímulo *m*; 2. *vt* aguijonear, picar; incitar, provocar.

goal, *n* fin *m*, objeto *m*, meta *f*; ambición *f*.

goat, *n* cabra *f*, macho *m* cabrío.

goatee, *n* barbas *f* de chivo.

goatskin, *n* piel *f* de cabra.

gobble, *vt* engullir; tragarse, engullirse ávidamente.

goblet, *n* copa *f*.

God, *n* dios *m*; Dios *m*.

goddaughter, *n* ahijada *f*.

goddess, *n* diosa *f*.

godfather, *n* padrino *m* (de).

godforsaken, *adj* dejado de la mano de Dios.

godless, *adj* impío, descreído.

godly, *adj* piadoso.

godmother, *n* madrina *f* (de).

godparents, *n* padrinos *m*.

godsend, *n* cosa *f* llovida del cielo.

godson, *n* ahijado *m*.

go-getter, *n* persona *f* emprendedora.

goggle, *vi* salírsele a uno los ojos de las órbitas.

goggles, *n* anteojos *m*.

going, *n* ida *f*, salida *f*, partida *f*.

gold, *n* oro *m*.

golden, *adj* de oro; dorado; áureo.

goldenrod, *n* vara *f* de oro.

goldfinch, *n* jilguero *m*.

goldfish, *n* pez *m* de colores.

goldfish bowl, *n* pecera *f*.

goldsmith, *n* orfebre *m*.

golf, *n* 1. golf *m*; 2. *vi* jugar al golf.

golf club, *n* 1. club *m* de golf; 2. palo *m* (de golf).

golf course, *n* campo *m* de golf.

golfer, *n* golfista *m/f*.

golly, *interj* ¡caramba!

gonad, *n* gónada *f*.

gondola, *n* góndola *f*; barquilla *f*.

gondolier, *n* gondolero *m*.

gong, *n* gong *m*, gongo *m*.

good, *adj* 1. bueno; 2. *n* provecho *m*; bien *m*; mercancías *f*; bienes *m*.

goodbye, *interj* ¡adiós!.

good-loocking, *adj* guapo, bien parecido.

goodness, *n* bondad *f*; buena calidad *f*.

goodwill, *n* buena voluntad *f*.

gooey, *adj* pegajoso, viscoso; empalagoso.

go off, *vi* 1. irse, marcharse; 2. dispararse; estallar, explosionar.

goof, *n* 1. bobo(d) *m/f*; 2. *vi* gandulear.

go over, *vt* 1. examinar, escudriñar; revisar, repasar; 2. pasar por encima (de); atravesar.

goose, *n* ganso *m* *m/f*.

gooseberry, *n* grosella *f* espinosa.

gopher, *n* ardilla *f* de tierra.

gorge, *n* 1. cañón *m*, barranco *m*, garganta *f*; 2. *vt* engullir; 3. *vi* hartarse, atracarse.

gorgeous, *adj* magnífico, brillante, vistoso.

gorilla, *n* gorila *m*.

gory, *adj* ensangrentado; sangriento.

gospel, *n* evangelio *m*.

gossip, *n* 1. chismoso(a) *m/f*; chisme; 2. *vt* chismear.

gouge, *n* 1. gubia *f*; 2. *vt* excavar con gubia; excavar.

gourd, *n* calabaza *f*.

gourmet, *n* gastrónomo(a) *m/f*.

gout, *n* gota *f*.

govern, *vt* gobernar; dominar; guiar, regir.

government, *n* gobierno *m*; régimen *m*.

governmental, *adj* gubernamental, gubernativo.

governor, *n* gobernador(a) *m/f*; alcalde *m*.

grab, *n* 1. arrebatiña *f*, agarro *m*; 2. *vt* asir, coger.

grace, *n* 1. gracia *f*, finura *f*; bendición; 2. *vt* embellecer.

gracefully, *adv* elegantemente, con garbo.

gracious, *adj* clemente; cortés, afable.

gradation, *n* gradación *f*.

grade, *n* 1. grado *m*; clase *f*, calidad *f*; 3. *vt* clasificar, calificar, dar nota a.

graded, *adj* graduado.

grading, *n* graduación *f*; gradación *f*; calificación *f*.

gradual, *adj* gradual; paulatino; progresivo.

gradually, *adv* gradualmente; poco a poco.

graduate, *n* 1. graduado(a) *m/f*, licenciado(a) *m/f*; 3. *vt* graduar.

graduated, *adj* graduado.

graduation, *n* graduación *f*.

graft, *n* corrupción *f*, chanchullos *m*.

grafter, *n* timador *m*, estafador *m*.

grain, *n* grano *m*.

gram, *n* gramo *m*.

grammar, *n* gramática *f*.

grammatical, *adj* gramatical.

granary, *n* granero *m*.

grand, *adj* magnífico, imponente, grandioso.

grandchild, *n* nieto(a) *m/f*.

granddaughter, *n* nieta *f*.

grandeur, *n* magnificencia *f*, grandiosidad *f*.

grandfather, *n* abuelo *m*.

grandiose, *adj* grandioso; ostentoso.

grandmother, *n* abuela *f*.

grandson, *n* nieto *m*.

grange, *n* cortijo *m*, alquería *f*.

granite, *n* granito *m*.

grant, *n* 1. otorgamiento *m*; concesión *f*; 2. *vt* otorgar, conceder; ceder; donar.

granular, *adj* granular.

granulated, *adj* granulado.

granule, *n* gránulo *m*.

grape, *n* uva *f*.

grapefruit, *n* toronja *f*, pomelo *m*.

grapevine, *n* vid *f*.

graph, *n* gráfica *f*, gráfico *m*.

graphic, *adj* gráfico; grafista *m/f*.

graphics, *n* artes *f* gráficas.

graphite, *n* grafito *m*.

grapple, *vt* 1. asir, agarrar; aferrar; 2. *vi* agarrarse.

grasp, *n* 1. asimiento *m*; alcance *m*; comprensión *f*; 2. *vt* asir, agarrar, comprender.

grasping, *adj* avaro, codicioso.

grass, *n* 1. hierba *f*; césped *m*; pasto *m*; 2. *vt* cubrir de hierba.

grasshopper, *n* saltamontes *m*, chapulín *m*.

grassland, *n* pradera *f*, dehesa *f*; pasto *m*.

grass roots, *n* 1. base *f* popular; 2. lo básico; popular; opinión *f* de las bases populares.

grassy, *adj* herboso, cubierto de hierba.

grate, *n* 1. parrilla *f*; reja *f*; 2. *vt* enrejar, (cheese, etc.) rallar.

grateful, *adj* agradecido; reconocido.

grater, *n* rallador *m*.

gratify, *vt* complacer; gratificar.

gratifying, *adj* gratificante, satisfactorio, grato.

grating, *n* 1. reja *f*, enrejado *m*, emparrillado *m*; 2. *adj* áspero.

gratitude, *n* agradecimiento *m*, gratitud *f*.

gratuitous, *adj* gratuito, innecesario.

gratuity, *n* gratificación *f*, propina *f*.

grave, *adj* 1. grave; serio; solemne; 2. *n* sepultura *f*; tumba *f*, sepulcro *m*.

gravedigger, *n* sepulturero *m*.

gravel, *n* grava *f*, cascajo *m*, recebo *m*.

graveness, *n* gravedad *f*.

gravestone, *n* lápida *f* (sepulcral).

graveyard, *n* cementerio *m*, camposanto *m*.

gravitate, *vi* gravitar; tender hacia.

gravitation, *n* gravitación *f*; tendencia *f*.

gravity, *n* 1. gravedad *f*; 2. gravedad *f*, seriedad *f*, solemnidad *f*.

grazing, *n* 1. pasto *m*. 2. apacentamiento *m*, pastoreo *m*.

grease, *n* grasa *f*; mugre *f*; sebo *m*.

greasy, *adj* grasiento: resbaladizo; graso.

great, *adj* grande, vasto, enorme; importante.

great-grandchild, *n* bisnieto(a) *m/f*.

great-grandfather, *n* bisabuelo *m*.

great-grandmother, *n* bisabuela *f*.

greatly, *adv* grandemente, mucho, muy.

greatness, *n* grandeza *f*.

greed, *n* codicia *f*, avaricia *f*; avidez *f* (de).

greedy, *adj* codicioso, avaro; ávido.

green, *adj* 1. verde; fresco; 2. *n* (color) verde *m*.

greenback, *n* billete *m* (de banco).

greenery, *n* verdura *f*.

greenhouse, *n* invernáculo *m*, invernadero *m*.

greet, *vt* recibir; saludar; dar la bienvenida a.

greeting, *n* saludo *m*, salutación *f*; bienvenida *f*.

gregarious, *adj* gregario.

grenade, *n* granada *f*.

grey, *adj* 1. gris *f*; 2. *vi* (cabello) encanecer.

grey-haired, *adj* canoso.

greyhound, *n* galgo *m*, lebrel *m*.

grid, *n* reja *f*; parrilla *f*; red *f*.

griddle, *n* 1. plancha *f*; 2. *vt* asar a la plancha.

gridlock, *n* atasco *m*, retención *f*, bloqueo *m*.

grief, *n* dolor *m*, pesar *m*, aflicción *f*.

grievance, *n* queja *f*; motivo *m* de queja; agravio *m*.

grieve, *vt* 1. dar pena a; 2. *vi* afligirse, acongojarse.

griffin, *n* grifo *m*.

grill, 1. *n* parrilla *f*; 2. *vt* asar a la parrilla.

grille, *n* rejilla *f*; reja *f*; verja *f*.

grim, *adj* severo; ceñudo; inexorable, inflexible.

grimace, *n* 1. mueca *f*; 2. *vi* hacer una mueca.

grime, *n* mugre *f*, suciedad *f*.

grimy, *adj* mugriento, sucio.

grind, *n* 1. trabajo *m* pesado; rutina *f*; 2. *vt* moler; pulverizar; 3. *vi* rechinar.

grinder, *n* 1. molendero *m*, amolador *m*; 2. amoladora *f*; molinillo *m*.

grinding, *adj* 1. rechinamiento *m*; 2. *n* molienda *f*; pulverización *f*; afilado *m*.

grindstone, *n* muela *f*.

grip, *n* 1. agarre *m*, asimiento *m*; 2. asidero *m*, agarradero *m*; 3. *vt* agarrar, asir.

griping, *adj* 1. retortijante; 2. *n* quejadumbre *m*.

gripping, *adj* absorbente, muy emocionante.

grisly, *adj* horripilante, espeluznante; repugnante.

gristle, *n* cartílago *m*, ternilla *f*.

grit, *n* 1. arena *f*, cascajo *m*; polvo *m*; 2. *vt* apretar los dientes.

gritty, *adj* arenisco, arenoso.

grizzled, *adj* gris, canoso.

groan, *n* 1. gemido *m*, quejido *m;* 2. *vt* gemir.

groceries, *n* comestibles *m pl*, provisiones *f*.

grocery, *n* tienda *f* de comestibles, abacería *f*.

groin, *n* ingle *f*.

groom, *n* 1. novio *m;* mozo *m* de caballos; 2. *vt* (horses) almohazar.

groove, *n* 1. ranura *f*, estría *f;* 2. *vt* estriar, acanalar.

grooved, *adj* estriado, acanalado.

grope, *vt* ir a tientas; avanzar a tientas hacia.

gross, *adj* grueso, enorme.

grossness, *n* gordura *f;* grosería *f*.

grotesque, *adj* grotesco.

grotto, *n* gruta *f*.

grouch, *n* 1. cascarrabias *m/f;* 2. *vi* refunfuñar, quejarse.

grouchy, *adj* malhumorado.

ground, *n* 1. suelo *m*, tierra *f*, terreno *m;* 2. (meat) molido, picado; (Elect) conectar con tierra.

grounding, *n* varada *f*.

groundspeed, *n* velocidad *f* respecto a la tierra.

groundwater, *n* agua *f* subterránea.

groundwork, *n* trabajo *m* preliminar, trabajo *m* preparatorio.

group, *n* 1. grupo *m;* 2. *adj* grupal; 3. *vt* agrupar.

grouper, *n* (pez) mero *m*.

grout, *n* 1. lechada *f;* 2. *vt* enlechar.

grove, *n* arboleda *f*, bosquecillo *m*.

grovel, *vi* arrastrarse; humillarse.

grovelling, *adj* rastrero, servil.

grow, *vt* 1. cultivar; dejar crecer; 2. *vi* crecer; cultivarse; aumentar, hacerse.

grower, *n* cultivador(a) *m/f*.

growl, *n* 1. gruñido *m;* 2. *vi* gruñir; rezongar.

grown, *adj* crecido, adulto.

grown-up, *adj* adulto; propio de persona mayor.

growth, *n* crecimiento *m;* aumento *m;* desarrollo *m*.

grub, *n* gusano *m*.

grubby, *adj* sucio, mugriento.

grudge, *n* 1. rencor *m;* inquina *f;* 2. *vt* escatimar, dar de mala gana.

gruel, *n* gachas *f*.

grueling, *adj* duro, penoso.

gruesome, *adj* horrible, horripilante.

gruff, *adj* bronco; brusco, malhumorado.

grumble, *n* 1. queja *f;* 2. *vi* refunfuñar, quejarse.

grumpy, *adj* gruñón, malhumorado.

grunt, *n* 1. gruñido *m;* 2. *vi* gruñir.

guano, *n* guano *m*.

guarantee, *n* 1. garantía *f;* 2. *vt* garantizar.

guaranteed, *adj* garantizado; asegurado.

guarantor, *n* garante *m/f*, fiador(a) *m/f*.

guard, *n* 1. guardia *f;* 2. guarda *f*, guarnición *f;* 3. *vt* guardar, proteger, defender.

guard dog, *n* perro *m* guardián.

guarded, *adj* cauteloso, circunspecto.

guardhouse, *n* cuartel *m* de la guardia.

guardian, *n* protector(a) *m/f*, guardián(ana) *m/f*.

guava, *n* guayaba *f*.

guerrilla, *n* guerrillero(a) *m/f*.

guess, *n* 1. conjetura *f*, suposición *f;* estimación *f* aproximada; 2. *vt/i* adivinar, conjeturar, suponer.

guesswork, *n* conjeturas *f*.

guest, *n* convidado(a) *m/f*, invitado(a) *m/f*.

guest-room, *n* cuarto *m* de huéspedes.

guffaw, *n* 1. risotada *f*, carcajada *f;* 2. *vi* reírse a carcajadas.

guidance, *n* dirección *f*, gobierno *m;* consejos *m*.

guide, *n* 1. guía *m/f;* 2. *vt* guiar; orientar; conducir.

guidebook, *n* guía *f*.

guide-dog , *n* perro-guía *m*.

guideline, *n* línea *f* directriz, pauta *f*.

guidepost, *n* poste *m* indicador.

guiding, *adj* principio *m* director.

guile, *n* astucia *f*, maña *f*.

guileless, *adj* inocente, candoroso.

guillotine, *n* 1. guillotina *f;* 2. *vt* guillotinar.

guilt, *n* culpa *f*, culpabilidad *f*.

guiltless, *adj* inocente, libre de culpa (de).

guilty, *adj* culpable (de).

guinea pig, *n* cobayo *m*, conejillo *m* de Indias.

guitar, *n* guitarra *f*.

gulf, *n* golfo *m;* abismo *m*.

gull, *n* gaviota *f*.

gullet, *n* esófago *m;* garganta *f*, gaznate *m*.

gullible, *adj* crédulo, simplón.

gully, *n* barranco *m*, torrentera *f*.

gulp, *n* 1. trago *m*, sorbo *m;* 2. *vt* tragarse.

gum, *n* (Anat) encía *f;* goma *f;* (chewing) chicle *m*.

gumboil, *n* flemón *m*.

gumdrop, *n* frutilla *f*.

gummed, *adj* engomado.

gun, *n* 1. arma *f* de fuego; 2. *vt* disparar sobre, atacar.

gunboat, *n* cañonero *m;* lancha *f* cañonera.

gunfight, *n* tiroteo *m*.

gunfire, *n* cañoneo *m*, fuego *m;* tiros *m*, tiroteo *m*.

gypsy, *n* gitano(a) *m/f*.

H

H, h , *n* (letra *f*) H, h.

haberdashery, *n* mercería *f*, prendas *f* de caballero.

habit, *n* costumbre *f*, hábito *m*.

habitation, *n* habitación *f*.

habitual, *adj* habitual, acostumbrado, usual.

habituate, *vt* acostumbrar, habituar.

hacienda, *n* hacienda *f*.

hack, *n* 1. caballo *m* de alquiler; hachazo *m*, corte *m;* 2. *vt* cortar, tajar.

hackneyed, *adj* trillado, gastado.

hacksaw, *n* sierra *f* para metales.

hackwork, *n* trabajo *m* de rutina.

Hades, *n* infierno *m*.

haft, *n* mango *m*, puño *m*.

hag, *n* bruja *f*.

haggard, *adj* ojeroso, trasnochado.

haggle, *vi* discutir, regatear.

hail, *n* 1. granizo *m*, pedrisco *m;* 2. grito *m;* saludo *m;* 3. *vt* llamar a, saludar; 4. *vi* granizar.

hailstone, *n* granizo *m*, piedra *f*.

hailstorm, *n* granizada *f*, granizal *m*.

hair, *n* pelo *m*, cabello *m;* pelo *m*.

hairbrush, *n* cepillo *m* para el pelo.

haircut, *n* corte *m* de pelo.

hairdo, *n* peinado *m*.

hairdresser, *n* peluquero(a) *m/f*.

hairless, *adj* sin pelo, pelón, calvo; lampiño.

hairpiece, *n* postizo *m*, tupé *m;* trenza *f* postiza.

hairpin, *n* horquilla *f*.

hairspray, *n* laca *f* (para el pelo).

hake, n merluza f.

hale, adj sano, robusto; sano y fuerte.

half, n 1. mitad f; 2. adj medio; 3. adv a medias.

half-dozen, n media docena f.

half-hour, n media hora f.

half-moon, n media luna f.

halfway, adv 1. a medio camino; 2. adj intermedio.

halibut, n halibut m, hipogloso m.

halitosis, n halitosis f.

hall, n vestíbulo m, hall m; sala f.

hallelujah, n aleluya f.

hallmark, n contraste m; sello m.

hallow, vt santificar.

hallowed, adj sagrado, santificado.

hallucinate, vi alucinar, tener alucinaciones.

hallway, n vestíbulo m, hall m.

halo, n halo m, aureola f, nimbo m.

halogen, n halógeno m; lámpara f halógena.

halt, n alto m, parada f; interrupción f.

halter, n cabestro m, ronzal m; dogal m.

halting, adj vacilante, titubeante.

halve, vt 1. partir por mitad; reducir en la mitad; empatar; 2. vi reducirse en la mitad.

ham, n jamón m; pernil m.

hamburger, n hamburguesa f; carne f picada.

hammer, n 1. martillo m; macillo m; percusor m; 2. vt martillar; batir; 3. dar una paliza a.

hammerhead, n pez m martillo.

hammering, n martilleo m.

hammock, n hamaca f, coy m.

hamper, n 1. cesto m, canasta f; 2. vt estorbar, impedir.

hamster, n hámster m.

hamstring, n tendón m de la corva.

hand, n 1. mano f; (clock) manecilla f; obrero m; 2. vt entregar, poner en manos de.

handbag, n bolso m, cartera f.

handbill, n prospecto m, folleto m.

handbook, n manual m; guía f.

handcraft, n productos m; hechos a mano.

handcream, n crema f para las manos.

handcuffs, n 1. esposas f; 2. vt esposar.

handful, n puñado m, manojo m; un puñado de gente.

handicap, desventaja f, estorbo m, obstáculo m; minusvalía f, discapacidad f.

handicapped, adj minusválido.

handicraft, artesanía f; destreza f manual.

handiwork, n obra f.

handkerchief, n pañuelo m.

handle, n 1. mango m; puño m; palanca f; manivela f; 2. vt tocar, manosear; tocar con la mano.

handler, n tratante m, comerciante m.

handling, n manejo m, manejar m; manipulación f.

handout, n distribución f, repartimiento m.

handrail, n pasamano m.

handshake, n apretón m de manos; coloquio m.

handsome, adj hermoso, bello; elegante.

handwriting, n escritura f, letra f.

handwritten, adj escrito a mano.

handy, adj a mano; próximo.

handyman, n factótum m; hombre m que tiene dotes prácticas.

hang, vt 1. colgar, suspender; pegar; manir; 2. vi colgar.

hangar, n hangar m.

hanging, adj 1. pendiente, colgante; 2. vt pender; (criminal) ahorcar.

hangover, n resaca f, cruda f.

hank, n madeja f.

hanker, vi añorar; anhelar, suspirar por.

hankering, n añoranza f; anhelo m.

haphazard, adj fortuito.

hapless, adj desventurado.

happen, vi pasar, suceder, ocurrir, acontecer.

happily, adv por fortuna, afortunadamente.

happiness, n felicidad f, dicha f, contento m; alegría f.

happy, adj feliz, dichoso, afortunado.

harangue, n 1. arenga f; 2. vt arengar.

harass, vt acosar, hostigar; hostilizar, picar.

harassment, n acoso m, hostigamiento m.

harbinger, n heraldo m, nuncio m; precursor m; presagio m; presagio m del desastre.

hard, adj duro; sólido, firme; endurecido.

hardback, adj empastado, de tapa dura.

harden, vt endurecer; solidificar.

hardening, n endurecimiento m.

hardly, adv apenas.

hardness, n dureza f; dificultad f; rigor m; severidad f.

hardship, n penas f; infortunio m; apuro m.

hardware, n ferretería f, quincalla f.

hardy, adj fuerte, robusto; resistente.

hare, n liebre f.

harelip, n labio m leporino.

harem, n harén m.

harlot, n ramera f.

harm, n daño m, mal m; perjuicio m peligro.

harmful, adj perjudicial, dañoso, nocivo; dañino.

harmless, adj inocuo, inofensivo.

harmonica, n armónica f.

harmonious, adj armonioso.

harmonize, n armonizar (con).

harmony, n armonía f.

harp, n arpa f.

harpist, n arpista m/f.

harpoon, n 1. arpón m; 2. vt arponear.

harpsichord, n clavicordio m, clavicémbalo m.

harpy, n arpía f.

harrow, n 1. grada f; 2. vt gradar.

harrowing, adj horrendo, horroroso, angustioso.

harry, n asolar; hostilizar.

harsh, adj severo, duro, cruel.

harshness, n severidad f, dureza f, aspereza f.

hart, n ciervo m.

harvest, n cosecha f, recolección f; siega f.

harvesting, n cosecha f, cosechado m.

hash, n picadillo m; embrollo m.

hasp, n pasador m, sujetador m.

hassle, n pelea f, riña f; lío m, problema m.

haste, n prisa f, precipitación f.

hasten, n acelerar; apretar el paso.

hastily, adv de prisa, precipitadamente.

hasty, adj apresurado, precipitado; imprudente.

hat, n sombrero m.

hatband, n cinta f de sombrero.

hatch, n 1. escotilla f; 2. vt (chick) empollar, encubar.

hatchery, n criadero m, vivero m.

hatchet, n hacha f (pequeña), machado m.

hate, n 1. odio m; 2. vt odiar, detestar, aborrecer.

hateful, adj odioso, repugnante.

hatrack, n percha f para sombreros.

hatred, n odio m aborrecimiento m.

hatter, n sombrerero m.

haughty, adj altanero, arrogante, altivo.

haul, n 1. tirón m, estirón m; recorrido m; 2. vt tirar, arrastrar, transportar.

haunch, n anca f; pierna f; es sentarse en cuclillas.

haunt, n 1. nidal m, guarida f, querencia f; 2. vt frecuentar, rondar.

haunted, adj obsesionado, embrujado.

have, vt 1. tener; poseer; 2. llevar.

haven, n puerto m; refugio m, asilo m.

havoc, n estragos m, destrucción f.

hawk, n 1. halcón m, gavilán m; 2. vt pregonar; 3. vi carraspear.

hawker, n vendedor m ambulante.

hawser, n guindaleza f, calabrote m, maroma f.

hay, n heno m.

haystack, n almiar m.

haze, n calina f, neblina f.

hazelnut, n avellana f.

hazing, n novatadas f.

hazy, adj calinoso, brumoso; confuso.

he, pron 1. él; 2. macho m, varón m.

head, n 1. cabeza f; cabellera f; 2. jefe m; director m, principal m; 3. vt encabezar, dirigir.

headache, n dolor m de cabeza.

headband, n cinta f (para la cabeza).

headboard, n cabecera f.

heading, n encabezamiento m, título m.

headlamp, n faro m.

headline, n encabezamiento m, cabeza f; titulares m.

headmaster, n director m.

headmistress, n directora f.

headphone(s), n auricular(es) m, audífono(s) m.

headstrong, adj voluntarioso, impetuoso, testarudo.

heal, vt 1. curar, sanar; curar, remediar; 2. vi cicatrizarse.

healer, n curador(ora) m/f.

healing, adj 1. curativo, sanativo; 2. curación f.

health, n salud f; sanidad f, higiene f.

healthy, adj sano, saludable.

heap, n 1. montón m; 2. vt amontonar.

hearer, n oyente m/f.

hearing, n oído m.

hearing-aid, n aparato m del oído.

hearken, vi escuchar.

hearsay, n rumores m, hablillas f.

hearse, n coche m fúnebre, coche m mortuorio.

heart, n corazón m.

heartache, n angustia f, pena f.

heart-attack, n ataque m cardíaco.

heartbeat, n latido m del corazón.

heartbroken, adj angustiado, acongojado.

heartburn, n acedia f.

heartening, adj alentador.

hearth, n hogar m, chimenea f.

heartily, adv sinceramente, cordialmente; enérgicamente.

heartless, adj cruel, inhumano.

hearty, adj person campechano, francote; sincero.

heat, n 1. calor m; calefacción f; ardor m; vehemencia f; 2. vt calentar; acalorar; 3. vi acalorarse.

heated, adj calentado.

heatedly, adv con vehemencia, con pasión.

heater, n calentador m.

heating, n calefacción f.

heatproof, adj termorresistente, a prueba de calor.

heatwave, n ola f de calor.

heave, n 1. esfuerzo m para levantar; tirón; 2. vi tener náuseas.

heaven, n cielo m; cielos m.

heavily, adv pesadamente; fuertemente, mucho; concentrate densamente.

heaviness, n peso m; pesadez f; lo fuerte, fuerza f.

heavy, adj 1. pesado; grueso, denso, oneroso; 2. forzudo m.

heavyweight, adj pesado, (Box) peso pesado.

heckle, vt interrumpir, molestar con preguntas.

heckling, n interrupciones f, gritos m de protesta.

hectare, n hectárea f.

hectic, adj febril; loco.

hectogram(me), n hectogramo m.

hedge, n 1. defensa f, protección f; 2. vi contestar con evasivas.

hedonist, n hedonista m/f.

heed, n 1. atención f; 2. vt prestar atención.

heedless, adj desatento, descuidado; hacer caso de.

heedlessly, adv sin hacer caso.

heel, n 1. talón m, calcañar m; tacón m; 2. vt poner tacón a.

hefty, adj object pesado; person fuerte, fornido.

hegemony, n hegemonía f.

heifer, n novilla f, vaquilla f.

height, n altura f, elevación f, altitud f.

heinous, adj atroz, nefando.

heir, n heredero(a) m/f.

heiress, n heredera f.

heirloom, n reliquia f de familia.

heist, n 1. robo m a mano armada; 2. vt robar a mano armada.

helicopter, n helicóptero m.

heliograph, n heliógrafo m.

helium, n helio m.

helix, n hélice f.

hell, n infierno m.

hellfire, n llamas f del infierno.

hellhole, n infierno m.

hellish, adj infernal; diabólico; horrible.

helm, n timón m; gobernar.

helmet, n casco m.

help, n 1. ayuda f; auxilio m, socorro m; favor m; 2. vt ayudar; auxiliar; 3. vi ayudar.

helper, n ayudante m/f, asistente m/f; auxiliar m/f.

helpful, adj útil, provechoso.

helpless, adj desamparado; desvalido; impotente.

helplessness, n desamparo m; impotencia f; incapacidad f.

helpmate, n buen compañero m, buena compañera f.

hem, n 1. dobladillo m, (edge) orilla f; 2. vt bastillar.

hematology, n hematología f.

hemisphere, n hemisferio m.

hemlock, n cicuta f.

hemoglobin, n hemoglobina f.

hemophilia, n hemofilia f.

hemorrhage, n hemorragia f; 2. vi sangrar.

hemorrhoids, n hemorroides f.

hemp, n cáñamo m; hachís m.

hen, n 1. gallina f; hembra f; 2. ad j el pájaro hembra.

hence, adv de aquí, desde aquí.

henceforth, adv de hoy en adelante.

henhouse, n gallinero m.

hepatitis, n hepatitis f.

heptagonal, adj heptagonal.

her, pron la; ella.

herb, n hierba f; tea infusión f de hierbas.

herbal, adj 1. herbario; tea; 2. infusión f de hierbas.

herbicide, n herbicida m.

herbivorous, adj herbívoro.

herd, n rebano m, hato m. manada f.

here, adv aquí; acá; presente.

hereabouts, adv por aquí.

hereafter, adv en el futuro.

hereby, adv por este medio.

hereditary, adj hereditario.

heredity, n herencia f.

herein, adv en esto.

hereinafter, adv más adelante, a continuación.

hereof, adv de esto.

heresy, n herejía f.

heretic, n hereje m/f.

hereto, adv a esto; las partes abajo firmantes.

heretofore, adv hasta ahora; hasta este momento.

hereupon, adv en seguida.

herewith, adv junto con esto.

heritable, adj heredable.

heritage, n herencia f; patrimonio m.

hermit, n ermitaño m; crab ermitaño m.

hermitage, n ermita f.

hernia, n hernia f.

hero, n héroe m; protagonista m.

heroic, adj heroico.

heroin, n heroína f.

heroine, n heroína f; protagonista f, personaje m principal.

heroism, n heroísmo m.

heron, n garza f (real).

herpes, n herpes m.

herring, n arenque m.

hers, poss pron suyo(a), (los/las) suyos(as), de ella.

herself, pron se; ella misma.

hesitant, adj vacilante, irresoluto, indeciso.

hesitantly, adv irresolutamente, indecisamente; con indecisión.

hesitate, vi vacilar, mostrarse indeciso.

hesitation, n vacilación f, irresolución f, indecisión f.

heterogeneous, adj heterogéneo.

heterosexual, adj heterosexual.

hew, vt cortar, tajar; labrar, tallar.

hex, 1. maleficio m; 2. bruja f; 3. vt embrujar.

hexagon, n hexágono m.

hey, interj ¡oye!; ¡eh!

hi, interj ¡oye!, ¡eh!, ¡hola!, ¡buenas!

hiatus, n hiato m; vacío m, laguna f, interrupción f.

hibernate, vi invernar, hibernar.

hibiscus, n hibisco m.

hiccup, n hipo m.

hick, adj 1. rústico, de aldea; 2. palurdo m, paleto m.

hickory, n nuez f dura, nogal m americano.

hidden, adj escondido; oculto, secreto.

hide, n 1. piel f, pellejo m; 2. cuero m; escondite m; 3. vt esconder; ocultar.

hideous, adj horrible.

hideout, n escondrijo m, guarida f.

hie, vi 1. apresurar; 2. vi ir volando, correr.

hierarchy, n jerarquía f.

hieroglyphic, adj jeroglífico.

high, adj alto, elevado; fuerte.

higher, adj más alto; superior.

highland, n tierras f altas, montañas f.

highlight, n claro m; realce m, toque m de luz.

highly, adv muy, muy bien, sumamente.

highness, n altura f; Su Alteza Real.

highway, n carretera f; autopista f.

hijack, n 1. secuestro; 2. vt piratear, secuestrar.

hijacker, n pirata m, secuestrador m.

hike, n caminata f, excursión f a pie; 2. aumento m; 3. vt dar una caminata; 4. aumentar, subir.

hiker, n excursionista m/f; caminador(a) m/f.

hilarious, adj divertido, regocijante; alegre.

hilarity, n regocijo m, alegría f.

hill, n colina f, cerro m, otero m; montaña f.

hillbilly, n rústico m montañés; palurdo(a).

hilliness, n montañosidad f.

hillside, n ladera f.

hilltop, n cumbre f.

hilly, adj montuoso, montañoso, accidentado.

hilt, puño m, empuñadura f.

him, pron le, lo; el

himself, pron se; él mismo.

hind, n 1. cierva f; 2. adj trasero, posterior.

hinder, vi estorbar, impedir, dificultar.

hindquarters, n cuartos m traseros.

hindrance, n estorbo m, obstáculo m.

hindsight, n percepción f retrospectiva.

hint, n 1. indirecta f, indicación f, insinuación f; 2. señal f, indicio m; 3. vi soltar indirectas.

hip, n cadera f.

hippodrome, n hipódromo m.

hippopotamus, n hipopotamo m.

hire, n alquiler m; salario m, jornal m.

hirsute, adj hirsuto.

his, poss, adj su, sus.

Hispanic, adj hispánico.

hiss, n 1. silbido m, siseo m; 2. vt silbar.

histology, n histología f.

historic(al), adj histórico.

history, n historia f.

hit, n 1. golpe m; tiro m certero; 2. éxito m, sensación f; 3. vi chocar; chocar con, dar contra; satirizar.

hitch, n 1. tirón m; 2. cote m; 3. vt mover de un tirón; 4. amarrar.

hitchhike, vi hacer autostop, hacer dedo.

hither, adv acá; acá y acullá.

hitherto, adv hasta ahora.

hives, n urticaria f.

hoard, n 1. acumulación f; 2. vt acumular.

hoarder, n acaparador m.

hoarfrost, n escarcha f.

hoarse, adj ronco; tener la voz ronca.

hoax, n trampa f, truco m, mistificación f.

hobble, n 1. cojera f; maniota f; cojear; 2. vt manear.

hobby, n pasatiempo m, afición f.

hobo, n vagabundo m; obrero m temporero, obrero m migratorio.

hock, n 1. corvejón m; 2. vt empeñar.

hockey, n hockey m.

hoe, n 1. azada f; azadón m, sacho m; 2. vt azadonar.

hog, n 1. cerdo m, puerco m, chancho m; 2. vt acaparar.

hoist, n 1. montacargas m; grúa f; 2. vt alzar, levantar; enarbolar.

hold, n 1. agarro m, asimiento m; presa f; 2. asidero m; 3. influencia f; 4. vt tener; agarrar, coger.

holder, n tenedor(ora) m/f.

holding, n tenencia f; posesión f, propiedad f.

holdup, n atraco m; atracador m.

hole, n 1. agujero m; hoyo m; cazoleta f; hueco m; 2. vt agujerear, perforar; abrir una brecha en.

holiday, n día de fiesta f, día m festivo.

holiness, n santidad f.

holistic, adj holístico.

hollandaise, adj salsa f holandesa.

hollow, adj 1. hueco, ahuecado; hundido; 2. n hoyo m, hueco m.

holly, n acebo m.

hollyhock, n malva f loca.

holocaust, *n* holocausto *m*.

hologram, *n* holograma *m*.

holster, *n* pistolera *f*, funda *f* (de pistola).

holy, *adj* santo; sagrado.

home, *n* casa *f*; domicilio *m*; hogar *m*.

homeland, *n* tierra *f* natal, patria *f*.

homely, *adj* casero, doméstico, familiar.

homesick, *adj* nostálgico.

homestead, *n* casa *f*, caserío *m*; granja *f*.

homeward, *adj* viaje *m* hacia casa.

homework, *n* deberes *m*, tarea(s) *f*.

homicide, *n* homicidio *m*; homicida *m/f*.

hominy, *n* maíz *m* molido.

homogenize, *vt* homogenizar.

homonym, *n* homónimo *m*.

homophobia, *n* homofobia *f*.

homosexual, *adj* 1. homosexual; 2. homosexual *m/f*.

hone, *n* 1. piedra *f* de afilar; 2. *vt* afilar.

honest, *adj* honrado, recto; franco, sincero.

honesty, *n* honradez *f*, rectitud *f*; franqueza *f*.

honey, *n* miel *f*.

honeybee, *n* abeja *f* (obrera).

honeycomb, *n* panal *m*.

honeymoon, *n* luna *f* de miel, viaje *f* de novios.

honeysuckle, *n* madreselva *f*.

honk, *n* 1. graznido *m*; bocinazo *m*; 2. *vi* graznar; tocar la bocina, bocinar.

honor, *n* 1. honor *m*; honra *f*; 2. *vt* honrar.

honorable, *adj* honorable; honrado.

honorarium, *n* honorarios *m*.

hood, capucha *f*; muceta *f*; capirote *m*.

hoodlum, *n* gorila *m*, matón *m*.

hoodwink, *vt* burlar, engañar.

hoof, *n* casco *m*; pezuña *f*; pata *f*.

hook, *n* 1. gancho *m*; garfio *m*; anzuelo *m*; 2. *vt* enganchar; pescar, coger.

hooked, *adj* ganchudo.

hookup, *n* acoplamiento *m*; transmisión *f* en circuito.

hookworm, *n* anquilostoma *m*.

hoop, *n* aro *m*; arco *m*.

hoot, *n* 1. ululato *m*; bocinazo *m*; 2. *vt* abuchear.

hop, *n* 1. lúpulo *m*; 2. salto *m*, saltito *m*, brinco *m*; 3. *vt* saltar con un pie.

hope, *n* 1. esperanza *f*; confianza *f*; 2. *vt* esperar.

hopeful, *adj* person lleno de esperanzas, optimista.

hopeless, *adj* desesperado, sin esperanza.

horde, *n* horda *f*; multitud *f*, muchedumbre *f*.

horizon, *n* horizonte *m*.

horizontal, *adj* horizontal.

hormonal, *adj* hormonal.

hormone, *n* hormona *f*.

horn, *n* cuerno *m*; asta *f*; bocina *f*.

hornbill, *n* búcero *m*.

horned, *adj* con cuernos, enastado; de cuernos .

hornet, *n* avispón *m*; avispero *m*.

horny, *adj* material córneo; calloso.

horrible, *adj* horrible.

horrid, *adj* horrible, horroroso.

horrify, *vt* horrorizar; escandalizar, pasmar.

horrifying, *adj* horroroso, horripilante.

horror, *n* horror *m*; tener horror a.

horse, *n* caballo *m*.

horseplay, *n* payasadas *f*, pelea *f* amistosa.

horsepower, *n* caballo *m* (de fuerza), caballaje *m*.

horticulture, n horticultura f.

hose, n 1. medias *f*; calcetines *m*; calzas *f*; manguera *f*; 2. *vt* regar con manga.

hosiery, *n* calcetería *f*.

hospice, *n* hospicio *m*.

hospitable, *adj* hospitalario; acogedor.

hospital, *n* hospital *m*.

hospitality, *n* hospitalidad *f*.

hospitalize, *vt* hospitalizar.

host, *n* 1. multitud *f*; 2. hueste *f*; huésped *m*, hospedador *m*; (Eccl) hostia *f*.

hostage, n rehén m.

hostal, n parador m; albergue *m* para jóvenes.

hostess, *n* huéspeda *f*; anfitriona *f*; azafata *f*.

hostile, *adj* enemigo, hostil; nada amistoso.

hostility, *n* hostilidad *f* hacia, enemistad *f*, antagonismo *m*.

hot, *adj* caliente, cálido; caluroso, de calor.

hotel, n hotel *m*.

hotelier, *n* hotelero *m*.

hothouse, *n* invernadero *m*.

hour, *n* hora; tiempo.

hourglass, *n* reloj *m* de arena.

hourhand, horario *m*.

hourly, *adj* de cada hora, por hora.

house, *n* 1. domicilio *m*, casa *f*; 2. *vt* alojar, hospedar.

housecleaning, *n* limpieza *f* de la casa.

housecoat, *n* bata de casa *f*.

household, *n* casa *f*, familia *f*.

housekeeper, *n* ama *f* de casa.

housewife, *n* ama *f* de casa; madre *f* de familia.

housework, *n* quehaceres *m* domésticos.

housing, *n* alojamiento *m*; provisión *f* de vivienda.

hovel, *n* casucha *f*, tugurio *m*.

hover, *vi* permanecer inmóvil (en el aire).

how, adv cómo.

however, adv comoquiera que lo haga; por (muy) ...; 2. conj sin embargo, no obstante.

howl, *n* aullido *m*, chillido *m*, grito *m*, alarido *m*.

hub, *n* cubo *m*; centro *m*, eje *m*.

hubcap, *n* tapacubos *m*.

huckster, *n* vendedor *m* ambulante, mercachifle *m*.

huddle, n 1. montón *m*, grupo *m*; corrillo *m*; 2. *vt* amontonar; 3. *vi* acurrucarse.

hue, n color m; matiz m, tono *m*; griterío *f*.

huffy, adj enojadizo; malhumorado, ofendido.

hug, n abrazo m.

huge, adj enorme, vasto, inmenso; descomunal.

hulking, *adj* grueso, pesado.

hull, *n* casco *m*.

hum, *n* 1. zumbido *m*; tarareo *m*; murmullo *m*; 2. *vt* tararear, canturrear; 3. *vi* zumbar; canturrear.

human, *adj* 1. humano; 2. *n* ser *m* humano; humano(a) *m/f*.

humanitarian, *adj* 1. humanitario; 2. n humanitario(a) m/f.

humanity, *n* humanidad *f*.

humanize, *vt* humanizar.

humankind, *n* género *m* humano.

humble, *adj* 1. humilde; 2. *vt* humillar; 3. *vr* humillarse.

humbleness, *n* humildad *f*.

humid , *adj* húmedo.

humidifier, *n* humectador *m*, humedecedor *m*.

humidify, *vi* humedecer.

humidity, *n* humedad *f*.

humiliate, *vt* humillar.

humiliating, *adj* vergonzoso, humillante.

humiliation, *n* humillación *f*.

humility, *n* humildad *f*.

humming, *n* zumbido *m*; tarareo *m*, canturreo *m*.

hummingbird, *n* colibrí *m* picaflor *m*.

humor, *n* 1. humorismo *m;* sentido *m* del humor; 2. *vt* complacer, seguir el humor a; mimar.

humorless, *adj* person sin sentido del humor.

humorous, *adj* person gracioso, chistoso.

hump, *n* 1. joroba *f,* corcova *f,* giba *f;* 2. *vi* encorvarse.

humpback, *n* jorobado(a) *m/f.*

humus, *n* humus *m.*

hunch, *n* 1. corazonada *f,* sospecha *f;* 2. *vt* encorvar.

hunchbacked, *adj* jorobado, corcovado.

hundred, *adj* ciento, cien.

hunger, *n* 1. hambre *f;* 2. *vi* tener hambre.

hunger strike, *n* huelga *f* de hambre.

hungrily, *adv* ansiosamente, ávidamente.

hungry, *adj* hambriento.

hunk, *n* pedazo *m* (grande), (buen) trozo *m.*

hunt, *n* 1. caza *f,* cacería *f;* partida *f* de caza; 2. *vt* animal cazar; buscar; perseguir.

hunter, *n* cazador(ora) *m/f.*

hunting, *n* caza *f,* montería *f.*

hurdle, *n* zarzo *m,* valla *f;* valla *f;* obstáculo *m.*

hurl, *vt* lanzar, arrojar; rechazar.

hurricane, *n* huracán *m.*

hurry, *n* 1. prisa, apuro *m;* 2. *vt* apresurar, dar prisa a, apurar, acelerar.

hurt, *n* 1. herida *f,* lesión *f;* daño *m,* mal *m,* perjuicio *m;* 2. *vt* herir, hacer mal a, hacer daño a, lastimar.

hurtful, *adj* dañoso, perjudicial.

hurtle, *vt* arrojar.

husband, *n* marido *m;* esposo *m.*

hush, *n* 1. silencio *m;* 2. *vi* callarse.

hushed, *adj* callado, muy bajo; silence profundo.

husk, *n* 1. cáscara *f,* vaina *f;* hollejo *m,* cascabillo *m;* 2. *vt* descascarar desvainar.

huskily, *adv* roncamente, en voz ronca.

huskiness, *n* ronquedad *f.*

husky, *adj* 1. ronco; fornido; 2. *n* perro *m* esquimal.

hussy, *n* pícara *f,* desvergonzada *f.*

hustle, 1. actividad *f* febril, bullicio *m;* empuje *m;* 2. *vt* empujar, codear.

hustler, *n* persona *f* dinámica; estafador *m.*

hut, *n* casilla *f;* barraca *f,* cabaña *f;* choza *f.*

hutch, *n* conejera *f.*

hyacinth, *n* jacinto *m.*

hybrid, *adj* 1. híbrido, 2. *n* híbrido(a) *m/f.*

hybridize, *vt/i* hibridar.

hydra, *n* hidra *f.*

hydrant, *n* boca *f* de riego.

hydrate, *n* 1. hidrato *m;* 2. *vt* hidratar.

hydraulic, *adj* hidráulico.

hydraulics, *n* hidráulica *f.*

hydrodynamics, *n* hidrodinámica *f.*

hydroelectric, *adj* hidroeléctrico.

hydrogen, *n* hidrógeno *m.*

hydroplane, *n* hidroavión *m.*

hygiene, *n* higiene *f.*

hygienic, *adj* higiénico.

hymnal, *n* himnario *m.*

hyperacidity, *n* hiperacidez *f.*

hyperactive, *adj* hiperactivo, hipercenético.

hyperactivity, *n* hiperactividad *f.*

hypertension, *n* hipertensión *f.*

hyphen, *n* guión *m.*

hyphenate, *vt* escribir con guión.

hypnosis, *n* hipnosis *f.*

hypnotize, *vt* hipnotizar.

hypoallergenic, *adj* hipoalérgeno.

hypodermic, *n* aguja *f* hipodérmica.

hypothermia, *n* hipotermia *f.*

hysteria, *n* histerismo *m,* histeria *f.*

hysterical, *adj* histérico; laughter risa *f* histérica.

hysterics, *n* histerismo *m,* paroxismo *m* histérico.

I

I, i, *n* (letra *f*) I, i.

I, *pron* yo.

iambic, adj yámbico.

Iberia, *n* Iberia *f.*

ibex, *n* cabra *f* montés, íbice *m.*

ibis, *n* ibis *m.*

ice, *n* 1. hielo *m;* 2.*vt* helar; enfriar; 3. *vi* helarse.

iceberg, *n* iceberg *m.*

icebreaker, *n* rompehielos *m.*

ice cream, *n* helado *m.*

ice-cube, *n* cubito *m* de hielo, cubeta *f* de hielo.

ice-hockey, *n* hockey *m* sobre hielo.

icepack, *n* compresa *f* de hielo.

ice pick, *n* piolet *m,* piqueta *f.*

ice-skate, *n* 1. patín *m* de hielo; 2. *vi* patinar sobre hielo.

ichthyology, *n* ictiología *f.*

icicle, *n* carámbano *m.*

icon, *n* icono *m;* símbolo *m* gráfico.

iconoclast, *n* iconoclasta *m/f.*

icy, *adj* helado, glacial.

ID card, *n* abbr carnet *m* de identidad.

idea, *n* idea *f;* concepto *m;* ocurrencia *f.*

ideal, *adj* ideal; perfecto; soñado.

idealistic, *adj* idealista.

idealize, *vt* idealizar.

ideally, *adv* idealmente; perfectamente.

identical, *adj* idéntico; gemelos *m.*

identifiable, *adj* identificable.

identification, *n* identificación *f.*

identify, *vt* 1. identificar; acertar; 2. *vr* identificarse.

identity, *n* 1. identidad *f;* 2. cédula *f* personal.

ideology, *n* ideología *f.*

idiocy, *n* imbecilidad *f;* estupidez *f.*

idiom, *n* idiotismo *m,* modismo *m,* lenguaje *m.*

idiomatic, *adj* idiomático.

idiosyncrasy, *n* idiosincrasia *f.*

idiot, *n* idiota *m/f,* imbécil *m/f,* tonto(a) *m/f.*

idle, *adj* 1. ocioso; holgazán, flojo; 2. *vi* haraganear, gandulear; marchar en vacío.

idleness, *n* ociosidad *f;* holgazanería *f;* flojera *f.*

idol, *n* ídolo *m.*

idolatry, *n* idolatría *f.*

idolize, *vt* idolatrar.

idyll, *n* idilio *m.*

if, *conj* (condicional) si.

iffy, *adj* dudoso, incierto.

igloo, *n* iglú *m.*

igneous, *adj* ígneo.

ignite, *vt* 1. encender, incendiar; 2. *vi* encenderse.

ignition, *n* ignición *f;* encendido *m.*

ignoble, *adj* innoble, vil.

ignominious, *adj* ignominioso, oprobioso.

ignorance, n ignorancia f.

ignorant, adj ignorante.

ignore, vt no hacer caso de, desatender.

iguana, n iguana f.

ill, adj enfermo, malo.

ill-advised, adj inconsiderado, imprudente.

ill-breeding, n mala educación f.

illegal, adj ilegal, ilícito.

illegally, adv ilegalmente, ilícitamente.

illegible, adj ilegible.

illegimacy, n ilegitimidad f.

illegitimate, adj ilegítimo.

illicit, adj ilícito.

illiteracy, n analfabetismo m.

illiterate, adj 1. analfabeto; sin instrucción, poco instruido; iletrado; 2. n analfabeto(a) m/f.

illness, n enfermedad f, mal m, dolencia f.

ill-nourished, adj malnutrido.

illogical, adj falto de lógica, ilógico.

illuminate, vt iluminar; poner luminarias en.

illuminating, adj aclaratorio; instructivo; revelador.

illumination, n iluminación f, alumbrado m.

illusion, n apariencia f; espejismo m; ilusión f.

illusionist, n prestidigitador(a) m/f, ilusionista m/f.

illustrate, vt ilustrar; aclarar; demostrar.

illustration, n ejemplo m; explicación f, aclaración f; grabado m.

illustrious, adj ilustre.

image, n 1. imagen f; 2. reputación f.

imaginary, adj imaginario.

imagination, n imaginacion f; inventiva f.

imagine, vt imaginar, imaginarse, figurarse.

imam, n imán m.

imbalance, n desequilibrio m, falta f de equilibrio.

imbecile, adj imbécil.

imitative, adj imitativo; imitador.

imitator, n imitador(a) m/f.

immaculate, adj limpísimo, perfectamente limpio, inmaculado.

immanent, adj inmanente.

immaterial, adj inmaterial, incorpóreo.

immature, adj inmaturo, no maduro; joven.

immaturity, n inmadurez f, falta f de madurez.

immeasurable, adj inmensurable, inconmensurable.

immediate, adj inmediato; urgente, apremiante.

immediately, adv inmediatamente, enseguida.

immemorial, adj inmemorial, inmemorable.

immense, adj inmenso, enorme.

immensity, n inmensidad f.

immerse, vt 1. sumergir, sumir, hundir; 2. vr sumergirse en.

immersion, n inmersión f, sumersión f.

immigrant, adj 1. inmigrante; 2. n inmigrante m/f.

immigrate, vi inmigrar.

immigration, n inmigración f.

imminent, adj inminente.

immobile, adj inmóvil, inmoble.

immobilize, vt inmovilizar.

immoderate, adj excesivo, inmoderado.

immodest, adj inmodesto.

immoral, adj inmoral.

immortal, adj inmortal.

immortality, n inmortalidad f.

immortalize, vt inmortalizar.

immovable, adj 1. inmoble, inmóvil; 2. n inmuebles m.

immune, adj inmune.

immunization, n inmunización f.

immunize, vt inmunizar.

immunodeficiency, n inmunodeficiencia

immure, vt emparedar; encerrar.

immutable, adj inmutable, inalterable.

impact, n 1. impacto m, choque m; 2. vt impactar.

impair, vt perjudicar, dañar, deteriorar, debilitar.

impaired, adj dañado, deteriorado.

impala, n impala m.

impale, vt empalar; espetar.

impart, vt comunicar, impartir, hacer saber.

impartial, adj imparcial.

impassable, adj intransitable; infranqueable.

impasse, n callejón m sin salida; cerrazón f.

impassioned, adj apasionado, exaltado.

impassive, adj impasible, imperturbable.

impatient, adj impaciente; intolerante.

impeachment, n denuncia f, acusación f; proceso m.

impeccable, adj impecable, intachable.

impecunious, adj inope, indigente, falto de dinero.

impede, vt estorbar; dificultar, impedir.

impediment, n obstáculo m, estorbo m.

impel, vt impulsar, mover.

impending, adj inminente; próximo.

impenetrable, adj impenetrable; insondable.

impenitent, adj impenitente.

imperative, adj imperioso, perentorio; esencial.

imperceptible, adj imperceptible, insensible.

imperfect, adj imperfecto, defectuoso.

imperfection, n imperfección f; desperfecto m.

imperial, adj imperial.

imperialism, n imperialismo m.

imperil, vt poner en peligro, arriesgar.

imperious, adj imperioso, arrogante; apremiante.

imperishable, adj imperecedero.

impermanent, adj impermanente.

impermeable, adj impermeable.

impersonal, adj impersonal.

impersonally, adv impersonalmente.

impersonate, vt imitar, personificar.

impertinence, n impertinencia f, insolencia f.

impertinent, adj impertinente, insolente.

imperturbable, adj imperturbable.

impervious, adj impermeable, impenetrable; insensible (a).

impetigo, n impétigo m.

impetuous, adj impetuoso, irreflexivo.

impetus, n ímpetu m; impulso m, incentivo m.

impiety, n impiedad f.

impinge, vi afectar a.

impious, adj impío.

impish, adj travieso, endiablado.

implacable, adj implacable.

implant, n 1. implante m; 2. vt implantar.

implausible, adj inverosímil; poco convincente.

implement, n 1. herramienta f, instrumento m; 2. vt poner por obra, llevar a cabo, realizar.

implementation, n realización f, ejecución f.

implicate, vt comprometer; implicar, involucrar.

implication, n complicidad f, implicación f.

implicit, adj implícito; incondicional, absoluto.

implied, adj implícito, tácito.

implore, vt implorar, suplicar.

imply, vt implicar, suponer, presuponer; querer decir.

impolite, adj descortés, mal educado.

imponderable, adj imponderable.

import, n 1. importación f, artículo m importado; 2. importancia f; 3. vt significar; 4. vi importar.

importance, n importancia f.

important, adj importante; de categoría; destacado.

importation, n importación f.

importer, n importador(a) m/f.

importunate, adj importuno; molesto, pesado.

importune, vt importunar, perseguir, fastidiar.

impose, vt 1. imponer; 2. vi abusar de.

imposing, adj imponente, impresionante.

imposition, n imposición f; molestia f; abuso m.

impossible, adj imposible; inaguantable, insufrible.

impost, n impuesto m.

impostor, n impostor(a) m/f, embustero(a) m/f.

impotence, n impotencia f.

impound, vt embargar, confiscar.

impractical, adj falto de sentido práctico, poco práctico; desmañado.

imprecation, n imprecación f.

imprecise, adj impreciso.

impregnable, adj inexpugnable.

impregnate, vt impregnar, empapar (de); fecundar.

impress, n 1. impresión f, señal f; sello m, huella f; 2. vt estampar; grabar, inculcar; impresionar.

impression, n impresión f.

impressionable, adj impresionable; influenciable.

impressive, adj impresionante.

imprint, n 1. impresión f, huella f, señal f; pie m de imprenta; 2. vt imprimir, estampar; grabar.

imprison, vt encarcelar, poner en la cárcel.

imprisonment, n encarcelamiento m, detención f.

improbability, n improbabilidad f.

improbable, adj improbable; inverosímil.

impromptu, adj improvisado.

improper, adj impropio, incorrecto, indebido.

impropriety, n falta f de decoro; deshonestidad f.

improve, vt 1. mejorar; perfeccionar; reformar; embellecer; 2. vi mejorar(se); perfeccionarse.

improvement, n mejora f, mejoramiento m.

improvident, adj impróvido, imprevisor.

improvise, vt/i improvisar, repentizar.

imprudent, adj imprudente.

impudence, n descaro m, insolencia f.

impudent, adj descarado, insolente, atrevido.

impugn, vt impugnar.

impulse, n impulso m; estímulo m; incitación f.

impulsive, adj irreflexivo, impulsivo.

impure, adj impuro; adulterado, mezclado.

impurity, n impureza f; deshonestidad f.

imputation, n imputación f; acusación f.

impute, vt imputar, achacar, atribuir; acusar.

in..., pref 1. in...; 2. adj interior; 3. adv dentro, adentro; 4. prep en, adentro de.

inability, n incapacidad f, falta f de aptitud.

inaccessible, adj inaccesible.

inaccurate , adj inexacto, incorrecto, erróneo.

inaction, n inacción f.

inactive, adj inactivo.

inadequate, adj inadecuado, insuficiente, incapaz.

inadmissible, adj inadmisible.

inadvertent, adj inadvertido; accidental.

inadvisable, adj no aconsejable.

inalienable, adj inalienable.

inanimate, adj inanimado.

inapplicable, adj inaplicable.

inappropriate, adj inoportuno, inconveniente.

inapt, adj impropio; inhábil.

inarticulate, adj incapaz de expresarse.

inasmuch, conj puesto que, ya que, por cuanto que.

inattention, n inatención f; desatención f.

inattentive, adj desatento, distraído.

inattentively, adv distraídamente.

inaudible, adj inaudible, que no se puede oír.

inaugurate, vt inaugurar.

inauguration, n inauguración f.

inauspicious, adj poco propicio, desfavorable.

inborn, adj innato, ingénito; instintivo.

incalculable, adj incalculable.

incandescent, adj incandescente.

incantation, n conjuro m, ensalmo m.

incapable, adj incapaz; incompetente.

incapacitate, vt incapacitar, inhabilitar.

incapacity, n incapacidad f; insuficiencia f.

incarcerate, vt encarcelar.

incarnate, vt encarnar.

incarnation, n encarnación f.

incautious, adj incauto, imprudente.

incendiary, adj 1. incendiario; 2. n incendiario m.

incense, n 1. incienso m; 2. vt indignar, encolerizar.

incensed, adj furioso, encolerizado.

incentive, n incentivo m, estímulo m.

inception, n comienzo m, principio m.

incertitude, n incertidumbre f.

incessant, adj incesante, constante, continuo.

incest, n incesto m.

incestuous, adj incestuoso.

inch, n pulgada f (= 2,54 cm).

incidence, n frecuencia f; extensión f; intensidad f.

incident, n incidente m, episodio m, suceso m.

incidental, adj incidental, fortuito; no esencial.

incinerate, vt incinerar, quemar.

incipient, adj incipiente, naciente.

incise, vt cortar; tallar; incidir, hacer una incisión en.

incision, n incisión f, corte m.

incisive, adj penetrante; mordaz; tajante, incisivo.

incisor, n incisivo m.

incite, vt incitar, estimular, provocar.

inclemency, n inclemencia f; intemperie f.

inclination, n 1. inclinación f; 2. propensión f.

incline, n 1. cuesta f, pendiente f; 2. vi inclinarse.

inclined, adj inclinado.

include, vt incluir; comprender, contener, encerrar.

including, prep incluso, inclusive, con inclusión de.

inclusive, adj inclusivo, completo.

incognito, adv de incógnito.

incoherent, adj incoherente, inconexo; ininteligible.

incombustible, adj incombustible.

income, n ingresos m, renta f, entrada f.

incoming, adj entrante, nuevo.

incommunicado, adj incomunicado.

incompatible, adj incompatible (con).

incompetence, n incompetencia f, inhabilidad f.

incompetent, adj incompetente, inhábil, incapaz.

incomplete, adj incompleto, sin terminar.

inconceivable, adj inconcebible.

inconclusive, adj poco concluyente.

incongruous, adj incongruo; disonante.

inconsequential, adj inconsecuente.

inconsiderable, adj insignificante.

inconsiderate, adj desconsiderado.

inconsistent, adj inconsecuente; incongruo; anómalo.

inconsolable, adj inconsolable.

inconspicuous, adj apenas visible, discreto,

inconstant, adj inconstante, mudable, veleidoso.

incontestable, adj incontestable.

incontinence, n incontinencia f.

incontrovertible, adj incontrovertible.

inconvenience, n 1. incomodidad f, molestia f, inconvenientes m; 2. vt incomodar, molestar.

inconvenient, adj incómodo, poco práctico, molesto.

incorporate, vt incorporar; incluir; comprender.
incorporation, n incorporación f; inclusión f.
incorrect, adj incorrecto, erróneo, inexacto.
incorrigible, adj incorregible.
incorruptible, adj incorruptible; insobornable .
increase, n 1. aumento m, incremento m (de); crecimiento m; 2. vt aumentar, 3. vi acrecentarse.
increasing, adj creciente.
incredible, adj increíble.
incredulous, adj incrédulo.
increment, n aumento m, incremento m.
incriminate, vt acriminar, incriminar.
incrimination, n acriminación f, incriminación f.
incrustation, n incrustación f; costra f.
incubate, vt 1. empollar, incubar; 2. vi incubarse.
incubator, n incubadora f.
inculcate, vt inculcar (en).
incumbent, adj incumbir a uno (hacer).
incur, vt incurrir en; contraer.
incurable, adj incurable; irremediable.
incursion, n incursión f, invasión f.
indebted, adj endeudado; estar en deuda con uno.
indebtedness, n endeudamiento m, deuda f.
indecent, adj indecente.
indecipherable, adj indescifrable.
indecisive, adj irresoluto, indeciso, vacilante.
indecorous, adj indecoroso.
indeed, adv en efecto; en verdad que ...
indefensible, adj indefendible; insostenible.
indefinable, adj indefinible.
indefinite, adj impreciso, indefinido; incierto.
indelible, adj indeleble, imborrable.
indelicacy, n indecoro m, falta f de decoro.
indelicate, adj indecoroso, inoportuno.
indemnification, n indemnización f.
indemnify, vt indemnizar, resarcir.
indent, vt endentar, mellar; sangrar.
indentation, n mella f, muesca f; sangría f.
indenture, n 1. escritura f, instrumento m; 2. vt obligar por contrato.
independence, n independencia f.
independent, adj independiente.
in-depth, adj a fondo, exhaustivo.
indescribable, adj indescriptible; indecible.
indestructible, adj indestructible.
indeterminate, adj indeterminado.
index, n 1. índice m; 2. vt poner índice a.
indicate, vt indicar.
indication, n indicación f, indicio m, señal f.
indict, vt acusar, encausar, procesar.
indictment, n acusación f, procesamiento m.
indifferent, adj indiferente; desinteresado, imparcial.
indigenous, adj indígena (de).
indigent, adj indigente.
indigestible, adj indigesto; indigerible.
indigestion, n indigestión f, empacho m.
indignant, adj indignado.
indignation, n indignación f; m de protesta.
indignity, n indignidad f; ultraje m, afrenta f.
indirect, adj indirecto.
indiscernible, adj imperceptible.
indiscreet, adj indiscreto, imprudente.
indiscretion, n indiscreción f, imprudencia f.
indiscriminate, adj indistinto, sin distinción.
indispensable, adj indispensable, imprescindible.
indisposed, adj estar indispuesto.
indisposition, n indisposición f, enfermedad f.
indisputable, adj incontestable, incuestionable.
indissoluble, adj indisoluble, irrompible.

indistinct, adj indistinto; confuso.
individual, adj individual; personal; particular.
individualize, vt individuar, individualizar.
indivisible, adj indivisible.
indoctrinate, vt adoctrinar (en).
indoctrination, n adoctrinamiento m, adoctrinación f.
indolence, n indolencia f, pereza f.
indolent, adj indolente, perezoso.
indomitable, adj indómito, indomable.
indoor, adj interior; de puertas adentro.
indubitable, adj indudable.
induce, vt inducir; producir, ocasionar.
inducement, n incentivo m, aliciente m, estímulo m.
induct, vt instalar; iniciar.
indulgence, n satisfacción f, gratificación f.
indulgent, adj indulgente.
industrialist, n industrial m.
industrialize, vt industrializar.
industrious, adj trabajador, laborioso; aplicado, diligente.
industry, n industria f.
inedible, adj incomible, no comestible.
ineducable, adj ineducable.
ineffable, adj inefable.
ineffaceable, adj imborrable.
ineffective, adj ineficaz, inútil; incapaz.
ineffectual, adj ineficaz, inútil.
inefficacy, n ineficacia f.
inefficient, adj ineficaz, ineflciente; incapaz, incompetente.
inelegant, adj inelegante, poco elegante.
inept, adj inepto; person incompetente, incapaz.
inequality, n desigualdad f.
inequity, n injusticia f.
inert, adj inerte, inactivo; inmóvil.
inertia, n inercia f, inacción f; pereza f.
inescapable, adj ineludible.
inestimable, adj inapreciable, inestimable.
inevitable, adj inevitable, ineludible; forzoso.
inexact, adj inexacto.
inexcusable, adj imperdonable.
inexhaustible, adj inagotable.
inexorable, adj inexorable, implacable.
inexpensive, adj económico; barato.
inexperienced, adj inexperto, falto de experiencia.
inexplicable, adj inexplicable.
infallible, adj infalible; indefectible.
infamous, adj infame.
infamy, n infamia f.
infancy, n infancia f; menor edad f.
infant, n infante m.
infantile, adj infantil.
infantry, n infantería f.
infantryman, n soldado m de infantería; infante m.
infatuated, adj encaprichado por.
infect, vt infectar, contagiar.
infection, n infección f, contagio m.
infectious, adj contagioso, infeccioso.
infelicitous, adj poco feliz, inoportuno, impropio.
infer, vt deducir, colegir, inferir (de).
inference, n deducción f, inferencia f, conclusión f.
inferior, adj inferior (a).
inferiority, n inferioridad f.
infernal, adj infernal; maldito.
inferno, n infierno m.
infertile, adj estéril, infecundo.
infest, vt infestar.
infidel, adj 1. infiel, pagano, descreído; 2. n infiel m/f.
infidelity, n infidelidad f.

infiltrate, *vt* infiltrarse en.

infinite, *adj* infinito; inmenso, enorme.

infinitive, *adj* infinitivo.

infinity, *n* infinito *m;* infinidad *f.*

infirm, *adj* enfermizo, achacoso, débil.

infirmary, *n* hospital *m;* enfermería *f.*

infirmity, *n* debilidad *f;* enfermedad *f,* achaque *m.*

inflammable, *adj* inflamable; explosivo.

inflammation, *n* inflamación *f.*

inflate, *vt* hinchar, inflar.

inflation, *n* inflación *f.*

inflect, *vt* torcer; doblar; modular.

inflection, *n* inflexión *f.*

inflexible, *adj* inflexible.

inflict, *vt* infligir, inferir; imponer.

influence, *n* 1. influencia *f,* influjo *m* (sobre); ascendiente *m;* 2. *vt* influir en, influenciar.

influential, *adj* influyente, prestigioso.

influenza, *n* gripe *f.*

inform, *vt* 1. informar; avisar; comunicar; 2. *vr* informarse sobre algo.

informal, *adj* afable, poco ceremonioso.

informant, *n* informante *m/f.*

informative, *adj* informativo.

infraction, *n* infracción *f,* violación *f.*

infra-red, *adj* infrarrojo.

infrastructure, *n* infraestructura *f.*

infrequency, *n* infrecuencia *f,* rareza *f.*

infrequent, *adj* poco frecuente, infrecuente, raro.

infringe, *vt* infringir, vulnerar, violar.

infringement, *n* infracción *f,* violación *f.*

infuriate, *vt* enfurecer, poner rabioso.

infuse, *vt* infundir (a).

infusion, *n* infusión *f.*

ingenious, *adj* ingenioso, inventivo.

ingenuity, *n* ingeniosidad *f,* inventiva *f,* habilidad *f.*

ingenuous, *adj* ingenuo, candoroso.

ingest, *vt* ingerir.

ingestion, *n* ingestión *f.*

ingratitude, *n* ingratitud *f,* desagradecimiento *m.*

ingredient, *n* ingrediente *m,* componente *m.*

ingress, *n* ingreso *m,* entrada *f.*

inhabit, *vt* habitar; vivir en; ocupar.

inhabitant, *n* habitante *m.*

inhalation, *n* aspiración *f;* inhalación *f.*

inhalator, *n* inhalador *m.*

inhale, *vt* aspirar; inhalar.

inherent, *adj* inherente, innato, inmanente.

inherit, *vt* heredar.

inheritance, *n* herencia *f;* patrimonio *m,* legado *m.*

inhibit, *vt* inhibir, impedir, imposibilitar.

inhibition, *n* inhibición *f.*

inhospitable, *adj* inhospitalario.

inhuman, *adj* inhumano.

inhumane, *adj* inhumano.

inhumanity, *n* inhumanidad *f.*

inimitable, *adj* inimitable.

iniquity, *n* iniquidad *f;* perversidad *f.*

initial, *adj* 1. inicial; primero; 2. *n* inicial *f,* letra *f* inicial; 3. *vt* marcar con sus iniciales.

initiate, *n* 1. iniciado(a) *m/f;* 2. *vt* iniciar, empeza.

initiation, *n* iniciación *f;* principio *m,* comienzo *m.*

initiative, *n* iniciativa *f.*

inject, *vt* inyectar; injertar, introducir.

injection, *n* inyección *f.*

injudicious, *adj* imprudente, indiscreto.

injunction, *n* mandato *m;* entredicho *m;* interdicto *m.*

injure, *vt* 1. herir, hacer daño a, lastimar; lesionar; 2. *vr* hacerse daño, lesionarse.

injured, *adj* herido; lesionado.

injury, *n* herida *f,* lesión *f.*

injustice, *n* injusticia *f.*

ink, *n* tinta *f.*

inkling, *n* indicio *m;* sospecha *f.*

inland, *adj* interior; del interior.

inlet, *n* ensenada *f;* cala *f,* entrante *m.*

inmate, *n* habitante *m/f,* ocupante *m/f,* residente *m/f;* internado(a) *m/f;* preso(a) *m/f.*

inn, *n* posada *f,* hostería *f,* mesón *m.*

innate, *adj* innato.

inner, *adj* interior, interno.

innkeeper, *n* posadero(a) *m/f,* mesonero(a) *m/f.*

innocence, *n* inocencia *f.*

innocent, *adj* inocente (de); honesto.

innocuous, *adj* innocuo, inofensivo.

innovate, *vi* introducir novedades.

innovation, *n* innovación *f,* novedad *f.*

innuendo, *n* indirecta *f,* insinuación *f.*

innumerable, *adj* innumerable.

inoculate, *vt* inocular (contra, de).

inoculation, *n* inoculación *f.*

inoffensive, *adj* inofensivo.

inoperable, *adj* inoperable.

inopportune, *adj* inoportuno.

inordinate, *adj* desmesurado, excesivo, desmedido.

inorganic, *adj* inorgánico.

input, *n* 1. contribución *f,* aportación *f;* inversión *f;* (Elect) entrada *f;* 2. *vt* introducir, entrar.

inquest, *n* investigación *f,* pesquisa *f* judicial.

inquire, *vt* 1. preguntar; informarse de, pedir informes sobre; 2. *vi* preguntar.

inquiry, *n* pregunta *f;* petición de informes, interrogación *f.*

inquisition, *n* investigación *f,* inquisición *f.*

inquisitive, *adj* inquiridor, curioso; preguntón.

inroad, *n* incursión *f,* irrupción *f;* invasión *f.*

inrush, *n* irrupción *f,* afluencia *f.*

insane, *adj* loco, demente; insensato.

insanity, *n* locura *f,* demencia *f.*

insatiable, *adj* insaciable.

inscribe, *vt* inscribir; dedicar.

inscription, *n* inscripción *f;* dedicatoria *f.*

inscrutable, *adj* inescrutable, enigmático.

insect, *n* insecto *m.*

insecticide, *n* insecticida *m.*

insecure, *adj* inseguro.

inseminate, *vt* inseminar.

insemination, *n* inseminación *f,* fecundación *f.*

insensitive, *adj* insensible (a).

insensitivity, *n* insensibilidad *f.*

inseparable, *adj* inseparable, indisoluble.

insert, *n* 1. cosa *f* insertada; hoja *f* suelta; 2. *vt* insertar, intercalar.

insertion, *n* inserción *f;* introducción *f.*

inset, *n* 1. grabado *m;* 2. *vt* insertar; imprimir.

inside, *adv* dentro; hacia dentro; por dentro.

insider, *n* persona *f* enterada.

insidious, *adj* insidioso; pernicioso; maligno.

insight, *n* penetración *f,* perspicacia *f,* intuición *f.*

insignia, *n* insignias *f.*

insignificant, *adj* insignificante.

insincere, *adj* poco sincero, insincero, nada franco.

insinuate, *vt* 1. insinuar, introducir; 2. *vr* insinuarse.

insinuation, *n* insinuación *f,* introducción *f.*

insipid, *adj* insípido, soso, insulso.

insist, *vt* 1. insistir; 2. *vi* porfiar, persistir.

insistent, *adj* insistente; porfiado, persistente.

insole, *n* plantilla *f.*

insolence, n insolencia f, descaro m, atrevimiento m.

insolent, adj insolente, descarado, atrevido.

insoluble, adj insoluble.

insomniac, adj insomne.

inspect, vt inspeccionar, examinar.

inspection, n inspección f, examen m; registro m.

inspector, n inspector(a) m/f.

inspiration, n inspiración f.

inspire, vt inspirar.

inspiring, adj inspirador.

instability, n inestabilidad f.

install, vt 1. instalar; 2. vr instalarse.

installation, n instalación f.

installment, n entrega f; plazo m.

instance, n ejemplo m; caso m.

instant, adj 1. inmediato, instantáneo; 2. n instante.

instantaneous, adj instantáneo.

instead, adv en cambio, en lugar de eso.

instigate, vt instigar.

instill, vt infundir, inculcar.

instinct, n instinto m.

instinctive, adj instintivo.

institute, n 1. instituto m; 2. vt instituir, establecer.

institution, n institución f, establecimiento m.

institutionalize, vt reglamentar; institucionalizar.

instruct, vt instruir (de, en, sobre); enseñar a uno.

instruction, n 1. instrucción f, enseñanza f; 2. orden f.

instructor, n instructor(a) m/f, profesor(a) m/f.

instrument, n instrumento m.

instrumental, adj instrumental.

insubordinate, adj insubordinado, desobediente.

insubordination, n insubordinación f.

insubstantial, adj insustancial.

insufferable, adj insufrible, inaguantable.

insufficient, adj insuficiente.

insular, adj insular; de miras estrechas.

insulate, vt aislar (de).

insulation, n aislamiento m.

insulator, n aislante m, aislador m.

insulin, n insulina f.

insult, n 1. insulto m, injuria f; 2. vt insultar, injuriar.

insulting, adj insultante, injurioso; ofensivo.

insupportable, adj insoportable.

insurance, n seguro m.

insure, vt 1. asegurar (contra); 2. vi asegurarse (contra).

insurgent, adj insurrecto, insurgente.

insurrection, n sublevación f, insurrección f.

intact, adj intacto; íntegro; ileso, entero, sano.

intake, n admisión f, toma f, entrada f.

intangible, adj intangible.

integer, n entero m.

integral, adj íntegro; integral.

integrate, vt integrar; combinar en un todo.

integration, n integración f.

intellect, n intelecto m.

intellectual, adj 1. intelectual; 2. n intelectual m/f.

intelligence, n inteligencia f.

intelligent, adj inteligente.

intelligensia, n intelectualidad f.

intelligible, adj inteligible, comprensible.

intemperance, n intemperancia f, inmoderación f.

intemperate, adj intemperante, inmoderado.

intend, vt intentar; tener intención de, querer decir, proponerse.

intense, adj intenso; muy grande, sumo, enorme.

intensify, vt intensificar; aumentar, reforzar f.

intensity, n intensidad f; fuerza f; exageración f.

intensive, adj intensivo; course intensivo, concentrado.

intent, adj 1. absorto; atento 2. n propósito m, intento m.

intention, n intención f; intento m, propósito m.

intentional, adj intencional, deliberado.

interact, vi obrar recíprocamente; interactuar.

interaction, n interacción f, acción f recíproca.

interbreed, vt 1. cruzar; 2. vi cruzarse.

intercalate, vt intercalar.

intercede, vi interceder.

intercept, vt interceptar; detener; cortar.

interception, n interceptación f.

intercession, n intercesión f, mediación f.

interchange, n intercambio m, cambio m; canje m.

interchangeable, adj intercambiable.

intercourse, n trato m, relaciones f, comercio m.

interest, n interés m; gran interés m.

interested, adj interesado m.

interfere, vi intervenir, entrometerse, mezclarse.

interference, n intervención f, intromisión f.

interior, adj interior, interno.

interject, vt interponer.

interjection, n interposición f.

intermittent, adj intermitente.

interminable, adj inacabable, interminable.

intermission, n intermisión f; intervalo m.

interlude, n intervalo m; interludio m.

intern, n 1. interno de hospital; 2. vt internar.

internal, adj interno, interior.

internalize, vt interiorizar.

international, adj internacional.

interpret, vt interpretar; traducir.

interpretation, n interpretación f; traducción f.

interpreter, n intérprete m/f.

interrogate, vt interrogar.

interrogation, n interrogación f.

interrogative, adj interrogativo.

interrupt, vt/i interrumpir.

interruption, n interrupción f.

intersect, vt cruzar, cortar.

intersection, n intersección f, cruce m.

interstate, adj interestatal; autopista f.

interval, n intervalo m.

intervene, vi intervenir; tomar parte, participar.

intervention, n intervención f.

interview, n 1. entrevista f; 2. vt entrevistar.

intertwine, vt 1. entrelazar; 2. vi entretejerse.

intestinal, adj intestinal.

intestine, n intestino m.

intimacy, n intimidad f.

intimate, vt dar a entender, indicar, intimar.

intimidate, vt intimidar, acobardar, amedrentar.

intimidation, n intimidación f.

into, prep en; a; dentro de; hacia el interior de.

intolerable, adj intolerable, inaguantable.

intolerance, n intolerancia f, intransigencia f.

intone, vt entonar; salmodiar.

intoxicate, vt embriagar.

intoxicated, adj ebrio, borracho.

intoxication, n embriaguez f, intoxicación f.

intractable, adj person intratable; difícil de trabajar.

intransigent, adj intransigente.

intransitive, adj intransitivo, neutro.

intravenous, adj intravenoso.

intravenously, adv por vía intravenosa.

intrepid, adj intrépido.

intricate, adj intrincado; complejo.

intrigue, n 1. intriga f; amoríos m; 2. vt intrigar, interesar.

intrinsic, adj intrínseco.

introduce, vt introducir, meter, insertar.

introduction, n introducción f, inserción f.

introductory, adj preliminar.

introspection, n introspección f.

introspective, adj introspectivo.

introvert, adj 1. introvertido; 2. n introvertido(a) m/f.

introverted, adj introvertido.

intrude, vt 1. meter en; 2. vi entrmeterse, estorbar.

intrusion, n intrusión f; invasión f.

intuit, vt intuir.

intuition, n intuición f.

inundate, vt inundar.

inundation, n inundación f.

invade, vt invadir.

invalid, adj 1. inválido, nulo; 2. n inválid(a)o m/f, enfermo(a) m/f, minusválido(a) m/f.

invalidate, vt invalidar, anular, quitar valor a.

invariable, adj invariable, inalterable.

invasion, n invasión f.

invective, n invectiva f; improperios m.

inveigh, vi vituperar, hablar en contra de, condenar.

invent, vt inventar; idear.

invention, n invención f, invento m.

inventor, n inventor(a) m/f.

inventory, n inventario m.

inverse, adj inverso.

inversion, n inversión f.

invert, n azúcar m invertido.

invertebrate, adj invertebrado.

invest, vt 1. invertir (en); 2. investir a uno.

investigate, vt investigar; examinar, estudiar.

investigation, n investigación f; pesquisa f.

investment, n 1. inversión f; inversiones f, fondos m invertidos; 2. investidura f.

investor, n inversionista m/f.

inveterate, adj inveterado, empedernido, habitual.

invidious, adj odioso, injusto.

invigorate, vt vigorizar; avivar, estimular.

invigorating, adj vigorizante, vigorizador.

invincible, adj invencible.

inviolate, adj inviolado.

invisibility, n invisibilidad f.

invisible, adj invisible.

invitation, n invitación f; convite m.

invite, n 1. invitación f; 2. vt invitar, convidar;

inviting, adj atractivo, atrayente, tentador.

invocation, n invocación f.

invoice, n 1. factura f; 2. vt facturar.

invoke, vt invocar; suplicar, implorar.

involuntary, adj involuntario.

involve, vt enredar, enmarañar.

inward, adj interior, interno; íntimo; espiritual.

inward(s), adv hacia dentro, para dentro.

iodine, n yodo m.

ion, n ion m.

ionize, vt ionizar.

ionosphere, n ionosfera f.

iota, n iota f; jota f.

irate, adj colérico, enojada, indignado.

iridium, n iridio m.

iris, n iris m; lirio m.

irk, vt fastidiar, molestar.

irksome, adj molesto, pesado, fastidioso.

iron, n 1. hierro m, fierro m; (clothing) plancha f; 2. vt planchar.

ironic(al), adj irónico.

ironing, n planchado m.

ironworks, n herrería f, fundición f.

irony, n ironía f.

irradiate, vt irradiar.

irradiation, n irradiación f.

irrational, adj irracional.

irreconcilable, adj irreconciliable, inconciliable.

irrecoverable, adj irrecuperable, incobrable.

irredeemable, adj irredimible; perpetuo.

irreducible, adj irreducible.

irrefutable, adj irrefutable, irrebatible.

irregular, adj irregular; anormal; desigual.

irregularity, n irregularidad f; anormalidad f.

irrelevant, adj impertinente, inoportuno, inaplicable.

irreligious, adj irreligioso.

irremediable, adj irremediable.

irremovable, adj inamovible.

irreparable, adj irreparable.

irreplaceable, adj insustituible, irreemplazable.

irrepressible, adj incontrolable, irrefrenable.

irreproachable, adj irreprochable, intachable.

irresistible, adj irresistible.

irresolute, adj irresoluto, indeciso.

irrespective, prep aparte de, sin consideración a.

irresponsibility, n irresponsabilidad f.

irresponsible, adj irresponsable, poco serio.

irretrievable, adj irrecuperable; irreparable.

irreverence, n irreverencia f; falta f de respeto.

irreverent, adj irreverente, irrespetuoso.

irreversible, adj irreversible; decision irrevocable.

irrevocable, adj irrevocable.

irrigate, vt regar; irrigar.

irrigation, n riego m; irrigación f.

irritability, n irritabilidad f.

irritant, n irritante m.

irritate, vt irritar, sacar de quicio, impacientar.

irritation, n irritación f, enojo m.

irruption, n irrupción f.

island, n isla f.

islander, n isleño(a) m/f.

isobar, n isobara f.

isolate, vt aislar.

isolated, adj aislado, apartado.

isometric, adj isométrico.

isosceles, adj triángulo m isósceles.

isotope, n isótopo m.

issue, n 1. resultado m, consecuencia f; 2. cuestión f, asunto m, problema m, 3. emisión f; edición f, tirada f; número m; 4. vt emitir; poner en circulación.

isthmus, n istmo m.

it, pron el, ella, ello; lo, la; le.

italicize, vt poner en bastardilla.

italics, n bastardilla f, cursiva f.

itch, vi picar.

itching, n picazón f, comezón f.

itchy, adj sentir comezón.

item, n artículo m; objeto m; partida f.

itinerant, adj ambulante.

itinerary, n ruta f, itinerario m; guía f.

itself, pron él mismo, ella misma, ello mismo.

ivory, n marfil m.

ivy, n hiedra f.

J

J, j, n (letra f) J, j.

jab, n 1. pinchazo m; codazo m; golpe m; 2. vt hurgonear; dar un codazo a; golpear.

jabber, n 1. farfulla f; 2. vi farfullar.

jack, n gato m.

jackal, n chacal m; paniaguado m, secuaz m.

jackboot, n bota f de montar, bota f militar.

jacket, n chaqueta f, americana f, saco m.

jackhammer, n taladradora f, martillo m picador.

jack-in-the-box, n caja f sorpresa, caja f de resorte.

jack plug, n enchufe m de clavija.

jackpot, n bote m; premio m gordo.

jack rabbit, n liebre f grande.

jacks, n cantillos m.

jade, adj 1. verde jade; 2. n jade m; 3. mujerzuela f.

jaded, adj cansado, hastiado.

jag, n punta f, púa f; diente m.

jagged, adj dentado, mellado, desigual.

jaguar, n jaguar m.

jail, n 1. cárcel f; 2. vt encarcelar.

jailer, n carcelero m.

jalopy, n cacharro m, armatoste m.

jam, n 1. mermelada f; 2. atasco m, obstrucción f; 3. vt atascar, obstruir; cerrar.

jamb, n jamba f.

jamboree, n francachela f, juerga f.

jamming, n interferencia f.

jam-packed, adj atestado, lleno a rebosar.

janitor, n portero m, conserje m; bedel m.

January, n enero m.

jar, n 1. tarro m, pote m; frasco m; jarra f; 2. sacudida f; choque m; vibración f; 3. vt tocar; mover; sacudir, hacer vibrar.

jargon, n jerigonza f; jerga f.

jasmine, n jazmín m.

jasper, n jaspe m.

jaundiced, adj desilusionado.

jaunt, n excursión f (corta); viajecito m.

jaunty, adj garboso, airoso; alegre; desenvuelto.

javelin, n jabalina f.

jaw, n 1. mandíbula f; quijada f; 2. vi charlar; cacharrear.

jawbone, n mandíbula f, maxilar m.

jay, n arrendajo m.

jazz, n 1. jazz m, palabrería f, disparates m; 2. vt sincopar; animar, avivar, exagerar.

jazz band, n orquesta f de jazz.

jealous, adj celoso; envidioso.

jealousy, n celos m; envidia f.

jeans, n (pantalones m) vaqueros m, tejanos m.

jeep, n yip m.

jeer, n 1. mofa f, befa f, grito m de sarcasmo; 2. vt mofarse de; 3. vi befar.

Jehovah, n Jehová m.

jell, vi convertirse en jalea, cuajar.

jelly, n jalea f, gelatina f.

jeopardize, vt arriesgar, poner en peligro.

jerk, n 1. tirón m, sacudida f; espasmo m muscular; 2. pelmazo m, memo m; 3. vt sacudir, tirar bruscamente.

jersey, n jersey m.

jest, n 1. chanza f, broma f; chiste m; 2. vi bromear.

jester, n bufón m.

Jesus, n Jesús; m, Jesucristo m.

jet, n 1. chorro m; surtidor m; mechero m; 2. vt lanzar en chorro; 3. vi chorrear.

jetty, n malecón m, muelle m, embarcadero m.

Jew, n judío(a) m/f.

jewel, n joya f, alhaja f.

jeweler, n joyero m; joyería f.

jewelry, n joyas f, alhajas.

jib, n foque m; aguilón m, brazo m.

jibe, n 1. pulla f; dicterio m; 2. vi mofarse.

jiffy, n instante m; momento m.

jigsaw, n 1. sierra f de vaivén; 2. rompecabezas m.

jingle, n 1. tintineo m, retintín m, cascabeleo m; 2. vi tintinear, retiñir, cascabelear.

jitters, n inquietud f, nerviosismo m.

jittery, adj muy inquieto, nervioso.

job, n trabajo m, tarea f; empleo m, oficio m.

jobber, n corredor(a) m/f, intermediario(a) m/f.

jobless, adj 1. sin trabajo; 2. desocupado.

jockey, n 1. jockey m, yóquei m; 2. vt persuadir mañosamente a uno a hacer algo.

jocose, adj alegre, de buen humor; guasón.

jocularity, n jocosidad f.

jog, n 1. empujoncito m, sacudida f (ligera; 2. trote m corto; 3. vt empujar (ligeramente), sacudir (levemente); estimular; 4. vi andar a trote corto.

join, n 1. juntura f; costura f; 2. vt unir, juntar, poner juntos; acoplar, ensamblar; 3. vi unirse, empalmar.

joint, adj 1. común; combinado; conjunto, colectivo; 2. n junta f, juntura f, unión f; ensambladura f; coyuntura f; 3. vt articular; juntar, ensamblar.

joist, n viga f; vigueta f.

joke, n 1. broma f, burla f; chiste m; 2. vi bromear, chancearse, hablar en broma; contar chistes.

joker, n bromista m/f.

jolly, adj alegre; divertido; character alegre, jovial.

jolt, n 1. sacudida f, choque m; 2. vt sacudir.

jolting, n traqueteo m.

jonquil, n junquillo m.

josh, vt tomar el pelo a.

jottings, n apuntes m.

journal, n periódico m; revista f; diario m.

journalism, n periodismo m.

journalist, n periodista m/f.

journey, n 1. viaje m; trayecto m; camino m; 2. vi viajar.

jovial, adj jovial.

joviality, n jovialidad f.

jowl, n quijada f; barba f.

joy, n alegría f, júbilo m, regocijo m, gozo m.

joyful, adj alegre; jubiloso, regocijado.

joyous, adj alegre.

jubilant, adj jubiloso.

jubilation, n júbilo m.

jubilee, n jubileo m.

Judaism, n judaísmo m.

judge, n 1. juez m/f; 2. vt juzgar; 3. vi opinar.

judg(e)ment, n 1. juicio m; sentencia f, fallo m; 2. opinión f, parecer m; criterio m; entendimiento m.

judg(e)mental, adj crítico.

judicial, adj judicial.

judicious, adj juicioso; prudente, sensato, acertado.

judo, n judo m, yudo m.

jug, n 1. jarro m; 2. chirona f.

juggle, vi 1. hacer juegos malabares; 2. vt falsificar.

juggler, n malabarista m/f.

jugular, n vena f yugular.

juice, n jugo m, zumo m.

juicer, n licuadora f.

juicy, adj jugoso, zumoso.

jukebox, n tocadiscos m automático, tocadiscos m.

July, n julio m.

jumbo, adj colosal, enorme; de tamaño extra.

jump, n 1. salto m, brinco m 2. alza repentina; 3. vt saltar, salvar.

jumper, n saltador(a) m/f.

jumping, n (Deporte) pruebas f de salto.

jumpsuit, n mono m.

jumpy, adj nervioso, asustadizo.

junction, n juntura f, unión f; cruce m, entronque m.

June, n junio m.

jungle, n selva f, jungla f; maraña f.

junior, adj 1. (edad) menor, más joven; (posición) subalterno; 2. n menor m/f, joven m/f; hijo m.

juniper, n enebro m.

junk, n 1. trastos m viejos; basura f; chatarra f; 2. vt echar a la basura, tirar, desechar.

junkshop, n tienda f de trastos viejos.

juridical, adj jurídico.

jurisdiction, n jurisdicción f; competencia f.

jurisprudence, n jurisprudencia f.

jurist, n jurista m/f.

juror, n jurado m (persona).

jury, n jurado m (conjunto).

just, adj 1. justo, recto, imparcial; 2. adv exactamente, precisamente.

justice, n justicia f.

justified, adj 1. justificado; 2. (margen) justificado.

justify, vt 1. justificar, vindicar; disculpar; 2. (margen) alinear, justificar.

justness, n justicia f; rectitud f.

jute, n yute m.

juvenile, adj 1. juvenil; de (o para) menores; infantil; 2. n joven m/f.

juxtapose, vt yuxtaponer.

K

K, k , n (letra f) K, k.

kafir, n cafre m/f.

kaftan, n caftán m.

kaleidoscope, n calidoscopio m.

kangaroo, n canguro m.

karate, n karate m.

kasbah, n casba(h) f.

kayak, n kayac m.

kebab, n kebab m, pincho m (moruno), broqueta f; brocheta f.

keel, n 1. quilla f; 2. vi zozobrar, dar de quilla, volcar(se).

keen, adj afilado; penetrante, agudo; astuto.

keep, vt 1. n, manutención f, subsistenca f; 2. vi quedar(se), permanecer; seguir, continuar.

keeper, n guardabosque m; conservador(a) m/f.

keg, n barrilete m, cunete m.

kelp, n quelpo m.

kennel, n perrera f, caseta f de perro; jauría f.

kerchief, n pañuelo m, pañoleta f.

kernel, n almendra f; núcleo m, meollo m.

kerosene, n keroseno m, queroseno m, querosén m.

ketch, n queche m.

ketchup, n salsa f de tomate, catsup m.

key, n 1. llave f; tecla f; clave f; 2. vt enchavetar, acuñar; templar, afinar; teclear.

keyboard, n teclado m.

keyhole, n ojo m de la cerradura.

keynote, n tónica f; idea f fundamental.

keypad, n teclado m numérico.

key-ring, n llavero m.

keystone, n piedra f clave; piedra f angular.

keyword, n palabra f clave.

kick, n 1. patada f, puntapié m; queja f; 2. vt dar un puntapié a; 3. vi quejarse; cocear.

kid, n 1. cabrito(a) m/f; 2. chiquillo(a) m/f; 3. vt tomar el pelo a; 4. vi bromearse.

kiddy, n chiquillo(a) m/f.

kidnap, vt secuestrar, raptar.

kidnapper, n secuestrador(a) m/f, raptor(a) m/f.

kidnapping, n secuestro m, rapto m.

kidney, n riñón m.

kill, vt 1. matar; dar muerte a; asesinar; 2. vr matarse.

killer, n matador(a) m/f; asesino(a) m/f.

killing, adj 1. que mata, mortal; 2. irresistible; divertidísimo; 3. n matanza f; ascesinato m.

kiln, n horno m.

kilo, n kilo m.

kilogram(me), n kilo(gramo) m.

kilometer, n kilómetro m.

kilowatt, n kilovatio m.

kilt, n falda f escocesa.

kimono, n quimono m, kimono m.

kin, n familia f, parientes m, parentela f.

kind, n 1. bondadoso; amable, bueno; 2. n clase f, género m, especie f.

kindergarten, n jardín m de infancia.

kindle, vt 1. encender; 2. vi encenderse.

kindliness, n bondad f, benevolencia f.

kindling, n leña f menuda, astillas f.

kindly, adj 1.bondadoso, benévolo; bueno, benigno; 2. adv bondadosamente, amablemente.

kindness, n bondad f, amabilidad f.

kindred, adj 1. emparentado; afín, semejante, análogo; 2. n parentesco m; familia f, parientes m.

king, n rey m.

kingdom, n reino m.

kingfisher, n martín m pescador.

king-size, adj de tamano extra, extra largo.

kink, n 1. coca f, enroscadura f; 2. vi formar cocas.

kinky, adj enroscado; rizado, ensortijado.

kinship, n parentesco m; afinidad f, relación f.

kinsman, n pariente m.

kinswoman, n parienta f.

kiosk, n quiosco m, kiosco m; cabina f.

kiss, n 1.beso m; roce m; 2. vt besar.

kit, n avíos m; equipaje m; herramientas f.

kitchen, n cocina f.

kitchenette, n cocina f pequeña.

kitchenware, n batería f de cocina.

kite, n 1. milano m rea; 2. cometa f.

kitten, n gatito(a) m/f.

klaxon, n claxon m.

kleptomania, n cleptomanía f.

knack, n tino m; maña f, destreza f.

knapsack, n mochila f.

knave, n bellaco m, bribón m.

knead, *vt* amasar, sobar; formar.

knee, *n* 1. rodilla *f;* 2. *vt* dar un rodillazo a.

kneebend, *n* flexión *f* de piernas.

kneecap, *n* rótula *f;* choquezuela *f.*

knee-deep, *adv* estar metido hasta las rodillas en.

knee-high, *adv* hasta las rodillas.

knee-joint, *n* articulación *f* de la rodilla.

kneel, *vi* arrodillarse, ponerse de rodillas.

kneepad, *n* rodillera *f.*

knife, *n* 1.cuchillo *m;* navaja *f;* cuchilla *f;* 2. *vt* acuchillar.

knifing, *n* cuchillazo *m,* navajazo *m.*

knight, *n* caballero *m.*

knit, *vi* hacer calceta, hacer media, hacer punto, tricotar.

knitting, *n* labor *f* de punto.

knob, *n* protuberancia *f,* bulto *m;* botón *m.*

knock, *n* 1. golpe *m;* choque *m;* llamada *f;* 2. *vt* golpear; 3. *vi* golpear; llamar a la puerta; martillear.

knocker, *n* aldaba *f.*

knocking, *n* golpes *m,* golpeo *m;* llamada *f.*

knot, *n* 1. nudo *m;* lazo *m;* 2. *vt* anudar, atar; 3. *vi* anudarse.

know, *vt* 1. saber, conocer; 2. *vi* reconocer, tener conocimiento de.

know-how, n saber hacer m, habilidad f, destreza *f.*

knowledge, *n* conocimiento *m.*

knowledgeable, *adj* entendido; erudito, informado.

knuckle, *n* nudillo *m.*

koala, *n* coala *f.*

kudos, *n* prestigio *m,* gloria *f.*

kummel, *n* cúmel *m.*

L

L, l, *n* (letra *f*) L, l.

lab, *n* laboratorio *m.*

label, *n* 1. etiqueta *f,* rótulo *m,* marbete *m;* 2. *vt* etiquetar, poner etiqueta a.

labial, *adj* 1. labial; 2. *n* labial *f.*

labor, *n* 1. trabajo *m;* labor *f,* faena *f,* tarea *f;* 2. *vt* trabajar, forcejar, estar de parto.

laboratory, *n* laboratorio *m.*

labored, *adj* fatigoso; torpe, penoso.

laborer, *n* peón *m;* labriego *m,* bracero *m,* peón *m,* afanador *m.*

laborious, *adj* penoso, difícil, penado.

labrador, *n* labrador *m.*

labyrinth, *n* laberinto *m.*

lace, *n* 1. encaje *m,* puntilla *f;* galón *m;* 2. cordón *m,* agujeta *f;* 3. *vt* guarnecer con encajes, atar.

lacerate, *vt* lacerar; (feelings etc) herir.

lack, *n* 1. falta *f,* ausencia *f,* carencia *f;* escasez *f;* 2. *vt* no tener; carecer de, necesitar.

laconic, *adj* lacónico.

lacquer, *n* 1. laca *f,* maque *m;* 2. *vt* laquear.

lacquered, *adj* barnizado con laca.

lactate, *vi* lactar.

lacy, *adj* de encaje; transparente, diáfano.

lad, *n* muchacho *m,* chico *m,* pibe *m,* chavo *m.*

ladder, *n* escalera *f,* escala *f.*

lading, *n* cargamento *m,* flete *m.*

lady, *n* señora *f;* dama *f.*

lag, *n* 1. retraso; 2. *vi* retrasarse; 3. *vt* revestir.

lagoon, *n* laguna *f.*

lair, *n* cubil *m,* guarida *f.*

lake, *n* lago *m.*

lamb, *n* cordero(a) *m/f;* borrego(a) *m/f,* cordero *m.*

lame, *adj* 1. cojo, lisiado; 2. poco convincente.

lament, *n* 1. lamento *m;* queja *f;* elegía *f;* 2. *vt* lamentar.

laminate, *n* 1. laminado *m;* 2. *vt* láminar.

laminated, *adj* laminado; plastificado.

lampoon, *n* 1. pasquín *m,* sátira *f;* 2. *vt* pasquinar.

lamppost, *n* farol *m,* farola *f.*

lamprey, *n* lamprea *f.*

lampshade, *n* pantalla *f* de lámpara.

lance, *n* 1. lanza *f;* 2. alancear, abrir con lanceta.

lancet, *n* lanceta *f.*

land, *adj* 1. terrestre; 2. *n* tierra *f,* región *f,* suelo *m;* 3. *vt* desembarcar; 4. aterrizar, arribar.

landfall, *n* recalada *f;* aterrada *f.*

landfill, *n* vertedero *m* de basuras.

landing, *n* desembarco *m,* desembarque.

landlord, *n* propietario *m,* dueno *m;* patrón *m.*

landmark, *n* marca *f,* señal *f* fija; mojón *m;* punto *m* destacado.

landscape, *n* 1. paisaje *m,* 2. *vt* ajardinar.

landslide, *n* corrimiento *m* de tierras.

lane, *n* vereda *f;* callejón *m;* (auto) carril *f.*

language, *n* lenguaje *m;* lengua *f,* idioma *m.*

languish, *vi* languidecer.

lanky, *adj* larguirucho, desmadejado.

lanoline, *n* lanolina *f.*

lantern, n linterna f; faro m; farol *m;* fanal *m.*

lap, *n* 1. (Anat) regazo *m;* (garment) traslapo *m;* (sport) vuelta *f;* 2. *vt* lamer, traslapar.

lapel, *n* solapa *f.*

lapidary, adj 1. lapidario; 2. n lapidario(a) m/f.

lapse, n 1. error m, desliz m, falta *f;* lapso *m;* 2. *vi* caer en el error; recaer, reincidir.

lard, *n* 1. manteca *f* de cerdo; 2. *vt* lardear, mechar.

large, *adj* grande; abultado, voluminoso; extenso; amplio.

larger, *adj* más grande, mayor; crecer.

largesse, *n* generosidad *f,* liberalidad *f.*

lariat, n lazo m.

lark, n alondra f; broma *f,* travesura *f.*

larkspur, n espuela f de caballero.

larva, n larva f.

laryngitis, *n* laringitis *f.*

larynx, *n* laringe *f.*

lasagna, *n* lasaña *f.*

lascivious, *adj* lascivo, lujurioso.

lasciviousness, *n* lascivia *f,* lujuria *f.*

laser, *n* 1. láser *m;* 2. rayo *m* láser.

lash, *n* 1. látigo *m,* azote *m;* tralla *f;* latigazo *m;* 2. *vt* azotar; dar latigazos a, fustigar.

lashing, *n* azotamiento *m.*

lassitude, n lasitud f.

lasso, n 1. lazo m; 2. *vt* lazar, coger con el lazo.

last, adj 1. último; final; 2. *n* último(a) *m/f;* 3. *adv* por último; 4. *vt* durar; 5. *vi* durar; perdurar.

lasting, *adj* duradero, perdurable, permanente.

latch, *n* 1. picaporte *m;* 2. *vt* cerrar con picaporte.

latchkey, *n* llavín *m.*

late, *adj* 1. tardío, atrasado; 2. fallecido, difunto, finado; 3. *adv* recién llegado.

latecomer, *n* recién llegado(a) *m/f;* llega tarde.

latent, *adj* latente.

later, *adj* 1. más tardío; más reciente; posterior; ulterior; 2. *adv* más tarde; luego.

lateral, *adj* lateral.

latest, *adj* 1. último; más reciente; 2. *adv* el último.

latex, *n* látex *m*.

lathe, *n* torno *m*.

lather, *n* 1. espuma *f*; 2. vt enjabonar; zurrar.

latin, *adj* 1. latino; 2. *n* latino(a) *m/f*; 3. (lang) Latín *m*.

latinize, *vt/i* latinizar.

latitude, *n* latitud *f*; libertad *f*.

latrine, *n* letrina *f*.

latter, *adj* más reciente; posterior; último; segundo.

lattice, *n* enrejado *m*; reja *f*, celosía *f*.

laudatory, *adj* laudatorio.

laugh, *n* 1. risa *f*; carcajada *f*; 2. *vi* reír, reírse.

laughable, *adj* ridículo, absurdo; cómico, divertido.

laughing, *adj* risueño, alegre.

laughter, *n* risa *f*, risas *f*.

launch, *n* 1. botadura *f*; lanzamiento *m*; 2. *vi* lanzar, (bote) echar al agua, comenzar.

launching, *n* botadura *f*; lanzamiento *m*, inauguración *f*.

launder, *vt* 1. lavar; 2. *vi* resistir el lavado.

laundress, *n* lavandera *f*.

laundry, *n* lavadero *m*, lavandería *f*.

laurel, *n* laurel *m*.

lava, *n* lava *f*.

lavatory, *n* excusado *m*, inodoro *m*; lavabo *m*.

lavish, *adj* profuso, abundante; lujoso.

law, *n* ley *f*; derecho *m*, jurisprudencia *f*.

lawbreaker, *n* transgresor.

lawful, *adj* legítimo, lícito, legal.

lawless, *adj* ilegal; rebelde, violento.

lawmaker, *n* legislador(a) *m/f*.

lawn, *n* césped *m*.

lawnmower, *n* cortacésped *m*, segadora *f*.

lawyer, *n* abogado(a) *m/f*.

lay, *n* 1. canción *f*; 2. *adj* laico, seglar, no experto; 3. *vt* poner, colocar, (plans) formar.

layer, *n* capa *f*; estrato *m*.

laying, *n* colocación *f*; tendido *m*; puesta *f*.

layman, *n* seglar *m*, lego *m*.

laziness, *n* pereza *f*, holgazanería *f*.

lazy, *adj* perezoso, holgazán, vago; lento.

lazybones, *n* gandul *m*, vago(a) *m/f*.

lead, *n* 1. (metal) plomo *m*; sonda *f*; 2. delantera *f*, cabeza *f*, ventaja *f*; 3. *vt* emplomar, dirigir, encabezar, sobresalir.

leader, *n* 1. líder *m/f*; caudillo *m*; 2. primero(a) *m/f*.

leadership, *n* jefatura *f*, dirección *f*; mando *m*; liderato *m*, liderazgo *m*.

leading, *adj* delantero; principal, importante; sobresaliente.

leaf, *n* 1. hoja *f*; 2. *vi* echar hojas.

leafless, *adj* sin hojas, deshojado.

leaflet, *n* folleto *m*, hoja *f* volante; prospecto *m*.

leafy, *adj* frondoso.

league, *n* liga *f*; sociedad *f*; (distancia) legua *f*.

leak, *n* 1. agujero *m*; gotera *f*; fuga *f*; 2. *vt* fugarse, gotear.

lean, *adj* 1. flaco; enjuto; magro; 2. *n* inclinación *f*.

leaning, *adj* 1. inclinado; 2. *n* inclinación *f*.

leap, *n* 1. salto *m*, brinco *m*; 2. *vt* saltar, saltar por encima de; 3. *vi* saltar, brincar, dar un salto.

learn, *vt/i* aprender; saber, enterarse de.

learner, *n* principiante *m/f*, aprendiz *m/f*; estudiante *m/f*.

learning, *n* el aprender, aprendizaje *m*, estudio *m*.

lease, *n* 1. arriendo *m*, contrato *m* de arrendamiento; 2. *vt* arrendar, tomar en arriendo; arrendar, dar en arriendo.

leaseholder, *n* arrendatario(a) *m/f*.

leash, *n* traílla *f*, cuerda *f*.

leasing, *n* alquiler *m*, arrendamiento *m*.

least, *adj* 1. menor; más pequeño; mínimo; menos importante; 2. *adv* menos; 3. *n* lo menos.

leather, *n* cuero *m*; piel *f*; gamuza *f*.

leather-bound, *adj* encuadernado en cuero,

leatherneck, *n* infante *m* de marina.

leave, *n* 1. permiso *m*; licencia *f*; 2. *vt* dejar, olvidar; legar; 3. *vi* irse, marcharse; salir.

leaven, *n* 1. levadura *f*; mezcla *f*; estímulo *m*; 2. *vt* leudar; penetrar e influenciar, servir de estímulo a.

leaving, *adj* 1. despedida; 2. *n* salida *f*.

lecher, *n* libertino *m*.

lecherous, *adj* lascivo, lujurioso.

lechery, *n* lascivia *f*, lujuria *f*.

lectern, *n* atril *m*.

lector, *n* lector(a) *m/f*.

lecture, *n* 1. conferencia *f*; clase *f*; explicación *f*; 2. *vt* sermonear; 3. *vi* dar una conferencia, dar una clase.

lecturer, *n* conferenciante *m/f*, conferencista *m/f*; profesor(a) *m/f*.

ledge, *n* repisa *f*, reborde *m*; retallo *m*.

ledger, *n* libro *m* mayor.

leech, *n* sanguijuela *f*.

leer, *n* 1. mirada *f* impúdica, mirada *f* maliciosa; sonrisa *f* impúdica; 2. *vi* mirar impúdico, mirar malicioso.

leery, *adj* cauteloso; sospechoso.

leeward, *adj* 1. a sotavento, de sotavento; 2. *adv* a sotavento.

leeway, *n* deriva *f*; libertad *f* de acción.

left, *adj* 1. izquierdo; 2. *adv* a la izquierda, hacia la izquierda; 3. *n* izquierda *f*.

left-handed, *adj* zurdo; person torpe desmañado.

leftist, *adj* 1. izquierdista; 2. *n* izquierdista *m/f*.

left-over, *adj* sobrante, restante.

left-wing, *adj* izquierdista.

leg, *n* pierna *f*; pata *f*.

legacy, *n* legado *m*; herencia *f*, patrimonio *m*.

legal, *adj* lícito, legítimo.

legalistic, *adj* legalista.

legality, *n* legalidad *f*.

legalization, *n* legalización *f*.

legalize, *vt* legalizar; autorizar, legitimar.

legate, *n* legado *m*.

legation, *n* legación *f*.

leg-bone, *n* tibia *f*.

legend, *n* leyenda *f*.

legendary, *adj* legendario.

leggings, *n* polainas *f*; pantalones *m* polainas.

legibility, *n* legibilidad *f*.

legion, *n* legión *f*.

legionary, *adj* legionario.

legionnaire, *n* legionario *m*; legionella *f*.

legislate, *vt/i* legislar.

legislation, *n* legislación *f*.

legislator, *n* legislador(a) *m/f*.

legislature, *n* cuerpo *m* legislativo, asamblea *f* legislativa.

legitimacy, *n* legitimidad *f*.

legitimate, *adj* 1. legítimo; admisible, justo; 2. *vt* legitimar.

legitimation, *n* legitimación *f*.

legroom, *n* espacio *m* para las piernas.

legume, *n* legumbre *f*; vaina *f*.

leguminous, *adj* leguminoso.

legwork, *n* trabajo *m* callejero.

leisure, *n* ocio *m*, tiempo *m* libre.

leisured, *adj* pace pausado; acomodado.

lemon, *n* limón m; limonero *m*.

lemonade, *n* limonada *f*.

lemon-grove, *n* limonar m,

lemonjuice, *n* zumo *m* de limón.

lend, *vt* prestar; dejar; dar.

lender, *n* prestador(a) *m/f;* prestamista *m/f.*

length, *n* 1. largo m, longitud *f;* eslora *f;* 2. espacio m, extensión *f*, duración *f.*

lengthen, *vt* 1. alargar, prolongar, extender; 2. *vi* alargarse, prolongarse, extenderse; crecer.

lengthy, *adj* largo, extenso; larguísimo.

lenience, *n* lenidad *f*, poca severidad *f;* indulgencia *f.*

lenient, *adj* poco severo, más bien blando; indulgente.

lens, *n* lente *f;* objetivo m, lupa *f;* cristalino *m.*

Lent, *n* cuaresma *f.*

lentil, *n* lenteja *f.*

leonine, *adj* leonino.

leopard, *n* leopardo *m.*

leotard, *n* leotardo *m.*

leper, *n* leproso(a) *m/f.*

leprosy, *n* lepra *f.*

leprous, *adj* leproso.

lesbian, *adj* 1. lesbiana; 2. *n* lesbiana *f.*

lesion, *n* lesión *f.*

less, *adj* 1. menor, inferior; inferior a; 2. menos.

lessee, n arrendatario(a) m/f, inquilino(a) *m/f.*

lessen, *vt* 1. disminuir, reducir, aminorar; 2. *vt* disminuir(se), reducirse, menguar.

lesson, *n* lección *f;* clase *f.*

lessor, *n* arrendador(a) *m/f.*

let, *n* 1. dejada *f*, let m; 2. *vt* dejar, permitir.

lethal, *adj* mortífero; mortal, letal.

lethargic, *adj* aletargado, letárgico.

lethargy, *n* letargo *m.*

let-out, *n* escapatoria *f;* cláusula *f* que incluye una escapatoria.

letter, *n* 1. letra *f;* 2. vt rotular, inscribir, estampar con letras.

letterbox, *n* buzón *m.*

letterhead, *n* membrete m, encabezamiento *m.*

lettering, *n* letras *f*, inscripción *f*, rótulo *m.*

letting, *n* arrendamiento *m.*

lettuce, *n* lechuga *f.*

leucocyte, *n* leucocito *m.*

leukemia, *n* leucemia *f.*

Levant, *n* Oriente *m* Medio.

level, *adj* 1. llano, plano; raso; a nivel, nivelado; 2. *adv* a nivel; 3. *n* nivel m; 4. *vt* nivelar, allanar; derribar.

level-headed, *adj* juicioso, sensato.

leveler, *n* persona en pro de la igualdad de derechos.

levelling-off, *n* nivelación *f.*

lever, *n* 1. palanca *f;* 2. *vt* apalancar.

leverage, *n* apalancamiento m; influencia *f;* fuerza *f;* ventaja *f.*

leveret, *n* lebrato *m.*

leviathan, *n* leviatán m; buque *m* enorme.

levitate, *vt* 1. elevar por levitación; 2. *vi* elevarse por levitación.

levitation, *n* levitación *f.*

levy, *n* 1. exacción *f;* impuesto m; sobrecarga *f*, sobretasa *f;* 2. *vt* exigir (o a), recaudar; imponer.

lewd, *adj* impúdico, obsceno.

lewdness, *n* impudicia *f*, obscenidad *f.*

lexicalize, *vt* lexicalizar.

lexicographer, *n* lexicógrafo(a) *m/f.*

lexicography, *n* lexicografía *f.*

lexicology, *n* lexicología *f.*

lexicon, *n* léxico *m.*

lexis, *n* vocabulario *m.*

liability, *n* 1. responsabilidad *f;* riesgo m; carga *f* onerosa; 2. obligaciones *f*, compromisos *m.*

liaison, *n* enlace m, conexión *f*, coordinación *f.*

liar, *n* mentiroso(a) *m/f*, embustero(a) *m/f.*

libation, *n* libación *f.*

libber, *n* liberacionista *f*, feminista *f.*

libel, *n* 1. difamación *f*, calumnia *f* (de); 2. *vt* difamar, calumniar.

liberal, *adj* liberal; generoso; abundante.

liberalization, *n* liberalización *f.*

liberalize, *vt* liberalizar,

liberate, *vt* libertar, librar; dejar escapar.

liberated, *adj* liberado.

liberation, *n* liberación *f.*

liberator, *n* libertador(a) *m/f.*

libertarian, *adj* 1. libertario, 2. *n* libertario(a) *m/f.*

libertinage, *n* libertinaje *m.*

libertine, *n* libertino *m.*

liberty, *n* libertad *f.*

librarian, *n* bibliotecario(a) *m/f.*

library, *n* biblioteca *f.*

libretto, *n* libreto *m.*

license, *n* 1. licencia *f*, permiso m; autorización *f;* 2. *vt* licenciar, autorizar, dar permiso (a; para).

licensed, *adj* autorizado, licenciado.

licensee, *n* concesionario(a) *m/f*, licenciatario *m.*

licensing, *n* licenciación *f;* autorización *f;* matrícula *f.*

licentious, *adj* licencioso.

lichen, *n* liquen *m.*

licit, *adj* lícito.

lick, *n* 1. lamedura *f*, lengüetada *f;* 2. *vt* lamer; besar.

licking, *n* lamedura *f.*

lid, *n* tapa *f;* cobertera *f;* techo *m.*

lidded, *adj* con tapa, con cobertera.

lie, *n* 1. mentira *f;* 2. *vt* salir del apuro mintiendo; 3. *vi* mentir.

lieu, *n* en lugar de, en vez de.

lieutenant, *n* lugarteniente m; teniente m; teniente *m* de navío.

life, *n* n vida *f;* ser m, existencia *f;* modo *m* de vivir.

lifebelt, *n* cinturón *m* salvavidas.

lifeblood, *n* sangre *f* vital; alma *f*, nervio m, sustento *m.*

lifeboat, *n* lancha *f* de socorro; bote *m* salvavidas.

lifebuoy, *n* boya *f* salvavidas, guindola *f.*

life-cycle, *n* ciclo *m* vital.

lifguard, *n* vigilante m, salvavidas *m.*

lifeless, *adj* sin vida, muerto, exánime.

lifelike, *adj* natural, vivo.

lifeline, *n* cuerda *f* salvavidas; alma *f*, sustento *m.*

lifelong, *adj* de toda la vida.

life-saver, *n* salvador(a) *m/f*, socorrista *m/f.*

life-style, *n* estilo *m* de vida.

lifetime, *n* 1. vida *f;* una vida entera; 2. eternidad *f*, mucho tiempo *m.*

lifework, *n* trabajo *m* de toda la vida.

lift, *n* 1. alzamiento m, levantamiento m, elevación *f;* 2. viaje *m* gratuito, viaje *m* en coche ajeno, aventón m; 3. ascensor m, elevador m; montacargas m; 4. estímulo m; 5. *vt* alzar, levantar, elevar; 6. *vi* levantarse, alzarse.

lift off, *vi* despegar.

lift-off, *n* despegue *m.*

ligament, *n* ligamento *m.*

ligature, n ligadura f; ligado m.

light, n 1. luz f; lumbre f; 2. adj claro; con mucha luz; 3. vi alumbrarse, iluminarse; encenderse.

light up, vt alumbrar, iluminar

light, adj ligero; poco denso; fácil.

light bulb, n bombilla f, foco m.

lighten, vt 1. iluminar; hacer más claro; 2. aligerar, hacer menos pesado; 2. vi clarear; relampaguear.

lighter, n encendedor m, mechero m.

lighting, n iluminación f; encendimiento m; alumbrado m.

lightness, n claridad f, luminosidad f; claridad f.

liyhtning, n relámpago m, rayo m.

lightweight, adj ligero, de poco peso.

light-year, n año m luz.

like, adj 1. parecido, semejante; 2. prep parecerse a uno; 3. vt querer, tener simpatía a, tener cariño a, apreciar; gustar.

likelihood, n probabilidad f.

liken, vt comparar (con), asemejar (a).

likeness, n parecido m, semejanza f.

likewise, adv asimismo, igualmente; además.

liking, n simpatía f, cariño m.

lilac, n lila f.

lilt, n ritmo m marcado, armonía f; canción f.

lilting, adj armonioso, melodioso.

lily, n lirio m, azucena f.

limb, n miembro m; rama f.

limber, adj 1. ágil; flexible; 2. vt hacer flexible.

limbo, n limbo m; estar olvidado; quedar en un estado indeterminado, quedar sin resolver.

lime, n 1. cal f; 2. vt abonar con cal.

lime kiln, n horno m de cal.

limelight, n luz m de calcio.

limerick, n especie de quintilla jocosa.

limestone, n piedra f caliza.

limit, n 1. límite m; 2. vt limitar, restringir; 3. vr limitarse a.

limitation, n limitación f, restricción f; prescripción f.

limited, adj limitado, restringido.

limitless, adj ilimitado, sin límites.

limousine, n limosina f.

limp, n 1. cojera f; cojear; 2. vi cojear.

limpet, n lapa f; persona f tenaz.

limpid, adj límpido, cristalino, transparente; diáfano.

limpness, n flojedad f; languidez f.

limy, adj calizo.

linchpin, n pezonera f; pivote m, eje m.

linctus, n jarabe m para la tos.

linden, n tilo m.

line, n 1. cuerda f; cuerda f de tender la ropa; sedal m; 2. línea f; raya f; 3. fila f, hilera f; 4. vt rayar; surcar.

lineage, n linaje m.

lineal, adj lineal, en línea recta; descent en línea directa.

linear, adj lineal; longitud.

lined, adj arrugado; reglado; forrado, con forro.

line fishing, n pesca f con caña.

linen, n 1. lino m, hilo m; lienzo m. 2. ropa f de casa; ropa f de cama; mantelería f; 3. adj de lino.

liner, n transatlático m, vapor m de línea.

lingerie, n ropa f blanca, ropa f interior (de mujer), ropa f íntima.

lingering, adj lento; prolongado; persistente.

lingo, n lengua f, idioma m; jerga f.

lingua franca, n lengua f franca.

linguist, n 1. políglota m/f; estudiante m/f de idiomas; 2. lingüista m/f.

linguistic, adj lingüístico.

linguistician, n lingüista m/f, especialista m/f en lingüística.

liniment, n linimento m.

lining, n forro m; revestimiento m; guarnición f.

link, n 1. eslabón m; enlace m, conexión f; vínculo m; 2. vt eslabonar; acoplar; enlazar, unir, vincular.

linkage, n unión f, conexión f, enlace m.

linked, adj relacionado, vinculado.

linking verb, n verbo m copulativo.

linnet, n pardillo m (común).

lino, n n linóleo m.

linseed, n linaza f.

lint, n hilas f.

lintel, n dintel m.

lion, n león m; celebridad f.

lion cub, n cachorro m de léon.

lioness, n leona f.

lip, n labio m; pico m.

lipid, n lípido m.

lipread, vt 1. leer los labios a; 2. vi leer en los labios.

lipstick, n lápiz m labial, rojo m de labios, barra f de labios.

liquefy, vt 1. licuar, liquidar; 2. vi licuarse, liquidarse.

liqueur, n licor m.

liquid, adj 1. líquido; 2. n líquido m; líquida f.

liquidate, vt liquidar.

liquidation, n liquidación f; entrar en liquidación.

liquidity, n liquide z f; relación f de liquidez.

liquidize, vt 1. licuar, liquidar; 2. vi licuarse, liquidarse.

liquor, n bebidas f fuertes; licor m espiritoso.

lira, n lira f.

list, n 1. lista f; listado m; relación f; catálogo m; 2. vt poner en una lista; registrar, inscribir.

listen, vi escuchar, ofr, escuchar, prestar atención.

listener, n oyente m/f; radioescucha m/f, radioyente m/f.

listening, n escuchar, oir.

listless, adj lánguido, desmayado, apático.

litany, n letanía f.

literacy, n alfabetismo m, capacidad f de leer y escribir.

literary, adj literario; agente m literario.

literate, adj alfabetizado, que sabe leer y escribir.

literature, n literatura f, impresos m.

lithograph, n 1. litografía f; 2. vt litografiar.

lithographer, n litógrafo m.

lithography, n litografía f.

litigant, n litigante m/f.

litigate, vi litigar, pleitear.

litigation, n litigio m, litigación f, pleitos m.

liter, n litro m.

litter, n 1. litera f; camilla f; 2. lecho m, cama f de paja; 3. camada f, cría f, críos m.

little, adj 1. pequeño, chico; poco; escaso; 2. adv poco.

littlenes, n pequeñez f; mezquindad f.

littoral, adj 1. litoral, 2. n litoral m.

liturgical, adj litúrgico.

liturgy, n liturgia f.

livable, adj llevadero, soportable.

live, vt 1. llevar, tener, pasar; 2. vi vivir; 3. seguir viviendo.

livelihood, n vida f; sustento m.

liveliness, n vida f, vivacidad f, viveza f; energía f; animación f; alegría f.

liver, n hígado m.

liverwort, n hepática f.

liverwurst, *n* embutido *m* de hígado.

livestock, *n* ganado *m*, ganadería *f*, hacienda *f*.

livid, *adj* 1. lívido; 2. estaba furioso.

living, *adj* 1. vivo, viviente; image; 2. *n* vida *f*.

lizard, *n* lagarto *m*, lagartija *f*.

llama, *n* llama *f*.

loach, *n* locha *f*.

load, *n* 1. carga *f*; peso *m*; 2. *vt* cargar; agobiar; 3. *vi* cargar, tomar carga; 4. *vr* cargarse de.

loaded, *adj* 1. cargado; lastrado; 2. intencionado, que sugiere una contestación.

loader, *n* cargador *m*.

loaf, *n* 1. pan *m*; hogaza *f*; barra *f*; 2. *vi* haraganear, gandulear.

loafer, *n* vago m, gandul *m*; azotacalles *m*.

loan, *n* 1. préstamo *m*; empréstito *m*; 3. *vt* prestar.

loath, *vt* abominar, detestar, aborrecer; odiar.

loathing, *n* aversión *f*; aborrecimiento *m*; odio *m*.

lob, *n* 1. voleo *m* alto, lob *m*, globo *m*; 2. *vt* volear por alto; 3. *vi* volear por alto.

lobby, *n* 1. vestíbulo *m*; pasillo *m*; antecámara *f*; 2. *vi* cabildear, ejercer presión.

lobbying, *n* cabildeo *m*.

lobbyist, *n* cabildero(a) *m/f*.

lobe, *n* lóbulo *m*.

lobster, *n* langosta *f*; bogavante *m*.

local, *adj* local.

locality, *n* localidad *f*.

localize, *vt* localizar.

localized, *adj* localizado, local.

locate, *vt* colocar, establecer, ubicar.

location, *n* situación *f*, posición *f*; ubicación *f*.

loch, *n* lago *m*; ría *f*, brazo *m* de mar.

lock, *n* cerradura *f*; retén *m*, tope *m*; 2. *vt* cerrar con llave; 3. *vi* cerrarse con llave; trabarse.

lock up, *vt* 1. encerrar; encarcelar; 2. *vi* echar la llave.

locker, *n* armario *m*; cajón *m* con llave; casillero *m*.

locker-room, *n* vestuario *m*.

locksmith, *n* cerrajero *m*.

locomotion, *n* locomoción *f*.

locomotive, *adj* locomotor.

locution, *n* locución *f*.

locutory, *n* locutorio *m*.

lodestar, *n* estrella *f* polar; norte *m*.

lodestone, *n* piedra *f* imán.

lodge, *n* 1. casa *f* del guarda; 2. *vi* alojarse, hospedarse.

lodging, *n* alojamiento *m*, hospedaje *m*.

loft, *n* desván *m*; pajar *m*; galería *f*.

lofty, *adj* alto, elevado, encumbrado; grandioso.

log in, *vt* 1. meter en el sistema; 2. *vi* entrar al sistema; 3. acceder, iniciar la sesión, tomar contacto.

log off, *vt* 1. sacar del sistema; 2. *vi* salir del sistema, terminar de operar, finalizar la sesión.

logbook, *n* cuaderno *m* de bitácora, diario *m* de navegación, diario *m* de a bordo.

logger, *n* maderero *m*, negociante *m* en maderas.

logic, *n* lógica *f*; lógicamente.

logical, *adj* lógico.

logician, *n* lógico *m/f*.

logistic, *adj* logístico.

logistics, *n* logística *f*.

logo, *n* logo *m*, logotipo *m*.

loin, *n* ijada *f*; lomo *m*; s lomos *m pl*.

lollipop, *n* pirulí *m*; chupachupa *f*, piruleta *f*.

lone, *adj* solitario; único, aislado; llanero *m* solitario.

lonely, *adj* solitario, solo; aislado, remoto; desierto.

loner, *n* individualista *m/f*, solitario(a) *m/f*.

lonesome, *adj* solitario, aislado.

long, *adj* largo; de cuerpo entero, prolongado.

long-distance, *adj* servicio interurbano; race de fondo, de larga distancia, de resistencia.

longevity, *n* longevidad *f*.

longing, *adj* 1. anhelante; 2. *n* anhelo *m*, ansia *f*, deseo.

longish, *adj* bastante largo.

longitude, *n* longitud *f*.

longitudinal, *adj* longitudinal.

longways, *adv* longitudinalmente, a lo largo.

look, *n* mirada *f*; vistazo *m*, ojeada *f*; 2. buscar algo; 3. aspecto *m*, apariencia *f*; aire *m*; 4. *vt* expresar con los ojos, expresar con la mirada.

look-alike, *n* parecido(a) *m/f*.

look-out, *n* atalaya *f*, puesto *m* de observación.

look-up, *n* consulta *f*; tabla *f* de consulta.

loom, *vi* surgir, aparecer, asomarse; amenazar.

looming, *adj* que amenaza, inminente.

loop, *n* 1. lazo *m*, gaza *f*; curva *f*, vuelta *f*, recodo *m*; 2. *vt* hacer gaza con; asegurar con gaza.

loophole, *n* aspillera *f*; escapatoria *f*; pretexto *m*.

loose, *adj* 1. suelto; desatado; flojo; movible, movedizo; 2. *n* estar en libertad; 3. *vt* soltar; desatar; aflojar.

loosen, *vt* 1. soltar; desatar; aflojar; 2. *vi* soltarse; desatarse; aflojarse.

loot, *n* botín *m*; presa *f*; ganancias *f pl*, botín *m*.

looter, *n* saqueador(ora) *m/f*.

looting, *n* saqueo *m*.

lop, *vt* mochar, desmochar.

loquacious, *adj* locuaz.

loquacity, *n* locuacidad *f*.

lord, *n* 1. señor *m*; 2. el Señor; Nuestro Señor; 3. *vr* hacer el señor, mandar despóticamente.

lordliness, *n* lo señorial, carácter *m* señorial.

lordship, *n* señorío *m*.

loro, *n* saber *m* popular; ciencia *f*, tradiciones *f pl*.

lorry, *n* camión *m*.

lose, *vt* 1. perder; quedarse sin; 2. perderse, quedar perdido; ahogado; 3. dejar atrás, adelantarse a; 4. *vi* perder; ser vencido; 5. *vr* perderse, extraviarse, errar el camino.

loser, *n* perdedor(ora) *m/f*; fracasado(a) *m/f*.

losing, *adj* team vencido, derrotado; perdedor.

loss, *n* pérdida *f*; inapetencia *f*; pérdida *f* de sueldo.

lost, *adj* perdido.

lot, *n* 1. echando suertes; mediante sorteo; echar suertes para decidir quién tendrá algo; 2. porción *f*, parte *f*.

lotion, *n* loción *f*.

lottery, *n* lotería *f*.

loud, *adj* 1. voice, alto; fuerte, recio; 2. *adv* decir algo en voz alta.

loudhailer, *n* megáfono *m*, bocina *f*.

loudness, *n* lo alto; fuerza *f*; ruido *m*; lo chillón; vulgaridad *f*.

loudspeaker, *n* altavoz *m*, altoparlante *m*.

lounge, *n* 1. salón *m*, cuarto *m* de estar; 2. traje *m* de calle; 3. *vi* pasearse despacito; gandulear, pasar un rato sin hacer nada.

lounger, *n* gandul *m*, haragán(ana) *m/f*.

louse, *n* piojo *m*; canalla *m*, mierda *m*.

lousy, *adj* piojoso; malísimo, horrible.

love, *n* amor *m*; cariño *m*; aflción *f*; 2. *vt* amar, querer; tener cariño a.

loveless, *adj* sin amor.

love-letter, *n* carta *f* amorosa, carta *f* de amor.

lover, *n* amante *m/f*; amante *m/f*, querido(a) *m/f*.

loving, *adj* amoroso; cariñoso; tierno.

low, *adj* 1. bajo; temperature, voice bajo; 2. *adv* bajo, cerca de la tierra; en voz baja; 3. *n* área *f* de baja presión, depresión *f*.

lower, *adj* 1. más bajo, menos alto; inferior; clase *f* baja; 2. *adv comp* más bajo; 3. *vt* bajar.

lowering, *adj* ceñudo; amenazador; encapotado.

lowing, *n* mugidos *m pl.*

lowland, *n* tierra *f* baja.

lowness, *n* bajeza *f*, lo bajo; escasez *f*; gravedad *f*.

loyal, *adj* leal; fiel.

loyalty, *n* lealtad *f*, fidelidad *f*.

lozenge, *n* pastilla *f*.

lubricant, *adj* lubricante.

lubricate, *vt* lubricar, engrasar.

lubricating, *adj* lubricante; aceite *m* lubricante.

lubrication, *n* lubricación *f*, engrase *m*.

lubricator, *n* lubricador *m*.

lucerne, *n* alfalfa *f*.

lucid, *adj* claro, lúcido, interval intervalo *m* lúcido.

lucidity, *n* lucidez *f*.

luck, *n* suerte *f*, fortuna *f*.

luckless, *adj* desdichado, desafortunado.

lucky, *adj* afortunado, feliz, que tiene suerte.

lucrative, *adj* lucrativo, provechoso,

lucubration, *n* lucubración *f*.

ludic, *adj* lúdico.

ludicrous, *adj* absurdo, ridículo.

luff, *n* 1. orza *f*; 2. *vi* orzar.

luffa, *n* esponja *f* de lufa.

lugage, *n* equipaje *m*.

lugger, *n* lugre *m*.

lughole, *n* oreja; oído *m*.

luysail, *n* vela *f* al tercio,

lugubrious, *adj* lúgubre, triste.

lugworm, *n* lombriz *f* de mar.

lukewarm, *adj* tibio, templado; tibio.

lumbago, *n* lumbago *m*.

lumbar, *adj* lumbar.

lumber, *n* 1. maderas *m pl*, maderas *f pl*; 2. *vt* obstruir; 3. *vi* cortar y aserrar árboles, explotar los bosques.

luminary, *n* lumbrera *f*.

luminous, *adj* luminoso.

lump, *n* 1. terrón *m*; masa *f* informe; trozo *m*, pedazo *m*; 3. *vt* aguantarlo.

lunacy, *n* locura *f*.

lunar, *adj* lunar.

lunatic, *adj* lunático, loco, demente.

lunch, *n* almuerzo *m*, comida *f*.

lung, *n* pulmón *m*.

lurch, *n* 1. sacudida *f*, tumbo *m*, movimiento *m* repentino; 2. *vi* dar sacudidas, dar tumbos, dar un tumbo.

lure, *n* 1. cebo *m*; señuelo *m*; 2. *vt* atraer (con senuelo); tentar; seducir.

lurid, *adj* misterioso, fantástico.

lurk, *vi* estar escondido, estar en acecho.

lurking, *adj* vago, indefinible.

luscious, *adj* delicioso, suculento, riquísimo, exquisito.

lush, *adj* lozano, exuberante; pasture rico.

lushness, *n* lozanía *f*, exuberancia *f*.

lust, n lujuria f, lascivia f; sensualidad *f*; codicia *f*, deseo *m* vehemente.

lustful, *adj* lujurioso, libidinoso; lascivo.

lustfulness, *n* lujuria *f*, lascivia *f*; sensualidad *f*.

lustre, *n* lustre *m*, brillo *m*.

lustrous, *adj* lustroso, brillante.

lusty, *adj* person vigoroso, fuerte, robusto.

luxuriance, *n* lozanía *f*, exuberancia *f*.

luxuriant, *adj* lozano, exuberante.

luxuriate, *vi* crecer con exuberancia; disfrutar.

luxurious, *adj* lujoso.

luxury, *n* lujo *m*; artículo *m* de lujo.

lyceum, *n* liceo *m*.

lye, *n* lejía *f*.

lying , *adj* 1. mentiroso, falso; 2. *n* mentiras *f*.

lymph, *n* 1. linfa *f*; 2. ganglio *m* linfático.

lynch, *vt* linchar,

lynching, *n* linchamiento *m*.

lynx, *n* lince *m*.

lyre, *n* lira *f*.

lyrebird, *n* ave *f* lira.

lyric, *adj* 1. lírico; 2. *n* poema *m* lírico, poesía *f*.

lyrical, *adj* lírico; elocuente, entusiasta.

M

M, m, *n* (letra *f*) M, m.

ma, *n* mamá *f*.

macabre, *adj* macabro.

macadam, *n* macadám *m*.

macadamize, *vt* macadamizar.

macaroni, *n* macarrones *m*.

macareon, *n* macarrón *m*, mostachón *m*.

macaw, *n* guacamayo *m*, avacanza *m*.

mace, *n* (spice) macis *f*; maza *f*.

macerale, *vt* macerar.

machete, *n* machete *m*.

machination, *n* maquinación *f*

machine, *n* máquina *f*; aparato *m*; coche *m*.

machinery, *n* 1. maquinaria *f*; mecanismo *m*; 2. organización *f*, sistema *m*.

machinist, *n* maquinista *m/f*; operario *m* de máquina.

machismo, *n* machismo *m*.

macho, *adj* 1. macho, masculino; 2. *n* macho *m*.

mackerel, *n* caballa *f*, berdel *m*, escombro *m*.

macramé, *n* macramé *m*.

macrobiolic, *adj* macrobiótico.

macrocosmo, *n* macrocosmo *m*.

macroscopic, *adj* macroscópico.

mad, *adj* loco; demente; rabioso; furioso.

madam, *n* señora *f*.

madcap, *n* tarambana *m/f*.

madden, *vt* volver loco; enfurecer, sacar de quicio.

madhouse, *n* manicomio *m*, casa *f* de locos.

madman, *n* loco *m*.

madness, *n* locura *f*; demencia *f*; furia *f*; rabia *f*.

madrigal, *n* madrigal *m*.

madwoman, *n* loca *f*.

maelstrom, *n* vórtice *m* remolino *m*.

maestro, *n* maestro *m*.

magazine, *n* revista *f*.

magenta, *n* 1. magenta *f*; 2. *adj* (color) magenta.

maggoly, *adj* agusanado, lleno de gusanos.

magic, *adj* 1. mágico; 2. *n* magia *f*.

magician, *n* mago *m*, mágico *m*, brujo *m*; prestidigitador *m*.

magistrate, *n* magistrado(a) *m/f*; juez *m/f*.

magnanimous, *adj* magnánimo.

magnate, *n* magnate *m*; potentado *m*.

magnesia, n magnesia f.

magnesium, n magnesio m.

magnet, n imán m.

magnetic, adj magnético; atractivo.

magnetism, n magnetismo m.

magnetize, vt magnetizar, imantar.

magneto, n magneto f.

magnification, n aumento m, ampliación f.

magnify, vt aumentar; exagerar; magnificar.

magnitude, n magnitud f; magnitud f, envergadura f.

magnolia, n magnolia f.

maharajah, n maharajá m.

mahogany, n caoba f.

maid, n criada f, doncella f suvienta f.

maiden, n 1. doncella f; 2. adj virginal.

mail, n 1. correo m, cartas f, correspondencia f; 2. cota de malla; 3. vt ecbar al correo.

mailbox, n buzón m; casilla f.

mailcarrier, n cartero(a) m/f.

mailing, n envío m.

mailman, n cartero m.

maim, vt mutilar, lisiar.

main, adj 1. más importante; principal; 2. n cañería f maestra, tubería f matriz, conducción f.

mainframe, n computadora f central.

mainland, n tierra f firme, continente m.

mainmast, n palo m mayor.

mainsail, n vela f mayor.

mainspring, n muelle m real; motivo m principal.

mainslay, n estay m mayor; sostén m principal.

maintain, vt mantener, sostener, aftrmar.

maintenance, n mantenimiento m; conservación f; entretenimiento m; manutención f.

maize, n maíz m, milpa f.

majestic, adj majestuoso.

majesty, n majestad f.

major, adj 1. mayor; principal; 2. n mayor m/f de edad; 3. comandante m/f; 4. vi estudiar como asignatura principal, especializarse.

majordomo, n mayordomo m.

majority, n mayoría f.

make, n 1. marca f; tipo m, modelo m; 2. vt hacer; fabricar; construir; elaborar; 3. vi crecer, subir.

maker, n hacedor(ora) m/f, creador(ora) m/f.

makeup, n 1. ccomposición f; estructura f; carácter m, naturaleza f; 2. maquillaje m, cosméticos m.

making, n fabricación f; construcción f; formación f; creación f; confección f; preparación f.

maladjusted, adj inadaptado.

maladjustment, n inadaptación f, desajuste m.

malady, n mal m, enfermedad f.

malaria, n paludismo m, malaria f.

malcontent, adj 1. malcontento, desafecto; 2. n malcontento m desafecto m.

male, adj macho; viril, masculino.

malediction, n maldición f.

malformation, n malformación f, deformidad f.

malformed, adj malformado, deforme.

malfunction, n funcionamiento m defectuoso.

malice, n malevolencia f, mala voluntad f.

malicious, adj malévolo, maligno; rencoroso.

malign, adj 1. maligno, enconoso; 2. vt calumniar, difaunar; tratar injustamente, ser inhjusto con.

malignancy, n malignidad f.

malignant, adj maligno.

malinger, vi fingirse enfermo, hacer la encorvada.

mall, n alameda f, paseo m; centro m comercial.

mallard, n pato m real, ánade m real.

malleable, adj maleable.

mallet, n mazo m.

mallow, n malva f.

malnourished, adj desnutrido.

malnutrition, n desnutrición f.

malodorous, adj maloliente, hediondo.

malpractice, n práctica f abusiva.

malt, n malta f.

maltreat, vt maltratar, tratar mal.

maltreatment, n maltrato m, maltratamiento m.

mam(m)a, n mamá f.

mammal, n mamífero m.

mammary, adj mamario.

mammoth, adj 1. gigantesco; 2. n mamut m.

man, n hombre m.

manage, vt manejar; manipular; conducur.

management, n manejo m; durección f; gerencia f.

manager, n director(a) m/f; gerente m/f.

manatee, n manatí m.

mandarin, n mandarí m.

mandate, n 1. mandato m; territorio m bajo mandato; 2. vt asignar como mandato.

mandatory, adj obligatorio; preceptivo.

mandible, n mandíbula f.

mandolin(e), n mandolina f, bandolina f.

mandrake, n mandrágora f.

mandrill, n mandril m.

mane, n melena f; (horse) crin f, crines f.

manganese, n manganeso m.

mange, n rona f sarna f.

manger, n pesebre m .

mangle, n 1. exprimidor m; 2. vt destrozar, mutilar.

mangrove, n mangle m.

mangy, adj ronoso, sarnoso.

manhandle, vt maltratar.

manhole, n registro m inspección.

manhood, n vurilidad f; edad f viril.

mania, n manía f.

maniac, adj maníaco.

manicure, n manicura f.

manifest, adj manifiesto, evidente, patente.

manifestation, n manifestación f.

manifesto, n poclama f, manifiesto m.

manipulate, vt manipular, manejar.

manipulative, adj manipulativo.

manipulator, n manipulador(a) m/f.

mankind, n humanidad f, género m humano, los hombres.

manna, n maná m.

manned, adj tripulado.

mannequin, n maniquí m; modelo f.

manner, n manera f, modo m; costumbres f.

mannerly, adj educado, bien criado, cortés.

manor, n feudo m; seóorío m; finca f.

manpower, n mano f de obra; personal m; recursos m humanos.

mansion, n palacio m, hotel m; mansión f.

manlilla, n mantilla f, velo m.

manual, adj manual.

manufacture, n 1. fabricación f; manufactura f, producto m; 2. vt fabricar, manufacturar.

manufacturer, n fabricante m/f.

manure, n estiércol m, abono m.

manuscript, adj manuscrito.

many, adj muchos, muchas.

map, n 1. mapa m; plano m; carta f; 2. vt trazar el mapa (or plano) de, levantar el plano de.

marathon, adj 1. maratónico; 2. n maratón m.

maraud, vi merodear.

marauder, n merodeador m; intruso m.

marble, adj 1. marmóreo; 2. n mármol m, canica f.

March, n marzo m.

march, n 1. marcha f; camunata f; 2. vt hacer marchar, llevar.

margarine, n margaruna f.

margin, n margen m; reserva f; excedente m.

marginal, adj marginal; dudoso, incierto.

marina, n centro m de deportes acuáticos.

marinate, vt escabechar, marinar.

marine, adj 1. marino; marítimo; 2. n marina f.

mariner, n marinero m, marino m.

marital, adj marital; matrimonial.

maritime, adj martríuno; código m marítimo.

marjoram, n mejorana f, orégano m.

mark, n 1. marca f; llamada f; señal f, indicio m; 2. vt señalar, marcar, poner una serial en; manchar.

mark-down, n reducción f.

marker, n marcador m, registro m, señal f.

market, n 1. mercado m; 2. vt vender, poner a la venta.

marketing, n mercadeo m.

marksman, n tirador m.

marksmanship, n puntería f.

mark-up, n margen m; valor m añdido.

marlin, n aguja f.

marmot, n marmota f.

maroon, adj 1. rojo oscuro; 2. vt abandonar.

marquee, n marquesina f.

marquess, n marqués m.

marriage, n matrunonio m; casamiento m.

married, adj casado.

marrow, n médula f, tuétano m, meollo m.

marry, vt casarse con.

marsh, n pantano m, ciénaga f; marism f.--

marshal, n mariscal m.

marshland, n pantanal m.

marsupial, adj 1. marsupial; 2. n marsupial m.

mart, n emporio m; mercado m.

martial, adj marcial; castrense.

marlyr, n mártir m/f.

marlyrdom, n martirio m.

marvel, n 1. maravilla f; prodigio m; 2. vi maravillarse.

marvelous, adj maravilloso.

marzipan, n mazapán m.

mascara, n rimel m, máscara f.

mascot, n mascota f.

masculine, adj 1. masculino; varonil; 2. n masculino m.

masculinily, n masculinidad f.

mash, n 1. mezcla f pasta f, amasijo m; 2. vt mezclar; amasar, despachurrar.

mask, n 1. máscara f; antifaz m; 2. vt enmascarar.

masked, adj enmascarado; encapuchado.

masochism, n masoquismo m.

masochisl, n masoquista m/f.

mason, n albañil m; cantero m; escultor m.

masonry, albañilería f; mampostería f.

masquerade, n baile m de máscaras, mascarada f.

mass, n 1. (Eccl) misa f; 2. masa f; bulto m; macizo m; 3. vt juntar en masa, reunir.

massacre, n matanza f, carnicería f, masacre f.

massage, n 1. masaje m; 2. vt dar masaje a.

masseur, n masajista m.

masseuse, n masajista f.

massive, adj macizo, sólido; grande, abultado.

massiveness, n macicez f, solidez f.

mast, n mástil m, palo m; torre f, mástil m.

mastectomy, n (Med) mastectomía f.

master, n 1. señor m, amo m; dueño m; capitán m; 2. vt vencer, aerrotar; domunar.

masterful, adj imperioso, autoritario; dominante.

mastermind, n inteligencia f genial, cerebro m.

masterpiece, n obra f maestra.

mastery, n dominio m; autoridad f; maestría f.

masthead, n tope m.

mastic, n masilla f.

masticate, vt/i masticar.

mastiff, n mastin m.

mastitis, n mastitis f.

mastodon, n mastodonte m.

mastoid, adj mastoides.

mat, n 1. estera f, esterilla f; ruedo m; 2. vt enmarañar, entretejer.

matador, n matador m, diestro m.

match, n 1. cerilla f, fósforo m; 2. n igual m/f, pareja f; hace juego; 3. partido m; 4. vt emparejar, igualar.

matchless, adj sun par, uncomparable.

matchmaker, n casaunentero(a) m/f;

matchstick, n fósforo m.

mate, n 1. conyuge m/f, compañero; 2. (ajedrez) mate; 3. vt/i casar, dar jaque mate a.

material, adj material; unportaulte, esencial.

materialize, vt materializar.

materiel, n material m bélico.

maternal, adj materno.

maternity, n maternidad f.

mathematical, adj matemático.

mathematician, n matemático(a) m/f.

mathematics, n matemáticas f.

matinée, n función f de tarde.

mating, n (Zool) apareamiento m, acoplamiento m; unión f.

matriarch, n matriarcal f.

matriarchy, n matriarcado m.

matricide, n matricidio m.

matriculale, vt matricular.

matrimonial, adj matrimonial; conyugal.

matrimony, n matrimonio m; vida f conyugal.

matrix, n matriz f; molde m.

matron, n matrona f; supervisora f.

matter, n 1. materia f; sustancia f; material m; 2. pus m; 3. asunto m, cuestión f; cosa f; 4. vi importar.

matting, n estera f.

mattress, n colchón m.

mature, adj maduro.

maturity, n madurez f.

maudlin, adj sensiblero; llorón.

maul, vt destrozar, magullar, herir.

mausoleum, n mausoleo m.

mauve, adj (de) color de malva.

maxilla, n maxilar m superior.

maxim, n máxima f.

maximize, vt maximizar, llevar al máximum.

maximum, adj 1. máximo; 2. n máximo m, tope m.

May, n 1. mayo m; 2. vi poder, ser posible; puede ser.

maybe, adv quizá, tal vez.

mayday, n señal f de socorro, s. o. s. m.

mayhem, n alboroto m; violencia f.

mayonnaise, n mayonesa f.

mayor, n alcalde m.

mayoress, n alcaldesa f.

maypole, n mayo m.

maze, n laberinto m.

me, pron me; mí.

meadow, n prado m, pradera f; vega f.

meager, adj escaso, exiguo, pobre.

meal, n harina f; comida f.

mealtime, n hora f de comer.

mean, adj 1. tacaño; mezquino; medio; promedio; 2. vt significar, querer decir.

meander, n 1. meandro m; 2. vi serpentear.

meaning, adj 1. significativo, sentido; 2. n intención f, propsito m.

meaningful, adj significativo, que tiene sentido.

meaningless, adj sin sentido.

meantime, adv entretanto, mientras tanto.

measurable, adj que se puede medir.

measure, n 1. medida f; compás m; 2. vi medir.

measurement, n medición f.

meat, n carne f; sustancia f, meollo m, jugo m.

mealball, n albóndiga f.

mechanic, n mecánico(a) m/f.

mechanics, n mecánica f; mecanismo m, técnica f.

mechanism, n mecanismo m; mecanicismo m.

medal, n medalla f.

medallion, n medallón m.

meddle, vi entrometerse.

meddler, n entrometido(a) m/f.

median, adj mediano.

mediate, vi mediar.

mediation, n mediación f.

mediator, n mediador(a) m/f, árbitro m/f.

medical, adj 1. médico; 2. n reconocimiento m médico.

medicate, vt medicar; impregnar.

medication, n medicación f.

medicine, n medicina f; medicamento m.

medieval, adj medieval.

mediocre, adj mediocre, mediano.

mediocrity, n mediocridad f.

meditate, vi meditar.

meditation, n meditación f.

medium, adj mediano, regular; médium.

medley, n mezcla f mezcolanza f; popurrí m.

medulla, n medula f.

meek, adj manso, dócil, sumiso.

meekness, n mansedumbre f, docilidad f.

meet, vt encontrar; encontrarse con; reunirse con.

meeting, n encuentro m, cita f, compromiso m.

megahertz, n megahercio m.

megaphone, n megáfono m.

melancholy, adj melancólico.

melanin, n melanina f.

melanoma, n melanoma m.

mellifluous, adj melifluo.

mellow, adj maduro, dulce; añejo.

melodious, adj melodioso.

melodrama, n melodrama m.

melody, n melodía f.

melon, n melón m.

melt, vt fundir; derretir; disolver.

meltdown, n fusión f de un reactor, fundido m.

member, n miembro m/f.

membranle, n membraula f.

membranous, adj membranoso.

memento, n recuerdo m.

memoir, n memoria f; biografía f, autobiografía f.

memorabilia, n cosas f memorables, recuerdos m.

memorable, adj memorable.

memorandum, n memorándum m.

memorial, adj conmemorativo.

memorize, vt aprender de memoria.

memory, n memoria f.

menace, n 1. amenaza f; 2. vt amenazar.

menacing, adj amenazador.

menagerie, n casa f de fieras, colección f de fieras.

mend, n 1. remiendo m; zurcido m; 2. vt reparar, zurcir.

mendacious, adj mendaz.

mendacity, n mendacidad f.

mendicant, adj 1. mendicante; 2. n mendicante m/f.

mending, n reparación f, compostura f; zurcidura f.

menial, adj doméstico; servil; bajo.

meningitis, n meningitis f.

menopause, n menopausia f.

menstruate, vi menstruar.

menslrualion, n menstruación f.

menswear, n ropa f de caballero.

mental, adj mental.

mentality, n mentalidad f.

menthol n mentol m.

mention, n 1. mención f, alusión f; 2. citación f; 3. vt mencionar, aludir a; hablar de.

mentor, n mentor m.

menu, n carta f lista f, menú m.

meow, n 1. maullido m, miau m; 2. vi maullar.

mercantile, adj mercantil.

mercenary, adj 1. mercenario; 2. n mercenario m.

merchandise, n mercancías f, géneros m.

merchandize, vt comerciar.

merchandizing, n comercialización f.

merchant, n comerciante m, negociante m.

merciful, adj person misericordioso, compasivo.

merciless, adj despiadado.

mercury, n mercurio m.

mercy, n misericordia f compasión f, clemencia f.

mere, adj mero, simple; solo.

merge, vt 1. unir; 2. vi unirse, converger.

merger, n fusión f, concentración f.

meridian, n meridiano m; cenit m, auge m.

meringue, n merengue m.

merino, adj 1. merino; 2. n merino m.

merit, n 1. mérito m; ventaja f, bondad f; virtud f; 2. vt merecer, ser digno de.

meritorious, adj meritorio.

merlin, n esmerejón f.

mermaid, n sirena f.

merriment, n alegría f; regocijo m, alborozo m.

merry, adj alegre; regocijado; alborozado.

mesa, n colina f baja, duna f.

mesh, n 1. malla f; (gears) engrane m, engranaje m; 2. vt enredarse; 3. vi engranar (con).

mesmerize, vt mesmerizar, hipnotizar.

mesomorph, n mesomorfo m.

mess, n 1. confusión f; revoltijo m; suciedad f; 2. vt desarreglar, hacer rancho.

messenger, n mensajero(a) m/f, mandadero(a) m/f.

Messiah, n Mesías m.

messianic, adj mesiánico.

messmate, n compañero m de rancho, comensal m.

messy, adj sucio; desaseado, desaliñado.

metabolism, n metabolismo m.

metabolize, vt metabolizar.

metal, n metal m.

metallic, adj metálico.

melallurgy, n metalurgia f.

metalwork, n metalistería f.

metamorphic, adj metamórfico.

metamorphosis, n metamorfosis f.

metaphor, n metáfora f.

metaphorical, adj metafórico.

metaphysical, adj metafísico.

metaphysics, n metafísica f.

metastasis, n metástasis f.

meteor, *n* meteorito *m*, bólido *m;* meteoro *m*.

meteorite, *n* meteorito *m*, bólido *m*.

meteorologist, *n* meteorólogo(a) *m/f*.

meteorology, *n* meteorología *f*.

meter, *n* contador *m*, medidor *m*.

methane, *n* metano *m*.

method, *n* método *m*.

methodical, *adj* metódico.

meticulous, *adj* meticuloso; minucioso.

meter, *n* metro *m;* (Mus) compás *m*, tiempo *m*.

metric(al), *adj* métrico.

metronome, *n* metrónomo *m*.

metropolis, *n* metrópolis *f*.

metropolitan, *adj* metropolitano.

mettle, *n* temple *m;* ánimo *m*, valor *m*.

mezzanine, *n* entresuelo *m*.

mezzo-soprano, *n* mezzosoprano *f*.

mica, *n* mica *f*.

microbe, *n* microbio *m*.

microbiology, *n* microbiología *f*.

microchip, *n* microchip *m*, micropastilla *f*.

microcosm, *n* microcosmo *m*.

microfilm, *n* 1. microfilme *m;* 2. *vt* microfilmar.

microorganism, *n* microorganismo *m*.

microphone, *n* micrófono *m*.

microscope, *n* microscopio *m*.

microscopic(al), *adj* microscópico.

microtechnology, *n* microtecnología *f*.

microwave, *n* microonda *f*.

mid, *adj* medio.

midday, *n* mediodía *m;* a mediodía.

middle, *adj* 1. medio, central; de en medio; intermedio; 2. *n* medio *m*, centro *m*, mitad *f*.

middleweight, *n* peso *m* medio.

midget, *adj* 1. en miniatura; 2. *n* enano(a) *m/f*.

midnight, *n* medianoche f.

midpoint, *n* punto *m* medio.

midst, *n* entre, en medio de.

midstream, *n* en medio de la corriente *f*.

midway, *adv* 1. a mitad del camino; 2. *adj* situado a medio camino.

might, *n* fuerza *f*, poder *m*, poderío *m*.

mighty, *adj* 1. fuerte; potente, poderoso; 2. enorme.

migraine, *n* jaqueca *f*.

migrant, *adj* 1. migratorio; 2. *n* peregrino(a) *m/f*, inmigrante *m/f;* ave *f* de paso.

migrate, *vi* emigrar, migrar; trashumar.

mildew, *n* moho *m;* añublo *m*.

mile, *n* milla *f*.

mileage, *n* distancia *f* recorrida en millas.

milestone, *n* piedra *f* miliaria, hito *m*.

militancy, *n* militancia *f;* actitud *f* belicosa.

militant, *adj* 1. militante; belicoso, agresivo; 2. *n* militante *m/f;* activista *m/f*.

militarist, *adj* 1. militarista; 2. *n* militarista *m/f*.

militarize, *vt* militarizar.

military, *adj* militar.

militia, *n* milicia(s) *f pl*.

milk, *n* 1. leche *f;* of magnesia leche *f* de magnesia; 2. *vt* ordeñar; chupar; 3. *vi* explotar.

milking, *adj* 1. lechero de ordeño; 2. *n* ordeño *m*.

milkman, *n* lechero *m*, repartidor *m* de leche.

milkshake, *n* batido *m* de leche.

mill, *n* 1. molino *m;* molinillo *m;* 2. fábrica *f*, hilandería *f;* 3. *vt* moler; abatanar; batir.

millennial, *adj* milenario.

miller, *n* molinero *m*.

millet, *n* mijo *m*.

milligram, *n* milígramo *m*.

millinery, *n* sombrerería *f*, sombreros *m* de señora.

milling, *n* molienda *f*.

million, *n* millón *m*.

millionaire, *n* millonario(a) *m/f*.

millstone, *n* piedra *f* de molino.

mime, *n* 1. pantomima *f*, mímica *f;* 2. *vt* remedar.

mimeograph, *n* 1. mimeógrafo *m;* 2. *vt* mimeografiar.

mimic, *adj* 1. mímico; fingido; 2. *n* remedador(a) *m/f*, imitador(a) *m/f;* 3. *vt* remedar, imitar.

mince, *n* 1. carne *f* picada; 2. *vt* desmenuzar; picar; 3. *vi* andar con pasos menuditos; hablar remilgadamente.

mind, *n* 1. mente *f;* inteligencia *f*, entendimiento *m* 2. *vt* hacer caso de; 3. *vi* cuidar, obedecer, fijarse en, sentur molstia por.

mindless, *adj* estúpido, fútil.

mine, *poss pron* 1. mío, mía; 2. *n* mina *f;* 3. *vt* explotar.

miner, *n* minero *m*.

mineral, *adj* mineral.

mineralogy, *n* mineralogía *f*.

minestrone, *n* minestrone *f*.

mingle, *vt* 1. mezclar (con); 2. *vi* mezclarse; confundirse (con).

miniature, *n* muniatura *f;* modelo *m* pequeño.

miniaturize, *vt* muniaturizar.

minimal, *adj* mínimo.

minimize, *vt* mununizar; aminorar, minorizar.

minimum, *adj* mínimo.

minion, *n* favorito(a) *m/f;* privado *m*, valido *m*.

minister, *n* ministro(a) *m/f*.

ministerial, *adj* munisterial.

minisyry, *n* mulisterio *m*.

mink, *n* visón *m;* piel *f* de visón.

minor, *adj* menor; menor de edad.

minority, *n* minoría, menor *m* de edad.

minstrel, *n* juglar *m;* cantor *m*.

minuscule, *adj* munúsculo.

minute, *adj* 1. diminuto, menudo, pequeño; 2. *n* minuto *m;* momentom, instante *m;* 3. **minuta** *f;* nota *f*, 4. *vt* minutar.

minx, *n* picaruela *f*, mujer *f* descarada.

miracle, *n* milagro *m*.

miraculous, *adj* milagroso.

mirage, *n* espejismo *m*.

mire, *n* 1. fango *m*, lodo *m;* 2. *vt* quedar atascado en.

mirror, *n* 1. espejo *m;* 2. *vt* reflejar.

misadventure, *n* desgracia *f*, percancem.

misapplication, *n* mala aplicación *f*.

misapply, *vt* aplicar mal; abusar de.

misapprehend, *vt* comprender mal.

misapprehension, *n* equivocación *f*, error *m*, concepto *m* erróneo.

misappropriate, *vt* malversar.

misappropriaton, *n* malversación *f*.

misbehave, *vi* portarse mal; ser malo.

misbehavior, *n* mala conducta *f*.

miscalculate, *vt/i* calcular mal.

miscalculation, *n* cálculo *m* erróneo; error *m*.

miscarriage, *n* l. aborto *m* espontaneo, malparto *m;* 2. fracaso *m*, malogro *m*.

miscarry, *vi* l. malparir, abortar; 2. fracasar, salir mal, frustrarse.

miscellaneous, *adj* vario, diverso.

miscellany, *n* miscelánea *f*.

mischief, *n* travesura *f*, diablura *f;* malicia *f*.

mischievous, *adj* malo, dañoso; malicioso, juguetón; travieso.

misconception, *n* concepto *m* erróneo, idea *f* falsa.

misconduct, n l. malaconducta f; 2. vr portarse mal.

misconstrue, vt interpretar mal; entender mal.

miscount, n l. cuenta f errónea; 2. vt contar mal.

misdemeanor, n ofensa f, delito m; delito m de menor cuantía, falta f.

misdirect, vt manejar mal, dirigir mal.

misdirection, n mal manejo m, mala dirección f.

miser, n avaro(a) m/f, tacaño(a) m/f.

miserable, adj l. indecente, vil; despreciable; sin valor; 2. triste, desdichado, desgraciado; abatido.

misery, n 1. sufrimiento m; pena f, tristeza f; aflicción f, desdicha f; 2. miseria f, sordidez f.

misfortune, n desgracia f, infortunio m, desventura f.

misgiving, n recelo m presentimiento m.

misgovern, vt/i gobernar mal; administrar mal.

misguided, adj mal aconsejado, equivocado.

mishandle, vt maneja mal, adminatrar mal.

mishap, n desgracia f contratiempo m, accidente m.

misinform, vt dar informes erróneos a.

misinterpret, vt malinterpretar; traducir mal.

misinterpretation, n mala iterpretación f.

misjudge, vt juzgar mal, equivocarse sobre.

mislay, vt extraviar; perder.

mislead, vt llevar a conclusiones erróneas, despistar.

misleading, adj erróneo; de apariencia engañosa.

mismanage, vt manejar mal, administrar mal.

mismanagenent, n mal manejo m, desgobierno m.

mismatch, vt emparejar mal, hermanar mal.

misplace, vt l. colocar mal; poner fuera de su lugar; 2. extraviar, perder.

misplaced, adj equivocado; inmerecido.

misprint, n l. errata f, error m de imprenta; 2. vt imprimir mal.

mispronounce, vt pronunciar mal.

misrepresent, vt desfigurar; falsificar; describir engañosamente; tergiversar.

misrule, n l. desgobierno m; 2. vt desgobernar.

miss, n señorita f.

missile, n proyectil m; arma f arrojadiza.

missing, adj ausente, desaparecido; perdido.

mission, n misión f.

missionary, adj l. misionero; 2. n misionero(a) m/f.

missive, n misiva f.

misspell, vt escribur mal.

misstate, vt declarar erróneamente.

misstatement, n declaración f errónea.

mist, n 1. neblula f; bruma f; 2. vt empañar, velar; 3. vi empañarse y elarse.

mistake, n l. equivocación f error m, falta f; 2. vt entender mal equivocarse.

mistaken, adj equivocado, erróneo; incorrecto.

mister, n señor m.

mistreat, vt maltratar, tratar mal.

mistreatment, n maltrato m, maltratamiento m.

mistress, n l. señora f, ama f de casa; 2. amante f.

mistrial, n juicio m viciado de nulidad.

mistrust, n 1. desconfianza f, recelo m; 2. vt desconfiar de, dudar de.

misty, adj nebuloso, b rumoso; vaporoso.

misunderstand, vt/i entender mal, comprender mal.

misunderstanding, n concepto m erróneo.

misuse, n l. abuso m, mal uso m; empleo m erróneo; malversación f; 2. vt abusar de; maltratar.

mite, n 1. ardite m; 2. ácaro m.

mitigate, vt mitigar.

mitten, n mitón m.

mix, n l. mezcla f; 2. vt mezcla, combinar; 3. vi mezclarse.

mixer, n batidora f, mezcladora f; licuadora f.

mixture, n mezcla f.

moan, n 1. gemido m, quejido m; 2. vi gemir.

moaning, n gemidos m; quejas f, protestas f

moat n foso m.

mob, n l. multitud f, muchedumbre f, gentío m; turba f; 2. vt acosar, atropellar; atacar en masa.

mobile, adj móvil, movible.

mobiliy, n movilidad f.

mobilize, vt l. movilizar; 2. vi movilizarse.

mobster, n gángster m, pamdillero m.

moccasin, n mocasín m.

mocha, n moca m.

mock, adj 1. fingido, simulado; imitado; 2. vt ridiculizar; burlarse de; 3. vi mofarse(de).

mockery, n mofas f, burlas f; parodia f.

mode, n modo m; manera f; moda f.

model, n l. modelo m; paradigma m; patrón m, pauta f; 2. (persona) modelo m/f; 3. vt modelar; fonmar, planear; 4. vi servur de modelo (a, para).

modem, n módem m.

moderate, adj 1. moderado, módico; 2. vt moderar; 3. vi moderarse.

moderation, n moderación f; temperancia f.

moderator, n árbitro m, asesor(a) m/f.

modern, adj l. moderno; 2. n modermo(a) m/f.

modernize, vt modernizar; actualizar.

modest, adj modesto; moderado.

modesty, n l. modestia f; moderación f; 2. pudor m.

modification, n modificación f.

modifier, adj modificante m.

modify, vt modificar.

modulate, vt/i modular.

modulation, n modulación f.

module, n módulo m.

moiré, n muaré m.

moist, adj húmedo; mojado.

moisten, vt 1. humedecer, mojar; 2. vi humedecerse.

moisture, n humedad f.

molar, n muela f.

mold, n 1. molde m, cosa f modelada; 2. (fungos) moho m; 3. carácter m; 4. vt moldear formar.

molecule, n molécula f.

molest, vt faltar al respeto a.

mollify, vt apaciguar, calmar.

molten, adj fundido, denretido.

mom, n mamá f.

moment, n momento m, instante m.

momentary, adj momentáneo.

momentous, adj trascendental, muy crítico.

momentum, n momento m; impulso m, ímpetu m.

monarch, n monarca m.

monarchy, n monarquía f.

monastery, n monasterio m, cenobio m.

monastic, adj monástico.

Monday, n lunes m.

monetary, adj monetario; política f monetaria.

money, n dinero m.

moneylender, n prestamista m/f.

moneymaking, adj l. provechoso, rentable, lucrativo; 2. n ganancia f, lucro m.

mongrel, adj mestizo; cruzado, callejero.

monitor, n 1. monitor m; 2. vt escuchar controlar; observar, monitorizar.

monitoring, n supervisión f; control m.

monk, n monje m.

monkey, n mono(a) m/f, mico(a) m/f.

monochrome, adj 1. monocromo; 2. n monocromo m.

monocle, n monóculo m.

monogamy, n monogamia f.

monogram, n monograma m.

monograph, n monografía f.

monolog(ue), n monólogo m.

monollucleosis, n mononucleosis f infecciosa.

monopolize, vt monopolizar, acaparar.

monopoly, n monopolio m.

monorail, n monorail m; monocarril m.

monotheism, n monoteísmo m.

monotone, n monotonía f.

monotonous, adj monótono.

monotony, n monotonía f.

monoxide, n monóxido m.

monsignor, n monseñor m.

monsoon, n monzón m/f.

monster, adj 1. monstruoso; 2. n monstruo m.

monstrous, adj 1. monstruoso, enorme; 2. injusto.

month, n mes m.

monthly, adj 1. mensual; 2. adv mensualmente.

monumental, adj monumental; colosal.

mood, n humor m; disposición f; modo m.

moody, adj caprichoso, cambiante, melancólico.

moon, n luna f.

moonbeam, n rayo m de luna.

moonlight, n 1. luz f de la luna; 2. vi tener un empleo secundario además del principal.

moonlighting, n pluriempleo m.

moonlit, adj iluminado por la luna.

moonshine, n luz f de la luna.

moose, n alce m de América.

mop, n 1. fregasuelos m, trapeador m; 2. mata f, grena f; 3. vt fregar, limpiar; enjugar.

moral, adj moral; virtuoso; honrado.

morality, n moralidad f.

moralize, v/i moralizar.

moratorium, n moratoria f.

moray, n (pez) morena f.

morbid, adj morboso, malsano; enfermizo.

mordacity, n mordacidad f.

mordant, adj mordaz.

more, adj más.

moreover, adv además, por otra parte; es más.

morgue, n depósito n de cadáveres; archivo m.

moribund, adj moribundo.

morn, n alborada f.

morning, n mañana f; madrugada f.

moron, n imbécil m/f.

morose, adj malhumorado, hosco, taciturno.

morphine, n morfina f.

mortadella, n mortadela f.

mortal, adj 1. mortal; 2. n mortal m/f.

mortality, n mortalidad f.

mortar, n mortero m.

mortgage, n 1. hipoteca f; 2. vt hipotecar y ender.

mortician, n director(a) m/f de pompas fúnebres.

mortify, vt mortificar; humillar.

mortifying, adj humillante.

mortise, n muesca f, mortaja f.

mosaic, n mosaico m.

mosey, vi pasearse; deambular.

mosque, n mezquita f.

mosquito, n mosquito m.

moss, n 1. musgo m; 2. pantano m.

mossy, adj musgoso, cubierto de musgo.

most, adj 1. más; la mayor parte; 2. adv muy, más, sumamente; 3. n el mayor número m de las veces.

mote, n átomo m, mota f.

motel, n motel m, hotel-garaje m.

moth, n mariposa; polilla f.

mother, n madre f.

motherhood, n maternidad f.

mother-in-law, n suegra f.

motherland, n patria f, madre patria f.

motherless, adj huérfano de madre, sin madre.

motherly, adj maternal.

mothproof, adj a prueba de polillas.

motif, n motivo m; tema m; adorno m.

motion, n movimiento m.

motionless, adj inmóvil.

motivate, vt motivar.

motivation, n motivación f.

motive, adj 1. motivo; 2. n motivo m.

motley, adj abigarrado.

motor, adj motor.

motorboat, n motora f, motorbote m.

motorcade, n desfile m de automóviles.

motorist, n automovilista m/f; conductor(a) m/f.

motorize, vt motorizar; adquirir un coche.

motto, n lema m; divisa f; consigna f.

mound, n montón m; terraplén m.

mount, n 1. monte m, montaña f; 2. montura f; 3. vt montar, subir a; 4. armar.

mountaineer, n montañero(a) m/f.

mountainous, adj montañoso; enorme; colosal.

mounting, n montaje m; armadura f, base f.

mourn, v 1. llorar, llorar la muerte de, lamentar; llevar luto por; 2. vi afligirse, lamentarse.

mourner, n doliente m/f; plañidero(a) m/f.

mournful, adj triste, afligido; triste, lúgubre.

mourning, n lamentación f; luto m, duelo m.

mouse, n ratón m.

mousetrap, n ratonera f.

mousse, n crema f batida.

mouth, n boca f; (river) embocadura f.

mouthful, n bocado m.

mouthpiece, n boquilla f; embocadura f.

mouthwash, n enjuague m (bucal).

move, n 1. movimiento m; 2. jugada f; (chess), movida f; 3. vt cambiar de sitio, trasladar; transportar.

movement, n movimiento m.

movie, n película f; el cine.

mow, vt segar; cortar.

mower, n segador(a) m/f; cortacésped m.

much, adj 1. mucho; 2. adv mucho; con mucho.

muck, n estiércol m; suciedad f.

muckraker, n escarbador(a) m/f de vidas ajenas.

mucous, adj 1. mucoso; 2. n moco m, mocosidad f; 3. membrana f mucosa.

mud, n lodo m, barro m, fango m.

mudbank, n banco m de arena.

muddle, n 1. desorden m, confusión f; 2. vt embrollar, confundir.

muddy, adj 1. lodoso, fangoso; 2. vt enlodar.

mudlark, n golopín m.

mudpack, n mascarilla f facial de barrro.

muffle, vt envolver; embozar, tapar.

muffled, adj sordo, apagado.

muffler, n bufanda f; sordina f; silenciador m.

mug, n 1. tarro m; taza f alta; 2. vt asaltar; 3. hacer muecas.

mugging, n asalto m, vapuleo m.

mulberry, n mora f; morera f moral m.

mule, n mulo(a) m/f; testarudo(a) m/f.

mulish, adj terco, testarudo.

multicolored, adj multicolor.

multicultural, adj multicultural.

multidimensional, adj multidimensional.

multidireccional, adj multidireccional.

multimillionaire, n multimillonario(a) m/f.
multiple, adj múltiplo.
multiplication, n multiplicación f.
multiply, vt multiplicar.
multiracial, adj multirracial.
multitude, n multitud f.
mum, adj callado.
mumble, vi musitar, hablar entre dientes.
mummification, n momificación f.
mummify, vt 1. momificar; 2. vi momificarse.
mummy, n momia f.
mumps, n paperas f, parótidas f.
munch, vt mascar, ronzar.
mundane, adj mundano; vulgar, trivial.
municipal, adj municipal.
municipality, n municipio m.
munitions, n municiones f pl; pertrechos m pl.
mural, adj mural.
murder, n 1. asesinato m; homicidio m; 2. vt asesinar;
  matar, dar muerte a.
murderer, n asesino m, homicida m.
murderess, n asesina f, homicida f.
murk, n oscuridad f, tinieblas f.
murkiness, n oscuridad f, lobreguez f.
murmur, n 1. murmullo m; 2. vt murmurar.
muscle, n músculo m.
muscular, adj muscular; musculoso; fornido.
mushroom, n seta f hongo m.
mushy, adj pulposo, mollar.
music, n música f.
musical, adj musical.
musicale, n velada f musical.
musician, n músico(a) m/f.
musicology, n musicología f.
musk, n almizcle m; perfume m de abnizcle.
musketeer, n mosquetero m.
muskrat, n rata f almizclera.
musky, adj almizcleño, almizclado.
muss, vt hair desarreglar, despeinar.
mussel, n mejillón m.
must, n 1. mosto m; moho m; 2. v/aux tener que.
mustache, n bigote.
mustang, n potro m mesteño, mustang(o) m.
mustard, n mostaza f.
musty, adj mohoso; rancio.
mutation, n mutación f.
mute, adj 1. mudo, silencioso; 2. n mudo(a) m/f; 3.
  vt ponersordinaa;apagar.
mutilate, vt mutilar.
mutilation, n mutilación f.
mutiny, n 1. motín m; 2. vi amotunarse.
mutter, n 1. murmullo m; unrumor de voces;
  2. vt munnurar, decir entre dientes.
mutton, n (carne f de) cordero m.
mutual, adj mutuo;común.
muzzle, n 1. hocico m; bozal m; boca f; 2. vt abozalar;
  amordazar, imponer silencio a.
myopia, n miopía f.
myriad, n miríada f.
myrtle, n arrayán m, muto m.
myself, pron yo mismo, yo misma.
mysterious, adj misterioso.
mystery, n misterio m.
mystic, adj 1. místico; 2. n místico m.
mysticism, n misticismo m.
mystincation, n misterio m; perplejidad f.
mystify, vt dejar perplejo, desorientar, desconcertar.
mystifying, adj inexplicable; desconcertante.
myth, n mito m.

mythic(al), adj mítico.
mythology, n mitología f.

N

N, n, n (letra f) N, n.
nacre, n nácar m.
nacreous, adj nacaruno, nacarado, de nácar.
nadir, n nadir m; punto m más bajo, nadir m.
nag, n 1. rocín m; 2. vt regañarcriticar.
nagger, n regañón(ona) m/f, criticón(ona) m/f.
nagging, adj reganón, criticón.
naiad, n náyade f.
nail, n 1. uña f; garra f; 2. clavo; 3. vt clavarenclavar;
  adomarconclavos,clavetear.
nailfile, n lima f para las uñas.
naive, adj ungenuo, cándido, sencillo.
naked, adj desnudo; desabrigado, indefenso.
nakedness, n desnudez f.
name, n 1. nombre m; designación f; apellido m;
  apodo m; 2. vi llamar;nombrar;designar.
nameless, adj anónimo, sin nombre, innominado.
namesake, n tocayo(a) m/f; homónimo(a) m/f.
nanny, n niñera f.
nap, n 1. lanilla f; sueñecito m, siesta f; 2. vi dormir
  lasiesta.
nape, n nuca f cogote m.
napkin, n servilleta f.
narcissus, n narciso m.
narcotic, adj 1. narcótico; 2. n narcótico m.
narrate, vi narrar, referir, contar.
narration, n narración f, relato m.
narrative, adj 1. narrativo; 2. n narrativa f, narración f.
narrator, n narrador(a) m/f.
narrow, adj 1. estrecho, angosto; 2. vt estrechar,
  angostar; reducir.
narrowness, n estrechez f.
nasal, adj 1. nasal; gangoso; 2. n nasal f.
nascent, adj naciente.
nasty, adj sucio, puerco; asqueroso.
natal, adj natal.
natality, n natalidad f.
nation, n nación f.
national, adj nacional.
nationality, n nacionalidad f.
nationalize, vt nacionalizar.
native, adj 1. natural, innato; indígena, 2. n natural
  m/f; nacional m/f.
nativity, n natividad f.
natural, adj natural; normal; instintivo.
naturalist, n naturalista m/f.
naturalization, n naturalización f.
naturalize, vt naturalizar.
nature, n naturaleza f; índole f; modo m de ser.
naturist, n narurista m/f, naturalista m/f.
naught, n nada f.
naughty, adj travieso, malo, pícaro; desobediente.
nausea, n náusea f, bascas f; asco m.
nauseate, vt dar náuseas a; dar asco a, repugnar.
nauseating, adj nauseabundo, repugnante, asqueroso.
nauseous, adj nauseabundo.

nautical, adj náutico, marítimo.

naval, adj naval, de marina.

nave, n nave f; cubo m; tapacubos m.

navel, n ombligo m.

navigate, vt gobernar; navegar.

navigation, n navegación f.

navy, n marina f de guerra, armada f, llota f.

nay, adv 1. no; más aun; 2. n negativa f; voto m negativo.

neap, n marea f muerta.

near, adj 1. cercano, próximo; 2. adv cerca; 3. prep acerca de; 4. vt/i acercarse.

nearly, adv casi, por poco.

nearness, n proximidad f, cercanía f, lo cercano.

near-sighted, adj corto de vista, miope.

neal, vt pulcro, esmerado, acicalado.

nebula, n nebulosa f.

nebulous, adj nebuloso.

necessary, adj necesario; forzoso, preciso.

necessitate, vt necesitar, exigir.

necessity, n necesidad f; cosa f necesaria.

neck, n 1. pezcueso; 2. vi acariciarse.

necklie, n corbata f.

necrology, n necrología f.

necromancy, n nigromancia f.

nectar, n néctar m.

nectarine, n nectarina f.

need, n 1. necesidad; 2. vt necesitar.

needle, n l. aguja f; 2. vt pinchar; provocar, fastidiar.

needless, adj innecesario, superfluo, unútil.

needlessly, adv innecesariamente, inútilmente.

needy, adj necesitado, pobre, undigente.

nefarious, adj vil, inicuo.

negate, vt anular, invalidar.

negative, adj 1. negativo; 2. n negativo(a) m/f.

neglect, n 1. negligencia f, descuido m; 2. vt descuidar, desatender.

neglectful, adj negligente, descuidado.

negligence, n negligencia f, descuido m.

negligent, adj negligente, descuidado; desatender.

negligible, adj insignificante; despreciable.

negotiavle, adj negociable.

negotiate, vt 1. negociar; gestionar, 2. vi negociar; negociar para obtener.

negotiation, n negociacóin f; gestión f.

negotiator, n negociador(ora) f/m.

neigh, n 1. relincho m; 2. vi relinchar.

neighbor, n vecuno(a) m/f.

neighborhood, n vecindad f; barrio m, sección f.

neither, adv 1. ni él ni yo; tampoco; ninguno (de los dos); 2. conj ni ,.... tampoco.

nemesis, n justo castigo m, justicia f.

neún, n neón m.

neonatal, adj neonatal.

nephew, n sobrino m.

nephritis, n nefritis f.

nepotism, n nepotismo m.

nerve, n nervio m; nervadura f; audacia f.

nervous, adj nervioso; tímido; miedoso.

nervousness, n nerviosidad f, nerviosismo m.

nest, n 1. nido m; nidal m; 2. vt anidarencajar.

nestle, vt arrimar afectuosamente; amdar.

nestling, n pajarito m (en el nido).

net, n 1. malla f, red m, tul; 2. adj neto, líquido; 3. enredar, producir.

nether, adj inferior, más bajo, de abajo.

netting, n red f, redes f.

nettle, n 1. ortiga f; 2. vt provocar, irritar.

network, n red f; cadena f.

neural, adj neural.

neuralgia, n neuralgia f.

neurasthenia, n neurastenia f.

neuritis, n neuritis f.

neurology, n neurología f.

neuron, n neurona f.

neurosis, n neurosis f.

neurotic, adj neurótico.

neuter, adj neutro.

neutral, adj neutral.

neutrality, n neutralidad f.

neutralize, vt neutralizar.

neutron, n neutrón m.

never, adv nunca, jaunás.

new, adj nuevo; reciente; fresco.

newborn, adj recién nacido.

news, n noticias f; nuevas f.

newsletter, n hoja f informativa, informe m.

newspaper, n periódico m, diario m.

next, adj 1. próximo, inmediato, contiguo, vecuno; 2. adv inmediatamente después.

nibble, n 1. mordisco m; 2. vi mordiscar.

nice, adj simpático; amable; guapo, mono, bonito.

niceness, n simpatía f, lo simpático; amabilidad f.

niche, n nicho m; honnacina f.

nick, n l. mella f, muesca f, corte m; 2. vt mellar, hacer muescas en, hacer cortes en.

nickel, n níquel m; moneda f de 5 centavos.

nickname, n l. apodo m, mote m; 2. vt apodar.

nicotine, n nicotina f.

niece, n sobrina f.

night, adj 1. nocturno m; 2. n noche f.

nightclub, n cabaret m boite f, sala f de fiestas.

nightly, adv todas las noches, cada noche.

nightmare, n pesadilla f.

nimble, adj ágil, ligero; listo.

nimbus, n nimbo m.

nine, adj nueve.

ninety, adj noventa.

ninth, adj noveno.

nip, n 1. pellizco m; mordisco m; 2. trago m; 3. vt pellizcar, pinchar; mordiscar.

nipple, n pezón m; tetilla f.

nirvana, n nirvana f.

nil, n liendre f.

nitrate, n nitrao m.

no, adv 1. no; 2. adj ninguno; 3. n no m, voto m negativo.

nobility, n nobleza f.

noble, adj noble; (title) de nobleza.

nobleman, n noble m, aristócrata m/f.

nobody, pron nadie.

nocturnal, adj nocturno.

nocturne, n nocturno m.

nod, n 1. cabezada f; señal f hecha con la cabeza; 2. vt inclinar, hacer una senal con la cabeza; 3. cabecear.

node, n nodo m; nudo m.

nodule, n nódulo m.

Noel, n Navidad f.

noise, n 1. ruido m; estrépito m; 2. vt divulgar.

noiseless, adj silencioso, sin ruido.

noisy, adj ruidoso, estrepitoso, clamoroso.

nomad, n nómada m/f.

nomenclature, n nomenclatura f.

nominal, adj nominal.

nominate, vt proponer (la candidatura de); nombrar.

nomination, n nombramiento m; propuesta f.

nominative, adj nominativo.

nominee, n candidato(a) m/f; persona f nombrada.

noodle, n 1. cabeza f; 2. fideos m, tallarines m.

nook, n rincón m; escondrijo m.

noon, n mediodía m.

none, pron indef nadie, ninguno.

noose, n lazo m; nudo m conedizo, dogal m.

nor, conj ni; tampoco.

norma, n norma f; pauta f; modelo m.

normal, adj 1. normal; regular; 2. n lo normal.

normalcy, n nonnalidad f.

normalize, n nonmalizar.

nonllally, adv normalmente.

norlh, n norte m.

northast, n nor(d)este m.

northern, adj del norte, septentrional, norteño.

northerner, n habitante m/f del norte.

northwest, n noroeste m.

nose, n nariz f.

nosebleed, n hemonragia f nasal.

nostalgia, n nostalgia f.

nostril, n nariz f, ventana f de la nariz.

nosy, adj curioso, husmedor.

not, adv no.

notable, adj notable; señalado, memorable.

notarize, vt autenticar (legalmente).

notary, n notario(a) m/f

notate, vt notar.

notalion, n notación f.

notch, n muesca f, mella f, corte m.

note, n 1. nota f; marca f, señal f; apunte m; cartita f; 2. vt notar, observar, advertir.

notebook, n libro m de apuntes, libreta f; cuaderno m.

noted, adj célebre, conocido, famoso.

nothing, n l. nada f; cero m; 2. adv de ninguna manera.

nothingness, n nada f.

notice, n 1. atención f, advertencia f, aviso m, letrero m; 2. vt notar, observar, reparar en, fjarse en.

notification, n notificación f, aviso m.

notify, vt notificar, comunicar, avisar.

notion, n noción f.

notoriety, n celebridad f; notoriedad f.

notorious, adj muy conocido, notorio.

notwithstanding, adv 1. no obstante, sin embargo; 2. prep a pesar de.

nought, n nada f; cero m.

nourish, vt nutrir, alimentar, sustentar.

nourishing, adj nutritivo.

nourishment, n sustento m; nutrición f.

novel, adj 1. nuevo, original; insólito; 2. n novela f.

novelette, n novela f corta; novela f.

novelist, n novelista m/f.

novelty, n novedad f.

November, n noviembre m.

novice, n principiante m/f, novato(a) m/f

now, adv ahora; actualmente, al presente, hoy día.

nowadays, adv hoy en día, actualmente.

nowhere, adv en ninguna parte.

noxious, adj nocivo, dañino.

nozzle, n tobera f, inyector m boquilla f.

nub, n pedazo m, protuberancia f; lo esencial.

nuclear, adj nuclear.

nucleus, n núcleo m.

nude, adj 1. desnudo; 2. n desnudo m.

nudge, n l. codazo m; 2. vt dar un codazo a.

nudity, n desnudez f, desnudo m.

nuisance, n molestia f, incomodidad f.

null, adj nulo, inválido.

nullify, vt anular, invalidar.

numb, adj entumecido; insensible.

number, n 1. número m, cifra f; 2. vt contar.

numeral, adj l. numeral; 2. n número m, cifra f.

numerical, adj numérico.

numerous, adj nuuneroso; muchos.

nun, n monja f, religiosa f.

nunnery, n convento m de monjas.

nuptial, adj l. nupcial; 2. n nupcias f.

nurse, n 1. enfermero(a) m/f; 2. vt cuidar, atender; 3. amamantar.

nursemaid, n niñera f, chacha f.

nursery, n 1. cuarto m de los niños; 2. vivero m, semillero m, plantel m.

nursing-home, n asilo m de ancianos.

nurture, n 1. nutrición f; educacón f, crianza f; 2. vt alimentar, nutrir.

nut, n 1. nuez f; 2. tuerca f; 3. chiflado (loco).

nutmeg, n nuez f moscada.

nutrient, adj l. nutritivo; 2. n nutriente m.

nutrition, n alinentación f.

nutritious, adj nutritivo.

nutshell, n cáscara f de nuez.

nylon, n nilón m.

nymph, n ninfa f.

O

O, ө, n (letter) O, o f.

oaf, n zoquete m, patán m.

oak, n roble m.

oaken, adj de roble.

oakum, n estopa f (de calafatear).

oakwood, n robledo m.

oar, n 1. remo m; 2. remero(a) m/f.

oared, adj provisto de remos.

oarlock, n tolete m, escálamo m, chumacera f.

oarsman, n remero m.

oarsmanship, n arte m de remar.

oasis, n oasis m.

oat bran, n salvado m de avena.

oatcake, n tortaf de avena.

oaten, adj de avena.

oatfield, n avenal m.

oath, n 1. juramento m; 2. blasfemia f, reniego m, palabrota f.

oatmeal, n harina f de avena.

oats, n avena f.

obbligato, n obligado m.

obduracy, n obstinación f, terquedad f; inflexibilidad f.

obdurate, adj obstinado, terco; inflexible.

obedience, n obediencia f; sumisión f; docilidad f.

obedient, adj obediente; sumiso, dócil.

obeisance, n reverencia f; saludo m.

obelisk, n obelisco m.

obese, adj obeso.

obesity, n obesidad f.

obey, vt obedecer; hacer caso a.

obituary, adj 1. necrológico; column sección f necrológica; 2. n necrología f, obituario m.

object, n 1. objeto m; cosa f, artículo m; mamarracho m; 2. vt objetar que ...; 3. vi hacer objeciones, oponerse.

objection, n objeción f, reparo m; protesta f.

objectionable, adj desagradable; molesto, pesado; indeseable; reprensible; censurable.

objective, adj 1. objetivo; 2. n objetivo m.

objectivism, n objetivismo m.

objectivity, n objetividad f.

objector, n objetante m/f.

objurgate, vt increpar, reprender.

oblation, n oblación f; oblata f, ofrenda f.

obligate, vt obligar a uno a hacer algo.

obligation, n obligación f; deber m; compromiso m.

obligatory, adj obligatorio.

obligue, vt 1. obligar, forzar; 2. complacer, hacer un favor a.

obligee, n tenedor m de una obligación.

obliging, adj servicial, atento, obsequioso.

oblique, adj oblicuo; indirecto, tangencial.

obliqueness, n n oblicuidad f; lo indirecto, lo tangencial.

obliterate, vt borrar, eliminar, destruir toda huella de.

obliteration, n borradura f, elliminación f; arrasamiento m.

oblivion, n olvido m.

oblivious, adj estar inconsciente de.

oblong, adj oblongo, apaisado.

obnoxious, adj detestable, repugnante, odioso.

oboe, n oboe m.

oboist, n oboe m/f.

obscene, adj obsceno, indecente, escabroso; procaz.

obscenity, n obscenidad f, indecencia f, escabrosidad f.

obscurantism, n oscurantismo m.

obscurantist, adj 1. oscurantista; 2. n oscurantista m/f.

obscure, adj 1. oscuro; 2. vt oscurecer; eclipsar.

obscurely, adv oscuramente.

obscurity, n oscuridad f; vivir en la oscuridad.

obsequies, n exequias f.

obsequious, adj servil.

obsequiousness, n servilismo m.

observable, adj observable, visible.

observance, n observancia f.

observant, adj observador, perspicaz; vigilante.

observation, n 1. observación f; observancia f; 2. observación f, comentario m.

observatory, n observatorio m.

observe, vt 1. rule, cumplir; 2. observar; examinar; vigilar.

observer, n observador(a) m/f.

obtrusive, adj importuno, molesto; intruso; indiscreto.

obtuse, adj 1. obtuso; 2. estúpido, duro de mollera.

obtuseness, n estupidez f, torpeza f, obtusidad f.

obverse, adj del anverso; 2. n anverso m; complemento m.

obviate, vt obviar, evitar, eliminar.

obvious, adj evidente, obvio, manifiesto, patente.

occasion, n 1. coyuntura f; oportunidad f, ocasión f; 2. razón f, motivo m; 3. vez f; 2. vt ocasionar, causar.

occasional, adj algo que pasa de vez en cuando, un acontecimiento poco frecuente.

occident, n occidente m.

occidental, adj occidental.

occipital, adj occipital.

occiput, n occipucio m.

occlude, vt obstruir.

occluded, adj oclusión f.

occlusion, n oclusión f.

occlusive, adj 1. oclusivo; 2. n oclusiva f.

occult, adj oculto, misterioso; sobrenatural, mágico.

occultism, n ocultismo m.

occultist, n ocultista mf.

occupancy, n ocupación f, tenencia f.

occupant, n ocupante m/f.

occupation, n tenencia f, inquilinato m; ocupación f

occupational, adj de oficio, relativo al oficio, profesional, laboral; ocupacional.

occupier, n inquilino(a) f/m.

occupy, vt ocupar; habitar, vivir en.

occur, vi ocurrir, suceder, acontecer, pasar.

occurrence, n acontecimiento m; incidente m; caso m.

oceanarium, n oceanario m.

Oceania, n Oceanía f.

oceanic, adj oceánico.

oceanographer, n oceanógrafo(a) m/f.

oceanographic, adj oceanográfico.

oceanography, n oceanografía f.

ocelot, n ocelote m.

ochre, n ocre m

ochreous, adj de color ocre.

octagon, n octágono m.

octagonal, adj octagonal.

octahedron, n octaedro m.

octal, adj 1. octal; 2. n octal m.

octane, n octano m; number grado m octánico.

octave, n octava f.

octavo, adj 1. en octavo; 2. n libro m en octavo.

octet, n octeto m.

October, n octubre m.

octogenarian, adj 1. octagenario; 2. n octagenario(a) m/f.

octopus, n pulpo m.

octosyllabic, adj octosílabo.

octosyllable, n octosílabo m.

ocular, adj ocular.

oculist, n oculista m/f.

odd, adj 1. sobrante, de más; suelto; sin pareja, desparejado; 2. impar.

oddball, adj raro, excéntrico.

oddity, n rareza f, singularidad f excentricidad f.

oddly, adj singularmente; extrañamente.

oddment, n artículo m suelto, artículo m que sobra.

oddness, n rareza.f, singularidad f.

odious, adj odioso, detestable.

odium, n odio m; oprobio m.

odometer, n cuentakilómetros m.

odoneologist, n odontólogo(a) m/f.

odontology, n odontología f.

odoriferous, adj odorífero.

odorous, adj oloroso.

odour, n olor m; fragancia f, perfume m.

odourless, adj inodoro.

Odyssey, n Odisea f.

oenologist, n enólogo(a) m/f.

oenology, n enología f.

oenophile, n enófilo(a) m/f.

oestrogen, n estrógeno m.

oestrous, adj en celo; ciclo m de celo.

oestrus, n estro m.

off, adv quitar; remover de; descuento; irse; estar fuera, no estar; estar libre, no trabajar.

offal, n asaduras f pl, menudencias f pl.

offbeat, adj excéntrico, insólito; inconformista, nada convencional.

offence, n ofensa f; ofender a.

offender, n ofensor(ora) m/f.

offending, *adj* delincuente, culpable.

offensive, *adj* 1. ofensivo, injurioso; repugnante; 2. *n* ofensiva *f*; la ofensiva.

offensively, *adv* injuriosamente; repugnantemente; groseramente.

offer, *n* oferta *f* ofrecimiento *m*; 2. *vt* ofrecer.

offering, *n* ofrecimiento *m*; ofrenda *f*.

offertory, *n* ofertorio *m*.

offhand, *adj* informal, brusco, descortés; poco ceremonioso.

office, *n* oficina *f*; despacho *m*.

officer, *n* oficial *m/f*; dignatario(a) *m/f*.

official, *adj* 1. oficial; autorizado; 2. *n* oficial *m/f*, oficial *m* público, oficial *f* pública.

officialdom, *n* burocracia *f*.

officialese, *n* lenguaje *m* burocrático, estilo *m* oficial burocrático.

officially, *adv* oficialmente; de modo autorizado.

officiate, *vi* oficiar (as de).

officious, *adj* oficioso.

officiously, *adv* oficiosamente.

officiousness, *n* oficiosidad *f*.

offing, *n* estar a la vista, estar cerca.

offset, *n* compensación *f*; acodo *m*, bulbo *m* reproductor; 2. *vt* compensar; contrarrestar, contrapesar.

offshore, *adv* a cierta distancia, a lo largo.

offside, *adv* 1. estar fuera de juego; 2. *adj* regla *f* de fuera de juego; trampa *f* de fuera de juego.

often, *adv* muchas veces, mucho, a menudo, con frecuencia.

ogival, *adj* ojival.

ogive, *n* ojiva *f*.

ogle, *vt* echar miradas amorosas a.

ogre, *n* ogro *m*.

oh, *interj* oh; ay!.

oik, *n* palurdo *m*, patán *m*.

oil, *n* aceite *m*, petróleo *m*.

oilwell, *n* pozo *m* de petróleo.

oily, *adj* aceitoso, oleaginoso; grasiento, grasoso..

ointment, *n* pomada *f*, ungüento *m*.

OhKay, *interj* ¡está bien!; sí!; comprendo!.

okapi, *n* okapi *m*.

old, *adj* 1. viejo; 2. *n* los viejos, los mayores, los ancianos.

oldish, *adj* algo viejo, más bien viejo, que va para viejo.

oldster, *n* viejo *m* vieja *f*.

olfactory, *adj* olfativo, olfatorio.

oligarchic, *adj* oligárquico.

oligarchy, *n* oligarquía *f*.

Oligocene, *adj* 1. oligocénico; 2. *n* el Oligoceno.

olive, *n* aceituna *f*, oliva *f*.

Olympiad, *n* olimpíada *f*.

Olympian, *adj* olímpico.

Olympic, *adj* olímpico.

omega, *n* omega *f*.

omelet(te), *n* tortilla *f*, tortilla *f* de huevo .

ominous, *adj* siniestro, de mal agüero, ominoso, amenazador.

omission, *n* omisión *f*; supresión *f*; olvido *m*.

omit, *vt* omitir; suprimir; olvidar, descuidar.

omnibus, *adj* 1. general, para todo; edition completo; 2. *n* autobús *m*.

omnipotence, *n* omnipotencia *f*.

omnipotent, *adj* omnipotente.

omnipresence, *n* omnipresencia *f*.

omnipresent, *adj* omnipresente.

omniscience, *n* omnisciencia *f*.

omniscient, *adj* omnisciente, omniscio.

on, *vi* 1. poner; seguir adelante; 2. *interj* ¡adelante! 4. *adj* abierto, en posición de abierto.

once, *adv* una vez.

oncologist, *n* oncólogo(a) *m/f*.

oncology, *n* oncología *f*.

oncoming, *adj* que se acerca, venidero.

one, *adj* 1. uno, una; 2. solo, único; 3. *indef pron* un, uno.

oneness, *n* unidad *f*; identidad *f*.

one-parent, *adj* familia *f* monoparental, hogar *m* sin pareja.

one-piece, *adj* enterizo, de una pieza.

onerous, *adj* oneroso.

oneself, *pron* uno mismo, una misma.

ongoing, *adj* que continúa; que sigue funcionando.

onion, *n* cebolla *f*.

only, *adv* 1. sólo, solamente, únicamente; no ... mas que; 2. *adj* único, solo.

onomatopoeia, *n* onomatopeya *f*.

onomatopoeic, *adj* onomatopéyico.

onrush, *n* arremetida *f*, embestida *f*; avalancha *f*.

onshore, *adv* 1. hacia la tierra, 2. *adj* breeze que sopla del mar hacia la tierra.

onside, *adj* izquierdo, derecho.

ontological, *adj* ontológico.

ontology, *n* ontología *f*.

onward, *adj* progresivo, hacia adelante.

onward, *adv* adelante, hacia adelante.

onyx, *n* ónix *m*.

ooze, *n* cieno *m*, lama *f*.

opacity, *n* opacidad f.

opal, *n* ópalo *m*.

opalescence, *n* opalescencia *f*.

opalescent, *adj* opalescente.

opaque, *adj* opaco.

open, *adj* 1. abierto; sin límites, no limitado; 2. *n* estar en el campo; estar al aire libre; 3. *vt* abrir; desplegar, extender.

opener, *n* abrelatas *m*.

opening, *adj* 1. primero; de apertura; horas *f* de abrir; 2. abertura *f*.

openness, *n* franqueza *f*.

opera, *n* ópera *f*.

operable, *adj* operable.

operate, *vt* 1. impulsar; machine hacer funcionar; 2. *vi* obrar, actuar; funcionar.

operatic, *adj* de ópera, operístico.

operating, *adj* operante; activo *m* operante.

operation, *n* funcionamiento *m*; manejo *m*; dirección *f*; operación *f*; actuación *f*.

operational, adj de operaciones.

operator, *n* operario(a); maquinista *m/f*; operador *m*.

ophthalmic, adj oftálmico.

ophthalmologist, *n* oftalmólogo(a) *m/f*.

ophthalmology, *n* oftalmología *f*.

opiate, *n* opiata, opiáceo *m*, narcótico *m*.

opine, *vi* opinar.

opinion, *n* opinión *f*, parecer *m*; juicio *m*; concepto *m*.

opinionated , *adj* terco, dogmático.

opium, *n* opio *m*.

opponent, *n* adversario(a) *m/f*.

opportune, *adj* oportuno, a propósito.

opportunism, *n* oportunismo *m*.

opportunist, *adj* 1. oportunista; 2. *n* oportunista *m/f*.

opportunistic, *adj* oportunista.

opportunity, *n* oportunidad *f*, ocasión *f*, chance *m*.

oppose, *vt* oponerse a; resistir, combatir.

opposeo, *adj* opuesto.

opposing, *adj* opuesto, contrario.

opposite, *adv* 1. en frente; se sentaran frente a frente; 2. *prep* enfrente de, frente a; 3. *adj* de enfrente; opuesto.

opposition, *n* oposición *f*; resistencia *f*; competencia *f*.

oppress, *vt* oprimir; agobiar; agobiar, ahogar.

oppression, *n* opresión *f*; agobio *m*.

oppressive, *adj* opresivo; tiránico, oprimente.

oppressor, *n* opresor(ora) *f/m*.

opprobrious, *adj* oprobioso.

opprobrium, *n* oprobio *m*.

optative, *adj* 1. optativo; 2. *n* optativo *m*.

optic, *adj* óptico; nervio *m* óptico.

optical, *adj* óptico.

optician, *n* óptico *m/f*.

optics, *n* óptica *f*.

optimal, *adj* óptimo.

optimism, *n* optimismo *m*.

optimist, *n* optimista *m/f*.

optimistic, *adj* optimista;

optimization, *n* optimización *f*.

optimize, *vt* optimizar.

optimum, *adj* óptimo.

option, *n* opción *f*.

optional, *adj* opcional.

optometrist, *n* optometrista *m/f*.

opulence, *n* opulencia *f*.

opulent, *adj* opulento.

opus, *n* opus *m*, obra *f*; obra *f*.

or, *conj* o.

oracle, *n* oráculo *m*.

oracular, *adj* profético, fatídico; sentencioso.

oral, *adj* oral; bucal; verbal, hablado.

orange, *n* naranja *f*; naranjo *m*; color *m* naranja.

orangeade, *n* naranjada *f*.

orange-juice, *n* zumo *m* de naranja, jugo *m* de naranja.

orate, *vi* perorar.

oration, *n* oración *f*, discurso *m*.

orator, *n* orador(a) *m/f*.

oratorical, *adj* oratorio; retórico.

oratory, *n* oratoria *f*.

orb, *n* orbe *m*; esfera *f*, globo *m*.

orbit, *n* 1. órbita *f*; 2. *vt* orbitar, girar alrededor de; 3. *vi* orbitar, girar.

orbital, *adj* orbital.

orchard, *n* huerto *m*.

orchestra, *n* orquesta *f*; platea *f*.

orchestral, *adj* orquestal.

orchestrate, *vt* orquestar, instrumentar.

orchestration, *n* orquestación *f*, instrumentación *f*.

orchid, *n* orquídea *f*.

ordain, *vt* 1. ordenar, decretar; 2. ordenar a uno de sacerdote o ministro; 2. *vi* mandar, disponer.

ordeal, *n* 1. ordalías *f*; 2. prueba *f* rigurosa, experiencia *f* penosa; sufrimiento *m*.

order, *n* 1. orden *m*; clase *f*, categoría *f*; 2. órdenes *f* sagradas; 3. orden *m*; clasificación *f*; método *m*; en orden, por orden; 4. *vt* disponer, arreglar, poner en orden; clasificar.

ordered, *adj* ordenado, metódico, disciplinado.

order-form, *n* hoja *f* de pedido, formulario *m* de pedido.

ordering, *n* pedido *m*; el pedir.

ordinance, *n* ordenanza *f*, decreto *m*.

ordinand, *n* ordenando *m*.

ordinary, *adj* corriente, común, normal.

ordination, *n* ordenación *f*.

ordure, *n* inmundicia *f*.

ore, *n* mineral *m*, mena *f*; mineral *m* de cobre.

oregano, *n* orégano *m*.

organ, *n* órgano *m*.

organdy, *n* organdí *m*.

organic, *adj* orgánico; análisis *m* orgánico.

organism, *n* organismo *m*.

organist, *n* organista *m/f*.

organization, *n* organización *f*.

organizational, *adj* organizativo.

organize, *vt* 1. organizar; organizarse, arreglárselas; 2. *vi* organizarse (para).

organized, *adj* 1. organizado; 2. metódico, ordenado.

organizer, *n* organizador(a) *m/f*.

organ pipe, *n* cañón *m* de órgano.

organza, *n* organza *f*, organdí *m* de seda.

orgasm, *n* orgasmo *m*.

orgasmic, *adj* orgásmico.

orgiastic, *adj* orgiástico.

orgy, *n* orgía *f*.

orient, *vt* oriéntate

oriental, *adj* oriental.

orientalism, *n* orientalismo *m*.

orientalist, *adj* orientalista.

orientate, *vt* 1. orientar (hacia); 2. *vr* orientarse.

orientated, *adj* orientado hacia una carrera.

orientation, *n* orientación *f*.

orifice, *n* orificio *m*.

origin, *n* origen *m*; procedencia *f*.

original, *adj* original, primero; prototipo; primitivo.

originality, *n* originalidad *f*.

originate, *vt* 1. producir, originar, dar lugar a; idear, crear; 2. *vi* originarse, nacer, surgir.

originator, *n* inventor(a) *m/f*, autor(a) *m/f*.

ornament, *n* 1. adorno *m*, ornato *m*, ornamento *m*; 2. *vt* adornar, ornamentar.

ornamental, *adj* ornamental; decorativo, de adorno.

ornamentation, *n* ornamentación *f*.

ornate, *adj* muy ornado, vistoso; florido.

ornithological, *adj* ornitológico

ornithologist, *n* ornitólogo(a) *m/f*

ornithology, *n* ornitología *f*.

orphan, *n* 1. huérfano; 2. *n* huérfano(a) *m/f*; 3. *vi* dejar huérfano.

orphanage, *n* orfanato *m*, orfelinato *m*, asilo *m* de huérfanos.

ortho, *pref* orto...

orthodontics, *n* ortodoncia *f*.

orthodontist, *n* ortodoncista *m/f*.

orthodox, *adj* ortodoxo.

orthodoxy, *n* ortodoxia *f*.

orthographic(al), *adj* ortográfico.

orthoyraphy, *n* ortografía *f*.

orthopedic, *adj* 1. ortopédico; 2. cirujano(a) *m* ortopédico(a) *m/f*.

orthopedics, *n* ortopedia *f*.

oryx, *n* orix *m*.

oscillate, *vt* 1. hacer oscilar; 2. *vi* oscilar, fluctuar, variar.

oscillating, *adj* oscilante.

oscillation, *n* oscilación *f*; fluctuación *f*, variación *f*; vacilación *f*.

oscillator, *n* oscilador *m*.

oscillatory, *adj* oscilatorio.

oscilloscope, *n* osciloscopio *m*.

osculate, *vt* 1. besar; 2. *vi* besar(se).

osculation, *n* ósculo *m*.

osier, *n* 1. mimbre *f*; 2. mimbrera *f*.

osmium, n osmio m.

osmosis, n ósmosis f.

osmotic, adj osmótico.

osprey, n águila f. pescadora, quebrantahuesos m.

osseous, adj óseo.

ossification, n osiflcación f.

ossify, vt 1. osificar; 2. vi osificarse.

ossuary, n osario m.

ostensible, adj pretendido, aparente.

ostensive, adj ostensivo.

ostentation, n ostentación f; aparato m, boato m; fausto m.

ostentatious, adj ostentoso; aparatoso; ostentativo.

osteopath, n osteópata m/f.

osteopathy, n osteopatía f.

osteoporosis , n osteoporosis f.

ostler, n mozo m de cuadra.

ostracism, n ostracismo m.

ostracize, vt condenar al ostracismo, excluir de la sociedad.

ostrich, n avestruz m.

other, adj otro; el otro; los otros.

otherness, n alteridadf;

otherwise, adv 1. de otra manera; 2. por lo demás, por otra parte; 3. conj si no; de lo contrario.

otiose, adj ocioso, inútil.

otitis, n otitis f.

otter, n nutria f.

ottoman, n otomana f.

ought, v aux deber.

ounce, n onza f.

our, adj nuestro(s), nuestra(s).

ourselves, pron nosotros mismos, nosotras mismas.

oust, vt desalojar; expulsar, echar; desahuciar.

out, adv fuera, afuera; hacia fuera.

outage, n apagón m, corte m.

outback, n despoblado m, interior m, campo m.

outboard, adj fuera de borda; motor m fuera de borda.

outbound, adv 1. hacia fuera, hacia el exterior; 2. adj que va hacia fuera, que va hacia el exterior.

outbreak, n erupción f; epidemia f, brote m.

outburst, n explosión f; arranque m; acceso m.

outcast, n paria m/f, proscrito(a) m/f; marginado(a) m/f.

outcome, n resultado m, consecuencia f.

outcry, n grito m, protesta f clamorosa.

outdated, adj anticuado, fuera de moda.

outdo, vt exceder, sobrepujar.

outdoor, adj al aire libre; actividades f al aire libre.

outdoors, adv al aire libre; fuera de casa.

outer, adj exterior; externo.

outermost, adj extremo, (el) más remoto.

outfit, n equipo m; herramientas f, juego m de herramientas; 2. unidad f, cuerpo m, equipo m; grupo m; organización f.

outgoing, adj saliente; cesante.

outlast, vt durar más tiempo que; sobrevivir a.

outlaw, n 1. proscrito m, forajido m; 2. vt proscribir; ilegalizar; declarar fuera de la ley.

outlay, n desembolso m, inversión f.

outlet, n salida f; concesionario m; desagüe m.

outline, n contorno m, perfil m; trazado m; esbozo m, bosquejo m; 2. vt perfilar; trazar, bosquejar.

outlive, vt sobrevivir a; durar mas tiempo que.

outlook, n perspectiva f, panorama m; pronóstico m.

outnumber, vt exceder en número, ser más numeroso que.

out-of-the-way, adj remoto, apartado, aislado; inaccesible.

outpace, vt dejar atrás.

outpatient, n paciente m externo.

outperform, vt hacer mejor que, superar a.

outpost, n avanzada f, puesto m avanaado.

outpouring, n efusión f.

output, n 1. producción f, volumen m de producción; 2. salida f.

outrage, n 1. atrocidad f; ultraje m, atropello m; 2. vt ultrajar, violentar, atropellar; violar.

outrageous, adj atroz, terrible; monstruoso; escandaloso; indignante.

outrank, vt ser de categoría superior a.

outrun, vt correr más que; exceder, rebasar.

outside, adv 1. fuera; estar fuera; 2. prep fuera de; al exterior de; más allá de; 3. adj exterior, externo.

outsider, n forastero m(a) m/f, desconocido(a) m/f, intruso(a) m/f.

outskirts, n afueras f; alrededores mpl; barrios m.

outsmart, vt ser más listo que, burlar; engañar, burlar.

outspoken, adj franco, abierto.

outstanding, adj destacado; excepcional, relevante, sobresaliente.

outvote, vt vencer en las elecciones; rechazar por votación.

outward, adj exterior, externo.

outward(s), adv hacia fuera; exteriormente.

outweigh, vt pesar más que, tener mayor peso que.

oval, adj oval, ovalado.

ovarian, adj ovárico.

ovary, n ovario m.

ovation, n ovación f.

oven, n horno m, cocina f.

ovenproof, adj refractario, (a prueba) de horno.

ovenware, n utensilios m para horno, utensilios m termorresistentes.

over, adv encima; por encima; arriba; por arriba.

overabundance, n sobreabundancia f.

overabundant, adj sobreabundante.

overact, vi sobreactuar, exagerar.

overacting, n sobreactuación f, exageración f.

overactive, adj demasiado activo.

overall, adv en conjunto, en su totalidad.

overbearing, adj imperioso, altivo; despotico.

overbill, vt cobrar demasiado a, presentar una factura excesiva.

overbook, vt sobrereservar, reservar con exceso.

overburden, vt sobrecargar; oprimir, agobiar.

overcapitalization, n sobrecapitalización f, capitalización f inflada.

overcapitalize, vt sobrecapitalizar.

overcast, adj encapotado, cubierto, nublado.

overcharge, n precio m excesivo, cargo m excesivo; 2. vt sobrecargar, cobrar demasiado a.

overcoat, n abrigo m, sobretodo m, gabán m.

overcome, vt 1. vencer; salvar; superar; 2. vi vencer, triunfar.

overcompensate, vi compensar algo excesivamente.

overcompensation, n compensación f excesiva.

overconfidence, n confianza f excesiva, exceso m de conflanza.

overcook, vt cocer demasiado, recocer.

overcrowd, vt atestar, superpoblar, congestionar.

overcrowded, adj atestado de gente, muy lleno.

overdependence, n dependencia f excesiva .

overdeveloped, adj superdesarrollado; sobreprocesado,

overdo, vt cocer demasiado, recocer; exagerar; usar demasiado; llevar a extremos, excederse en.

overdone, adj exagerado; demasiado asado.

overdose, n 1. sobredosis f; 2. vi tomar una sobredosis (de).

overdraft, n sobregiro m, (en) descubierto m; saldo m deudor.

overdress, vi vestirse con demasiada elegancia.

overdrive, n sobremarcha f, superdirecta f.

overdue, adj vencido y no pagado; atrasado, con retraso.

overeat, vi comer con exceso.

overeating, n comida f excesiva,

overelaborate, adj demasiado complicado; demasiado detallado; rebuscado.

overemphasize, vt sobreenfatiza f.

overestimate, n 1. sobreestimación f estimación f excesiva; 2. vt sobre(e)stimar, apreciar en una cantidad excesiva; estimar en valor excesivo.

overexcite, vt sobre(e)xcitar.

overexcited, adj sobre(e)xcitado; sobre(e)xcitarse.

overexpenditure, n gasto m excesivo.

overexpose, vt sobre(e)xponer.

overexposure, n sobre(e)xposición f.

overfeed, vt 1. sobrealimentar; dar demasiado de comer a; 2. vi sobrealimentarse; comer demasiado, atracarse.

overfeeding, n sobrealimentación f.

overflow, n 1. exceso m de líquido, líquido m derramado; rebosadero m; 2. vt desbordarse de, salir de; inundar.

overfly, vt sobrevolar.

overfull, adj demasiado lleno (de), más que lleno, rebosante.

overgrown, adj (demasiado grande para su edad.)

overhaul, n 1. repaso m general, revisión f; 2. vt revisar, repasar, dar un repaso general a.

overhead, adv 1. por lo alto, en alto, por encima de la cabeza; 2. adj de arriba, encima de la cabeza.

overhear, vt oír, oír por casualidad; acertar a oír.

overheat, vt 1. recalentar, sobrecalentar, recalentarse; 2. vi recalentarse, sobrecalentarse.

overheating, n sobrecalentamiento m .

overjoyed, adj llenos de alegría, alegrarse muchísimo.

overlap, n 1. traslapo m, solapo m; coincidencia f parcial; superposición f; 2. vt traslapar.

overlay, n 1. capa f sobrepuesta; incrustación f; 2. vt cubrir (con).

overload, n 1. sobrecarga f; 2. vt sobrecargar.

overlook, vt 1. dominar; dar a, mirar hacia, tener vista a; 2. vigilar; inspeccionar, examinar; 3. pasar por alto; olvidar; no hacer caso de; dejar pasar, disimular.

overnight, adv 1. (que) ocurrió durante la noche, ocurrió de la noche a la mañana; 2. pasar la noche, pernoctar.

overpass, n paso m superior, paso m a desnivel.

overpay, vt pagar demasiado a.

overpayment, n pago m excesivo.

overplay, vt exagerar.

overpopulated, adj superpoblado.

overpopulation, n superpoblación f.

overpower, vt sobreponerse a, vencer, subyugar; dominar.

overpowering , adj abrumador, arrollador.

overpraise, vt elogiar demasiado.

overprice, vt cargar demasiado sobre el precio de.

overproduction, n superproducción f, exceso m de producción.

overprotect, vt proteger demasiado

overprotection, n sobreprotección f.

overqualified, adj sobrecualificado

overrate, vt supervalorar sobre(e)stimar

overrated, adj sobre(e)stimado

overreact, vi reaccionar demasiado, sobrereaccionar.

overreaction, n sobrerreacción f

override, vt (ignorar) no hacer caso de; anular, invalidar.

overripe, adj demasiado maduro, pasado.

overrule, vt desautorizar, anular; denegar, rechazar.

oversee, vt superentender, vigilar.

overseer, n superintendente mf; inspector(a) m/f; capataz m.

oversell, vt hacer una propaganda excesiva a favor de; insistir demasiado en.

oversensitive, adj hipersensible, demasiado sensible.

overshadow, vt sombrear, ensombrecer; eclipsar.

oversight, n 1. descuido m, inadvertencia f, equivocación f; 2. superintendencia f, vigilancia f.

oversimplification, n simplificación f excesiva.

oversimplify, vt simplificar demasiado.

oversized, adj demasiado grande, descomunal.

oversleep, vi dormir demasiado, no despertar a tiempo.

overspend, vi gastar demasiado, gastar más de la cuenta.

overspending, n gasto m excesivo.

overspill, n desparramamiento m.

overstate, vt exagerar.

overstatement, n exageración f.

overstep, vt exceder, pasar de, traspasar; pasarse de la raya.

overstock, vt abarrotar; tener existencias excesivas de.

overstrike, n 1.superposición f; 2. vt superponer.

overt, adj abierto, público; evidente.

overtake, vt 1. alcanzar; adelantar, rebasar; pasar, sobrepasar; 2. vi adelantar, pasar.

overtaking, n adelantamiento m, paso m.

overtax, vt oprimir con tributos, exigir contribuciones excesivas a.

overthrow, n 1. derrumbamiento m, derrocamiento m; 2. vt echar abajo, tumbar, derribar; volcar.

overtime, n horas f extra(ordinarias); tiempo m suplementario.

overturn, vt 1. volcar; trastornar; derrumbar, derrocar; 2. (decisión) revocar, anular; 3. vi volcar, capotar, dar una vuelta de campana.

overuse, vt usar demasiado.

overvalue, vt sobrevalorar, sobre(e)stimar.

overview, n visión f de conjunto.

overweight, adj demasiado pesado; pesar demasiado, ser gordo.

overwhelm, vt arrollar, aplastar; fundir, vencer, postrar; abrumar.

overwhelming, adj arrollador, aplastante, contundente; abrumador; irresistible.

overwork, n 1. trabajo m excesivo; 2. vt hacer trabajar demasiado; exigir un esfuerzo excesivo a; 3. vi trabajar demasiado, cansarse trabajando demasiado.

overwrite, vt 1. exagerar; cargar los efectos literarios de; 2. sobreescribir.

ovine, adj ovino.

oviparous, adj ovíparo.

ovoid, adj ovoide.

ovulate, vi ovular.

ovulation, n ovulación f.

ovule, n óvulo m.

owe, vt 1. deber; 2. vi tener deudas; estar en deuda con.

owing, adj 1. deuda; 2. prep debido a, por causa de.

owl, n lechuza f; mochuelo m.

owlet, *n* mochuelo *m*.

own, *adj* 1. propio; 2. *pron* lo suyo; 3. *vt* poseer, tener; ser dueño de.

owner, *n* dueño(a) *m/f*, propietario(a) *m/f*.

ownerless, *adj* sin dueño.

ownership, *n* posesión *f*; propiedad *f*.

ox, *n* buey *m*.

oxalic, *adj* ácido *m* oxálico.

oxcare, *n* carro *m* de bueyes

oxford, *n* zapato *m* (de tacón bajo).

oxhide, *n* cuero *m* de buey.

oxidation, *n* oxidación *f*.

oxide, *n* óxido *m*.

oxidize, *vt* 1. oxidar; 2. *vi* oxidarse

oxtail, *n* cola de buey

oxygen, *n* oxígeno *m*.

oxygenate, *vt* oxigenar.

oxygenation, *n* oxigenación *f*.

oxygen-mask, *n* máscara *f* de oxígeno, mascarilla *f* con oxígeno.

oxygen-tent, *n* tienda *f* de oxígeno.

oyster, *n* ostra *f*.

oysterbed, *n* criadero *m*. (o vivero) de ostras

oystercatcher, *n* ostrero *m*.

oyster-shell, *n* concha *f* de ostra

ozone, *n* ozono *m*.

ozonosphere, *n* ozonosfera *f*.

P

P, p , *n* (letra *f*) P, p.

pa, *n* papá *m*.

pace , *n* 1. paso *m*; 2. velocidad *f*; ritmo *m*; 3. *vt* medir apasos;pasearsepreocupadopor.

pachyderm , *n* paquidermo *m*.

pacific, *adj* pacífico.

Pacific Ocean, *n* Océano *m* Pacífico.

pacifier, *n* chupete *m*.

pacifist, *adj* 1. pacifista; 2. *n* pacifista *m/f*.

pacify, *vt* pacificar; apaciguar, calmar.

pack, *n* 1. lío *m*, fardo *m*; carga *f*; 2. jauría *f*; manada *f*; 3. *vt* llenar.

package, *n* 1. paquete *m*; 2. *vi* empaquetar;envasar.

packet, *n* paquete *m*.

packing, *n* embalaje *m*, envase *m*, envasado *m*; relleno *m*.

pact, *n* pacto *m*; convenio *m*.

pad, *n* 1. almohadilla *f*, cojinete *m*; 2. *vt* acolchar, almoiladillar; rellenar; 3. *vi* andar;pisar.

padding, *n* relleno *m*, almohadilla *f*.

paddle, *n* 1. canalete *m*, zagual *m*; raqueta *f*; 2. *vt* umpulsar con canalete, remar con canalete.

padlock, *n* candado *m* .

pagan, *adj* 1. pagano; 2. *n* pagano(a) *m/f*.

paganism, *n* paganismo *m*.

page, *n* 1. paje *m*; 2. (ofabook)página *f*; 3. *vt* paginar, buscar llamando.

pageantry, *n* pompa *f*, boato *m*.

pager, *n* localizador *m*, busca *m*.

paid, *adj* 1. asalariado; 2. pagado.

pail, *n* cubo *m*, balde *m*.

pain, *n* 1. dolor *m*; 2. *vt/i* doler.

painful , *adj* doloroso, dolorido; difícil, penoso.

painstaking , *adj* laborioso, concienzudo, esmerado.

paint, *n* pintura *f*; colorete *m*.

painter, *n* pintor(a) *m/f*.

painting, *n* pintura *f*; cuadro *m*.

pair, *n* 1. par *m*; pareja *f*, yunta; 2. *vt* aparear.

pajamas, *n* pijama *m*.

pal, *n* camarada *m/f*, compañero(a) *m/f*.

palace, *n* palacio *m*.

palatable, *adj* sabroso, apetitoso.

palate, *n* paladar *m*.

pale, *adj* 1. pálido; color claro; tenue; 2. *vi* palidecer, ponerse pálido; 3. *n* estaca *f*.

pall, *n* 1. paño *m* de ataúd; 2. (Ecl) palio *m*; 3. *vt* empalagar; 4. *vi* perdersusabor.

palladium, *n* paladio *m*.

pallbearer, *n* portador *m* del féretro.

pallet, *n* jergón *m*; paleta *f*, plataforma *f*.

pallid, *adj* pálido.

palm , *n* palma *f*; palmera *f*.

palmistry, *n* quuomancia *f*.

palpitate, *vi* palpitar.

palpitating, *adj* palpitante.

palpilation, *n* palpitación *f*.

palsy, *n* parálisis *f*.

paltry, *adj* insignificante, baladí

pamper , *vt* mimar.

pamphlet, *n* folleto *m*, impreso *m*; panfleto *m*.

pan , *n* 1. cazuela *f*, cacerola *f*; perol *m*; sartén *f*; 2. *vi* lavar con batea para obtener el oro.

panacea, *n* panacea *f*.

panache , *n* aire; garbo *m* brío *m* brillantez *f*.

pancake , *n* crepé *m*, hojuela *f*, tortita *f*, panqueque *m*.

pancreas, *n* pancreas *m*.

panda, *n* panda *m/f*.

panel, *n* 1. panel *m*; artesón *m*; entrepaño *m*; 2. *vt* poner paneles a, adornar con paneles.

paneling, *n* paneles *m*; artesonado *m*.

panelist, *n* miembro *m* del jurado, panel *m*.

pang, *n* punzada *f*, dolor *m* súbito, dolor *m* agudo.

panic, *n* 1. pánico *m*; 2. *vt* infundirpánicoa.

panorama, *n* panorama *m*.

panoramic, *adj* panorámico.

pant, *n* 1. jadeo *m*; resuello *m*; 2. *vt* decijadeando.

pantheism, *n* panteismo *m*.

pantheon, *n* panteón *m*.

panther, *n* pantera *f*.

panties, *n* calzonsillas *f pl* de mujer.

panting, *n* jadeo *m*; respiración *f* difícil.

pantomime, *n* pantomima *f*.

pantry, *n* despensa *f*.

pants, *n* calzoncillos *m*; pantalones *m*.

pap, *n* papilla *f*, gachas *f*.

papa, *n* papá *m*.

papacy, *n* papado *m*, pontificado *m*.

papal, *adj* papal, pontificio.

papaya, *n* papaya *f*, mamón *m*.

paper, *n* 1. papel *m*; 2. periódico; 3. *vt* empapelar.

paprika, *n* pimienta *f* húngara, paprika *f*.

parable, *n* parábola *f*.

parachute, *n* 1. paracaídas *m*; 2. *vt* lanzar;en;paracaídas.

parachutist, *n* paracaidista *m/f*.

parade, *n* 1. desfile *m*, parada *f*; 2. *vt* formar;en parada; recorrer, desfilar por.

paradise, *n* paraíso *m*.

paradox, *n* paradoja *f*.

pararfin, *n* petróleo *m*, queroseno *m*.

paragraph, *n* párrafo *m*, acápite *m*.

parakeet, *n* perico *m*, periquito *m*.

parallel, adj 1. paralelo; 2. n paralela f, línea paralela; 3. vt ser paralelo a, ser análogo a.

paralysis, n parálisis f; paralización f.

paralyze, vt paralizar.

paramedic, n paramédico(a) m/f.

paramounl, adj supremo, de la mayor importancia, primordial.

paranoia, n paranoia f.

parapet, n parapeto m.

paraphernalia, n parafernalia f.

paraphrase, n 1. paráfrasis f; 2. vt parafrasear.

paraplegic, adj 1. parapléjico; 2. n parapléjico(a) m/f.

parapsychology, n parapsicología f.

parasite, n parásito m.

parasol, n sombrilla f, quitasol m, parasol m.

paratrooper, n paracaidista m.

parcel, n paquete m; parcela f.

parch, vt secar, resecar; agostar; quemar.

parchment, n pergamino m.

pardon, n 1. perdón m; indulto m; indulto m absoluto; 2. vt perdonar, dispensar.

pardonable, adj perdonable.

pare, vt cortar; mondar; adelgazar, pelar.

parent, n 1. padre m, madre f; 2. adj madre, matriz.

parentage, n familia f, linaje m.

parenthesis, n paréntesis m; entre paréntesis.

pariah, n paria m/f.

parish, n parroquia f.

parisbioner, n feligrés(esa) m/f.

parity, n paridad f, igualdad f; paridad f.

park, n 1. parque m; jardines m; campo m; 2. vt estacionar, aparcar.

parkway, n carretera f principal, alameda f.

parliament, n parlamento m.

parlor, n sala f de recibo, salón m.

parochial , adj parroquial; estrecho, limitado.

parody, n 1. parodia f; 2. vt parodiar.

parole, n 1. palabra f, palabra f de honor; libertad f bajo palabra; 2. vt dejar libre bajo palabra.

parricide, n parricidio m.

parrot, n loro m, papagayo m.

parse, vt analizar.

parsley, n perejil m.

parson, n clérigo m, cura m; párroco m.

parsonage, n casa f del párroco; casa f del pastor.

part, n 1. parte f; porción f; trozo m; número m; 2. adj parcial; 3. vt separar, dividir, romper, partir.

partial , adj parcial.

partiality, n parcialidad f; predisposición f.

participant, n partícipe m/f, participante m/f.

participate, vi participar, tomar parte.

participle, n participio m.

particle, n partícula f.

particular, adj 1. particular; especial; concreto; de terminado; 2. n detalle m, pormenor m, dato m.

partition, n 1. partición f, división f; 2. vt compartir, dividir.

partner, n compañero(a) m/f; socio m; pareja f.

partnersbip, n asociación f, sociedad f.

party, n partido m; festa f.

paschal , adj pascual.

pass, n 1. permiso m, pase m; 2. desfiladero m; 3. vt pasar; pasar por delante de.

passable, adj pasable; tolerable, admisible.

passage, n paso m, tránsito m; viaje m.

passenger, n 1. pasajero m/f; 2. vi ajero(a) m/f.

passing, adj 1. pasajero; rápido, superficial; 2. n paso m; aprobación f; desaparición f.

passion, m pasión f; cólera f, arranque m de cólera.

passionate, adj apasionado.

passive, adj pasivo; inactivo, inerte.

passkey, n llave f maestra.

Passover, n Pascua f (de los judíos).

passport, n pasaporte m.

past, adv 1. por delante; pasar; 2. prep por delante de; más de; 3. adj pasado; antiguo, ex.., que fue.

paste, n 1. pasta f; goma; 2. vt engrudar, pegar, engomar, pegar.

pastel , n pastel m; lápiz m de color.

pasteurize, vt pasteurizar.

pastille, n pastilla f.

pastime, n pasatiempo m.

pastor, n pastor m.

pastoral, adj pastoral.

pastry, n pasta f; pastas f, pasteles m pl.

pasture, n pasto m; prado m.

pal , n 1. palmadita f, golpecito m; palmada f; 2. vt tocar, pasar la mano por.

patch, n 1. pedazo m; parche m, guarache m; 2. vt remendar, poner remiendo a.

patella, n rótula f.

patena, n patena f.

patent, adj 1. patente, evidente; 2. n charol m.

paternity, n paternidad f.

path, n camino m, senda f, sendero m.

pathetic, adj patético, lastimoso, conmovedor.

pathfinder, n explorador m, piloto m; pionero m.

pathology, n patología f.

patience, n paciencia f.

patio, n patio m.

patriarch, n patriarca m.

patrimony, n patrimonio m.

patriot, n patriota m/f.

patriotism, n patriotismo m.

patrol, n 1. patrulla f; 2. vt patrullar por.

patron, n cliente m/f; patrocinador m.

patronize, vt cliente de, comprar en.

patter, n 1. chapaleteo m; 2. jerga f; 3. pasos m ligeros; 4. vi charlar; 5. aundar con pasos ligeros.

pattern, n 1. modelo m; muestra f; diseño m, dibujo m; 2. vt modelar, diseñar.

patterned, adj material estampado.

paunch, n panza f, barriga f.

pauper, n pobre m/f, indigente m/f.

pause, n 1. pausa f; 2. vt hacer una pausa.

pave, vt pavimentar; enlosar, solar.

pavement, n pavimento m.

pavilion, n pabellón m.

paw, n 1. pata f; garra f; 2. vt tocar con la pata.

pawn, n 1. (chess) peon m; 2. vt empeñar, pignorar, dejar en prenda.

pay, n 1. paga f; remuneración f, retribución f; 2. vt pagar.

paying, adj provechoso, que rinde bien; rentable.

payment, n pago m; remuneración f, retribución f.

payroll, n nómina f.

pea, n guisante m, arveja f, chícharo m.

peace, n paz f.

peaceful, adj pacífico.

peach, n melocotón m, durazno m.

peacock, n pavo m real.

peak, n 1. punta f; cumbre f, cima f; apogeo m; 2. vi alcanzar su punto más alto.

peaked, adj pálido, enfermizo.

peal, n 1. repique m, campanillazo m; 2. vi repicar.

pear, n pera f.

pearl, n perla f.

peasant, n campesino(a) m/f.

peal, n turba f.

pebble, *n* guija *f* guijarro *m*, china *f*.

pecan, *n* pacana *f*.

peck, *n* 1. picotazo *m*; besito *m*, medida de áridos *m*; 2. *vr* picotear.

pectin, *n* pectina *f*.

pectoral, *adj* 1. pectoral; 2. *n* pectorales *m*.

peculiar, *adj* peculiar; propio.

pedagogue, *n* pedagogo(a) *m/f*.

pedal, *n* pedal *m*.

pedant, *n* pedante *m/f*.

pedantic, *adj* pedante; pedantesco.

peddle, *vi* vender como buhonero, vender por las casas.

peddler, *n* buhonero *m*.

pedestal, *n* pedestal *m*, basa *f*.

pedestrian, *adj* 1. prosaico, pedestre; 2. *n* peatón *m*.

pediatrician, *n* pediatra *m/f*.

pediatrics, *n* pediatría *f*.

pedicure, *n* pedicura *f*, quuropedia *f*.

peek, *n* 1. mirada *f* rápida, mirada *f* furtiva; 2. vi mirar a hurtadillas.

peep, *n* 1. mirada *f* rápida, mirada *f* furtiva; 2. pío *m*; 3. vi mirar rápidamente, mirar furtivamente; 4. *vi* piar.

peer, *n* 1. par *m*; 2. *vi* mirar con ojos miopes.

peerless, *adj* sin par, incomparable.

peeve, *vt* enojar, irritar.

peevish , *adj* malhulllorado, displicente.

peg , *n* 1. clavija *f*, claveta *f*; estaca *f*, estaquilla *f*; 2. *vt* enclavijar.

pejorative, *adj* peyorativo.

pelican, *n* pelícano *m*.

pell, *n* 1. pellejo *m*; piel *f*, 2. *vt* tirar, arrojar.

pelvis, *n* pelvis *f*.

pen, *n* 1. corral *m*; redil *m*, aprisco *m*; pluma *f*; 2. *vi* encerrar, acorralar; 3. *vi* penar; perjudicar.

penalty, *n* pena *f* castigo *m*; multa *f*.

penance, *n* penitencia *f*.

penchant, *n* predilección *f*; inclinación f

pencil, *n* lápiz *m*.

pendant, *n* pendiente *m*, medallón *m*.

pending, *adj* pendiente.

pendulum, *n* péndulo *m*.

penetrate, *vt* penetrar (por).

penetrating, *adj* penetrante.

penguin, *n* pingüino *m*.

penicillin, *n* penicilina *f*.

peninsula, *n* península *f*.

peninsular, *adj* peninsular.

penis, *n* pene *m*.

penitent, *adj* 1. penitente; arrepentido, compungido; 2. *n* penitente *m/f*.

penitentiary, *n* cárcel *f*, presidio *m*, penitenciaría *f*.

pennant, *n* banderola *f*; bandera *m*.

penny, *n* centavo *m*.

penology, *n* ciencia *f* penal, criminología *f*.

pension, *n* pensión *f*; retiro *m*.

pensive, *adj* pensativo, meditabundo; preocupado.

pentagon, *n* pentágono *m*.

Pentecost, *n* Pentecostés *m*.

penthouse, *n* cobertezo *m*; ático *m*; casa *f* de azotea.

penultimate, *adj* penúltimo.

penumbra, *n* penumbra *f*.

penury, *n* miseria *f*; pobreza *f*.

peon, *n* peón *m*.

people, *n* pueblo *m*; ciudadanos *m*; nación *f*; gente *f*.

pepper, *n* pimienta *f*; pimiento *m*.

perceive, *vt* percibir; notar, observar.

percentage, *n* porcentaje *m*.

perceptible, *adj* perceptible; sensible.

perception, *adj* percepción *f*; perspicacia *f*.

perceptiveness, *n* penetración *f*; sensibilidad *f*.

perch, *n* 1. perca *f*; percha *f*; 2. *vt* encaramar;colocar (enunaposiciónelevada,pocosegura).

perchance, *adv* por ventura, acaso.

percolator, *n* percolador *m*.

percussion, *n* percusión *f*.

perdition, *n* perdición *f*.

peregrination, *n* peregrinación *f*.

peregrine, *n* halcón *m* común, neblí *m*.

peremptory, *adj* perentorio; imperioso, autoritario.

perennial, *adj* 1. perenne; 2. *n* planta *f* vivaz.

perfect, *adj* 1. perfecto; 2. *n* perfecto *m*; 3. *vt* perfeccionar.

perfidy, *n* perfidia *f*.

perforate, *vt* perforar, horadar, agujerear.

perforation, *n* perforación *f*; agujero *m*; trepado *m*.

perform, *vt* hacer, cumplir, realizar.

performance, *n* cumplimiento *m*, ejecución *f*, realización *f*; resultado *m*; representación *f*; interpretación *f*; funcionamiento *m*.

performer, *n* actor *m*, actriz *f*; artista *m/f*.

perfume, *n* perfume *m*.

pergola, *n* pérgola *f*.

perhaps, *adv* tal vez, quizá(s), puede que.

peril, *n* peligro *m*, riesgo *m*.

perilous, *adj* peligroso, arriesgado.

perimeter, *n* perínetro *m*.

period, *n* período *m*; época *f*, edad *f*; hora *f*, clase *f*.

periodical, *adj* periódico.

periphery, *n* periferia *f*.

periscope, *n* periscopio *m*.

perish, *vt* deteriorar, estropear, echar a perder.

perjure, *vt* perjurar, perjurarse.

perjury, *n* perjurio *m*; jurar en falso.

perk, *vt* 1. reanimar a uno, infundir nuevo vigor a uno; 2. *vi* filtrarse.

perkiness, *n* alegria *f*, buen humor *m*; despejo *m*.

permanence, *n* permanencia *f*.

permanent, *adj* permanente.

permeable, *adj* permeable.

permeate, *vt* penetrar; calar; saturar, impregnar.

permission, *n* permiso *m*; licencia *f*; autorización *f*.

permit , *n* 1. permiso *m*, licencia *f*; 2. *vt* permitir; autorizar; tolerar, sufrir.

permute, *vt* permutar.

pernicious, *adj* pennicioso; nocivo, dañoso.

peroxide, *n* peróxido *m*.

perpendicular, *adj* 1. perpendicular; 2. *n* perpendicular *f*.

perpetrate, *vt* cometer; perpetrar.

perpetrator, *n* autor(a) *m/f*; responsable *m/f*.

perpetual, *adj* perpetuo; incesante, constante.

perpetuate, *vt* perpetuar.

perplex, *vt* dejar perplejo, confundir.

perplexity, *n* perplejidad *f*, confusión *f*.

persecute, *vt* perseguir; atormentar, importunar.

persecution, *n* persecución *f*.

persecutor, *n* perseguidor(a) *m/f*.

perseverance, *n* perseverancia *f*, tenacidad *f*.

persevere, *vi* perseverar, persistir; continuar con.

persist, *vi* persistir; continuar.

persistent, *adj* persistente; continuo porfiado.

person, *n* persona *f*; particular *m*; en persona.

personal, *adj* 1. personal; privado, íntimo; 2. *n* nota *f* de sociedad; mensaje *m* personal.

personality, *n* personalidad *f*.

personify, *vt* personificar.

personnel, *n* personal *m*.

perspective, *n* perspectiva *f*.

perspicacious, *adj* perspicaz.

perspiration, *n* transpiración *f*; sudor *m*.

perspire, *vi* transpirar, sudar.

persuade, *vt* persuadir, convencer.

persuasiveness, *n* persuasiva *f*.

pert, *adj* impertinente, respondón, fresco.

pertain, *vi* tener que ver con, estar relacionado con.

pertinacious, *adj* pertinaz.

pertinent, *adj* pertinente, oportuno, a propósito.

pertinently, *adv* oportunamente, a propósito, atinadamente.

pertness, *n* unpertinencia *f*, frescura *f*, elegancia *f*.

perturb, *vi* perturbar, inquietar.

perturbation, *n* perturbación *f* inquietud *f*.

pervade, *vt* extenderse por, difundirse por, empapar (de); impregnar.

pervasive, *adj* penetrante; omnipresente.

perverse, *adj* perverso, terco, contumaz.

perversion, *n* perversión *f*.

pervert, *n* pervertido(a) *m/f*.

perverted, *adj* pervertido.

pervious, *adj* permeable.

peseta, *n* peseta *f*.

pessimism, *n* pesimismo *m*.

pessimist, *n* pesimista *m/f*.

pessimistic, *adj* pesimista.

pest, *n* plaga *f*; insecto *m* nocivo, animal *m* dañino.

pester, *vt* molestar, acosar, importunar.

pesticide, *n* pesticida *m*.

pestilence, *n* pestilencia *f*, peste *f*.

pet, *adj* 1. doméstico, domesticado, de casa, familiar; 2. *n* animal *m* doméstico, animal *m* de casa; 3. *vt* acariciar.

petal, *n* pétalo *m*.

petite, *adj* chiquita.

petition, *n* petición *f*, instancia *f*, demanda *f*.

petrified, *adj* petrificado.

petrify, *vt* petrificar.

petroleum, *n* petróleo *m*.

petticoat, *n* enaguas *f*, combunación *f*; falda *f*.

pettiness, *n* insignificancia *f*, pequeñez *f*; nimiedad *f*.

petting, *n* caricias *f*.

petty, *adj* insignificante, pequeño, nimio.

petulant, *adj* malhumorado, irritable.

petunia, *n* petunia *f*.

pew, *n* banco *m*.

pewter, *n* peltre *m*.

phantom, *n* fantasma *m*.

pharmacist, *n* farmacéutico(a) *m/f*.

pharmacy, *n* farmacia *f*.

pharynx, *n* faringe *f*.

phase, *n* 1. fase *f*; etapa *f*; 2. *vt* proyectar en una serie de etapas, escalonar.

phenol, *n* fenol *m*.

phenomenal, *adj* fenomenal.

phenomenon, *n* fenómeno *m*.

philanderer, *n* tenorio *m* mariposón *m*.

philanthropist, *n* filántropo(a) *m/f*.

philanthropy, *n* filantropía *f*.

philharmonic, *adj* filarmónico.

philosopher, *n* filósofo(a) *m/f*.

philosophize, *vi* filosofar.

philosophy, *n* filosofía *f*.

phobia, *n* fobia *f*.

phone, *n* 1. telefono *m*; 2. *vt* telefonear.

phonograph, *n* fonógrafo *m*, tocadiscos *m*.

photo, *n* foto *f*.

photocopier, *n* fotocopiadora *f*.

photocopy, *n* fotocopia *f*.

photograph, *n* 1. fotografía *f*; 2. *vt* fotografiar.

photographer, *n* fotógrafo(a) *m/f*.

photography, *n* fotografía *f*.

phrase, *n* 1. frase *m*; 2. *vt* frasear.

phrasing, *n* redacción *f*; estilo *m*; fraseología *f*.

physical, *adj* físico.

physician, *n* médico(a) *m/f*.

physicist, *n* físico(a) *m/f*.

physics, *n* física *f*.

physiological, *adj* fisiológico.

physique, *n* físico *m*, complexión *f*.

pianist, *n* pianista *m/f*.

piano, *n* piano *m*.

pick, *n* 1. pico *m*; 2. selección *f*, elección *f*; 3. *vt* escoger.

picking, *n* recolección *f*; cosecha *f*.

pickle, *n* 1. encurtido *m*; escabeche *m*; adobo *m*; 2. *vt* encurtir; escabechar; adobar; conservar.

picnic, *n* 1. jira *f*, excursión *f* campestre; 2. *vt* merendar en el campo.

pictorial, *adj* 1. pictórico; ilustrado; 2. *n* revista *f* ilustrada.

picture, *n* 1. cuadro *m*, pintura *f*; 2. *vt* pintar; describir.

picturesque, *adj* pintoresco.

piddling, *adj* de poca monta, insignificante.

pie, *n* pastel *m*, tarta *f*.

piece, *n* pedazo *m*, trozo *m*; obra *f*, pieza *f*.

piecrust, *n* pasta *f* de pastel.

pier, *n* pilar *m*; columna *f*; malecón *m*, embarcadero *m*.

pierce, *vt* penetrar; atravesar, traspasar; agujerear; oradar, perforar; taladrar.

piercing, *adj* cortante; agudo, desgarrador.

piety, *n* piedad *f*, devoción *f*; beatería *f*.

pig, *n* cerdo *m*, puerco *m*, cochino *m*.

pigeon, *n* paloma *m/f*.

pigmentation, *n* pigmentación *f*.

pigmy, *adj* pigmeo.

pigtail, *n* trenza *f*; coleta *f*.

pike, *n* pica *f*, chuzo *m*; lucio *m*.

piker, *n* cicatero *m*; persona *f* de poco fuste.

pilaf(f), *n* plato *m* oriental a base de arroz.

pilaster, *n* pilastra *f*.

pilchard, *n* sardina *f*.

pile, *n* 1. montón *m*, pila *f*, rimero *m*; 2. *vi* aunontonarse, apilarse; acumularse.

piles, *n* hemorroides *f*.

pilfer, *vt* 1. ratear, hurtar; 2. *vi* ratear, robar cosas.

pilferage, *n* hurto *m* robo *m*.

pilgrim, *n* peregrino(a) *m/f*.

pilgrimage, *n* peregrinación *f*, romería *f*.

pill, *n* gragea *f*, píldora *f*.

pillage, *n* 1. pillaje *m* saqueo *m*; 2. *vt* pillar, saquear.

pillar, *n* pilar *m*, columna *f*; sostén *m*.

pillory, *n* 1. picota *f*; 2. *vt* poner en ridículo, satitizar.

pillow, *n* almohada *f*.

pillowcase, *n* funda *f* de almohada.

pilot, *adj* 1. piloto; 2. *n* piloto *m/f*, aviador(a) *m/f*; 3. *vt* pilotar.

pimento, *n* pimiento *m*.

pimple, *n* grano *m*.

pin, *n* 1. alfiler *m*; perno *m*, chaveta *f*; arandela *f*; 2. *vt* prender con alfiler, prender con alfileres.

pinball, *n* millón *m*, fliper *m*.

pincer, *n* 1. pinzas *f pl*; 2. tenazas *f pl*; 3. *vt* pellizcar.

pinch, n 1. pellizco m; 2. pizca f; 3. aputo m; 4. vt pellizcar, apretar.

pinched, adj 1. tener la cara pálida; estar aterido, estar chuprdo; 2. andar escaso de dinero.

pine, n 1. pino m; 2. vi languidecer,consumirse; suspuar por, perecer por.

pineapple, n piña f, ananás m.

pinion, n 1. ala f; piñón m; 2. vt cortar las alas a;atar los brazos a.

pink, n 1. clavel m, clavellina f; 2. color m de rosa.

pinnacle, n pináculo m, remate m; chapitel m.

pinpoint, n 1. punta f de aifiler, punto m muy pequeño; 2. vt indicar con toda precisión;concretar.

pint, n pinta f.

pioneer, n pionero(a) m/f; explorador(a) m/f.

pious, adj piadoso, devoto.

pipe, n 1. tubo m, caño m, conducto m, tubería f, cañería f; 2.pipa f; 3. vt conducir en cañerías.

pipeline, n tubería f de distribución.

piper, n flautista m/f; gaitero m.

piquancy, n picante m, lo picante.

piquant, adj picante.

pique, n 1. pique m, resentimiento m; 2. vt picar.

piracy, n piratería f; publicación f pirata.

piranha, n piraña f.

pirate, n pirata m.

pirouette, n 1. pirueta f; 2. vi piruetear.

pistol, n pistola f, revólver m.

pit, n l. hoyo m, fosa f; 2. hueco m; 3. vt hacer hoyos en; 4. deshuesar.

pitch, n 1. brea f; 2. (ball) tiro m, lanzamiento m; 3. pendiente m; 4. (Mus) tono m; 5. vt embrear, arrojar, lanzar.

pitcher, n cántaro m, jarro m; lanzador m.

pitchfork, n horca f, bielda f.

pitfall, n escollo m, peligro m; trampa f.

pith, n médula f; meollo m, médula f, jugo m.

pitifull, adj lastimero, lastimoso; conmovedor.

pitiless, adj despiadado, implacable, inmisericorde.

piton, n pitón m; clavija f de escala.

pituitary, adj pituitario.

pity, n 1. compasión f, piedad f; 2. lástima f; 3. vt compadecerse (de), tener lástuma a.

pivot, n 1. pivote m; eje m, punto m central; 2. vi girar sobre, depender de.

pizza, n pizza f.

placard , n cartel m; letrero m.

placate, vt aplacar, apaciguar.

place, n 1. sitio m, lugar m; local m, 2. vt poner, colocar; fijar; situar, emplazar,

placebo, n placebo m.

placement, n colocación f.

placenta, n placenta f.

placid , adj plácido; apacible; tranquilo, sosegado.

plagiarize, vt plagiar.

plague, n 1. peste f; plaga f; 2. vt plagar,infestar.

plaid, n tela f a cuadros, tartán m.

plain, adj 1.claro, evidente, 2. franco, abierto, 3.sencillo, llano; sin adornos; 4. adv claro, claramente; 5. n llano m, llanura f.

plaintiff, n demandante m/f, querellante m/f.

plaintive, adj lastimero, dolorido, quejumbroso.

plait, n 1. trenza f; 2. vt trenzar.

plan, n 1. plano m; 2. programa m; 2. vt planear, planificar; proyectar; preparar.

plane, adj 1. plano; 2. n plano m; 3. vt acepillar;4. vi planear,aquaplanear.

planet, n planeta m.

planetarium , n planetario m.

plank, n 1. tabla, tablón m; 2. vt entablar,entarimar.

plankton, n plancton m.

planning, n planificación f; proyectos m.

plant, n 1. planta f; 2. equipo m, maquinaria; 3. vt plantar,sembrar.

plantation, n hacienda f; arboleda f.

planter, n plantador(a) m/f.

plaque, n placa f; sarro m.

plasm, n plasma m.

plaster, n 1. yeso m; enlucido m; 2. emplasto m, parche m; 3. vt enyesar,enlucir;emplastar.

plastic, adj 1. plástico; 2. n plástico m.

plate, n 1. plato m, lámina f; 2. vt planchear,chapear.

plated, adj chapeado; niquelado.

platform, n plataforna f.

platitude, n lugar m común, perogrullada f.

platonic, adj platónico.

platoon, n pelotón m, sección f.

play, n 1. juego m, recreo m, diversión f; 2. vt representar,poner, dar; hacer,hacer el papel de;3. vi jugar;divertirse,retozar.

playwright, n dramaturgo m/f, autor m dramático, autora f dramática.

plaza, n zona f de servicios.

plea, n 1. pretexto m, disculpa f; 2. ruego m, súplica f, petición f; 3. vi suplicar, rogar.

pleasant, adj agradable; grato; ameno; simpático.

please, vt/i 1. dar gusto a, dar satisfacción a, agradar, contentar; 2. vr hacer lo que le da la gana.

pleased, adj alegre, contento; estar contento.

pleasing, adj agradable; grato.

pleasure, n placer m, gusto m, satisfacción f.

pleat, n 1. pliegue m, doblez f; 2. vt plegar,plisar.

pledge, n 1. prenda f; promesa f, voto m; garantía f; 2. vt empeñar,pignorar,dejar en prenda.

plenitude, n plenitud f.

plenty, vt contaminar; ensuciar; corromper.

pollution, n contaminación f.

polygamy, n poligamia f.

polygraph, n polígrafo m.

pomade, n pomada f.

pomp, n pompa f; fausto m, boato m, ostentación f.

pompous, adj pomposo; fastuoso, ostentoso; ampuloso, hinchado.

poncho, n poncho m.

pond, n charca f; estanque m; vivero m.

ponder, vt 1. ponderar, meditar, considerar con especial cuidado; 2. vi reflexionar, pensar.

pontifical, adj pontificio, pontifical.

pontificate, n pontificado m.

pontoon, n 1. pontón m; 2. puente m de pontones.

pony, n caballito m, jaca f, poni m, poney m.

poodle, n perro m de lanas, caniche m.

pool, n 1. charca f, piscina f, alberca f; 2. polla f; 3. vt mancomunar.

pooped, adj estar hecho polvo.

poor, adj pobre; estéril.

pop, n 1. taponazo m; 2. bebida f gaseosa; 3.(Pop) papá m; 4. vt reventar.

popcorn, n rosetas f pl, palomitas f pl (de maíz).

pope, n papa m; el Papa m.

poplar, n chopo m, álamo m; álamo m blanco.

poplin, n popelina f.

popular, adj popular.

popularity, n popularidad f.

popularize, vt popularizar.

population, n población f; habitantes m/f pl.

populous, adj populoso.

porcelain, n porcelana f.

porch, n pórtico m.

porcupine, n puerco m espín.

pork, n cerdo m, chancho m; tocinero m.

pornography, n pornografía f.

porosity, n porosidad f.

porous, adj poroso.

porpoise, n marsopa f, puerco m de mar.

port, n 1. puerto m, portilla f; babor m; 2. vino oporto; 3. vt virar a babor.

portable , adj portátil,

portal, n puerta f.

portend, vt presagiar, anunciar.

portent, n presagio m, augurio m, señal f.

porter, n portero m, conserje m.

portfolio, n cartera f, carpeta f.

portion, n porción f, parte f; ración f; dote f.

portliness, n gordura f, corpulencia f.

portly, adj gordo, corpulento,

portrait , n retrato m.

portray, vt retratar; puntar, describir; representar.

portrayal, n retrato m; descripción f.

pose, n 1. postura f, actitud f; 2. vt colocar.

posh, adj elegante, de lujo, lujoso.

position, n posición f, situación f; postura f.

positive, adj 1. positivo; definitivo; 2. n positiva f.

possess, vt poseer; tomar posesión de.

possession, n posesión f.

possibility, n posibilidad f; perspectiva f.

possum, n zarigüeya f; fingir.

post, n 1. poste m; estaca f; 2. puesto m; 3. vt anunciar; fijar.

postage, n porte m, franqueo m.

postal, adj postal, de correos,

postcard, n tarjeta f postal, postal f.

poster, n cartel m; póster m.

posterior, adj posterior.

posterity, n posteridad f.

postern, n postigo m.

posting, n destino m.

postpone, vt aplazar; diferir.

postponement, n aplazamiento m.

postscript, n posdata f; añadidura f.

postulate, n postulado m.

posture, n postura f, actitud f.

pot, n 1. olla f, puchero m, marmita f; tarro m, pote m; 2. vt conservar; enmacetar.

potable, adj potable.

potash, n potasa f.

potassium, n potasio m.

potato, n patata f, papa f.

potency, n potencia f; fuerza f; eficacia f.

potent, adj potente, poderoso; fuerte,

potentate, n potentado m.

potential, adj 1. potencial; 2. n potencial m; capacidad f.

potion, n poción f, pócima f.

potter, n alfarero m; ceramista m/f.

pottery, n alfar m, alfarería f.

potty, n orinal m de niño, bacinica f.

pouch, n bolsa f.

poulterer, n pollero(a) m/f.

poultice, n 1. cataplasma f, emplasto m; 2. vt emplastar.

poultry, n aves f pl de corral; pollos m pl, volatería f.

pound, n 1. libra f; corral m de conejo; 2. vt machacar, majar.

pounding, n palpitación f; martilleo m, golpeo m.

pour, vt verter, echar; derramar; llover a torrentes.

powder, n 1. polvo m; polvos m; 2. vt reducir a polvo, pulverizar.

power, n 1. poder m; fuerza f energía f, vigor m; 2. vt accionar impulsar.

powerful, adj poderoso.

powerless, adj impotente; ineficaz.

practical, adj práctico; en la práctica.

practice, n 1. costumbre f, uso m; 2. ejercicio m; adiestramiento; 3. práctica f; 4. vt practicar tener por costumbre.

pragmatist, n pragmatista m/f.

prairie, n pradera f, llanura f, pampa f.

praise, n 1. alabanza f, elogio m; alabanzas f pl; 2. vt alabar elogiar.

prance, vi hacer cabriolas, hacer corvetas.

prank, n travesura f; broma f.

prawn , n gamba f; quisquilla f camarón m.

pray, vt 1. rogar, suplicar; 2. rezar, orar.

prayer, n oración f, rezo m.

preach, vt predicar.

preacher, n predicador(a) m/f; pastor m.

preamble, n preámbulo m.

prearrange, vt arreglar de antemano, predeterminar.

precarious, adj precario.

precaution, n precaución f.

precede, vt /i preceder.

precedence, n precedencia f; priondad f; primacía f.

precedent, n precedente m.

preceding, adj precedente.

precept, n precepto m.

precinct, n precinto m; barrio m; distrito m electoral.

precious, adj precioso; precioso.

precipice, n precipicio m, despeñadero m.

precipitate, n 1. precipitado m; 2. vt precipitar.

precipitation, n precipitación f.

precipitous, adj escarpado, cortado a pico.

precise, adj preciso, exacto; claro.

precision, n precisión.

preclude, vt excluir; imposibilitar.

precocious, adj precoz.

preconceived, adj preconcebido.

preconception, n preconcepción f.

precondition, n condición f previa.

precursor, n precursor(a) m/f.

predator, n depredador m.

predatory, adj rapaz, de rapiña; agresivo.

predecessor, n predecesor(a) m/f.

predetermine, vt predeterminar.

predicament, n apuro m, situación f difícil.

predict, vt pronosticar, profetizar, predecir.

prediction, n pronóstico m, profecía f, predicción f.

predilection, n predilección f.

predispose, vt predisponer.

predominant, adj predominante.

predominate, vi predominar.

prefabricate, vt prefabricar.

prefabricated, adj prefabricado.

preface, n prólogo m, prefacio m.

prefect, n prefecto m; tutor m, monitor m.

prefer, vt preferir.

preference, n preferencia f, prioridad f.

prefix, n prefijo m.

pregnancy, n embarazo m, preñez f.

pregnant, adj embarazada; estar embarazada.

prejudice, n 1. parcialidad f; prejuicio m; 2. vt prevenir, predisponer.

prejudicial, adj perjudicial.

prelate, n prelado m.

preliminary, adj preliminar.

prelude, n preludio m.
premature, adj prematuro.
premeditate, vt premeditar.
premeditated, adj premeditado.
premenstrual, adj premenstrual.
premier, adj primero, principal.
premise, n premisa f.
premium, n (prize) premio m; (insur) prima f.
premonition, n presentimiento m, premonición f.
prenatal, adj prenatal, antenatal.
preoccupation, n preocupación f.
preoccupy, vt preocupar.
preordain, vt predestinar.
preparation , n preparación f.
prepare, vt preparar, disponer, aparejar.
prepay, vt pagar por adelantado.
preponderance, n preponderancia f; predominio m.
preposition, n preposición f.
preposterous, adj absurdo, ridículo.
prerequisite, n requisito esencial.
preschool, adj preescolar.
prescient, adj presciente.
prescribe, vt prescribir; ordenar.
presealed, adj precintado (de antemano).
presence, n presencia f; asistencia f.
present, adj 1.presente; 2. n presente m, actualidad f; 3. regalo m; 4. vt presentar.
presentation, n presentación f, exposición f.
presentiment, n presentimiento m.
preservation, n conservación f; preservación f.
preservative, adj preservativo.
preserve, n 1. conserva f; confitura f; compota f; 2. vt conservar.
preside, vi presidir.
presidency, n presidencia f.
president, n presidente(a) m/f.
press, n 1. presión f; apretón m; 2. prensa f; 3. vt apretar,pulsar,presionar,empujar;4. planchar.
pressing, adj urgente, apremiante, acuciante.
pressure, n presión f; peso m; urgencia f, apremio m.
pressurize, vt presionar,hacer presión sobre, ejercer presión sobre.
pressurized , adj cabin a presión, presurizado.
prestidigitation, n prestidigitación f.
presligious, adj prestigioso.
presume, vt presumir; suponer.
presumption, n presunción f; atrevimiento m.
presuppose, vt presuponer.
presupposition , n presuposición f.
pretend, vt aparentar; simular; pretender.
pretender, n pretendiente m/f.
pretension, n pretensión f.
pretentiousness, n pretenciosidad f; presunción f.
preterite, n pretérito m.
preterm, adj prematuro.
pretext, n pretexto m.
pretty, adj guapo, bonito, lindo.
prevail, vi prevalecer, umponerse.
prevailing , adj reinante, imperante; vigente; predominante.
prevalent , adj predominante; frecuente, común.
prevaricate, vi tergiversar, mentir.
prevent, vt impedir, estorbar; evitar.
prevention, n prevención f; el impedir, el evitar.
preventive, adj preventivo, impeditivo.
preview, n preestreno m; vista f anticipada.
previous, adj previo, anterior.
prey, n 1. presa f, víctima f; 2. vi atacar,alimentarse de,comer,devorar.

price, n 1. precio; valor; 2. vt estimar,valuar,valorar.
pricing, n fijación f de precios.
prick, n 1. pinchazo m, punzada f; picadura f; 2. vt pinchar,punzar,picar.
prickle, n 1. púa f; escozor m; 2. vt picar; 3. vi hormiguear.
pride, n orgullo m; soberbia f, arroganciaf
priest, n sacerdote m; cura m.
priesthood, n sacerdocio m; clero m.
prim, adj etiquetero, esturado; remilgado.
primacy, n primacía f.
primal, adj original; principal.
primary, adj primario; principal; central.
primate, n primado m.
prime, adj 1. primo; 2. primero, principal.
primer, n cartilla f, libro m de texto elemental.
priming, n preparación f; cebo m; primera capa.
primitive, adj primitivo; anticuado; rudimentario.
prince, n príncipe m.
princess , n princesa f.
principal , adj principal.
principle , n principio m.
print, n 1. marca f, señal f, impresión f; 2. letra f de molde; 3. vt imprimir,grabar,imprimir.
printed, adj impreso; estampado.
printing, n tipografía f; imprenta f.
prior, adj 1. anterior, previo; preferente; 2. n prior m.
prioritize, vt priorizar.
priority, n prioridad f; anterioridad f, antelación f.
prism, n prisma m.
prison, n cárcel f, prisión f.
prisoner, n detenido(a); prisionero(a) m/f.
privacy, n soledad f.
private, adj 1. privado; particular; propio, personal; 2. n soldado m raso.
privater, n corsario m.
privation, n privación f, miseria f.
privet, n ligustro m, alhena f.
privilege, n privilegio m; prerrogativa f.
privileged, adj privilegiado; confidencial.
privy, adj estar enterado secretamente de algo.
prize, n 1. premio m; galardón m; 2. vt apreciar, estimar.
probability, n probabilidad f.
probable, adj probable.
probate, n verificación f oficial.
probation, n libertad f condicional.
probe, n 1. sonda f, tienta f; cohete m, proyectil m; 2. vt sondar,tentar,explorar.
problem, n problema m.
procedure, n procedimiento m; proceder m.
proceed, vi proceder.
process, n 1. proceso m; 2. método m, sistema m; 3. vt preparar,tratar.
processing, n preparación f; tratamiento m.
procession, n desfile m; procesión f; cortejo m.
proclaim, vt proclamar.
proclamation, n proclamación f; proclama f.
procrastinate, vi aplazar una decisión.
procrastination, n dilación f, falta f deresolución.
procreate, vt procrear.
procreation, n procreación f.
procure, vi obtener, conseguir; lograr; gestionar.
prodigal, adj pródigo.
prodigy, n prodigio m; portento m.
produce, n 1. producto m; productos m; 2. vt presentar,mostrar,producir.
product, n producto m.
productivity, n productividad f.

profane, adj 1. profano; 2. vt profanar.

profanity, n profanidad f; blasfemia f, impiedad f.

profess, vt profesar.

profession, n profesión f, declaración f.

professional, adj profesional,

proressor, n profesor(a) m/f; catedrático(a) m/f.

proficiency, n pericia f, habilidad f.

profile, n perfil m.

profit, n 1. ganancia f; provecho m, beneficio m; 2. vt servir a, aprovechar a, ser de utilidad a.

profound, adj profundo.

profundity, n profundidad f.

profuse, adj profuso; pródigo.

profusion, n profusión f; abundancia f.

progenitor, n progenitor m.

progeny, n progenie f, prole f.

progesterone, n progesterona f.

prognosis, n pronóstico m.

program, n programa m.

programmed, adj programado.

progress, n 1. progreso m; progresos m; 2. vi hacer progresos progresar avanzar.

progression, n progresión f.

progressive , adj progresivo; progresista.

prohibit, vt prohibir.

prohibition, n prohibición f.

prohibitive, adj prohibitivo; imposible.

project, n 1. proyecto m; 2. vt proyectar.

projectile, n proyectil m.

projection, n proyección f.

proletarian, adj 1. proletario; 2. n proletario(a) m/f.

proliferate, vi multiplicar; extender.

prolific, adj prolífico.

prologue, n prólogo m.

prolong, vt prolongar, extender; alargar, extender.

prolonged, adj prolongado.

promenade, n 1. paseo m; 2. vt pasean

prominence, n prominencia f.

prominent, adj prominente, saliente, eminente.

promiscuous, adj promiscuo.

promise, n 1. promesa f; 2. vt prometer.

promising, adj prometedor, que promete.

promontory, n promontorio m.

promote, vt promover, fomentar.

promotion, n promoción f, fomento m.

prompt, adj 1. pronto; inmediato; 2. vt mover a uno a hacer algo.

promulgate, vt promulgar.

prone, adj estar postrado (boca abajo); propensa a.

pronoun, n pronombre m.

pronounce, vt pronunciar.

pronouncement, n declaración f; opinión f.

pronunciation, n pronunciación f.

proof, n 1. prueba f; comprobación f; prueba f concluyente; 2. vt impermeabilizar.

prop, n 1. apoyo m; puntal m; 2. vt apoyar.

propaganda, n propaganda f.

propagation, n propagación f.

propane, n propano m.

propel, vt impulsar.

propeller, n hélice f.

propensity, n propensión f.

proper, adj 1. propio; característico; 2. verdadero, exacto, apropiado.

property, n propiedad f.

prophecy, n profecía f.

prophesy, vt profetizar.

prophet, n profeta m.

prophetic, adj profético.

propitiate, vt propiciar.

propitious, adj propicio, favorable.

proponent, n defensor(a) m/f.

proportion, n proporción f; parte f, porción f.

proportionate, adj proporcionado.

proposal, n propuesta f, proposición f; oferta f.

propose, vt proponer; ofrecer.

propound, vt proponer, exponer, presentar.

proprietor, n propietario(a) m/f.

propriety, n decoro m, decencia f, corrección f.

propulsion, n propulsión f.

prorate, n 1. prorrata f; 2. vt prorratear.

prosaic, adj prosaico.

proscenium, n proscenio m.

proscribe, vt proscribir.

prose, n prosa f.

prosecute, vt procesar; enjuiciar.

prosecution, n proceso m, causa f, juicio m.

prosecutor, n acusador(a) m/f.

proselyte, n prosélito(a) m/f.

proselytize, vi ganar prosélitos.

prospect, n vista f, panorama m.

prospective, adj anticipado, prospectivo, esperado.

prospector, n explorador m.

prospectus, n prospecto m; folleto m informativo.

prosper, vt favorecer, fomentar.

prosperity, n prosperidad f.

prosperous, adj próspero.

prostate, n próstata f.

prosthesis, n prótesis f.

prostitute, n 1. prostituta f; 2. vt prostituir.

prostrate, adj 1. postrado; procumbente; 2. vt postrar.

prostration, n postración f.

protagonist, n protagonista m/f.

protect, vt proteger, amparar.

protection, n protección f.

protector, n protector(a) m/f.

protein, n proteína f.

protest, n 1. protesta f; 2. vi protestar.

protestation, n protesta f.

protester, n protestador(a) m/f.

protocol, n protocolo m.

protoplasm, n protoplasma m.

prototype, n prototipo m.

protractor, n transportador m.

protuberance, n protuberancia f, saliente m.

proud, adj orgulloso; soberbio, arrogante, altanero.

prove, vt demostrar; probar; comprobar.

proven, adj probado.

proverb, n refrán m, proverbio m.

provide, vt suministrar, surtir; dar, proporcionar.

providence, n providencia f.

provider, n proveedor(a) m/f.

province, n provincia f.

provincial, adj provincial, de provincia,

provision, n 1. provisió f; suministro m; 2. vt aprovisionar abastecer.

provoke, vt provocar, causar, producir, motivar.

provoking, adj provocativo; irritante, fastidioso.

prowess, n destreza f, habilidad f.

prowl, n 1. ronda f; 2. vi rondar.

prowler, n rondador m.

proximity, n proximidad f; cerca de, junto a.

prudent, adj prudente.

prune, n 1. ciruela f pasa; 2. vt podar; recortar.

pry, vi curiosear; entrometerse.

prying, adj fisgón, curioso; entrometido.

psalm, n salmo m.

psalter, n salterio m.

psoriasis, *n* soriasis *f.*
psyche, *n* psique *f.*
psychiatrist, *n* psiquiatra *m/f.*
psychiatry, *n* psiquiatría *f.*
psychic(al), *adj* **1.** psíquico; **2.** *n* medium *m/f.*
psychoanalysis, *n* psicoanálisis *m.*
psychoanalyze, *vt* psicoanalizar.
psychology, *n* psicología *f.*
puberty, *n* pubertad *f.*
public, *adj* público.
publication, *n* publicación *f.*
publicity, *n* publicidad *f.*
publicize, *vt* publicar, dar publicidad a, anunciar.
publish, *vt* publicar; correr.
publisher, *n* editor(a) *m/f.*
publishing, *n* publicación *f* (de libros).
pudding, *n* pudín *m;* postre *m.*
puddle, *n* **1.** charco *m;* **2.** *vt* pudelar.
puff, *n* **1.** soplo *m;* **2.** *vt* soplar.
pugilist, *n* púgil *m,* pugilista *m.*
pulchritude, *n* belleza *f.*
pull, *n* **1.** tirón *m;* jalón *m,* jalada *f;* **2.** influencia *f;*
    3. *vt* tirar de, jalar.
pullet, *n* polla *f,* pollita *f.*
pulley, *n* polea *f.*
pulmonary, *adj* pulmonar.
pulp, *n* **1.** pulpa *f;* carne *f;* pasta *f;* **2.** *vt* hacerpulpa.
pulpit, *n* púlpito *m.*
pulsate, *vi* pulsar, latir.
pulsation, *n* pulsación *f,* latido *m.*
pulse, *n* legumbre *f,* legumbres *f pl.*
pulverize, *vt* **1.** pulverizar; **2.** *vi* pulverizarse.
pump, *n* **1.** bomba *f;* pompa *f;* zapatilla *f;* **2.** *vt* sacar,
    elevar.
pumpkin, *n* calabaza *f;* calabacera *f.*
punch, *n* **1.** sacabocados *m,* taladro *m,* ponche *m;*
    2. *vt* punzar,taladrar;perforar;picar.
punctual, *adj* puntual.
punctuate, *vt* puntuar; interrumpir.
punctuation, *n* puntuación *f.*
puncture, *n* **1.** perforación *f;* puntura *f* punzada *f;*
    2. *vt* perforar.
pundit, *n* lumbrera *f,* erudito *m.*
pungent, *adj* (smell)acre; picante; mordaz, acerbo.
punish, *vt* castigar.
punishment, *n* castigo *m.*
punitive, *adj* punitivo; punitorio.
punk, *adj* malo; baladí, de baja calidad.
pupil, *n* **1.** alumno(a) *m/f;* **2.** (eye) pupila *f.*
puppet, *n* tíere *m;* marioneta *m/f.*
puppeteer, *n* titiritero(a) *m/f.*
puppy, *n* cachorro(a) *m/f;* perrito(a) *m/f.*
purchase, *n* **1.** compra *f;* adquisición *f;* **2.** *vt* comprar.
purchaser, *n* comprador(a) *m/f.*
pure, *adj* puro.
pureness, *n* pureza *f.*
purgative, *adj* purgativo, purgante.
purgatory, *n* purgatorio *m.*
purge, *n* **1.** purga *f;* purgante *m;* **2.** *vt* purgar, purificar.
purification, *n* purificación *f,* depuración *f.*
purifier, *n* depurador *m.*
purify, *vt* purificar.
puritan, *adj* **1.** puritano; **2.** *n* puritano(a) *m/f.*
purity, *n* pureza *f.*
purple, *adj* purpúreo.
purport, *n* **1.** significado *m;* **2.** *vt* significar.
purpose, *n* propósito *m,* intención *f,* objeto *m.*
purse, *n* bolsa *f;* monedero *m,* portamonedas *m.*
purser, *n* contador *m,* comisario(a) *m/f.*

pursue, *vi* seguir, seguir lapista de, perseguir, cazar.
pursuit, *n* caza *f;* perseguimiento *m,* persecución *f.*
purvey, *vt* proveer, suministrar, abastecer.
push, *n* **1.** empuje *m,* empujón *m;* de un empuje;
    2. *vt* empujar;pisar.
put, *vt* poner; colocar; meter.
putative, *adj* supuesto; putativo.
putrefy, *vt* pudrir.
putrid, *adj* podrido, putrefacto.
putt, *n* pun *m,* pat *m,* golpe *m* corto.
putter, *n* **1.** putter *m;* **2.** *vi* ocuparseenfruslerías.
puzzle, *n* **1.** rompecabezas *m,* acertijo *m;* cruci-
    grama *m;* **2.** *vt* dejar perplejo, confundir.
pylon, *n* pilón *m,* poste *m.*
pyramid, *n* pirámide *f.*

Q

Q, q, *n* (letter *f*) Q,q.
quack, *n* graznido *m;* charlatán *m.*
quadrangular, *adj* cuadrangular.
quadrant, *n* cuadrante *m.*
quadrille, *n* cuadrilla *f.*
quadrophonic, *adj* cuadrafónico *m.*
quadruped, *n* cuadrúpedo *m.*
quadruple, *adj* cuadruple, cuádruplo.
quaff, *vt* beber(se).
quail, *n* **1.** codroniz *f;* **2.** *vi* acobardarse.
qualm, *n* **1.** bascas *f,* náusea *f;* mareo *m;* **2.** escrúpulo
    m, duda *f.*
quandary, *n* dilema *m,* apuro *m.*
quantifiable, *adj* cuantificable.
quantifier, *n* cuantificador *m.*
quantify, *vt* cuantificar.
quantitative, *adj* cuantitativo.
quantitatively, *adv* bajo el aspecto cuantitativo.
quantity, *n* cantidad *f.*
quantum, *n* cuanto *m,* quántum *m.*
quarantine, *n* **1.** cuarentena *f;* **2.** *vt* poner en cuaren-
    tena.
quark, *n* cuark *m.*
quarrel, *n* **1.** riña *f,* disputa *f;* reyerta *f,* pendencia *f,*
    pelea *f;* **2.** *vi* reñir, pelearse; disputar.
quarreling, *n* disputas *f;* altercados *m.*
quarrelsome, *adj* pendenciero, discutón, peleón.
quarrier, *n* cantero *m.*
quarry, *n* presa *f;* víctima *f.*
quarry, *n* **1.** presa *f;* víctima *f;* **2.** cantera *f;* mina *f;*
    3. *vt* sacar, extraer; **4.** *vi* explotar una cantera,
    extraer piedra de una cantera.
quarryman, *n* cantero *m,* picapedrero *m.*
quart, *n* cuarto de galón.
quarter, *n* cuarto *m,* cuarta parte *f.*
quartering, *n* cuartel *m.*
quarter, *n* ventanilla *f* direccional.
quartermaster, *n* furriel *m,* comisario *m.*
quartet(te), *n* cuarteto *m;* grupo *m* de cuatro.
quartile, *n* cuartil *f.*
quartz, *n* cuarzo *m.*
quartzite, *n* cuarcita *f.*
quasar, *n* cuasar *m.*

quash, *vt* anular, invalidar.

quaver, *n* 1. temblor *m;* vibración *f;* trémolo *m;* 2. *vi* temblar, vibrar.

quay, *n* muelle *m,* desembarcadero *m.*

queasy, *adj* vascoso; delicado; escrupuloso.

queen, *n* reina *f.*

queer, *adj* raro, extraño, misterioso.

quell, *vt* reprimir; calmar; dominar.

quench, *vt* apagar, matar, sofocar.

query, *n* 1. pregunta *f;* interrogante *m;* duda *f;* 2. *vt* preguntar, dudar de, interrogar.

quest, *n* 1. busca *f;* búsqueda *f;* demanda *f;* 2. *vt/i* buscar.

question, *n* 1. pregunta *f;* interrogante *m;* 2. asunto *m;* cuestión *f;* problema *m;* 3. *vt* hacer preguntas, interrogar, examinar; 4. cuestionar, dudar de.

questionnaire, *n* cuestionario *m;* encuesta *f.*

quick, *adj* rápido, veloz; ligero; listo.

quicken, *vt* 1. acelerar, apresurar, avivar; 2. *vi* acelerarse, apresurarse, avivarse.

quicksand, *n* arena *f* movediza.

quiet, *adj* 1. silencioso, callado; 2. *n* silencio *m;* 3. *vt* clamar, hacer callar, acallar.

quilt, *n* 1. colcha *f,* edredón *m;* 2. *vt* acolchar.

quinine, *n* quinina *f.*

quintet(te), *n* quinteto *m.*

quintuplet, *n* quintillizo(a) *m/f.*

quit, *vt* 1. dejar, abandonar; salir de; 2. *vi* irse, marcharse, retirarse.

quite, *adv* 1. totalmente; 2. bastante.

quiver, *n* 1. temblor *m,* estremecimiento *m;* 2. *vi* temblar, estremecerse.

quiz, *n* 1. interrogatorio *m;* examen *m;* test *m;* 2. *vt* mirar con curiosidad, interrogar.

quorum, *n* quórum *m.*

quota, *n* quota *f;* contingente *m;* cupo *m.*

quotation, *n* cita *f;* comillas *f;* cotización *f.*

quote, *vt* 1. citar; dar, expresar; 2. *vi* cotizar.

quotient, *n* cociente *m.*

R

R, r, *n* (letra *f*) R, r.

rabbi, *n* rabino *m;* rabí *m.*

rabbit, *n* 1. conejo *m;* 2. *vi* cazar conejos.

rabble, *n* canalla *f,* chusma *f.*

rabies, *n* rabia *f.*

raccoon, *n* mapache *m.*

race, *n* 1. carrera *f,* prueba *f,* regata *f;* 2. raza *f;* casta *f,* estirpe *f,* familia *f;* 3. *vt* hacer correr, competir con uno en una carrera; 4. *vi* correr de prisa, ir a máxima velocidad.

racetrack, *n* pista *f,* hipódromo *m;* autódromo *m.*

racial, *adj* racial; racista.

racing, *n* carreras *f.*

racis, *n* racismo *m.*

racist, *adj* 1. racista; 2. *n* racista *m/f.*

rack, *n* 1. estante *m,* anaquel *m;* 2. *vt* atormentar.

racket, *n* 1. (Sport) raqueta *f;* ruido *m,* estrépito *m;* barahúda *f;* 2. *vt* hacer ruido.

racketeer, *n* estafador *m,* timador *m;* chantajista *m.*

radar, *n* radar *m.*

radiance, *n* brillantez *f,* brillo *m,* resplandor *m.*

radiant, *adj* radiante, brillante, resplandeciente.

radiate, *vt* 1. radiar, irradiar; difundir; 2. *vi* irradiar, radiar, salir (de).

radiation, *n* radiación *f.*

radiator, *n* radiador *m.*

radical, *adj* radical.

radio, *n* 1. radio *f,* radiofonía *f;* 2. *vt* radiar, transmitir por radio.

radioactivity, *n* radiactividad *f.*

radiography, *n* radiografía *f.*

radiology, *n* radiología *f.*

radius, *n* (curcunferencia) radio *m.*

raffle, *n* 1. rifa *f,* sorteo *m;* 2. *vt* rifar, sortear.

rag, *n* 1. trapo *m;* pano *m;* 2. *vt* tomar el pelo.

rage, *n* 1. rabia *f,* furor *m,* ira *f;* 2. *vt* rabiar.

ragged, *adj* andrajoso, harapiento; desigual.

raging, *adj* rabioso, furioso; violento.

raid, *n* 1. incursión *f,* correría *f,* ataque *m;* 2. *vt* invadir, atacar.

rail, *n* 1. baranda *f,* barandilla *f,* pasamanos *m;* 2. carril *m,* raíl *m,* riel *m;* 3. *vt* poner barandillaa; 4. *vi* demostrar.

railing, *n* baranda *f,* barandilla *f,* pasamanos *m.*

railway, *n* ferrocarril *m;* vía *f* férrea; línea *f* (de ferrocarril).

rain, *n* 1. lluvia *f;* 2. *vt/i* llover.

rainbow, *n* arcoiris *m.*

raincoat, *n* impermeable *m,* gabardina *f.*

rainfall, *n* precipitación *f;* lluvia *f.*

rainy, *adj* lluvioso; día *m* de lluvia, tiempo *m.*

raise, *n* 1. aumento *m,* subida *f,* 2. *vt* levantar, alzar elevar; 3. (children) criar.

raised, *adj* en relieve.

raisin, *n* pasa *f,* uva *f* pasa.

rake, *n* 1. rastrillo *m;* rastro *m;* 2. libertino *m;* 3. *vt* rastrillar, hurgar.

rally, *n* 1. reunión *f,* mitin *m,* manifestación *f;* 2. *vt* reunir; rehacer; 3. *vi* reunirse, recobrarse.

ram, *n* 1. carnero *m,* morueco *m;* 2. *vt* chocar con; 3. *vt* apisonar, apretar, rellenar.

ramification, *n* ramificación *f.*

ramp, *n* rampa *f;* desnivel *m.*

rampage, *n* 1. alboroto *m;* 2. *vi* desmandarse.

rampant, *adj* rampante; exuberante, lozano.

rampart, *n* terraplén *m,* defensa *f.*

ranch, *n* hacienda *f;* estancia *f,* rancho *m.*

rancher, *n* ganadero *m,* estanciero *m,* ranchero *m.*

rancor, *n* rencor *m.*

random, *adj* fortuito, casual; hecho al azar, hecho sin pensar.

range, *n* 1. línea *f;* alcance *m;* escala *f;* (voice) extensión *f;* (mountain) sierra *f;* dehesa *f;* 2. *vi* extenderse, recorrer.

ranger, *n* guardabosque *m.*

rank, *adj* 1. lozano; 2. maloliente; 3. *n* hilera *f;* posición *f;* categoría; 4. *vt* clasificar.

ransom, *n* 1. rescate *m,* redención *f;* 2. *vt* rescatar; redimir.

rap, *n* 1. golpecito *m,* aldabada *f;* 2. *vt* dar un golpecito en, tocar.

rape, *n* 1. rapto *m;* violación *f,* estupro *m;* 2. *vt* violar, estuprar.

rapid, *adj* rápido.

rapids, *n* rápido(s) *m* rabión *m.*

rapine, *n* rapiña *f.*

rapist, *n* violador *m.*

rapport, *n* buena relacíon *f;* entenduniento *m.*

rapt, *adj* arrebatado; absorto, ensimismado.

rapture, *n* éxtasis *m,* rapto *m,* arrobamiento *m.*

rare, adj raro, poco común; (carne) poco hecho, algo crudo.

rascal, n pillo m. pícaro m.

rash, adj temerario; imprudente; precipitado; n erupción f (cutánea); sarpullido m.

rasp, n 1. escofina f, raspador m; 2. vt escofinar, raspar.

raspberry, n frambuesa f.

rat, n rata f; canalla m.

ratchet, n trinquete m; rueda f de trinquete.

rate, n 1. proporción f, relación f, razón f; 2. vt estimar, tasar, merecer.

rather, adv 1. antes, más bien; mejor dicho; 2. algo, un poco, bastante.

ratify, vt ratificar.

rating, n 1. tasación f, valuación f; valor m; 2. clasificación f; puesto m posición f.

ratio, n razón f, relación f, proporción f.

ration, n 1. ración f; suministro m; 2. vt racionar.

rational, adj racional; lógico, razonable; sensato.

rationality, n racionalidad f; lógica f.

rationalize, vt racionalizar.

rationing, n racionamiento m.

rattan, n rota f, junco m (o caña f) de Indias.

rattle, n 1. golpeteo m; traqueteo m; tableteo m; 2. vt agitar, sacudir; 3. vi traquetear.

rattlesnake, n serpiente f de cascabel.

raunchy, adj lascivo, verde; cachondo.

ravage, n 1. estrago m, destrozo m; destrucción f; 2. vt estragar, destruir, destrozar.

rave, vi delirar, desvariar.

raven, n cuervo m.

ravenous, adj famélico, hambriento; voraz.

raver, n juerguista m/f; persona f totalmente desinhibida.

ravine, n barranco m, garganta f, quebrada f.

raving, adj loco m de atar.

ravish, vt 1. encantar, embelesar; 2. raptar, robar; violar.

raw, adj 1. crudo; puro, sin mezcla; 2. novato, inexperto; tosco, grosero.

ray, n rayo m; rayo m de luz; (pez) raya f.

rayon, n rayón m.

raze, vt arrasar, asolar.

razor, n navaja f, chaveta f; maquinilla f de afeitar.

razorblade, n hoja f de afeitar, cuchilla f de afeitar.

re, prep 1. respecto a, con referencia a; 2. (Mus) re m.

reabsorb, vt reabsorber.

reach, n 1. alcance m; extensión f; distancia f; 2. vt alargar, extender; 3. vi alcanzar; llegar; 4. tender la mano.

react, vi reaccionar.

reaction, n reacción f.

reactionary, adj 1. reaccionario; retrógrado. 2. n reaccionario(a) m/f.

reactivate, vt reactivar.

reactor, n reactor m.

read, vt 1. leer; 2. vi leer en voz alta.

reader, n lector(a) m/f, usuario(a) m/f.

readiness, n prontitud f; disponibilidad f; buena disposición f, buena voluntad f.

reading, n lectura f; recitación f.

readjust, vt 1. reajustar, reorientar; 2. vi reorientarse.

ready, adj 1. listo, preparado; dispuesto; 2. vt preparar, disponer.

reappear, vi reaparecer, volver a aparecer.

reapply, vt 1. aplicar de nuevo; dar otra capa de; 2. vi volver a presentarse.

rear, adj 1. trasero, posterior, de cola; de retaguardia; 2. n parte f trasera, parte f posterior; cola f; 3. vt levantar, criar.

reason, n 1. razón f; motivo m, causa f; 2. vt razonar que, calcular que; 3. vi razonar.

reasonable, adj razonable; sensato, juicioso; tolerante.

reasoning, adj 1. racional; 2. n razonamiento m.

reassemble, vt volver a reunir; montar de nuevo.

reassert, vi reafirmar, reiterar.

reassertion, n reafirmación f reiteración f.

reassess, vt tasar de nuevo, revalorar.

reassure, vt tranquilizar; alentar; estar más tranquilo.

reassuring, adj tranquilizador; alentador.

rebate, n 1. rebaja f, descuento m; 2. vt rebajar.

rebel, adj 1. rebelde; 2. n rebelde m/f; 3. vi rebelarse, sublevarse.

rebellion, n rebelión f, sublevación f.

rebellious, adj rebelde; revoltoso, díscolo.

rebound, n 1. rebote m; de rebote, de rechazo; 2. vi rebotar, dar un rebote; repercutir.

rebuild, vt reconstruir, reedificar.

rebuke, n 1. reprensión f; 2. vt reprender.

rebut, vt rebatir, refutar, rechazar.

recalcitrant, adj reacio, refractario, recalcitrante.

recall, n 1. aviso m, llamada f; retirada f; 2. vt llamar, hacer volver.

recap, n 1. recapitulación f, resumen m; 2. vt/i recapitular, resumir.

recapitulate, vt/i recapitular, resumir.

recapture, n 1. recobro m; reconquista f; 2. vt recobrar, volver a prender; reconquistar.

recast, vt refund m.

receipt, n recepción f, recibo m.

receivable, adj recibidero; por (a) cobrar.

receive, vt recibir; cobrar, aceptar.

receiver, n recibidor(a) m/f; destunatario(a) m/f.

receiving, n recepción f; receptación f.

recent, adj reciente; nuevo.

reception, n recepción f recibimiento m; acogida f.

receptionist, n recepcionista f.

receptive, adj receptivo.

recess, n 1. vacaciones f; descanso m; recreo m; 2. vi prorrogarse, suspenderse la sesión.

recession, n retroceso m , retirada f.

recharge, vt volver a cargar, recargar; reponerse.

rechargeable, adj recargable.

recipe, n receta f.

recipient, n recibidor(a) m/f, recipiente m/f.

reciprocal, adj recíproco, mutuo.

reciprocate, vt 1. intercambiar, devolver; corresponder a; 2. vi oscilar, alternar.

recital, n relación f, narración f; recital m.

recite, vt narrar, referir; enumerar; recitar,

reckless, adj temerario, imprudente.

reckon, vt 1. contar, calcular; computar; calcular, estumar; 2. considerar, estimar; 3. pensar; creer.

reclaim, vt reclamar; recoger.

recline, vt 1. apoyar, recostar, reclinar; descansar; 2. vi reclinarse, recostarse, apoyarse.

reclining, adj acostado; tumbado; yacente.

recognize, vt reconocer, identificar.

recognized, adj reconocido como tal; conocido; acreditado.

recoil, n 1. retroceso m; (de un ara m de fuego), rebufo m; 2. vi recular, retroceder; rebufar.

recollect, vt recordar, acordarse de.

recommend, vt recomendar.

recommendation, n recomendación f.

recompense, n 1. recompensa f; 2. vt recompensar.
reconcilable, adj conciliable, reconciliable.
reconcile, vt 1. reconciliar; 2. vr resignarse a algo.
reconciliation, n reconciliación f; conciliación f.
recondite, adj recóndito.
recondition, vt reacondicionar.
reconnaissance, n reconocimiento m.
reconquer, vt reconquistar.
reconsider, vt volver a considerar, volver a examinar; reconsiderar, repensar.
reconsideration, n reconsideración f.
reconstitute, vt reconstituir.
reconstitution, n reconstitución f.
reconstruct, vt reconstruir; reedificar; reconstruir.
reconstruction, n reconstrucción f; reedificación f.
record, n 1. documento m; registro m; relación f; 2. vt registrar apuntar grabar.
recorded, adj música f grabada.
recorder, n registrador(a) m/f, archivero(a) m/f.
recount, n 1. recuento m; 2. vt recontar.
recoup, vt recobrar, recuperar; indemnizarse por.
recourse, n recurso m. .
recover, vt 1. recobrar, recuperar; 2. vi restablecerse, reponerse; reactivarse; 3. vr reponerse.
recovery, n recobro m, recuperación f.
recreate, vt recrear.
recreation, n 1. recreación f; 2. recreo m.
recreational, adj recreativo.
recreative, adj recreativo.
recruit, n 1. recluta m; 2. vt reclutar; restablecer.
recruiting, n reclutamiento m.
rectal, adj rectal.
rectangle, n rectángulo m.
rectangular, adj rectangular.
rectify, vt rectificar.
rectilinear, adj rectilíneo.
rectitude, n rectitud f.
rector, n párroco m, rector(a) m/f, director(a) m/f.
rectory, n casa f del párroco.
recuperate, vt 1. recuperar; 2. vi restablecerse.
recuperation, n recuperación f; restablecimiento m.
recur, vi repetirse, producirse de nuevo.
recurrent, adj repetido; constante; recurrente.
recyclable, adj reciclable.
recycle, vt reciclar.
recycling, n reciclado m, reciclaje m.
red, adj 1. rojo, colorado; encarnado; 2. n rojo m.
redbreast, n petirrojo m.
redcurrant, n grosella f roja, grosellero m rojo.
reddish, adj rojizo.
redecorate, vt renovar, volver a decorar.
redeem, vt 1. redimir, rescatar; amortizar; 2. vr salvarse, expiar su falta.
redeemable, adj redimible; amortizable.
redefine, vt redefinir.
redemption, n redención f, rescate m; amortización f; desempeño m.
redevelop, vt reorganizar.
redevelopment, n reorganización f.
redhead, n pelirroja f.
redial, vt/i volver a marcar.
rediscover, vt volver a descubrir, redescubrir.
rediscovery, n redescubrimiento m.
redistribute, vt distribuir de nuevo.
redistribution, n redistribución f.
redo, vt rehacer, volver a hacer.
redolence, n fragancia f, perfume m.
redouble, vt redoblar, intensificar, redoblar.
redoubt, n reducto m.

redraft, vt volver a redactar.
redskin, n piel roja m/f.
reduce, vt 1. reducir, disminuir; rebajar; 2. vi reducirse, disminuir.
reduction, n reducción f, disminución f; rebaja f.
redundant, adj excesivo, superfluo; redundante.
redwood, n secoya f.
reed, n carrizo m, junco m, caña f.
re-edit, vt reeditar.
re-educate, vt reeducar.
re-education, n reeducación f.
reef, n 1. rizo m; 2. escollo m, arrecife m; 3. vt arrizar.
reek, n 1. mal olor m, hedor m, 2. vi vahear; oler, heder.
reel, n 1. carrete m; bobina f; broca f; 2. vt devanar; 3. vi tambalear, tambalearse; cejar, retroceder.
re-elect, vt reelegir.
re-enact, vt volver a promulgar; decretar de nuevo.
re-enter, vt reungresar en, volver a entrar en.
re-establish, vt restablecer.
re-examine, vt reexaminar.
refer, vt 1. remitir; 2. vi referirse a, aludir a, mencionar, hacer referencia a.
referee, n 1. árbitro m/f; 2. vt dirigir, arbitrar en.
refill, n repuesto m, recambio m; mina f.
refinance, vt refinanciar.
refine, vt 1. refinar; purificar; hacer más culto; 2. vi refinar algo, mejorar algo.
refinement, n 1. refinamiento m; refinación f; purificación f; 2. finura f, cultura f, educación f.
refinery, n refinería f.
reflect, vt 1. reflejar; 2. vi reflexionar pensar.
reflection, n reflexión f, reflejo m.
reflector, n reflector m; reflectante m, captafaros m.
reflex, adj 1. reflejo; 2. n reflejo m.
reflexive, adj reflexivo.
reflux, n reflujo m.
reforest, vt repoblar de árboles.
reforestation, n repoblación f forestal.
reform, n 1. reforma f; reformatorio m; 2. vt reformar; 3. vi reformarse.
reformatory, n reformatorio m.
reformed, adj reformado.
reformer, n reformador(a) m/f.
refract, vt refractar.
refraction, n refracción f.
refrain, n 1. estribillo m; 2. vi abstenerse de algo.
refresh, vt 1. refrescar; recordar algo a uno; 2. vr refrescarse.
refreshing, adj 1. refrescante; 2. estimulante.
refrigerate, vt refrigerar.
refrigerator, n frigorífico m; refrigerador m.
refuel, vt reabastecer (o rellenar) de combustible.
refuge, n refugio m, asilo m; albergue m.
refugee, n refugiado(a) m/f.
refund, n 1. devolución f; reembolso m; 2. vt devolver, reuntegrar, reembolsar.
refurbish, vt restaurar; renovar; retundir.
refurnish, vt amueblar de nuevo.
refusal, n negativa f, denegación f.
refuse, n 1. basura f, desperdicios m, desecho m; 2. vt rehusar, rechazar, denegar; negar.
refute, vt refutar, rebatir.
regain, vt cobrar, recobrar, recuperar.
regal, adj regio, real.
regalia, n insignias f.

regard, n 1. mirada f; 2. respecto m; aspecto m; 3. atención f; 4. respeto m, consideración f; estimación f; 5. vt mirar; observar; 6. considerar.

regarding, prep en cuanto a, por lo que se refiere a.

regardless, adj 1. indiferente a; insensible a; 2. adv a pesar de todo; pese a quien pese.

regatta, n regata f.

regenerate, adj 1. regenerado; 2. vt regenerar.

regeneration, n regeneración f.

regime, n régimen m.

region, n región f; comarca f; zona f.

regional, adj regional.

register, n 1. registro m; lista f; matrícula f; 2. vt registrar; declarar; matricular; 3. vi inscribirse, matricularse.

registered, adj certificado; matriculado; legalizado.

registrar, n registrador(a) m/f, archivero(a) m/f.

registration, n registro m; inscripción f matrícula f; declaración f; certificación f.

regret, n 1. sentimiento m, pesar m; remordimiento m; 2. vt sentir, lamentar; arrepentirse de.

regroup, vt 1. reagrupar; reorganizar; 2. vi reagruparse; reorganizarse.

regular, adj regular.

regulate, vt regular; arreglar, ajustar; reglamentar.

regulation, n 1. regulación f; arreglo m; 2. regla f; reglamento m.

regulator, n regulador m.

rehabilitate, vt reliabilitar.

rehabilitation, n rehabilitación f.

rehearsal, n enumeración f, repetición f; ensayo m.

reign, n 1. reinado m; 2. vi reuna.

reimburse, vt reembolsar.

reimbursement, n reembolso m.

rein, n rienda f.

reincarnate, vi reencarnar; volver a encarnar.

reincarnation, n reencarnación f.

reindeer, n reno m.

reinforce, vt reforzar; armar.

reinforced, adj reforzado; armado.

reinforcement, n reforzamiento m; refuerzos m.

reintegrate, vt reuntegrar; reunsertar (en).

reinvest, vt reunvertur, volver a invertir.

reiterate, vt reiterar, repetir; subrayar.

reiteration, n reiteración f, repetición f.

reject, n 1. cosa f rechazada, cosa f defectuosa; 2. vt rechazar; denegar; desestunar.

rejection, n rechazamiento m, rechazo m.

rejoice, vt 1. alegrar, regocijar, causar alegría a; 2. vi alegrarse, regocijarse.

rejoin, vt replicar, contestar; reunirse con.

rejuvenate, vt rejuvenecer.

rejuvenation, n rejuvenecuímieno m.

rekindle, vt volver a encender, reencender.

relapse, n 1. recaída f; reuncidencia f; 2. vi recaer.

relate, vt 1. contar, narrar, relatar; 2. relacionar (con); 3. vi refrersea.

relation, n 1. narración f; relato m, relación f; 2. conexión f, relación f, nexo m.

relationship, n relación f, conexión f, afinidad f; parentesco m.

relative, adj 1. relativo (a); respectivo; 2. n relativo m; 3. pariente(a) m/f, familiar m/f.

relatively, adv relativamente.

relax, vt relajar.

relaxed, adj relajado, tranquilo, sosegado.

relaxing, adj relajante.

relay, n 1. tanda f; 2. carrera f de relevos; 3. (Elec) relé m; 4. vt retransmitir.

release, n 1. liberación f; excarcelación f; libertad f; emisión f; 2. vt soltar, libertar; excarcelar; absolver; 3. lanzar; despedir, arrojar, emitir; 4. publicar; poner a la venta; estrenar.

relegate, vt relegar (a).

relent, vi ablandarse, apiadarse, ceder.

relentless, adj implacable, inexorable; despiadado.

relevant, adj pertunente; conexo, relacionado.

reliable, adj fidedigno, fehaciente.

reliance, n confianza f; dependencía f.

relic, n reliquia f, vestigio m; reliquia f.

relief, n 1. alivio m; desahogo m; consuelo m; 2. socorro m; 3. relevo m.

relieve, vt 1. aliviar, mitigar; desahogar; 2. vr hacer del cuerpo, hacer su necesidades.

religion, n religión f.

religious, adj 1. religioso; 2. n religioso(a) m/f.

relinquish, vt abandonar, renunciar a.

reliquary, n relicario m.

relish, n 1. sabor m, gusto m; 2. salsa f, condimento m; 3. vt paladear, saborear; gustarde.

relive, vt vivir de nuevo, volver a vivir.

reload, vt recargar, volver a cargar.

relocate, vi moverse (a otro domicilio), trasladarse.

reluctance, n desgana f, renuencia f, reticencia f.

reluctant, adj renuente, poco dispuesto.

rely, vi confiar en, contar con, fiarse de.

remain, vi 1. sobrar; quedar; 2. permanecer; 3. vt saldar.

remaining, adj que queda.

remains, n restos m; sobras f, desperdicios m.

remark, n 1. observación f; comentario m; 2. vt observarnotar.

remarkable, adj notable, singular; extraordinario.

remedy, n 1. remedio m; recurso m; 2. vt remediar; curar.

remember, vt 1. acordarse de, recordar; conmemorar; 2. tener presente, no olvidar.

remembrance, n recuerdo m.

remind, vt 1. recordar; 2. vr recordarse que.

reminder, n recordatorio m; notifcación f.

reminisce, vi contar los recuerdos.

remission, n remisión f.

remit, vt remitir, enviar.

remittance, n remesa f envío m.

remnant, n resto m, residuo m.

remodel, vt modelar de nuevo, remodelar.

remorse, n remordumiento m.

remorseless, adj implacable, despiadado,

remote, adj remoto; distante, lejano; aislado.

removable, adj separable, amovible; desmontable.

remove, vt quitar; llevarse; quitar de en medio.

remuneration, n remuneración f.

renaissance, n renacimiento m.

renal, adj renal.

renascence, n renacimiento m.

renascent, adj renaciente, que renace.

render, vt 1. derretir; 2. entregar; 3. hacer, prestar (servicio).

rendezvous, n 1. cita f; lugar m de una cita; 2. vi reunirse, verse; efectuar una reunión.

rendition, n interpretación f, ejecución f.

renegade, adj renegado.

renew, vt renovar; reuludar; extender, prorrogar.

renewal, n renovación f; reanudación f; extensión f.

renounce, vt/i renunciar.

renovate, vt renovar, restaurar.

renovation, n renovación f, restauración f.

renown, n renombre m, nombradra f, fama f.

renowned, *adj* renombrado; famoso por.

rent, *n* 1. alquiler *m*, arriendo *m;* 2. *vt* alquilar, rentar.

repair, *n* 1. reparación *f*, compostura *f;* remiendo *m; 2. vt* reparar.

reparation, *n* reparación *f;* satisfacción *f;* indemnización *f*.

repatriate, *n* 1. repatriado(a) *m/f,* 2. *vt* repatriar.

repay, *vt* devolver, reembolsar, reintegrar.

repeal, *n* 1. revocación *f;* abrogación *f;* 2. *vt* revocar, abrogar.

repeat, *n* 1. repetición *f;* 2. *vt* repetir;reiterar.

repel, *vt* 1. rechazar, repeler; 2. *vi* repelerse.

repellent, *adj* 1. repugnante; 2. *n* repelente *m*.

repent, *vt* 1. arrepentirse de; 2. *vi* arrepentirse.

repentance, *n* arrepentimiento *m*.

repentant, *adj* arrepentido; contrito, compungido.

repercussion, *n* repercusión *f*.

repertory, *n* repertorio *m*.

repetition, *n* repetición *f;* recitación *f*.

rephrase, *vt* expresar de otro modo.

replace, *vt* reponer; reemplazar, sustituir.

replay, *n* 1. repetición *f;* desempate *m.* 2. *vt* repetir.

replenish, *vt* rellenar; reaprovisionar, repostar.

replete, *adj* repleto, totalmente lleno (de).

replica, *n* copia *f*, reproducción *f* (exacta); réplica *f*.

reply, *n* 1. respuesta *f*, contestación *f;* 2. *vi* responder, contestar.

report, *n* 1. relato on relación *f;* parte *m;* uniforme *m; 2. vt* relatar, narrar, dar cuenta de; 3. *vi* hacer informe, presentar un informe.

reporter, *n* reportero(a) *m/f*, periodista *m/f*.

reporting, *n* reportaje *m*.

repose, *n* 1. reposo *m; 2. vt* reposar;descansar.

repossess, *vt* 1. recobrar; 2. *vt* recobrar algo.

repossession, *n* recuperación *f* de un artículo no pagado.

reprehend, *vt* reprender.

reprehensible, *adj* reprensible, censurable.

represent, *vt* representar; ser apoderado de.

representative, *adj* 1. representativo; 2. *n* representante *m/f* apoderado *m;* diputado(a) *m/f*.

repress, *vt* reprimir.

repression, *n* represión *f*.

reprimand, *n* 1. reprimenda *f*, reprensión *f;* 2. *vt* reprender;reconvenir.

reprint, *n* 1. reimpresión *f;* tirada *f* aparte, separata *f; 2. vt* reimprimir.

reproach, *n* 1. reproche *m*, censura *f;* oprobio *m; 2. vt* reprochar algo a uno, censurar.

reprocess, *vt* reprocesar.

reproduce, *vt* 1. reproducir; 2. *vi* reproducirse.

reproduction, *n* reproducción *f*.

reproof, *n* represión *f*, reconvención *f*.

reprove, *vt* reprender, reconvenir.

reptile, *n* reptil *m*.

republic, *n* república *f*.

republican, *adj* republicano.

republication, *n* reedición *f*.

republish, *vt* reeditar.

repudiate, *vt* rechazar, negar, desechar.

repudiation, *n* rechazamiento *m;* repudio *m*.

repugnance, *n* repugnancia *f*.

repugnant, *adj* repugnante.

repulse, *n* 1. repulsa *f*, repulsión *f;* rechazo *m; 2. vt* rechazar.

repulsive, *adj* repelente.

reputable, *adj* acreditado, de toda confianza.

reputation, *n* reputación *f*, fama *f*.

request, *n* 1. ruego *m*, petición *f;* 2. *vt* pedir, rogar, solicitar.

require, *vt* necesitar; exigir; pedir, requerir.

requirement, *n* requisito *m;* necesidad *f*.

requisite, *adj* requisito *m*.

requisition, *n* 1. requisición *f;* 2. *vt* requisar.

reread, *vt* releer, volver a leer.

rescind, *vt* rescindir, anular, revocar.

rescue, *n* 1. rescate *m;* 2. *vt* salvar;rescatar.

rescuer, *n* salvador(a) *m/f*.

research, *n* 1. investigación *f;* 2. *vi* investigar.

researcher, *n* investigador(a) *m/f*.

resemblance, *n* semejanza *f*, parecido *m*.

resemble, *vt* parecerse a.

resent, *vt* resentirse de (por).

resentment, *n* resentimiemo *m* (por).

reservation, *n* 1. reserva *f;* salvedad *f;* 2. (booking) reservación *f*.

reserve, *n* 1. reserva *f;* coto *m* (de caza); 2. *vt* reservar.

reserved, *adj* reservado.

reservoir, *n* depósito *m*, represa *f;* depósito *m*, cisterna *f*.

reset, *vt* reajustar; recomponer; reinicializar.

resettle, *vt* 1. restablecer; 2. *vi* restablecerse.

reshape, *vt* reformar, formar de nuevo, rehacer.

reside, *vi* residir, vivir.

residence, *n* 1. residencia *f;* permanencia *f*, estancia *f;* 2. domicilio *m*.

resident, *adj* 1. residente; 2. *n* residente *m/f*.

residual, *adj* residual.

residue, *n* resto *m*, residuo *m;* saldo *m*.

resign, *vt* 1. dimitir, renunciar a; 2. *vi* resignarse.

resignation, *n* 1. dimisión *f;* 2. resignación *f*.

resin, *n* resina *f*.

resist, *vt* 1. resistir; oponerse a; 2. *vi* resistirse.

resistant, *adj* resistente.

resistor, *n* resistor *m*, (Elec) resistencia *f*.

resole, *vt* sobresolar, remontar.

resolute, *adj* resuelto.

resolution, *n* 1. resolución *f;* mostrarse resuelto; 2. propósito *m*.

resolve, *n* 1. resolución *f;* 2. *vt* resolver; 3. *vi* resolverse.

resolved, *adj* resuelto.

resonance, *n* resonancia *f*.

resonate, *vi* resonar (de).

resort, *n* 1. recurso *m;* 2. *vi* frecuentar, concurrir a, acudir a.

resound, *vi* resonar, retumbar.

resource, *n* recurso *m*, expediente *m*.

resourceful, *adj* inventivo, ingenioso.

respect, *n* 1. respecto *m;* 2. *vt* respetar;acatar.

respectable, *adj* respetable; decente, honrado.

respectful, *adj* respetuoso.

respecting, *prep* (con) respecto a; en cuanto a; por lo que se refiere a.

respective, *adj* respectivo.

respiration, *n* respiración *f*.

respire, *vt/i* respirar.

respite, *n* respiro *m*, respiradero *m;* plazo *m*.

resplendent, *adj* resplandeciente, refulgente.

respond, *vi* responder; reaccionar, atender (a).

response, *n* respuesta *f*.

responsibility, *n* responsabilidad *f*.

responsive, *adj* que reacciona con entusiasmo.

rest, *n* 1.descanso *m*, reposo *m;* paz *f;* 2. (Mus) pausa; 3. *vi* descansar;dejardescansar;4. apoyar

restate, *vt* repetir, reafirmar; volver a exponer.

restaurant, *n* restaurante *m* restorán *m*.

restful, *adj* descansado, repósado, sosegado.

restitution, *n* restitución *f*.

restless, *adj* inquieto, intranquilo, desasosegado.

restlessness, *n* inquietud *f*, intranquilidad *f*.

restoration, *n* restauración *f*; devolución *f*.

restore, *vt* devolver; restablecer; volver a imponer.

restraint, *n* freno *m*, control *m*; restricción *f*.

restrict, *vt* restringir, limitar (a).

restricted, *adj* restringido; limitado.

restriction, *n* restricción *f*, limitación *f*.

restroom, *n* cuarto *m* de descanso; aseos *m*, sanitarios *m*.

restructure, *vt* reestructurar; sanear.

restyle, *vt* remodelar.

result, *n* 1. resultado *m*; 2. *vi* resultar de; producir, motivar, terminar en.

resume, *vt* 1. reanudar, continuar; reasumir; 2. *vi* continuar; comenzar de nuevo.

resumé, *n* resumen *m*; curriculum *m* (vitae).

resurrect, *vt* resucitar.

resurrection, *n* resurrección *f*.

resuscitate, *vt/i* resucitar.

resuscitation, *n* resucitación *f*.

retail, *n* 1. venta *f* al por menor, venta *f* al detalle; 2. *vt* vender al por menor, vender al detalle.

retailer, *n* detallista *m/f*, menorista *m/f*.

retain, *vt* retener; conservar; guardar, quedarse con.

retaliate, *vi* desquitarse, tomar represalias.

retaliation, *n* desquite *m* , represalia *f*, revancha *f*; venganza *f*.

retard, *vt* retardar, retrasar.

retarded, *adj* retardado, retrasado.

retention, *n* retención *f*; conservación *f*.

reticence, *n* reticencia *f*, reserva *f*.

reticent, *adj* reticente, reservado.

retina, *n* retina *f*.

retire, *vt* 1. jubilar; 2. *vi* retirarse.

retirement, *n* retiro *m*; pension *f*, jubilación *f*.

retort, *n* 1. réplica *f*; 2. *vt* devolver.

retrace, *vt* volver a trazar; recordar.

retract, *vt* 1. retractar, returar; 2. *vi* retractarse.

retrain, *vt* recapacitar, reciclar, reeducar.

retraining, *n* recapacitación *f*, reeducación *f*.

retread, *n* 1. recauchutado *m*; 2. *vt* recauchutar.

retreat, *n* 1. retiro *m*; refugio *m*, asilo *m*; 2. *vi* retirarse, batirse en retirada.

retrial, *n* nuevo proceso *m*.

retribution, *n* justo castigo *m*, pena *f* merecida.

retrieve, *vt* cobrar, recobrar, recuperar.

retriever, *n* perro *m* cobrador *m*, perdiguero *m*.

retroactive, *adj* retroactivo.

retrograde, *adj* retrógrado.

retrospect, *n* restrospección *f*.

retrospective, *adj* retrospectivo.

retry, *vt* procesar de nuevo.

retune, *vt* afinar de nuevo.

return, *n* 1. vuelta *f*, regreso *m*; 2. *vt* devolver, regresar; restituir; 3. *vi* volver, revertir.

reunification, *n* reunificación *f*.

reunion, *n* reunión *f*.

reunite, *vt* 1. reunir; reconciliar; 2. *vi* reunirse.

revamp, *vt* remendar; renovar; modernizar.

reveal, *vt* revelar; desplegar, demostrar.

revealing, *adj* revelador.

revelation, *n* revelación *f*.

revenge, *n* 1. venganza *f*; 2. *vt/i* vengar; vengarse.

revenue, *n* ingresos *m*; renta *f*; rédito *m*.

reverberate, *vi* resonar, retumbar; reverberar.

revere, *vt* reverenciar, venerar.

reverence, *n* 1. reverencia *f*; 2. *vt* reverenciar.

reversal, *n* inversión *f*; cambio *m* completo.

reverse, *adj* 1. order inverso, invertido; 2. *n* marcha atrás; 3. *vt* invertir, trastrocar; volver al revés; 4. *vi* dar marcha atrás.

revert, *vi* revertir (a).

review, *n* 1. revisión *f*; 2. *vt* rever; repasar; examinar.

reviewer, *n* crítico(a) *m/f*; reseñante *m/f*.

revile, *vt* injuriar, llenar de injurias, vilipendiar.

revise, *vt* revisar.

revision, *n* revisión *f*; repaso *m*; modificación *f*.

revitalize, *vt* revivificar; vigorizar.

revival, *n* resucitación *f*; reanimación *f*.

revivalist, *n* evangelista *m/f*.

revive, *vt* 1. resucitar; reanimar; restablecer; 2. *vi* resucitar; reponerse, restablecerse.

revocation, *n* revocación *f*.

revoke, *n* 1. renuncio *m*; 2. *vt* revocar.

revolt, *n* 1. rebelión *f*, sublevación *f*; 2. *vt* repugnar, dar asco a; 3. *vi* rebelarse, sublevarse (contra).

revolting, *adj* asqueroso, repugnante.

revolution, *n* revolución *f*.

revolutionize, *vt* revolucionar.

revolve, *vt* 1. girar, hacer girar; dar vueltas a, revolver, meditar; 2. *vi* girar; dar vueltas; revolverse.

revolver, *n* revólver *m*.

revue, *n* revista *f*.

reward, *n* 1. recompensa *f*, premio *m*; 2. *vt* recompensar, premiar.

rewarding, *adj* remunerador; provechoso, útil.

rewind, *vt* dar cuerda a; devanar; rebobinar.

rewrite, *vt* 1. nueva versión *f*, refundición *f*; 2. *vt* volver a escribir, escribir de nuevo.

rhetoric, *n* retórica *f*.

rheumatism, *n* reumatismo *m*.

rheumatology, *n* reumatología *f*.

rhinestone, *n* diamante *m* de imitación.

rhinocerous, *n* rinoceronte *m*.

rhyme, *n* 1. rima *f*; 2. poesía *f*, versos *m*; 3. *vt/i* rimar.

rhymed, *adj* rimado.

rhythm, *n* ritmo *m*.

rib, *n* costilla *f*.

ribbon, *n* cinta *f*; galón *m*.

rice, *n* arroz *m*.

rich, *adj* rico; costoso, precioso.

rickety, *adj* 1. raquítico; 2. tambaleante.

rid, *vt* librar un lugar de, eliminar.

riddle, *n* acertijo *m*, adivinanza *f*; enigma *m*.

ride, *n* 1. paseo *m*; (horse) cabalgata *f*; 2. *vi* montar, cabalgar.

rider, *n* jinete(a) *m/f*, caballero *m*; ciclista *m/f*.

ridge, *n* cadena *f*, sierra *f*; estribación *f*.

ridicule, *n* 1. irrisión *f*; 2. *vt* poner en ridículo, mofarse de.

ridiculous, *adj* ridículo, absurdo.

riding, *n* equitación *f*, montar a caballo.

rifle, *n* 1. rifle *m*, fusil *m*; 2. *vt* robar, saquear.

rifleman, *n* fusilero *m*.

rift, *n* hendedura *f*, grieta *f*, rendija *f*; claro *m*.

rig, *n* 1. aparejo *m*; 2. *vt* aparejar, enjarciar.

right, *adj* 1. justo, debido, undicado; derecho, exacto; 2. *n* (justice) derecho *m*; 3. *vt* rectificar.

righteous, *adj* justo, honrado, recto.

rightful, *adj* legítimo; verdadero.

rigid, *adj* rígido; yerto; inflexible.

rigidity, *n* rigidez *f*; inflexibilidad *f*, severidad *f*.

rigorous, *adj* riguroso.

rim, *n* borde *m*, canto *m*.

rime, *n* rima *f*; escarcha *f*.

rimmed, *adj* con un borde de ..., bordeado de ...

rind, n corteza f, cáscara f, piel f.

ring, n 1. aro m; argolla f; anillo m; 2. vt cercar, rodear; anillar.

ring binder, n carpeta f de anillos.

ringing, adj 1. resonante, sonoro; 2. n repique m, tañido m.

ringleader, n cabecilla m.

ringlet, n rizo m, bucle m, tirabuzón m.

rinse, n 1. enjuague m; aclarado m; 2.vt enjuagar; aclarar; lavar, limpiar.

riot, n 1. motín m, disturbio m; tumulto m; 2. vi amotinarse.

rioter, n amotiado(a) m/f, manifestante m/f.

rip, n 1. rasgón m, rasgadura f; 2. vt rasgar, desgarrar; 3. vi rasgarse, romperse.

ripe, adj maduro.

ripen, vt/i madurar.

ripple, n 1. rizo m, onda f; murmullo m; 2. vt rizar; 3. murmurar.

rise, n 1. subida f, ascensión f, elevación f; 2. vi levantarse, subir, crecer, ascender.

rising, adj 1. creciente; naciente; 2. n sublevación f; rebelión f.

risk, n 1. riesgo m, peligro m; 2. vt arriesgar; atreverse a, exponerse a.

risky, adj peligroso, arriesgado, aventurado.

rite, n rito m; exequias f.

ritual, adj 1. ritual; 2. n ritual m, ceremonia f.

rival, adj 1. rival, opuesto; competidora; 2. n rival m/f; 3. vt rivalizar con, competir con.

rivalry, n rivalidad f; competencia f.

river, n río m.

riverbank, n orilla f del río, margen f del río.

riverbed, n lecho m, cauce m(del río).

rivet, n 1. roblón m, remache m; 2. vt remachar.

roach, n escarcho m; cucaracha f.

road, n camino m.

roadmap, n mapa m de carretera.

raodway, n calzada f.

roam, vt 1. vagar por, recorrer; 2. vi vagar.

roamer, n hombre m errante, andariego m; vagabundo m.

roar, n 1. rugido m, bramido m; 2. vt rugir.

roast, n 1. carne f asada, asado m; 2. vt asar; tostar.

roaster, n asador m, tostador m.

rob, vt robar; atracar.

robber, n ladrón m; atracador m; salteador m.

robbery, n robo m; latrocinio m.

robe, n 1. manto m; túnica f; hábito m; sotana f; 2. vt vestir a uno.

robin, n petirrojo m.

robot, n robot m, autómata m.

robust, adj robusto; fuerte, vigoroso.

rock, n 1. roca f; peria f, periasco m; 2. vi mecerse, balancearse;sacudirse.

rocker, n balancín m; mecedora f.

rocket, n 1. cohete m; 2. vt atacar con cohetes.

rocky, adj 1. que se bambolea, inestable; 2. rocoso.

rod, n vara f, varilla f, barra f.

rodeo, n rodeo m.

roe, n corzo(a) m/f; hueva f; lecha f.

rogue, n pícaro m, pillo m; picaruelo m.

roll, n 1. rollo m; pieza f; rodete m, rosca f; 2. (bread) panecillo m; 3. lista f, 4.vt hacer rodar.

roller, n rodillo m; rueda f.

romantic, adj 1. romántico; 2. n romántico(a) m/f.

romanticize, vt hacer romántico.

roof, n 1. techo m, tejado m; 2. vt techar, poner techo a.

rookie, n bisoño m, novato m.

room, n 1. cuarto m; habitación f; espacio m; cupo m; 2. vi alojarse.

roomy, adj amplio, espacioso; holgado.

root, n 1. raíz f; radical m; 2. vt hacer arraigar;3. (pig)hocicar.

rope, n 1. cuerda f, mecate m; soga f; 2. vt atar con cuerda;coger con lazo.

rosary, n rosario m.

rose, n 1. rosa f; 2. adj color de rosa, rosado.

roseate, adj róseo, rosado.

roster, n lista f.

rosy, adj rosado, sonrosado.

rot, n 1. putrefacción f, podredumbre f; 2. vt pudrir, corromper, descomponer.

rotate, vt hacer girar; dar vueltas a.

rotating, adj rotativo; giratorio.

rotten, adj podrido, putrefacto, corrompido.

rotting, adj podrido, que se está pudriendo.

rotund, adj rotundo; gordo.

rotunda, n rotonda f.

rouge, n 1. colorete m, carmín m; 2. vt ponerse colorete.

round, adj redondo.

rouse, adj despertar; emotion excitar, susciar.

rousing, adj emocionado, entusiasta.

route, n ruta f; camino m; itinerario m.

routine, n encaminameinto m.

rover, n vagabundo m, andariego m; purata m.

row, n 1. fila f, hilera f; 2. (fuss) bronca f, lío m; 3. vt (boat) remar; 4. reñir.

royal, adj 1. real; regio; 2. magnífico, espléndido.

rub, n 1. frotamiento m; roce m rozadura f; 2. vt frotar, friccionar.

rubber, n goma f; juego m; coto m.

rubbing, n frotamiento m.

rubbish, n basura f; desperdicios m, desechos m.

rubella, n rubéola f.

rudder, n timón m, gobernalle m.

rude, adj grosero, descortés, ofensivo.

rudimentary, adj rudunental.

ruffian, n matón m. cruninal m.

ruffle, n 1. arruga f; volante m fruncido; rizo m; 2. vt arrugar; molestar, agitar.

rug, n tapete m, alfombrilla f; manta f(de viaje).

rugged, adj terrain escabroso, áspero.

ruin, n 1. ruína f; s ruinas f; restos m; 2. vt arruinar.

ruined, adj arruinado, en ruinas, ruinoso.

rule, n 1. regla f; nomma f; costumbre f; decisión f; 2. vt gobemar; mandar, regir.

rum, n ron m.

rumble, n 1. retumbo m, ruido m sordo, rumor m; 2. vi retumbar; redoblar.

ruminate, vt/i rumiar.

rummage, vi hurgar; revolverlo todo.

rumor, n rumor m.

rump, n ancas f, grupa f; rabadilla f; trasero m.

rumple, vt ajar, arrugar, chafar.

rumpus, n lío m, jaleo m; batahóla f, revuelo m.

run, n 1. corrida f, carrera f; acarraladura f, 2. paseo m; 3. vt correr; llevar; 4. vt dirigir, funcionar, manejar.

runaway, adj 1. fugitivo; 2. n fugitivo(a) m/f.

runner, n corredor(ora) m/f; mensajero(a) m/f.

running, adj 1. corriente; corredizo; cursivo; 2. n el correr, administración f, funcionamiento m.

runt, n redrojo m, enano m.

rupture, n 1. hernia f, quebradura f; 2. vt causar una hernia en; quebrarse.

rush, n 1. ímpetu m; ataque m; 2. prisa f precipitación f, apuro m; 3. vt dar prisa a, apresurar.

rust, *n* 1. oxidación *f*, corrosión *f*; 2. *vt* oxidar, corroer; aherrumbrar.

rustic, *adj* rústico.

rustler, *n* ladrón *m* de ganado.

rustless, *adj* inoxidable.

rusty, *adj* oxidado, herrumbroso, aherrumbrado.

rut, *n* rodera *f*, rodada *f*; bache *m*; (Bio) celo *m*, brama *f*.

ruthless, *adj* despiadado; sin piedad; implacable, inexorable.

rye, *n* centeno *m*.

S

S, s, *n* (letra *f*) S, s.

sabbatical, *adj* 1. sabático; dominical; 2. *n* sabático *m*.

saber, *n* sable *m*.

sable, *n* marta *f*; negro *m*; sablem.

sabotage, *n* 1. sabotaje *m*; 2. *vt* sabotear.

saccharine, *adj* 1. sacaruna; 2. *n* sacaruna *f*.

sacerdotal, *adj* sacerdotal.

sachet, *n* almohadilla *f* perfumada.

sack, *n* 1. saco *m*, costal *m*; 2. saqueo *m*, 3. *vt* ensacar, meter en sacos; 4. saquear.

sacrament, *n* sacramento *m*; Eucaristía *f*.

sacred, *adj* sagrado; santo; consagrado.

sacrifice, *n* 1. sacrifcio *m*; víctima *f*; 2. *vt* sacrificar.

sacristy, *n* sacristía *f*.

sad, *adj* triste; melancólico; lamentable.

sadden, *vt* entristecer; afligir.

saddle, *n* 1. silla *f* (de montar); asiento *m*, sillín *m*; 2. *vt* ensillar.

sadism, *n* sadismo *m*.

sadness, *n* tristeza *f*, melancolía *f*.

safe, *adj* 1. seguro; salvo, fuera de peligro; 2. *n* caja *f* de caudales; caja *f* fuerte.

safely, *n* seguridad *f*.

saffron, *n* azafrán *m*.

sag, *n* 1. comba *f*; 2. *vi* combarse, hundirse, pandear.

sagacious, *adj* sagaz.

sagacity, *n* sagacidad *f*.

sage, *adj* 1. sabio; 2. *n* sabio *m*; salvia *f*.

said, *adj* dicho, antedicho.

sail, *n* 1. vela *f*; 2. aspa *f*; 3. paseo *m*; 4. *vt* gobernar; manejar navegar.

sailing, *n* navegación *f*.

sailor, *n* marinero *m*, marino *m*.

sainted, *adj* santo; bendito.

sainthood, *n* santidad *f*.

sake, *n* por; por motivo de; en consideración a.

salad, *n* ensalada *f*.

salamander, *n* salamandra *f*.

salami, *n* salatmi *m*.

salary, *n* sueldo *m*.

sale, *n* venta *f*.

salient, *adj* saliente; sobresaliente, destacado.

salinity, *n* salunidad *f*.

saliva, *n* saliva *f*.

salivary, *adj* salival; glándula.

salivate, *vi* salivar.

salmon, *n* salmón *m*.

salon, *n* salón *m*.

saloon, *n* cantuna *f*.

salt, *n* sal *f*.

saltines, *n* galletas *f* saladitas.

salty, *adj* salado.

salubrious, *adj* salubre, sano.

salutation, *n* salutación *f*, saludo *m*.

salute, *n* saludo *m*; salva *f*.

salvage, *n* 1. salvamento *m*; recuperación *f*; 2. *vt* salvar; recuperar.

salvation, *n* salvación *f*.

salve, n 1. unguento *m*, bálsamo; 2. *vt* curar (con ungüento); aliviar.

Sabbath, *n* domingo *m*; sábado *m*.

samba, *n* samba *f*.

same, *adj* 1. mismo; igual; idéntico; 2. *pron* el mismo, la misma.

sample, *n* 1. muestra *f*; 2. *vt* probar.

sanatorium, *n* sanatorio *m*.

sanctification, *n* santificación *f*.

sanctify, *vt* santificar.

sanction, *n* 1. sanción *f*, autorisación *f*, aprobación *f*; 2. *vt* sancionar, autorizar, aprobar.

sanctuary, *n* santuario *m*; sagrario *m*; sagrado *m*, refugio *m*; asilo *m*.

sand, *n* 1. arena *f*; 2. *vt* enarenar.

sandal, *n* sandalia *f*; alpargata *f*.

sandwich, *n* sándwich *m*, emparedado *m*.

samba, *n* samba *f*.

same, *adj* 1. mismo; igual; idéntico; 2. *pron* el mismo, la misma.

sample, *n* 1. muestra *f*; 2. *vt* probar.

sanatorium, *n* sanatorio *m*.

sanctification, *n* santificación *f*.

sanctify, *vt* santificar.

sanction, *n* 1. sanción *f*, autorisación *f*, aprobación *f*; 2. *vt* sancionar, autorizar, aprobar.

sanctuary, *n* santuario *m*; sagrario *m*; sagrado *m*, refugio *m*; asilo *m*.

sand, *n* 1. arena *f*; 2. *vt* enarenar.

sandal, *n* sandalia *f*; alpargata *f*.

sandwich, *n* sándwich *m*, emparedado *m*.

sane, *adj* person cuerdo, sensato, de juicio sano.

sanguine, *adj* optimista.

sanitarium, *n* sanatorio *m*.

sanitary, *adj* higiénico.

sanity, *n* cordura *f*, sensatez *f*, juicio *m* sano.

sap, *n* 1. (Bot) savia *f*; jugo *m*, vitalidad *f*; tonto *m*; 2. *vt* debilitar, agotar

sapphire, *n* zafiro *m*.

sarcasm, *n* sarcasmo *m*.

sarcastic, *adj* sarcástico.

sardine, *n* sardina *f*.

sartorial, *adj* relativo al vestido.

satan, *n* satanás *m*.

satanic, *adj* satánico.

satchel, *n* bolsa *f*, cartera *f*.

sate, *vt* saciar, hartar.

sateen, *n* satén *m*.

satellite, *n* satélite *m*.

satiate, *vt* saciar, hartar.

satin, *n* raso *m*.

satire, *n* sátira *f*.

satirize, *vt* satirizar.

satisfaction, *n* satisfacción *f*.

satisfy , *vt* satisfacer.

satisfying, *adj* satisfactorio, que satisface.

saturate, *vt* saturar, empapar.

saturation, *n* saturación *f*.

Saturday, *n* sábado *m*.

sauce, n salsa f; crema f; compota f.

saucepan, n cacerola f, cazo m.

saucer, n platillo m.

saucy, adj fresco, descarado, coqueta.

sauna, n sauna f.

saunter, n 1. paseo m; 2. vi pasearse.

sausage, n embutido m; salchicha f.

sauté, adj 1. salteado; 2. vt saltear.

savage, adj 1. salvaje; 2 n salvaje m/f; 3. vt embestir.

savant, n sabio m, erudito m, intelectual m.

save, prep, conj 1. salvo, exepto, con exepción de; 2. vt salvar; rescatar; 3. guardar, reservar; 4. vi ahorrar, economizar.

saver, n ahorrador(ora) m/f.

saving, adj 1. económico; tacaño; 2. n salvamento m, rescate m.

savior, n salvador m.

savor, n 1. sabor m, gusto m; 2. vt saborear, paladear.

savory, adj 1. sabroso, apetitoso; 2. n plato m salado.

saw, n 1. sierra f; 2. proverbio m; 3. vt serrar; 4. escalar.

saxophone, n saxofón m, saxófono m.

say, n 1. tener voz y voto; 2. vt decir.

scab, n 1. costra f; 2. roña f.

scaffold, n andamio m.

scald, n 1. escaldadura f; 2. vt escaldar.

scalding, adj hirviendo, hirviente.

scale, n 1. (Fish) escama f; 2. balanza f, báscula f; 3. (Mus, Math) escala; 4. vt escamar; 5. vi pesar.

scallion, n cebolleta f.

scallop, n venera f, vieira f.

scalp, n cuero m cabelludo, cabellera f.

scalpel, n escalpelo m.

scam, n estafa f, timo m.

scamp, n tunante m/f, bribon(ona) m/f.

scan, vt escudriñar, explorar con la vista.

secession, n secesión f, separación f.

secluded, adj retirado, apartado.

seclusion, n retiro m.

second, adj 1. segundo; otro; 2. n segundo m; segundero m; muy inferior al que gana.

secrecy, n secreto m; reserva f, discreción f.

secret, adj 1. secreto; 2. n secreto m.

secretary, n secretario(a) m/f.

secrete, vt esconder, ocultar.

secretive, adj reservado, callado; sigiloso.

sect, n secta f.

sectarian, adj 1. sectario; 2. n sectario(a) m/f.

section, n sección f; parte f, porción f.

secular, adj secular, seglar.

secure, adj 1. seguro; firme; 2. vi asegurar; fijar, afianzar.

security, n seguridad f; protección f.

sedate, adj 1. tranquilo, sosegado; serio; 2. vt administrar sedantes a.

sedative, adj 1. sedante, calmante; 2. n sedante m, calmante m.

sediment, n sedimento m; poso m.

sedimentation, n sedimentación f.

seduce, vt seducir; apartar a uno de su deber.

seducer, n seductor m.

seduction, n seducción f.

seductive, adj seductor.

see, n 1. sede f; 2. vt ver; acompañar; comprender; entender; 3. mirar; observar; percibir.

seed, n 1. semilla f, simiente f; 2. vt sembrar; 3. despepitar.

seeing, n vista f, visión f.

seem, vi parecer; así parece.

seeming, adj 1. aparente; 2. n apariencia f.

seep, vi filtrarse, rezumarse.

seepage, n filtración f.

seer, n vidente m/f, profeta m/f.

segment, n segmento m.

segregate, vt segregar, separar.

segregation, n segregación f, separación f.

seize, vt agarrar, asir, coger; detener, prender, embargar, secuestrar.

seizure, n asimiento m; detención f; convulsión f.

select, vt escoger, elegir; seleccionar.

selection, n selección f; elección f; surtido m.

selective, adj selectivo.

self, pron 1. se; sí mismo; 2. n uno mismo, una misma.

sell, vi vender a.

seller, n vendedor(a) m/f.

selling, n venta f, el vender.

selvage, n orillo m, borde m.

semantic, adj semántico.

semaphore, n semáforo m.

semantic, adj semántico.

semaphore, n semáforo m.

semen, n semen m.

semester, n semestre m.

seminar, n seminario m.

senator, n senador(a) m/f.

send, vt 1. enviar, mandar; despachar; remitir; 2. lanzar; 3. vt mandar.

sender, n remitente m/f.

send, vt 1. enviar, mandar; despachar; remitir; 2. lanzar; 3. vt mandar.

sender, n remitente m/f.

senile, adj senil.

senility, n senilidad f.

senior, adj mayor, más viejo; más antiguo.

sensation, n sensación f.

sensational, adj sensacional.

sense, n 1. sentido m; 2. juicio m; 3. inteligencia f; 3. vt sentir, percibir, barruntar, intuir.

senseless, adj insensato, estúpido, sin sentido.

sensibility, n sensibilidad f; sensibilities.

sensible, adj juicioso, prudente, sensato.

sensitize, vt sensibilizar; mentalizar.

sensor, n sensor m.

sensory, adj sensorio, sensorial.

sensual, adj sensual.

sentence, n 1. frase f; oración f; 2. vt condenar.

sentient, adj sensitivo, sensible.

sentiment, n sentimiento m.

sentimental, adj sentimental.

sentinel, n centinela m.

sentry, n centinela m, guardia m.

separable, adj separable.

separate, adj 1. separado; distinto; 2. n separata f; 3. vt separar, separarse.

separation, n separación f.

September, n septiembre m.

septet, n septeto m.

septic, adj séptico.

sequel, n consecuencia f, resultado m; desenlace.

sequence, n sucesión f, orden m de sucesión.

sequential, adj secuencial.

sequester, vt aislar.

sequestered, adj aislado, remoto.

sequin, n lentejuela f.

seraph, n serafín m.

serendipity, *n* serependismo *m.*

serene, *adj* sereno, tranquilo.

serenity, *n* serenidad *f.*, tranquilidad *f.*

serf, *n* siervo *m.*

sergeant, *n* sargento *m.*

serial, *adj* consecutivo, en serie.

serialize, *vt* serializar.

series, *n* serie *f.*; sucesión *f.*

serious, *adj* serio; character serio, formal.

sermon, *n* sermón *m.*

serpent, *n* serpiente *f.*, sierpe *f.*

serrated, *adj* serrado, dentellado.

serum, *n* suero *m.*

servant, *n* criado(a) *m/f.*

serve, *vt* servir; estar al servicio de.

service, *n* 1. servicio *m;* 2. *vt* revisar, mantener.

servile, *adj* servil.

servitude, *n* servidumbre *f.*

session, *n* sesión *f.*; curso *m.*

set, *adj* 1. rígido, inflexible, fijo; (time) señalado; 2. *n* (tools, etc.) juego *m;* (drums, utensils) batería *f.*; equipo; 3. *vt* poner, colocar, engastar, fijar; 4. *vi* (sun) ponerse.

setting, *n* 1. (sun) puesta *f.*; (jewel) montadura *f.*; (Theat) escena *f.*; ambiente *m.*

settlement, *n* liquidación *f.*, arreglo *m;* acuerdo; establecimiento *m;* pueblo *m.*

seven, *adj* 1. siete; 2. *n* siete *m.*

seventeen, *adj* diecisiete.

sever, *vt* cortar, separar; dividir.

several, *adj* varios, algunos; diversos.

severance , *n* corte *m;* separación *f.*, división *f.*

severe, *adj* severo; riguroso, fuerte; duro.

severity, *n* severidad *f.*; rigor *m;* gravedad *f.*

sew, *vt* 1. coser; 2. *vi* coser.

sewer, *n* albañal *m,* alcantarilla *f,* cloaca *f.*

sex, *n* sexo *m.*

sexist, *adj* 1. sexista; 2. *n* sexista *m/f.*

sextant, *n* sextante *m.*

sexton, *n* sacristán *m;* sepulturero *m.*

sexual, *adj* sexual.

sexuality, *n* sexualidad *f.*

shabby, *adj* pobremente vestido, desharrapado.

shack, *n* chabola *f,* choza *f,* jacal *m.*

shackle, *n* 1. grillete *m;* 2. *vt* encadenar; poner grilletes a.

shade, *n* 1. sombra *f;* 2. *vt* dar sombra a, sombrear.

shadow, *n* sombra *f.*

shadowy, *adj* oscuro; indistinto.

shaft, *n* flecha *f,* dardo *m,* saeta *f;* astil *m.*

shake, *n* 1. sacudida *f,* sacudimiento *m;* 2. batido *m;* 3. *vt* sacudir.

shaky, *adj* inestable, poco firme, poco sólido.

shale, *n* esquisto *m.*

shall, *v aux* se usa para formar el futuro.

shallow, *adj* poco profundo, (pers) superficial, frívolo.

sham, *adj* 1. falso, fingido, simulado; 2. *n* impostura *f,* fraude *m,* engaño *m.*

shamble, *vi* andar arrastrando los pies.

shambles, *n* escombrera *f,* caos *m,* desorden; matanza *f.*

shame, *n* 1. vergüenza *f;* deshonra *f;* 2. *vt* avergonzar; deshonrar.

shameful, *adj* vergonzoso.

shameless, *adj* desvergonzado, descarado.

shampoo, *n* 1. champú *m;* 2. *vt* person lavar la cabeza a, dar un champú a.

shamrock, *n* trébol *m.*

shank, *n* caña *f;* zanca *f;* tallo *m.*

shanty, *n* choza *f,* chabola *f.*

shape, *n* 1. forma *f;* figura *f;* configuración *f;* corte *m;* 2. *vt* formar, dar forma a; moldear.

shapeless, *adj* informe, sin forma definida.

shapely, *adj* bien formado, bien proporcionado.

shard, *n* tiesto *m,* casco *m,* fragmento *m.*

share, *n* 1. parte *f,* porción *f;* cuota *f;* (stock) acción; 2. *vt* compartir, poseer en común.

shared, *adj* compartido; facilities etc comunitario.

shark, *n* tiburón *m.*

sharp, *adj* 1. afilado, cortante; puntiagudo; 2. listo, despierto; 3. *n* (Mus) sostenido.

sharpen, *vt* afilar; aguzar; amolar.

sharpener, *n* afilador *m,* máquina *f* de afilar.

shatter, *vt* 1. romper, hacer anicos, hacer pedazos; 2. *vi* romperse, hacerse anicos.

shattered, *adj* destrozado; abrumado, confundido.

shave, *n* 1. afeitado *m,* rasurado *m;* 2. *vt* afeitar.

shawl, *n* chal *m.*

she, *pron* 1. ella; 2. *n* hembra *f.*

shear, *vt* 1. esquilar, trasquilar; 2. *n* tijeras *f* (grandes).

sheathe *vt* envainar; enfundar.

shed, *n* 1. cobertizo *m,* alpende *m;* barraca *f;* 2. *vt* despojarse de; mudar; desprenderse de.

sheen, *n* lustre *m;* brillo *m.*

sheep, *n* oveja *f;* carnero *m.*

sheer, *adj* 1. transparente; escarpado; absoluto; 2. *vi* desviarse.

sheet, *n* sábana *f;* hoja *f,* sábana *f.*

shelf, *n* tabla *f,* anaquel *m;* repisa *f.*

shell, *n* cáscara *f,* cascarón *m;* concha *f.*

shelter, *n* 1. abrigo *m,* asilo *m,* refugio *m;* 2. *vt* abrigar, proteger, amparar.

shepherd, *n* pastor *m.*

sherbet, *n* sorbete *m.*

sheriff, *n* sheriff *m,* alguacil *m.*

shield, *n* escudo *m;* rodela *f;* capa *f* protectora.

shift, *n* 1. cambio *m;* turno *m;* 2. *vt* cambiar mover.

shin, *n* espinilla *f;* jarrete *m,* corvejón *m.*

shine, *n* 1. brillo *m,* lustre *m;* 2. *vt* sacar brillo a.

shingle, *n* 1. ripia *f;* 2. *vt* cubrir con ripias

ship, *n* 1. buque *m,* barco *m,* navío *m;* 2. *vt* embarcar.

shipment, *n* embarque *m;* transporte *m.*

shirt, *n* camisa *f.*

shiver, *n* 1. temblor *m,* estremecimiento *m;* 2. *vi* temblar, estremecerse; vibrar.

shoal, *n* banco *m,* cardumen *m;* banco *m* de arena, bajío *m.*

shock, *n* 1. descarga *f;* sacudida *f,* sobresalto *m,* susto *m;* 2. *vt* sobresaltar, dar un susto a.

shocked, *adj* sorprendido; ofendido; escandalizado.

shoe, *n* zapato *m.*

shoot, *n* 1. renuevo *m,* retoño *m,* vástago *m;* 2. *vi* disparar, tirar, descargar.

shop, *n* tienda *f,* negocio *m;* (work) taller.

shoplifter, *n* mechera *f,* ratero *m* de tiendas,

shopping, *n* ir de tiendas.

shore, *n* playa *f;* orilla *f,* ribera *f;* estribo *m.*

short, *adj* 1. corto, breve, sucinto; insuficiente; 2. *n* (Elect) cortocircuito *m;* calzoncillos *m.*

shoreline, *n* línea *f* de la costa.

shortage, *n* escasez *f,* falta *f.*

shorten, *vt* 1. acortar; abreviar; reducir; 2. *vi* acortarse.

shortening, *n* 1. acortamiento *m;* 2. manteca *f.*

shot, *n* bala *f;* proyectil *m;* tiro *m,* disparo *m.*

shoulder, n 1. hombro m; espaldas f pl; espalda f; 2. vt llevar al hombro.

shout, n 1. grito m, voz f; 2. vt gritar.

shove, n 1. empujón m; empujar a uno; 2. vt empujar.

shovel, n 1. pala f; 2. vt traspalar, mover con pala.

show, n 1. demostración f; 2. exposición f; 3. función f, espectáculo m; 4. vt mostrar, enseñar.

showcase, n vitrina f.

shower, n 1. ducha; 2. (rain) aguacero m; 3. vi tomar una ducha; llover.

showing, n exposición f; proyección f; presentación f.

shred, n 1. fragmento m, pedazo m; triza f, jirón m; 2. vt hacer trizas, hacer tiras; desmenuzar.

shrew, n musaraña f; arpía f, fiera f.

shrewd, adj sagaz; perspicaz; listo.

shriek, n 1. chillido m, grito m agudo; 2. vt gritar.

shrill, adj 1. chillón, agudo; estridente; 2. vt gritar.

shrimp, n camarón m.

shrine, n sepulcro m (de santo), lugar m sagrado.

shrink, vt encoger; contraer; reducir, disminuir.

shrivel, vt secar, marchitar; arrugar.

shroud, n 1. sudario m, mortaja f; velo m; 2. vt amortajar; velar, cubrir.

shrub, n arbusto m.

shrubbery, n arbustos m, plantío m de arbustos.

shrug, n 1. encogimiento m de hombros; 2. vt encogerse de hombros.

shuffle, n 1. a caminar arrastrando los pies; 2. vt arrastrar; (cards) barrajar.

shun, vt evitar, esquivar, rehuir.

shunt, vt maniobrar; apartar.

shut, vt cerrar.

shutter, n celosía f, persiana f, contraventana; (camera) obturador m.

shuttle, n 1. lanzadera f; 2. vt mandar a uno de acá para alla; hacer viajes cortos.

shy, adj 1. tímido; vergonzoso; reservado; 2. vi espantarse, respingar.

sibling, n hermano m (hermana f).

sick, adj enfermo.

sicken, vt dar asco a.

sickening, adj nauseabundo; asqueroso, repugnante.

sickness, n enfermedad f.

side, n 1. costado m, lado m; 2. vt tomar partido.

sidetrack, n 1. apartadero m; 2. vt desviar.

sidewalk, n acera f, vereda f.

siege, n cerco m; sitio m.

sift, vt tamizar, cerner, cribar.

sigh, n 1. suspiro m; susurro m; 2. vi suspirar.

sight, n 1. vista f; visión f; 2. vt ver, divisar, avistar.

sighted, adj vidente, que ve, de vista normal.

sightseeing, n excursionismo m, turismo m.

sign, n 1. señal f, seña f; letrero m; 2. vt firmar.

signal, n 1. señal f, seña f; 2. vt hacer una seña.

signature, n firma f; signatura f.

significance, n significación f, significado m.

significant, adj significativo; trascendente.

signify, vt significar, querer decir.

silage, n ensilaje m.

silence, n 1. silencio m; 2. vt hacer callar, acallar.

silent, adj silencioso; callado.

silicone, n silicona f.

silk, n seda f.

sill, n antepecho m; alféizar m, repisa f.

silly, adj tonto, bobo, necio; insensato.

silt, n sedimento m, aluvión m.

silver, n 1. plata f; monedas f de plata; 2. vt platear; azogar; blanquear.

silverware, n plata f, vajilla f de plata.

similar, adj parecido, semejante.

simile, n símil m.

simmer, vt cocer a fuego lento.

simper, n 1. sonrisa f afectada; 2. vi sonreir bobamente.

simple, adj sencillo; fácil.

simplicity, n sencillez f; simpleza f, ingenuidad f.

simplification, n simplificación f.

simplify, vt simplificar.

simplistic, adj simplista.

simply, adv sencillamente; simplemente.

simulate, vt simular.

simulated, adj simulado.

simulation, n simulación f, fingimiento m; simulación f.

simulator, n simulador m.

simultaneous, adj simultáneo.

sin, n 1. pecado m; 2. vi pecar.

since, adv desde entonces, después.

sincere, adj sincero.

sincerity, n sinceridad f.

sinew, n tendón m.

sinful, adj pecador.

sing, vt cantar.

singe, vt chamuscar, socarrar.

singer, n cantor(a) f.

single, adj 1. único, solo; simple, sencillo; 2. n billete m sencillo.

singular, adj 1. singular; 2. n singular f.

sink, n 1. fregadero m; pila f; 2. vt hundir, sumergir.

sinless, adj libre de pecado, puro, inmaculado.

sinner, n pecador(a) m/f.

sinuous, adj sinuoso.

sinus, n seno m.

sinusitis, n sinusitis f.

sip, n 1. sorbo m; 2. vt sorber, beber a sorbito.

siphon, n 1. sifón m; 2. vt sacar con sifón.

sir, n señor m.

sire, n 1. padre; 2. caballo m semental; 3. vt engendrar.

siren, n sirena f.

sirloin, n solomillo m, diezmillo m.

sister, n hermana f.

sister-in-law, n cuñada f, hermana f política.

sit, vt 1. sentar; 2. vi posar; (hen) echarse, sentarse.

sitting, adj 1. sentado; 2. n sesión f; nidada f.

situate, vt situar.

situation, n situación f.

six, adj 1. seis; 2. n seis m.

sixteen, adj dieciséis.

sixty, adj sesenta.

size, n 1. tamaño m; dimensiones f; talla f; 2. apresto m; 3. vt clasificar según el tamaño; 4. aprestar.

sizeable, adj bastante grande, considerable.

sizeably, adv considerablemente.

sizzle, vi chisporrotear, churruscar, crepitar.

skate, n 1. patín m; 2. vi patinar.

skateboard, n monopatín m.

skater, n patinador(a) m/f.

skating, n patinaje m.

skating-rink, n pista f de patinaje.

skein, n madeja f.

skeletal, adj esquelético.

skeleton, n esqueleto, esquema m, plan m; armazón f.

sketch, n 1. esbozo m, boceto m, bosquejo m, croquis m; 2. vt esbozar; bosquejar; 3. vi dibujar.

sketch(ing)-pad, n bloc m de dibujo.

sketchy, adj incompleto, superficial, somero.

skewed, *adj* sesgado, torcido.

skewer, *n* 1. broqueta *f*, espetón *m*; 2. *vt* espetar.

ski, *n* 1. esquí *m*. 3. *vi* esquiar.

skid, *n* 1. patinazo *m*, derrape *m*, deslizamiento *m*; 3. *vi* patinar, derrapar; resbalar.

skier, *n* esquiador(a) *m/f*.

skill, *n* habilidad *f*, destreza *f*; pericia *f*.

skilled, *adj* hábil, diestro; cualificado.

skillet, *n* sartén *f*; cacerola *f* de mango largo.

skim, *vt* espumar; desnatar, descremar.

skimp, *vt* escatimar; chapucear, frangollar.

skimpy, *adj* escaso, pequeño; mezquino.

skin, *n* 1. piel *f*, pellejo *m*, corteza *f*; 2. *vt* despellejar, desollar; pelar, quitar la piel a.

skin-deep, *adj* epidérmico, superficial.

skindiver, *n* buceador(a) *m/f*.

skindiving, *n* exploración *f* submarina.

skinny, *adj* flaco, magro, escuálido, descarnado.

skin-tight, *adj* muy ajustado, muy ceñido.

skip, *n* 1. brinco *m*, salto *m*; 2. *vt* omitir, pasar por alto; 3. *vi* brincar, saltar.

skipper, *n* 1. capitán *m*; patrón *m*; 2. *vt* patronear.

skirmish, *n* escaramuza *f*; roce *m*; 2. *vi* escaramuzar.

skirt, *n* falda *f*, pollera *f*.

skit, *n* sátira, parodia; número *m* corto satírico.

skulduggery, *n* trampas *f*, embustes *m*.

skulk, *vi* procurar no ser visto.

skull, *n* calavera *f*; cráneo *m*.

skullcap, *n* casquete *m*, solideo *m*.

skunk, *n* mofeta *f*.

sky, *n* cielo *m*.

sky-blue, *adj* 1. azul celeste; 2. *n* azul *m* celeste.

sky-dive, *n* 1. caída *f* libre; 2. *vi* saltar en caída libre.

sky-diver, *n* paracaidista *m/f* de caída libre.

skyjacking, *n* atraco *m* aéreo; piratería *f* (aérea).

skylark, *n* alondra *f*.

skylight, *n* tragaluz *m*, claraboya *f*.

skyline, *n* horizonte *m*, línea *f* del horizonte.

skyscraper, *n* rascacielos *m*.

skywriting, *n* escritura *f* aérea, publicidad *f* aérea.

slab, *n* bloque *m*; plancha *f*, tabla *f*.

slack, *adj* 1. flojo; 2. descuidado, negligente; vago, inactivo; 3. *n* lo flojo, parte *f* floja.

slacken, *vt* 1. aflojar; disminuir; 2. *vi* aflojarse.

slagheap, *n* escorial *m*, escombrera *f*.

slake, *vt* apagar; cal *f* muerta.

slam, *n* 1. golpe *m*; portazo *m*; 2. golpear; dar un portazo; 3. *vi* cerrarse de golpe.

slander, *n* 1. calumnia *f*, difamación *f*; 2. *vt* calumniar, difamar; decir mal de, hablar mal de.

slanderous, *adj* calumnioso, difamatorio.

slang, *n* argot *m*; jerga *f*.

slant, *n* 1. inclinación *f*, sesgo *m*; 2. *vt* inclinar, sesgar; 3. *vi* inclinarse, sesgarse.

slanting, *adj* inclinado, oblicuo, sesgado.

slap, *n* 1. palmada *f*, manotada *f*; bofetada *f*; 2. *vt* dar una palmada (o bofetada) a; pegar, golpear.

slapdash, *adj* person descuidado; chapucero.

slash, *n* 1. cuchillada *f*; 2. *vt* acuchillar.

slat, *n* tablilla *f*, hoja *f*, listón *m*.

slate, *n* pizarra *f*; (Pol) lista *f* de candidatos.

slatted, *adj* de tablillas, hecho de listones.

slaughter, *n* 1. matanza *f*, sacrificio *m*; carnicería *f*; 2. *vt* matar, sacrificar, hacer una carnicería.

slaughterhouse, *n* matadero *m*.

slave, *n* 1. esclavo(a) *m/f*; 2. *vi* trabajar como un esclavo.

slavery, *n* esclavitud *f*.

slave-trade, *n* comercio *m* de esclavos, tráfico *m* de esclavos.

slavishly, *adv* servilmente.

slay, *vt* matar, asesinar.

slayer, *n* asesino *m*.

sled, *n* 1. trineo *m*; 2. *vi* ir en trineo.

sleek, *adj* 1. liso y brillante, lustroso; 2. *vt* alisar.

sleep, *n* 1. sueño *m*; 2. *vi* dormirse, quedarse dormido; dormir.

sleepiness, *n* somnolencia *f*; letargo *m*.

sleeping, *adj* durmiente, dormido.

sleeping-bag, *n* saco-manta *m*, saco *m* de dormir.

sleeping-pill, *n* comprimido *m* para dormir.

sleeplessness, *n* insomnio *m*.

sleepwalker, *n* sonámbulo(a) *m/f*.

sleepwear, *n* ropa *f* de dormir.

sleepy, *adj* soñoliento; soporífero.

sleet, *n* 1. aguanieve *f*; cellizca *f*; 2. *vi* cellisquear.

sleeve, *n* manga *f*; portada *f*, funda *f*.

sleeved, *adj* con mangas.

slender, *adj* delgado, tenue; fino, esbelto.

slenderize, *n* adelgazar.

slew, *n* 1. montón *m*; 2. *vt* torcer, girar.

slice, *n* 1. tajada *f*, lonja *f*, raja *f*, rebanada *f*; 2. *vt* cortar, tajar, cortar en rodajas, rebanar.

sliced, *adj* rebanado, en rebanadas; en rodajas.

slick, *adj* hábil, diestro; rápido.

slide, *n* 1. resbaladero *m*; deslizadero *m*; resbalón *m*; (Photo) diapositiva *f*; 2. *vt* correr, deslizar; 3. *vi* resbalar.

sliderule, *n* regla *f* de cálculo.

slight, *adj* 1. delgado, fino; pequeño; 2. *n* desaire *m*, insulto *m*; 3. *vt* desairar, ofender, insultar.

slim, *adj* 1. delgado, esbelto; 2. *vt* adelgazar.

slime, *n* limo *m*, légamo *m*, cieno *m*.

slimy, *adj* limoso, legamoso; baboso; viscoso.

sling, *n* 1. honda *f*; cabestrillo *m*; 2. *vt* lanzar, tirar.

slingshot, *n* honda *f*, tirador *m*; tirachinas *m*.

slink, *vi* andar furtivamente.

slinky, *adj* seductor, provocativo; sinuoso.

slip, *n* 1. resbalón *m*; traspié *m*, tropezón *m*; 2. falta *f*, error *m*, equivocacion *f*; 3. estaca *f*; papeleta *f*; 4. *vt* deslizar; 5. *vi* deslizarse, tropezar, resbalar.

slipknot, *n* nudo *m* corredizo.

slippage, *n* deslizamiento *m*; pérdida *f*.

slipper, *n* zapatilla *f*; babucha *f*, pantufla *f*.

slippery, *adj* resbaladizo; viscoso.

slipshod, *adj* descuidado, poco correcto.

slit, *n* 1. hendedura *f*, raja *f*; resquicio *m*; corte *m*; 2. *vt* hender, rajar; cortar.

slither, *vi* deslizarse; ir rodando.

sliver, *n* raja *f*; astilla *f*.

slobber, *n* 1. baba *f*; 2. *vi* babear; besuquear.

slogan, *n* slogan *m*, eslogan *m*.

sloop, *n* 1. balandra *f*; corbeta *f*.

slope, *n* inclinación *f*; cuesta *f*, pendiente *f*.

sloping, *adj* inclinado; en pendiente, en declive.

sloppy, *adj* desaseado; descuidado.

slot, *n* muesca *f*, ranura *f*.

sloth, *n* pereza *f*, indolencia *f*, desidia *f*.

slouch, *n* 1. postura *f* relajada; 2. *vi* caminar con los hombros caídos.

slough, *n* 1. fangal *m*, cenegal *m*; camisa *f*, piel *f* vieja (que muda la serpiente); escara *f*; 2. *vt* mudar, echar de sí; 3. *vi* desprenderse, caerse.

sloven, *n* 1. persona *f* desgarbada, desaseada *f*.

slovenliness, *n* desaseo *m*; descuido *m*, chapucería *f*.

slow, *adj* 1. lento; pausado; torpe; 3. *vt* retardar; reducir la velocidad.

slowdown, n huelga f de manos caídas.

slowly, adv despacio, lentamente; poco a poco.

slowness, n lentitud f.

sludge, n lodo m; fango m; sedimento m fangoso.

slug, n 1. babosa f; posta f; lingote m; ficha f; 2. vt pegar, aporrear.

sluggard, n haragán(ana) m/f.

sluggish, adj perezoso; lento; inactivo, inerte.

sluice, n compuerta f, esclusa f; dique m de contención.

slum, n barrio m bajo, barrio m pobre.

slumber, n 1. sueño m; inactividad f, inercia f; 2. vi dormir; estar dormido; permanecer inactivo, estar inerte.

slump, n 1. depresión f, declive m económico, retroceso m; 2. vi hundirse, bajar repentinamente.

slurred, adj indistinto, poco correcto.

slush, n nieve f a medio derretir.

sly, adj astuto; taimado; furtivo, disimulado, sigiloso.

smack, n 1. manotada f, palmada f; golpe m; 2. beso m sonado; 3. vt dar una manotada a.

small, adj pequeño; chico; menudo.

smallish, adj más bien pequeño.

smallpox, n viruela f, viruelas f.

smart, adj 1. elegante; pulcro, aseado; 2. listo, vivo, inteligente; 3. pronto, rápido, vivo.

smash, adj 1. exitazo; 2. n choque m (violento), colisión f; 3. vt romper, quebrar; hacer pedazos; 5. vi romperse.

smashing, adj imponente, bárbaro, pistonudo.

smattering, n conocimientos m elementales.

smear, n 1. mancha f; calumnia f; 2. vt manchar (de), untar (de); 3. calumniar.

smell, n 1. olfato m; 2. olor m; 3. vi oler.

smelling-salts, n sales f (aromáticas).

smelly, adj de mal olor, apestoso, hediondo.

smelt, n fundir.

smelting, n fundición f.

smile, n 1. sonrisa f; 2. vi sonreír, sonreírse (de).

smiling, adj sonriente, risueño.

smirk, n 1. sonrisa f satisfecha; sonrisa f afectada; 2. vi sonreírse satisfecho; sonreírse afectadamente.

smock, n 1. bata f corta; 2. vt fruncir, adornar.

smocking, n adorno m de frunces.

smoke, n 1. humo m; 2. vi humear; 3. fumar.

smoked, adj ahumado.

smokestack, n chimenea f.

smolder, vi arder sin llama, requemarse.

smooth, adj 1. liso, terso; suave; llano; 2. vt alisar; allanar, igualar.

smother, n ahogar, sofocar, asfixiar.

smudge, n 1. mancha f, tiznón m; 2. vt manchar.

smug, adj pagado de sí (mismo); presumido.

smuggle, vt pasar géneros de contrabando.

smuggler, n contrabandista m/f.

smut, n tizne m.

smuttiness, n obscenidad f.

smutty, adj tiznado; atizonado.

snack , n bocadillo m, tentempié m, piscolabis.

snaffle, n bridón m.

snag, n 1. nudo m; tocón m; obstáculo m; 2. vt enganchar, coger.

snail, n caracol m.

snake, n culebra f, serpiente f.

snap, n 1. castañetazo m; chasquido m; estallido m; golpe m seco, ruido m seco; 2. adj repentino; 3. vt castañetear; chasquear.

snare, n 1. lazo m, trampa f; 2. vt coger con trampas.

snarl, n 1. gruñido m; 2. vt gruñir; 3. enmarañar, enredar.

snatch, n 1. arrebatamiento m; arrancada f; 2. vt asir, coger, agarrar.

snazzy, adj elegante.

sneak, n 1. soplón(ona) m/f; 2. vt a hurtadillas, afanar, birlar.

sneakers, n zapatos m de lona, zapatillas f.

sneaking, adj furtivo, sigiloso.

sneaky, adj furtivo, sigiloso.

sneer, n 1. visaje m de burla y desprecio; 2. vi hacer un visaje de burla y desprecio.

sneeze, n 1. estornudo m; 2. vi estornudar.

snide, adj despreciativo, sarcastico.

sniff, n 1. sorbo m por las narices; inhalación f; 2. vt sorber por las narices; inhalar.

sniffle, n hacer ruido con las narices.

snigger, n 1. risa f disimulada; 2. vi reírse con disimulo.

snip, n 1. tijeretada f, tijeretazo m; 2. vt tijeretear.

snipe, n 1. agachadiza f, becacina f; 2. vi tirar a uno desde un escondite.

snitch, n 1. napias f; soplón m; 2. vi soplarse.

snivel, vi lloriquear.

snob, n (e)snob m/f.

snobbery, n (e)snobismo m.

snoop, n 1. fisgón(ona) m/f; 2. vi curiosear, fisgonear.

snooze, n 1. siestecita f, sueñecillo m; 2. vi echar un sueñecito.

snore, n 1. ronquido m; 2. vi roncar.

snoring, n ronquidos m.

snorkel, n 1. tubo m snorkel, esnórquel m, tubo m de respiración; 2. vi nadar respirando por un tubo.

snort, n 1. bufido m; 2. vt bufar.

snout, n hocico m, morro m.

snow, n 1. nieve f; 2. vi nevar.

snub, n desaire m; repulsa f.

snuff, n rapé m, tabaco m en polvo.

snuffle, n 1. ruido m de la nariz; 2. vi respirar con ruido, hacer ruido con la nariz.

snug, adj cómodo; abrigado, al abrigo.

so, adv 1. tan; 2. así; de este modo, de esta manera.

soak, vt remojar algo en un líquido.

soap, n 1. jabón m; 2. vt enjabonar.

soapy, adj jabonoso.

soar, vi remontarse, encumbrarse, subir muy alto.

sob, n 1. sollozo m; 2. vt sollozar.

sobbing, n sollozos m.

sober, adj sobrio, serio, moderado; no embriagado.

sobriquet, n apodo m, mote m.

soccer, n fútbol m.

sociable, adj sociable; afable; amistoso.

social, adj 1. social; sociable.

socialism , n socialismo m.

socialize, n 1. socializar; 2. vi alternar con la gente.

society, n sociedad f.

socioeconomic, adj socioeconómico.

sociology, n sociología f.

sock, n 1. calcetín m; 2. tortazo m. 3. vt pegar.

socket, n cuenca f, alvéolo m; fosa f; enchufe m.

sod, n césped m.

soda, n 1. sosa f; 2. soda f, agua f gaseosa.

sodden, adj empapado, mojado, saturado.

sodium, n sodio m.

sofa, n sofá m.

soft, adj blando; muelle; flojo; suave.

soften, n 1. ablandar, reblandecer; debilitar; 2. vi ablandarse, reblandecerse; debilitarse.

softener, n descalcificador m; suavizante m.

softening, n reblandecimiento m; mitigación f.

soft-hearted, adj compasivo, bondadoso.

softness, *n* blandura *f;* flojedad *f;* suavidad *f.*

software, *n* elementos *m* de programación.

soggy, *adj* empapado, saturado; esponjoso.

soil, *n* 1. tierra *f,* suelo *m;* 2. *vt* ensuciar; mancha.

soiled, *adj* sucio.

sojourn, *n* 1. permanencia *f,* estancia *f;* 2. *vi* permanecer, residir, morar; pasar una temporada.

solace, *n* 1. consuelo *m;* 2. *vt* consolar.

solar, *adj* solar, del sol.

solarium, *n* solario *m,* solárium *m,* solana *f.*

solder, *n* 1. soldadura *f;* 2. *vt* soldar.

soldering-iron, *n* soldador *m.*

soldier, *n* 1. soldado *m/f;* 2. *vi* militar, ser soldado.

sole, *adj* 1. solo, único; 2. *n* (foot) planta *f;* (fish) lenguado *m;* 3. solar.

solemn, *adj* solemne.

solemnly, *adv* solemnemente.

solenoid, *n* solenoide *m.*

solicit, *n* 1. solicitar; implorar, pedir insistentemente; 2. *vi* importunar.

solicitation, *n* solicitación *f.*

solicitor, *n* representante *m/f,* agente *m/f;* abogado.

solicitude, *n* solicitud *f;* preocupación *f,* ansiedad *f.*

solid, *adj* sólido.

solidarity, *n* solidaridad *f.*

solidify, *n* 1. solidificar; 2. *vi* solidificarse.

solidly, *adv* sólidamente; densamente.

soliloquy, *n* soliloquio *m.*

solitaire, *n* solitario *m.*

solitary, *adj* solitario, solo; retirado, apartado.

solitude, *n* soledad *f.*

solo, *n* solo.

soloist, *n* solista *m/f.*

solstice, *n* solsticio *m.*

soluble, *adj* soluble.

solution, *n* solución *f.*

solve, *n* resolver, solucionar; adivinar.

solvent, *adj* 1. solvente; 2. *n* solvente *m.*

some, *adj* alguno, algún; unos, unos cuantos.

somebody, *pron* alguien;algún otro, otra persona.

someday, *adv* algún día.

somehow, *adv* de algún modo, de un modo u otro.

somersault, *n* 1. salto *m* mortal; 2. *vi* dar un salto mortal; dar una vuelta de campana.

something, *pron* algo; alguna cosa.

sometime, *adv* algún día; alguna vez.

sometimes, *adv* algunas veces, a veces; ocasionalmente.

somewhat, *adv* algo, algún tanto.

somewhere, *adv* en alguna parte; a alguna parte.

somnambulist, *n* sonámbulo(a) *m/f.*

somnolence, *n* somnolencia *f.*

somnolent, *adj* soñoliento.

son, *n* hijo *m.*

sonar, *n* sonar *m.*

sonata, *n* sonata *f.*

song, *n* canción *f;* canto *m.*

songwriter, *n* compositor(a) *m/f* de canciones.

sonic, *adj* sónico.

son-in-law, *n* yerno *m,* hijo *m* político.

sonnet, *n* soneto *m.*

sonority, *n* sonoridad *f.*

soon, *adv* pronto, dentro de poco; temprano.

sooner, *adv* más temprano, antes.

soothe, *n* tranquilizar, calmar; aliviar.

soothing, *adj* tranquilizador, calmante; analgésico.

soothsayer, *n* adivino(a) *m/f.*

sop, *n* sopa *f.*

sophist, *n* sofista *m/f.*

sophisticated, *adj* sofisticado.

sophomore, *n* estudiante *m/f* de segundo año.

sopping, *adj* empapado, totalmente mojado.

soprano, *n* soprano *f,* tiple *f.*

sorbet, *n* sorbete *m.*

sorcerer, *n* hechicero *m,* brujo *m.*

sorceress, *n* hechicera *f,* bruja *f.*

sorcery, *n* hechicería *f;* brujería *f.*

sordid, *adj* sórdido, asqueroso, sucio.

sore, *adj* inflamado, dolorido, enojado con.

soreness, *n* inflamación *f,* dolor *m.*

sorority, *n* hermandad *f* de mujeres.

sorrel, *adj* 1. alazán; 2. *n* acedera *f,* 3. caballo *m* alazán.

sorrow, *n* 1. pesar *m,* pena *f,* dolor *m;* tristeza *f;* 2. *vi* apenarse, afligirse, dolerse.

sorrowful, *adj* afligido, triste, pesaroso.

sorry, *adj* arrepentido; triste, afligido, apenado.

sort, *n* 1. tipo *m,* clase *f,* género *m;* 2. *vt* ordenar, clasificar.

sot, *n* borrachín *m.*

sotto voce, *adv* en voz baja.

sough, *n* 1. susurro *m;* 2. *vi* susurrar.

soul, *n* alma *f.*

soulless, *adj* person sin alma, desalmado.

soul-searching, *n* examen *m* de conciencia.

sound, *adj* 1. sano, firme; 2. *n* sonido *m,* ruido *m;* 3. estrecho *m;* 4. sonda *f;* 5. *vt* sonar, ausultar, entonar.

soundless, *adj* silencioso, sin ruido; insonoro.

soundly, *adv* sólidamente; razonablemente, lógicamente, prudentemente.

soundness, *n* firmeza *f,* solidez *f;* robustez *f;* solvencia *f;* formalidad *f.*

soundproof, *adj* 1. insonorizado; 2. *vt* insonorizar.

soup, *n* caldo *m,* consomé *m;* sopa *f.*

soupspoon, *n* cuchara *f* sopera.

sour, *adj* 1. agrio, acre; 2. *vt* agriar; amargar; 3. *vi* agriarse, volverse agrio; malearse.

source, *n* fuente *f,* nacimiento *m;* fuente *f,* origen *m.*

sourdough, *n* pan *m* de masa fermentada.

south, *n* sur *m;* mediodía *m.*

southern, *adj* del sur; meridional.

southerner, *n* habitante *m/f* del sur; meridional *m/f,* sureño(a) *m/f.*

southpaw, *n* zurdo *m.*

South Pole, *n* Polo *m* Sur.

souvenir, *n* recuerdo *m.*

sovereign , *adj* soberano.

sovereignty, *n* soberanía *f.*

soviet, *n* soviet *m;* soviético(a) *m/f.*

sow, *n* 1. puerca *f;* 2. *vt* sembrar.

sowing, *n* siembra *f.*

soy, *n* soya *f,* n soja *f.*

spa, *n* balneario *m,* estación *f* termal.

space, *n* 1. espacio *m;* 2. *vt* espaciar.

space-bar, *n* barra *f* espaciadora, espaciador *m.*

spacecraft, *n* nave *f* espacial, astronave *f.*

space-flight, *n* vuelo *m* espacial.

spaceman, *n* astronauta *m,* cosmonauta *m.*

spaceship, *n* nave *f* espacial, astronave *f.*

space-shuttle, *n* transbordador *m* espacial.

spacesuit, *n* traje *m* espacial.

spacewoman, *n* astronauta *f,* cosmonauta *f.*

spacing, *n* espaciamiento *m;* espaciado *m.*

spacious, *adj* espacioso, amplio; extenso.

spade, *n* pala *f,* laya *f.*

spadework, *n* trabajo *m* preliminar.

spaghetti, *n* espaguetis *m.*

span, n **1.** lapso m, espacio m; duración f; envergadura f; **2.** vt extenderse sobre, cruzar.

spaniel, n perro m de aguas.

Spanish-speaking, adj hispanohablante, hispanoparlante, de habla española.

spank, n azote m, manotada f; **2.** vt zurrar, manotear.

spar, n **1.** palo m, verga f; **2.** vi entrenarse en el boxeo.

spare, adj **1.** sobrante, que sobra, de más; disponible; **2.** de repuesto, de recambio; **3.** vt excusar; escatimar.

spark, n **1.** chispa f; chispazo m; **2.** vt hacer estallar; precipitar, provocar; **3.** vi chispear, echar chispas.

spark-plug, n bujía f, chispero m.

sparkle, n **1.** centelleo m, destello m; brillo m; **2.** vi centellear, destellar, chispear; brillar.

sparkler, n bengala f; diamante m.

sparkling, adj centelleante; brillante, reluciente.

sparrow, n gorrión m.

sparrowhawk, n gavilán m.

sparse, adj disperso, esparcido; poco denso; escaso.

spasm, n espasmo m; acceso m, arranque m.

spasmodic, adj espasmódico; irregular.

spastic, adj **1.** espástico, **2.** n espástico(a) m/f.

spate, n avenida f, crecida f; torrente m; avalancha f.

spatial, adj espacial.

spatter, n salpicar, rociar.

spatula, n espátula f.

spawn, n **1.** freza f, hueva f; semillas f; **2.** vt engendrar, producir; **3.** vi desovar, frezar.

spawning, n desove m, freza f.

spay, n sacar los ovarios a.

speak, n **1.** decir, hablar; **2.** vi hablar.

speaker, n el (o la) que habla; orador(a) m/f.

speaking, adj hablante.

spear, n **1.** lanza f; arpón m; **2.** vt alancear, herir (o matar) con lanza; arponear.

speargun, n harpón m submarino.

spearhead, n **1.** punta f de lanza; **2.** vt encabezar.

spearmint, n menta f verde, menta f romana.

special, adj especial, particular.

specialist, n especialista m/f.

specialize, vi especializarse (en).

specialty, n especialidad f.

species, n especie f.

specific, adj específico.

specification, n especificación f.

specify, vt/i especificar; designar; concretar.

specimen, n ejemplar m, espécimen m, muestra f.

speck, n manchita f; grano m; mota f.

speckle, n **1.** punto m, mota f; **2.** vt salpicar, motear.

spectacle, n espectáculo m.

spectacular, adj espectacular; aparatoso; impresionante.

spectator, n espectador(a) m/f.

spectral, adj espectral.

specter, n espectro m, fantasma m.

spectrum, n espectro m; gama f.

speculate, n especular (en).

speculation, n especulación f.

speech, n habla f; palabra f; lenguaje m.

speechless, adj mudo, estupefacto.

speed, n velocidad f; rapidez f; prisa f.

speedboat, n motora f, lancha f rápida.

speed bump, n banda f de frenado.

speeding, n exceso m de velocidad.

speed-limit, n velocidad f máxima.

speedometer, n velocímetro m, cuentakilómetros m.

speedy, adj veloz, rápido.

spell, n **1.** encanto m, hechizo m; **2.** turno m, tanda f; **3.** rato m; **4.** vt/i escribir; **5.** deletrear.

spellbinder, n orador(a) m/f fascinante.

spellbound, adj embelesado, hechizado.

spelling, n ortografía f.

spend, n **1.** gastar (en); **2.** invertir (en), dedicar; **2.** vi gastar dinero.

spender, n gastador(a) m/f; derrochador(a) m/f.

spendthrift, adj derrochador, pródigo.

sperm, n esperma f.

spew, n vomitar, arrojar, echar fuera.

sphagnum, n esfagno m.

sphere, n esfera f.

spherical, adj esférico.

sphincter, n esfínter m.

sphinx, n esfinge f.

spice, n **1.** especia f, olor m; **2.** vt condimentar.

spicy, adj condimentado, picante.

spider, n araña f.

spike, n **1.** punta f; escarpia f; pico m; (Bot) espiga f; **2.** vt sujetar con un clavo.

spiked, adj claveteado.

spikenard, n nardo m.

spill, n **1.** derrame m; caída f; vuelco m; **2.** vertido m, **3.** vt derramar, verter; **4.** vi derramarse.

spin, n **1.** vuelta f, revolución f; **3.** vi girar, dar vueltas.

spina bifida, n espina f bífida.

spinach, n espinaca f; espinacas f.

spindle, n huso m; eje m.

spine, n espinazo m, columna f vertebral.

spine-chilling, adj escalofriante.

spineless, adj débil, rojo, sin carácter.

spinet, n espineta f.

spinnaker, n balón m, espinaquer m.

spinner, n hilandero(a) m/f.

spinning, n rotación f, girar m.

spinning-wheel, n torno m de hilar, rueca f.

spinster, n soltera f; solterona f.

spiny, adj con púas, erizado de púas; espinoso.

spiral, adj **1.** espiral; **2.** vi dar vueltas en espiral.

spire, n aguja f, chapitel m.

spirit, n espíritu m, alma f; ánima f.

spiritual, adj espiritual.

spiritualist, n espiritista m/f.

spirituality, n espiritualidad f.

spit, n **1.** (culin) asador m, espetón m; **2.** (land) lengua f; **3.** saliva f, esputo m; **4.** vt espetar, escupir.

spite, n **1.** rencor m, ojeriza f, despecho m; **2.** vt mortificar, herir, causar pena a.

spiteful, adj rencoroso, malévolo; tratar a uno con malevolencia.

spitfire, n fierabrás m.

spittle, n saliva f, baba f.

spittoon, n escupidera f.

splash, n **1.** salpicadura f, rociada f; **2.** vt salpicar.

splashdown, n amaraje m, chapuzón m.

spleen, n bazo m; esplín m.

splendid, adj espléndido; ¡magnífico!

splendor, n esplendor m; magnificencia f.

splice, n **1.** empalme m, junta f; **2.** vt empalmar, juntar.

splicer, n máquina f de montaje.

splint, n **1.** tablilla f; sobrecaña f; **2.** vt entablillar.

splinter, n **1.** astilla f; espigón m; **3.** vt astillar, hacer astillas; **4.** vi astillarse, hacerse astillas.

split, adj 1. hendido, partido, dividido; 2. n hendidura f, raja f, grieta f; 3. vt partir, hender, dividir; 4. vi rajarse, henderse.

splutter, n 1. chisporroteo m; farfulla f; 2. vt decir balbuceando; farfullar.

spoil, n 1. despojo m, botín m; trofeo m; 2. vi echarse a perder, estropearse; arruinarse.

spoiled, adj pasado, malo; cortado.

spoke, n rayo m, radio m.

spoken, adj hablado, oral.

spokesperson, n portavoz m/f.

sponge, n 1. esponja f; 2. vt lavar con esponja.

spongecake, n bizcocho m.

sponginess, n esponjosidad f.

sponsor, n 1. patrocinador(a) m/f; 2. vt patrocinar.

sponsorship, n patrocinio m.

spontaneous, adj espontáneo.

spoof, n trampa f; truco m, mistificación f.

spook, n espectro m; espía m/f.

spooky, adj fantasmal, espectral; escalofriante.

spool, n carrete m; canilla f.

spoon, n cuchara f; cucharilla f.

spoonful, n cucharada f.

spoor, n pista f, rastro m.

sporadic, adj esporádico.

spore, n espora f.

sport, n deporte m.

sporting, adj deportivo.

sportsman, n deportista m.

sportswear, n ropa f de deporte.

sportswoman, n deportista f.

spot, n 1. sitio m, lugar m, mancha f; 2. vt manchar, descubrir.

spotless, adj nítido; sin manchas, inmaculado.

spotlight, n foco m; reflector m, proyector m.

spotted, adj manchado; moteado.

spouse, n cónyuge m/f.

spout, n 1. pico m; pitón m, pitorro m; conducto m; 2. vt arrojar en chorro.

sprawl, n 1. postura f desgarbada; 2. vi arrellanarse.

sprawling, adj desmadejado; desgarbado.

spray, n 1. rociada f; riego m por aspersión ramita f; ramo m; 2. vt rociar, regar, atomizar, pulverizar.

spread, n 1. extensión f; diseminación f, difusión f; 2. vt esparcir, extender, diseminar, propagar.

spreader, n esparcidor m.

spree, n juerga f, parranda f; excursión f.

sprig, n ramita f; espiga f.

sprightliness, n viveza f, energía f, animación f.

spring, n 1. fuente f, manantial f; 2. primavera f; 3. salto m, brinco m; 4. elasticidad f; 5. resorte m; muelle m; 6. vt saltar, saltar por encima de; 7. vi brotar, nacer; salir en chorro.

spring fever, n desasosiego m primaveral.

springtime, n primavera f.

sprinkle, n 1. rociada f; salpicadura f; 2. vt salpicar, rociar; 3. vi lloviznar

sprinkler, n rociadera f; aspersor m.

sprinkling, n rociada f; salpicadura f; aspersión f.

sprinter, n velocista m/f.

sprocket, n rueda f de espigas.

sprout, n 1. brote m, retoño m; 2 vi brotar, retoñar, echar retoños.

spruce, adj aseado, acicalado, pulcro.

spry, adj ágil, activo.

spud, n 1. escarda f; 2. patata f, papa f; vt escardar.

spume, n espuma f.

spunk, n agallas f; arrojo m, coraje m.

spunky, adj valiente, arrojado.

spur, n 1. espuela f; espolón m; 2. vt espolear, picar con las espuelas; estimular, incitar.

spurious, adj falso, espurio.

spurn, n desdeñar, rechazar.

spurt, n 1. esfuerzo m supremo; 2. chorro m repentino; 3. vi hacer un esfuerzo supremo; 4. salir en chorro.

spy, n 1. espía m/f; 2. vt divisar, columbrar; lograr ver; observar; 3. vi espiar, ser espía.

spyglass, n catalejo m.

spying, n espionaje m.

squabble, n 1. riña f, disputa f; 2. vi reñir, disputar.

squad, n pelotón m; escuadra f; brigada f.

squadron, n escuadrón m; escuadra f.

squalid, adj miserable, vil, asqueroso.

squall, n 1. chillido m, berrea f; 2. ráfaga f; tempestad f; 3. vi chillar, berrear.

squalor, n miseria f; suciedad f.

squander, n malgastar, derrochar, despilfarrar.

square, adj 1. cuadrado; 2. n cuadrado m; cuadro m; 3. plaza f, zócalo m; 4. vt cuadrar; escuadrar.

square dance, n baile m de figuras.

squarely, adv en cuadro.

squash, n 1. calabacín m, calabacita f; 2. vt aplastar; confutar; 3. vi aplastarse.

squat, adj 1. rechoncho, achaparrado; 2. vi agacharse, sentarse en cuclillas.

squatter, n colono m usurpador, intruso(a) m/f.

squawk, n 1. graznido m, chillido m; 2. vi graznar.

squeak, n 1. chirrido m, rechinamiento m; crujido m; 2. vi chirriar, rechinar; crujir; chillar.

squeaky, adj chirriador; que cruje; chillón.

squeal, n 1. chillido m; 2. vi (inform on) soplar a; 3. dar un chillido.

squeamish, adj remilgado, delicado, susceptible.

squeeze, n 1. estrujón m, presión f, apretón m; 2. vt estrujar, apretar.

squeezer, n exprimelimones m, exprimidor m.

squelch, n aplastar, despachurrar.

squid, n calamar m.

squiggle, n garabato m.

squint, n 1. estrabismo m; mirada f bizca; 2. vi bizquear, ser bizco.

squire, n 1. propietario m, hacendado m; escudero m; 2. vt acompañar.

squirm. vi retorcerse, revolverse.

squirrel, n ardilla f.

squirt, n 1. chorro m, jeringazo m; jeringa f; 2. vt arrojar un chorro de, arrojar a chorros.

stab, n 1. puñalada f; 2. vt apuñalar.

stability, n estabilidad f.

stabilize, n 1. estabilizar; 2. vi estabilizarse.

stable, adj 1. estable, firme; estacionario; 2. n cuadra f, caballeriza f; 3. vt poner en una cuadra, guardar en una cuadra.

stableboy, n mozo m de cuadra.

stack, n 1. montón m; rimero m, pila f; 2. vt amontonar, apilar; recoger en un montón.

stadium, n estadio m.

staff, n 1. palo m; bastón m, bordón m; 2. personal m; 3. vt proveer de personal.

stag, n ciervo m, venado m.

stage, n 1. plataforma f, tablado m; 2. escenario m, teatro m; 3. etapa f, jornada f; 4. vt play representar, escenificar.

stagecoach, n diligencia f.

stagger, n 1. tambaleo m; modorra f; 2. vt asombrar, consternar, sorprender; 3. vi tambalear, titubear.

staggering, adj asombroso, pasmoso.

staging, n 1. andamiaje m. 2. escenificación f.

stagnate, vi estancarse; estar estancado, quedar estancado; estar paralizado.

stagnation, n estancamiento m; paralización f.

staid, adj serio, formal.

stain, n 1. mancha f; tinte m; 2. vt manchar; teñir; 3. vi mancharse.

stainless, adj inmaculado; inmanchable; inoxidable.

stain-remover, n quitamanchas m.

stair, n peldaño m; escalón m; escalera f.

staircase, n escalera f; caja f de escalera.

stake, n 1. estaca f, poste m; rodrigón m; 2. vt estacar; cercar con estacas, señalar con estacas.

stalactite, n estalactita f.

stalagmite, n estalagmita f.

stale, adj no fresco, pasado, rancio.

stalemate, n 1. paralización f, estancamiento m; 2. vt ahogar; paralizar.

stalk, n 1. tallo m; 2. vt acechar; seguir los pasos a; 3. vi andar con paso majestuoso.

stall, n 1. casilla f de establo, pesebre m; 2. vt parar, atascar; 3. vi pararse, atascarse.

stallion, n caballo m padre, semental m.

stalwart, adj 1. fornido, robusto; leal; valiente; 2. n partidario(a) m/f leal.

stamina, n resistencia f, aguante m; nervio m.

stammer, n 1. tartamudeo m; balbuceo m; 2. vt balbucir, decir tartamudeando; 3. vi tartamudear; balbucir.

stammering, adj 1. tartamudo; 2. n tartamudeo m.

stamp, n 1. patada f; 2. estampilla f; cuño m; troquel m; 3. sello m (de correos), estampilla f; 4. vt patear, golpear con el pie; 5. estampar, imprimir.

stamp-collecting, n filatelia f.

stamped, adj sellado, timbrado; con sello.

stampede, n 1. estampida f; 2. vt hacer huir en desorden.

stand, n 1. posición f, postura f; pedestal m; (mus) atril m; 2. (market) puesto m; 3. vt tolerar, aguantar; 4. estar de pie; levantarse.

standard, adj 1. regular, normal; 2. n estandarte m, bandera f; 3. nivel m, grado m.

standardization, n normalización f, estandarización f.

standardize, n normalizar, regularizar, estandarizar.

standing, adj derecho; de pie, en pie.

standpoint, n punto m de vista.

standstill, n parada f; paro m; alto m; paralización f.

stanza, n estrofa f, estancia f.

staple, adj 1. principal; establecido; corriente; 2. n producto m principal; materia f prima 3. grapa f, corchete m; 4. vt grapar.

stapler, n grapadora f.

star, n 1. estrella f, astro m; 2. vt estrellar; 3. vi lucirse, sobresalir.

starboard, n estribor m.

starch, n 1. almidón m; fécula f; 2. vt almidonar.

stare, n 1. mirada f fija; mirar fijamente.

starfish, n estrella f de mar.

stark, adj completo, puro; escueto, severo.

stark-naked, adj en cueros, en pelota.

starkness, n desolación f, severidad f.

starless, adj sin estrellas.

starlight, n luz f de las estrellas.

starry, adj estrellado, sembrado de estrellas.

start, n 1. susto m, sobresalto m; 2. principio m, comienzo m; salida f, partida f; 3. vt comenzar, empezar; iniciar; principiar.

starting-line, n línea f de salida.

starting-point, n punto m de partida.

startle, n asustar, sobrecoger; alarmar.

startling, adj asombroso, sorprendente; alarmante.

starvation, n hambre f, inanición f; muerte f por hambre.

starve, n hacer morir de hambre.

starving, adj hambriento, famélico.

stash, n 1. escondite m; alijo m. 2. vt ir acumulando.

state, adj 1. estatal; 2. n estado m, condición f; circunstancias f pl; 3. (político) estado m; nación f; 4. vt declarar, afirmar, decir; 5. exponer, explicar.

stated, adj dicho; indicado; fijo, establecido.

stateless, adj desnacionalizado, apátrida, sin patria.

statement, n declaración f, afirmación f, manifestación f; informe m; estado m de cuenta.

state-of-the-art, adj moderno, al día; de vanguardia.

stateroom, n camarote m.

statesman, n estadista m, hombre m de estado.

static, adj 1. inactivo, inmóvil, estancado; estático; 2. n estática f; parásitos m.

station, n 1. puesto m, sitio m; situación f; 2. estación f; (Rad TV) emisora f; 3. vt colocar, situar; estacionar, destinar; emplazar.

stationary, adj estacionario; inmóvil.

stationer, n papelero(a) m/f; papelería f.

stationery, n papelería f, papel m de escribir.

station wagon, n urgoneta f, camioneta f.

statistic, n estadística f, número m.

statistical, adj estadístico.

statistician, n estadístico m/f.

statuary, adj estatuario.

statue, n estatua f.

statuesque, adj escultural.

stature, n 1. estatura f, talla f; 2. valor m, carácter m.

status, n posición f, condición f; rango m, categoría f.

status quo, n statu m quo.

statute, n ley f, estatuto m.

stave, n duela f; peldaño m; pentagrama m; estrofa f.

stay, n 1. estancia f, permanencia f, visita f; 2. sostén m, soporte m; 3. vt detener, controlar, sostener, poyar; 4. vi esperar.

steadfast, adj firme, resuelto; constante; tenaz.

steadfastness, n firmeza f, resolución f; constancia f; tenacidad f.

steady, adj 1. firme, fijo; estable; regular, constante; 2. vt mantener firme, sujetar en posición firme; estabilizar.

steak, n biftec m.

steal, vt/i robar, hurtar.

stealing, n robo m, hurto m.

stealth, n cautela f, sigilo m.

steam, n 1. vapor m; vaho m, humo m; 2. vt cocer al vapor; 3. vi echar vapor.

steamboat, n vapor m; buque m de vapor.

steamer, n 1. buque m de vapor; 2. vaporera f.

steaming, adj 1. humeante; 2. furioso.

steamy, adj vaporoso; lleno de vapor.

steed, n corcel m.

steel, n acero m.

steel mill, n acería f, fábrica f de acero; fábrica f siderúrgica, fundidora f.

steely, adj acerado; inflexible, duro.

steep, adj 1. escarpado, abrupto; 2. (price) excesivo; 3. vt (soak) empapar, remojar.

steeple, n aguja f, campanario m, torre f.

steeplechase, n carrera f de obstáculos.

steeplejack, n reparador m de chimeneas, torres etc.

steer, n 1. buey m; novillo m; 2. vi conducir, manejar; gobernar.

steering, n dirección f, conducción f; gobierno m.

steering-wheel, n volante m (de dirección).

stellar, adj estelar

stem, n 1. tallo m, pie m; cañón m; 2. vi provenir de, proceder de, resultar de; 3. vt (stop) refrenar, detener; represar.

stench, n hedor m.

stencil, n 1. patrón m picado, estarcido m; plantilla f; 2. vt estarcir; hacer un cliché de.

stenographer, n taquígrafo(a) m/f.

stenography, n taquigrafía f, estenografía f.

step, n 1. paso m; pisada f; huella f; 2. peldaño m, escalón m, grada f; 3. escalinata f; 4. vt escalonar; 5. vi dar un paso; ir, andar, caminar.

stepbrother, n hermanastro m.

stepchild, n hijastro(a) m/f.

stepfather, n padrastro m.

stepladder, n escalera f de tijera, escalera f doble.

stepmother, n madrastra f.

steppe, n estepa f.

stepsister, n hermanastra f.

stepson, n hijastro m.

stereo, pref estereo…

stereophonic, adj estereofónico.

stereotype, n clisé m, estereotipo m

sterile, adj estéril.

sterilization, n esterilización f.

sterilize, n esterilizar.

sterling, adj 1. verdadero, excelente; 2. plata f de ley; 3. n libras f esterlinas.

stern, adj 1. severo; duro; austero; 2. n popa f.

sternly, adv severamente; duramente.

sternum, n esternón m.

steroid, n esteroide m.

stet, vt vale, deje como está.

stethoscope, n estetoscopio m.

stevedore, n estibador m.

stew, n 1. cocido m; estofado m, guisado m; 2. vt estofar; guisar; cocer; 3. vi pasarse.

steward, n administrador m; mayordomo m; portero m, auxiliar m/f de vuelo; azafata f.

stewardship, n administración f, mayordomía f.

stewpot, n cazuela f, cacerola f, puchero m.

stick, n 1. palo m, vara f, (cane) bastón m; (shift) palanca f; 2. vt clavar, hincar; picar; pegar; 3. vi pegarse, atascarse.

stickiness, n pegajosidad f; viscosidad f; humedad f.

stickler, n rigorista m/f.

stick-on, adj adhesivo.

stick-up, n atraco m, asalto m.

sticky, adj pegajoso; viscoso; engomado.

stiff, adj rígido, inflexible, tieso.

stiffen, n hacer mas rígido, atiesar; endurecer.

stiff-necked, adj terco, obstinado; estirado.

stiffness , n rigidez f, inflexibilidad f, tiesura f.

stifle, n 1. ahogar, sofocar; suprimir; 2. vi ahogarse, sofocarse.

stifling, adj sofocante, bochornoso.

stigma, n estigma m; tacha f, baldón m.

stigmatize, n estigmatizar.

stiletto, n estilete m; pinzón m.

still, adj 1. inmóvil; quieto; tranquilo, silencioso; 2. adv todavía, aún; aun más, mejor aun; 3. conj sin embargo; con todo, a pesar de todo; 4. n silencio m, calma f; 5. vt tranquilizar; aquietar; acallar.

stillborn, adj nacido muerto, mortinato.

stillness, n inmovilidad f; quietud f; silencio m.

stilt, n zanco m; pilar m, soporte m; pilote m.

stilted , adj afectado, hinchado, artificial.

stimulant, adj estimulante.

stimulate, n estimular; favorecer; fomentar.

stimulus, n estímulo m.

sting, n 1. aguijón m; 2. vi picar; escocer.

sting-ray, n pastinaca f.

stingy, adj tacaño.

stink, n 1. hedor m, mal olor m; tufo m; 3. vi heder, oler mal.

stinking, adj hediondo, fétido.

stint, n 1. destajo m; tarea f; 2. vt limitar, restringir; escatimar.

stipend, n estipendio m, sueldo m.

stipple, n puntear; granear.

stipulate, n 1. estipular, poner como condición; especificar. 2. vi estipular algo.

stir, n 1. acto m de agitar; hurgonada f; chirona f; 2. vt remover, agitar, revolver, menear.

stir-fry, n 1. sofreir; 2. n sofrito m .

stirring, adj emocionante, conmovedor; inspirador.

stirrup, n estribo m.

stitch, n puntada f, punto m.

stitching , n puntadas f, puntos m.

stoat, n armiño m.

stock, adj 1. común, usual; 2. n ganado m; (family) linaje m, raza f; provisión f, surtido m, existencia f; 3. vt surtir, proveer, tener existencia de.

stockade, n estacada f; prisión f militar.

stockbreeder, n ganadero m.

stockbroker, n bolsista m/f, agente m/f de bolsa.

stock exchange , n bolsa f.

stockholder, n accionista m/f.

stocking, n media f; calceta f.

stockpile, n 1. reservas f (de materias primas) 2. vt acumular, poner en reserva.

stocktaking, n inventario m, balance m.

stocky, adj rechoncho, bajo pero fuerte.

stockyard, n corral m de ganado.

stoic, adj estoico.

stoke, n 1. cargar, cebar; echar carbón a; 2. vi cebar el hogar, echar carbón a la lumbre; atiborrarse.

stole, n estola f.

stolid, adj impasible, imperturbable; flemático.

stomach, n 1. estómago m; vientre m; m, apetito m; 2. vt tragar, aguantar.

stomach-ache, n dolor m de estómago,

stone, n 1. piedra f; lápida f; 2. vt apedrear, lapidar.

stonework, n cantería f, obra f de sillería; piedras f.

stony, adj como piedra, pedregoso.

stool, n taburete m, escabel m; silla f de tijera.

stoop, n 1. encorvada f, inclinación f; 2. pequeña veranda f; 3. vi encorvarse; 4. vt/i inclinar, bajar.

stooping, adj encorvado; cargado de espaldas.

stop, n 1. parada f; alto m; pausa f, interrupción f; 2. vt tapar; cegar; 3. vi parar, pararse; detenerse.

stoppage, n parada f, cesación f, detención f.

stopper, n tapón m; taco m, tarugo m.

stopping-place, n paradero m; parada f.

storage, n almacenaje m, depósito m.

store, n 1. tienda f, reserva f; 2. vt almacenar, guardar.

storm, n 1. tormenta f, tempestad f, temporal m; 2. vt asaltar, tomar por asalto.

stormy, adj tempestuoso, borrascoso.

story, n 1. historia f, relación f, relato m; 2. cuento m.

stoup, n copa f, frasco m; pila f.

stout, adj 1. sólido, robusto, macizo, fuerte.

stove, n estufa f; hornillo m, cocina f.

stow, n 1. meter, poner, colocar; estibar, arrumar; 2. vi viajar de polizón.

straddle, vt estar con una pierna a cada lado de; montar a horcajadas.

strafe, n bombardear, canonear, atacar.

straggle, vi rezagarse; extraviarse; extenderse, estar esparcido.

straight, adj 1. derecho, recto; 2. honrado; franco, directo; 3. adv en línea recta.

straighten, vt enderezar, poner en orden.

strain, n 1. tensión f; esfuerzo m; deformación f; linaje m; genio m; 2. torcedura f; 3. vt estirar, poner tirante, ténder con fuerza.

strained, adj forzado; relations tenso, tirante.

strainer, n colador m; filtro m, coladero m.

strait, n 1. estrecho m; 2. situación f apurada.

strand, n 1. playa f, ribera f; 2. ramal m; hebra f; 3. vt varar, encallar.

strange, adj desconocido; nuevo, extraño.

stranger, n desconocido(a) m/f; forastero(a) m/f.

strangle, n estrangular; abuse, ahogar.

strap, n 1. correa f; tira f, banda f; tirante m, hombrera f; 2. vt atar con correa.

strategic(al), adj estratégico.

strategy, n estrategia f.

stratify, n estratificar.

stratosphere, n estratosfera f.

stratum, n estrato m.

straw, n paja f; (drink) pajita f, pitillo m.

strawberry, n fresa f.

stray, adj 1. extraviado; mostrenco; perdido; 2. vi extraviarse, perderse; vagar.

streak, n 1. raya f, lista f; 2. vt rayar.

stream, n 1. arroyo m, riachuelo m; río m; 2. vt correr, fluir.

streamer, n flámula f; gallardete m; serpentina f.

street, n calle f.

strength, n fuerza f; resistencia f.

strengthen, n fortalecer, reforzar, hacer más fuerte.

strenuous, adj enérgico, vigoroso; arduo.

stress, n 1. fuerza f, compulsión f; presión f; tensión f; estrés m; 2. vt acentuar; 3. subrayar, recalcar.

stressful, adj lleno de tensión (nerviosa).

stretch, n 1. extensión f; estirón m; 2. vt extender, estirar, alargar.

stretcher, n bastidor m; camilla f.

strew, n derramar, esparcir; cubrir, sembrar.

stricken, adj herido; condenado; afligido.

strict, adj estricto, exacto, riguroso.

stricture, n constricción f.

stride, n 1. zancada f, tranco m, paso m largo; 2. vi andar a trancos, andar a pasos largos.

strident, adj estridente.

strife, n lucha f; contienda f; disensión f.

strike, n 1. huelga f, paro m; 2. vt golpear; pegar.

striking, adj notable, impresionante; chocante.

string, n 1. cuerda f, mecate m; cordel m, bramante m; guita f; 2. cuerda f; 3. vt ensartar; encordar; desfibrar.

stringent, adj riguroso, severo.

strip, n 1. tira f; banda f, faja f; 2. vt desnudar.

stripe, n 1. raya f, lista f, banda f; galón m; 2. vt rayar, listar.

striped, adj listado, rayado.

strive, vi esforzarse, afanarse, luchar.

stroke, n 1. (golf, etc.) golpe, (lightning) rayo, (bell) campanada, pincelada f; 2. ataque m fulminante; 3. caricia f; 4. vt acariciar, frotar suavemente.

stroll, n 1. paseo m, vuelta f; 2. vi pasear(se), dar un paseo, deambular, callejear.

strong, adj fuerte; recio, robusto; enérgico.

structure, n 1. estructura f; construcción f; 2. vt estructurar.

structured, adj estructurado.

struggle, n 1. lucha f; contienda f, conflicto m; 2. vi luchar; esforzarse.

strum, n (guitar) rasguear; tocar distraídamente.

strut, n 1. puntal m, riostra f, tornapunta f; 2. vi pavonearse, contonearse.

strychnine, n estricnina f.

stub, n 1. tocón m; colilla f; cabo m; 2. vt dar con el dedo del pie contra algo, dar un tropezón.

stubble, n rastrojo m; barba f de tres días.

stubborn, adj tenaz, terco.

stud, n 1. taco m; tachón m, clavo m; lleguada f; sementa m; 2. vt tachonar; adornar con clavos.

student, n alumno(a) m/f; estudiante m/f.

studious, adj estudioso; aplicado, asiduo.

study, n 1. estudio m; 2. vt estudiar; investigar; examinar.

stuff, n 1. materia f; material m, sustancia f; 2. vt llenar, hinchar, atiborrar; meter sin orden, meter de prisa; atracarse.

stuffing, n relleno m, borra f.

stumble, n 1. tropezón m, traspié m; 2. vi dar un traspié.

stump, n 1. cabo m, fragmento m; tocón m; 2. vt desconcertar, dejar perplejo.

stun, n dejar sin sentido; aturdir de un golpe.

stunned, adj aturdido, atontado; pasmado.

stunt, n 1. vuelo m acrobático, ejercicio m acrobático; 2. vi hacer vuelos acrobáticos.

stupid, adj atontado; estúpido.

stupidity, n estupidez f.

stupor, n estupor m.

sturdy, adj robusto, fuerte; vigoroso.

sturgeon, n esturión m.

stutter, n 1. tartamudeo m; 2. vt balbucir.

stuttering, adj 1. tartamudo; 2. n tartamudeo m.

sty, n pocilga f, zahurda f; orzuelo m.

style, n 1. estilo m; moda f; 2. vt cortar a la moda, estilizar; hair marcar.

stylish, adj elegante; a la moda; garboso, estiloso.

stylist, n estilista m/f.

styptic, adj 1. estíptico; 2. n estíptico m.

suave, adj afable, cortés, fino.

subject, adj 1. subyugado, esclavizado; 2. n súbdito(a) m/f; 3. tema m; materia f, asunto m; (gram) sujeto m; 4. vt sojuzgar, dominar.

subjugate, n subyugar.

subjunctive, adj subjuntivo.

sublime, adj 1. sublime; 2. n lo sublime.

submarine, n submarino m.

submerge, n sumergir.

submit, n someter.

sobordinate, adj 1. subordinado; 2. vt subornidar.

subscribe, n suscribir, contribuir.

subsequent, adj subsiguiente.

subside, vi (water) bajar; (wind) amainar; disminuir.

subsidize, vt subvencionar.

subisidy, n subvención f.

subsist, vi subsistir, sustentarse.

substance, n sustancia f; esencia f.

substantial, adj sustancial.

substantiate, n establece.

substitute, n 1. sustituto(a) m/f; 2. vt sustituir.

substitution, n sustitución f.

subtle, adj sutil; fino, delicado.

subtlety, n sutileza f; finura f, delicadeza f.

subtract, n sustraer, restar.

subtraction, n sustracción f, resta f.

subway, n paso m subterráneo.

succeed, n suceder a.

succession, n sucesión f.

succulence, n suculencia f.

succulent, adj suculento; carnoso.

succumb, vi sucumbir.

such, adj 1. tal; semejante; parecido; tal como; 2. pron los que, las que.

suck , n 1. chupada f; sorbo m; 2. vt chupar; sorber.

sucker, n 1. ventosa f; 2. vt estafar, timar, embaucar.

suckle , n amamantar, dar el pecho a.

suction, n succión f.

sudden, adj repentino, súbito; imprevisto, impensado.

suds, n jabonaduras f, espuma f.

sue, n demandar a uno, llevar a uno ante el tribunal.

suet, n sebo m.

suffer, n sufrir, padecer.

suffering, adj 1. que sufre; doliente, enfermo; 2. n sufrimiento m, padecimiento m.

sufficient, adj suficiente, bastante.

suffix, n 1. sufijo m; 2. vt añadir como sufijo.

suffocate, n ahogar, asfixiar, sofocar.

suffocating, adj sofocante, asfixiante.

suffocation, n sofocación f, asfixia f.

suffrage, n sufragio m; derecho m de votar.

suffragette, n sufragista f.

suffusion, n difusión f.

sugar, n azúcar m.

suggest, n sugerir; indicar; aconsejar, indicar.

suggestible, adj sugestionable.

suggestion, n sugerencia f; indicación f; insinuación f.

suggestive, adj sugestivo; indecente.

suicidal, adj suicida.

suit, n 1. traje m; 2. pleito m, litigio m, proceso m; 3. petición f; 4. vt adaptar, ajustar, acomodar.

suitable, adj conveniente, apropiado; adecuado.

suitcase, n maleta f, valija f.

suitor, n pretendiente m/f.

sulk, n 1. murria f; 2. vi amorrarse.

sulky, adj mohíno; malhumorado; resentido.

sullen, adj hosco, malhumorado; resentido.

sulphate, n sulfato m.

sultan, n sultán m.

sultana, n sultana f.

sultry, adj bochornoso; sofocante.

sum, n 1. suma f, total m; 2. vt sumar.

summarize, vt/i resumir.

summary, adj 1. sumario; 2. n resumen m.

summation, n adición f; recapitulación f.

summer, n verano m.

summit, n cima f, cumbre f.

summon, vt llamar; convocar.

summons, n 1. llamamiento m, citación f; requerimiento m; 2. vt citar, emplazar.

sumptuous, adj suntuoso.

sun, n 1. sol m; 3. vt asolear.

Sunday, n domingo m.

sunder, n romper, dividir, hender; separar.

sunglases, n gafas f para el sol.

sunken, adj hundido.

sunny, adj place, soleado; expuesto al sol.

super, adj 1. estupendo, bárbaro, súper; 2. n figurante(a) m/f.

supervise, n supervisar.

supervision, n supervisión f.

supper, n cena f.

supplant, n suplantar.

supple , adj flexible.

supplement, n 1. suplemento m; apéndice m; 2. vt suplir, complementar.

supplicate, vt/i suplicar.

supplication, n súplica f.

supplier, n suministrador(a) m/f.

supply, n 1. suministro m, provisión f, abastecimiento m; provisiones f, víveres m; 2. vt suministrar, facilitar, proporcionar.

support, n 1. **soporte** m, **apoyo** m; **pilar** m; 2. vt apoyar, sostener.

supportive, adj soportante; amable, compasivo.

suppose, n suponer; figurarse, imaginarse.

supposed, adj supuesto, pretendido.

suppository, n supositorio m.

suppress, n suprimir; ahogar; contener.

suppressed, adj suprimido.

suppurate, vi supurar.

suppuration, n supuración f.

supremacy , n supremacía f.

supreme, adj supremo.

sure, n 1. seguro; cierto; certero; firme; 2. seguro; 3. adv sí; ¡claro!; ¡naturalmente!.

surface , n 1. superficie f; exterior m; 2. vt poner superficie a.

surfing, n surf m, acuaplano m.

surge, n 1. oleada f; 2. (Elect) **sobretensión** f; 3. vi agitarse, ondular.

surgeon, n cirujano(a) m/f.

surgery, n cirugía f.

surly, adj hosco, malhumorado; maleducado.

surmise, n 1. conjetura f, suposición f; 2. vt suponer, conjeturar.

surmount, n superar, vencer.

surname, n apellido m.

surpass, n sobrepasar; superar, exceder.

surplus, n excedente m; sobrante m, exceso m.

surprise, n 1. sorpresa f, asombro m; 2. adj inesperado; 3. vt sorprender, asombrar, extrañar.

surprising, adj sorprendente, asombroso.

surrender, n 1. rendición f, capitulación f; 2. vt rendir.

surrogate, n sustituto m, suplente m.

surround, n 1. marco m; borde m; 2. vt rodear, cercar, circundar.

surveillance, n vigilancia f.

survey, n 1. inspección f, examen m; estudio m; 2. vt mirar, inspeccionar, examinar.

surveying, n agrimensura f; planimetría f.

survival, n supervivencia f.

survive, n sobrevivir a.

susceptible, adj susceptible, sensible; propenso.

suspect, adj, n 1. sospechosos m; 2. vt sospechar.

suspected, adj presunto.

suspend, vt suspender.

suspense, n incertidumbre f, duda f; ansiedad f.

suspension, n suspensión f.

suspicion, n sospecha f; recelo m.

suspicious , adj suspicaz, desconfiado, receloso.

sustain, vt sostener, apoyar; (life) sustentar.

sustaining, adj nutritivo; pedal m de sostenido.

sustenance, n sustento m.

suture, n 1. sutura f; 2. vt suturar, coser.

swab, n 1. estropajo m, trapo m, lampazo m; 2. vt limpiar.

swaddle, n envolver; empanar, fajar.

swain, n zagal m; pretendiente m, amante m.

swallow, n 1. trago m; (ornith) golondrina f; 2. vt tragar.

swamp, n 1. pantano m, marisma f, ciénaga f; 2. vt sumergir, cubrir de agua.

swan, n cisne m.

swap, n 1. intercambio m, canje m; duplicados m; 2. vt intercambiar, canjear.

swarm, n 1. enjambre m; multitud f, muchedumbre f; 2. vi enjambrar.

swarthy, n moreno m.

swat, n aplastar; matar.

sway, n 1. balanceo m; dominio m; 2. vt disuadir, balancear; hacer tambalear.

swear, vt 1. prestar, jurar; 2. vi jurar; maldecir.

sweat, n 1. sudor m; 2. vi sudar.

sweater, n suéter m, jersey m.

sweating, adj 1. sudoroso; 2. n transpiración f.

sweep, n 1. barredura f; escobada f; 2. vt barrer.

sweet, adj 1. dulce; azucarado; 2. n dulce m, caramelo m; golosina f.

sweetheart, n novio(a) m/f; enamorado(a) m/f.

sweetness, n dulzura f; lo dulce, lo azucarado.

swell, n 1. marejada f, oleaje m; 2. adj magnífico; 3. vt hinchar; inflar; aumentar.

swelling, n hinchazón f; protuberancia f.

swerve, n 1. desvío m brusco, viraje m repentino; 2. vt desviar bruscamente, torcer.

swift, adj rápido, veloz.

swig, n 1. trago m, tragantada f; 2. vt beber.

swill, n 1. bazofia f; aguachirle f; 2. vt lavar.

swim, n 1. nadada f; 2. vi nadar.

swimmer, n nadador(ora) m/f.

swimming, n natación f.

swindle, n 1. estafa f; 2. vt estafar, timar.

swindler, n estafador m, timador m.

swine, n cerdos m, puercos m.

swing, n 1. balanceo m, oscilación f, vaivén m; 2. vt balancear; hacer oscilar; menear.

swipe, n 1. golpe m fuerte; 2. vt golpear.

swirl, n 1. remolino m, torbellino m; 2. vi arremolinarse; girar.

swish, n 1. silbido m; crujido m; 2. vt agitar produciendo un silbido.

switch, n 1. vara; (Elect) llave f interruptora; 2. vt azotar, commutar.

swivel, n 1. eslabón m giratorio; pivote m; 2. vt girar.

swoop, n 1. calada f; 2. vi calarse.

sword, n espada f.

sybarite, n sibarita m/f.

syllable, n sílaba f.

syllabus, n programa m (esp de estudios).

symbol, n símbolo m.

symbolize, vt simbolizar.

symmetry, n simetría f.

sympathetic, adj compasivo con, compadecido.

sympathize, vi compadecerse, condolerse.

sympathy, n simpatía f; solidaridad f.

symphony, n sinfonía f; orquesta f sinfónica.

symptom, n síntoma m; indicio m.

synagogue, n sinagoga f.

synchronization, n sincronización f.

synchronize, n sincronizar.

syndicate, n sindicato m.

syndrome, n síndrome m.

synonym, n sinónimo m.

synopsis, n sinopsis f.

synthesize, n sintetizar.

synthesizer, n sintetizador m.

synthetic, adj sintético.

syphillis, n sífilis f.

syrup, n jarabe m; almíbar m.

system, n sistema m.

systematic, adj sistemático, metódico.

systematize, n sistematizar.

T

T, t, n (letra f) T, t.

tab, n oreja f, lengüeta f; etiqueta f; resguardo m.

Tabasco, n tabasco m.

tabby, n gato m atigrado.

tabernacle, n tabernáculo m.

table, n 1. mesa f; tablero m; (Math) tabla f; 2. vt aplazar la discusión.

tablet, n tableta f, comprimido m.

taboo, adj tabú, prohibido.

tabulate, vt disponer en tablas, tabular.

tacit, adj tácito.

tack, n 1. tachuela f; hilván m; (Naut) virada f; 2. vt clavar con tachuelas, 3. virar.

tackle, n aparejo m; polea f; 2. vt agarrar, asir; atacar.

tacky, adj pegajoso; de pacotilla, malísimo.

tact, n tacto m; discreción f.

tactfully, adv discretamente, diplomáticamente.

tactic, n táctica f; maniobra f; táctica f.

taffeta, n tafetán m.

taffy, n toffee.

tag, n 1. etiqueta f, marbete m; pingaja f; 2. vt poner una etiqueta; jugar al "tócame tu", seguir de cerca.

tail, n 1. cola f, rabo m; cabo m; trenza f; 2. vt seguir, seguir y vigilar.

tailoring, n corte m, hechura f.

taint, n 1. infección f; mancha f, tacha f; 2. vt contaminar; manchar.

tainted, adj viciado; pasado, contaminado.

take, n 1. toma f, vista f; 2. ingresos m; recaudación f; 3. vt tomar; coger, agarrar; 4. vi pegar; cuajar.

talc, n talco m.

tale, n cuento m; historia f, relación f.

talent, n talento m.

talk, n 1. conversación f, charla f; 2. vt hablar.

talkative, adj locuaz, hablador, platicón.

tall, adj alto; grande.

tallow, n sebo m.

tally, n 1. cuenta f; número m; total m; 2. vi concordar, corresponder.

talon, n garra f.

tambourine, n pandereta f.

tame, adj 1. domesticado; manso, dócil; 2. vt domar, domesticar; amansar.

tamper, vi estropear, manosear, descomponer; ajar.

tampon, n tapón m; tampón m.

tan, n 1. bronceado m, tostado m; casca f; 2. adj color café claro, color canela; 3. vt broncear, tostar.

tandem, n 1. tándem m; 2. adj en tándem.

tangerine, n mandarina f, clementina f.

tangible, adj tangible; palpable.

tangle, n 1. nudo m; enredo m, maraña f; 2. vt enredar, enmarañar.

tangled, adj enredado, enmarañado.

tank, n tanque m.

tankard, n bock m, pichel m.

tanker, n petrolero m; camión-tanque m.

tanner, n curtidor m.

tannin, n tanino m.

tantalize, vt/i tentar (con cosas imposibles).

tantrum, n rabieta f, berrinche m.

tap, n 1. grifo m, llave f, canilla f; 2. golpecito m; 3. vt barrel espitar; dar golpecitos.

tape, n 1. cinta f; cinta f simbólica; cinta f adhesiva; 2. vt poner una cinta a; 3. grabar.

tapered, adj ahusado, que termina en punta; cónico.

tapestry, n tapiz m; tapicería f.

tappet, n alzaválvulas m.

tar, n 1. alquitrán m, brea f; 2. vt alquitranar, embrear.

tarantula, n tarántula f.

tardy, adj tardío; lento.

target, n 1. blanco m; 2. vt elegir como blanco.

tariff, n tarifa f, arancel m.

tarnish, n 1. deslustre m; 2. vt deslustrar, empañar.

tarot, n tarot m.

tarpaulin, n alquitranado m, encerado m.

tarpon, n tarpón m.

tarry, adj 1. embreado; 2. vi quedarse; quedarse atrás.

tart, n 1. tarta f; pastelillo m de fruta; 2. adj ácido, agrio.

tartar, n tártaro m; sarra m.

tartness, n acidez f, agrura f; aspereza f.

task, n tarea f, labor f; empresa f, cometido m.

tassel, n borla f.

taste, n 1. sabor m; gusto m; 2. vt probar.

tasteless, adj sin sabor, soso; de mal gusto.

tasty, adj sabroso, apetitoso.

tattered, adj person andrajoso, harapiento.

tattle, n 1. charla f; chismes m, habladurías f; 2. vi charlar, parlotear; chismear; contar chismes.

tattoo, n 1. tatuaje m; 2. vt tatuar.

taunt, n 1. mofa f, pulla f, dicterio m; 2. vt mofarse de; insultar, reprochar con insultos.

taunting, adj insultante, mofador, burlón.

taut, adj tieso, tenso, tirante; tirante.

tauten, vt tensar, estirar; tesar.

tavern, n taberna f.

tax, n 1. impuesto m, contribución f; 2. vt imponer contribuciones a, gravar con un impuesto.

taxable, adj imponible, gravable.

taxi, n 1. taxi m; 2. vi ir en taxi.

taxicab, n taxi m.

taxidermy, n taxidermia f.

taxing, adj dificilísimo; duro, agotador.

tea, n té m.

teach, vt 1. enseñar; 2. vi enseñar; ser profesor(a).

teacher, n profesor(ora) m/f; maestro(a) m/f.

teaching, n ensenanza f.

team, n equipo m, grupo m.

tear, n 1. rasgón m, desgarrón m; 2. lágrima f; 3. vt rasgar, desgarrar.

tease, n 1. embromador(a) m/f; 2. vt jorobar; embromar.

technical, adj técnico.

technicality, n tecnicidad f.

technician, n técnico(a) m/f.

technique, n técnica f.

technology, n tecnología f; técnica f.

tedious, adj aburrido, pesado.

teem, vi abundar; llover a cántaros.

teenage, adj de los adolescentes, de los jóvenes.

teenager, n adolescente m/f, joven m/f.

teens, n edad f de adolescencia.

teeter, vi balancearse, oscilar; columpiarse.

teethe, vi endentecer, echar los dientes.

teething, n dentición f.

teetotaller, n abstemio m; que no toma alcohol.

telegram, n telegrama m.

telepathic, adj telepático

telepathy, n telepatía f.

telephone, n 1. teléfono m; 2. vt telefonear.

telescope, n telescopio m.

television, n televisión f.

tell, vt decir; contar; narrar, informar.

teller, n narrador(a) m/f, (bank) cajero(a) m/f.

temper, n 1. disposición f, natural m; humor m, genio m; 2. vt templar; moderar, mitigar.

temperament, n temperamento m, disposición f.

temperate, adj templado; moderado; abstemio.

temperature, n temperatura f; calentura f, fiebre f.

tempered, adj templado.

tempestuous, adj tempestuoso; borrascoso.

template, n plantilla f.

temple, n templo m; (forehead) sien f; patilla f.

temporal, adj temporal.

temporary, adj temporáneo, provisional.

temporize, vi contemporizar.

tempt, vt tentar; atraer; seducir.

temptation, n tentación f; atractivo m; aliciente m.

tempting, adj tentador; atractivo.

ten, adj diez.

tenable, adj defendible, sostenible.

tenacious, adj tenaz; porfiado.

tenacity, n tenacidad f; porfía f.

tenancy, n tenencia f; inquilinato m, ocupación f.

tenant, adj inquilino.

tend, vi 1. tender; inclinarse a, 2. vt cuidar; atender; cattle guardar.

tendency, n tendencia f, inclinación f; propensión f.

tender, adj 1. tierno, blando; (pain) adolorido; 2. n (Naut) gabarra f; oferta f; 3. vt ofrecer, presentar.

tenderize, vt ablandar.

tenderness, n ternura f; lo delicado; sensibilidad f.

tendon, n tendón m.

tenement, n vivienda f; habitación f; casa f de pisos.

tenet, n principio m, dogma m.

tennis, n tenis m.

tenor, adj 1. de tenor; para tenor; 2. n tenor m.

tense, adj 1. tirante, estirado; tieso; 2. n (Gram) tiempo m; 3. vt tensar, tesar; estirar.

tension, n tirantez f; tensión f.

tent, n tienda f, carpa f.

tentacle, n tentáculo m.

tentative, adj experimental; tentativo.

tenth, adj 1. décimo; 2. n décimo m.

tenuous, adj tenue; sutil; poco fuerte.

tenure, n posesión f, tenencia f; permanencia f.

tepid, adj tibio.

term, n 1. término m, límite m; 2. período m; duración f; plazo m; 2. vt llamar; nombrar, denominar; calificar de.

terminal, adj 1. terminal, final; 2. n terminal m.

terminate, vt terminar; interrumpir.

termination, n terminación f; interrupción f.

terminology, n terminología f.

termite, n termita f, termes m, comején m.

terrace, n 1. terraza f; terraplén m; 2. vt aterrazar, formar terrazas en.

terrain, n terreno m.

terrestrial, adj terrestre.

terrible, adj terrible; horrible, malísimo, fatal.

terrier, n terrier m.

terrific, adj tremendo; bárbaro, fabuloso.

terrify, vt aterrar, aterrorizar.

terrifying, adj aterrador, espantoso.

territory, n territorio m.

terror, n terror m, espanto m.

terrorize, vt aterrorizar.

terse, adj breve, conciso, lacónico; brusco.

tertiary, adj terciario; producción f, terciaria.

test, n 1. examen, prueba; 2. criterio m; 3. vt probar, poner a prueba, someter a prueba; examinar.

testament, n testamento m.

testicles, n testículos m.

testify, vt atestiguar.

testimonial, n certificado m; recomendación f.

testimony, n testimonio m, declaración f.

tetanus, n tétanos m.

tether, n 1. atadura f, traba f; 2. vt atar.

text, n texto m; tema m.

textile, adj 1. textil; industria f textil; 2. n textil m.

texture, n textura f.

thankful, adj agradecido.

thankless, adj ingrato.

that, adj dem 1. (pl those) ése, aquel; 2. pro rel que, quien, el cual, el que; 3. adv tan; 4. conj que, para que.

than, conj que; de (más, menos); de lo que.

thank, vt dar las gracias a uno.

thank you, n gracias f.

thaw, n 1. deshielo m; 2. vt deshelar, derretir.

the, art 1. el, la; 2. los, las.

theatrical, adj teatral.

theft, n hurto m, robo m.

them, pron los, las; les; ellos, ellas.

theme, n tema m.

themselves, pron ellos mismos, ellas mismas.

then, adv 1. entonces; por entonces; en ese momento; 2. luego, después; 3. adj de entonces.

theology, n teología f.

theorize, vi teorizar.

theory, n teoría f.

therapist, n terapeuta m/f.

therapy, n terapia f, terapéutica f.

there, adv allí; allá; ahí.

thereafter, adv después, después de eso.

therefore, adv por tanto, por lo tanto.

thermal, adj termal; térmico.

thermometer, n termómetro m.

Thermos, n termos m, termo m.

thermostat, n termostato m.

these, (plural of this) 1. dem, adj m estos; f; estas.

thesis, n tesis f.

they, pron ellos, ellas.

thick, adj espeso; grueso; abultado.

thicken, vt espesar, hacer más espeso.

thickness, n espesura f; densidad f; grueso m.

thief, n ladrón(ona) m/f.

thigh, n muslo m.

thighbone, n fémur m.

thimble, n dedal m.

thin, adj 1. delgado; ligero; 2. vi aguar.

thing, n cosa f; objeto m; artículo m; creatura f; asunto m.

think, vt pensar, creer; considerar.

thinker, n pensador(a) m/f.

thinking, adj 1. pensante, que piensa; inteligente; 2. n pensamiento m; pensamientos m.

thinner, n 1. disolvente m, diluyente m; 2. adj comp más flaco.

third, adj 1. tercero; 2. n tercio m.

thirsty, adj sediento; árido.

this, dem adj 1. este m; esta f; 2. dem pron éste m, ésta f.

thong, n correa f.

thoracic, adj torácico.

thorax, n tórax m.

thorn, n espina f.

thorny, adj espinoso.

thorough, adj completo, cabal; acabado; minucioso, concienzudo, meticuloso.

those, dem adj esos, aquellos; esas, aquellas.

thought, n pensamiento m; idea f; concepto m.

thoughtfulness, n seriedad f; carácter m; reflexivo.

thoughtless, adj descuidado, inconsiderado.

thousand, adj mil.

thrash, vt golpear; apalear.

thread, n 1. hilo m; 2. vt enhebrar.

threat, n amenaza f.

threaten, vt amenazar, proferir amenazas contra.

three, adj 1. tres; 2. n tres m.

thresh, vt (Agr) trillar.

threshold, n umbral m.

thrift, n economía f, frugalidad f.

thrifty, adj económico, frugal, ahorrativo.

thrill, n 1. emoción f viva; 2. vi emocionar, conmover.

thriller, n novela f de suspenso.

thrive, vi prosperar, medrar; florecer; crecer mucho.

thriving, adj próspero, floreciente.

throat, n garganta f; cuello m.

throb, n 1. latido m, pulsación f; palpitación f; 2. vi latir; palpitar; vibrar; estremecerse.

throbbing, adj 1. palpitante; vibrante; 2. n latido m, pulsación f; palpitación f; vibración f.

throes, n agonía f; dolores m; angustia f, agonía f.

thrombosis, n trombosis f.

throne, n trono m; corona f, poder m real.

throng, n 1. multitud f, tropel m, muchedumbre f; 2. vt atestar, llenar de bote en bote.

throttle, n 1. gaznate m; regulador m, válvula f reguladora; 2. vt ahogar, estrangular.

through, adv 1. a través, de un lado al otro; 2. adj directo, sin paradas, terminado; 3. prep por, a través de, por medio de.

throw, n 1. echada f, tirada f, tiro m; jugada f; derribo m; 2. vt echar, tirar, lanzar, arrojar.

thrum, vt piano teclear en; guitar rasguear.

thrush, n zorzal m, tordo m; (Med) afta f.

thrust, n 1. empuje m; avance m; 2. vt empujar; impeler, impulsar; introducir.

thud, n 1. ruido m sord; 2. vi hacer un ruido sordo.

thug, n asesino m, gángster m; bruto m.

thumb, n 1. pulgar m; 2. vt manosear.

thump, n 1. golpazo m, porrazo m; 2. vt golpear; (heart) latir con golpes pesados.

thunder, n 1. trueno m, tronido m; 2. vt fulminar amenazas contra uno; 3. tronar.

Thursday, n jueves m.

thus, adv así; de este modo; hasta aquí.

thyroid, adj 1. tiroideo; 2. n tiroides m.

tic, n tic m.

tick, n 1. tic-tac m; 2. momento m, instante m; 3. n garrapata f.

ticket, n 1. billete m; boleto m; 2. vt rotular, poner etiqueta a.

ticket window, n taquilla f, ventanilla f.

tickle, n 1. cosquilla f; 2. vt cosquillear.

tidal, adj de marea.

tide, n marea f; corriente m; marcha f, progreso m.

tidiness, n buen orden m; limpieza f.

tidings, n noticias f.

tidy, adj 1. ordenado; limpio, aseado; 2. vt arreglar, poner en orden, limpiar.

tie, n 1. atadura f, lazo m; (neck) corbata f; empate m; 2. vt atar, enlazar, empatar.

tier, *n* grada *f*, piso *m;* nivel *m*.

tiger, *n* tigre *m/f*.

tight, *adj* **1.** estrecho, bien cerrado, apretado; estanco; **2.** tieso, tirante; estirado; estricto.

tighten, *vt* atiesar, estirar; estrechar; apretar.

tilde, n tilde *f*.

tile, *n* **1.** teja *f;* baldosa *f;* azulejo *m;* **2.** *vt* tejar; cubrir de tejas; embaldosar.

till, *prep* **1.** hasta; **2.** *conj* hasta que; **3.** *n* cajón *m* de dinero; **4.** *vt* cultivar.

tilt, *n* **1.** inclinación *f;* ladeo *m;* **2.** *vt* inclinar, ladear.

timber, *n* **1.** madera; árboles *m pl;* **2.** *vt* enmaderar.

timbre, *n* timbre *m*.

time, *n* **1.** tiempo *m;* período *m*, rato *m;* **2.** (occasion) vez *f;* **3.** *vt* medir el tiempo.

timeless, *adj* eterno; atemporal.

timely, *adj* oportuno.

timer, *n* avisador *m*, reloj *m* automático.

timid, *adj* tímido.

timidity, *n* timidez *f*.

timing, *n* medida *f* del tiempo.

tin, *n* **1.** estaño *m;* hojalata *f;* **2.** lata *f;* **3.** *vt* estañar; envasar en lata, conservar en lata, enlatar.

tinfoil, *n* papel *m* (de) estaño, papel *m* (de) aluminio.

tingle, *n* **1.** comezón *f;* hormigueo *m* (de la piel); **2.** *vi* sentir comezón, sentir hormigueo.

tingling, *n* hormigueo *m*.

tinkle, n **1.** tilín *m*, retintín *m;* **2.** *vt* hacer retiñir; hacer tintinar.

tinsel, *adj* **1.** de oropel; **2.** *n* oropel *m*.

tint, *n* **1.** tinte *m*, matiz *m*, color *m;* **2.** *vt* teñir.

tiny, *adj* pequeñito, chiquitín, diminuto, minúsculo.

tip, *n* **1.** propina *f*, gratificación *f;* **2.** aviso *m*, advertencia *f;* consejo *m;* **3.** extremidad *f*, punta *f;* **4.** *vt* dar una propina a; **5.** *vi* inclinarse.

tipped, *adj* cigarette emboquillado, con filtro.

tipsy, *adj* achispado, bebido, tomado.

tiptoe, *vi* caminar de puntillas.

tirade, *n* invectiva *f*, diatriba *f*.

tire, *n* **1.** goma *f;* **2.** *vt* cansar, fatigar; aburrir; **3.** *vi* cansarse, fatigarse.

tired, *adj* cansado.

tissue, *n* tisú *m*, lama *f;* pañuelo *m* de papel.

titillate, *vt* estimular, excitar, encandilar.

title, n **1.** título *m;* **2.** *vt* titular, intitular.

to, *prep* **1.** a; **2.** a; hacia; **3.** hasta; **4.** para.

toad, *n* sapo *m*.

toast, *n* **1.** pan *m* tostado, tostada *f;* **2.** brindis *m;* **3.** *vt* tostar; **4.** brindar por, beber a la salud de.

toaster, *n* tostador *m*.

tobacco, *n* tabaco *m*.

today, *adv* **1.** hoy; hoy día; **2.** *n* hoy *m*.

toddle, *vi* empezar a andar, dar los primeros pasos.

toe, *n* dedo *m* del pie; punta *f* del pie.

together, *adv* junto; juntos.

toil, *n* **1.** labor *f*, trabajo *m;* **2.** *vi* trabajar.

toilet, *n* **1.** tocado *m;* atavío *m;* **2.** inodoro *m*.

toiletries, *n* artículos *m* de tocador.

token, *n* **1.** señal *f*, muestra *f*, indicio *m;* **2.** prenda *f*, recuerdo *m*.

tolerance, *n* tolerancia *f;* paciencia *f*, indulgencia *f*.

tolerate, *vt* tolerar, soportar, aguantar.

toll, *n* **1.** peaje *m*, portazgo *m;* pontazgo *m;* **2.** mortalidad *f;* **3.** *vt* (campanas) tañer.

tomato, *n* tomate *m*.

tomb, *n* tumba *f*, sepulcro *m*.

tome, *n* librote *m*.

tomorrow, *adv* **1.** mañana; **2.** *n* mañana *f*.

ton, *n* tonelada *f*.

tone, *n* **1.** tono *m;* **2.** *vt* entonar; virar.

tongue, *n* lengua *f*.

tonic, *adj* **1.** tónico; **2.** *n* tónica *f*.

tonight, *adv* esta noche.

too, *adv* **1.** demasiado; **2.** también; además, por otra parte.

tool, *n* herramienta *f;* utensilio *m*.

toot, n **1.** sonido *m* breve; **2.** *vt* sonar, tocar.

tooth, *n* teeth diente *m*.

top, *n* **1.** cumbre *f*, cima *f;* ápice *m;* copa *f;* coronilla *f;* **2.** (juguete) peonza *f;* **3.** *vt* exceder, superar.

topaz, *n* topacio *m*.

topcoat, *n* sobretodo *m*.

topic, *n* asunto *m*, tema *m*.

topknot, *n* mono *m;* cabeza *f*.

topmast, *n* mastelero *m*.

topmost, *adj* más alto, el más alto.

top-notch, *adj* de primerísima categoría.

topographic(al), *adj* topográfico.

topography , *n* topografía *f*.

topple, *vt* **1.** derribar, volcar; **2.** *vi* caerse.

topsail, *n* gavia *f*.

top-secret, *adj* ultrasecreto, de reserva absoluta.

topside, *n* lado *m* superior, superficie *f* superior.

topsoil, *n* capa *f* superficial del suelo.

torch, *n* antorcha *f*, tea *f*, hacha *f*.

toreador, *n* torero *m*.

torment, *n* **1.** tormento *m;* **2.** *vt* atormentar.

tormentor, *n* atormentador(a) *m/f*.

tornado, *n* tornado *m*.

torpedo, *n* **1.** torpedo *m;* **2.** *vt* torpedear.

torpid, *adj* aletargado, inactivo; torpe, apático.

torrent, *n* torrente *m;* llover a cántaros, diluviar.

torrid, *adj* tórrido.

torso, *n* torso *m*.

tortilla, *n* tortilla *f*.

tortoise, *n* tortuga *f*.

tortuous, *adj* tortuoso.

torture, *n* **1.** tortura *f;* tormento *m;* **2.** *vt* torturar.

toss, *n* **1.** echada *f;* **2.** *vt* mover bruscamente, sacudir, menear; **3.** *vi* echar.

tot, n **1.** trago *m*, copita *f;* **2.** nene *m/f*.

total, *adj* **1.** total; completo, entero; **2.** *n* total *m;* suma *f;* cantidad *f* global; **3.** *vt* sumar.

totalitarian, *adj* totalitario.

totality, *n* totalidad *f*.

tote, *vt* acarrear, llevar (con dificultad).

totem, *n* tótem *m*.

totter, *vi* bambolearse, tambalearse.

tottering, *adj* tambaleante; nada seguro; ruinoso.

touch, *n* **1.** tacto *m;* **2.** toque *m;* contacto *m;* roce *m;* **3.** *vt* tocar, afectar, lindar.

touched, *adj* chiflado, tocado.

touching, *adj* conmovedor, patético.

touchstone, *n* piedra *f* de toque.

touchy, *adj* susceptible, quisquilloso.

tough, *adj* **1.** materials duro, fuerte, resistente; **2.** *n* machote *m;* forzudo *m*.

toughnesss, *n* dureza *f*, resistencia *f;* inflexibilidad.

toupée, *n* peluca *f*.

tour, *n* **1.** viaje *m* excursión *f;* **3.** *vt* viajar por.

tourism, *n* turismo *m*.

tourist, *n* turista *m/f*.

tournament, *n* torneo *m;* concurso *m*, certamen *m*.

tourniquet, *n* torniquete *m*.

tousle, *vt* ajar, desarreglar; hair despeinar.

tow, *n* **1.** remolque *m;* grua *f;* **2.** *vt* remolcar.

toward(s), *prep* hacia; cerca de; con, para con.

towaway zone, *n* zona de aparcamiento prohibido.

towboat, n remolcador m.

towel, n 1. toalla f; 2. vt secar con toalla.

towel-rack, n toallero m.

tower, n torre f; campanario m.

towering, adj encumbrado; elevado, elevadísimo.

town, n ciudad f; pueblo m, población f.

townsfolk, n ciudadanos m.

township, n municipio m.

townspeople, n ciudadanos m.

towrope, n remolque m, cable m de remolque.

tow truck, n (camión m) grúa f.

toxemia, n toximia f.

toxic, adj tóxico; alga f tóxica; sustancia f tóxica.

toxicology, n toxicología f.

toxin, n toxina f.

toy, n 1. juguete m; 2. vi jugar con.

toyshop, n juguetería f.

trace, n 1. rastro m, huella f, indicio m; 2. vt trazar, (with paper) calcar, 3. seguir.

trachea, n tráquea f.

track, n 1. huella f; pista f, rastro m; 2. vt seguir la huella de.

tracker, n rastreador m.

tracking, n rastreo m.

tract, n 1. región f, zona f; extensión f; 2. folleto m; tratado m.

tractable, adj person tratable, dócil; soluble.

traction, n tracción f.

tractor, n tractor m.

trade, n 1. comercio m; negocio m; trueque m; 2. vt vender; cambiar, trocar; 3. vi comerciar.

trademark, n marca f registrada, marca f de fábrica.

trader, n comerciante m; traficante m.

tradition, n tradición f.

traditional, adj tradicional; clásico, consagrado.

traduce, vt calumniar, denigrar.

traffic, n 1. circulación f, tráfico m, tránsito m; movimiento m; 2. vi traficar, comerciar.

traffic-jam, n embotellamiento m, atasco m.

traffic-light, n semáforo m, luces f.

tragic, adj trágico.

trail, n 1. cola f; 2. rastro m, pista f; 3. vt arrastrar, rastrear, seguir la pista de.

trailblazer, n pionero m/f.

trailer, n remolque m; caravana f.

trailing, adj colgado; rastrero.

trailer truck, n tráiler m.

train, n 1. tren m; ferrocarril m; 2. vt adiestrar; preparar, formar; 3. vi adiestrarse; prepararse, formarse; educarse.

trained, adj cualificado, capacitado.

trainee, n aprendiz m, aprendiza f; recluta m/f.

trainer, n entrenador(a) m/f.

training, n adiestramiento m; preparación f.

trait, n rasgo m.

traitor, n traidor(a) m/f.

trajectory, n trayectoria f.

trammel, vt poner trabas a, trabar, impedir.

tramp, n 1. pasos m pesados; 2. vagabundo m; 3. vt pisar con fuerza; recorrer a pie; 4. vi marchar pesadamente.

trample, vt pisotear.

trampoline, n trampolín m, cama f elástica.

trance, n rapto m, arrobamiento m, éxtasis m.

tranquil, adj tranquilo.

tranquility , n tranquilidad f.

tranquilize, vt tranquilizar.

tranquilizer, n tranquilizante m.

transact, vt hacer, despachar; tramitar.

transaction, n negocio m, transacción f.

transatlantic, adj transatlántico.

transcend, vt exceder, superar, rebasar.

transcendent, adj superior; sobresaliente.

transcontinental, adj transcontinental.

transcribe, vt transcribir, copiar.

transcript, n trasunto m, copia f; transcripción f.

transfer, n 1. transferencia f, traspaso m; 2. vt transferir, traspasar, pasar; 4. vi trasladarse, cambiar, hacer transbordo.

transferable, adj transferible.

transfigure, vt transfigurar, transformar (en).

transfix, vt traspasar, pasar de parte a parte.

transform, vt transformar (en), convertir.

transformation, n transformación f, conversión f.

transformer, n transformador m.

transgress, vt 1. traspasar, exceder, violar; 2. vi pecar, cometer una transgresión.

transgression, n pecado m, transgresión f; infracción f.

transgressor, n transgresor(a) m/f; pecador(a) m/f.

transient, adj pasajero, transitorio, fugaz.

transistor, n transistor m.

transit, n tránsito m, paso m; de tránsito, de paso.

transition, n transición f, paso m de, a; transformación f, evolución f (en).

transitional, adj transicional, de transición.

transitive, adj transitivo.

transitory, adj transitorio.

translate, vt traducir (de, a); interpretar.

translation, n traducción f; versión f.

transliterate, vt transcribir.

transliteration, n transliteración f, transcripción f.

translucence, n translucidez f.

translucent, adj translúcido.

transmigrate, vi transmigrar.

transmission, n transmisión f.

transmit, vt transmitir.

transmitter, n transmisor m; estación f transmisora, emisora f.

transmute, vt transmutar (en).

transom, n travesaño m; abanico m.

transparency, n transparencia f.

transparent, adj transparente, diáfano; claro.

transpire, vt transpirar; 2. vi revelarse.

transplant, n 1. trasplante m; 2. vt trasplantar.

transport, n 1. transporte m; acarreo, transporte; 2. vt transportar; llevar, acarrear.

transportation, n transporte m, transportación f.

transporter, n transportista m, transportador m.

transpose, vt transponer, cambiar (a); transportar.

transship, vt tra(n)sbordar.

transverse, adj transverso, trasversal.

transvestite, adj travestido; 2. n travestido(a) m/f.

trap, n 1. trampa f; lazo m; 2. vi coger (agarrar) en una trampa, entrampar, atrapar.

trapeze, n trapecio m.

trapezoid, n trapezoide m.

trapper, n cazador m, trampero m.

trappings, n adornos m; jaeces m.

trappist, adj, n trapense.

trash, n 1. pacotilla f, hojarasca f; basura f; 2. vt hacer polvo, destrozar.

trash-can, n cubo m de la basura.

trash-heap, n basurero m.

trauma, n trauma m.

traumatic, adj traumático.

traumatize, vt traumatizar.

travail, n esfuerzo m penoso; dolores m del parto.

travel, n 1. viajes m, el viajar; 2. vt recorrer; 3. vi viajar.

traveler, n viajero(a) m/f; viajante m.

traverse, n 1. travesaño m; través m; escalada f oblicua; 2. vt atravesar, cruzar; recorrer.

travesty, n 1. parodia f; 2. vt parodiar.

trawl, n 1. red f barredera; 3. vi pescar al arrastre.

tray, n bandeja f, charola f.

treacherous, adj traidor, traicionero; falso.

treachery, n traición f, perfidia f; falsedad f.

tread, n 1. paso m, pisada f; andar m; 3. vi pisar.

treadle, n pedal m.

treadmill, n rueda f de andar; rutina f, monotonía f.

treason, n traición f.

treasonable, adj traidor, desleal.

treasure, n 1. tesoro m; 2. vt atesorar; guardar.

treasurer, n tesorero(a) m/f.

treasury, n tesoro m, tesorería f, fisco m, erario m.

treat, n 1. convite m; regalo m; 2. placer m; gusto m; 3. vt tratar.

treatise, n tratado m.

treatment, n tratamiento m; tratamiento m, cura f.

treaty, n tratado m.

tree, n árbol m.

tree-covered, adj arbolado.

treeless, adj pelado, sin árboles, desarbolado.

tree-planting, n repoblación f forestal.

treetrunk, n tronco m de árbol.

trek, n 1. migración f; jornada f; viaje m largo y difícil; 2. vi emigrar; viajar; caminar (penosamente).

trellis, n enrejado m; espaldera f, espaldar m.

tremble, n 1. temblor m, estremecimiento m; 2. vi temblar, estremecerse; vibrar, agitarse.

trembling, adj tembloroso.

tremendous, adj tremendo, inmenso, formidable.

tremolo, n trémolo m.

tremor, n temblor m; estremecimiento m.

tremulous, adj trémulo, tembloroso; tímido.

trench, n 1. zanja f, foso m; trinchera f; 2. vt atrincherar.

trenchant, adj mordaz, incisivo.

trenchcoat, n trinchera f, guerrera f.

trend, n tendencia f; curso m, dirección f, marcha f.

trendsetter, n persona f que inicia la moda.

trepidation, n turbación f, agitación f.

trespass, n 1. intrusión f, entrada f ilegal; 2. vi entrar sin derecho (en), entrar ilegalmente.

trespasser, n intruso(a) m/f.

tress, n trenza f; cabellera f, pelo m.

trestle, n caballete m.

triad, n tríada f.

trial, n proceso m, juicio m, vista f de una causa.

triangle, n triángulo m.

tribe, n tribu f; tropel f, masa f; ralea f.

tribulation, n tribulación f; aflicciones f.

tribunal, n tribunal m.

tributary, adj 1. tributario; 2. n tributario m.

tribute, n tributo m; homenaje m; elogio m.

triceps, n tríceps m.

trick, n 1. engaño m, truco m; estafa f; 3. vt engañar; trampear; burlar; estafar, timar.

trickery, n astucia f, mañas f; fraude m.

trickle, n 1. hilo m, chorro m delgado, goteo m; 2. vi salir en chorro delgado.

tricky, adj astuto; mañoso, tramposo; situation.

tricycle, n triciclo m.

trident, n tridente m.

tried, adj probado, de toda garantía.

trifle, n friolera f, bagatela f, fruslería f.

trifling, adj insignificante, sin importancia.

trigger, n 1. gatillo m; disparador m, tirador m; 2. vt hacer estallar; hacer funcionar, poner en movimiento.

trigonometry, n trigonometría f.

trill, n 1. trino m, gorjeo m; trino m, quiebro m; 2. vi trinar, gorjear.

trim, adj 1. aseado, arreglado; elegante; en buen estado; 2. vt recortar, arreglar, ordenar; disponer.

trimester, n trimestre m.

trimming, n adorno m, guarnición f; orla f.

trinity, n trinidad f.

trinket, n dije m, chuchería f; baratijas f.

trip, n 1. viaje m; excursión f; 2. vt hacer tropezar, hacer caer; 3. vi andar airosamente.

tripe, n callos m; guata f, mondongo m.

triple, adj 1. triple; 2. n triple m; 3. vt triplicar; 4. vi triplicarse.

triplicate, adj 1. triplicado; 3. vt triplicar.

tripod, n trípode m.

trisect, vt trisecar.

trisyllable, n trissílabo m.

trite, adj vulgar, trivial; gastado, trillado y llevado.

triumph, n 1. triunfo m; éxito m; 2. vi triunfar.

triumphant, adj triunfante; victorioso; jubiloso.

trivial, adj trivial, insignificante; banal; superficial.

triviality, n trivialidad f, insignificancia f; banalidad f.

trivialize, vt trivializar, banalizar.

trolleycar, n tranvía m.

trolling, n pesca f a la cacea.

trombone, n trombón m.

troop, n 1. banda f, grupo m, compañía f; tropa f; 2. vi marchar.

trophy, n trofeo m.

tropic, n trópico m; trópicos m, zona f tropical.

tropic(al), adj tropical.

trot, n 1. trote m; 2. vt hacer trotar; 3. vi trotar, ir al trote.

trotting, n trote m.

troubadour, n trovador m.

trouble, n 1. aflicción f; pena f, angustia f; desgracia f, desventura f; 2. vi molestarse.

troublemaker, n alborotador(a) m/f, buscarruidos m, elemento m perturbador.

troublesome, adj molesto, fastidioso; importuno.

trough, n depresión f, hoyo m; seno m; canal m.

trounce, vt pegar, zurrar, dar una paliza a.

troupe, n compañía f, grupo m, conjunto m.

trouser, n pantalones m, pantalón m.

trout, n trucha f; arpía f, bruja f.

trowel, n desplantador m, transplantador m.

truancy, n ausencia f sin permiso.

truant, adj 1. ausente; 2. n gandul m, vago m; novillero m; 3. vi ausentarse.

truce, n tregua f; suspensión f, cesación f.

truck, n 1. carro m; vagón m; 2. vt llevar, transportar.

truck-driver, n camionero m.

trucking, n acarreo m, transporte m.

truckload, n carretada f; vagón m (lleno).

truculent, adj agresivo; malhumorado, áspero.

trudge, n 1. caminata f difícil; 2. vt recorrer a pie penosamente.

true, adj verdadero.

truffle, n trufa f.

truism, n perogrullada f, tópico m.

truly, adv verdaderamente; exactamente.

trumpet, n trompeta f.

truncate, vt truncar.

truncheon, n porra f.

trunk, n tronco m; baúl m; maletero m.

truss, n 1. lío m, paquete m; haz m, 2. vt liar, atar.

trust, n 1. confianza f; 2. vi confiar; esperar.

trustee, n síndico m; fideicomisario(a) m/f, administrador(a) m/f.

trustful, adj confiado.

trustworthiness, n formalidad f, honradez f, confiabilidad f.

trustworthy, adj formal, honrado, confiable.

truth, n verdad f; realidad f; verosimilitud f.

truthful, adj verídico, exacto; veraz.

truthfulness, n veracidad f; verdad f, exactitud f.

try, n 1. tentativa f; probar suerte; 2. vt intentar, probar, ensayar; 3. vi esforzarse.

trying, adj molesto; cansado; difícil.

tryst, n cita f; lugar m de una cita.

tub, n tina f, cubo m.

tuba, n tuba.

tube, n tubo m; cámara (tubo de aire dentro de un neumático.

tubeless, adj sin cámara.

tuber, n tubérculo m.

tuberculosis, n tuberculosis f.

tubing, n tubería f, cañería f.

tubular, adj tubular, en forma de tubo.

tuck, n 1. alforza f; pliegue m; 2. vt alforzar; plegar.

tucker, vt cansar, agotar.

Tuesday, n martes m.

tuft, n copete m; mechón m; cresta f.

tufted, adj copetudo.

tug, n 1. tirón m; estirón m; tirar de algo; 2. vt tirar de; dar un estirón a; arrastrar algo.

tuition, n enseñanza f; costo m de la enseñanza.

tulip, n tulipán m.

tulle, n tul m.

tumbler, n 1. vaso m. 2. seguro m, fiador m; interruptor m de resorte; 3. volteador(a) m/f.

tummy-ache, n dolor m de tripas.

tumor, n tumor m.

tumult, n tumulto m, alboroto m.

tun, n tonel m.

tuna, n tuna f, atún m.

tundra, n tundra f.

tune, n 1. aire m, melodía f, tonada f; tono m; 2. vt afinar, acordar, templar (cuerdas).

tuneful, adj melodioso, armonioso.

tuner, n 1. afinador m; 2. botón m sintonizador.

tungsten, n tungsteno m.

tunic, n túnica f; guerrera f, blusa f.

tuning, n sintonización f; afinación f.

tuning-coil, n bobina f sintonizadora.

tuning-fork, n diapasón m.

tunnel, n 1. túnel m; (mining) galería f; 2. vt construir un túnel.

tunny, n atún m; bonito m.

turban, n turbante m.

turbid, adj túrbido.

turbine, n turbina f.

turbojet, n turborreactor m.

turbulence, n turbulencia f; desorden m.

turbulent, adj turbulento; revoltoso.

turkey, n pavo m, guajolote m.

turmoil, n confusión f, desorden m; alboroto m.

turn, n 1. vuelta f, revolución f; espiral f; 2. vt girar, hacer girar; dar vueltas.

turncoat, n renegado(a) f.

turning, n vuelta f; ángulo m; recodo m.

turnkey, n llavero m (de una cárcel),

turnover, n volumen m de negocios.

turnpike, n autopista f de peaje.

turntable, n giradiscos m.

turpentine, n aguarrás m, trementina f.

turquoise, n turquesa f.

turret, n torreón m; torre f, torrecilla f.

turtle, n tortuga f marina.

turtledove, n tórtola f.

turtleneck, n (jersey m de) cuello m de cisne.

tussle, n 1. lucha f (por); pelea f, agarrada f; 2. vi luchar (con); pelearse, reñir.

tutor, n 1. ayo m; preceptor(a) m/f; profesor(a) m/f particular; 3. vt enseñar, instruir; dar clase particular a.

tuxedo, n esmoquin m.

twaddle, n tonterías f, bobadas f.

twang, n 1. tañido m, punteado m; 2. vt puntear; estirar y soltar repentinamente.

tweak, n 1. pellizco m; 2. vt pellizcar.

tweeter, n altavoz m para altas audiofrecuencias.

twelve, adj doce.

twenty, adj veinte.

twice, adv dos veces.

twilight, n crepúsculo m.

twill, n tela f cruzada.

twin, adj 1. gemelo; 2. n gemelo(a) m/f.

twine, n 1. guita f, hilo m, bramante m; 2. vt tejer; ceñir, rodear; enrollar.

twin-engined, adj bimotor.

twinkle, n 1. centelleo m, parpadeo m; 2. vi centellear, parpadear, titilar.

twirl, n 1. vuelta f (rápida), giro m; pirueta f; 2. vt girar rápidamente, dar vueltas rápidas a.

twist, n 1. torzal m; mecha f; trenza f; 2. torcedura f; 3. vt torcer, retorcer; 4. vi torcerse, retorcerse; enroscarse.

twisting, n retorcimiento m.

twitch, n 1. sacudida f repentina, tirón m; contracción f nerviosa; tic m; 2. vt tirar bruscamente de.

twitter, n 1. gorjeo m; agitación f, inquietud f; 2. vi gorjear; agitarse, estar inquieto.

two, pron, adj, n dos m.

tycoon, n magnate m.

tympanum, n tímpano m.

type, n 1. tipo m; 2. sujeto m; 3. género m; 4. tipo m (de letra) letra f, carácter m; 5. vt escribir a máquina, mecanografiar.

typeface, n área f de texto impreso, tipografía f.

typeset, vt componer.

typesetter, n (persona) cajista m; máquina f de componer.

typewriter, n máquina f de escribir.

typewriting, n mecanografía f.

typhoid, n tifoidea f, fiebre f tifoidea.

typhoon, n tifón m.

typhus, n tifus m.

typical, adj típico; característico; clásico.

tipify, vi simbolizar.

typist, n mecanógrafo(a) m/f.

typo, n errata f.

typography, n tipografía f.

tyrannize, vt tiranizar.

tyranny, n tiranía f.

tyrant, n tirano(a) m/f.

tzar, n zar m.

tzarina, n zarina f.

U

U, u, n (letra f) U, u.
ubiquitous, adj ubicuo, omnipresente.
ubiquity, n ubicuidad f, omnipresencia f.
udder, n ubre f.
UFO, n (abbr) of unidentified flying object objeto m volante (o volador) no identificado, OVNI m.
ugly, adj feo; repugnante, asqueroso.
ukulele, n ukulele m.
ulcer, n úlcera f; llaga f.
ulcerate, vt 1. ulcerar; 2. vi ulcerarse.
ulterior, adj ulterior; motivo m oculto, segunda intención f.
ultimate, adj más remoto, extremo; último, final.
ultimatum, n ultimata, ultimátum m.
ultrafine, adj ultrafino.
ultrasonic, adj ultrasónico.
ultrasound, n ultrasonido m.
ultraviolet, adj ultravioleta.
umber, n tierra f de sombra.
umbilical, adj umbilical.
umbilicus, n ombligo m.
umbrage, n resentimiento m; resentirse (de).
umbrella, n paraguas m; quitasol m; sombrilla f.
umlaut, n metafonía f; diéresis f.
umpire, n 1. árbitro m/f; 2. vt/i arbitrar.
unabashed, adj descarado, desvergonzado.
unabated, adj sin disminución, no disminuido.
unabbreviated, adj íntegro, completo.
unable, adj ser incapaz de hacer algo.
unabridged, adj íntegro, integral.
unaccented, adj inacentuado, átono.
unacceptable, adj inaceptable.
unaccompanied, adj sin acompañamiento, no acompañado.
unaccountable, adj inexplicable.
unaccustomed, adj desacostumbrado.
unacquainted, adj desconocer algo, ignorar algo.
unadorned, adj sin adorno, sencillo.
unadulterated, adj sin mezcla, puro.
unadvisable, adj poco aconsejable.
unaffected, adj sin afectación.
unaffiliated, adj no afiliado.
unafraid, adj sin temor, impertérrito.
unaided, adv sin ayuda, por sí solo.
unalike, adj no parecido.
unalterable, adj inalterable.
unamiable, adj poco simpático.
unanimity, n unanimidad f.
unanimous, adj unánime.
unannounced, adj llegar sin dar aviso.
unanswerable, adj incontestable; irrebatible.
unappealable, adj inapelable.
unappealing, adj poco atractivo.
unappreciative, adj desagradecido.
unapproachable, adj inaccesible; intratable.
unarguable, adj indiscutible, incuestionable.
unarmed, adj que no lleva armas, desarmado.
unassailable, adj inexpugnable; inatacable.
unassisted, adj sin ayuda, por sí solo.
unattached, adj suelto, separable; disponible.
unattainable, adj inasequible; inalcanzable.

unattended, adj descuidado; sin guardia.
unattractive, adj poco atractivo.
unauthorized, adj no autorizado.
unavailable, adj indisponible, inasequible.
unavoidable, adj inevitable, ineludible.
unaware, adj inconsciente.
unawares, adv de improviso, inopinadamente.
unbalanced, adj desequilibrado; trastornado.
unbearable, adj inaguantable, insufrible.
unbeatable, adj insuperable; imbatible.
unbeaten, adj imbatido; invicto; no mejorado.
unbelievable, adj increíble.
unbend, vt 1. desencorvar, enderezar; 2. vi suavizarse.
unbending, adj inflexible, rígido; poco afable.
unbias(s)ed, adj imparcial.
unbind, vt desatar; desvendar.
unborn, adj no nacido aún, nonato.
unbound, adj sin encuadernar, en rústica.
unbounded, adj ilimitado, infinito.
unbreakable, adj irrompible, inquebrantable.
unbribable, adj insobornable.
unbroken, adj entero, intacto; no interrumpido.
unbuckle, vt deshebillar.
unburden, vt desahogarse de algo.
unburied, adj insepulto.
unbutton, vt desabotonar, desabrochar.
uncanny, adj misterioso, extraño, extraordinario.
uncap, vt destapar.
uncaring, adj poco compasivo.
unceasing, adj incesante.
uncensored, adj no censurado.
unceremonious, adj descortés, poco formal.
uncertain, adj incierto, dudoso; indeciso, vacilante.
uncertainty, n incertidumbre f, duda f; indecisión f.
unchallenged, adj incontestado, no desafiado.
unchangeable, adj inalterable, inmutable.
uncharitable, adj poco caritativo, duro.
uncharted, adj inexplorado, desconocido.
unchecked, adv libremente, sin estorbo.
uncivilized, adj incivilizado, inculto.
unclaimed, adj sin reclamar, sin dueño.
uncle, n tío m.
unclean, adj sucio, inmundo; deshonesto; impuro.
unclear, adj poco claro, nada claro.
unclog, vt desobstruir, desatrancar.
unclothe, vt desnudar.
unclothed, adj desnudo.
uncollected, adj sin recoger; no recaudado.
uncomfortable, adj incómodo; molesto.
uncommitted, adj no comprometido; no alineado.
uncommon, adj poco común, nada frecuente.
uncommunicative, adj poco comunicativo.
uncompleted, adj incompleto, inacabado.
uncomplicated, adj sin complicaciones, sencillo.
uncompromising, adj intransigente, inflexible.
unconcern, n calma f, tranquilidad f, sangre f fría.
unconditional, adj incondicional, sin condiciones.
unconfirmed, adj no confirmado.
unconnected, adj inconexo.
unconquerable, adj inconquistable, invencible.
unconscious, adj inconsciente, desmayado.
unconsciousness, n inconsciencia f; insensibilidad f, pérdida f de conocimiento.
uncontrolled, adj incontrolado, libre, desenfrenado.
unconventional, adj poco convencional.
uncooked, adj sin cocer, crudo.
uncoordinated, adj incoordinado.
uncork, vt descorchar, destapar.
uncorrected, adj sin corregir.

uncorroborated, *adj* no conifirmado, sin corroborar.

uncorrupted, *adj* incorrupto.

uncouth, *adj* grosero, mal educado.

uncover, *vt* descubrir; destapar.

uncultivated, *adj* inculto.

uncut, *adj* sin cortar; sin labrar; sin tallar.

undamaged, *adj* indemne, intacto.

undecided, *adj* question pendiente, no resuelto.

undefeated, *adj* invicto, imbatido.

undemocratic, *adj* antidemocrático.

undeniable, *adj* innegable.

undependable, *adj* poco formal, poco confiable.

under, *adv* 1. debajo; abajo, inferior; 2. *prep* debajo de, de acuerdo con, según.

underage, *adj* menor de edad.

underarm, *n* sobaco *m*, axila *f*.

undercharge, *vt* cobrar menos del precio justo a.

underclothing, *n* ropa *f* interior, ropa *f* íntima.

undercover, *adj* secreto, clandestino.

underdeveloped, *adj* infradesarrollado, subdesarrollado.

underdog, *n* desvalido *m*; perdidoso *m*.

underdone, *adj* poco hecho.

underestimate, *n* 1. estimación *f* demasiado baja; 2. *vt* subestimar; infraestimar, infravalorar.

underfed, *adj* subalimentado, desnutrido.

undergo, *vt* sufrir, experimentar; someterse a.

undergraduate, *n* estudiante *m/f* (no licenciado).

underground, *adj* subterráneo.

underhanded, *adj* taimado, clandestino.

underline, *vt* subrayar.

underling, *n* subordinado *m*, inferior *m*.

underlying, *adj* subyacente; fundamental.

undermine, *vt* socavar, minar.

underneath, *adv* debajo, por debajo.

undernourished, *adj* desnutrido.

undernourishment, *n* desnutrición *f*.

underpaid, *adj* insuficientemente retribuido.

underpay, *vt* pagar mal.

underpin, *vt* apuntalar.

underprivileged, *adj* desvalido, desfavorecido, desamparado.

underrate, *vt* subestimar.

underripe, *adj* poco maduro, verde.

underscore, *vt* subrayar, recalcar.

undersea, *adj* 1. submarino; 2. *adv* debajo del mar.

undersell, *vt* vender a precio más bajo que.

undershirt, *n* camiseta *f*.

underside, *n* superficie *f* inferior; envés *m*.

undersigned, *n* abajofirmante, el infraescrito.

understand, *vt* comprender, entender.

understandable, *adj* comprensible.

understanding, *adj* 1. comprensivo, compasivo; 2. *n* entendimiento *m*, comprensión *f*; acuerdo *m*.

understate, *vt* minimizar.

understatement, *n* atenuación *f*.

understood, *adj* comprendido.

undertake, *vt* emprender; acometer.

undertaker, *n* director *m* de pompas fúnebres.

undertaking, *n* empresa *f*; tarea *f*.

undertone, *n* voz *f* baja, sonido *m* suave.

undervalue, *vt* subvalorar, minusvalorar.

underwear, *n* ropa *f* interior, ropa *f* íntima.

underweight, *adj* de peso insuficiente.

underwrite, *vt* asegurar, asegurar contra riesgos.

undeserved, *adj* inmerecido.

undesirable, *adj* indeseable.

undeveloped, *adj* subdesarrollado.

undiagnosed, *adj* sin diagnosticar.

undigested, *adj* indigesto.

undiluted, *adj* sin diluir, puro.

undiscernible, *adj* imperceptible.

undisciplined, *adj* indisciplinado.

undiscovered, *adj* no descubierto.

undisputed, *adj* incontestable, indiscutible.

undistinguished, *adj* más bien mediocre.

undisturbed, *adj* tranquilo, sin molestar.

undivided, *adj* indiviso, íntegro, entero.

undo, *vt* deshacer, anular, arruinar.

undoubted, *adj* indudablemente.

undress, *n* 1. traje *m* de casa, desabillé *m*; 2. *vt* desnudar, 3. *vi* desnudarse.

undrinkable, *adj* no potable, imbebible.

undue, *adj* indebido, excesivo.

undulate, *vi* ondular, ondear.

unearned, *adj* no ganado.

unearth, *vt* desenterrar; descubrir.

uneasiness, *n* inquietud *f*; desasosiego *m*.

uneatable, *adj* incomible, que no se puede comer.

uneconomical, *adj* antieconómico.

unedited, *adj* inédito.

uneducated, *adj* inculto, ignorante.

unemotional, *adj* impasible, reservado.

unemployed, *adj* parado, sin empleo, desempleado.

unemployment, *n* paro *m* (forzoso), desempleo *m*.

unending, *adj* interminable, sin fin.

unendurable, *adj* inaguantable, insufrible.

unenviable, *adj* poco envidiable.

unequal, *adj* desigual; desproporcionado.

unescorted, *adj* sin escolta; sin compañía.

unethical, *adj* inmoral; poco honrado.

uneven, *adj* desigual; quebrado, ondulado.

unexpected, *adj* inesperado, inopinado.

unexpired, *adj* no vencido; no caducado.

unexplained, *adj* inexplicado.

unexplored, *adj* inexplorado.

unexposed, *adj* no descubierto; inexpuesto.

unfailing, *adj* indefectible; infalible; inagotable.

unfair, *adj* injusto, no equitativo; improcedente.

unfaithful, *adj* infiel (to a).

unfaithfulness, *n* infidelidad *f*.

unfamiliar, *adj* desconocido, nuevo.

unfashionable, *adj* pasado de moda, fuera de moda.

unfasten, *vt* desatar; desabrochar, abrir.

unfavorable, *adj* desfavorable, adverso.

unfeeling, *adj* insensible.

unfinished, *adj* incompleto, inacabado, inconcluso.

unfit, *adj* incapaz, incompetente.

unfold, *vt* 1. desplegar, 2. *vi* desplegarse.

unforeseeable, *adj* imprevisible.

unforeseen, *adj* imprevisto.

unforgettable, *adj* inolvidable.

unforgivable, *adj* imperdonable, indisculpable.

unfortunate, *adj* desgraciado, desdichado.

unfounded, *adj* infundado.

unfriendliness, *n* hostilidad *f*.

unfurnished, *adj* desamueblado, sin muebles.

ungracious, *adj* descortés, grosero.

ungrammatical, *adj* incorrecto, agramatical, antigramatical.

ungrateful, *adj* desagradecido, ingrato.

unhappy, *adj* person infeliz, desdichado.

unharmed, *adj* ileso, incólume; indemne.

unhealthy, *adj* enfermizo; malsano, insalubre.

unheard-of, *adj* inaudito.

unhitch, *vt* desenganchar.

unholy, *adj* impío; atroz.

unhook, vt desenganchar; descolgar.

unhoped-for, adj inesperado.

unhurried, adj lento, pausado, parsimonioso.

unhurt, adj ileso, incólume.

unicorn, n unicornio m.

unidentified, adj sin identificar, no identificado.

unification, n unificación f.

uniform, adj 1. uniforme; igual, constante; 2. n uniforme m.

uniformity, n uniformidad f.

unify, vt unificar, unir.

unilateral, adj unilateral.

unilingual, adj monolingüe.

unimpeachable, adj irrecusable, intachable.

unimportant, adj sin importancia, insignificante.

uninformed, adj desinformado, poco instruido, ignorante.

uninhabited, adj deshabitado, inhabitado; desierto.

uninjured, adj ileso.

uninspired, adj sin inspiración, soso, mediocre.

uninsured, adj no asegurado.

unintelligent, adj ininteligente, poco inteligente.

unintended, adj involuntario, no intencional.

uninterrupted, adj ininterrumpido.

uninvited, adj no invitado.

union, n unión f; sindicato m, gremio m obrero.

unionize, vt 1. sindicar, agremiar; 2. vi sindicarse.

unique, adj único.

uniqueness, n unicidad f.

unison, n unisonancia f; cantar al unísono.

unit, n unidad f.

unite, vt 1. unir, juntar; casar; 2. vi unirse, juntarse.

united, adj unido.

United States, n (Los) Estados m Unidos (de América).

unity, n unidad f; unión f; armonía f.

universal, adj universal.

universe, n universo m.

university, n universidad f.

unjust, adj injusto.

unjustly, adv injustamente.

unkempt, adj desaseado, descuidado; despeinado.

unkind, adj poco amable, nada amistoso.

unknown, adj desconocido, ignorado; ignoto.

unlatch, vt abrir, alzar el pestillo de.

unlawful, adj ilegal, ilícito.

unleaded, adj 1. sin plomo; 2. n gasolina f sin plomo.

unleash, vt desatraillar, soltar; desencadenar.

unless, conj a menos que...

unlettered, adj indocto.

unlicensed, adj sin permiso, sin licencia.

unlike, adj 1. desemejante, distinto; 2. prep a diferencia de.

unlikely, adj improbable, poco probable; difícil.

unlimited, adj ilimitado, sin límite.

unload, vt 1. descargar; 2. vi descargar.

unloading, n descarga f.

unlock, vt abrir (con llave).

unlovable, adj antipático, poco amable.

unloved, adj no amado; sentirse rechazado.

unlucky, adj desgraciado; funesto, nefasto.

unmanageable, adj inmanejable, difícil de manejar.

unmannerly, adj descortéz, malcriado.

unmarked, adj sin marcar; camuflado.

unmarried, adj soltero.

unmask, vt 1. desenmascarar; 2. vi descubrirse.

unmerciful, adj despiadado.

unmistak(e)able, adj inconfundible, inequívoco.

unmotivated, adj inmotivado, sin motivo.

unmoved, adj impasible; insensible a.

unnatural, adj antinatural, no natural.

unnecessary, adj innecesario, inútil.

unnerve, vt acobardar; trastornar.

unnoticed, adj inadvertido, desapercibido.

unobserved, adj desapercibido.

unobtainable, adj que no se puede conseguir.

unobtrusive, adj discreto, modesto.

unoccupied, adj deshabitado; despoblado.

unofficially, adv de modo extraoficial.

unopened, adj sin abrir.

unorganized, adj no organizado.

unorthodox, adj nada convencional.

unpack, vt desembalar, desempaquetar.

unpaid, adj por pagar, no pagado.

unpardonable, adj imperdonable, indisculpable.

unpaved, adj sin pavimentar.

unplanned, adj sin planear; imprevisto.

unpleasant, adj desagradable; repugnante.

unplug, vt desenchufar, desconectar.

unpolished, adj sin pulir; en bruto; grosero, tosco.

unpolluted, adj impoluto; no contaminado.

unpopular, adj impopular, poco popular.

unprecedented, adj sin precedente.

unpredictable, adj imprevisible, incierto.

unprejudiced, adj imparcial.

unpremeditated, adj impremeditado.

unprepared, adj no preparado; improvisado.

unpresentable, adj mal apersonado.

unpretentious, adj modesto, nada pretencioso.

unprofitable, adj improductivo; infructuoso.

unprompted, adj espontáneo.

unpronounceable, adj impronunciable.

unproved, adj no probado.

unprovoked, adj no provocado, sin provocación.

unpublished, adj inédito, sin publicar.

unpunished, adj impune; sin castigo.

unqualified, adj incompetente; sin título; no cualificado.

unquestionable, adj incuestionable, indiscutible.

unravel, vt deshebrar, desenredar.

unreadable, adj ilegible; imposible de leer.

unreal, adj irreal; imaginario, ilusorio.

unrealistic, adj ilusorio, fantástico; irrealista.

unrealized, adj no realizado.

unreasonable, adj irrazonable, poco razonable.

unrecognizable, adj irreconocible, desconocido.

unregistered, adj no registrado; sin certificar.

unrehearsed, adj improvisado; imprevisto.

unrelated, adj inconexo, no relacionado.

unreliable, adj informal, de poca confianza.

unremarkable, adj ordinario, corriente.

unrepentant, adj impenitente.

unresolved, adj problem no resuelto, pendiente.

unresponsive, adj insensible, sordo (a).

unrest, n malestar m, inquietud f.

unrestrained, adj desenfrenado, desembarazado.

unrestricted, adj sin restricción, libre.

unrevealed, adj no revelado.

unrewarded, adj sin recompensa, sin premio.

unrighteous, adj malo, perverso.

unripe, adj verde, inmaturo.

unroll, vt 1. desenrollar; 2. vt desenrollarse.

unromantic, adj poco romántico.

unsafe, adj inseguro; peligroso, arriesgado.

unsaid, adj sin decir, sin expresar.

unsalted, adj sin sal.

unsatisfactory, adj insatisfactorio.

unsatisfied, *adj* insatisfecho.

unsaturated, *adj* no saturado, insaturado.

unscheduled, *adj* no programado; no previsto.

unscrew, *vt* destornillar.

unscrupulous, *adj* sin escrúpulos.

unseal, *vt* desellar, abrir.

unsecured, *adj* no respaldado, sin aval.

unseen, *adj* oculto, invisible.

unselfish, *adj* desinteresado; abnegado; altruista.

unselfishness, *n* desinterés *m;* abnegación *f.*

unsettle, *vt* perturbar, agitar, inquietar.

unsettled, *adj* inquieto, intranquilo; variable.

unshak(e)able, *adj* inquebrantable.

unshaven, *adj* sin afeitar.

unshrinkable, *adj* inencogible.

unsinkable, *adj* insumergible.

unskilled, *adj* no cualificado; no especializado.

unsociable, *adj* insociable; poco sociable, huraño.

unsolicited, *adj* no solicitado.

unsolved, *adj* no resuelto.

unsophisticated, *adj* sencillo, cándido, ingenuo.

unspeakable, *adj* indecible; incalificable.

unspecified, *adj* no especificado.

unspoiled, *adj* intacto; no estropeado; no mimado.

unspoken, *adj* no expresado, tácito.

unstable, *adj* inestable.

unsteady, *adj* inestable, inseguro; inconstante; movedizo.

unstop, *vt* desobstruir, desatascar.

unstructured, *adj* sin estructura, no estructurado.

unsubmissive, *adj* insumiso.

unsuccessful, *adj* fracasado; infructuoso, inútil.

unsuitable, *adj* inapropiado; inconveniente.

unsure, *adj* inseguro, poco seguro.

unsurmountable, *adj* insuperable.

unsurpassed, *adj* insuperado, sin par.

unsuspecting, *adj* nada suspicaz, sin recelo.

unsweetened, *adj* sin azucarar.

untainted, *adj* inmaculado, no corrompido.

untamed, *adj* indomado.

untangle, *vt* desenmarañar.

untapped, *adj* sin explotar.

untaxed, *adj* libre de impuestos.

unthinkable, *adj* inconcebible, impensable.

untidiness, *n* desaliño *m;* desorden *m.*

untie, *vt* desatar.

untold, *adj* nunca contado, inédito; nunca revelado.

untouched, *adj* intacto; incólume, indemne.

untrained, *adj* inexperto.

untransferable, *adj* intransferible.

untroubled, *adj* tranquilo, sosegado.

untrue, *adj* falso; ficticio, imaginario.

untruthful, *adj* mentiroso, falso.

unused, *adj* nuevo, sin usar; sin estrenar.

unusual, *adj* insólito, poco común, inusual.

unveil, *vt* quitar el velo a; descubrir.

unveiling, *n* descubrimiento *m* (de una estatua); inauguración *f.*

unverified, *adj* sin verificar.

unwanted, *adj* superfluo; no deseado.

unwary, *adj* incauto, imprudente.

unwed, *adj* soltero.

unwelcome, *adj* importuno, molesto.

unwilling, *adj* desinclinado; no querer.

unwillingly, *adv* de mala gana.

unwind, *vt* 1. desenvolver; desovillar; 2. *vi* desenvolverse; desovillarse; esparcirse, relajarse.

unwise, *adj* imprudente, desaconsejado.

unworldly, *adj* poco mundano, poco realista.

unworthy, *adj* indigno (de).

unwrap, *vt* desenvolver; deshacer, desempaquetar.

unwritten, *adj* no escrito.

unyielding, *adj* inflexible.

upbraid, *vt* reprender, censurar.

upbringing, *n* educación *f,* crianza *f.*

upcoming, *adj* venidero, futuro; que se acerca,

update, *n* 1. actualización *f;* 2. *vt* actualizar.

upgrade, *n* 1. cuesta *f,* pendiente *f;* 2. *vt* ascender; asignar a un grado más alto.

uphill, *adv* cuesta arriba.

uphold, *vt* sostener, apoyar.

upholster, *vt* tapizar, entapizar.

upholsterer, *n* tapicero(a) *m/f.*

upholstery, *n* tapicería *f,* tapizado *m.*

upkeep, *n* conservación *f;* mantenimiento *m.*

uplift, *n* 1. inspiración *f;* 2. *vt* inspirar, edificar.

upper, *adj* superior, más alto; de arriba.

upper-case, *n* mayúsculo *m,* de letra *f* mayúscula,

uppermost, *adj* más alto; principal.

upraise, *vt* levantar.

upright, *adj* vertical; derecho; plano vertical, recto.

uprising, *n* alzamiento *m,* sublevación *f.*

uproar, *n* alboroto *m,* tumulto *m;* escándalo *m.*

uproot, *vt* desarraigar, arrancar; eliminar, extirpar.

upset, *n* 1. vuelco *m;* revés *m,* contratiempo *m;* trastorno *m; 2. vt* volcar, trastornar; derramar; 3. *vr* acongojarse, apurarse; preocuparse.

upsetting, *adj* inquietante, desconcertante,

upstairs, *adv* arriba.

upstart, *adj* 1. advenedizo; 2. *n* advenedizo(a) *m/f.*

upstream, *adv* aguas arriba, río arriba.

up-to-date, *adj* moderno, actual; al día.

up-to-the-minute, *adj* de última hora.

upward, *adj* ascendente, ascensional.

uranium, *n* uranio *m.*

Uranus, *n* Urano *m.*

urban, *adj* urbano; zona *f* urbana.

urbane, *adj* urbano, cortés, fino.

urbanization, *n* urbanización *f.*

urbanize, *vt* urbanizar.

urchin, n galopín *m,* pilluelo *m,* golfillo *m.*

urea, *n* urea *f.*

urethra, *n* uretra *f.*

urge, *n* 1. impulso *m;* 2. *vt* instar; incitar.

urgent, *adj* urgente; apremiante, perentorio.

urinal, *n* urinario *m;* orinal *m.*

urinary, *adj* urinario.

urinate, *vt* 1. orinar. 2. *vi* orinarse.

urine, *n* orina *f,* orines *m.*

urology, *n* urología *f.*

usage, *n* uso *m,* costumbre *f.*

use, *n* 1. uso *m,* empleo *m;* manejo *m;* 2. *vt* usar, emplear; servirse de, utilizar, consumir.

used, *adj* 1. usado; gastado, viejo; 2. acostumbrado.

useful, *adj* útil; provechoso.

usefulness, *n* utilidad *f;* valor *m;* provecho *m.*

useless, *adj* inútil; inservible; inoperante.

user, *n* usuario(a) *m/f.*

usher, *n* 1. ujier *m,* portero *m;* acomodador *m;* 2. *vt* hacer pasar.

usherette, n acomodadora *f.*

usual, *adj* usual; acostumbrado, habitual.

usurp, *vt* usurpar.

usurpation, *n* usurpación *f.*

usury, *n* usura *f.*

utensil, *n* utensilio *m.*

uterus, *n* útero *m.*

utilitarian, *adj* 1. utilitario; 2. *n* utilitarista *m/f.*

utility, n 1. utilidad f; 2. empresa f de servicio m público.

utilization, n utilización f.

utilize, vt utilizar.

utmost, adj supremo, mayor.

utopia, n utopía f.

utter, adj 1. completo, total; 2. vt proferir, decir; 3. vi saltar.

utterly, adv completamente, totalmente, del todo.

V

V, v, n (letra f) V, v.

vacancy, n vaciedad f, vacuidad f; vacante m.

vacant, adj libre, desocupado; disponible.

vacate, vt house desocupar; dejar.

vacation, n vacaciones f.

vaccinate, vt vacunar.

vaccination, n vacunación f.

vaccine, n vacuna f.

vacillate, vi oscilar; vacilar, dudar.

vacuum, n 1. vacío m; 2. vt pasar la aspiradora por.

vacuum-cleaner, n aspiradora f.

vagabond, adj 1. vagabundo; 2. n vagabundo m.

vagary, n capricho m, extravagancia f.

vagina, n vagina f.

vagrancy, n vagancia f, vagabundaje m.

vagrant, adj vagabundo, vagante; errante.

vague, n vago; indistinto, incierto; impreciso.

vain, adj vano, inútil.

vale, n valle m.

valence, n valencia f.

valiant, adj esforzado, denodado, valiente.

valid, adj válido; valedero.

validate, vt convalidar.

valise, n valija f, maleta f.

valley, n valle m.

valor, n valor m, valentía f.

valuable, adj 1. valioso; estimable; 2. n objetos m de valor, valores m.

value, n 1. valor m; estimación f; importancia f; 2. vt valorar, valorizar, tasar; estimar.

valve, n válvula f; lámpara f.

vampire, n vampiro m.

van, n camioneta f, furgoneta f.

vandalism, n vandalismo m, gamberrismo m.

vandalize, vt destruir, estropear, arruinar.

vanilla, n vainilla f.

vanish, vi desaparecer, desvanecerse.

vanity, n vanidad f.

vapor, n 1. vapor m; 2. vi fanfarronear; decir disparates de.

vaporize, vt vaporizar, volatilizar.

variable, adj variable.

variation, n variación f.

varied, adj variado.

variety, n variedad f.

various, adj vario, diverso.

varnish, n 1. barniz m; 2. esmalte m para las uñas; 3. vt barnizar; laquear, esmaltar.

vascular, vi variar.

vascular, adj vascular.

vase, n florero m, jarrón m.

vast, adj vasto; inmenso, enorme; dilatado.

vastness, n inmensidad f.

vat, n tina f, tinaja f, cuba f.

vault, n 1. bóveda f; bodega f; sótano m, cámara f acorazada; tumba f; salto m; 2. vt abovedar; 3. vi saltar.

veal, n ternera f.

veer, vi virar; girar, cambiar.

vegetable, n vegetal f; legumbre f.

vegetarian, adj 1. vegetariano; 2. n vegetariano(a) m/f.

vegetate, vi vegetar.

vegetation, n vegetación f.

vehemence, n vehemencia f; violencia f, pasión.

vehement, adj vehemente; violento, apasionado.

vehicle, n vehículo m.

vehicular, adj de vehículos, para coches.

veil, n 1. velo m; 2. vt velar.

vein, n vena f.

veined, adj veteado, jaspeado.

velocity, n velocidad f.

velvet, n terciopelo m.

venal, adj venal.

venality, n venalidad f.

vend, n vender.

vendetta, n enemistad f mortal, odio m de sangre.

vendor, n vendedor(a) m/f.

venerable, adj venerable.

venerate, vt venerar.

venereal, adj venéreo.

vengeance, n venganza f.

vengeful, adj (liter) vengativo.

venom, n veneno m; virulencia f, malignidad f.

venomous, adj venenoso; virulento.

venous, adj venoso.

vent, n 1. abertura f; válvula f; 2. vt purgar.

ventilate, vt ventilar.

ventilation, n ventilación f.

ventricle, n ventrículo m.

ventriloquist, n ventrílocuo(a) m/f.

venture, n 1. aventura f, empresa f (arriesgada); 2. vt aventurar; jugar; expresar.

veracity, n veracidad f.

veranda, n veranda f, terraza f, galería f.

verb, n verbo m.

verbal, adj verbal.

verbalize, vt expresar en palabras.

verbatim, adj palabra por palabra, literal.

verdict, n veredicto m, fallo m, sentencia f, juicio m.

verge, n borde m, margen m.

verification, n comprobación f, verificación f.

verify, vt comprobar, verificar.

versatile, adj versátil.

versatility, n versatilidad f.

verse, n estrofa f; versículo m; verso m.

versed, adj versado en.

version, n versión f.

versus, prep contra.

vertebra, n vértebra f.

vertebral, adj vertebral.

vertebrate, adj vertebrado.

vertical, adj 1. vertical; 2. n vertical f.

verve, n energía f, empuje m; brío m.

very, adv 1. muy; mucho; 2. adj mismo, mero.

vesicle, n vesícula f.

vespers, n vísperas f.

vessel, n vaso m; vasija f, recipiente m; barco, bote.

vest, n camiseta f; (US) chaleco m.

vestal, adj 1. vestal; 2. n vestal f.

vestige, n vestigio m, rastro m.

vetch, n arveja f.

veteran, adj 1. veterano; 2. n veterano m.

veterinarian, n veterinario m/f.

veterinary, adj veterinario.

veto, n 1. veto m; tener veto; 2. vt vedar, vetar.

vex, vt molestar.

via, prep vía, por vía de, por medio de.

viable, adj viable.

viaduct, n viaducto m.

vial, n frasquito m.

vibrant, adj 1. vibrante; 2. n vibrante f.

vibrate, vt/i vibrar.

vibration, n vibración f.

vicarious, adj experimentado por otro; indirecto.

vice, n vicio m.

vice-versa, adv viceversa.

vicinity, n vecindad f, región f.

vicious, adj vicioso; depravado, perverso.

viciousness, n viciosidad f; perversidad f.

victim, n víctima f.

victimize, vt victimizar; escoger y castigar.

victorious, adj victorioso.

victory, n victoria f; triunfo m.

video, n 1. vídeo m; 2. vt hacer un vídeo de.

view, n 1. vista f; panorama m; perspectiva f; 2. vt mirar; ver, contemplar; examinar.

viewer, n espectador(a) m/f.

viewpoint, n punto m de vista.

vigil, n vigilia f.

vigilant, adj vigilante; desvelado, alerta.

vigor, n vigor m, energía f, pujanza f.

vigorous, adj vigoroso, enérgico, pujante.

vile, adj vil; infame, detestable.

village, n aldea f, pueblecito m.

vindicate, vt vindicar, justificar.

vindictive, adj vengativo; rencoroso.

vine, n vid f.

vinegar, n vinagre m.

vineyard, n viña f, viñedo m.

vintage, n vendimia f; cosecha f.

vinyl, n vinilo m; acetate acetato m de vinilo.

viola, n viola f; viola f de gamba.

violate, vt violar.

violation, n violación f.

violent, adj violento.

violet, n violeta f.

violin, n violín m.

viper, n víbora f.

virgin, adj virgen.

virility, n virilidad f.

virology, n virología f.

virtual, adj virtual.

virtue, n virtud f.

virtuoso, n virtuoso m/f.

viscera, n vísceras f.

viscose, adj 1. viscoso; 2. n viscosa f.

vise, n torno m de banco.

visibility, n visibilidad f.

visible, adj visible.

vision, n visión f.

visionary, adj 1. visionario; 2. n visionario(a) m/f.

visit, n 1. visita f; 2. vt visitar, hacer una visita a.

visitor, n visitante m/f.

visor, n visera f.

visualize, vt representarse (en la mente), imaginarse.

vital, adj 1. esencial; imprescindible; 2. crítico; 3. enérgico, vivo, lleno de vida.

vitality, n vitalidad f, energía f.

vitalize, vt vitalizar, vivificar.

vitamin, n vitamina f.

vivacious, adj animado, vivaz, alegre, lleno de vida.

vivacity, n animación f, vivacidad f, vida f.

vivid, adj vivo; color, intenso; súbito.

vividness, n viveza f; intensidad f; vivacidad f.

vixen, n zorra f, raposa f; arpía f.

vocabulary, n vocabulario m, léxico m.

vocal, adj 1. vocal; 2. n voz f, canto f.

vocalist, n cantante m/f; vocalista m/f.

vocalize, vt vocalizar.

vocation, n vocación f.

vociferate, vt/i vociferar, gritar.

vogue, n boga f, moda f.

voice, n 1. voz f; 3. vt expresar, hacerse eco de.

voiceless, adj mudo.

void, adj 1. vacío; desocupado; vacante; 2. nulo, inválido; 3. n vacío m; hueco m, espacio m.

volatile, adj volátil.

volcanic, adj volcánico.

volcano, n volcán m.

volition, n volición f.

volley, n 1. descarga f, (Dep) voleo m; 2. vt volear.

volt, n voltio m.

voltage, n voltaje m.

voluble, adj person locuaz, hablador.

volume, n volumen m.

voluminous, adj voluminoso.

voluntarily, adv voluntariamente, espontáneamente.

voluntary, adj voluntario, voluntariamente.

volunteer, n 1. voluntario m; 2. vt ofrecer; hacer.

vomit, n 1. vómito m; 2. vt vomitar, arrojar.

voracious, adj voraz.

voracity, n voracidad f.

votary, n devoto m.

vote, n 1. voto m; 2. vt votar.

voter, n votante m/f.

votive, adj votivo.

vow, n 1. voto m; promesa f solemne; 2. vt jurar.

vowel, n vocal f.

voyage, n 1. viaje m; 2. vt viajar.

voyager, n viajero(a) m/f.

vulcanize, vt vulcanizar.

vulgar, adj vulgar.

vulgarity, n vulgaridad f; ordinariez f.

vulnerable, adj vulnerable (to a).

vulture, n buitre m.

W

W, w, n (letra f) W, w.

wad, n 1. taco m, tapón m; bolita f de algodón; 2. vt rellenar; acolchar.

waddle, n 1. anadeo m; 2. vi anadear.

wade, n 1. vadear; 2. vi caminar por el agua.

wafer, n galleta f; oblea f; (Eccl) hostia f.

wag, n 1. meneo m, movimiento m; coleada f; 2. bromista m/f; 3. vt mover, menear, agitar.

wage, n 1. salario m; jornal m; pago m; premio m; 2. vt (guerra) hacer; proseguir.

wagon, n carro m; vagón m; camioneta f.

waif, n niño m abandonado, niña f abandonada.

wail, n 1. lamento m, gemido m; 2. vi lamentarse, gemir.

wailing, n lamentación f, lamentaciones f; gemidos m.

waist, n cintura f, talle m.

wait, n 1. espera f; pausa f, intervalo m; 2. vt esperar; aplazar; guardar para después.

waiter, n camarero m, mesero m.

waitress, n camarera f, mesera f.

waive, vt renunciar a; prescindir de.

wake, n 1. vela f, velatorio m; 2. vt despertar; 3. vi despertarse.

wakeful, adj despierto; vigilante; desvelado; insomne.

waken, vt/i despertar.

walk, n 1. paseo m; caminata f, excursión f a pie; 2. vi llevar a paseo, pasear; 3. vi andar, caminar.

walker, n paseante m/f; peatón m; marchador(a) m/f; andarín m.

walk-out, n huelga f.

wall, n 1. muro m; pared f; muralla f; 2. vt murar.

wallet, n cartera f, billetera f.

wallop, n 1. golpe m, golpazo m; 2. vt golpear.

wallow, n 1. revuelco m; 2. vi revolcarse.

wallpaper, n 1. papel m de empapelar; 2. vt empapelar.

walnut, n nuez f; nogal m.

walrus, n morsa f.

waltz, n 1. vals m; 2. vi valsar.

wan, adj pálido, débil.

wand, n vara f.

wander, vt 1. vagar por, recorrer; 2. vi vagar.

wanderer, n nómada m/f; errante m/f.

wane, n decaer, menguar, disminuir.

waning, adj 1. menguante; 2. n menguante f.

want, n 1. falta f; ausencia f; carencia f; escasez f; 2. miseria f, pobreza f; 3. necesidad f; 4. vt necesitar; exigir, requerir.

wanton, adj inconsiderado, licensioso.

war, n 1. guerra f; 2. vi guerrear.

ward, n 1. tutela f, custodia f; 2. distrito m electoral; 3. (Hosp) sala f, crujía f.

warden, n guardián m; vigilante m/f.

wardrobe, n vestidos m, vestuario m.

warehouse, n 1. almacén m; 2. vt almacenar.

wares, n mercancías f.

warm, adj 1. caliente; templado, tibio; cálido; 2. vt calentar; alegrar, acalorar.

warming, n recalentamiento m.

warmth, n calor m; ardor m.

warn, vt avisar, advertir; amonestar; prevenir.

warning, n 1. aviso m, advertencia f.

warp, n 1. urdimbre f; 2. deformación f, alabeo m, comba f; 3. vt deformar, alabear, torcer; pervertir.

warped, adj deformado, torcido.

warrant, n 1. autorización f, justificación f; 2. cédula f, certificado m; 3. mandato m, orden f; 4. vt autorizar, justificar.

warranty, n garantía f.

warrior, n guerrero m.

wart, n verruga f.

wary, adj cauteloso, cauto.

wash, n 1. lavado m; baño m; 2. vt lavar; fregar.

washable, adj lavable.

washer, n arandela f; lavadora f.

washing, n lavado m, el lavar.

washbowl, n jofaina f, palangana f.

washroom, n lavabo m, sanitarios m.

wasp, n avispa f.

waspish, adj irascible; de prontes enojos.

wastage, n desgaste m, desperdicio m; pérdida f.

waste, adj 1. sobrante; 2. n derroche m, desgate m; despilfarro m; desperdicios m; 3. vt malgastar, derrochar.

wasted, adj desaprovechado; inútil, vano.

watch, n 1. vigilancia f; vigilia f, vela f; 2. vt guardar, vigilar; proteger.

watchful, adj vigilante; observador; desvelado.

water, n 1. agua f; 2. vt regar; abrevar; aguar.

watered, adj aguado.

watering, n riego m.

watt, n vatio m.

wattage, n vataje m.

wave, n 1. ola f; onda f; 2. vt agitar, blandir; señalar con la mano.

wavelength, n longitud f de onda.

waver, vi oscilar; dudar, vacilar.

wax, n 1. cera f; 2. vt encerar; 3. vi crecer; ponerse, hacerse.

way, n 1. camino m, vía f; carretera f; calle f; 2. medio m; forma; manera f, modo m.

weak, adj débil; flojo.

weaken, vt debilitar; disminuir, reducir.

weakness, n debilidad f; flojedad f; tenuidad f.

wealth, n riqueza f; abundancia f.

wealthy, adj rico; acaudalado, pudiente.

wean, vt destetar.

weaning, n destete m, ablactación f.

weapon, n arma f.

wear, n 1. uso m; 2. deterioro m, desgaste m; 3. ropa f; prenda f; 4 vt llevar, usar, gastar; traer, traer puesto.

weariness, n cansancio m, fatiga f; abatimiento m.

weary, adj 1. cansado, fatigado; abatido, hastiado; 2. vt cansar, fatigar; aburrir.

weasel, n comadreja f.

weather, n 1. tiempo m; 2. vt aguantar, hacer frente a; superar, sobrevivir a.

weathered, adj maduro, curado.

weave, n 1. tejido m; textura f; 2. vt tejer; trenzar; entretejer, entrelazar.

weaver, n tejedor(a) m/f.

weaving, n tejeduría f.

web, n tela f, tejido m; telaraña f; (duck) membrana f.

wed, vt casarse con; casar.

wedded, adj casado.

wedding, n boda f; casamiento m; bodas f.

wedge, n 1. cuña f; calce m, calza f; 2. vt acuñar; calzar.

Wednesday, n miércoles m.

wee, adj pequenito, diminuto.

weed, n 1. mala hierba f; 2. vt escardar, desherbar.

weeding, n escarda f.

week, n semana f.

weekday, n día m laborable; on a entre semana.

weekend, n fin m de semana.

weep, vi llorar, derramar.

weeping, adj 1. lloroso; willow sauce m llorón; 2. n llanto m, lágrimas f.

weevil, n gorgojo m.

weigh, vt pesar.

weight, n peso m; pesadez f.

weird, adj misterioso, fantástico, sobrenatural.

welcome, adj 1. bienvenido; 2. n bienvenida f; 3. vt dar la bienvenida a.

weld, vt soldar.

welder, n soldador m.

welding, *n* soldadura *f.*

welfare, *n* **1.** bienestar *m,* bien *m;* **2.** asistencia *f* social, beneficencia *f* social.

well, *adv* **1.** bien; muy bien; también; **2.** *n* pozo *m;* fuente *f,* manantial *m.*

welt, *n* **1.** vira *f;* verdugón *m;* **2.** *vt* poner vira a.

wen, *n* lobanillo *m,* quiste *m* sebáceo.

west, *n* oeste *m,* occidente *m.*

western, *adj* occidental.

westerner, *n* habitante *m/f* del Oeste.

westernize, *vt* occidentalizar.

wet, *adj* **1.** húmedo; **2.** mojado; **3.** *n* humedad *f;* **4.** *vt* mojar, humedecer.

whack, *n* **1.** golpe *m* grande; **2.** *vt* golpear, aporrear.

whale, *n* ballena *f.*

wharf, *n* muelle *m.*

what, *adj* **1.** el ... que, la ... que, lo ... que; **2.** qué; cuál de ...; **2.** *pron* el que, la que, lo que.

whatever, *pron* **1.** lo que; todo lo que; **2.** *adj* qualquiera que.

wheat, *n* trigo *m.*

wheedle, *vt* engatusar.

wheel, *n* **1.** rueda *f;* torno *m;* timón *m;* **2.** *vt* hacer girar; hacer rodar; empujar.

wheeze, *n* **1.** resuello *m,* resuello *m* asmático; respiración *f* sibilante; **2.** *vi* resollar (con ruido), jadear.

whelp, *n* **1.** cachorro *m;* **2.** *vi* parir (la perra etc).

when, *adv* **1.** cuándo; **2.** *conj* cuando.

whenever, *conj* siempre que; cada vez que.

where, *adv* **1.** ¿dónde?, ¿a dónde? **2.** *conj* donde adonde.

whereas, *conj* visto que, por cuanto, mientras.

wherever, *conj* dondequiera que.

whet, *vt* afilar, amolar; estimular, despertar, aguzar.

whether, *conj* si.

which, *adj* **1.** ¿qué?; ¿cuál?; **2.** *pron* ¿cuál?; **3.** que; lo que.

whichever, *adj* cualquier.

while, *conj* **1.** mientras, mientras que; **2.** *n* rato *m.*

whim, *n* capricho *m,* antojo *m,* manía *f.*

whimper, *n* quejido *m,* gemido *m;* **2.** *vi* lloriquear.

whimpering, *adj* **1.** que lloriquea; **2.** *n* lloriqueo *m.*

whine, *n* **1.** quejido *m,* gimoteo *m,* **2.** *vi* quejarse, gimotear.

whip, *n* **1.** látigo *m;* azote *m,* zurriago *m;* **2.** *vt* azotar.

whiplash, *n* **1.** tralla *f,* latigazo *m.*

whipped, *adj* cream etc batido.

whipping, *n* azotamiento *m;* flagelación *f;* derrota *f.*

whir, *n* **1.** zumbido; **2.** *vi* girar zumbando.

whirl, *n* **1.** giro *m,* vuelta *f;* rotación *f;* el girar; **2.** *vt* hacer girar, hacer dar vueltas, dar vueltas a.

whisk, *n* **1.** escobilla *f;* mosqueador *m;* espumadera *f,* batidor *m;* **2.** *vt* batir.

whisker, *n* pelo *m* (de la barba).

whisper, *n* **1.** cuchicheo *m;* **2.** *vt* susurrar; **3.** *vi* cuchichear, hablar muy bajo.

whispering, *n* cuchicheo *m;* susurro *m.*

whistle, *n* **1.** silbido *m,* silbo *m,* pitido *m;* **2.** *vt* silbar.

white, *adj* **1.** blanco; **2.** *n* blanco *m.*

whiten, *vt/i* blanquear.

whiting, *n* pescadilla *f.*

whittle, *vt* cortar pedazos a, tallar.

whizz, *n* **1.** silbido *m,* zumbido *m;* **2.** *vi* silbar.

who, *pron* ¿quién?; que; el que, quien.

whoever, *pron* quienquiera que, cualquiera que; quién.

whole, *adj* **1.** todo, entero; total: íntegro; **2.** sano; ileso, intacto **3.** *n* todo *m.*

wholesale, *n* venta *f* al por mayor.

wholesaler, *n* comerciante *m/f* al por mayor.

wholly, *adv* enteramente, completamente.

whom, *pron* a quién.

whopper, *n* cosa *f* muy grande; mentirón *m.*

whose, *pron* **1.** de quién; **2.** *adj* ¿quién?.

why, *adv* **1.** ¿por qué?, ¿para qué?; ¿por qué razón?; **2.** *interj* ¡cómo!, ¿qué pasa?; **3.** *n* porqué *m;* causa *f,* razón *f.*

wick, *n* mecha *f.*

wicked, *adj* malo, malvado; perverso; inicuo.

wicker, *n* mimbre *m.*

wide, *adj* **1.** ancho; extenso; **2.** *adv* lejos.

widen, *vt* **1.** ensanchar; ampliar, extender; **2.** *vi* ensancharse.

widow, *n* **1.** viuda *f;* **2.** *vt* dejar viuda (o viudo).

widower, *n* viudo *m.*

width, *n* anchura *f;* extensión *f,* amplitud *f.*

wield, *vt* manejar; ejercer, poseer.

wife, *n* mujer *f,* esposa *f;* parienta.

wig, *n* peluca *f.*

wiggle, *n* **1.** meneo *m;* contoneo *m;* a contonearse; **2.** *vt* menear.

wild, *adj* salvaje; silvestre.

wilderness, *n* desierto *m,* yermo *m,* tierra *f* virgen.

wilful, *adj* voluntarioso; testarudo.

will, *n* **1.** voluntad *f;* albedrío *m;* deseo *m;* **2.** *vt* querer; ordenar, disponer.

will, *v* aux para formar el tiempo futuro.

willing, *adj* servicial; complaciente.

willingness, *n* buena voluntad *f,* complacencia *f.*

willow, *n* sauce *m.*

wilt, *vt* marchitar; debilitar, hacer decaer.

win, *n* **1.** victoria *f,* éxito *m;* **2.** *vt* gana.

wince, *n* **1.** mueca *f* de dolor; **2.** *vi* hacer una mueca de dolor.

wind, *n* **1.** viento *m;* **2.** *vt* dar cuerda al reloj, enrollar.

winding, *adj* tortuoso, sinuoso, serpentino.

windmill, *n* molino *m* de viento.

window, *n* ventana *f;* ventanilla *f.*

windproof, *adj* a prueba de viento.

windshield, *n* parabrisas *m.*

windshield wipers, *n* limpiaparabrisas *m.*

windy, *adj* ventoso; de mucho viento.

wine, *n* vino *m.*

winery, *n* lagar *m.*

wing, *n* **1.** ala *f;* **2.** *vt* tocar, herir en el ala.

wink, *n* pestañeo *m;* guiño *m;* **2.** *vt* eye guiñar.

winking, *n* pestañeo *m.*

winkle, *n* **1.** bígaro *m,* bigarro *m;* **2.** *vt* hacer salir a uno.

winner, *n* ganador(a) *m/f.*

winning, *adj* triunfante; atrayente, simpático.

winter, *n* invierno *m.*

wipe, *n* **1.** limpión *m;* **2.** *vt* limpiar; enjugar.

wire, *n* **1.** alambre *m;* **2.** *vt* instalar el alambrado de; alambrar; telegrafiar.

wiring, *n* alambrado *m,* cableado *m.*

wisdom, *n* sabiduría *f;* saber *m;* prudencia *f.*

wise, *adj* sabio; prudente, juicioso.

wish, *n* **1.** deseo *m;* ruego *m;* **2.** *vt* desear, querer.

wishful, *adj* deseoso.

wistful, *adj* triste, melancólico; pensativo.

wit, *n* **1.** agudeza *f;* **2.** inteligencia *f,* entendimiento *m,* juicio *m;* talento *m.*

witch, *n* bruja *f.*

witchcraft, *n* brujería *f.*

with, *prep* con; en compañía de; con.

withdraw, *vt* retirar, sacar, quitar.

withdrawal, *n* retirada *f;* retiro *m;* abandono *m.*

withhold, *vt* retener; negar, suspender.

within, *adv* 1. dentro; 2. *prep* dentro de, al alcance de.

without, *adv* fuera; por fuera; desde fuera.

witness, *n* 1. testimonio *m;* en fe de; 2. *vt* asistir a, presenciar; testimoniar.

wittiness, *n* agudeza *f,* viveza *f* de ingenio.

wizard, *n* hechicero *m,* brujo *m,* mago *m.*

wobble, *n* 1. bamboleo *m,* tambaleo *m;* 2. *vi* bambolear, tambalearse; vacilar, oscilar.

wobbly, *adj* inseguro, poco firme, cojo.

wodge, *n* trozo *m.*

woe, *n* aflicción *f,* dolor *m;* mal *m.*

wolf, *n* lobo *m.*

wolverine, *n* carcayú *m,* glotón *m.*

woman, *n* mujer *f.*

womb, n matriz *f,* útero *m.*

wonder, *n* 1. maravilla *f;* prodigio *m;* portento *m,* milagro *m;* 2. *vt* desear saber, preguntarse.

wonderful, *adj* maravilloso; estupendo.

wood, *n* bosque *m;* madera.

wooden, *adj* de madera.

wool, *n* lana *f;* pelo *m.*

word, *n* 1. palabra *f;* vocablo *m;* voz *f;* 2. *vt* redactar; expresar.

work, *n* 1. trabajo *m;* empleo *m,* ocupación *f;* 2. *vt* hacer trabajar, trabajar.

worker, *n* trabajador(a) *m/f;* obrero(a) *m/f.*

workshop, *n* taller *m.*

world, *n* mundo *m,* tierra *f.*

worldliness, *n* mundanería *f.*

worm, *n* 1. gusano *m;* lombriz *f;* 2. *vi* serpentear.

worn, *adj* roto, raido, gastado.

worrier, *n* aprensivo *m/f.*

worry, *n* 1. inquietud *f,* preocupación *f;* 2. *vt* inquietar, preocupar.

worsen, *vt* agravar, hacer peor; hacer más difícil.

worship, *n* 1. adoración; 2. *vt* adorar, venerar.

worst, *adj* 1. peor; 2. *adv* peor; 3. *n* lo peor;.

worth, *adj* 1. equivalente a, que vale, del valor de; 2. digno de, que merece; 3. *n* valor *m.*

worthless, *adj* sin valor; inútil.

worthy, *adj* digno, meritoso.

would, *v aux* para formar el modo condicional.

worthwhile, *adj* valioso, útil.

wound, *n* 1. herida *f;* 2. *vt* herir.

wounding, *adj* remark, hiriente, mordaz.

wraith, *n* fantasma *m.*

wrangle, *n* 1. altercado *m,* riña *f,* pelea *f;* 2. *vi* reñir pelear; regatear.

wrap, *n* 1. bata *f,* abrigo *m;* 2. *vt* envolver; arropar.

wreak, *vt* ejecutar; hacer, causar.

wreath, *n* guirnalda *f,* corona *f.*

wreathe, *vt* ceñir, rodear; trenzar; entrelazar.

wreck, *n* 1. naufragio *m;* ruina *f,* desastre *m;* 2. *vt* hundir, destruir.

wreckage, *n* ruina *f,* destrucción *f.*

wrench, *n* 1. arranque *m,* tirón *m;* torcedura *f;* 2. *vt* arrancar, tirar violentamente.

wrestle, *n* 1. lucha *f;* partido *m* de lucha; 2. *vt* luchar.

wretch, *n* desgraciado(a) *m/f.*

wretched, *adj* desgraciado, desdichado; miserable.

wring, *vt* torcer, retorcer; escurrir; 2. *n* exprimir.

wrinkle, *n* 1. arruga *f;* pliegue *m.*

wrist, *n* muñeca *f.*

writ, *n* escritura *f;* orden *f,* mandato *m* judicial.

write, *vt* escribir; redactar; poner por escrito.

writer, *n* escritor(ora) *m/f;* autor(ora) *m/f.*

writhe, *vi* retorcerse, contorcerse; debatirse.

writing, *n* el escribir, escritura *f;* in por escrito.

wrong, *adj* 1. malo, inicuo; injusto; 2. erróneo, incorrecto, inexacto; 3. *n* mal *m;* injusticia *f;* agravio *m,* entuerto *m;* 4. *vt* agraviar; ser injusto con; hacer daño a.

wrongful, *adj* injusto.

wry, *adj* torcido.

X, x, *n* (letra *f*) X, x.

Xmas, *n* Christmas *f.*

X-ray, *n* radiografía *f.*

xylophone, *n* xilófono *m.*

Y

Y, y, *n* (letra *f*) Y, y.

yacht, *n* yate *m,* velero *m,* balandra *f.*

yachting, *n* deporte *m* de la vela, balandrismo *m.*

yank, *n* 1. tirón *m;* 2. *vt* tirar de.

yap, *n* 1. ladrido *m* agudo; 2. *vi* dar ladridos agudos.

yard, *n* patio *m;* corral *m;* (measure) yarda *f.*

yardage, *n* metraje *m.*

yardstick, *n* vara *f* de medir; criterio *m.*

yarn, *n* hilo *m* hilaza *f.*

yawn, *n* 1. bostezo *m;* 2. *vt* decir bostezando.

year, *n* año *m.*

yearbook, *n* anuario *m.*

yearling, *adj* 1. primal, 2. *n* primal.

yearn, *vi* suspirar; to for anhelar, añorar, ansiar.

yearning, *adj* 1. anhelante; 2. *n* anhelo *m,* añoran- za *f.*

yeast, *n* levadura *f.*

yell, *n* 1. grito *m,* alarido *m,* chillido *m;* 2. *vt* gritar.

yelling, *n* gritos *m,* alaridos *m,* chillidos *m.*

yellow, *adj* amarillo.

yelp, *n* 1. gañido *m;* 2. *vi* gañir; gritar, dar un grito.

yes, *adv* sí.

yesterday, *adv* 1. ayer; 2. *n* ayer *m.*

yet, *adv* todavía, aún; as hasta ahora, todavía.

yew, *n* tejo *m.*

yield, *n* 1. producción *f;* productividad *f;* cosecha *f;* 2. *vt* producir, dar; rendir; 3. *vi* rendirse, someterse; ceder.

yielding, *adj* flexible, blando.

yoke, *n* 1. yunta *f;* balancín *m,* percha *f;* horquilla *f;* 2. *vt* uncir, acoplar.

yokel, *n* palurdo *m,* patán *m.*

yolk, *n* yema *f* (de huevo).

yon, *adv* aquel.

yore, *n* de antaño, de otro tiempo, de hace siglos.

you, *pron* (informal) tú, vosotros, vosotras, (formal) usted, ustedes; le, la, les.

young, *adj* joven; nuevo, reciente.

youngster, *n* joven *m/f*, jovencito(a) *m/f*.

your, *adj* tu(s), vuestro(s), vuestra(s); su, sus.

yours, *poss pron* (el) tuyo, (la) tuya; (el) vuestro.

yourself, *pron* (informal) tú mismo, tú misma; te; ti; (formal) usted mismo, usted misma.

youth, *n* juventud *f*.

yowl, *n* **1.** aullido; **2.** *vi* aullar.

Z

Z, z, *n* (letra *f*) Z z.

zeal, *n* celo *m*, entusiasmo *m*.

zealous, *adj* celoso (de), entusiasta (de).

zebra, *n* cebra *f*.

zenith, *n* cenit *m*.

zephyr, *n* céfiro *m*.

zeppelin, *n* zepelín *m*.

zero, *adj* cero, nulo.

zest, *n* entusiasmo *m;* gusto *m*, sabor *m*.

zestfully, *adv* con entusiasmo.

zinc, *n* cinc *m*.

zip, *n* silbido *m*, zumbido *m;* energía *f;* brío *m*.

zipper, *n* **1.** cierre *m* cremallera; **2.** *vt* abrir o cerrar cierre de cremallera.

zippy, *adj* enérgico, vigoroso; pronto, rápido.

zircon, *n* circón *m*.

zirconium, *n* circonio *m*.

zodiac, *n* zodíaco *m*.

zone, *n* **1.** zona *f;* **2.** *vt* dividir por zonas, distribuir en zonas.

zoning, *n* división *f* por zonas.

zoo, *n* zoo *m*, jardín *m* zoológico.

zoological, *adj* zoológico.

zoologist, *n* zoólogo(a) *m/f*.

zoom, *n* **1.** zumbido *m;* empinadura *f;* **2.** *vi* zumbar.

zucchini, *n* calabacín *m*, calabacines.

Weights and Measures - Pesos y Medidas

Metric System
Sistema Métrico

The following prefixes are used to form measures units.

deca-	10 times	10 veces
hecto-	100 times	100 veces
kilo-	1000 times	1000 veces
deci-	one tenth	una décima
centi-	one hundredth	una centésima
mili-	one thousandth	una milésima

Linear measures - medidas longitudinales

1 millimeter (milímetro)	=	0.039373 inch (pulgada)
1 centimeter (centímetro)	=	0.03937 inch (pulgada)
1 meter (metro)	=	39.37 inches (pulgadas)
		1.094 yards (yardas)
1 kilometer (kilómetro)	=	0.6214 mile (milla)

Square measures - medidas cuadradas (de superficie)

1 sq. centimeter (centímetro cuadrado)	=	0.0155 sq. inch (pulgada cuadrada)
1 sq. meter (metro cuadrado)	=	1.764 sq. feet (pies cuadrados)
		1.196 sq. yards (yardas cuadradas)
1 sq. kilometer (kilómetro cuadrado)	=	0.3861 sq. mile (milla cuadrada)
		247.1 acres (acres)
1 are	=	100 sq. meter (área)
		119.6 sq. yards (yardas cuadradas)
1 hectare	=	100 ares (hectárea)
		2.471 acres (acres)

Cubic measures - medidas cúbicas (de volumen)

1 cu. centimeter (centímetro cúbico)	=	0.161 cu. inch (pulgada cúbica)
1 cubic meter (metro cúbico)	=	35.315 cu. feet (pies cúbicos)
		1.308 cu. yards (yardas cúbicas)

Measures of capacity - medidas de capacidad

1 liter (litro)	=	100 cu. centimeter
		1.76 pints (pintas)
		0.22 gallon (galón)

Weights - pesos

1 gram (gramo)	=	15.4 grains (granos)
1 kilogram (kilogramo)	=	2.2046 pounds (libras)
1 quintal (quintal métrico)	=	100 kilograms
		220.46 pounds (libras)
1 metric ton (tonelada métrica)	=	1000 kilograms
		0.9842 ton (tonelada)

US Measures - Medidas de Estados Unidos
Linear Measures - medidas longitudinales

1 inch (pulgada)	=	2,54 cetímetros)
1 foot (pie)	=	12 inches
		30,48 centímetros
1 yard (yarda)	=	3 feet
		91,44 centímetros

1 mile (milla)	=	170 yards
		1.609,33 metros
		1,609 kilómetro

Square measures - medidas cuadradas

1 sq. inch (pulgada cuadrada)	=	6,45 cm^2
1 sq. foot (pie cuadrado)	=	144 sq. inches
		929,03 cm^2
1 sq. yard (yarda cuadrada)	=	9 sq. feet
		0,836 m^2
1 acre	=	480 sq. yards
		40,47 áreas
1 sq. mile (milla cuadrada)	=	640 acres
		2,59 km^2

Cubic measures - medidas cúbicas

1 cu. inch (pulgada cúbica)	=	16,387 cm^3
1 cu. foot (pie cúbico)	=	178 cu. inch
		0,028 m^3
1 cu. yard (yarda cúbica)	=	27 cu. feet
		0,765 m^3

Measures of capacity - medidas de capacidad

1 US liquid gill	=	0,118 litro
1 US liquid pint (pinta)	=	0,473 litro
1 US liquid quart (cuarto)	=	2 pints
		0,946 litro
1 US liquid gallon (galón)	=	4 quarts
		3,785 litros

Weights - Pesos

1 hundredweight (or short hundredweight)	=	100 pounds
		45,36 kilogramos
1 ton (or short ton)	=	2000 pounds
		20 hundredweight
		907,18 kilogramos

Traditional Spanish Weights and Measures - Pesos y Medidas Españolas Tradicionales
Linear measures - medidas lineares

1 vara	=	0.836 meter
1 braza	=	1.67 meters
1 milla	=	1.852 kilometers
1 legua (league)	=	5.5727 kilometers

Square measures - medidas cuadradas

| 1 fanega | = | 640 sq. meters |
| | | 1.59 acres |

Measures of capacity - medidas de capacidad

1 cuartillo	=	0.504 liter
1 azumbre	=	4 cuartillos
		2.016 liters
1 cántara	=	8 azumbres
		16.128 liters

Weights - pesos

1 onza	=	28.7 grams
1 libra	=	16 onzas
		460 grams
1 arroba	=	25 pounds
		11.502 kilograms
1 quintal	=	4 arrobas
		100 pounds
		46 kilograms